Developmental Psychology

Patrick Leman, Andy Bremner
Ross D. Parke, Mary Gauvain

Mc
Graw
Hill
Education

Developmental Psychology, Second Edition
Patrick Leman, Andy Bremner, Ross D. Parke, Mary Gauvain
ISBN-13 9780077175191
ISBN-10 0077175190

Published by McGraw-Hill Education
338 Euston Road
London
NW1 3BH
Telephone: +44 (0) 203 429 3400
Website: www.mheducation.co.uk

British Library Cataloguing in Publication Data
A catalogue record for this book is available from the British Library

Library of Congress Cataloging in Publication Data
The Library of Congress data for this book has been applied for from the Library of Congress

Content Developer: Nicola Cupit
Content Product Manager: Adam Hughes
Production Manager: Ben King
Marketing Manager: Lauren Ward

Text design by Kamae Design
Cover design by Adam Renvoize
Printed and bound by Ashford Colour Press Ltd, Gosport, Hants PO13 0FW

ISBN-13 9780077175191
ISBN-10 0077175190
eISBN-13 9781526847454

Brief table of contents

Detailed table of contents

Preface

We were all young once. It follows that every psychological phenomenon you will study in adults has a developmental history. For this simple reason, developmental psychology comprises one of the largest sub-divisions within psychology, with huge numbers of scientific papers dedicated to attempting to answer the questions it poses. The journal *Developmental Psychology* receives the second highest number of submitted articles out of all of the American Psychological Association (APA) journals.

Developmental psychology is a dynamic area of research; it continually combines with, integrates and informs other subdivisions of psychology to provide frequent, novel insights into how children grow and learn about the world around them. To provide some examples of this kind of synergy of developmental psychology with other disciplines and domains: advances in cognitive neuroscience enable advances in understanding of cognitive development and cognitive functions; likewise, changes in society have an important impact on the social and emotional development of gender identity and peer relationships. The impact of developmental psychology is equally wide; it stimulates new developments in educational practice for typically and atypically developing children, and informs health care for people of all ages across the lifespan. Importantly, though, it is an intrinsic interest in what makes us mature, and in how that relates to almost every other area of psychological understanding, that has kept developmentalists committed to researching and teaching developmental psychology. This is why we have written this book.

This revised edition of one of the world's leading developmental psychology textbooks adopts an international outlook. It is with this in mind that we have looked to develop a text that encompasses a broader range of theories and research. The book also combines classic and up-to-date research across the broad span of developmental psychology.

The book is designed with first- and second-year undergraduate students in mind. The structured and topical approach provides teachers and students alike with a systematic introduction to the latest international research in the area, building upon knowledge in a progressive way throughout. It also means that each chapter serves as a standalone introduction to an area, with links through to other chapters throughout.

OUR APPROACH IN THIS BOOK

Balanced theoretical perspectives

The topical approach of the book allows for a sophisticated presentation of the theories that guide research in the many areas of developmental psychology. We have attempted to show in each chapter how thinking about important questions has changed through critiques and revisions of classic theories in accordance with up-to-date empirical findings. We aim to provide a balanced presentation of the grand and classic theories, with acknowledgement of the more specialized theories that are important in particular areas.

While the theoretical approaches that are most popular vary from region to region, we have attempted as far as is possible to portray the field in a balanced way, offering at the same time a holistic overview of the major topics for developmental psychology. In order to achieve this we have added new topics and chapters to the original US format of the book and have extensively revised other areas. Also, to highlight the importance of how research in different areas and different theoretical approaches can influence and inform one another we have therefore included cross-links in every chapter to highlight some of the main ways in which students and instructors can think about linking material across the book.

Basic and applied research

Throughout the book you will see a focus on a data-driven approach to understanding development. We believe that this is important if university education is to stimulate new generations of researchers who will apply their scientific acumen to investigating new questions about development. You will see this empirical emphasis particularly in the methods chapter (Chapter 3), but we have also taken the opportunity to remind students about the methods developmentalists use through our coverage of each individual topic. Perhaps the clearest way in which this is achieved is through the Research Close-Up boxes (detailed below). While this book covers research methods that are employed across psychology as a discipline, there are of course some methodological approaches that are unique to developmental psychology. Particular emphasis is therefore placed on developmental methodologies.

Thus, we advocate a consideration of 'basic' developmental psychology research throughout the book. However, we also place particular emphasis on how understanding the broadest implications and applications of this research can provide further insights. Basic research can enable us to understand real-life problems and, conversely, insights gained from applying the results of scientific investigation can help improve research and sharpen theoretical understanding. This emphasis of basic research and application is brought into focus by the pedagogical features we employ throughout the book. Each chapter contains two types of pedagogical boxes: Research Close-Up (these boxes present single research studies in detail, giving students a sense of how research is carried out) and Applied Developmental Psychology (these boxes discuss instances of how developmental research has been applied outside of the purely academic domain).

International approach

Developmental psychology is an international discipline. As such, we have opted not to focus explicitly on any particularly region with regard to theories and research. Our aim is to provide students with an international and holistic introduction to the discipline; this means using the most appropriate research and examples for a given topic. Based on our location, there is some natural bias towards the European region and local research, but we do not offer this at the expense of key US or broader international research.

This approach is reflected in both the research and theoretical presentation across the book. There are certain theories and topics that were not covered in the US edition but are deemed important by a wider international community. These topics and theories have been included in our revised edition. We provide more detail regarding the adaptation next.

HIGHLIGHTS OF THE NEW EDITION

In our original adaptation of Parke and Gauvain, we undertook a number of structural changes as well as updating and expanding the coverage in a number of areas. We introduced new chapters on developmental research methods and theoretical approaches, as well as consolidating coverage of developmental psychology into a topic based approach via new chapters on brain development, physical development, perceptual and sensorimotor development, and adult development. We think that the structural changes which we introduced in the new edition have been effective and have retained these for the new edition, whilst undertaking a thorough revision of content. We have highlighted some of the key changes to the second edition below:

Chapter 2: Theories in Developmental Psychology

- Significant expansion of coverage of modern nativist theories of development (e.g., those of Spelke and Gopnik).
- Increased coverage of computational models of development, incorporating connectionist, Bayesian models of development as well as dynamical systems accounts.

Chapter 3: Research Methods in Developmental Psychology

- Updated Applied Developmental Psychology box on delayed gratification in response to recent and significant findings in this area.
- Updated Applied Developmental Psychology box on research addressing the effects of television use in children to include the latest perspectives and data on the use of social media and tablets.
- A new structure and a thorough updating of the 'Methods for Data Collection' section.

Chapter 4: Physical Development: Growing a Body

- Thorough updates and additions to the section on 'Risks in the Prenatal Environment' to incorporate the latest developments in this area of research. This includes new subsections on 'Principles of teratogenesis', and 'How do teratogens have their effects?'
- A new Applied Developmental Psychology box examining the effects of tactile contact on brain development in preterm infants.
- A new section on embodied approaches to development.
- A new section on the effects of puberty on brain development.

Chapter 5: The Biology of Development: Genes, Nervous System, Brain and Environment

- Updated and more extensive coverage of polygenicity.
- An extensive update of the behavioural genetics section, including an analysis of critiques of behavioural genetics methods.
- New Research Close-Up box on use of functional near infrared spectroscopy (fNIRS) for investigating the social brain in infancy.
- A substantially updated section on brain plasticity.

Chapter 6: Perceptual and Sensorimotor Development

- Completely restructured chapter which captures current trends in the discipline, emphasizing the development of a wider range of senses including touch and chemosensation, as well as multisensory interactions among the senses.
- New material on the origins of an ability to perceive material properties of objects in infancy.
- New section capturing a wide range of research findings regarding how infants perceive their social world.
- New Research Close-Up box on human foetus's *in utero* face preferences.
- New section on the development of self and body perception in infancy.

Chapter 7: Emotional Development and Attachment

- Expanded coverage of children's understanding of facial expressions.
- Revised attachment coverage.

Chapter 8: Language and Communication

- Increased coverage of pointing, joint attention and crying.
- Additional coverage of phonological development, including research on dyslexia.

Chapter 9: Cognitive Development: Origins of Knowledge

- Enhanced coverage of Bruner and scaffolding.
- Updated coverage of language and internal speech.
- Updated coverage of perspective taking in children.
- Updated coverage of children's trust in testimony.
- New coverage of recent controversies around early false belief abilities in infants.

Chapter 10: The Development of Cognitive Functions

- Substantially updated coverage of the development of imitation, controversies surrounding neonatal imitation and rational imitation.
- Rewritten and updated section on models of cognition, with an increased emphasis on the working memory model.
- New section on the relevance and use of cognitive models.
- Considerable restructuring of the sections on the development of cognitive strategies and functions, placing a greater emphasis on the development of executive function and the role of executive functions across domains.

Chapter 11: Intelligence, Achievement and Learning

- Expanded assessment coverage to include the Cognitive Assessment System and Raven's Matrices.
- Individual differences in intelligence expanded.
- New coverage of executive functions and working memory in education.
- Expanded achievement coverage.

Chapter 12: Parents, Peers and Social Relationships

- Revised parents and family section.
- Expanded coverage of parental versus peer influence.
- Coverage of bullying included.

Chapter 13: Social Identities: Gender, Gender Roles and Ethnicity

- Extended biological coverage of gender differences.
- Revised section on media impact on gender identity.
- New coverage of ethnicity.

Chapter 14: Morality, Altruism and Aggression

- Extended section on Piaget's theory.
- Neuropsychological and socioemotional approaches.
- Revised section on prosocial behaviour.

Chapter 15: Atypical Development

with Alice Jones

- This chapter has been renamed 'atypical development' (whereas previously it was developmental psychopathology) to reflect a rebalancing of the coverage towards cognitive developmental disorders.
- Updated section on the principles of atypical development.
- Updating of all coverage to reflect revised diagnostic criteria and classification of disorders in DSM-5 (2013).

Chapter 16: Development in Adulthood

- Focus on the cognitive decline in intelligence, problem solving and memory.
- Social focus on relationships and happiness in later life, particularly with regard to romantic relationships.

Guided tour

The primary means by which researchers investigate causal connections among factors is with an experiment. An experiment can be carried out in a laboratory or in natural situations. In a laboratory experiment, researchers are able to control factors that may influence the variable they are interested in, and therefore their results allow them to draw conclusions about cause and effect. Researchers will control or hold constant, or equate, every possible influence except the one factor they have hypothesized to be the cause of the variable they want to study. They then create two groups of participants. One group, called the experimental group, is exposed to the proposed causative factor; the second group, the control group, does not experience this factor. Researchers put people in these two groups by using random assignment, which helps to rule out the possibility that the people in each of the groups differ from one another in some systematic way that could distort the results of the experiment.

To understand how these various controls enable the laboratory experimenter to determine causality, let's look at a classic study of the relation between watching violent television programm...

> All **key terms** are defined in the margin near where they are first mentioned in the text. Use these at-a-glance definitions to learn the important terms in developmental psychology as you go through the course. They are also collected together in the Glossary at the back of the book and online.

Applied Developmental Psychology

BOX 3-2   How can we make better use of research on childre...
television/internet use?

The impact on children of the amazing growth of communications me...
radio, movies and comic books to television and its more recent cousir...
internet, social media, smartphones and tablets – children have been bom...
experiences via the media.

What has the wealth of research on children and television revealed?...
shown that some television programmes do help young children learn, but...
on children of watching programmes filled with violence and sex as well...
young child's limited understanding (Comstock & Scharrer, 2006).

Research on children's and adolescents' use of the internet and soc...
positive effects, such as improved reading scores (Jackson et al., 2006)...
increasing adolescents' awareness of dangerous behaviours such as various f...
& Eckenrode, 2006). More worryingly, social media use seems to, under some...
negative effects on mental well-being such as increased depressive symptom...

With the advent of media equipment which is becoming ever more acces...

> **Applied Developmental Psychology** boxes bring research, theories and concepts to real-world, practical situations.

Research close-up

BOX 4-2   The impact of pubertal timin...
environment on delinquenc...

Source: Based on Caspi et al. (1993)

Introduction:

In 1993, results of several longitudinal investigations of the affect of l...
ing) on various behaviours and social outcomes in adolescent girls...
message about early puberty. Simmons and Blyth (1987) reported that...
than their peers experienced more body image problems, and lower aca...
Magnusson (1990) reported more sexually precocious and delinquent...
Caspi and Moffitt (1991) showed that early-menarche girls produce m...
in adolescence. Particularly striking was the fact that these converging...
number of different countries (the US, New Zealand and Sweden). The r...
the causal developmental pathways linking sexual maturation to these...

> **Research Close-Up** boxes introduce you to the format of real research in developmental psychology. Each box summarizes an important research paper, explaining the methods the authors used, the results they obtained and a discussion to help you think critically about the significance of the study.

, but all of our senses depend on what our bodies can do. We can only
 right directions. We can only touch them if we bring our bodies into
hapes and sizes and abilities of our bodies determine what we perceive.
nt now. In the infant and child, the body and
stent and constant as they are in an adult.
d sometimes grow perceptibly even overnight
Our abilities to use their bodies in the service
not just in infancy, but throughout early life
l., 2017). If we agree with the embodied cogni-
er that infants' and children's ways of thinking

> In Chapters 6 and 9 we
> will look at some of the
> ways in which changes
> in the body influence our
> cognitive and perceptual
> abilities.

Making Connections margin notes will help you to relate topics explored in different chapters. They provide a link to relevant content covered in other chapters to help you draw associations between different topics.

male and female partners of the mother can play important roles
ven what we have discussed in this chapter, what do you think
negative influences partners can have on the early development

Explore and Discuss

nall preterm infants to survive, but some of these children face physical,
ere things that can be done to improve these problems?

ng increasingly obese. What factors do you think account for this trend?

:h sexual maturation can impact on social and cognitive development?

Explore and Discuss study questions at the end of the chapter prompt you to think critically about some of the issues discussed in the chapter. These questions can be either undertaken individually or used as a focus for group discussion in seminars or tutorials.

:gor, N. A., & Smotherman, W. P. (1995). *Fetal development:*
lale, NJ: Lawrence Erlbaum.
formant. In J. W. Fagen & H. Hayne (eds) *Progress in infancy*
ce Erlbaum.
4). Puberty and psychological development. In R. M. Lerner &
scent psychology*, 2nd edn. New York: John Wiley & Sons.

Recommended Reading

Use the **Recommended Reading** list at the end of each chapter as a starting point for further research.

CHRONOLOGY OF DEVELOPMENT
An overview of prenatal development

	No. of months gestational age	Approximate size & weight (millimetres & grammes)	Central nervous system and peripheral sensory systems
Zygote	0–1	5 mm, 0.2 g	Neural tube forms,

Chronology of Development charts show the typical ages at which children develop abilities.

SUMMARY

Developmental psychologists use the *scientific method* in their researc
basis of theories. Hypotheses are tested using replicable techniques t
Researchers collect data from a number of different sources. These i
reports from others who know the child – such as parents, teachers and p
challenges to collecting data from individuals at different ages, from infa
the competency of individuals at different ages varies enormously. Thus a
employed in the field, and researchers tailor these methods to answer the
ages. For instance, biological and psychophysiological measures inclu(

Use the **Summary** at the end of the chapter to check your understanding of the core theory.

McGraw-Hill Connect Psychology is a learning and teaching environment that improves student performance and outcomes whilst promoting engagement and comprehension of content.

You can utilize publisher-provided materials, or add your own content to design a complete course to help your students achieve higher outcomes.

PROVEN EFFECTIVE

With Connect   Without Connect

MORE As and Bs
WITH CONNECT

A   B   C   D

INSTRUCTORS

With McGraw-Hill Connect Psychology, instructors get:

- Simple **assignment management,** allowing you to spend more time teaching.
- **Auto-graded** assignments, quizzes and tests.
- **Detailed visual reporting** where students and section results can be viewed and analysed.
- Sophisticated **online testing** capability.
- A **filtering and reporting** function that allows you to easily assign and report on materials that are correlated to learning outcomes, topics, level of difficulty, and more. Reports can be accessed for individual students or the whole class, as well as offering the ability to drill into individual assignments, questions or categories.
- **Instructor materials** to help supplement your course.

Get Connected. Get Results.

Available online via Connect is a wealth of instructor support materials, including:

- Fully updated PowerPoint Slides to use in lectures.
- Fully updated instructor's manual to support your course preparation.
- Image library of artwork from the book to personalise your lectures and tutorials.

STUDENTS

With McGraw-Hill Connect Finance, students get:

Assigned content

- Easy **online access** to homework, tests and quizzes
- **Immediate feedback** and 24-hour tech support

With McGraw-Hill SmartBook, students can:

- Take control of their learning with a personalized and adaptive reading experience.
- Identify gaps in their knowledge by working through the stages of reading and practice in a completely personalized way.
- Gain the maximum return on their study time as SmartBook adapts to their own particular knowledge base and provides them with the information they need at the right time to help them progress.
- Focus on concepts they are most likely to forget, ensuring that knowledge is retained into the long term memory.

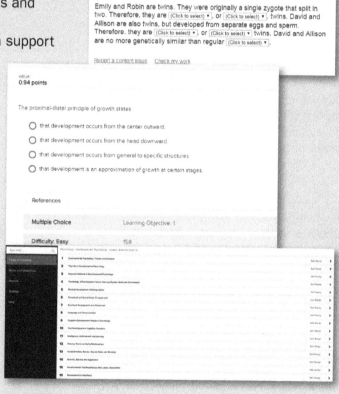

Mc Graw Hill Education **connect**®

Connect is an online assignment and assessment solution that offers a number of powerful tools and features that make managing assignments easier, so faculty can spend more time teaching. With Connect, students can engage with their coursework anytime and anywhere, making the learning process more accessible and efficient.

Interactives

Encourage students to illustrate a concept in an engaging and stimulating activity format with step-by-step guidance, to ensure conceptual understanding is tested, applied and reinforced. The activities provide seamless assignability and automatic grading capabilities.

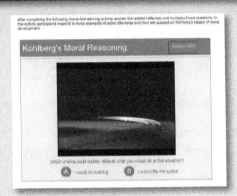

Milestone videos

Allow students to experience life as it unfolds from infancy to late adulthood. The video series tracks the development of real children as they progress through the early stages of physical, social and emotional development in their first few weeks, months and years of life.

Auto-gradable questions

Check students' knowledge and conceptual understanding through multiple choice and true or false questions. Provides students with immediate feedback and enables lecturers to have further insight into student performance.

Testbank

Comprehensive auto-gradable questions which can be used for testing and as homework assignment.

SmartBook™

Fuelled by LearnSmart—the most widely used and intelligent adaptive learning resource—SmartBook is the first and only adaptive reading experience available today. Distinguishing what a student knows from what they don't, and honing in on concepts they are most likely to forget, SmartBook personalizes content for each student in a continuously adapting reading experience. Valuable reports provide instructors with insight as to how students are progressing through textbook content, and are useful for shaping in-class time or assessment.

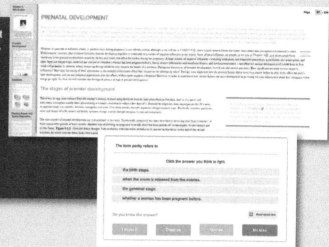

LearnSmart™

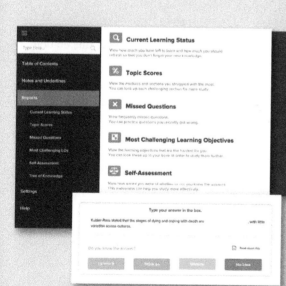

McGraw-Hill LearnSmart is an adaptive learning program that identifies what an individual student knows and doesn't know. LearnSmart's adaptive learning path helps students learn faster, study more efficiently, and retain more knowledge. Now with integrated learning resources which present topics and concepts in different and engaging formats, increases student engagement and promotes additional practice of key concepts. Reports available for both students and instructors indicate where students need to study more and assess their success rate in retaining knowledge.

Acknowledgements

Any publication is a team effort, and not just the product of work solely by the authors. Throughout our careers, and in the here and now we have been lucky that so many friends and colleagues have guided and supported us; sometimes in a general sense, sometimes in showing particular patience or providing particular insights and information, to help us produce what we believe is a fine, international textbook! We would like also to thank all those developmental psychologists – professors, lecturers and students – who have helped us to hone our writing and who continue to inspire us with new and exciting research. Those people are too numerous to list, but your time, energy and enthusiasm is always appreciated. Thank you.

Natalie Jacobs and Nicola Cupit at McGraw-Hill have put a huge amount of time and effort into persuading us to write this book, coaxing us into making it better, and firmly but kindly cajoling us to deliver the revised manuscript on time. Their input and advice has been both helpful and creative throughout the process. In many ways this book is as much their work as it is ours.

Publisher's acknowledgements

We would like to thank Alice Jones at Goldsmiths, University of London, and Paula Lacey at Royal Holloway, University of London, for their contributions to the first edition of this text.

Our thanks go to the following reviewers for their comments at various stages in the text's development:

Claire Monks, University of Greenwich
Mark Mon-Williams, University of Leeds
Kempie van Rooyen, Nelson Mandela Metropolitan University
Jo Saunders, University of Strathclyde
Eilis Hennessy, University College Dublin
Niamh Stack, University of Glasgow
Angela Veale, University College Cork

Andrew Dunn, Nottingham Trent University
Maurits van der Molen, University of Amsterdam
Hanneke van Mier, Maastricht University
Marcel van Aken, Utrecht University
Annerieke Oosterwegel, Utrecht University
Fiona MacCallum, University of Warwick
Emily Mather, University of Hull
Richard Jolley, Staffordshire University

Our thanks also go to the digital contributors who helped to updated the Connect package for this edition including the SmartBook, testbank and interactive questions.

Every effort has been made to trace and acknowledge ownership of copyright and to clear permission for material reproduced in this book. The publishers will be pleased to make suitable arrangements to clear permission with any copyright holders whom it has not been possible to contact.

About the authors

Patrick Leman Patrick is Professor of Psychology and Dean of Education at the Institute of Psychiatry, Psychology and Neuroscience, King's College London. He completed his undergraduate degree in Psychology, Philosophy and Physiology (PPP) at the University of Oxford, followed by a PhD at the University of Cambridge in children's understanding of authority and moral reasoning. Patrick's research spans several areas of social developmental psychology in childhood and adolescence including gender and ethnic identity, social relationships, refugee children, positive youth development, and peer group communication and learning. He is a Fellow of the British Psychological Society, and formerly British Academy Senior Research Fellow, Chair of the British Psychological Society Developmental Psychology Section, and Editor of the *British Journal of Developmental Psychology*.

Andy Bremner Andy completed his first degree and DPhil in experimental psychology at the University of Oxford supervised by Professor Peter Bryant, F.R.S. Following some postdoctoral appointments Andy spent 13 years at Goldsmiths, University of London, where he was latterly Head of Psychology. In 2018 Andy was appointed as a Reader in Psychology in the School of Psychology, University of Birmingham, where he conducts research into a variety of questions surrounding perceptual and cognitive development and developmental cognitive neuroscience. Particular research interests include multisensory development, the development of body representations and object representations. Andy is Co-Editor with Robin Banerjee of *Infant and Child Development*.

Ross D. Parke Ross D. Parke is Professor Emeritus at the University of California, Riverside.

Mary Gauvain Mary Gauvain is a Professor of Psychology at the University of California, Riverside.

Let us help make our **content** your **solution**

At McGraw-Hill Education our aim is to help lecturers to find the most suitable content for their needs delivered to their students in the most appropriate way. Our custom **publishing solutions** offer the ideal combination of content delivered in the way which best suits lecturer and students.

Our custom publishing programme offers lecturers the opportunity to select just the chapters or sections of material they wish to deliver to their students from a database called CREATE® at

http://create.mheducation.com/createonline/index.html

CREATE™ contains over two million pages of content from:

- textbooks
- professional books
- case books – Harvard Articles, Insead, Ivey, Darden, Thunderbird and BusinessWeek
- Taking Sides – debate materials

Across the following imprints:

- McGraw-Hill Education
- Open University Press
- Harvard Business Publishing
- US and European material

There is also the option to include additional material authored by lecturers in the custom product – this does not necessarily have to be in English.

We will take care of everything from start to finish in the process of developing and delivering a custom product to ensure that lecturers and students receive exactly the material needed in the most suitable way.

With a **Custom Publishing Solution**, students enjoy the best selection of material deemed to be the most suitable for learning everything they need for their courses – something of real value to support their learning. Teachers are able to use exactly the material they want, in the way they want, to support their teaching on the course.

Please contact your local **McGraw-Hill representative** with any questions or alternatively contact Marc Wright, email: marc.wright@mheducation.com

CHAPTER 1
Developmental Psychology: Themes and Contexts

Introduction

Every adult was once a child; every individual has a developmental history. If you can recall your first memory, you might also be able to remember what you felt like when you were younger, how you are no longer excited or alarmed by the same things that you were back then. You might also have a sense that your social relationships, how you feel about other people, and how you approach and understand your friends, acquaintances and family members, are very different at different points in your life.

Developmental psychology seeks to identify and describe *changes* in the way we think and behave, and to uncover the *developmental processes* that drive these changes. In other words, developmental psychologists are interested in *what* things change as we get older and *how* these changes come about. Developmental psychologists are scientists. And so, to understand the changes and processes that underlie child development, developmental psychology researchers devise theories of development and carry out empirical studies to test these theories (see Chapters 2 and 3). These advances in research make possible practical applications that can help to promote effective development and change, and remove some of the obstacles to them.

Throughout this book, we will discuss different areas of developmental psychology in turn. In each chapter we explore the key observations and research findings which have shaped the field. We will also describe the theories that have been proposed to account for these findings and explain development.

This might all sound rather abstract so far. But let's look at some examples. In Chapter 4 we examine how the very earliest influences before a child's birth can have a profound effect on psychological functioning during childhood, adolescence and even into adulthood. In Chapters 4 and 6 you'll see how our first abilities to sense the world around us emerge *in utero* and continue to develop significantly in the first years of life. Later, in Chapter 8 we look at how children learn to communicate with others, how they acquire an understanding of the self through communication and social interaction. In the last chapters, Chapters 15 and 16 respectively, we describe what happens when there are problems with the normal development process, and also consider the developmental changes that may occur across adult life and into old age.

But before we launch into these topics there's some groundwork to do first. In the remainder of this chapter we are going to describe some of the themes and perspectives which run through developmental psychology. Many of these themes are in common with those seen in psychology more widely. One particularly important issue is that developmental psychology, like psychology more generally, is studied and explained at multiple 'levels of explanation'. And so we can investigate how development happens at numerous levels: at the level of our social interactions (e.g., between an infant and a parent), at the level of our thought processes (e.g., improvements in memory), and at a more biological level (e.g., the maturation of particular brain areas or connections between brain areas).

The development of the biological apparatus that underpins our psychological abilities and social interactions is a focus of study which has been gaining in importance in recent years as more and more methods are developed to examine changes in the brain and nervous functions. We shall focus on this particularly in Chapters 4 and 5. However, it is crucial to remember that all levels of explanation are needed if we are to have the full picture of how development works. This is an important aspect of the approach that we adopt in this textbook.

So in this first chapter we introduce the field of developmental psychology by discussing some of the central themes and concerns that pervade it. In Chapters 2 and 3 we will continue the groundwork, outlining developmental theories and research methods in order to provide you with the necessary contexts for understanding development in the different domains we will discuss in the remainder of the book.

Throughout the book we will introduce both classic and contemporary research in developmental psychology. While we cannot of course include the entire literature of developmental psychology (it would definitely take us substantially more than a whole book to describe all of the advances made even over the last year!),

developmental psychology A field of study that seeks to understand and explain change in individuals' cognitive, social and other capacities, first by describing changes in the child's observed behaviours and second by uncovering the processes that underlie these changes.

we aim to cover the discipline as thoroughly as possible from an internationally representative perspective. More specifically, each 'topic' chapter will describe a topic and its associated literature as thoroughly as possible, at the same time drawing out some of the central themes and emerging issues. In order to bring the research and theory to life we have included *Research Close-Up* boxes to describe some of the empirical research in more detail and *Applied Developmental Psychology* boxes to highlight the impact that developmental research has made beyond the discipline itself. In each chapter you'll also see definitions boxes and connections boxes to link themes that emerge across different topic areas and chapters. Lastly, we also summarize each chapter, and provide some further classic and contemporary readings for each chapter.

Questions about the origins of psychological abilities have fascinated philosophers for many years. As we shall describe in Chapters 2 and 7, there was great tension between accounts of human perception and thought which relied on the influence of experience (Locke, 1960) or innate understanding brought into the world before experience (Rousseau, 1762). However, it was not until just over a century ago that researchers began to investigate development using empirical scientific methods. Possibly the first scientific observation of human development was made by Charles Darwin, who reports an observational biography of his own child 'Doddy's' sensory capacities and emotions (Cairns & Cairns, 2006; Darwin, 1877).

Some have argued that Darwin's 'biography' of his son Doddy is the first empirical scientific study in developmental psychology (Bornstein & Kessen, 2017). Interestingly, it was not until around the time of Darwin's work that scholars truly began to view childhood as a different phase of life from adulthood. For most of recorded history, little was written about children or childhood (Aries, 1962). By and large, people viewed children as miniature adults – a view that affected the way adults treated children at the time. For example, in earlier historical periods, children were often labourers in the fields, factories and mines. It was not until the late nineteenth century that child labour laws were introduced to protect children from this kind of exploitation. Today, in the twenty-first century, research in developmental psychology affects people's everyday experiences, from pre-birth to old age. For instance, developmental psychologists have influenced social policy and legislation relevant to children, families and the care of the elderly (Renninger & Sigel, 2006).

To understand the scientific study of human development, it is important to appreciate the central themes that underlie current

Proposing one of the first theories of children's emotional development, Charles Darwin (1809–1882) based much of his theorizing on his infant son's earliest emotional expressions. Although Darwin is more widely known for his theory of evolution, his work on children's emotional behaviour has had a considerable influence on the field of developmental psychology.
© Library of Congress Prints and Photographs Division [LC-USZ62-52389]

theory and research in the field. It is also important to be familiar with the main theoretical views that guide this research and the methods that are used. Throughout our exploration of contemporary developmental psychology, we discuss how we can use what we learn to improve psychological and social functioning, and opportunities for development in important areas of their life such as relationships with family, friends and peers; academic pursuits; and personal development.

THEMES OF DEVELOPMENT

As scientists have studied development, they have examined and debated a number of recurring and key themes relating to psychological growth. We are going to focus on some of the most important of those themes here: those concerning the origins of human behaviour, the specificity or generality of change (that is, whether changes happen to all of a child's thinking or behaviour at the same time, or just one part of it), and the individual and contextual forces that define and drive development. We will encounter these three themes repeatedly throughout the book as we discuss the many aspects of development: biological, cognitive, linguistic, emotional and social.

Origins of behaviour: inheritance and environment

Historically, developmental psychologists have argued fiercely about whether natural (hereditary, genetic) forces shape psychological development, or whether the ways in which a child is nurtured (for instance, upbringing and environmental influences) are more fundamental to understanding the drivers of developmental change. The question of how we should understand the relationship between inheritance and environment is sometimes referred to as the nature versus nurture debate. Broadly speaking, these nature and nurture positions are referred to, respectively, as nativism and empiricism. As we shall see in Chapter 2, most contemporary theories recognize that both environment and inheritance influence human development. However, developmental theorists disagree about the relative importance of each of these factors in various domains of development. Today, there are almost no theories that support extreme positions in any simplistic way. Instead, modern developmental psychologists explore how hereditary and environmental factors, or nature and nurture, interact or work together to produce developmental change.

> **nativism** The idea that development is primarily determined by inherited factors (i.e. genetics).
>
> **empiricism** The idea that development is primarily determined by environmental influences.

Let's have a look at an example of how nature–nurture (or gene–environment) interactions can occur. Research on child maltreatment finds that children with certain genetic characteristics are more likely to exhibit behaviour problems than are children who do not have these characteristics (e.g., McCrory, Puetz, & Viding, 2017; Yaylaci et al., 2017). When children with these genetic dispositions live in abusive environments, they are more likely to be maltreated than other children. Thus, the *combination* of the child's inherited characteristics, the way he or she expresses these characteristics behaviourally, and the abusive environment itself, puts a particular child at risk.

In the above example we see how genetic variations between different individuals can lead to different developmental outcomes because of the different ways in which individual children's genetic inheritance interacts with the environments in which they are placed. However, there are also some more general principles concerning the ways in which our (genetic) inheritance interacts with our environments.

> In Chapter 2 we will introduce Piaget's constructivist theory of development in which he argues that infants and children play an active role themselves in their own development.

Humans are not merely passive recipients of information: they try to understand and explore the world about them. The active nature of the human organism supports interaction between inherited propensities and the environment which those propensities exposes them to over the course of development (Kuczynski, 2003). Thus, the interaction between inheritance and environment is an active, dynamic process to which the developing children themselves make an active and vital contribution.

Describing developmental change: continuity versus discontinuity

Another major question that confronts developmental psychologists is how to describe patterns of developmental change. Two broad kinds of pattern are often debated and put at tension with one another.

Some psychologists view development as a continuous process (continuous development) whereby each new event builds on earlier experiences (Figure 1-1a). According to this view, development is a smooth and gradual accumulation of ability. Developmental changes add to or build on earlier abilities in a cumulative or quantitative way, without any abrupt shifts from one change to the next. For many behaviours, this seems like a suitable explanation. For example, as we learn a new skill – let's say, how to swim – we usually observe gradual improvement from day to day.

> **continuous development** A pattern of development in which abilities change in a gradual and smooth way.

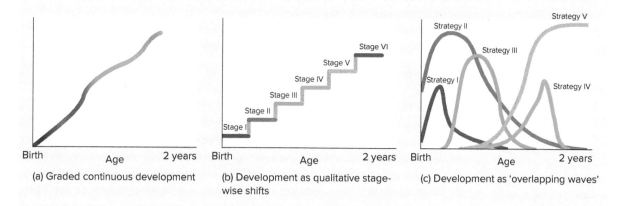

Figure 1-1   Continuity and discontinuity in the child's development

The continuous view (a) sees development as a gradual series of shifts in capacities, skills and behaviour with no abrupt changes. A discontinuous view (b) proposes abrupt, step-like changes that make each stage qualitatively different from the one that precedes it. An influential and more contemporary third view, holds that development is fundamentally continuous, but because the development of a range of abilities and tendencies is happening in parallel, overall developmental change in ability can appear to be interspersed with sudden or discontinuous/ qualitative shifts. Siegler's 'overlapping waves' model (c) suggests that children use a variety of strategies in thinking and learning at any given age. The use of each strategy ebbs and flows with increasing age and expertise, and only gradually do the most successful strategies predominate. As a result, from a long-range perspective, development can appear to be discontinuous, but using a closer examination, we can observe gradual quantitative changes in the use of certain ways of thinking.

Source: Part (c) based on Siegler (1996).

However, sometimes we notice an abrupt change in our ability. Whereas yesterday we were swimming competently, today it seems as if some big improvement has occurred – all our practice seems to have finally paid off. Compared with the earlier more incremental changes, our more recent changes seem more qualitative in nature, and our smoother or more rapid swimming stroke now bears little resemblance to the choppy, halting strokes we had when we first began to swim. This latter type of change is of interest to developmental psychologists who view development as discontinuous (discontinuous development). This view likens development to a series of discrete steps or stages in which behaviours get reorganized into a qualitatively new set of behaviours (Figure 1-1b).

A very influential and more contemporary view on the continuity-discontinuity debate is offered by Siegler (1996; 2016) who sees development as basically continuous or quantitative, but argues that because development of a range of abilities and tendencies is happening in parallel, overall developmental change in ability can appear to be interspersed with sudden or discontinuous/qualitative shifts (Figure 1-1c). We will look more closely at this issue in Chapter 9.

Critical and sensitive periods

Developmental psychologists have investigated whether some experiences are particularly important at specific ages. A critical period of development is an age range during which certain experiences are required for development to proceed in a typical way. A sensitive period is an age range at which specific experiences are optimal for development to occur in a typical way. This consideration is obviously of critical importance and interest in the field as both critical and sensitive periods imply that there are certain things which we can

discontinuous development
A pattern of development in which changes occur suddenly, resulting in qualitatively different stages (periods) of development.

critical period
A period of development (age range) at which specific experiences are vital for development to occur in a typical way.

sensitive period
A period of development (age range) at which particular experiences are important for typical development. If those experiences do not occur during that period, typical development may still occur.

do in order to optimize the environment for fostering the best outcomes we can for developing children. We will discuss the matter of critical and sensitive periods in Box 1-1.

Domain-general or domain-specific development

domain-general development The idea that developments can have an impact on a wide range of abilities.

domain-specific development The idea that the development of various abilities occurs independently (separately) and has little impact on skills in other domains.

level of explanation The way in which we choose to describe psychological abilities (and the developments of those abilities). Levels of explanation can include biological, behavioural, social and emotional.

One question that has intrigued many developmental psychologists concerns the extent to which the development of a new ability or skill has impacts in other domains. Let's go back again to the example of learning how to swim. When we learn a new way of swimming (e.g., a new stroke like backstroke), that new skill might impact on our other motor abilities. Taking our example of backstroke, this new way of swimming involves bringing the arms up over the head in order to move us in the water. One might wonder whether practising this raised-arm posture might help us in other domains – for example, when serving over-arm in tennis or for lifting weights above our head. These could be considered as a domain-general influence. Psychologists differ in the extent to which they consider development to be domain general. Piaget is perhaps the clearest example of a developmental psychologist who argued that development is domain general. As we shall see in Chapter 9, he thought that when children developed a new way of logical thinking, this impacted on a variety of different skills (e.g., thinking about space, number, categorization). Other developmental psychologists have tended to take a more domain-specific viewpoint in which development proceeds relatively independently in different domains (e.g., Karmiloff-Smith, 1995; Siegler, 2016). This viewpoint thus suggests that if a child makes some progress on, let's say, mathematics, these new abilities have little influence on other domains. It is useful to note that there is some alignment between the domain-general/domain-specific argument and the question of nature versus nurture. Theorists arguing for innate cognitive abilities have often characterized such abilities as being domain specific (e.g., Pinker, 1994). However, this is not inevitably the case, and other researchers have argued that domain-specific development does not necessarily imply a strong influence of inheritance (Karmiloff-Smith, 1995).

Locus of developmental change

An important question to ask concerns what changes when development occurs. When an infant learns to smile on eye contact for the first time we have observed a change in his facial behaviour. Should we stop there or should we describe the change in other terms – for instance, maybe it is more appropriate to describe the change in terms of the social interactions between the infant and his parent, or indeed other people in general. We could of course go to a more fine level of description and consider changes in the brain areas subserving smiling, or even the neurons which are involved. Perhaps the most important thing to say about this is that these different 'levels of explanation' are not mutually exclusive. Change is happening at all of these levels at once. The more controversial matter concerns which level of explanation or locus of change

Infants learn to smile on eye contact.
© *Terry Vine/Blend Images LLC*

is the most informative for us. Can we learn more about development if we consider behavioural changes than if we consider changes in the brain? One way of answering this question is in trying to determine whether the factors that influence developmental change are primarily at one level or another (e.g., are biological or environmental factors more important). Perhaps in the case of an infant smiling we should acknowledge that the social interactions infants have play an important role in the development of smiling on eye contact; in which case perhaps the social interaction is the most useful level at which to describe developmental change. However, to complicate matters, developmental scientists are increasingly acknowledging that development is probably caused by a multitude of factors at all levels (Mareschal et al., 2007).

PERSPECTIVES ON DEVELOPMENT

As we have just discussed, it is possible to describe developmental change at several different levels of explanation, and perhaps at more than one level of explanation at once. This means that developmental psychologists have sometimes chosen very different ways to explain psychological development. In this section we describe some of the more influential perspectives and debates you will encounter throughout this book.

Individual characteristics and contextual influences

As well as studying how we all develop as humans, developmental psychology has to try to account for individual variations in development. Different paths through development can occur to the extent that individuals are considered to be developing atypically (see Chapter 15). However, individual variation also occurs within typical (and atypical) development. In Chapter 5 we will describe how the field of behavioural genetics has attempted to understand how the role of genes and environment (and their interactions) can explain individual differences in the way we grow up.

To illustrate the factors which play a role in the development of the individual consider how development occurs in a variety of settings. Do we behave similarly across a broad range of situations, or do the contexts in which we live affect how we behave and even how development occurs? Developmental psychologists differ in their emphasis on individual characteristics (which might be due to our inheritance) versus situational or contextual influences. As we shall see in Chapter 5, it is appropriate to think of the development of the individual as an *interaction* between genes and environment (Knopik et al., 2016). For example, children with aggressive personality traits may often seek out contexts in which they can display these characteristics; thus, they are more likely to join a gang or enrol in a karate class than to opt for the church choir or chess club. But these same children, in settings that do not allow or promote aggressive behaviour, such as a choir or chess club, may be less likely to behave aggressively and perhaps may even be friendly and cooperative.

One important way in which individual characteristics have been studied is by examining how different children respond when they are confronted with situational challenges or risks to healthy development. Risk can come in many forms. Some risks are biological or psychological – for example, a serious illness or a less resilient genetic inheritance. Other risks are environmental, such as family income or the child's experience at school. Individual children respond to such risks in different ways. Many seem to suffer permanent developmental disruptions. Others show 'sleeper' effects; they seem to cope well initially but exhibit problems later in life (perhaps in adolescence or even in adulthood). Still others exhibit resilience and are able to deal with the challenge with little or no effect on behaviour later in life. And some children, when they confront new risks later in life, appear to have learned in childhood strategies and mechanisms for coping with similar adversity, sometimes such that they seem better able to adapt than those who have experienced little or no risk as children (Cummings et al., 2000; Luthar et al., 2000; Masten, 2015; Masten & Labella, 2016).

BOX 1-1   The significance of early deprivation: findings from the English and Romanian Adoptee Project

Research close-up

Source: Based on Beckett et al. (2006).

Introduction:

The English and Romanian Adoptee Project (ERA) adopted a longitudinal approach to assess the development of children adopted in the United Kingdom from Romania in the early 1990s. These children had grown up during years of extreme economic hardship in Romania, many were without parents and had been placed in institutions in Romania where they experienced extreme levels of deprivation from an early age (up to 42 months). Deprivation included lack of social contact or even stimulation, and sometimes physical abuse and malnutrition. Children were adopted into UK families before their 4th birthday.

In a series of studies, the ERA research team explored the consequences of this early deprivation for social, emotional and cognitive functioning. In this particular study, the researchers were interested in how these early experiences of deprivation affected cognitive functions at age 11 years.

Method:

Participants (total 324) were Romanian children who had experienced deprivation, who were subsequently adopted into families in the United Kingdom between February 1990 and September 1992. Of this group, 165 of these children were adopted before they were 43 months of age. A comparison group of 52 UK-born adoptees had not experienced institutional deprivation. These children were tested again at 11 years of age.

In the study, children were identified as belonging to three groups based on the extent of early deprivation that they had experienced (that is, the age at which they had been adopted and the deprivation ended). These are: (i) a < 6 months group, (ii) a < 24 months group, and (iii) a 24 months and over group. Measures at or before the time of adoption included birth weight, head circumference and an assessment of developmental status.

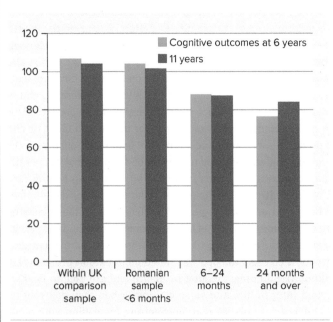

Figure 1-2   Test scores of each group (UK comparison; Romanian adoptee sample < 6 months, 6–24 months, 24 months and over at age of adoption) on cognitive tests at 6 and 11 years
Source: Adapted from Beckett et al. (2006).

At 6 years of age the same groups had completed a general measure of cognitive ability (McCarthy test). At 11 years they completed the Wechsler Intelligence Scale for Children (WISC).

Results:

Among several other analyses, the researchers compared performance at 6 and 11 years for each of the different groups. These findings are shown in Figure 1-2. Statistical analyses revealed few differences between the UK sample and Romanian children who had experienced institutional deprivation, but had been adopted when young (< 6 months). However, Romanian children who had been adopted after 6 months fared worse, and particularly badly if they had been adopted when over 2 years old. Although there was some evidence from this and other analyses suggesting that this group, who had experienced deprivation for the longest, showed some 'catch up' at 11 years (again see Figure 1-2).

Discussion:

The findings from this study point to the importance of enduring deprivation in the early years. For the youngest adoptees from Romania, the effects of deprivation appeared less marked. However, children who had been adopted later (after 6 months) were profoundly affected by deprivation in terms of cognitive functioning (specifically, performance on intelligence tests) up to 10 years later! Not only does this demonstrate how important a caring and stimulating social environment is for child development, it also suggests that before 6 months the child may be less affected by the social aspects of this environment at least, and that after 6 months a sensitive period of development ensues in which children ideally need a supportive and stable socioemotional environment.

Note: For discussion of some applications and implications of this research, see Rutter et al. (2009).

Cultural contexts

Researchers who emphasize contextual influences on development have studied a range of settings, including the home, the neighbourhood and the school. Examination of the contribution that context makes to child development has also led to increased interest in how culture relates to development. We know that children who grow up on a farm in China, in a kibbutz in Israel, or in a suburb of a city like Berlin have very different kinds of experiences that could influence their development. For example, in some cultures, children are encouraged to walk very early and are given opportunities to exercise their new motor skills. In other cultures, infants are carried or swaddled for long periods of time, which reduces their chance to walk until they are older. Examining development across cultures provides information about variation in the range of human potential and expression that may emerge in different circumstances of growth (Rogoff, 2003).

Comparing development across cultures, as well as being a valuable way of understanding how development can vary, also provides big clues to the role of the (cultural) environment on the development of our psychological abilities (Neilsen & Haun, 2016). It turns out that even some of the basic abilities which we take for granted vary considerably across different cultures (Bremner et al., 2016; Caparos et al., 2012; Linnell et al., 2018; Varnum et al., 2010).

The biological perspective

Whenever we develop, in whatsoever way, something biological is changing. Put another way, without a biological body, brain and nervous system, we could not develop at all! Given this you might be surprised to hear that up until rather recently, many developmental psychologists rejected the idea that we could learn much about development by considering biology. This kind of opinion is becoming less and less frequent as more technologies become available for advancing our understanding of the development of brain structure and function (we will discuss this in Chapter 5). However, even with the advent of new brain imaging techniques, some resistance remains. This is, to some extent quite understandable. Is it really meaningful to describe the emerging attachment relationship between a parent and a child at the level of neurons and chemical neurotransmitters? In one sense, no, and certainly you might find it hard to persuade a new parent of the importance of this particular perspective.

These days, however, developmental psychologists are much more ready to acknowledge that a biological perspective on development is crucial. This is because, as we have already stated, development and the interaction of our inheritance and environment does happen at the level of neurons and patterns of functional brain activity. And because there are certain ways in which brains and neurons behave and develop, these 'biological constraints' exert an influence on the development of our behaviour, our social relationships and our cognitive abilities.

The ecological perspective

One approach that has sought, from a psychological perspective, to connect the influence of different spheres of life is the ecological perspective. The ecological perspective stresses the importance of understanding not only the relationships between the developing organism (e.g., the child) and various environmental systems (e.g., the family and the community), but also the relationships among these environmental systems.

Urie Bronfenbrenner (1979; Bronfenbrenner & Morris, 2006), a major advocate of the ecological perspective, provides a theoretical framework that describes the layers of environmental or contextual systems that impact child development. Environmental systems range from the most direct or immediate settings in the child's experience, such as the family or peer group, to more remote contexts of the child's life, such as the society's systems of values and of law. The *microsystem* is the setting in which the child lives and interacts with the people and institutions closest to her. The *mesosystem* comprises the interrelations among the components of the microsystem. Thus, parents interact with teachers and the school system,

> **ecological perspective**
> A perspective that stresses the importance of understanding not only the relationships between organisms and various environmental systems but also the relations among such systems themselves.

both family members and peers may maintain relations with a religious institution, and so forth. The *exosystem* is composed of settings that impinge on a child's development but with which the child has largely indirect contact. For example, a parent's work may affect the child's life if it requires the parent to travel a great deal or work late into the night. The *macrosystem* represents the ideological and institutional patterns of a particular culture or subculture. Finally, these four systems change over time, a process that Bronfenbrenner refers to as the *chronosystem*. Over time, both the child and his environment undergo change, and change can originate within the individual (e.g., puberty, severe illness) or in the external world (e.g., the birth of a sibling, parental divorce or even war). For Bronfenbrenner, development involves the interaction of a changing child with the changing ecological context in all of its complexity.

The lifespan perspective

Another relatively recent perspective considers development across the lifespan. In the early years, most developmental psychologists focused their research efforts on understanding the changes in infants' and children's behaviour and reasoning. This was partly because it was assumed that in the childhood years change was most pronounced, so to study development through childhood maximized the chances of finding change and identifying the processes that underlie it. However, increasingly, many researchers have felt that the focus on the early years of development is too narrow and may neglect some aspects of development that happen beyond childhood and through an individual's adult life. In Chapter 16, we discuss some of the main features of adult development.

> **lifespan perspective**
> A view of development as a process that continues throughout the life cycle, from infancy through adulthood and old age.
>
> **age cohort** People born within the same generation.

The lifespan perspective also incorporates historical factors that may influence psychological development (Baltes et al., 2006). This phenomenon is generally referred to as an *age cohort effect*; the term age cohort means a group of individuals who were born in the same year or during the same general historical period of time. As cohorts develop, they share the same historical experiences. For instance, children born at certain times may have experienced their teenage and early adult years against a backdrop of considerable social upheaval. These shared experiences may lead to specific and distinctive problems for that cohort, such as PTSD (post-traumatic stress disorder) in former servicemen who have experienced conflict, or societies where there has been rapid social change that has led to subsequent changes in family structures, relationships and roles. Thus a lifespan perspective points to the need to consider a different sort of context – a historical one – when conducting and evaluating research.

Psychology and developmental psychology

The lifespan approach looks at the continued social and cognitive development through later life.
© Radius Images/Alamy

A final and important context for developmental psychology is within research in psychology as a discipline. Developmental psychology is one of the central areas of research and interest in the discipline and as a consequence there is often a symbiotic relation between developmental and other research.

In many ways it makes little sense for developmental psychologists to study development if we do not know where that is heading. Without an understanding of the mature (adult) state of our abilities, a careful scientific study of development can end up going down blind alleys. The bigger picture of psychology more generally is required to make sense of what we study and observe.

However, developmental psychology is also crucial for other domains of psychology. For instance, social psychologists who have studied how people behave in groups have often used children as participants to explore how processes operate (e.g., Sherif & Sherif, 1953). Many contemporary developmental psychologists who study children's knowledge of groups use social psychological theories to better understand developmental processes (e.g., Killen & Rutland, 2011). Models of language processing from cognitive psychology have informed developmental research aimed at improving children's reading and language skills, and advances in neuroscience demonstrate how the developing brain processes and encodes experiences to produce more advanced, adult-like psychological functioning. Developmental psychology is central to so much in psychology because, just as every person has a developmental history, so almost every psychological process has developed over time. Understanding development therefore offers a unique and fundamentally important perspective on human understanding and behaviour.

SUMMARY

Developmental psychology attempts to uncover the processes that underlie age-related change in growth, behaviour, knowledge and learning. In the past developmental psychologists often aligned themselves with either an empiricist or a nativist position. However, most modern developmentalists recognize the importance of both inheritance and environmental influences. Many psychologists are concerned with discovering the ways in which inheritance and environmental factors interact to produce developmental change.

Developmental psychologists address a number of questions about development, considering whether development should be described as a continuous process, whereby change takes place smoothly and gradually over time, or as a series of qualitatively different steps or stages. Additional questions concern whether development is domain general or domain specific in its influence, where development occurs, and whether there are particularly sensitive or critical periods of development.

Given that there are various different ways in which we can describe development, a number of different perspectives on development are available. Particularly important debates concern whether individual or contextual influences are more important in determining individual development. Most developmentalists agree that cultural contexts are important to consider.

Considering development at a biological level of explanation has not always been popular in developmental psychology. However, it is increasingly acknowledged that biology is a crucial part of the puzzle of how and why development happens the way it does.

A useful way to consider development is from an ecological perspective. This stresses the importance of understanding the relationship between the organism and various environmental systems, such as the family, school, community and culture. An ecological theoretical framework provided by Bronfenbrenner describes development as involving the interplay between children and their changing relationships with these different ecological systems – the microsystem, mesosystem, exosystem, macrosystem and chronosystem. The child's subjective experience of, or understanding of, the environment and the child's active role in modifying the environment are important aspects of this perspective.

Recently, historical perspectives have examined the contribution of cohort events to development. Psychologists who view development from a lifespan perspective are particularly interested in the effects of historical events on human development. In closing we emphasize that it is particularly important to take into account what we know about mature psychological functioning from domains such as cognitive and social psychology. If we do not know where development is heading to it is difficult to make sense of it!

1. What themes of development do you think are most important and why?

2. Pick a psychological ability and consider it from the ecological perspective. Can you work out what the most important ecological systems will be in the context of Bronfenbrenner's theory?

Explore and Discuss

Recommended Reading

Classic

Bronfenbrenner, U. (1986). Ecology of the family as a context for human development: research perspectives. *Developmental Psychology, 22*, 723–742.

Contemporary

Masten, A. S. (2015). *Ordinary magic: Resilience in development*. New York: Guilford Press.

Rutter, M. (2006). *Genes and behavior: Nature–nurture interplay explained*. Oxford: Blackwell Publishing.

Siegler, R. S. (2016). Continuity and change in the field of cognitive development and in the perspectives of one cognitive developmentalist. *Child Development Perspectives, 10*(2), 128–133.

CHAPTER 2
Theories in Developmental Psychology

Introduction

'If you want to get ahead, get a theory.'

This quotation is actually the title of a paper written by Annette Karmiloff-Smith and Barbel Inhelder (1975). Rather than instructing psychologists on how to conduct scientific investigations, this paper actually addresses how young children develop theories in order to take an active role in shaping their own learning until they settle on the best one (in this case the children try several different approaches to solving how to balance a set of scales). But the point is well taken with respect to both children's own development and the process of undertaking research into children's development. Rather than passively observing and measuring the world around us (we might be waiting for ever for something interesting to occur), developmental scientists propose theories that can be tested in order to make the progress in understanding of development quicker.

THE ROLE OF THEORIES IN DEVELOPMENTAL PSYCHOLOGY

As we explained in Chapter 1, developmental psychologists undertake their work in order to answer two key questions: (i) to describe developmental change, and (ii) to explain developmental change. The job of theories of developmental psychology is to advance coherent and plausible solutions to these questions about how and why developmental change occurs. Such theories can then be taken out into the world or into the research lab to investigate their validity. As is the practice in other branches of psychology, and indeed other scientific disciplines, developmental scientists draw out predictions from theories and then empirically test those predictions in experiments or observations in order to determine whether or not the theory is correct. If the theory stands up well to this empirical testing, then further predictions are drawn out and tested. If the empirical test indicates that the theory is incorrect, then the theory is adapted or rejected altogether. Thus, developmental theories do two important things. First, they help organize and integrate existing information into coherent, interesting and plausible accounts of how children develop. Second, they generate testable hypotheses or predictions about children's behaviour.

Because theories stand or fall on the basis of scientific (empirical) findings, there is a sense in which they can be construed as ephemeral (short-lived) things, which are rejected and replaced as soon as research shows them to be incorrect. There is some truth to this, as developmental scientists are quick to place their bets on the view that is best supported by current empirical data, and as empirical data are accumulated, this frequently changes our understanding of development. However, in some situations alternative theories can be more long-lasting or co-exist. Theories which have a longer relevance often have a broader scope that attempts to account for or describe more than one developmental phenomenon (e.g., if it explains aspects of both language development and mathematical development). Piaget's constructionist argument is a good example of this. As we shall describe later, Piaget attempted to explain a great many aspects of cognitive development as being due to a process of active construction by the child. Because such broader-scope theories do not stand or fall on the basis of a single empirical observation they outlast findings that show just one element to be incorrect.

There are, however, reasons other than scope for why some theories outlast others. One of these reasons is the novelty of the explanatory approach that they offer. Across the history of developmental psychology there have been several novel theoretical contributions in which a theorist has offered a new way of describing or explaining developmental change, which had not been considered before. An example of this might be the relatively recent emergence of connectionist and dynamic systems models of development. Before the emergence of these explanatory models, stage-changes in development (of the sort described by Piaget) were explained in terms of qualitative changes in knowledge or thought (e.g., sudden insights). The mildly troubling question concerns where these qualitative shifts come from.

Piaget and others, of course, had answers to this question. However, the emergence of dynamic systems and connectionist models demonstrated for the first time that stage-wise shifts can come about due to the interaction of several small-scale quantitative developments in learning and other factors (e.g., learning interacting with the physical sizes of the limbs). Because these new advances in conceptualizing the how and why of developmental change are novel and deserve to be considered among the alternatives when seeking to explain any given development, they continue to be referred to as important and influential theories.

In addition, it is not uncommon for contrasting developmental theories to co-exist. For instance, we have invoked Theory of Mind or executive function explanations to account for children's failures to understand others' false beliefs (a false belief is a belief that someone thinks something that is incorrect, perhaps because they lack some knowledge information that the child has). Contrasting theories may provide different accounts for the same observation or phenomenon, and in such cases researchers will often develop experiments to test out which of the two competing explanations is more adequate. Often, however, contrasting theories may co-exist because they account for different elements of a broader phenomenon or aspect of behaviour. Co-existing theories can, eventually, be compared and evaluated once more information is gathered or known, or once researchers can agree on specifics or have agreed and reliable observations.

For the next part of this chapter we will describe the key aspects of some of the most influential theoretical approaches to explaining human development. Because theories themselves develop out of the current state of knowledge in which they exist, we have ordered them in this chapter according to a rough chronology of the influence they have had on the field of developmental psychology over the past 120 years.

ORIGINS OF THOUGHT ABOUT HUMAN DEVELOPMENT

Philosophers had been considering questions about psychological development well before the origins of psychology as a scientific field of study. An important question among philosophers in the seventeenth century concerned whether humans require experience of the world in order to perceive and understand it. John Locke (1632–1704), in a similar vein to other 'British empiricist' philosophers like Berkeley and Hume, argued that infants are born into the world *tabula rasa* – that is, as a 'blank slate'. This metaphor is meant to suggest that because they have been unable to learn from the outside world, newborn infants understand nothing of it when they emerge from their mother's uterus. On the other side of the argument were 'rationalist' philosophers (including Leibniz and Descartes), who argued that the mind imposes some kind of order on the environment in order to be able to comprehend it. This argument closely resembles the tension between 'nativist' accounts of development, which emphasize nature and inheritance, and more 'empiricist' positions, which emphasize the role of nurture and environment in development.

Important foundational figure in developmental psychology: William James.
© Universal History Archive/Getty Images

At the end of the nineteenth century, when psychology became established as a scientific discipline in its own right, the question of nature and nurture was similarly on the minds of the early psychologists. William James (1890) famously took a rather empiricist position on the origins of perceptual abilities in babies (see Chapter 6), stating that newborn infants perceive only 'a blooming buzzing confusion'. This 'blank slate' assumption was later echoed in the behaviourist school, which we will discuss next. As we shall see, the principal opponents to this empiricist view were the maturationists who, drawing much on Charles Darwin's ideas about human evolution and natural selection (see Chapter 1), suggested that development is shaped more by a genetic blueprint than the environment.

BEHAVIOURISM AND MATURATIONISM IN THE EARLY TWENTIETH CENTURY

Behaviourism

> In Chapter 1, we described how a major discussion in developmental psychology concerns whether development is characterized as continuous (gradual) or discontinuous (sudden). Behaviourism argued that development was characterized by continuous and gradual changes in behaviour.

behaviourism A school of psychology prominent in the early twentieth century, which emphasized the role of learning in human behaviour and attempted to describe behaviour in such terms.

classical conditioning A type of learning in which two stimuli are repeatedly presented together until individuals learn to respond to the unfamiliar stimulus in the same way they respond to the familiar stimulus.

The behaviourist approach to development is exemplified in the work of John B. Watson, Edward Lee Thorndike, Ivan Pavlov and B.F. Skinner. Behaviourism emerged as an important school of thought in psychology in the early twentieth century. Behaviourists focused on the learning of behaviours in animals and humans. As such their approach is not specifically a developmental one. In fact, perhaps the most well-cited behaviourists spent more of their time working with mature animals (rats, dogs, pigeons) than with human children. Nonetheless, the behaviourists (John Watson is a particularly prominent example) argued that the principles of learning which they observed in mature adults (animal or human) also play a fundamental role in development. The key tenet of their position is that changes in behaviour are driven by experience, and that these changes in behaviour happen gradually and continuously (rather than in shifts or stages, such as when we have sudden insight into a problem). The behaviourist position on development is perhaps best summed up by the following quote from John Watson:

> *Give me a dozen healthy infants . . . and I'll guarantee to take any one at random and train him to become any type of specialist I might select – doctor, lawyer, artist . . . even beggar man and thief, regardless of his talents, penchants, and race of his ancestors. (Watson, 1930, p. 104)*

But what were these learning principles that the behaviourists considered so important? The two key forms of learning they advocated were classical conditioning and operant conditioning. Classical conditioning was first discovered by Pavlov, in the early twentieth century, while he was investigating the physiology of digestion in dogs. He was presenting food to dogs and measured their salivary response, when he made an accidental but important discovery. He noticed that, with repeated testing, the dogs began to salivate before the food was presented, such as when they heard the footsteps of the approaching experimenter. Pavlov concluded from this and further investigations that the dog was able to learn an association between two stimuli (in this case food and arriving footsteps) and behave accordingly.

Rather infamously, Watson and Rayner (1920) used Pavlov's concept of classical conditioning to examine whether other behaviours, and even emotions such as fear, could be conditioned in children. They worked with an 11-month-old infant named Albert. Watson and Rayner presented Albert with a white rat to which he displayed no sign of fear. Later, in the learning phase of their experiment at the same time as presenting the rat to Albert they hit a steel bar with a hammer, making a loud clang. The noise of course scared Albert and made him cry. After several of these learning episodes even the sight of the rat on its own made Albert cry.

Unfortunately for Watson and Rayner, in addition to their having conducted a particularly unethical experiment, their results were not very conclusive. After several attempts to condition fear in Albert to several animals (including the rat again, but also a rabbit and a dog), Albert showed little reaction to all of these animals in a different room (Harris, 1979). Records do not tell us whether Albert went on to experience phobias in later life.

Watson and Rayner examine how Little Albert reacts to a furry mask.
Source: Courtesy of Professor Benjamin Harris

Edward Thorndike and B.F. Skinner examined another form of learning, which is most commonly referred to as operant conditioning (you will sometimes hear it referred to as instrumental conditioning). Operant conditioning is a type of learning in which new behaviours are learned in response to a specific stimulus. Importantly, operant conditioning is controlled by a manipulation of the consequences of behaviour. Thorndike and Skinner found that by providing a reward for a particular behaviour in response to a stimulus, they could encourage that 'stimulus-response' pairing later. It was first studied in animals (e.g., cats, rats and pigeons), but was later applied to children's behaviour. There are different kinds of reward. Positive reinforcement could be a food pellet, or something else with positive connotation for the participant. On the other hand, punishment or withdrawal of privileges can decrease the chance that the same behaviour will be produced in a given context.

Inspired by their success with animals, Skinner and Thorndike went on to advocate the use of operant conditioning to guide the way children develop. Indeed Skinner predicted positive changes in society if such conditioning was introduced in a widespread way. Behaviourism continues to have an important influence on modern developmental psychology. An instance of operant conditioning being used to change the behaviour of children is provided by Patterson and his colleagues (Patterson, 1982; Patterson & Capaldi, 1991). They showed that punishment of children's aggressive behaviour by 'time out' – a brief period of isolation away from other family members – can help diminish aggressive behaviour. Operant conditioning has been incorporated into many applied programmes to help teachers and parents change children's behaviour, including hyperactivity (restlessness, inattention, impulsivity) and aggression.

> As we shall describe in Chapter 10 it has been possible to demonstrate classical conditioning in human infants in a much more humane way than that which Watson and Rayner attempted.

> **operant conditioning**
> A type of learning that depends on the consequences of behaviour; rewards increase the likelihood that a behaviour will recur, whereas punishment decreases that likelihood.

> **maturational approach**
> An early approach to explaining development in terms of maturational timetables, predetermined by genetic inheritance.

Maturational theory

At the beginning of the twentieth century, the major opposition to the behaviourist school of thought concerning children's development had come to be known as the maturational approach. 'Maturationists' argued that, far from being entirely shaped by experience (as suggested by John Watson), the emergence of infants' and children's abilities are to a large extent determined by our genetic inheritance. Inspired by Darwin, Arnold Gessell and Myrtle McGraw (both key figures in the maturational approach) they examined the directions (or trajectories) of development of certain skills. Observing that skills appear to unfold developmentally in particular orders, they argued that these 'biological timetables' of development were set out in advance by the genes of our species.

> The maturationists mapped out the developmental trajectories of growth and of developing motor skills (see Chapters 4 and 7).

As we will see in Chapters 4 and 7, the body, and our ability to undertake certain motor skills, develops in certain directions or trajectories (e.g., an ability to control the hands develops after an ability to control the neck and torso). Gessell (Gessell & Ames, 1940) argued that this was due to a maturational timetable inherited in our genetic code. Further evidence for this important role of inheritance was supplied by an influential study of two identical twins (Jimmy and Johnny) by McGraw (1935). McGraw observed that, even though one of the twins was given additional motor stimulation, Jimmy and Johnny's motor development nonetheless remained closely linked. Maturational explanations have been applied throughout developmental psychology. For instance, maturational theories have been very influential in explaining the emergence of children of different temperaments (see Chapter 7).

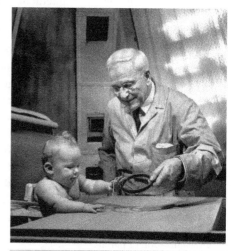

Arnold Gessell – a maturational theorist.
© Herbert Gehr/Getty Images

Even though the maturationists and the behaviourists represent quite different sides of the nature–nurture argument, it is important to acknowledge that they, like modern developmental scientists, adopted variations on a moderate position, acknowledging that nature and nurture have a role, but varying as to how much importance they placed on those relative roles. As we shall see, perhaps the most important advance on this position was that of Piaget, who next attempted to understand exactly how nature and nurture interact. However, before moving on to Piaget we will discuss some important theoretical approaches in developmental psychology that were being formulated at the same time as the maturational and behaviourist positions.

PSYCHODYNAMICS AND ETHOLOGY

The psychodynamic approach

In the early 1900s, Sigmund Freud introduced his theory of psychodynamics. Freud's theory of psychodynamics is best known in the context of treatment of psychological disorders. Freud was particularly concerned with attempting to solve mental turmoils, and psychoanalysis – a particular tradition in the study and treatment of psychological disorders – emerged from his work. Freud's psychodynamic theory, rather than addressing particular behaviours and abilities, attempts to discern and describe the more internal motivations and personalities of individual people. Importantly for us, he took the view that adults' motivations and personalities were largely formed through the experiences of infancy and childhood. This theory is very complex and covers many aspects of psychological functioning. Here we concentrate on the parts of this theory that have influenced developmental psychology.

For Freud, the developing personality consists of three interrelated parts: the id, the ego and the superego. The roles of these three components of personality change across development as the infant, who is largely under the control of the id, or instinctual drives, gradually becomes more controlled by the ego. The ego is the rational and reality-bound aspect, and attempts to gratify needs through socially appropriate behaviour. With further development, the third component of personality, the superego, emerges when the child *internalizes* – that is, accepts and absorbs – parental or societal morals, values and roles, and develops a *conscience*, or the ability to apply moral values to her own acts.

To Freud, personality development – that is, changes in the organization and interaction of the id, ego and superego – involves five stages (see Table 2-1). In the first, the *oral* stage, the young infant is preoccupied with pleasurable activities such as eating, sucking and biting. In the second to third year, the child enters the *anal* stage and learns to postpone personal gratification, such as the pleasure of expelling faeces, as he is trained to use the toilet. Following the anal stage, the *phallic* stage begins, and curiosity about sexual anatomy and sexuality appears. Freud saw this stage as critical to the formation of gender identity. During the *latency* period, from about 6 years of age to puberty, sexual drives are temporarily submerged and children avoid relationships with peers of the other gender. In the last stage, the *genital* period, sexual desires emerge and are directed towards peers, a topic we return to in Chapter 12. The genital period encompasses much of later life. We include some later periods of life in the table to give you an idea of progression across the lifespan.

One of Freud's primary contributions to developmental psychology is his emphasis on how early experiences, especially in the first 6 years of life, influence later development. For him, the way in which the child negotiates the oral, anal and phallic stages has a profound impact on emotional development and the adult personality. For example, infants who have unsatisfied needs for oral stimulation may be more likely to smoke as adults. Although current developmental theory does not adopt

psychodynamic theory In this view of development, which is derived from Freudian theory, development occurs in discrete stages and is determined largely by biologically based drives shaped by encounters with the environment and through the interaction of the personality's three components: the id, ego and superego.

id In Freudian theory, the person's instinctual drives; the first component of the personality to evolve, the id operates on the basis of the *pleasure principle*.

ego In Freudian theory, the rational, controlling component of the personality, which tries to satisfy needs through appropriate, socially acceptable behaviours.

superego In Freudian theory, the personality component that is the repository of the child's internalization of parental or societal values, morals and roles.

Table 2-1 Freud's and Erikson's developmental stages

Stage of development		
Age period	Freudian	Eriksonian
0–1	**Oral.** Focus on eating and taking things into the mouth	**Infancy.** Task: to develop *basic trust* in oneself and others Risk: *mistrust* of others and lack of self-confidence
1–3	**Anal.** Emphasis on toilet training; first experience with discipline and authority	**Early childhood.** Task: to learn self-control and establish *autonomy* Risk: *shame* and *doubt* about one's own capabilities
3–6	**Phallic.** Increase in sexual urges arouses curiosity and alerts children to gender differences; period is critical to formation of gender identity	**Play age.** Task: to develop *initiative* in mastering environment Risk: feelings of *guilt* over aggressiveness and daring
6–12	**Latency.** Sexual urges repressed; emphasis on education and the beginnings of concern for others	**School age.** Task: to develop *industry* Risk: feelings of *inferiority* over real or imagined failure to master tasks
12–20		**Adolescence.** Task: to achieve a sense of *identity* Risk: *role confusion* over who and what individual wants to be
20–30	**Genital.** Altruistic love joins selfish love; need for reproduction of species underlies adoption of adult responsibilities	**Young adulthood.** Task: to achieve *intimacy* with others Risk: shaky identity may lead to avoidance of others and *isolation*
30–65		**Adulthood.** Task: to express oneself through *generativity* Risk: inability to create children, ideas or products may lead to *stagnation*
65+		**Mature age.** Task: to achieve a sense of *integrity* Risk: doubts and unfulfilled desires may lead to *despair*

Freud's exact views about early experience, the idea that Freud introduced – namely, that events in infancy and childhood have a formative impact on later development – remains an important theme in the study of social and emotional development. Psychodynamic theory has also been particularly influential in certain areas of applied and clinical psychology, as discussed in Chapter 15.

Freud had many followers who went on to devise their own theories of development, many of which contain concepts that stem from Freud's ideas. Erik Erikson devised one of the most prominent of these theories in his **psychosocial theory** of human development. In Erikson's theory, development is seen as proceeding through a series of eight stages that unfold across the lifespan. Each stage is characterized by the personal and social tasks that the individual must accomplish, as well as the risks the individual confronts if she fails to proceed through the stages successfully (see Table 2-1). Of these ideas, the most influential for current research in child development is the stage of adolescence, in which the child focuses on identity development and seeks to establish a clear and stable sense of self.

Another central contribution that Freud's thinking makes to contemporary developmental psychology is the vital role that emotional attachment early in life, especially to the mother, has in socioemotional development. We will cover this in more detail in Chapter 7 but we will here cover an important figure who played an important role in shaping the psychoanalytic approach to address our understanding of early attachment – John Bowlby.

> **psychosocial theory**
> Erikson's theory of development, which sees children developing through a series of stages largely through accomplishing tasks that involve them in interaction with their social environment.

Sigmund Freud (1865–1939) and Erik Erikson (1902–1990). Freud was the father of psychodynamic theory. Erikson studied psychology in Vienna with Freud. His psychosocial theory continues to be influential today, especially for those who hold a lifespan perspective on development.
© Time & Life Pictures/Getty Images (L) © Corbis Historical (R)

Ethological theory and John Bowlby

ethological theory
A theory which holds
that behaviour must be
viewed and understood
as occurring in a
particular context and
as having adaptive or
survival value.

Ethological theory, which was developed by biologists, contends that behaviour must be viewed and understood as occurring in a particular context, and as having adaptive or survival value. Since Charles Darwin introduced evolutionary theory (the idea that we have evolved as a species to be well suited to survive in our environment), other scientists have sought to understand both the evolution of behaviour and its adaptive, or survival, value to the species exhibiting it. You may have heard of a behaviour exhibited by young ducklings in which they appear to follow around an adult of an entirely different species (see photo). German ethologist Konrad Lorenz (1937) named this behaviour imprinting.

Lorenz described imprinting as a sudden, biologically primed form of attachment. It occurs in some bird species, including ducks and geese, and in a few mammals, such as shrews. Imprinting involves a critical period. In mallard ducklings, the strongest imprinting occurs within a day after hatching, and by two days the capacity to imprint is lost (Hess, 1959). Thus, in some species, offspring must be exposed to parents within hours or days after entering the world in order to attach to them. The important point about imprinting for ethologists is that despite the fact it can go wrong in some instances, it is a highly adaptive behaviour in that it serves to create a strong proximity between infant and parent.

Psychologists have also adopted ethological theory by also including mental processes like perception, cognition and emotion in this list of 'behaviours' which are adaptive and have survival value (Hinde, 1994; Bjorklund & Pelligrini, 2002). And as we will discuss in Chapter 7, some 'evolutionary' approaches to developmental psychology have suggested that some maladaptive behaviours (like adolescent risk taking) might also be explained by historical ethological pressures (Machluf & Bjorklund, 2015).

Central to the ethological line of thought is the necessity to view and understand the behaviour and mental processes of an organism in relation to its biology and the ecosystem in which it functions. So it is important to take into account environment and needs at different stages of development. For instance, the needs of a newborn baby in the arms of a parent are very different from those of a young child in a playground.

*Konrad Lorenz and a group of ducklings
who have imprinted to him.*
© Thomas D. McAvoy/Getty Images

Ethologists' basic method of study is the observation of children in their natural surroundings, and their goals are to develop detailed descriptions and classifications of behaviour. For developmental psychologists, ethological theory is useful for understanding that many behaviours seen across a range of cultures, such as smiling and crying, may have a biological basis and play an important role in ensuring that caregivers meet children's needs. For example, crying can be viewed as an 'elicitor' of parental behaviour; it serves to communicate that a child is distressed or hungry. It thus has clear survival value, for it ensures that parents give the young infant the kind of attention she needs for adequate development.

Although human ethologists view many elicitors, such as crying, as biologically based, they also assume that these types of behaviour are modified by environmentally based experiences. For example, children may learn to mask their emotions by smiling even when they are unhappy (Kromm, Färber, & Holodynski, 2015; McDowell, O'Neil, & Parke, 2000). Thus, modern ethologists view children as open to learning and using input from the environment; they are not solely captives of their biological roots.

One particular focus of ethological theory has been the behaviours in human infants and children that are 'species specific' (unique to the human species) and that may play an important role in ensuring that others meet children's basic needs, which are critical to survival. Studies have found, for example, that emotional expressions of joy, sadness, disgust and anger are similar across a wide range of cultures (Ekman et al., 1987; LaFreniere, 2000). Others have argued that imitation is a behaviour which humans are specialized in, and which enables us to learn particular things from our environment (Csibra & Gergely, 2009; Meltzoff & Prinz, 2002), although this idea is rather controversial (Farmer, Ciaunica, & Hamilton, 2018; Heyes, 2016).

Perhaps the area of developmental psychology that has been most greatly influenced by the ethological approach is the study of early relationships. The key ethological theorist who considered the adaptive value of early human relationships was John Bowlby (see Research Close-Up). Bowlby proposed the maternal deprivation hypothesis, in which he suggested that attachment bonds between infant and parent in the first years of life are vital to ensure well-adjusted socioemotional development. As you will see in Chapter 7, although some of the details of Bowlby's account have been challenged, his ideas continue to be very important in our understanding of early emotional bonds.

> Bowlby's maternal deprivation hypothesis took a great deal of inspiration from ethology. Bowlby's approach set the scene for modern empirical research into parent–infant attachment (see Chapter 7).

As well as being rooted in the psychoanalytic tradition beginning with Freud, Bowlby's maternal deprivation hypothesis took much inspiration from ethological theory. The idea that a certain kind of experience (bonding with a parent) at a critical stage in development is vital for the normal development of attachment relationships can be traced back to ethologists like Lorenz's observations concerning imprinting.

BOX 2-1   44 Thieves

Research close-up

Source: Based on Bowlby (1944).

Introduction:

In 1944 John Bowlby, a famous psychoanalyst, was following up his ideas about how maternal deprivation early in life could result in problems in forming close relationships with others. Bowlby was particularly interested in, and had worked a great deal with, young adults who had difficulty with giving or receiving affection from others, and those who demonstrated delinquent behaviour. At the time in Britain, the vast majority of indictable criminal offences were for theft of some kind, and many (about half) of those offences were committed by people under 21 years of age. In order to examine whether there was any evidence for his view that delinquent behaviour was caused by maternal deprivation of some kind, Bowlby conducted a study of the backgrounds of 44 juvenile delinquent thieves.

Method:

Bowlby conducted clinical interviews with 44 juveniles who had been referred to a 'child guidance' programme in London because they had been suspected of theft (not all had actually been convicted). Bowlby also selected a control group of children who had also been referred to the child guidance programme, but not because of theft. The control group were similarly composed in terms of age and intelligence to the 'theft' group. Bowlby reported his observations concerning the psychopathology of 44 juvenile delinquent thieves, and examined the links between their delinquency, their psychopathology and the environment in which they had grown up. Bowlby specifically attended to long separations from the children's mother early in life.

Results:

The central finding was that a substantial proportion of the juvenile thieves (17 of 44) had been separated from their mothers for longer than six months in the first five years of their life. In the control group only two of the children had had such a separation. Bowlby also reported that several children in the thieving group showed 'affectionless psychopathy' and, of those, 12 had experienced maternal deprivation for longer than six months before the age of five.

Discussion:

This study, among other observations, reinforced Bowlby's view that maternal deprivation in early life leads to socioemotional difficulties, particularly in forming relationships with others. He was particularly concerned with the strong relationship between maternal deprivation and affectionless psychopathy.

Although this study is an important contribution to the literature, there are a number of problems of interpretation. Could there be a different direction of causation at play than the one Bowlby thought important? For instance, it is possible that the affectionless psychopaths had inherited those traits from their parents (including their mother). In which case it might not be surprising that their mothers spent time apart from them early in life. In current theoretical approaches, researchers tend to consider how genetic and environmental contributions can work together in these kinds of situations. Perhaps the affectionless psychopathy Bowlby observed was due to both maternal deprivation and inherited traits (Price & Jaffee, 2008). Also, as we shall see in Chapter 7, although Bowlby's maternal deprivation hypothesis has been influential, a number of aspects of it have been challenged and revised.

GRAND THEORIES OF COGNITIVE DEVELOPMENT

Researchers interested in cognitive development attempt to describe the development of internal mental processes such as memory, logic and language. In the early to mid-twentieth century, behaviourism was the dominant force in explaining not just development, but behaviour in young and mature animals and humans alike. However, whilst behaviourism placed little importance on internal mental processes, more and more psychologists began to argue that there was more to psychology than simple associative learning mechanisms such as classical and operant conditioning.

One set of observations which were a particular problem for behaviourists concerned more creative kinds of learning which cognitive psychologists would now call spontaneous (or insightful) problem solving. Some researchers (e.g., Köhler, 1947) even began to demonstrate that animals could solve problems by thinking about them (rather than by being shaped by their experiences, which was the basic tenet of the behaviourist position). This movement towards a consideration of internal mental processes led to the birth of cognitive psychology (Neisser, 1967). However, perhaps the most important figure in sealing the doom of behaviourism as an all-encompassing explanation for psychology came from a developmental perspective. Jean Piaget, as we shall see, described sudden (insightful) shifts in knowledge in young children in which he argued that they moved from one developmental stage to the next.

Sudden developments in ability or behaviour were not well accounted for by mainstream behaviourist positions in the mid-nineteenth century. However, before we discuss Piaget's explanation for qualitative (stage-wise) developmental change, we will cover one approach to explaining development which emerged straight out of behaviourism, and was able to account for a wider range of developmental phenomena: social learning theory.

Social learning theory

According to social learning theory, children learn not only through classical and operant conditioning but also by observing and imitating others in what has been called observational learning (Bandura, 1989, 1997). In his classic studies, Albert Bandura showed that children exposed to the aggressive behaviour of another person were likely to imitate that behaviour. For example, after a group of nursery school children watched an adult punch a large Bobo doll (an inflated rubber doll that pops back up after being pushed), the children were more likely to attack and play aggressively with the doll than were a group of children who had not seen the model. Neither the adult model nor the children had received any reinforcement, yet the children learned specific behaviours.

social learning theory
A learning theory that stresses the importance of observation and imitation in the acquisition of new behaviours, with learning mediated by cognitive processes.

observational learning
Learning that occurs through observing the behaviour of others.

Further research on how the process of imitation aids learning has revealed the important contribution of cognition to observational learning. Children do not imitate the behaviours of others blindly or automatically; rather, they select specific behaviours to imitate, and their imitation relies on how they process this information. According to Bandura, four cognitive processes govern how well a child will learn a new behaviour by observing another person (Figure 2-1). First, the child must *attend* to a model's behaviour. Second, the child must *retain* the observed behaviours in

Figure 2-1 Bandura's model of observational learning

According to Bandura, to produce a behaviour that matches that of a model, a child goes through four sets of processes. Her ability to attend to the modelled behaviour is influenced by factors in her own experience and in the situation; her skill in retaining what she has observed reflects a collection of cognitive skills; her reproduction of the behaviour depends on other cognitive skills, including the use of feedback from others; and her motivation to produce the behaviour is influenced by various incentives, her own standards and her tendency to compare herself with others.
Source: Based on Bandura (1989).

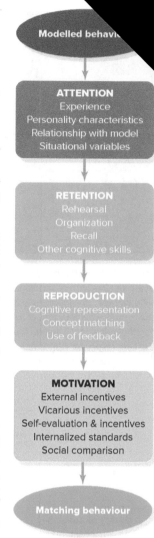

memory. Third, the child must have the capacity, physically and intellectually, to *reproduce* the observed behaviour. Fourth, the child must be *motivated*, that is, have a reason to reproduce the behaviour.

As we shall see in Chapter 10, observational learning, and particularly imitation, continues to be a topic of much debate and controversy. As an important means by which we can learn from our social and cultural environments, these learning processes have wide-reaching implications across and beyond developmental psychology. As well as debating questions about precisely when and how imitation becomes available to infants and children as a learning mechanism (e.g., Meltzoff & Prinz, 2002; Heyes, 2016a), researchers and theorists have also argued about whether there is more to imitation than is suggested in Bandura's model (e.g., Gergely, Bekkering, & Király, 2002; Heyes, 2016b).

Piaget's constructionism

As we have already mentioned, perhaps the most famous theoretical account of cognitive development was proposed by Jean Piaget, a developmental psychologist based in Geneva. The body of work Piaget published as a result of his research led him to become probably the most influential developmental psychologist of the twentieth century. As we will be discussing Piaget's theories in great detail in Chapter 9 we will only briefly introduce his ideas here.

Piaget began his own scientific research at a considerably younger age than most other people do. His primary interest was biology, and at the age of 10 he published his first scholarly article on the rare albino sparrow. As Piaget continued his studies, his interest in biology continued. However, he also became interested in philosophy, especially the study of knowledge, or *epistemology*. As a young man, Piaget pursued these interests by studying in Paris with Alfred Binet, who was working on the development of the first intelligence test (discussed in Chapter 11). As he helped Binet develop standardized IQ tests for children, Piaget made two important observations. First, he noticed that children of the same ages tended to get the same answers wrong. Second, he noticed that the errors of children of a particular age differed in systematic ways from those of older or younger children. Piaget's theory of cognitive development began to take shape as he thought about these errors; in particular, he thought they revealed distinct age-related ways of thinking and understanding the world. The key to understanding how children think, Piaget believed, was not whether they got the right answers but *how* they arrived at their answers.

Piagetian theory
A theory of cognitive development that sees the child as actively seeking new information.

A developmental psychologist at the Universities of Geneva and Lausanne, Switzerland, Jean Piaget (1896–1980) framed a theory of the child's cognitive development that has had great impact on developmental scientists, educators, and others concerned with the course and determinants of children's development.
© AFP/Getty Images

Lev Vygotsky (1895–1934) was a Byelorussian born psychologist who worked, predominantly in the former Soviet Union, at the Psychological Institute and founded the Laboratory for Abnormal Childhood in Moscow. He developed many ideas in developmental science including the idea of a 'zone of proximal development' for understanding children's psychological growth.
© Fine Art Images/Heritage Images/ Getty Images

sociocultural theory
A theory of development, proposed by Lev Vygotsky, that sees development as emerging from children's interactions with more skilled people, and the institutions and tools provided by their culture.

Piaget introduced a constructionist theory to describe intellectual development (e.g., Piaget, 1951). The origins of this theory can be observed from early in Piaget's career when he was working with Alfred Binet. He proposed that children's thinking changes *qualitatively* with age and that it differs from the way adults think. Piaget believed that cognitive development results from a process of development in which children actively construct their own development by coming up with theories and testing them. He believed that this predilection to actively acquire the environment (to construct abilities and knowledge) interacted with the experiences brought about by this activity in order to determine how the child develops. In a nutshell Piaget viewed children as 'little scientists' who actively seek to understand their world.

Piaget proposed that all children go through three periods of cognitive development, each characterized by qualitatively different ways of thinking. We outline these periods in detail in Chapter 9. In brief, though, Piaget described that infants rely on their sensory and motor abilities to learn about the world, preschool children rely more on mental structures and symbols, especially language. In the school years, children begin to rely more on logic and, in adolescence, children can reason about abstract ideas. According to Piaget, cognitive development is a process in which the child shifts from a focus on the self, immediate sensory experiences and simple problems, to a more complex, multifaceted and abstract understanding of the world.

Vygotsky and sociocultural development

One of the major criticisms of Piaget's approach was that he did not take enough into account the social environment of the child. Sociocultural theory places particular emphasis on the impact of social and cultural experience on child development. This approach traces many of its roots to the writings of Lev S. Vygotsky, a Russian psychologist who worked in the early part of the twentieth century (at a similar time to Piaget).

Vygotsky grew up in the early twentieth century, which was a time of tumultuous social change in Russia (Kozulin, 1990). In 1917, the year Vygotsky graduated from Moscow University, the Russian Revolution began and the entire society was in upheaval. After the Revolution, as Vygotsky launched his career as a psychologist and developed his theory, civil war and famine ravaged the country, and the entire social structure of the nation changed dramatically. Although some aspects of Vygotsky's life improved, others did not. At the time of his death at age 37 from tuberculosis, he had fallen into political disfavour in Stalinist Russia and his work was banned. As a result, it wasn't until the late 1970s that psychologists in the United States and other parts of the world began to explore Vygotsky's ideas (Wertsch & Tulviste, 1992).

Vygotsky's theory (e.g.,Vygotsky, 1978) proposes that the child's development is best understood in relation to social and cultural experience. Social interaction, in particular, is seen as a critical force in development. Through the assistance provided by more experienced people in the social environment, the child gradually learns to function intellectually on her own. Thus, the social world mediates individual cognitive development.

By emphasizing the socially mediated nature of cognitive processes, this approach offers new ways of assessing children's cognitive potential and of teaching reading, mathematics and writing (Brown & Campione, 1997; Hyson, Copple, & Jones, 2006). A vivid example in the classroom is peer tutoring, in which an older child helps a younger pupil learn to read, write, add, subtract, and so on.

Sociocultural theory has also increased our appreciation of the profound importance of cultural variation in development. The ways in which adults support and direct child development are influenced by culture, especially the values and practices that organize what and how adults and children think and work together, and use cultural tools to understand the world and solve cognitive problems. These tools are devised by cultures and they take a variety of forms, including language, mathematical symbols, literacy and technology. As children develop, different tools help them function more effectively in solving problems and understanding the world. Thus, tools of thinking, which are products of culture, become incorporated into the ways individuals think about and act in the world. We discuss this theory at greater length in Chapter 8. Throughout the book, many culturally based examples will touch back to this theory.

Nativist theories of cognitive development

Another group of modern theories of cognitive development have appealed to the idea that (some of) our cognitive abilities are innate, provided by our genetic inheritance. This is a direct extension of the arguments of the rationalist philosophers who we discussed at the outset of this chapter. One of the most important figures among nativist theories is Noam Chomsky, who argued that we inherit an innate mental structure which helps us to learn language.

> In Chapter 8 we will discuss how children learn language. Chomsky has argued that our inheritance provides us with a mental structure which enables us to do this.

Another kind of nativist account argues that we not only inherit a particular *mental structure*, but we are also born with innate *knowledge* about specific aspects of our worlds. This argument has been made particularly forcefully by Elizabeth Spelke in her 'core knowledge' account (see Chapter 9), which proposes that infants are born with knowledge of, among other things, the permanence and solidity of objects.

Nativist accounts of cognitive development obviously owe a lot to Darwin's theory of evolution, as the argument is that our inherited knowledge (and/or mental structure) has been provided through evolutionary selective forces. However, it is important to realize that Darwin and the theory of evolution play central roles in all modern theories of development, not just the modern nativist theories of Spelke and Chomsky. For instance, although one might consider behaviourism's emphasis on the role of experience in shaping development to be at odds with concepts of inheritance and evolution, behaviourism actually owes much to Darwin; behaviourism appeals to evolution as a means of explaining the learning mechanisms with which animals and humans adapt to their environments (Costall, 2004). As we have already seen, ethological theory also owes much to Darwin's theory of evolution as it seeks to understand how our inheritance provides us with adaptive behaviours.

Nativist theories of cognitive development can be described as having a particular relationship to evolutionary theory as they fall under the somewhat more narrow umbrella of evolutionary psychology. Evolutionary psychological theories can be contrasted with ethology as, rather than describing inherited behaviours, evolutionary psychologists have examined how our inheritance can play a role in the development of internal *cognitive processes*. Indeed, some of the leading proponents of evolutionary psychology argue that the critical components of human evolutionary change are in the areas of brain changes underlying cognitive functioning (Cosmides & Tooby, 1987).

> **evolutionary psychology**
> An approach which holds that critical components of psychological functioning reflect evolutionary changes and are critical to the survival of the species.

A number of modern nativist developmental theories are strongly influenced by an argument developed by Jerry Fodor in his book *Modularity of Mind* (Fodor, 1983). In this book, Fodor argued that many of the cognitive functions humans possess are subserved by modules that are especially designed to process specific kinds of information. A good example of such a module might be a specialized system for learning language, like the 'language acquisition device' proposed by Noam Chomsky (see Chapter 8). Fodor argued that such modules are 'computationally encapsulated', that is, they process information in the way they have been designed, but autonomously and out of the influence of other aspects of mental functions (and other modules).

In developmental terms it is easy to see how such modules could fit well with a nativist account of cognitive development. Our inheritance could specify cognitive modules, meaning that we just have to wait until the brain and body mature until such modules come into action and help us to think about the world in ways which evolution has prepared us for. A number of such arguments have been made. For example, evolutionary developmental theorists have argued that we have an innate (i.e., inherited) ability to acquire language (Chomsky, 1965; Pinker, 1994; Pinker & Jackendoff, 2005), that we have innate cognitive modules that help

Alison Gopnik has argued that our inheritance provides us with a propensity to learn about the world around us by forming theories and testing them.
© Alison Gopnik

us understand others' minds (Leslie & Thaiss, 1992; Leslie, Friedman, & German, 2004), and innate knowledge about objects, number, and our spatial environment (Carey, 2009; Spelke et al., 1992; Shusterman, Lee, & Spelke, 2008).

So where does development fit into the picture? If we have so many cognitive modules provided by our inheritance, then why do children take so long to develop mature cognitive abilities? Actually a number of these evolutionary theories of development argue that while some aspects of cognitive functioning are innate, some are acquired through experience (e.g., Spelke et al., 1992). Also, rather like the maturationists of the early twentieth century, many modern evolutionary developmental psychologists also argue that innate modules emerge according to maturational timetables (Carey, 2009; Diamond, 1988; Bjorklund & Pelligrini, 2002).

Many developmental psychologists argue that it is going too far to say that we are born with knowledge or cognitive modules as such (e.g., Elman et al., 1996; Mareschal et al., 2007). But the Chomskyan idea that we are born with a particular *mental structure* to think about the world is perhaps a little more accepted. One account of this kind has been advanced by Alison Gopnik. Gopnik (e.g., Gopnik, 2017) argues that we are born with the means to think about the world around us, to form theories about why we have observed certain things, and to gather evidence to check whether or not our theories are true. Her argument is that we are all born to be scientists, prepared to think about and test our ideas about the world around us. In some ways this brings us back to Piaget, and his idea that we are given the tendencies to actively acquire and learn from our environments.

Another account which proposes that we have some specific innate tendencies, rather than knowledge as such, is put forward by Csibra and Gergely (2011). As we shall see in Chapter 9, they argue that there is an innate, or natural, pedagogy, in which we are born with predispositions to attend to and draw in the social world around us in a way which will best help us learn from the teachers which it offers up; even those teachers, like carers, parents, or siblings who do not have a formal teaching qualification!

INFORMATION PROCESSING AND COMPUTATIONAL ACCOUNTS OF COGNITIVE DEVELOPMENT

Information processing approaches to development are a broad grouping of theoretical accounts that have been inspired from a tradition of models of cognitive abilities in adult humans. At the same time that Piaget and Vygotsky's approaches to describing the origins of knowledge were becoming popular, a movement among researchers studying cognitive abilities in adults, called the 'information processing' approach, was trying to characterize the flow of information through the cognitive system, beginning with an input or stimulus, proceeding to processing of that information (e.g., perceptual elaboration, attention, memory storage) and ending with an output or response, much like the way computers process information (Munakata, 2006). In human information processing, output may be in the form of an action, a decision or simply a memory that is stored for later use.

And so the information processing approach to development attempts to understand how the cognitive processes that an adult uses (memory, attention, perception, motor control) develop over the lifespan. One particular question raised concerns what cognitive processes children of different ages can use. For instance, a question

information processing approaches Theories of development that focus on the flow of information through the child's cognitive system and particularly on the specific operations the child performs between input and output phases.

that has received particular attention concerns when we first develop the ability to store long-term episodic memories. This approach has been applied to a wide range of topics in cognitive development, including attention, memory, problem solving and planning. Information processing theory has also proved valuable in studying how children develop an understanding of reading, mathematics and science (Siegler, 2000; Siegler & Alibali, 2005) as well as social behaviours, such as social problem solving and aggression (Lemerise & Arsenio, 2000; Kupersmidt & Dodge, 2004).

In Chapter 10, we examine the information processing approach more closely in relation to the development of thinking and problem solving. However, here let's look at a few broad classes of information processing accounts.

Neo-Piagetian information processing accounts

Neo-Piagetian theories of information processing attempt to integrate Piaget's ideas with an information-processing perspective. According to Case (1992, 1998), the proponent of one of these theories, the stage-like development of cognition described by Piaget is based on improvements in memory capacity and executive control, two features of an information-processing system. Like Piaget, Case divides development into stages. Each of the proposed stages entails an increasingly sophisticated executive control structure, which is a 'mental blueprint or plan for solving a class of problems'. An executive control structure has three components (Case, 1984): a representation of the problem, a representation of the goal of the problem, and a representation of a strategy for attaining the goal. Case and his colleagues applied this theory to a variety of tasks and domains, including scientific reasoning, the analysis of social problems and mathematics (see Case, 1998, for a review of this research).

> **neo-Piagetian theories** Theories of cognitive development that reinterpret Piaget's concepts from an information-processing perspective.
>
> **executive control structure** According to Case, a mental blueprint or plan for solving a class of problems.
>
> **connectionist models** Connectionist models are a class of computational model used to make explicit theoretical accounts of human cognition and development.

Computational accounts of development

A criticism of developmental psychology which has come to the fore in the twenty-first century (Munakata & Johnson, 2005) has been that we are finding out relatively little about the processes by which developmental change happens. How precisely do nature and nurture interact? Piaget of course had his ideas about this which we've talked about already. He proposed that the child plays an active role in constructing her/his development through exploring their own environment. But then if we probe any further, it is difficult to get to a very precise account of the mechanisms by which this might work. The neo-Piagetians' ideas are perhaps even more difficult to pull out. Why is it exactly that children develop increasingly sophisticated control structures, as Case argued? These challenges have led information processing theorists to try to develop more precise models of how cognitive development happens, models which attempt to specify how the mind/brain computes information, and how those computations can drive developmental change. These are 'computational models' of development (Bonawitz et al., 2014; McClelland et al., 2010; Perfors et al., 2011; Shultz, 2013).

CONNECTIONIST MODELS OF DEVELOPMENT

A particular type of computational developmental account which gained a great deal of attention around the turn of the century is connectionist modelling (Elman et al., 1997; Mareschal et al., 2007; McClelland et al., 2010; Shultz, 2013). Connectionist models consist of a large set of interconnected nodes, rather like a network of neurons in the brain (connected together through their synapses). These nodes and connections (see Figure 2-2) are not usually put together in physical form. They are typically simulated in a virtual environment on a computer. Connectionist models process information; a pattern of input activations is fed in to the network at one end and that pattern is then transformed into an output at the other end. As such these networks represent precise theories of how information might be processed in a neural network. Some connectionist theorists (or 'modellers') attempt to emulate exactly how the brain

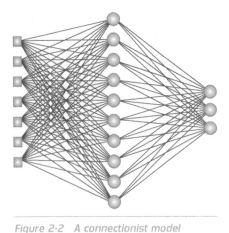

Figure 2-2   A connectionist model

This particular model has seven input nodes (the squares on the left), fully connected to three output nodes, through a large middle 'hidden' layer of ten nodes. Connectionist models learn via changes in the strengths of connection between each layer of nodes.

processes information (by programming the computer to simulate how neurons would function in the brain; e.g., Rolls & Treves, 1998). Other modellers are less concerned with simulating exactly how the brain works, but more with using connectionist models to show how cognitive computations can be made (Rumelhart & McClelland, 1986).

But how do these connectionist models simulate development? The way these models learn is again similar to how networks of neurons in the brain learn. They learn by altering the strengths of connections between the nodes, rather like synapses between neurons change strength in the nervous system and brain. Changes in these connection strengths result in sensory input being processed and transformed in new ways, leading to new ways of the network responding to that input. Imagine a network that is learning to read. It has to transform a pattern on the page (the input) into some appropriate speech sounds (the output). If the network's connections are changed in such a way to respond to the errors it makes and improve its performance then it will eventually find a set of connection strengths that enable it to read. We can imagine the same scenario in human development. Initially the networks of neurons in our brains are naive, the connections between various neurons mean that our responses to stimuli in the environment will produce a naive response (if you ask a pre-reading child to name a word written on the page you are likely to get an odd response). But gradually, as we are exposed to reading practice and tuition, the neural networks in our brain retune in order to produce accurate reading. In the Research Close-Up box, we show how a connectionist model can explain early visual categorization in young infants.

The connectionist modelling approach typically places a lot of emphasis on how the environment to which we are exposed shapes our learning and development (Elman et al., 1997; Mareschal et al., 2007). Usually, models learn by changing weights in specific response to the input patterns that are provided to the models (and sometimes the subsequent outputs that models produce). Thus the input to which the model is exposed shapes its development. In that sense, connectionism is rather similar to behaviourism. The similarity does not end there, as connectionist models learn by associating inputs with particular outputs. These are more complicated versions of the associative learning mechanisms that the behaviourists advocated. However, a particular contribution of modern connectionism is that it has shown us that associative learning in such networks can result in sudden, stage-like changes in behaviour over time. In that sense they represent a link between behaviourism and Piaget – like Siegler's overlapping waves model (which we discussed in Chapter 1) they show how insightful shifts in development can arise from gradual shaping of behaviour.

Research close-up

BOX 2-2   A connectionist model of early categorization

Source: Based on French et al. (2004).

Introduction:

As we shall see in Chapter 9, a puzzle that has interested developmental psychologists for a long time concerns how we come to be able to form categories. Imagine if you were not able to do this. Every object you saw would be entirely new. Without the knowledge that the new animal you see on your way to lectures is a cat, you would have no point of reference from which to predict its behaviour – should you stroke it, say hello, or might that be a fatal mistake? Thankfully we try to place animals and objects we see into categories so that we can learn that animals that fit a certain set of criteria behave in similar ways (we know that medium small furry animals with tails, whiskers, large eyes and meowing calls are cats and so we can predict that they will, usually, respond well to a stroke). Infants are no exception. Studies measuring young infants' visual fixations show that they form separate categories. In one study, infants were shown a series of pictures of different cats. Over time their interest in them declined (as shown by a decline in their visual fixation of the pictures). A dog picture was then introduced, paired with another new cat picture. The infants showed a preference to look at the dog even though they had not seen either the dog or the cat before (Quinn, Eimas, & Rosenkrantz, 1993). This shows that infants formed a visual category of cats which excluded the dog.

However, an unusual finding was observed with this study. Quinn et al. (1993) found that when 3- to 4-month-olds are initially exposed (habituated) to a series of pictures of dogs (rather than being initially exposed to cats) they will not perceive a new cat as being more novel than a new dog. So, when learning about cats, young infants appear to treat dogs as new, but when learning about dogs, they treat cats as the same as dogs.

Method:

Mareschal and colleagues (Mareschal, French, & Quinn, 2000; Mareschal & French, 2000) set out to explain this strange finding, and to understand infant categorization behaviour more generally by constructing a connectionist model. They used a particular kind of model called an 'auto-encoder'. Auto-encoder networks attempt to find a set of connection strengths that enable them to form representations of any input pattern presented to them. After training, the auto-encoder manages to do this better with some patterns than with others. Typically, it is the patterns that are least similar to what the network has learned from in the past that it makes the most errors in reproducing. So, we can imagine that the error the network makes when reproducing corresponds to the novelty of the stimulus to which it has been exposed. Mareschal et al. used the encoder in this way to model a looking preference in infants. They used the model's error in reproducing a pattern as corresponding to the amount of looking that infants direct towards a given stimulus.

Results:

So the auto-encoder was trained up on cats and dogs, just like the infants were in Quinn et al.'s experiments. The way Mareschal et al. exposed the auto-encoder to the pictures was to measure a set of dimensions in each of the pictures (e.g., nose length, leg length, distance between the ears) and present the figures to networks for categorization. Interestingly the networks developed CAT and DOG categories with the same asymmetry as the 3- to 4-month-olds in Quinn et al.'s study; if trained on cats, the networks showed error when presented with a novel dog, but if trained on dogs, the networks were more accurate at reproducing a representation of a novel cat.

A closer look at the network allowed Mareschal and French to explain why the networks behaved like this. Most cat features (ear length, nose length, etc.) fell within the range of the dog values to which the network had been trained, but the converse was not true (i.e. there is more variation between dogs in these features than there is between cats). The auto-encoder had learned to categorize on the basis of the statistical distribution of features of the stimuli to which they had been presented. Mareschal and French (2000) argue that the same is true for infants.

Discussion:

Here we see quite clearly how a particular class of connectionist model (an auto-encoder) helped explain confusing behavioural findings, by forming an explicit mechanistic theory of that behaviour with testable hypotheses. In this case the model helped demonstrate that infants form categories for visual objects on the basis of the statistics to which they are exposed, rather than by using any 'top down' knowledge.

BAYESIAN MODELS OF DEVELOPMENT

A group of computational accounts of development which have gained particular interest in the last decade or so involve what is called Bayesian modelling (Bonawitz et al., 2014; Gopnik & Tenenbaum, 2007; Perfors et al., 2011). Thomas Bayes, who these models are named after, was an eighteenth-century statistician who came up with Bayes's theorem.

Bayes's theorem describes something called conditional probability – the probability that something is the case given the knowledge that something else is true (e.g., the probability that a young child has chicken-pox given that she has lots of spots appearing on her face). Bayesian modellers construct networks of conditional probabilities in order to provide explicit theories of why we believe certain things, or for instance why we perceive objects in particular ways, based on our knowledge of the world around us or at least our knowledge of what is happening right now.

The broad idea of Bayesian models is that our brains/minds use prior knowledge and conditional probabilities to form our understanding of the world around us. In developmental psychology, Bayesian modelling has been used to explain how children develop in their knowledge of the world. Theorists such as Gopnik (2017) have argued that children develop their understanding of the world through a 'scientific' Bayesian 'sampling'. She argues that children have naive theories about the work, which they then test out by applying to novel situations. When their predictions turn out to be true or false they update their Bayesian predictions accordingly, so that next time they encounter something similar they can predict what will happen more precisely.

Bayesian modelling
A form of computational modelling which rests on conditional probabilistic relationships between items of information. Bayesian modelling is used to model the development of children's understanding of the relationships between many things, including events, words and objects.

Bayes's theorem
Bayes's theorem describes conditional probability; that is, the probability of an event based on prior knowledge that something else which might be related to the event is the case or has occurred.

dynamic systems accounts of development
Dynamic systems are an area of study in mathematics which attempts to describe complex systems with many inputs which interact in complex ways. Developmental psychologists have tried to explain development in this way.

Let's think about Bayesian learning in the context of word learning. If a child hears an adult refer to a bunch of paper as a 'newspaper', he or she might, when they next see a newspaper or a magazine, test out their idea of this, waiting to hear what an adult will call the object (or even trying the word newspaper out themselves). They might turn out to be right or wrong, but if they learn to update their predictions, then they will have learned.

This all might sound a bit like the kinds of 'associative' learning which the behaviourists were so fond of, and it might also sound rather like the connectionist computational models which we were just discussing (where the strength of the connection is changed based on associations in a learning episode). There are certainly some similarities. However, the key thing about Bayesian modelling is that it provides a straightforward way to capture how a brain or mind makes predictions on the basis of what it knows. Gopnik (Gopnik & Wellman, 2012) argues that this is what children do. In fact, it is reasonable to say that Piaget said this too. The difference is that Piaget argued that children constructed their own ability to do this through development, whereas Gopnik (2017) argues that children are born with this ability.

DYNAMIC SYSTEMS ACCOUNTS OF DEVELOPMENT

Working with babies is chaos! Honestly, who would be a developmental psychologist? The beauty of dynamic systems accounts of development is that that they embrace this chaos, treating it as a natural part of development. Dynamic systems are an area of study which comes from mathematics. The idea is to be able to describe change in a complex system which has many inputs to its behaviour. Think of a 6-month-old baby. Not long from being a newborn muddle of reflexive motor behaviours, the baby is bombarded with sensory information from across all of its senses. It also has a bunch of desires (biscuit, Daddy, remote control) all vying for its attention. All of these desires, behaviours, sensory inputs are happening at once, with different time courses, and different strengths of action in the baby. Dynamics systems modelling can be used to describe how a baby's or a child's behaviour might result from the chaotic interactions of all of these inputs to the system (Smith & Thelen, 2003).

As well as describing the time course of behaviour, dynamic systems accounts can describe how development unfolds over time. Given that developmental processes are also fundamentally to do with change over time, this can be a very helpful conceptual tool. Think of how one developmental outcome (for instance, learning first words) feeds into other outcomes (e.g., the development of conversation and communication skills) which in turn feed into learning further words. In this way development can be viewed as part of a dynamic system where change in a process (e.g., language development) is not linear and depends upon previous developmental change and the broader developmental and environmental context.

Like connectionist models, one of the great benefits of the dynamic systems approach is that it can explain how sudden (stagewise) developmental changes can result from the complex interactions of multiple quantitative changes. Also, as we shall see in Chapter 6, dynamic systems accounts have helped highlight the importance of thinking about all potentially relevant inputs to the developing system. In the 1980s, Esther Thelen's renowned research helped show how things you might not immediately think of, like increases in the weight of an infant's legs, were just as (if not more) important in explaining the development of their motor abilities than were things which might more typically spring to the developmental psychologist's mind (like the maturation of motor cortex, for instance).

> In Chapter 6 we describe how a dynamic systems approach has been used to explain motor development in young infants.

NEUROSCIENCE AND DEVELOPMENTAL THEORIES

In recent years, developmental psychologists have begun turning their attention towards methods that can tell us about the development of the neural processes that underlie our psychological abilities. As we discuss in Chapter 3, the refinement of non-invasive techniques for studying neural responses in infants and children (e.g., EEG, fMRI, fNIRS) has led to a substantial increase in what we know about the development of human brain function.

These methods have revealed some exciting and interesting patterns of development in how infants' and children's brains respond while they are perceiving and processing information. The key debate, though, is how developmental changes in neural function arise. Mark Johnson at the University of Cambridge proposes some alternative ways of envisaging changes in brain function over development (Johnson, 2011). One approach, the 'maturational' account of brain development, suggests that the development of perceptual and cognitive abilities is held up by the maturation of relevant parts of the brain (for example, children may take a long time to master tasks where they have to inhibit a behaviour because their frontal cortex – responsible for inhibition – takes longer to grow than some other parts of the brain). Nativist theorists who, as we have discussed, take the view that many of our cognitive abilities are provided by our inheritance (e.g., Spelke, 1998; Leslie, Friedman, & German, 2004), generally adhere to a maturational position. This view thus implies that brain areas are specialized for particular tasks (e.g., face perception or Theory of Mind) but that the functioning of these brain areas occurs without the need for a major input of information from the environment.

Another approach, favoured by Johnson (2011), is the 'interactive specialization' account. Unlike the maturational account, interactive specialization suggests that particular parts of the brain are not predesigned for specific tasks, but rather that the brain becomes gradually specialized into different areas and networks that specialize at different tasks. Importantly, interactive specialization also argues that the environment to which infants and children are exposed plays an important role in shaping brain specialization.

But which approach is the correct one? It is certainly early days in answering this question, and it is important to acknowledge that maturation and interactive specialization could both be going on at once. However, evidence showing that the regions involved in particular tasks (e.g., in face perception; Halit, de Haan, & Johnson, 2003; Cohen-Kadosh et al., 2013) change substantially over development provides support for Johnson's interactive specialization account.

SUMMARY

As we stress throughout this book, the understanding of children's development can be approached from many perspectives. You can see from even the brief descriptions of the theories we have covered in this chapter that they have differing positions on several fundamental aspects of development (e.g., continuity vs stages, the role of nature vs nurture).

Although the presence of different theories adds a layer of complexity to studying child development, many questions about development benefit from these multiple theoretical perspectives. As well as giving us much to think about via these multiple perspectives on the same problem, it is important to realize that theories do not have to be mutually exclusive. While Freud and Piaget chose to describe development in quite different ways (Freud placing emphasis on needs and motivations, and Piaget focusing on logic and understanding), their different emphases do not necessarily contradict each other. Nonetheless, it is increasingly clear that different aspects of development, such as language and emotional and social behaviour, are interlinked. For instance, children's learning takes place in social contexts, and the experiences and relationships children have with other people affect what and how they learn from them. To understand such complex processes, several theoretical points of view are needed.

Many developmental psychologists today draw on some of the assumptions of several different approaches. It seems that several theories can tell us a great deal more about the causes and course of children's development than any single one can alone.

Explore and Discuss

1. What do you think the hallmarks of a good theory of development are?

2. Can you compare the theories of development discussed in this chapter in terms of their emphasis on nature vs nurture?

Recommended Reading

Classic

Flavell, J. H. (1963). *The developmental psychology of Jean Piaget.* Princeton, NJ: D. Van Nostrand.

Karmiloff-Smith, A., & Inhelder, B. (1974). If you want to get ahead, get a theory. *Cognition, 3*, 195–212.

Contemporary

Crain, W. (2015). *Theories of development: Concepts and applications.* Hove: Psychology Press.

Gopnik, A. (2017). How babies think. *Scientific American, 26*, 48–53.

Mareschal, D., Johnson, M. H., Sirois, S., Spratling, M., Thomas, M., & Westermann, G. (2007). *Neuroconstructivism: Vol. I. How the brain constructs cognition.* Oxford: Oxford University Press.

CHAPTER 3
Research Methods in Developmental Psychology

Introduction

Psychology is an empirical discipline: what counts as good or bad evidence for a psychological phenomenon, a developmental process, or a theory depends on what can be observed or recorded from individuals' behaviour. In this fundamental respect, developmental psychology is no different from other areas of the discipline. However, observing or recording the behaviour of infants and children presents particular challenges for researchers. For instance, a social psychologist might give a simple questionnaire to an adult participant to establish her attitudes on a topic, and ask the participant to complete the paper questionnaire with a pen or pencil and return it. Clearly, this will be impossible for a child or infant who cannot yet write or even understand the language terms or instructions used. In fact, even if they do understand the instructions young children are not always very compliant!

Although researchers may try to adapt their methods to allow comparable tests to be conducted across age groups (for instance, by having an adult ask questions and complete a questionnaire for a child), there may be further problems with using even subtly different measures or research procedures with different age groups of participants in a study. Differences in the methods used in the different age groups can cause problems because they may limit a researcher's ability to draw clear comparisons between these different ages. This may make it difficult to identify whether or not an ability is developing. Moreover, in some cases, it is simply impossible to get the same sort of information from individuals at different ages. For instance, the concept of attitude, as understood by most social researchers, carries little meaning when studying infants. From a conceptual perspective, researchers may need a different set of ideas to explain psychological processes at different points across the lifespan.

Another important difference between research in developmental psychology and other areas of psychology is that the study of development fundamentally involves identifying change over time. As we shall see, sometimes researchers examine behaviour or cognition at different ages and *infer* how psychological processes develop. However, a very important approach in developmental psychology is to study how changes occur in an individual or sample of individuals longitudinally; that is, how things change over time. Longitudinal research studies not only take time but also require considerable resources to conduct.

Although developmental psychologists face some unique research challenges, many innovative methods have been developed to explore psychological development from before birth up to the end of life. These include a range of different research designs, techniques and measures for capturing how infants, children and adults think, feel and behave.

When conducting research, developmental psychologists also need to be mindful of the particular set of ethical issues that they face when studying children. Just as the methods sometimes need to be adapted to fit the different types and forms of responses that infants, children and adults can give, the level of consent that can be given in studies is also a concern. More specifically, in everyday life children and other young people (up until the age of 16 or 18 years, depending on the country one lives in) are usually deemed not to be able to make fully informed decisions for themselves. For instance, there are usually restrictions on voting age and the age at which young people become legally fully responsible for their actions. In a similar vein, care needs to be taken to ensure that children always consent to participate in every aspect of research and are not doing so merely to please an adult researcher, or because they think they have no option. Normally parental consent (agreement from the adult responsible for a child's welfare) is required as a further safeguard, to ensure that children are protected from any potential harmful effects of participation in research studies.

METHODOLOGICAL APPROACHES TO STUDYING HUMAN DEVELOPMENT

There are many approaches to studying development. Researchers have used self-reports, observations and even in some instances computer modelling to seek to understand how children acquire knowledge and understanding of the world. The data that are gathered can be quantitative (that is, in some way to do with measurement and numbers) or qualitative (focusing more on understanding individual's experiences of a situation or issue). Often, the methods that researchers use will be influenced both by their theoretical orientation and by the topic or phenomenon under study. For instance, if an entirely new topic is being explored for the first time, it may be more appropriate to collect information to help build a theory and understanding of the topic first, and this may involve more exploratory, qualitative methods. After these initial investigations, a theory can be developed and then explored, possibly using quantitative methods, to see how appropriate the theory is for explaining behaviour in the general population. In more established areas of research, any new work needs to be developed in the context of existing theories. In this case, experimental methods that allow clear connections between causes and effects to be established, may be more suitable.

Most contemporary developmental psychologists use scientific methods in their research; that is, they formulate hypotheses on the basis of a theory and use measurable and replicable techniques to collect, study and analyse data. It is important that research findings of this nature are robust and reliable, and that similar outcomes could be reproduced if another researcher collected the same data, from a similar sample, in the same way. The main issues in a scientific approach to psychological development include selecting a sample, designing a study that taps into developmental processes in some meaningful way, using appropriate statistical tests to establish the significance of findings, and ensuring that all ethical protections are in place. Different forms of scientific (experimental) approach are explored in more detail later in this chapter.

> **scientific methods**
> The use of measurable and replicable techniques in framing hypotheses, and collecting and analysing data to test a theory's usefulness.

Even when scientific and experimental techniques are used, it is important for researchers to remember that particular issues may exist when collecting data with children. For instance, the experimental situation – often where an adult researcher asks a child questions or to perform a task – is a rather unusual one in many respects, and may be understood differently by children and adults. Box 3-1 gives an example of how this experimental context might lead children to give responses that do not reflect their full ability or understanding. Good researchers always need to be sensitive both to the context of study and to a child's likely interpretation and understanding of the testing situation.

> The development of conservation skills is discussed in further detail in Chapter 9.

BOX 3-1   When questions can confuse ...

Research close-up

Source: Based on Rose and Blank (1974).

Introduction:

One of Piaget's key tasks, which he used when studying children's reasoning, concerned children's ability to conserve. However, one criticism of Piaget's research in this area was that he underestimated children's competence and understanding.

There are many different types of conservation task – for example, conservation of number, mass, volume – but a typical feature of the ability to solve a conservation task is that a child can understand that a certain property of an object remains the same if nothing is added or taken away from it. For instance, if a child can conserve number he can appreciate that a row of five counters will remain five counters providing a counter is not added or taken away from the row. Grasping this understanding is a key achievement during the concrete operational period (around 2 to 11 years, spanning both the preoperational subperiod and concrete operations).

Piaget's ideas about conservation were developed through his observations in a series of interviews with children and quasi-experiments – little tasks that he asked children to complete. By exploring the errors that younger children made, Piaget speculated that children were seduced by differences in appearance into making conservation errors. In other words, even if no counters had been added to a row, if they were moved around so that one looked longer than another then younger children might think the number had changed in some way.

However, although Piaget's experiments were doubtless innovative and led to important insights, subsequent research has suggested that his method of testing could lead to problems in eliciting information about what children really thought. For example, Rose and Blank (1974) explored whether the form of questioning had an influence on children's responses.

Method:

In the standard conservation of number test, Piaget asked a child if two identical rows of counters included the same or a different number. Children answered that they were the same. Then, Piaget moved counters in one of the lines so it looked longer than the other (although the number of counters in each row remained the same) and asked the child once again if the numbers in each row were the same or different.

Rose and Blank argued that, by asking the same question twice, Piaget may inadvertently have led children to think their initial answer was wrong. So when they answered the second question by saying there were different numbers of counters in each row, maybe children were merely trying to give what they thought was a better answer second time around.

To evaluate their argument, Rose and Blank conducted two studies. In the first, they placed 84 children into one of three equal-size groups (average age 6 years, 3 months). Groups were tested on conservation ability using (1) a standard task, (2) a one-judgement task where children saw the counters being rearranged but were asked the question about equality only once, (3) a fixed-array task where children just saw the counters in the final state (i.e., the same number of counters in each row, arranged into different lengths).

Results:

Mean error scores on questions about equality and inequality are show in Figure 3-1. There were significantly fewer errors on the single-judgement task for both types of judgement.

A second study ruled out the possibility that the one-judgement task was easier or required fewer cognitive demands. In other words, children who were only asked the question once performed better than children who had also been asked the question prior to moving the counters.

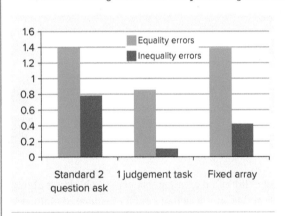

Figure 3-1   Mean errors in equality and inequality judgements by experimental group
Source: Adapted from Rose and Blank (1974)

Discussion:

Piaget's studies of conservation are still very important, yet Rose and Blank's study demonstrates how children can misunderstand the experimental situation or what is required of them. Researchers need to be very sensitive to how children may understand a situation when collecting data because they may respond in ways that are different from how adults would respond. This may, in turn, limit the confidence with which conclusions can be drawn from a study.

METHODS FOR DATA COLLECTION

Essentially, there are three methods of gathering such data: we can ask children about themselves; we can ask people who are close to these children about them; or we can observe the children directly. However, within these three broader approaches there are further refinements that have been devised to avoid some of the limitations, while building on the advantages, of each approach.

Self reports

A self report is information that a person provides about himself or herself, typically by answering a set of questions devised by a researcher. Soliciting such information from a child, as you may imagine, often presents particular problems in developmental research. Compared with adults, children – especially younger ones – are apt to be less attentive, slower to respond, and to have more trouble understanding the questions that researchers ask. Despite these limitations on children's self reports, some kinds of information, such as how a child feels about an experience or another person, are difficult to obtain in any other way (Cowie et al., 2018; Cummings, Davies, & Campbell, 2000).

> **self-report** Information that people provide about themselves, either in a direct interview or in some written form, such as a questionnaire.

Reports by family members, teachers and peers

A second way of collecting data on child development is to solicit information from people who know a child or children well. Most commonly, researchers seek this information from family members, teachers and peers.

A strength of collecting data from parents and other family members is that these reports are generally based on many observations made over time in a variety of situations. Another advantage of reports by family members is that even if parents and siblings are not totally accurate in their reporting, their perceptions, expectations, beliefs, and interpretations of events and behaviour may be just as important as what we can only assume is objective reality (Collins & Repinski, 2001; Bugental & Grusec, 2006). For example, whether or not a young girl's parents explicitly insist on exceptionally good academic performance, the child's belief that her parents want her to do very well in school may greatly influence her behaviour or self-esteem.

There are some clear disadvantages in soliciting parental and other family reports about a child's growth and development. Human memory is not completely reliable. Also, because people often are motivated to remember themselves in the best light possible, parents can remember themselves as more consistent, patient and even-tempered with their children than more objective assessments might have revealed them to be. Of course, parents and others may also make a choice to present themselves in a certain light, and answer dishonestly.

In an effort to increase the accuracy of parents' reports about their children, investigators have devised a number of strategies. For example, they may have parents report only very recent events so as to ensure more reliable memories, they may phone parents every evening and ask which of a list of specific behaviours (e.g., crying or refusing to comply) their children have exhibited in the past 24 hours (Patterson & Bank, 1989; Patterson, 1996), or they may ask parents to keep a structured diary in which they record the child's behaviours at regular intervals (e.g., every hour; Hetherington, 1991). Child development researchers have even texted parents at random intervals, asking them to record their activities or feelings, or those of their children (Larson & Richards, 1994). This approach allows for a random sampling not only of behaviour but also of the situations in which this behaviour occurs.

To learn about a child's behaviour in school and other settings researchers can ask people outside the immediate family, such as teachers and peers. Investigators may ask teachers to rate children on a specific series of dimensions such as attentiveness, dependability and sociability in the classroom or on the playground. One technique researchers often use is to ask children, such as classmates, to rate how well a particular child's peers accept him. For example, investigators might ask all the youngsters in a classroom to rate each of their peers in terms of 'how much I like to play with' him or her. The researchers then combine all the ratings to yield a picture of each child's social status in the classroom (Ladd, 2005; Rubin, Bukowski, & Parker, 2006).

> **observation** A method in which researchers go into settings in the natural world or bring participants into the laboratory to observe behaviours of interest.

Naturalistic observation

There is often no substitute for researchers' own direct observation of people, and students of child development may make such observations in naturalistic settings, such as participants' own homes, or in laboratories where they give children

> In Chapter 7 we discuss one famous form of structured observation of infant attachment: the Strange Situation.

Child undergoing an assessment.
© Shutterstock/CandyBox Images

and sometimes parents a structured task to perform. Observational data are valuable resources in examining human behaviour. However, such data are valid only to the extent that the presence of an observer or other demands of the situation do not distort the participants' behaviour and responses. It is also important to remember that entirely objective observation (that is, observation without an observer's bias or preconceptions influencing how he or she interprets behaviour) can be difficult to achieve without robust and well-established procedures and measures.

These distorting factors are sometimes hard to avoid because children and parents often behave differently in different kinds of settings or when they know they are being watched. Both adults and children tend to express less negative emotion and to exhibit more socially desirable behaviour when observations are conducted in unfamiliar settings, such as a laboratory, compared with at home (Lamb, Suomi, & Stephenson, 1979). Even in home observations, customary behaviour can be distorted by the presence of an outside observer. Parents, for instance, tend to inhibit negative behaviour when they are watched (Russell, Russell, & Midwinter, 1991). Attempts to minimize such distortions in studies in people's homes include the use of less obtrusive observational methods, such as camera or sound recordings without the observer present (e.g., Tapper & Boulton, 2002), and by conducting many regular visits from an observer – for example, an observer being at a family's home each dinner hour over a period of several weeks (Feiring & Lewis, 1987).

As surprising as it may seem, people can get used to observational techniques; as observations proceed, one sees gradual increases in less socially accepted behaviours, such as quarrelling, criticizing and punishing (Boyum & Parke, 1995). However, it is important to remember that there is always a balance to be struck between gaining high-quality observations of behaviour, and conducting research which maintains respect for individuals' privacy. For this reason among many others, ethical concerns are often at the forefront of researchers' minds when conducting observational research.

In order to try to avoid observer bias, when researchers decide to observe children and their families directly, they must decide what kinds of behaviours to record (Bakeman & Gottman, 1997). For instance, they need to decide how detailed the observations will be, perhaps how to code or classify certain types of action, or how frequently they will be recorded. When a developmental researcher is interested in a specific behaviour, he may arrange a situation to observe the behaviour using a method called structured observation. Suppose a researcher is interested in the way mothers instruct their children about how to solve problems. The researcher may invite mothers and children to the laboratory to participate in a joint problem-solving session, perhaps one that involves putting together different types of puzzles, and observe how their interaction changes as the child attains skill and understanding of the task.

> **structured observation**
> A form of observation in which researchers structure a situation so that behaviour(s) they wish to study is/are more likely to occur.

Interviews

Another popular means of conducting research with children and adolescents, used very widely in the social sciences and educational research, is the interview. In fact, many psychological studies include an interview component – that is, an adult researcher will ask the participant a series of questions and then examine the responses. While interviews in some form are relatively common in psychology the degree to which these are 'scripted' does vary somewhat across disciplines. Often, researchers in psychology will conduct interviews following a tightly prescribed set of questions, where an interview format is used to elicit children's responses to a questionnaire that they cannot complete themselves. However, other less structured interviews are used to explore children's reasoning in greater depth.

One distinctive form of interview method was employed by Piaget (e.g., Piaget, 1923) to explore the underlying structure and processes involved in children's reasoning. Piaget devised his 'clinical interview technique' to probe a child's reasoning about a number of different topics and, in turn, to reveal errors or notable features of a child's thinking. Piaget used his clinical interview findings to complement experimental and observational data, and make inferences about developmental processes.

Consider the following two examples from Piaget's work on the features of reasoning and judgement at different stages of development. Piaget (1926) was seeking to explore how children who are at the pre-operational stage reasoned in semi-logical ways:

> *6 year old child: How did the sun begin?* – It was when life began. – *Has there always been a sun?* – No. – *How did it begin?* – Because it knew that life had begun. – *What is it made of?* – Of fire. – *But how?* – Because there was fire up there. – *Where did the fire come from?* – From the sky. – *How was the fire made in the sky?* – It was lighted with a match. – *Where did it come from, this match?* – God threw it away.
> *(Piaget, 1926, pp. 258–259)*

> *6 year old child:* Does the sun move? – Yes, when one walks it follows. When one turns round it turns round too. Doesn't it ever follow you? – *Why does it move?* – Because when one walks, it goes too (il marche). – *Why does it go?* – To hear what we say. – *It is alive?* – Of course, otherwise it couldn't follow us, it shouldn't shine.
> *(Piaget, 1929/1952, p. 215)*

In these cases, as in others, Piaget's technique was to conduct an interview on a certain topic but, rather than following a pre-set script, he sought to probe a child's answers further. Thus, as an interviewer he reacted to his participants' answers to develop a line of questioning that revealed immature reasoning. Interviews such as these can be helpful in establishing new information on a new topic and can help to build up ideas for further, more systematic study using experimental methods.

We discuss Piaget's theory in much greater detail in Chapter 9.

Participatory research

Another form of data collection and approach to research in developmental psychology can be described under the broad category of participatory research. Participatory research involves the research participants themselves being actively engaged in the research process, perhaps designing the study, collecting data (on) themselves, and sometimes analysing and reporting the findings (Groundwater-Smith, Dockett, & Bottrell, 2015).

Participatory research is well suited to studies that seek to articulate a developmental phenomenon in a community or contextualized setting, where the perspectives of research participants or a community are central to the questions being explored. For example, Roshanfekr et al. (2017) examined children's development across communication, motor skills, cognitive and social domains in a suburb of Tehran, Iran, to record progress according to a set of predefined measures. The mothers screened and recorded data on their children from 5 years of age, assisted by others in the local community. The results demonstrated how participatory research often overlaps with interventions to promote positive development. In Roshanfekr et al.'s study, the children of mothers participating in the study showed improved developmental outcomes compared with a comparison group of children where data were collected previously, elsewhere in Tehran, and who had not engaged in research using the participatory approach.

While it may be the case that participatory research studies can influence research outcomes, that is often an intended goal of the study. Moreover, researchers argue that such approaches can empower participants and break down some of the imbalance in status, or more general wariness, between researchers and research participants. However, participatory research does not guarantee that traditional imbalances between researchers and research participants are not replaced by other biases and influences. Inferences drawn from participatory research need to be regarded with caution and contextualized before considering how they may be generalized to other populations or used to inform theory. Additionally, language and cognitive ability limit how far children may be able to participate in designing and conducting robust and reliable research studies. Developmental researchers need to consider carefully what the goals and intended outcomes of any participatory research study might be (Waller & Bitou, 2011).

Eliciting behavioural responses in experiments

However much we ask questions of children, or observe their behaviour, this might not necessarily provide a window onto their internal mental processes. Take a 5-month-old infant – 5-month-olds have typically just learned to sit upright. They're not usually able to pick up objects by themselves, let alone speak, and yet they look a lot at the world around them, and clearly understand something of it. Because their behavioural repertoire is more limited, it may take more time than there is available to investigate the mental processes of young babies through naturalistic observation alone. However, researchers have come up with lots of ways to elicit behavioural responses from infants and children in experiments, in order to gain more immediate insight into their internal mental processes.

One of the most obvious examples of researchers' use of elicited behaviour is the measurement of infants' visual preferences. As we'll see in Chapter 6, if we give young babies a choice of two things to look at they will typically show a visual preference for looking at one of these. Those visual preferences are remarkably consistent within any given age group of babies, and so experimenters can use these preferences to determine whether infants of a particular age can discriminate between the stimuli presented.

Other instances of elicited behaviour in infants include manual responses, where experimenters make use of infants' tendencies to want to get their hands on interesting looking objects. For instance, Piaget and many researchers after him used reaching behaviours to examine infants' understanding of object permanence (see Chapter 9). Others have observed infants' reaches under certain experimental manipulations to determine which sensory cues they use to guide their movements (e.g., Keen et al., 2003; see Chapter 6).

Beyond infancy, experimenters can start to elicit behaviour by giving children task instructions. For instance, the false belief task used to test young children's theory of mind abilities (see Chapter 9), acts out a story scenario to children and then asks them to respond to specific questions about those scenarios. Once we are able to tell children to respond to experimental stimuli quickly, then we can start to measure their speed of processing in a way which is more comparable with adult performance (e.g., Kail et al., 2013; see Chapter 10).

Biological and psychophysiological measures

Many developmental psychologists are interested in the biological basis of psychological development. While our understanding of this is at a relatively early stage (certainly as compared to our understanding of behavioural development), scientists are now asking quite a range of questions about how our brains and nervous systems develop, and what this can tell us about psychological development.

Previously, researchers interested in psychological development on a biological level were restricted to a relatively small number of measures that tapped in to physiological correlates of behaviour. These were typically linked to the functioning of the peripheral nervous system (PNS) rather than the central nervous system (CNS). Examples of measures of the PNS include heart rate, sweating responses on the skin, and muscle activity. The measures available for investigating the functioning of the CNS, which comprises the brain and spinal cord, the main physical machinery of psychological functions, were much more restricted, and researchers interested in the functioning of the CNS had to resort to studying the development in non-human animals with more invasive methods. While some important questions about the development of the nervous system can still only be addressed invasively in animals, recent years have witnessed a revolution in non-invasive methods available for studying the functioning of the CNS in infants and young children. These new methods have enabled researchers to investigate how neural anatomy develops in humans, from the cellular level to larger-scale shape of particular parts of the brain, and how the functions of neural anatomy develop (i.e., how the kinds of neural activity supported by specific brain areas or networks of neurons change). We now discuss some of the psychophysiological methods used by developmental psychologists.

MEASURES OF THE PERIPHERAL NERVOUS SYSTEM

The PNS is made up of the neural tissue in the body outside of the brain and spinal cord. The PNS directly senses the environment before passing information to the CNS. It also directly controls movements including both voluntary actions (e.g., movement of the arm) and involuntary actions (e.g., heart rate or sweating). A range of methods have been used to investigate activity in the PNS. Responses in the PNS have been linked with and are thus used to measure emotional cognitive and even behavioural processes. For instance, changes in heart rate have been used to identify everything from perceptual discrimination to emotional changes in young infants (e.g., Lewkowicz & Turkewitz, 1980). Measurement of electrical activity in the muscles (electromyography; EMG) has been used to investigate the precise timing of movements in young infants and children (Thelen & Fisher, 1982).

FMRI, FNIRS AND PET

Functional magnetic resonance imaging (fMRI) has been a very important method for neuroscientists over the past 20 years, not least for neuroscientists interested in development (e.g., Decety, Michalska, & Akitsuki, 2008; Deen et al., 2017; Houdé et al., 2010). Without going into the details of this method, which are complex, fMRI uses strong magnetic fields to detect the level of oxygenated blood present across the brain. Because the brain pumps oxygenated blood to parts of the brain that are in use, this allows researchers to determine what parts of the brain are involved in whatever a person is doing while they are being 'scanned'. fMRI has good spatial resolution and so it can tell us quite precisely which parts of the brain are active. fMRI has been used to investigate a wide range of questions concerning the brain areas involved in cognitive functions across development (see Chapters 5, 9 and 10). The downside of fMRI is that, as well as being very expensive, participants are required to keep very still, and put up with lots of rather loud noises and a claustrophobic environment. Because of this, the majority of developmental fMRI studies have been conducted with children older than 5 or 6 years. In order to test younger children or infants who are more sensitive to the strange and loud environment of an fMRI scanner, researchers often have to sedate the participant, or wait until they are asleep. However, there are a number of notable exceptions to this in which researchers have managed to scan infants while they are awake (e.g., Dehaene-Lambertz, Dehaene, & Hertz-pannier, 2002; Deen et al., 2017).

More recently, a new method for detecting levels of oxyhaemoglobin in the brain has come to light. FNIRS (functional near infrared spectroscopy) capitalizes on the fact that infrared light passes through the skull and is refracted in different ways by oxygenated and deoxygenated blood (infrared rays from the sun are probably passing through your head right now!). By measuring the way infrared light shines at young children's and infants' brains and is refracted it is possible to identify which parts of the brain are active. Although this method does not provide quite as good spatial resolution as fMRI or PET it is much more tolerable for young children and infants, and so is gaining ground (Lloyd-Fox et al., 2009; Gervain et al., 2011).

Another way of measuring brain function through blood flow to the brain is positron emission tomography (PET). PET involves injecting a radioactive isotope into the bloodstream, which has the effect of labelling blood in different ways, enabling researchers to measure brain function through the chemicals that are pumped to it in order to sustain its activity (see, e.g., Baron-Cohen et al., 1994). PET is of course more invasive than fNIRS or fMRI, but it has the advantage that a wider range of chemicals used by the brain can be traced (by injecting different kinds of radioactive isotopes).

EEG

Perhaps the most widely used brain imaging technique with young infants has been to measure electrical activity on the scalp (EEG). This electrical activity arises from the neurons that fire when the brain is active. EEG does not provide very good spatial resolution as the electrical activity in EEG spreads across the scalp rather than remaining localized. On the other hand, it is a very good method for measuring rapid changes in neural activity over time. Researchers use EEG to measure 'event related potentials' (ERPs; brain activity timelocked to a particular stimulus or behaviour). ERPs give us clues as to how neural processes unfold from millisecond to millisecond (e.g., Halit et al., 2003; Rigato et al., 2017). EEG can also be used to measure oscillations in brain activity. Certain speeds of oscillatory neural activity have been linked to particular cognitive processes in adults and so we can track the emergence of such processes in infants and children (e.g., Csibra et al., 2000; Kaufman et al., 2003; Southgate et al., 2009). Perhaps the key benefit of EEG is that it is relatively tolerable for young infants as there is no claustrophobic or noisy environment associated. Some might argue that the most important advances in this technique for developmental scientists have been those that make the electrode cap (or net) comfier so that the infant stays contented during the experiment and does not try to pull it off!

MARKER TASKS

Lastly, it is important to mention that there are ways to track the development of brain function without taking physiological measurements. Many researchers interested in brain development make use of behavioural tasks that have been linked to the activity of certain brain areas or networks in typical adults, neuropsychological patients and animal studies. Developmental researchers can adapt these 'marker' tasks for use with children and trace the development of the associated brain region or network. An example of this is the Dimension Change Card Sort (DCCS) task (see Chapter 10), which is a measure of executive function linked to the prefrontal cortex (Zelazo, 2004).

In Chapters 4 and 6 we discuss several studies that have employed psycho-physiological measures in studies with infants.

The development of methods for researching the function of the brain and CNS in very young infants and children has led to a recent and substantial increase in the number of studies of functional brain development. However, research into brain development is not without controversy or conceptual difficulties. Historically, a number of developmental psychologists have suggested that development is best understood by observing changes in behaviour, and that attempting to reduce our understanding of development to physiological process does not add useful information. However, revelations that both brain structure and function change dramatically right into adulthood and beyond (e.g., Blakemore, 2008; Cohen-Kadosh et al., 2013) imply that changes in the brain may have an important bearing on emerging abilities. It is therefore becoming more important to understand cognitive development at the level of neural processes (Nelson & Luciana, 2001; Mareschal et al., 2007; Johnson, 2011).

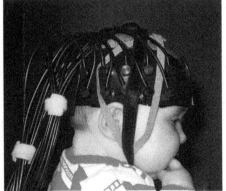

Infants taking part in EEG and fNIRS experiments.
Source: © Audrey van der Meer, reproduced with permission (L); Reproduced with the permission of Dr Sarah Lloyd-Fox (R)

Table 3-1 Techniques for studying human brain function and structure

Technique	What it shows	Advantages and disadvantages
EEG *(electroencephalograph):* multiple electrodes are placed on the scalp	Electrical fields resulting from the activity of billions of neurons	Detects very rapid changes in electrical activity, allowing analysis of stages of cognitive processing
		Provides poor spatial resolution of the source of electrical activity
PET *(positron-emission tomography) and SPECT (single photon emission computed tomography):* positrons and photons are emissions from radioactive substances	An image of the amount and localization of any molecule that can be injected in radioactive form, such as neurotransmitters, drugs or tracers for blood flow or glucose use (images indicate specific changes in neuronal activity)	Allows functional and biochemical studies
		Provides visual image corresponding to anatomy
		Requires exposure to low levels of radioactivity
		Provides spatial resolution better than that of EEG but poorer than that of MRI
		Cannot follow rapid changes (faster than 30 seconds)
fMRI *(functional magnetic resonance imaging):* exposes the brain to a magnetic field and measures radio frequency waves	Traditional MRI provides high-resolution image of brain anatomy. Functional MRI (fMRI) provides images of changes in blood flow (which indicate specific changes in neural activity). A new variant, diffusion tensor imaging (DTI), shows water flow in neural fibres, thus revealing the 'wiring diagram' of neural connections in the brain	Requires no exposure to radioactivity
		Provides high spatial resolution of anatomical details (under 1 mm)
		Provides low temporal resolution (slower than one second)
fNIRS *(functional near infrared spectroscopy):* measures flow of oxygenated blood to regions of the brain by detecting refraction of infrared light shone into the brain	Like fMRI, fNIRS provides information about blood flow to regions of the brain	Not invasive as infrared light is at levels that the brain is normally exposed to in sunlight

QUALITATIVE RESEARCH METHODS

A great deal of research in developmental psychology is concerned with collecting quantitative data. Researchers use the quantitative data that is generated in experiments, surveys and systematic observations to conduct statistical tests and generalize findings to a wider group or population. An advantage of quantitative data is that it is often associated with robust and reliable measures and outputs of the data collection process that are easy to handle, analyse and interpret in larger numbers and regular ways. However, sometimes researchers may wish to explore a new area of research or understand better how a child experiences or understands a situation. Additionally, a researcher may wish to capture the influence of cultural or contextual factors on development, conduct a more in-depth case study, or explore the ways in which language and meaning affect behaviour. In these cases, researchers may choose to employ qualitative methods.

Qualitative methods can focus on specifics of the interactions, language or discourse children use, or on the complex meanings that research participants draw from their experiences. In much qualitative research, the role or perspective of the researcher is considered as an important factor in understanding the phenomenon. For instance, in a qualitative analysis of an interview researchers may seek to identify themes from a child's responses, but would also be careful to try to understand how they might have influenced those responses. Acknowledging and understanding the influence of the researcher on data collection, analysis and interpretation should be a feature of all good research in developmental psychology, including experimental studies. However, it is arguably more important in qualitative research where there may be fewer of the standardized measures and procedures that experimental and quantitative researchers often use.

While there are many different forms of qualitative method, not all are suitable for developmental research. For instance, *discourse analysis* (e.g., Potter & Wetherell, 1987) is used in some social psychological research where the aim is to understand how individuals use language to construct or represent an understanding of the world. However, extending this approach to developmental studies is not straightforward because young children's language abilities and vocabulary do not match those of adults. Studies of discourse and children's conversations typically need to be adapted to focus more on developing loose 'themes' from children's talk.

A more widely used qualitative approach for studying children's social interactions is *ethnography*. Ethnographic research seeks to get inside a particular group or culture to understand aspects of the relationships between its members, and the values and beliefs that exist as a result. For instance, an ethnographic researcher or ethnographer might join a community or group in a particular culture for a number of weeks to study a process. Barbara Rogoff's studies of how children in a Mayan community learned how to become skilled weavers from their mothers (Rogoff et al., 2016) is one such example of an ethnographic study. By living with and closely observing processes of communication, Rogoff was able to chart how these skills were taught and learned, and how the broader context for learning framed this process. Although, in theory, ethnographic research could extend to many contexts including studying at-risk groups such as delinquent children and peer relationships in a nursery school (e.g., Corsaro, 1990). However, there can be problems with access, and questions about how far a researcher can ever fully participate in the life of a group given that her primary aims are observation and academic study. Nevertheless, ethnographic and other qualitative research methods can reveal important perspectives about developmental processes, and are especially useful when exploring a new issue or complex context.

SELECTING A SAMPLE

If you wanted to study the typical play activities of preschoolers, how would you go about collecting your data? A key concern, possibly the first one to consider, is how to select a sample, or a group made up of individuals who, you hope, are representative of the entire population of preschoolers that you want to describe.

Representativeness of a sample

If we want our research conclusions to be applicable to the population our sample is designed to reflect, we must ensure the representativeness of that sample. That is, the individuals we choose to study must possess nearly the same characteristics evidenced by the larger population in which we are interested. Also, depending on that population, we may need a very broad sample in which many cultures, social classes or ethnic backgrounds are represented. Consider the following example:

> A researcher wants to study the way children's vocabularies change over time. Living near a private nursery school in an affluent suburban community, she selects thirty 3 year olds and thirty 5 year olds from the school population and tests their vocabulary levels. Based on the performance of these children, the investigator reports that she has a set of norms or guidelines for what may be expected of preschoolers' vocabulary knowledge. What's wrong with the researcher's conclusion?

sample A group of individuals who are representative of a larger population.

representativeness The degree to which a sample actually possesses the characteristics of the larger population it represents.

The investigator has chosen her sample poorly because, other things being equal, the parents of these children are likely to be well educated and to have verbal skills that surpass those of less educated parents. It's also possible that experiences at the school, where the ratio of teachers to students may be more favourable than in public schools, facilitate children's learning. Clearly, we can't generalize about the average vocabulary accomplishment of all children of ages 3 and 5 unless we sample a range of children from different backgrounds and in different instructional settings.

This example illustrates one of the major problems that researchers face when selecting a sample – namely, to try to recruit a group of people representative of the larger population about which the researcher wishes to hypothesize. Of particular concern is obtaining a sample that represents the diverse population of many nations.

The question is even more important if researchers are seeking to draw implications from their studies about universal developmental laws or norms, because context and culture can be a very important aspects of development and psychological functioning. This is a problem across psychology as a whole, rather than one limited to developmental psychology (Henrich, Heine, & Norenzayan, 2010).

Of course, researchers also need to make sensible, practical decisions when selecting a sample. It would usually be prohibitively expensive and time-consuming to conduct many research studies in different countries purely to explore whether a particular result holds true across cultures. However, more practical steps – such as ensuring equal gender representation – should be included as part of a balanced research design (Denmark et al., 1988). Thus sample selection is something that researchers need to consider carefully when drawing up a study. It is important that core characteristics of samples (gender, ethnicity, social class) are reported when disseminating research findings. It is also important that researchers are careful when making claims about how far findings from a study can be applied to other populations.

RESEARCH DESIGN IN DEVELOPMENTAL PSYCHOLOGY

Selecting a sample and a method of gathering information enables us to describe some aspect of human development, but what will this information do for us? To make use of it, we need to design a study to determine how the various factors of development that we have described are related to and interact with one another, with the goal of identifying the reasons that development occurs as it does. In this section, we offer a brief discussion of the most common research designs – the correlational method, the experimental method and the case study – that are used by psychologists to study the nature and process of child development. In describing these methods, we have chosen illustrations that pertain to a single topic: the effect on children's behaviour of viewing violent television programmes. Our aim is to show how different designs yield different approaches and answers to this question.

Correlational designs

Many questions in child development reflect an interest in whether some experiences of childhood are related to other experiences of childhood in a regular or systematic way. For example, how does watching aggression on television or playing aggressive computer games relate to the levels of aggression children show at school or towards siblings and peers? To illustrate the correlational method of research, a design that enables researchers to establish that certain experiences or factors are related to each other and to assess the strength of the relations, let's examine a study that addressed this question. John Wright and Aletha Huston (1995) studied the TV-viewing behaviour of preschool children in more than 250 families, all from low-income areas. The children were either 2 or 4 years old at the start of the study and either 5 or 7 at its conclusion. The parents were asked to make detailed reports on how their preschoolers spent their time, including which TV shows they watched and for how long each day, and every year, the children were given a variety of cognitive achievement tests, such as measures of mathematical skill and word knowledge. The researchers found that the more educational programmes the children watched, the higher they scored on the tests (Figure 3-2).

> **correlational method**
> A research design that permits investigators to establish relations among variables as well as assess the strength of those relations.

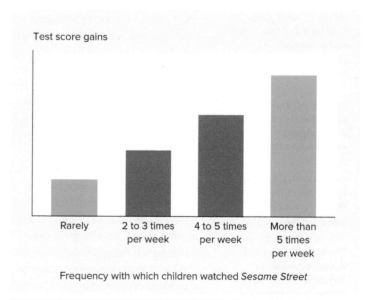

Test score gains

Frequency with which children watched *Sesame Street*

Figure 3-2   Watching Sesame Street *makes scores rise*

In one of the first studies of the effects of watching *Sesame Street*, researchers found that on tests of identification of body parts; recognition of letters, numbers, and geometric forms; and classifying and sorting, preschoolers who frequently watched the show performed significantly better than those who watched rarely.

Frequency of watching *Sesame Street* and gains in test scores were positively correlated with each other because both measures increased in step with one another: so, children who viewed more educational TV shows showed more improvement on the academic tests. It is very important to be careful when describing correlational findings because this finding does not mean that watching educational TV necessarily led to increases in test scores. An alternative possibility is that as children's test scores improved they became more interested in educational TV, perhaps finding it more interesting once they were better able to grasp all the content. Interestingly, the researchers also found that the more time children spent watching cartoons or adult programmes (that is, not educational TV), the lower they scored on these tests. This is a negative correlation; that is, as one score increased the other score decreased.

The critical point to remember about correlational research is that a correlation does not indicate causal relations between factors; it simply tells us that two factors are related to each other and indicates the strength or magnitude of that relation. Thus, the correlations found by Wright and Huston (1995) do not indicate that watching educational programmes caused higher test scores. Any number of factors other than watching educational shows could have improved the children's test scores. For example, suppose that children whose parents give them a great deal of encouragement and guidance in academic subjects are the same ones who watch the educational programmes.

If correlational research doesn't allow us to determine causation, why do we use it? For one thing, many questions are difficult to study in a controlled laboratory design. For example, the effect of viewing educational programmes on cognitive development is cumulative, meaning it happens over a long period of time. An experiment to study such long-term exposure would be difficult to design. Also, understanding causal processes is not the goal of all developmental research. Many investigators are primarily interested in describing the patterns and path of development as it naturally occurs, which is what the correlational method describes.

Experimental designs

laboratory experiment
A research design that allows investigators to determine cause and effect by controlling variables and treatments, and assigning participants randomly to treatments.

experimental group
In an experiment, the group that is exposed to the treatment, or the *independent variable*.

control group In an experiment, the group that is not exposed to the treatment, or the *independent variable*.

random assignment
The technique by which researchers assign individuals randomly to either an *experimental* or *control group*.

The primary means by which researchers investigate causal connections among factors is with an experiment. An experiment can be carried out in a laboratory or in natural situations. In a laboratory experiment, researchers are able to control factors that may influence the variable they are interested in, and therefore their results allow them to draw conclusions about cause and effect. Researchers will control or hold constant, or equate, every possible influence except the one factor they have hypothesized to be the cause of the variable they want to study. They then create two groups of participants. One group, called the experimental group, is exposed to the proposed causative factor; the second group, the control group, does not experience this factor. Researchers put people in these two groups by using random assignment, which helps to rule out the possibility that the people in each of the groups differ from one another in some systematic way that could distort the results of the experiment.

To understand how these various controls enable the laboratory experimenter to determine causality, let's look at a classic study of the relation between watching violent television programmes and aggressive behaviour. Liebert and Baron (1972) randomly assigned 136 boys and girls ranging in age from 5 to 9 to either an experimental group or a control group. The children in both groups first saw two brief commercials selected for their humour and attention-getting value. Then half the children – those in the experimental group – saw 3.5 minutes of a TV programme about crime that contained a chase, two fist-fights, two shootings and a knifing. In contrast, the children in the control group watched a highly active but non-violent sports sequence of the same time length. Finally, the children in both groups watched another 60 seconds of a tyre commercial. The only difference between the two groups was the 3.5-minute video they watched – that is, whether they were exposed or not exposed to the violent TV episodes. This is the independent variable, or the factor the researchers deliberately manipulate. The researchers thus hypothesized that if the children in the experimental group later behaved differently from those in the control group, it would be reasonable to conclude that exposure to TV violence was the cause.

In the second phase of the study, the experimenters told each of the children that they were to play a game with another child in an adjoining room (whom they could not see and who, in fact, was purely imaginary). The researchers seated each child before a panel that had two buttons labelled 'Hurt' and 'Help', and told the child that the buttons were connected to a handle in the other room that their play partner would use. The experimenter explained that if the child wanted to make it easier for her 'play partner' to turn the handle, she could press the Help button. But if the child wanted to hinder her 'play partner' she could press the Hurt button, which would turn the handle burning hot. Of course, this entire scenario was a deception, and nothing a child did hurt anyone else. (The issue of deception raises ethical questions that we discuss shortly.) The amount of aggressiveness the children display is the dependent variable, or the factor that researchers expect to change due to the independent variable. The researchers believed that by measuring how long and how often children depressed the Hurt button, they could find out how aggressively children in the experimental and the control groups would behave towards another child. Liebert and Baron discovered the causal relation they predicted. Children who had seen the violent TV segment were more willing to harm or behave aggressively towards their 'play partner' than were children who had watched the non-violent sports programme.

Although this study was carefully designed, it has limitations that may prevent generalization from the experimental situation to the natural world. Ensuring a study's ecological validity, or its accurate representation of events and processes that occur in the natural environment, is often difficult. For example, Liebert and Baron edited their violent TV programme to include more acts of violence in 3.5 minutes than would normally occur in a randomly chosen TV segment of this length, even in a show that has a lot of violence. Despite these limitations, experimenters can gain important insights about human behaviour from laboratory experiments. For instance, finding out the softest ranges of sound a child can hear requires controlling all outside noise, which is rare if not impossible in everyday experience. When scientists want to use an experiment yet study behaviour in a more ecologically valid way, they conduct experiments in the field.

In a field experiment, investigators deliberately introduce a change, called a manipulation, in a person's normal environment and then measure the outcome of their manipulation. As an illustration, let's consider a field experiment about the impact of viewing TV violence on aggressive behaviour in children (Friedrich & Stein, 1973). Preschoolers enrolled in a summer programme were the participants in this study. During the first three weeks of the study, the researchers observed the children during their usual play sessions to determine how much aggressive behaviour each child displayed under normal circumstances. This is called a baseline measure. Then, for the next four weeks, they showed the children, who were randomly assigned to one of three groups, a half-hour TV programme each day. Some children always saw programmes depicting interpersonal aggression, such as cartoons; others saw programmes with a message of caring and kindness towards others; and others watched neutral shows, such as nature programmes.

The researchers found that children who had been rated high in aggressive behaviour before the TV-watching manipulation behaved even more aggressively after repeated exposure to aggressive cartoons but not after exposure to the other two kinds of show. For children who were rated low in aggression during the initial assessment period, watching aggressive TV shows had no effect; they were still less likely to behave aggressively. Children who watched neutral shows did not change either. The researchers concluded that exposure to TV violence can increase aggression in children, but only among children already likely to behave aggressively. These findings were especially interesting in that the researchers took care to minimize observer bias – that is, the tendency of observers who are knowledgeable about a hypothesis to be influenced in their

independent variable
The variable, or factor, that researchers deliberately manipulate in an experiment.

dependent variable
The variable, or factor, that researchers expect to change as a function of change in the independent variable.

ecological validity
The degree to which a research study accurately represents events or processes that occur in the natural world.

field experiment An experiment in which researchers deliberately create a change in a real-world setting and then measure the outcome of their manipulation.

observer bias The tendency of observers to be influenced in their judgements by their knowledge of the hypotheses guiding the research.

> Chapter 15 discusses some of the other sources of aggressive and antisocial behaviour.

observations by that knowledge. The observers who assessed the children's behaviour after the TV viewings did not know which types of programme the different children had seen.

One advantage of the field experiment over the laboratory experiment is that the results can be generalized more readily to real-life experiences and settings. Friedrich and Stein did not edit the TV programmes the children saw in any way, and these programmes were among those that many of the children watched in their homes. Moreover, the children's aggressive behaviour was measured in an everyday setting, not in a situation that allowed or encouraged them to behave aggressively. At the same time, the field experiment retains some important features of a laboratory experiment. Because the independent variable – the type of TV programme – was under the control of the researchers, and the participants were randomly assigned to the various groups, Friedrich and Stein could be reasonably confident that they had demonstrated a causal connection – namely, that exposure to TV violence may encourage aggressive children to behave even more aggressively.

natural experiment
An experiment in which researchers measure the results of events that occur naturally in the real world.

There is yet another type of experiment that developmental psychologists use that you will see discussed in the text. For ethical or practical reasons, researchers may not be able to introduce changes into the natural world. In these instances, they may conduct a natural experiment, in which they measure the effects of events or changes that occur naturally in the real world. Unlike a laboratory or field experiment, the research participants are not randomly assigned to experimental conditions. Instead, the researchers select the children they study because the children are already exposed to a set of conditions that are of interest to the researcher, such as enrolment in day care or a nutritional supplement programme. A natural experiment differs from the correlational approach because it allows for some assessment of cause and effect, for instance by examining differences between a group where one aspect differs, clearly and systematically, from a control group. One example of a natural experiment is a study that investigated the way the introduction of television into a community affected aggressive behaviour among children (MacBeth, 1996). By monitoring the level of aggressiveness in children's play both before and after the debut of television in a small town in Canada, the investigator was able to show that aggressive behaviour did in fact increase after TV arrived in town. As our examples suggest, a great deal of research has been devoted to children's television viewing and, more recently, internet, smartphone and tablet use. Box 3-2 discusses some of this research and its impact on legislation.

Applied Developmental Psychology

BOX 3-2   How can we make better use of research on children and television/internet use?

The impact on children of the amazing growth of communications media cannot be denied. From early radio, movies and comic books to television and its more recent cousins – video games, computers, the internet, social media, smartphones and tablets – children have been bombarded with new information and experiences via the media.

What has the wealth of research on children and television revealed? Research on the effects of TV has shown that some television programmes do help young children learn, but it has also shown negative effects on children of watching programmes filled with violence and sex as well as advertisements that prey on the young child's limited understanding (Comstock & Scharrer, 2006).

Research on children's and adolescents' use of the internet and social media has also revealed some positive effects, such as improved reading scores (Jackson et al., 2006), and some negative effects, such as increasing adolescents' awareness of dangerous behaviours such as various forms of self-injury (Whitlock, Powers, & Eckenrode, 2006). More worryingly, social media use seems to, under some circumstances, predict more general negative effects on mental well-being such as increased depressive symptoms (Nesi & Prinstein, 2015).

With the advent of media equipment which is becoming ever more accessible for younger age groups, such as touchscreen tablets, research in this area is moving even into the effects of media exposure on infants in the first two years of life. There the evidence also points to both benefits and problems. Researchers have wondered whether children can transfer what they learn on a touchscreen app to a real world task, and the answer there is yes (Huber et al., 2016). Of concern though, it seems that increased touchscreen use in infants and toddlers is associated with reduced duration of sleep overall (with an increase in sleep during the day but a decrease in sleep at night), as well as a later onset of sleep (the greater the touchscreen use, the longer the infants took to get to sleep).

If certain media exposure is unsuitable for children or adolescents, what can parents and others do beyond seeking stricter laws and government policies?

Huston and Wright (1998) stress that parents need to recognize and act on their own enormous influence on children's use of media. It is obviously easier to enforce boundaries in infants and toddlers, but this can be more difficult with older children and adolescents. Setting an example, co-viewing programmes, navigating internet sites with their children and setting household limits are possible approaches.

© Blend/Image Source

It is incumbent upon families, educators, government and the media themselves to take responsibility for considering the effects of children's exposure to media, both positive and negative, and to act accordingly. It is also important for developmental psychologists to take this area of research seriously in order to best inform everyone involved in this ever-increasing aspect of infants', children's and adolescents' experiences (Hirsh-Pasek et al., 2015).

The case study approach

Can we learn anything about development by studying a single child or perhaps a single group, such as a particular classroom? The close study of individual persons or a group, called the case study method, is sometimes used in developmental research. The case study allows investigators to explore phenomena they do not often encounter, such as an unusual talent, a rare developmental disorder or a model classroom. As we have already mentioned earlier in this book, Charles Darwin (1872) kept a highly detailed diary of his infant son's emotional expressions, a record that became the basis for his theory of emotional development in infants and children.

> case study A form of research in which investigators study an individual person or group very intensely.

Sometimes, a case study provides insights or hypotheses that later investigations pursue in a more systematic fashion. For example, careful observation of one child who experiences a new treatment for child conduct problems may shed light on how the treatment works for children with certain behavioural patterns. However, the chief limitation of the single-case approach is that, without further study or a larger sample, it is difficult to know if the results of the case study generalize from one individual to other people or situations.

One distinctive form of the case study approach is the Microgenetic Method (e.g., Siegler & Crowley, 1991; Kuhn, 1995). The Microgenetic Method involves studying changes in an individual's behaviour over time on the same or similar set of tasks. Thus the Microgenetic Method constitutes an exploration of performance or knowledge of a particular skill or use of a strategy to solve a problem. Researchers who use microgenetic methods are interested in studying 'change as it is occurring'. Flynn, Pine and Lewis (2006) identify three key principles for conducting research using this approach:

1. Any observations that researchers make need to identify some sort of change (i.e., from before to after the acquisition of a skill or understanding).
2. There need to be frequent and a high number of observations to be sure to capture the processes of change as they are happening. Thus the Microgenetic Method involves more than simply collecting pre- and post-test methods and then inferring how any changes came about.
3. Observations need to be analysed very closely and in detail in order to identify how any change came about.

For instance, Siegler (1995) used the Microgenetic Method to study how 5-year-old children came to understand conservation of number: that is, appreciating that, even if things look different, the number of objects remains the same if nothing is added or taken away. After a pre-test, non-conservers (children who gave incorrect answers) were placed in four intervention or treatment conditions: a control condition, a condition where an experimenter gave children feedback on their performance, a condition where children were given feedback and then asked to explain their answers, and finally a condition where children were given feedback but were also asked to explain why the experimenter gave a different (correct) response. Not only was Siegler able to demonstrate that children learned best when they were asked to explain the experimenter's reasoning, but the careful analysis of children's talk and answers revealed how children came to learn. This included grasping that appearance was relatively unimportant, and adding or taking away something was important to answer the questions correctly. The Microgenetic Method also allowed Siegler to demonstrate that understanding was achieved through a gradual process, and sometimes children continued to give wrong answers even when they appeared to grasp some of the key principles involved in conservation.

Mixing methods in developmental research

The research method that a developmental scientist uses depends both on the question being asked and the ages of the children studied. (Table 3-2 summarizes the differences among the research designs that have been examined so far.) Researchers may also combine these designs over a series of studies on the same topic. For example, a researcher may start off in an unexplored area by using a correlational approach to establish some possible relations among the factors studied. Then she may use an experimental approach to achieve a clearer view of the causal links among these factors. Finally, she may examine closely a single-case study, either of an individual or a group, to provide more details about the process under study. In the field of child development, the use of multiple methods is becoming increasingly common because each area may help to illuminate different aspects of a problem, or help a researcher to see the same problem from different perspectives. Of course, using multiple methods can be expensive and time-consuming so, when conducting research in developmental psychology, careful attention needs to be paid to balancing the strengths and limitations of different approaches, and to what methods are most appropriate to address a particular research question.

Table 3-2 Research designs: strengths and limitations

Design	Control over independent variable	Control over dependent variable	Generalizability of findings
Correlational method	Low	Low	Medium
Laboratory experiment	High	High	Low
Field experiment	Medium	Low	High
Natural experiment	Low	Low	High

STUDYING CHANGE OVER TIME

Recall that the main concerns of research in developmental psychology are to chart and understand change over time. To study developmental change, the field makes use of certain methods intended to measure this type of change. The main research methods used to study time are the cross-sectional, longitudinal and sequential methods.

The cross-sectional method

cross-sectional method
A research method in which researchers compare groups of individuals of different age levels at approximately the same point in time.

The most common strategy for investigating age-related differences in development is the cross-sectional method, in which researchers compare different individuals of different ages at the same point in time. Cross-sectional research compares different age groups of children on a topic, such as a behaviour or cognitive performance, to determine how changes associated with age may unfold over the course of development.

Consider the cross-sectional research done by Rheingold and Eckerman (1970), who examined how children grow and develop independence from their mother. They observed mothers and their children, aged between 12 and 60 months. There were six children (three boys and three girls) at each of the 6-month intervals between 12 and 60 months of age; for example, six children were 12 months old, six children were 18 months old, and so on. The researchers observed the children's behaviours in a controlled outdoor setting. They positioned the mothers and children at one end of a large lawn; the mothers sat in chairs and the children were free to roam. Observers were stationed nearby, and they recorded the paths the children took. A positive correlation between child age and distance travelled from mother was found. The average furthest distance from mothers for 1-year-olds, the youngest age group, was about 23 feet (6.9 metres); by 2 years of age, children ventured about 50 feet (15.1 metres); 3-year-olds went 57 feet (17.3 metres); and 4-year-olds went 68 feet (20.6 metres).

Using the cross-sectional method, the researchers were able to determine how independence differs across age levels. However, this approach yields no information about the causes that lie behind these age-related changes because we cannot know what the children in the study were like at younger ages. For example, we do not know if the child who is very independent at 1 year is likely to be more independent at age 5 than a peer who exhibited little independence when he was 1 year old. Another research design, the longitudinal method, is better suited to tackling the issue of individual change over time.

The longitudinal method

The Fels Longitudinal Study began in 1929 and continued until the 1970s. It followed the same groups of children from birth to age 18. Parents who enrolled their newborns in this study agreed to have the child weighed, measured, observed and tested until he or she was old enough to graduate from high school. One conclusion of this study, which could only be obtained by studying the same children over time, was that certain behaviours are stable over time and that in some cases the stability of behaviour was affected by the child's gender. For instance, boys were more likely to show stable patterns of aggressive behaviour from childhood to adulthood (Kagan & Moss, 1962; see also Chapter 13).

> **longitudinal method**
> A method in which investigators study the same people repeatedly at various times in the participants' lives.

This type of research uses the longitudinal method, in which researchers study the same individuals repeatedly at various points in their lives to assess patterns of stability and change over time. A longitudinal design allows researchers to follow the development of individuals and, as a result, it can explore possible causes of any observed pattern. It is a powerful method for evaluating the impact of earlier events on later behaviour.

The longitudinal method also has disadvantages. It can take years to collect longitudinal data, and researchers often want to obtain information more quickly. In addition, there is the problem of losing participants. Over time, people move, become ill, or simply lose interest and no longer participate in the study. In addition, the questions and concerns that inspired the research may not be of interest later in the study. Another problem arises from what we call *practice effects*, or the effects of repeated testing. Since the same measures may be used in several successive years, participants' answers may be the result of their familiarity with the items or questions.

A common approach in much research is the short-term longitudinal study. Here researchers track the same group of people but for a limited time period, usually a few months or a few years. Their focus is usually limited to a few key questions, often questions that this relatively brief time period can address adequately. Such research has the advantage of shortening the period of data collection and thereby avoiding dropouts in the sample.

A different kind of drawback to lengthy longitudinal studies is the problem of generalizing to generations other than the one studied. Children today grow up with many experiences unknown to children growing up in their parents' or grandparents' generations – for example, computers or the widespread use of day care. Findings from a longitudinal study may lose relevance as society changes and be descriptive of only a particular age cohort – that is, members of the same generation.

Applied Developmental Psychology

BOX 3-3   Deferred gratification: the Stanford Marshmallow Experiment

The advantages of following a group of individuals over a long time period, and some of the difficulties involved in testing individuals at different ages, are nicely highlighted by a famous study conducted by Walter Mischel. In 1972, Mischel invited a group of 4-year-old children who had just started at the Bing Nursery in Stanford University, to sit on their own at a table. In front of each child was a single marshmallow (or in some cases, an Oreo cookie, or pretzel stick). Mischel's experimental instructions to the children were clear and simple. If the child could resist eating that marshmallow for 15 minutes, she or he could have two rather than one. Mischel's interest was in whether and for how long children could resist the temptation to eat the single treat.

This simple task was an excellent, and child-friendly, method for collecting data about children's ability to delay gratification. And Mischel's results were striking. Only 30% of children were able to hold out and resist eating the marshmallow. Of those who gave way to temptation and ate the treat, most did so within 3 minutes of the study starting.

The Stanford Marshmallow Experiment revealed some interesting (and occasionally amusing) aspects of children's ability to delay gratification. Mischel recorded children's behaviour while trying to resist temptation – covering their eyes and turning the tray away, among other distraction activities.

However, perhaps even more interesting were the findings from a study conducted by Mischel's team some years later (Shoda, Mischel, & Peake, 1990). The researchers were intrigued by anecdotal evidence that some of the 4-year-old children who were able to delay gratification were outperforming their peers who were not able to do so. So Shoda and colleagues contacted as many of the initial participants in Mischel's original study as they could, and looked at their school performance. In adolescence, some 10 years after the initial study, those children who delayed gratification outperformed their classmates who had not. Clearly, the ability to resist eating a marshmallow and to earn greater rewards later was associated with positive outcomes into adolescence. Mischel's initial cohort of participants were followed throughout their lives and into adulthood.

Many people in developmental psychology and the media pounced on Shoda et al.'s findings. Perhaps if we can teach young children more self control then that will improve their school performance further down the line. What a triumph for developmental psychology! However, it is important that we don't get too carried away about this possibility. As we will explain, some care and more research is needed.

Firstly, more recent findings indicate that the strength of Shoda et al.'s (1990) findings may have arisen by chance. Watts, Duncan, and Quan (2018) replicated Shoda et al.'s study with a much larger sample of participants. They found that the correlations between marshmallow test performance at 4 years of age and academic performance at 15 were only half the strength of those observed by Shoda et al. And in fact the correlations disappeared altogether once factors like intelligence and family background were controlled for.

Another more methodological problem is faced by researchers who want to follow up research on the role of self-gratification in development. Nowadays, the Stanford Marshmallow test is probably a lame duck. It is now well known – certainly those individuals who participate in it, or their parents/teachers, know that it is a study about delayed gratification. This knowledge could clearly influence behaviours.

And so researchers have had to explore the processes associated with self-gratification with some different tasks. They are also faced with the possibility that the basis of the current focus on delayed gratification may not be as solid as once assumed. Certainly more research is needed to understand this important area of study, but the road from science to application does not seem to be easy in this case.

The sequential method

A creative way around the problem of separating age-related changes from changes caused by the unique experiences of a particular age cohort is to use the sequential method, which combines features of both cross-sectional and longitudinal studies. In this method, researchers begin by select-ing samples of children of different ages, as they would in cross-sectional research. Suppose, for example, that we wanted to study the change in the development of children's reading skills throughout childhood. We might begin by recruiting and test-ing three samples of children: 2-year-olds, 4-year-olds and 6-year-olds. We would then test these same children again at periodic intervals, let's say every two years. Then, at each of the two-year measuring points, we would add a new sample of 2-year-olds to

sequential method
A research method that combines features of both the *cross-sectional* and the *longitudinal methods*.

the study, which would enable us to compare a larger number of age cohorts. Figure 3-3 displays the design of this study.

There are several advantages of the sequential method. First, the longitudinal aspect of the study allows researchers to examine age-related changes in children. Second, the cross-sectional aspect allows researchers to examine the impact of the year of evaluation and testing or practice effects. Third, in following each age cohort, the design can explore generational effects, or effects of the particular time period in which each group of children was born and raised. For example, perhaps the 6-year-olds originally recruited for this study entered kindergarten when mathematics curricula in the primary grades underwent much change. By comparing these and other age cohorts, we might be able to assess changes in children's mathematics abilities as instructional techniques changed. Finally, the design has a time-saving advantage. Six years after the start of the study, in 2006, the study would include data on changes in mathematics ability that span a period of 10 years (look again at Figure 3-3). This is a 4-year saving over a traditional longitudinal study.

This combination of the cross-sectional and longitudinal designs yields a third dimension of measurement that compares cohorts,

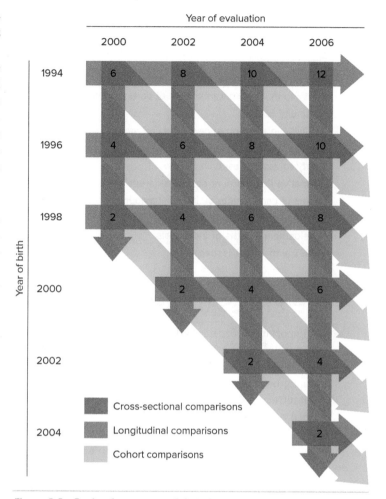

Figure 3-3   Design for a sequential study

or people of the same age, at different points in time. The numbers within the arrows are the ages of the groups of children to be studied. For example, in the year 2000, we would do a cross-sectional study of three groups of children, aged 2, 4 and 6. In 2002, we would add a new group of 2-year-olds and we would again measure the earlier groups of children, who would now be 4, 6 and 8. A number of different types of comparison are possible from such a design.

When studying change over time, developmental researchers have a choice of design and method (see Table 3-3 for a comparison of the pluses and minuses of all three approaches). From a practical point of view, it makes sense to select a research method that is ideal for answering the questions posed in a particular study. However, theoretical perspectives do tend to favour some methods over others, largely because particular methods are better suited to the kinds of questions that stem from a particular perspective. For example, early researchers in the psycho-dynamic tradition often use case studies because they provide the sort of personal detail they seek. Piaget focused on the systematic observation of children, typically in a laboratory. Researchers who use a learning perspective have relied heavily on observational techniques in both the field and the laboratory. Observational analysis permits close inspection of behavioural changes to determine if any learning has occurred. Sociocultural theorists and qualitative researchers also tend to rely on observational techniques. These techniques may provide evidence of how interactions between a child and her social partner or the cultural or physical environment influence a change in behaviour. Lifespan researchers tend to use interview techniques, surveys and objective demographic data such as health and longevity statistics. These techniques capture broader social and historical patterns than are available in first-hand observations.

Table 3-3   Comparison of methods of studying developmental change over time

	Cross-sectional	Longitudinal	Sequential
Time required	Short	Long	Moderate
Ability to control costs	High	Low	Moderate
Ability to maintain potential pool of participants	Excellent	Problematic	Moderate to good
Continuity of staff	High	Moderate to low	Moderate to high
Flexibility in adapting to new tests and measures	High	Low	Moderate
Likelihood of practice effects	Low	High	Moderate
Ability to assess research issues:			
Normative development data at different ages	Excellent	Excellent	Excellent
Impact of early events on later behaviour	Poor	Excellent	Good
Stability vs instability of behaviour	Poor	Excellent	Good
Developmental paths of individuals	Poor	Excellent	Good
Historical or cohort issues	Excellent	Poor	Good

THE ETHICS OF RESEARCH WITH CHILDREN

It is important to consider ethical issues in all research involving human participants. There are some particular ethical issues that exist when conducting research with infants, children and young people. Many of these issues are a consequence of a need to consider carefully how to present some themes in some research that may be unfamiliar, unsuitable or even frightening to children. Others arise because children may often find it difficult to assert their wishes if these conflict with those of an adult, or because children are typically deemed not to be able to give fully informed consent. Research organizations now give clear guidance about appropriate ethical issues to help researchers, participants and others fully understand the issues involved in conducting research with children, and to act appropriately.

informed consent
Agreement, based on a clear and full understanding of the purposes and procedures of a research study, to participate in that study.

Perhaps the foremost ethical issue when considering research with children is informed consent. In all psychological research, agreement to participate in research is based on a clear understanding of the purposes and procedures to be employed in the study, and so all research with human subjects requires that researchers obtain informed consent from all participants before being included in a study. When participants are young children, most ethical guidelines stipulate that parents or legal guardians must provide informed consent on their behalf. It is also generally considered important not only to secure parental or caregiver consent for younger participants, but also to seek positive assent from the young participants themselves. This is not only important from an ethical point of view, but also makes good practical sense, too.

Research participants also have the unarguable right to protection not only from physical harm but also from psychological and emotional harm, such as feeling uncomfortable or embarrassed. Such experiences are of particular concern in research that involves deception. Recall the experiment by Liebert and Baron (1972), discussed earlier, on the effects of viewing violent TV programmes on children's later aggressive behaviour towards other children in a 'mock' game situation. Even though no child was actually harmed, how might the children have viewed themselves after they participated in the study? Might they have felt ashamed of themselves? Laboratory research involving deception is becoming less common. However, such questions remain important, and careful scrutiny of all ethical issues in research with children is critical.

Of course, many ethical issues that exist for children also need to be considered carefully when conducting research with adults. The core challenge for the developmental researcher is to judge how far any procedure may affect children differently or in ways in which adults would not be affected. For instance, it would be inappropriate for a researcher to show a child violent images or videos in order to establish whether this led to subsequent aggressive behaviour, whereas some such material might be suitable for adults, who are better able to judge what is acceptable to them. For this reason, institutional ethical committees often look especially carefully at research proposals to study children, to ensure standards are met and guidelines are being followed.

It is also important to consider arrangements for communicating the findings of research or 'debriefing' children and adolescents who participate in research. Ideally, both children and their caregivers (those who may have formally provided consent on their child's behalf) should be given information about a study both before and afterwards, to inform them of the findings. When testing has been conducted at school, teachers may also need to be informed. Clearly, when explaining findings to children, care needs to be taken to ensure that this is done in a way that children will understand.

Developmental research is a tool for increasing our knowledge about children, and it is hoped that the lives of children will benefit from this knowledge. Recently, some investigators and child advocates have called for more stringent criteria regulating the participation of children in psychological research. Others worry that too many additional restrictions will seriously impede the ability of psychologists to learn more about issues that may ultimately lead to benefits for children. The ethics of research in child psychology continue to comprise a topic of much debate.

Providing information to children and their caregivers is important both before and after research is conducted.
© Lisa F. Young/Alamy

debriefing Communicating the findings of research, or its purpose, to participants after a study has been completed.

SUMMARY

Developmental psychologists use the *scientific method* in their research, formulating hypotheses on the basis of theories. Hypotheses are tested using replicable techniques to collect, study and analyse data. Researchers collect data from a number of different sources. These include self-reports from children, reports from others who know the child – such as parents, teachers and peers – and observations. There are challenges to collecting data from individuals at different ages, from infancy through to adulthood, because the competency of individuals at different ages varies enormously. Thus a wide range of approaches is often employed in the field, and researchers tailor these methods to answer their research questions at different ages. For instance, biological and psychophysiological measures include fMRI, fNIRS and PET scans, and EEG. Researchers can also use qualitative methods such as discourse analysis and ethnography.

There are important questions that all developmental psychologists need to consider in terms of research design. It is important for researchers to select an appropriate sample to ensure that this sample is representative of the wider population under study. The *correlational method* involves examining the relationship between two variables, but a correlation does not tell us whether one factor causes the other. In contrast, a *laboratory experiment* permits researchers to establish cause-and-effect relationships in a controlled setting. While this is a great strength of experimental designs, a laboratory experiment cannot easily be generalized to real-world settings. A *field experiment* or a *natural experiment* are alternatives. The *case study method* and *Microgenetic Method* take a more in-depth look at a single individual or group, to observe a particular process.

The most common strategy for investigating developmental change over time is the *cross-sectional method*, in which researchers compare groups of different ages at a given point in time. This approach is economical both in terms of time and money, but yields no information about change or about the causes of any observed age-related differences in participants. The *longitudinal method* overcomes these two drawbacks of cross-sectional research because the researcher examines the same individuals at different points in their lives. But longitudinal research has a high cost, and there may be problems if there is a gradual loss of participants as the research progresses. To overcome some of these limitations, researchers can use the *sequential method*, which combines features of both cross-sectional and longitudinal studies.

A major consideration when deciding on a research strategy is the effects the procedures will have on participants. Government and institutional review boards, in addition to professional organizations, are involved in setting and maintaining guidelines for the proper treatment of human subjects in research. These guidelines include the right to *informed consent* before participating, and special care needs to be taken to ensure that children (or their care-givers/parents) have provided this.

Explore and Discuss

1. What research methods should you use if you want to determine what causes a particular behaviour or event?

2. Explain the difference between causation and correlation.

3. What are some of the limitations of longitudinal methods as a way of studying children? Do you think these methods are worth the effort or not? Explain your answer.

4. Are some research measures appropriate for one age group but not for another? Why or why not? What problems might arise from using different measures or methods with different age groups?

5. How do the ethical issues one might encounter when researching with young children differ from those with adults?

Recommended Reading

Classic

Bryant, P. E. (1974). Experiments. In P. E. Bryant, *Perception and understanding in young children*. London: Methuen.

Schaie, K. W. (1965). A general model for the study of developmental problems. *Psychological Bulletin, 64,* 92–107.

Contemporary

Grieg, A. D., Taylor, J., & MacKay, T. (2012). *Doing research with children* (3rd edn). London: Sage.
Jeličić, H., Phelps, E., & Lerner, R. M. (2009). Use of missing data methods in longitudinal studies: The persistence of bad practices in developmental psychology. *Developmental Psychology, 45,* 1195–1199.
Reznick, J. S. (2017). *The developmental scientist's companion.* Cambridge: Cambridge University Press.
Teti, D. M. (ed.) (2005). *Handbook of research methods in developmental science.* Oxford: Blackwell.

CHAPTER 4
Physical Development: Growing a Body

Introduction

At first encounter, it may seem strange that a textbook on developmental psychology would choose to devote an entire chapter to physical development. Surely we should be more interested in the development of mental growth? However, psychologists believe that psychological functions and the physical form of our bodies (our selves), are intrinsically bound up with one another, both in terms of the way our body shapes the way we think about the world (and our experience of it), and also because our psychological processes are underpinned by a physical biological substrate – the brain and nervous system (which we consider partly here, but in more detail in Chapter 5). Developmental psychologists are no exception. Take for instance, Piaget's approach to cognitive development – under this view, infants develop cognitive abilities by learning through their own patterns of action in the environment. These patterns of action are themselves dependent upon the physical development of the body and limbs. More rapid development of the body and nervous system will thus lead to earlier cognitive advances. However, rapid growth is not necessarily the gold standard of development. If an infant grows at a slower rate, this does not mean that he or she will not eventually catch up with his/her peers. On the other side of the coin, early maturation (physical and sexual) can lead to a number of problems. Notably, as we will see later, early maturers, especially girls, can end up getting into more difficulties of a socioemotional nature (negative body images and more risk-taking behaviours, to name just two).

Thus, physical development is very important for understanding developmental psychology, as it can impact significantly on the development of cognitive, emotional and social processes (just as these processes can impact on physical development). In this chapter, we will examine children's physical growth from conception, through to adolescence. First, we will describe the development of the human being from conception to delivery (i.e., prenatal development), considering some of the factors that can threaten normal development of the body and brain during pregnancy. We will look at childbirth and at some of the complications of labour and delivery, including the problems of prematurity and low birth weight. We will also review the research that has explored the long-term effects of complications during pregnancy and birth. In the second part of the chapter we explore the physical growth patterns that infants and children follow after birth, and the factors that speed up or slow down these patterns. Finally, we will also consider sexual maturation, and in particular puberty, its characteristics and the factors that influence its course.

PRENATAL DEVELOPMENT

From outside, prenatal development can seem a little underwhelming. A pregnant woman simply grows a big belly. However, this external view certainly doesn't give due credit to the fantastically complex biological processes that are happening below the surface. Perhaps it is knowledge of how incredible the process of making a new life is that can make waiting for the birth of a child a very emotionally charged period of people's lives. Expectant mothers, and their partners if they have them, often look forward to becoming parents and enjoy preparing for their baby's arrival. They may even try to influence the development of the new family member by playing favourite music or reading to their unborn child. In other, less fortunate situations, pregnancy can be a more stressful period – this can be the case for example when it has been preceded by several unsuccessful attempts to have a child, or when the pregnancy is unexpected.

Whether it's possible to influence a baby in positive ways during pregnancy is not entirely certain, although as we will see in Chapter 6, there is quite some evidence that babies learn about their perceptual environment *in utero*. Unfortunately, however, clear evidence indicates that the developing organism is vulnerable to a variety of negative influences in the womb. Some of these influences are genetic, as we see in Chapter 5, and others result from variations in the prenatal environment caused by factors and events that affect the mother during her pregnancy. A large number of negative influences – including medications and diagnostic procedures; prescription, non-prescription, and other legal and illegal drugs;

maternal age and *parity* (whether a woman has been pregnant before); illness, dietary deficiencies and emotional distress; and environmental toxins – can affect the normal development of a child from its first weeks of gestation. In addition, events occurring during childbirth may threaten the health of a newborn.

In this section, we will consider several questions about negative influences on prenatal development. How significant are these various influences? How does the timing of their appearance in the prenatal environment affect their impact on the developing infant? How do perinatal factors (events occurring shortly before, during, or after birth) affect later development? And perhaps most importantly we will ask whether any postnatal experiences alter or mitigate the effects of these early negative influences?

In order to understand how certain prenatal and perinatal factors can cause development to go awry, as we do later in this chapter, we need information about how development happens in the typical scenario. So, first, we will consider the biological process of typical prenatal development.

The stages of prenatal development

The ovum (or egg), once released from the mother's ovaries, only lives for about three to five days unless it is fertilized. And so if a sperm cell intervenes, conception usually takes place within a few days of a woman's ovulation. Prenatal development encompasses the 38 weeks, or approximately nine months, between conception and birth. Over these months, the new organism changes in many ways. The kinds, numbers, positions, sizes and shapes of cells, tissues and bodily systems change, usually through increases in size and complexity.

The nine months of prenatal development are characterized in two ways. Traditionally, pregnancy has been described as occurring over three trimesters (the trimesters are three consecutive periods of three months). Another way of dividing up pregnancy is to talk about the three periods of: (a) the zygote, (b) the embryo, and (c) the foetus. Figure 4-1 illustrates these changes, from ovulation, when the ovum embarks on its journey to the uterus, to the end of the second trimester, by which time the foetus looks like a miniature human.

THE ZYGOTE

The period of the zygote (often referred to as the germinal stage) is approximately the first two weeks of post-conceptual life. The germinal stage begins when a sperm fertilizes the ovum, which is then referred to as a zygote, or fertilized egg, which then proceeds down the mother's Fallopian tube, undergoing rapid cell divisions all that time, and implants in the wall of the uterus. Despite the increase in size due to cell division, when the zygote implants in the uterine wall about seven days after conception, it is very small: 100 to 200 zygotes placed side by side would measure only an inch, and some 5 million would weigh only 30 grams. Gradually, tendrils or stems from the zygote penetrate the blood vessels in the wall of the uterus. At this point, the zygote begins a physiological dependence on the mother that will continue throughout the course of prenatal development.

THE EMBRYO

Once the zygote is firmly implanted in the mother's uterus, the second prenatal period, the embryonic stage, begins. This is a stage that lasts from the beginning of the third week of gestation, the term for the entire period of development in the uterus, until the end of the eighth week, when the embryo's most important physiological structures and systems become distinct or differentiated, and it becomes recognizable as

> Human development begins almost from the moment of conception. In Chapter 5 we describe how genes and environment interact at a biological level to determine the course of development. We also describe how the central nervous system develops *in utero*.

germinal stage The stage of pregnancy beginning with the zygote being formed by the fertilization of the egg, and finishing when the zygote is implanted in the wall of the uterus (about seven days later).

zygote The developing organism from the time sperm and egg unite to about the second week of gestation, during which the zygote undergoes rapid cell division.

embryonic stage The period of prenatal development lasting from the second to around the eighth week of gestation.

gestation The carrying of an embryo/foetus during pregnancy, usually for nine months in humans.

embryo The developing organism, which, implanted in the uterus wall, undergoes rapid cell division resulting in the differentiation of the major physiological structures and systems.

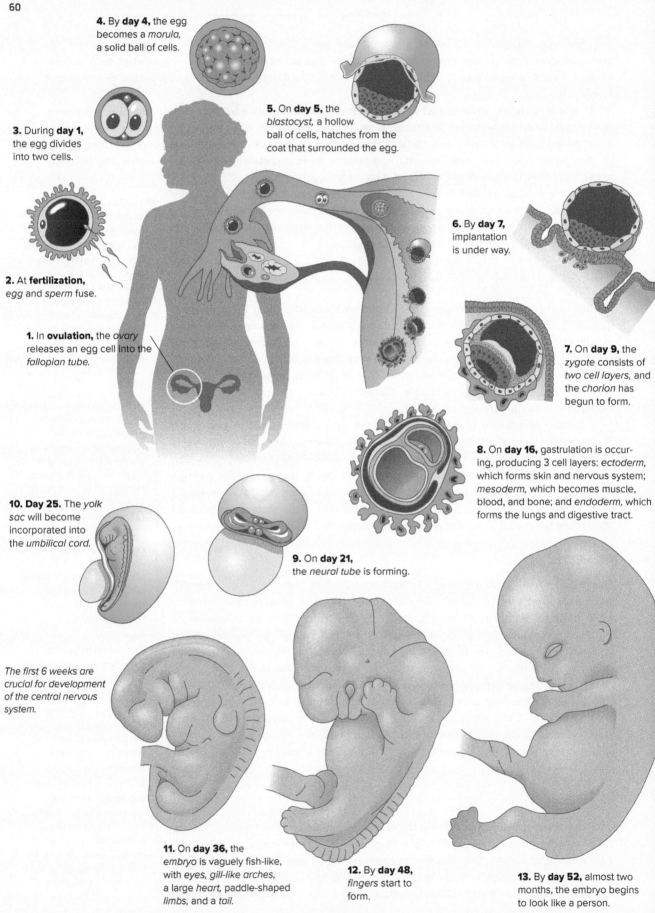

4. By **day 4,** the egg becomes a *morula,* a solid ball of cells.

3. During **day 1,** the egg divides into two cells.

5. On **day 5,** the *blastocyst,* a hollow ball of cells, hatches from the coat that surrounded the egg.

2. At **fertilization,** *egg* and *sperm* fuse.

6. By **day 7,** implantation is under way.

1. In **ovulation,** the *ovary* releases an egg cell into the *fallopian tube.*

7. On **day 9,** the *zygote* consists of *two cell layers,* and the *chorion* has begun to form.

8. On **day 16,** gastrulation is occurring, producing 3 cell layers: *ectoderm,* which forms skin and nervous system; *mesoderm,* which becomes muscle, blood, and bone; and *endoderm,* which forms the lungs and digestive tract.

10. Day 25. The *yolk sac* will become incorporated into the *umbilical cord.*

9. On **day 21,** the *neural tube* is forming.

The first 6 weeks are crucial for development of the central nervous system.

11. On **day 36,** the *embryo* is vaguely fish-like, with *eyes, gill-like arches,* a large *heart,* paddle-shaped *limbs,* and a *tail.*

12. By **day 48,** *fingers* start to form.

13. By **day 52,** almost two months, the embryo begins to look like a person.

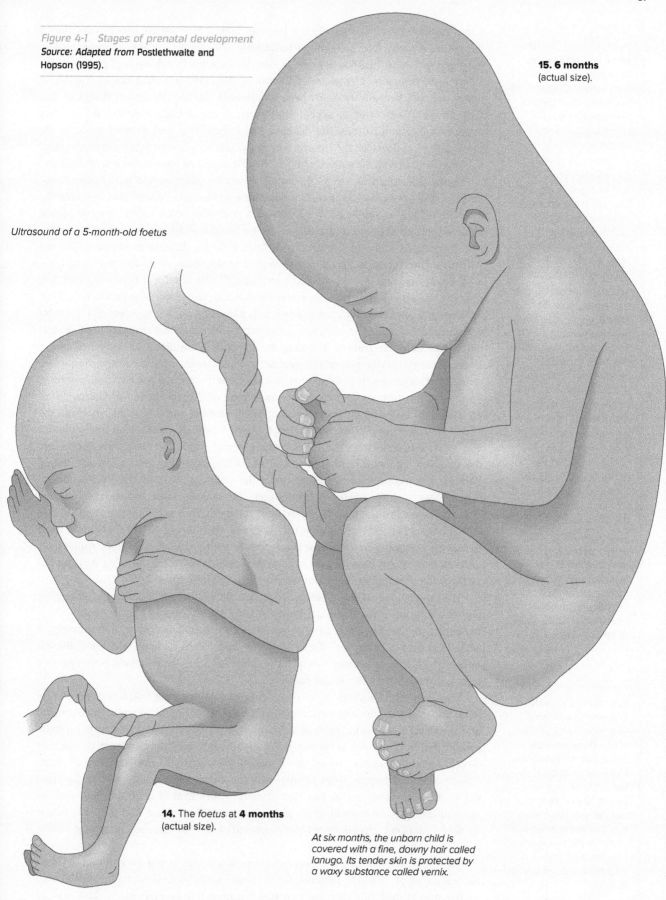

Figure 4-1   Stages of prenatal development
Source: Adapted from Postlethwaite and
Hopson (1995).

Ultrasound of a 5-month-old foetus

15. 6 months
(actual size).

14. The *foetus* at **4 months**
(actual size).

*At six months, the unborn child is
covered with a fine, downy hair called
lanugo. Its tender skin is protected by
a waxy substance called vernix.*

amniotic sac A membrane that contains the developing organism and the amniotic fluid around it; sac and fluid protect the organism from physical shocks and temperature changes.

placenta A fleshy, disk-like structure formed by cells from the lining of the uterus and from the zygote that, together with the *umbilical cord*, serves to protect and sustain the life of the growing organism.

umbilical cord A tube that contains blood vessels connecting the growing organism and its mother by way of the *placenta*; it carries oxygen and nutrients to the growing infant, and removes carbon dioxide and waste products.

cephalocaudal The pattern of human physical growth in which development begins in the area of the brain and proceeds downwards to the trunk and legs.

proximal-distal The pattern of human physical growth wherein development starts in central areas, such as the internal organs, and proceeds to more distant areas, such as arms and legs.

In Chapter 6 we will describe how infants' motor skill acquisition also follows proximal-distal and cephalocaudal trajectories of development. Maturationist psychologists used this as evidence that motor development is determined by the same processes of physical maturation which we are discussing here.

a tiny human being (following which it becomes known as a foetus). Development during this period is rapid: from the time of fertilization until the end of the embryonic stage, the infant increases 2 million per cent in size. At about the fourth week of gestation, the baby's head begins to take shape, followed by the eyes, nose and mouth. The blood vessel that will become the heart begins to pulsate. By the fifth week, buds that will form arms and legs begin to appear. By the end of the embryonic period, the growing organism's face and features are detailed, and fingers, toes and external genitalia are present. Even at 6 weeks, the embryo is recognizable as a human being, although rather out of proportion with the mature adult; the head is almost as large as the rest of the body.

During the embryonic stage, the amniotic sac, the placenta and the umbilical cord develop. The amniotic sac is a thin membrane around the embryo that contains the amniotic fluid, a watery liquid that serves as a protective buffer for the embryo against physical shocks and temperature changes. The tendrils that attach the embryo to the uterine wall increase in size and complexity to form a fleshy disc-like structure called the placenta. The embryo is joined to the placenta at the abdomen by the umbilical cord, a tube that contains the vessels that carry blood back and forth between infant and placenta. Because semipermeable membranes within the placenta separate the bloodstreams of mother and child, some substances pass from mother to infant. The placenta and umbilical cord transmit oxygen and nutrients to the infant, and remove carbon dioxide and waste products from it, but they do not permit the direct exchange of blood. Unfortunately, certain potentially destructive substances, such as drugs, hormones, viruses and antibodies from the mother, can also pass through the placenta to the embryo.

During the embryonic period, the inner mass of the developing organism differentiates into three layers: the endoderm, the mesoderm and the ectoderm. From the *endoderm* come the gastrointestinal tract, trachea, bronchi, Eustachian tubes, glands, and vital organs such as the lungs, pancreas and liver. The *mesoderm* forms into the muscles, skeleton, circulatory and excretory systems, and inner skin layer. Perhaps the most important layer, from the point of view of the developmental psychologist, is the *ectoderm*, from which the sensory cells and nervous system develop (as well as the hair, nails, parts of the teeth, the outer layer of the skin and skin glands). The nervous system first appears when the ectoderm folds in on itself to form the neural tube (at about the fourth or fifth week of gestation), which later differentiates along its length to become the brain and spinal cord. We pick up the story of the developing brain and nervous system in Chapter 5.

The especially rapid development and differentiation that occur during the embryonic period make the organism particularly susceptible to environmental assault. As a result, it is the period when most gross congenital anomalies occur. For example, if something occurs to prevent the neural tube from closing completely, the child will have *spina bifida*, a disorder in which the spinal cord and the membranes that protect it may protrude from the spinal column.

Some important aspects of developmental psychology that characterize both prenatal and postnatal development first emerge in the embryonic stage: cephalocaudal and proximal-distal trajectories of development. Cephalocaudal (the term *cephalocaudal* derives from the Latin words for 'head' and 'tail') development means that development proceeds from the head downwards to the trunk and legs. Proximal-distal (again, from Latin words for 'toward the centre' and 'away from the centre') development means that growth occurs first in central areas, such as internal organs, and then in more distant areas, such as arms and legs. We return to these physical directions of development when we discuss postnatal motor development in Chapter 6.

Most miscarriages, or spontaneous abortions, occur during the embryonic stage; for a number of different reasons, the embryo can become detached from the wall of the uterus and will then be expelled through the vaginal canal. The rate of miscarriage has been estimated to be as high as one in four pregnancies, but many miscarriages are not detected because they occur in the first few weeks of pregnancy. A great number of embryos aborted in this manner have gross chromosomal and genetic disorders.

THE FOETUS

The developing baby is referred to as a foetus from the beginning of the third month of gestation to delivery. During the foetal period, the organism experiences rapid development of its muscles and central nervous system. At the start of the third month, the foetus has all of its organs, though some may not yet be in their final position. By the end of the third month, all of the foetus's body parts, including the external genital organs, are clearly delineated. By the end of the fourth month,

miscarriage The natural or spontaneous end of a pregnancy before the infant is capable of survival outside the womb. Human infants are generally unable to survive outside the uterus prior to 20 weeks' gestation.

foetus The developing organism from the third month of gestation through delivery; during the foetal period, bodily structures and systems develop to completion.

CHRONOLOGY OF DEVELOPMENT
An overview of prenatal development

	No. of months gestational age	Approximate size & weight (millimetres & grammes)	Central nervous system and peripheral sensory systems	Behaviour	Other points of note
Zygote	0–1	5 mm, 0.2 g	Neural tube forms, forebrain and primordial eyes and ears develop		
Embryo	1–2	28 mm, 2.6 g	Touch receptors develop	The foetus moves if the lips are touched	Hands develop
Foetus	2–3	81 mm, 45 g	Olfactory and taste receptors develop	Hands move	The foetus is now recognizably human in form
	3–4	135 mm, 142 g	Vestibular sense system develops		
	4–5	230 mm, 482 g	Myelination of the spinal cord	Evidence of a range of 'reflex' behaviours, including sucking, hiccoughing, grasping	
	5–6	284 mm, 737 g	Brain now responds to light; inner ear is now mature	Visual tracking behaviours possible; foetus startles in response to sounds	Survival outside womb now possible but relatively rare
	6–7	368 mm, 1219 g	Laminar structure appears in the cortex	The foetus opens and closes eyes	Eyelids open; Survival outside womb not uncommon
	7–8	406 mm, 1984 g			
	8–9	508 mm, 3232 g			Full term birth at 9 months

Source: Adapted from Moore, Persaud, and Torchia (2016)

mothers usually report that they can feel the foetus move (note though that it has been moving for a long time before this point). At around 5 months, reflexes such as sucking, swallowing and hiccoughing usually become observable via ultrasound. In the case of hiccoughing the mother can usually feel this quite plainly without ultrasound! After the fifth month, the foetus develops nails and sweat glands, and a coarser, more adult-like skin. By 6 months, the foetus's eyes start to open and close.

> **age of viability** The age of 22 to 26 weeks from conception, at which point the foetus's physical systems are advanced enough that it has a chance to survive if born prematurely.

The age of 22 to 26 weeks, sometimes referred to as the age of viability, is an important point in foetal development. By this time, the foetus's physical systems are sufficiently advanced that the child, if born prematurely, has a reasonable probability of surviving. However, if an infant is born prematurely before 26 weeks or so, the regulatory processes and nervous and respiratory systems are usually not mature enough for survival without intensive intervention. With the exceptional resources available in modern neonatal care units, infants as immature as 22 weeks can sometimes live. Bear in mind however that, as shown in the Chronology of Development chart, many systems are still developing at this point; the respiratory system in particular continues to evolve into the ninth month of gestation. Thus, babies born before 28 weeks can have many difficulties, especially if they encounter other adverse environmental conditions (Moore, Persaud, & Torchia, 2016).

RISKS IN THE PRENATAL ENVIRONMENT

> **teratology** The study of abnormalities in physical development and how they arise. Teratologists often investigate the influence of teratogens on prenatal and postnatal development.
>
> **thalidomide** A drug once prescribed to relieve morning sickness in pregnant women but discontinued when found to cause serious foetal malformations. Current controversy surrounds its possible use in treating symptoms of such diseases as AIDS, cancer and Hansen's disease (leprosy).
>
> **teratogen** An environmental factor, such as a drug, medication, dietary imbalance or polluting substance, that may cause developmental deviations in a growing human organism; teratogens are most threatening in the embryonic stage but are also capable of causing abnormalities in the foetal stage.

Children are occasionally born with physical malformations which can affect their body, organs or central nervous system. The study of the origins of such abnormalities is referred to as teratology. Up until about the 1930s and 40s medical scientists and teratologists were largely of the belief that abnormalities in newborn infants were due to genetic defects. However, experiments with animals from the 1930s began to show that environmental interventions such as nutritional deprivation of an important vitamin, or the introduction of an external toxic agent, could lead to congenital defects. In the 1960s a medical disaster, in which pregnant mothers were prescribed with thalidomide, resulting in a wide range of deformities, brought sharp focus to the harmful effects of environmental agents on prenatal development.

Teratogens

Environmental factors which can lead to congenital abnormalities are referred to as teratogens. A wide range of environmental agents, including prescription and non-prescription medications, drugs taken by the mother, and environmental toxins such as pollution, are teratogenic. In addition to these introduced environmental agents a number of factors which are internal to the mother are also teratogenic: For instance, the mother's age, her diet and her emotional state can all affect development. In this section, we consider these teratogenic hazards in the prenatal environment, along with the specific risks which these pose to the developing child.

Teratogens have a range of different effects on prenatal development. As we are primarily concerned with psychological development we will focus particularly on those teratogens which affect the development of the brain and nervous system. Nonetheless, it is crucial to note that teratogens can have an impact on psychological development independently of their specific effects on the nervous system. Even teratogenic factors which do not directly influence the development of the brain and nervous system can have deleterious effects on a child's psychological development. For instance, if an infant is ill in early life, the emotional bond between a parent and child can be affected by the stress of this situation and the infant's longer stay in hospital. Such socioemotional considerations are particularly important because early socioemotional experiences may play key roles in sustaining or minimizing the long-term effects of early difficulties.

ENVIRONMENTAL TOXINS

Dangerous substances in the everyday environment can be harmful to the developing baby. Teratogenic environmental toxins include radiation (pregnant women are advised to avoid X-rays), lead, mercury, herbicides, pesticides, household cleaners, and even food additives and cosmetics. Lead is a particularly well-documented toxin for the developing foetus. Women and babies may be exposed to lead by inadvertently inhaling automobile exhaust fumes, drinking water contaminated with industrial waste, or living near lead-based paint. Exposure to lead during pregnancy has been associated with prematurity and low birth weight, brain damage and physical defects, as well as with long-term problems in cognitive and intellectual functioning (Dietrich et al., 1993; Evans, 2004).

Fathers' exposure to environmental toxins can also have harmful effects on a developing foetus. Men who work in occupations that expose them to toxic substances such as radiation, anaesthetic gases, mercury or lead may develop chromosomal abnormalities that may affect their fertility or increase the risk that their partners will miscarry or bear infants with birth defects (Merewood, 2000). It is quite clear that both men and women planning to have a child should monitor their exposure to environmental toxins.

DISEASES AND DISORDERS

A considerable number of maternal diseases and disorders can affect an infant's development prenatally or during the birth process. The viral disease *rubella* can lead to cardiac disorders, cataract formation, deafness and cognitive delay in children if contracted by their mother during pregnancy. Viral infections can be passed on *in utero* and at birth, but they bear special consideration as the risks they pose to the infected newborn can be very much out of proportion to the risks they pose to mature adults. One of the most harmful viruses that can be passed to the newborn is genital herpes. The risk of this passing is especially great if the mother is having an active outbreak of herpes at the time of birth. Because an infected infant does not have a fully developed immune system before 5 weeks of age the disease is much more serious and can cause blindness, motor abnormalities, cognitive delay and a number of neurological disorders.

A teratogenic disease which has recently come to prominent attention, following an outbreak and epidemic in 2015–2016 in the Americas, is the Zika virus. The Zika virus can be transmitted to the mother in a variety of ways, including via blood transfusion, sexual contact and mosquito bites. From the mother it can spread to the baby via the placenta during pregnancy or at delivery. Although the symptoms of the Zika virus can be very mild in adults who contract it, it can cause very severe brain malformations in prenatal babies, the most notable of which is microcephaly (see Figure 4-2).

Other maternal conditions that may increase rates of foetal abnormalities, miscarriage and death include *hypertension*, also known as high blood pressure, and *diabetes* (see Table 4-1 for more details). Parasitic and bacterial infections can also pass to the infant (either prenatally or during birth – see Table 4-1). With their underdeveloped immune systems, infants are much more vulnerable to the toxic effects of these diseases which can then have significant effects on their psychological development.

genital herpes
A common viral infection spread primarily through sexual contact; if contracted by an infant during birth, it can cause blindness, motor abnormalities, cognitive delay and a wide range of neurological disorders.

Zika virus A teratogenic virus which can be passed from mother to foetus. Infants born with the Zika virus can have microcephaly, severe brain malformations and other birth defects.

microcephaly A condition in which an infant is born with a head and brain which are smaller than normal.

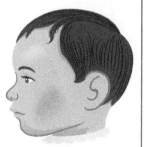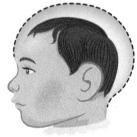

Figure 4-2 Microcephaly
Microcephaly is a physical abnormality in which an infant is born with a head and brain which are smaller than normal. Microcephaly can be caused by teratogenic influences of diseases borne by the mother (such as the Zika virus), and drugs taken by the mother (such as cocaine).
Source: © Shutterstock/Luciano Cosmo

Table 4-1   Diseases and disorders that can have a negative impact on development through their potential prenatal teratogenic effects

Diseases and disorders with potential teratogenic effects	
Rubella (German measles)	Infant may be born with a range of impairments including cardiac disorders, deafness, cataracts, and cognitive delay.
Hypertension (high blood pressure)	Can lead to foetal abnormalities, miscarriage, and foetal death.
Syphilis	Can lead to miscarriage; if the infant survives, she/he may be born blind, cognitively delayed and/or may have other physical abnormalities.
Zika virus	Can lead to microcephaly (a smaller than normal head and brain), brain malformations, and other physical abnormalities.
Genital herpes	Infected infant may become blind, cognitively delayed, develop motor abnormalities and a wide range of neurological disorders.
Toxoplasmosis	Eye and brain damage in the developing baby.

MEDICAL INTERVENTIONS IN PREGNANCY

As already mentioned, the modern focus on teratogens came about largely because of some medical disasters from the 1960s onwards. The best known of these was surrounding the use of thalidomide. Thalidomide was prescribed in the 1960s by many physicians to relieve pregnant women's symptoms of morning sickness. As a result, their children were sometimes born with abnormalities that included deformations of the eyes, nose and ears; cleft palate; facial palsy; and fusing of fingers and toes; as well as dislocations of the hip joint and malformations of the heart and the digestive and genitourinary tracts. The most characteristic deformity was something called *phocomelia*, in which limbs were missing and the feet and hands were attached directly to the torso (Moore, Persaud, & Torchia, 2016) (see Figure 4-3.)

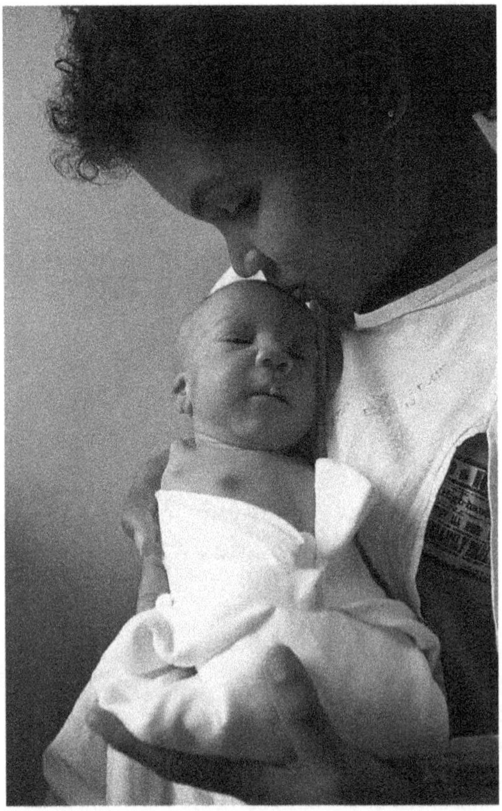

When these types of abnormality appeared initially, it was extremely difficult for doctors and scientists to discover their cause. The role of the drugs was not at all obvious, as the pregnant women themselves showed no adverse effects from them, and in the case of thalidomide only a small percentage of the mothers who took the drug bore children with abnormalities.

Following the thalidomide disaster, many precautions have been taken to avoid unintended harm to prenatal development through therapeutic interventions. Not all drugs are teratogenic of course, and it is crucial to remember that therapeutic interventions during pregnancy are a crucially important aspect of modern medical practice which helps avoid potential harm to parent and foetus. However, it is important to know that even some over-the-counter (non-prescription) drugs may have adverse effects on the foetus. For example, heavy use of aspirin has been associated with low birth weight, lower IQ and poor motor control (Barr et al., 1990; Briggs et al., 2017). Furthermore, many pregnant women take legal and illegal recreational drugs. Indeed, nearly 90 percent of women take some sort of recreational or therapeutic drug during pregnancy (Cunningham et al., 1993; Briggs et al., 2017).

Despite the high incidence of prenatal exposure to drugs, it is important for all to be aware of the potential dangers so that pregnant women can make well-informed choices, but always bearing in mind that exposure of the prenatal infant to harmful drugs could occur because the mother does not yet realize that she is pregnant.

Figure 4-3   A newborn infant whose development, in utero, was affected by thalidomide.
Source: © John Maier, Jr/The Image Works

LEGAL AND ILLEGAL RECREATIONAL DRUGS

Both illegal and legal recreational drugs have been shown to have teratogenic effects (Woodward, McPherson, & Volpe, 2018). As well as exerting specific physical injuries to the developing body and nervous system, drugs of dependency (e.g., opioids, cocaine, nicotine) pose another problem. If mothers are addicted to a drug (illegal or legal) during pregnancy, their babies are also often born addicted to these drugs – this is known as neonatal abstinence syndrome Following birth, such babies often undergo withdrawal symptoms: irritability, minimal ability to regulate their state of arousal, trembling, shrill crying, rapid respiration and hyperactivity. Moreover, because these infants are often premature and of low birth weight due to the teratogenic influence of the drugs, and possibly also the associated lifestyle of the mother, it is even more difficult for them to cope with the trauma of withdrawal (Lester et al., 2000; Messinger & Lester, 2006).

Among illegal drugs, the prenatal effects of opioids (heroin, morphine), methamphetamine, and cocaine are of particular concern. As a result of the crack cocaine epidemic in the 1980s–90s, we now know rather a lot about the immediate and long-term effects of *in utero* exposure to cocaine (Woodward et al., 2018). There is very strong evidence that maternal cocaine use during pregnancy can lead to many physical and behavioural problems which often persist into adolescence and adulthood (Buckingham-Howes et al., 2013; Woodward et al., 2018). Research shows, however, that the long-term effects of maternal cocaine use on children's school performance depend on how supportive the child's environment turns out to be, and not all infants show detrimental effects on later academic achievement (Messinger & Lester, 2006).

Among legal recreational drugs, the effects of tobacco smoking and alcohol are particularly significant. The rate of prematurity and low birth weight in babies is also higher for mothers who smoke or drink than for those who do neither (Mills, 1999; Gilliland et al., 2001).

Even passive smoke – that is, smoke breathed in by non-smokers – can contribute to low birth weight among the babies of mothers who don't smoke. Studies have shown that babies exposed *in utero* to passive smoke are at increased risk for a variety of illnesses (Charlton, 1994). In Chapter 15 we will discuss how parental smoking before the birth of the child has been linked to attention deficit hyperactivity disorder (ADHD; Thapar et al., 2003; Altink et al., 2009).

Foetal alcohol syndrome (FAS) occurs in about 6% of infants of alcoholic mothers (Day & Richardson, 1994). Infants with this disorder have a high incidence of facial, heart and limb defects; they are 20% shorter than the average child of their age, demonstrate abnormal behaviour patterns and are often cognitively delayed (Streissguth, 1997, 2007; Woodward et al., 2018).

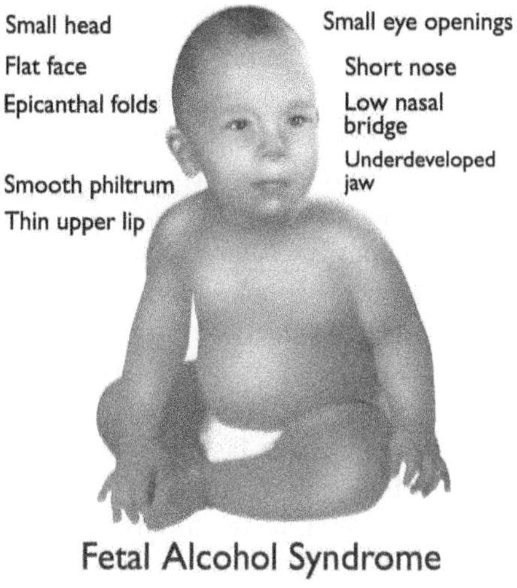

Abnormal behaviour patterns of children with foetal alcohol syndrome include excessive irritability, distractibility and hyperactivity. They may also engage in repetitive behaviours such as repeatedly banging their heads or rhythmically rocking their bodies (Jacobson & Jacobson, 1996; Streissguth, 1997).

Studies of older children indicate that many children whose mothers drank during pregnancy have a range of cognitive problems involving particularly language and attention (Burden, Jacobson, & Jacobson, 2005; Connor et al., 2001; Woodward et al., 2018), and in young adulthood (age 25) are at higher risk for alcohol problems and psychiatric disorders (Streissguth, 2007). Negative effects of alcohol on prenatal development may not be limited to maternal drinking because men who drink heavily may also sustain genetic damage that leads to birth defects in their offspring (Cicero, 1994).

> **neonatal abstinence syndrome** A withdrawal syndrome in newborn infants experienced following exposure to drugs of dependence *in utero*.

> Parental smoking (including passive smoking by the mother) is known to be linked to dangers for the foetus and for later development. In Chapter 15 we will discuss how attention deficit hyperactivity disorder has been linked to exposure to smoking in the prenatal environment.

> **foetal alcohol syndrome** A disorder of the developing foetus caused by the ingestion of alcohol by the foetus's mother during gestation. It is characterized by stunted growth, a number of physical and physiological abnormalities and, often, mental retardation.

Small head
Flat face
Epicanthal folds

Small eye openings
Short nose
Low nasal bridge
Underdeveloped jaw

Smooth philtrum
Thin upper lip

Fetal Alcohol Syndrome

Figure 4-4   Children who suffer from foetal alcohol syndrome not only look different but also can have delays in the development of their nervous systems.
Source: © Gwen Shockey/Science Source

Although the worst cases of foetal alcohol syndrome are seen in babies born to alcoholic mothers, it is possible that even moderate drinking by a pregnant woman can cause abnormal behaviour patterns in the baby (Abel, 1998; Willford et al., 2006). As we will see, the extent of damage inflicted by teratogens may depend substantially on the baby and/or the mother's genetics and this is particularly the case with alcohol. With alcohol, it certainly seems wise to err on the side of caution.

PARENTAL FACTORS

Some factors affecting the foetus are directly related to characteristics of the parents (and in particular, the mother). Many parental factors are strongly associated with one another. For instance, it is difficult to separate the effects of maternal malnourishment from those of a variety of other harmful factors. Malnourished mothers often live in environments characterized by poverty, poor education, inferior sanitation and shelter, and inadequate medical care (Evans, 2004).

Nonetheless, studies have shown that gross deficiencies in the diets of pregnant women, especially of some vitamins, minerals and proteins, are related to prematurity, physical and neural defects, and smaller size in neonates (Shonkoff & Phillips, 2000). Researchers have found that prenatal malnutrition is detrimental for children's social and motor development and cognitive abilities (Riciutti, 1993; Sigman, 1995; Lozoff, Jimenez, & Smith, 2006). Cognitive difficulties may not only be the result of long-term biological changes in the brain but may also be driven by more immediate behavioural aspects of continued malnutrition following birth; for example, lowered energy, inattention, and lack of motivation and responsiveness.

> As we will see later in Chapter 4 in the section on physical growth, a current new direction of research is attempting to determine the effects of postnatal malnutrition on functional brain development.

A woman's age may influence the development of her foetus. Children of both younger and older mothers are at higher risk of developing abnormalities. The incidence of chromosomal abnormality increases with the age of the mother and her reproductive system. Furthermore, among older mothers emerging health risks – such as increases in hypertension and alcoholism – rather than age *per se* can contribute to teratogenic effects. Evidence also suggests that older fathers may also contribute to poor birth outcomes: as they age men tend to have more infants with birth defects due to the deteriorating quality of sperm (Lowe et al., 2001; Wyrobek et al., 2006).

The children of teenage mothers are at risk for delays in developing intellectual, language and social skills (Moore & Brooks-Gunn, 2002). Why is this? Firstly, teenage mothers may have teratogenic problems with their pregnancies because their reproductive systems are immature. However, many of the potential teratogenic outcomes of teenage parenthood seem to be driven by associations with other risk factors. Teenage mothers are less likely to have healthy personal habits (e.g., an increased use or abuse of drugs). In addition, younger mothers are more likely to live in poverty and thus can lack good nutrition and prenatal care, and are more likely to live in environments with higher rates of disease and pollution. An indication that teratogenic outcomes are not primarily due to the age of young mothers, but rather to associations of other risk factors with this, comes from the finding that when the infants of teenage mothers are raised in supportive environments, their infants do not show a higher rate of developmental delay (Smith, 1994; Moore & Brooks-Gunn, 2002). (See Chapter 12 for more discussion of teen parenthood.)

Pregnancy can be a particularly stressful time, especially for young mothers, but in some unfortunate cases, mothers can encounter particularly severe additional stressors like marital discord or the death of a close one. A pregnant woman's emotional state can lead to metabolic or biochemical changes that affect the foetus. In fact, it is now known that foetal stress hormones reflect those of the mother (DiPietro, 2004; DiPietro et al., 2006).

Sadly, maternal stress can be teratogenic. Mothers who are stressed during pregnancy tend to give birth to infants who demonstrate behavioural differences. They tend to be more hyperactive and irritable. They cry more, and exhibit more feeding and sleep problems (Van Den Bergh, 1992). Behavioural differences in these babies persist into later postnatal development. They are less attentive at 8 months than other babies (Huizink, Mulder, & Buitelaar, 2004), and even at the age of 7 years, they are more likely to exhibit behavioural difficulties, depression and anxiety (O'Connor et al., 2005). A poignant example of how stress during pregnancy may have affected later development comes from infants born in the

Netherlands to mothers who were pregnant during the German invasion of the country in the Second World War. These infants were more likely to develop later schizophrenia than adults born in earlier or later years (van Os & Selton, 1998). Similarly, Huttunen and Niskanen (1978) have demonstrated that prenatal loss of a father has a significant impact on the likelihood of developing mental illness or social conduct problems in later life.

PRINCIPLES OF TERATOGENESIS

As we have seen teratogens can take many forms, from environmental toxins and therapeutic and recreational drugs, to parental factors such as age, nutrition and stress. But how do teratogens work? How and why do they have their effects? In this section, we will detail some general principles about how teratogens exert their effects on development. We will illustrate these principles with some specific examples from the teratogens we have already discussed.

The following principles of teratogenesis were largely laid out by Wilson (1973), and are widely accepted today (e.g., Moore et al., 2016; Briggs et al., 2017).

- *Atypical development resulting from the effects of teratogens manifests in different levels of severity.*

Effects of teratogens can range from mildly impaired function, and the delayed growth of the structure of the body and its organs, to malformation and, in the worst cases, death. The effects of foetal alcohol exposure are a good illustration of this principle. Given the wide distribution of severity of such problems, researchers have defined a spectrum of maternal alcohol consumption-related problems in the child as 'foetal alcohol spectrum disorders' (FASD). Foetal alcohol syndrome (FAS) is at the most severe end of this spectrum and includes abnormal facial features, poor body growth and abnormalities of the central nervous system. At the less severe end of the spectrum is Alcohol Related Neurodevelopmental Disorder, in which exposure of the foetus to alcohol has been confirmed and behavioural abnormalities and cognitive delays are seen, but without the more visually obvious physical symptoms of FAS.

- *The longer a foetus is exposed to a teratogen and the greater the intensity of the teratogen, the more likely it is that the foetus will be harmed.*

An example of this principle can be seen in the effects of malnutrition. Impairment of a child's intellectual development due to prenatal malnutrition is most likely when the mother's malnutrition has been severe and long lasting, and when dietary deprivation continues after childbirth (Sigman, 1995; Lozoff et al., 2006).

- *Teratogens have specific effects.*

Different teratogens influence different developmental processes. For example, rubella in the mother affects mainly the foetus's heart, eyes and brain. The drug thalidomide causes malformations of the limbs. Cocaine's effects include microcephaly (a smaller than typical brain and head), and brain haemorrhages.

- *A teratogen exerts its effects largely during critical periods of development.*

The timing at which an embryo or foetus is exposed to teratogens has an important bearing on outcomes. This depends on the specific teratogen involved. For example, if a woman contracts *rubella* during the first month of her pregnancy, her foetus risks cardiac disorders, cataract formation, deafness and mental retardation; if she contracts this illness in her third month or later, however, the likelihood that her infant will suffer disability declines substantially (Cochi et al., 1989; Eberhart-Phillips et al., 1993). As another example, the foetal damage from alcohol appears to be greatest in the last trimester. If women can stop drinking during this period, their babies tend to be longer, weigh more and have a larger head circumference than those of women who continue heavy drinking (Streissguth, 1997, 2007).

The timing of teratogenic influence is also due to critical periods of development for particular organs and systems. As Figure 4-5 shows, the organism as a whole is most vulnerable to teratogens during the embryonic stage. However, each organ system has a different critical period. For example, the most vulnerable period for the heart is between 20 and 40 days after conception.

- *Maternal or foetal genotypes and physiological status may promote vulnerability to or resilience against a teratogen's effects.*

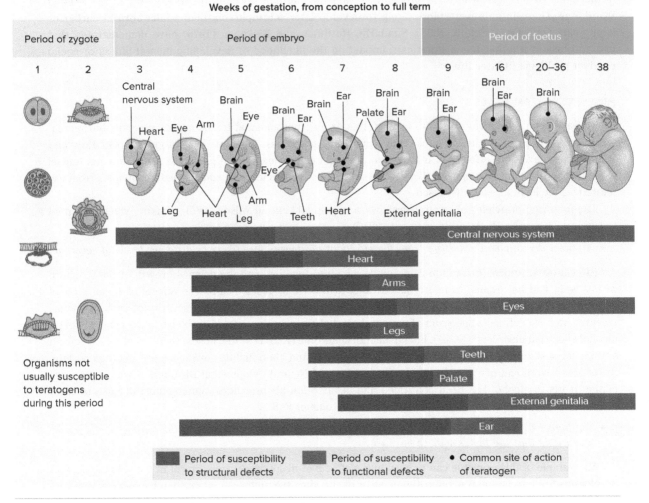

Figure 4-5   *The child's prenatal susceptibility to teratogenic agents*

Sensitivity of the growing embryo to teratogens is greatest in the first 4 to 8 weeks of gestation, peaking about the fifth week. Normally, the zygote is not susceptible to specific teratogens, but teratogenic agents may cause it to die. The defects that occur early in development, when critical organs are being formed, are generally structural (i.e., they produce physically obvious changes); teratogenic agents that affect the foetus in later weeks are more likely to stunt growth or cause functional problems (problems with the function of organs in the absence of an obvious structural problem).
Source: Adapted from Moore (1989).

The influence of a mother's genes on teratogenic influence is very well illustrated by the case of alcohol. If mothers have a certain genetic make-up which means that they metabolize alcohol quickly, then this is a protective factor against the teratogenic influence of prenatal alchol on her child (Dodge et al., 2014). The mother's age, nutrition and hormonal balance also modify the impact of a teratogen. For example, nutritional deficiencies in the foetus, which interfere with healthy prenatal development, also intensify the adverse effects of drugs that the mother has ingested. Also, if the mother's ability to metabolize harmful teratogens is compromised by poor nutrition, then this presents a greater harmful exposure to the foetus or embryo.

> In Chapter 5 we outline in more detail how genes and environment interact in development. The interaction of maternal and foetal genotype with environmental teratogenic factors is an instance of gene–environment interaction.

HOW DO TERATOGENS HAVE THEIR EFFECTS?

Teratogens can have their effects in a range of ways. Some of these pathologies seem intuitive and direct, but there are many ways in which teratogens can have complicated and non-obvious effects on development. Let's look at some examples.

With cocaine, the primary physical injuries to the central nervous system include microcephaly (a smaller than typical brain and head), and brain haemorrhages. Both of these are likely due in large part to abnormal growth of the brain during prenatal development, and if we look at the brain tissue of affected infants, there is evidence of structural abnormalities in both grey and white matter neural tissue, and these abnormalities seem to be due substantially to the way cocaine disturbs how neurons differentiate for different purposes in brain development (Woodward et al., 2018) (see Chapter 5).

However, cocaine can also have effects on brain development due to a reduction in blood flow from the mother to the foetus as a result of poorer blood flow to the placenta and through the umbilical cord. Similarly, smoking and drinking are associated with disturbances in placental functioning, and with changes in maternal physiology that lead to oxygen deprivation and thus to changes in the foetus's brain (Woodward et al., 2018). The cognitive delays seen in children with foetal alcohol spectrum disorders may be related to the loss of oxygen in the foetal brain when the foetus's breathing ceases temporarily. Some evidence for this explanation comes from research showing that if in their last trimester women who are not heavy drinkers consume just 28 millilitres of 80-proof vodka, the respiratory actions of their foetuses may stop for more than half an hour (Fox et al., 1978).

Teratogens can influence development in a range of complicated ways during pregnancy, but also beyond birth and well into later development. A clear illustration of effects beyond birth is provided by neonatal abstinence syndrome. Although neonatal abstinence syndrome is transient, dissipating soon after birth, it can nonetheless have longer-term consequences on later behavioural and socioemotional development. At a time when an infant needs particular attention and care, the behaviour of infants exposed to these drugs, and their parents (who may still be using drugs), may contribute towards problems in the formation of secure attachment relationships (Phillips et al., 1996, Tronick et al., 2005; see Chapter 7). Although addicted babies' irritable behaviour is likely to get the attention of a caregiver, such infants are often not as alert, and may not maintain the visual or physical contact. These behaviours are the main ways in which infants interact with their caregivers (Lester et al., 2000). So the absence of these behaviours in addicted newborns may disrupt parenting and have long-term adverse outcomes for attachment relationships. Figure 4-6 shows the myriad ways in which teratogens have their influences on development.

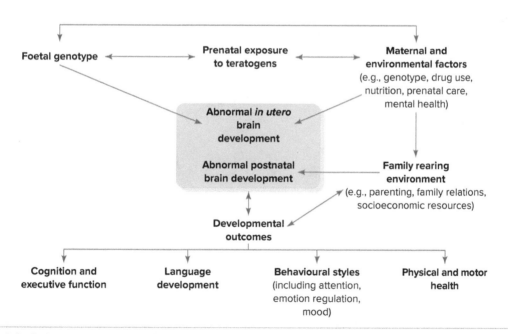

Figure 4-6   Pathways to teratogenesis
The myriad and complex ways in which teratogenesis can occur reflect the complexity of development itself.
Source: Adapted from Woodward et al. (2018).

CHILDBIRTH

For parents, the last few weeks of pregnancy are typically characterized by joyous anticipation and, especially in first births, by apprehension about labour and childbirth. Parents can experience a great deal of anxiety about whether the child will be normal, and whether the labour will be difficult. Although the process of birth exhausts both parents, most are exhilarated, even awestruck, in seeing and holding their newborn for the first time. Birth is also a momentous physical and social transition for the infant. Like the parents, a newborn baby arrives into the world exhausted from the effort involved in getting out into the world. Not only that, but he/she also has to learn to exercise wholly new behaviours such as breathing air, and also undergoes a huge change in their environment: The baby moves from the warm, wet environment of the uterus to the cooler, dry, bright environment of the external world, full of lights, objects, movements, touches, voices and faces (see Chapter 6 where we discuss some of the challenges which the infant faces in perceiving and understanding their new world).

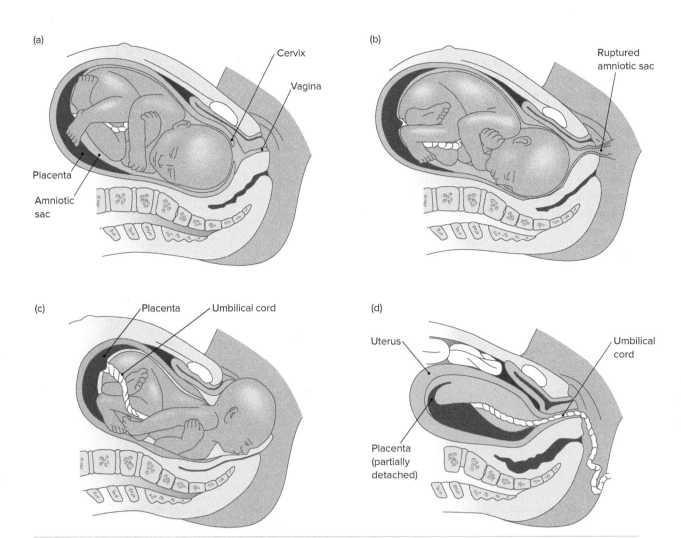

Figure 4-7   The stages of the birth process
With arms and legs folded and head pointed toward the birth canal, the foetus is ready to be born (a). In stage 1, the foetus moves toward the cervix as it gradually dilates (b). In stage 2, the foetus moves through the vaginal opening (c). In stage 3, the placenta detaches from the uterine wall in preparation for its expulsion (d).
Source: Adapted from Vander, Sherman, and Luciano (1994).

The three stages of childbirth

Birth involves a series of changes in the mother that permit the infant to move from the womb out into the external world. Figure 4-7 shows the way the foetus appears and is positioned in the uterus just before labour begins as well as the three stages in the birth process.

The first stage of labour begins as the mother experiences regular uterine contractions that are usually spaced at 10- to 15-minute intervals; these contractions become more intense and frequent as labour progresses. This first stage, which generally lasts between 8 and 14 hours for first-born children and half that for later-born children, concludes when the cervix is dilated sufficiently to permit the infant's head to pass through it and into the vaginal canal. In the second stage of labour, which usually lasts less than an hour, the infant descends through the birth canal and is delivered through the vaginal opening. The third and final stage of birth takes only a few minutes, as the uterus expels the placenta.

CAESAREAN DELIVERY

The Caesarean delivery, in which a baby is removed from the mother's uterus through an incision in her abdomen, is performed in a variety of situations. Labour may be unusually slow or prolonged, the baby may be in difficulty, there may be vaginal bleeding, or the baby's position may make a normal vaginal delivery impossible (e.g., the baby's feet may be in position to deliver first, or the baby may lie horizontally in the uterus). Caesarean is performed in approximately 20% of childbirths in the UK (with similar rates in other industrialized countries).

> **Caesarean delivery**
> The surgical delivery of a baby; the baby is removed from the mother's uterus through an incision made in her abdomen and uterus in a procedure also known as Caesarean section.

Despite the benefits of this procedure, Caesarean births place mothers at greater risk of infection and involve longer hospital stays (Liu, 2007), as well as other problems such as an increased risk of preterm and low-birth-weight infants with a subsequent pregnancy (Kennare, 2007). In addition, Caesarean babies are exposed to more maternal medication during delivery; as a result, they have somewhat more trouble breathing, and are less responsive and wakeful than other newborns, and in turn, breast-feeding may be more difficult (Emory, Schlackman, & Fiano, 1996). However, short-term studies of Caesarean births suggest that this method of delivery has few effects on infants' cognitive or neurological development (Entwisle & Alexander, 1987). Moreover, recent longer-term evidence indicates that babies delivered by Caesarean did not have higher rates of hospitalization or outpatient visits during their first 18 months of life (Leung et al., 2007). Although early mother–child interactions may be adversely affected, by the time the children are a year old, these relationships are positive (Reilly, Entwisle, & Doering, 1987). In many cases of course, the mother's partner may become more involved than they otherwise would have been following Caesarean births, because of the longer recovery period for the mother (Parke, 1996).

Perinatal complications

Although labour and childbirth are normal processes in human development, and in the majority of cases go smoothly, sometimes there are complications (these are known as perinatal complications). The factors which can contribute to perinatal complications are known as perinatal risk-factors. We've seen that diseases can be passed to the infant as it moves through the birth canal. In addition, the process of birth can lead to anomalies by itself. Of interest here, it has been found that more males than females are born with physical anomalies. Although this can be attributed in part to the role of the sex chromosomes (see Chapter 5), another important possibility is that this is due in part to the larger size of, and hence greater pressure on, a male's head during birth. The majority of infants do not suffer serious impairment at birth, however. Fewer than 10% have any type of abnormality, and many of these difficulties disappear during subsequent development.

> **perinatal complications**
> Difficulties surrounding the birth of a child, which can lead to developmental difficulties.
>
> **perinatal risk factors**
> Factors that can contribute to perinatal complications.

To assess the condition of the newborn infant after birth and check for any problems, doctors often use the Apgar scoring system (see Table 4-2). At 1 minute and 5 minutes after birth, the doctor or nurse measures the heart rate, respiratory effort, reflex irritability, muscle tone and body colour of the infant. Each of the

Table 4-2   Apgar evaluation of the newborn infant

Sign	Score 0	Score 1	Score 2
Heart rate	Absent	Less than 100 beats per minute	100 to 140 beats per minute
Respiratory effort	No breathing for more than 1 minute	Slow and irregular	Good respiration with normal crying
Muscle tone	Limp and flaccid	Some flexion of the extremities	Good flexion, active motion
Reflex irritability	No response	Some motion	Vigorous response to stimulation
Colour	Blue or pale body and extremities	Body pink with blue extremities	Pink all over

Source: Adapted from Apgar (1953).

five signs is given a score of 0, 1 or 2; the higher the score attained, the more favourable the baby's condition. A total score of 7 to 10 indicates that the newborn is in good condition, whereas a score of 4 or lower alerts medical staff to the need for immediate emergency procedures.

One particular problem that can arise during childbirth is the deprivation of oxygen to the infant (or foetal anoxia). Because of the transition to the outside world, the foetus has to switch from relying on oxygen supplied by the placenta to oxygen supplied by breathing air into the lungs. If the start of breathing is delayed in some way, the resulting anoxia can lead to brain damage. One situation that puts children at risk of anoxia is *breech birth*, in which the infant does not turn around to exit the uterus head first, and labour begins with the infant exiting buttocks first. Because of the danger of anoxia, breech-birth infants are often delivered by Caesarean. A delay in the onset of breathing can also occur when infants are delivered particularly early (preterm). Infants born more than 6 weeks preterm can experience *respiratory distress syndrome*. This occurs because the babies are not strong enough to inflate their own lungs properly. These days, when respiratory distress occurs, mechanical respirators are used to artificially present oxygen to the infant's lungs.

Prematurity and low birth weight

preterm A term describing a premature baby that is born before its due date and whose weight, although less than that of a full-term infant, may be appropriate to its gestational age.

low birth weight A term describing a premature baby who may be born close to its due date but who weighs significantly less than would be appropriate to its gestational age.

Premature or preterm babies are those born before they have completed the normal or full-term gestational period (37 weeks after conception). About 9% of infants are born prematurely, and the extent to which they are born premature can vary a great deal from babies just two to three weeks early to *extremely preterm infants* (EPIs) born more than ten weeks early, who as a result might be under a kilogramme in weight! Infants whose weight is less than 2,500 g at full term or less than appropriate for their time *in utero* are called low birth weight (or small-for-date) babies. Although babies who weigh less than 1,500 g, because they are preterm or because they are small for date, have many difficulties, modern medicine is increasingly successful in enabling them to survive (Wolke, 1998; McIntire et al., 1999; Goldberg & DeVitto, 2002). (See Table 4-3 for a summary of types of preterm and low-birth-weight babies.)

Being born prematurely can be a risk for developmental delays, but does not necessarily mean that the child will have significant long-term problems. As we shall discuss later, if at-risk infants (including those prematurely born) receive high-quality care and a stimulating environment, the prognosis for development can be good (Saigal & Doyle, 2008; Werner & Smith, 1982). However, infants who are born very (<32 weeks) or extremely preterm (<26 weeks) are more at risk than other preterm babies for long-term difficulties (Wolke, 1998). Likewise, having a very low birth weight despite full-term birth, is more strongly associated with prolonged impairment. Although most low-birth-weight babies (full term or preterm) catch up on motor and intellectual development by the time they are 4 years old, problems in academic achievement, hyperactivity, motor skills, and speech and hearing disorders occur more often in very low-birth-weight and very preterm babies (Goldberg & DeVitto,

Table 4-3   Preterm and low-birth-weight babies

Description	Timing of delivery	Weight at delivery
Full term	Average of 38 weeks from conception	~3,500 g (7.7 lb)
Preterm (premature)	>2 weeks before due date	
– Very pre-term infant (VPI)	<32 weeks of gestational age	~1,700 g (3.7 lb)
– Extremely pre-term infant (EPI)	<26 weeks of gestational age	~700 g (1.5 lb)
Low birth weight (small for date)	Full term or preterm	If full term, usually classified low birth weight if <2,500 g (5.5 lb). If preterm, can be classified low birth weight if lighter than would be expected for time spent *in utero* (see above)
– Very low birth weight (VLBW)		<1,500 g (3.3 lb)
– Extremely low birth weight (ELBW)		<1,000 g (2.2 lb)

2002; Anderson et al., 2003), and also in preterm babies who are subject to other prognostic risk factors such as being male, and having a lower level of parental education (Linsell et al., 2015). Although the greater perinatal risk factors in these groups of infants decrease in their importance relative to social environmental factors across the first years of life, they can still play a significant role in cognitive and motor problems at 6 years (Marlow et al., 2007), and in social adjustment at 11 years (Tessier et al., 1997).

Behavioural genetics researchers have asked whether genetic inheritance can play a role in infants' susceptibility to perinatal risks surrounding preterm birth (Koeppen-Schomerus et al., 2000). These researchers examined the influence of the shared genes of monozygotic compared to dizygotic twins (for more details of these methods see Chapter 5) in early measures of cognitive development at 2 years. In the children who experienced mild perinatal risks (>32 weeks' gestation), shared environmental factors and genetic factors appeared to play a role. However, in the children who experienced greater perinatal risks (born at less than 32 weeks' gestation), the shared environmental factors (presumably those surrounding the problematic birth) greatly overshadowed any genetic contribution. This indicates that genes can only protect infants from (or set them at risk for greater) cognitive impairment when the perinatal risk factors are relatively mild.

As advances in medical science are now enabling extremely preterm babies to survive on a much more regular basis, it has become increasingly important to find ways of improving the prognosis for such infants (Jaekel et al., 2015; Wolke, 1998).

STIMULATION PROGRAMMES FOR PREMATURE BABIES

In the 1960s it was common practice to isolate low-birth-weight babies from the outside world for weeks, with the view that this restriction of stimulation would help prevent infection of the vulnerable infant. In the late 1960s and early 1970s, however, researchers in infant development began to question whether such deprivation could have potentially debilitating effects on newborn development (particularly in vulnerable preterm babies). Researchers like Lewis Lipsitt (2002) argued that, in particular, the reduced physical contact and opportunities for stimulation that come along with such contact might delay the development of the important motoric behaviours that an infant needs in order to cope with the outside world (more about these in Chapter 6). In order to find a good solution to these problems, researchers have worked with health care professionals to explore ways to improve the environments of premature and low-birth-weight babies by administering extra stimulation. Some have provided stimulation that approximates the conditions the baby would have experienced *in utero* – for example, tape-recorded heartbeats (Barnard & Bee, 1983), rocking hammocks (Neal, 1968) and waterbed mattresses (Burns et al., 1983; which presumably simulate the rotation, movement and rhythmic activity the foetus would have experienced within the amniotic sac). Other investigators have used stimulation characteristic of the experiences of full-term infants, such as mobiles, tape recordings of the mother's voice, talking and singing, and cuddling and stroking (Field, 2001b; Goldberg & DeVitto, 2002; Field et al., 2007).

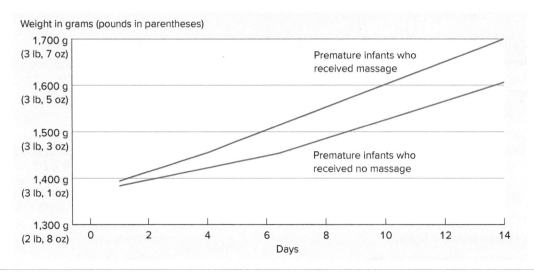

Weight in grams (pounds in parentheses)

Figure 4-8 Improvement in weight of premature babies receiving massage every day
A group of premature infants were given three 15-minute massages daily for 10 days, while another group received no massage. The infants given extra stimulation averaged 47% more weight gain per day, were awake and active more of the time, showed more mature motor behaviours, and were in the hospital for 6 days fewer than the other infants. Moreover, 6 to 8 months later, the first group weighed more and performed better on the behavioural and cognitive indices than the second group.
Source: Adapted from Field et al. (1986).

> Here we have explained how increased stimulation can improve the outcomes of premature babies. In Chapter 6 we will describe how young infants provided with practice at certain motor behaviours like stepping are quicker to master such motor skills later in development. Could the same developmental mechanisms be playing a role in each of these cases?

As Figure 4-8 shows, some evidence indicates that premature infants gain benefits in their physical development from early stimulation (Field et al., 1986). There are also arguments that these benefits extend to the later development of sensorimotor and motor skills, and exploratory behaviour (Lipsitt, 2002; Field et al., 2007). Stimulation clearly has at least a short-term positive effect on the development of premature infants (Field et al., 2007; Korner, 1989), and perhaps these early experiences give children a longer-lasting leg-up for their development.

However, although some studies like that described in Figure 4-8 have indicated that such approaches produce significant positive results in newborns (Klaus & Kennell, 1976), there remains some controversy over whether these programmes work in the way they are intended, and the extent of their effectiveness more long term (Ohlsson & Jacobs, 2013; Spittle et al., 2015). We can also ask whether early tactile stimulation has benefits on brain development as well as the well-documented increases in weight and sleep patterns (Field et al., 2007). In Box 4-1 we examine some recent findings which suggest that the kinds of tactile stimulations which preterm infants experience make a difference to early brain development.

PREMATURE BABIES AND PARENTAL CONTACT

Another type of intervention to help premature and low-birth-weight infants is to facilitate parents' contact with their infants. Some mothers of premature babies can be apprehensive about handling and caring for their fragile-appearing infants. When mothers of premature infants are eventually able to take their babies home from the hospital, they tend to show less emotional involvement with them than do mothers of full-term babies (Goldberg & DeVitto, 2002). Their infants sometimes fail to gain normal weight and height, and they are at risk for adverse circumstances in later development (Bugental & Happaney, 2004). Premature babies' typical physical appearance, small size, high-pitched cry, feeding difficulties and low responsiveness may make them less appealing and more frustrating to parents. It is thus important to familiarize parents with the appearance and behaviour of their premature baby as early as is possible, so that they have time to adjust before they become the sole carers when the baby is released from hospital.

BOX 4-1   Early tactile experiences predict functional brain development in preterm newborns

Preterm newborns often spend several of their first weeks in neonatal intensive care units where their first sensory experiences can be quite different to those of a full-term newborn without perinatal complications.

Most full-term babies go home from the hospital to brightly decorated rooms and cots containing stuffed toys. They also likely receive a great deal of body-to-body and skin-to-skin contact from their doting parents. In contrast, preterm newborns, even in recent years, experience a much depleted environment in which tactile contact with others (including their parents) is rather less frequent. Indeed, tactile experiences in the first weeks of a preterm newborn's life may well be more typified by noxious (painful) touch as medical interventions are undertaken as part of preterm neonatal care.

In prenatal development, touch is the first of our senses to develop and become functional (see Chapter 6), and so we might consider that tactile experiences are foundational in the development of our sensory abilities. So what effects do the different tactile inputs which preterm babies experience in neonatal care units have on their development? In a recent study (Maitre et al., 2017) researchers examined whether the kinds of tactile experiences which preterm babies get, predicted the ways in which their neural responses to touch developed.

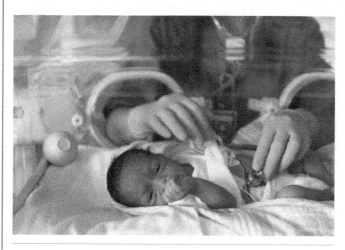

A newborn infant in a neonatal intensive care unit.
© ERproductions Ltd/Blend Images LLC

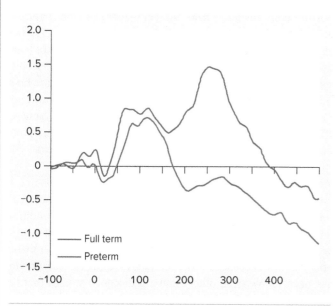

Preterm newborns show smaller (attenuated) brain responses to light touches. This is shown here through somatosensory evoked potentials recorded from the infants' EEG.
Source: Based on Maitre et al. (2017).

Maitre and colleagues (2017) tracked a group of preterm newborns during their neonatal care, examining records of the number of 'supportive' and 'painful' tactile experiences which they were exposed to. Painful tactile experiences include Td surgical procedures, the 'heel lance' method for taking blood, and tube insertions. Supportive tactile experiences included skin-to-skin care from a parent, and massage from physical/occupational therapists.

When the preterm babies were discharged from hospital, Maitre and colleagues measured their brain responses to light touches, using electroencephalography. The 'somatosensory evoked potentials' (the brain's response to touches measured over somatosensory cortex) of the preterm babies were significantly smaller in amplitude to a comparison group of full-term newborns. However, the finding of particular interest was that the more supportive tactile experiences the preterm babies had received, the more their somatosensory evoked potentials resembled those of the full-term neonates. On the other side of the coin, the more painful tactile events which the preterm babies had experienced during neonatal care, the smaller and more atypical were their brains' responses to light touches. Maitre and colleagues concluded that the nature of early tactile experiences determines how effectively the brain develops in its ability to respond to touches.

Because touch plays a range of important roles in our perceptual, cognitive and social abilities, Maitre and colleagues' findings and claims are important, and have important implications for the way in which we look after preterm babies, and newborn infants more generally. It may be that our first tactile experiences are foundational in development.

However, might there be other interpretations of these findings? One possibility is that those infants who experienced more painful tactile experiences in preterm neonatal care might also have experienced a wider range of more negative experiences and events (e.g., they may have been more unwell, necessitating more painful interventions). Maitre and colleagues attempted to control for some of these possibilities in the measurements and statistical tests which they ran, but it is unlikely that they were able to exhaust all possibilities of this kind. Given that recent reviews of tactile interventions in neonatal care suggest that such programmes may have limited efficacy for long-term developmental outcomes (e.g., Ohlsson & Jacobs, 2013), we certainly need to do more research to understand the effects of early tactile experience on development.

When hospital personnel increase the amount of contact, particularly skin-to-skin contact, that mothers have with their premature infants, this can improve mother–child relations (Klaus & Kennell, 1982), increase maternal self-confidence and sensitive parenting (Klebanov et al., 2001), and improve infant sleep patterns and cognitive development (Feldman & Eidelman, 2003; Tessier et al., 2003).

Vulnerability and resilience in children at risk from prenatal and perinatal complications

In this chapter, we have discussed a number of events and conditions that can cause things to go wrong during pregnancy and surrounding childbirth. At this point, you could be forgiven for wondering if things ever go right! Thankfully, they do; most pregnancies proceed without major disruptions, and many parents find the period of waiting and preparing for the arrival of a child one of the happiest times of their lives. Among *all* children, about 10% are born with any kind of disability or anomaly. That percentage is of course high enough that researchers have attempted to determine how the effects of adverse prenatal and perinatal events are either compounded or compensated for by subsequent conditions. They have also tried to uncover the reasons behind why some children with early problems develop *resilience*, or the capacity to achieve competence in life despite initially challenging circumstances.

In trying to understand the resilience of children to prenatal and perinatal complications, researchers have found that both the biological features of the child resulting from the complications, and features of their subsequent environment, can play roles in determining how successfully a child develops (Provenzi, Guida, & Montirosso, 2018). The kinds of complications that can demonstrate themselves in a child's behaviour can range from relatively minor perceptual, attentional, intellectual, motor and behavioural disabilities to gross abnormalities. The environmental situation the infant enters can range from a healthy intact family with good caregiving skills and adequate financial support to a family or parent struggling with highly adverse conditions, including poverty, drug abuse, divorce and violence (Sameroff & Chandler, 1975; Sameroff, 2007). Resilience – the ability to overcome difficulties – results from the interaction between risk and protective factors in the child (i.e., genetic inheritance) and the environment (Selman & Dray, 2006; Luthar, 2007; Rutter, 2007).

In a longitudinal study of the development of the entire population of 698 children born in 1955 on the Hawaiian island of Kauai, Werner and colleagues (Werner et al., 1971; Werner, 1995; Werner & Smith, 2001) assessed the long-term consequences of birth complications and adverse early rearing conditions. The researchers discovered that the effects of adverse perinatal complications often lessen in intensity or disappear with age. This is in large part a function of the caregiving environment in which children mature. The Kauai study offered 'a more hopeful perspective', according to Werner (1984), than did the previous literature on children with problems, and it has been followed by other similarly designed studies that tend to support its findings. More than one of these studies showed that a close and continuing relationship with another caring person is a significant factor in the development of resilience. It is informative to note that the caring person was not always a parent but a grandparent, an older sibling, a neighbour, a day care provider, a teacher, a youth worker or an older mentor. Such findings lend hope to the view that environmental circumstances can help alleviate problems experienced pre- and perinatally. Indeed, birth complications, unless they involved serious damage to the central nervous system, were consistently related to impaired physical or psychological development only if they were combined with chronic poverty, parental psychopathology or persistently poor rearing conditions (Selman & Dray, 2006; Aldwin & Werner, 2007; Luthar, 2007). Clearly, the environment can play an important role in helping children overcome a difficult beginning.

PHYSICAL GROWTH

As we have already discussed, the growth of the body has profound developmental implications beyond purely physical development. The physical sizes and shapes of the body and limbs, determine the ways in which infants and children can interact with and learn from their environments. Changes in the body size and distribution will require that infants and children adapt to the new demands of their bodies, but will also facilitate the acquisition of new skills (e.g., reaching, crawling), which will have important consequences for development in other domains (social cognitive and emotional). We will discuss some of the consequences of physical growth and motor development across the next few chapters, but in this chapter we will examine the factors that influence infants' and children's growth, beginning with genetic factors and then turning to environmental factors such as nutrition, sanitation and poverty. We will also look at the evidence that people – at least in more developed countries – are growing taller and are putting on more weight. First, however, let's look at the reasons why it is crucial to consider the role of the changing physical body in the development of our psychological abilities.

The embodied approach to development

The idea that our intelligence is rooted in not just our brains/minds, but also our bodies is gaining respect among many scientists. We see this, not just in developmental psychology, but throughout psychology, cognitive neuroscience, and even in the fields of robotics and artificial intelligence (Varela, Thompson & Rosch, 2017; Wilson, 2002).

The embodied cognition approach in psychology argues that our thought processes and behaviours are often determined by the nature of our bodies and the possibilities that our bodies afford. One of the most clear examples of this comes from multisensory perception. It is easy to forget about the ways in which we perceive the world. We touch, hear, see and taste the things around us. These ways of sensing determine the ways we encounter our environments, but all of our senses depend on what our bodies can do. We can only see things if we move our eyes in the right directions. We can only touch them if we bring our bodies into contact with them, and so on. So the shapes and sizes and abilities of our bodies determine what we perceive.

But let's come back to development now. In the infant and child, the body and its abilities are not nearly as consistent and constant as they are in an adult. Infants' bodies change by the day, and sometimes grow perceptibly even overnight (Lampl, Veldhuis, & Johnson, 1992)! Our abilities to use their bodies in the service of action also change dramatically, not just in infancy, but throughout early life (Adolph & Berger, 2006; D'Souza et al., 2017). If we agree with the embodied cognition approach then we have to consider that infants' and children's ways of thinking change considerably in development as their bodies and abilities change (Smith & Gasser, 2005). As we shall see in later chapters there is lots of evidence that this is indeed the case. For instance, our abilities to sense our environment through touch change dramatically in the first year of life as we become better at manipulating objects (Begum Ali, Spence & Bremner, 2015).

> In Chapters 6 and 9 we will look at some of the ways in which changes in the body influence our cognitive and perceptual abilities.

Next, in this chapter, we consider the physical changes which infants and children go through as their bodies grow, and some of the factors which affect those changes.

Height and weight: genetic and environmental influences

Perhaps the aspects of physical development that have the most immediate implications to the developing child are his or her height and weight. As children get taller, breakable items have to be put further out of reach; and this of course challenges children to learn new ways to get their hands on these interesting objects!

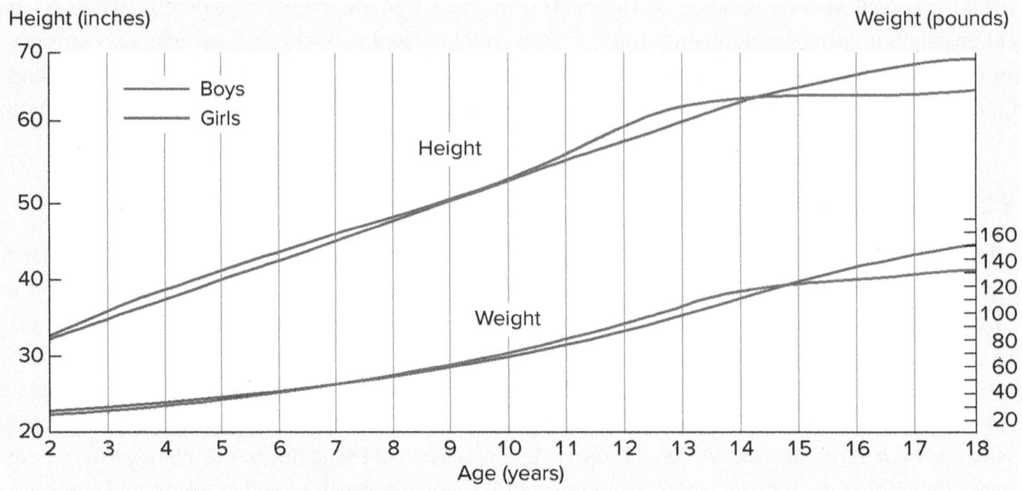

Figure 4-9   Male and female growth in height and weight
As they approach puberty, girls tend to gain height and, to a lesser degree, weight, faster than boys, but by the age of 14 or 15, boys surpass girls on both dimensions.
Source: National Centre for Health Statistics.

As height and weight are the most convenient measures of physical development we will focus largely on research that has investigated the influences of these dimensions of growth. However, it is important to bear in mind that some more subtle physical changes – for example, the distribution of weight across the body – also take place across development. If we take a look at newborns' bodies, these are initially top-heavy but change across the first year to become increasingly cylindrical, with the centre of mass moving down the body, allowing the child to eventually balance on two legs and walk (Adolph, Vereijken, & Denny, 1998; Adolph & Eppler, 2002).

Babies grow faster in their height and weight within their first half year of life than at any other age. They nearly double their weight in the first 3 months and triple their weight by the end of the first year. From then on, infants' growth rate slows down, but they still increase their weight by five or six times by 3 years of age. If we trace growth year by year, it appears to follow a smooth and gradual pattern, as shown in Figure 4-9. Daily observations, on the other hand, reveal that growth is episodic rather than continuous (Lampl et al.; 2001). Dramatic growth spurts can occur across a few days followed by days or weeks of no change (Adolph & Berger, 2006).

Research suggests that genetic factors strongly influence height and weight (Tanner, 1990; Rutter, 2006a). Data from the Colorado Adoption Project, a longitudinal study that compares adoptive and biological parents and their adopted and natural children, indicate that genetic factors may determine as much as two-thirds of the variance in height and weight (Cardon, 1994). In other research, too, scientists have found a strong relation between the weights of adopted children and their biological parents, but no relation between adoptees' and adoptive parents' weights (Stunkard et al., 1986b). Similarly, identical twins are twice as likely to resemble each other in weight as are fraternal twins (Stunkard, Foch, & Hrubeck, 1986a). Twins reared apart who did not share a common environment still show marked similarity in weight (Bouchard, 1994).

Gender (itself determined by genes) has a clear effect on children's height and weight, as you can see in Figure 4-9. Girls tend to be a bit taller than boys from the age of 2 until about the age of 9, when boys catch up. At about 10½, girls experience a growth spurt, shooting up above boys of their own age. At about age 14, however, girls' height almost plateaus, whereas boys continue to grow taller until they are about 18. The pattern for weight is similar; girls tend to weigh less than boys in the early years and then to exceed them in weight until about age 14, when their weight gain slows down, while boys' gain continues to accelerate (Tanner, 1990).

There are also wide individual differences in maturation rates. Because these differences become particularly obvious at adolescence, it is often assumed that they begin at that point. In fact, however, these differences are present at all ages, so that early maturers are almost always ahead of late-maturing peers.

Tanner (1978, 1990), a pioneer in the study of physical growth, coined the term *tempo of growth* to describe this difference between individuals in the speed of changes across development.

However, growth is not just determined by genetic factors but also by environmental influences such as nutrition, physical and psychological disorders, and climate (Tanner, 1990; Bradley et al., 1994; Pollitt, 1994). There are fairly wide variations across regional areas; for example, people in north-western and western European countries are taller than those in southern Europe. Within the continent of Africa and among the countries of Central America, there are also substantial variations in height and weight. For example, in one African tribe, adults typically grow to 7 feet tall, whereas the bushmen of Zaire, Rwanda, Burundi and the western coastal areas are on average about 4 feet tall. Of course it is difficult to determine whether such geographic differences are due to environmental or genetic factors. However, people also vary in growth within the same country, and in ways which suggest that environment is important. For example, in Brazil and India, people in urban areas, where nutrition and standards of living are high, tend to be taller than rural dwellers. In the United States, children in upper-middle-class families are both taller and heavier than children of families living in poverty (Martorell, 1984).

Nutrition and growth

Good nutrition is critical for healthy physical development from infancy to adolescence. In this section, we examine nutrition's part in normal growth and under adverse conditions such as famine. The effects of over- and under-eating are examined as well.

EFFECTS OF BOTTLE- VERSUS BREAST-FEEDING

An important choice parents face is whether to feed their baby breast milk or bottled formula milk. Although over the last century ideas about the relative virtues of each have fluctuated – in some decades, experts promoted the bottle, and in other periods, breast-feeding was more popular – it is pretty clear today that breast-feeding offers the best nutrition for young babies' healthy development (Blum, 2000). As Table 4-4

Table 4-4 Advantages of breast-feeding for infants and mothers

Infants	
Short-term benefits of breast-feeding	*Long-term benefits of breast-feeding*
Breast milk contains nutritionally balanced ingredients, including proteins, cholesterol, and lactose that together support development of the brain and nervous system	Breast-fed children have slightly higher IQs than bottle-fed children.
Supports appropriate weight gain	Breast-fed children demonstrate better reading comprehension.
Strengthens infant's immune system and reduces risk of diarrhoea and infectious diseases	Breast-fed children are less likely to have childhood cancer, allergies, or diabetes.
Promotes more efficient absorption of iron, lessening likelihood of iron deficiencies	Breast-fed children have denser bones in preadolescence.
Reduces likelihood of SIDS (Sudden Infant Death Syndrome)	
Lessens likelihood of allergies	
Builds denser bones	
Facilitates the shift to solid food	
Mothers	
Breast-feeding	
Builds closeness to her baby	
Promotes faster weight loss after baby's birth	
Delays ovulation (but is not a reliable form of birth control)	
Is convenient for some parents	

Sources: Lifshitz, Finch, and Lifshitz (1991); Fredrickson (1993); Newman (1995); Harwood and Fergusson (1998); Blum (2000); Jones, Riley, and Dwyer (2000); Dewey (2001); Hoppu et al. (2001); Caspi et al. (2007).

The amount and type of food a child consumes can have a direct effect on their growth, in conjunction with genetic and biological influences.
© David Buffington/Getty Images

outlines, a host of benefits for both infants and mothers are associated with the choice to breast-feed. These include protection against infectious disease, better development of the brain and nervous system, and a reduction in the likelihood of sudden infant death syndrome (SIDS). One important study has shown that young children in the UK (age 5) and in New Zealand (ages 7–13) who had been breast-fed demonstrated higher intelligence than children who had been bottle-fed, but only if they had a specific genetic makeup (Caspi et al., 2007). Specifically, children who were genetically predisposed to benefit from fatty acids present in breast milk showed the advantage in IQ; those without this genetic makeup did not benefit from breast-feeding.

On first inspection, we might explain this result by arguing that mothers who are better off socioeconomically are more likely to breast-feed as well as have smarter children. However, Caspi et al.'s findings were evident even after statistically controlling for the contribution of socioeconomic factors. Nevertheless there remains some controversy concerning the relationship between breast-feeding and cognitive development (Von Stumm & Plomin, 2015).

It is important to remember that some mothers are unable to breast-feed because of medical conditions, such as AIDS or tuberculosis, or because they are being treated for illnesses. Sometimes breast-feeding is difficult for parent and child, even in the absence of a medical condition. Although evidence indicates that breast-feeding confers advantages, it is important to note that babies who receive appropriate formula-based bottle nutrition develop normally, especially in countries where bottle-feeding is safe.

EFFECT OF NUTRITION ON TEMPO OF GROWTH

Nutrition plays a controlling role in physical growth. Wartime restrictions on food consumption provide clear evidence of this fact. In Europe during the First and Second World Wars, for example, there was a general trend towards less growth. In contrast, in the period between these wars, there was a general increase in growth, especially in weight (Tanner, 1990). Nutritional factors can also affect the age at which children enter puberty; during the Second World War, girls in occupied France on average did not achieve menarche (the onset of menstruation) until they were 16 years old, approximately 3 years later than the prewar norm (Howe & Schiller, 1952). Of course, stress could have contributed to this delay as well.

Studies of people during times of peace have also demonstrated the role of nutrition in growth. In a study in Bogotá, Colombia, researchers found that the provision of food supplements for entire families from midgestation until a child was 3 years old effectively prevented severe growth retardation in children at risk for malnutrition (Super, Herrera, & Mora, 1990). Moreover, the children who received the food supplements remained taller and heavier than control children at 6 years of age, 3 years after the intervention ended. Equally impressive were the results of a study in rural Bangladesh in which researchers found that changing traditional unhygienic practices by means of educational and supportive interventions improved children's health, growth and nutrition (Ahmed et al., 1993). When parents used safer methods of food preparation and waste disposal, they lessened food contamination and reduced the incidence of diarrhoea, which interferes with the absorption of essential minerals and vitamins.

Finally, research on the effects of poverty also highlights the importance of providing nutritional supplements and controlling disease (Pollitt, 1994). Iron-deficiency anaemia, a condition in which insufficient iron in the diet causes listlessness and may retard children's physical and intellectual development, is common among poor minority children and children in low-income countries, especially countries with little meat in their diets (Conrad, 2006). Interventions in Kenya and Zanzibar involving iron or meat supplements were found to improve these children's rates of growth as well as their motor and mental development (Olney et al., 2006; Neumann et al., 2007).

CATCH-UP GROWTH AFTER MALNUTRITION

A corrective principle, referred to as catch-up growth, operates after children are born: children who are born small or who experience early environmental injury or deprivation are usually able to catch up to normal physical growth (Emons et al., 2005). If they are deflected from their genetically governed growth trajectory by acute malnutrition or illness, when the missing food is supplied or the illness terminated they catch up towards their original curve (Tanner, 1970). However, the degree of catch-up growth the child can achieve depends on the duration, severity and timing of the original deprivation and the nature of the subsequent treatment or therapy. In a study of the effects of nutritional supplements following severe malnutrition, researchers found that malnourished infants who had a 5% deficit in height were able to catch up, but infants with a 15% deficit remained significantly shorter (Graham, 1966). Catch-up growth following severe malnutrition may also be limited to only some aspects of growth. In a 20-year longitudinal study of severely starved children, a programme of nutritional intervention failed to enable full development in head circumference (and presumably brain development) and produced only some catch-up in height (Stoch et al., 1982).

Timing is also critical in determining the degree of catch-up growth. Pathology and undernutrition early in life can have serious consequences, and children starved *in utero* usually show only partial catch-up (Tanner, 1990; Pollitt, Gorman, & Metallinos-Katsaras, 1992). In general, the earlier and more prolonged the malnutrition, the more difficult it is for interventions to be fully effective in helping children achieve normal growth.

This impact of malnutrition on brain development may, in part, account for the intellectual and attentional deficits shown by malnourished children (Shonkoff & Phillips, 2000; Neumann et al., 2007). Recent research has focused on attempting to better understand the impact of malnutrition on brain function in deprived rural Africa (e.g., Lloyd-Fox et al., 2017). Because behavioural assessments often do not provide useful information about development until two or three years of age, it may be that brain imaging studies of young babies will provide the best means of identifying infants in need of special care and intervention following possible prenatal malnutrition (Tomalski et al., 2013).

Secular trends in growth

A secular trend is a shift that occurs in the normative pattern of a particular characteristic over some historical time period, such as a decade or a century. There have been secular trends towards increased height and weight over centuries and even millennia. In the developed world, increases in height are levelling off. However, there is a particularly exaggerated recent trend for weight to increase further, although this is particularly obvious in quite recent history (since the 1960s). Why are we growing larger?

PEOPLE ARE GROWING TALLER

According to scientists who have measured bones exhumed from grave sites, between the eleventh and fourteenth centuries, the average Englishman was about 5 feet 6 inches tall, whereas today the average adult British male is 5 feet 9 inches tall (Figure 4-10). However, this increase in height is not necessarily still occurring (and indeed has levelled off in many developed countries; in the UK, Norway and Japan

iron-deficiency anaemia A disorder in which inadequate amounts of iron in the diet causes listlessness, and may retard a child's physical and intellectual development.

catch-up growth The tendency for human beings to regain a normal course of physical growth after injury or deprivation.

secular trend A shift in the normative pattern of a characteristic, such as height, that occurs over a historical time period, such as a decade or century.

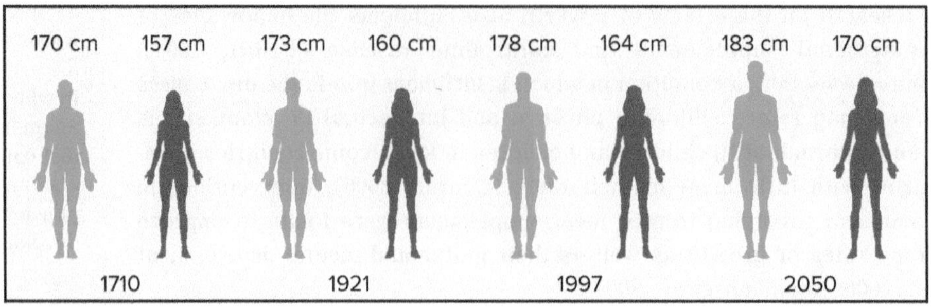

Figure 4-10 Gains in average height across the centuries.
Source: Adapted from Richard Steckel, Ohio State University, 1997.

increases in stature have apparently come to a halt; Tanner, 1990; Murata, 2000). It is possible, for example, that people in higher socioeconomic ranges have reached their maximum growth potential. People in less advantaged segments of society will probably continue to make gains as, hopefully, their conditions improve. Accordingly, in the so-called 'less developed world', people are currently experiencing the kinds of height increase that were seen across the western countries during the twentieth century (Cole, 2000; Jaruratanasirikul & Sriplung, 2015). In other countries, there are different patterns of change. In the Netherlands, for instance, people are continuing to gain in height and weight regardless of socioeconomic level: the average Dutch male is now 6 feet 1 inch, and Dutch women average 5 feet 8 inches in height (Bilger, 2004).

There are several reasons for these historical trends towards greater height. First, health and nutrition have improved in many countries of the world. Growth-retarding illnesses have come under control, particularly those that strike in the first 5 years of life, such as *marasmus* (caused by insufficient protein and calories) or *kwashiorkor* (caused by insufficient protein). In many areas, nutritional intake has improved in terms of both quantity of food consumed and balance among essential food groups (Tanner, 1990). Medical care and personal health practices have also improved. Second, socioeconomic conditions have generally improved; child labour is less common, and living conditions such as housing and sanitation have improved. Third, the influence of genetic factors has been affected by such things as intermarriage among people of different racial and ethnic backgrounds, which produces increases in height in offspring. In the future, if we experience major changes in the environment brought about by spectacular medical discoveries, natural disasters like famine or global warming, or substantial increases or decreases in pollution levels, the average height of the population could shift again.

There are reasons to believe that the most dramatic increases in height are attained during infancy. Reviewing the literature, Cole (2000) points out that increased developments of leg length during the first two years of life can for the most part account for the secular trends in height. As mentioned earlier, the first years are the most rapid period of growth across development, and Cole suggests that secular trends in height are due to a reduction in the stunting of growth achieved through better quality (rather than quantity) of nutrition during this period.

WHY ARE WE GROWING HEAVIER?

obesity A condition in which a person's weight is significantly in excess of the average weight for his or her height and frame. In the UK, childhood obesity is defined as being above the 95th centile compared to norms in 1990.

Children and adults across the industrialized world are growing heavier. Obesity, the condition in which a person's weight is significantly above average for his or her height and frame, has been on the rise since the early 1960s (Raynor & Epstein, 2001) when about 5% were obese. In 2016 in the UK, 10% of 5- to 6-year-olds and 20% of 10- to 11-year-olds were classified as obese. This trend towards obesity varies across different nations, ethnic groups and genders. In Europe adult obesity prevalence varies between 5 and 23% for men and 7 and 36% for women. Percentages of the population who are defined as overweight (but not obese) vary between 27 and 57% for men, and 18 and 43% for women. Uzbekistan and Kazakhstan are among the countries demonstrating the lowest levels of obesity, while the UK and Bosnia-Herzegovina have some of the highest (WHO Summary, 2007). In the United States, more than 20% of Mexican American boys and African American girls are overweight (National Center for Health Statistics, 2006a, 2006b); Asian Americans are the least likely to be overweight.

The generational increases in weight, and also the variations in obesity across different nations seem to indicate that our cultural environment plays a large role in our weight. An emerging lifestyle in which we eat more high energy foods, have less exercise, and spend more time in sedentary activities, such as using smartphones, or watching TV is likely to be responsible at least in part for the secular trend for increasing weight (Rao, 2006). Evidence shows that weight-gaining lifestyles can start early. Children's eating behaviour imitates their parents' food choices and eating behaviour (Ray & Klesges, 1993). Parents of obese children encourage them to eat more than their thinner siblings. In Chapter 15 we will consider obesity, and potential treatments for it in more detail, in the context of a discussion about eating disorders more generally.

Genetic inheritance also seems to play an important role in obesity. Genetic variation explains the stability in children's body mass index (BMI) around a particular weight profile (Cardon, 1994). A genetic influence also explains why adopted children are more likely to be obese if their biological parents are obese, regardless of their adoptive parents' weights (Stunkard et al., 1986b). Other evidence of an influence of heredity comes from a study by Milstein (1980), who found that newborn infants with two overweight parents were more responsive to the contrast between a sweet-tasting solution and plain water than were infants of normal-weight parents. This stronger sensitivity to taste predicted the children's weight at 3 years of age, suggesting that a preference for sweetness early in life increases the risk for obesity. Thus, even babies' predispositions to suck in particular patterns predicts later obesity (Agras, 1988).

SEXUAL MATURATION

Whereas physical growth occurs across the whole of early development and past adolescence (although, admittedly, with one or two growth spurts), sexual maturation (puberty) occurs relatively suddenly. The most important signs of puberty are: in girls, the first menstruation; in boys, the first ejaculation. These occurrences indicate that the individual is now capable of reproduction. Puberty, or the onset of sexual maturity, has long been held as a time of stress for the adolescent, when the intensity of new drives and the social pressures for new behaviours and new responsibilities may cause conflict and confusion. Whether this somewhat negative view of puberty is correct is a matter of some debate. In this section, we describe the actual changes that occur with puberty and then explore the question of whether young people are experiencing puberty earlier and earlier. We discuss whether maturing earlier or later than one's peers has a significant effect on a young person.

Puberty

Puberty is marked by the sudden bodily growth and changes that take place when the hypothalamus, at the base of the brain, stimulates the pituitary gland (see Figure 4-11) to secrete certain hormones. Hormones are powerful and highly specialized chemical substances that are produced by the cells of certain body organs and that have a regulatory effect on the activities of certain other organs. In this case, the pituitary gland's hormones cause the *adrenal cortex* (the outer layer of an adrenal gland) and the *gonads* (in males, the testes, and in females, the ovaries) to initiate a growth spurt. In girls, pubertal changes begin with breast development, and in both sexes the appearance of pubic hair is an early sign of puberty. These characteristics, along with voice change in boys, are considered *secondary sex characteristics*, which are not directly involved in sexual reproduction. *Primary sex characteristics*, which are involved in the reproductive process and evolve a few years after the first secondary characteristics, include male spermarche, or the capability of the testes and associated internal organs to produce sperm-containing ejaculate. In females, primary sex characteristics include the changes in the reproductive organs that culminate with menarche, or the beginning of *ovulation*.

puberty The onset of sexual maturity.

pituitary gland A so-called master gland, located at the base of the brain, which triggers the secretion of hormones by all other hormone-secreting (endocrine) glands.

hormones Powerful and highly specialized chemical substances that are produced by the cells of certain body organs and that have a regulatory effect on the activity of certain other organs.

spermarche In males, the first ejaculation of sperm-containing ejaculate.

menarche In females, the beginning of the menstrual cycle.

oestrogens Hormones that, in the female, are responsible for sexual maturation.

progesterone A hormone that, in females, helps regulate the menstrual cycle, and prepares the uterus to receive and nurture a fertilized egg.

testosterone A hormone that, in males, is responsible for the development of primary and secondary sex characteristics, and is essential for the production of sperm.

In both female and male adolescents, the rising concentrations of hormones stimulate the development of both primary and secondary sex characteristics. In females, oestrogens are crucial to the maturation of the reproductive system, including the ovaries, Fallopian tubes and uterus, and to the onset of ovulation and menstruation. Progesterone helps regulate the menstrual cycle and readies the uterus for the reception and nurturing of a fertilized egg. In males, testosterone, the most important of several *androgens*, is essential to the maturation of the penis, testes and other organs of the reproductive system, and to the production of sperm.

Even the attainment of secondary sex characteristics is gradual, with menarche and spermarche occurring two to three years after the beginning of the maturation process. Nevertheless, it is because these two later events signal such a marked change in the person, not only physically and physiologically but also psychologically, that they are considered primary characteristics.

> We discuss the development of grey and white matter in the brain in more detail in Chapter 5.

EFFECTS OF PUBERTY ON THE BRAIN

It is widely accepted that the hormonal changes which children go through at puberty not only lead to changes in their bodies and sexual characteristics, but also to changes in their mental abilities and the ways in which they think and behave. At least some of these changes seem likely to be due to the influence of hormones on brain development (Blakemore, 2008). There has been rather a lot of work undertaken in this area over the last two decades, in order to understand how changes in the brain and behaviour come about during adolescence. As is shown in Figure 4-12, changes in the brain structure seem to be determined both by age and puberty. This suggests that hormonal changes at puberty have a causal role in influencing developmental changes in brain structure (Blakemore, 2008; Giedd et al., 1999).

More recent findings have supported the idea that hormones play a role in brain development, indicating that both grey matter (connections or synapses between neurons), and white matter (the parts of neurons which conduct signals from one brain area to another) are associated with puberty (Herting & Sowell, 2017; Goddings et al., 2014; Menzies et al., 2015). However, it is important to emphasize that brain changes during adolescence are the

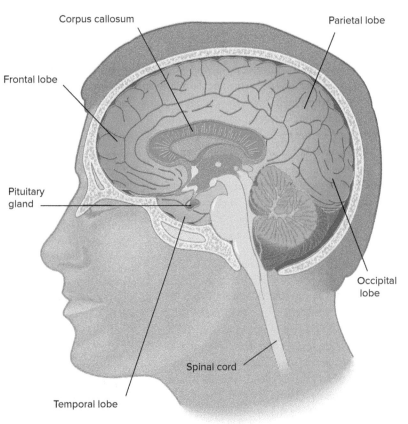

Figure 4-11 The pituitary gland

In this mid-saggital section of the brain, we can see the location of the pituitary gland, which controls the secretion of important human hormones, including those that stimulate cell growth and replication.
Source: Adapted from Postlethwait and Hopson (1995).

result of a highly complex interaction of a range of factors, including environmental factors as well as age and hormonal changes. Indeed, the most recent research indicates that we must take environmental factors including socioeconomic status, sociocultural environment, and even the child's peer group into account if we are to understand how any individual child's brain develops (Foulkes & Blakemore, 2018).

So maturational changes like puberty and also environmental factors like one's peer group seem to drive changes in the structure and function of the brain in adolescence (Blakemore, 2008; Burnett et al., 2011; Foulkes & Blakemore, 2018). However, our picture of what it is that drives brain development in adolescence becomes even more complex when we consider that environmental factors can also influence the onset of puberty, as we shall see next.

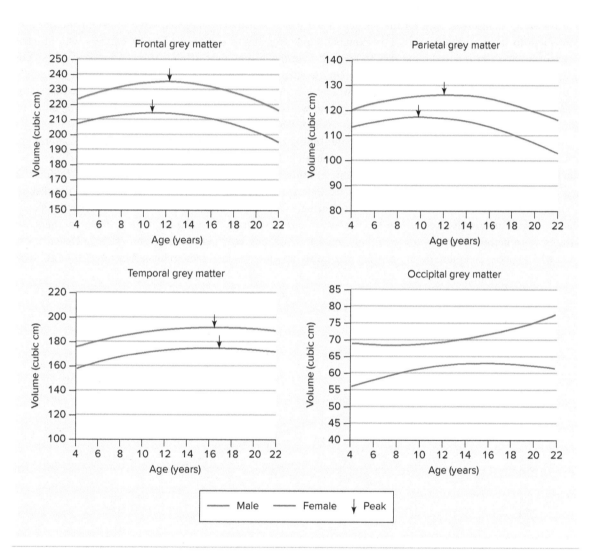

Figure 4-12 Changes in brain grey matter volume in male and female development

There is a characteristic rise and fall in grey matter across child development with the peak typically occurring within adolescence. The developmental schedule of grey matter volume changes in the brain varies across brain areas, and depends on whether a child is male or female. There is generally a lag of the brain volume between males and females, which seems to mirror the onset of puberty, particularly in frontal and parietal cortex. These findings suggest that structural changes in the brain may have as much to do with hormonal changes linked to puberty as with age.

Source: Adapted from Giedd et al. (1999).

SECULAR CHANGES IN PUBERTAL TIMING

In line with the secular increases in height detailed in the last section, young women in Western countries have demonstrated a decrease in the attainment of menarche. As Figure 4-13 shows, in the countries of Finland, Norway and Sweden, the age of menarche dropped about 3.5 years in a little over a century. This trend to earlier menarche is slowing down in many Western European countries and in the United States (Wyshak & Frisch, 1982; Wellens et al., 1990; Helm & Grolund, 1998). The reduction in age at menarche has not been uniform around the world, however. In certain developing countries, such as some parts of New Guinea, the median age of menarche is still very late – 18 years (Malcolm, 1970).

WHAT DETERMINES THE TIMING OF PUBERTY?

Inheritance plays some role in the timing of menarche; young women whose mothers matured early tend to mature early themselves. But, as the secular trend described above suggests, environmental factors also contribute to this important event. For example, gymnasts, figure skaters and ballet dancers who practise intensively, perform regularly and diet to keep fit may delay the onset of menstruation by as much as one year (Brooks-Gunn & Warren, 1985). After young women reach menarche, their periods may not be regular if they exercise strenuously and keep their weight low; for example, runners and gymnasts sometimes stop menstruating, or become *amenorrheic*. Such young women can modulate their menstrual cycles by stopping and restarting their training regimen (Brooks-Gunn & Warren, 1985).

Parent–child relationships can also alter the timing of sexual maturation (Ellis, 2004). In a longitudinal study, Steinberg (1987) found that systematic changes in family systems around the time of puberty affected the timing of young people's sexual maturation, and this maturation affected family relationships by increasing conflicts between youth and parents. In families where parents and children were emotionally distant, young people tended to reach sexual maturity earlier, whereas the closer parent and child were, the slower the process of maturation seemed to be. Recent research confirms these findings: girls whose mothers and fathers were more supportive towards them in early childhood reached puberty later (Ellis & Essex, 2007); girls who experienced more family conflict and father absence reached menarche earlier (Moffitt et al., 1992;

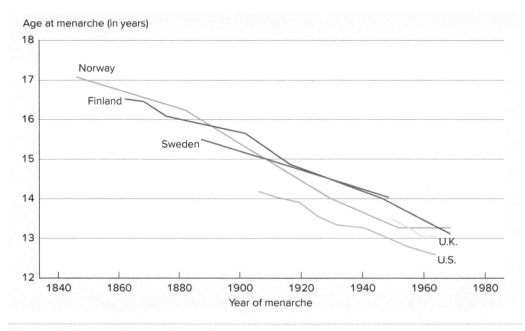

Figure 4-13   Decline in the age of menarche
In the Scandinavian countries represented here, the age of first menstruation declined considerably over a little more than a century and a half. Although the data for the United Kingdom and the United States do not cover the same time period, their trend suggests that the rate of change in menarche in all these countries is similar.
Source: Adapted from Roche (1979).

Ellis et al., 1999; Belsky et al., 2007). These findings may be explained by suggesting that stress leads to earlier maturation. Indeed, Belsky, Steinberg, and Draper (1991) have suggested that achieving menarche at an earlier age may be an evolutionarily adaptive response to a stressful environment, as it enables young women to mate at an earlier age and pass their genes on to as many others as is possible. Belsky et al. (1991) argue that this 'quantity over quality' approach is the best evolutionary response to a stressful environment in which it may not be possible to invest time into nurturing the development of just one or two children. However, it is also possible that the relation between childhood stress and onset of menarche is governed by a shared genetic factor in both children and parents, which leads to both early maturation and stress following childbirth. For example, statistics show that women who mature early and have children early are likely to become single parents, which exposes their children to more stressful conditions and father absence. Thus, the link between early maturation of the child and the stressful situation during childhood may be because the mother also matured early. At the moment it appears that the data support an explanation of the relationship between stressful conditions and early menarche in terms of a shared genetic factor (Moffitt, 1993).

Effects of early and late maturation

Does variation in the rate of maturation make a psychological difference for children? To some extent it depends on gender. For boys, there are some risks and some advantages in maturing early, but for girls the disadvantages clearly outweigh the advantages.

Boys who mature early have the advantage of being considered by their peers to be more physically attractive, athletic, masculine and popular; late maturing boys are viewed as less attractive and masculine, more childish, bossy, talkative and attention seeking (Jones & Bayley, 1950). However, there is a downside for boys who reach maturity early: early-maturing boys, owing to their obvious physical maturity, are often accepted by, and associate with, older males – leading them to more risk taking and more externalizing problems such as aggression and delinquent behaviour (Ge, Conger, & Elder 2001a, 2001b; Ge et al., 2002). Moreover, these boys are more likely to experience depressive symptoms during adolescence, although these symptoms decrease after several years. It seems that too many temptations before they are ready to evaluate the risks associated with these more mature activities can lead to trouble and elevated sadness for early-maturing boys.

For girls, the effects of early maturing can be more negative, dramatic and long lasting. Early-maturing girls may not be as prepared for the changes in their bodies and body functions as girls reaching puberty on time because their development typically occurs before schools offer health classes, and their mothers are less likely to discuss these changes with them (Brooks-Gunn, 1988; Mendle et al., 2007). They tend to have a poorer body image than on-time or late maturers, in part because the weight gains accompanying the onset of maturation violate the cultural ideal of thinness for girls (Mendle et al., 2007). As you can see from Figure 4-14, the trends for positive body image for young men and young women are almost opposite: early-maturing boys have a far more positive body image than late maturing boys; early-maturing girls tend to have negative body images, whereas late-maturing girls have positive self-images. Notice, however, that like boys who mature late, the latest-maturing girls also tend to have some problems with body image. Early-maturing girls have been found to have more adjustment or behavioural problems, including higher and more sustained levels of depression (Ge et al., 2001a, 2001b; Mendle et al., 2007), higher levels of eating disorders such as bulimia nervosa

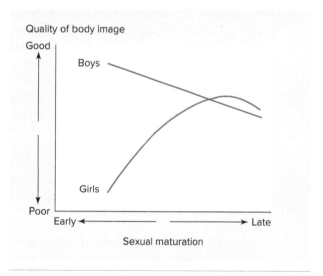

Figure 4-14 Body image in adolescent girls and boys
For boys, the relation between body image and timing of puberty is a straight line: the sooner, the better. Girls tend to have more positive body images the later they mature, but if maturity comes exceedingly late, their body images may suffer.
Source: Adapted from Tobin-Richards, Boxer, and Petersen (1983).

(Kaltiala-Heino et al., 2001), earlier initiation of substance use such as smoking and drinking (Stice et al., 2001), poorer academic achievement (Stattin & Magnusson, 1990), earlier initiation of sexual activity (Stattin & Magnusson, 1990; Stice et al., 2001) and higher rates of delinquent behaviour (Haynie, 2003). Longitudinal studies in Sweden (Magnusson, 1988, 1996; Stattin & Magnusson, 1990; Stice et al., 2000) suggest the causes of these patterns. Early-maturing girls had smaller networks of close friends and were more likely to engage in adult behaviours such as smoking, drinking and sexual intercourse at a younger age than late maturers because they tended to associate with older peers who were closer to them in terms of physical status and appearance.

> Research shows that physical development can have important impacts on social and emotional development. Take a look at Chapters 12, 13 and 14, and see if you can consider some ways in which these influences might occur.

Of course, although early maturation entails risks, not all early maturers have a poor body image, or date, smoke or drink earlier. Individuals differ in whether they perceive early maturation as 'on time' (normal) or 'off time' (deviant) depending on the attitudes, beliefs and behaviours of their particular reference group. In the final analysis, both girls' and boys' adjustment to the changes of puberty possibly depends significantly on the kinds of support, encouragement and guidance they receive from parents, and the values and expectations of her own particular peer group, as well as whether maturation is early, average or late (Conger & Petersen, 1984).

The impact of the transition to sexual maturity cannot be fully appreciated in isolation from other changes in young people's lives. For example, some researchers have shown that attending a mixed-sex school also increases problems for early-maturing girls (Caspi et al., 1993; Ge, Conger, & Elder, 1996). These findings underscore the idea that the impact of the timing of puberty can best be understood in the context of other transitions, and illustrate the ability of the environmental context to help or hinder children's abilities to cope with biological change (see Box 4-2).

Research close-up

BOX 4-2 The impact of pubertal timing and social environment on delinquency in adolescent girls

Source: Based on Caspi et al. (1993)

Introduction:

In 1993, results of several longitudinal investigations of the affect of late vs early puberty (pubertal timing) on various behaviours and social outcomes in adolescent girls were converging on a depressing message about early puberty. Simmons and Blyth (1987) reported that girls going though puberty earlier than their peers experienced more body image problems, and lower academic success later on. Stattin and Magnusson (1990) reported more sexually precocious and delinquent behaviour in early-maturing girls. Caspi and Moffitt (1991) showed that early-menarche girls produce more socially disruptive behaviours in adolescence. Particularly striking was the fact that these converging findings were gathered across a number of different countries (the US, New Zealand and Sweden). The next important question concerns the causal developmental pathways linking sexual maturation to these poor social outcomes. Is there a direct link between physical maturation and delinquent behaviour, or is this mediated by particular kinds of social context (like the presence of delinquent peers)? Caspi et al. (1993) conducted a further longitudinal study to investigate this question.

Method:

Caspi et al. (1993) tracked a cohort of girls in New Zealand who had been born in Dunedin, New Zealand, between 1972 and 1973. These girls and their parents and teachers had been given questionnaires to fill in at regular intervals between the ages of 3 and 15 years. Particular data of relevance to this study concerned:

- the age at which girls had reached their menarche (the sample was divided into: early maturers – menarche before 12½ years; on-time maturers – menarche between 12½ and 13½ years; and late maturers – menarche after 13½ years)
- self-report questionnaires concerning delinquent behaviour (the Early Delinquency Scale at age 13, and a Delinquency Scale at age 15)
- self-report questionnaires concerning their familiarity with peers who were involved in delinquent behaviour (completed at age 13).

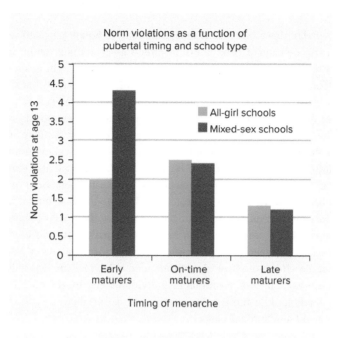

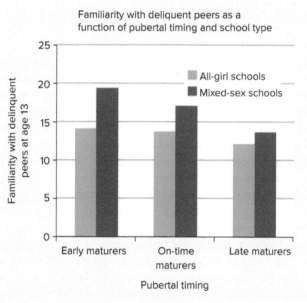

Figure 4-15   Pubertal timing
Source: Based on Caspi et al. (1993).

Because of some unique conditions in New Zealand there remains a school system in which roughly half of secondary school attendees go to single-sex (in this case, all-girl) schools, with the other half attending mixed-sex schools.

Results:

Caspi et al. (1993) replicated the previously reported findings that early maturers are more at risk of delinquent behaviour at age 13. However, it was very interesting that this effect was particularly pronounced in a mixed-sex environment (see Figure 4-15). In examining 13-year-old girls' association with delinquent peers, a similar finding was revealed: early maturers were particularly likely to associate with delinquent peers, and this was also particularly the case in a mixed-sex environment.

Discussion:

Caspi et al. (1993) interpreted these findings as indicating that, although physical sexual maturation plays an important role in early delinquent behaviours in girls, this effect is strongly mediated by the social environmental context; in this case, early maturers were particularly likely to be involved in delinquent behaviours in a mixed-sex environment. Their explanation of this was that, because boys are generally more delinquent than girls, the more delinquent environment in mixed-sex schools provides a social context for heightened delinquency in early-maturing girls. This explanation is reinforced by the data indicating that early-maturing girls in mixed-sex schools are more familiar with delinquent peers. They argue that, in the case of the girls in the mixed-sex schools, 'Physical maturation was thus their [the girls'] ticket of entry into the delinquent world of boys' (p. 28). Caspi et al. also examined whether earlier 'dispositional' factors in children's behaviour (in particular, aggressive behaviour at age 9) interacted with the effects of early puberty and the school environment. They found that the influence of early puberty on delinquent behaviour was particularly pronounced for girls without a history of aggression at age 9. For girls who were aggressive at age 9, puberty appeared to make little difference to their delinquent behaviour – they would seek out delinquent peers and behaviours irrespective of their maturational status.

Thus, it appears that the effects of physical maturation on behaviour are certainly not straightforward – they are mediated by the particular dispositions of individuals and by the social environment in which they find themselves. Findings like these help practitioners to predict, and potentially divert negative outcomes on an individual-by-individual basis.

SUMMARY

After conception, the prenatal human develops through three distinct periods (zygote, embryo, foetus) during which the new human grows, protected and sustained by the amniotic sac, the placenta and the umbilical cord. Prenatal development is a marvel of nature in which a new human is created in a rapid and complex cascade of events in which cells in the body and nervous system become differentiated for different functions.

During prenatal development, *teratogens*, agents that produce developmental abnormalities, may affect the growing organism, resulting in physical and mental deviations. Several general principles summarize the effects of teratogens on prenatal development, indicating that the type, timing and duration of the teratogen, as well as the genotypes of the mother and child, determine the outcome.

Birth involves a series of changes in the mother that permit the child to move from the womb to the outside world. Birth complications occur in only about 10% of deliveries. Some important birth factors related to developmental problems and infant mortality are prematurity and low birth weight. *Preterm* birth and low birth weight have been associated with physical, neurological, cognitive and emotional deficits. Most of these negative effects diminish with age, except in extreme cases. Stimulation programmes have been successful in protecting infants from these risk factors. Researchers who have studied newborn development have shown that often more favourable early environmental conditions can compensate to some extent for adverse pre-natal and perinatal complications.

As we grow, the most obvious physical changes are in weight and height. Both of these are influenced by genetic inheritance (infants of tall parents tend to be tall themselves), and environmental factors (most notably, nutrition during prenatal development and the first years of life). Inadequate nutrition may result in severely depressed growth rates. Other environmental factors that may affect growth rates include illness and disease.

Secular trends in many countries show that people have developed to become taller and heavier over centuries. The secular trend in height has been largely explained by the increase in the quality of nutrition, especially prenatally and in the first two years postnatally.

Puberty, the onset of sexual maturity, is triggered when the *pituitary gland* stimulates other endocrine glands to secrete *hormones*, including *oestrogens* and *progesterone* in females and *testosterone* in males, which initiate a growth spurt. This milestone in growth is marked by changes such as the start of breast develop-ment and *menarche* in girls, and the enlargement of the testes and *spermarche* in boys. Inheritance is a strong factor in the timing of menarche, although environmental conditions such as conflict within the family and the absence of the father may also exert an influence on when a young girl reaches menarche. The hormonal changes which take place during puberty not only lead sexual development but also play an important role in brain development, in interaction with environmental factors.

The timing of physical maturation can affect the child's social and emotional adjustment. Research indicates that the effects for late-maturing boys and early-maturing girls are largely negative. In general, the impact of the timing of puberty is best understood in the context of other transitions, such as school transitions and family disruptions, which may help or hinder the child's ability to cope with biological changes.

Explore and Discuss

1. Although men cannot bear children, male and female partners of the mother can play important roles during pregnancy and after birth. Given what we have discussed in this chapter, what do you think are the most important positive and negative influences partners can have on the early development of a child?

2. Medical science has permitted very small preterm infants to survive, but some of these children face physical, social and cognitive problems. Are there things that can be done to improve these problems?

3. Children and adolescents are becoming increasingly obese. What factors do you think account for this trend?

4. Can you describe three ways in which sexual maturation can impact on social and cognitive development?

Recommended Reading

Classic

Lecanuet, J.-P., Fifer, W. P., Krasnegor, N. A., & Smotherman, W. P. (1995). *Fetal development: A psychobiological perspective.* Hillsdale, NJ: Lawrence Erlbaum.

Lipsitt, L. (2002). The newborn as informant. In J. W. Fagen & H. Hayne (eds) *Progress in infancy research*, Vol. 2. Mahwah, NJ: Lawrence Erlbaum.

Susman, E. J., & Rogel, A. (2004). Puberty and psychological development. In R. M. Lerner & L. Steinberg (eds) *Handbook of adolescent psychology*, 2nd edn. New York: John Wiley & Sons.

Contemporary

Volpe, J. J. (ed.) (2018). *Volpe's neurology of the newborn* (6th edn). Philadelphia, PA: Elsevier.

Wolke, D. (2011). Preterm and low birth weight babies. In P. Howlin, T. Charman, & M. Ghaziuddin (eds), *The SAGE handbook of developmental disorders* (pp. 497–527). London: Sage.

CHAPTER 5
The Biology of Development: Genes, Nervous System, Brain and Environment

Introduction

When we think about human psychological make-up, there is a tendency to consider this in terms of the ways in which we behave and the ways in which we think. But stop. *Everything we think and do is biological.* All of our thought processes and behaviours are underpinned by some kind of biological substrate. Nonetheless, in their quest to understand the developmental origins of behaviour and thinking, developmental psychologists have mainly tended to ignore biology. After all, does it really make any sense to try to explain a complex behaviour like moral reasoning via the action of networks of neurons and brain regions? However, as the techniques and methods available for investigating biological development have improved, developmental psychologists have begun to make more serious attempts to draw connections between biological and cognitive/behavioural development. As we will try to make clear in this chapter, it is becoming increasingly clear that we cannot fully understand development without considering biology. Specific aspects of our biological development determine and influence psychological development in ways which cannot be explained just by our behavioural and cognitive interactions with our environments.

Where does biological development start? With the formation of the reproductive cells (called gametes): the sperm and egg cells. Then in the woman's oviduct, at the point of conception, sperm and egg unite to create a new living organism with the potential to develop into a human being. The first key focus of this chapter on biological development is how we inherit (at conception) from our parents the biological material which not only makes us human, but which also bestows us with a range of our own individual characteristics. This is the process of genetic transmission, and it is over even before the new zygote has undergone one cell division (i.e., when the new human is still only one cell big). The genetic inheritance which a new organism receives at this point is passed on to every other cell that will ever be formed in the human body.

> **genetic transmission**
> The biological process in which genetic material from both parents is combined into a new organism's genetic inheritance at conception via the conjoining of reproductive cells (gametes).

After genetic transmission, an individual's genes are fixed. This gives the false impression that the way in which genes exert their influence is a relatively straightforward process. However, after genetic transmission comes gene expression. Gene expression is an incredibly complex process, and probably the most important message about it is that it depends substantially on environmental context: the way a cell expresses its genetic material depends on the physical/chemical environment in which it exists. This influence of the environment extends naturally to how inheritance works at the level of the organism also: the environmental contexts in which we live (for example, our social, perceptual and nutritional environments) have very important roles in shaping how our inheritance is expressed in our behaviour and psychology.

In the second part of this chapter we will consider how our brain and nervous system develops. These organs, of course, underlie all of our psychological functions, from our motor, perceptual, and cognitive abilities, to our social interactions, emotions, and personality traits. Understanding how the brain and nervous systems develop to serve these functions is perhaps one of the greatest puzzles in psychology today, and current research indicates that we are only just peeping under the surface. The ways in which our genetic inheritance becomes expressed to form our neural anatomy and functions are incredibly complex! Another factor that makes it difficult to study brain development is that it is difficult to observe how a baby's or child's nervous system develops. In recent years, however, a number of brain imaging techniques (see Chapter 3) have been adapted for use with young children. This has allowed us to understand a great deal more about brain development than we could previously have hoped for. At the end of this chapter, we will describe some of the general principles of brain development that these techniques have uncovered.

THE PROCESS OF GENETIC TRANSMISSION

Chromosomes, meiosis, sexual reproduction and mitosis

> **Chromosomes**
> Threadlike structures, located in the nucleus of a cell, that carry genetic information to help direct development.

Chromosomes are located inside the nucleus, a microscopic organ at the centre of every human cell. Chromosomes carry the genes that code the aspects of ourselves that we inherit. Most cells contain a full complement of 46 chromosomes,

ovum The female reproductive cell, or egg.

sperm The male reproductive cell.

meiosis The process by which a cell divides to produce new reproductive cells with only half the normal complement of chromosomes; thus male and female reproductive cells (sperm and ovum) each contain only 23 chromosomes so that, when they unite, the new organism they form will have 46 chromosomes, half from each parent.

sexual reproduction The production of a new living organism by the combination of genetic material from two individuals of different sexes (the biological mother and father). This occurs via the fusion of two gametes originating from the mother (ovum) and the father (sperm).

crossing over The process by which equivalent sections of homologous chromosomes switch places randomly, shuffling the genetic information each carries.

zygote The developing organism from the time sperm and egg unite to about the second week of gestation, during which the zygote undergoes rapid cell division.

mitosis The process in which a body cell divides in two, first duplicating its chromosomes so that the new daughter cells produced each contain the usual 46 chromosomes.

which contain enough genetic material to provide the foundation for a typical human. The key exceptions to this rule are the egg and sperm cells, which contain only half of this material (23 chromosomes).

The egg, or ovum, is very small, only just visible to the naked eye and somewhat smaller than the full stop at the end of this sentence. Nonetheless, it is the largest type of cell in a woman's body. The nucleus of the ovum contains half the genetic information needed to construct a new person. The sperm, the smallest cell in a man's body, is microscopically small and about 90,000 times lighter than the egg. It comprises a head, which contains the other half of the genetic information, and a whip-like tail, which propels it through the woman's reproductive system in search of the ovum.

The process by which the genetic material of a new person is formed begins when the egg and sperm cells are formed in the reproductive organs of the mother and father (the ovaries and the testes). This happens by a special form of cell division, called meiosis. In meiosis, the 46 chromosomes in total (23 chromosome pairs) are split or halved (see Figure 5-1). When the egg and sperm unite in a process called sexual reproduction, 23 chromosomes from the sperm combine with 23 chromosomes from the egg to produce the full typical quota of 46 chromosomes for a new person.

The new individual's 46 chromosomes are thus in 23 pairs, with one half of each pair from the father and the other half from the mother. This pairing is possible because each chromosome contributed by the father's sperm is homologous (similar in shape and function) to one of the chromosomes contributed by the mother's egg. Copies of these original 23 homologous pairs of chromosomes are passed on to every cell in a person's body apart from the reproductive cells, which, as we have already described, have 23 single chromosomes.

Crucial aspects of both meiosis and sexual reproduction are that each of these processes facilitates the production of a tremendous diversity of genetic combinations. During meiosis, when a parent male's or a female's set of chromosomes is halved to produce a reproductive cell – sperm or egg – that halving process mixes chromosomes that originated from the parent's father with chromosomes that originated from the parent's mother. Further genetic variability is added during meiosis by a process called crossing over, in which equivalent sections of homologous chromosomes randomly switch places (Figure 5-1), so that genetic information is shuffled even more. The upshot of all of these shuffling and sorting processes is that there are a huge range of possible ways in which a child's genetic inheritance can arise from the genetic contributions of his or her parents.

In Chapter 4, where we will deal with aspects of biological development which are at a larger scale, we will follow the progress of the fertilized egg, or zygote, as it develops within the mother's body, becoming an embryo, then a foetus, and finally, at birth, an infant. Here we describe briefly how this process happens at the smaller scale (cellular) level. Following the fusion of the egg and sperm in sexual reproduction, the new human consists of a single-celled zygote. The developmental process by which the zygote eventually becomes the hugely complex multicellular human adult is underpinned by a form of cell division called mitosis. During mitosis, a cell duplicates its chromosomes and then divides into daughter cells that have the exact same number of chromosomes as their parent cell (see Figure 5-2). Thus, the zygote divides and continues to divide, each time producing new cells that have the full complement of 46 chromosomes. Because each new cell can also undergo mitosis, cell populations in the developing organism grow exponentially (e.g., 1 cell becomes 2, and then 2 cells become 4, 8, 16, 32, 64, 128 and so on).

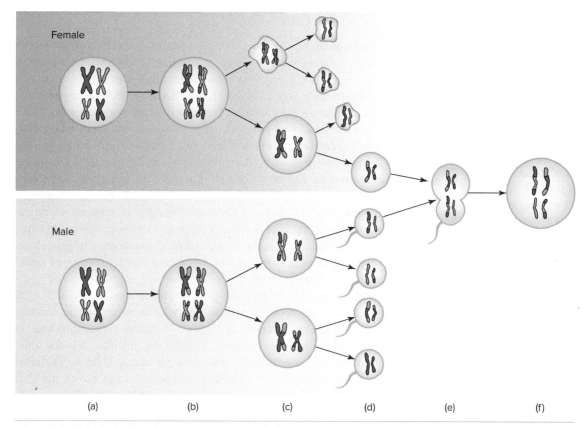

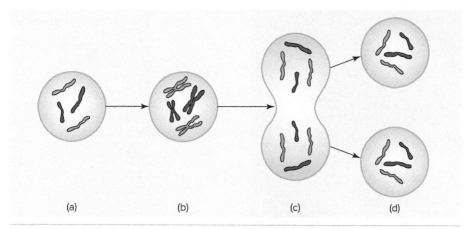

Figure 5-1   Meiosis (a-d) and sexual reproduction (e-f)

In (a) all the 46 chromosomes from a parent's cell are duplicated. In (b) crossing over between chromosomes facilitates diversity of genetic inheritance between reproductive cells. In (c) the chromosome pairs separate to form two cells. In (d) the chromosomes separate once again to form reproductive cells with 23 chromosomes. When a sperm cell fertilizes an ovum (e), a zygote is formed (f), with 23 chromosome pairs, or 46 in all.

Figure 5-2   Mitosis: the process of cell division which underpins the transformation of a zygote into the multicellular adult

In (a) we see a zygote (only 4 chromosomes are represented rather than the 46 each cell normally contains). In (b), each chromosome splits in half (lengthwise) to produce a duplicate of itself. Next, in (c), the duplicates move away from each other as the cell begins to divide. Finally, in (d), the cell has divided in two, and each new cell has the same set of chromosomes as the other and as the original parent cell (a).

Genes, DNA and proteins

deoxyribonucleic acid (DNA) A ladder-like molecule that stores genetic information in cells and transmits it during reproduction.

gene A portion of DNA located at a particular site on a chromosome and that codes for the production of specific kinds of proteins.

nucleotide A compound containing a nitrogen base, a simple sugar and a phosphate group. The order in which the 4 types of nitrogen base contained within the nucleotide is sequenced in our DNA is the genetic code which contains our inheritance.

Chromosomes are made up of one long, thin molecule of deoxyribonucleic acid, or DNA. These DNA molecules are made up of building blocks called nucleotides that are held together by two long, twisted parallel strands that resemble the two side rails of a spiral staircase (see Figure 5-3). How does the DNA in chromosomes carry the units of hereditary information? Portions of a chromosome's DNA molecule, called genes, are located at particular sites on the chromosome, where they code for the production of various kinds of proteins. It is these proteins which then go on to build the machinery of our bodies and nervous systems. Each of the many different types of proteins serves a different function. Some proteins give cells their characteristic physical properties. For example, bone cells get their hardness, skin cells their elasticity and nerve cells their capacity to conduct electrical impulses from the different kinds of proteins they possess. Other proteins do many other jobs within the body, such as triggering chemical reactions, carrying chemical messages, fighting foreign invaders and regulating the expression of genes (we will discuss this in the next section).

So that you can get a sense of how the genetic code works, let's look in a bit more detail at the way genes code for proteins. As we just mentioned, nucleotides are lined up along the DNA molecule. Each nucleotide contains a nitrogen base of which there are four kinds: adenine, cytosine, guanine, and thymine. It is the order in which these nitrogen bases occur in the DNA molecule which codes for proteins.

As you will see in Figure 5-3, the nitrogen bases of each nucleotide project out from one of the DNA strands towards the base opposite it on the other strand. Only bases that are compatible with each other will bond together. Figure 5-3 shows that adenine and thymine form a bond, as do cytosine and guanine. No other combination of the four nitrogen bases is possible.

Genes trigger the production of proteins only when a particular change in the environment signals them to activate. When it is activated, the gene splits down the middle of its section of DNA so that its pairs of

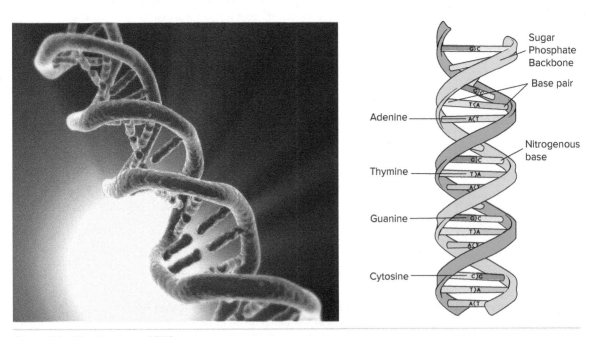

Figure 5-3   The structure of DNA

The two twisted strands of DNA form a kind of spiral structure that is composed of the complementary base pairs of nucleotides, adenosine–thymine or guanine–cytosine.

© MedicalRF.com (L)

bases are no longer joined. According to the rules by which the four bases bond with one another, 'free' nucleotides surrounding the gene connect to the exposed bases to form new pairs. The resulting copy of the gene containing the protein code in the sequence of nitrogen bases (called mRNA, or messenger ribonucleic acid) then travels from the cell nucleus to the body of the cell, where protein synthesis takes place. The copy acts as a template for building protein molecules: each sequence of three bases codes for one of the many amino acids (organic compounds) that combine to form different kinds of proteins. When the protein molecule is assembled, it is ready to begin its work in the body.

> **messenger ribonucleic acid (mRNA)** Molecules that transcribe the genetic code in DNA in the nucleus of the cell, and then travel to the body of the cell, where they are then used to synthesize protein.

So, as you can see, we gain our human inheritance, and also our unique characteristics passed onto us by our parents, via a sequenced code of nitrogen bases in DNA contained within our chromosomes. Incredibly, this transcription of this sequence code in our DNA into protein molecules is what underpins our growth from single cell zygotes into multicellular human adults with particular psychological and behavioural characteristics and traits. However, it is crucial to understand that the environment plays a huge role in this process of development also. In the next sections we will discuss what we know about how genes come to code for traits and behaviours. As we shall see, the ways in which genes are expressed into proteins are hugely affected by environmental signals and other bits of DNA. Thus, as soon as a new cell is created, the environment it finds itself in starts to determine how our genetic inheritance is realized.

INHERITANCE AND GENE EXPRESSION

Early in the twentieth century, geneticists made the important distinction between *genotype*, the specific genetic makeup of the individual, and *phenotype*, the individual's observable characteristics (e.g., her eye colour, tendency to start brawls etc.). As we have seen, genes direct the process of development by programming the formation of protein molecules. However, some of the genes' directives are used on one occasion, some on another. Some are never used at all, possibly because they are contradicted by other code in the DNA or because the environment never calls them forth. For example, geneticists discovered that hens have retained the genetic code for teeth (Kollar & Fisher, 1980). Yet, because the code is prevented from being phenotypically expressed (converted into a particular protein), you won't find any hens biting postmen (at least not outside of genetics laboratories!). Genotype is present from conception, but the expression of genotype into phenotype can be affected both by the environment and other parts of our genetic inheritance.

Scientists are learning more and more about how genotype comes to be expressed in phenotype. The central lesson is that genes almost always act in combination with one another and with environmental influences (Turkheimer, 2000; Rutter, 2006a). The way a gene is 'expressed' (whether, when and how quickly it comes to synthesize protein) depends on context. This context could be where the given cell is in the body, what other genes and DNA are present, how they have been expressed and when they have been expressed. The study of how genes come to be expressed is known as epigenetics (Armstrong, 2013).

How does gene expression occur at the level of DNA? Recall what we said earlier about how DNA exerts its influence on development – DNA is transcribed into mRNA, which in turn is used to synthesize proteins. As it turns out though, only 2% of our DNA actually consists of traditional genes which code for proteins. For a long time, scientists were unsure what the other 98% of non-protein-coding DNA was for. Some suggested that this was 'junk DNA', which had be retained in our inheritance by chance (Doolittle, 2013; Ohno, 1972). But more recently it has become clear that much of the rest of the DNA regulates the extent to which protein-coding DNA is expressed (or transcribed into mRNA for protein synthesis). One way this regulatory DNA can work is by inhibiting transcription into mRNA until some substance in the environment (called a regulation factor) switches off this inhibition. This environmental regulation of genes has incredibly wide-ranging implications. It means that gene expression can be altered by a huge array of different environmental chemicals – be these transmitted to the cell from outside of it (e.g., from nearby cells or hormones, or from the outside world) or from inside of it.

> **epigenetics** The study of how genetic material is expressed.
>
> **regulation factor** A substance that influences non-protein-coding DNA to regulate transcription of protein-coding DNA into mRNA and, later, protein.

One particular current focus of interest in the field of epigenetics is the role of non-protein-coding RNA. Non-protein-coding RNA is synthesized from non-protein-coding sequences of DNA, and various types of this RNA are now known to play key roles in regulating gene expression (Kosik, 2006; Rinn & Chang, 2012). The evolution of these roles of non-protein-coding RNA have been argued to have played an important role in the evolution of higher order cognitive abilities in humans, and some have actually suggested that this has been even more important than increases in brain size and complexity (Barry & Mattick, 2012).

We will now describe a basic model of how individual genes interact and are expressed, to determine what characteristics (or traits) an organism inherits. Following that, we will explain some further general principles that determine gene expression and which make the story very complex! Lastly, in this section, we will discuss how some genetic disorders arise through gene expression.

You could be forgiven for feeling a bit lost at this stage. And you might reasonably ask what exactly all of this means for understanding developmental psychology. The key messages for the moment are that: (i) environment plays a very important role in the ways our genetic inheritance influences development, and (ii) the complex ways in which gene expression works means that the interaction of our inheritance (nature) with the environment we grow up in (nurture) is also very complex.

The transmission of traits: a basic model

Let us run through some of the basics of how inheritance works. First, at any given gene's position on two homologous chromosomes, there can be more than one form of that gene; these alternate forms are called the gene's alleles. One of these alleles comes from the person's mother and the other from the person's father. Second, if the alleles from both parents are the same, the person is said to be homozygous for that particular gene or for the trait associated with it. If the two alleles are different, the person is heterozygous for that particular trait.

Let's try to work this out a bit more systematically. So, if 'A' represents one allele and 'a' another, the individual can have one of three possible combinations: AA, aa or Aa/aA. When a person has one of the first two of these combinations (AA or aa), she or he is homozygous for the trait because it is coded by the two identical alleles. Thus, for example, a person with two alleles for dark skin will have dark skin, and a person with two alleles for light skin will have light skin. When a person has a variant of the third combination (Aa), however, he or she is heterozygous for the trait for which each allele codes, and the result of this combination may vary.

Now let's look at heterozygous genes a bit more. Sometimes, the combination of two dissimilar alleles will produce an outcome intermediate between the traits for which each single allele codes. For instance, a light-skinned parent and a dark-skinned parent may produce a child of intermediate skin colour. A second possibility is that both alleles will express their traits simultaneously; that is, the two traits will combine but will not blend. For example, the allele for blood type A in combination with the allele for blood type B produces the blood type AB, which has both kinds of antigens, A and B, on the surface of the red blood cells. This pattern is called codominance of the two alleles.

A third possibility is that, in a heterozygous combination, the characteristic associated with only one of the alleles may be expressed. The more powerful allele is said to be dominant over the weaker, recessive allele. An example is the dominant allele for wet earwax combined with the recessive allele for dry earwax; this combination produces a person whose earwax is wet (Table 5-1). Also both blood types A and B are dominant over blood type O; this means that only someone who inherits the gene for blood type O on both alleles will have O antigens on their blood cells. Fortunately, many deleterious alleles – those that result in serious disorders – are recessive, which greatly reduces the incidence of genetic abnormalities. One of the reasons many societies prohibit marriage between close blood relatives is that a harmful recessive allele possessed by one relative is more apt to be possessed by

allele Alleles are alternative forms of a gene. An individual typically has two alleles – one from the mother and one from the father.

homozygous The state of an individual whose alleles for a particular trait from each parent are the same.

heterozygous The state of an individual whose alleles for a particular trait from each parent are different.

codominance A genetic pattern in which heterozygous alleles express the variants of the trait for which they code simultaneously and with equal force.

dominant The more powerful of two alleles in a heterozygous combination.

recessive The weaker of two alleles in a heterozygous combination.

Table 5-1   Some common dominant and recessive traits

Dominant	Recessive
Blood type A	Blood type O
Blood type B	Blood type O
Normal skin colouring	Albinism (lack of skin pigmentation)
Wet earwax	Dry earwax
Normal blood clotting	Haemophilia (failure of blood to clot)
Normal protein metabolism	Phenylketonuria
Normal red blood cells	Sickle-cell anaemia

other relatives as well, thus increasing the chances that children of their intermarriage will be homozygous for the harmful trait.

The sex chromosomes

The genes on the sex chromosomes provide some exceptions to the rules we've just discussed, because not all of these genes have two alleles. In every human being, 22 of the pairs of chromosomes are autosomes, while chromosome pair number 23 are called sex chromosomes. The sex chromosomes determine the individual's sex, and they differ in males and females (see Figure 5-4). A female has two large, homologous sex chromosomes, the XX chromosomes. A male, on the other hand, has one X chromosome from his mother and a smaller Y chromosome from his father; this pattern is referred to as XY. Because an X chromosome is about five times longer than a Y chromosome, it carries more genes. This means that some genes on a male's X chromosome will have no equivalent genes on his Y chromosome and, as a result, any recessive X-linked genes will automatically be expressed; the male's Y chromosome has no counteracting dominant genes.

Because of these differences between the sex chromosomes, genetic disorders that occur in the sex chromosomes vary in incidence between men and women. One sex chromosome abnormality is fragile X syndrome. People with this syndrome carry an X chromosome with a particular mutation which is visible as a 'pinching' of the end of the chromosome. Because females are more likely to have at least one normal X chromosome, the syndrome is more frequent in males than

autosomes   The 22 paired non-sex chromosomes.

sex chromosomes   In both males and females, the 23rd pair of chromosomes, which determine the individual's sex and are responsible for sex-related characteristics; in females, this pair normally comprises two X chromosomes, in males an X and a Y chromosome.

X-linked genes   Genes that are carried on the X chromosome and that, in males, may have no analogous genes on the Y chromosome.

fragile X syndrome A form of chromosomal abnormality, more common in males than in females, in which an area near the tip of the X chromosome is narrowed and made fragile due to a failure to condense during cell division. Symptoms include physical, cognitive and social problems.

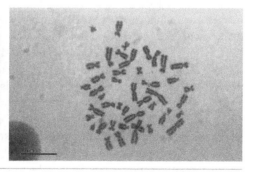

Figure 5-4   Karyotypes

Karyotypes show the appearance and number of chromosomes in a cell. On the left you can see a schematized depiction of the normal line-up of chromosomes in the male and female. Whereas the 23rd pair of chromosomes is XX in the female, it is XY in the male. On the right you can see how a male karyotype looks under the microscope.

© Science Photo Library/Alamy Stock Photo (L); Doc. RNDr. Josef Reischig, CSc. (R)

autism spectrum disorder (ASD) A lifelong disorder in which children's ability to communicate and interact socially is seriously impaired; children with ASD often have communicative and social difficulties, and often engage in repetitive and stereotyped kinds of behaviours.

dopamine A neurohormone involved in the motivation of motor behaviour.

females. People with fragile X syndrome typically have physical, cognitive and social problems. Cleft palate, seizures, abnormal brain activity and disorders of the eyes are some of the more common physical symptoms. Psychological and social problems include anxiety, hyperactivity, attention deficits and abnormal communication patterns (Garrett et al., 2004; Karmiloff-Smith et al., 2016).

As well as developmental disorders with a very clear genetic basis on the X chromosome, such as fragile X syndrome, a number of other developmental disorders have higher prevalence in males than females. Autism spectrum disorder (ASD) is perhaps the most well-known of these. ASD is known to have a genetic basis as it is very heritable, but it is not known precisely what that genetic basis is, as genetic studies point to hundreds of genes which may play a role (Burbach, 2016). Nonetheless, the predominance of ASD diagnosis in males points to the importance of X-linked genes in the disorder, giving scientists one way to focus their efforts to more clearly delineate its genetic basis (Jamain et al., 2003; Marco & Skuse, 2006).

The increased prevalence of certain psychological disorders in men due to their origins in X-linked genetic inheritance is perhaps one of the clearest examples of how biology plays a crucial role in psychological development. In the case of fragile X syndrome we have a clear causal role of a genetic mutation in atypical psychological development. The precise location of that abnormality on the X chromosome dictates the fact that this disorder is more likely to develop in males than females. We need this understanding of biological processes, as development in this case cannot be explained by reference to behavioural or thought processes alone.

Candidate genes, pleiotropy and polygenicity

So far, we have mostly focused on a relatively simple genetic model in which a single allele or a single pair of alleles determines a particular characteristic. Although this model applies to certain human traits, many other characteristics are determined not by one pair of alleles but by many pairs acting together. We know that this is the case with ASD for instance. In fact, it is becoming increasingly clear that most characteristics of greatest interest to psychologists, such as intelligence, creativity, sociability, style of emotional expression, are influenced by multiple genes and their interactions (e.g., Plomin & Deary, 2015). This involvement of many genes with one trait is what geneticists refer to as *polygenicity*.

A popular approach in attempting to identify the basis of heritability of certain traits is to look for associations between certain alleles of candidate genes and the trait of interest. However, in line with what we said above about traits often being polygenic, the more data are gathered using the candidate gene approach, the more complex the story seems to become. For instance, Bobb et al. (2006), in a review of searches for candidate genes involved in attention deficit hyperactivity disorder (ADHD) noted that 93 different polymorphisms of 33 different genes had been implicated in ADHD. The strongest evidence for an association came from a gene called DRD4, which codes for a receptor of the neurotransmitter dopamine (a neurotransmitter involved in the motivation of motor behaviour). However, even DRD4, the strongest associated candidate gene, accounted for only about 25% of the hyperactivity observed in children with ADHD. Why is this association so small? The answer, of course, is that genes do not work in isolation, but in combination with one another and with environmental influences. It seems likely that hyperactivity in children with ADHD is governed by more than just DRD4. The other 32 candidate genes Bobb et al. reviewed could all be involved.

This interaction between genes in determining traits may help explain why some traits influenced by genes do not tend to run in families. Development of such traits usually depends on a certain configuration of many genes, and that particular configuration is not likely to be passed on from parent to child. One other example of this is intelligence. Why are individuals described as geniuses sometimes born to parents of quite typical intelligence? This starts to make more sense if you consider intelligence to be a trait that emerges not from one or two genes, but from complex configurations of many genes which interact with one another (Lykken et al., 1992; Plomin & Deary, 2015; Turkheimer, 2000).

Hopefully by this stage, this theme of 'complexity' is ringing a bell for you. For instance, if we cast our minds back to the description earlier in this section of how gene expression takes place in the cells of our body, our conclusion then was that the ways in which genes interact with one another and the cellular environment are incredibly complex. Here we are picking up a similar picture. The ways in which our genetic inheritance leads to certain kinds of behavioural, social and cognitive traits are also highly complex. The complexity of how inheritance works at the biological level goes on to characterize the ways in which we inherit behaviours.

Let's bring in even more complexity. It turns out that genes rarely do only one thing. They are often pleiotropic, that is they code for many traits rather than just one. A good example of this is phenylketonuria, or PKU (see below). PKU is caused by a recessive allele of a gene called PAH that fails to produce an enzyme necessary to metabolize the protein phenylalanine present in milk, the basic diet of infants. This causes a wide number of different outcomes including reduced skin and hair pigmentation, and also cognitive impairment.

> **pleiotropy** A gene is pleiotropic if it is expressed differently in different parts of the brain.

GENETIC DISORDERS

As we've seen, genes can have both positive and negative effects on development. People can inherit harmful alleles of certain genes, which can interfere with normal physical and psychological development. Table 5-2 summarizes the chief characteristics of some of the psychological disorders these abnormalities cause. As we've already discussed, whereas some disorders have a known genetic basis (e.g., PKU and fragile X are due to

Table 5-2 Some psychological disorders that are caused by genetic defects

Disorder and its nature	Incidence	Cause	Method of diagnosis	Current methods of treatment and prevention
Phenylketonuria (PKU)				
Inability to convert phenylalanine to tyrosine; untreated, leads to mental retardation	0	Heredity: recessive allele of a single gene	Blood tests prenatally or at birth	Genetic counselling can indicate the risk that a couple will have a PKU child. Modern genetic techniques can detect recessive alleles before such a child's birth, and immediately after birth, a special diet can be instituted to prevent the disorder's toxic effects
Down syndrome (trisomy 21)				
Physically and mentally retarded development; sometimes, cardiovascular and respiratory abnormalities	1/999	Heredity: extra full or partial chromosome 21	Amniocentesis, alphafetoprotein assay, chorionic villi sampling, chromosome analysis	Special physical training; special education, including speech therapy. Surgical correction of problems with the heart and hearing are sometimes necessary
Turner (XO) syndrome				
Underdeveloped secondary sex characteristics; infertility; short stature; social immaturity; webbed neck; cardiovascular and renal abnormalities	1/1200–4000 females	Chromosomal abnormality: only one X chromosome instead of two	Blood tests	Hormone therapy can promote development of secondary sex characteristics. Counselling; special education to lessen deficits in spatial understanding
Fragile X syndrome				
Physical abnormalities; mental retardation that deepens with time; psychological and social problems	1/2000–4000 males 1/5000 females	Heredity: silenced single gene	Blood tests	Special education; medications for easing some of the physical abnormalities such as seizures
Autism spectrum disorder				
Social and communicative impairments; restricted behavioural repertoires	1/50 males 1/200 females	Heredity: polygenic	Behavioural tests	Special education and behavioural interventions

Sources: Nightingale and Meister (1987); Lin et al. (1993); Money (1993); Martini (1995); Postlethwait and Hopson (1995); Lambert and Drack (1996).

phenylketonuria (PKU)   A disease caused by a recessive allele that fails to produce an enzyme necessary to metabolize the protein phenylalanine; if untreated immediately at birth, damages the nervous system and causes mental retardation.

problems on single genes), others are more complex. ASD for instance, is known to be genetic as it is highly heritable. However, a clearly prescribed genetic basis has not been identified and it is considered to have a polygenic cause.

Phenylketonuria (PKU)

A major reason why potentially harmful alleles survive is that they are not harmful in the heterozygous state – that is, when a person inherits both a normal allele and a recessive one. A good example of this phenomenon is the allele that causes phenylketonuria, or PKU. PKU is an example of a disorder with a genetic determinant on a single gene: it is caused by a recessive allele that fails to produce an enzyme necessary to metabolize the protein phenylalanine present in milk, the basic diet of infants. As long as a person also possesses a normal allele, the PKU allele has no ill effects. In fact, about 1 of every 20 Europeans (and European Americans) carries the recessive PKU allele and doesn't even know it. Problems arise only in infants who are homozygous for the recessive gene. After birth, when these babies start ingesting milk, their bodies cannot break down phenylalanine. If these infants are not treated, toxic substances accumulate in their bodies, damaging the nervous system and causing mental retardation. Figure 5-5 shows that two heterozygous parents have a one in four chance of producing an infant who is homozygous for PKU. Most people who carry the PKU allele also have a normal allele, so they do not succumb to the disorder. Because these individuals survive and reproduce, however, the defective allele also survives from generation to generation, even though its effect may be seen only 25% of the time (when these individuals mate).

Some potentially harmful alleles may survive because they are actually beneficial in combination with a normal allele. For example, sickle-cell anaemia, a disease to which some people of African descent are subject, is determined by an allele that helps some people survive another life-threatening disease: malaria.

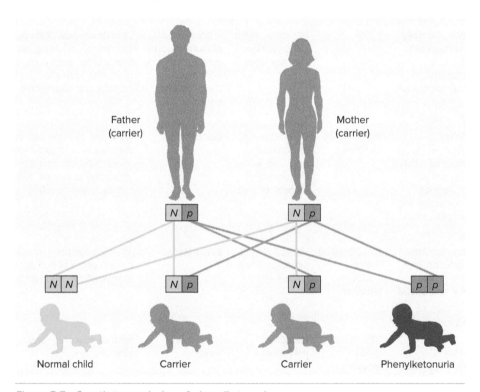

Figure 5-5   Genetic transmission of phenylketonuria

When both parents carry the recessive allele for phenylketonuria, they have a one in four chance of producing a child with the disorder. If their dominant genes for normality (N) are passed to their offspring, the child will be normal. If the child receives one dominant and one recessive gene (p) it will be a 'carrier'; that is, the child will not have the disorder, but it may pass the recessive allele to its own children. And, of course, if the child receives recessive genes from both parents, it will have phenylketonuria.

In considering these genetic abnormalities, it is important to remember what we learned earlier in the chapter – that the environment influences the way genes are expressed. It is also important to remember that, with special therapeutic and educational methods, some manifestations of these abnormalities may be modified. For instance, although PKU has a single gene inheritance, inheriting the disorder does not necessarily lead to mental retardation. As we'll see in the next section, a simple intervention of reducing phenylalanine in affected individuals' diets lessens this behavioural outcome of the disorder (Guthrie & Bickel, 1996). Furthermore, recent studies with animals show promise of developing enzyme-inhibiting therapies that may be able to lessen or even reverse the symptoms of fragile X syndrome (Franklin et al., 2014; Hayashi et al., 2007). Studies such as this not only improve the outcomes of people with debilitating disorders, but also inform us about how our environment and genetic inheritance interact in the course of typical development.

More generally, the severity of the symptoms that arise from hereditary disorders is often related to the degree to which the person has a supportive environment (Evans & Gray, 2000; Hodapp, 2002). We will return to the topic of how environmental conditions can interact with both typical and atypical genetic inheritance later in this chapter. However, we will first discuss more dramatic ways in which knowledge about genetic makeup can be used to change developmental outcomes.

BOX 5-1   Gene counselling, genetic engineering, gene therapy and the human genome project

Applied Developmental Psychology

Advances in biology and genetics have opened new opportunities for shaping and controlling some aspects of development. For some time now, it has been possible to sample cells from a developing foetus to determine whether the foetus carries genes for any of the disorders we have discussed as well as for many others. With this knowledge, gained through genetic counselling, parents may choose either to abort the birth of a child with abnormalities or to prepare for the arrival of such a child, who will need special care. For many people, this is a very difficult choice. Compounding this dilemma, because environmental factors can affect genetic predispositions, we cannot know for sure whether the anomalies we detect will inevitably result in serious problems. For example, although some XYY males (Klinefeldter's syndrome) engage in criminal activity, such men are relatively few. What would be the ethical implications, then, of a parental decision to abort a foetus with this chromosomal pattern?

The new availability of genetic information also raises issues of ethics and policy in such areas as employment and personal insurance, and among people who oppose abortion (Plomin & Rutter, 1998). For example, it is conceivable that employers might employ a liberal eugenics, in deciding to require genetic screening for potential employees and reject individuals who have a gene that may someday put them at risk for cancer, heart trouble or other diseases, or might indicate that they might have a predisposition for certain undesirable behaviours. The film *Gattaca* envisages such a utopia, and takes a rather dim view of the effects that this kind of information will have on the quality of life for humans generally. Countries are increasingly creating legislation in order to protect against the possibility that insurance companies might decide to use information about the genetic risks people may have for certain diseases or behaviours to exclude such individuals from insurance protection or to adjust rates for insurance coverage (Murray, 1996; Kass, 2002).

Scientists hope not only to locate the genes responsible for inherited disorders but also to use gene therapy to ameliorate or even cure these problems. Gene therapy involves inserting normal alleles into patients' cells to compensate for defective alleles (see Figure 5-6). The most effective current technique uses modified viruses (viruses from which harmful properties have been removed) to carry the new genes into the patient's cells. Scientists have adopted this strategy because viruses are by nature adapted to penetrate another organism's cells. Most often, target cells in the patient are first removed from the person's body, infused with the new gene by way of the virus, and then returned to the body.

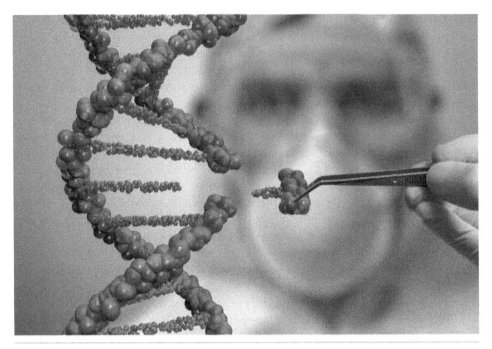

Figure 5-6   Gene therapy

This is not exactly how gene therapy works. The DNA molecules are much smaller. However, it gives a sense of the aims of gene therapy – to replace defective alleles in an affected individual's cells. By introducing alleles which manufacture helpful proteins which are missing or suppress the manufacture of harmful proteins, gene therapists hope to ameliorate the effects of debilitating hereditary diseases.

© vchal/Shutterstock

It may take some time before gene therapy is perfected, but much information has been gathered to assist scientists in their work. In particular, it is hoped that the Human Genome Project (HGP), whose aim was to map the identities and locations of all human genes, will aid us in preventing or treating diseases with a genetic basis. It will also provide us with important insights into genetic diseases such as fragile X syndrome, Turner syndrome and Williams syndrome. These and several hundred other diseases are carried on single genes, but most inherited illnesses, such as cancer, heart disease, or ASD are polygenic and determined by interactions among multiple genes; figuring out the origins of most genetically caused illnesses is a truly daunting task (Benson, 2004; Knopik et al., 2016; Trouton et al., 2002).

Finally, this information is also shedding new light on the interplay between genes and the environment. For instance, Moffitt and Caspi (2006) have studied a gene identified through the HGP that affects the breakdown and uptake of neurotransmitters in the brain. Interestingly, these pioneering researchers discovered that although this gene has effects on antisocial behaviour, these effects are seen only in people exposed to abuse during childhood. Once again, we are reminded that genes do not act alone; their impact on human behaviour depends on the particular environmental factors that also affect the individual.

So far we have discussed how our genetic code arises and functions at the level of biomolecules and cellular biology. By way of illustration we have also described how very simple combinations of genes can lead to specific traits such as type A blood or the disorder of PKU. Of course, developmental psychologists are typically interested not just in the genes which play causal roles in the development of certain traits. They are interested in how our genetic inheritance can interact with our environment to lead to behavioural and psychological outcomes. This is the field of behavioural genetics. In the next section we will describe how behavioural geneticists have attempted to unravel the relationship between genetic inheritance and human behaviour.

behavioural genetics
The field of study that examines the role of genetics in human (and animal) behaviour.

BEHAVIOURAL GENETICS

In the past, many scientists took up opposing positions on what was familiarly referred to as the nature–nurture issue. Some scholars, often referred to as maturationists (see Chapter 2), emphasized the role of heredity and biological maturational factors in human development (e.g., Gessell & Ilg, 1949), whereas others emphasized the role of learning and experience (e.g., behaviourists such as Skinner, Thorndike and Watson).

As we argued in Chapters 1 and 2, contemporary psychologists see neither nature nor nurture as wholly responsible for the development of a human being. Instead, researchers today investigate how heredity and environment interact to shape the developing person. Although they see genetic inheritance as to some extent limiting what a person can do, think and become, most psychologists believe that social and environmental experiences exert a substantial influence on the developing child. Moreover, gene–environment interactions are typically acknowledged to be highly complex. Not only do environments influence how genes are expressed, but genes can also help shape the environments to which people are exposed. Much of this kind of thinking has been inspired by findings in the field of behavioural genetics (Knopik et al., 2016).

Behavioural geneticists attempt to quantify the ways in which genes and environment interact in order to determine human behavioural traits. Behavioural geneticists, largely because of the methods and techniques available to them, have usually focused on the role of genetics in *individual differences* between humans. One of the main ways in which behavioural genetics addresses questions about nature and nurture is by measuring those differences and attempting to determine how they have come about through the interaction of genes and environment.

> **behavioural genetics**
> The study of the relative influences of heredity and environment on the evolution of individual differences in traits and abilities.
>
> **range of reaction** The notion that the human being's genetic makeup establishes a range of possible developmental outcomes, within which environmental forces largely determine how the person actually develops.

How environment and genes interplay

The concept of range of reaction helps explain how environments influence genes (Gottesman, 1963; Gottlieb, 2003; Plomin, 1995). According to this concept, heredity does not rigidly fix behaviour but instead establishes a range of possible developmental outcomes that may occur in response to different environments. As you might expect, individuals with different genetic make-ups also have different ranges of reaction; their particular sets of genes set boundaries on their range of developmental possibilities. Of course, some traits, such as earwax wetness, appear to be explained entirely by genetic variation, but for the complex behaviours that concern developmental psychologists, models that stress the interplay between genes and environment are more useful.

A hypothetical example of the interaction between range of reaction and the environment is provided in Figure 5-7. Each of the three children represented by curves A, B

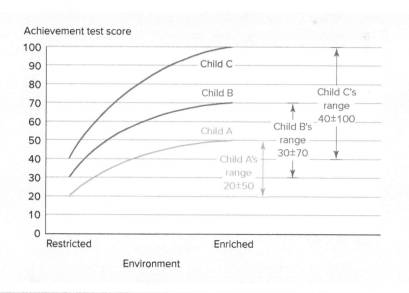

Figure 5-7 Interaction between environment and genotype

Providing any child with an enriched, stimulating environment can substantially improve the child's performance on various measures of achievement. However, each child's genotype – in this hypothetical illustration, the genotypes are represented by the labels child A, child B and child C – will determine the limits within which his or her performance may vary.
Source: Adapted from Gottesman (1963).

> **canalization** The genetic restriction of a phenotype to a small number of developmental outcomes, permitting environmental influences to play only a small role in these outcomes.

and C has a different range of possible scores on an achievement test. If all three children experience exactly the same kind of environmental input, child C will always outperform the other two. However, child B could achieve a substantially higher score than C if B experiences a more enriched environment than does C. (In this hypothetical case, an enriched environment may have been a high level of physical and mental stimulation, such as a wide array of toys and books; more optimal social-emotional stimulation, such as the presence of highly responsive and attentive caregivers; or more optimal social-cognitive-linguistic stimulation, such as caregivers who talk and read a lot to a child.) Notice, too, that child C has the widest range of reaction; that is, the difference between child C's potential performance in either restricted or enriched environments is much greater than the analogous difference for child B and child A. Child A has both the lowest and the most limited range of reaction. This child not only scores below average (50) whether raised in a stimulating or unstimulating setting, but also shows less ability to respond to environmental enrichment.

When a reaction range for a trait is extremely narrow, even narrower than child A's, it is said to show strong canalization (Waddington, 1962, 1966). The development of a highly canalized trait is restricted to just a few pathways, and more intense or more specific environmental pushes are required to alter the course of development. For example, a baby's tendency to repetitively utter consonant–vowel combinations (called babbling) is strongly canalized because babbling occurs even in babies who are born deaf and have never heard a human voice (Lenneberg, 1967). In contrast, numeracy is less highly canalized, for it can be modified by a variety of physical, social and educational experiences.

Gilbert Gottlieb (1991, 1992, 2007; Gottlieb & Lickliter, 2004) has offered a view of gene–environment interaction in which genes play a less deterministic role in shaping development. Gottlieb argues that individual development is organized into multiple levels – genetic activity, neural activity (activity of the nervous system), behaviour and environment – all of which influence one another. As Figure 5-8 shows, this influence is bidirectional; that is, it is directed both from bottom to top and from top to bottom. Consequently, genes and environment mutually influence each other; for example, the prenatal environment could alter the expression of the genes, and the postnatal environment could, in part, determine whether a genetic predisposition found full expression in behaviour. Thus, although each of the figure's levels generally influences the level directly above or below it, other interactions across non-adjacent levels are possible. In his work on mallard ducklings, Gottlieb found that ducklings' usual preference for the sounds of other ducks – a genetically governed preference – could be modified if the duckling were exposed before birth to sounds made by chickens. The duckling exposed to chicken sounds preferred these sounds to duck sounds.

The most important point of this view is the recognition that genes are part of an overall system and that their activity – that is, the expression of the characteristics they carry – is affected by events at other levels of the system, including the organism's environment. The message is clear: both genes and environment are inextricably linked and always operate in a mutually dependent fashion in shaping development. It is impossible to

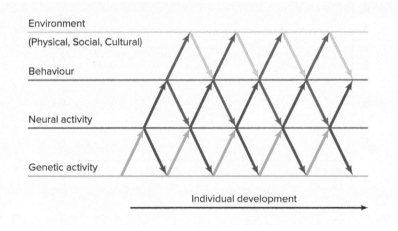

Figure 5-8 Bidirectional influence in gene–environment interactions
In the developmental systems view, the influence each of the four levels of individual development wields is bidirectional; that is, each level influences both the one above and the one below it. Any level may also influence non-adjacent levels.
Source: Adapted from Gottlieb (1992).

treat genes and environment as truly separable. Both need to be considered together (Manuck & McCaffery, 2014).

Another factor in gene–environment interaction is the stage of the child's development. Both the developmental stage and the environment determine the likelihood that a genetically based trait or characteristic will be influenced by environmental forces. An example of the importance of a critical period like this can be seen in the treatment for PKU, the genetic disorder we discussed earlier. Babies today are routinely tested for

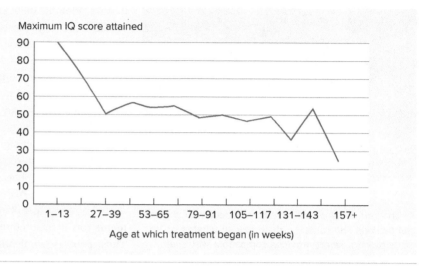

Maximum IQ score attained

Age at which treatment began (in weeks)

Figure 5-9   Diet and intelligence in PKU children
Clearly, delaying the age at which a special diet begins for the child born with phenylketonuria can have seriously negative effects on the child's intellectual functioning. If the diet begins at birth, however, the child can eventually achieve an IQ score close to average (which would be 100; see Chapter 11).
Source: Adapted from Baumeister (1967).

PKU, and if they are found to be homozygous for the trait, they are placed on a special diet low in phenylalanine to prevent the buildup of toxins that results in mental retardation. In Figure 5-9, we see once again that, in the interaction between genotype and environment, there is a window of opportunity. The special PKU diet must begin immediately after birth, for delays of even a few months can have devastating effects on a child's intellectual development. If this diet begins at once and continues until the nervous system is mature, a child with PKU can develop intellectual abilities close to normal. This example illustrates not only the importance of the timing of environmental influences but also the complex way in which developmental outcomes – even those involving a genetically based predisposition – arise from the interaction between genes and environment.

How genetic makeup helps to shape environment

It is now widely accepted that the environment influences gene expression. However, the idea that the environment can be shaped by genes is relatively new and is less commonly acknowledged. Scientists have proposed several ways in which people's genetic makeup can influence their environments (Scarr, 1996; Moffitt & Caspi, 2006; Rutter, 2006a). In one of these pathways, known as the passive genetic–environmental correlation, parents with certain genetic predispositions may create a home environment that suits those predispositions, and that may also suit and encourage the inherited predispositions of their children. Intelligent, well-educated parents may provide a home with books and stimulating conversation, enhancing their children's inherited tendencies to be bright, and encouraging them to learn. On the other side of the coin, antisocial parents increase the risk for conduct problems in their offspring who have already inherited that risk in their genetic inheritance (see Box 5-2; Jaffee et al., 2003).

In another pathway, known as the evocative genetic–environmental correlation, genes can influence the environment through people's inherited tendencies to evoke certain responses from others; that is, from their social environment. For instance, babies with an inborn tendency to smile often will probably elicit more positive stimulation from others than do very sombre, unresponsive

critical period A period of development (age range) at which specific experiences are vital for development to occur in a typical way.

passive gene–environment correlation The associations between the genetic inheritance a child receives and the environment in which they are raised.

evocative gene–environment correlation Genetic influence on the environment through an individual's inherited tendencies to evoke certain environmental responses; for example, a child's smiling may elicit smiles from others.

As children develop and have more freedom to choose companions and contexts, they may, in what is called niche picking, select activities compatible with their genetic predispositions. They give expression to these predispositions by choosing endeavours that support them.
© McGraw-Hill Education/Jill Braaten

infants (Plomin, 1995; LaFreniere, 2000; Elam et al., 2017). In this pathway, the environment that has been altered by genetic expression has reciprocal effects on genetic makeup: the evoked stimulation reinforces the babies' smiling and ultimately, by a circular process, tends to magnify the babies' genetic predisposition.

Finally, genes can influence environment in a third way – namely, through an active genetic–environmental correlation. People's genetic makeup may encourage them to actually seek out experiences compatible with their inherited tendencies (Scarr & McCartney, 1983; Scarr, 1996; Zwicker, Denovan-Wright, & Uher, 2018). In a process called niche picking, people search for, select or build environments or niches compatible with their predispositions. Thus, people genetically predisposed to be extroverted or gregarious actively seek the company of other people and become involved in a wide range of social activities. Or perhaps aggressive children are more likely to sign up for martial arts classes than a chess club (Bullock & Merrill, 1980). These experiences, in turn, enhance the expression of their genes for aggression. The importance of niche picking probably increases from childhood to adolescence and adulthood, as people gain more freedom to choose their activities and companions.

active gene–environment correlation
A situation in which people's genes encourage them to seek out particular kinds of experiences.

niche picking Seeking out or creating environments compatible with one's genetically based predispositions.

These influences of genes on environment underscore the difficulty of determining the relative contributions of heredity and environment to individual differences in development. If genes influence environmental experiences, which in turn influence genes, it is difficult to separate the factors involved in these complex feedback loops. In fact, most view the issue as a search for how genes and environment operate together in shaping development rather than assigning responsibility to one or the other source (Rutter, 2006a). As we will see in the next section, researchers have attempted to demonstrate the influence of both heredity and environment on individual differences in a large number of characteristics.

Heredity, environment and individual differences

As we have already made clear, a central question in behavioural genetics research is why people develop in such widely different ways. Why, for example, does one child achieve an IQ score of 105, whereas his sister has a score of 150? Why is one child so outgoing and sociable, and another more introverted and shy? How can we explain why some children and adults are chronically aggressive, whereas others seek to cooperate and avoid confrontation? For years, psychologists interested in human personality have struggled with questions like these. However, in the 1960s behavioural geneticists began to focus their attention particularly on the relative contributions that heredity and environment make to the array of individual differences observed in human behaviour (Knopik et al., 2016; Rutter, 2006a).

Behavioural geneticists have addressed the roles of genes and environment in IQ development. We return to intelligence in Chapter 11.

It is possible for behavioural geneticists to conduct their research without ever directly measuring chromosomes, DNA or genes. Using sophisticated statistical techniques, they can calculate what are called heritability factors, or percentage estimates of the contribution that heredity makes to a particular ability or type of behaviour. We will cover the methods which are used to calculate heritability factors shortly. First, let's address some popular misconceptions about the field of behavioural genetics.

heritability factor
A statistical estimate of the contribution heredity makes to a particular trait or ability.

UK psychiatrist Sir Michael Rutter (1992, 2006a) argues that people have many misconceptions about what the study of genetics contributes to our knowledge of human development (see Table 5-3). Rutter makes the point that the field of behavioural genetics has as much to say about environmental influences as it does about genetic effects on human development. With the right research strategies, Rutter claims, it is possible not only to reveal the interaction between these two forces but also to distinguish between them and to estimate the extent to which each contributes to any given trait or ability.

Table 5-3   Some misconceptions about behavioural genetics

• **Genes limit potential.** Wrong. Genetic factors do affect potential, but that potential is also affected by a child's environment. Change the environment and the potential changes too.
• **Strong genetic effects mean that environmental influences are not important.** Wrong. Although genetic effects account for individual variability, the environment may nonetheless affect changes in the expression of a characteristic across individuals. For example, the range of individual differences in IQ of children from disadvantaged families who are adopted into more advantaged families is more closely related to the IQ range of the children's biological parents. Nevertheless, these children show a general rise in IQ levels, demonstrating the effects of a stimulating environment.
• **Nature and nurture are separate.** Wrong. Both genes and environment are necessary for an individual to develop: 'No genes, no organism; no environment, no organism' (Scarr & Weinberg, 1983, p. 265).
• **Genetic influences diminish with age.** Wrong. The relation between genes and ageing is highly complex. Some hereditary characteristics are most evident in early stages of development; some are more evident in later stages. For example, variations in the age at which puberty occurs is largely under genetic control, whereas the contribution of genetic factors to individual differences in intelligence is more evident in older than in younger children.
• **Genes regulate only static characteristics.** Wrong. Genes affect developmental changes as well. Deviations in the normally expected environment can upset the timetable for the child's physical and psychological development, producing gross delay. However, the time at which particular characteristics emerge and the sequence in which they appear are influenced by the child's genetic inheritance.

Sources: Rutter (1992, 2006a); Schaffer (1996).

Methods of studying individual differences

The method used most often to investigate the contributions of heredity and environment to individual differences is the study of family members whose degrees of biological relatedness are known. Studies of this type generally compare adopted children with their biological and adoptive parents, examine similarities and differences between fraternal and identical twins, or explore the effects of similar and different environments on twins and on ordinary siblings (Knopik et al., 2016; Rutter, 2006a).

ADOPTION AND TWIN STUDIES

In adoption studies, researchers usually compare characteristics of adopted children with those of both their adoptive and biological parents. Although the adoptive parents exert environmental influences on their adopted children, investigators can assume that there is no genetically determined similarity between these adoptive parents and their children. Adopted children, of course, have genes in common with their biological parents, but the latter exert minimal postnatal environmental influences on the children. (These kinds of studies typically include only adopted children who have no contact with their biological parents.) Based on these assumptions and conditions, researchers reason that any similarity of adopted children to their adoptive parents must be due to their environment, whereas any similarity of the children to their biological parents must be the result of similar genetic makeup (Moffitt & Caspi, 2006; Rutter, 2006a), or influences of their biological parents on their prenatal environment (Loehlin, 2016). Adoption studies sometimes investigate the similarities and differences between biological siblings and adopted children who live in the same home. To cite one example, researchers have found that a biological parent's educational level is a better predictor of an adopted child's intelligence test scores than is similar information about the child's adoptive parents (Scarr & Weinberg, 1983). This suggests that genetic factors (or the prenatal environment) make an important contribution to intelligence.

monozygotic Characterizing identical twins, who have developed from a single fertilized egg.

dizygotic Characterizing fraternal twins, who have developed from two separate fertilized eggs.

In twin studies, researchers take a different approach to uncovering the contributions of heredity and environment to human differences. Often, these studies involve comparing the similarities between identical and fraternal twins raised together in the same home. Identical, or monozygotic, twins are created when a single zygote splits in half and each half becomes a distinct embryo with exactly the same genes; both embryos come from one zygote (mono means 'one'). In contrast, fraternal, or dizygotic, twins develop from two different eggs that have been fertilized by two different sperm, producing two different zygotes (di means 'two').

Because they are conceived independently of each other, fraternal twins are no more similar genetically than any other pair of siblings; on average, they have half their genes in common. When comparing sets of identical and fraternal twins, researchers assume that each set has been raised in essentially the same type of environment. Thus, if identical twins show more resemblance on a particular trait than fraternal twins do, we can assume that the resemblance is strongly influenced by genes. We will see many examples in later chapters of the greater resemblance of identical twins compared with fraternal twins on such characteristics as IQ, altruism and aggression (see Chapters 11 and 14). On the other hand, if on a given trait the two kinds of twins resemble each other almost equally, we can assume that the resemblance is strongly influenced by the environment.

Research close-up

BOX 5-2   Genes and environment interact in childhood conduct problems

Source: Based on Jaffee et al. (2003).

Introduction:

Whether fathers spend enough time at home with their children has been a matter of great social and political concern across several countries. Many political parties take the view that fathers should be more involved in child care, and some have even attempted to encourage this by providing tax breaks specifically for married couples with children. Is this the right thing to do? Jaffee et al. (2003) set out to investigate what kind of effect the presence of the father in the home has on the conduct of young children. However, an important factor for consideration when asking this kind of question is what role genes play. For instance, it might be possible to find a relationship between the father being around and better behaviour in the child, but then this might simply be because both the father and the child have genes in common that do not predispose them to antisocial behaviour (i.e., the father is more often at home, and the child is well behaved because of the well-behaved genes they both share). In order to examine the importance of heredity, Jaffee et al. undertook a twin study.

Method:

Jaffee et al. (2003) collected data from a large sample of twins born in England and Wales in 1994 and 1995 (Trouton, Spinath, & Plomin, 2002). They focused specifically on families in which the children had been born before the mother's 21st birthday. This resulted in 1,116 families who participated, of whom 56% of the twins were identical (monozygotic) and 44% were fraternal (dizygotic). The mothers were interviewed about the father's and the mother's antisocial behaviour, the presence of the father in the home and his involvement in caretaking. Information about the child's level of antisocial (delinquent) behaviour was gathered from both the interview with the mother and from questionnaires sent to the children's teachers. All of this information was gathered within 120 days of each child's 5th birthday. Jaffee et al. examined genetic contributions to conduct problems by comparing concordance (resemblance) in levels of antisocial behaviour between monozygotic and dizygotic twins. If there is a higher concordance between monozygotic twins then this indicates a genetic contribution.

Results:

As Figure 5-10 shows, the effect of the father being at home on conduct problems in his children was very different according to whether he was high or low in antisocial behaviours himself. If he was low in antisocial behaviour his presence in the home was associated with lower levels of conduct problems in his children. But if he was more antisocial, his presence in the home was associated with increased antisocial behaviours in his children. But what is causing this relationship? Is it the presence of the father in the home or just something to do with the shared genetic material between father and children? Jaffee et al., found that conduct problems are highly heritable (i.e., they observed that monozygotic twins were more similar in their levels of antisocial behaviour than dizygotic twins). However, they also found that, even

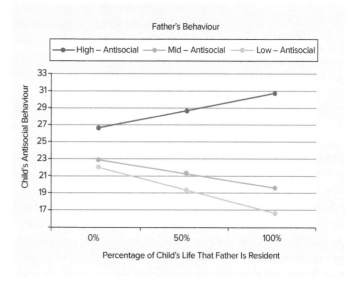

Figure 5-10   *The relationship between antisocial behaviour and the presence of the father in the home*
The graph shows that children of antisocial fathers are more antisocial if their father spends more time with them. But if the father is low in antisocial behaviours, his presence reduces the amount of antisocial behaviour.

discounting the genetic contribution to antisocial behaviour, the fathers' presence in the home still had an important influence on behaviour (in the same way that we see in Figure 5-10, but somewhat reduced). So both genes and environment play a role.

Discussion:

Jaffee et al. concluded that both the genetic contribution from the father and his presence in the home contribute to levels of antisocial behaviour in children. If the father is low in antisocial behaviour then his children will be less at risk for antisocial behaviours themselves because they have inherited genetic material that predisposes them to less antisocial behaviour. Furthermore, the presence of the father in the home is a positive influence on these children. However, if the father is high in antisocial behaviour he passes on these antisocial genes to his children *and* his presence in the home will also increase levels of antisocial behaviour in his children. Jaffee et al. describe this as a 'double whammy' of genetic and environmental effects. So, in answer to the question of whether it is better for the father to be around in the home and contribute to caretaking – the answer depends on how antisocial the father is.

SHARED AND NON-SHARED ENVIRONMENTS

Behavioural genetics research does not often find that behavioural traits in humans are explained more than 50% by genes (genetic variance). The environment is more responsible than genes for individual differences between humans, and no complex behavioural trait is 100% explained by genetic inheritance (Plomin et al., 2016). Plainly it is crucial for us to study how the environment influences the development of behavioural traits (Plomin, 2011). So, how do behavioural geneticists investigate environmental influences on development?

There are two broad kinds of environmental contributions considered by behavioural genetics: those from shared and non-shared environmental factors. Shared environmental contributions to behaviour are those experiences which

shared environment
A set of conditions or experiences shared by children raised in the same family; a parameter commonly examined in studies of individual differences.

non-shared environment A set of conditions or activities experienced by one child in a family but not shared with another child in the same family.

are shared by children in the same family. Shared environmental conditions would include such factors as being poor or well off, living in a good or a bad neighbourhood, and having parents who are employed or unemployed, in good health or physically or mentally ill (Reiss et al., 2000; Towers et al., 2003). Non-shared environments are the experiences which one sibling in the same family has but the other sibling does not have.

It is possible to use twin studies to estimate shared and non-shared environmental contributions to behaviour by making comparisons between the concordance of behavioural traits between identical and fraternal twins. One of the biggest lessons from behavioural genetics has been that non-shared environmental factors appear to be significantly more important than the shared environment in determining most of our behaviours through development (Knopik et al., 2016; Plomin, 2011; Polderman et al., 2015).

What are these non-shared environmental factors? The friends which different siblings make and their different educational experiences might be one contribution. However, it turns out that siblings in the same family don't have to leave the home in order to experience different environments. In fact the prenatal environment in the uterus can be different for siblings, and even for identical twins (Stromswold, 2006). In postnatal development, parents do not treat their children in the same ways. Furthermore, in both deliberate and unintentional ways, people help to shape the many experiences they're exposed to. With this in mind, consider whether two siblings who live together in the same home encounter exactly the same family environment (Dunn & Plomin, 1991; Feinberg & Hetherington, 2001). There are differences in people's experiences even within the same setting, differences based in part on who the people are as individuals.

Essentially, non-shared environments would include factors or events related to the individual characteristics of a particular child; for example, what specific activities that child engages in or how he or she is treated because of age, gender, temperament, illness, or physical and cognitive abilities. Studies show that siblings, even twins, have many non-shared experiences that affect their development (Plomin, 1995, 2011). Even siblings' perceptions that their experiences – for example, the way their parents treat them – are different can affect their behaviour, whether or not these perceptions are accurate. A consideration of non-shared environment helps explain why adoptive siblings, and even biologically related ones, often show only a modest similarity on behavioural traits.

Critique of behavioural genetics

The field of behavioural genetics has been around for quite some time now, over a century. In that time, as well as currently, it has not gone without significant critique. This is partly due to its origins. Perhaps the most significant figure in the emergence of behavioural genetics was Sir Francis Galton (1822–1911) who developed the initial basis for the twin method, comparing twins raised in similar or distinct environments. Galton's findings led him to come down heavily with the view that heredity plays an important role in behaviour and ability. This prompted the emergence of a new field of eugenics which promoted the selective breeding of humans in order to promote the genetic quality among the human population. Quite apart from the horrific ways in which such arguments were used by Nazism in the Second World War, such an approach is these days tempered by the general view from behavioural genetics studies that heredity typically accounts for less than 50% of variations in behaviour. In the excitement about genetic influences on behaviour, we should not forget that the environment plays a greater role (Plomin et al., 2016).

equal-environment assumption Twin methods in behavioural genetics assume that monozygotic and dizygotic twins receive equal exposure to environmental influences which determine their behaviour. Some researchers have criticized this assumption, but most research demonstrates that it holds up.

Some modern critiques of behavioural genetics raise methodological concerns. The twin method is the mainstay of behavioural genetics research, but sources of environmental influence on development raise some questions about how we should interpret twin studies. Twin studies assume that monozygotic and dizygotic twins receive equal exposure to environmental effects which determine their behaviour. This is known as the equal-environment assumption. However, there is the possibility that identical twins, because of their identical genes and inherited predispositions, are treated more similarly by their parents, evoke more similar responses from people outside the family, and select more similar settings, companions and activities than do fraternal twins (Scarr & McCartney, 1983; Scarr, 1996). This brings into question whether heritability estimates represent just the effects of genes or also environmental contributions. Future research designs will attempt to address this limitation, but in the meantime it is worth noting that studies testing whether differences in environment could distort heritability estimates find little evidence that this is the case (Derks et al., 2006; Kendler et al., 1993).

Another concern regarding behavioural genetics is the extent to which heritability estimates from twin studies have been found to be traceable to specific contributions from the genotype. However, rather than seeing this as a weakness, researchers are more and more taking this to be a 'law' of behavioural genetics research which tells us something important about how inheritance works (Chabris et al., 2015). It seems that most human behavioural traits are not strongly associated with single, so-called 'candidate', genes, but rather have a much wider range of weaker associations across the genome. The phenomenon, where many genes influence a trait is called polygenicity. Another phenomenon which we have discussed already, and which, on face value, can seem confusing and complex, is the pleiotropic nature of genes – the fact that individual genes are associated with lots of different traits. For instance, Kovas and Plomin (2006) have hypothesized that the reason we see high correlation between attainment in school across a wide range of academic tasks (reading, maths etc.) is that many genes for academic achievement (and learning disability) are generalist across domains of learning. Overall then, there is no straightforward link between genes and behaviour (between genotype and phenotype). But crucially, this does not mean that such a link does not exist – behavioural genetics has shown convincingly that inheritance matters. Rather, the message here is that the relationships between genes and behaviour are going to be complex to uncover.

DEVELOPMENT OF THE BRAIN AND NERVOUS SYSTEM

At the beginning of this chapter we described how the genetic code of a new human is formed in the fertilized ovum. In the previous chapter (Chapter 4), we described the process of physical development which occurs as the ovum rapidly undergoes a process of cell division, which after nine months brings forth a fully developed foetus, ready for birth into the outside world. Here, however, we will describe a particular aspect of this process of biological development: we will consider how a new baby's brain and nervous system develop.

From neural tube to central nervous system

Just after conception, cell division quickly leads to a human embryo, which first resembles a disk with three layers of cells in it: the endoderm, the mesoderm and the ectoderm. These differentiated layers of cells all carry the same DNA, but it is the different processes of gene expression going on in different parts of the embryo that allow the layers of cells to become differentiated from one another in appearance and function. This process of cell differentiation will continue right through the new human's life to produce a complex human adult with all of the differentiated parts that compose him or her.

However, at this early stage, the first obvious differentiations are between the three layers of cells in the new embryo. From the endoderm come later the gastrointestinal tract, the trachea, bronchi, glands, and vital organs such as the lungs, pancreas and liver. The mesoderm forms into the muscles, skeleton, circulatory and excretory systems, and the inner skin layer. Perhaps the most important layer from the point of view of the developmental psychologist, is the ectoderm, from which the sensory cells and nervous system develop (as well as the hair, nails, parts of the teeth, the outer layer of the skin and skin glands). The nervous system first appears when the ectoderm folds in on itself to form the neural tube

> **neural tube** This structure, which is formed by the ectoderm (a layer of cells in the embryo) folding in on itself, develops into the nervous system, via a process of cell differentiation, along its extent.

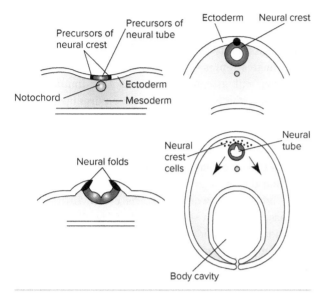

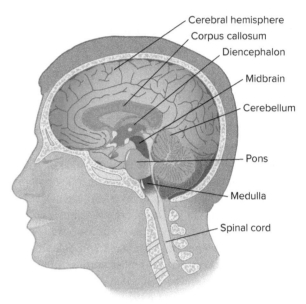

Figure 5-11   Formation of the neural tube from the embryonic disc

The neural tube (highlighted in purple), which in the adult forms the main structure of the central nervous system, originates as a differentiated portion of the ectoderm which folds over on itself. Neural crest cells in turn differentiate from the neural tube and later form the basis of the peripheral nervous system (Bronner & Simões-Costa, 2016).

Figure 5-12   The major subdivisions of the adult central nervous system

(at about the fourth or fifth week of gestation), which will later become the brain and spinal cord (see Figure 5-11).

Through gestation, the neural tube differentiates along its length, around its circumference and across its radius. The differentiations along the length lead to the various subdivisions in brain structures that we see in the mature adult brain (e.g., between the cortex, midbrain, hindbrain and spinal cord, which you can see in Figure 5-12). Differentiation around the circumference leads to distinct sensory input (in dorsal cells) and motor output (in ventral cells) areas of the CNS. Differentiation in the radial dimension leads to a layered structure later seen in the mature brain.

As the brain develops, the front part (the forebrain), expands to form the cerebrum, the large, convoluted upper mass that in the adult dominates the upper and side portions of the brain. The cerebrum is covered by the cerebral cortex (see Figure 5-13), specific areas of which are devoted to particular functions such as motor, visual or auditory processes.

Cellular development in the central nervous system

NEURAL PROLIFERATION, DIFFERENTIATION AND MIGRATION

During the embryonic period, neurons multiply at a very rapid pace, in a process called neural proliferation (Poduri & Volpe, 2017). At birth, a baby's brain has most of its neurons, or nerve cells – 100 to 200 billion of them (Nash, 1997; LeDoux, 2002). In fact, most neurons are present in the brain by the seventh month of gestation (Rakic, 1995). Neurologists had assumed that the brain did not grow new neurons after birth, but studies suggest that the adult brain has the capacity to regenerate some nerve cells (e.g., Rosenzweig, Leiman, & Breedlove, 1996; Gould et al., 1999).

neural proliferation
The rapid formation of neurons in the developing organism's brain.

neuron   A cell in the body's nervous system, consisting of a cell body, a long projection called an axon and several shorter projections called dendrites; neurons send and receive neural impulses, or messages, throughout the brain and nervous system.

Glial cells, which surround and protect the neurons, also proliferate. These cells eventually provide the neurons with structural support, regulate their nutrients and repair neural tissue.

During brain development it is not enough for neurons simply to multiply. Neurons are very long cells, sometimes over a metre in length, and so they have to reach across and connect up the correct areas of the CNS and peripheral nervous system. Thus, neurons, at least during embryonic development, are always on the move (Breedlove & Watson, 2013) as they migrate to their eventual locations in the brain. This neural migration ensures that the relevant parts of the brain and nervous system are networked together by a sufficient number of neurons. Some migration

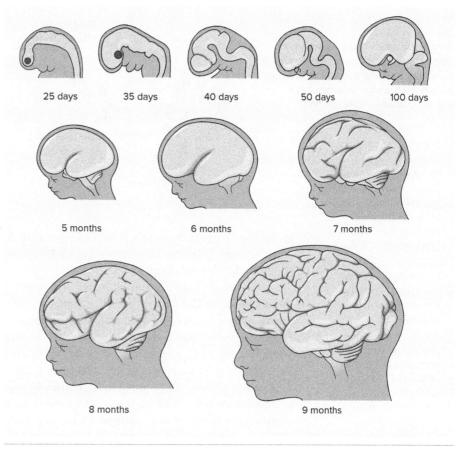

25 days   35 days   40 days   50 days   100 days

5 months   6 months   7 months

8 months   9 months

Figure 5-13   Foetal brain development. The first five of the drawings in this figure have been enlarged to make the details more clear
Source: Adapted from Papalia and Olds (1996, p. 172).

occurs by cells being pushed from the proliferative regions to new places in the developing organism. However, some cells migrate actively, guided by chemical signals. Researchers have also proposed and shown that glial cells play an important role in providing neurons with a structure to migrate along (Rakic, 1988; Franco & Muller, 2013).

POSTNATAL DEVELOPMENT OF THE CNS: SYNAPTOGENESIS, PRUNING AND MYELINATION

After birth, even though neuronal proliferation slows, the brain still increases in size. It gets bigger because existing neurons grow, and the connections between them proliferate. Perhaps as essential as neurons themselves are the junctions between neurons, known as synapses. At these specialized junctions, the extended axon of one neuron transmits a message to the projected dendrites of another neuron, usually by means of chemicals that cross the small space between the neurons (Figure 5-14). This activity is crucial to survival and learning, for as the brain's neurons receive input from the environment, they create new synapses, allowing for increasingly complex communications. Synaptogenesis, or the forming of synapses, begins early in prenatal life, as soon as neurons appear (Kinney & Volpe, 2017). The brain forms many more synapses than neurons; for example, at birth, in the brain's visual cortex, there are 2,500 synapses for every neuron; when the child is about 2 years old, there are about 15,000 synapses for every neuron (Huttenlocher, 1994). By adulthood, each

glial cell   A nerve cell that supports and protects neurons, and serves to encase them in myelin sheaths.

neural migration   The movement of neurons within the brain, which ensures that all brain areas have a sufficient number of neural connections.

synapse   A specialized site of intercellular communication where information is exchanged between nerve cells, usually by means of a chemical neurotransmitter.

synaptogenesis   The forming of synapses.

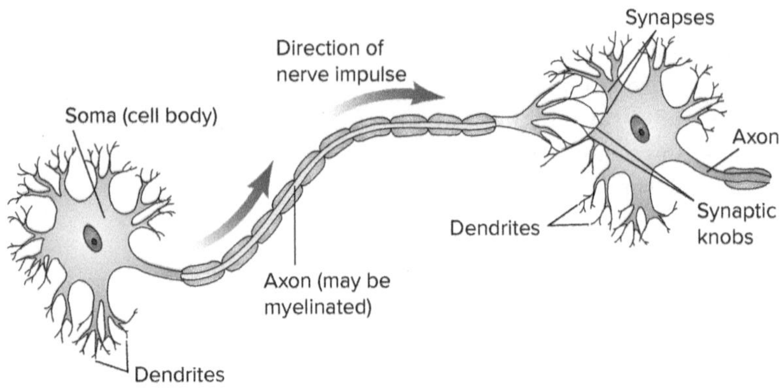

Figure 5-14   Synaptic connection between two neurons

Across the small space between one neuron's synaptic knobs and another's dendrites or soma a chemical substance effects the transfer of information.
Source: Adapted from Martini (1995)

neuronal death
The death of some neurons that surround newly formed synaptic connections among other neurons; also called programmed cell death.

synaptic pruning   The brain's disposal of the axons and dendrites of a neuron that is not often stimulated.

myelination   The process by which glial cells encase neurons in sheaths of the fatty substance myelin.

of the brain's approximately 1 trillion neurons makes 100 to 1000 connections with other neurons. That adds up to about 1 quadrillion synapses in the adult human brain (Huttenlocher & Dabholkar, 1997).

Are all these neurons and synapses necessary? Do they continue to function throughout life? The answer to both questions is no. The brain is programmed to create more neurons and connections than are needed. With development, two processes reduce the number of neurons and connecting fibres (Sowell et al., 2003). When new synapses are formed, some surrounding neurons die in what is called neuronal death, or programmed cell death (Kandel, Schwartz, & Jessell, 2000; Kristiansen & Ham, 2014), apparently to provide more space for these crucial loci of information transmission. In synaptic pruning, the brain disposes of a neuron's axons and dendrites if that particular neuron is not often stimulated (Abitz et al., 2007; Kinney & Volpe, 2017). The goals of both neuronal death and synaptic pruning are to increase the speed, efficiency and complexity of transmissions between neurons as the ways in which they are connected are shaped by experience (Huttenlocher, 1994; Kolb et al., 2003). Brain development is not simply an additive process but one that increases in efficiency and specialization. Loss of cells and connections in this case leads to adaptive gains for the developing organism.

Another feature of neurons that continues to change beyond birth and even into middle childhood is the amount of myelin that covers the neuronal axon. Myelin, thought to be produced for neurons by glial cells, is a fatty, membranous wrapping (Figure 5-15). The insulation provided by myelin makes the neuron more efficient in transmitting information, increasing the speed at which neural signals are transmitted along the axon (Johnson & De Haan, 2011). Most myelination occurs during the first two years of life,

Figure 5-15   A myelinated neuron
The neuron's axon terminates in synaptic knobs that, in synaptic connection with the dendrites of another neuron (see Figure 5-14) or with other types of cells, transmit messages through the nervous system. The myelin sheaths that encase much of the axon facilitate the transmission of signals rapidly and efficiently. Neurons are the longest cells in the human body, sometimes reaching more than 3 feet in length.
Source: Adapted from Martini (1995)

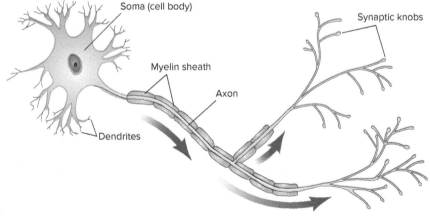

but some continues into adulthood, a reminder that change in the brain is a lifelong process (Kinney & Volpe, 2018).

As we have seen, there are a great many changes in the structure of the brain both pre-natally and postnatally, leading right up beyond childhood. These changes are physically notice-able. As Figure 5-16 dramatically illustrates, in the postnatal period the brain grows very rapidly espe-cially in the first 3 years of life. It continues to grow at a considerable pace right up until adult-hood. Although at birth an infant's brain weighs only about one-fourth as much as a mature brain, by the time the baby is about 6 months old, its brain weighs half what an adult brain weighs, and the brain of the 2-year-old child weighs three-quarters as much as an adult brain (Figure 5-16; Shonkoff & Phillips, 2000).

So far we have mainly discussed the develop-ment of the structures of the brain and nervous system. In the next section we go on to discuss the development of brain function.

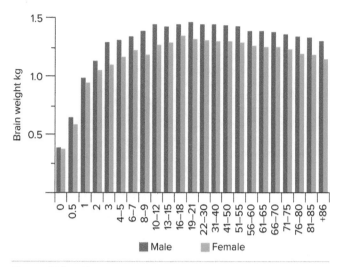

Figure 5-16   How brain weight increases with age
In this figure, the age scale for the early years has been expanded to show this period of rapid growth more clearly. As human beings mature, male brains tend to be heavier than female brains because of men's larger body sizes.
Source: Based on data from Dekaban and Sadowsky (1978).

DEVELOPMENTAL COGNITIVE NEUROSCIENCE

What happens in the brain that allows our cognitive abilities to develop? This is a question that has begun to take centre stage in developmental psychology in recent years. But why should we concern ourselves with the brain? Do we really learn anything useful by considering how neurons and regions of nervous tissue underpin our developing abilities? Psychologists, including developmental psychologists, have not always considered biological processes to be very relevant in understanding cognitive abilities (e.g., Mehler, Morton, & Jusczyk, 1984). Perhaps we can understand development simply by considering the interaction between inherited abilities and the environment to which we are exposed, without having to think about how this works in the brain.

Nonetheless, over the last 20 years or so, developmental psychology has become more and more influ-enced by methods and ideas from the field of cognitive neuroscience. Developmental researchers, as well as being interested in brain development for its own sake, now frequently argue that we cannot fully under-stand development without understanding the role of the brain and biological processes more generally in development (Johnson & De Haan, 2015). The crucial point to appreciate here is that the brain and nervous system are the organs of our psychological abilities and traits. As such, any developmental changes in the biology of these organs has important implications for the development of psychological abilities. In this section, we will see how this argument can be justified. However, let's first discuss the development of perhaps the most crucial part of the brain underlying the devel-opment of cognitive abilities: the cerebral cortex.

The cerebral cortex

The largest portion of the human brain consists of the two connected hemispheres that make up the cerebrum, a mass of tissue that governs mental functions which humans share with other vertebrate animals (e.g., sensory perception, motor abilities and memory) as well as functions which are thought to be particular to humans

cognitive neuroscience
The field in which scien-tists study the biological machinery and pro-cesses which underpin cognition.

cerebrum   The two connected hemispheres of the brain.

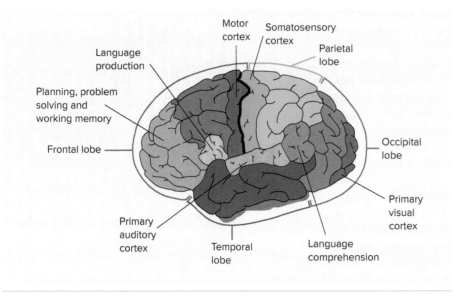

Figure 5-17   The cortex

The cortex is divided into four lobes – frontal, temporal, occipital and parietal – and specific areas within these lobes typically specialize in particular functions. For instance, the left hemisphere of the cortex (the hemisphere which is shown here), is generally associated with the processing of language, whereas the right hemisphere (not seen here) plays a greater role in visual and spatial processing.

(e.g., speech and self-awareness). The covering layer of the human cerebrum, the cerebral cortex (Figure 5-17), is a highly folded surface containing about 90% of the brain's cell bodies. In the last few years, significant progress has been made in learning how these most sophisticated areas of the central nervous system are involved in cognitive functions, such as seeing, hearing, smelling, moving, planning and speaking. In many cases specific sensory, emotional and cognitive functions have been traced to particular regions of the cerebral cortex.

BRAIN MATURATION

There is an orderly sequence to brain development during infancy and childhood. We know from neuro-anatomical studies that the parts of the brain that are furthest from the spinal cord develop last. The cerebral hemispheres, which are right at the top of the brain, in fact develop much slower in humans than they do in other primates (Johnson & De Haan, 2015). As the cerebral hemispheres mature, a range of cognitive functions unfold.

In the visual cortex, synaptogenesis takes place, multiplying the number of synapses per neuron by six times within the first two postnatal years. In accordance with this, infants' visual capabilities are greatly enhanced; for example, they become more able to resolve fine detail in their visual field up to about 6 months of age (Dobson & Teller, 1978), and they also become more skilled at following visual stimuli with their eyes ('smooth tracking') and orienting their eyes towards visual events (Johnson & De Haan, 2015; Nelson, Thomas, & de Haan, 2006).

The last areas of the cerebrum to develop are the prefrontal areas. Prefrontal cortex is particularly involved in a range of skills which are often grouped together under the umbrella term 'executive function'. Executive functions include planning actions, inhibiting behaviours and working memory. In the prefrontal cortex, the main maturational changes beyond 2 years of age are not synaptogenesis, but rather synaptic pruning and myelination (as covered in the previous section, synaptic pruning is a process in which synapses are removed, and in myelination the axons of neurons are insulated to make them more efficient). In line with the protracted maturation of prefrontal areas, it is perhaps unsurprising by now that executive functions have perhaps the longest developmental trajectories across childhood, with, for instance, working memory abilities developing substantially during toddlerhood, and continuing well into early adolescence (Blakemore, 2008; Conklin et al., 2007; Crone, 2009). In Chapter 10 we will discuss the development of executive functions in more detail.

So, what we are seeing here is that our cognitive abilities seem to develop in line with the maturation of the specific brain areas which govern those abilities. It seems that the biological process of brain maturation constrains the development of our cognitive and behavioural abilities. As such, developmental cognitive neuroscientists

cerebral cortex The covering layer of the cerebrum that contains the cells that control specific functions such as seeing, hearing, moving and thinking.

executive function A cognitive system that is presumed to control and manage other cognitive processes.

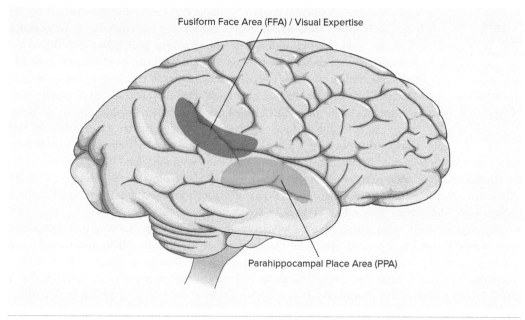

Fusiform Face Area (FFA) / Visual Expertise

Parahippocampal Place Area (PPA)

Figure 5-18   The fusiform face area and the parahippocampal place area
(Shown here in the right hemisphere of the cerebral cortex.)

have argued that understanding biological development is crucial to understanding how, when and why our cognitive abilities and psychological traits emerge.

BRAIN SPECIALIZATION

As we have just seen, the frontal lobes are specialized for certain tasks, including inhibition, working memory and planning. This is an example of what is referred to as functional specialization in the brain. Through various methods, including studies of brain-damaged patients and functional brain-imaging methods, neuroscientists have identified in great detail how the human brain is specialized into different areas and networks of areas that subserve specific functions. One of the most obvious ways in which the brain is subdivided into different functional areas is in its division into two halves, or brain hemispheres. The left and right hemispheres, which are connected by a set of nerve fibres called the corpus callosum, are quite different anatomically and, in many ways, control different functions (Kandel et al., 2000). Later we will describe how the left hemisphere comes to control specifically language-related skills, and the right hemisphere spatial abilities.

However, the brain is also subdivided into much more fine-grained functional regions. Good examples of this are the fusiform face area (FFA) and the parahippocampal place area (PPA). Functional imaging studies have indicated that the FFA is particularly important in recognizing faces (Kanwisher et al., 1997), and the PPA is involved in encoding information about visual scenes (Epstein et al., 1999). Figure 5-18 shows where these areas are in the brain. While researchers have disagreed over whether these areas are specialized just for processing faces and places, they are certainly important in these tasks.

DEVELOPMENT OF FACE RECOGNITION IN THE BRAIN

How does this specialization come about? Some developmental theorists consider these kinds of specialized brain areas to be the result of a strong genetic influence (e.g., Sugita, 2009). On the other hand, others have argued that brain specialization comes about because the perceptual input we receive from our environment shapes the functional organization of the brain (Johnson, 2011). We will discuss much of the research on the development of face perception in Chapter 6, but here we will describe

brain hemispheres
The two halves of the brain's cerebrum, left and right.

corpus callosum The band of nerve fibres that connects the two hemispheres of the brain.

fusiform face area
An area of the temporal lobes that is strongly involved in face recognition.

parahippocampal place area An area in the temporal lobe (surrounding the hippocampus), which is strongly involved in forming representations of visual scenes.

The brain changes substantially in both structure and function in infancy. In Chapter 4 we discussed how these considerable changes continue well into adolescence.

some of the brain imaging studies in infants that have informed us about the development of the brain areas and networks subserving this particularly important skill.

Early brain imaging studies of the development of functioning in the areas of the brain that are specialized for face recognition used the event related potential (ERP) technique, which measures electrical activity across the scalp in response to sensory stimulation (in this case the presentation of a face). Halit et al. (2003) examined changes in a specific brain wave (ERP) called the N170, which in adults has been shown to be related to detection of faces (specifically upright, human faces). Halit et al. (2003) showed that between 3 and 10 months of age, the N170 became progressively more responsive, specifically to upright human faces. Theorists have suggested that these changes in the N170 represent the gradual tuning of brain regions, which will later subserve face recognition (including the FFA; Johnson, 2011). Research using fMRI even shows that the networks of neurons involved in face recognition continue to develop into early adolescence (Cohen-Kadosh et al., 2013).

In many ways it seems unsurprising that the human brain would develop in a way that specializes it for processing faces. Faces are a part of the social environment of the human infant, and humans and their brains are particularly adapted to live in social circumstances (Dunbar & Shultz, 2007; Frith, 2007). More recently, researchers have gone beyond faces to look at a wider range of ways in which the brain is specialized for processing social information. In Box 5-3 we describe a study by Lloyd-Fox et al. (2015), which has used a technique called functional Near Infrared Spectroscopy (fNIRS) to investigate the specialization of the infant brain for perceiving other people's actions. As you will see the authors' findings seem to indicate that experience (in this case the infants' own experiences of acting on the world themselves) may play an important role in the development of the specialized social brain.

Research close-up

BOX 5-3 Using near infrared spectroscopy to examine the developmental origins of the social brain in infancy

Source: Based on Lloyd-Fox et al. (2015).

Introduction:

Adults' brains are specialized so that we can perceive and navigate our way around our social world (Frith, 2007); for instance they are specialized for recognizing faces and voices (e.g., Belin et al., 2000; Cohen-Kadosh et al., 2011). A number of studies have examined the development of the brain regions which govern infants' emerging abilities to perceive faces and voices, but until recently few had examined whether there are specialized regions in the infant brain for perceiving human actions.

When you watch someone carrying out an action you can easily perceive their movements and usually divine their intentions (i.e., you can figure out what they are trying to do). When adults are shown visual presentations of humans carrying out actions, this has been found to be associated with activity in a range of brain areas known as the Action Observation Network. Two areas in particular in this network are the posterior Superior Temporal Sulcus (pSTS), and the Temporal-Parietal Junction (TPJ), which sit adjacent to each other around the border between the temporal and parietal lobes (see Figure 5-16). Historically, it has proved difficult to localize functional brain activity in human infants. Functional Magnetic Resonance Imagining (fMRI) is a difficult technique to use with infants when they are awake, as they do not like the enclosed environment of the MRI scanner. Infants do tolerate Electroencephalography (EEG), but this is not a good method for localizing brain activity to small regions. Another, more recently developed method for localizing brain activity in human infants is functional Near Infrared Spectroscopy (fNIRS) which is tolerated by infants and is superior to EEG at localizing brain activity.

Method:

Lloyd-Fox and colleagues used fNIRS to measure blood flow to the cortex directly under a large array of sensors with its centre placed over the infants' temporal lobes. They tested 24 four- to six-month-old infants (10 were female, a further 12 infants were tested but did not complete the study). FNIRS measures blood flow to particular parts of the brain by (safely!) shining infrared light into the brain and then measuring the reflection of that light by oxygenated and deoxygenated blood. As we explained in Chapter 3, infrared light can pass through the skull and is shining into your brain all the time when you sit in daylight. Lloyd-Fox et al. did this while the infants were watching videos of an actor moving their hand (manual condition) or moving their eyes (eye-gaze condition), and measured the amount of oxygenated and deoxygenated blood flow to the frontal lobe while this was happening. After the fNIRS experiment, the authors also looked at how competent infants were at using their own hands to pick up objects.

Results:

Lloyd-Fox et al. compared the infants' brain activity in the manual and eye-gaze conditions to a 'baseline' condition in which the infants viewed pictures of cars. They found more activity to the eye gaze and manual videos over a range of areas including at the fNIRS sensors which were placed over the pSTS and the TPJ (the brain areas known to be important for action perception in adults; you can see these marked by a green box in Figure 5-19). Importantly though, they found a significant correlation between the infants' ability to use their own hands to pick up objects and activity in pSTS-TPJ whilst the infants viewed the actions in the manual condition. The better the infants were at picking up objects, the greater the activity which was observed in pSTS-TPJ. This correlational relationship was not found for the eye-gaze condition or over any other brain regions.

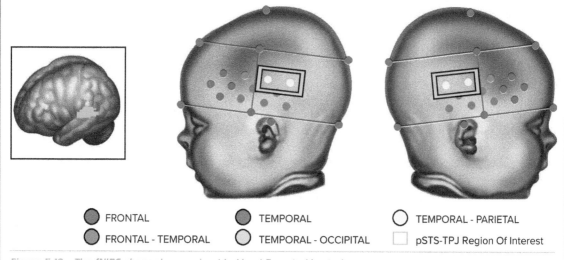

| ● FRONTAL | ● TEMPORAL | ○ TEMPORAL - PARIETAL |
| ● FRONTAL - TEMPORAL | ○ TEMPORAL - OCCIPITAL | ▢ pSTS-TPJ Region Of Interest |

Figure 5-19   The fNIRS channels examined in Lloyd-Fox et al.'s study
**The authors were particularly interested in establishing whether they could record activity in pSTS and TPJ (high-
lighted in green) whilst the infants were viewing human actions (hand movements and movements of the eyes).**

Discussion:

Lloyd-Fox et al. concluded that, at 4–6 months of age it is possible to measure the brain's responses to observed actions over a range of different areas including the specific areas known to be involved in processing observed actions in adults (pSTS and TPJ). Interestingly, the extent to which these areas respond to observed actions seems to depend on the expertise which any individual infant has at carrying out actions themselves. Infants who were better at picking up objects showed stronger brain responses to observed actions in pSTS-TPJ. This may indicate that

> Functional Near Infrared Spectroscopy (fNIRS) is a method which is increasingly used to localize brain activity in infants. In Chapter 3 we cover this method in more detail.

in early life, our experience of acting on the world plays a role in shaping how our brain becomes specialized for perceiving and interpreting others' actions when we observe them. We'll discuss how experience is involved in brain specialization further down.

LEFT- AND RIGHT-HEMISPHERE SPECIALIZATION

hemispheric specialization Differential functioning of the two cerebral hemispheres; the left controlling the right side of the body, the right controlling the left side.

lateralization The process by which each half of the brain becomes specialized for certain functions – for example, the control of speech and language by the left hemisphere and of visual-spatial processing by the right.

Hemispheric specialization begins early in life (Stephan et al., 2003). The left hemisphere of the motor cortex controls simple movement in the right side of the body, and the right hemisphere controls the body's left side. Lateralization describes the specialization of each hemisphere in specific perceptual and cognitive tasks.

Handedness is to some extent determined by hemispheric specialization and lateralization. About 90% of adults are right-handed and a majority of young infants show right-hand dominance (Maurer & Maurer, 1988; Dean & Anderson, 1997); even 90% of foetuses prefer to suck their right thumbs, which suggests that handedness develops in the womb (Hepper, 2004).

The right hemisphere is generally thought to be specialized for processing visual-spatial information, non-speech sounds like environmental noises, and the perception of faces (Nelson & Bosquet, 2000; Nelson et al., 2006). When damage occurs to the right side of the brain, people may have difficulty attending to a task requiring visual-spatial perception, their drawing skills may deteriorate, they may have trouble following a map or recognizing friends, and they may become spatially disorientated (Carter, Freeman, & Stanton, 1995). The right hemisphere is also involved in processing emotional information, as shown by the fact that people with right-brain damage can have difficulty interpreting facial expressions (Dawson, 1994; Nelson et al., 2006). At the same time, right-hemisphere damage can sometimes make people indifferent to or even cheerful about things that would normally upset them. This is thought to be because the right hemisphere is activated in emotional expressions that causes the person to turn away or withdraw from that environment, such as distress, disgust and fear. In contrast, the left hemisphere is thought to be specialized to subserve the expression of emotions with which we approach the external environment, such as joy, interest and anger (see Figure 5-20, as well as Fox, 1991; Davidson, 1994; Demaree et al., 2005).

The left hemisphere of the brain is associated with language processing; although people with left-hemisphere damage can recognize a familiar song and tell a stranger's face from an old friend's, they may have trouble understanding what is being said to them or speaking clearly (Springer & Deutsch, 1993). Evidence of a genetic basis of lateralization is seen in the positive association of the degree of language lateralization between parents and children (Anneken et al., 2004). Interestingly, however, in people who are deaf and use sign language to communicate – a language that involves motor movements of the hands – the right side of the brain can take over language functions (Neville & Bruer, 2001; Sanders et al., 2007).

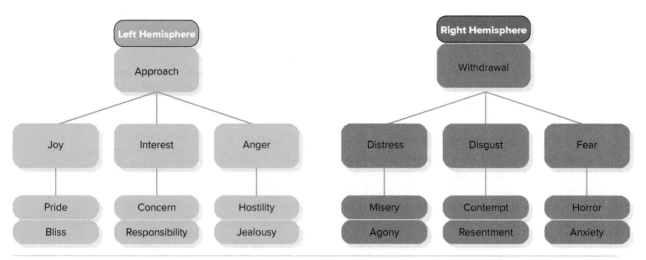

Figure 5-20   Emotions associated with left- and right-hemisphere activity
Both hemispheres are involved in emotional expression, but evidence indicates that the left focuses on feelings that trigger an approach to the environment and the right on feelings that cause a person to turn away from the environment.
Source: Adapted from Fox (1991).

These and other findings demonstrate that the brain is capable of adapting to external change. If brain injury occurs in the early years of life, because the young brain is not fully developed and hemispheric specialization is not yet complete, infants and young children often recover their functioning (Fox et al., 1994; Stiles et al., 2012). For instance, when the left hemisphere is damaged in early infancy, a child can still develop language ability close to normal (Stiles et al., 2012). Even in adults, there is still a great deal of modifiability, and lost function can often be partially recovered through treatment (Briones et al., 2004).

The degree to which a newborn's brain is prone to use one hemisphere rather than the other for processing speech (i.e., lateralized) has consequences for the child's language ability three years later. Infants whose left hemisphere differentiates among speech sounds and whose right hemisphere differentiates among non-speech sounds exhibit better language skills at age 3 (Molfese & Molfese, 1985; Hoff, 2005). However, infants' brain responses to hearing speech and matching it with concrete objects are multidimensional and involve a variety of processes, some of which are lateralized and some of which are not (Molfese et al., 1990). Clearly, brain functioning between the hemispheres is highly complex and requires continued study.

Maturation or plasticity?

An important question for developmental cognitive neuroscientists concerns *how* the brain develops. Much evidence, as we have just described, points to protracted development of the brain and nervous system. But is this development simply growth (or 'maturation') according to an unfolding genetic plan, or is the environment and other experiences involved in shaping changes in brain structure and function? Changes in the brain as a result of experience are referred to as brain plasticity. Just as we can see all across the discipline of developmental psychology, contemporary developmental cognitive neuroscientists are fairly uniform in their acceptance that both maturational and environmental factors are important in brain development. The question is one of emphasis and determining exactly how inheritance and experience interact to shape the biological machinery of our psychological abilities. It is difficult to determine whether changes in brain function are due to maturation or experience. Take face recognition. The changes in the N170 and the networks of neurons involved in face recognition could be due to either the influence of sensory input on brain structure and function, or it could be that these changes represent the influence of the maturation of the various brain areas involved in face processing.

> **plasticity** The capacity of the brain, particularly in its developmental stages, to respond and adapt to input from the external environment.

Some research on human infants demonstrates the brain's plasticity. As we have already heard, infants with significant brain damage manage to recover well. Some have even developed language after losing their entire left hemisphere (Lenneberg, 1967; Stiles et al., 2012). However, perhaps some of the clearest clues that the environment plays an important role come from animal research, which shows that the size, structure and even the biochemistry of the brain can be modified by experience. There is now a great deal of evidence that the kind of environment which animals are exposed to can have measurable effects on their brains. In particular, if rats and mice are exposed to more complex and interesting (enriched) environments, this has a number of positive outcomes for their brains (Garthe et al., 2016; Pysanenko et al., 2018). This kind of work on the effects of enriched environments, was pioneered by Rosenzweig and his colleagues (Benloucif et al., 1995; Rosenzweig, 2003). They placed young rats in two very different environments. The 'enriched' environment consisted of large, brightly lit, communal cages with wheels, ladders, platforms and other toys that were changed daily to ensure that the rats had a steady stream of new learning experiences. In the 'impoverished' environment, each rat was alone in a bare, isolated cage located in a quiet, dimly lit room. When the researchers compared the brains of the young rats after nearly three months, they discovered that the weight of the cerebral cortex, which controls higher-order processes, was about 4% heavier for the rats in the enriched environment, and the weight of the occipital region, which controls vision, was 6% heavier.

One reason the enriched rats had bigger brains was that enriched environments tend to increase the complexity of neurons as measured by the number of dendrites (Jones & Greenough, 1996; Black et al., 1998). A greater number of dendrites means that more synapses formed with other neurons, which in turn means that more information can be sent via these synaptic connections. At the same time, the activity of key chemicals in the brain, especially in the cerebral cortex, increases significantly as a result of enriched rearing environments.

It may not be only the young who can benefit from enriched experiences. Adult rats and mice exposed to impoverished or enriched environments after being reared in normal laboratory conditions show changes like those in young rats (Black et al., 1998; Brione et al., 2004; Garthe et al., 2016). Still, the effects of differential experience tend to be greater during the earlier periods of life.

Lack of stimulation or exposure to traumatic events, in contrast, can damage the brain and cause it to malfunction. In abused children, both the cortex and the limbic system – centres in the brain that are involved with emotions and infant–parent attachment – are 20% to 30% smaller and have fewer synapses than in non-abused children (Perry, 1997).

Techniques for studying brain function and activity, such as fMRI and EEG (see Chapter 3), also show the effects on the developing brain of early deprivation. One programme of research, led by Nelson and colleagues (Nelson, 2007; Troller-Renfree et al., 2018) has examined the effects on the brain of the profound deprivation experienced by children placed in Romanian orphanages around the fall of the tyrant Nicolae Ceauşescu in 1989. Studies of such unfortunate children (many of whom are now adults of course) show that this deprivation results in reduced connectivity or communication between a range of regions of the brain (Eluvathingal et al., 2006), as well as reduced cortical brain activity during tasks such as memory tasks or face processing (Parker et al., 2005). Not only do these studies illustrate the malleability of the developing brain and its responsiveness to environmental conditions, they also help inform about the circumstances which can lead to developmental improvements in deprived individuals. Troller-Renfree et al. (2018) report on an investigation of the effects of foster-care intervention on deprived children in Bucharest, Romania, identifying neural markers which can help explain why some children are resilient to deprivation and able to benefit from intervention while others are not.

SUMMARY

During the course of development, the *genotype* interacts with the environment in complex ways to produce the *phenotype*. Developmental scientists study the phenotypic expression of individual physical and behavioural characteristics in an effort to understand how genes and the environment interact to produce each unique human being. In this chapter we have described how the genetic code is first created in a new human life. We then went on to describe how our genetic code comes to be expressed via interactions with other genes and environmental influences.

Behavioural geneticists attempt to understand how the behaviours we produce across our lifespan are the result of interactions between our heredity and environmental influences. The concept of the *range of reaction* helps shed light on how environments and genes interact. According to this concept, heredity does not rigidly fix behaviour but instead establishes a range of possible developmental outcomes that may occur in response to different environments. Not only does environment influence genetic expression, but genes also influence the environments to which people are exposed.

Behavioural geneticists also ask why significant differences exist in individual development. Commonly, researchers examine family members with known degrees of biological relatedness, such as *monozygotic* and *dizygotic* twins, and adopted children. From these groups they can draw conclusions about the extent to which a given trait is heritable.

Following on from this discussion about the process of inheritance and the influence of inheritance with the environment we went on to describe how this might happen at a biological level in the brain. We first described the structural development of the brain *in utero* and following birth, and then how the field of developmental cognitive neuroscience has addressed how the brain comes to be specialized in terms of its functioning across early life. Brain imaging studies have shed a great deal of light on this question.

While the brain is undoubtedly shaped substantially by our genetic inheritance, the environment plays a critical role in brain development. The brain has great *plasticity*, which allows it to compensate for defects or damage in one area or even one whole hemisphere. The fact that the environment influences our development at all levels of biological explanation, in gene expression, and in structural and functional brain development means that development is a process in which our inheritance interacts with our environments in truly complex ways.

---

1. Two friends ask you about the heredity versus environment debate. One is a strong believer in the influence of the environment and the other is committed to a belief in the importance of heredity. In light of our discussions in this chapter, what would you tell your friends to convince them that there are problems with both of these positions?

2. The development of the brain can be modified by environmental factors that range from useful stimulation to the extreme deprivation suffered by some children reared in orphanages. What implications does this plasticity of the brain have for the heredity–environment debate?

3. Neuroscientific approaches to understanding development are on the increase. Do you think neuroscience can tell us important things about development? Explain your position.

Explore and Discuss

Contemporary

Johnson, M. H., & de Haan, M. (2015). *Developmental cognitive neuroscience* (4th edn). Oxford: Wiley-Blackwell.

Nelson, C. A. (2007). A neurobiological perspective on early human deprivation. *Child Psychology Perspectives, 1,* 13–18.

Knopik, V. S., Neiderhiser, J. M., DeFries, J. C., & Plomin, R. (2016). *Behavioral genetics.* New York: Macmillan Higher Education.

Classic

Gottlieb, G. (2007). Probabilistic epigenesis. *Developmental Science, 10,* 1–11.

Lenneberg, E. H. (1967). *Biological foundations of language.* Oxford: Wiley.

Recommended Reading

CHAPTER 6
Perceptual and Sensorimotor Development

Parents are sometimes quite surprised at the appearance of their newborns. At the moment of birth and for a little while afterward, most newborns, or neonates, can look very frail, and not just a little bit alien. Their noses, ears and entire heads often bear the marks of the pressure exerted on them as they passed through the birth canal, and their skin is typically wrinkled and blotchy, partly as the result of floating for nine months in amniotic fluid. Their heads appear very large in proportion to their small bodies and newborns have difficulty supporting their heads with their necks (from childhood to adulthood, the head goes from a quarter to an eighth of total body size). Their legs appear weak, even useless, and their arms do not appear to move with any great purpose.

This portrayal of the newborn infant as a frail and rather helpless little being is an idea which philosophers and psychologists alike extended to infants' psychological makeup, until about 50 years ago. As we discussed in Chapter 2, John Locke (1632–1704), one of the 'British empiricist' philosophers argued that infants are born into the world *tabula rasa*; that is, as a 'blank slate'. Newborns were thought to be naive in more than just their knowledge of the world. William James (1842–1910), acknowledged by many as the father of modern psychology, wrote about the perceptual experience of the newborn infant in his seminal book *The Principles of Psychology* (1890). He speculated that, 'The [newborn] baby, assailed by eye, ear, nose, skin and entrails all at once, feels it all as one great blooming, buzzing confusion' (James, 1890).

But are infants really born in a state of multisensory confusion? These days, most developmental psychologists would answer with a resounding 'No'. The advent of new methods for examining the perceptual abilities of even the youngest of infants (and even before their birth) has demonstrated perceptual abilities that go well beyond what Locke or James thought possible.

In this chapter we will tackle the question of how our sensory and motor behaviours emerge. It may seem odd that we are considering what has traditionally been considered as the *input* to the human information processing system (sensory perception) in the same chapter as the *output* (motor behaviour). However, it is increasingly acknowledged that there is such an inextricable link between these aspects of psychological life that it makes no sense to consider them in isolation (e.g. Gibson, 1979). This opinion is based largely on the consideration that our perceptual abilities subserve our ability to act on the world (perception is for action). Hence our decision to cover the emergence of motor abilities under the heading 'sensorimotor development'.

Thus, as we progress through this chapter we will consider the development of perceptual abilities in various sensory modalities, and also in combination, from birth, though infancy and into childhood. In the second section of the chapter we will move on to cover the development of overt sensorimotor behaviour in infants and young children: that is, when, how and why infants and children learn about the links between sensory stimuli and motor movements in order to coordinate complex actions in and on their environment.

LEARNING TO PERCEIVE

As we just described, the British empiricist philosophers, including John Locke and George Berkeley, argued that the *tabula rasa* state of the human newborn included their ability to perceive. This is quite a striking idea. Imagine being transported to a new world where you not only have to learn all about that world for the first time, but you have to learn how to see, feel, hear, and smell it also!

Newborns as naive perceivers: Molyneux's question

Locke and Berkeley based their argument on some specific ideas. For instance, they argued that it was impossible to perceive one's visual world properly without first learning how visual stimuli were related to the tactile senses of touch and movement (kinematics). Locke came to this idea through a discussion of a famous question (known as Molyneux's question; see Richardson, 2015) posed to him by another

neonate A newborn baby.

Molyneux's question William Molyneux asked the seventeenth-century British philosopher John Locke whether a blind person who had their sight restored might be able to see and recognize objects which they had previously learned about through touch alone.

George Berkeley and John Locke (as seen in Chapter 2). These eminent philosophers and early psychologists argue that the newborn infant had a lot to learn before he or she could perceive the outside world.
© Pictorial Press Ltd/Alamy Stock Photo (L)/image courtesy National Gallery of Art (R)

philosopher, William Molyneux. Molyneux asked Locke whether a blind man who had learned to distinguish objects through touch would then be able to recognize those objects if sight were restored to him. Locke's answer (which Molyneux agreed with) was that this was not possible without the man first being able to touch and see the environment simultaneously, and thus learn the relations between the senses.

There are three ideas which arise from Locke's consideration of Molyneux's question (Locke, 1894) which it is useful for us to think about here. First Locke suggests that in order to perceive properly, we have to gain perceptual experience through development. We will certainly get some idea of the extent to which this is true in the following sections of this chapter. What are your preconceptions?

Second, Locke seems to consider that *multisensory* experience is particularly important in perceptual development. He indicates that we have to learn about multisensory correspondences, or how the senses are related to one another (e.g., how what an object looks like is related to how it feels when touched and explored). As multisensory development is an important and current focus of debate in developmental psychology, we have devoted a whole section to this.

The last idea which comes from Locke's thoughts on Molyneux's question is that he seems to think that babies need to learn to perceive by actively exploring their world through motor behaviour. Do we need to explore the world with our hands in order to bring the senses into contact with one another and learn about the links between them? We will explore this question throughout this chapter.

Newborns as competent perceivers

Locke's and Berkeley's view that human newborn babies must be perceptually naive has been commonly shared since their time. Charles Darwin, the renowned naturalist was of the view that newborns could see little other than light and dark (this was also based partly on his observations of one of his own children; Darwin, 1877). And as we've already said, William James the early psychologist, thought newborns inhabited a 'blooming, buzzing confusion'. However, research over the past 50 years or so has revealed that newborns are actually far from blind or perceptually naive. It seems that when they emerge from the uterus they already possess many of the perceptual abilities they need to make sense of the outside world, even in the absence of many of the motor skills which Locke presumed they would require in order to learn how to perceive.

Themes in perceptual development

As you can see in this chapter's Chronology of Development chart below, the newborn infant is quite capable of distinguishing many features of their sensory environment. Nonetheless there are considerable developmental achievements in perception over the first year of life, particularly in the first 6 months.

The idea that babies need to act on the world in order to develop perceptual abilities is closely related to the ideas which Piaget had about cognitive development which we will discuss in Chapter 9.

Examining perceptual abilities in young infants has been a particular challenge for developmental psychologists. In Chapter 3 we describe many of the methodologies they have used, and so you may find it useful to refer to the section on infant methods there. Many of the methods we use for examining perceptual abilities in young infants make use of the fact that when infants distinguish different stimuli in their environment, they behave differently towards those different stimuli (e.g., they may show a visual preference for one stimulus over another). However, as we shall see, even if we determine that infants possess a certain sensory discriminative capability (e.g. distinguishing between the shapes of square and circle, or the tastes of sweet and sour), we cannot be sure they experience the same sensations or discriminate them in the same way as older children and adults. Throughout the next sections we will indicate how developmental psychologists have employed clever experiments to get around this problem.

As you will see, children's and particularly infants' early perceptual abilities are especially sensitive to the social environment (e.g. the world of human voices, faces and smells). This suggests that a baby's sensory and perceptual systems may be biologically prepared in some way to process and respond to social stimuli.

CHRONOLOGY OF DEVELOPMENT

The development of multisensory perception in infancy

Birth

Competencies

- The newborn baby can distinguish visual forms, and differentiate between sounds; prefers to follow faces with their gaze than other visual stimuli, and prefers to hear their mother's voice over that of a stranger; newborns demonstrate size and shape constancy, and also imitate facial gestures; they can locate sounds within the visual field, and process and respond to tactile stimuli

Limitations

- Eye movements are jerky and reactive as newborns do not smoothly track moving stimuli or anticipate visual events; poor visual acuity

2 Months

Developmental Achievements

- Smooth visual tracking develops and the infant begins to anticipate visual events

Limitations

- 2 month olds occasionally demonstrate so-called 'sticky fixation', in which they cannot divert their attention away from an object they have gazed upon

4 Months

Developmental Achievements

- Begins to appear more alert to their perceptual surroundings than previously; can distinguish a range of colours, shapes, sizes; differentiates objects on the basis of their configural shape in preference to simple features; can discriminate between different faces (of both humans and monkeys); sticky fixation disappears; distinguish speech sounds (phonemes) that are differentiated both in native language and in non-native languages

Limitations

- Responds to touches as if they are only located on the body and not in the external spatial world also

- Responds more to the patterns of visual lightness reflected by objects' surfaces to their eyes, rather than differentiating surfaces on the basis of their material properties (e.g. gold vs matt yellow)

6 Months

Developmental Achievements

- Visual acuity approximates normal adult vision

Limitations

- Do not appear to take account of changes in the positions of their own arms when in less familiar postures

12 Months

Developmental Achievements

- When spoken to, no longer needs to look at speakers' mouths to decode speech and looks at eyes also

Developing Limitations

- No longer discriminates speech sounds that are not in parents' language(s); no longer discriminates between different monkey faces (NOTE: these 'developing limitations' may actually be helpful as a means of simplifying perception (and reducing the 'blooming, buzzing confusion')

Note: Developmental events described in this chart represent several trends identified in research studies. Individual children vary greatly in the ages at which they achieve these developmental changes.

Such preparation is clearly adaptive: a baby's responsiveness to other human beings enhances both their learning about the social environment and also caregivers' interest in their child (thereby improving the child's well-being and chances of survival).

Interestingly, another salient theme in perceptual development research, albeit one that is a little counterintuitive, is that over the first year of life infants gradually reduce the number of perceptual discriminations they make (e.g. they learn to treat speech sounds that are not differentiated in their own language as being the same). Although it might seem odd that infants reduce the number of perceptual discriminations they make as they get older, this may be one of the ways in which they move beyond the blooming buzzing confusion!

THE DEVELOPMENT OF THE SENSORY SYSTEMS

Before considering how our senses develop we should first try to give an idea of what our senses are. Since the time of Aristotle the classical Greek philosopher, we have tended to divide our perceptual abilities up, conceptually speaking, into five different senses (sight, hearing, smell, taste and touch). However, a close look at the physiological systems which underpin sensation and perception shows us that the reality is considerably more complex. For instance, our inner ear includes not just the cochlear which enables us to hear, but also our vestibular system for determining the direction of gravity and our movements with respect to the world. It is difficult to decide which of Aristotle's classical five senses the vestibular system belongs to. Even though it is located in the ear, it probably does not constitute hearing as it provides rather different information. Perhaps it has more to do with touch.

> **vestibular system**
> A sensory system residing in the inner ear which provides cues to gravity and movement which enable us to balance and coordinate our movements.

We run into similar difficulty when looking at touch. The somatosensory system which contributes to our sense of touch can be broken down into lots of different kinds of sense information. We have receptors in the skin which tell us about pressure, temperature and vibration, and noxious (painful) stimuli among other things. But somatosensation does not reside just in the skin. We also have receptors in the muscles and internal organs which help us keep track of our body and what it is doing. Are these separate senses or all part of the same sense system? Philosophers, psychologists and neuroscientists alike change their minds about these issues on a regular basis (Macpherson, 2011; Matthen, 2015; Smith, 2015).

As it turns out, we can also run into some difficulties when thinking about our senses as separate systems. The more we learn about perception in adults, the more it becomes apparent that our senses work together, and often a sensation or perception which we might assume is coming from one sense turns out to originate from several (Spence, 2017).

How do our sense organs and the connections between them develop? In Chapter 4 we described the physical physiological development of the human foetus in the mother's uterus. Some of the most obvious events in prenatal development are the emergence of various aspects of our sensory anatomy (e.g., the eyes, ears and hands) as well as the behaviours which indicate that those systems have become functional. For instance, the 'righting reflex' in which a foetus will correct the orientation of its body when moved out of its normal position, is known to be driven by information from the vestibular system. Human foetuses show this from around

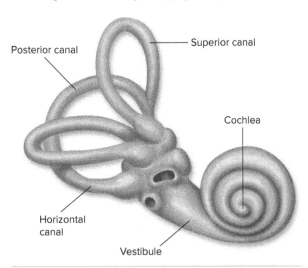

Posterior canal
Superior canal
Cochlea
Horizontal canal
Vestibule

The inner ear contains not just the cochlea which supports hearing, but also the semicircular canals which make up the vestibular system which supports balance and the coordination of movement.
© McGraw-Hill Education

18 weeks gestational age (Bremner, Lewkowicz, & Spence, 2012a; Gottlieb, 1971), and so we can infer that the vestibular system is functional from at least this point onwards. An inspection of post-mortem tissues from foetuses can also give us an idea of the development of prenatal sensory anatomy.

So when do our various senses develop prenatally? And which is first? The most dominant sense in the adult brain is certainly vision, occupying way more of the brain than each of the other senses. And so you could be forgiven for assuming that vision would develop first. And yet, even though there is enough light in the uterus to stimulate the foetus's visual system (Del Giudice, 2011), vision is one of the last senses to become anatomically mature and functional. Actually, in the developmental race of the senses, it is a dead heat between touch and chemosensation (taste and smell) for first place (Bremner et al., 2012a). Figure 6-1 gives an idea of the timing of the development of our sensory systems.

In the next few sections, we will cover the development of our sensory systems. Rather than starting with vision, however, we'll start right at the beginning of ontogeny, with touch. As you will see, many of our

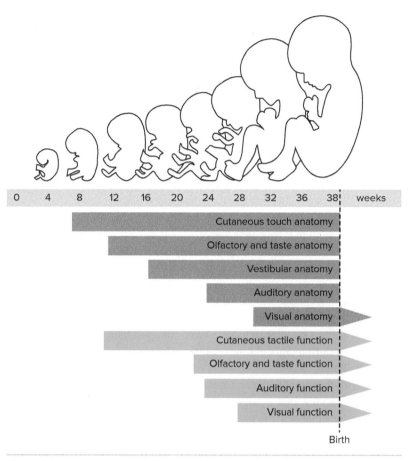

Figure 6-1   *The ontogeny of the senses in prenatal development*
Our senses do not mature and become functional all at once. During prenatal development, touch and chemosensation (smell and taste) lead the way, followed by hearing and then vision. In the figure, the pink bars indicate the development of anatomy and the green bars, the point at which these senses become functional (this is usually determined by observing the foetus's behaviour).
Source: © Dragana Gerasimoski/Alamy Stock Vector (T) Adapted from Bremner et al. (2012a) (B)

sensory systems are functional at birth, and, in many cases, much earlier. Here we will discuss the evidence which indicates that the senses have this early functionality. In later sections we will examine how infants and children develop in their use of the senses to perceive their worlds.

Touch and haptics

Think of a sense. What is the first sense you think of? Most likely it is not touch. However, touch is probably the first means by which we sense anything. And even in adulthood, touch probably plays a much greater role in our perception than we think. Touch includes a very considerable variety of different receptor channels that each provide quite distinct kinds of information, including pressure, temperature, painful stimuli and limb position (or proprioception). The more you think about touch, the more you'll realize that it is pervasive – it helps us sense the world around us, our own bodies (our selves) (Bremner & Spence, 2017; Gallace & Spence, 2014).

When we use touch to sense the world of objects and surfaces around us this is called **haptic perception**. Haptics makes use of tactile sensors in the skin, but

haptic perception
The active use of touch to encode and recognize objects and surface properties, which relies on inputs from both cutaneous (skin) receptors and proprioception (muscle receptors).

also in the muscles and joints to feel properties of objects (e.g., if we feel our hand enclosed around an object this gives us some clues to its shape and size). Although early studies of infant haptics tended to focus on oral exploration (exploration of objects in the mouth), it is now clear that newborns (e.g., Jouen & Molina, 2005) and, astonishingly, preterm infants of only 28 weeks' gestational age (Marcus et al., 2012) can extract and remember information about object shape with their hands alone. Nonetheless, newborns are more limited in the active aspects of haptics, and infants show substantial improvements in the ways they manually explore objects.

Touch also plays a crucial role in interpersonal relationships and bonding in early development. Babies are clearly responsive to different types of touch, and new evidence indicates that they are particularly sensitive to the kinds of touch given to them by a caregiver or parent. They show positive reactions to gentle stroking (e.g., Fairhurst, Löken, & Grossmann, 2014; Maitre et al., 2017 – see Chapter 4) and usually negative reactions to sudden changes in temperature or texture, and to uncomfortable pressure on the body – for example, when blood is drawn for testing (Gray, Watt, & Blass, 2000).

Although it was once assumed that newborns were indifferent to pain, it is almost universally accepted now in developmental psychology that this is untrue. Evidence of the infant's sensitivity to painful procedures comes from studies of infant stress reactions; for example, male infants have shown higher levels of plasma cortisol (a stress marker) after a circumcision than before the surgery (Gunnar et al., 1985). Although it was once standard practice to perform circumcision and other invasive medical procedures on infants without using any pain-relieving drugs, advances in our understanding of the newborn's sensitivity to pain have changed these practices. In fact, some measures, such as facial expressions during innoculations, suggest they may be more sensitive to pain than older infants (Axia, Bonichini, & Benini, 1999).

Interestingly, recent research on functional brain imaging of pain processing in newborn infants backs up the view that newborns feel pain in a similar way to adults. FMRI reveals that the majority of the brain regions that respond to painful stimuli in adults are activated by painful stimuli in full term newborns (Goksan et al., 2015). However, work with preterm newborns indicates that earlier in prenatal development foetuses do not differentiate as clearly between painful and non-painful tactile stimuli. Cortical responses to painful stimuli have been observed using EEG in preterm newborns from as early as 28 weeks' gestational age (Bartocci et al., 2006), but we now know that there is a switch around 35 weeks' gestational age, when non-specific brain responses are replaced by responses which differentiate painful and non-painful tactile stimulation for the first time (Fabrizi et al., 2011).

Chemosensation: taste and olfaction

Taste (gustatory perception) and smell (olfactory perception) are often grouped together under the heading of *chemosensation*. Chemosensations tell us about the chemical composition of stimuli in our environment that impinge on our bodies either through odours (in the air or in the amniotic fluid) in the case of smell, or through solids and liquids entering the mouth in the case of taste. Interest in chemosensation in developmental psychology is certainly on the increase (Bremner et al., 2012b). As food choice and food preferences become an increasingly important social issue, researchers are beginning to investigate how taste and smell are involved in the development of these kinds of behaviours.

Some researchers have also argued that the chemical senses are among the most useful for early development, particularly as they function *in utero* well before birth (Schaal, 2015; Schaal & Durand, 2012). Newborns can discriminate among a variety of odours, and they show appropriate facial expressions in response to odours that adults rate as either pleasant or aversive (see Figure 6-2). In one particularly nice study, Benoist Schaal and colleagues (Schaal, Marlier, & Soussignan, 2000) showed that the odours which foetuses are exposed to *in utero* affected their behaviour at birth. Schaal and colleagues asked one group of pregnant mothers to consume anise flavoured food and drinks during pregnancy, and another group to abstain. The newborn infants whose mother had eaten anise during pregnancy were much more accepting of the smell of anise (as seen in their facial expressions) than those whose mother had not (see Figure 6-2).

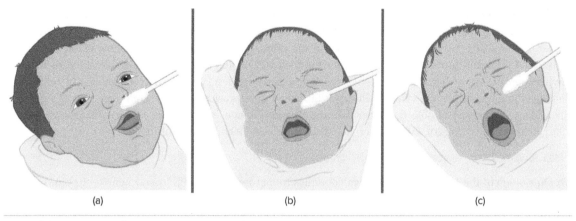

(a) (b) (c)

Figure 6-2 Newborn infants remember smells from the womb
Newborn infants only 3 hours old showed accepting responses to the smell of anise (a) if their mother had eaten anise during pregnancy, but showed aversive responses from the same smell (b and c) if their mother had not eaten anise during pregnancy.
Source: Based on Schaal et al. (2000).

Hearing

An infant's hearing can be tested shortly after birth, and these tests show that the newborn is able to detect a wide range of different sounds (Saffran, Werker, & Werner, 2006). We also know that hearing is functional before birth. The earliest evidence of auditory processing is around 23–24 weeks of gestational age when foetuses start to respond to sounds with gross movements of the body *in utero*. Furthermore, auditory brain responses have been observed in infants born prematurely from these ages also (Weitzman & Graziani, 1968).

In the physiological sense, there appear to be relatively few limitations of newborn audition, at least in comparison to vision, which continues to be limited in terms of its acuity until 6 months of age. Nonetheless a newborn's hearing is not as sensitive as an adult's. Adults can detect sounds about 10 to 15 decibels quieter than the quietest that newborns notice (Hecox & Deegan, 1985). In addition, compared with adults, babies are less sensitive to low-pitched sounds relative to higher frequencies (Saffran et al., 2006). This may help explain why adults so often raise the pitch of their voices during *infant-directed speech*, also called *motherese* (Hoff, 2005). In speaking to babies, mothers and other adults – and even older children (Shatz & Gelman, 1973) – somehow know or quickly detect that a high-pitched voice is more likely to capture the child's attention. Over their first 2 years, however, babies rapidly improve in their ability to discriminate sounds of different pitch, until eventually they reach adult levels of discrimination (Saffran & Griepentrog, 2001).

As well as answering the question of whether infants can detect sounds *per se*, we also need to examine what auditory discrimination babies can make. Kisilevsky and Muir (1991) investigated the foetus's responses to sounds in the outside world by monitored changes in foetal body movements and heart rates. These changes indicated that, even before birth, foetuses can detect and discriminate different sounds presented outside the mother's body (Kisilevsky & Muir, 1991). For instance, they were able to discriminate pure tones from complex speech sounds. As we will see later in this chapter, researchers have also shown that infants may learn and remember voices and speech that they heard before they were born (see also Box 6-2).

Vision

Vision is frequently assumed to be the most important of the human sensory modalities, as it provides in many cases the most detailed information about our perceptual environment. We should certainly not assume that this is always the case (e.g., in comparison to audition, vision tells us almost nothing about what is happening in another room whereas hearing, smell, and even touch can). However, there are many cases in which vision is our most helpful sense (for example, when exploring a landscape in the distance). From a developmental point of view, vision is particularly interesting because it is probably the most underused sensory modality prior to birth. There are significant tactile, chemosensory and even auditory stimuli in the womb. And whilst light does reach the foetus in the uterus (Del Giudice, 2011) it seems unlikely that this reflected light would provide enough detail for the foetus to be able to learn much of use about their visual environment. Despite this lack of visual experience, newborn humans can detect changes in brightness, distinguish movements in the visual field, track faces and objects with their eyes and they can even perceive the real size and shape of objects (rather than the sizes and shapes cast on their retina) (Johnson & Morton, 1991; Kellman & Arterberry, 2006; Slater, Mattock, & Brown, 1990; Slater & Morison, 1985).

EARLY PHYSIOLOGICAL LIMITATIONS OF INFANT VISION

Th physiology of the infant's visual system continues to mature postnatally. Visual acuity, the sharpness or clarity with which a person can detect visual details, is quite significantly limited at birth. If you examine Figure 6-3, you should be able to distinguish parallel vertical black and grey lines (what is referred to in the literature as a grating stimulus). Because young infants' visual acuity is poorer, those lines would blur together into a uniform grey. However, because patterns like this become larger on the retina if they are closer to us, the problems caused by this decreased acuity can be made better by presenting stimuli closer to the infants. This is why visual acuity is measured in visual angle rather than the size of the stimuli. Try for yourself. If you move away from the black and grey lines there will come there a point at which the lines will be such a small visual angle with respect to your eye that you would no longer be able to resolve them, and thus they would appear as uniform grey.

> **visual acuity**
> Sharpness of vision; the clarity with which fine details can be detected.

The smallest visual angle that newborn infants can resolve is about 30 times that which adults can perceive. Researchers have been able to establish this because newborns prefer to look at grating patterns (like that in Figure 6-3) than uniform grey. This preference disappears when the visual angle of the grating is reduced to 30 times the size that adults can resolve (Atkinson & Braddick, 1981). This means that most objects that are not held close to a baby's face appear as quite blurry and indistinct. Visual acuity improves rapidly over the next few months, however, and seems to be within the normal adult range by the time a child is between 6 months and a year old (Banks & Shannon, 1993). Gradually, babies develop the ability to detect more detailed patterns; thus, little by little, they are able to detect stripes that are closer together (Maurer & Maurer, 1988). To appreciate this ability to see details more clearly, examine Figure 6-4, which shows how well an infant can see a human face at birth compared to adult acuity.

Figure 6-3   Spatial resolution sensitivity in infants
At 1 week of age, infants can discriminate black stripes of this size from a grey field when they are a foot away from the target. Any further and they only see a uniform grey. This is only about one-thirtieth as fine a discrimination as an adult with normal vision can make.
Source: Based on Maurer & Maurer, 1988

Figure 6-4   How newborns see faces?
The first photo estimates the level of acuity with which a newborn infant can see a face. In this case, one of the authors' faces. By 6 months of age, infants have visual acuity which matches that of adults. Come to think of it, perhaps newborn vision is best.
© Andrew J. Bremner.

MULTISENSORY DEVELOPMENT

Human foetuses and infants develop in a startlingly complex sensory world where their central nervous systems are bombarded with information from touch, taste, smell, proprioception, vestibular input, audition, and vision. All of these sources of information provide cues to objects, events, people, limbs etc., but in very different ways. How do infants learn to integrate the sensations coming from vision, hearing, taste, smell and touch? Or is it the case that these multisensory abilities are innate?

As you will see in this chapter, much of the research on perceptual development has focused on the development of abilities within one sense or another, with a particular emphasis on vision and hearing. However, when we, as adults, use our sensory apparatus in the everyday environment, we make use of all modalities simultaneously – we explore and perceive a multisensory world.

The more multisensory abilities are investigated in adults, the more it seems that we rarely, if ever, use our senses separately, and that interactions between the senses are the rule rather than the exception (Shi & Muller, 2013; Spence, 2017; Stein, 2012). And so it is becoming more and more important for developmental researchers to start to make progress in addressing how our multisensory (rather than unisensory) abilities develop. We will consider this question throughout this chapter but will focus on it particularly in this section.

Multisensory perception: how we come to integrate the senses

In almost all ecological situations, sensory information about the world arrives to our brains through more than one sense modality at the same time. As adults we are able to synthesize this information into a unified representation of the world. For instance, when we perceive a ball bouncing or grasp a handle, there are multiple sources of information telling us about these events, and we usually link the unisensory (single sense) inputs together. In the case of the ball we perceive the visual and auditory bounce of the ball as one and the same event. Likewise we perceive the tactile feel of moving towards and grasping the handle, and the visual stimulus of that movement and contact as being one and the same event. The question of interest to developmental psychologists of course concerns whether infants and children can do this also or whether they have to learn to make these links (Bremner, 2017). Multisensory perception (sometimes referred to as intermodal, intersensory or crossmodal perception) is this process by which we combine sensory information across more than one modality.

> **multisensory perception** The process of perceiving objects and events in a unified way across more than one modality.

At the beginning of the chapter we described the problem that William Molyneux posed to John Locke – he asked whether a blind man who had learned to distinguish objects through touch would then be able to recognize those objects if sight were restored to him. Locke's answer was that this was not possible without the man first being able to simultaneously touch and see the environment, and thus learn the relationships between the senses. And so Locke was arguing that multisensory perception is something that occurs through a process of learning from experience in development, in which we come to be able to link together the senses in the appropriate ways. A casual consideration of young babies' behaviour does sometimes suggest that they do not integrate senses in an adult-like way. Take, for example, G. Stanley Hall's description of a 4-month-old baby's behaviour:

> *Sometimes the hand would be stared at steadily, perhaps with growing intensity, until interest reached such a pitch that a grasping movement followed as if the infant tried by an automatic action of the motor hand to grasp the visual hand, and it was switched out of the centre of vision and lost as if it had magically vanished. (Hall, 1898, p. 351)*

This anecdote seems to suggest that this 4-month-old infant was unable to understand that the hand which he could see was the very same thing as the tactile felt hand with which he was trying to grasp the thing he had seen. This kind of observation chimes with Locke's account, indicating that infants have much to learn about how different aspects of their sensory worlds should be combined.

However, another, quite different, view of how multisensory perception develops was advanced by Eleanor Gibson (1969). Gibson suggested that newborn infants perceive commonalities among the senses from birth, and that the problem for development is one in which the infant must learn to differentiate between which aspects of sensory stimulation belong to which senses. So, according to this account, a newborn infant would perceive a bouncing ball as one unified sensory event but over development would have to learn what aspects of that event are sounds (e.g., the occasional regular thud) and what aspects are sights (e.g., the up–down movements of the ball). This account of multisensory development is known as a 'differentiation' account.

A number of empirical investigations of multisensory abilities in young children appear to indicate that Gibson's 'differentiation' account of multisensory development correct in a number of cases. Researchers have explored babies' ability to perceive multisensory links using crossmodal matching paradigms. In one of the first uses of a crossmodal matching task with infants, Spelke (1976) found that 4-month-old infants perceive some crossmodal *temporal* correspondence between sound and vision. Spelke constructed two animated films of balls bouncing on a screen, with each ball bouncing out of phase with the other. At the same time as showing these films side by side to 4-month-old infants, a soundtrack was played that produced bounces in synchrony with only one of the balls, from a speaker positioned between the two screens. The 4-month-olds looked more at the screen that was bouncing in synchrony with the sound being played.

> **crossmodal matching paradigms** Tasks that examine whether participants can match an object according to its unimodal properties. For instance, one could examine if an infant can match a cube presented to his hands with a visual cube by examining where he looks when presented with both a cube and a distracter stimulus, such as a triangle.

Other studies using crossmodal matching tasks have shown that even newborn babies will, when they are shown two videos of faces speaking, prefer to look at the facial movements which correspond to the speech or vocalizations which they are hearing (Aldridge et al., 1999; Lewkowicz, Leo, & Simion, 2010). Perhaps the most remarkable early multisensory skill demonstrated by newborns though, is an ability to match visual displays of a number of objects with auditory sequences of the same number of objects. Izard and colleagues (2009) have shown, for instance, that newborns, if they hear a sequence of 4 separate sounds will prefer to look at 4 rather than 12 objects. And vice versa, if they hear 12 sounds will prefer to look at 12 rather than 4 objects.

Although the majority of studies investigating multisensory abilities in young infants have examined audiovisual abilities, some studies have also investigated links with other senses. Exploring crossmodal matching of touch and vision, Meltzoff and Borton (1979) designed two different dummies, one smooth and one knobbly (Figure 6-5), and gave 4-week-old infants a chance to suck one or the other. Later, when the researchers let their small participants look at both dummies – but not suck on them – the infants looked longer at the dummy that they had sucked on earlier than at the unfamiliar one.

There remains some doubt over early abilities to match objects between sight and touch. For instance, other studies have found it difficult to reproduce Meltzoff and Borton's findings with dummies (Maurer, Stagner, & Mondlach, 1999). However, more recently, Streri and colleagues have shown that infants seem to perceive crossmodal matches between objects which they have explored with their hands, and objects they are looking at visually even in the first few days after birth (Streri & Gentaz, 2003, 2004; Sann & Streri, 2007).

And so the overall picture which emerges seems to be that very young infants are able to perceive crossmodal matches between a number of the senses. Such findings support the view (Gibson, 1969) that the senses are united from an early stage of development. But in this case, how does multisensory perception develop? Despite the evidence (discussed above) of early abilities in both audiovisual and visual-tactile multisensory perception there remains little doubt that there is considerable development in infants' and children's multisensory skills. For instance, when an unseen touch is presented to one of an infant's hands, infants do not appear to know where to look for those touches in the visual field (i.e., they don't know which hand to look at) until around 8 to 10 months of age (Bremner et al., 2008; Somogyi et al., 2017).

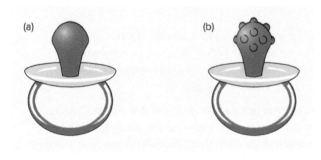

(a)   (b)

Figure 6-5   Testing a baby's multisensory perceptual abilities
Source: From Meltzoff and Borton (1979).

So what aspects of multisensory abilities are easy for a newborn? Bahrick and Lickliter (2000; Bahrick, 2010) have an interesting developmental theory concerning multisensory development which draws on Eleanor Gibson's differentiation theory. They argue that some crossmodal abilities are straightforward for young infants to acquire or demonstrate because the senses provide equivalent information across that match. Take the bouncing ball example that we discussed earlier. Bahrick and Lickliter (2000; 2014) think that there are aspects of auditory bounces and visual bounces that are the same: they argue that rhythm of the bouncing is the same whether you are seeing it or hearing it, as is the timing with which those bounces happen. They call this 'intersensory redundancy' and argue that intersensory redundancy directs infants' attention towards crossmodal events and allows them to learn more about the unisensory and multisensory aspects of the stimulus (e.g., the colour of the ball, the particular sound it makes when it bounces).

Bahrick and Lickliter (2000) provide some convincing evidence in favour of their intersensory redundancy account. They presented 5-month-old infants with a video display of a hammer tapping an irregular rhythm on a table. The infants either saw this visual unisensory rhythm without sound or with an accompanying and synchronous soundtrack of the hammer-hits. Afterwards they showed that the infants who saw the visual–auditory rhythm were better able to recognize the rhythm when it was paired with a new rhythm. And so it seems that multisensory stimulation (or in Bahrick and Lickliter's terms, intersensory redundancy) may play an important role in driving perceptual development.

INFANTS' AND CHILDREN'S PERCEPTION OF THEMSELVES AND THE WORLD AROUND THEM

Now that we've covered how sensory systems develop and discussed how infants come to use their senses together, let's take a closer look at how infants and children use their senses to perceive important aspects of their experience: the spatiotemporal world of objects, events, and people. We will also examine a more neglected but perhaps equally important aspect of perception: how infants perceive themselves – their own bodies – in relation to the world around them.

To some extent it is unfortunate that developmental psychologists have tended to explore the development of perceptual abilities by focusing on ability with respect to one sense at a time. This has happened, probably for practical scientific reasons, because as an experimental researcher it is easier to design well-controlled experiments by reducing the perceptual information which is presented to young participants in a given experimental scenario. As such, you will notice that the majority of studies of perceptual development covered here only consider visual or auditory abilities. However, it is important to bear in mind that even the youngest infants are being presented with several sources of information about the world simultaneously. This may have important implications for the development of their perceptual abilities which may go beyond what we can tell from studies of visual or auditory perceptual development alone (Bremner et al., 2012b).

How babies perceive patterns and objects

Perhaps the single most important advance in the scientific study of infant development came when Robert Fantz (1961) developed the visual prefer-ence method for determining whether the newborn baby can see and discriminate visual patterns (see Figure 6-6). Fantz observed that infants of only a few days of age would look for different amounts of time at dif-ferent patterns. The more complex the pattern, the longer the infants would tend to look at them. And indeed, they seemed to prefer to look at sche-matic faces more than any other visual stimulus. So for the first time developmental psychologists had a means of determining what visual patterns infants could differentiate.

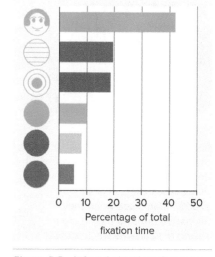

Figure 6-6 *Infants' visual preferences*
Whether 2 days old or 2 to 3 months old (the data shown here), infants prefer to look at complex patterns more than simple patterns or solid colours.
Source: Based on Fantz (1961).

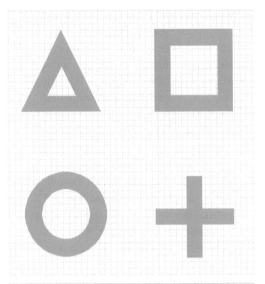

Figure 6-7 Visual habituation in newborns
If habituated to any one of the four shapes shown here (e.g. the circle), infants of only a few days old will demonstrate a novelty preference for any of the other three stimuli (e.g., the cross, the triangle or the square) when they are paired with the habituated stimulus (in this case the circle).
Source: Based on Slater, Morison and Rose (1983).

FORM AND SHAPE PERCEPTION

Since Fantz's discoveries, we have also determined that very young babies are able to sense patterns and forms, not just through vision of 2D displays, but also through active use of touch for exploring 3D objects, what is known as haptic perception.

Researchers have found that 2-day-old infants show different patterns of haptic exploration for different kinds of shapes and patterns of objects (Streri, Lhote, & Dutilleul, 2000). Incredibly, more recent research has shown that even preterm babies of only 28 weeks' gestational age can differentiate different object shapes with their hands (Marcus et al., 2012).

Using the visual habituation technique (also developed by Fantz, 1964), Alan Slater at the University of Exeter has shown that newborn infants are able to make an even wider variety of perceptual discriminations between different visual stimuli. Figure 6-7 shows some of the visual form discriminations that newborns can make. With visual habituation, infants are shown one stimulus until they have habituated to it (until the amount of time they are looking at it has declined below a criterion – e.g., 50% of what it was to start with). They are then shown the familiar (habituated) stimulus and a novel stimulus sequentially or together. If they can remember the familiar stimulus and discriminate between the novel and familiar stimuli then they should look longer at the novel stimulus. The visual habituation technique allows us to investigate more perceptual discriminations than the visual preference method as it is less subject to the intrinsic preferences that infants bring to the testing room.

Despite the success of the visual preference and visual habituation techniques for investigating visual perceptual abilities in very young infants, they are not completely without their complications. One particular problem lies in what we can conclude from a perceptual discrimination. Take, for instance, Slater, Morison and Rose's (1983) demonstration of form discrimination (see Figure 6-7). Do newborn infants discriminate between these stimuli in the same way we might – by comparing the configural shapes of the stimuli? From Slater and colleagues' evidence alone we cannot be sure. It is possible that the infants are focusing on some much more simple perceptual cues, such as the orientation of component lines. For example, they might discriminate the triangle from the other shapes by simply registering that it contains a diagonally orientated line. Or maybe they discriminate the figures by attending to only one small feature (e.g., the corner of the square vs the curvature of one side of the circle).

Do infants see patterns? This baby seems quite fascinated by the mobile. A question that has occupied, and still challenges, infant researchers is what exactly infants see when they look at patterns. Is this little girl seeing the patterns we perceive, or is she perceiving something less unified, like the orientations of the lines or the contours of light-to-dark that make up the patterns we discriminate?
Shutterstock/Lifebrary

Support for this more basic interpretation of young infants' perceptions of patterns comes from eye-tracking studies of how young infants inspect visual figures. Researchers, using eye-tracking techniques, reflect infrared light off infants' eyes to determine precisely where they are directing their eyes. In one classic eye-tracking study, Salapatek and Kessen (1966) found that when newborn infants were looking at a triangle figure, their gaze was not distributed over the whole triangle as an adult's would be. The typical newborn centred attention on one of the triangle's angles but sometimes also scanned part of an edge in a limited way. This suggests that, although certain elements of a complex pattern attract a newborn's attention (angles, edges, boundaries), babies this young do not necessarily perceive the whole form.

Cohen and Younger (1984) conducted an elegant habituation-novelty study that seems to support this conclusion. In this study they examined whether

Figure 6-8 *Can young infants discriminate between acute and obtuse angles?*

Cohen and Younger tested this ability by habituated infants to an acute angle (labelled 'habituation'), and then examined whether they would show a novelty preference for each of the test figures A–D. The 1.5 month olds showed a novelty preference for B and D, which are both made of lines that differ in orientation from the habituation stimulus, but they showed no increase in looking towards A and C. It is unsurprising that the infants showed no novelty preference for A, which is exactly the same as the habituation stimulus. However, while test C contains exactly the same orientations as the habituation figure, it is a completely new configural shape. Thus, 1.5 month olds discriminate between objects on the basis of orientation and not configural shape; 3.5 month olds, on the other hand, showed a novelty preference for C and D, but not for A and B, indicating that, by this age, they discriminate on the basis of configural shape.
Source: Adapted from Cohen & Younger (1983).

young infants could discriminate shapes (in this case acute and obtuse angles) on the basis of the configuration of their component lines (acute angles are those under 90 degrees, and obtuse angles are those over 90 degrees – see Figure 6-8). They found that while 4-month-old infants could discriminate on the basis of the configuration of the lines in such figures, 1.5 month olds seemed only to notice changes in the orientation of component lines of the figures and not the overall, configural shape. From these findings it seems that newborn infants do not perceive configural shapes – rather they may be perceiving their basic features. Infants' scanning of forms improves quickly with age. By the age of 2 months, babies visually trace both the edges of a pattern and the internal areas (Aslin, 1987; Kellman & Arterberry, 2006). This increase in the scope of visual tracking behaviour may be driving changes in the ability to discriminate different configural shapes observed by Cohen and Younger in 4 month olds.

However, this was not the end of the story. A subsequent experiment by Slater and colleagues (1991) showed that, under certain conditions, even babies of only a few days of age can discriminate angles on the basis of their configural shape. Slater et al. employed a method in which the orientation of an angle figure (let's say an acute angle) was altered several times during the course of the habituation phase. This had the effect of desensitizing infants to the line orientation, because they subsequently preferred to look at an obtuse angle in preference to an acute one, even though the orientations of their component lines were exactly the same. Thus, it seems that infants can perceive configural shape at birth. But how, then, do we explain Cohen and Younger's (1983) findings? Perhaps their 1.5-month-old infants did not discriminate configural shapes, not because they could not perceive them, but because they had not yet learned to differentiate between visual stimuli on that basis.

One of the lessons we can draw from Slater et al.'s (1991) study is that young infants may be more sophisticated at perceiving patterns when a stimulus changes orientation, or moves. It is possible that this is because that helps them to ignore simple features such as orientation. Another alternative is that, when stimuli move, this helps them overcome the limits imposed by their immature visual scanning behaviour (described above). In any case, there are a number of observations of young infants being very capable of seeing patterns in moving forms (Bertenthal & Clifton, 1998; Booth, Pinto, & Bertenthal, 2002a).

OBJECT CONSTANCY

Objects frequently appear to us in many different guises: at different distances in different orientations, and under very different lighting conditions. So it is certainly an interesting puzzle how infants come to be able to recognize objects across these widely varying situations. This ability is known as object constancy.

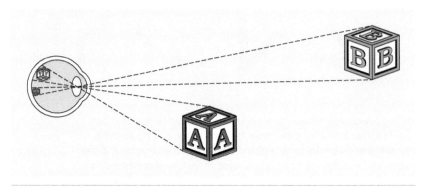

Figure 6-9   Size constancy

The two blocks pictured here are exactly the same size, and the viewer perceives them as the same size. However, because they are placed at different distances from the viewer, they cast retinal images of different sizes. Under certain circumstances, newborn infants are able to ignore retinal size and discriminate between objects on the basis of their real 'physical' size.

We've already looked at shape constancy to some extent. As we discussed above, even newborns seem to be able to perceive the configural shape of visual forms across changes in their orientation (Slater et al., 1991). In fact other studies show that this ability to recognize the configuration of shapes across different orientations is also seen in regard to real solid objects (Bremner et al., 2007; Kraebel & Gerhardstein, 2006; Slater & Morison, 1985).

Let's also consider size constancy: the ability to perceive an object as being the same thing regardless of changes in the distance from which it is viewed and so regardless of the associated changes in the size of the object's image on the retinas of the eyes (see Figure 6-9). For example, even though a truck viewed from far away can cast the same size on our retina as a toy truck close-up we still perceive the truck as being a normal-sized vehicle.

Research with newborns suggests that this basic ability may be present from birth. Slater and colleagues familiarized newborn infants to an object of a particular size, but they varied the distance of the object from the infant (and thus its retinal size) across the familiarization phase. The reason for varying the object's retinal size like this was to desensitize them to retinal size (by changing the retinal size, infants are unable to attend to it), so that they might have more chance of attending to the object's real size. When at test they presented this object again, but at a distance the newborns had not seen during familiarization, the newborns preferred it to a different-sized object that was casting exactly the same size on the retina because it was at a different distance. As these infants were only a few days of age, it seems that size constancy is either an innate ability or is acquired very quickly.

However, another aspect of object constancy may develop more gradually in infancy. Recent research from Japan (Yang et al., 2015) shows that up until around 8 months of age, infants may have difficulty perceiving the constant material properties of objects across different lighting conditions. Imagine the difference between an object carved out of wood versus the same shape created from a polished metal. Although these different material properties (one matt, one glossy) are very easy for adults to distinguish with vision, it turns out that this is by no means a straightforward ability, as the different patterns of light reflected by these different material properties are much more subtle than the different patterns of light caused by variations in lighting conditions.

As adults, we have become attuned to the subtle variations in light patterns created by different materials (e.g., wood vs gold), and even though there are often substantial visual differences between objects which are illuminated in different ways, adults do not notice these differences as much as smaller differences which are produced when an image of an object is changed (by computer) from a matt to a shiny version (Fleming, 2014). However, Yang and colleagues (2015) found that this is not the case with 3- to 4-month-old infants who in some situations respond more strongly to the difference between the same shiny object across different conditions of illumination than they do to changes in the material properties of objects. More research is needed to determine how object constancy develops in early infancy.

PERCEIVING OBJECTS AND SURFACES IN DEPTH

The ability to perceive depth has much practical value. Besides preventing us from walking off precipices, it also helps us to accomplish many everyday skills such as distinguishing objects from their backgrounds, and making accurate reaches towards objects.

Depth perception was thought by the empiricist philosophers to be an accomplishment that required environmental experience. Berkeley (1709), for instance, thought that without learning about how vision and touch link together, we would only be able to perceive a 2D environment corresponding with the pattern projected to the backs of our retinas. He surmised that by learning about the relationships between visual stimuli and tactile experience we can learn what in the retinal image signals depth. However, it was not until 1960 that researchers investigated this question empirically. To investigate whether young infants are able to perceive depth, Gibson and Walk (1960) developed an apparatus called the visual cliff (see photo). The visual cliff consists of an elevated glass platform with a pattern of some type directly beneath the glass on one side (the 'shallow' side) and the same pattern several feet below the glass on the other (the 'deep' side). Gibson and Walk found that babies who were able to crawl (their sample ranged from 6 to 14 months old) would not cross from the shallow to the deep side to get to their mothers even

This baby doesn't take chances: he is hesitant to venture beyond the safety of the visual cliff's 'shallow' side, despite being coaxed to (by a parent, out of frame). Clearly, the child perceives a problem with walking across the 'deep' side.
© Science History Images/Alamy Stock Photo

when the mother encouraged the child to do so. Thus, crawling babies were fearful enough of heights to avoid them. Gibson and Walk (1960) concluded that infants have an innate ability to perceive depth. But, can we agree with this? The infants here were all able to crawl, and had at least six months' experience, which could have taught them about depth.

Joe Campos and colleagues (see Campos et al., 2000) developed a way of examining depth perception in the visual cliff in much younger children. They placed 1.5-month-old babies first on the shallow side of a visual cliff and then on the deep side, while measuring their heart rates. The 1.5-month-old infants' heart rates decreased, which generally indicates interest rather than fear (fear is normally accompanied by an increase in heart rate). In contrast, when researchers placed older infants who could crawl on the deep side, these babies showed heart-rate accelerations, suggesting that they had learned to be afraid of heights (Campos et al., 1978). Apparently, experience with locomotion is involved in the development of a fear of heights. Baby animals that are able to walk shortly after birth avoid the deep side of the visual cliff when they are only 1 day old. And when human infants who are unable to crawl are provided with 30 to 40 hours of experience in wheeled walkers, they begin to show fear of high places (Campos, Bertenthal, & Kermonian, 1992; Bertenthal, Campos, & Kermoian, 1994; Dahl et al., 2013).

So, fear of heights appears to develop in a way that is dependent upon experience of movement around and physical interaction with the environment. However, this does not go to show that Berkeley was correct to state that touch tutors depth vision. Even though Campos et al.'s youngest participants did not appear to fear heights, their heart rates showed that they nonetheless distinguished between the shallow and the deep sides of the cliff. This shows that some form of depth perception is available well before the onset of locomotion and very early in life. However, as with our discussion of pattern perception in the previous section, once we have established a perceptual skill in young babies we then have to ask how they made that perceptual discrimination. In the case of the depth we can ask what particular depth cues the infants were using.

As adults, we use a variety of depth cues that can be roughly divided into monocular and binocular cues. Monocular cues are those that are available even if we were viewing the world with only one eye. Among these are motion parallax, which is displayed when we move. You may have noticed that when you are seated in a moving

visual cliff
An apparatus that tests an infant's depth perception by using patterned materials and an elevated, clear glass platform to make it appear that one side of the platform is several feet lower than the other.

motion parallax A cue to depth emerging from the fact that, when we move, objects that are further away move across our visual field more slowly than do objects that are closer to us.

binocular disparity
The sense of a third spatial dimension, that of depth, produced by the brain's fusion of the separate images contributed by each eye, each of which reflects the stimulus from a slightly different angle.

interposition The sense that one object is in front of another, provided by the partial occlusion of the further object by the nearer object.

linear perspective
The manner in which patterns of light fall on the eye from objects that recede in depth.

vehicle, such as a train or a car, objects closer to you move faster across your visual field than objects further away. This motion parallax helps us judge the distance of objects from us. Other monocular cues include interposition (the fact that when one object is closer to us it covers those that are further away) and linear perspective of the sort that we can see in renaissance Italian paintings.

On the other hand, binocular cues to depth require two eyes. Chief among the binocular depth cues is binocular disparity. Binocular disparity arises because of the distance between our eyes. Because our eyes view the world from a slightly different vantage point there are slight spatial disparities between objects that vary with respect to how far away they are from us in depth. These disparities allow us to perceive depth.

So which cues do infants use, and how does depth perception develop? We know that newborns' eyes do not work together in the way that the eyes of older children and adults do. The eyes of newborns move in the same direction only about half the time (Slater & Findlay, 1975; Maurer & Maurer, 1988), so early in life this makes it difficult for young infants to rely on binocular depth cues. By 3 to 5 months of age, babies can coordinate their two eyes, and they can begin to see depth as adults do, using retinal disparity. We know this because infants of this age make more accurate judgements of the depth of an object when reaching for it if they are allowed to inspect the object with both eyes. Proper use of the two eyes together at an early age is necessary for normal stereoscopic vision to develop. Babies born with crossed eyes (a condition called *convergent strabismus*) usually do not develop normal stereoscopic vision unless the eyes are surgically corrected before the age of 2 (Banks, Aslin, & Letson, 1975; Banks & Salapatek, 1983).

The development of infants' use of monocular cues is a bit more complicated. There are several monocular cues to depth. As mentioned above, motion parallax is a cue about depth emerging from the fact that, when we move, objects that are further away move across our visual field more slowly than do objects that are closer to us. Although motion parallax seems to be available in very young infants (Campos et al., 1970, argue that the 1.5 month olds in their visual cliff study were using motion parallax), other monocular cues such as interposition (Granrud & Yonas, 1984) and linear perspective (Arterberry, Bensen, & Yonas, 1991) appear to develop much later, at around 6 and 7 months of age. Interposition cues are those provided when one object comes in front of another (see Figure 6-10); the partial covering up of the object it comes in front of tells the eye which object is closer.

Figure 6-10 demonstrates the design of a study by Granrud and Yonas (1984) who examined whether infants would perceive depth through interposition cues. When different depths of object were specified by

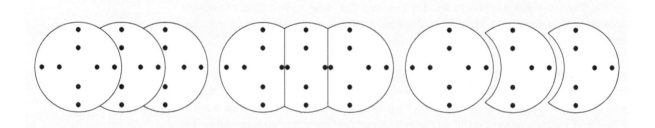

Figure 6-10   Learning to perceive depth through interposition cues
The 7-month-old but not the 5-month-old infants reach to the left-hand square more than the other squares in pattern A, but not in patterns B or C. This is likely because the left-hand square in A appears to be closer because of cues to interposition. So it seems that an ability to see depth through interposition develops between 5 and 7 months of age.
Source: Adapted from Granrud and Yonas (1984).

interposition cues, 7-month-old infants (but not 5-month-old infants) tended to reach more to the closer looking object. But without such cues, they showed no reaching preferences.

How babies perceive people and their social world

What are the most important objects for newborn infants to perceive? Given that they will not be able to successfully reach for and grasp objects which they might use for any kind of functional purpose until 5 months of age, it seems likely that perceiving people is going to be more important. People are of course a very special kind of object, and there is evidence that newborn infants come to perceive people early on and quickly become specialized at making sense of people and their social environments more generally (Csibra & Gergely, 2011).

A PREFERENCE FOR FACES

Faces are complex patterns. As adults we are able to perceive these patterns in order to recognize a person as human. Although all human faces are arranged similarly, there are many differences across individual faces, and adults are also able to capitalize on these differences in order to recognize individual people. Importantly, adults are able to do this quite effortlessly, even though faces are experienced from various angles and with different expressions. Fantz's (1961) demonstration of an early preference (between 2 days and 3 months) for faces was thus considered very important, as such a preference could represent an innate ability to perceive some aspect of these complex patterns. Since Fantz's work, other studies have shown that infants appear to perceive and orientate to faces with very limited experience of them.

Mark Johnson and colleagues (Johnson et al., 1991) made use of a straightforward adaptation of the visual preference technique – preferential tracking – in which they measured infants' preferential tendencies to follow a stimulus with their eyes as it is moved through their visual field. In order to examine whether preferences were innate, they tested infants who were only an hour old at the most.

The newborns were placed on their backs on the experimenter's knee and shown a single stimulus of the three in Figure 6-11 directly above them and at their midline. The experimenter then moved the stimulus slowly into the periphery of the infant's visual field. The number of degrees though which the infants followed each of the stimuli shown in Figure 6-11 was compared.

Figure 6-11 shows that the infants tracked (with their eyes and head) the face-configured stimuli further into the periphery than both the scrambled stimuli and the blank stimuli. In addition they tracked the scrambled face stimulus further than the blank stimulus. The fact that the infants preferred the face stimulus over the scrambled face stimulus is quite convincing evidence of a preference for faces over other stimuli as both the face stimulus and the scrambled face stimulus contain exactly the same features, and both are symmetrical in their configuration. The only difference is the configural layout of the features.

And so Johnson and colleagues had demonstrated that newborn infants of only 30 minutes of age preferred to track face-like stimuli with their eyes than other stimuli. At the time, this finding was amazing for the field, partly because of the audacious nature of the investigation (looking at abilities within 30 minutes of birth) and partly because since William James and Charles Darwin, few had sincerely thought that an ability to perceive faces could be provided to infants independently of experience.

However, more recent findings have pushed the boundaries of visual face perception even earlier in development, into prenatal life (Reid et al., 2017). We discuss this research in Box 6-1.

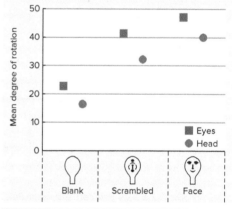

Figure 6-11 Newborns preferential tracking of face-like stimuli

This graph shows the mean number of degrees through which the newborn infants rotated their eyes and heads when following three different stimuli (a normally configured schematic face, a scrambled, but symmetrical schematic face, and a black face outline).
Source: Based on Johnson et al. (1991).

Research close-up

BOX 6-1   Face preferences in *in utero* human foetuses in the third trimester

Source: Based on Reid et al. (2017).

Introduction:

Recent advances in the modelling of how light sources pass through human tissue have indicated that more light reaches the eyes of the human foetus *in utero* than was previously thought (Del Giudice, 2011). Making use of these advances, as well as new developments in 4D ultrasound (which can provide a moving rendered 3D image of the foetus's face and behaviour), Vincent Reid and colleagues asked the question of whether newborn preferences to track faces into the periphery of vision might also have their origins prior to birth and prior to any visual experience of faces whatsoever.

Method:

The final sample of participants was 39 pregnant mothers and their *in utero* foetuses. The mean gestational age of the foetuses at the time of testing was 241 days (infants are born at about 280 days' gestational age on average).

The experimenters first measured the depth of the maternal tissue between the uterus and the foetus using 2D ultrasound. With this information they calculated the strength of the light which was needed to present a face-like configuration to the foetus. They then presented either upright or inverted face-like configurations of light dots (see Figure 6-12) to the pregnant mother's skin, next to the location of the foetus's head. The lights emitted red light as this is the most likely to make it through human tissue. They moved the light dots slowly across the skin and, via 4D ultrasound, observed whether the foetuses moved their heads towards or away from the lights.

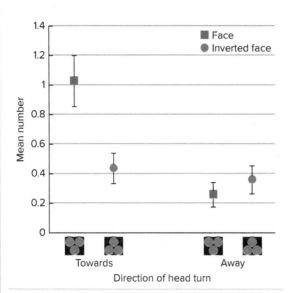

Figure 6-12   Preferential orienting to face-like stimuli in foetuses

On the x axis you can see what Reid et al. (2017) think the lights will have looked like to the foetuses (taking into account estimations of how the light sources will have been blurred by the maternal tissue and the foetal visual system. The graph shows that the foetuses looked towards the upright (face-like) configuration of dots more often than they looked away from it. But this pattern was not seen for the inverted (non-face-like) stimuli. Reid et al. (2017) concluded that the foetuses showed a visual preference for faces. The error bars show the standard error of the mean.
Source: Based on Reid et al. (2017).

configurations of light dots (see Figure 6-12) to the pregnant mother's skin, next to the location of the foetus's head. The lights emitted red light as this is the most likely to make it through human tissue. They moved the light dots slowly across the skin and, via 4D ultrasound, observed whether the foetuses moved their heads towards or away from the lights.

Results:

As Figure 6-12 shows, the foetuses looked towards the upright (face-like) configuration of dots more often than they looked away from it. But this pattern was not seen for the inverted (non-face-like) stimuli. This indicates that the foetuses had a visual preference for face-like configurations of dots.

Discussion:

These findings not only indicate that human foetuses appear to show preferences for face-like configurations in the absence of any visual experience of face, they also open up an entirely new vista of research into visual perceptual abilities prior to birth. However, Reid et al.'s findings are not without controversy. In a comment on their study, Scheel et al. (2018) argue that the light would have spread out so much before it reached the foetuses' eyes that it would no longer have looked anything like a face configuration, and they raise some concerns that the authors' findings could have arisen by chance. In a response, Reid et al. (2018) nonetheless stick by their conclusions and provide additional support for them. Further work will clearly be needed in this area for us to get a firmer grip on the nature of foetal visual abilities. Regardless, this study has opened up a fascinating new debate and avenue of research into the developmental origins of humans' perceptual abilities.

Despite these amazing findings, we certainly would not be likely to conclude that newborns are able to see faces and distinguish between them in the way that we do as adults. Even the discovery that newborns prefer their mothers' faces to the faces of strangers (Walton, Bower, & Bower, 1992) needs some careful consideration. It turns out that this ability may reflect the baby's focus on one particular feature of their mother's face. For instance, Pascalis and his colleagues (1995) found that 4-day-old newborns looked longer at their mothers' faces than at those of strangers only when the mother was not wearing a head scarf. This may suggest that the hairline and the outer contour of the face play a crucial role in the newborn's face recognition.

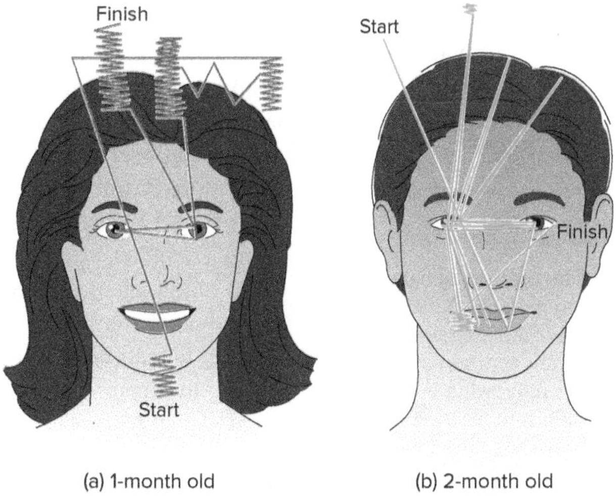

Another reason to believe that newborn infants do not perceive faces in the same way as older infants and adults is that there are rapid changes in how babies scan faces in the first months. As you can see in Figure 6-13, infants 1 month old tend to scan the outer contours of the face; however, by 2 months of age, infants concentrate on internal features (Maurer & Salapatek, 1976).

Johnson and Morton (1991) explain early face preferences in newborns as reflecting something akin to a sensorimotor reflex (see below), governed by subcortical brain areas. Later as the infant acquires perceptual experience of faces over the first days of life, higher, cortical areas of the brain take over, and begin driving stronger and more detailed processing of human faces.

(a) 1-month old   (b) 2-month old

Figure 6-13   How infants scan the human face

A 1-month-old baby fixates mainly on the outer perimeter of the face, although he shows some interest in the eyes. An infant who is 2 months old scans more broadly and focuses on the features of the face. She pays a lot of attention to the eyes and mouth, which suggests that some pattern detection may be occurring.
Source: Based on Maurer and Salapatek (1976).

> Johnson and Morton (1991) explain the development of face perception by appealing to the gradual specialization of brain areas (see Chapter 5).

Evidence reported by Pascalis, de Haan, & Nelson (2002) supports this idea. They examined whether 6-month-old and 9-month-old infants and adults will show looking preferences for novel faces when these are paired with faces their participants had inspected for a few seconds. Both 9 month olds and adults could discriminate between pictures of human faces. However, neither of these groups was able to distinguish between different faces of monkeys. In contrast, 6 month olds are able to discriminate facial information for both human and monkey faces. Essentially, these findings seem to demonstrate that face processing by human infants becomes specialized to human faces over the first year of life.

As discussed in Chapter 5, Johnson and colleagues have also demonstrated the gradual specialization of face perception in infancy, showing significant changes in the neural correlates of face recognition in cortical areas of the brain (the N170 event-related potential measured with an EEG net) over the first year of life (de Haan, Johnson, & Halit, 2003).

PERCEIVING EYES, THE MOUTH AND HUMAN MOVEMENT

There is more to people, however, than just their faces. Within the faces, features such as the eyes and mouth carry powerful communicative information. Observing the movements of the mouth can, for instance, help infants to decode the auditory signal specifying information carried in speech. Lewkowicz and Hansen-Tift

(2012) show that as infants are gaining expertise with the speech sounds in their own language, or in a novel language, they have more of a tendency to look towards the mouth, as if using the visual information there to help figure out what speech sounds are being uttered.

Attending to the eyes seems to be an important aspect of social perception from early on. Newborn infants prefer to look at faces which are looking directly towards them rather than faces where the eyes are averted away from them (Farroni et al., 2002). What does this tell us? Csibra and Gergely (2011) argue that infants prefer to look at faces which are looking at them because they have an innate preference to orient towards situations in which someone is attempting to communicate with them. They call this natural pedagogy and suggest that it is an evolution that has prepared infants to learn from their social environment.

Young infants can also attend to aspects of their social environment by singling out 'biological' motion. This ability has been investigated by showing infants 'point-light displays'. If 10 or 12 points of light are attached to a walking person's head and major joints, and then an image of the person moving in a dark space is presented, adults quickly recognize this moving display as depicting a person. Bertenthal and colleagues (Bertenthal, Proffitt, & Cutting, 1984; Bertenthal, Proffitt, & Kramer, 1987; Bertenthal & Davis, 1988) tested babies with this same kind of stimulus, and found that infants of 3, 5 and 7 months of age were able to discriminate between random displays (Figure 6-14, panel c) and coherent motion displays containing dynamic information about human form (Figure 6-14, panel a). Interestingly, if the motion depicted a walking human upside-down (Figure 6-14, panel b), only the 3 month olds discriminated this from random motion. The 5 and 7 month olds appeared to treat an upside-down walker as being just as novel as random motion. Perhaps this was due to their accrual of experiences, which told them that humans normally only appear upright. Despite these developmental changes, there is also evidence that even newborn infants discriminate human biological motion from random motion (Simion, Regolin, & Bulf, 2008), suggesting some degree of preparation for isolating humans from the moving visual world.

> The perceptual narrowing in infants' ability to discriminate faces of different species parallels the narrowing in their ability to discriminate speech sounds that are made only in nonnative languages (see Chapter 8).

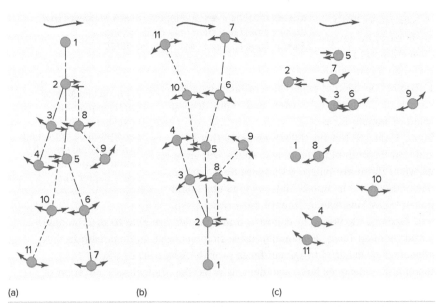

(a) (b) (c)

Figure 6-14 Extracting information about form from movement
Very young infants are able to discriminate human motion specified by 11 points of light. Newborns, and 3- to 7-month-old infants discriminate a from c. Interestingly, only younger infants appear to discriminate upside-down human motion from random motion (b from c). It seems that perceptual experience tunes infants' experience to lead them to expect humans to appear upright.
Source: Adapted from Bertenthal, Proffitt, and Kramer (1987).

PERCEIVING HUMAN VOICES AND SPEECH

Early in development the human auditory system appears especially sensitive to the sound of human voices (Saffran et al., 2006). Babies as young as 2 days old prefer to hear the human voice over other sounds, particularly a voice that is high in pitch with exaggerated pitch contours – the exact type of sound that makes up much of motherese, or infant-directed speech (Fernald, 1992). This preference for infant-directed speech, which is discussed at greater length in Chapter 7, plays an important role in language development and in the development of social relationships early in life. Infant caregivers often speak in a high-pitched voice and sing in a high-pitched and melodic fashion. The preference by infants for melodic songs (which we discuss later), especially songs that are repetitive and have simple musical structures, may help explain why lullabies are sung throughout the world and are effective in soothing infants (Trainor, 1996; Winner, 2006).

Perhaps because infants have an innate preference for the human voice as well as substantial experience with the human voice from early in life, babies learn to discriminate among voices very quickly. Indeed, evidence has indicated for some time now that even foetuses can learn about the differences between voices and patterns of speech *in utero* (Box 6-2).

BOX 6-2   Can infants learn about voices *in utero*?

Research close-up

Source: DeCasper and Fifer (1980) and DeCasper and Spence (1986).

Introduction:

The fact that human foetuses can hear sounds in the womb prompted DeCasper and colleagues (DeCasper & Fifer, 1980; DeCasper & Spence, 1986) to examine whether we are able to learn about sounds and, in particular, voices *in utero*. In previous studies the sounds presented to foetuses had been presented outside of the mother's body. Such sounds presented outside the body are carried through the amniotic fluid to the foetus. However, DeCasper and colleagues reasoned that the loudest sounds in the uterus were likely to be the sound of the mother's voice travelling through the diaphragm (a membrane between the chest cavity and the uterus). In a series of papers, DeCasper and colleagues asked several questions concerning what the human foetus was able to learn about their mother's voice, including: (i) Whether they could learn the sound of a particular voice (that of their mother compared to the voice of a stranger), and (ii) whether foetuses are able to learn about the patterns of speech being uttered by their mother.

Methods and results:

DeCasper and Fifer (1980) used a procedure in which babies could suck to control what they heard on a tape recorder: either their mother or a strange woman speaking to them (DeCasper & Fifer, 1980). As we will describe in Chapter 8, newborns can learn to vary their sucking patterns, and will do so in order to preserve the presentation of something they like.

Experiment 1

In the first study (DeCasper & Fifer, 1980), which we will call Experiment 1, ten infants in the first few days of life were presented with different voices reading a passage of text from 'To Think That I Saw It On Mulberry Street' by Dr Seuss. When infants sucked in one pattern of bursts, they activated their mother's voice on the tape recorder; a different sucking pattern activated the stranger's voice. The researchers found that infants adjusted their sucking patterns in order to hear their own mother's voice in preference to the voice of the stranger. DeCasper and Fifer (1980) concluded that the newborns were able to recognize their mother's voice.

Experiment 2

It could be argued, of course, that the infants heard their mother's voice from the time of birth and thus could have learned to prefer it in their first hours of life. To rule out this familiarity hypothesis, Spence and DeCasper designed another study in which 16 pregnant women were asked to read Dr Seuss's famous children's book, *The Cat in the Hat*, to their foetuses twice a day for the last 6.5 weeks of pregnancy. After birth, the infants of these women were presented with either their mother's tape-recorded voice reading *The Cat in the Hat* or an entirely new passage from *The King, the Mice and the Cheese*. They adapted their sucking patterns in order to hear *The Cat in the Hat* rather than the novel passage. Because in this test condition the mothers read not just one of the poems but both of them, it seems pretty clear that the babies preferred not their mothers' voices per se but their mothers' voices reading the poem to which the infants had been exposed prenatally.

Experiment 3

In the next study, DeCasper and Spence (1986) wanted to examine whether the newborns could recognize the particular speech patterns they had been exposed to prior to birth, but independently of the voice in which they heard these utterances. They again exposed 16 unborn infants to their mothers reading a passage from *The Cat in the Hat*. Later they compared infants' sucking preferences for the familiar passage (over a novel one) across two conditions. In one condition (containing nine infants) the passages were read by the newborn's mother. In the second condition (containing seven infants) the passages were read by a strange mother. Both groups sucked in patterns to switch on the familiar passage. This shows that the infants must have been able to extract some information about the speech patterns their mother was producing independently of the sound of their mother's own voice.

Discussion:

It is clear from these studies that unborn babies are able to learn about the sound of their mother's voice, and the patterns of speech she utters. However, although these studies give us evidence that prenatal auditory experiences influence postnatal auditory preferences, we don't have a clear understanding of the exact mechanisms involved in prenatal learning. The sounds babies hear *in utero*, filtered through the mother's body and the amniotic fluid, must be different from the sounds of their mothers' voices as they hear them after birth. It may be that the component of speech to which the foetus responds is *prosody*. Prosody includes the rhythm, intonation and stress of speech, and is carried by the sound frequencies that are the least altered in the prenatal environment. Because both of the books the mothers in DeCasper and Spence's studies read to their babies are long poems but of very different meters, the infants may also have been expressing a preference for the familiar prosody.

Participants in experiments on foetal sensitivity to sound read The Cat in the Hat *to their unborn babies. Whether such reading would give the baby a head start on learning language is still unknown, but the research showed that newborn babies prefer to hear not only their own mothers' voices but also the specific pieces of poetry or prose their mothers read to them before they were born.*
© Photographee.eu/Shutterstock (L); Westend61 GmbH/Alamy Stock Photo (R)

The evidence is accumulating that newborns may exhibit a postnatal preference for a specific passage or melody experienced prenatally (Saffran et al., 2006). However, it is currently unclear whether these learning experiences influence the development of mature speech perception after the baby is born.

PERCEIVING MUSIC

Young babies are also remarkably sensitive to other qualities of sound which emanate from their social environment. Newborns will alter their sucking patterns if doing so allows them to hear music instead of general noise (Butterfield & Siperstein, 1972). By the time they are 2 months old, infants can distinguish among some types of musical sounds, such as those produced by bowing or by plucking the strings of a violin (Jusczyk et al., 1977). By the age of 6 months, infants can even distinguish changes in melodies

(Trehub & Trainor, 1993). And infants who are 4 to 6 months old seem to prefer music composed of common chords to music composed of tone combinations not found in common chords (Schellenberg & Trehub, 1996).

Infants' attention to music, however, has been useful for learning about auditory abilities. Researchers have found that 6-month-old infants are able to distinguish melodies whether they are based on Western musical scales or on Javanese (*plog*) scales, whereas adults perform better with the Western scales (Lynch et al., 1990). It appears that, early in development, infants are able to process either type of scale, but with experience in their culture, they become more skilled at processing one type of scale over another (Aslin, Jusczyk, & Pisoni, 1998). As we will see in Chapter 8, research has revealed a similar shift in the infant's response to speech sounds. Although infants initially respond to the speech sounds of many languages, by the end of the first year infants respond only to the sounds of the language the people around them speak.

How babies perceive themselves in the world

Since Fantz's discovery of methods which could reveal infants' perceptual abilities, a great deal of research has been directed at what infants can perceive of the external world outside themselves, and comparably little has been done to understand how they perceive themselves and how they fit into the world (Bremner, 2016; 2017).

Perhaps one of the reasons why relatively little research has addressed infants' perceptions of themselves and their own bodies is that this requires stepping away from studies of purely visual perception to the perceptual realms of touch, where we have fewer methods available to help researchers. However, some important steps have been made in this direction, particularly in recent years.

THE ROUGE TEST AND SELF PERCEPTION IN INFANCY

For years, the most important test of self perception or self recognition in human infants has been the rouge test, first reported by Amsterdam (1972). In this task a dab of rouge (red makeup) is surreptitiously placed just below an infant's eye and they are then placed in front of a mirror. If an infant can successfully locate the mark of rouge on their own face, after seeing it in the mirror then they are classed as a self recognizer. Some children manage this by 18 months of age, and the majority pass the test at 2 years. But does this really mean that infants cannot perceive themselves below 18 months of age? This seems somewhat unlikely, and there are certainly doubts about the rouge test, and whether it might not be indexing a number of abilities which go beyond self perception (such as understanding of mirrors for instance). It is certainly not clear that the rouge test can provide a reliable index of all aspects of self perception. Since the advent of methods for examining perception in younger infants, some researchers have tried to find evidence of self perception in younger infants.

Some of the seminal research in this area has investigated infants' visual preferences for video displays of their own moving legs versus those of another child, or of their own legs but delayed in time. Infants as young as 4 months of age appear to be able to identify when they are seeing their own legs moving (Bahrick & Watson, 1985; Rochat, 1998). More recently, a study by Filippetti and colleagues (Filippetti et al., 2013) has shown that newborns will look longer at a video of a face which is being stroked on a cheek at the same time that they themselves are being stroked on the cheek, rather than a face which is being stroked out of synchrony. This seems to indicate that some aspects of body perception are in place from birth. However, a number of other findings indicate that there are considerable developments in infants' perceptions of their own bodies across the first years of life.

PERCEIVING TOUCH ON THE BODY AND IN THE OUTSIDE WORLD

Bremner et al. (2008) have documented developments in the ability to localize touch sensations across the first year of life (see Figure 6-15). They tested two age-groups of infants (6.5 month olds and 10 month olds), and examined the ability to localize vibrotactile stimuli presented to their hands (the set of little buzzers attached to the infants' palms). Strikingly, they observed that the younger infants, although they moved the hands which were touched, seemed very limited in the extent to which they could locate the touch on their hands with their eyes. It is as if younger infants (before about 8 to 10 months of age) had difficulty locating

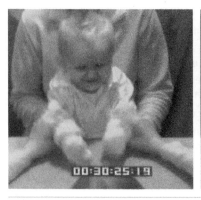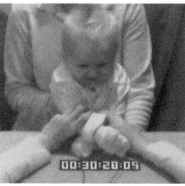

Figure 6-15   Do infants know where touch stimuli come from even when their hands are crossed?

Bremner and colleagues tested this ability by presenting mild tactile 'buzzes' to infants' hands using vibrating 'tactors' – one placed in the palm of each hand. One hand was buzzed at a time and Bremner et al. examined whether the infants looked towards and moved the hand that was buzzed. The youngest age group were better at orientating towards the buzzed hand if their hands were in their normal 'uncrossed' positions, but made more errors in responding towards the buzzed hand when their hands were on a different side of the body to that they were used to (when the hands were crossed). The 10 month olds were equally good at orientating towards the buzzed hand in both postures. It seems that infants get better at keeping track of their arms across different postures as they get older.

Source: Bremner, Mareschal, Lloyd-Fox, Spence (2008).

the tactile world of the body in their field of vision.

As well as having difficultly at moving their eyes to touches, younger infants tended to make mistakes when their hands were in unfamiliar positions. When the infants were presented with a touch to their hands, both 6.5 and 10 month olds were good at responding to the 'buzzed' hand when their hands were uncrossed. But when their hands were crossed over (see Figure 6-15), the younger babies were unable to respond correctly (even with hand movements), whereas the 10 month olds were equally good as when their hands were uncrossed. This research illustrates two points: first, that it is a complex task for infants to localize touch stimuli, especially when their bodies and limbs move around with respect to one another; second, babies seem to get better at keeping track of where tactile locations are when their limbs move around.

Recent research has also shown that there are changes in the way the touch areas of the brain respond to touches between 6 and 10 months of age, which may explain improvements in the ability to keep track of the body across changes in the way it is positioned (Rigato et al., 2014). Interestingly, movement of the limbs across the body midline increases between 6 and 10 months, too. Perhaps it is this experience that enables the infants to keep track of their limbs when they move into new postures.

When you or I feel a touch on our hands or feet, we feel that touch at a place on our bodies, but we can also locate it in a place in the outside world. Begum Ali, Spence, and Bremner (2015) have investigated whether this is also the case in young infants by tickling their feet and crossing their legs!

When adults are given difficult touch localization tasks where they have to move the hand or foot which was touched, crossing their arms or legs can lead to a greater number of mistakes (Schicke & Röder, 2006). This is because the hands and feet are not where they would usually be in the outside world. This will ring true to any of you who have tried riding a bike with your arms crossed (this not advisable to those of you who have not). However, the important point to consider here is that there is no need for this to be the case in tactile localization. If we can simply learn to move the limb which felt a touch then it should not matter where our hands or feet are in space – we should be equally good whether our hands or feet are crossed or not. But this is not the case. It seems that, as adults, we automatically locate touches in the external world, and the decrease in performance which is seen when we cross our hands or feet is a good measure of this.

Begum Ali et al. (2015) set out to find out whether infants also show worse touch localization when their feet are crossed. They placed vibrating tactile stimulators on 4- and 6-month-old infants' feet. The older age group of children were able to locate touches (through little movements of their feet or toes) fairly accurately when their feet were uncrossed (about 70% accuracy). But when their feet were crossed over their accuracy declined to 50%, which is a chance level of performance (i.e., they could not reliably locate touches in this condition).

By striking contrast the 4-month-old infants matched the best performance of the 6-month-olds both when their feet were uncrossed and when they were crossed. Begum Ali et al. (2015) concluded that before 6 months of age, infants do not locate touches in the external world, but only on the body. Think about this for a moment. If newborn babies only locate touches on their body and do not relate them to what they are seeing or hearing in the external world, this would be a very strange perceptual experience compared to our own. It certainly seems to show that there is a lot of postnatal developments in the ways infants learn to perceive themselves in relation to the external world.

SENSORIMOTOR DEVELOPMENT

At the beginning of the chapter we argued that it makes little sense to consider the development of motor abilities in isolation from emerging perceptual skills, as these abilities are intrinsically bound up in one another. This point rings true when we consider many of our motor behaviours in more detail. On closer inspection, the skills involved in many of our motor tasks turn out to be in understanding how to best link together perception and action. Take for example the task of walking. When we walk we are constantly using information from multiple sensory modalities. Proprioception (a sensory input deriving from our muscles) tells us how our body is arrayed; for example, it tells us which foot is in front of the other, and thus which one to swing. Our distance senses, vision, hearing and smell, guide us in our decisions about what to walk towards (and what to avoid). Vision, as we shall see later, also plays a crucial role in helping us maintain an appropriate posture with respect to gravity while walking. In this sense motor development, rather than being a sequence of motor attainments, may concern the emerging ability to control motor behaviour with respect to specific sensory information.

This said, one might argue that the newborn's motor behaviours are perhaps less linked to sensory perception than at any other stage in development. Indeed, the traditional view of newborn sensorimotor abilities is that they are structured in terms of a set of 'reflexes', which they produce in a relatively inflexible way. One example of these is the suck reflex. Sucking – a behaviour that provides the infant with her first means to feed herself is frequently produced in non-nutritive situations – to put it bluntly, newborn babies, and even babies several months older, will suck anything that they can get in their mouth. In newborns, sucking is certainly not as linked to specific sensory situations as they will be in later life; adults tend only to suck objects when that provides some kind of utility.

The pattern of development in sucking can be seen in other behaviours too. And so motor development can be described as a process in which infants and children become increasingly specific in regard to the ways and contexts in which they produce particular behaviour patterns. We will next cover how this process unfolds in the context of skilled sensorimotor behaviours.

Another aspect of newborn behaviour that is not always tied to an appropriate sensory environmental situation, and which we will cover at the end of this chapter, is sleeping behaviour. Newborns frequently produce vigorous patterns of motor behaviour (crying perhaps principal among these) when the rest of the world prefers to sleep, they wake themselves (and usually their parents) in the middle of the night.

Neonatal reflexes

Newborns have a range of sensorimotor reflexes with which they can respond to the environment from the first moments after birth. Reflexes are typically characterized as being involuntary responses to external stimuli. Some researchers challenge the idea that early reflexes are involuntary and suggest that the infant behaves purposefully (von Hofsten, 2004). Table 6-1 describes the newborn's

> reflex An involuntary response to external stimulation.

major reflexes, some of which are permanent (e.g., eye-blink). Other reflexes disappear during the first year, and in some cases, these are replaced by voluntary behaviours that the baby learns early in life (e.g., rooting and sucking reflexes). Many of these reflexes help ensure the newborn's survival. For example, the eye-blink helps to shield the eyes from strong light, and the rooting and sucking reflexes help the newborn to locate and obtain food. The functions of other newborn reflexes are less obvious. Researchers have speculated that some of the less obviously functional reflexes may have had survival benefits for the infants of our evolutionary ancestors. Another way that we can think about newborn

Table 6-1   The newborn's major reflexes

Reflex	Method	Baby's response	Function/significance of response	Developmental course of reflex
	TESTING THE REFLEX			
Permanent				
Biceps reflex	Tap on the tendon of the biceps muscle	Baby displays short contraction of muscle	Absent in depressed babies or those with congenital muscular disease	Brisker in first few days
Eye blink	Flash bright light in baby's eyes	Baby blinks or closes eyes	Protects baby from high intensity visual stimuli	Relatively unchanging
Patellar tendon reflex ('knee jerk')	Tap on the tendon below the kneecap, or patella	Baby quickly extends or kicks leg	Weak or absent in depressed babies or those with muscular disease; exaggerated in hyperexcitable babies	More pronounced in first 2 days than later
Withdrawal reflex	Prick sole of baby's foot gently with a pin	Baby withdraws foot and pulls leg up, bending knee and hip	Absent when there is damage to the sciatic nerve, the largest nerve of the body	Constantly present during first 10 days; less intense later
Temporary				
Babinski reflex	Stroke bottom of foot from heel to toes	Baby's big toe curves up and other toes fan and curl	Absent in defects of the lower spine	Usually disappears near end of first year; replaced in normal adult by plantar flexion of big toe
Babkin or palmar reflex	With baby lying on his back, apply pressure to both of baby's palms	Baby opens mouth, closes eyes, and moves head to midline position	Inhibited in general depression of the central nervous system	Disappears at 3–4 months
Moro reflex	Suddenly allow baby's head to drop back a few inches; lower baby's overall position about 6 inches or make sudden, loud noise	Baby throws arms outward and extends legs; then brings both arms back toward centre of body, clenching fists	Absent or consistently weak reflex indicates serious problem in central nervous system	Disappears at 6–7 months
Palmar grasp	Press a finger or cylindrical object against baby's palm	Baby grasps finger or object	Weak or absent in depressed babies	Initially strong; disappears by 3–4 months; replaced by voluntary grasp within a month or so
Plantar or toe grasp	Press on the ball of the baby's foot	Baby curls all toes, as if grasping	Absent in defects of the lower spinal cord	Disappears between 8 and 12 months
Rooting response	Stroke baby's cheek lightly	Baby turns head toward finger, opens its mouth, and tries to suck	Absent in depressed babies	Disappears at about 3–4 months and becomes voluntary
Stepping reflex	Support baby in upright position and move her forward, tilting her slightly to one side	Baby makes rhythmic stepping movements	Absent in depressed infants	Disappears at 3–4 months
Sucking response	Insert finger 1–1.5 inches into baby's mouth	Baby sucks finger rhythmically	Weak, slow, interrupted sucking found in apathetic babies; maternal medication during childbirth may depress sucking	Often less intensive and regular in first 3–4 days; disappears by 6 months

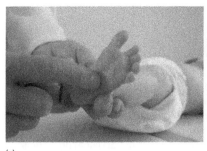  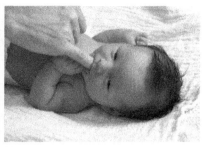

(a)   (b)   (c)

Babies have lots of reflexes (many are described in Table 6-1) that serve as important indicators of physical well-being. The 6 week old's Babinski reflex (a) tells the examiner that the child's lower spine is fully functional; the infant's palmar grasp (b) and rooting response (c) at 4 weeks of age are also important tests.
© Custom Medical Stock Photo/Alamy Stock Photo (L), Ingram Publishing (M), Shutterstock/Science Photo Library (R)

reflexes is as the building blocks of later behaviour. As infants develop they will need to form increasingly complex ways of interacting with their environments. It is difficult to develop a complex sensorimotor skill from nothing. Reflex behaviours almost certainly make this task easier by providing infants with a set of behaviours that can be adapted to new behaviours and can be linked together in increasingly complex ways to form the skills adults possess.

> In Chapter 3, we described how *in utero* exposure to harmful substances can cause neurological defects. The severity of such effects can be tested by observing newborns' reflex responses.

Abnormalities in a baby's reflexes during the first days or weeks after birth can be useful in identifying visual and hearing problems, and can even help predict abnormal functions that don't appear until months or years later (Dubowitz & Dubowitz, 1981; Francis, Self, & Horowitz, 1987; Swaiman & Phillips, 2017). Reflexes that are either weak, absent, unusually strong or that fail to disappear when expected can be a sign of neurological problems. At birth, physicians often test the newborn for certain reflexes to evaluate the baby's central nervous system (e.g., Phillips et al., 1996). For example, babies exposed to cocaine show abnormal patterns in the intensity of the sucking and rooting reflexes.

USING REFLEXES TO EVALUATE THE NEWBORN'S HEALTH AND CAPABILITIES

To find out about the health, maturity and capabilities of the newborn, tests of the baby's reflexes (see Table 6-1) may be combined with other assessment techniques. One of the most widely used tests for newborns is the Brazelton Neonatal Assessment Scale (Brazelton, Nugent, & Lester, 1987). This test measures many of the capabilities of the infant we discuss in this chapter: sensory and perceptual abilities (including orientation to sights and sounds); early learning capabilities (e.g., familiarity or habituation to sensory stimuli); motor development (e.g., muscle tone); infant states and the ability to regulate them (including soothability); and signs that the brain is properly controlling involuntary responses (e.g., the startle reflex).

> **Brazelton Neonatal Assessment Scale**
> A scale containing a battery of tests used to measure an infant's sensory and perceptual capabilities, motor development, range of states and ability to regulate these states, as well as whether the brain and central nervous system are properly regulating involuntary responses.

The Brazelton scale has been used for a variety of purposes. It is used to identify infants at risk for developmental problems, and it can aid in diagnosing neurological impairment (Eldredge & Salamy, 1988; Black, Schuler, & Nair, 1993). The scale is also useful in predicting later development. For instance, newborns who score high on it in some cases tend to score higher on later measures of cognitive, motor or social development (Keefer et al., 1991). Finally, the Brazelton scale has been used as an intervention technique, teaching parents about their newborn's capacities either by having them watch a health-care professional administer this test to their baby or by having them try the same tests with their baby themselves (Wendland-Carro, Piccinini, & Miller, 1999).

Applied Developmental Psychology

BOX 6-3 Preventing sudden infant death syndrome (SIDS)

Each year many babies die in their sleep from causes classified as sudden infant death syndrome (SIDS), also known as *cot death*. It is most common between the ages of 2 and 4 months, and rarely occurs after 6 months.

It's most likely victims are low-birth-weight male babies with a history of respiratory problems, who were hospitalized longer than usual after birth and who have abnormal heart-rate patterns and night-time sleep disturbances (Rovee-Collier & Lipsitt, 1982; Mitchell et al., 1993; Sadeh, 1996). Their mothers are more likely to be anaemic, use narcotics and to have received little prenatal care. Parental smoking has also been suggested as a contributing factor (Fleming & Blair, 2007). It is important to stress, however, that most babies of women with these characteristics are not affected.

sudden infant death syndrome (SIDS)
The sudden, unexplained death of an infant while sleeping; also called *cot death*.

The cause of SIDS is still a mystery (Hunt, 2001). Indeed it seems likely that there are multiple causes. However, we do now know that it is not due to mucus or fluid in the lungs or to choking on regurgitated food. Nor has there been any success in finding a virus associated with SIDS, although this is still a possibility. Another possibility is that *apnoea*, the spontaneous interruption of breathing that sometimes occurs during sleep, may be a factor (Steinschneider, 1975). The brainstem, which controls breathing, may not be developed well enough in some infants to overcome brief cessations in breathing.

One hypothesis about the cause of SIDS is that its victims may have failed to develop adequate responses to nasal blockage and other threats to breathing (Lipsitt, 2003). Although newborns have reflexes that provide them with built-in defensive reactions to respiratory threats (e.g., when a cloth is placed over a baby's face, she will use her hands to try to remove it), between 2 and 4 months of age, these reactions change from reflexive behaviours to voluntary ones. Cot death is most common during this same age period. Perhaps failure of some infants to make a smooth transition from reflexive to voluntary defences puts them at greater risk for SIDS.

Some have argued that monitors that sound an alarm to alert parents when an infant's breathing is interrupted may be useful in preventing SIDS. However, it is not conclusive that interruptions in breathing are strongly related to SIDS (Moon, Horne, & Hauck, 2007). As the false alarms of these devices may place stress on the parents this is a matter of some controversy. In the eight years following a recommendation from the American Academy of Pediatrics that babies sleep on their backs (the Back-to-Sleep Movement), there was a 50% decline in infant deaths attributable to SIDS. Lipsitt (2002) argues that sleeping infants on their backs helps protect more vulnerable infants when their motor reflexes for preventing suffocation begin to wane. The success of this movement is encouraging.

Developing new sensorimotor behaviours

As adults we interact with the world and its objects in highly skilled ways – our sensorimotor behaviours are very skilled. So much so, that it is easy to forget how skilled we are. Daniel Wolpert, a researcher investigating sensorimotor functioning at the University of Cambridge uses a very useful anecdote to bring this point home.

> *Taking the game of chess, we can pit a grandmaster against the best chess computers in the world and usually the computer will win. In fact, if the computer were to play the entire population of the world perhaps only a handful of people would be able to ever win a single game. Therefore, when compared to the majority of players this problem is effectively solved. However, if we consider the skills of dexterously manipulating a chess piece it is clear that if we pit the best robots of today against the skills of a young child, there is no competition. The child exhibits manipulation skills that outstrip any robot.*

Wolpert's point is that human movement is much more complex than many of us assume, and he goes on to explain why moving and manipulating an object is so difficult a task to implement: 'Unlike the game of chess where the state of the board and the consequences of each move are known, the control of movement requires interaction with a variable and ever-changing world.'

Next we will discuss the course of sensorimotor development – in particular focusing on the development of hand skills, as infants reach and grasp and pick up objects, and locomotion skills, as infants learn to balance, crawl and then to walk.

FROM REFLEXES TO SKILLED BEHAVIOUR

Reflexes change rapidly over the first months of life. Initially, very strong reflexes such as the stepping reflex and the grasping reflex actually begin to wane, such that by 2 months of age many of them have disappeared entirely. Later still, many of these early behaviours re-emerge, but this time in the form of more purposeful and controlled motor behaviours. Figure 6-16 demonstrates this U-shaped developmental pattern.

Why do reflexes disappear at around 2 months? Traditionally, maturational theorists (e.g., McGraw, 1940) have argued that early reflexes are governed by subcortical areas of the brain and spinal cord, which are mature at birth. They argue that, as higher, cortical areas of the brain develop (in this case, the motor cortex), these areas inhibit the functioning of the subcortical reflex systems. Gradually, as the infant matures, the cortex replaces subcortical reflexes with more voluntary and controlled behaviours.

The maturationist position rests largely on the view that the development of motor behaviour occurs according to a fixed maturational timetable, which is prescribed by our genetic inheritance. This U-shaped trajectory is part of such a timetable. Other evidence that the maturationists cited concerned the fixed spatial patterns of development of motor abilities. You may recall from Chapter 4 that the developing embryo matures according to proximo-distal (from the core outwards) and cephalo-caudal (from the head to toe) directions. The maturationists argued that a similar principle holds for postnatal motor development. For instance, as an infant gets older the skills she masters begin with the head. Balancing the head on the neck is one of the earliest achievements. Next the infant manages to sit up straight; later still, she may begin to move her legs in crawling and then walking. This describes the cephalo-caudal trajectory. At the same time that this is going on, proximo-distal

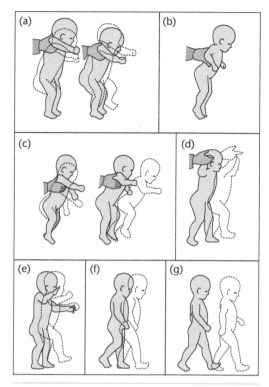

Figure 6-16   The developmental course of the stepping reflex

At birth, the stepping reflex is strong when a baby is placed above a platform (a). Yet, in the same situation, a 2-month-old produces no such behaviour (b). Later as the infant gets older the stepping returns, but this time in the guise of purposeful learned and controlled behaviour (d, e, f, g).

Source: Adapted from McGraw (1940).

development is also taking place. Take the task of reaching for an object in a sitting position. Whereas in young infants movements of the torso are the primary means whereby an object is reached, later infants learn to move the arms on the shoulder to contact an object. Later, mastery moves to the elbow, wrist and fingers as the child acquires more and more complex manipulative skills. The maturationists argued that these invariant sequences of development (we never see an infant learn to walk before she can hold her head straight on her shoulders) are due to the unfolding maturational timetable prescribed by our genetic inheritance.

But are genetics the only important factor in sensorimotor development? This seems unlikely. First, we know that environmental factors can affect sensorimotor development. For instance, cross-cultural research has shown that a baby's behaviour during the Brazelton assessment may differ across cultures due to parent–child interactions. Using the Brazelton scale, researchers identified superior motor performance by infants in the Gusii community of West Africa in comparison with American babies (Nugent, Lester, & Brazelton, 1991). This superior ability was found to be related to more vigorous handling by caregivers early in the child's life, including carrying the child on the mother's body in a sling, which has the effect of strengthening various muscles in the infant's body as she grips the mother (Keefer et al., 1991).

A number of studies have also shown that practice in sensorimotor behaviour can hasten the development of a number of skills. Zelazo, Zelazo, and Kolb (1972) asked mothers of newborns to give their infants practice in the stepping reflex a few minutes a day. Not only did these babies make more walking responses at

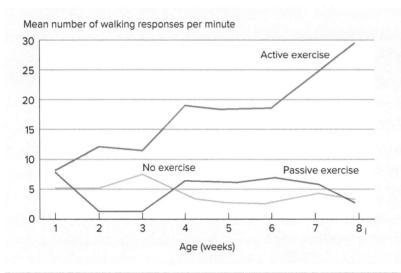

Mean number of walking responses per minute

Figure 6-17 Can practice really make perfect?
Newborns who engaged in the active exercise of the walking reflex showed a clear increase in this response over babies who took part in passive exercise or no exercise at all. The practised babies also walked earlier than the other children in this experiment.
Source: Adapted from Zelazo, Zelazo, and Kolb (1972).

2 to 8 weeks of age, but they also walked earlier than a control group of babies who were given no practice (see Figure 6-17). In another study, these investigators found that practice in sitting yielded similar results: babies who were given practice in sitting for three minutes a day were able to sit upright longer than infants in a no-practice control group (Zelazo et al., 1988). Karen Adolph and her colleagues (Adolph, 2005; Adolph & Berger, 2006) collected diary records of infants' walking activities. These records showed that walking infants practised keeping balance in an upright stance and locomotion for more than six hours a day, averaging between 500 and 1500 walking steps per hour, so that by the end of each day, they had taken 9000 walking steps and travelled the length of 29 football fields.

Not surprisingly, infants with more walking experience were the most skilled walkers. But practice does not necessarily make perfect.

There are limits to how far infants' motor development can be pushed. No stepping-trained baby has walked at 3 or 4 months of age, for example (Zelazo et al., 1988). Likewise, the invariant sequence the maturationists proposed seems to place some constraints on sensorimotor development, as deviations from the cephalocaudal and proximodistal trajectories of development are not typically seen. However, there are some questions over whether these fixed trajectories and limits of sensorimotor attainment are determined by genetically prescribed timetables. In the next sections we will show how some researchers have demonstrated that much more basic factors may account for these timetables of development.

HAND SKILLS

Learning to reach out and grasp an object is one of the most important achievements of the first two years of life. Reaching enables infants to inspect objects, and manipulate them in entirely new ways. In addition to this it seems likely that learning to act on objects will have knock-on influences on the way they perceive them. While newborn infants do not often manually contact objects, their reaches are more often directed towards an object if they are looking at it (von Hofsten, 2004). This rudimentary form of reaching – called 'prereaching' – is gradually replaced by more sophisticated sensorimotor coordination in which the reaches are more specifically integrated with particular visual aspects of the object.

From 3 to 4 months of age, reaches gradually become more 'goal directed' in nature (Spencer & Thelen, 2000). Grasps that

As adults we adjust our grasp to suit the size and orientation of the object we are trying to reach. This is something which infants, like this 7-month-old begin to master from 5 months onwards.

anticipate the orientation of an object, with changes in the orientation of the hand, begin to emerge at around 5 months (von Hofsten & Fazel-Zandy, 1984). Grasps that anticipate the size of an object are first observed from 9 months of age (von Hofsten & Rönnquist, 1988). Beyond this stage, infants increasingly hone their reaching and hand and arm movements so that they are increasingly efficient at carrying out the intended action. One recent study shows that from 9 to 12 months of age infants manage to reduce the number of irrelevant movements which they make with non-acting arms and legs when they are carrying out an action (D'Souza et al., 2017).

But what drives these developmental changes? Accurate reaching requires muscle growth, control of body posture, and of the movement of arms and hands, which in turn require that the infant learns about how to link motor behaviours to specific sensory inputs (e.g., learning to turn the hand to the correct orientation in order to connect efficiently with a handle in a particular orientation). Only when all parts of the system are ready to work together can infants become competent in reaching and grasping objects (Adolph, 2005; Thelen & Smith, 2006).

Another component involves the motor ability to grip an object. The frequency and skill with which infants employ various grips improve with age (Siddiqui, 1995; Adolph & Berger, 2010). Grips also depend on the size and shape of the object. Infants vary their grip according to the size and shape of an object and the size of their own hands relative to the object's size (Newell et al., 1989). They use a grip involving the thumb and index finger for small objects, but, for large objects, they use either all the fingers of one hand or both hands. Four-month-olds rely on touch to determine their grip; 8-month-olds use vision of the object as a guide so they can preshape their hand as they reach for it.

Over the first year of life, infants' progress in controlling their hands enables a number of important attainments. They not only become skilled reachers and graspers, but they also begin to use objects as tools – for example, a spoon (McCarty et al., 2001). Although at first they often use the object incorrectly (grabbing a spoon by the bowl instead of the handle), by 18 months they know which end to grab and how to use a spoon to feed themselves. Moreover, they learn to use hand and finger gestures in social communication – for example, pointing and using their hands to show objects to others (Franco & Butterworth, 1996; Goldin-Meadow, 2006). By age 2, they use their hands skilfully in play (e.g., building a tower of blocks) and, by age 3, they use their hands to scribble with crayons or copy vertical lines on a page.

BALANCE AND LOCOMOTION

When you think of the development of locomotion you most likely think of a baby's first steps, or the emergence of crawling. But, as Karen Adolph points out (e.g., Adolph, 2008), there are actually a lot of ways that a baby can learn to get around: they can crawl like a bear on all fours, or like a commando on their belly. They might miss out crawling altogether and go straight to walking. They might first learn to move by rolling around, or by bum-shuffling on a potty. This rich variation in the development of locomotion gives us a clue about how sensorimotor development happens. It happens in a rich variety of different ways, and it happens according to individual motivations and trajectories of development (Adolph, Hoch, & Cole, 2018).

Nonetheless, there are some regularities which are worth considering. For instance, the development of walking follows a U-shaped pattern. The first reflexive form of stepping does not actually allow the infant to walk, but nonetheless seems to be preparation for a later stage: when you hold a young baby upright and let its feet touch a flat surface, tilting the baby's body slightly from side to side, the baby responds by reflexively moving the legs in a rhythmic stepping motion that resembles walking. But this stepping reflex disappears by the time the infant is about 2 months old. Not until the second half of the baby's first year does the second transition occur, with the reappearance of stepping movements. At about 1 year of age, infants begin to walk without support.

As we hinted earlier, maturational theorists suggested that this kind of U-shaped pattern of development was due to the maturation of the motor cortex (McGraw, 1940). Others have suggested that it may be driven by the emergence of an ability to plan sequences of movement, or as a consequence of watching other people walk (Zelazo, 1983). A more recent, and very influential, explanation has come from dynamic systems theory (Thelen, 1995; Thelen & Smith, 2006), which suggests that walking skills are determined by the interaction

Taking your first steps must be an emotional experience; the excitement on the face of this baby is contagious. Perhaps these positive motivations are also contributing to the baby's slightly advanced ability; on average, children walk alone at about 12 months.
© redpepper82/123RF.com

of multiple factors, including genetic, environmental and also physical factors, such as the changing shape of the body. According to this theory, the newborn's stepping response disappears for a ten-month interval before true walking emerges, not because of inhibition by the motor cortex, but because of simpler physical factors; in this case, the baby's legs become too heavy! The size and weight of the legs become too much of a load on the emerging motor system, masking the child's stepping capability (Thelen, 1995). Thelen et al. (Thelen, 1995; Thelen & Smith, 2006) tested this explanation by examining whether infants between the ages of 2 months and 12 months should be able to step as long as they're given the stability and postural support necessary to stretch each leg forward and back while in an upright position. They provided such support by holding infants on a motorized treadmill. Immediately, they performed alternating stepping movements that were remarkably similar to more mature walking.

Upright walking is only the beginning, of course, and by the time children are about 7 years old, they have acquired the more complex skills of running and hopping (Cratty, 1999; Adolph & Berger, 2006). Running is well established by the time the child is a year and a half old, and galloping emerges at about the same time (Whitall & Clark, 1994). Hopping, which requires balance and strength, emerges between 2 and 3 years (Halverson & Williams, 1985). These skills depend on improvements in balance and coordination and on the opportunity for practice (Bertenthal & Clifton, 1998; Adolph & Berger, 2006).

HOW THE ACQUISITION OF NEW SENSORIMOTOR BEHAVIOURS INFLUENCES OTHER ASPECTS OF DEVELOPMENT

One important consequence of locomotor development is increased independence. Babies who can crawl or walk can explore their environments more fully and initiate more contact with other people. This newfound independence, in turn, changes the way people respond to the child. No longer can parents place their infants on a blanket in the middle of the floor, expecting that they will be there when they turn around. Infants can now move at will, leaving behind them a trail of mayhem – torn magazines, overturned coffee cups, broken glass. To prevent this chaos, parents must intervene with distractions or prohibitions. Researchers have observed that early walking is related to increased parent–child interaction (Biringen et al., 1995).

> The sensorimotor attainment of learning to walk or crawl may have an important influence on the development of cognitive abilities – see Chapters 9 and 10.

The onset of locomotion also affects the way babies perceive and react to the world (Adolph & Berger, 2006). After they begin crawling, infants develop a fear of heights (Campos & Bertenthal, 1989; Bertenthal et al., 1994), perhaps partly because they are now able to perceive depth in terms of what it actually means – the potential for a nasty fall. In one study of the influence of crawling on spatial cognitive development (Campos et al., 2000), researchers compared pre-crawling infants, belly crawling infants, and babies who crawled on hands and knees, at a spatial hiding task. All the babies watched while a toy was hidden in one of two containers. Then the researchers rotated each infant 180 degrees and left him or her to find the toy.

Good crawlers were more likely to solve the problem than infants who did not crawl or infants who crawled on their bellies, suggesting that locomotion helps infants deal with changes in spatial orientation.

Along similar lines, more recent studies also indicate that if infants are given experience of self-propelled locomotion in vehicles which they can use themselves, then this speeds the development of wariness of heights. It seems that experience of movement gives new meaning to perceptual information which is relevant to movement.

Thus, the attainment of new sensorimotor abilities may be important in the development of a range of perceptual and cognitive abilities. In Chapter 9 we will describe research and theory that has suggested why action may be so important in cognitive development.

THE ROLE OF CULTURE IN SENSORIMOTOR DEVELOPMENT

Although overall limits to motor development are set by physical maturation, within these limits the timing of various skills is affected by environmental factors (Bradley et al., 2001). Cross-cultural studies have provided us with information about how specific ways of caring for infants can alter their motor development. In general, it seems that when parents or other caregivers pay special physical attention to babies, including manipulation, massage, exercise and specific practice of skills, the infants achieve motor milestones somewhat earlier than children not given such care and opportunities. For example, in Zambia, mothers carry their new babies with them everywhere in a sling on their backs; then, when they are able to sit, the mothers leave their infants sitting alone for considerable periods of time, giving them plenty of opportunity to practise motor skills. Zambian babies show early development of motor skills (Hopkins & Westra, 1988). Jamaican mothers regularly massage their infants, stretch their arms and legs, and give them practice in stepping, and their children, too, are motorically advanced (Hopkins & Westra, 1990). In contrast, among the Zinacantecos of Mexico, infants are tightly swaddled for the first 3 months of life; they have less advanced motor skills (Greenfield & Childs, 1991). In Chinese families living in small, cramped apartments with uncarpeted floors, parents put their infants on soft featherbeds and pillows to prevent them from hurting themselves, and the babies' crawling is restricted by the lack of room to roam (Campos et al., 2000). Some of these infants fail to develop adequate strength in muscle groups critical for crawling, and their crawling is delayed.

STATE CHANGE AND SLEEP IN INFANCY

Patterns of sleep and wakefulness are one example of the several ways in which human motor behaviour is structured through predictable temporally regulated patterns of activity. As adults, if this temporal pattern is disturbed in some way (e.g., as a result of long-haul air travel across multiple time zones, of shift work, or just through lack of sleep) we very quickly notice the deleterious effects on our day-to-day performance.

States in the newborn infant

Just like adults, newborn babies have alternating patterns of sleep and wakefulness. These patterns are referred to as the infant state, which is defined as the recurring pattern of arousal that ranges from alert, vigorous, wakeful activity, to quiet, regular sleep.

Infant states tell us about some important characteristics of human behaviour (Table 6-2). First, they indicate that, from early in life, human behaviour is *organized* and *predictable*. Newborn states do not occur in a random, haphazard manner.

infant state A recurring pattern of arousal in the newborn, ranging from alert, vigorous, wakeful activity to quiet, regular sleep.

Table 6-2 Newborn infant states

State	Typical duration	Characteristics
Regular sleep	8–9 hours	Infant's eyes are closed, and body is completely still. Respiration is slow and regular. Baby's face is relaxed, with no grimacing, and eyelids are still.
Irregular sleep	8–9 hours	Baby's eyes are closed, but baby engages in gentle limb movements and general stirring. Grimaces and other facial expressions are frequent.
Drowsiness	½–3 hours	Baby's eyes open and close intermittently and display recurrent rapid eye movements. Baby is relatively inactive. Respiration is regular, though faster than in regular sleep.
Alert inactivity	2–3 hours	Infant's eyes are open, have a bright and shining quality, and can pursue moving objects. Baby is relatively inactive; face is relaxed and does not grimace.
Waking activity	2–3 hours	Baby's eyes are open but not alert, and respiration is irregular. Baby frequently engages in diffuse motor activity involving the whole body.
Crying	1–3 hours	Baby makes crying vocalizations and engages in diffuse motor activity.

Source: Wolff (1966, 1987).

Rather, they recur in a regular fashion. Second, human beings are not passive creatures that merely react to the environment. Internal forces regulate much of our behaviour and explain many of the changes in our activity levels (Schaffer, 1996). The observation that regular state changes are present early in life indicates that internal regulation of behaviour is a fundamental component of the human species. This is an important consideration for developmental psychologists. Indeed, a number of developmental theorists (e.g. Piaget, 1952; Mareschal et al., 2007) argue that as internally generated activity is vitally important in driving psychological development (a view which is opposed to the idea that the infant is a 'blank slate' or a *tabula rasa*, on which the environment makes its imprint). Nonetheless, both internal and external influences are important in shaping early behavioural regulation. As we shall see, despite clear indications that state-change is internally regulated from before birth, cross-cultural studies have revealed that differences in child-rearing practices can lead to quite different kinds of behavioural regulation.

Studies of foetal activity tell us that state change in arousal patterns begin to form well before birth (Prechtl, 1984). Indicators of distinct behavioural states prenatally come from observations that increases or decreases in various distinct behaviours are correlated. The earliest observations of such state changes have been taken from foetuses at around 28 weeks of gestational age (Curzi-Dascalova, Giganti, & Salzarulo, 2008). Studies of premature babies also indicate that state changes develop prior to 9 months' gestation. For example, babies born 2 months prematurely demonstrate regular changes in state that develop and become more organized as the infants grew older (Holditch-Davis, 1990). And so it is perhaps likely that the organization of behaviour into distinct states is part of our genetic inheritance. In line with this interpretation, behavioural genetics research (see Chapter 5) shows us that inherited individual differences in a state of arousal and the ability to regulate states are important components of temperament.

The development of sleep states in infancy

There are two basic infant states: waking and sleeping. Each of these states includes several variations. When infants are in the waking state they may be quiet, active or distressed, as in fussing and crying. The state of sleeping also includes variations in activity; notably the differentiation between REM and NREM sleep, which we will describe shortly. Let us first consider changes in state between sleep and waking.

The newborn, on average, sleeps about 13 hours of the day (55% of the time) across a series of long and short naps during the day and night (Curzi-Drascalova et al., 2008). This percentage decreases dramatically as the child ages, and particularly so during the first year of life. By the end of the first year the global amount of sleep has decreased to around 10 hours per day (about 42% of the time). Another important change in sleep patterns during the first year concerns the length of the individual periods of waking and sleeping. The newborn sleeps in short naps throughout the night and day. However, by the time an infant is 4 weeks old, her periods of sleep tend to be fewer but longer (moving towards a 'monophasic' sleep pattern), and by the time she is 8 weeks old, she is sleeping more during the night and less during the day ('diurnal sleep'). This shift towards diurnality is observable in Figure 6-18. By the end of the first year, most infants sleep through the night, much to the relief of their parents. It seems likely that these changes in the infants' internal biorhythms play a role in reducing the fussiness of infants' behaviour during the night-time hours.

Sleep phases in infancy

Researchers have used brain-recording techniques (more specifically EEG – see Chapter 3) when infants sleep in order to examine different phases of the infant sleep cycle, focusing in particular on the distinction between rapid eye movement (REM) and non-REM phases of sleep. REM sleep is characterized by the sleeper's eyes darting around in rapid, jerky movements under closed eyelids. This phase of sleep has often been associated with dreaming in adults because it is after this type of sleep that adults report having dreamt. Although infants also have REM sleep, it is obviously difficult to know whether they are dreaming.

REM sleep REM, or rapid eye movement, sleep is characterized by rapid, jerky movements of the eyes and, in adults, is often associated with dreaming.

In addition to rapid eye movement, REM sleep is characterized by fluctuating heart rate and blood pressure. The precise function of REM sleep (and indeed dreaming) is unknown, but we do know that it has functional value. For example, if people

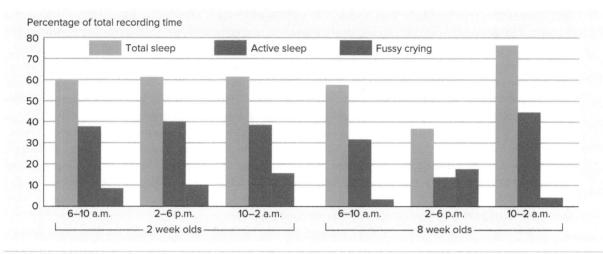

Figure 6-18   Infants' sleep patterns

At 2 weeks of age, infants tend to maintain about the same ratio of total sleep, active sleep and fussy crying in the morning, afternoon and at night, but by the time they're 8 weeks old, they have begun to spend appreciably more time in quiet sleep during the night-time hours.
Source: Adapted from Sostek and Anders (1981).

are awakened repeatedly as they begin REM sleep and thus are prevented from obtaining this type of sleep, they tend to be irritable and disorganized during their later waking hours. Compared to adults and older children, newborns undergo a lot of REM sleep. In newborns, 50% of sleep is characterized by REM patterns. As children age, though, REM sleep declines to about 20% (Ingersoll & Thoman, 1999). And so by the age of 18 and onward through adulthood (when most people sleep about 8 hours a day) only about an hour and a half of sleep is spent in REM sleep.

The role of sleep in development

Some researchers have suggested that the high level of REM sleep in newborns plays an important role in early brain development. Quite some time ago, Roffwarg, Muzio, and Dement (1966) proposed that REM sleep is self-stimulating; that is, it stimulates the infant's brain and thereby contributes to the development of the central nervous system. But how might this process happen? The idea here is that neural activity (in this case generated by REM sleep) is required in some sense for brain development. As we discussed in Chapter 5 several studies now point to the fact that environmental stimulation can influence the development of neural connections between different brain areas (e.g., Stellwagen & Shatz, 2002).

Have you ever wondered why babies seem to twitch when they sleep? Recent research in neuroscience has examined the link between REM sleep in young animals, twitching during sleep and sensorimotor development. Mark Blumberg argues that REM sleep gives rise to twitching. This stimulation of movement provides sensory information which may teach the brains of developing animals and humans about the layout of their bodies and potential uses of their limbs for action (Blumberg, Marques, & Iida, 2013).

Developmental drivers of diurnal sleep patterns

As we have described, children's sleep patterns change significantly across development (and particularly in the first year of life); infants become progressively more diurnal (sleeping through the night), the total amount of time that children spend sleeping continues to decrease through adolescence, and the percentage of sleep they spend in the REM state also declines. But what drives these changes? Are they due purely to the continued maturation of the central nervous system, or does the environment play a role? The fact that the major changes in sleep patterns happen during the first year of life – the period when the neuronal systems responsible for sleep are undergoing most development – shows us that biological maturation plays a very important role. However, researchers have also shown that additional external stimulation when awake reduces the amount of REM sleep that infants require, and this seems to be a convincing demonstration that environmental input has an important role to play in the development of sleep behaviours (Boismier, 1977).

What environmental factors might be most important in changing the ways in which children sleep? One way we can answer this question is by examining what factors cause the individual differences in infants' sleeping patterns. As every parent knows, young infants can differ dramatically in the extent to which they sleep through the night. You may know some new parents or may be one yourself. If a new parent always looks tired, the chances are that they have a baby who wakes them up several times during the night (rather than one who sleeps right through). Sadeh (2008) examined the determinants of these individual differences in sleep patterns during early life. In addition to factors intrinsic to the infant, he has argued that the most established external factor is parental behaviours (Sadeh, Tikotzky, & Scher, 2010); it is now well established that a reduction in parental intervention during the night leads to faster development of diurnal sleep (increases in night-time sleep and decreases in daytime napping).

Differences in the development of sleep patterns can also be observed cross-culturally. While most Western cultures tend to foster diurnal behaviour by keeping infants awake during the day and putting them to bed at night, other cultures are less concerned with this. For example, among the Kipsigis of rural Kenya, infants are constantly with their mothers and regularly take naps throughout the day. In contrast to Western babies, who undergo the shift towards diurnality in the first few months, Kipsigis babies continue to take shorter and more frequent naps. Although these Kenyan babies eventually sleep through the night, in one study by Super and Harkness (1981) they show this pattern much later than US babies.

Overall then, there are considerable changes in the ways in which infants sleep and wake across the first years of life. There is considerable current interest in the nature of sleep, and the ways in which sleep develops in early life. This is partly because we are gaining a greater understanding of sleep and the ways in which it works in adulthood (e.g., Gregory, 2018). But it is probably mostly because the ways in which infants and children sleep has profound implications for their parents or carers! However, the relevance of sleep research is made particularly important by findings that the quality of sleep which infants get in early life has implications for their later development, with both cognitive and socioemotional effects (Mindell et al., 2017; Sadeh et al., 2015).

SUMMARY

In this chapter we have tackled the question of how we come to be able to perceive and act on the world around us. This matter has intrigued developmental psychologists and philosophers alike for centuries. To study infants' *sensations* and *perceptions*, investigators often make use of the infant's tendency to *habituate* to, or become used to, a given stimulus. Another technique is to use the *visual preference method*, in which researchers pinpoint a baby's preference for looking at one of two alternative stimuli. Newborns can distinguish among different kinds of sounds, sights, touches, tastes and smells, and can also, in some cases, tell where these sensations are. They are particularly responsive to human voices and faces. They prefer to look at faces minutes after birth and are able to learn about the sound of voices even before birth. From a very early age, using their capacity for crossmodal perception, babies can integrate information from two different senses, such as the sounds that go with a certain sight. It seems that young infants are particularly sensitive to amodal crossmodal relations, and that their attention to these may have important influences on their perceptual development.

Babies experience predictable changes in state, or recurring patterns of alertness and activity level, ranging from vigorous, wakeful activity to quiet, regular sleep. Two significant *infant states* are sleeping and crying. Changes in these states over the first years of life have important implications for the way the infant's sensorimotor behaviour is structured. The newborn has a repertoire of *reflex* responses to external stimuli. Many of these reflexes, some of which have obvious value in helping the newborn survive, disappear during the first year of life. Researchers have disagreed over whether these early reflexes represent purposeful actions or involuntary responses to stimulation. Dynamic systems theory has offered perhaps the most exhaustive explanation of the developmental changes observed in infant reflexes over the first years of life.

Sensorimotor skills (using perception to guide action) often develop according to a U-shaped pattern. Initial reflexes disappear at around 2 months, and then gradually re-emerge in a more voluntary and controlled form. A dynamic systems approach to explain this pattern suggests that the development of walking depends on genetic, environmental and physical factors. The particular physical factor of importance in the waning of the step reflex is the weight of the legs, which overcomes the infant's ability to express their stepping reflex. The attainment of new sensorimotor abilities across the lifespan can have widespread effects on perceptual, emotional and cognitive development.

Explore and Discuss

1. What is the practical value of knowing about the young infant's sensory abilities? How might this information help in the early detection of problems and in the design of useful interventions to help children?

2. Based on your newly gained knowledge of infants' sensory and perceptual capacities, do you think 'the amazing newborn' is an appropriate description? Explain your answer.

3. How do you think infants' visual and auditory abilities help them form relationships with their caregivers?

4. The senses give us different kinds of information. Discuss what these are and how they might interact.

5. Sensorimotor development is influenced by a variety of factors. What role may culture play in the timing of children's walking?

6. Dynamic systems theorists suggest that a variety of factors interplay in the development of sensorimotor abilities, including genetics, environment and physical factors. What do you think the most significant physical factors will be in the first years of life?

Recommended Reading

Classic

Thelen, E., & Fisher, D. M. (1982). Newborn stepping: An explanation for a 'disappearing' reflex. *Developmental Psychology*, 18, 760–775.

Von Hofsten, C. (2004). An action perspective on motor development. *Developmental Science*, 8, 266–272.

Contemporary

Bremner, A. J., Lewkowicz, D. J., & Spence, C. (2012). *Multisensory development*. Oxford: Oxford University Press.

Moon, R. Y., Horne, R. S. C., & Hauck, D. R. (2007). Sudden infant death syndrome. *Lancet*, 370, 1578–1587.

CHAPTER 7
Emotional Development and Attachment

Children display a wide range of emotions from the time they are infants. The smiling infant tells others that something is pleasurable, while a frown communicates displeasure. Older children may use smiling as a sign of welcome and express anger as a way of deterring a potential aggressor. Adolescents can display a range of emotions, or learn to suppress them in more strategic ways. In addition to using emotions to communicate with and regulate their worlds, children and adolescents learn to read the emotional signs that other people display. Both processes – the production and the recognition of emotion – are essential to useful interactions with other people, and they enable babies to begin to exert some control over their social world.

Introduction

The chapter starts by examining why emotions are important. It introduces theories that have been proposed to explain emotional development and then explores children's earliest expressions of emotion by examining several of the earliest emotional expressions – smiling, laughter, fear, anger and sadness – followed by later-developing emotions such as pride, shame, guilt and jealousy. It then considers how emotions link to temperament and how the social context can influence emotional expression. Then the chapter turns to examine how infants and children learn to recognize emotions in others, and learn to regulate and think about their emotions.

The second part of the chapter considers the development of attachment – the close bond between infant and caregiver. Key theories of how attachment relationships form are reviewed, and then research is discussed describing how relationships develop between infants, children, adolescents and parents, siblings and others. The chapter concludes with an exploration of the nature and quality of attachment relationships, considering the causes and effects of attachment quality, including issues about parental and institutional child care, on cognitive and social development.

EARLY EMOTIONAL DEVELOPMENT

Emotions, such as joy, anger, fear and surprise, are (a) subjective reactions to the environment, (b) usually experienced as either pleasant or unpleasant, (c) generally accompanied by some form of physiological arousal, and (d) often communicated to others (deliberately or unintentionally). Emotions have a wide variety of functions for children: they are an important means of letting others know how they feel, and success in communicating emotional states and in learning to interpret other people's emotions is linked with social success. Being able to express and interpret emotions is important, and being able to navigate successfully in the world of your own and other people's emotions is a critical ingredient of everyday life. Just as we have intellectual or cognitive intelligence, children develop their capacity for emotional intelligence as well.

> **emotions** Subjective reactions to the environment that are usually experienced cognitively as either pleasant or unpleasant, generally accompanied by physiological arousal, and often expressed in some visible form of behaviour.

Emotions are also linked to mental and physical health. As we explore in greater detail in Chapter 15, children who become depressed or despondent may develop other problems such as poor concentration and withdrawal from social interaction, impoverished relationships and low self-worth. Children reared in environments in which they are emotionally and socially deprived develop later problems with the management of stress and anxiety when compared with peers who grow up in emotionally richer environments. Even children from ostensibly normal homes may suffer impaired physical health when they are exposed to emotional hostility between their parents (Gottman, Katz, & Hooven, 1996). Thus, emotional development is a central and important area of developmental psychology.

When considering research in the area it is important to distinguish primary and secondary emotions. Primary emotions – such as fear, joy, disgust, surprise, sadness and interest – emerge early in life and do not require introspection or self-reflection. Another set of emotions are secondary, or self-conscious, emotions – such as pride, shame, guilt, jealousy and embarrassment. These emerge later in development and rely in part on our sense of self and our awareness of other individuals' reactions to our actions (Lewis, 1998; Saarni, Campos, & Camras, 2006).

Perspectives on emotional development

A child's emotional development is influenced by many factors: genetic inheritance, the conditions of the environment into which the child is born, their interactions with family members and, later, with peers. These and other factors all play important roles in determining an individual's emotional responses, reactions and temperament. Three overlapping theoretical perspectives on emotional development – the genetic-maturational, learning and functionalist perspectives – may be useful in explaining aspects of development at different stages of life.

The average age for a baby to begin smiling is 6 weeks, based on a baby carried to full term.
© Shutterstock/leungchopan

According to the *genetic-maturational view*, emotions are products of biology. Individual differences play a central role in how intensely children react to emotionally arousing situations and in how well they are able to regulate their reactions. A key source of evidence for this view comes from twin studies. In Chapter 5 we introduced how studies of identical and fraternal twins can provide compelling evidence for establishing the importance of biology (genes) and environment on development. In terms of emotional development, identical twins show greater similarity than fraternal twins in both the earliest times of their first smiles and the amount of smiling in which each engages (Plomin et al., 1997). Studies of smiling in premature infants support the role of genetic-maturational factors in the onset of smiling. Most full-term babies begin to smile about 6 weeks after they are born, or at a conceptual age (the age after the infant's conception) of 46 weeks. Premature infants who are born at 34 weeks often do not smile until 12 weeks after birth, which for them is also 46 weeks since conception (Dittrichova, 1969). A certain amount of physical maturation and social stimulation, or both, must therefore occur before a baby is ready to start smiling. Most researchers agree that the interplay between genetics and the environment accounts for the timing and form of this behaviour.

A genetic-maturational basis for negative emotions, such as fear, is also supported by twin studies. Again, identical twins are more similar than fraternal twins in their fear reactions to strangers and in their general degree of inhibitedness (Robinson et al., 1992; Plomin et al., 1997; Rutter, 2006a).

> Parent–child interactions in infancy are important not only for a child's emotional development, but also for the development of language and communication skills as we discuss in Chapter 8.

An alternative view is the *learning perspective*, which is particularly useful in explaining individual differences in emotional expression. Different emotions, and the way in which children express them, have different ages of onset, different frequencies and different intensities in different children. Many researchers suggest that the frequency with which children smile or laugh seems to vary with the nature of the environment in which they are raised. Parents can help their children learn to manage and understand their emotions by rewarding only certain emotional displays. On the other hand, parents can negatively impact the normal development and expression of emotions by dismissing or ignoring their children's emotional expressions and experiences (Gottman et al., 1996). Common sense suggests that parents who respond with enthusiasm to their smiling infant will tend to encourage him to smile more. This has in fact been verified in studies showing that when adults, particularly familiar caregivers, respond to a baby's smile with positive stimulation, the child's rate of smiling increases (e.g., Denham, Bassett, & Wyatt, 2007).

Learning experiences can also elicit and reinforce fear responses. Children may learn to be afraid of certain situations or objects through operant conditioning when one of their own behaviours, such as climbing up a high ladder, is followed by a harmful or distressing consequence, such as a painful fall. And they can learn still other fears simply by observing others. For example, a child may watch her mother react fearfully to a bee or to a large dog and later imitate her mother's reaction (Bandura, 1989; Denham et al., 2007). In all these cases, the child's particular set of fears depends on what they have learned.

The *functionalist perspective* (e.g., Saarni et al., 2006) contends that emotions serve to help us achieve our goals and adapt to our environment, and emphasizes the role of emotions in establishing and maintaining social relationships, as well as the role that social cues play in regulating our emotional perceptions and expressions. This approach incorporates many features of the learning perspective in a unified view of emotional development.

The functionalist perspective argues that the purpose of emotion is to help us achieve goals. Goals arouse emotions – for example, fear may lead us to flee the dangerous situation, enabling us to achieve the goal of self-preservation. In this respect emotions have an important social component: we use information provided by others' emotional signals to guide our own behaviour. For instance, the way someone you view as a potential friend reacts emotionally to your conversation will be a critical determinant of how you feel. If he responds positively and smiles, you'll be happy and carry on, but if he frowns, you'll probably stop or in some cases reconsider the basis of the friendship. In this way past experiences also guide and shape how the child will respond emotionally to future situations. Children who have routinely been rebuffed by potential friends will be more wary, whereas children who have been socially successful will be more confident in a similar situation. In both cases, emotions regulate children's behaviour and enhance their adaptation to their environment.

Emotions are complex things – sometimes very complex! – that can involve a very intimate and personal experience. So a single theoretical perspective is unlikely to integrate all aspects of emotional development. And while genes play a likely role as well as environment, fundamentally our emotions are triggered and developed in relation to or in the context of others and of events. So, often, different theories are more or less useful in answering different sorts of research questions. Emotional responses are shaped by a complex interplay between biological factors and the many social and developmental experiences that the child encounters.

The development of emotional expressions

Many parents believe that infants display a wide range of emotions at a very early age. When asked, 95% of mothers say that their 1 month olds clearly display joy, 85% anger, 74% surprise, 58% fear and 34% sadness (Johnson et al., 1982). These mothers based their judgements not only on their babies' behaviours (facial expressions, vocalizations, body movements) but also on the nature of the situations in which those behaviours occurred. For example, a mother who watched her baby staring intently at the mobile above her crib was likely to label the infant's emotion 'interest', whereas she might call the emotion expressed by a gurgling, smiling baby 'joy'. As adults we rarely judge the emotions of others outside of a broader context in which the behaviour is expressed; context is a vital ingredient of interpretation in terms of understanding others' emotions.

However, relying on mothers' judgements may not be the best or most scientific way to approach the issue. Mothers may be more motivated to see certain behaviours or may by subject to biases of interpretation or observation that all of us are. A more objective means of assessing emotion involves using coding schemes where independent observers assign finely differentiated scores to different parts of the face (e.g. lips, eyelids, forehead) and to specific infant movement patterns. Researchers then use these scores to judge whether an infant has displayed a particular emotion. Izard et al. (1995) have developed an elaboration of the coding system for infant emotional expressions now in use: the Maximally Discriminative Facial Movement, or MAX, coding system.

Of course, as children get older and learn more about their own (and others') emotions, they also learn more about social norms, behaviours, and managing social situations (Darling-Churchill & Lippman, 2016). Older children and adolescents learn more about how to mask negative emotions, manufacture positive ones, or how different 'audiences' (e.g., adults, peers, friends) might react in different situations (Burkitt & Watling, 2013). While primary emotions develop throughout life, older children and adolescents also understand more about more complex secondary emotions and the social context in which these occur. Secondary emotions often require more subtle or more complex methods to accurately code behaviour or rely more on self-reports from young people themselves.

Individual differences and temperament

There are wide individual differences among infants and young children in their readiness to express positive or negative emotions. Babies who are more sociable show less wariness in encounters with strangers than do less sociable infants (Bohlin & Hagekull, 1993). Some babies smile more readily and laugh more heartily (LaFreniere, 2000). Other babies react more fearfully to novel people and events, and are more easily angered than other infants. Perhaps differences in temperament contribute to these differences in emotional reactions. For instance, Kagan (1998) has identified a subset of children whom he calls 'behaviourally inhibited'. These children tend to be shy, fearful and introverted, often avoiding even their peers, and they are more anxious and upset by mildly stressful situations than are other children (Kagan, 1998). Behaviourally inhibited youngsters tend to show atypical physiological reactions – such as rapid heart rates – in stressful situations, and their fearful responses and shyness tend to endure across time, from toddlerhood on into the early school years. However, warm, supportive parents can reduce fearfulness and reduce the likelihood that their children will continue to be abnormally shy and fearful (Gunnar, 1998; Kagan, 1998; Kagan & Snidman, 2004).

Individual differences in positive and negative emotionality are related to children's adjustment (Lengua, 2002). For example, 10 year olds who exhibited high levels of negative emotionality (fearfulness and irritability) were more likely to have adjustment difficulties. They tended to be depressed and to have conduct problems. Children who were judged emotionally positive (rated high on smiling and laughing) had high self-esteem and social competence, indicating better adjustment.

Temperament is a term often used to characterize sets of personality characteristics across groups of infants and children in terms of various behaviours and tendencies including activity level, attachment to others, mood, responsiveness and attention span. Chess and Thomas (1987) suggested there are three different types of child or clusters of temperament: easy, difficult, and slow-to-warm-up. Easy children eat and sleep regularly, adapt to change well and show a good mood most of the time. Difficult children eat and sleep irregularly, show a negative response to new situations and may throw frequent tantrums. Slow-to-warm-up children respond negatively to new situations but slowly come to accept them. As might be expected, fewer behavioural or social problems are associated with easy children, whereas difficult children may encounter difficulties socially and behaviourally, especially when encountering new situations. Problems or outcomes for slow-to-warm-up children can be more varied in nature, and may depend on a variety of other factors specific to a situation or the child.

Of course, many parents (and others) will seek to understand their child's temperament and may adjust their parenting style accordingly. An analysis of the structure of infant temperament (the Revised Infant Temperament Questionnaire, RITQ) with a large sample of Australian babies suggested that *rhythmicity* and *persistence* were core factors that distinguished temperament based on parents' reports. Persistence is the extent to which a baby can stop a task or how strong-willed they appear to be. Rhythmicity describes the patterning or regularity of infants' behaviours: for instance, a baby may regularly go to sleep at 7 pm each evening, or may settle to sleep at 5 pm, 7 pm, or 1 am on different nights. In the early stages of a baby's life, one core aspect of parenting (and one of the most disruptive to a new parent) can be the extent to which an infant sleeps. In chapter 6 we discussed how sleep patterns can change across development, and clearly if a child sleeps poorly this will impact on the parents' sleep and perhaps also their parenting approaches and capacities over a period of time.

Infant temperament also has an influence on the development of attachment relationships, which we will discuss later in this chapter. In this respect the interplay between infant, child, adolescent and parent is a two-way street and individual and environmental factors can have a bearing on how the relationship (and emotions and well-being) of both parent and child develop over the course of time. Thus, again, emotions are often understood and forged within social contexts and can relate to and be influenced by social situations in myriad ways. How far temperament augments or inhibits normal emotional development therefore depends both on factors affecting the individual child as well as those around her or him.

Temperament appears relatively stable, certainly across the years of infancy and early childhood. It also connects with parents' behaviour and other characteristics, although, as we have seen, disentangling parenting styles or practices that may be a consequence of a child's temperament is not straightforward. Bornstein et al. (2018) explored the temperament of 10,000 children from 3 to 6 years of age in the Avon Longitudinal Study of Parents and Children. This large-scale study identified many stable and consistent factors in temperament including child age, term status (whether born prematurely) and mothers' anxiety, and depression. However, while gender, birth order, mother's age and level of education are still associated with temperament, they were found to have only small moderating effects.

PRIMARY AND SECONDARY EMOTIONS
The development of primary emotions

If you watch closely, you can see smiles even in newborn infants. These reflex smiles (also known as simple smiles) (Wolff, 1987; Fogel et al., 2006) are usually spontaneous and appear to depend on the infant's internal state, but the exact nature of the internal stimulus remains unknown. Whether or not researchers can shed light on the origin of the baby's reflex smiles, these smiles serve a good purpose. Most caregivers interpret these smiles as signs of pleasure, and this gives the caregivers pleasure and encourages them to cuddle and talk to the baby. In this sense, these smiles may have adaptive value for the baby, ensuring critical caregiver attention and stimulation. Overall, early as well as later smiling helps keep caregivers nearby and thus becomes a means of communication and an aid to survival.

> **reflex smile** A smile seen in the newborn that is usually spontaneous and appears to depend on some internal stimulus rather than on something external such as another person's behaviour.

Between 3 and 8 weeks of age, infants begin to smile in response not only to internal events but also to a wide range of external eliciting stimuli, including social stimuli such as faces, voices, light touches and gentle bouncing (Sroufe, 1996). Infants are particularly interested in people and faces, and a high-pitched human voice or a combination of voice and face are reliable smile elicitors for babies between 2 and 6 months old. When 3-month-old infants were shown a human face and puppets whose faces varied in their resemblance to a human face, the infants smiled almost exclusively at the human face (Ellsworth, Muir, & Hains, 1993).

As infants grow older, they tend to smile at different aspects of the human face (Saarni et al., 2006). When 4-week-old babies look at human faces, they tend to focus on the eyes, but by the time they are 8 or 9 weeks old, they examine the mouth as well. Smiling behaviour follows a similar pattern: at first, babies smile at the eyes, then the mouth, and finally the entire face and the facial expression. By the time they are about 3 months old, babies also start to smile more selectively at familiar faces (Camras, Malatesta, & Izard, 1991; Saarni et al., 2006), suggesting that smiling has begun to signal pleasure and not just arousal. There is other evidence that smiling takes on a social dimension as infants get older: 3 month olds show greater increases in smiling when their smiles are reinforced by reciprocal smiles and vocalizations from their mothers than when they are reinforced by equally responsive women who are strangers (Wahler, 1967). These findings are consistent with the learning and functionalist perspectives, and suggest that infant smiling becomes more discriminating as babies develop.

> Being able to perceive faces is an important skill for infants and serves an important function in the early development of social interactions. The development of these fundamental perceptual processes is discussed in Chapter 6.

A baby's pleasure at watching a familiar face is revealed in other ways as well. For instance, one study found that 10 month olds generally reserved a special kind of smile for their mothers, rarely offering it to strangers (Fox & Davidson, 1988). These special smiles (called *Duchenne smiles* after Guillaume Duchenne, the French physician who noticed this pattern more than 100 years ago) are likely to involve not just an upturned mouth but wrinkles around the eyes as well, making the whole face seem to light up with pleasure (Ekman, Davidson, & Friesen, 1990; Ekman, 2003). Finally, babies display genuine smiles more in interacting with caregivers than when smiling alone (Messinger, Fogel, & Dickson, 2001). Babies show other kinds of smiles during play, too – including the display smile, which is a combination of the Duchenne smile and a jaw

CHRONOLOGY OF DEVELOPMENT
The evolution of emotional expression and the sense of self

Early weeks	Shows distress by crying
1 month	Generalized distress; may be irritable by late afternoon
2 months	Shows pleasure; mildly aroused by sight of toy; social smile
3 months	Excitement and boredom appear; smiles broadly and often; cries when bored; may show wariness and frustration
4 months	Laughs, especially at certain sounds; crying lessens; gurgles with pleasure; shows beginnings of anger
5 months	Usually gleeful and pleased but sometimes frustrated; shows primitive resistant behaviours; turns head from disliked food; smiles at own image in mirror; some babies may begin to show wariness of strangers
6 months	Matches emotions to others, e.g. smiles and laughs when mother does; fear and anger may appear now or later
7 months	Fear and anger; defiance; affection; shyness
8 months	More individuality in emotional expression
9 months	Shows negative emotions when restrained; frowns when annoyed; actively seeks others' comfort when tired; night-time crying may reappear; recognizes self in mirror; most babies display real fear of strangers
10 months	Intense positive and negative emotions; occasionally testy; uses reflection in mirror – e.g. seeing toy in mirror, may move towards toy
11 months	Greater variability in emotions; individual temperament is more evident; learning to associate names of body parts; may insist on feeding self
12 months	Becomes distressed when others are distressed; cries when something is not to liking; may show signs of jealousy; laughs often at own cleverness; struts/preens when walking; loves to look at self in mirror; wants to show mastery; plays on own
15 months	More mood swings; is more caring to age-mates; annoyed by dirty hands; strongly prefers certain clothing; may fret or cry often, but usually briefly
18 months	Can be restless and stubborn; may sometimes have tantrums; sometimes shy; shows shame; uses adjectives to refer to self; uses objects like a blanket or a favourite stuffed animal to soothe self
21 months	Makes some efforts to control negative emotions; can be finicky and exacting; makes more efforts to control situations; begins to understand parents' values; refers appropriately to self as good or bad
24 months	Can be contrary but also appropriately contrite; responds to others' moods; very intense; may be overwhelmed by changes; can be upset by dreams; refers to self by name; identifies self by gender; talks about self by using I and a verb, such as hurt or need; keen to experience world on own terms; begins to understand emotional display rules
30 months	Begins to show shame, embarrassment
36 months	Shows pride, guilt
48 to 60 months	Shows increased understanding and use of emotional display rules
72 months	Begins to understand how two or more emotions can occur simultaneously

Note: developmental events described in this and other turning point charts represent overall trends identified in research studies. Individual children vary greatly in the ages at which they achieve these developmental changes.

Source: Kopp (1994); Sroufe (1996); Saarni et al. (2006).

drop. This is evident in later phases of tickle games and peek-a-boo where there is a build-up of excitement, followed by completion of the play bout (Fogel et al., 2006).

Of course, there are individual differences in the amount of smiling a baby does. Some of these differences have to do with the social responsiveness of the baby's environment. Cultural norms may be an important factor here, For example, Israeli infants reared in a family environment smiled more often by the second half-year than infants raised in either a kibbutz (a communal living arrangement – described in more detail in the section on attachment later in this chapter) or an institution, where the level of social stimulation (or at least individual attention) is presumed to be lower (Gewirtz, 1967). Gender is related to babies' smiling, too: in the newborn period at least, girls generally show more spontaneous smiles than boys (Korner, 1974). Nor are gender differences in smiling restricted to infants; teenage girls smile more than teenage boys (LaFrance, Hecht, & Levy Paluck, 2003). This higher rate of smiling has led some observers to suggest that girls may be genetically better prepared for social interaction than boys because their greater tendency to smile more often draws others to them (Saarni et al., 2006). This view supports the genetic-maturational perspective. On the other hand, parents generally elicit and expect more emotions from girls than boys, which suggests that both genetic and environmental factors need to be considered. Indeed, social forces must at least play a part because there are widespread cultural, ethnic and gender differences in smiling (LaFrance et al., 2003). Compared with their peers in the UK, children and adults in North America show larger gender differences in smiling. These differences may stem from different stereotyped views of gender differences in the different societies.

Duchenne smiles (or 'smizing', smiling with the eyes) are generally viewed as indicating a more authentic emotional response than smiles without changes in the eyes.
© Science History Images/Alamy Stock Photo

Laughing, at which infants become quite skilled by the time they are 4 months old (Sroufe, 1996), is, if anything, even more useful in maintaining the baby's well-being (Nwokah et al., 1994). If smiling gradually becomes a sign of pleasure, laughter leaves us with little doubt of a baby's positive emotion, and it plays a very important role in caregiver–infant interaction.

Sroufe and Wunsch (1972) asked mothers to record the amount of laughter elicited in babies between 4 and 12 months of age using different visual, tactile, auditory and social-behavioural stimuli – for example, a human mask or a disappearing object; bouncing the child on an adult's knee or blowing on the baby's hair; making whispering or whinnying sounds; and playing peek-a-boo, covering the baby's face or sticking out the tongue.

As Figure 7-1 shows, up to about 7 months of age, babies are increasingly likely to laugh at visual, tactile and social events, but their reactions to auditory stimulation remain stable. Note, however, that the nature of the stimuli that elicit laughter changes as the child develops. From 7 months on, both social and tactile stimuli begin to be less effective, but response to visual stimuli continues to increase. Towards the end of the first year, babies respond more to social games, visual displays and other activities in which they can participate, such as covering and uncovering the mother's face with a cloth or playing tug-of-war with a blanket. By the end of the first year and throughout the second year, infants increasingly smile and laugh in response to activities that they create themselves (Sroufe, 1996),

Simple games, like peek-a-boo, can easily invoke laughter in babies; they are particularly responsive to social games from towards the end of the first year.
© JGI/Jamie Grill/Blend Images LLC

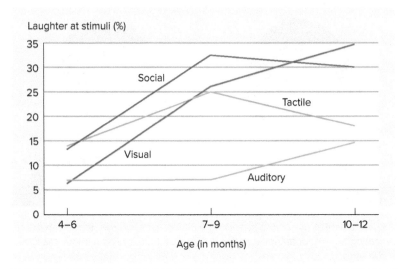

Between the ages of 4 months and a year, children were most consistently likely to laugh at visual and social stimuli, such as a disappearing object or playing peek-a-boo.
Source: The development of laughter in the first year of life, Child Development, Sroufe and Wunsch © 1972. Reproduced with permission of John Wiley & Sons, Inc.

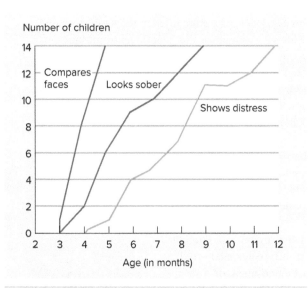

Figure 7-2 The onset of stranger distress
At 8 months of age, half of the children studied were showing distress at the appearance of strangers and, within a month or two, this distress reaction was clearly dominant.
Source: Adapted from Emde, Gaensbauer, and Harmon (1976).

such as practising their motor accomplishments by pulling themselves to a standing position or laughing after making a jack-in-the-box pop up. As children grow older, laughing increases and becomes more of a social event (LaFreniere, 2000; Saarni et al., 2006). In one study of 3 to 5 year olds, nearly 95% of laughter occurred in the presence of other children and adults (Bainum, Lounsbury, & Pollio, 1984). 'Acting silly' was most often the elicitor of laughter among the nursery school set!

Negative primary emotions: fear, anger and sadness

At the same time that babies are beginning to display signs of positive emotion in smiles and laughter, they are also learning to be fearful of some events and people, especially unfamiliar ones (LaFreniere, 2000; Saarni et al., 2006).

The negative emotional response called *fear of strangers* evolves more slowly than the positive emotional expressions we've just discussed. Sroufe (1996) distinguishes two phases in the emergence of fear. At about 3 months of age, Sroufe maintains, infants show *wariness*, in which they respond with distress to an event that includes both familiar and unfamiliar aspects and which they therefore cannot comprehend and assimilate. This argument is consistent with the cognitive perspective of emotional development. By the time they are 7 to 9 months old, babies show true *fear*, which is an immediate negative reaction to an event that has specific meaning for them, such as seeing the face of a total stranger (e.g., 'I don't know what this is, and I don't like it').

Even at 4 months of age, babies smile less at unfamiliar adults than their mothers, showing early signs that they recognize familiar people. But they are not yet distressed by the presence of a stranger. In fact, they show great interest in novel people as well as novel objects. Often, they look longer at a stranger than at a familiar person and, if the mother is present, they will frequently look back and forth between her face and the stranger's, as if comparing them. Then, at about 5 months of age, this earlier reaction of gaze and interest starts to be replaced largely by giving a stranger a sober stare. At 6 months, although babies still are most likely to react to strangers with a sober expression, they're also likely to display distress. A distress reaction then gradually increases in frequency over the next half year, and by 7 to 9 months, the earlier wary reactions give way to clear expressions of fear. Figure 7-2 summarizes this progression from interest and exploration to fear over the first year of life (Emde, Gaensbaruer, & Harmon, 1976).

Fear of strangers, or stranger distress, has become enshrined in the psychological literature as a developmental milestone and at one time was thought to be both inevitable and universal. Researchers now know that it is neither (LaFreniere, 2000; Saarni et al., 2006). Stranger distress emerges at about 7 to 9 months of age in several cultures, including the Hopi Indians (Dennis, 1940) and in Uganda (Ainsworth, 1963). However, in other cultures, such as the Efe (Africa), that emphasize shared caregiving among relatives, babies show little stranger fear (Tronick, Morelli, & Ivey, 1992). Moreover, babies are not all alike in their reactions to strangers. For some, greeting and smiling may be a frequent reaction, and fear is not typical, but others show fear (Rheingold & Eckerman, 1973).

Whether a baby is fearful of a stranger depends on a host of variables, including who the stranger is, how he or she behaves, the setting in which the person is encountered, and the child's age (Mangelsdorf, Watkins, & Lehn, 1991; Saarni et al., 2006), as shown in Table 7-1. Consistent with the functionalist perspective on emotional development, contextual factors help determine the way an infant will react to a stranger. When babies meet strangers in their own homes, they show less stranger fear than when encountering unfamiliar people in an unfamiliar setting such as a researcher's laboratory (Sroufe, Waters, & Matas, 1974). Similarly, babies who sit on their mothers' laps while a stranger approaches rarely show any fear, but when not in physical contact with their caregiver they may show fear when a stranger approaches (Morgan & Ricciuti, 1969; Bohlin & Hagekull, 1993). And it depends on how the mother reacts to the stranger, too. When a baby sees his mother reacting positively to a stranger, he tends to follow suit and responds much more positively, smiling more, approaching the stranger and offering toys (Feinman & Lewis, 1983). Conversely, when the mother adopts a worried look in the presence of a stranger, her baby is apt to cry more and smile less (Boccia & Campos, 1989; Mumme, Fernald, & Herrera, 1996).

> **stranger distress**
> A fear of strangers that typically emerges in infants around the age of 9 months.

> ▼ Fear of strangers has been proposed as an important factor in the development of ethnic group prejudice from a young age. We discuss this theory in Chapter 13. ▲

Table 7-1 Factors that alter infant fear of strangers

	More fear	Less fear
Context	Unfamiliar setting (e.g., lab)	Familiar setting (home)
	No physical contact with familiar figure; distant from mother or familiar person	Close physical proximity to familiar figure
	Sober or negative emotional reactions to stranger from familiar figure	Positive or encouraging reactions to stranger from familiar figure
Characteristics of stranger	Adult size and features	Child size and features
Behaviour of stranger	Passive and exhibits sober expression	Active, friendly, smiling
Degree of control over strange person or object	Low control and unpredictability	High control and predictability

These studies illustrate social referencing in infants – that is, the process of 'reading' emotional cues in other people to help determine how to act in an uncertain situation (Saarni et al., 2006). Much of this work has been stimulated by the functionalist perspective on emotional development. This social referencing undergoes clear changes over time (Walden, 1991). As infants develop, they are more likely to look at the mother's face than at other parts of her body. Babies between 14 and 22 months old were clearly more aware that their mother's face was the best source of information than were babies 6 to 9 months old (Walden, 1991). Infants grow also in their tendency to check with their mothers before they act. Younger infants often act first and look later – a strategy that could lead to

> **social referencing** The process of 'reading' emotional cues in others to help determine how to act in an uncertain situation.

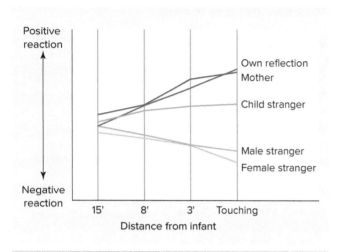

Figure 7-3 Proximity and age of a stranger affect babies' reactions

In this study of stranger distress, the gender of a stranger had no effect, but his or her age did. The infants did not perceive the 4-year-old stranger as threatening but reacted very negatively to both adults. Distance from the infants had relatively little effect on the way they perceived the young stranger, but the closer the adult strangers got, the more intensely the babies showed their distress. In comparison, the infants reacted quite positively both to their own reflections and to their mothers', and this tendency increased with proximity.

Source: Adapted from Lewis & Brooks (1974).

> **separation protest**
> An infant's distress reaction to being separated from his or her mother, which typically peaks at about 15 months of age.

trouble in a dangerous situation. The fact that even infants learn to use others' emotional expressions as a guide to their own actions underscores the importance of emotion for regulating social behaviour (Saarni et al., 2006). Another contextual factor is the degree to which the situation allows the infant some control over the extent and pace of the interaction (Mangelsdorf et al., 1991). When babies could control the noise and movement of a toy monkey or the predictability of the noise (regular vs erratic), 1 year olds were less fearful (Gunnar, 1980; Gunnar et al., 1984). The characteristics of the stranger matters, too. Infants are less afraid of children than they are of adults, as Figure 7-3 indicates.

A stranger's behaviour also affects the degree of stranger distress an infant displays (Mumme et al., 1996; Saarni et al., 2006). When confronted by an active, friendly stranger who talks, gestures, smiles, imitates the baby and offers toys, most 12 month olds show little fear. In contrast, infants are more apprehensive when confronted by a passive and sober-looking stranger.

Some kinds of fear do appear to be universal and are present in all cultures. A common fear in childhood is associated with being separated from one's mother or other familiar caregivers. This fear, called separation protest, tends to peak in western infants at about 15 months and displays a remarkably similar timetable in such diverse cultures as those of Guatemala and the Kalahari Desert region in Botswana. As we will see later in the chapter, separation protest also occurs in infants in child care when working parents drop them off at a child-care centre. Although *separation anxiety*, as this fear is also called, generally becomes less and less common in childhood, it sometimes reappears in other forms. Box 7-1 describes a study of homesickness among children at camp and suggests some useful ways of coping with this kind of distress.

Applied Developmental Psychology

BOX 7-1 Coping with homesickness

Homesickness, which is common in the middle and later childhood years, usually arises when children are away from home for periods of more than a day. Summer camps, boarding schools, colleges, foster homes and hospitals are among the sites in which researchers have studied homesickness in children (Thurber & Weisz, 1997). Homesickness – a longing to be with one's family or regular caregivers – may be expressed in depressive or anxious behaviour; in acting up, as in aggressive behaviour; or in complaints about physiological problems, such as headache, stomach ache and other pains of an ill-defined nature.

How do children cope with homesickness? According to Thurber and Weisz (1997), a child's beliefs about his ability to exert control over a situation strongly determine his choice of coping mechanism. If a child who is sent to live with relatives because of economic distress at home believes he can change his situation, he may exert primary control by running away from his aunt's house and returning to his own home. Often, however, a child is unable to change his situation or finds that attempts to do so are unsuccessful and lead only to feelings of helplessness and depression. In this event, a child may instead elect secondary control, changing himself or his behaviour to adapt to the unwanted situation. Thus, a child placed in a boarding school many miles from home might write letters home every day to feel in touch with his family, or he might join specific activities in which he had participated at home. A third way of dealing with homesickness is to relinquish control, or to give up trying to change things and seek solace in expressing sadness through a means such as crying or withdrawing from others.

Because some stressors are controllable and others are not, coping is often a mix of primary and secondary measures, with the child trying first one and then another. The choice of coping measure depends on the specific constraints of the situation, such as camp rules, as well as on individual characteristics, such as age, perceived ability to control events, and cognitive sophistication.

To study homesickness, Thurber and Weisz (1997) chose two summer camps, one for girls and one for boys, and found that, overall, both boys and girls tended to use secondary control methods to cope with homesickness, most often doing something that was fun in order to forget their negative feelings. Among these youngsters, who ranged in age between 8 and 16 but who were on average 12.5, the most homesick were those most likely to relinquish control, making little effort to cope with their unhappiness. On the other hand, the least homesick were those who appeared to know how to use different combinations of both primary and secondary methods to cope with their unpleasant feelings; this group was also the least likely to relinquish control.

Girls were more likely to call upon specific coping devices than were boys. However, there was also a significant gender difference in respect to the use of the primary control device of seeking out 'someone who could talk with me and help me feel better, like a leader or one of my friends'. Although 8- to 10-year-old boys and girls differed little on this parameter, from 11 on, girls were far more likely than boys to use this social support approach to solving the problem of homesickness (Figure 7-4). As we have suggested earlier in the book, and will discuss at greater length in Chapter 13, girls seem to be more socially orientated from early on.

Thurber and Weisz (1997) conclude that useful intervention in homesickness involves helping children to understand that being homesick isn't just an unhappy emotion but an emotional reaction to circumstances, some of which they can control and some of which they can't. It is important to help children distinguish these components of the problem and to help them develop specific coping methods at both the primary and secondary levels. Then one can show children how to apply each type for maximum benefit and help them understand why relinquishing control is not effective.

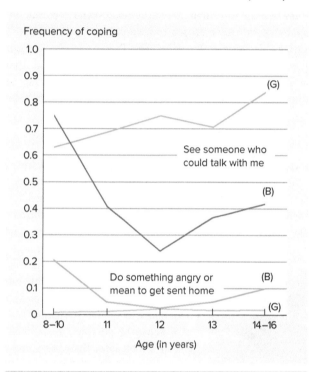

Figure 7-4   Coping with homesickness
When they were homesick at camp, both girls (G) and boys (B) preferred to talk with someone about it rather than act up in the hope of being sent home. However, this trend was much stronger in girls than boys.
Source: Adapted from Thurber and Weiss (1997).

Alongside fear, other common negative emotions are *anger* and *sadness*. Young infants' emotional expressions are clearly the same as what seem to be analogous adult expressions and it may not even be the case that infants are expressing the same sets of feelings. For example, what looks like anger in a baby may actually represent a generalized state of distress (Camras et al., 1991; Saarni et al., 2006). Izard, a pioneer in the study of infant emotion, holds that newborns do express specific emotions (Izard, 1994; Izard et al., 1995). According to Izard, the first negative expressions to appear are *startle, disgust* (as in response to bitter tastes) and *distress* (in response to pain) that seem unrelated to external events. However, Izard proposes, not until babies are about 2.5 or 3 months old do they begin reliably to display facial expressions of anger, interest, surprise and sadness (Izard et al., 1995). For example, although few 1 month olds show anger expressions when their arms are gently restrained, by the time infants are 4 to 7 months old, some 56% show clear expressions of anger at this restriction (Stenberg & Campos, 1989). These kinds of early emotions are probably influenced at the outset by genetic-maturational factors. Over time, learning and functional perspectives come into play.

Not unlike adults, infants usually display anger in response to particular external events (Sroufe, 1996; Saarni et al., 2006). For example, researchers have evoked anger in 7 month olds by offering them a teething biscuit and then withdrawing it just before it reaches the baby's mouth (Stenberg, Campos, & Emde, 1983). Two month olds respond with a distress expression to being inoculated by a physician, whereas 6-month-old babies respond to the same stimulus with an expression of anger (Izard, Hembree, & Huebner, 1987). It seems that babies respond to emotional provocations in predictable ways at specific ages (Denham et al., 2007), and anger is elicited by pain and frustration.

Sadness, too, is a reaction to pain, hunger or lack of control, but it occurs less often than anger. Babies become sad when there are breakdowns in parent–infant communication. For example, when a usually responsive caregiver ceases to respond to the babies' social overtures, the infant will exhibit distress and sadness (Weinberg & Tronick, 1998; Tronick et al., 2005). In older infants, separation from their mothers or other familiar caregivers can lead to sadness as well. Again, just as we saw with positive emotions, anger and sadness are effective emotional signals for eliciting care and comfort from adults and therefore serve an important function that evolutionary psychologists believe serves to promote the infant's survival.

The development of secondary emotions

To appropriately display more complex emotions, such as pride, shame, guilt and jealousy, a child requires the ability to differentiate and integrate the roles of multiple factors in a situation, including the role of personal responsibility. Often called secondary, or 'self-conscious', emotions because they rely on the development of self-awareness, these emotions begin to emerge towards the middle of the second year (Tangney & Fischer, 1995; Saarni, 1999; Saarni et al., 2006). For example, children may show embarrassment by blushing and turning away, and they may express envy or jealousy by pouting or crossing their arms when other children

receive more desirable toys (Lewis, 1995; Lewis & Ramsey, 2002). When children are pleased with their accomplishments, they show pride, but when they perceive that someone finds them wanting or deficient – perhaps having failed an easy task – they may show evidence of shame. The feeling of guilt, which requires the development of a sense of personal responsibility and the internalization of moral standards, emerges a bit later than pride and shame (Tangney, 1998).

A sense of the differences between 'easy' and 'difficult', and between 'success' and 'failure', is crucial for distinguishing between children's experiences of *pride* or *shame* (Lewis, 2000). Lewis and his colleagues (Lewis, 1992; Lewis, Alessandri, & Sullivan, 1992) found that, by the time they were 3 years old, children were more likely to express pride if they succeeded at difficult tasks than at easy ones. They also expressed more shame if they failed an easy task but expressed little if any shame if they failed a difficult task. Solving a problem that was not particularly difficult elicited joy in these youngsters, but succeeding on a difficult task produced pride. Failing a difficult task caused sadness, but failing an easy task aroused shame.

Shame and pride are both complex emotions that require additional abilities in a child, not least the ability to understand personal responsibility.
© Shutterstock/Onjira Leibe (T);
© Shutterstock/iofoto (B)

Children's understanding of pride also depends on their ability to entertain multiple emotions – such as pleasure at doing a task well and happiness that others appreciate the accomplishment (Saarni et al., 2006) – and on their sense of personal agency or effort. To evaluate this understanding, Thompson (1989) told stories to 7, 10 and 18 year olds involving accomplishments that individuals achieved either by their own efforts or by luck, and then asked them questions about the stories. The 7 year olds used the term proud in discussing good outcomes regardless of whether the actors in the stories had succeeded through their own efforts. More discriminating, the 10 and 18 year olds realized that 'feeling proud' can occur only when the good outcomes that occur are the result of a person's own effort, not of luck or chance.

It is only gradually that children develop an appreciation of the central role of personal responsibility in their behaviour and thus an understanding of *guilt*. According to Graham, Doubleday, and Guarino (1984), this understanding emerges in middle childhood. Asking 6- and 9-year-old children to describe situations in which they had felt guilty, these researchers found that only the older children had a clear understanding of this emotion and its relation to personal responsibility. Even when they had little control over the outcome of a situation, 6 year olds often described themselves as feeling guilty – so, for example, harm caused by an accident leads to a sense of guilt in a younger child. In contrast, 9 year olds recognized that, to feel guilty, it is critical to be responsible for the outcome of a situation, so the intentions of the actor are important. Young children focus on simple outcomes, whereas older children understand that unless they themselves caused the outcome they need not feel guilty. A sense of shame and guilt also plays an important role in moral development, especially in terms of regulating behaviour.

Jealousy can occur as early as 1 year of age. In one study, children showed signs of jealousy (e.g., sadness, seeking maternal attention, anger) when mothers directed their attention away from their child towards an infant-size doll, a newborn infant or a peer (Case et al., 1988; Hart et al., 1998). Jealousy is a social emotion; it occurs among three people who have established important social relationships. Generally speaking, two people who have been friends for many years don't experience jealousy in interacting with a new acquaintance.

Volling, McElwain, and Miller (2002) explored jealousy among younger (12 months old) and older (2 to 6 years old) children. When mothers or fathers played with one child and encouraged her or his sibling to play alone, both younger and older children expressed jealousy of the sibling who received parental attention. Not surprisingly, the way that children express their jealousy changes across development. Volling and colleagues found that, in response to a jealousy-provoking scenario, younger children displayed distress, whereas older siblings showed sadness and anger. And jealousy reactions are costly: children who react with jealousy may be less able to focus on their play activities than children who show less jealousy. As in the case of other complex emotions, such as pride and shame, cognitive understanding of emotions helps modify children's jealous reactions. Especially in older siblings, a more sophisticated understanding of emotions may be associated with less jealousy and less disturbed behaviour.

CHILDREN'S UNDERSTANDING OF THEIR OWN AND OTHERS' EMOTIONS

Recognizing emotions in others

A significant developmental challenge for the child is to learn how to recognize the emotions that other people express. According to Malatesta (1982), between the ages of 3 and 6 months, babies are exposed to others' facial expressions some 32,000 times. Learning to interpret these expressions of emotion is a formidable task for an infant, but during this peak period for face-to-face interaction, facial expressions are an effective way for parents to communicate their feelings and wishes to a child who cannot yet understand speech.

The joy–anger recognition sequence is also consistent with the course of the infant's own emotional displays. As we saw earlier, smiling and laughter emerge before fear (LaFreniere, 2000). Review the Chronology of Development chart on page 172 for an emotional development time frame.

Children, of course, become more discriminating as they develop; 9 to 10 year olds can discriminate between Duchenne (or authentic) smiles and non-Duchenne smiles more reliably than can 6 to 7 year olds (Gosselin et al., 2002). Others suggest that adults are even better than children in recognizing Duchenne smiles (Del Giudice & Colle, 2007).

The nature of early experience alters children's ability to recognize emotions, as the learning perspective on emotional development would predict. For example, 3.5-month-old infants recognize their mothers' emotional expressions earlier than they recognize such expressions in either fathers or strangers. Moreover, when mothers spent more time interacting directly with their babies, their infants were more successful at recognizing their mothers' emotional expressions (Montague & Walker-Andrews, 2002). However, both the quality and the quantity of interactions between parents and infants make a difference in children's ability to recognize emotions. Abused children who experience high levels of threat and hostility are able to identify anger expressions more easily than children who have not been abused, but are less capable of detecting expressions of sadness (Pollak & Sinha, 2002). The early family environment clearly plays a role in shaping children's abilities to recognize emotions. And culture matters, too. Both Mexican and Chinese children were better than either Euro-American or Australian children in recognizing vocal and/or facial emotional expressions (Cole & Tan, 2007). Both China and Mexico are societies that value group harmony, and a focus on others' feelings is one way to achieve this goal.

It is probably harder for babies to learn to recognize expressions of emotions in others than it is for them to learn to express emotions accurately themselves. Citing the fact that around the world people use similar facial expressions of emotion, some researchers believe that the production of these expressions is, at least in part, genetically determined (Ekman, 1994; Izard, 1994). If this were so, it would help to explain also why both babies and children are more accurate at producing emotional expressions than at interpreting them (Field, 1990; Denham, 1998; Denham et al., 2007). Nevertheless, by the time they are 2 or 3, children show production and recognition skills that are positively correlated: toddlers who send clear emotional signals also tend to be good at identifying emotions (Magai & McFadden, 1995). Both these abilities continue to improve with age, probably contributing to the older child's ability to participate more often and more successfully in peer group activities as well as to his more sustained and sophisticated social interactions (Saarni et al., 2006; Denham et al., 2007).

Emotional regulation and emotional display rules

Learning how to regulate the expression of their emotions is a major challenge for infants and children (Cole, Martin, & Dennis, 2004; Saarni et al., 2006; Thompson, 2006a). In this section, we trace the developmental changes in emotional regulation and shifts in children's use of display rules that govern expression of emotions.

Often, humans get their first clue from something they began learning even before they were born: they found that putting their thumbs in their mouths helps soothe them. From this unintentional act of control, infants move to the more deliberate regulation of their emotions. For example, when they encounter a frightening event, they may turn away, place their hands over their faces, or distract themselves by some form of play (Bridges & Grolnick, 1995). Children's methods of emotional control continue to change as they grow older. Mangelsdorf, Shapiro, and Marzolf (1995) found that 6 month olds who confronted a stranger typically looked away or became fussy, whereas 18 month olds were more likely to use self-soothing and self-distraction to cope with uncertain or arousing situations.

As infants become toddlers and in turn preschoolers, parents and others typically require them to exert even more control over how they express their emotions. This greater self-control over emotions is evident in several ways: emotional expressions become less frequent, less distinct, less intense and exaggerated, and less variable and more conventionalized (LaFreniere, 2000; Saarni et al., 2006). For example, a hungry baby may cry in uncontrollable frustration, whereas an older child whose mealtime is delayed will merely pout and complain. Adolescents may employ yet more complex ways of expressing their displeasure (Morris et al., 2017). And emotional regulation abilities are important predictions of later adjustment (Fox & Calkins, 2003). Children in preschool who were better at regulating their anger showed less externalizing behaviour when they entered school; those who were able to distract themselves by shifting attention away from the frustrating situation were less aggressive and disruptive in kindergarten (Gilliom et al., 2002).

At the same time, children begin to learn emotional display rules that dictate what emotions to show under what circumstances. This often means learning to separate the visible expression of an emotion from its inner experience. Conforming to various social norms, children 8 to 10 years old learn to smile even when they feel unhappy, to feign distress that is not really felt, or to mask amusement when they know they shouldn't laugh (Garner & Power, 1996; Saarni et al., 2006). But children as young as 2 may show an understanding of display rules for emotions (Lewis & Michaelson, 1985). In their earliest attempts to follow these rules, children typically mirror others' behaviour by

emotional display rules Rules that dictate which emotions one may appropriately display in particular situations.

simply exaggerating or minimizing their emotional displays. Moreover, children acquire knowledge about display rules before they are proficient regulators of their own emotional displays (Saarni, 1999).

Perhaps unsurprisingly, culture plays a very important role in how children appraise situations, communicate emotions and act on their feelings. Studying three cultural groups – Brahman and Tamang societies in rural Nepal, and a rural town in the United States – Cole, Bruschi, and Tamang (2002) compared the reactions of children to difficult, emotionally arousing situations. They interviewed children about how they would react to a difficult interpersonal situation, such as someone spilling a drink on their homework or accusing them falsely of stealing. Among the Tamang, a Buddhist group who endorse interpersonal harmony, children were more likely than the other two groups to respond to difficult situations with shame. In contrast, children of the Brahman society, which teaches self-control in social interactions and the careful control of emotions, did not reveal anger or shame in response to their emotionally upsetting problem. Different again were the American children, who were more likely to endorse the display of anger. Clearly, cultural and religious customs and values shape the ways that children react to emotionally upsetting events. Learning to follow cultural display rules appears to be an important developmental accomplishment. It seems that competence in implementing these rules is linked with better social relationships with peers (Parke et al., 2005; Valiente & Eisenberg, 2006).

BOX 7-2   Do young children understand the use of false facial expressions when they are used to manipulate other people's evaluations of a person?

Research close-up

Source: Based on Banerjee and Yuill (1999).

Introduction:

Children as young as 3 years are able to mask negative emotions and, by 6 years, they are able to understand that the emotions people show are not always the same as they are really feeling. People may hide their emotions for different reasons. One reason may be prosocial – that is, they do not want to hurt another person's feelings. A second reason is self-presentational; they may want to control other people's evaluation of them to preserve their self-esteem. For example, they may put on a brave face after being hurt, to avoid looking like a cry-baby. Banerjee and Yuill argued that the different motives for using false facial expressions required different levels of cognitive understanding. Prosocial display rules only require an appreciation that an individual's expressive behaviour affects the emotions of another person. However, self-presentational display rules require an understanding that the individual intends to manipulate the way he or she is evaluated by others. This requires an understanding of second-order representations – the ability to understand or appreciate that other people have intentions or differing perceptions from you. Second-order representations develop at around 5 years of age. The present study was carried out by Banerjee and Yuill to test the hypothesis that there is an association between understanding second-order mental states and comprehending self-presentational display rules, but no such relation with prosocial display rules.

Method:

Sixty-seven children, aged between 4 and 6 years, participated in this study. Each child heard eight different stories, each accompanied by a series of three pictures. In three of the stories, the aim of the protagonist was to conceal their feelings for prosocial reasons. For example, in one story children were told about a child who was having a birthday, and a relative gives an unwanted gift. Children were asked how the child should look if s/he wanted to conceal their disappointment from the relative. In a further three stories, the aim was to conceal their feelings for self-presentation reasons; for example, a story about a child who concealed that s/he was upset after being hurt when playing a game with older children. In two stories, the protagonist aimed to show their true feelings (to help assess children's general emotion awareness).

After the child had heard the story and the aim of the protagonist, they were asked to choose a picture showing the facial expression that the protagonist should have. They were also asked questions to assess their understanding of the situation. Finally, children completed a second-order false-belief task in which they listened to another story and answered questions about the beliefs of the characters involved.

Results:

Children who passed the second-order false-belief task performed significantly better in understanding the self-presentational display rule stories than those who didn't; however, there was no such effect of second-order false-belief task performance on prosocial display rule performance. However, even children who did not pass the second-order false-belief task were good at understanding what the audience would believe from the facial expression shown. The researchers also found that performance was better if the motivation in the self-presentational stories was phrased negatively ('he wanted to avoid looking stupid') rather than positively ('he wanted to look clever').

Discussion:

As predicted, this study showed that children need to develop a comprehension of second-order representations before they can understand the motivation behind self-presentation display rules. However, even without this understanding, they are able to understand the effect of this type of display rule. They do not need this cognitive comprehension to be able to understand the motivation underlying prosocial display rules. The finding that children seem to understand negatively phrased motivations better than those that are positively phrased is interesting; it suggests that our motivation in using self-presentational false facial expressions is to avoid making a bad impression rather than to impress.

Cognition and emotion

Not only do children act on their emotions, but they also think about those emotions as well. As children develop, there are shifts in the ways they express their emotions. With age, children acquire a more complete understanding of the meanings of emotion terms and of the situations that evoke different kinds of feelings.

> **emotional script**
> A complex scheme that enables a child to identify the emotional reaction likely to accompany a particular sort of event.

According to Saarni et al. (2006), this understanding can be seen as a collection of emotional scripts, or complex schemes that enable the child to identify the type of emotional reaction likely to accompany a particular kind of event.

From a young age, children create a number of such emotional scripts. In a classic study, Borke (1971) told 3- and 4-year-old children simple stories about such things as getting lost in the woods or having a fight or going to a party, and asked the children to tell her the emotions they thought the characters in the different stories would be likely to feel. The children easily identified situations that would lead to happiness, and they were reasonably good at identifying stories that were linked with sadness or anger. Other research (Levine, 1995; Cole & Tan, 2007) showed that 3- and 4-year-old children could also describe situations that evoked other emotions, such as excitement, surprise and fear. Clearly, even young children can often know which primary emotions go with which situations.

Children's emotional scripts gain in complexity as they mature. For example, 5 year olds generally understand only those situations that lead to emotions with a recognizable facial display (e.g., anger, displayed in frowning) or that lead to a particular kind of behaviour (e.g., sadness, displayed in crying or moping about). By the time they are 7, however, children can describe situations that elicit more complicated emotions with no obvious facial or behavioural expressions, such as pride, jealousy, worry and guilt. And by the time they reach 10 or 14, children can describe situations that elicit relief and disappointment (Harris et al., 1987). A similar developmental sequence is found in a variety of cultures, including Great Britain, the United States, the Netherlands and Nepal, although there are cultural differences in the content of emotions and responses to different situations (Harris, 1989, 1995).

Another aspect of emotional understanding that develops only gradually is the awareness that one can have more than one feeling at a time and that one can even experience two or more conflicting feelings at the same time. Although toddlers and even young infants show signs of experiencing conflicting feelings, children's ability to understand and express their knowledge of emotions emerges slowly and lags well behind their capacity to experience ambivalent emotions (Arsenio & Kramer, 1992; Wintre & Vallance, 1994; Pons, Harris, & deRosnay, 2004). According to Harter (Harter & Buddin, 1987; Harter, 2006), children show a clear developmental sequence in their ability to understand multiple and conflicting feelings. From their study of children between the ages of 4 and 12, Harter and Buddin (1987) derived the five stages of emotional understanding shown in Table 7-2. As you can see, it is not until the fourth stage, at about the age of 10, that children acquire the ability to conceive of opposite feelings existing simultaneously.

Table 7-2   Children's understanding of multiple and conflicting emotions

Approximate ages	Children's capabilities
4 to 6	Conceive of only one emotion at a time: 'You can't have two feelings at the same time.'
6 to 8	Begin to conceive of two emotions of the same type occurring simultaneously: 'I was happy and proud that I hit a home run.' 'I was upset and mad when my sister messed up my things.'
8 to 9	Describe two distinct emotions in response to different situations at the same time: 'I was bored because there was nothing to do and mad because my mom punished me.'
10	Describe two opposing feelings where the events are different or different aspects of the same situation: 'I was sitting in school worrying about the next soccer game but happy that I got an A in math.' 'I was mad at my brother for hitting me but glad my dad let me hit him back.'
11 to 12	Understand that the same event can cause opposing feelings: 'I was happy that I got a present but disappointed that it wasn't what I wanted.'

Source: Based on Harter and Buddin (1987); Harter (2006).

As they develop, children learn to consider more and more aspects of an emotion-related situation, such as the desires, goals and intentions of the people involved. Children realize that people's emotional expressions are produced by inner states and that these expressions are not responsive solely to the characteristics of the situation. For example, young children often get angry when someone thwarts, wrongs or frustrates them, regardless of whether the wrongful act was intentional, but children 7 years and older, like adults, tend to reserve their anger for situations in which they think a person intended to upset them (Levine, 1995).

> Being able to control and regulate emotions is important for the control of aggression, which we discuss in Chapter 14.

Family and peer influences on emotional development

Families play a major role in children's emotional development. Denham (1998) outlined three ways in which families influence children's emotions. First, family members' own patterns of emotional expressiveness serve as models for the child's emotional expressiveness. Second, parents' and siblings' specific reactions to children's emotions encourage or discourage certain patterns of emotional expressiveness. Third, parents often act as 'emotional coaches' by talking about emotions, and explaining and exploring children's understanding of their own and other people's emotional responses.

Families vary in their emotional expressiveness. Some are subdued and restrained in their emotional reactions; others are more demonstrative and engage in more intense and frequent emotional displays. Many studies have shown similarities between parents and their children in both level of emotional expressiveness and types of emotion typically displayed (Eisenberg, Zhou, & Koller, 2001; Halberstadt, Denham, & Dunsmore, 2001). Children who grow up in a positive emotional home with lots of happiness and joy are more likely to exhibit positive emotions (Halberstadt et al., 2001). However, children reared in a negative family environment characterized by hostility and conflict are more likely to display negative emotions, such as anger and sadness (Halberstadt et al., 2001; Denham et al., 2007).

Children whose parents help them with their emotions are better able to manage emotional upset on their own and are also more accepted by their peers (Gottman et al., 1996). When parents are punitive or dismissive of their children's emotions, the children are hampered in regulating their own emotions (McDowell & Parke, 2000; Parke et al., 2005; Valiente & Eisenberg, 2006). Dismissive parents may belittle the child's emotion or show little interest in how the child is feeling. Punitive parents may scold or punish their child for expressing emotions, especially negative ones such as anger or sadness. Dismissive or punitive parents 'fail to use emotional moments as a chance to get closer to the child or to help the child learn lessons in emotional competence' (Goleman, 1995, p. 191).

Parents who are good emotional coaches value emotional expression, are aware of their own emotions, and are willing to help their children with theirs. Help often takes the form of talking about feelings, for children whose parents discuss emotions are better at taking the perspective or viewpoint of others and at understanding their own and others' emotions. For example, Dunn and her colleagues (Dunn, Brown, & Maguire, 1995; Dunn & Hughes, 1998) found that 3-year-old children's conversations with their mothers and siblings about feeling states were closely related to the same children's ability, at the age of 6, to understand other people's emotions. Children from families in which there was more discussion of feelings were better able to recognize others' emotions than children raised in families in which feelings were less often discussed (Dunn, 2004). In general, the better a child understands emotions, the more skilled he is at such social behaviours as problem solving and conflict resolution, and the more likely he is to be accepted by peers and to form and maintain friendships (Parke & O'Neil, 2000; Dunn, 2004; Denham et al., 2007).

In a similar vein, Morris et al. (2017) argues that parents are important for developing children's emotion regulation skills through observation of parents' own emotion regulation, emotion-related parenting practices (such as discussing feelings and resolving conflicts), and the broader emotional climate of the family. Additionally, parenting may influence the neural circuitry of the developing brain into adolescence which can act as a protective force or source of vulnerability in dealing with emotions inside and outside of the family environment. In adolescence, there is heightened sensitivity to social and emotional information; not only does the social and emotional landscape for the individual change but there is increasing evidence that neural mechanisms may be implicated in responses to others' emotion expression and to psychopathology (e.g., Rosen et al., 2018).

It is important to remember that not only parents but also peers and siblings function as socializers of emotion. When children display anger, their peers often respond with anger or rejection (Fabes et al., 1996; Denham et al., 2007). Similarly, siblings often shape children's emotional reactions by their positive or negative responses or by alerting a parent to their siblings' angry emotional outbursts (Dunn, 1988, 2004; Denham et al., 2007). Interactions with siblings also contribute to a child's development of emotional understanding. Pretend play with siblings or friends, often characterized by conflict and other intense emotional experiences, is associated with increased understanding of other people's feelings and beliefs (Dunn & Hughes, 2001).

ATTACHMENT

attachment A strong emotional bond that forms between infant and caregiver in the second half of the child's first year.

The development of attachment, a strong emotional bond that forms in the second half of the first year between an infant and one or more of the child's regular caregivers, is closely related to emotional development. Visible signs of attachment are the warm greetings a child gives their parents when they approach, smiling broadly, active efforts to make contact when picked up, touching a parent's face and snuggling close. Attachment can also be seen in a child's efforts to stay near their parents in an unfamiliar situation, crawling or running to them and holding on to a leg. Attachment can also be seen in the distress that older babies show when their parents leave them temporarily; its negative counterpart is expressed in the separation protest discussed earlier.

The emergence of attachment is one of the developmental milestones in the first year of life. It is of great interest to researchers not only because it is so intense and dramatic but also because it is thought to enhance the parents' effectiveness in the later socialization of their children. Children who have developed an attachment to their parents presumably want to maintain their parents' affection and approval and so are motivated to adopt the standards of behaviour the parents set for them.

Attachment is a widely studied topic and we begin this section with several theories of why attachment develops, including psychoanalytic, learning and ethological theories. We next look at the way attachment evolves over the first two years of life, and then consider the special characteristics of attachment to fathers and to peers. In the last section of the chapter, we discuss variations in the quality of attachment and in the consequences of such variations.

Theories of attachment

A variety of theories have been offered to explain the development of attachment, including psychoanalytic, learning, and ethological theories. Each position makes different assumptions about the variables that are important for the development of attachment and about the processes underlying the development of an attachment relationship.

According to Freud's classic psychoanalytic theory of attachment, babies become attached to their caregivers because the caregivers are associated with gratification of the infant's innate drive to obtain pleasure through sucking and other forms of oral stimulation. This argument from traditional psychoanalytic theory, focusing on innate drives and pleasure-seeking, is generally not supported by research evidence. However, the theory's emphasis on a person's inner needs and feelings, and its focus on mother–infant interaction remain important influences in the study of infant attachment. Although specific Freudian interpretations may be seen as fanciful nowadays, the contribution of psychoanalytic work lies in helping to open up ground for research in the area.

> **psychoanalytic theory of attachment** Freud's theory that babies become attached first to the mother's breast and then to the mother herself as a source of oral gratification.
>
> **learning theory of attachment** The theory that infants become attached to their mothers because a mother provides food, or primary reinforcement, and thus becomes a secondary reinforcer.
>
> **secondary reinforcer** A person or other stimulus that acquires reinforcing properties by virtue of repeated association with a primary reinforcer.

There has also been recent work that has sought to demonstrate concordance between neuroscience and psychoanalytic approaches. Although there do appear to be some associations between some brain processes and adult attachment style (e.g., Birnbaum & Reis, 2019; Young & Wang, 2004) these may be associated with orientations towards adult relationships and their developmental significance is not well understood. While not well understood, how far childhood experiences affect neural functioning (and vice versa) or connections is a potentially fertile field for further study, although how far these may connect with traditional psychoanalytic approaches remains an open question (Fonagy, 2018).

Other theories are better supported by empirical evidence. Like psychoanalytic theory, the learning theory of attachment has traditionally associated the formation of mother–infant attachment with the mother's reduction of the baby's primary drive of hunger. Because the mother provides the infant with food, a *primary reinforcer*, she herself becomes a secondary reinforcer. Presumably, this ability to satisfy the baby's hunger forms the basis for infant attachment to the mother or any other caregiver linked to feeding.

Many studies, however, have challenged the view that feeding is critical for the development of attachment. In what is probably the most famous of these, Harlow separated infant monkeys from their real mothers and raised them in the company of two surrogate mothers. One 'mother' was made of stiff wire and had a feeding bottle attached to it; the other was made of soft terrycloth but lacked a bottle (Harlow & Zimmerman, 1959). Especially in moments of stress, the baby monkeys preferred to cling to the cloth mother, even though she dispensed no food. Attachment to this surrogate mother clearly did not require the reduction of hunger.

Research on humans tells a similar story. Schaffer and Emerson (1964) found that babies formed attachments to their fathers and other frequently seen adults who played little or no role in the child's feeding. They found that babies whose mothers were relatively unresponsive and distant, except for routine physical care, but whose fathers were attentive and stimulating tended to form paternal attachments, even though they actually spent more time with their mothers.

The central point of the learning theory explanation is that attachment is not automatic; it develops over time as a result of satisfying interactions with responsive adults. Some learning theorists suggest that the visual, auditory and tactile stimulation that adults provide in the course of their daily interactions with an infant are the basis for the development of attachment (Gewirtz, 1969). According to this view, babies are initially attracted to their regular caregivers because they are the most important and reliable sources of this type of stimulation. As interactions with these caregivers continue over weeks and months, infants learn to depend on and to value these special adults in their lives, becoming attached to them.

cognitive developmental view of attachment
The view that to form attachments infants must differentiate between mother and stranger, and understand that people exist independent of the infant's interaction with them.

ethological theory of attachment Bowlby's theory that attachment derives from the biological preparation of both infant and parents to respond to one another's behaviours in such a way that parents provide the infant with care and protection.

imprinting The process by which birds and other infrahuman animals develop a preference for the person or object to which they are first exposed during a brief, critical period after birth.

Cognitive developmental approaches suggest that, before specific attachments can occur, the infant not only must be able to differentiate between her mother and a stranger but also must be aware that people still exist even when she cannot see them. That is, she must have developed what Piaget terms *object permanence*, or the knowledge that objects, including people, have a continuous existence apart from her own interaction with them.

Advances in the infant's cognitive development may also account, in part, for the gradual shift in the ways attachment is expressed. Physical proximity to attachment figures becomes less important as children grow older. With age, children become increasingly able to maintain psychological contact with a parent through verbal and non-verbal communication. In addition, because they are also better able to understand that parental absences are sometimes necessary and usually temporary, they are less upset by separations. Parents can reduce their children's distress over separations further by explaining the reasons for their departures. In one study, for instance, 2 year olds handled separation from their mothers much better when the mothers gave them clear information ('I'm going out now for just a minute, but I'll be right back') than when the mother left without a word (Weinraub & Lewis, 1977).

Another approach that has emphasized the reciprocal nature of the attachment process is John Bowlby's **ethological theory of attachment** (1958, 1969, 1973). Both evolutionary theory and observational studies of animals helped shape this theory, and an important early demonstration of the value of the ethological approach was provided by Lorenz's (1952) classic studies of **imprinting**, see Chapter 2. Bowlby suggested that attachment has its roots in a set of instinctual infant responses that are important for the protection and survival of the species. The infant responses of crying, smiling, sucking, clinging and following (visually at first, and later physically) both elicit the parental care and protection that the baby needs and promote contact between the child and the parents. Just as the infant is biologically prepared to respond to the sights, sounds and nurturing provided by the parents, so the parents are biologically prepared to respond to the baby's behaviour. As a result of these biologically pre-programmed responses, both parent and infant develop a mutual attachment.

The value of Bowlby's position lies in its emphasis on the active role in the formation of attachment played by the infant's early social signalling systems, such as smiling and crying. Another attractive feature is the theory's stress on the development of mutual attachment, whereby both partners, not just one, become bonded to each other (Cassidy, 1999; Thompson, 2006a). From this perspective, attachment is a relationship, not simply a behaviour of either the infant or the parent (Sroufe et al., 2005). More controversial is Bowlby's suggestion that these early behaviours are biologically programmed. As we have seen, for example, there is considerable evidence that smiling has social as well as biological origins.

The development of attachment

Attachment does not develop suddenly and unheralded, but rather emerges in a series of steps, moving from a baby's general preference for human beings to inanimate objects to a child's real partnership with its parents. Schaffer (1996) proposes four phases in the development of attachment; these are outlined in Table 7-3.

Table 7-3   Phases in the development of attachment

	Age range (months)	Principal features
1. Preattachment	0–2	Indiscriminate social responsiveness
2. Attachment-in-the making	2–7	Recognition of familiar people
3. Clear-cut attachment	7–24	Separation protest; wariness of strangers; intentional communication
4. Goal-corrected partnership	24 on	Relationships more two-sided: children understand parents' needs

Source: Social Development, Schaffer © 1996. Reproduced with permission of John Wiley & Sons, Inc.

In the first phase, which lasts only a month or two, the baby's social responses are relatively indiscriminate. In the second phase, the baby gradually learns to distinguish familiar from unfamiliar people. As you learned in Chapter 5, even very young infants can distinguish their mothers' faces, voices, and even smells from those of other women. However, although a baby under 6 months of age can discriminate between their mother and other caregivers, and prefers familiar caregivers to strangers, they do not yet protest when familiar caregivers depart; the baby is not yet truly attached to these people.

In the third phase, which begins when the baby is about 7 months old, specific attachments develop. Now the infant actively seeks contact with certain regular caregivers, such as the mother, greeting them happily and often crying when those people temporarily depart. The baby does not behave like this with just anyone – only to *specific* attachment figures. When the child passes the 2-year mark and enters toddlerhood (from about 2 to 5), the attachment relationship moves into the final phase – the so-called goal-corrected partnership (Bowlby, 1969). At this point, owing to advances in cognitive development, children become aware of other people's feelings, goals and plans, and begin to consider these things in formulating their own actions. As Colin (1996) noted, 'the child becomes a partner in planning how the dyad will handle separations' (p. 72).

Infants develop attachments not only to their mothers but also to their fathers and to a variety of other persons with whom they regularly interact. When children are a little older, for example, they often develop attachments to siblings or other peers. Moreover, according to anthropologists (Weisner & Gallimore, 1977; Harkness & Super, 2002), mothers are exclusive caregivers in only about 3% of human societies. In as many as 40% of societies, mothers are not even the major caregivers. And, as we will see later, the quality of attachment relationships can vary greatly (Sroufe et al., 2005).

In one study, older babies showed similar patterns of attachment to their mothers and fathers in a situation in which a friendly but unfamiliar visitor observed the children in their homes with both parents present (Lamb, 1997, 2004). In this non-stressful situation, the babies showed no preference for either parent in their attachment behaviour. They were just as likely to touch, approach and be near their fathers as their mothers. In other, stressful situations, however, babies generally look to their mother for security and comfort if she is available (Belsky & Cassidy, 1994; Lamb, 1997, 2004). This is probably because the mother has most often served this role in the past.

In some cultures, particularly hunter-gatherer societies where the search for food and other necessities requires the efforts of both men and women, fathers may be more likely to share in child care. According to Hewlett (2004), fathers among the Aka, who live in the southern part of the Central African Republic and the northern reaches of the Democratic Republic of Congo, provide more direct care to their babies than fathers in any other known society. Among the Efe, however, another forager society, in Congo, child care is considered a woman's responsibility, and although Efe fathers spend a great deal of time with their infants, a relatively small percentage of that time goes into direct child care (Morelli & Tronick, 1992). Among the Agta, in Cagayan, Philippines, a hunter-gatherer society in which women and men share work and subsistence activities almost equally, mothers remain the primary caregivers (Griffin & Griffin, 1992; Lamb, 2004).

In many cultures, fathers have a special role in the infant's development – that of playmate. The quality of a father's play with a baby generally differs from a mother's: fathers engage in more unusual and physically arousing games (especially with their sons), whereas mothers tend to stimulate their babies verbally and to play quieter games such as peek-a-boo (Parke, 1996, 2002). Even when fathers have assumed the role of their babies' primary caregiver, they tend to display this physically arousing style of interaction (Field, 1978; Hwang, 1986). Although fathers in countries such as Australia, Great Britain and Israel spend four to five times more time playing with their infants than caring for them, apparently not all fathers engage in rough-and-tumble play with their children (Roopnarine, 2004). Fathers in India, Central Africa and Sweden are apparently less likely to engage in this style of play (Hewlett, 2004). Fathers who enter parenthood at a later age (over 35) tend to be less physical in their play than younger men (Neville & Parke, 1997).

Clearly, culture is important in shaping fathering roles, but biology may play a role in preparing men for their fatherhood role as well. Mothers, as well as fathers, undergo a variety of hormonal changes during pregnancy and childbirth that makes them sensitive to infant cries and primed for parenthood. Men experience changes in several hormones, including a drop in testosterone after the birth of the baby, when the father has the first opportunity to interact with his new offspring (Storey et al., 2000). Men with lower testosterone were more responsive to infant cues such as crying and held baby dolls longer than men who did not show these hormonal decreases (Fleming et al., 2002). These shifts are especially true for men who were closely involved with their wives during pregnancy, which suggests that intimate ties between partners during pregnancy may stimulate hormonal changes. This is an important reminder that hormones may alter social behaviour, but social relationships may modify hormonal levels as well.

Although infants' most significant attachment relationships are usually with fathers and mothers, a variety of other individuals are important in the infant's social world, including peers, siblings, and relatives such as grandparents, aunts and uncles (Berlin & Cassidy, 1999; Smith & Drew 2002). Peers can become important attachment figures, even for very young children. For example, one investigator found that in a preschool/kindergarten where some children were transferring to new schools, both those who were leaving and those who were staying behind experienced a variety of reactions, including increased fussiness, heightened activity level, illness and changes in eating and sleeping patterns (Field, 1986). These reactions were viewed as separation stress associated with the loss of familiar peers. As children reach adolescence, they develop attachment relationships with friends and with romantic partners (Furman et al., 2002; Collins & Van Dulman, 2006).

The nature and quality of attachment

Like most aspects of human development, the formation of early attachments is not uniform from one child to another or from one relationship to the next. Many children form what appear to be highly secure attachments. The important adults in their lives seem to serve as a source of support and affection that gives children confidence to explore the world and become more independent. For others, however, attachments seem much less secure and dependable. Researchers describe such variations as differences in the *quality* of attachments.

secure base According to Ainsworth, a caregiver to whom an infant has formed an attachment, and whom the child uses as a base from which to explore and as a safe haven in times of stress.

Strange Situation A testing scenario in which mother and child are separated and reunited several times; enables investigators to assess the nature and quality of a mother–infant attachment relationship.

Mary Ainsworth's studies, based on her concept of the *secure base* and using the so-called Strange Situation, have been replicated many times and in many parts of the world. She proposed that infants organize their attachment behaviour around a particular adult so that they seem to be using the adult as a secure base for exploration or a safe haven in the event of distress. Ainsworth made valuable observations of infants' attachment and exploratory behaviour at about 1 year of age (Ainsworth, 1973; Posada et al., 1995). The striking differences in the infants' behaviours in what is known as the Strange Situation, a carefully worked-out scenario in which a mother twice leaves her baby alone or with a stranger and returns twice to be reunited with her child (see Table 7-4), enabled Ainsworth to assess the infant–mother relationships, and to classify them according to their nature and quality. This procedure is typically used with infants at 8 or 9 months of age. Subsequent research both expanded on Ainsworth's work and added a longitudinal feature, comparing children's behaviour from infancy to young adulthood (Solomon & George, 1999; Main, Hesse, & Kaplan, 2005; Sroufe et al., 2005).

Table 7-5 summarizes four categories of attachment relationship: secure, insecure-avoidant, insecure-resistant and insecure-disorganized attachment. As we note here,

Table 7-4   The Strange Situation scenario

Episode number	Persons present	Duration	Brief description of actions
1	Mother, baby and observer	30 seconds	Observer introduces mother and baby to experimental room, then leaves. (Room contains many appealing toys scattered about.)
2	Mother and baby	3 minutes	Mother is non-participant while baby explores; if necessary, play is stimulated after 2 minutes.
3	Stranger, mother and baby	3 minutes	Stranger enters. First minute: stranger silent. Second minute: stranger converses with mother. Third minute: stranger approaches baby. After 3 minutes: mother leaves unobtrusively.
4	Stranger and baby	3 minutes or less	First separation episode. Stranger's behaviour is geared to that of baby.
5	Mother and baby	3 minutes or more	First reunion episode. Mother greets and/or comforts baby, then tries to settle the baby again in play. Mother then leaves, saying 'bye-bye'.
6	Baby alone	3 minutes or less	Second separation episode.
7	Stranger and baby	3 minutes or less	Continuation of second separation. Stranger enters and gears behaviour to that of baby.
8	Mother and baby	3 minutes	Second reunion episode. Mother enters, greets baby, then picks baby up. Meanwhile, stranger leaves unobtrusively.

Table 7-5   Children's attachment behaviour in the Strange Situation: a typology

1 YEAR OLD	6 YEARS OLD
Secure attachment	
On reunion after brief separation from parents, children seek physical contact, proximity, interaction; often try to maintain physical contact. Readily soothed by parents and return to exploration and play.	On reunion, children initiate conversation and pleasant interaction with parents or are highly responsive to parents' overtures. May subtly move close to or into physical contact with parents, usually with rationale such as seeking a toy. Remain calm throughout.
Insecure-avoidant attachment	
Children actively avoid and ignore parents on reunion, looking away and remaining occupied with toys. May move away from parents and ignore their efforts to communicate.	Children minimize and restrict opportunities for interaction with parents on reunion, looking and speaking only as necessary and remaining occupied with toys or activities. May subtly move away with rationale such as retrieving a toy.
Insecure-resistant attachment	
Although infants seem to want closeness and contact, their parents are not able effectively to alleviate their distress after brief separation. Child may show subtle or overt signs of anger, seeking proximity and then resisting it.	In movements, posture, and tones of voice, children seem to try to exaggerate both intimacy and dependence on parents. They may seek closeness but appear uncomfortable (e.g. lying in parent's lap but wriggling and squirming). These children sometimes show subtle signs of hostility.
Insecure-disorganized attachment	
Children show signs of disorganization (e.g. crying for parents at door and then running quickly away when door opens; approaching parent with head down) or disorientation (e.g. seeming to 'freeze' for a few seconds).	Children seem almost to adopt parental role with parents, trying to control and direct parents' behaviour either by embarrassing or humiliating parents or by showing extreme enthusiasm for reunion or overly solicitous behaviour towards parents.

Source: Adapted from Ainsworth et al. (1978); Main and Cassidy (1988); Main and Hesse (1990); Solomon and George (1999).

secure attachment
A kind of attachment displayed by babies who are secure enough to explore novel environments, who are minimally disturbed by brief separations from their mothers, and who are quickly comforted by their mothers when they return.

insecure-avoidant attachment A type of attachment shown by babies who seem not to be bothered by their mothers' brief absences but specifically avoid them on their return, sometimes becoming visibly upset.

insecure-resistant attachment A kind of attachment shown by babies who tend to become very upset at the departure of their mothers and who exhibit inconsistent behaviour on their return, sometimes seeking contact, sometimes pushing their mothers away.

insecure-disorganized attachment A type of attachment shown by babies who seem disorganized and disorientated when reunited with their mothers after a brief separation.

Attachment Q Sort (AQS) An assessment method in which a caregiver or observer judges the quality of a child's attachment based on the child's behaviour in naturalistic situations, often including brief separations from parents.

the importance of these classifications lies in their value in predicting differences in infants' and children's later emotional, social and cognitive development. Of the white, middle-class children studied, Ainsworth classified some 60% to 65% as displaying secure attachment to their mothers because they readily sought contact with her after the stress of her departure in an unfamiliar setting and were quickly comforted by her, even if initially quite upset. These babies also felt secure enough to explore a novel environment when the mother was present. They did not whine and cling to her but actively investigated their surroundings, as if the mother's presence gave them confidence. In familiar situations, such as the home, these children are minimally disturbed by minor separations from the mother, although they greet her happily when she returns.

Ainsworth classified the remaining children she studied as insecure in one of several ways. Exhibiting insecure-avoidant attachment were children who typically showed little distress over the mother's absence in the Strange Situation, at least on her first departure. However, these children actively avoided their mothers on their return: they turned away from mothers, increased their distance from them and paid them no attention. After the mother's second departure, during which time many of these babies became visibly upset, they again avoided her on her return. Later researchers found that this first insecure pattern typically characterizes about 20% of American samples.

A second type of insecure relationship is called insecure-resistant attachment. Researchers have found that infants who display this type of attachment (and who make up about 10% to 15% of American samples) often become extremely upset when the mother leaves them but are oddly ambivalent towards her when she returns. Intermittently, they seek contact with her and then angrily push her away.

The third type of insecure relationship, identified by later researchers, is called insecure-disorganized attachment (Solomon & George, 1999). When babies who display this kind of behaviour are reunited with their mothers in the Strange Situation scenario, they seem disorganized and disorientated. They look dazed, they freeze in the middle of their movements or they engage in repetitive behaviours, such as rocking. These children also seem apprehensive and fearful of their attachment figures, and are unable to cope in a consistent and organized way with distress in the presence of their caregivers. Note that all these attachment classifications reflect the quality of the relationship between the child and the parent, not traits of either the child or the parent. Interestingly, as Table 7-5 shows, similar child–parent relationship patterns can be observed in these children and parents when the children are 6 years old (Main & Cassidy, 1988).

New methods for assessing attachment have been developed in recent years. Relying on the judgements of caregivers who are familiar with the child's behaviour, the Attachment Q Sort (AQS) (Waters, 1995; Solomon & George, 1999; van IJzendoorn et al., 2004) calls for the mother or other caregiver to sort a set of cards containing phrases that describe the child's behaviour (e.g., 'rarely asks for help', 'keeps track of mother's location while playing around the house', 'quickly greets mother with a big smile when she enters the room') into sets ranging from those that are most descriptive of the child to those that are least descriptive. The method, which is useful for children between the ages of 1 and 5, was designed to facilitate making ratings, in naturalistic settings, of a broad variety of attachment-related behaviours (e.g., secure-base behaviour, attachment-exploration balance and affective responsiveness). Often used with older children (6–12 years) the Attachment Insecurity Screening Inventory (AISI) can be a helpful screening tool in pre-clinical settings (Spruit et al., 2018). As we will see later, other investigators (Solomon & George, 1999; Bretherton, 2005) have developed later-age assessments of attachment that closely resemble the Strange Situation and permit across-time comparisons between children in infancy and at later ages.

Finally, other innovative procedures for assessing attachment have been developed that do not rely on mother–child separations. The California Attachment Procedure (CAP) focuses on how mothers manage children's fear and upset in response to stressful events such as loud noises or a scary robot instead of maternal separations (Clarke-Stewart et al., 2000). This approach has been used with children at 18 months and more accurately classifies the attachment of children who are accustomed to routine separations from their parents, such those involved in child care.

BOX 7-3   Attachment types in different cultures

Applied Developmental Psychology

Can Ainsworth's Strange Situation be used across cultures to assess the character of children's relationships with their parents? If mothers and fathers in Norway encourage their young children to develop independence earlier than Italian parents, how may this affect the interpretation of 'avoidant' behaviour on a child's reunion with parental figures? A number of researchers have addressed these and other questions relating to the universality of Ainsworth's concepts. They have found that although the attachment categories seem to have considerable applicability across cultural groups overall, important variations do occur in the way infants of different ethnic groups express secure and insecure attachment relationships.

Another important question is the origin of particular attachment behaviours and relationships. According to Thompson (2006b), parental solicitude is affected not only by personality factors and personal belief systems but also by such things as the availability of environmental resources and a parent's degree of freedom to care for a child rather than be stressed or exhausted by the effort to obtain the necessities for survival. On this view, all three major types of attachment can be seen as adaptive responses by infants to parental investment patterns.

Secure attachment relationships

When babies are accustomed to almost constant contact with their mothers, they may react differently to reunion in the Strange Situation, either not seeking contact or failing to be comforted by it, and because behaviour at reunion is the primary basis for determining attachment classifications, understanding cultural variations in caregiving is crucial. Secure attachments may be present even when infants' behaviour in the Strange Situation at first seems to indicate otherwise.

For example, the Ganda infants Ainsworth studied showed more distress in response to brief separations from their mothers than US babies, but on investigation it was revealed that separations of only a brief period of time are infrequent in this African society. Ganda mothers leave their babies for hours at a time while they work in their gardens, and other relatives look after the children in their absence (Colin, 1996). Thus, when they left their babies in the experimental situation, the infants expected a long absence and reacted accordingly.

In the United States, most 1 year olds are encouraged to engage in activities by themselves – to play with toys, exercise motor skills and even to nap alone. Few US parents bring their babies into their own beds, but in many parts of the world, it is common for infants to sleep with their parents. For example, babies in Japan usually sleep in the same bed with their mothers, and parents don't hesitate to take a child into their bed when the youngster cries or asks to be fed (van IJzendoorn & Sagi, 1999). Infants in Japan show much stronger reactions to the departure of the mother than US babies do.

Resistant attachment relationships

Japanese and Israeli babies seem more likely than Western infants to show resistant behaviour in both phases of the Strange Situation. In the case of the Japanese infants, this may well be because they are in close contact with their mothers from the time they are born, including, as we've noted, sharing their parents' beds (Rothbaum et al., 2000b). For these infants, the stress of separation seems much greater than it is for Western babies.

Babies living on Israeli kibbutzim probably show resistant attachment behaviour in the Strange Situation for different reasons. Although an infant Israeli 'kibbutznik' is usually raised by a hired caregiver (in Hebrew, a metapelet), this person is not always highly motivated to engage in infant care and, typically having responsibility for three children, may be unable to respond sensitively to each of them in optimal fashion (Aviezer et al., 1999; Sagi-Schwartz & Aviezer, 2005). The child customarily spends only a few hours with her parents, at supper time, and unless she sleeps at home, she may be watched at night by a person who must monitor all the babies in the nursery building. As a result, 'even secure attachments might be expected often to be tinged with resistance and/or preoccupation with the caregiver, who may often have been unavailable' (Colin, 1996, p. 155).

Can we rely on the Strange Situation in cross-cultural contexts?

In view of the foregoing findings, we may ask whether the Strange Situation is truly applicable to assessing attachment relationships in babies of other cultures. Given the cultural practices we've described that either neutralize the effects of separation or make it excessively threatening, it can be argued that this measurement device needs revision or replacement.

Does the fact that children from Germany and Sweden who may be well adjusted in terms of their upbringing nevertheless appear to have avoidant – and thus, by definition, insecure – attachment relationships undermine the usefulness of the assessment in those cultures? And perhaps the test situation is just too stressful for Japanese and Israeli babies. Several researchers have argued that as long as the experimenter shortens separation episodes for babies who are highly distressed by the scenario, the procedure probably produces valid classifications across cultures.

The newer Attachment Q Sort (AQS) allows for more input by infants' caregivers into the assessment process, but even this device may be culture bound. Although Posada and colleagues (1995) found considerable overall cross-cultural consistency in their study of mothers' Q sorts in China, Colombia, Germany, Israel, Japan, Norway and the United States, they report that sociocultural similarity both within and across cultural groups was modest and that there is considerable diversity in the ways that children behave in separation situations. The issue of multicultural applicability of attachment assessment measures may remain unresolved until researchers undertake multiple naturalistic observations of infant–caregiver dyads in many cultures and social contexts (van IJzendoorn & Sagi, 1999; Sagi-Schwartz & Aviezer, 2005).

Influences on attachment quality

Ainsworth was the first to describe how parents' styles of interacting with their infants are linked with the kinds of attachment relationships that infants and parents develop. Mothers of securely attached infants, for instance, usually permit their babies to play an active role in determining the onset, pacing and end of feeding early in life. This behaviour is not sufficient to promote a secure attachment, but it serves a positive purpose because it identifies a mother as generally responsive to her baby's needs. The mother of a securely attached infant is also consistently available to her baby; she does not sometimes ignore her baby when he or she signals a genuine need for her (Belsky, 1999; Braungart-Rieker et al., 2001). This style of parenting, called sensitive care, is widely associated with the formation of secure attachments. Moreover, this link between sensitive parenting and attachment security is evident in many cultures, such as Australia, Brazil and South Africa (Harrison & Ungerer, 2002; Posada et al., 2002; Tomlinson, Cooper, & Murray, 2005).

A number of parenting styles are associated with insecure attachments. Cassidy and Berlin (1994), for example, have found that mothers of babies with an insecure-avoidant type of attachment tend to be *unavailable* and *rejecting*. These mothers are generally unresponsive to their infants' signals, rarely have close bodily contact with them, and often interact with them in an angry, irritable way. And the parents of infants with insecure-resistant attachments exhibit an *inconsistently available* parenting style (Belsky, 1999; Thompson, 2006b). Mothers who display this style respond to their babies' needs at times, but at other times, they do not, and in general, they offer little affection and are awkward in their interactions with their infants.

The most problematic forms of parenting are found among parents whose attachment with their infants is of the insecure-disorganized type; these parents often neglect their babies or abuse them in other ways. The approach/avoidance behaviour – the tendency to show an alternating pattern of approaching a person or object and retreating or escaping from it – that infants with this type of attachment display when reunited with their caregivers in the Strange Situation may actually be an adaptive response; these babies do not know what to expect, given the abuse they have already suffered (Solomon & George, 1999). Carlson et al. (1989) found that mistreated infants were significantly more likely to develop insecure-disorganized attachments (82%) than were children who were not

sensitive care
Consistent and responsive caregiving that begins by allowing an infant to play a role in determining when feeding will begin and end, and at what pace it will proceed.

approach/avoidance behaviour A pattern of interaction in which the infant or child shows an inconsistent pattern of approaching and retreating from a person or an object.

mistreated (19%). Another factor often associated with this pattern of attachment is maternal depression. Babies of depressed mothers show not only approach/avoidance behaviour but also sadness upon reunion. Observations of such mothers with their 6-month-old babies have revealed little mutual eye contact and minimal mutual responsiveness; instead, mother and baby each tend to avert their gaze (Field, 1990; Greenberg, 1999; Isabella, 1993; Belsky, 1999). The presence of a non-depressed caregiver such as a father can, in part, mitigate the negative effects of maternal depression on the infant's development (Hossain et al., 1994). Studies of the Dogan, who live in Mali, West Africa, suggest that frightening or frightened maternal behaviour is linked with disorganized attachment patterns – a finding similar to those reported in the Netherlands (Lyons-Ruth & Jacobvitz, 1999; True, Pisani, & Oumar, 2001). In this situation, as in the case of abuse, the parent is seen as a source of both comfort and fear, which leads to the infant's disorganized behaviour.

The longer term implications of early attachment problems can be severe. Hoeve et al. (2012) conducted a meta-analysis of 74 published papers and over 55,000 participants, to identify a link between poor attachment to parents and delinquency for both boys and girls. The link was stronger for poor attachment to mothers than to fathers and, interestingly, there were stronger effects if the parent and child were the same sex. Effects were also stronger for younger than for older participants. This comprehensive study demonstrates that although there may be debate about the theoretical basis of attachment, the identification or bond with a parent is an important determining factor in child development.

Being reared in an institution or orphanage may lead to high levels of disorganized attachment as well (Zeanah, Smyke, & Settles, 2006). The style of caregiving, which includes a lack of eye contact, mechanical interaction patterns with little talking, slow responsiveness to child distress, and ineffective soothing, probably contributed to these unhealthy attachment classifications.

Although the consequences of early attachment problems are deemed particularly problematic, attachment processes do not cease in infancy but continue to be important in later phases of development such as adolescence. Just as infants gain comfort from using the mother as a secure base, adolescents continue to find value in the quality of the attachment relationship with their parents. When the mother was supportive and attuned to the adolescent's needs and self-perceptions, and when the mother and adolescent were able to maintain their relationship through disagreements, the adolescents' attachment relationship with their mother was more secure (Allen et al., 2003). Just as a secure base allows the infant to begin to explore her physical world, a secure base as expressed by a positive and supportive mother–adolescent relationship allows the adolescent to explore independence in ideas and behaviours. The forms of attachment relationships shift across development, but the fundamental dynamics remain the same.

Attachment is not a process that is only influential in infancy; it continues all through the development into adolescence. The attachment relationship with a parent can continue to be an important influence, whether that is negative or positive.
© Blend Images/Image Source

Attachment in adolescence is grounded in a relationship which is very different in many ways from parent–infant interaction, although fundamental features (e.g., love, nurturance) remain. As children grow parents may begin to offer not only direct support but also assistance to adolescents in managing increasing complex peer and other relationships and demands. Laible (2007) suggested that although attachment was related to aspects of social and emotional competence, adolescents' social behaviour was mediated through an adolescent's social competence. In other words, positive attachment relationships tended to lead to adolescents with higher levels of emotional competence, and this in turn led to more positive social behaviour. Other studies (e.g., Guedes et al., 2018) identify similar mechanisms for adolescent victims of aggression who, similarly, may be lacking social and emotional competence or peer support networks to buffer against negative outcomes.

What can we learn about attachment quality from infant–parent interactions in other cultures? An interesting example is the parenting styles of Israeli parents, some of whom live with their families in a kibbutz, or communal village, where they generally rear their infant children in group-care arrangements.

In all kibbutzim (plural of kibbutz), babies stay in the infant-care centre during the day and, in some, they stay in the centre even at night, but in others, they spend the night with their families. Sagi and his colleagues (Sagi et al., 1994) examined the effects of these contrasting child-rearing arrangements on attachment relationships. Some of their results are summarized in Table 7-6, which shows that infants who slept at home with their families were more likely to develop secure attachments than babies who spent the night in the infant centre. Among the children who spent the night at home, the secure and insecure-resistant attachment groups represented proportions similar to those observed in most other studies. Note that no infants were classified as having insecure-avoidant attachments. Babies reared in kibbutzim rarely exhibit such attachments because kibbutzim caregivers seldom exhibit rejecting behaviour or pressure children to act independently (Sagi-Schwartz & Aviezer, 2005). The differences observed between the sleep-at-home and sleep-at-the-kibbutz babies were not related to any other factors, for the researchers equated their young participants on such things as temperament, early life events, mother–infant interaction in play, quality of day-care environment, and maternal characteristics such as job satisfaction and anxiety about separation from children. The researchers suggest, therefore, that it may have been the mothers' greater opportunity to respond sensitively to their babies' needs during the evening and night-time hours that increased the mothers' overall sensitivity to their infants (Sagi-Schwartz & Aviezer, 2005).

Table 7-6   Attachment in children raised in an Israeli kibbutz

Attachment type	CHILDREN WHO SPENT THE NIGHT		
	In the care centre	At home	All children
Secure	6 (26%)	15 (60%)	21 (44%)
Insecure-avoidant	0	0	0
Insecure-resistant	7 (30%)	2 (8%)	9 (19%)
Insecure-disorganized	10 (44%)	8 (32%)	18 (37%)

Source: Adapted from Sagi et al. (1994).

More evidence of the impact of maternal sensitivity on the attachment relationship comes from an experimental study by Anisfeld and co-workers (1990). Lower-income inner-city mothers of newborns were divided into two groups: an experimental group received soft baby carriers and a control group was given rigid carriers of the 'car seat' type. The researchers predicted that the soft infant carriers would increase physical contact between infants and mothers, and facilitate the development of maternal responsiveness; in fact, the mothers given the soft carriers were indeed more responsive to their infants' vocalizations at 3.5 months. Moreover, attachment measured at 13 months was affected as well: 83% of the babies in the experimental group were securely attached to their mothers, whereas only 39% of the control group babies were securely attached to their mothers.

Of course, relationships between parents and infants do not develop in a vacuum. They are affected by and affect other relationships among family members, as well as relationships outside the home. For example, there is a link between marital adjustment and infant–parent attachment: secure attachment is more likely when marital adjustment is good (e.g. Belsky, 1999; Thompson, 2006b). Although the birth of a child is generally associated with a decline in marital satisfaction (Cowan & Cowan, 2000), mothers whose infants become securely attached usually report less dissatisfaction with their marriages than mothers whose children are insecurely attached (Belsky, 1999).

internal working model According to Bowlby, a person's mental representation of himself as a child, his parents and the nature of his interaction with his parents, as he reconstructs and interprets that interaction; also referred to as an *attachment representation*.

The kind of care that parents received when they were infants is another influence on the quality of attachment that develops between them and their own children (Bretherton & Munholland, 1999; Thompson, 2006b). From our mothers and fathers, we all acquire what Bowlby (1973) calls internal working models of the self and parents. According to Bowlby, these models are mental representations about oneself, one's own parents and the styles of interaction one experienced as a child. Working models are also often referred to as *attachment representations*. Note that it is not the actual experience of the parent when she was an infant that forms this model but rather how she reconstructs or interprets these early experiences. Because of these internal working models, people tend to re-create their own childhood relationships when they themselves become mothers or fathers (Bretherton, 2005).

To investigate this notion of intergenerational continuity, Main and her colleagues (Main, Kaplan, & Cassidy, 1985; Main, Hesse, & Kaplan, 2005) interviewed 40 middle-class mothers about recollections of their own relationships with their mothers during infancy and childhood. Supporting Bowlby's theory, the mothers' memory patterns did relate to the quality of their current attachment relationships with their own infants. As Table 7-7 shows, Main classified the women into three groups: autonomous, dismissing and preoccupied. The *autonomous* group, who had developed secure attachment relationships with their infants, revealed in their interviews that although they valued close relationships with their parents and others, they were at the same time objective. They tended not to idealize their own parents but had a clear understanding of their relationships with them and were able to describe both their positive and negative aspects even if the relationship was strong enough to overcome any weaknesses. The *dismissing* group, who had avoidant attachment relationships with their babies, had a different set of memories; they dismissed and devalued attachment and frequently claimed that they couldn't recall incidents from their childhoods. The third, *preoccupied* group was made up of the parents of resistant infants. Preoccupied with earlier family attachments, these mothers recalled many conflict-ridden incidents from childhood but couldn't organize them into coherent patterns.

Table 7-7   Relationships between mothers' and children's attachment status

ATTACHMENT CATEGORY		
Mother	Child	Mother–child relationship
Autonomous	Secure	Mother's mind not taken up with unresolved concerns about her own experience; mother thus able to be sensitive to child's communications
Dismissing	Insecure-avoidant	Mother reluctant to acknowledge her own attachment needs and thus insensitive and unresponsive to child's needs
Preoccupied	Insecure-resistant	Mother confused about her attachment history and thus inconsistent in her interactions with her child

Source: Main, Kaplan, and Cassidy (1985); Schaffer (1996); Hesse (1999).

Intergenerational continuity is not always straightforward, for some children and adults are able to overcome early adversity and insecure attachments, and eventually develop satisfying interpersonal relationships with their spouses, partners and offspring. Several cross-sectional studies have supported the existence of this resilient group of individuals, now called 'earned secure' people (Paley et al., 1999). Roisman and colleagues (2002), who used data from a 23-year longitudinal study, showed that individuals can indeed overcome early problems and develop 'secure' attachment relationships. Even though these young adults had negative childhood experiences, those who overcame their past and developed secure internal working models of attachment relationships had high-quality romantic relationships in their early twenties. The romantic ties of these earned secure young adults were comparable to those of individuals who were continuously secure and of higher quality than those of individuals with insecure attachments.

> In Chapter 16 we discuss how adult social relationships develop across the lifespan. The individual's approach to relationships may well be grounded in early family and caregiver experiences.

Additional support for intergenerational continuity comes from a study in Germany where Grossmann and colleagues (Grossman, Grossman, & Kindler, 2005) found strong links between adults' recollections and their attachment relationships with their infants. In Israel, Scharf (2001) found that adolescents who had been reared in a kibbutz communal setting, including overnight sleeping in the kibbutz, differed from family-raised adolescents in their attachment representations or working models of relationships. The kibbutz group had a higher incidence of non-autonomous attachment representations and were less competent at coping with imagined separations than family-reared adolescents. Adolescents in the kibbutz, whose parents had switched to family sleeping arrangements when the children were between age 3 and 6, did not differ from family-reared adolescents in terms of attachment representations. This suggests that children's working models can shift in response to changing circumstances (Bretherton, 2005).

Research close-up

BOX 7-4   Transmission of attachment security across three generations

Source: Based on Cassiba et al. (2017).

Introduction:

Perhaps it is unremarkable to think that parents can transmit a particular style of parenting to their children. Indeed, parents typically serve as a source of values and beliefs for their children as they bring them up and seek actively to communicate and instil those in their offspring. However, just as positive parenting values can be transmitted from parent to child, so too can some of the negative aspects of parenting that lead to poor or dysfunctional attachment styles. A study of the inter-generational attachment in adults suggests that it is not just across two, but three generations, that this transmission of attachment styles can occur.

Method:

The researchers gave the Adult Attachment Interview (AAI; Main & Goldwyn, 1985/1991) to members of three generations of 32 middle-class families without a history of divorce. They were also given a brief questionnaire about their current mental health and well-being. Recruitment of the sample was initiated from students at an urban Italian university studying psychology. The youngest generation in the study, therefore, were arguably a somewhat unrepresentative sample in terms of broader demographic characteristics. The AAI has high predictive validity (van IJzendoorn, 1995) and is a semi-structured interview that probes alternately for descriptions of relationships, current relationships with parents, and memories relating to attachments from early childhood until the present. The sample included one adult offspring, two parents, and four grandparents, giving a total sample size of 224 individuals.

Results:

The study resulted in several interesting outcomes. First, as previous research might have indicated, experiencing two secure parents led to offspring who also had secure attachment relationships into adulthood. Second, transmission across two generations (i.e., grandparent to parent, or parent to child) was stronger in the presence of a female caregiver (i.e., mother or maternal/paternal grandmother). Third, and arguably more striking, the study found that the transmission of any particular attachment style was only found to be significant in the presence of two female caregivers (i.e., paternal/maternal grandmother to mother to child).

Discussion:

These findings therefore suggested that attachment follows a female 'lineage'. However, it is important to note that such long-term effects are based on participant reports at a particular point in time, in a particular culture. A lot may have happened to individuals, families, and in broader Italian society in the intervening years that span three generations of a family. For instance, standards, methods and approaches to parenting and children and perhaps also changes to male and female care-giving roles in a specific culture have demonstrably changed in many countries over the 60 or more years that span three generations. In that respect, it is important to recognize how different and changing cultural norms across a range of areas might affect how we transmit attachment styles and advance positive means of childcare across society. So the study demonstrates an association across generations and an intriguing finding worthy of future investigation: but correlation is not causation!

Some babies are more difficult to interact with and care for than others. Yet although attachment is a process of mutual influence, researchers have paid less attention to the infant's contribution than to the parental one. Some, however, have found a link between certain temperament characteristics in infants and the kinds of relationships they develop with their parents. For instance, irritable newborns or those with difficulties orientating to people and to objects may be more apt to develop insecure attachments (Spangler & Grossman, 1993; Susman-Stillman et al., 1996). Perhaps these early difficulties reflect underlying problems in adaptive mechanisms that continue to influence a child's behaviour and interactions with others as he grows. Similarly some (Stevenson-Hinde, 2005) suggest that children who are shy and fearful may fail to develop secure attachment due to their inability to openly express their emotions while interacting with their caregivers. We must be cautious in drawing such conclusions, however, because many other researchers have failed to find clear links between early infant temperament and later infant–parent attachment (Vaughn & Bost, 1999; Thompson, 2006b).

If infant temperament does have some influence on the development of attachment, that influence is probably mediated by many other factors. A 'difficult' infant is not necessarily destined to have a poor relationship with her parents. Parents who have a difficult or irritable baby can usually cope successfully if they receive help and support from others. When adequate social support is available to the mother, an irritable baby is no more likely to become insecurely attached than a non-irritable one (Crockenberg, 1981; Van den Boom, 1994). If a mother is socially isolated or has poor relationships with other adults, however, she is more likely to have problems fostering secure attachment in a difficult infant (Levitt, Weber, & Clark, 1986). Thus, the effect of temperament on attachment cannot be separated from the influence of the total social context in which the baby is developing (Sroufe, 1996; Vaughn & Bost, 1999; Thompson, 2006b).

Stability and outcomes of quality of attachment

There is substantial stability in the quality of attachment from one period of time to another. As was discussed earlier in the chapter, among infants tested with their mothers in the Strange Situation, the same attachment patterns were detected both at 12 months and at 6 years of age (Solomon & George, 1999). Although the correlation was not perfect between attachment behaviour in these children at different points in time – for example, 100% of the children rated securely attached at 12 months were rated similarly at 6 years of age, but only 66% of the children rated insecure-disorganized at 12 months were rated similarly at 6 years of age – the overall findings support the notion that attachment behaviour is highly stable. A German study found that first-year attachment classifications predicted 78% of sixth-year classifications (Wartner et al., 1994). Moreover, Waters and colleagues (2000) found that 72% of their sample classified as secure versus insecure in infancy were similarly rated 20 years later – an impressive level of stability of attachment across the lifespan. Even in adulthood, attachment representations tend to be relatively stable: 78% of couples received similar Adult Attachment Interview classifications before marriage and 18 months later (Crowell, Treboux, & Waters, 2002).

But general stability in the quality of parent–child relationships does not mean that change is impossible (Waters et al., 2000). Substantial minorities of children with insecure attachments as infants manage to develop better relationships with their parents by school age. This is particularly likely when a child's parents begin to experience less stress in their lives (e.g., fewer financial worries or less marital tension) and so are able to become more available to their child and to interact in ways more responsive to the child's needs (Thompson, Lamb, & Estes, 1982). Alternatively, secure infant–parent attachment relationships can become insecure if the life circumstances of the family deteriorate due to job loss, divorce, illness or abuse. More infants (44%) who later experienced negative life events changed attachment classifications from infancy to adulthood than children (22%) in families with no significant negative events (Waters et al., 2000).

Professional intervention can help improve a troubled parent–child relationship (Bakermans-Kranenburg, van IJzendoorn, & Juffer, 2003). In the Netherlands, mothers who were taught to be more sensitive to their infants developed better attachment relationships with them than did the mothers of a control group of infants (van den Boom, 1994). Whereas 68% of the experimental group were classified as securely attached at 12 months of age, only 28% of the control group were securely attached. Another 58% were insecure-avoidant and 16% were insecure-resistant. Clearly, attachment relationships continue to develop and are responsive to changes in the behaviour of both parent and child (Waters et al., 2000; Thompson, 2006b).

There are many outcomes and consequences of different attachment relationships. Early secure attachment appears to be related to more complex exploratory behaviour at 2 years of age (Main, 1973). Moreover, as the child continues to develop, this intellectual curiosity is reflected in an intensified interest and enjoyment in solving problems. This positive approach to problem solving is seldom seen in toddlers who were insecurely attached as infants. Matas, Arend, and Sroufe (1978) found that securely attached 2 year olds were more enthusiastic, persistent, cooperative and effective in solving problems than their insecurely attached peers. The former group showed less frustration, less negative affect, less crying and whining, and less aggression towards their mothers. In addition, the securely attached toddlers engaged in more symbolic or pretend play – for example, transforming a block of wood into an imaginary car or a stick into a witch's broom. Nor are the effects of attachment status on cognitive outcomes restricted to infants and toddlers. High-quality parent–child relationships and higher early maternal sensitive responsiveness were linked with better cognitive development at age 7. In turn, attachment disorganization was linked with poorer cognitive outcomes (Stams, Juffer, & van IJzendoorn, 2002). In this case, the relations were not due to shared genetic factors because the children were all adopted at an early age. In a longitudinal study in Iceland, Jacobsen and Hofmann (1997) found that children who at age 7 were securely attached were likely to be more attentive and participative in the classroom at the ages of 9, 12 and 15. They maintained higher grades than children judged avoidant, ambivalent or disorganized in their attachment.

It is not only mothers' and fathers' relationships with their child that are important to her or his cognitive development but the child's relations with other significant caregivers as well. Marinus van IJzendoorn and colleagues in Netherlands and Israel (e.g. van IJzendoorn, Sagi, & Lamberman, 1992; van IJzendoorn & Sagi, 1999) found that the quality of the whole attachment network (mother, father, others) in infancy predicted the children's intelligence scores when they were 5 years old; the greater the attachment security, the higher the test score.

Many studies support the idea that the quality of the caregiver–infant relationship is important for later social development (Sroufe et al., 2005; Thompson, 2006b). A recent longitudinal study in which children were traced from infancy to age 19 illustrates the importance of the early attachment for later social behaviour (Carlson, Sroufe, & Egeland, 2004; Sroufe et al., 2005). Securely and insecurely attached youngsters developed very different social and emotional patterns. At 4 to 5 years of age, teachers rated securely attached children as showing more positive emotions and as having greater empathy for others and more ability to initiate, respond to and sustain interactions with other people. Securely attached children also whined less, were less aggressive and displayed fewer negative reactions when other children approached them. Not surprisingly, their teachers rated them more socially competent and socially skilled and as having more friends than other children, and their classmates considered them more popular than others.

At 8 and 12 years of age, the securely attached continued to be rated as more socially competent, more peer orientated and less dependent on adults. Moreover, they were more likely to develop close friendships than their less securely attached peers. Attachment history also predicted friendship choices: children with secure attachment histories were more likely to form friendships with other securely attached peers. At age 19, the socioemotional functioning of those adolescents with a history of secure attachment was rated higher as well. In comparison with peers who had a history of insecure attachment, these young adults were more likely to have close family relationships, long-term friendships, sustained romantic involvement, higher self-confidence and greater determination regarding personal goals. Others have found similar links between the quality of early attachment and later school-age peer competence and friendship patterns (Contreras et al., 2000; Schneider, Atkinson, & Tardif, 2001). The long-term consequences of attachment security are evident not just in biologically related families but also in families of adopted children. Infants who were adopted before 6 months of age and who developed high-quality infant–mother relationships and secure attachments were better adjusted socially at age 7 (Stams et al., 2002). This work underscores the importance for later adjustment of good early caregiving and suggests that the effect is not simply due to a shared genetic history.

Just as Bowlby argued, the links between attachment and social outcomes are forged by children's internal working models. In his longitudinal study, Sroufe (2005) assessed children's cognitive working models of relationships at various times throughout childhood and adolescence. For example, in the pre-school years, these researchers evaluated children's relationship expectations, attitudes and feelings. Securely attached children's relationship models were characterized by expectations of empathy between play partners, a high expectation of sharing during play and constructive approaches to conflict resolution (e.g., taking turns, seeking adult acceptance, getting another toy). During adolescence (age 12), securely attached children construed their friendships as close, emotionally connected and skilled in conflict resolution. These investigators showed that cognitive working models and social behaviour mutually influence each other across time. In other words, cognitive representations in the preschool period predict social behaviour in middle childhood; in turn, the representations in middle childhood predict social behaviour at 12 years of age, and these cognitive models predict social outcomes at 19 years of age. Moreover, across time, social behaviour at one point predicts later cognitive representations. For example, social behaviour in middle childhood influences a child's cognitive working models in early adolescence. Other studies find similar links between working models and social behaviour with peers (Cassidy et al., 1996). Together, these studies illustrate the interplay among attachment, cognitive understanding and children's social outcomes.

Emotions play a role in accounting for the links between attachment and social competence, too. For example, attachment to his mother affects the way a child processes emotional information and understands and regulates his emotions. Securely attached children tend to remember positive events more accurately than negative events, whereas insecurely attached children do the opposite (Belsky, Spritz, & Crnic, 1996). And securely attached preschoolers are better at understanding emotions than insecurely attached children (Laible & Thompson, 1998). Finally, Contreras et al. (2000) found that securely attached children are better at regulating their emotions, which in turn accounted for their superior social relationships with peers.

In trying to understand children's social behaviour, it is also important to consider both infant–mother and infant–father attachment relationships (Berlin & Cassidy, 1999; Lamb, 2004). Even very young children may develop different relationships with each parent. In a study of 1-year-old infants, Main and Weston (1981) classified babies according to whether they were securely attached to both parents, to their mothers but not their fathers, to their fathers but not their mothers, or to neither parent. To determine whether the infants' relationships with their mothers and fathers affected their social responsiveness to other people, Main and Weston then observed the infants' reactions to a friendly clown. The infants who were securely attached to both parents were more responsive to the clown than those who were securely attached to only one parent and insecurely attached to the other, and the babies who were insecurely attached to both parents were the least responsive of all. These results suggest that a less-than-optimal relationship with one parent is offset by a better relationship with the other parent – and that therefore it is not enough to study just mothers or fathers alone. Viewing the parents as part of a family system is the best way to understand their role in child development (Parke & Buriel, 2006).

In summary, a healthy attachment to parents facilitates exploration, curiosity and mastery of the social and physical environment. Early healthy attachment also increases the child's trust in other social relationships and permits the later development of mature affectional relationships with peers. Longitudinal studies aimed at defining the links between early parent–infant interaction and later relationships in adolescence and adulthood suggest the long-term stability of the cognitive and social effects of early attachment. Clearly, developmental history leaves its mark (Thompson, 2006b).

Child care and attachment

Although many children of working parents are cared for entirely by their parents, siblings and other relatives, many children under 5 spend some hours a week in some form of day care – that is, care provided by one or more non-family members in the child's own home, in the caregiver's home or in an organized child care facility (Clarke-Stewart & Allhusen, 2005). Often, but not always, this is because parents are forced to work to maintain the economic well-being of the family, thus placing an infant or child in outside care is often a necessity rather than a choice. However, child care norms do vary across cultures due to different traditions and family practices, as well as different economic conditions and social practices, such as shorter or extended maternity (and paternity) leave.

According to John Bowlby, having a number of caregivers other than a child's parents who share in caring for an infant may impair the quality of infant attachment. This proposition has been central to the controversy surrounding the advantages and disadvantages of child care for development. There is no evidence that being in child care actually prevents the formation of an attachment between infants and their parents. Children who spend time in child care form close relationships with their mothers and fathers, just as children raised at home do (Clarke-Stewart & Allhusen, 2002, 2005; Lamb & Ahnert, 2006). As we saw earlier, children do show separation protest in response to being left by their parents even when they are clearly attached to them.

Some studies have suggested that infants who are in day care because their mothers are employed full-time – especially babies who begin full-time day care before they are 1 year old – are more likely to be classified as insecurely attached than infants of non-employed or part-time working mothers (Barglow, Vaughn, & Molitor, 1987; Belsky & Rovine, 1988; Belsky & Cassidy, 1994). Again, however, the correlations were not strong. Moreover, in a review of day-care studies, Clarke-Stewart (1989) found that although on average 36% of the infants of full-time working mothers became insecurely attached, 29% of the infants of non-employed or part-time working mothers also developed insecure attachments.

How might we explain why roughly a third of the babies of working mothers, regardless of whether they are in day care or are cared for at home, develop insecure attachments? It is of course possible that day-care babies are somewhat more apt to develop an insecure attachment because their mothers are less available to them or because they interpret her absence as rejection (Barglow et al., 1987; Belsky & Rovine, 1988). However, other explanations are also possible (Clarke-Stewart & Allhusen, 2005; Lamb & Ahnert, 2006). For instance, mothers who dislike caring for a baby (and who thus tend to be less sensitive caregivers) may be more inclined than other mothers to take full-time jobs. Or, possibly, the stress associated with handling both a baby and work interferes with a working mother's ability to promote secure attachment. These alternative explanations suggest that day care itself may not exert an influence on attachment but rather that something associated with a parent's use of day-care facilities, such as holding a full-time job, may reduce parental effectiveness at being a consistently sensitive and responsive caregiver.

Thus, even with the latest findings on day care, it seems unlikely that day care alone is responsible for a lesser degree of security in these relationships (Clarke-Stewart & Allhusen, 2002). What's more, good day-care providers can sometimes compensate for less than optimal care from parents by giving children an opportunity to form secure attachments outside the home (Howes, 1999; Howes & Ritchie, 2003). Research shows that children with an insecure attachment to their mothers, but a secure attachment to a day-care provider, tend to be more socially competent than insecurely attached children who have not formed such a strong compensatory relationship outside the family.

Stability of staff may be an important determinant of the relationship quality that emerges between care providers and children in day care. Barnas and Cummings (1994) found that 21-month-old toddlers more frequently sought out caregivers who had been on staff for longer periods of time and who were rarely absent and could thus be relied upon to be there for them. When the children were distressed, these familiar figures were able to soothe them more effectively than were caregivers whose employment records were unstable.

Good-quality child care tends to enhance children's language abilities and cognitive skills, and infants with child-care experience adapt more quickly and explore more in an unfamiliar setting (Clarke-Stewart & Allhusen, 2005). These children play more with peers and are more socially competent, and they exhibit more self-confidence and are less fearful of unfamiliar adults, especially when they have a secure infant–care provider relationship (Howes & Ritchie, 2003).

The effects of day care quality continue even after children reach school age. In one study, high-quality preschool day care was related to less child hostility and better orientation to tasks in kindergarten.

Poor-quality day care, however, coupled with early entry into day care (before the age of 1), was related to a higher level of destructiveness and less consideration for others (Howes, 1999; Howes & Ritchie, 2003). In another study, even 4 years after being enrolled in high-quality day care, children were rated friendlier, more inclined towards positive emotions, more competent and better at resolving conflicts (Vandell, Henderson, & Wilson, 1988).

BOX 7-5 Does early child care affect the quality of attachment between a mother and her infant?

Research close-up

Source: Based on NICHD Early Child Care Research Network (1997).

Introduction:

The effect of early child care (being in a nursery or kindergarten) on the quality of attachment between a mother and her infant has been the subject of much debate, and a number of early studies suggested that it could lead to insecure attachment as assessed by the Strange Situation. However, a study of 105 infants by Roggman et al. (1994) found no significant relationship between child care experience and security of attachment. The NICHD Study of Early Child Care therefore set out to investigate this issue in more depth. The study provided an excellent source of evidence because it was based on a well-established prospective, longitudinal study with a large sample size of over 1,000 children. The present study looked at whether being a child in child care would increase the likelihood of insecure attachment and whether various features of the child care were particularly important. It also considered how these features of child care would interact with characteristics of the mother and of the child itself. In such cases, poor-quality child care might further increase the likelihood of insecure attachment, whereas good-quality child care could provide a compensatory function. Finally, some researchers have suggested that the Strange Situation is not a useful measure for children who have experience of child care, because they are accustomed to the situation used in this assessment method; therefore this study also set out to investigate whether this is, in fact, the case.

Method:

Visits were made to the children's homes when they were 1, 6 and 15 months old. Children were also observed in their child care arrangements when they were 6 and 15 months old and were assessed in the Strange Situation at 15 months. Various different methods of assessment were used, including questionnaires, observations and interviews and, from these, a number of composite measures were obtained. For the mother, these included measures of psychological adjustment, sensitivity in play and overall sensitivity and responsiveness. For the child, a measure of temperament was obtained. For the child care arrangements, measures of type of care, amount of care, age of entry and stability of care were obtained; there were also measures of amount and frequency of positive caregiving. Finally, the type of attachment of each child was assessed using the Strange Situation procedure.

Results:

The researchers found that the Strange Situation gave consistent and reliable results, regardless of the amount of child care experience a child might have. Findings also showed that attachment security was related to the mother's sensitivity and overall responsiveness, but was not related to the child's temperament. With regard to child care, the results showed that, overall, there was no effect of child care on attachment security, even if the child care was rated as early, extensive, unstable or poor quality. However, interactions between maternal and child care factors were found. Children with less sensitive mothers, who were also in poor-quality child care, experienced more than minimal amounts of child care or had more than one care arrangement showed the highest rates of insecure attachment. On the other hand, among children with poor maternal care, those in high-quality child care showed a higher proportion of secure attachment than those in low-quality child care.

Discussion:

The Strange Situation remains an important and valid method of assessing attachment, regardless of the amount of child care experience a child might have. It also shows that, overall, child care does not seem to adversely affect the security of attachment. The reasons why these results are different from earlier studies is not clear but it may be that a different type of family uses child care from the families included in earlier studies, or that parents have begun to make special efforts to compensate for any effects of child care. However, the study has also shown that the effects of poor mothering can be made worse by poor child care or partly compensated for by good child care. Overall, it confirms that the nature of the attachment relationship itself, as well as the effect upon it of child care, depends primarily upon the interaction between the child and its mother.

SUMMARY

Expression of emotions forms an important part of communication, while their development also influences the child's physical and mental well-being as well as social success. Primary emotions such as surprise and joy, which do not involve introspection, emerge early in life, while others, such as pride and shame, take longer to develop.

Three different theoretical perspectives are useful in explaining aspects of emotional development. The *genetic-maturational* view suggests that biological factors underpin emotions, while the *learning perspective* explains their development in terms of learning experiences. Finally, the *functionalist perspective* argues that emotions help us to adapt to our environment and achieve our goals; it emphasizes the importance of the role of emotions in establishing and maintaining social relationships.

The first sign of emotion is the *reflex* or simple smile, which is seen even in newborn babies. Over time, the use of this smile develops and it is seen in response to a variety of internal and external elicitors. Babies also show increasing interest in other people and smiling begins to perform a social function. During the same period, babies also begin to develop negative emotions and use *social referencing* to learn about emotions by 'reading' emotional cues in other people. One example of this is *stranger distress*, which is common but not found in all cultures; however, *separation protest* is universal. A child's temperament may also influence emotional development and its expression throughout life.

Primary emotions are more basic whereas secondary emotions are more complex and require self-awareness. These emotions begin to emerge towards the middle of the second year. Learning to recognize emotions in others takes longer but, by the age of about 2 or 3 years, most children show a positive correlation of ability in the production and recognition of emotion.

Learning to regulate emotions presents another major challenge to children and this ability develops as they learn appropriate emotional *display rules*, which dictate which emotions are appropriate in different circumstances. These have been shown to vary with culture.

With increasing age, children also develop a more complete cognitive understanding of emotions. This understanding can be seen as a collection of *emotional scripts* that allow the child to identify the feeling that typically accompanies a given situation. Such scripts begin to develop as early as the age of 2 years and become gradually more complex with children learning that it is possible to experience more than one feeling at any one time.

Families have a major influence on the development of emotions. They can act as models for emotional expressiveness, can encourage or discourage different patterns of emotional expression and can provide 'emotional coaching' by talking about feelings. As well as parents, siblings and peers can function as socializers of emotion.

The development of attachment is an important aspect of emotional development. This intense bond between the infant and one or more of their regular caregivers is a developmental milestone that occurs in the first year. A variety of theories have been offered to explain the development of attachment, including *psychoanalytic*, *learning* and *ethological* theories. However, the most widely accepted is John Bowlby's ethological theory of attachment, which emphasizes the importance of attachment as an actively formed relationship between infant and caregiver. Attachment develops gradually in a series of stages where the infant develops a preference for familiar individuals, followed by a specific attachment to the primary caregiver and a fear of strangers; the child also protests at being separated from the primary attachment figure. Although the primary attachment figure is usually the mother, this is not always the case, and the infant also develops secondary attachments to other people such as the father and siblings.

Many children form a very *secure attachment* and this provides a *secure base* for both physical exploration and emotional development. However, there is variation in the quality of attachment, and this was demonstrated by the classic *Strange Situation* study by Mary Ainsworth. Some children are *insecurely attached* and this may be further classified as insecure-avoidant, insecure-resistant or insecure-disorganized.

As with many aspects of emotional development, considerable cultural variation is seen in attachment, but the types of attachment are universal and there is consistency in the type of parenting style associated with each. Mothers of securely attached infants demonstrate a type of parenting known as *sensitive care*, while insecure attachment is associated with a variety of parenting styles which include a lack of availability, rejection and abuse. Other factors also affect the quality of the attachment relationship and there is an intergenerational continuity of attachment type.

An infant develops an *internal working model*, which represents all aspects of their attachment, and this forms a stable basis for the interpretation of future relationships and behaviour. Securely attached children tend to show greater cognitive development and better social skills than those who are insecurely attached. However the quality of attachment can be improved in some cases with appropriate intervention.

The effect of day care on attachment has been the subject of considerable research, with suggestions that it may lead to less secure attachments. However, the evidence for this is not strong and there a number of different factors that can combine to affect the quality of the attachment. In some cases, good day care might compensate for less than optimal parental care.

---

1. The focus of this chapter has been on the development of emotion. How do you think friends compare with family in their influence on emotional development?

2. In some areas of emotional development, variations between different cultures have been noted. How would you explain the role of culture in emotional development? What can cultural differences tell us about the different theories of emotional development?

3. What strategies can you suggest to help a child whose poor social understanding is causing them to be rejected by their peers?

4. Security of attachment has been shown to be related to sensitivity and responsiveness in the mother (or primary caregiver). Write a description of the personality and behaviour of a mother who you would expect to have a securely attached child.

5. Imagine you have a friend who is worried about putting her child into day care. What advice would you give her?

Explore and Discuss

Classic

Ainsworth, M. D. S., Blehar, M. C., Waters, E., & Wall, S. (1978). *Patterns of attachment: A psychological study of the Strange Situation.* Hillsdale, NJ: Lawrence Erlbaum.

Bowlby, J. (1969). *Attachment and Loss: Vol. 1. Attachment.* London: Hogarth.

Carroll, J. J., & Stewart, M. S. (1984). The role of cognitive development in children's understandings of their own feelings. *Child Development*, 55(4), 1486–1492.

Recommended Reading

Contemporary

Saarni, C. (2007). The development of emotional competence: Pathways for helping children to become emotionally intelligent. In R. Bar-On, J. G. Maree, & M. J. Elias (eds), *Educating people to be emotionally intelligent* (pp. 15–37). Westport, CT: Praeger.

Schore, A. N. (2015). *Affect regulation and the origin of the self: The neurobiology of emotional development.* New York: Routledge.

Schultz, D., Izard, C. E., Stapleton, L. M., Buckingham-Howes, S., & Bear, G. A. (2009). Children's social status as a function of emotionality and attention control. *Journal of Applied Developmental Psychology, 30*(2), 169–181.

Weinfield, N. S., Sroufe, A. L., Egeland, B., & Carlson, E. (2008). Individual differences in infant–caregiver attachment: Conceptual and empirical aspects of security. In J. Cassidy & P. R. Shaver (eds), *Handbook of attachment: Theory, research and clinical applications* (pp. 78–101). New York: Guilford Press.

CHAPTER 8

Language and Communication

Introduction

Language is one of the most complex systems of rules a person learns, yet children in a wide range of different environments learn to understand and use their native languages quite rapidly. Their ability to do this suggests that human infants are prepared in some way to acquire language skills.

However, biological preparation alone is insufficient because the language abilities the child develops must fit with the community in which he or she lives. Thus, a crucial part of language learning is the social support provided by others as children learn to speak and use language to accomplish their own goals.

Language serves a wide range of purposes for the developing child: it helps her to interact with others, communicate information, and express her feelings, wishes and views. Children can use language to influence other people's behaviour, to explore and learn about their environment, and to use their imaginations (Halliday, 1975). Language helps children to organize their perceptions and thinking, control their actions and even to modify their emotions.

language A communication system in which words and their written symbols combine in rule-governed ways and enable speakers to produce an infinite number of messages.

productive language The production of speech.

receptive language Understanding the speech of others.

An important part of children's language learning is the development of *communicative competence,* which is the ability to convey thoughts, feelings and intentions in a meaningful and culturally patterned way (Hymes, 1972; Schaffer, 1974; Haslett & Samter, 1997; Tomasello, 2006). Communication is by definition a two-way process: we send messages to others and receive messages from them. Thus, using productive language, we produce communications, and using receptive language, we receive communications from others.

We start this chapter with an overview of the developing processes of communication and the antecedents of language; next we explore the dominant theories of how language develops in the infant and young child. Then we discuss the structure of language, including words, sentences and grammar. After this discussion, we examine how children begin to understand and use language to communicate. Finally, we consider language development for children who are bilingual and learn two languages and how adults can facilitate language development.

THE ANTECEDENTS OF LANGUAGE DEVELOPMENT

Communication is not achieved solely by using words. If, as developmental psychologists, we restricted our focus to verbal communication only, we could easily underestimate how early in life communication begins. To understand the development of human communication fully we must consider the many sounds babies make as well as the many looks, movements and gestures by which they convey meaning before they can begin to talk. These prelinguistic achievements are important precursors to actual language use (Adamson, 1995).

Preverbal communication

Some of infants' earliest communications take place during interactions with their first caregivers (Uzgiris, 1989; Fogel, 1993). Parent and infant often engage in a kind of dialogue of sounds, movements, smiles and other facial expressions. Smiles, in particular, seem important in helping infants learn how to coordinate vocalizations and to translate expressions into effective communication (Yale et al., 2003). Although these early transactions may seem at first glance to be 'conversations', a closer look suggests that they be described as 'pseudo-conversations' because the adult alone is responsible for maintaining their flow (Schaffer, 1977). Babies have limited control over the nature and timing of their responses, so adults insert their behaviour into the infants' cycles of responsiveness and unresponsiveness. For instance, a baby gurgles and her mother replies by speaking to the infant. She first waits for the child's response, but if none is forthcoming, she may prompt the baby by changing her expression, speaking again or gently touching the child. Such interactions help the infant become a communicative partner by the end of her first year (Schaffer, 1977, 1996; Golinkoff, 1983).

Gestures such as pointing and touching can help children connect a physical object with the word being pronounced.
© Design Pics/Ross Germaniuk

Gestures and expressions play an important role in this process (Goldin-Meadow, 2006). Between 3 and 12 months of age, infants improve greatly in their ability to use gestures to communicate (Fogel, 1993). By at least the time babies are 3 or 4 months old adults offer and show things to them, and 6-month-old infants respond with smiles, gestures, movements and sounds. When babies are about 6 months old they begin to use a pointing gesture to guide others' attention to particular objects. Although able to track object movements from early in infancy, it's not until children are a year old that they can follow the point of another person. Through pointing, children can receive labels for objects that interest them and learn a great deal about the world around them (Golinkoff & Hirsh-Pasek, 1999). Some researchers argue that when 12 month olds point, they are attempting to influence the thinking and action of another person and, thus, reveal an effort to share their intentions with this person (Tomasello, Carpenter, & Liszkowski, 2007).

This type of gesture also helps set the stage for learning about language and the communicative process (Goldin-Meadows, 2007). When a preverbal infant uses a gesture to call an object to someone's attention, her action is called a protodeclarative because it functions like a declarative statement (Bates, 1976). When babies can also use gestures to get another person to do something for them, it is called a protoimperative; for example, a child may point to a teddy bear on a high shelf to get someone to give it to her (Bates, 1976; Bates et al., 1989). When two communicative partners attend to the same visual information, this behaviour is referred to as *joint visual attention* (Adamson & Bakeman, 1991).

> **protodeclarative** A gesture that an infant uses to make some sort of statement about an object.
>
> **protoimperative** A gesture that either an infant or a young child may use to get someone to do something she or he wants.

BOX 8-1 What's the point of pointing? How shared experience helps infants to understand the meaning of gestures

Research close-up

Source: Based on Liebal et al. (2009).

Introduction:

Tomasello, Carpenter, and Liszkowski (2007) have argued that understanding pointing is a crucial developmental advance because not only does pointing pick out objects in the world, it also signals shared attention or focus on those objects. Pointing therefore amounts to one of the building blocks of social interaction because it is a way of establishing a 'shared ground' (Goldin-Meadow, 2007) between people and, in turn, a joint system for representing the world and establishing meaning (i.e. language). Liebal et al. (2009) explored at what age infants could understand the meaning of pointing gestures.

Methods and results:

In two experimental studies, Liebal and colleagues assessed how infants aged 14 and 18 months responded to pointing from two experimenters who had previously played with the infants in a puzzle (study 1) or a 'tidy up' (study 1 and 2) game. In both studies the dependent measure was whether a child turned to the game in question or put a target object into a basket (tidy-up game). These observations of infants' actions were made by a judge who observed videotapes of the infants, and then subsequently coded for type of action by another judge, who was unaware of the experimental details. This allowed for a check of whether the judges were in agreement, and helped to establish that the observations of infants' behaviour were reliable. In both studies, both judges agreed.

Study 1:

A first study sought to test whether infants can link particular experiences that they have with particular adults to clarify the context and meaning of the adults' gestures (pointing). Twenty-four 14- and twenty-four 18-month-old infants first played a puzzle game with an experimenter (E1) that involved putting differently shaped objects into holes on a small table. This was followed by a 'tidy-up game' with another experimenter (E2) where objects were thrown into a basket to clear them away. Towards the end of this activity, out of sight of the child, E2 placed a target object (an orange cardboard triangle) behind the child before leaving the room. The orange triangle had featured in both the puzzle and tidy-up games. In order to test if the child connected gesture with a specific activity and adult, an experimenter (either E1 or E2) then entered the room. The adult then said, 'Oh, there' and pointed at the orange triangle for 4 seconds, looking in turn at the object and the child's face. The researchers expected that children would respond to E1 by placing the object in the puzzle table and to E2 by placing it in the basket. The results indicated that this was the case for older infants (18 months) but not for the younger infants (14 months). Hence, at 18 months infants placed the object in the puzzle significantly more than not when interacting with E1 at the test phase, and they tidied up the object significantly more often than not when interacting with E2.

Study 2:

The researchers speculated that the failure of 14 month olds to respond to experimenters in expected ways was due to the relatively high memory demands of the task. Therefore, in a second study, the researchers used just one game (tidying up) to see if infants responded appropriately or did not. This second study involved thirty 18 month olds and thirty 14 month olds. Infants played with both E1 and E2, then E2 left and the infant played the tidy-up game with E1. Then E2 re-entered the room and either E1 or E2 pointed at the target object and said 'There!' at one of three possible objects that again had been placed in the room without the infant knowing. In this simpler version of the task, both 18- and 14-month-old infants gave more appropriate responses when E1 pointed at the object, indicating that they appreciated the intent and meaning of the gesture from E1.

Discussion:

The two studies together demonstrate that infants as young as 14 months can interpret an adult's pointing gestures as a result of a shared experience with them. Importantly, it appears that not only can infants understand what an adult is pointing to, but also they can infer messages about these based on previous experiences. The ability to share attention and incorporate prior experiences is an important precursor to the development of language and a pragmatic understanding of human communication.

As children learn language, they often combine words and gestures for more effective communication (Adamson, 1995). A child may point to an object and then comment verbally to emphasize the meaning of the words. However, children's ability to use and understand gestures may develop independently of verbal language. It is only in the third year of life that children begin to recognize that gestures and language can be part of the same message and that, if they are, they require an integrated response (Shatz, 1983; Bates, 1999). Across time, children reduce their use of gestures as they rely increasingly on their verbal skills to communicate their needs and wishes (Adamson, 1995). However, use of gestures can help children, particularly those experiencing difficulties with language, such as Specific Language Impairment (SLI), to infer meaning from speech (e.g. Kirk & Pine, 2011). Gestures complement and sometimes add meaning to speech (Doherty-Sneddon, 2003).

Early language comprehension

The foundations for receptive language skills emerge early. Well before they are able to speak themselves babies can attend selectively to certain features of others' speech. In fact, newborns prefer listening to speech or to vocal music than to instrumental music or other rhythmic sounds (Butterfield & Siperstein, 1972). As we saw in Chapter 4, infants quickly become skilled listeners. Even before birth a foetus may be able to distinguish his mother's voice from the voice of an unfamiliar woman. Moreover, like adults, infants respond with different parts of their brains to speech and non-speech sounds. Electrical activity, for example, increases in the left half of the infant's brain in response to speech, whereas the right side responds to music (Molfese, 1973; Molfese & Betz, 1988; Neville, 1991).

CATEGORICAL SPEECH PERCEPTION

Infants perceive some consonants categorically (Werker & Polka, 1993; Aslin, Jusczyk, & Pisoni, 1998), that is, they hear 'one range of acoustic signals all as /p/ and a different range of acoustic signals as /b/ but no acoustic signal is perceived as something in between a /p/ and a /b/' (Hoff, 2005, p. 109). This phenomenon is known as categorical speech perception, or the *phoneme boundary effect*. In a classic study of discriminatory ability, one group of 5-month-old babies listened to 60 repetitions of the sound *bah*, followed by 10 repetitions of *gah*; a second group listened to 60 repetitions of *gah*, followed by 10 *bah* repetitions; and a third group heard only 70 repetitions of *bah* (Moffitt, 1971). The babies in the first two groups showed a marked heart-rate response when the experimenters suddenly presented the new consonant sound, *gah* or *bah*, respectively, which is evidence that the infants perceived the change. Babies in the third group showed no change in heart rate, suggesting that this sort of change as seen in the babies of the first two groups was not simply a reaction to the continuation of sounds. This ability to discriminate speech sounds is evident from as early as 1 month of age and holds true for a variety of other consonants, such as *m*, *n* and *d* (Aslin, 1987; Miller & Eimas, 1994; Aslin et al., 1998). Infants' discrimination abilities rapidly improve; by the time they are 2 months old, infants can tell the difference between /a/ and /i/. Even more remarkably, 2- to 3-month-old infants can recognize the same vowel even when it is spoken by different people at different pitches (Marean, Werner, & Kuhl, 1992).

> **categorical speech perception** The tendency to perceive as the same a range of sounds belonging to the same phonemic group.

Findings such as these seem to suggest that infants are indeed born with some innate mechanism for perceiving oral language. However, although evidence suggests that infants have an innate tendency to find the boundaries in sound patterns the tendency to organize and group incoming information into patterns is not unique to processing the sounds of speech. In addition, research by Miller and colleagues (1976) revealed that chinchillas show categorical speech perception and can discriminate between /b/ and /p/! This research casts further doubt on the notion that humans are uniquely prepared for language acquisition. Instead of being a specifically linguistic property of auditory perception, categorical speech perception may be a property of the mammal's aural system that language simply utilizes (Miller & Eimas, 1994; Kuhl et al., 1997).

BEYOND CATEGORICAL PERCEPTION

Categorical speech perception is not the only skill babies exhibit that may help them learn language. In Box 6-2, we discussed studies by DeCasper suggesting that infants may learn some features of language prenatally; recent evidence suggests that infants can identify key properties of their native language's rhythmic organization either prenatally or during the first few days of life (Saffran et al., 2006). For example, 4-day-old French babies increased their sucking rate when listening to French speech as opposed to Russian (Mehler et al., 1988).

Whatever innate abilities infants have for perceiving speech sounds, these abilities constantly interact with experience over the language-learning period. Research suggests that, as babies develop, they lose their ability to distinguish the sounds of languages to which they haven't been exposed (Werker, 1989). For example, one study found that infants of English-speaking parents could distinguish between sounds that are unique to Swedish only until the age of 6 months (Kuhl et al., 1992). Similar findings occur for other languages as well. Jusczyk and colleagues (1993) found that by the time American infants were 9 months old, they 'tuned out' Dutch words, and Dutch infants were similarly unresponsive to English words. Findings such as this provide strong support for a dual role of innate and experiential or environmental factors in the early recognition of speech sounds.

Although babies become highly skilled at discriminating the speech sounds of their native language at an early age, it takes time for them to learn to focus on important sound distinctions in everyday speech. As we've seen, 1-month-old infants can detect the differences between the consonant sounds of *bah* and *gah*, and 2- and 3-month-old infants are able to recognize the consistency of a speech sound, for example /i/, even when pronounced by different speakers (Marean et al., 1992). Learning a language also requires learning which of the many discriminable differences in speech sounds actually signal differences in meanings. Further evidence suggests that infants can segment fluent speech and recognize words in ongoing speech better and much earlier than we had thought possible – by the end of their first year (Saffran et al., 2006) and perhaps even as early as 6.5 to 7 months of age (Thiessen & Saffran, 2003). Research suggests that infants have the capacity to make the kinds of distinctions that indicate word boundaries in the flow of speech (Hohne & Jusczyk, 1994; Morgan & Saffran, 1995; Saffran, Aslin, & Newport, 1996) and they use a variety of cues such as strong syllables (e.g., *tar* in *gui•TAR*), stressed monosyllables (e.g., *cup, dog* or *bike*), a strong syllable followed by a weak one (e.g., *TALK•er, TUR•ban*), and rhythmic properties to help define the boundaries of words, including pitch and pauses (Jusczyk et al., 1993; Morgan, 1994; Jusczyk, Houston, & Newsome, 1999; Thiessen & Saffran, 2003).

> **habituation** A form of learning instantiated in a decrease in the strength of response to a repeated stimulus.

According to other research (Saffran et al., 1996), 8-month-old infants can detect new words in unfamiliar artificial language even when they have no idea what the words mean. Researchers had infants listen to 2 minutes of nonsense syllables mixed with 'words' from an artificial language, which the researchers devised to eliminate the possibility that the infants were picking out words based on what they had already learned at home. Using a habituation paradigm, the researchers noted that when the tape was played a second time, the babies did not pay attention to the words – an indication that they had already learned them. This suggests that, in the second half of the first year, babies are capable of detecting words in ongoing speech (Aslin et al., 1996). Fortunately, infants have the ability to detect words in sentences because this is how most words are introduced to the young language learner. When Woodward and Aslin (1990) asked mothers to teach new words to their 12 month olds, the mothers presented their infants with most of the words in sentences. They presented only 20% of the words as words alone.

Crying

Crying is one of the infant's earliest means of communicating needs to caregivers. Three different patterns of crying, reflective of the infant's varying needs, have been identified (Schaffer, 1971, p. 61).

Newborns typically cry because of some form of physiological distress, such as hunger, the need for a nappy change, or digestive problems. By 3 or 4 months of age, a baby's crying – a clear form of communication – will often be related to psychological needs, such as his wish to be picked up and hugged or caressed, or to be played with.
© Shutterstock/Irina Rogova

Most mothers can distinguish among these different types of crying, but only when listening to the cries of their own babies (Wiesenfeld, Malatesta, & DeLoache, 1981). In general, fathers are less skilled than mothers at distinguishing among types of cry, and non-parents are less skilled than parents (Holden, 1988). These differences are probably related to varying amounts of experience with babies and differences in the amount of time spent caring for them.

In the early months of life, crying is usually related to the infant's physiology; hunger, hiccups, or digestive problems may disturb him and lead to crying. By 3 or 4 months, however, crying is less associated with physiological distress and increasingly related to the baby's psychological needs, such as wanting to be picked up

Table 8-1 Characteristics of crying

Pattern	Characteristics
Basic	Starts arrhythmically and at low intensity; gradually becomes louder and more rhythmic; sequence is cry–rest–inhale–rest. Linked to hunger, among other factors.
Angry	Same as basic pattern except that segments of crying, resting and inhaling vary in length, and crying segments are longer. Causes include removing a pacifier or toy.
Pain	Sudden in onset, loud from the start, and made up of a long cry followed by a long silence that includes holding the breath and then by a series of short, gasping inhalations. Causes include discomfort from soiled nappy or a stomach ache.

or played with. Also, by this age, most infants spend less of their days crying, and their concerns are easier to interpret (Kopp, 1994).

Crying often leads to a response from the caregiver. In one study, 77% of 2,461 episodes of crying that were observed were followed by some intervention by the mother (Moss, 1967). This intervention becomes an opportunity for social interaction, so the caregiver is rewarded in two ways: the crying stops, and the caregiver and child engage in a mutually enjoyable exchange (Lester, 1988).

Babbling and other early sounds

It is not just receptive language abilities that develop rapidly in infancy. Babies are actively producing sounds – even though not language – from birth onwards. Anyone who has been woken up in the middle of the night by the sound of a baby happily 'talking' to herself knows that infants are neither quiet nor passive in the process of early language learning. They make a great many sounds, as if 'gearing up' for their ultimate production of speech.

The production of sounds in the first year of life follows an orderly four-stage sequence summarized in Table 8-2. Crying, which begins at birth, is an important way of indicating distress and serves as a rudimentary means of communication. *Cooing*, the production of vowel-like sounds, starts at the end of the first month. Cooing, so named because it consists of *oo* sounds that resemble the sounds pigeons make, often occurs during social exchanges between infant and caregiver. *Babbling*, or producing strings of consonant–vowel combinations, begins in the middle of the first year. Finally, at the close of the first year, *patterned speech* appears. In this pseudo-speech, the child utters strings of 'words' made up of phonemes in his native language that sound very much like real speech – even in intonation – but are not. These various stages overlap, and even patterned speech and true speech may occur together as the child's first meaningful words begin to appear.

Table 8-2 Stages of sound production in the infant's first year

Stage	Begins	Description
Crying	At birth	Signals of distress
Cooing	At about 1 month	*Oo* sounds that occur during social exchanges with caregiver
Babbling	Middle of first year	Strings of consonant–vowel combinations
Patterned speech	Close of first year	Strings of pseudo-words, made up of phonemes in native language, that sound like words

Not only does the early production of sounds follow an orderly sequence, but the kinds of sounds made at each of the first three stages are quite similar across different language communities. For instance, young Chinese, American and Ethiopian babies all babble similar consonant–vowel combinations, even though they are exposed to different phonemes in their native languages (Thevenin et al., 1985). Even the early babbling of deaf babies sounds similar to the babbling of babies who can hear (Lenneberg, Rebelsky, & Nichols, 1965). Deaf infants born to deaf parents who sign (rather than speak) babble with their hands and fingers at the same age as hearing children babble vocally; moreover, their movements show similar structure in terms of syllabic and phonetic patterning (Bloom, 1998; Petitto et al., 2001). These similarities between manual and vocal babbling suggest 'a unitary language capacity that underlies human signed and spoken language acquisition' (Petitto & Marenette, 1991, p. 1495). Overall, these findings suggest that the pattern of development of early sounds that infants make is a function of maturational changes in vocal structures and in the parts of the brain that control producing sound.

In the middle of the second half-year, however, cultural differences in the prespeech sounds that babies make begin to emerge. For instance, babies exposed to one of two different native languages, Arabic or French, which contrast significantly in voice quality and pitch, may begin to show differences in their babbling at around 8 months of age (Ingram, 1989). Japanese and French words contain more nasal sounds than Swedish and English words, and in the latter part of the first year, French and Japanese babies' babbling contains more nasal sounds than that of their Swedish and English counterparts (De Boysson-Bardies et al., 1992). It is as if the babies are now starting to 'tune in' to the language they hear spoken around them. Interestingly, the amount of time exposed to language, not just the baby's physical maturation, appears to be an important factor. Babies who are born prematurely, and who are therefore exposed to language earlier (in terms of their gestational age) than full-term babies are, begin complex babbling sooner than full-term infants (Eilers et al., 1993).

Thus, although historically linguists have argued that there is no relation between babies' early vocalizations and their later speech (Jakobson, 1968), other evidence challenges this view. The babblings of infants over their first year resemble the child's first meaningful words in a variety of ways (Oller et al., 1976; Elbers & Ton, 1985; Carroll et al., 2003). Evidently, a child's early vocalizations are not only orderly in their development but also related to later speech. In terms of the foundations for both receptive and productive language skills, the infant is very well prepared for learning to talk.

THEORIES OF LANGUAGE DEVELOPMENT
The components of language

Children learn about the sounds, meaning, structure and use of language simultaneously. However, for the purposes of understanding how children learn language, researchers typically divide the study of language into four main components or areas: phonology, semantics, grammar and pragmatics.

Phonology, the system of sounds that a particular language uses, includes not only the language's basic units of sound, or *phonemes*, but also rules about how we put phonemes together to form words and rules about the proper intonation patterns for phrases and sentences. Phonemes are considered basic units of sound because they are the smallest sound units that affect meaning; changing a phoneme changes the meaning of a word. For example, by changing the initial phoneme in the word *bat*, we can make the very different word *cat*. By changing the middle phoneme, we can make yet another word, *bit*. A very important feature of phonologic rules is that they are *generative*; that is, they can be applied beyond the specific cases on which they are based. For example, a native English speaker knows that *kib* is not a word in English, but it is nonetheless a possible sound pattern in the language's system. In contrast, *bnik* is not possible in English.

> **phonology** The system of sounds that a language uses.
>
> **semantics** The study of word meanings and word combinations.
>
> **grammar** The structure of a language; consists of *morphology* and *syntax*.
>
> **morphology** The study of morphemes, language's smallest units of meaning.
>
> **syntax** The part of grammar that prescribes how words may combine into phrases, clauses and sentences.
>
> **pragmatics** A set of rules that specify appropriate language for particular social contexts.

The study of word meanings and word combinations is called semantics. Comprehension of language requires not only knowledge of specific words and their definitions but also an understanding of how we use words and how we combine them in phrases and sentences. Thus, as children mature intellectually, their semantic knowledge continues to grow. Even adults continue to expand their vocabularies as they obtain new knowledge. For example, a student who begins to study psychology for the first time has to learn a whole new vocabulary of psychological terms and their meanings.

Grammar describes the structure of a language and consists of two major parts: morphology and syntax. The subfield of grammar studies called morphology concentrates on the smallest units of meaning in a language, such as prefixes, suffixes and root words. These units are called *morphemes*. Rules for altering root words to produce such things as plurals, past tenses and inflections are part of a language's morphological system. Syntax is the aspect of grammar that specifies how words are combined into sentences. For example, each language has syntactic rules for expressing grammatical relations such as negation, interrogation, possession, and the arrangement of subject and object in a statement. The rules of syntax allow us to vary word order so that we are not limited to one way of saying what we mean, provided that what we say is still syntactically correct. For example, we can say, 'After school, I went to the library and listened to some music', but the syntactically incorrect sentence, 'I listened to some music after school and I went to the library', is ambiguous and less clear.

> The debate between learning and nativist approaches to language development corresponds to the nature versus nurture theme in developmental psychology, discussed in Chapter 1.

The fourth component of language, pragmatics, consists of rules for the use of language in particular contexts (Bates, 1999). Thus, pragmatics directly concerns effective and appropriate communication. For example, a child learns that certain forms of language are more appropriate in some situations. A child may have a better chance of getting what she wants if she asks a schoolmate, 'Please may I have one of your crayons?' instead of demanding, 'Give me the crayon!' Researchers in pragmatics study these and other issues, such as how children learn to take turns speaking, to remain silent while others speak, and to speak differently in such different settings as the classroom and the playground.

As in many other subfields of child psychology, those who study language development debate how much heredity contributes to the development of language and how much children's experiences contribute to the ability to use language and communicate effectively. Most theorists today hold an interactionist view. This view recognizes that biological and environmental factors are frequently intertwined and both play an important role in language development. To gain a full understanding of this interactionist approach, we first explore the environmental, or learning, view and then the biological, or nativist, view.

The learning approach: claims and limitations

Traditional learning explanations use the principle of *reinforcement* to account for language development. The learning theorist B.F. Skinner (1957) suggested that parents or other caregivers selectively reinforce the child's babbling sounds that are most like adult speech. He argued that by giving attention to these particular sounds and showing approval when their baby utters them, parents encourage the child to repeat them. When the child repeats the sounds, the parents or caregivers approve again, and the child, in turn, vocalizes these particular sounds more often. Thus, according to Skinner, by giving their greatest approval to the infant's closest approximations to adult speech sounds, parents shape their child's verbal behaviour into what increasingly resembles adult speech. Other learning theorists (e.g., Bandura, 1989) propose that children learn through *imitation* or observational learning. According to this view, children pick up words, phrases and sentences directly by imitating what they hear. Then, through reinforcement and *generalization*, or applying what they have learned to new situations, children learn when to use particular words and phrases.

There is no doubt that the environment plays a part in language development. Learning theory accounts, however, have not fared well as a singular explanation of language acquisition, for several reasons. First, the number of stimulus-response connections – that is, specific linkages between a baby's vocalization and a parent's reinforcing response – that would be needed to explain language, even the language of a very young child, is so enormous that is seems unfeasible that a child could learn them in a lifetime, let alone a few short years. Second, naturalistic studies of parent–child interaction fail to support the learning theory account. For example, mothers are just as likely to reward their children for truthful but grammatically incorrect statements as they are to reinforce the children for grammatically correct utterances (Brown & Hanlon, 1970). Parents are concerned to teach their children acceptable behaviour as well as the correct use of language. It is difficult to see, then, how reinforcement alone might account for children's grammar learning (Brown, 1973; Pinker, 1994).

A third argument against a learning explanation is that we cannot predict the vast majority of language utterances from opportunities to observe specific utterances by others. For example, utterances that are closely tied to environmental cues, such as 'Hello' or 'Watch out!', are relatively rare. For most sets of circumstances, language entails more creative responses than can be accounted for by a learning view. Fourth, learning theory accounts have not explained the regular sequence in which language develops. Children across cultures seem to learn the same types of grammatical rule in the same order. For example, they learn active constructions before passive constructions: they learn to say, 'Jonas and Martin made cakes for the party' before they learn to say 'The cakes for the party were made by Jonas and Martin'. Finally, the learning explanation portrays the child as playing a rather passive role in language development. However, as evidence we discuss later shows, the child often plays an active and creative role in discovering and applying general rules of language.

The nativist view: claims and limitations

An alternative explanation to learning accounts – the nativist view – suggests that language acquisition unfolds as a result of the unique biological properties of humans. Linguist Noam Chomsky (1968) proposed that children are born with an innate mental structure that guides their acquisition of language and, in particular, grammar. Chomsky termed this structure a language acquisition device (LAD).

language acquisition device (LAD)
Chomsky's proposed mental structure in the human nervous system, which incorporates an innate concept of language.

Nativists argue that the human child is biologically predisposed to acquire language and that, because language ability is an inherited species-specific characteristic, all languages of the species must display universal features; that is, they must share certain basic characteristics. By examining features such as the sounds used in speaking, the way words are organized in sentences, and how meaning is determined in various languages, investigators have concluded that a set of common principles does underlie all human languages (Slobin, 1985, 1992). For instance, speakers of all languages create a vast number of spoken words by combining a relatively small set of the possible vocal sounds humans can make. Finally, all languages have grammars, and nativists claim these grammars share certain formal properties as well (e.g., the subject–predicate relationship).

Also, in support of their position, nativists point out that, in many different cultures, normal children acquire language relatively quickly and learn it well (Maratsos, 1989; Pinker, 1994; Meisel, 1995). Even in situations in which children receive fragmented and incomplete environmental input, they can learn language. Thus, nativists argue that the child must be biologically prepared to acquire language. As Box 8-2 suggests, some of the most striking evidence for the possibility of an innate predisposition for language comes from the study of children who learn language even with restricted input.

Applied Developmental Psychology

BOX 8-2 Can children create new languages?

The most striking evidence that children may possess an innate programme or template for grammar comes from the work of Derek Bickerton (1983, 1990, 2008), who has studied creole languages around the globe. The *creole language* often arises in a context in which people who speak different languages for some reason end up together in a single culture. We see this, for instance, in Hawaii, the south-east coast of North America, New Orleans, the Caribbean, north-eastern South America, Africa, islands in the Indian Ocean, Indonesia and the Philippines, where peoples from countries of Asia, Africa, Europe and the Americas came together and formed polyglot societies. Although the adults in these situations crafted a common language that could be used to communicate, this language, called pidgin, lacked grammatical structure. However, the children in these cultures, regardless of their parents' native languages, used a language derived from *pidgin*, called *creole*, which had a single structure and linguistic system. Moreover, the creole languages persisted into succeeding generations in similar form. How could the children of these different cultural groups have evolved languages that resemble one another if they did not possess some sort of inner template of a universal grammar?

In these multicultural societies, many of which were made up of people who were moved, often against their will, to work on colonial plantations, communication began with the development of a pidgin language, a simplified linguistic system created out of two languages that suddenly come into contact with each other. Pidgin lacks grammatical complexity: its sentences are often no more than strings of nouns, verbs and adjectives. For this reason and because pidgin is highly individualistic, varying from speaker to speaker, its usefulness is limited. Such limitations may be what led the children of pidgin speakers to develop the more complex type of communication represented by creole languages.

The language children in polyglot societies develop is much richer in grammatical structure than pidgin (Bickerton, 1983). And, interestingly, creole languages that develop in different places throughout the world are very similar in their structure, regardless of the contributing languages! Even more remarkably, the speech of first-generation creole-speaking children does not differ from that of later generations of speakers, which suggests that the acquisition of this new language happens very rapidly. Together, the uniformity of language across speakers and geographical locales, and the speed of language acquisition, argue against any simple explanation that children who learn creole are simply borrowing from the contact languages in a haphazard fashion.

What are the implications of these observations for theories of language acquisition? According to Bickerton (1983):

> The evidence from creole languages suggests that first-language acquisition is mediated by an innate device ... the device provides the child with a single and fairly specific grammatical model. It was only in pidgin-speaking communities, where there was no grammatical model that could compete with the child's innate grammar, that the innate grammatical model was not eventually suppressed. The innate grammar was then clothed in whatever vocabulary was locally available and gave rise to the creole languages heard today. (p. 121)

A similar process appeared in the language development of a group of deaf children in Nicaragua. In 1977, Nicaragua opened its first school for deaf people. Before the school opened, the lack of an organized school system prevented the deaf from much interaction. In the school, children and adults were taught to lip-read and to speak Spanish. This approach yielded little success, but the students were also able to freely engage in gestural communication. Slowly, a rudimentary sign language emerged among the students. As new children of various ages entered the school, they learned this sign language from their peers. Senghas and Coppola (2001) investigated the complexity of this gestural language in relation to how long children were at the school and the age at which they entered the school. If the complex grammar of language was found only among the children, then they could conclude that the knowledge stemmed from innate abilities available to the child until he or she reaches the critical period. If the most complex components of the language were found only in adults learning the new sign language, they could conclude that higher cognitive levels are needed to grasp the hardest parts of language. The investigators found that the most complex patterns of speech originated in children under the age of 10 and that adults were unable to make use of these structures in either comprehension or production. Thus, children were able to create and learn gestures that conveyed complex linguistic structures, whereas adults who were past the critical period were unable to do so. This conclusion provides powerful support for the theory that humans are designed to learn language at an early age.

Our understanding of these processes is not complete, however. Some critics, like Tomasello (1995), have argued that adult influences may play a role in the emergence of creole. And others argue that creole languages reveal the common uses of language across cultures rather than simply reflecting properties of the human mind (Jourdan, 1991). Finally, as Hoff (2005) points out, the fact that creole languages developed a long time ago makes it difficult to know exactly what processes underlie them. At this point, it seems that the interactionist view (see below), which suggests that both biological factors and environmental influences provide the best account of language acquisition, may offer a viable alternative explanation for the creole languages.

Another source of support for the nativist view is evidence that human beings learn language far more easily during a certain critical period of biological development. The critical period for language stretches from infancy to puberty. Before puberty, a child may achieve the fluency of a native speaker in any language without special training but, after puberty, it is extremely difficult to learn a first language.

> **critical period** A period of development (age range) at which specific experiences are vital for development to occur in a typical way.

Dramatic examples come from several famous case studies. In 1800, a 12-year-old boy was discovered living on his own in the woods near Aveyron, France. The boy had no language, and in spite of efforts by Jean Itard at the National Institute for Deaf-Mutes in Paris, the boy was able to learn only a few words. Although no one knows why the boy had such difficulty (e.g., he may have been impaired at birth), his case raises the question of whether language can be acquired only before puberty (Lane, 1976). In another modern case, 13-year-old 'Genie' was discovered to have been kept locked in a room by her mentally ill father from the time she was 18 months of age (Curtiss, 1989; Rymer, 1993). Although Genie was more successful in learning to communicate than the wild boy in France, she never acquired normal language. These cases strongly suggest a critical period for language acquisition (Hoff, 2005). Further support for the idea of a critical period of language learning is found among young children whose speech is disrupted by brain injury and who often recover their language capacity rapidly and completely. If the brain damage occurs after puberty, however, the prognosis for the recovery of language is poorer. Nevertheless, the fact that there is considerable variation, even among adults, suggests that despite the existence of a critical period, other contributions are also important (Goodglass, 1993).

Often, people have cited the ability of animals to learn language as evidence against the nativist viewpoint, but the conclusions are mixed (Gomez, 2004). Determining whether animals other than humans learn language depends on the definition of language a scientist uses as well as on the assumptions about what goes on in the human mind when people use language. If one is to define language as a use of symbols as referents, then the average sheepdog is able to learn a language when it learns dozens of whistles for various actions. However, linguists consider many features when defining language, including the understanding of word order ('Bob hit Jim' as opposed to 'Jim hit Bob'), and the creation of novel yet understandable speech – for example, by putting together two known words to create a novel meaning. Using these guidelines, there does seem to be some evidence of language in many species, ranging from the African grey parrot (Pepperberg, 2000) to dolphins (Herman & Uyeyama, 1999) and various primate species (Savage-Rumbaugh & Shanker, 1998). Some researchers, such as Kako (1999), argue that their language abilities place these animals at about the level of a 2-year-old human. They are still lacking crucial aspects of language learning such as the use of prepositions and conjunctions. Finally, the assumption that using human language effectively entails understanding the mind and its properties, whether such abilities exist in non-human primates, such as chimpanzees, is difficult to determine (Povinelli, Bering, & Giambrone, 2000; Hermann et al., 2007).

Like the learning view, the nativist explanation of language development has its limitations. First, few theorists agree about the exact nature of the types of grammatical rules that children learn. In fact, several theorists have offered alternative explanations of the early grammar acquisition process that differ from Chomsky's original formulation (Slobin, 1985; Maratsos, 1989, 1998; Pinker, 1994). Second, language learning is a gradual process and is not completed as early as nativist accounts would predict. As we will see later in the chapter, specific aspects of grammar continue to develop in the elementary school years and even beyond.

Third, this perspective makes it very difficult to account for the many languages human beings speak throughout the world. Despite the nativist claim that languages possess universal features, it is difficult to envision features that produce such different grammatical structures and the enormous variety of sound combinations in the world's languages. Fourth, the nativist view gives the social context of language little recognition. We now know from research that takes an interactionist approach to language development that social influences play a much larger role in language development than is proposed in a nativist view (Nelson, 2007). Additionally, the theoretical assertion that language milestones are acquired in a universal stage sequence is not supported by empirical research stemming from an interactionist approach (Nelson, 1998). The communicative context of language development, especially adult–child communication, plays a significant role in the pacing of this developmental process.

It seems likely that human beings are biologically prepared *in some way* for learning language. However, it seems quite unlikely that biological principles alone can account for all aspects of language development.

The interactionist view

Most modern theorists of language development take the interactionist view, recognizing that language is learned in the context of spoken language, but assuming as well that humans are in some way biologically prepared for learning to speak (Tomasello, 2003). The child's own active role in language development complements the role played by socializing agents like parents (Morgan, 1990; Gallaway & Richards, 1994). In addition, language acquisition is not separate from other aspects of development (Bloom & Tinker, 2001). Rather, language learning takes place in a rich behavioural and developmental context in which children engage in relationships with others and try to accomplish meaningful goals.

In the interactionist view, normal language develops as a result of a delicate balance between parent and child understanding: when parents speak to children in a way that recognizes how much the children already know and understand, they increase enormously their children's chance of comprehending a novel message (Ninio & Snow, 1996; Bloom, 1998; Tomasello, 2006). In this respect, children can only really learn language from someone who communicates with them.

From an interactionist perspective, biology is also considered an important contributor to language development. One strand of evidence for a genetic component in language development comes from studies of children whose language development is impaired or delayed in some way. These impairments are often better understood using theoretically defined, cognitive approaches which also better explain links to genetic factors than do clinical descriptions of symptoms. However, as Bishop (2006) notes, the group of children with some impairment to language are highly heterogeneous. For instance, some children may show only language problems (for instance, semantic-pragmatic difficulties where there are problems in understanding what others say and communicating a child's own beliefs and intentions appropriately) but in many other cases these are co-morbid (i.e., co-occur) with psychological disorders such as autism (which is also associated with language problems). As such, it seems probable that different genetic mutations are implicated in different cases. And that these may interact in a plethora of ways with environmental influences to create observable language problems.

Further evidence for the interplay of environment and genes in language development (consistent with the interactionist approach) comes from twin studies in children with typical language development. Reznick, Corley, and Robinson (1997) examined language and cognitive development in twins at 14, 20 and

24 months using a longitudinal research design. Monozygotic (identical) twins showed a higher concordance for non-verbal cognitive and intellectual functions than dizygotic (fraternal) twins, indicating a strong genetic component. However, in terms of language, genetic influence emerged only at 14 months for receptive language (the ability to understand words and speech) and only at 20 months for expressive language (the ability to communicate verbally). It is around 20–24 months that some key skills rapidly emerge, such as using more sophisticated word combinations. This suggests that genes play a part in language development, but these are reliant on maturing, underlying cognitive processes and that progress in each area is linked to environmental variation.

BOX 8-3   Wh...? Fathers' questions matter for toddlers' language development

Research close-up

Source: Based on Rowe, Leech, & Cabrera (2017).

Introduction:

Interactionists argue that biology and experience (environmental factors) inter-relate to facilitate language development. In this way the play, early conversations and interactions between parents and children help a child's language skills and understanding to develop. Much work has explored how mothers' interactions can facilitate language development in children. Fewer have focused on how others, and notably fathers, can have a positive influence on language development. Moreover, it is important to recognize that it is not just the quantity of interaction but also the quality of interaction, and the responses that parents can elicit from children, that promotes development.

Method:

The 24-month-old children (n = 41) of low-income, African American fathers were assessed on several verbal measures and then videotaped interacting with their fathers at home. The sessions were semi-structured in that the pair were given three bags with different contents. In the first bag was a child's book, in the second a toy pizza and phone, and in the third a toy farm and some animals. Fathers were told to play with the contents in each bag in order, for a total of 10 minutes for all three bags. The 10-minute sessions were then transcribed and analysed to assess the total amount of talk, and different types of talk including the questions that fathers asked. The researchers also evaluated how children responded (or attempted to respond) to questions. The proportion of different types of questions asked was calculated for each dyad (i.e., father-child unit). A year later, when the child was 36 months old, the researchers returned to assess the child's verbal reasoning skills and vocabulary knowledge.

Results:

The researchers found that the overall quantity (amount) of fathers' talk with their child did not relate to their child's verbal or reasoning skills a year later. In other words, it was not the *amount* of talk that matters. Rather, fathers' use of wh- questions (who, what, when, why, where and how?) but not other questions (e.g., 'yes/no' questions) did relate to development of vocabulary and reasoning measures a year later. It is important to note that it was likely not the session of interaction itself, but rather the father's more general approach to interacting to his child that was picked up by the video-observations at 24 months. The researchers also observed that children's responses to *wh-* questions tended to be more complex (and more frequent), suggesting that they offer more of a challenge to children than other types of question.

Discussion:

Clearly, parent–child interaction is a fundamental ingredient in child language development. This study suggests that fathers' interactions can stimulate their child's language development by actively engaging children in conversation by asking certain types of question that challenge the child a little to produce more complex responses. It is not, then, just the quantity but the quality of interaction that is likely to get the child actively engaged in interaction and in language to produce and understand more. From an interactionist perspective, it is the child's rehearsal and use of language, in interaction, that can promote both language and cognitive development. It is also important to note that this study was conducted with low-income African American fathers; not a typical group studied in much developmental psychology research and a group where, perhaps, a child's language skills and cognitive development are important factors for promoting child development. Thus, the quality of father–child interaction is just as important in what may be a more challenging developmental and educational set of circumstances than, say, those in a white, middle-class family. This sort of research with diverse samples that are under-represented in much developmental research is important if we are to gain a comprehensive understanding of developmental process. It is also vital if we wish to apply our research understanding to promote social change.

SEMANTIC DEVELOPMENT

Despite children's early skills in both receptive and productive language, research suggests that children's understanding of language far exceeds their capacity to express themselves clearly (see Figure 8-1). These findings may help to explain the fact that children don't develop their vocabularies in a strictly linear fashion. Like other aspects of development, vocabulary acquisition proceeds in bursts. The *naming explosion* (Bloom, Lifter, & Broughton, 1985) is the rapid increase in vocabulary that most children begin to show at the age of about 1.5, when typically they can comprehend between 50 and 100 words. Children usually utter their first words between 10 and 15 months (Fenson et al., 1994).

By 2 years of age the average child knows approximately 900 root words, and by 6 they know around 8000. Some research suggests that although some children – about 20% – display a spurt or explosion in vocabulary, most children add words gradually (Ganger & Brent, 2004). Whatever development is gradual or a consequence of several periods of intensive development the remarkable growth of vocabulary over the first 5 years of life is a dramatic example of the human capacity for language and communication.

How children acquire words

How do children learn words? Imagine that you have taken a job in a foreign country, and your first task is to learn the language. A native of the country points to a dog lying on a rug and says, '*xitf*'. How do you know whether *xitf* refers to the dog, the dog's twitching ear, the dog's name, the dog's fur, the fact that the dog is sleeping on the rug, the fact that the dog is the speaker's pet, or the rug? Clearly, the acquisition of object names is no simple matter.

There are many different views of how children create a linguistic link between the mind and the world (Waxman & Lidz, 2006). Some theorists argue that children simply form an association, others contend that the social aspect of this process is important, and still others take the middle ground. According to Smith (2000), word learning is based on associations combined with attention to perceptual similarity. Through experience, children realize that words label categories based primarily on similarity of overall object shape. If a child sees many tables that are often given the label *table*, over time he will realize that most things with a flat top and four legs get the label of *table*.

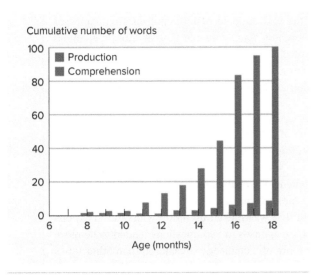

Figure 8-1 Receptive and productive language in infants
Children's comprehension outpaces their production of words. On average, children understood nearly 100 words by the time they were 18 months old, but could produce only 8 to 10.
Source: Based on Huttenlocher (1974)

Another view is that children use mainly social cues from adults to learn what a word labels (Tomasello, 1998; Bloom, 2000). Many findings show that simply hearing a label in the presence of an object is not enough for an infant to learn that the word is a symbol for the object. For example, seeing a novel toy on a table and hearing an automated voice saying *glorp* will not cause the child to attach the label *glorp* to the object. Children depend on social cues such as pointing and the speaker's eye gaze.

Still other theorists claim multiple cues are available to infants for word learning, but how much they depend on each type of cue changes with age (Hollich, Hirsh-Pasek, & Golinkoff, 2000). In this viewpoint, younger children do rely on perceptual similarity to realize when a word is the correct label for an object, but as they get older, they become more dependent on social and linguistic cues. There is evidence that 16 month olds will not accept a common label for two objects that look extremely different, but 20-month-old infants are willing to trust the speaker and give two perceptually distinct objects the same label (Nazzi & Gopnik, 2001).

Although the task of word learning may seem difficult, infants appear to come into the task with some constraints or principles that aid them. (See Box 8-4 for a discussion of how children with mental retardation can learn to use words.) Markman (1989) was the first to introduce the idea of word-learning principles. For example, the *whole object constraint* involves the assumption that a new word refers to the entire object and not to one of its parts or properties. Children as young as 18 months appear to make use of this constraint. For example, when 2-year-old Jamal visits the zoo and hears the word *anteater* for the first time, he assumes that anteater refers to the animal, not its nose, body or behaviour. Even 12 month olds associate novel words with whole objects rather than parts of the object (Hollich, Golinkoff, & Hirsch-Pasek, 2007).

BOX 8-4   Children at risk for failure to develop language

Applied Developmental Psychology

Youth with moderate or severe mental retardation often need extensive and ongoing support in more than one major life activity; one of the most important is communication. Youth with moderate and severe retardation range from those who do learn to speak, although slowly and often with limited success, to those who are unable to develop spoken communicative skills at all, even with considerable speech and language instruction.

Using one of the methods developed by investigators of non-human primate communication, Mary Ann Romski and Rose Sevcik (1996) have shown that such youth who have never developed oral speech can learn to communicate intelligibly with adults and peers. In an approach based on Vygotskian concepts, each of 13 young boys with moderate to severe retardation worked with a partner (a teacher or a parent) who demonstrated and encouraged the child in using a computerized device that enabled him to select a particular symbol or lexigram, referred to as the System for Augmenting Language (SAL), on a keyboard to produce a single word or phrase (Figure 8-2). When the child presses a given key, the computer produces a synthesized voicing of the word or phrase and also prints it on a screen. The literature on children with severe retardation had claimed that such children could learn only with continuous prompting. Romski and Sevcik found, however, that a majority of their participants, 12 years old on average, who used the SAL device rapidly learned to associate symbols with words and phrases. By the end of the 2 years, most of the participants could both comprehend and produce a majority of the vocabulary words presented to them in instruction sessions. More than half of the participants even demonstrated the skill of fast-mapping, immediately associating a new name with a new object/symbol.

Romski and Sevcik chose to use arbitrary visual-graphic symbols rather than representational pictures in this work in part because they wanted to study 'the process of learning to communicate symbolically' (1996, p. 61). They introduced only a small number of symbols at a time to participants, beginning with a set of 12 symbols relevant to mealtime – symbols for specific foods, drinks and utensils. The next group of words introduced related to leisure-time activities – for example, *ball, game, magazine, television* – and the third group were social-regulative words and phrases such as *hello, excuse me, I want* and *thank you*. A final group consisted of words tailored to individual participants' needs; for example, they added the word *work* to the lexicon of a participant who had a part-time job.

By the end of the two-year period, all participants had acquired 53 single words or two-word phrases in the first two categories, 16 words or phrases in the third group, and additional words or phrases in the final category. Moreover, many used their lexicons to engage in communication with people in the community without the use of the computer and synthesized speech. Thus, the participants' speech production had to stand on its own. For instance, one youth, classified as severely retarded, went to a mall music store and requested the

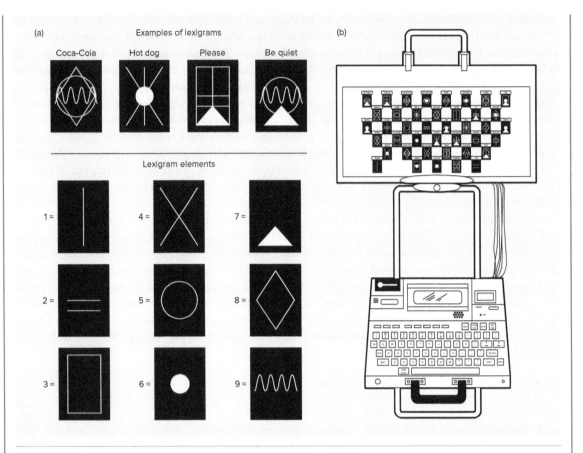

Figure 8-2 Communicating with a computer and lexigrams
(a) Lexigrams like these, each made up of some combination of the nine elements shown, appear on the upper keypad of the computerized device (b). When a child presses the key for, say, hot dog, the words are sounded in synthetic speech and are also printed on the display screen of the computer.
Source: Adapted from Romski and Sevcik (1996)

assistance of a clerk by asking 'HELP TAPE' and then showing the clerk a photograph of the tape he wanted. With tape in hand, the youth then said 'THANK YOU' (Romski & Sevcik, 1996, p. 145).

According to Romski and Sevcik, some parents have been reluctant to offer SAL training to their children because they fear it will impede the children's efforts to learn to speak. Very few data, in fact, are available on the outcome of the early use of intervention with speech-output communication devices. Clearly, there is room for a great deal more research in this area. Among other things, we need to know what early predictors, such as specific behaviours or difficulties, may differentiate children who will not develop speech from those who will. We also need to determine whether early intervention with SAL could not only help children who are at risk for failure to develop language to communicate, but perhaps also help provide the cognitive stimulation and trigger the motivation that might facilitate their learning of oral speech. Whatever its ultimate usefulness, SAL training has revealed the presence of cognitive capacities in children with mental retardation who, by traditional measures, had been considered only minimally functional. The work suggests that such young people can learn language under the right conditions and can apply it in social interaction.

After Markman introduced the concept of constraints, researchers began to notice other constraints that children seem to follow in word learning (Merriman & Bowman, 1989; Markman & Hutchinson, 1994). As a result, Hollich and colleagues (2000) have compiled a set of six principles deemed necessary and sufficient to account for how children get word learning 'off the ground' within the framework of their Emergentist Coalition Model (ECM). These principles are less strict than the more nativist view Markman proposed because the principles themselves undergo change with development and because the use of these principles depends on a combination of both inborn biases and word-learning experience.

These six principles begin with the basic necessity to understand language. For example, the first thing a child must understand is the principle of *reference*, or the idea that words stand for objects, actions and events. Later in development, children come to understand more complex principles such as the *Novel Name-Nameless Category* (abbreviated as *N3C*). Similar to Markman's (1994) *mutual exclusivity bias*, N3C states that, upon hearing a novel label, infants assume it labels a novel object over a familiar one. In a representative experiment, the researcher placed four objects in front of a 28 month old (Golinkoff et al., 1992). Three of the objects were familiar (a ball, a shoe and keys) and one was unfamiliar (a tea strainer). The experimenter asked for the *glorp*. Consistent with N3C, children in this experiment selected the unnamed object as the referent for *glorp*. In a control condition in which no label was used, but children were asked to retrieve an object, children selected the unnamed object only at a chance level.

The ECM places a strong emphasis on the necessity for social interaction in word learning. According to Nelson (1998), to acquire a full understanding of semantic development, we must look more closely at the social context in which word learning occurs. Some researchers have found, for example, that parents clearly influence vocabulary growth. In one example, the amount of time parents spent reading to their 2 year olds was significantly related to the children's language skills when they were 4 years old (Crain-Thoreson & Dale, 1992). Another study found that the more parents talked to their children, the larger the children's vocabularies became (Huttenlocher et al., 1991).

Some of the strongest support for the social environmental approach comes from studies of vocabulary development in children of differing socioeconomic classes and in relation to parental education (Huttenlocher et al., 2007). Hart and Risley (1999) studied the language environments of 42 children, ranging in age from 10 months to 3 years, by observing them in their homes. These investigators found that social class, language environment and children's vocabulary were all highly correlated: The higher the social class, the richer the language environment, and the greater the growth in the child's vocabulary. A large study conducted by Weizman and Snow (2001) extended these results by investigating the home language environments of children in low-income families at age 5 and the vocabulary performance of these same children in kindergarten and second grade. Two important findings emerged. First, the researchers found substantial variation in these children's homes in language experience; not all low-income mothers communicate with their children in the same way. Some mothers produced a much richer language experience for children than others did. Second, children's language experience at home at age 5 was positively related to their later vocabulary performance in school. The context of language learning also appears to be important (Hsaio & Nation, 2018); the more diverse the contexts in which a child hears a word, the quicker children respond to and learn to use it accurately.

What kinds of words do children learn first?

Analysing the kinds of words children acquire, and the ways in which they use them, can give us important information about children's cognitive development and concept formation. Studying the first 50 words learned by a group of 18 young children, Nelson (1973), in a classic study of early word acquisition, classified these words into six categories. Mothers kept diaries of each new word their children produced until the children produced 50 words. On average, children reached the 50-word level by the time they were 1.5, but there was a great deal of individual difference. Some infants learned their first 50 words by 15 months, whereas others took 24 months. As Figure 8-3 illustrates, about 65% of the 50 words were naming or object words, whereas words denoting action made up only about 14%. Schwartz and Leonard (1984) found about the same proportion of action words, and other research has determined that nouns are learned more easily than verbs (Childers & Tomasello, 2002).

One explanation for why children may learn object words first is that the concepts to which object words refer are simpler than those to which action words refer (Gentner, 1982; Huttenlocher & Smiley, 1987). To learn object words, children must match objects with their appropriate linguistic referents (Gentner, 1982), but to learn action words, or verbs, children must also form an understanding of the connections between objects and actions (Huttenlocher & Lui, 1979). However, some action words are learned more readily than others. Huttenlocher, Smiley and Charney (1987) found that children are better at learning action words for things they can actually do themselves. For example, a 2 year old is more likely to

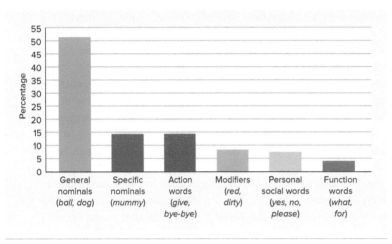

Figure 8-3 Words that children use first

According to the classic work illustrated here, naming or object words make up almost two-thirds of the vocabularies of children between 1 and 2 years old.
Source: Based on data from Nelson (1973)

learn the word *walk* than *skip* because she is physically able to perform the action of walking.

Some researchers (e.g., Bloom, 1993, 1998) have challenged the assumption that object names predominate in early vocabularies. Studying children who ranged in age from 9 months to 2 years, Bloom found that object words represented only a third of the words the children learned. Similarly, Tardif (1996) found that 21-month-old children learning Mandarin Chinese used equal numbers of verbs and nouns in their speech. In part, this is because in some Asian languages verbs play a more prominent role in speech and often occur in a prominent place at the end of a sentence (Hoff, 2005). The fact that Japanese mothers spend less time labelling objects than American mothers may also account for the less pronounced bias towards noun production among Japanese children (Fernald & Morikawa, 1993).

It is important to note that the principles and constraints discussed in object learning must also apply to verb learning. With this in mind, Merriman et al. (1996) investigated children's use of the *mutual exclusivity* bias in verb learning. Two year olds watched a TV screen that on one side had an actor doing an action that the children had a word for, like clapping, while on the other side a different actor did something that the children had no word for, like rolling his arms in circles. Overall, both actions were equally interesting to the infants, but when the children were asked to 'Look at the person glorping', they were more likely to look at the novel action. This is similar to Golinkoff and colleagues' (1992) finding, in which children assumed a novel label applied to a novel object.

Errors in early word use

Errors in children's early word use can help illuminate the learning process. Two such errors are overextension and underextension. In overextension, children use a single word to refer to many different things. For example, a young child may use the word *doggie* for horses, cows, giraffes, and all sorts of four-legged animals or *light* for pointing at a house light, the moon, or a reflection in a mirror.

Rescorla (1980) investigated how and when children between 1 year and 18 months overextend words. She found that although about a third of young children's utterances involve overextensions, a relatively small number of different words are included. Rescorla also found that children's overextensions usually show one of three themes or characteristics. First, overextensions can be categorical, meaning children will use one word within a category for another closely related word; for example, they will use the name of one colour for another. Second, the words are used for something perceptually similar, as when a child calls all round objects *balls*. Finally, overextensions can reflect a relationship. For example, a child might use the word *doll* for an empty crib where the doll should be. As children's vocabularies increase, they use fewer overextended words (deVilliers & deVilliers, 1992; Bloom, 1993).

In underextension, a less common type of error, children use a single word in a highly restricted and individualistic way. For example, a child may use the word *car* only when she sees her father's yellow Volkswagen and may call all other vehicles, including her mother's green Volvo, *trucks* (Bloom, 1993, 1998). The use of underextensions suggests that a child's understanding of a word is too restrictive, or limited to a small set of meanings. In speaking with their young children, parents may not

overextension The use, by a young child, of a single word to cover many different things.

underextension The use, by a young child, of a single word in a restricted and individualistic way.

initially give every instance of a class of objects its correct name and may thus trigger some word errors. Mervis and Mervis (1982) found that mothers tended to use single nouns to label certain toys and objects; for example, they called both lions and leopards *kitty cats*.

According to some researchers, errors like over- and underextension in early word use are not really errors in the usual sense of the term. As a child's vocabulary is limited, she may try to find a linguistic form that fits with an element of experience (Bloom, 1993, 1998). As Bloom notes, gradually, as the child's vocabulary improves and her conceptual categories become stabler, her accuracy in word use increases.

It seems entirely reasonable for the child to use an available word to represent different but related objects – it is almost as if the child were reasoning, 'I know about dogs; that thing is not a dog. I don't know what to call it, but it is like a dog.' (Bloom, 1976, p. 23)

THE ACQUISITION OF GRAMMAR

Can one word express a complete thought?

Are first words simply words? Or are they early attempts to express complete thoughts? When a young child points to a toy plane on a high shelf and says 'Down', or when he takes a spoon from his mother and says 'Me', is there more to his utterance than meets the ear? In the first case, parents may assume that the child is requesting that the toy be taken down off the shelf; in the second example, they might guess that the child is letting them know that she wants to do it herself.

Dale (1976) has noted, 'First words seem to be more than single words. They appear to be attempts to express complex ideas – ideas that would be expressed in sentences by an adult' (p. 13). The term holophrase has been given to such single words that appear to represent a complete thought. Whether or not children are really expressing in these single-word utterances thoughts that could be expressed in sentences – thoughts that include subjects, objects and actions – remains an unanswered question.

> **holophrase** A single word that appears to represent a complete thought.
>
> **telegraphic speech** Two-word utterances that include only the words essential to convey the speaker's intent.

Two-word sentences

Some time between 1.5 and 2 years of age, the child begins to put two words together in what is often called telegraphic speech. Like telegrams, these two-word utterances include only the crucial words needed to convey the speaker's intent. Although children generally use nouns, verbs and adjectives, they are likely to omit other parts of speech such as articles and prepositions. Thus, the child's speech is creative and is not merely a copy of adult language. Table 8-3 shows some two-word sentences used by young children speaking either English or one of several other languages (Slobin, 1985). Notice how these two-word phrases resemble one another in terms of the relationships between the words, or the basic structure or grammar of language, no matter how different the languages in which they were spoken. This similarity in relations extends to the sign language many deaf people use.

Why are the early utterances of children similar in terms of the meaning of what they talk about? Language can be viewed as a way of expressing what one knows or understands about the world. As children's capacity for understanding events in the world around them continues to grow, and because children around the world tend to have encounters with similar kinds of basic situations in life, their learning of language is tied to their cognitive development. Such fundamental experiences include the distinction between self and other, the concept of causality and an understanding of objects. Thus, wherever they live, in whatever society, children beginning to speak express similar relations between objects and between events, such as agent–action relations, possessives, and person and object identity. The development of cognitive capacity and the development of language are closely related (Clark, 1983; Carey, 1994).

> In Chapters 9 and 10 we introduce some of the broader issues and theories in cognitive development.

Table 8-3   Two-word sentences in several languages

Function of utterance	LANGUAGE					
	English	German	Russian	Finnish	Luo	Samoan
Locate, name	there book	buch der [book there]	Tosya tam [Tosya there]	tuossa Rina [there Rina]	en saa [it clock]	Keith lea [Keith there]
Demand, desire	more milk	mehr milch [more milk]	yeshchë moloko [more milk]	anna Rina [give Rina]	miya tamtam [give-me candy]	mai pepe [give doll]
Negate	no wet	nicht blasen [not blow]	vody net [water no]	ei susi [not wolf]	beda onge [my-slasher absent]	le' ai [not eat]
Describe event or situation	Bambi go	puppe kommt [doll comes]	mam prua [mama walk]	Seppo putoo [Seppo fall]	odhi skul [he-went school]	pá u pepe [fall doll]
Indicate possession	my shoe	mein ball [my ball]	mami chashka [mama's cup]	täti auto [aunt car]	kom baba [chair father]	lole a' u [candy my]
Modify, qualify (attributive)	pretty dress	milch heiss [milk hot]	mama khoroshaya [mama good]	rikki auto [broken car]	piypiy kech [pepper hot]	fa'ali'i pepe [headstrong baby]
Question	where ball	wo ball [where ball]	gde papa [where papa]	missä pallo [where ball]		Fea Punafu [where Punafu]

Notes: Luo is spoken in Kenya. The order of the two words in each 'sentence' is generally fixed in all languages but Finnish, in which children are free to use both orders for some types of utterances.

Source: Slobin (1979, Table 4-2, pp. 86–87). Copyright © 1979. Adapted by permission of Professor Dan Slobin.

Learning the rules

One of the most interesting aspects of early grammar acquisition is the way children learn how to modify the meanings of the words they use; an accomplishment that also illustrates the close ties between semantic and grammar development. Roger Brown (1973), in his classic longitudinal study of Adam, Eve and Sarah, followed these three children from 2 to 4 years of age and noted, among many other things, that they acquired certain morphemes in a regular order. For example, during this period, the children began to use qualifiers that indicate plurality or a possessive relationship. Table 8-4 lists the 14 morphemes that Brown studied in the order in which his young participants acquired them. Although Adam, Eve and Sarah each acquired these morphemes at a different rate of speed, the order in which each child acquired them was the same.

Notice that the order in which these morphemes are acquired is sensible: Simpler morphemes are acquired earlier than more complex ones. For example, plural forms, like -s, are learned before the copula (meaning a linking word) be. Similarly, Golinkoff, Hirsh-Pasek, and Schweisguth (2001) found that children began to understand morphemes – for example, they learn that -ing is a morpheme generally used with actions – much earlier than they can produce the same morphemes. In Chapters 9 and 10, we will see that this same general principle of progressing from the simple to the more complex characterizes children's cognitive development as well.

Slobin (1985) suggests that children go through four phases in their application of grammatical rules like the use of plurals. In phase 1, they try but fail. In phase 2, they succeed in memorizing some of the irregular verbs, such as broke and went, but do not yet acquire a grammatical rule. This kind of learning, of course, is quite inefficient. Imagine how time-consuming it would be if children had to learn separate, specific rules for each new word that they encountered. They might learn, for example, that two dogs is expressed as dogs, but they would have to learn in a separate lesson how to pluralize other words, such as house. In Slobin's third phase, children learn general grammatical rules that can be used with new as well as familiar words. Only in the fourth phase do children – at 7 or 8 years – finally approach language that resembles adult usage, recognizing when to apply these rules. A crucial achievement of this last phase is learning when not to apply a rule.

Table 8-4 English-speaking children's first 14 morphemes in order they were acquired

Form	Meaning	Example
1. Present progressive: -ing	Ongoing process	He is sitting down.
2. Preposition: in	Containment	The mouse is in the box.
3. Preposition: on	Support	The book is on the table.
4. Plural: -s	Number	The dogs ran away.
5. Past irregular: e.g. went	Earlier in time relative to time of speaking	The boy went home.
6. Possessive: -'s	Possession	The girl's dog is big.
7. Uncontractible copula be: e.g. are, was	Number; earlier in time	Are they boys or girls? Was that a dog?
8. Articles: the, a	Definite/indefinite	He has a book.
9. Past regular: -ed	Earlier in time	He jumped the stream.
10. Third person regular: -s	Number; earlier in time	She runs fast.
11. Third person irregular: e.g. has, does	Number; earlier in time	Does the dog bark?
12. Uncontractible auxiliary be: e.g. is, were	Number; earlier in time; ongoing process	Were they at home? Is he running?
13. Contractible copula be: e.g. -'s, -'re	Number; earlier in time	That's a spaniel.
14. Contractible auxiliary be: e.g. -'s, -'re	Number; earlier in time; ongoing process	They're running very slowly.

Source: Based on Brown (1973).

Adult language is full of irregularities and other exceptions to the rules. When children are first learning a language, they ignore these irregularities and rigidly apply the rules they learn. In overregularization of rules, children apply a rule for forming regularities in cases where the adult form is irregular and does not follow the rule. For instance, a young child may start out using the words *went* and *came* correctly, but after learning that *-ed* forms the past tense for many verbs, he may begin to use this ending for all verbs, producing *goed* and *comed* (Slobin, 1985). Similarly, a child often uses the word *feet* until she learns the regular plural ending; then she may switch to *foots* or sometimes *feets*. Overregularization is found across cultures and different language groups where children applied the rules they learned broadly to form novel 'regularized' words and phrases that did not occur in adult speech (Slobin, 1982).

> **overregularization**
> The application of a principle of regular change to a word that changes irregularly.

Despite great interest in overregularization among researchers, questions remain about why and how often children overregularize language in their speech. Additionally, it has been shown that some children are more likely than others to overregularize language (Maratos, 1993), which suggests that children's interest in or skill at the rules of language may vary individually. Finally, some researchers suggest that it is not language development per se that explains overregularization. Rather, memory development may contribute to this behaviour because learning all the complexities and rules of language places great demands on memory. Because young children are developing memory skills at the same time they are developing language, these processes may influence one another, and behaviours such as overregularization may be a result (Marcus, 1995).

Approaching formal grammar

In the third year of life comes 'a grammatical flowering' (deVilliers & deVilliers, 1992, p. 378). Simple sentences start to become subtle and more complex as children show early signs of understanding the rules of adult grammar (Valian, 1986). Among children's many achievements is the beginning use of auxiliary and modal verbs (deVilliers & deVilliers, 1992). *Mode*, or 'mood', is the capacity of verbs to convey factual

Animated conversations like this one are a sign of the 'grammatical flowering' that generally characterizes the third year of life.
© Shutterstock/Olga Enger

statements, expressions of possibility (e.g., the subjunctive), or imperatives. One of the auxiliary verbs children begin to use at this stage is the verb *to be* (or its equivalent in different languages), which appears in many sentence structures and thus opens up the possibility of many new forms of expression. Children begin to use tenses other than the present: 'I kicked it.' And they begin to use pronouns and articles, and even begin to create complex sentences: 'The teddy and doll are gonna play' (deVilliers & deVilliers, 1992, p. 379). Let us take a closer look at two of these grammatical milestones: questions and negatives.

Questions

To express a question, young children may first use an assertion such as 'sit chair' by simply raising their voices at the end to indicate that they are asking a question (deVilliers & deVilliers, 1979). In the latter part of the third year, children begin to ask 'wh' questions – those that start with the words *what, when, who, why* and *which* – as well as questions that begin with *how*.

Between ages 2 and 3, children's 'wh' constructions may fail to include the auxiliary verb, and they can be heard to say things such as 'Where you going?' A little later, they include the auxiliary without inverting it – for example, 'Where you are going?' Finally, they incorporate all the rules for producing a 'wh' question – for example, 'Where are you going?'

As we saw earlier, an important feature of 'wh' questions is that they enable children to learn new things. Callanan and Oakes (1992) asked parents of 3-, 4- and 5-year-old children to keep diaries over a 2-week period of their children's 'why' and 'how' questions. They found, as every parent knows, that the frequency of these questions increases over these years. They also found that at all ages these questions tended to be complex; that is, children rarely asked about the world just by stating 'why' or 'how'. Rather, these questions usually included referents, ideas and observations – for example, 'Why is the sky blue?' or 'How does the telephone know which house to call?' Children use their emerging skill at questioning as an important tool for obtaining knowledge. Again, we see that language and cognitive development are closely linked in promoting the child's overall progress.

NEGATIVES

Some of the earliest evidence of children's expression of negation (disagreement) comes in non-verbal form, for example, by shaking their heads. The simplest verbal forms involve the word 'no' either alone or affixed to the beginning of a phrase; for example, a child may say 'No doggie' to mean the dog is not here. As children develop, they learn to form different kinds of negatives, and three distinct types of negation appear in a particular developmental order (Bloom, 1970; Tager-Flusberg, 1997). First, children are able to express the non-existence of something (e.g., 'All gone'), then they become capable of rejecting something (e.g., 'No wash hair'), and lastly they are able to deny that something is true (e.g., 'That not Daddy').

Language researchers have found that these same types of negations appear in a different order in Japanese and English (Clancy, 1985; Bloom, 1991). As children's language skills develop, more complex forms of negation appear that include auxiliary verbs – for example, 'I didn't do it' or 'He isn't my friend.'

The development of questions and negatives is only part of a wide range of grammatical accomplishments during the preschool years. By 3 years of age, children begin to use complex sentences, and progress is gradual but orderly. At first, children tack on relative clauses – for example, 'See the ball that I got.' It's only later that they interrupt a main clause with a subordinate clause: 'The owl who eats the candy runs fast' (Slobin, 1985; Maratsos, 1998), and they compose complex utterances like, 'Where did you say you put my doll?' (deVilliers & deVilliers, 1992, p. 379). Although most fundamental forms of grammar are acquired by 4.5 to 5 years, the process of grammar acquisition continues to develop through the school years (Maratsos, 1998).

How children make sense of what they hear

Although we have been discussing language production, it is important to remember that productive and receptive language are closely linked. Several researchers have shown that, at a very early age, children are able to understand sentences that are more complex than those they can produce. This understanding is aided by syntax, which provides clues about the meanings of nouns (or object words) and verbs (or action words). For example, some types of verbs appear in some sentences and not others (Hoff, 2005). Verbs such as *hit* and *hug* refer to an action that one person does to another, and therefore, such verbs usually appear in sentences in which the verb is preceded by a noun, the doer of the action, and followed by a different noun, the recipient of the action (e.g., *David hugged Maria*). Other verbs, such as those that refer to an action with no recipient, such as *laugh* or *slip*, appear in sentences in which there is just one noun, the doer (e.g., *Paul laughed*). According to Gleitman and her colleagues (Gleitman, 1990; Fisher et al., 1994), children use a kind of 'syntactic bootstrapping' to figure out word meaning. According to this theory, once children learn how to parse utterances into syntactic units, they use this knowledge to distinguish the meanings of verbs they may not yet understand. In other words, they use what they already know about syntax to support, or bootstrap, their learning and comprehension (Naigles, 1990).

According to Goodman (1989), even 1.5- to 3.5-year-old children use semantic and syntactic cues to identify spoken words. In a sentence completion task, Goodman presented children with spoken sentences and asked them to fill in a final missing noun. For example, to the utterance 'Mummy feeds the ____ ', children responded 'baby'. In a word identification task, children listened to complete sentences and pointed to pictures to identify the final word in each sentence. In one condition of this task, the word called for by the sentence meaning was among those pictured, but the word actually spoken was represented by another picture. For example, children listened to the sentence 'Anja drives the duck' and then looked at pictures of a duck, a truck, a dog and a book. Although the word spoken was *duck*, children chose the truck. When the children heard the sentence 'The man sees the duck', however, they chose the duck picture.

Does the ability to use semantic and syntactic information improve with age? Entwisle and Frasure (1974) demonstrated that this is very probably so. Using a 'noisy telephone' technique, in which background noise was used to make auditory material difficult to hear, these researchers asked groups of children 6, 7, 8 and 9 years old to listen to three sentences. The children were then asked to repeat the sentences as accurately as possible. Because the noise blocked out parts of the sentence, the children had to rely on their knowledge of how sentences are generally formed to fill in the missing words. The sentences were:

> *Bears steal honey from the hive.*
>
> *Trains steal elephants around the house.*
>
> *From shoot highways the passengers mothers.*

In the *meaningful* first sentence, both semantics and syntax are correct. The *anomalous* second sentence is syntactically correct, although it makes no sense. In the *scrambled* last sentence, both syntax and semantics are jumbled, making this presumably the most difficult sentence for children to reproduce. As you can see from Figure 8-4, the older the child, the more he or she was able to benefit from the available syntactic and semantic clues. At all ages, the more such clues the children had, the better they did; all age groups experienced similar difficulties with the sentence in which these clues were totally absent.

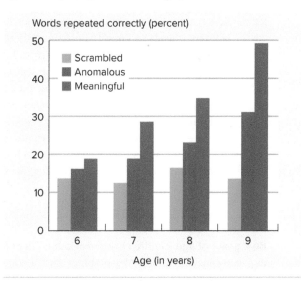

Figure 8-4 *Learning to use semantic and syntactic clues*
The more syntactic and semantic clues offered by sentences heard against background noise, the more successful children were at repeating the sentences. All children had difficulty with the scrambled sentence that lacked any clues, but when clues were present, as in the meaningful and anomalous sentences, older children made better use of them than younger children.
Source: Adapted from Entwisle & Frasure (1974)

However, children's comprehension of many complex constructions remains poorly understood (Maratsos, 1983). Children continue to develop in both their production and understanding of complex syntax well beyond the early school years; both comprehension and usage of language continue to develop for many years and into adulthood.

The rules of pragmatics

Language, by its very nature, is a social phenomenon; it enables the child to communicate with other people. What becomes very important as children develop, therefore, is the decision as to what words and phrases to use in differing social situations. The rules for this usage, which we have already identified, are known as *pragmatics*. Speakers have a variety of pragmatic forms, such as getting people to do things for them and thanking people for their help, and they need to know how to express these forms appropriately depending on the situation and the other people involved. When verbal expressions clearly refer to situations rather than to just one object or action, we call these expressions *speech acts*.

Communication becomes *discourse*, or conversation, when children are able to listen to and respond to another's speech. The latter achievement includes the ability to recognize one's own lack of understanding and to request additional information. In this section, we begin by looking at some of the rules of pragmatics, and then turn to the ways children learn first to communicate and then to be good listeners.

Even when a child has mastered meaning and syntax, she is not yet fully equipped to be an effective communicator. She must learn another set of rules – namely, how to use language appropriate to a given situation. To be an effective speaker requires a complicated set of skills. First, the child must engage the attention of her listeners so they know that she wants to address them and that they should listen. Second, effective speakers have to be sensitive to listeners' feedback. If children are unaware that others fail to understand them, or do not know how to change their messages to make themselves clear, they are not going to be very successful communicators. Third, speakers must adjust their speech to the characteristics of their listeners, such as age and cultural and social background. For example, the 10 year old must learn that in talking to his peers he can use words and concepts that he cannot use when he speaks with a 3 year old. Being a good communicator requires that you adapt your message to consider 'who the listener is, what the listener already knows, and what the listener needs to know' (Glucksberg, Krauss, & Higgins, 1975, p. 329).

A fourth rule requires that children learn to adjust their speech to suit the situation. Children and adults learn to talk differently on a playground or street than they do in a church or a classroom. A fifth guideline points out that communication is a two-way process. To participate in a conversation, one must be not only an effective speaker but also a skilled listener; learning to listen is just as important as learning to speak. A sixth rule underlines the importance of understanding one's own communicative skills; that is, children must learn to evaluate both their own messages and the messages they receive from others for clarity and usefulness. They must also learn to correct their own messages when necessary and to let another speaker know when they do not understand the speaker's communication (Glucksberg et al., 1975).

Learning to adjust speech to audience

By 2 years of age, children are remarkably adept both at engaging the attention of a listener and at responding to listener feedback. Videotaping ten 2 year olds in their day-to-day interactions in a nursery school, Wellman and Lempers (1977) recorded 300 referential communicative interactions in which the communicator's intent was to point out, show or display a particular object or referent to another child. The results were striking in their demonstration of these children's competence as speakers. The toddlers addressed their listeners when both were either interacting or playing together (82%) or when the listeners were at least not involved with someone else (88%). The children also directed communications to others when they could see each other (97%), when they were physically close to each other (91%), and to a lesser extent, when the listeners were looking directly at them (41%). Similarly, the children made sure that, when they spoke, they were close to the thing they were talking about (92%) and that the listener was also close to the thing referred to (84%) to make it more likely that the listener would understand the message.

CHRONOLOGY OF DEVELOPMENT
Language milestones from infancy to middle childhood

Birth	Cries Perceives others' speech Prefers human voices
1–6 months	Decreases crying Makes soft sounds Coos, laughs, gurgles Imitates short string of vowel sounds; alternates making sounds with another person Makes consonant sounds; 'says' consonants increasingly often Responds to prosodic features of speech (e.g., inflection and pitch) Intonations move toward speech patterns heard most often Recognizes own name
6–12 months	Babbles strings of consonant–vowel combinations May babble more in familiar than unfamiliar settings Sounds resemble speech Shows increasing preference for own language over unfamiliar language Produces sound for familiar toy or object; experiments with sounds Babbling develops a sentence-like quality May 'say' a word – bah for 'bottle', mah for 'mother' May say no but doesn't always mean no May say two or three words; uses same word for category, such as wah for both 'water' and 'milk' Intentional communication begins
12–18 months	Forms one-word sentences at first Tries hard to make self understood Makes symbolic gestures Imitates words; may repeatedly use a new word May use a few two-word sentences May use adjective to refer to self (good boy) Understands naming processes
18–24 months	Begins naming explosion; average child goes from 50 to 900 words in about 6 months Uses two-word sentences Rapidly expands understanding
24–36 months	Decreases gesturing Gives up babbling Increases use of plurals, past tense, definite and indefinite articles, some prepositions Uses three-word combinations Shows excellent comprehension Gradually increases use of sentences to communicate
36–48 months	Uses yes/no questions, why questions, negatives, and imperatives Embeds one sentence within another (using clauses) Uses overregularizations Vocabulary increases by about 1000 words Coordinates simple sentences and uses prepositions
48–60 months	Uses pragmatic rules of communication in increasingly sophisticated way Uses humour and metaphor
5 years and beyond	Uses more complex syntax Further expands vocabulary (to about 14,000 words) Develops metalinguistic awareness

Note: Developmental events described in this and other Chronology of Development charts represent overall trends identified in research studies. Individual children vary greatly in the ages at which they achieve these developmental changes.

Sources: Kopp (1994); Hoff (2005); Tomasello (2006); Waxman and Lidz (2006).

In light of these precautions, it is not surprising that these young speakers were very effective in engaging their listeners. In fact, 79% of messages met with an adequate response from listeners. Moreover, speakers showed an awareness that certain situations were particularly difficult and adjusted their communications accordingly. They communicated more in difficult situations – for example, when there was an obstacle between the listener and the thing referred to. Finally, these children were responsive to feedback from their listeners; more than half the time, when the speakers received no response, they repeated their messages in some form, but they repeated messages only 3% of the time when they received an adequate response. In sum, these 2 year olds were surprisingly sophisticated speakers.

Children as young as 2 years of age learn to adjust their speech when talking with other children of different ages. In several studies (Dunn & Kendrick, 1982; Dunn, 1988), 2 and 3 year olds used more repetitions and more attention-eliciting words (*hey, hello* and *look*) when talking to their baby brothers and sisters than they did when addressing their mothers. Researchers (Gelman & Shatz, 1977; Shatz, 1983, 1994) have also found that children make the same kinds of adjustments when they speak to people outside the family.

Despite the sophisticated level at which children can communicate, children's communicative competence does face some limitations. Preschoolers, for example, are more effective in a one-to-one conversation; they do less well when they must compete for their turn with adults and other children (Ervin-Tripp, 1979). Young children also are more competent when speaking about single familiar objects that are present in their immediate environment than when speaking about absent objects (absent in time or space) or their own feelings, thoughts or relationships (Shatz, 1983, 1994; Dunn, 1988).

How do children acquire the ability to converse on an increasingly sophisticated level? Learning the social aspects of language is similar to learning other forms of social behaviour. Children learn by observing people and through direct instruction from parents and teachers (Dunn, 1988; Bandura, 1989). They also learn by listening to people talk about conversations – who said what to whom and how this or that person responded (Miller & Sperry, 1987).

Much of what children learn from parents about the appropriate use of language involves the acquisition of social conventions. For example, one of the child's first lessons in formal communication involves learning how to use polite words and phrases, such as *hello, goodbye, please* and *thank you* (Grief & Gleason, 1980); these simple social routines are common to all cultures (Schieffelin & Ochs, 1987). Children must also learn when, where and to whom it is appropriate to express negative feelings and thoughts, such as anger (Miller & Sperry, 1987).

Learning to listen critically

Young children are often unaware that they do not understand a message. In one experiment, Markman (1977) gave 6 and 9 year olds instructions to a game that left out critical information essential to playing the game. The 9 year olds noticed the inadequacy of the instructions more readily than the younger children; indeed, the latter were generally unaware that information was missing and had to be urged to try to play the game before realizing that they didn't know enough to do so.

However, if the task is simple, even 3 year olds can recognize an ambiguous message when they hear one and can act in appropriate ways to resolve the communication gap. In one study (Revelle, Wellman, & Karabenick, 1985), an adult made a variety of requests of 3 and 4 year olds during a play session. Sometimes, the requests were ambiguous – for example, the investigator might ask for a cup without specifying which of four different cups she or he wanted. In other cases, a request was impossible – 'Bring me the refrigerator' (the only refrigerator available was a real and very large one). Even the 3 year olds showed clearly that they recognized when a request was problematic, and preschoolers knew how to remedy the communication problem by requesting more information. For example, when asked to bring the refrigerator, more than one 3 year old asked, 'How? It's too heavy.' Revelle and associates suggest that the essential skills in monitoring communication are realizing that problems can arise, recognizing problems when they do occur and knowing how to fix them. Three and four year olds seem to possess all of these fundamental monitoring skills; as we'll see later, all are important in the development of metalinguistic awareness.

Children can be taught to be more effective listeners, but there may be a minimal age at which children can learn to listen critically. Research has shown that when 6- to 10-year-old children were encouraged to ask a speaker questions to clarify his or her communication, they performed more effectively than children who were not given this lesson in listening (Cosgrove & Patterson, 1977; Patterson & Kister, 1981). Because 4 year olds did not benefit from this instruction, this type of listening strategy may be a moderately advanced communication skill.

Non-verbal communication

Non-verbal communication complements or adds to (and sometimes replaces) verbal communication. Understanding and reproducing non-verbal aspects of communication are important skills that can have a positive impact for development generally, and language development specifically. Certainly even preschoolers can recognize non-verbal signals relating to emotion (e.g., Buck, 1975) and requests for attention or action (Doherty-Sneddon, 2003). Four year olds can also infer intentions and beliefs, over time, from another person's non-verbal signals (Fusaro & Harris, 2008).

In some clinical groups, where non-verbal skills (or their cognitive antecedents) may be disrupted, the failure to employ adequately non-verbal skills is associated with problems and difficulties in interaction. For instance, Mundy et al. (1987) found that better language skills in autistic children were associated with greater and more effective use of various non-verbal correlates of language, such as using gestures to coordinate attention during interaction. Non-verbal skills are particularly useful when trying to direct someone's attention to an object, in order to secure joint attention. Thus the lack of non-verbal skills may, for autistic children, arise as a consequence of other cognitive deficits (Chiang et al., 2008). Inhibited use of non-verbal communication such as non-verbal requests for objects was also evident in infants and preschoolers diagnosed with Down Syndrome (Mundy et al., 1988), a group often associated with deficits in the use of expressive language.

The link between non-verbal communication skill and social and cognitive development has been identified for normally developing children, too. For instance, Pine et al. (2007) explored the gestures and talk that children produced as they tried to solve a balance-beam task. Surprisingly, gestures were rarely used without accompanying speech and, in around a third of cases, gestures appeared to contradict or conveyed different information from what was spoken. Often, children conveyed an idea about how the beam might balance non-verbally (pointing to a spot or direction in which the beam might move), before articulating an explanation verbally. The authors conclude that, for many aspects of children's communication, and for certain types of manual or object-related tasks in particular, gestures are an important means of adding to or helping with thinking and problem solving.

KNOWING ABOUT LANGUAGE

An important achievement in language development, and one of the latest to develop, is the understanding of how language works. That is, children become aware that they know language and can think and talk about language itself.

Metalinguistic awareness is the understanding that language is a rule-bound system of communicating. It includes the ability to talk about the various properties and uses of language as well as to monitor language as it is used (Whitehurst & Lonigan, 1998). This understanding and ability emerge well after children are proficient at producing language (Bullinger & Chatillon, 1983).

> metalinguistic awareness The understanding that language is a rule-bound system of communicating.

To test children's understanding of grammar, for instance, we can ask them to judge between grammatical and ungrammatical sentences, and acceptable and unacceptable syntax. In one investigation, de Villiers and de Villiers (1992), using the technique of asking children to teach a puppet to talk correctly, tested children's ability to judge and to correct word order in sentences describing specific actions. Sometimes, the puppet spoke in the correct word order; for example, 'Eat the cake.' At other times, the puppet reversed word order: 'Dog the pat.' And at still other times, the puppet used correct syntax but described actions that were impossible: 'Drink the chair.' The children both told the puppet whether the sentence was right or wrong and then helped the puppet rephrase it the 'right way'. The researchers found a clear relation between the children's level of language development and their metalinguistic awareness; as their ability to produce and comprehend sentences increased, their awareness increased as evidenced by their ability to correct the puppet's 'wrong' utterances (de Villiers & de Villiers, 1992).

Phonological awareness is the specific aspect of metalinguistic awareness related to the sounds of language. This understanding includes knowledge of the sounds of language and of properties related to these sounds, such as how many sounds are in a word. Rhyming is a particularly interesting instance of phonological awareness because of the delight children seem to take in discovering that words can rhyme and in learning how to make this happen. Children as young as 2 years of age have been observed making rhymes. Learning and passing on oral rhymes are common in the preschool and early school years.

> **phonological awareness**
> The understanding of the sounds of a language and of the properties, such as the number of sounds in a word, related to these sounds.
>
> **dyslexia** A learning disability that impairs the ability to read and spell fluently.

Children's interest in and use of rhymes reflect phonological awareness and can help create social connections and enjoyment for children. Phonological awareness also has significance for learning to read. Research has shown that children's phonological awareness before they enter school is positively related to success in reading both in the early grades and later (Goswami & Bryant, 1990).

The distinction between phonological and metalinguistic aspects of speech is an important one in terms of diagnosing and addressing the problems that children may experience with reading. When learning to read, children have difficulties with decoding information (letters and words on the page), which is often referred to as dyslexia, or they may have difficulties understanding or comprehending what they are reading (Cain, 2010).

In a review of interventions, Snowling and Hulme (2011) argue that decoding difficulties appear to be due to problems with phonological processing, whereas comprehension problems are caused by problems with metalinguistic capabilities, morphology and syntax. Hence interventions that are targeted at addressing these phonological deficits – for instance, training children in understanding how printed letters and words map onto spoken sounds – appear to be most effective at improving the reading skills of dyslexic children. In contrast, programmes that help children to develop inferencing skills such as drawing out the meaning from the story structure or linking a sequence of events, improved the reading of children who experienced comprehension difficulties (Yuill & Oakhill, 1988).

Research close-up

BOX 8-5 Is dyslexia associated with neural deficits in Chinese children who learn English as a second language?

Source: Based on You et al. (2011).

Introduction:

Dyslexia is a developmental disorder of reading, where children (and adults) have difficulty recognizing and reading words. Research evidence suggests that at its core may be difficulties experienced by the dyslexic individual in phonological processing in alphabetic languages (i.e., processing the sounds of words and letters). This evidence is based on experimental behavioural studies, and also on neurobiological information about brain activity during reading and language processing. However, an important question is whether the same underlying problems are evident for individuals whose original language is not alphabetic and who are learning English as a second language? For instance, in Chinese (Mandarin and Cantonese) the character symbols are word forms and not based on phonology. The present study compared the brain activity of Chinese students who were learning English with success or were experiencing reading impairments in English.

Method:

The researchers used functional magnetic resonance imaging (fMRI) to investigate the neural responses on a letter rhyming (phonological) judgement task and an orthographic task with 36 Chinese school children (4–6 years) with or without impairments in reading English and Chinese. In the phonological task participants were asked to judge whether two letters rhymed (e.g., D and T) or did not rhyme (e.g., D and A). They responded, while in the scanner, by pressing a button. In the orthographic task children had to judge whether letters were the same (e.g., D and D) or different (e.g., D and A).

Results:

Behavioural measures included accuracy and reaction time (the time taken to press the button to indicate a decision had been made). Behavioural measures were better for typical children than those with reading impairment. Analysis of fMRI scans suggested several differences between typical and impaired readers both on orthography and phonology tasks. Specifically, there was reduced activation within the left lingual/calcarine gyrus and in occipitotemporal regions during orthographic processing in children with reading impairment compared to typical readers. There was reduced activation in parietotemporal regions during phonological processing for the impaired group, a finding that was consistent with previous work involving English native speakers.

Discussion:

Activation in the left parietotemporal region has been found in other studies of individuals with reading impairments. It is a region of the brain often associated with phonological processing and as part of the brain default network that is connected to the generation of spontaneous thoughts and 'mind wandering'. The authors suggest that impaired readers may have an abnormal brain default network that adversely affects phonological processing and, in turn, leads to language learning problems.

The brain activation patterns associated with differences between typical and impaired readers on the orthographic task could be a consequence of problems with the retrieval of visual graphic images or more complex integration of systems concerned with linking orthography and phonology.

Taken together these findings suggest that similar neural deficits underlie the difficulties experienced by impaired readers whether they are native (first language) English speakers or not. In other words, there is a common neural mechanism for learning English for native and second language learners.

Bilingualism

Bilingualism is the acquisition of two languages. For some children, bilingualism involves learning two languages simultaneously, such as when one parent speaks one language and another parent speaks a second language to the child. For other children, bilingualism entails learning two languages sequentially – for instance, when one language is spoken at home when the child is young and a second language is acquired when the child goes to school.

What are the implications of bilingualism for the language acquisition process? Although some have expressed concern that learning two languages interferes with children's language learning more generally, this may not be the case. Children who learn two languages may learn both languages more slowly than some of their peers learn one language; however, this gap disappears as children develop. Additionally, studies of children between 8 months and 2.5 years of age found that bilingual and monolingual children had comprehension vocabularies of about the same size (Pearson, Fernandez, & Oller, 1993). In contrast, children who are 5 or older when they learn to speak two languages appear to have smaller comprehension vocabularies than monolingual children (Hakuta, 1986; de Houwser, 1995; Bialystok, 1997). Although a bilingual child may have in each of her languages a vocabulary that's smaller than a monolingual child's vocabulary, her total production vocabulary – her vocabularies in both languages combined – may be equal in size to the monolingual child's production vocabulary (Pearson et al., 1993).

The way two languages are learned differs depending on whether children learn the languages simultaneously or in sequence. When very young children learn two languages simultaneously, they rely on language sounds, such as consonants, longer than monolingual children do (Fennell, Byers-Heinlein, & Werker, 2007). The researchers think that this process may be adaptive in that bilingual children can use the distinct language sounds to help them deal with the cognitive load of learning words in two languages. In addition, research (Hirsch & Kim, 1997) has suggested that when children learn two languages simultaneously, from infancy, the languages share the same brain region (called *Broca's area*) that is responsible for the execution of speech as well as for some grammatical aspects of language. However, when children learn a second language later in childhood or adulthood, this brain region is divided, with a distinct area reserved for the second language. If these findings are valid, we might speculate that they underlie the apparent greater ease of learning a second language early in childhood. Perhaps future studies will shed more light on this issue.

One important determinant of how well children master each of two languages is how often they are exposed to each one. Very few children, for example, are exposed to equal inputs of Spanish and English. As researchers found in Miami, a city that is home to a large Cuban population, children who received less than 25% of their language input in Spanish were unlikely to become competent Spanish speakers (Pearson et al., 1997). As in the case of many other kinds of lessons, exposure is an important determinant of how well children will learn.

Learning a second language often has specific benefits. Studies have shown that children who learn two languages are more cognitively advanced than monolingual children. Children skilled in two languages have better concept formation, are more flexible in their thinking, have greater morphological awareness and have better attentional control (Diaz, 1983, 1985; Rosenblum & Pinker, 1983; Goncz & Kodzopeljic, 1991; Bialystok, 1999; Deacon et al., 2007). Bilingualism also appears to facilitate the development of metalinguistic awareness (Bialystok, 1991). Not only do language and cognitive development benefit from bilingualism, but children's social behaviour may also improve. Lambert (1987) studied English-speaking children who participated in a French language immersion programme in Quebec, Canada. In comparison to control pupils, the 'immersion' students had less stereotyped attitudes toward French Canadian peers. Moreover, the immersion experience resulted in more mature and productive 'social perspectives'. For example, these children offered more sophisticated solutions to solving cultural differences between French and English Canadians.

In sum, learning two languages may not be as problematic as some thought but rather an advantage and an opportunity. Evidence of the benefits of bilingualism must be interpreted with caution, however. Children who are successful at multiple languages may be a select group (Diaz, 1983). We do not know how many children try to learn several languages and fall short of becoming bilingual. In other words, we don't know whether the samples used to date in studying the benefits of bilingualism are fully representative.

Research close-up

BOX 8-6   Bilingualism and executive control: evidence from Canada and India

Source: Based on Bialystok and Viswanathan (2009).

Introduction:

Research has pointed to generalized academic benefits for bilingual children. Specifically, many bilingual children appear to perform better than monolingual children (children who speak only one language). Bialystok and colleagues have argued that one explanation for this may be that learning two languages promotes executive control – that is, the ability to plan and control cognitive operations such as the ability to suppress responses, control inhibition, and cognitive flexibility. The present experiment aimed to explore executive control in these three areas among bilingual and monolingual children.

Method:

Ninety 8-year-old children were involved in the study. These included monolingual English-speaking Canadians, bilingual Canadian children who spoke English plus one of several other languages including Cantonese, Croatian, Hebrew, French, Hindi, Russian and Urdu, and bilingual children in India who spoke English and either Tamil or Telugu. All the children were being educated in English and spoke the other language at home.

Children were asked to complete a Faces Task (Bialystok, 2006). In the task children are asked to pay attention to a monitor. They then saw a cartoon/schematic face and, after 1000 ms, the eyes turned either red or green. After that, an asterisk appeared in one of two boxes, and children were asked to press a button on the computer on the same side as the asterisk if the eyes had been green, but on the other side from the asterisk if the eyes had been red. The task repeated for 24 trials (i.e., 24 faces) and the direction of gaze of eyes changed on the schematic face for different trials. This allowed different aspects of executive control to be assessed. For instance, inhibitory control was assessed comparing reaction times on the straight versus averted gaze versions of the schematic faces.

Results:

Both groups of bilingual children were faster than the monolingual children on tasks involving inhibitory control and shifting sets (cognitive flexibility). However, there were no differences between bilingual and monolingual children on tasks involving response suppression or in a control condition.

Discussion:

Bialystok argues that these findings provide further support for the association between bilingualism and enhanced executive control. However, specific features of executive control are implicated. Moreover, the findings extend to bilingualism in two cultures (Canada and India), suggesting that it is not merely features of a specific language or languages, but the mastery of two (rather than one) language that is associated with these benefits.

FACILITATING CHILDREN'S LANGUAGE DEVELOPMENT

Bruner (1983) proposed that the environment provides the language-learning child with a language acquisition support system, or LASS. This view emphasizes the parents' or caregivers' role as facilitators of language acquisition (Snow, 1989). When children are very young, parents support their language development with several strategies. For example, parents often introduce objects to a child to provide a basis for their mutual play and speak about objects and events that are present and easily visible to the child. They also monitor their child's apparent goals or intentions closely, often commenting on them. Although parents don't usually conceive of these practices as deliberate teaching techniques but as conversations with their children, they are facilitating their children's language learning.

Adults use many techniques to stimulate and facilitate language development including playing non-verbal games, using simplified speech, and elaborating on and rewording children's own utterances to help them sharpen their communicative skills. These techniques may also stimulate many other aspects of development, and often form part of naturally occurring parent–child interactions from infancy onwards.

Parents make some of their first efforts to 'converse' with their children in early non-linguistic games like peek-a-boo or pat-a-cake. Children learn some structural features of spoken language, such as turn-taking, from these games. And because these kinds of games involve regular, repetitive and thus predictable behaviour, they may also lay a foundation for the rules of language. At first, young babies aren't capable of either initiating or responding in these playful 'conversations'. Parents help them learn these social skills by carrying more than their share of early dialogues and by waiting for pauses in the infant's vocal or motor behaviour and then inserting an appropriate response. This supportive activity of parents may contribute not only to later give-and-take in conversation but also to social turn-taking in play and other more complex games (Garvey, 1990).

Using simplified speech

Parents often modify their speech when they talk to infants and children. Typically, they use a simplified style, called infant-directed, or child-directed, speech (also called *motherese*), in which they speak in short, simple sentences that refer to concrete objects and events, and that often repeat important words and

language acquisition support system (LASS) A collection of strategies and tactics that environmental influences – initially, a child's parents or caregivers – provide to the language-learning child.

infant-directed, or child-directed, speech A simplified style of speech parents use with young children, in which sentences are short, simple and often repetitive, and the speaker enunciates especially clearly, slowly and in a higher-pitched voice, often ending with a rising intonation. Also called *motherese*.

Many games that parents and siblings play with young children help them learn words as well as pragmatic features of language such as turn-taking and the meaning of pauses.
© Hero/Corbis/Glow Images

phrases. In this style of speech, parents also talk more slowly and in higher-pitched voices, enunciate more clearly, and often end sentences with a rising intonation (Fernald, 1992; Fernald & Morikawa, 1993). The simplified grammar and syntax may help children learn the relationships between words and objects, and may also give them some understanding of the rules of segmentation – that is, how speech is divided into words, phrases and sentences. The acoustic variations can help highlight important words. For example, in reading to 14 month olds, mothers consistently positioned a word that identified a picture ('that's a *shirt*' or 'that's a *boy*') at the end of a phrase and spoke in exaggerated pitch, thus capturing their infants' attention (Fernald & Kuhl, 1987; Fernald & Mazzie, 1991).

Research has shown that newborns and 4 week olds prefer to listen to infant-directed speech than to adult-directed talk (Cooper & Aslin, 1990), and that babies are equally responsive to this style of communication whether it is used by men or women (Pegg, Werker, & McLeod, 1992). In addition, infants show a preference for infant-directed speech even when speech is in a non-native language. For example, even when English-learning infants listened to Cantonese, they still appeared to prefer infant-directed speech (Werker, Pegg, & McLeod, 1994).

Exaggerating speech, placing important words at the ends of sentences, and raising pitch and intonation help adults gain infants' attention, but does the use of simplified speech actually facilitate children's language learning? In fact, simplified speech may not always be helpful. In one study, children who had progressed beyond the one-word stage were more likely to respond appropriately to an adult form of a command ('Throw me the ball') than to a simplified form ('Throw ball'). As we have seen in other areas of development, a level of complexity that is slightly ahead of children may maximize their learning (Hoff-Ginsberg & Shatz, 1982; Sokolov, 1993). When infants or children show signs that they do not understand something, adults often revert to simpler speech (Bohannon & Warren-Leubecker, 1988). In general, parents adjust their speech to a child's level of linguistic sophistication, using a wider and wider range of words and parts of speech as children mature (Shatz, 1983; Hoff, 2005).

Other techniques

Parents facilitate early communication in several other important ways. Consider the following exchanges between a mother and her child:

> **expansion** A technique adults use in speaking to young children in which they imitate and expand or add to a child's statement.

> **recast** A technique adults use in speaking to young children in which they render a child's incomplete sentence in a more complex grammatical form.

> Parents' help with children's language development is one of the most important features of parental involvement from a young age. In Chapter 13 we discuss other ways in which parents play a vital role in other aspects of development, too.

Child: *Daddy juice.*
Adult: *Daddy drinks juice.*
Child: *Give Mama.*
Adult: *Give it to Mama.*

In the technique of expansion illustrated here, the adult imitates and expands or adds to the child's statement. Expanding on children's statements facilitates language development, including vocabulary (Weizman & Snow, 2001). And parents are especially likely to use this expansion strategy after a child has made a grammatical error (Bohannon & Stanowicz, 1988). Moreover, following up on the child's interests and attention is more supportive of learning than switching the child's attention to another topic (Tomasello & Farrar, 1986; Dunham, Dunham, & Curwin, 1993). Brown (1973) has estimated that, among middle-class families, about 30% of the time parents' speech to their children is composed of such expansions, but that lower-class parents use this technique much less often.

In the technique called recast, the adult listener reframes the child's incomplete sentence in a more complex grammatical form. For example, when the child says, 'Kitty eat', the adult may recast the sentence as a question: 'What is the kitty eating?' Through recasting, adults are, in effect, both correcting children's utterances and guiding them towards more appropriate grammatical usage. Some researchers have shown that children whose parents have recast their utterances appear to develop linguistically at a faster rate, using questions and complex verb forms at an earlier age than is common (Nelson, Carskadden, & Bonvillian, 1973; Nelson, 1989; Nelson et al., 1995). As we do not know how often parents use recasts, we cannot yet say how powerful a role recasting plays in normal language acquisition.

We do know, however, that children often imitate their parents' expansions and recasts, especially when the children's utterances are incorrect. When children's speech is correct, they are unlikely to imitate the adult's speech (Bohannon & Stanowicz, 1988). Perhaps children are more aware of their mistakes than we realize!

Is social interaction crucial to language development?

Some theorists hold that although social interaction is necessary for language acquisition, the specific devices of expansion and recasting, together with children's imitation, may not be necessary. First, no universal pattern of social linguistic support characterizes all parents within or across cultural groups (Hoff, 2005). In fact, there are impressive individual differences among the linguistic environments that parents within a given cultural group provide for their children (Shatz, 1983; Hart & Risley, 1999). In addition, not all cultures use the devices typical of the American middle class (Peters, 1983; Minami & McCabe, 1995). For example, among the Kaluli of New Guinea and in Samoa, people speak to the very youngest children as if they were adults (Schieffelin & Ochs, 1987; Ochs, 1988). Evidently, there are forms of interaction that we do not yet entirely understand but that nevertheless ensure that children around the world (including the Kaluli and Samoans) develop language at the same general pace.

Those who advocate the interactionist view hold that, although the child is biologically prepared for learning language, there is also strong support for the role of environmental input in the child's development of language. For instance, longitudinal research exploring the relation between maternal responsiveness and the achievement by children of language milestones indicates that a mother's responsiveness to her child's activity at 9 and 13 months of age predicts language development (Tamis-LeMonda, Bornstein, & Baumwell, 2001). Maternal responsiveness was defined as any meaningful, positive change in the mother's behaviour within 5 seconds of a child's action – for example, if the child picked up a cup and the mother said, 'That's a cup.' Such research suggests that social contributions play an important facilitative role in language acquisition.

SUMMARY

Language serves a variety of purposes for the developing child. It facilitates interpersonal communication, helps organize thinking and aids in learning. The development of *communicative competence* is an important part of children's language learning. Communication requires us to use both *productive language*, transmitting messages to others, and *receptive language*, receiving and understanding messages others send us.

We can divide the study of language into four areas. *Phonology* describes a language's systems of sounds, or the way basic sound units, called *phonemes*, are connected to form words. *Semantics* is the study of the meaning of words and sentences. *Grammar*, which describes the structure of a language, includes *syntax* and *morphology*; *morphemes* are a language's smallest units of meaning. *Pragmatics* consists of rules for the use of appropriate language in particular social settings.

The learning view explains language development by the principles of reinforcement and imitation. In contrast, Chomsky's nativist approach argues that children have an innate *language acquisition device (LAD)* that enables them to learn language early and quickly. Most modern theorists take an interactionist view, recognizing that children are biologically prepared for language but require extensive experience with language and communication for adequate development. In proposing a *language acquisition support system (LASS)*, Bruner emphasizes the critical roles parents and other early caregivers play in the child's language development.

Infants' capacity for receptive language begins as early as the first month of life, as demonstrated in their *categorical speech perception*, the ability to discriminate among consonant sounds as well as their ability to recognize some vowel sounds by the age of 2 months. As children are exposed to their native languages, their abilities to distinguish and categorize phonemes are refined and specialized for the sounds of their own languages. Language is a social phenomenon, so children must learn to raise their level of communication beyond *speech acts* to true *discourse*, which includes a complicated set of skills such as engaging the listener, sensitivity to listeners' feedback, adjusting speech to characteristics of listeners and to particular situations, being a good listener, and how to let others know that their messages are unclear. Children improve their conversational sophistication through direct instruction and by observing and listening to others speak.

When children achieve *metalinguistic awareness* at about the age of 10, they can both understand that language is a system of rules for communication and discuss the properties and uses of language. Although they can use many rules at an earlier age, they have difficulty separating words from the objects or events they represent, and grasping the concept that words are elements of language. The evidence indicates that *bilingualism*, in which children learn two languages either simultaneously or sequentially, does not place children at a disadvantage in terms of language proficiency. In fact, learning two languages may have benefits, such as advanced cognitive skills, more flexibility of thought, and greater acceptance of peers from other cultural backgrounds.

Explore and Discuss

1. How do you think language development affects a child's social and emotional development?

2. Why is it important for a child's language development that she or he talk to adults as well as to other children?

3. Preschool children ask lots of why questions, sometimes even exhausting parents by the sheer number of their queries. If a child asked you a why question, such as 'Why don't doggies cry?' or 'Why are circles round?' how would you answer?

4. Is there an upper limit on the number of languages a child can learn to speak fluently? If so, what do you think this limit is, and why is there a limit?

5. How should we teach children to read?

Recommended Reading

Classic

Brown, R. (1958). How shall a thing be called? *Psychological Review, 65,* 14–21.

Chomsky, N. (1972). *Language and the mind.* New York: Harcourt Brace Jovanovich.

Nelson, K. (1973). Structure and strategy in learning to talk. *Monographs for the Society for Research into Child Development, 38.*

Contemporary

Cain, K. (2010). *Reading development and difficulties.* Oxford: Wiley-Blackwell.

Chapman, R. S. (2000). Children's language learning: An interactionist perspective. *Journal of Child Psychology and Psychiatry, 41,* 33–54.

Pinker, S. (1991). Rules of language. *Science, 253,* 530–535.

CHAPTER 9

Cognitive Development: Origins of Knowledge

Introduction How do we make sense of the world around us, all the people, objects and places in it? As adults, we take what we know about the world for granted. For example, when was the last time you wondered if an object continues to exist even when you can't see it? Or when did you last stop to think about how to understand the gestures that people use to communicate with one another?

> **cognition** The mental activity through which human beings acquire and process knowledge.

Cognition is the term used to describe the mental activity through which human beings acquire, remember and learn to use knowledge. Cognition includes many mental processes, such as perception, attention, learning, memory and reasoning. It is such a broad concept that most of the topics covered in this book have some relation to cognition and its development. After all, human beings are thinking creatures, and much of our behaviour reflects this fact. Research on cognitive development focuses specifically on how and when intellectual abilities and knowledge of the world first emerge in childhood and then change as a person grows older.

In this chapter and its companion, Chapter 10, we discuss several different approaches to the study of cognitive development. This chapter focuses on questions concerning the emergence of knowledge and ways of thinking about (conceptualizing) the world and people. Much of the groundwork concerning these questions was inspired by the classic theories of Piaget and Vygotsky, and we will spend quite a lot of time in this chapter discussing these theories, and more recent alternatives which have been proposed. In contrast, Chapter 10 will focus more on the emergence of *cognitive functions*. By *cognitive functions* we mean the specific cognitive abilities that we know humans possess, such as memory, attention, planning, decision making and so on. While Piaget's and Vygotsky's approaches touch on the development of these cognitive functions, they were more concerned with the structures of knowledge that children possess, and how these emerge. However, perhaps the most important frameworks for understanding the development of *cognitive functions* have emerged from cognitive psychology, rather than developmental theory. This is why we have decided to treat these matters in separate chapters.

First of all in this chapter, we explore Jean Piaget's theory of cognitive development, which emphasizes the child's own role in developmental changes in the organization or structure of their thinking processes. Then we consider Lev Vygotsky's sociocultural theory of cognitive development, which suggests that a child's interactions with the social world produce advances in thinking and understanding. Next we will cover some more modern accounts of the development: notably those which take a more nativist approach, arguing that we inherit structures of knowledge. Last of all we will address what has become a central topic for consideration by cognitive developmentalists: the emergence of knowledge about our social world.

PIAGET'S THEORY OF COGNITIVE DEVELOPMENT

One of the most influential theories of cognitive development is that of the Swiss scientist Jean Piaget (see Chapter 2 for a more extensive discussion of Piaget's life and background). Piaget's theory is not without controversy, and many developmentalists have challenged both his methods and his conclusions. However, despite these many criticisms Piaget's approach still has a significant legacy of influence on the field of cognitive developmental research. Part of the longevity of Piaget's perspective comes from the fact that his theory was the first to raise a great many of the most interesting questions about intellectual development that are still addressed today (Piaget, 1926, 1929, 1950, 1985). Furthermore, he was particularly skilled in applying his theoretical account of cognitive development across a very wide range of different scenarios. And so, even though he may have come to some incorrect conclusions, researchers are still pondering answers to the questions he raised, and using his framework to consider new questions (e.g., Hammond, 2014; Karmiloff-Smith, Thomas, & Johnson, 2018). First, we describe Piaget's theory, and then we turn to the main criticisms of this approach.

Piaget's theory, which became popular in English-speaking countries in the 1960s – largely through the influence of carefully written explanations by John Flavell (1963) – proposed that, over the course of development, the child undergoes qualitative changes in the ways in which he thinks and understands the world. For developmental psychologists at the time, this theory was an attractive alternative to behaviourism, which was the dominant account; rather than treating children's development as an extension of adult learning processes Piaget focused on how infants, children and adults faced very different developmental constraints from one another, and used these constraints to understand how development proceeds.

PIAGET'S CONSTRUCTIVISM

Piaget argued that children play an active role in acquiring knowledge. In contrast to behaviourism, he argued that development occurs in the way it does because children actively seek out information from their environments. Furthermore, he argued that when children encounter new information, they actively try to understand it by fitting it into the structures of knowledge they already possess. In other words, children construct their own understanding. This is why Piaget's theory is referred to as a constructivist theory of development (you will also hear people refer to it as *constructionism* or constructivism.

There is a lot of knowledge about the world that children have to gain. Piaget was particularly interested in the development of knowledge about properties of the world. He set out to discover precisely how children at different points in their development think about how objects work and are related to one another. He also focused on how children become able to think beyond solid objects in a more abstract way, focusing particularly on the development of logical thought in childhood. Despite acknowledging that children vary in the timing of how they develop these abilities and knowledge, Piaget argued that children develop according to a fixed order of developmental stages. As a result, he provided approximate ages at which these developmental achievements occur. The Chronology of Development chart covers many topics discussed in this chapter (see below) and includes a summary of Piaget's descriptions of the milestones of cognitive development.

> **constructivism** The idea that children actively create their understanding of the world as they engage with new information and attempt to understand it.
>
> **schema** An organized unit of knowledge that the child uses to try to understand a situation; a schema forms the basis for organizing actions and thoughts in response to the environment.
>
> **operations** Schemas based on internal mental activities.

Schemas and their organization

Piaget believed that, over the course of development, children's knowledge of the world gets organized into increasingly more complex cognitive structures. A *cognitive structure* is not a physical entity in the brain but an organized group of interrelated memories, ideas and strategies that the child uses in trying to understand a situation. Piaget built much of his theory around the notion of the schema, which is much like a concept. A schema is an organized unit of knowledge and, collectively, schemas form the knowledge base that a person uses to understand and interact with the environment.

A key feature of children's developing knowledge according to this account is that schemas become increasingly organized into more complex structures of knowledge. Schemas become organized and reorganized over time because of the ways in which children integrate new experiences with their current knowledge structure.

For instance, newborns possess many reflexes, such as sucking, grasping and looking, all of which help the infant engage with and learn about the world. Initially, these reflexes are used in very specific ways. However, over time and with experience at sucking, for example, this schema changes and the newborn sucks differently on different objects and uses this schema for different purposes, such as exploring objects. So the schema of sucking changes and becomes more complex.

Organization between schemas is also an important developmental change. According to Piaget, many schemas are initially separate (for example, looking and sucking), but as the infant realizes that he can look and suck at the same object, those schemas become linked (or reciprocal, in Piaget's terms).

As children grow older and gain experience, they shift gradually from using schemas based on overt physical activities to those based on internal mental activities. Piaget called these mental schemas operations. With development, cognitive operations are altered and combined to form more complex behaviours and ways of thinking. When a substantial number of changes in schemas or operations occur, Piaget claimed that children change from one organized way of understanding to an entirely new way of approaching the world. He described these large-scale organizational changes as stages. There are four of Piaget's major stages, described in detail in the next section.

Stagewise development through assimilation and accommodation

A crucial aspect of understanding Piaget's approach is in grasping his account of the processes of development; his description of *how* infants and children adapt their schemas and thereby progress to the next developmental stages. Piaget described two mechanisms involved in this, which he called assimilation and accommodation.

> **assimilation** Applying an existing schema to a new experience.
>
> **accommodation** Modifying an existing schema to fit a new experience.

To understand a new experience, Piaget stated that children assimilate that experience; that is, they try to apply what they already know, their existing schemas, to the new experience. For example, as babies are confronted with new objects, they try to assimilate those objects to their looking–grasping–sucking schema. In most cases, they are successful, and object after object gets seen, grasped and placed in the mouth.

However, sometimes babies encounter an object that is hard to assimilate. For example, a large beachball is very difficult to grasp and suck. Now the infant must modify her strategy for exploring objects (her looking–grasping–sucking schema) and adopt a new approach. This is where accommodation comes in. She may hold the ball in her arms instead of her hands and lick it with her tongue instead of suck on it. In this way, she has modified an existing schema to fit the characteristics of the new situation.

An example of assimilation and accommodation in older children comes into play when children attempt to name things they have not named before. Let's say a child sees a squirrel, points to it and says 'mouse'. This is assimilation in action – the child is assimilating squirrels into her linguistic schema for mice. However, when the parent corrects the child, by saying 'no, that's a squirrel', the child has to accommodate their schema for naming furry animals to include this new category. Assimilation and accommodation work together to organize children's knowledge and behaviour into increasingly complex structures.

CHRONOLOGY OF DEVELOPMENT

The child's cognitive development from infancy through late childhood

1 to 2 months	The child becomes more efficient in the use of reflexes and can invite stimulation that allows this use; begins to adapt reflexive behaviours to different environmental conditions (e.g., sucks differently when nurses, drinks from a bottle, and has thumb or pacifier in mouth); shows recognition memory and can learn basic associations; can anticipate: crying stops at sight of mother's breast or the bottle; expects and shows interest in animate behaviour from humans; gradually develops organized and selective looking
3 to 4 months	Becomes more focused on specific objects; quiets at sight of interesting toy; investigative type of attention; has more voluntary control of looking; makes eye contact; social looking time increases; face-to-face play becomes common; repeats body actions that are pleasurable and satisfying; can reach out and gently probe objects; may be capable of simple grouping or categorization; reacts differently to some usual and unusual physical events
5 to 6 months	Visually follows an object as it moves out of direct line of vision; remembers pictures of faces; looking time increases; increasingly focuses attention on objects as well as people; learns behaviours of familiar people; reacts to changes in familiar events

7 to 8 months	Explores objects by manipulation; drops objects from heights; may understand the notion of physical support; is more attentive when playing; likes to make things happen and combines learned behaviours in this effort (e.g., shaking, banging and dangling toys); displays basic problem-solving abilities; attends to play; often mouths toys as a way of exploring; uncovers hidden objects
9 to 10 months	Uses knowledge to solve problems; seems aware of some cause-and-effect relations; recognizes that own actions may affect outcomes; gets other people to make things happen; able to look at more distant objects or images; exerts increased control over own actions; begins to show goal-orientated attention; can alternate attention between a person and an object; explores inside and outside surfaces of toys; repeats play sequences with different toys; investigates textures, designs or parts of toys; looks intently at pictures
11 months to 1 year	Uses tools to accomplish goals (e.g., uses a chair to stand up); begins to put knowledge of containment to use (e.g., tries to stack cups); examines objects comprehensively; uses imitative learning; deliberately introduces variations into play sequences; recognizes self in mirror; shows increased tendency to inspect complex visual stimuli; frequently looks at partner's face; follows the glances and points of others towards objects that are currently out of sight
15 months	Continues to use systematic trial-and-error learning; is more aware of the functions of objects; may use dolls in play; recognizes and uses more cause-and-effect relationships; shows clear evidence of social referencing; some research now suggests that infants of this age understand others' perspectives
18 months	Likes to experiment with the properties of objects; has better recall memory; has basic idea of 'what should be' (e.g., puts lids on jars); recognizes that others have possessions; can use language to direct attention
21 months	To some degree, understands past, present and future; uses scripts to organize activities into episodes; has some understanding of the idea of categories (e.g., colours)
2 years	Can think symbolically and use language to direct attention and regulate behaviour; can remember behaviours and reproduce an action long after observing it; can plan how to solve a problem mentally rather than use trial and error; begins to understand conservation; engages in fantasy play; recognizes that family members have specific roles; shows creative problem solving
3 to 4 years	Becomes better at reasoning about others' perspectives; may be able to understand part–whole relations
5 years	Has improved language and problem-solving skills; can use certain mental operations to solve problems but does this intuitively, without a clear understanding of how and why they work
7 years	Has achieved conservation of number, mass, liquid, length; begins to describe self in more abstract terms
8 to 10 years	Can anticipate and consider the thoughts of others; achieves conservation of weight and area
11 to 12 years	Achieves conservation of volume; begins to think deductively; can sort things in complicated combinations of attributes
12 and beyond	Thinking becomes more flexible and abstract; can apply logic to ideas and problems that violate reality; can entertain many possible solutions to a problem

Note: This table represents an approximation of what infants and children can do at various ages. As more research enlightens our understanding, we may come to find that infants or children can accomplish some of these tasks earlier or later than stated here.

Sources: Flavell (1963); Kopp (1994); Gauvain (2001); Siegler and Alibali (2005).

A STAGE THEORY OF COGNITIVE DEVELOPMENT

Piaget viewed intellectual growth in terms of progressive changes in children's cognitive structures. According to Piaget's theory, small changes in understanding and interacting with the world eventually result in large-scale changes as children move between what are referred to as stages of development. Each stage is qualitatively different from the one that precedes it. Because stages are built through individuals' experiences, children do not necessarily reach these stages at exactly the same ages. However, an important aspect of Piaget's argument is that all children pass through the stages in the same order, and no stage can be skipped. This is because the attainments of earlier stages are the building blocks of the later stages and thus are essential for these later developments to emerge.

Piaget laid out his stage theory of intellectual development as occurring across three major periods: the *sensorimotor period*, the *concrete operational period* (which is itself divided up into two sub-periods, the *pre-operational period* and *concrete operations*), and the *formal operational period* (see Table 9-1). As children pass through these stages, Piaget's theory describes them in increasingly sophisticated terms; they change from infants who are incapable of mental operations and depend on sensory and motor activities to explore and learn about the world, into emerging young adults capable of great flexibility of thought and abstract reasoning. In many ways infants have more to learn in the initial periods of development than they do in later childhood. Consequently the developments Piaget described are somewhat more detailed in the earlier periods of development (particularly the sensorimotor period). For the same reason we dedicate more time to this period here.

Table 9-1   Piaget's stages of cognitive development

Stage	Age range (years)	Major characteristics and achievements according to Piaget
Sensorimotor period	0–2	The infant's thought is confined to action schemas and sensory experiences. He seeks stimulation by prolonging interesting sights and experiences; through this active experience he gradually differentiates himself from objects and other people, develops a concept of what an object is (including object permanence and causal relations among objects). He develops concepts of time, and space; comes to grasp means–end relationships; begins to imitate behaviours; and late in the stage, shows the beginnings of symbolic thought, and begins to engage in imaginative play.
Preoperational representations (concrete operational period)	2–7	The child begins to use symbols to represent objects and experiences, and to use language symbolically; shows intuitive problem solving. Her thinking is pre-logical, characterized by irreversibility, centration, egocentrism and animism. She begins to think in terms of classes, sees relationships, and starts to grasp a concept of numbers.
Concrete operations (concrete operational period)	7–11	The child becomes capable of logical reasoning, but this ability is limited to a consideration of physical objects; he grasps concepts of the conservation of mass, length, weight and volume; his thinking is now characterized by reversibility, decentration, and the ability to take the role of another; he can organize objects into hierarchical classes (classification) and place objects into ordered series (seriation).
Formal operational period	11 plus	The child acquires flexibility in thinking as well as the capacities for abstract thinking and mental hypothesis testing; she can consider possible alternatives in complex reasoning and problem solving.

sensorimotor period
Piaget's name for the first stage of cognitive development that he described, during which children's abilities are rooted in their physical interactions with objects.

The sensorimotor period

Perhaps the most dramatic achievements in children's intellectual development take place during the sensorimotor period, which spans approximately the first two years of life. Piaget wrote about the sensorimotor period in two of his most famous books: *The construction of reality in the child* (Piaget, 1954) and *The origins of intelligence in the child* (1952). In these books he described how, by interacting with their environment in active ways, children build on their basic reflexes and, from these origins, formulate increasingly more sophisticated ways of interacting with and understanding the world.

The newborn child is described by Piaget as being fundamentally egocentric. He argued that their early actions demonstrate that, early in the sensorimotor period, they only understand the world from the perspective of those particular reflexes and actions, and are unable to consider the world from the standpoint of the object or objects which they are acting on or with. The culmination of the sensorimotor period, at around 2 years of age, is the ability to overcome this egocentrism and form mental representations of objects and events that are independent of the child's own actions. From that attainment they can progress into the concrete operations period and begin thinking about and imagining objects such that they can solve problems in a logical way. Piaget built up and illustrated his theoretical account of the sensorimotor period with observations of his own three children, Laurent, Lucienne and Jacqueline.

Because so many cognitive changes occur in the first two years, Piaget divided the sensorimotor stage into six substages. According to the sensorimotor theory, one of the major cognitive achievements during the sensorimotor stage is the development of the object concept. Piaget argued that we are not born with knowledge of objects. He thought that the infant must construct this knowledge over the course of her or his experience with objects.

One of the attainments in the sensorimotor period that Piaget particularly emphasized was an understanding of object permanence – the realization that objects continue to exist even when out of sight or touch (Table 9-2). However, Piaget also considered knowledge of spatial layouts and causal interactions between objects to be particularly important in the first two years. We discuss Piaget's thinking about development in the first two years of life, as we outline his description of the six stages of the sensorimotor period. We will focus mainly on his discussion of the object concept. While reading our account of Piaget's description, try to notice how the organization of schemas becomes more and more complex as the sub-stages progress. Also consider how infants are using assimilation and accommodation to achieve this developmental progression. Bear in mind of course, that this description is Piaget's interpretation rather than a statement of fact!

> **egocentrism** The tendency to view the world from one's own perspective and to have difficulty seeing things from another's viewpoint.
>
> **object permanence** The notion that entities external to us, such as objects and people, continue to exist independent of our seeing or interacting with them.

> Piaget considered motor reflexes to be of foundational importance in starting children's cognitive development. We discuss some reflex behaviours in infants in Chapter 6.

Table 9-2 Piaget's description of how infants in the sensorimotor period acquire the object concept and an understanding of object permanence, illustrated by some of the observations he made

Stage	Age (months)	Observational evaluation of infant's behaviour
1 Basic reflex activity	0–1	Focuses only on objects directly in front of her
2 Primary circular reactions	1–4	Begins to operate on objects with action schemes; initially, this occurs accidentally and then becomes less accidental; looks a long time at place where an object disappeared but does not search visually or manually for the object
3 Secondary circular reactions	4–8	Can operate on objects and repeats actions towards objects; can visually anticipate where an object may be; searches for partially concealed objects
4 Coordination of secondary circular reactions	8–12	Will search for completely hidden objects but has tendency to repeat old actions by searching where objects were previously hidden (A-not-B error)
5 Tertiary circular reactions	12–18	Lots of trial-and-error experimentation with objects and how they move; searches for objects that have been concealed while he was watching but has difficulty if an object is displaced more than once
6 Internalization of schemes – the origins of symbolic thought	18–24	Object concept is fully developed; child searches and finds objects easily, even if the object has been hidden and displaced several times in a row before he is allowed to search

STAGE 1: BASIC REFLEX ACTIVITY (0 TO 1 MONTH)

basic reflex activity
An infant's exercise of, and growing proficiency in, the use of innate reflexes.

primary circular reactions Behaviours focused on the infant's own body that the infant repeats and modifies because they are pleasurable and satisfying.

secondary circular reactions Behaviours focused on objects outside the infant's own body that the infant repeatedly engages in because they are pleasurable and satisfying.

coordination of secondary circular reactions An infant's combination of different schemas to achieve a specific goal (sometimes referred to as means–end coordination).

In the substage of basic reflex activity, infants become more skilled in the use of their innate reflexes, such as grasping and sucking. Much of their initial exploration of objects occurs through involuntary reflexive behaviours. However, over the first month of life, many of these involuntary behaviours are replaced by behaviours that are similar in form but are controlled voluntarily. For example, between birth and 1 month of age, the grasping reflex gradually subsides, and in its place, the infant begins to use her hands voluntarily to grab on to objects that come within reach. Infants look only at objects that are directly in front of them. At this stage, Piaget thought the infant carried out all of these actions for their own sake (e.g. they were not grasping or looking at an object for any other reason than grasping or looking alone).

STAGE 2: PRIMARY CIRCULAR REACTIONS (1 TO 4 MONTHS)

This substage is called primary circular reactions because, from 1–4 months, infants produce repetitive behaviours that are focused on the infant's own body. Babies repeat and modify actions they find pleasurable. Often, these actions begin by chance. For example, a baby may accidentally bring a finger close to her mouth and start sucking on it. Finding this behaviour pleasurable, the infant may attempt to reproduce the exact behaviour – in this case, by seeking the finger to suck on it again and again. With regard to objects infants display an expectation that an object may reappear, but they seem to have no comprehension that objects have an existence when out of sight or touch. When a toy vanishes, they don't look for it. In fact, if the toy drops from a child's hand, he may stare at his hand rather than follow the falling object's path to the floor.

STAGE 3: SECONDARY CIRCULAR REACTIONS (4 TO 8 MONTHS)

Not until the infant enters the substage of secondary circular reactions, at about 4 months of age, does he become interested in making things happen in the world outside his own body. Secondary circular reactions involve repetitive behaviours focused on objects. The child's reactions are still circular; that is, he repeatedly engages in behaviours that please him. For example, the infant may shake a rattle, hear an interesting sound, shake the rattle again, and so on. But the baby now is capable of combining schemas, such as looking and shaking, to produce more complex behaviours. It is the gradual linking of separate schemas that Piaget thought was the basis of a more objective (i.e. less egocentric) understanding of the world. Realizing that an object can be both grasped and looked at enables infants to appreciate that an object is an entity that is independent of those actions (Bremner & Spence, 2008). These developmental processes enable the infant to begin to show some awareness of the permanence of objects: The child will search for a partially visible object, but not a covered one. Even if she watches as an object is covered, she will not attempt to retrieve it.

STAGE 4: COORDINATION OF SECONDARY CIRCULAR REACTIONS (8 TO 12 MONTHS)

In this substage (coordination of secondary circular reactions), the infant develops more sophisticated combinations of behaviours towards objects and these begin to appear intentional in nature. According to Piaget, at this sub-stage the child first becomes able to plan deliberately to attain a goal. He or she does this by combining schemas in order to reach these goals (this is often referred to as means–end coordination). For example, the child can now combine a hitting schema with her reaching and grasping schemas to move one toy out of the way (the 'means') so she can reach another (the 'end'). Thus, this substage marks the beginning of problem-solving behaviour. Although infants can sometimes achieve means end–coordination prior to 8 months, Piaget argued that this was fortuitous rather than reflecting an intentional action (Willatts, 1999).

The child now begins to search for completely concealed objects. However, although the child will search successfully for an object hidden in one location, if the object is moved to another location as the child watches, the child will continue to search in the first hiding place. This type of error is referred to as the A-not-B error because the child continues to search in the first hiding place, identified as A, even after, in the child's presence, the object is put in a second spot, identified as B. Piaget argued that this error represents a failure to understand the relationship between permanent objects and spatial locations. More specifically, he argued that the infant comprehends the permanence of objects as being intrinsically tied to their own actions; for the infant, the uncovering reaches they make actually re-create the object.

STAGE 5: TERTIARY CIRCULAR REACTIONS (12 TO 18 MONTHS)

In the substage of tertiary circular reactions, children begin to experiment with external objects. Children use trial-and-error methods to learn more about the properties of objects and to solve problems. Again they are concerned with means–end actions, but unlike the earlier substages they now begin to experiment with finding new means to reach their goals. Because of this kind of novel exploration, Piaget referred to infants at this stage as 'little scientists' (see also Gopnik, 2017). An example of this kind of experimentation might be for an infant to deliberately drop objects from different heights to see the effect these slightly different actions have on the way the object contacts with the ground.

This 7-month-old child is quite absorbed in shaking her rattle. Using its different parts, she may get the rattle to make more than just one intriguing sound; this means–end coordination illustrates the substage of secondary circular reactions.
© McGraw-Hill Education/Jill Braaten

In this substage, the infant solves the AB task (i.e., they no longer make the A-not-B error), but despite this new awareness Piaget found that children still have difficulty following more than one displacement of an object. While playing a hiding game with his son, Laurent, Piaget hid his watch repeatedly behind one of two cushions, and Laurent consistently searched for the watch under the correct cushion. However, as Laurent watched, Piaget then placed the watch in a box, put the box behind a cushion, and then secretly removed the watch from the box and put the watch behind the cushion. He then handed the box to Laurent, who opened it and found it empty. Laurent did not search for the watch behind the cushion. This type of hiding problem has been referred to as *invisible displacement*, and was clearly not within Laurent's grasp during sub-stage 5.

The subtle ways in which Piaget complicates the tasks that he uses each time a child reaches a given level of understanding is testament to his extraordinary inventiveness in researching cognitive abilities in young children. Although these are not experiments in the strict meaning of the word, this kind of subtle complication is one of the hallmarks of Piaget's clinical observation method (see Chapter 3).

STAGE 6: INVENTING NEW MEANS BY MENTAL COMBINATION (18 TO 24 MONTHS)

It is not until the sixth and last substage of inventing new means by mental combination (sometimes referred to as 'internalization of schemas') that the beginnings of symbolic thought appear. Children begin to think symbolically and engage in internal (mental) problem solving. The child can now invent ways to attain a goal by *mentally* combining schemas; his cognitive schemas are no longer limited to physically exploring, manipulating, and acting on objects. Symbolic capabilities are evident in the child's emerging ability to use language and in deferred imitation in which the child mimics an action some time after observing it.

tertiary circular reactions Behaviours in which infants experiment with the properties of external objects and try to learn how objects respond to various actions.

inventing new means by mental combination Children begin to combine schemas mentally, and rely less on physical trial and error.

symbolic thought The use of mental images and concepts to represent people, objects and events.

deferred imitation Mimicry of an action some time after having observed it; requires that the child have some sort of mental representation of the action.

Finally, at this last substage, children fully acquire the concept of object permanence. They are able to make inferences about the positions of unseen objects even when the objects have been hidden or displaced several times.

Alternative explanations of the development of knowledge in infancy

In the late 1960s developmental scientists began in earnest to investigate the validity of Piaget's ideas about the development of knowledge in infancy with more rigorous experimental methodologies. It was of course important to determine whether Piaget's observations and conclusions were borne out across a more representative sample than just Laurent, Lucienne and Jacqueline (his own three children), but researchers also wanted to confirm his observations in more strictly controlled experimental settings. Interestingly, cross-cultural research on the sensorimotor stage supports Piaget's general framework. A longitudinal study conducted with Baoulé children between 6 and 30 months of age in Côte d'Ivoire revealed the same six substages Piaget described (Dasen et al., 1978).

However, most of the subsequent research activity concerning Piaget's sensorimotor period focused on the emergence of the object concept. Bower and Wishart (1972) investigated whether infants' failure to search for hidden objects might be due to a difficulty in completing the required motor movements to uncover the object, rather than a lack of understanding about permanence. They did this by investigating whether infants would uncover an object if they could see it through a transparent cover. They found that 6-month-old infants would uncover a hidden object behind a transparent cover but not behind an opaque cover, and so concluded, consistent with Piaget's account, that motor or means–end difficulties were not responsible for a failure to search for objects (Shinskey & Munakata, 2001).

A great deal of research has investigated the A-not-B error made by infants after they have first begun to uncover fully hidden objects (at about 8 months). Remember that Piaget explained this as being due to the infants' thinking that their own egocentric actions summoned up the object. An alternative explanation was that infants kept responding at A because they thought that the object existed permanently at only that place (A), rather than because they were egocentric in their representations of hidden objects and space. Bremner and Bryant (1977) tested that idea by running the AB task as usual but, with one group of infants, moving them around the table just before the B trials. They found that, when the infants were moved around the table, they still reached to the same (egocentric) location with respect to the body such that they actually responded to a new place in objective space (location B). Even though the infants passed the AB test in this condition, this finding confirmed that the infants made the error due to an egocentric response. However, researchers still debate the question of exactly why infants seem unable to break out of the habit of responding to that egocentric location (e.g., Clearfield & Niman, 2012; Marcovitch & Zelazo, 2009; Topal et al., 2008).

Despite several examples of research studies that confirmed aspects of Piaget's account, his theory of sensorimotor development has met with a number of important challenges. Perhaps the biggest sticking point is that, in most of Piaget's tasks for studying the object concept in infants, he relied on infants' manual (hand) search behaviour. Many investigators have argued that we can gain better understanding of what the infant really knows about the world by investigating their patterns of looking behaviour.

A method that has been used a lot over the last three decades is the *violation of expectation* paradigm (Baillargeon, Spelke & Wasserman, 1985). In a violation of expectation study, the experimenter typically presents infants with contrasting visual events, one of which demonstrates an impossible scenario (e.g., one object appearing to pass straight through another one), with the other event being as similar as possible in appearance to the impossible event, but possible. The infants' looking at these events is used to determine whether they notice that the impossible event violates a physical principle of some kind (e.g., object permanence); if the infants look longer, then researchers typically conclude that they understand that physical principle. More recently, researchers have also used other measures of infant behaviour to measure violation of expectation like pupil dilation (Jackson & Sirois, 2009), looking towards the parent (Dunn & Bremner, 2017), and looking towards particular parts of the display where the violation took place (Southgate, Senju, & Csibra, 2007).

Renée Baillargeon (1986, 1993, 2004) has been particularly prolific in using violation of expectation to assess infants' understanding of objects. For instance, in one task Baillargeon (1986) presented 6- and 8-month-old infants with an event in which one solid object appeared to move through the space occupied by another solid object. The infant sat in front of a platform on which there was an inclined ramp (see Figure 9-1a). At the bottom of the ramp, directly in front of the infant, was a small screen that could be raised and lowered. After the screen had been lowered, a small car rolled down the ramp along a track, disappearing behind the screen and reappearing at the other side of the screen. This event was repeated until the infant became habituated to it and stopped looking at the display.

Next the infant saw one of two test events (Figures 9-1b and 9-1c). Both of these events were identical to the habituation event except that, when the screen was raised, the infant saw a box placed behind it and then hidden by the lowered screen. The two test events differed by the placement of the box. In the possible event (Figure 9-1b), the box was placed behind the track and therefore out of the car's path. In the impossible event (Figure 9-1c), the box was placed on top of the track, directly in the car's path. This time when the car disappeared behind the screen and then reappeared, it appeared to have rolled right through the box. (During the impossible event, the box was secretly removed through a door in the back of the stage.)

Baillargeon found that infants looked longer at the impossible event than at the possible event. And in later studies using the same basic experimental procedure, Baillargeon and her colleagues (see Baillargeon & Wang, 2002) found that even infants as young as 3.5 months of age could demonstrate an awareness of object permanence under these conditions. These findings suggest that infants of only 3–4 months of age (Piaget's substage of primary circular reactions) have object permanence and appear to hold in mind objects' locations and solidity. Baillargeon argues that Piaget substantially underestimated infants' cognitive abilities when he stated that object permanence does not start emerging until they are able to manually retrieve a hidden object at 8 months. In Box 9-1 we describe another looking-time study, which has shown that Piaget also underestimated young infants' ability to represent spatial layouts.

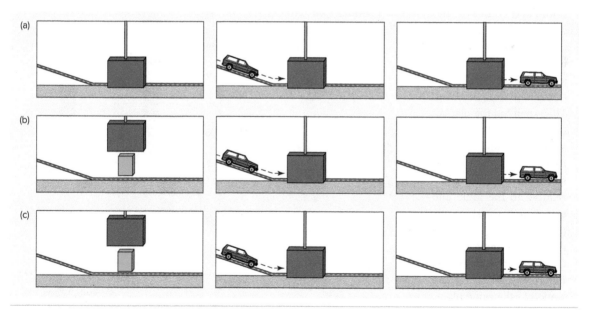

Figure 9-1 Testing infants' understanding of object permanence
As 6- to 8-month-old babies watched, a car rolled down a ramp, disappeared behind a screen and reappeared at the other side (a). After infants saw a box placed behind the ramp, the car again rolled down the ramp, disappearing and reappearing once again (b; a possible event). After infants saw the box placed on the ramp, where it would obstruct the car's passage, the car once again rolled down the ramp, disappearing and reappearing as before (c; an impossible event). Babies looked longer at the event in (c) than at the event in (b).
Source: Adapted from Baillargeon (1986).

Research close-up

BOX 9-1   6.5 month olds think about the layout of a space, independently of how they see it

Source: Based on Kaufman and Needham (1999).

Introduction:

Piaget considered infants' difficulties with object permanence to be partly due to their inadequate understanding of space. He considered infants to be egocentric – that is, he argued that they understand the spatial layout of the world only from their own egocentric perspective. This spatial egocentrism should have a profound effect on how they understand spatial arrays. For instance, if they know that a hidden object is on their left, they will only be able to relocate it if it always stays on their left. If they move relative to the object so that it is in a new place with respect to them, then by Piaget's account they should not be able to relocate it. This was borne out by studies using object search tasks (Acredolo, 1978; Bremner, 1978): If infants are moved around a room, then they will not update the way in which they search for hidden objects – they will still search where the object last was with respect to them, rather than with respect to where it is in the room. Because the infant is in a new place, this means that they will search in the wrong place!

But, as we have seen, infants tend to demonstrate much more competence in looking-time tasks. Kaufman and Needham (1999) set out to see if infants might be better at this kind of task but using visual habituation rather than object search (see Chapter 6 for more detail on visual habituation).

Method:

Kaufman and Needham (1999) tested forty 6.5-month-old infants. In the task they designed, infants were habituated to an object at a particular place on a table in front of them (in this case it was a furry pig-puppet in a cage on the near right-hand corner of the table). Remember that habituation means that the researchers waited until the infants were looking less at the object (the pig) than they were initially. They then hid the display from the infants and then split them into one of four groups. One group stayed in the same place relative to the table and saw exactly the same display with the pig on the near right-hand corner (called 'No change' in Figure 9-2). Another group stayed in the same place, but saw the pig in a new place with respect to the table (the top-left corner; 'Pig Moves' in Figure 9-2). Both of the other groups of infants were moved around to the other side

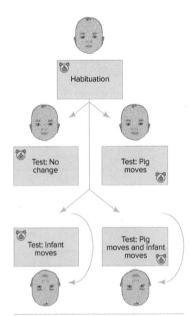

Figure 9-2   The experimental conditions in Kaufman and Needham's experiment

Source: Adapted from Kaufman and Needham (1999).

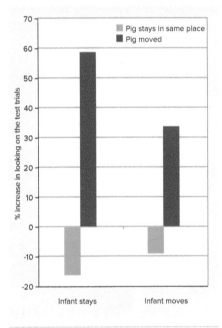

Figure 9-3   The results from Kaufman and Needham's (1999) experiment

The infants' looking recovered only in the conditions where the pig had moved with respect to the table. They continued to habituate even when the object was in a new egocentric location (but an old location on the table).

Source: Adapted from Kaufman and Needham (1999).

of the table before the pig was revealed. In one of these groups ('Infant Moves' in Figure 9-2) the pig remained in the same place with respect to the table, but was now in a new place relative to the infant because the infant had moved. In the last group ('Pig Moves and Infant Moves' in Figure 9-2) the pig was in a new place with respect to the table, but in the same place with respect to the infant as it was before (i.e., on his near-right side). By examining how much the infants looked at the pig in these conditions Kaufman and Needham were able to determine whether they noticed the change in location of the pig.

Results:

The infants' looking increased with respect to the end of the habituation phase in two of the four conditions: the 'Pig Moves' condition, and the 'Pig Moves and Infant Moves' condition (see Figure 9-2). This shows that the infants noticed the change in location of the pig with respect to the table, even in the condition where they themselves had also moved to another place.

Discussion:

These results indicate quite clearly that infants notice where objects are with respect to an 'external' layout (in this case, a table), even when they themselves move with respect to that layout. Kaufman and Needham (2011) have since demonstrated that even 4 month olds are able to achieve this. But why, then, do infants have such trouble in tasks like the AB task where they have to retrieve objects from particular spatial locations (Bremner, 1978)? Again we are faced with the challenge of explaining why looking-time tasks give us different results from tasks involving active responses with the hand.

Research has demonstrated that infants represent several aspects of the world much earlier than Piaget thought. There may be some other understandings about the world so fundamental to cognitive development that these appear very early in life. Evolutionary developmental theorists (see Chapter 2) have referred to these types of understanding as core knowledge (Spelke, 2000, Spelke & Kinzler, 2007), and examples include some understanding of physical laws, such as the solidity and continued existence of objects when out of sight. As we will see later in this chapter, violation of expectation studies have more recently been used to demonstrate that quite young infants seem to have an early understanding of other people's mental states (e.g., Onishi & Baillargeon, 2005), which certainly goes a long way beyond what Piaget thought was possible in the sensorimotor period!

> ▼ Some theorists have suggested, contrary to Piaget's account, that knowledge of objects is provided by innate 'core' knowledge (e.g., Spelke & Kinzler, 2007). We discuss such evolutionary accounts of development in more detail in Chapter 2. ▲

Despite violation of expectation studies indicating that some kinds of knowledge are available very early in infancy, other pieces of the puzzle seem to develop more gradually. For instance, Hespos and Baillargeon (2001; Baillargeon & Wang, 2002) have shown that infants seem to be relatively slow in learning about what happens during containment events, when one object is placed inside another. Baillargeon (2004) has suggested that infants may understand some general principles quite early (such as solidity and permanence), perhaps due to innate *core knowledge* (Spelke & Kinzler, 2007) but take longer to learn about the specifics of particular classes of event.

> core knowledge Ways of reasoning about ecologically important objects and events, such as the solidity and continuity of objects.

However, it is important to add that other researchers have raised some quite robust criticisms of violation of expectation studies of infant cognitive abilities. Some have argued that while longer looking time indicates that the infant can discriminate between two events, it does not tell us why the infant looks longer at one event (Haith & Benson, 1998). Indeed, some developmental psychologists have argued that perceptual differences between *possible* and *impossible* displays rather than conceptual processes explain an infant's longer looking (Rivera, Wakeley, & Langer, 1999; Bogartz, Shinskey, & Schilling, 2000; Cashon & Cohen, 2000; Sirois & Mareschal, 2002).

Finding objects that have moved into a hidden space. When a ball rolled down a ramp and into one of the spaces behind the screen with the small doors, children had to open the door behind which they thought they'd find the ball. The movable barrier that protruded above the screen, and that stopped the ball rolling, gave them a clue as to which door led to the ball.
Source: Berthier et al. (2000).

The concern that violation of expectation studies may not be telling us exactly what we want to know is corroborated by the findings showing that knowledge identified in infants in such tasks is occasionally not clearly evident in other behaviours even by 2 and 3 years of age (Hood, Carey, & Prasada, 2000; Keen, 2003). For instance, in one study, toddlers were asked to find a ball after it rolled down a ramp and stopped behind a screen (Berthier et al., 2000), as depicted in the photo. The ball could be stopped at any one of several locations behind the screen by a movable barrier that protruded above the screen and therefore served as a cue as to where the ball had stopped. To find the ball, the child opened one of the small doors in the screen. Children under 3 years of age were unsuccessful at finding the ball. Moreover, changes to the display, such as making the small doors transparent, did not help 2 year olds perform any better on this task (Butler, Berthier, & Clifton, 2002). However, 2.5 year olds performed better with the transparent doors than they had with the opaque doors.

Researchers have more recently attempted to understand the biological basis of sensorimotor development in specific areas of the brain and nervous system. We discuss the development of the brain in Chapter 5. Can you think of some changes in the brain that might account for the acquisition of object permanence?

A more recent focus of research has been to determine why young infants demonstrate knowledge in looking-time tasks, and yet are unable to use that knowledge in actions (like the actions in Piaget's tasks, and in the Berthier et al. study above) until much later (Keen, 2003; Bremner & Mareschal, 2004). A number of explanations have been offered. Some researchers appeal to the executive means–end requirements of manual tasks (Diamond, 1988; Marcowitz & Zelazo, 2009). Other explanations suggest that different knowledge is required for looking-time and manual tasks (Munakata et al., 1997; Mareschal & French, 2000; Bremner & Spence, 2008). One explanation offered by Munakata et al. (1997) was that *stronger* representations of objects are required for success on manual as opposed to visual object permanence tasks (see also Shinskey & Munakata, 2010). An alternative has been suggested by Mareschal (2000), who has argued that the kinds of knowledge required for manual and looking-time tasks are quite different. For instance, to succeed at the Baillargeon task described in Figure 9-4, the infant needs to keep track of where several objects are and how they interact. However, keeping track of what the objects are, or which object is which is not required to notice that something impossible has happened. On the other hand, infants intentionally search for objects with manual actions only when they desire to uncover that particular object, and so they have to keep track of both the identity and the location of an object. Mareschal suggests that the parts of the brain that process object identity and object location (the ventral and dorsal visual pathways) do not integrate properly until late in infancy. Because integration of object location and object identity is required for manual retrieval of hidden objects, but not for success at looking-time tasks, this may go some way to explaining why infants are much slower to demonstrate object permanence in manual tasks than they are in looking-time tasks.

It is clear that the account of infant cognition outlined in Piaget's six sensorimotor substages cannot explain many of the recent findings on early infant capabilities. Although Piaget did not capture the entirety of the young infant's early cognitive capacities, he provided the first detailed description of cognitive development in the first two years of life. Nonetheless, in many cases Piaget set more stringent criteria for the attainment of object permanence than many of the researchers who have challenged his work. One wonders whether or not he would be surprised at the findings from looking-time research (Bremner & Mareschal, 2004).

The concrete operational period: preoperational representations

The concrete operation period is a long period spanning 2 to 11 years, which Piaget subdivided into two subperiods, *preoperational representations*, which we will discuss first, and *concrete operations*. Concrete operations are mental representations and abilities which allow children to think about and, crucially, to *imagine* objects in a logical way. Piaget characterized preoperational representations as being a sub-period in which children are preparing for the logical abilities which characterize concrete operations. The major characteristic of preoperational representations is the child's ability to form symbolic representations. Symbolic representations enable children to use symbols, such as words in their thinking and behaviour. Remember that symbolic representation was the culmination of the sensorimotor period.

The emergence of symbolic capabilities is evident in children's rapid development of language, their great interest in imaginative play and their increasing use of deferred imitation. However, despite this big advance, there remain some important ways in which preoperational children's thinking is immature. The limitation that Piaget focused on was childhood egocentrism.

Childhood egocentrism

Piaget claimed that children in the preoperational substage tend to view the world from their own perspective and to have difficulty imagining the world from another person's point of view. Piaget considered this to have wide-reaching consequences. Specifically, he suggested that an inability to consider other points of view meant that the child could not understand that other perspectives exist, or that there is a difference between what is objectively correct and what is subjective. Piaget called this type of reasoning egocentrism. He also later referred to this as children's inability to *decentre* (or shift their focus away) from their own perception.

To test the child's ability to see things from another person's perspective, Piaget designed what is known as the three-mountains test (see Figure 9-4). Models of three mountains of varying sizes are placed on a square table, and chairs are placed at all four sides of the table. The child is seated in one chair, and the experimenter places a doll in each of the other three chairs, one at a time, and each time asks the child to describe what the doll sees from the three different positions. The child may select one of a set of drawings or use cardboard cutouts of the mountains to construct the doll's views. Piaget found that preoperational children could not consistently identify the doll's view from each of the three locations. The youngest children tended to select their own view of the mountains; 7- to 8-year-old children managed some kind of reversal (e.g., they might realize that the mountain at the front in their view is at the back in the doll's view), but still selected the wrong viewpoint. Piaget found that children were not completely successful until later in the stage of concrete operations, when they were 9 or 10 years old.

Piaget argued that egocentrism had an impact on the preoperational child's thinking in lots of different situations. One of these impacts was animistic thinking. Animistic thinking is the tendency to attribute life to inanimate objects. For example, preoperational children may believe that the wind and rivers have feelings. Piaget asked questions about these beliefs and often found that children assumed this because they saw that rivers and wind move. Piaget argued that this was because egocentrism made it difficult for children to distinguish between the physical and psychological world: because their egocentric world is psychological and active, they assume that activity produced by anything else is also psychological.

However, Piaget's views on both animism and egocentrism have been challenged. In contrast to Piaget's observations on animacy, Massey and Gelman (1988) found that when they used simple and familiar objects, children as young as 4 were quite good at deciding whether animate objects, such as mammals,

preoperational representations In this subperiod, the ability to use symbols facilitates the learning of language; this stage is also marked by pre-logical reasoning, egocentricity – in which the child sees the world from her own point of view – and intuitive behaviour, in which the child can solve problems using mental operations but cannot explain how she did so.

symbolic representation The ability to use symbols, such as images, words and gestures, to represent objects and events in the world.

egocentrism The tendency to view the world from one's own perspective and to have difficulty seeing things from another's viewpoint.

animistic thinking The attribution of life to inanimate objects.

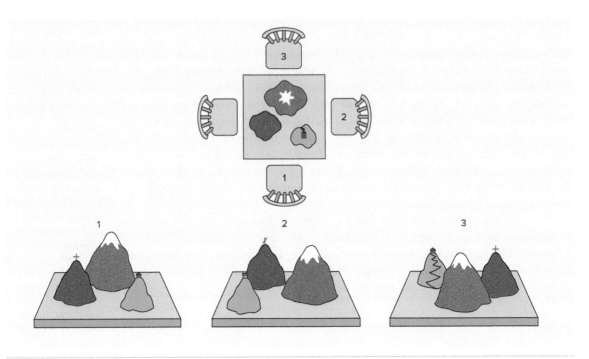

Figure 9-4   Understanding different perspectives: Piaget's three-mountains test

We show Piaget's classic test, which used a tabletop model to represent three mountains. As we shortly discuss, contemporary researchers have found that young children can understand the perspectives of others, represented by dolls or imaginary people, better under a number of conditions: when the mountains look more realistic, when the children are allowed to rotate small models of the mountains, and when the reason for taking another's perspective is made more meaningful or sensible to children.

or inanimate objects, such as statues, could move on their own. Since this work, researchers have also argued quite contrary to Piaget's ideas, that an understanding of animacy or an ability to differentiate animacy versus inanimacy is something which we inherit without experience (e.g., Mahon & Caramazza, 2009; Schultz et al., 2005). These kinds of argument are supported by findings that infants and even newborns seem to respond differently to the visual appearance of animate versus inanimate objects (for instance, they appear particularly interested in objects which are self-propelled; Luo & Baillargeon, 2010; Di Giorgio et al., 2017).

Piaget's three-mountains task and his interpretations of when children develop perspective-taking skills have been challenged by many researchers on several grounds. Hughes (1975, cited in Donaldson, 1978) tried to make the purpose of the task more understandable to the children. Rather than having three mountains, he sat the children at a table on which there were two 'walls' that intersected in the middle. Thus, there were four areas or corners of the table, each set off from each other by these walls (see Figure 9-5). Hughes then introduced two dolls, a boy doll and a policeman doll, and asked the child a series of questions about where the boy doll could hide so that the policeman could not find him. Most of the children between 3.5 and 5 years of age were able to provide correct answers. But, is this task testing the same thing that Piaget was interested in? Some authors have suggested that it gets at quite a different skill (Cox, 1991; Harris & Butterworth, 2002). Rather than examining how children can perform mental transformations to determine how the world will look from someone else's perspective, Hughes's task really examines whether children can follow someone else's line of sight to determine whether they can see something or not (not how that something will look to them).

In another critique of Piaget's methods, Borke (1975) made two simple changes to Piaget's design, and obtained very different results: (a) The investigator placed familiar things, such as snowcaps, trees or houses, on the sides of the mountains to make them more distinctive, and (b) he asked children to rotate a scaled-down duplicate model of the display to present the appropriate view rather than reconstruct the display or

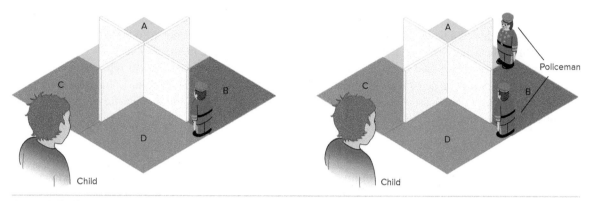

Figure 9-5 Another way to study children's perspective-taking abilities

In this model, Hughes devised four small rooms (A, B, C and D) from among which a boy doll could choose a hiding place where the policeman doll, from various positions around the model, could not find him. Most children between 3.5 and 5 years of age were able to provide correct answers to questions about this scenario.
Source: Adapted from Donaldson (1978).

choose from drawings. Children as young as 3 were then able to identify the correct perspective from each of the three different positions.

More recently, Piaget's inferences about the development of perspective taking in childhood have been challenged by some remarkable revelations about some of the skills which infants appear to possess in this domain. As we shall see later in this chapter, it seems that even before a year of age infants may be able to represent belief states in adults (like a perspective) even when that belief state is different to their own (Luo, 2011; Onishi & Baillargeon, 2005). More recent techniques examining perspective taking in children and adults indicate that even though performance at tasks like the three mountains task improves across development, the extent to which an egocentric bias drives our errors (i.e., Piaget's explanation of development at perspective taking) is fairly constant from 6 years of age (preoperational operations) through childhood and even into adulthood (Surtees & Apperly, 2012).

Preoperational problems with logic

Piaget argued that the main limitation in preoperational thinking is that the child is pre-logical. We will illustrate this with two examples of tasks Piaget set young children: class inclusion and conservation. As we shall see, quite a deal of criticism has been levelled at Piaget's claims.

CLASS INCLUSION

Piaget showed that the child has difficulty understanding part–whole relations, as illustrated in class-inclusion problems, such as the following: a child is given seven toy dogs and three toy cats, a total of ten animals. If the child is asked whether there are more dogs or more cats, he can answer correctly that there are more dogs. However, if the child is then asked if there are more dogs than there are animals, the child responds that there are more dogs. Piaget proposed that the child is responding incorrectly because he is unable to focus simultaneously on a part of the set of animals (the subset of dogs) and on the whole set of animals.

Developmentalists have criticized Piaget's research on part–whole relations, suggesting that the way he posed his questions confused young children. When Smith (1979) used simpler questions that still addressed children's ability to use part–whole relations, such as, 'A pug is a kind of dog, but it's not a shepherd. Is a pug an animal?', she found that children as young as 4 displayed knowledge of the part–whole relation between dogs and animals by correctly answering that a pug is an animal.

And although Piaget thought that the ability to classify develops during the preoperational and concrete operational periods, we now have evidence that even infants can place objects into categories (Oakes &

Madole, 2003; Althaus & Plunkett, 2015). Researchers have shown that babies as young as 3 to 4 months old can form categories of animals, such as a category with dogs and cats but not with birds (Haith & Benson, 1998; Hoehl, 2016; Quinn & Eimas, 1998; Westermann & Mareschal, 2014). In addition, they are able to categorize animals and vehicles based on perceptual similarities and also based on different types of motion – for example, the motion of a dog versus the motion of a car (Arterberry & Bornstein, 2001; Rakison, 2007). Apparently, children can classify objects at a much earlier age and in a more sophisticated fashion than Piaget believed possible.

CONSERVATION

We see one of the most vivid examples of pre-logical thinking when preoperational children perform conservation tasks. To understand conservation, the child must recognize that even when an object's appearance is altered in some way, the object's basic attributes or properties remain the same. For example, we present the child with two identical glasses, each of which contains the same amount of liquid. The liquid in these glasses is then poured into two other glasses of different sizes, such that one glass is tall and thin and the other glass is short and wide. The result of the pouring is that although the liquid remains the same quantity – nothing has spilled or been taken away – the water levels in the tall and short glasses are now different.

> **conservation** The understanding that altering an object's or a substance's appearance does not change its basic attributes or properties.
>
> **reversibility** The understanding that the steps of a procedure or operation can be reversed, and that the original state of the object or event can be obtained.

Two basic attributes of a physical object, in this case, the liquid, are at issue here. One attribute pertains to the identity of the object, which is a qualitative property. To probe a child's understanding of identity in this example, we can ask her: is the water in the different-shaped glasses the same water that was in the two original glasses of the same shape? Preoperational children have no difficulty with this question and therefore understand *object identity*, a qualitative attribute of objects. The second attribute of a physical object that can be assessed is the quantity of the object – in this case, whether the amount of the liquid before and after the pouring is the same. Preoperational children have great difficulty with object quantity questions and respond that the amounts of liquid in each of the two different-shaped glasses, though previously the same, are now different. Thus, these children understand the identity or quality but not the amount or quantity of objects.

This pre-logical pattern of reasoning among preoperational children has been demonstrated on a wide range of conservation tasks, such as those involving liquid, mass, volume and area (see Figure 9-6). What processes of reasoning may lead the child to make this error in judgement? Piaget emphasized two particular characteristics of this pre-logical thinking: the inability to understand reversibility, and centration, which as we have already described is closely related to egocentrism.

According to Piaget, the child's inability to understand reversibility means that the child cannot mentally reverse or undo an action. For example, preoperational children presented with the liquid-conservation task that we have outlined do not understand that if the water in the tall, thin glass is poured back into the short, wide glass it will reach the same height it had before. Potential problems with reversibility can be seen elsewhere in children's responses to tasks and questions between 2 and 7 years old. For example, an investigator asks a 4-year-old boy:

This child's decision as to whether the two glasses hold equal amounts of coloured water will reveal whether she's attained an understanding of the conservation of liquid.
© Marmaduke St. John/Alamy Stock Photo

'Have you a brother?'
The child replies, 'Yes.'
'What's his name?'
'Jim.'
'Does Jim have a brother?'
'No.' (Phillips, 1969, p. 61)

1. **Number**

Experimenter shows child two rows of plastic chips. Child agrees there are the same number of chips in each row.

Experimenter increases length of one row by adding space between chips (or by squeezing other row) and asks child whether each row still has the same number of chips.

2. **Mass, or substance**

Experimenter presents child with two identical balls of clay or plasticine. Child agrees that each has the same amount of clay.

Experimenter rolls one ball into breadstick or sausage form and asks child whether the two objects still have the same amount of clay.

3. **Length**

Experimenter places two sticks of equal length before child, who agrees they are of the same length.

Experimenter moves one of the sticks to the right and asks child whether sticks are still of the same length.

4. **Liquids**

Experimenter fills two glasses of the same size and shape to the same level with water. Child agrees each glass has the same amount of water.

Experimenter pours the water in one of the glasses into a taller, thinner glass and asks child if each glass with water in it now contains the same amount of water.

5. **Area**

Experimenter shows child two sheets of cardboard, on each of which square blocks are placed in identical positions. Child agrees that each sheet has the same amount of open (uncovered) area.

Experimenter then scatters the blocks about one of the cardboard sheets and asks child whether the two sheets now have the same amount of open area.

6. **Weight**

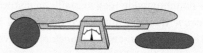

Experimenter places two balls of clay of the same size on a scale and asks the child if they weigh the same.

Experimenter then reshapes one ball and, before replacing it on the scale, asks the child if the two pieces of clay still weigh the same or if one weighs more.

7. **Volume**

Experimenter drops each of two balls of clay of the same size into two glasses of water; the child has already agreed that the glasses have the same amount of water.

Experimenter removes one piece of clay, reshapes it, and, before putting it back into the glass, asks the child if the water level will be higher or lower than or the same as the water level in the other glass.

Figure 9-6   Some Piagetian tests of conservation
These tests are discussed at further length in the text.
Source: Based on Lefrancois (1973).

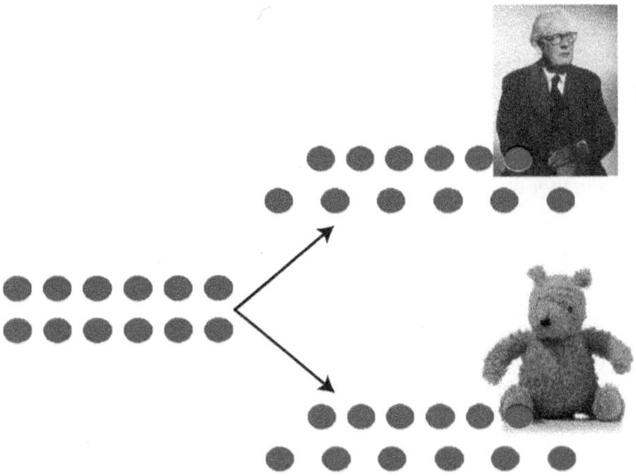

Piaget's original number conservation experiment

Accidental transformation

Figure 9-7   The 'naughty teddy' experiment

McGarrigle and Donaldson (1975) adapted Piaget's original conservation of number task to examine whether children would be better able to conserve number following accidental rather than purposeful transformations.
Photos: © AFP/Getty Images (T); © Rubberball/Mike Kemp/Getty Images (B)

Researchers have also presented strong criticisms regarding Piaget's conservation tasks. A particularly influential criticism was raised by McGarrigle and Donaldson (1975), who focused on Piaget's number conservation task. In the number conservation task the experimenter spreads out one row of counters and asks the child which row has more. Piaget found that preoperational children get the answer to this wrong because they are unable to reverse the change and centrate on the length of the row. However, McGarrigle and Donaldson (1975) asked whether the children could be using the action of spreading out one of the rows as a social cue to respond that the longer row had more counters? In other words it is possible that 4-year-old children might be able to conserve number, but their ability may be masked by their immature understanding of the language the experimenter is using, and a desire to respond in the way they think the experimenter wants them to. McGarrigle and Donaldson (1975) tested this alternative interpretation, by changing the way in which the transformation was made. They reasoned that if the transformation was made accidentally then the child would ignore the transformation and their true conservation abilities would be revealed. They achieved the accidental transformation by introducing a 'naughty teddy' (a toy manipulated by the experimenter) in the middle of the task. The naughty teddy rampaged across the table and lengthened one of the rows of counters. The experimenter would then take the teddy away and ask the crucial conservation question, 'Are the number of counters in the two rows the same or different?' Under these circumstances McGarrigle and Donaldson (1975) found that 4 year olds responded more accurately, suggesting that preoperational children do have conservation abilities, but that the social contexts of Piaget's original experiments were leading them into responding inaccurately (see Figure 9-7).

Piaget's conservation experiment has remained controversial, as some other researchers (notably Moore and Fry, 1986) have pointed out that, rather than helping children to respond on the basis of what they know, the naughty teddy may actually be distracting children from the transformation so that they answer correctly because they did not notice the change in one of the rows. And so, despite some doubts, the conservation task remains somewhat important in developmental psychology, particularly with regard to the development of numeracy abilities (e.g., Lambert & Spinath, 2018)

TRANSITIVE INFERENCES

Piaget also investigated children's ability at a more traditional test of logical reasoning – the ability to make transitive inferences. By way of illustration, suppose we present a child with three children of varying heights in differently composed pairs. In pair 1, the child sees that Miranda is taller than Zoe, and in pair 2 she sees that Zoe is taller than Georgina. Without seeing Miranda and Georgina together, Piaget found that preoperational children have difficulty reasoning that Miranda is taller than both Zoe and Georgina. Again, Piaget explains this in terms of a difficulty with reversibility. According to his account, the preoperational child cannot reverse the size relation which Zoe (the medium-sized child) from one of her comparators (Miranda) to another (Georgina); the child cannot understand that the middle term in the inference holds two size relations simultaneously.

Again, however, developmentalists have questioned whether the solution of such problems is based on the underlying changes in mental operations that Piaget proposed. Some investigators have suggested that in tests of transitive inference like that described above, what poses difficulty for the concrete operational child is not the logical comparison, but an inability to remember the premises of the inference. In our example, if, when the child is asked the transitive inference question, they cannot remember that Miranda is taller than Zoe and that Zoe is taller than Georgina, they will not be able to work out the difference between Miranda and Georgina. To test this idea, Bryant and Trabasso (1971) trained children up on the premises of the inference until they were sure that they could remember those. They then found that preoperational children could make transitive inferences.

> In Chapter 10 we will discuss how children's ability to remember information can help them with problem solving (such as transitive inferences).

An important aspect of Piaget's theory is that it argues that logical mental operations have impacts across a wide range of different skills. Here we have seen a range of tasks which Piaget used to assess the development of an ability to reason logically about imagined objects and scenarios (class inclusion, perspective taking, conservation, transitive inference). Crucially, Piaget argued that reversibility, an ability to imagine transformations both forwards and in reverse, plays a key role in children's success at all of these tasks. This theme is important for Piaget's theory – his view is that there are some central revolutions in the way children's thinking changes from one stage to the next, and that these revolutions have widespread impacts across many domains. As we shall see, this argument also has not remained unchallenged.

Concrete operations

The concrete operations subperiod extends from about the age of 7 to the age of 11 or 12. At this time, children understand reversibility and are able to *decentre* and attend to more than one dimension of a problem at a time. According to Piaget they are now able to conserve quantity and to classify or group things in a logical way, make inferences, and they also progress in their perspective-taking. However, their thinking at this point is tied to concrete reality (hence *concrete* operations); that is, they can solve problems only if the objects necessary

> concrete operations
> Subperiod in which the child is able to reason logically about materials that are physically present.

for problem solution are physically present. So if we give a concrete operations child a transitive inference problem with abstract items – let's say we do not show them Miranda, Zoe and Georgina, we just tell them, in hypothetical terms, that Miranda is taller than Zoe, and Zoe is taller than Georgina, then this will be more difficult for them. Likewise with even less concrete items – for example, if A>B and B>C, which is greater out of A and C?

Another limitation at concrete operations is a difficulty in performing more than one kind of mental operation at once. As we shall see in Chapter 10, before formal operations children have difficulty balancing a beam. In such a task they have to take account of both weight and distance from the fulcrum. Piaget argued that the concrete operations child had difficulty with the combination of two separate dimensions.

CULTURE AND CONCRETE OPERATIONS

Researchers who have undertaken cross-cultural studies of Piagetian concepts associated with concrete operations have demonstrated the importance of culture in determining what concepts will be learned and when. This research indicates that cognitive competence is related to the cultural context in which development occurs (Rogoff, 2003; Cole, 2006; Shweder et al., 2006). If we define intelligence as adaptation to the environment, as did Piaget, it is not surprising that cognitive development differs in some ways in cultures with different environments, expectations and needs. Some cultures emphasize the need to learn certain kinds of concepts, while other cultures stress other kinds. Even when cultures emphasize similar concepts, the timing of this emphasis – in terms of when opportunities are provided for children that support the development of these skills – may vary.

Pierre Dasen (1984) has examined these ideas by comparing the performance of children of two very different cultures on tasks of the conservation of liquids and of horizontality (the latter requires the child to understand that when a vessel containing a liquid is tilted at various angles, the surface plane of the water

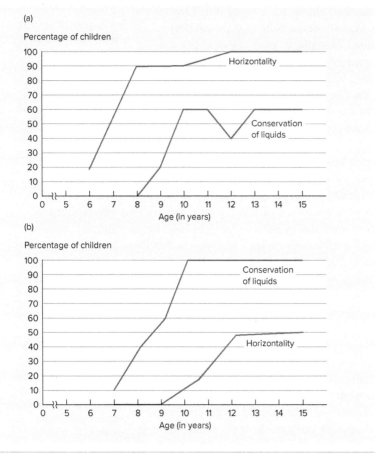

Figure 9-8 Conservation among Inuit and Baoulé children
Achievement of the concepts of horizontality and the conservation of liquids between the ages of 6 and 15 among (a) Inuit children of the Canadian Nunavut Territory and (b) Baoulé children of Côte d'Ivoire.
Source: Adapted from Dasen (1984).

will always be horizontal). Dasen found interesting differences on these tasks across the two groups. Whereas 90% of Inuit children, of Cape Dorset (in Canada's Nunavut Territory above Hudson Bay), understood horizontality by the age of 8 (100% by age 12), only 60% grasped the conservation of liquids even by the age of 15 (see Figure 9-8a). In contrast, only 50% of Baoulé children, of Côte d'Ivoire, understood horizontality by age 15, but 100% had an understanding of the conservation of liquids by the age of 10 (Figure 9-8b). Commenting on these results, Dasen suggests that people develop 'those skills and concepts that are useful in the daily activities required' in their ecocultural settings. The Inuit, who are nomadic hunter-gatherers, value spatial skills and, as a result, acquire ideas like horizontality quite quickly, but they have less experience with quantitative comparisons. The Baoulé, on the other hand, are an agricultural people who, because they produce food, store it and exchange it in the markets, have considerable experience with quantitative concepts, especially those concepts involved in measurement.

As these results suggest, culture alters the cognitive experiences children have and the *rate* at which children learn certain types of knowledge, including the concepts Piaget described in relation to the stage of concrete operations.

Formal operations

How do thought processes in the period of formal operations, which begins at age 11 or 12, differ from those typical of the concrete operations stage? As we have already hinted at, Piaget considered the most significant changes to be in the use of purely mental (abstract) logic, and the ability to involve many different sources of variation when solving problems. These advances enable formal operations children to think in an increasingly more complex way (Kuhn & Franklin, 2006).

One particularly interesting change is the ability to think abstractly and understand and even solve problems that have no basis in reality. For example, consider the problem, 'If all blue people live in red houses, are all people who live in red houses blue?' According to Piaget's account, the concrete operational child would have difficulty getting beyond the fact that no people are blue. In contrast, the child, or more accurately the young adolescent, in the stage of formal operations can move beyond the unrealistic content to focus on applying logical solutions to the question posed. This is an example of further decentration. Consequently, in the stage of formal operations, the thinker's understanding and examination of the world are not confined to reality. Rather, the young adolescent is able to think of and contrast both real and ideal states of the world. They can consider different ways of arranging the world; for instance, they can think about and discuss philosophical issues such as truth and justice, and they can imagine alternative lifestyles and universes. Interestingly, this is the stage when science fiction becomes of interest.

Children in this stage are also able to review several possible alternatives or hypotheses in a problem-solving situation. Inhelder and Piaget (1958) used a task involving a problem in physics to illustrate the differences in problem solving in the stages of concrete and formal operations. In this task, participants are shown an assortment of objects and a container of water and asked to use these materials to find an explanation for why some objects float and others do not. What the children are actually being asked is to derive Archimedes' law of floating bodies, which states that an object will float if its weight per unit (or density) is less than that of water. Thus, if two objects are of equal weight, the larger object is more likely to float than the smaller object. Concrete operational children may focus on weight or size as a reason things float or sink; for instance, they may say that the heavier or bigger objects are more likely to sink. They may even arrive at a double classification that involves the categories large and heavy, large and light, small and heavy, or small and light. However, they are still unable to consider alternatives that violate what is usually observable in the physical world. For example, they cannot predict that a large and heavy piece of wood will float even though it is bigger and heavier than a small lead weight.

In contrast, in the formal operations stage, the child can free herself from the obvious cues of weight and size and conceptualize a variety of possible alternatives to arrive at the concept of density. Piaget describes the comments of a child who has just entered the period of formal operations grappling with this kind of problem: 'It sinks because it is small, it isn't stretched enough. You would have to have something larger to stay at the surface, something of the same weight and which would have a greater extension' (Inhelder & Piaget, 1958, p. 38).

Developmentalists continue to debate Piaget's notions about cognitive development in this last stage and to search for the best ways to describe the child's thinking at this time (Keating, 1990; Overton & Byrnes, 1991; Kuhn & Franklin, 2006). Actually, not all adolescents or, for that matter, all adults in all societies reach the stage of formal operations and achieve the flexibility in problem solving that Piaget associated with this period (Kuhn & Franklin, 2006). Unlike concrete operational thought, which seems to be acquired to some degree in all societies, the eventual attainment of formal operations is strongly influenced by culture (Bond, 1998; Rogoff et al., 2003). In cultures that do not emphasize symbolic skills or in which educational experiences are limited, the stage of formal operations may occur late in development or may even be absent (Moshman, 1998). Even in Western communities in which symbolic skills and educational attainment are highly valued and available, adolescents and adults are more likely to achieve the capacity for logical abstract reasoning within their particular areas of interest or expertise than in other domains. For instance, abstract thinking has been documented in traditional cultures in tasks of much importance to the group, such as court cases related to land disputes and navigating on the open seas (Gladwin, 1970; Hutchins, 1980). Thomas Gladwin found that seafarers in traditional communities in Micronesia use star charts and other complex techniques to construct elaborate and sophisticated routes that enable them to transverse the ocean and even cross the equator. In addition, scientific training in such subjects as physics, chemistry, and the philosophy of logic has been found to be associated with greater ability to use formal operations (Kuhn & Franklin, 2006). Thus, formal operational thinking is strongly tied to social and cultural experiences.

EVALUATION OF PIAGET'S THEORY

Piaget's theory has an invaluable place in the study of cognitive development as it sets the framework for deriving new questions to ask about how children's cognitive abilities emerge. However, as we have already seen, there are some significant limitations in how it can explain the current state of our knowledge about cognitive development, and in particular the significant cognitive abilities which researchers have demonstrated in infants in recent years. Let's take a look at the strengths and limitations of Piaget's constructivism.

In Chapter 2, we pointed out that theories are useful for two reasons: they integrate a wide array of information, and they lead to new research by stimulating hypotheses and defining new areas of study. Piaget's theory achieved both of these goals. With his stage model and his underlying concepts such as schemas, assimilation and accommodation, Piaget integrated a broad spectrum of issues regarding concepts of the physical world – such as the object concept, conservation, classification and number – into a single *domain general* theory. In addition, Piaget's theory has stimulated an enormous amount of research.

According to Miller (2002), the most important ideas that Piaget introduced to the field are that cognitive development unfolds over a series of qualitatively distinct stages, that in the first two years of life, cognition is based on the child's sensorimotor system, and that the child actively seeks and constructs knowledge. In many ways this last point is the essence of what will survive from Piaget's account. Piaget was the first theorist to really take the developmental process seriously in all its potential complexity, showing how simple aspects of an active behavioural repertoire, such as reflexes, could be the basis for a cascading emergence of schemas of increasing sophistication and adaptability. This was of course Piaget's aim – to capture how knowledge and thinking could be created from development, what he called genetic epistemology.

genetic epistemology
The genesis of knowledge; this was the term which Piaget used to describe what he was attempting to study and to capture in his constructivist theory of development.

In addition to his rich theory, Piaget was an extraordinary observer of human behaviour. His observations described behaviours that continue to intrigue developmental psychologists. Why do infants behave as if objects disappear when they go out of sight? Why do preschoolers not conserve the quantities of substances when their shapes or appearances are altered? Why is it that school-age children can think logically about problems, even difficult problems, but when these problems are abstract (concrete materials are not available), they cannot use their skills at logical thought?

Limitations of the theory

DID PIAGET JUDGE THE CHILD'S ABILITIES ACCURATELY?

As we discussed, a great deal of research has suggested that infants and children may know a lot more than Piaget thought. In other words, Piaget may have underestimated the timing or onset of children's cognitive abilities. For instance, infants seem to understand some aspects of object permanence, and even other people's perspectives quite early (e.g., Spelke & Kinzler, 2007; Buttelmann, Baillargeon, & Southgate, 2018), and many children in the preoperational and concrete operational periods seem to be more cognitively advanced than Piaget's theory would suggest (Halford & Andrews, 2006).

A particularly important criticism in this regard is that Piaget tested abilities in ways that did not take into account the kinds of social contexts in which the child might view his enquiries (e.g., McGarrigle and Donaldson, 1975; Donaldson, 1978). This point is well taken. The social context of experiments must be taken into account if we are to know what we are measuring when we place children in an experimental situation. For example, Piaget certainly thought that the conservation experiment measures cognitive abilities, whereas McGarrigle and Donaldson argue that it measures children's sensitivities to the social cues which the experimenter makes (in this case the action of spreading one of the rows might be interpreted as a cue to say that one row has more counters). It is thus vitally important for developmental psychologists to consider the ways in which children of different ages may interpret social cues in the context of an experiment.

However, despite the argument that Piaget underestimated children's abilities, it is not always clear that showing cognitive abilities at an earlier age than Piaget proposed represents a major challenge to his theory. After all, Piaget was less concerned with the age of onset of the abilities he studied than with their order and nature of appearance. Nonetheless, it seems likely that Piaget would have been particularly surprised at recent findings of infants' abilities to represent other people's perspectives (e.g., Buttelmann et al., 2018).

DOES COGNITIVE DEVELOPMENT PROCEED IN STAGES?

According to Piaget, children's cognitive development undergoes qualitative shifts from one stage to another, and these stages are presumed to follow each other in an invariant order. Moreover, the child cannot proceed to the next stage until she has mastered the ways of thinking characteristic of the current one.

More recent evidence and accounts (Siegler & Alibali, 2005) suggest that cognitive development may not occur in the stage-like steps that Piaget proposed. However, how we describe changes in children's thinking, and whether or not they are called stages or considered to be more continuous patterns of development, depends in large measure on the way in which a change is studied. The focus of a study and especially the length of time between two or more measurement points are important. For example, if we evaluate a child's abilities at 6-month intervals or even years apart, changes in these abilities may seem discontinuous, as Piaget found. However, if we look closely at the changes that occur within a shorter period of time, an hour or a day or even across several weeks – let's say as a child tries to solve a particular problem – we may find that the child's progress appears more gradual and continuous. As we have described in Chapter 1, Siegler's overlapping waves model of cognitive developmental change may be a more accurate characterization of cognitive development than Piaget's domain general stage changes.

> In Chapter 1 we discussed how more recent accounts of development have tended to emphasize continuous rather than qualitative changes in ability; an example of this is Siegler's 'overlapping waves' model.

One difficulty in knowing for sure whether cognitive development is best described as a series of stages is due to the fact that children in the concrete operational stage do not acquire the ability to conserve all types of substances at the same age. This unevenness in development, which Piaget called horizontal décalage (the French word *décalage* can be translated as 'time lag'), is problematic for the idea that his stage theory described domain general attainments. The idea of a domain general stage implies that the child in a particular stage should be consistent in her thinking across similar types of problems. Piaget proposed that horizontal décalage reflects the differing degrees of abstraction required to understand the conservation of particular objects or substances. For example, he suggested that conserving mass requires the fewest abstract operations, whereas conserving volume requires the most; as a result, conservation of mass is acquired earlier. This perhaps indicates that Piaget's theory is rather more adaptable than might be good for it. At some point, the weight of adaptations to take account of variations from one situation to another undermines the validity and explanatory power of the uniting theory.

> **horizontal décalage**
> The term Piaget used to describe unevenness in children's thinking within a particular stage; for example, in developing an understanding of conservation, children conserve different objects or substances at different ages.

Interestingly, findings from studies in which conservation tasks have been changed to be more accessible to children show that if we present children with simpler versions of these tasks or teach them to attend to all the relevant aspects of the task, they can often demonstrate their understanding of conservation. For instance, in a study in Mexico of the children of potters, children who initially performed poorly on conservation tasks that were conducted with materials unfamiliar to them went on to perform quite well on a test of conservation of mass when they were dealing with familiar materials, such as the clay and other substances used in making pottery (Price-Williams, Gordon, & Ramirez, 1969). To test the notion that failure to conserve may occur because the child attends to some irrelevant aspect of the stimulus, such as shape, length or height, Jerome Bruner (1966) presented preoperational children with a modification of Piaget's liquid-conservation task. As the experimenters poured the water from the short glass to the tall glass, they placed a screen in front of the tall glass. When the distracting changes in the height and width of the water column were not visible to the children, most were able to conserve. In sum, if a task is simplified or made more comprehensible, children can conserve at earlier ages than Piaget suspected.

THE SOCIOEMOTIONAL AND CULTURAL CONTEXT OF DEVELOPMENT AND PIAGET'S THEORY

Although Piaget's theory did not include social, emotional and cultural contributions to cognitive development in any central way, research indicates that cognitive development, including Piagetian-based concepts, may be modified by cultural, social and other experiential factors (Dasen, 1984; Cole, 2006). We discussed contributions of the social and cultural context to many aspects of Piaget's theory. Except in his theory of children's moral development (Chapter 14), Piaget rarely considered the significance of children's social relations and emotional development in relation to cognitive change. Although it would be inaccurate to describe Piaget as disregarding the role of social and cultural processes in development, his theory has certainly been characterized as emphasizing individual processes at the expense of social ones (e.g., Beilin, 1992; Lourenço & Machado, 1996). As we will see next, there has been a great deal of work since Piaget addressed the role of social context in development, and the development of social cognitive abilities. You will see that the social world of the infant and child is much richer than captured in Piaget's account.

Additionally, in spite of Piaget's pessimism about the child's ability to proceed more quickly through the stages as a result of instruction, the evidence is now clear that active intervention, such as training in problem-solving strategies – a specialized form of social experience – can accelerate cognitive development (Gelman & Baillargeon, 1983; Siegler & Alibali, 2005).

Despite these theoretical limitations, Piaget's ideas have relevance to both education and counselling, which may in turn affect children's social and emotional functioning. There is a long history of connections between Piaget's theory and educational practice. Piaget admired the ideas of Maria Montessori, especially her views on the close relation between thought and action (Lillard, 2005). He drew on these ideas in his theory, and even conducted many of his observations of young children's thinking at a modified Montessori school in Switzerland. In addition, approaches to child counselling may be informed by Piaget's ideas. Consider how Piaget's theory could be helpful in counselling a young child who is struggling with his parents' divorce or a parent's death. Would a preoperational child be likely to interpret such situations egocentrically and perhaps blame himself for his parents' divorce? Or would a preoperational child, because of limited understanding of the distinction between what is real and what is not, be prone to wishful thinking, perhaps believing that if he just wished hard enough, his deceased parent would come back to life? Although Piaget did not deal directly with such issues, clearly an understanding of the capabilities and limitations associated with the different stages of thinking that he described could help guide an educator or therapist who works with children in need.

Overall assessment

Despite new findings and their resulting criticisms, Piaget's theory has had an enormous impact on the study of the child's development of cognitive skills. In fact, his theory was a major force in introducing cognition into developmental research in the latter half of the twentieth century (Beilin, 1992). Although his methods, and more occasionally his theorizing, can be criticized, Piaget asked and answered important questions in innovative ways, and his ideas have stimulated a vast amount of research and theorizing among other behavioural scientists. If one test of the worth of a theory is its ability to generate interesting ideas for further study, Piaget's theory, without question, is among the best ever articulated in psychology.

VYGOTSKY'S SOCIOCULTURAL THEORY OF COGNITIVE DEVELOPMENT

As we have seen, for many developmentalists, an enduring concern with Piaget's approach has been a perceived failure fully to explore the importance of social and cultural processes in his theory. For Piaget, development was largely a matter of constructing knowledge through interactions with the world – be it the physical or 'social' world. Critical researchers have argued that culture and social context plays a far greater and more fundamental role in development than Piaget suggested. The principal theorist who articulated this contrasting approach was the Russian psychology, Lev S. Vygotsky.

The developmental theory introduced by Vygotsky focuses on the influence of the social and cultural world on cognitive development (Vygotsky, 1978). Vygotsky grew up in the early twentieth century, which was a time of tumultuous social change in Russia (Kozulin, 1990). In 1917, the year Vygotsky graduated from Moscow University, the Russian Revolution began and the entire society was in upheaval. After the revolution, as Vygotsky launched his career as a psychologist and developed his theory, civil war and famine ravaged the country, and the entire social structure of the nation changed dramatically. Although some aspects of Vygotsky's life improved, others did not. At the time of his death at age 37 from tuberculosis, he had fallen into political disfavour in Stalinist Russia and his work was censored. As a result, it wasn't until the late 1970s that psychologists in the United States and other parts of the world began to explore Vygotsky's ideas (Wertsch & Tulviste, 1992).

Vygotsky's view of cognitive development is called a sociocultural approach because it proposes that cognitive development is largely the result of children's interaction with more experienced or expert members of their culture, such as parents, teachers and older children. As the child and her partners solve problems together, the child has opportunities to participate in actions that extend beyond her current individual capabilities. Through these experiences, the child learns to function on her own in a more advanced intellectual way. Although Vygotsky held that each child is born with a set of innate capabilities, such as attention, perception and memory, he believed that input from the child's social and cultural worlds, in the form of interactions with more experienced adults and peers, directs these basic capabilities towards more complex, higher-order cognitive capabilities. Because this theory puts great emphasis on the role of social interaction in cognitive development, Vygotsky held that language has a particularly important role in the child's intellectual development.

Vygotsky was especially interested in the social and cultural processes that support cognitive development. He described changes in the ways that children interact with other people as well as with the psychological tools and symbol systems of a culture that can be used to support and extend cognition, which he called mediators. Across development, children learn to use different types of mediators – such as language, counting, mnemonic devices, algebraic symbols, art and writing. Mediators permit the child to function more effectively in solving problems and understanding the world. For Vygotsky, what was particularly important about mediators is that they come from and thereby represent the social and cultural context of development. As the child develops competence with these mediators and comes to use them in his or her thinking, the child's thinking is increasingly aligned with the social and cultural context in which growth occurs. This enables children to act effectively in their environment, and interact in understandable and meaningful ways with other people in their culture.

We begin by discussing Vygotsky's notion of mental functions. Here we see how mediators enable the child to move to new levels of psychological processing. We then examine Vygotsky's concept of the *zone of proximal development*, a concept that expands on his idea that children learn through social interaction, and that has given rise to such concepts as scaffolding and guided participation. We next explore the influence of culture on children's cognitive development, learning and use of language.

Elementary and higher mental functions

In Vygotsky's theory, an important change in children's cognitive development occurs between elementary and higher mental functions. Elementary mental functions, such as basic attention, perception and involuntary memory, are biological and emerge spontaneously. With development, elementary mental functions are transformed into higher mental functions, such as voluntary attention and intentional remembering. These functions involve the coordination of several cognitive processes.

mediators Psychological tools and signs – such as language, counting, mnemonic devices, algebraic symbols, art and writing – that facilitate and direct thinking processes.

elementary mental functions Psychological functions with which the child is endowed by nature, including attention, perception and involuntary memory, which emerge spontaneously during children's interaction with the world.

higher mental functions Psychological functions, such as voluntary attention, complex memory processes and problem solving, that entail the coordination of several cognitive processes and the use of *mediators*.

They also involve the use of mediators, such as language and other cognitive tools and symbol systems that children learn to use as they interact with other people in their culture.

Vygotsky's discussion of memory illustrates the difference between these two types of mental functions. The elementary form of memory is constructed of images and impressions of events. It is very similar to perception; it is also unintentional and the environment directly influences its content. The higher form of memory involves the use of signs to mediate memory functions; for instance, the child may write something down to help her remember it. Thus, the child uses literacy as a tool to extend basic memory processes. Mediational systems, like language and other tools that aid intelligent action, such as literacy, are products of culture (Cole, 2006). Children learn how to use these tools through the assistance of people in their culture who are more experienced than the child in their use. For Vygotsky, culture provides children with mediators that enable them to transform elementary mental functions into higher-level cognitive skills.

The zone of proximal development

Vygotsky's interest in the social origins of cognitive development led him to be less concerned with children's individual intellectual capabilities at a particular point in time than he was with the child's potential for intellectual growth through social experience (Daniels, Cole, & Wertsch, 2007). To describe and assess this potential, Vygotsky proposed the notion of the zone of proximal development (ZPD). The ZPD is defined as the difference between a child's 'actual developmental level as determined by independent problem solving' and his 'potential development as determined through problem solving under adult guidance or in collaboration with more capable peers' (Vygotsky, 1978, p. 86). The child's zone is, essentially, his region of sensitivity to learning in a particular area of cognitive development. When support for learning is targeted at the child's zone of proximal development, the child's level of competence in this area changes through this social experience. The concept of the zone of proximal development is twofold. First, it describes how cognitive development may arise from social interaction with more skilled partners. Second, it provides a method of assessing children's intellectual potential under optimal conditions – that is, conditions that are tailored to the child's specific learning needs and that build on the child's present capabilities.

> **zone of proximal development (ZPD)**
> The region of sensitivity for learning characterized by the difference between the developmental level of which a child is capable when working alone and the level she is capable of reaching with the aid of a more skilled partner.

Developmental researchers have demonstrated the value of this approach to cognitive development in studies of children's learning in many areas, including attention, memory, problem-solving skills and planning. This research shows that children's understanding and cognitive skills can indeed be improved when adults or more skilled peers provide children with appropriate support for learning (Rogoff, 1998; 2003; Gauvain, 2005). This is because when a child and a more skilled partner work together within a child's zone of proximal development, the child has the opportunity to engage in more advanced cognitive activities than she could undertake on her own

More experienced partners are able to describe or break down a cognitive activity, such as planning a series of errands, in ways that make it more understandable and accessible to the learner. More experienced partners also may model new strategies for solving the problem and encourage and support the child's involvement in the more difficult parts of the problem. Finally, the more experienced partner may take on or assume some of the more difficult parts of the problem so that the learner can concentrate on other aspects. For example, when an adult and child work together on a task that involves planning and carrying out errands in a model grocery store, the adult may keep track of how many errands have been planned, thereby allowing the child to concentrate on the best way to organize the remaining errands (Gauvain, 1992).

In the classic study described in Box 9-2, children planned a series of errands with the help of an adult or a peer. Children learn different things when they collaborate with an adult versus a peer partner. Whereas adults provide children with more opportunities to learn about a task, peers can help children learn how to negotiate and share activities. The skills that can be obtained from both adult–child and peer interactions are important to social and cognitive development.

BOX 9-2   Who is better at helping children develop efficient plans: adult or peer partners?

Do children plan more efficiently when they work with an adult or a same-age peer? To find out, Radziszewska and Rogoff (1988) asked 9 year olds to plan an errand in collaboration with either another 9 year old or a parent as a partner.

Partners were given a map of an imaginary town (see Figure 9-9) and two lists of errands, and were asked to plan a trip to obtain materials for a school play (e.g., to buy uniforms from the theatrical supplies store, paintbrushes from the paint shop). Partners were asked to be efficient to save fuel, which required that they develop a plan that incorporated all these stores in sequence and minimized backtracking or other unnecessary travel.

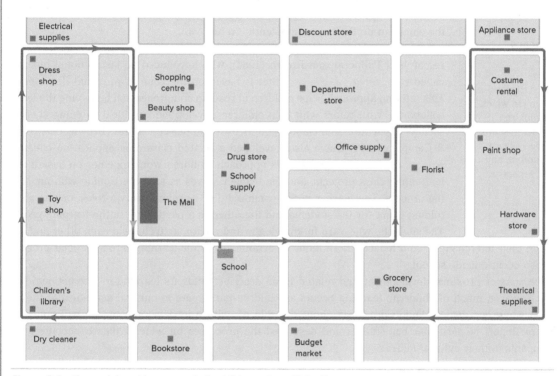

Figure 9-9   How adult guidance can help children plan efficiently
This map of an imaginary town shows the efficient route an adult–child pair planned for acquiring all the materials they would need to prepare for and stage a school play.
Source: Radziszewska and Rogoff (1988).

Adult–child dyads were better planners than peer dyads. The adult–child dyads planned longer sequences of moves (average of 4.9 stores per move) than the peer dyads (average of 1.3 stores per move). Nearly half of the adult–child dyads planned the whole route at the outset, whereas none of the peer dyads did so. Children learned other helpful strategies when they worked with an adult, such as examining the map of the town carefully before making any moves and marking stores where they needed to shop with particular colours. Of great importance was the children's active involvement in the planning decisions, which the adults often verbalized and explained to their child partners. In contrast, peer partners often dominated the decision-making process, ignored their co-workers and communicated very little.

Not only did children plan better with an adult, but they were also able to transfer what they had learned to later planning tasks that they did by themselves. In a later independent planning task, children who had worked with adults planned more efficient routes (20% shorter) than children who had previously planned with a peer.

As Vygotsky predicted, 'children appear to benefit from participation in problem-solving with the guidance of partners who are skilled in accomplishing the task at hand' (Rogoff, 1990, p. 169).

scaffolding An instructional process in which the more knowledgeable partner adjusts the amount and type of support he offers to the child to fit with the child's learning needs over the course of the interaction.

reciprocal instruction A tutoring approach based on the ideas of the *zone of proximal development* and *scaffolding*.

community of learners An approach to classroom learning in which adults and children work together in shared activities, peers learn from one another, and the teacher serves as a guide.

Vygotsky's theory has had considerable impact in the fields of psychology and education. Scaffolding, a form of instruction inspired by Vygotskian thinking, is a process by which the teacher adjusts the amount and type of support he offers to fit with the child's learning needs over the course of an interaction. In a classic demonstration, Wood, Bruner, and Ross (1976) taught 3 and 5 year olds to build a pyramid out of interlocking wooden blocks through both verbal and physical scaffolding. This scaffolding involved modelling the steps, encouraging the child to put the blocks in the right places, and segmenting the task into more easily understood steps. By careful monitoring of the child's progress, the teacher was able to constantly adjust the task to make it manageable for the child and provide assistance when needed. During the scaffolded learning experience, the teacher gradually reduces the amount of support he provides as the child becomes more skilled, so that eventually the child can do the task competently on her own.

One example of the application of these ideas to the classroom comes from the research of Palincsar and Brown (1984), who introduced an instructional technique called reciprocal instruction that is based on the zone of proximal development. This tutoring approach helps children in reading comprehension by having the learner collaborate with tutors who help children develop skills critical to comprehension, such as explication and elaboration. Brown and her colleagues (Brown, 1994; Brown & Campione, 1997) have also developed a related classroom application called the community of learners. In this approach, children work together on sustained or long-range class projects, and the teacher serves as an expert guide who facilitates the process. The teacher in the community of learners has two roles: one as a scaffolding agent for the students and the other as a participant in the learning process. The students, who vary in knowledge and ability, actively help each other and learn through their interchanges. And indeed, these kinds of arrangements for learning through social processes can also occur outside school.

The zone of proximal development and related ideas describe children's learning in instructional situations. However, much of children's learning occurs as children participate in cultural activities. In the next section where we discuss Vygotsky's ideas about the role of culture in development, we will cover how Barbara Rogoff in particular has studied and described the processes by which children become guided participants in their cultural milieux.

The role of culture

An important feature of Vygotsky's approach is his emphasis on the role of culture in cognitive development (Cole, 2006). Cultures provide the institutions and social settings that support and direct cognitive development. Social institutions, such as schools, can significantly alter the ways in which people think.

CULTURAL TOOLS

In these settings, particular ways of identifying and solving problems are emphasized, along with the tools that aid problem solving. In every culture, both symbolic tools, such as language and mathematics, and material tools, such as pencil, paper and computers, are used to support intelligent action. Once certain cultural tools become incorporated into intelligent action, it is difficult to imagine how the activity would occur without such tools. Think for a moment about how you would remember your class material without the cultural tool of literacy, which mediates your learning and remembering in the classroom. There is cultural variation in the tools that support cognitive development. For example, in cultures in which verbal explanation is highly valued, activities such as oral narratives and storytelling assume much importance and are part of children's cognitive development in that community (Heath, 1998).

Vygotsky stressed that any attempt to assess children's cognitive development must consider the cultural context. He claimed that if we ignore the culturally specific nature of children's learning, we run the risk of seriously underestimating children's intellectual capabilities. Indeed, many cross-cultural studies have documented that children learn highly sophisticated and complex cognitive skills important in their culture (Rogoff, 2003; Cole, 2006). These skills are conveyed to children largely through social experiences. Social interactions with more experienced cultural members are especially important because these people are the most immediate representatives in children's lives of culturally organized ways of thinking and acting (Gauvain & Perez, 2007).

Researchers have studied several social processes that promote children's learning of culturally valued skills, such as observational learning (Morelli, Rogoff, & Angellio, 2003), the social regulation of attention in infancy (Martini & Kirkpatrick, 1981; Bornstein, Tal, & Tamis-LeMonda, 1991), deliberate efforts to transfer knowledge from more to less experienced partners (Serpell & Hatano, 1997), social coordination during joint cognitive activity (Rogoff, 1998), and cognitive socialization through conversation and joint narratives (Mullen & Yi, 1995). Taken together, this research suggests that social opportunities for children's learning appear in many forms and that culture determines the frequency and manner with which these processes occur.

GUIDED PARTICIPATION

To describe this type of culturally mediated learning, Rogoff (1990) introduced the concept of guided participation. This approach highlights the fact that adults regularly support learning in the context of everyday activities by directing children's attention to, and involvement in, these activities. Sometimes these activities are child focused, such as in play or an organized game, but often they are adult activities in which the primary purpose is not to instruct children but to carry out the activity itself.

In one form of guided participation, learning through intent community participation, Rogoff and her colleagues (2003) describe how children seek out ways to participate in authentic activities of their community alongside more experienced cultural members. For example, as a mother tries to make a cake, her child may ask if he can help. The mother may agree and then structure the task in a way that gives the child some real responsibility in the activity, such as stirring the ingredients that the mother has assembled. The mother then carefully supervises the child and provides assistance when needed. In this example, the child initiates participation and engages in the activity as a meaningful participant; that is, his actions, though guided by the adult, contribute in meaningful ways to the activity. Over time, if the child remains interested in and continues to be involved in making cakes with his mother, the child's roles and responsibilities change with his competence and understanding of the activity.

> **guided participation**
> Learning that occurs as children participate in activities of their community and are guided in their participation by the actions of more experienced partners in the setting.
>
> **intent community participation**
> Children's participation in the authentic activities of their community with the purpose of learning about the activity.

For Rogoff (2003), intent community participation is one of the most prevalent forms of children's learning.

Most recently, Rogoff has updated her conception of the ways in which children are participants in their social worlds. Rogoff (2016) raises concerns about overly narrow definitions of culture and cultural differences, arguing that culture should not be reduced to individual/group characteristics such as race, ethnicity, or nationality, but should rather be seen as the collaborative transactions of members of communities across generations. Arguing that an aspect of many cultural communities across the world is the prioritization of children's participation in family and community activities, Rogoff puts forward a model for this prioritized inclusion of children in cultural practices called *Learning by Observing and Pitching In*. Under this framework culture is seen more as a way of life between members of a community across generations rather than static characteristics of groups.

CULTURAL SPECIFICITY OF COGNITIVE ABILITIES

Vygotsky's theory not only leads us to an appreciation of different cultures and their values, but it also connects cultural values and practices directly to cognitive development. Mathematics provides an interesting example of this kind of link. Findings from research of the mathematics skills of children in Brazil who work as street vendors are discussed in Box 9-3. As this box shows, the children's daily interaction with addition and subtraction, as well as their lack of formal schooling, has led them to develop ways of performing mathematical functions that work for them in their daily activities. If, as Vygotsky insisted, we take culture into account in evaluating such children's cognitive skills, we must recognize the sophistication of their competence, which certainly exceeds what we might have expected. Studies such as these underscore the importance of considering the cultural context in our examination and evaluation of children's cognitive development.

Applied Developmental Psychology

BOX 9-3 Street maths and school maths in Brazil

Most human beings use mathematics and numerical reasoning every day of their lives. People calculate the costs of items in the supermarket, divide a snack equally among friends, and estimate how far it is to school and other destinations. In most cases, people learn the necessary skills to accomplish these mental acts in primary school, but not all children or adults have the opportunity to acquire a formal education. How do those without that opportunity perform such daily tasks? As the study we discuss here illustrates, even without formal training and in the face of hardship and risk, children demonstrate an amazing ability to develop the cognitive skills needed for their everyday functioning.

Carraher, Schliemann, and Carraher (1988) studied young vendors on the streets of Brazilian cities. These children, who are usually between 9 and 15 years of age, sell all kinds of goods, including coconuts, oranges and other fruits, as well as candy and sweets, to pedestrians and riders of public transportation. The researchers were interested in the ability of these children to solve mathematical problems. After all, they reasoned, success at their trade relied on mathematical skill. Often, the children sold items in bulk, such as three oranges for 10 cruzados (the monetary unit in Brazil), but if a customer only wanted two oranges, the seller would need to figure out a fair price or risk losing the sale (Saxe, 1991). Also, because inflation is rampant in Brazil, the prices of one day may be different from the prices yesterday. As a result, there is no fixed pricing scheme for the children to memorize. To study these children's skill at mathematical calculations, the experimenters presented five young vendors, who ranged in age from 9 to 15 years old, with either a familiar commercial transaction between a vendor and a customer or a similar mathematics problem presented as it would be in school.

The young vendors revealed striking differences in their abilities to perform the two different types of problem. On the familiar commercial transaction, the children were correct 98% of the time, but when the same problems were presented in the form of a school exercise, the percentage of correct answers dropped to 37. One notable difference in the children's solutions to the two types of problems was in the method they used: the children solved the commercial problem mentally but resorted to pencil and paper to solve the school like problem. They also used different problem-solving strategies in the two situations. The following protocol from one of the children illustrates these differences (Nunes & Bryant, 1996):

Commercial transaction problem
Customer: *I'll take two coconuts. (Each coconut costs 40 cruzados, and the customer pays with a 500-cruzado bill.) What do I get back?*
Child vendor (before reaching for the customer's change): *Eighty, ninety, one hundred, four hundred and twenty.*

School-type problem
Test question: *What is 420 plus 80?*
Child's response: *The child writes 42 on one line and 8 underneath and obtains 130 as the result. She apparently proceeds as follows: She adds the 8 and the 2, carries the 1, and then adds 1 1 4 1 8, obtaining 13. With the 0 already in the sum, she gets 130. (Note that the child is confusing multiplication and addition rules.)*

The child has approached the same problem (420 + 80) in two distinctly different ways. On the street, she uses an 'add-on' strategy efficiently to arrive at the correct answer, whereas in the academic setting, she applies strategies learned in school incorrectly. As Vygotsky would have predicted, this study shows the importance of context for understanding cognitive development. It also illustrates how cognitive tools or mediators – in this case, mathematical symbols and strategies – are integrated with thinking. Finally, it demonstrates the resilience of children at risk and their ability to survive and learn even complex cognitive skills despite the lack of opportunity for formal schooling.

The role of language

Language plays a central role in Vygotsky's approach to cognitive development. Language provides children with access to the ideas and understandings of other people. It also enables children to convey their own ideas and thoughts to others. Moreover, language, which is a cultural product, is the primary cultural tool that mediates individual mental functioning. Once children learn to use language, it gradually becomes incorporated into their thought processes.

EGOCENTRIC SPEECH AS A COGNITIVE AID

For Vygotsky, thought and speech are independent in early development. However, around the second year of life, they begin to join together when children start to use words to label objects. Within a year, speech assumes two forms: social, or communicative, speech and egocentric speech (also called *private speech*). For Vygotsky, egocentric speech is a form of self-directed monologue by which the child instructs herself in solving problems. For example, in her efforts to solve a dinosaur puzzle, a child might say, 'First I'll put the tail piece here, then the claw goes over here and the head right there.' By age 7 or 8, this form of speech becomes internalized in the thought process and becomes inner speech, a form of internal monologue that, according to Vygotsky, guides intelligent functioning. This view is quite different from Piaget's ideas about egocentrism and egocentric speech.

> **egocentric speech**
> According to Vygotsky, a form of self-directed dialogue by which the child instructs herself in solving problems and formulating plans; as the child matures, this becomes internalized as *inner speech.*
>
> **inner speech**
> Internalized egocentric speech that guides intellectual functioning.

For Piaget, egocentric speech is a mental limitation of the preoperational stage in which the child's self-focused way of thinking leads children to explain natural phenomena in reference to the self – for example, by claiming that the moon follows the child home at night because it always appears when he is around (unless, of course, it is cloudy). The egocentric child, in Piaget's view, makes no effort to adapt his point of view in a way that makes it understandable to others. Moreover, unlike Vygotsky, who considered egocentric speech as one step in the path of the development of internalized knowledge, Piaget thought that egocentric speech served no useful cognitive function. Egocentric speech was merely a consequence or symptom of underlying cognitive egocentrism. Finally, Piaget suggested that egocentric speech diminishes at the end of the preoperational period, as the child's perspective-taking abilities improve, whereas Vygotsky thought that this kind of speech becomes internalized as thought. Thus Vygotsky argued that egocentric (private) speech served a vital developmental function, whereas Piaget felt it was more of an obstruction to development, or at least served no developmental role.

Who is right? Most of the evidence favours Vygotsky's position. For example, children use more private or self-speech when they work on a difficult cognitive task; as a result, their performance improves, suggesting that children use this form of speech as a cognitive aid to 'narrate' and support actions (Berk, 1992: Berk, Mann, & Ogan, 2006; Fernyhough & Fradley, 2005). In addition, in a longitudinal study of the developmental sequence of this kind of speech, Bivens and Berk (1990) found that egocentric speech does shift from external (audible, self-directed speech) to internal (silent, self-directed speech) between 7 and 10 years of age, supporting Vygotsky's view.

Although there is some debate over the functions of internal speech there is increasing evidence that it plays important roles in supporting emerging cognitive functions such as in working memory, in task-switching and planning (Alderson-Day & Fernyhough, 2015; Cragg & Nation, 2010). We will discuss the development of these abilities in the next chapter. As Vygotsky stated, and despite Piaget's lack of interest, language, as well as being a vital tool for communicating effectively with others, does also seem to serve important roles in supporting and regulating other cognitive functions and processes.

BOX 9-4 How mothers help their children to solve a puzzle by themselves …

Research close-up

Source: Based on Wertsch et al. (1980).

Introduction:

A key feature of the zone of proximal development (ZPD) is that it is through joint action (e.g., solving a problem together) that children learn to solve problems on their own. Thus, according to Vygotskians, social interaction is a prerequisite for the development of knowledge and related skills. In this study, Wertsch and colleagues were interested in exploring how children learned to solve a puzzle through joint activity with their mother.

Method:

Eighteen mother–child dyads (i.e., pairs comprising a mother and her child) were divided into three age groups, based on the child's age. These three groups had average ages of 33 months, 43 months and 53 months respectively. After a warm-up, simple task, mothers were asked, together with their child, to complete a puzzle of a truck to match a model completed puzzle by fitting the appropriate coloured pieces into the correct place (see Figure 9-10).

Researchers recorded the talk between mother and child as well as direction of gaze – whether mother or child looked towards the model, the puzzle, the child or mother, and so on – as well as gestures such as pointing.

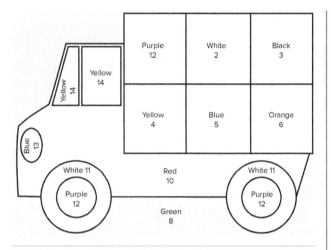

Figure 9-10   Truck puzzle

Results:

The researchers' main interest was to explore how far gazes towards the model were regulated, and by whom. Gazes were described as 'other regulated' when the child looked at the model after the mother pointed to the model, or said something about the model (e.g., 'Where is the red piece on the other puzzle?'). Gazes were self-regulated when children did not receive any of these 'prompts' to look at the model from the mother.

As can be seen in Figure 9-11, the proportion of other regulated gazes decreased progressively with age, indicating that mothers of the older children did not need to frame their child's activity so much as the mothers of the younger children.

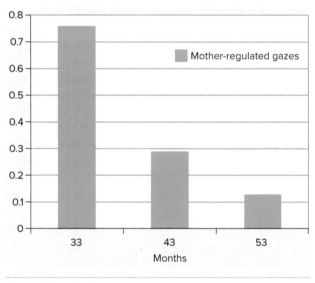

Figure 9-11   Mother-regulated gazes

Discussion:

The decrease in mother-guided gazes with age suggests that the role of each participant in the mother–child dyad is changing with age. Specifically, children are more independent in generating and using a strategic approach to solving a simple puzzle completion task such as this. Mothers also intervened less in other ways as children became better able to devise ways to solve the task efficiently themselves.

EVALUATION OF VYGOTSKY'S THEORY

Vygotsky's approach offers a perspective on cognitive development that emphasizes the culturally organized and socially mediated nature of this development. As such, it overcomes some of the limitations of Piaget's focus on cognitive development as an individual or solitary endeavour.

Strengths of the theory

Vygotsky's theory has helped to make developmental psychologists more aware of the importance of the immediate social contexts of learning and cognition. In particular, through the notion of the zone of proximal development and the related concepts of scaffolding and guided participation (Rogoff, 2003), this approach has pointed to new ways of assessing children's cognitive potential, and of teaching reading, mathematics and writing.

Vygotsky's approach has increased our appreciation of the importance of culture in cognitive development. This approach is particularly useful in multi-ethnic and diverse modern societies, because it provides a theoretical base for examining the ways that children of different cultural and ethnic traditions approach cognitive tasks and schooling. Vygotsky's theory also provides a way of conceptualizing the role played by tools of thinking in cognitive development. This theory addresses how tools such as literacy and numerical systems, which are products of culture, get passed on across generations and become incorporated into the ways children learn to think and solve problems as they grow.

Does Vygotsky's theory describe developmental change?

Although Vygotsky's theory has recently inspired a great deal of research, the theory has several limitations, largely pertaining to its explanation of development. Although the approach emphasizes change over time in a specific learning experience, or microgenetic change, and the role of long-term historical influences on intellectual development as embodied in cultural practices and tools, this approach is not very specific in relation to age-related, or *ontogenetic*, change. Vygotsky, somewhat in contrast to Piaget, did not provide a detailed description of how children's thinking changes with age and precisely what developmental processes are responsible for these changes (Miller, 2002). This approach also does not describe how changes in physical, social and emotional capabilities contribute to changes in children's cognitive abilities.

microgenetic change
Changes associated with learning that occur over the time of a specific learning experience or episode.

Overall assessment

In a sense, Vygotsky left developmental psychology a unique framework for thinking about cognitive development rather than a fully specified theory. Filling in the details of this theoretical position remains a challenge for the future. However, for now, most developmentalists agree that this approach offers a crucial perspective on human cognition and that it has particular value as a way of thinking about cognitive development in social and cultural contexts.

SOCIAL COGNITIVE DEVELOPMENT: UNDERSTANDING AND LEARNING FROM OTHERS

As we have seen, Vygotsky provided the field of cognitive development research with some crucial ideas concerning the role of social factors in the emergence of cognitive abilities. These ideas have stimulated a great deal of research into what has become known as social cognitive development – the study of how infants and children come to be able to make sense of and learn from the social world around them. Researchers have focused specifically on how children come to be able to understand others' behaviours, their mental states and also, in the same vein as Vygotsky, how they learn from others.

Although Piaget concentrated on the individual's cognitive development, a number of his ideas have stimulated research on the development of social cognition. His concept of object permanence, for example, has relevance for the development of self-recognition – conceiving of the self as separate from the environment and other people. Piaget's views on egocentrism also have implications for the development of social cognition, and in particular, social perspective taking.

And so, on the one hand there is Vygotsky and Rogoff who argue rather strongly that cognitive development is scaffolded and led by the sophisticated sociocultural transactions in which the child is engaged.

On the other hand there is Piaget's domain-general account which implies that changes in cognitive abilities will underlie increasing sophistication of social interactions and skills (though there are some indications that Piaget considered that social interactions might bring about cognitive developmental change via other children challenging egocentrism; Piaget, 1950). Let's explore developmental interactions between social and cognitive development in this section addressing the emergence of children's ability to think about themselves and others.

The self among others

In Chapter 6 we considered how infants come to perceive their own body, and also their emerging understanding of how their body as an object relates to the world around them. However, as well as understanding their own bodies, infants and children also need to learn about how their body and ways of thinking are differentiated from those of other people. This emerging ability is considered by many to be a central component in the development of social cognition (Harter, 2006; Fonagy et al., 2002; Rochat, 2010). The beginning of this differentiation is evident in early infancy when babies expect people and objects to behave differently (Di Giorgio et al., 2017). From an early age, babies seem to expect certain kinds of behaviours from people. For example, if you face a 2-month-old baby without moving or speaking, the infant will become distressed (Adamson & Frick, 2003). Later in infancy, as children come to pass the mirror test around 18–24 months (see Chapter 6), we start to see what many would describe as 'self consciousness', evident, for instance, in their embarrassment in certain situations (Rochat, 2010).

With development, the child's view of herself includes more information about the self, such as values, motives, intentions, and other psychological experiences. Whereas preschool children (5 or younger) tend to define themselves mainly by physical attributes or favourite activities (e.g., 'I'm 4 years old; I like to swim'), increasingly with age children begin to describe themselves in more complex terms that focus on abilities and interpersonal characteristics, such as *smart* and *nice* (Harter, 2006). In adolescence (from 11 or 12 on) children gradually create a more complex and integrated view of the self and their role in society (Harter, 2006). One of the skills underlying these developments in self awareness and understanding is an ability to flexibly adopt different perspectives, to see the world and one's self from other people's perspectives as well as one's own perspective.

Understanding others' perspectives

Very early in development, infants will respond to the emotional and perceptual states of others. Contagious crying, for instance, is often seen in neonatal care wards, and even premature babies will show imitation of emotional facial expressions (Field et al., 1982). Recent findings show that, as is seen in adults, when infants observe another person being touched, tactile responses in their brains are affected – as if they themselves perceive the tactile feeling to some extent (Rigato et al., 2017).

In these early behaviours and responses it is clear that infants are able to sense other's feelings and perceptions, but it is unclear to what extent the infant perceives those perceptions and feelings as belonging to someone else – is he able to separate self from other? Regardless, with development, children become increasingly able to understand the thoughts and desires of others as distinct from their own (Yuill & Pearson, 1998). In line with Piaget's framework, some researchers argue that these developments are due to a cognitive shift away from an egocentric orientation and that this leads also to improved communication skills as well as the development of moral standards and prosocial behaviours (Eisenberg, Fabes, & Spinrad, 2006; Harter, 2006). The development of these abilities is basic to the child's developing participation in her community, and we will return to this topic in greater detail in Chapter 14.

So what cognitive abilities underlie the development of self knowledge and the ability to take social perspectives? As we saw earlier, Piaget, with his relatively socially impoverished three mountains task, identified some orderly developmental improvements in children's abilities to identify other people's viewpoints on the world. Subsequently, Selman and colleagues constructed a more explicit stage theory of perspective taking in which they examined the role of cognitive changes in a wider *social* consideration of perspective taking (see Table 9-3) (Selman & Byrne, 1974; Selman & Jacquette, 1978; Selman, 1980). Interviewing children about

Table 9-3   Role taking: developing the ability to take different perspectives

Stage 0 Egocentric perspective
The child does not distinguish his own perspective from that of others or recognize that another person may interpret experiences differently.
Stage 1 Differentiated perspective
The child realizes that she and others may have either the same or a different perspective. Although she is concerned with the uniqueness of each person's cognitions, she can't judge accurately what the other person's perspective may be.
Stage 2 Reciprocal perspective
Because the child can see himself from another's perspective and knows the other person can do the same thing, he can anticipate and consider another's thoughts and feelings.
Stage 3 Mutual perspectives
Now the child can view her own perspective, a peer's perspective, and their shared, or mutual, perspective from the viewpoint of a third person. For example, she can think of how a parent, teacher or other peer might view both her and her friend's perspectives as well as their mutual perspective.
Stage 4 Societal or in-depth perspectives
Children (and adults) can see networks of perspectives, such as Societal, Conservative, or Immigrant points of view. People understand that these varying perspectives not only exist in awareness but involve deeper, perhaps unconscious representations, such as feelings and values.

Source: Adapted from Selman and Jacquette (1978).

their thoughts on short vignettes of social situations, Selman and Byrne (1974) identified stages beginning with the child's egocentric behaviour and then proceeding into more complex social understanding and reasoning. As children move through these stages, they learn not only to differentiate between their own perspectives and those of others but also to understand others' views and the relations between those views and their own (see Figure 9-12).

But can we really explain social development of this level of complexity by decreases in the extent to which children take egocentric perspectives on the world and other people? To some extent this seems

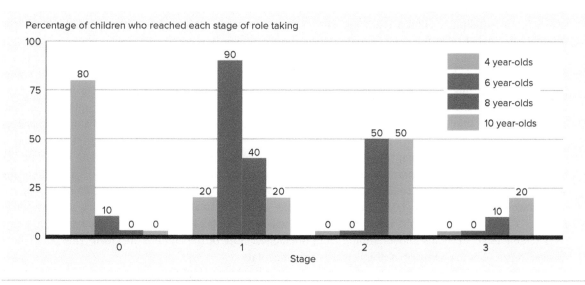

Figure 9-12   Social perspective taking at different ages

When children are asked to describe social vignettes, younger children tend to focus more on egocentric aspects of their understanding. Between the ages of 4 and 6, children shift from an egocentric perspective to a more differentiated one. From here on, progress in appreciating others' views gradually becomes increasingly complex.
Source: Based on Selman and Byrne (1974).

unlikely, as the rich tapestry of social awareness described at Stage 4 of Selman's account involves more than just ignoring one's own perspective. It requires rich knowledge of different situations, cultures, psychological motivations, opinions and groups. Indeed, as we saw in the last section, there are some doubts over whether children's shedding of egocentric perspectives took as long as Piaget's three mountains task seemed to demonstrate. In fact, the latest research on the development of perspective taking indicates that children of all ages, as well as adults, have some difficulty decentring from their own view of a visual scene (Samson et al., 2010). But children's ability to ignore their own perspective and identify what someone else can see seems to be fully mature by 6 years of age at the latest (Surtees & Apperly, 2012).

In sum, the development of social perspective taking may require more than an ability to ignore one's own egocentric perspective. So what does it require? Interestingly, although there are normative patterns in the development of perspective taking, some children develop these abilities earlier than others. Factors which relate to these individual differences might give us a clue as to how they develop. As we discuss in Chapter 14, some studies have found positive relations between prosocial behaviour, such as helping and sharing, and role-taking skills (Eisenberg, 1992; Eisenberg et al., 2006).

Theory of mind

> **theory of mind** A person's beliefs about the 'mind' and the ability to understand mental states.

The area of study known as theory of mind focuses on when and how children come to understand mental states that are different from their own current mental state. Although the term *theory of mind* came from researchers investigating these abilities in non-human primates (Premack & Woodruff, 1978), there is a clear link between understanding of other people's mental states and the kinds of perspective-taking abilities that Piaget and Selman considered important. However, whereas Piaget is perhaps most famous for his focus on the more spatial aspects of perspective taking (e.g., in his three-mountains task), modern research into theory of mind attempts to examine more closely infants' and children's ability to think about other people's mental states. As such, theory of mind research covers topics ranging from the development of the ability to distinguish appearance from reality to children's understanding of dreams, beliefs, intentions, desires, and deception (Harris, 2006).

A number of studies have explored when children begin to understand the thinking of other people. A task that has been used often to study this question is the *false-belief task* (Wimmer & Perner, 1983), which involves telling a child a story and then asking him what a character in the story thinks. In the original false belief task, the child is told a story about a young boy named Maxi who puts his chocolate in a cupboard in the kitchen and then goes into another room to play. When Maxi is off playing, his mother moves his chocolate from the cupboard to a drawer. After a while, Maxi returns and wants his chocolate. At this point, the researcher would ask the child where Maxi will look for his chocolate. Older preschoolers, 4- to 5-year-old children, typically say that Maxi will search in the cupboard, indicating they assume that Maxi will look where he believes the chocolate is (even though they themselves understand that it is not there). In other words, they attribute to Maxi a belief, or mental state, that is different to their own and they use this belief as a basis for their response. To answer in this way, the child needs to hold two understandings or representations of the situation in his mind simultaneously: what the child himself knows to be true and what Maxi believes to be true. Three-year-old children respond quite differently; they say that Maxi will look for the chocolate in the drawer where his mother put it. In other words, the child has his own belief about where the chocolate is based on his knowledge, and he is unable to separate his understanding from the mental state of the child in the story. Thus, the child's answer represents his own belief about where the chocolate is.

Are changes in children's understanding of mind universal; that is, do these changes appear in all cultures? Avis and Harris (1991) conducted a study of children's reasoning about people's beliefs and desires in the Baka community, hunter-gatherers who live in central Africa. These researchers found that by 5 years of age, most of the children they studied were able to predict correctly what an adult would find in a container that they had left for a moment and that, while they were gone, had been emptied. These results are consistent with other findings that show successful performance by preschool-age children in non-Western communities on theory of mind tasks (Harris, 2006). Although variation both within and across cultures in the development of theory of mind have been shown (Lillard, 1998), the research indicates that during childhood an important set of capabilities known as theory of mind develops and that cultural experiences around the world support this process.

Interestingly, research has shown that the presence of older siblings in the home environment can speed children's progression from success to failure on false belief tasks. In one study of 2- to 6-year-old English and Japanese children, those over the age of 3 who grew up with older brothers and sisters performed better on a false belief task than children who grew up alone or with younger brothers and sisters (Ruffman et al., 1998). But children under the age of 3 performed poorly regardless of how many older siblings they had: the task was simply beyond their cognitive capacity.

UNDERSTANDING ONE'S OWN MIND

The term *theory of mind* can also refer to the ability to understand one's own mental state. Some of the earliest studies to examine this address children's understanding of the tension between the appearance of something and what it really is. Think about this for a moment in your own experience. Imagine going into a shop to buy some new household implements, let's say some new cutlery. You spot some nice shiny knives and forks which you like the look of, and go over to pick them up. On doing so you discover that the cutlery only looks like it is made of stainless steel, but its weight in your hand tells you that it is made of something else, plastic. This sort of experience is quite commonplace of course, as it is financially expedient for manufacturers to make items which look good on the shelf. But once you've discovered an object's 'real' properties or quality, it is often difficult to disregard these; the shiny cutlery no longer appears so solid and substantial, and certainly not nearly as appealing as it did before.

So adults under some circumstances seem to have difficultly separating appearance from reality. Our perceptions of the appearance of objects can change in response to new knowledge, despite no physical changes in appearance. This kind of mental phenomenon is even more difficult for young children to master. Three year olds, when presented with a deceptive object, such as a fake rock (which looks like a rock but is actually a sponge), will initially correctly identify the object's appearance, but once they know what the object really is, they will often have difficulty with subsequent questions about what the object looks like and what it really is, ascribing its appearance to what they know it to be and, in some cases, vice versa (Flavell, Green, & Flavell, 1986).

Although some studies have shown considerable correlation between performance on appearance-reality tasks and other theory of mind tasks such as false belief tasks (Gopnik & Astington, 1988), this is not always apparent and some authors have questioned whether the appearance-reality task is related to children's theory of mind abilities. Deák (2006) for instance, has argued that the questions put to children in the appearance reality task are odd, and that early difficulties are driven more by children's problems with understanding the nature of their dialogue with the experimenter.

Nonetheless, Perner, Leekam, and Wimmer (1987) present evidence that an ability to accurately remember and report one's own state of mind does indeed develop between 3 and 4 years. The task they devised to assess this ability was called the 'deceptive box' task. In this task, an experimenter shows a child a box of 'Smarties' (a brand of sweets that all children recognized). They ask them, 'What do you think is in this box?' Both 3 and 4 year olds tend to guess 'Smarties!' Unfortunately for them this is not the case, and when the experimenter opens the box to reveal pencils the children often express dismay. The test of metacognition comes in the next question however, when the experimenter asks the children, 'What did you think was in the box when I first showed it to you?' At this point 4 year olds will typically answer correctly ('Smarties'), but 3 year olds will often fail to reflect on their past state of mind and answer 'pencils'.

So, both false belief tasks and deceptive box tasks seem to indicate that, before 4 years of age, children have difficulty with understanding the mental states (those of others as well as themselves), specifically when those mental states differ with respect to their own current knowledge or beliefs. This appears to indicate an important conceptual change at this age in children's understanding of themselves and their social world

(Doherty, 2008; Gopnik & Astington, 1988; Oktay-Gür, Schulz, & Rakoczy, 2018). However, as we shall see, subsequent research has questioned this conclusion.

PROBLEMS WITH THE FALSE BELIEF TASK

Although this basic progression to passing theory of mind tasks at age 4 has been replicated in a wide range of studies (Wellman, Cross, & Watson, 2001), the findings have been contested on a number of grounds (Mitchell, 1997). For instance, some investigators have pointed out that there may be a difference between the development of a theory of mind in relation to fictional information, as in pretend play, and the development of an understanding of states of knowledge, such as false beliefs (Lillard, 1993).

Another important question concerns whether the change in children's success at this task is due to developments in understanding other people's minds or, as we discussed in relation to the appearance-reality task above, whether there is some other artefact driving success, such as children's understanding of the question (Lewis & Osborne, 1990). Lying and deception also provide evidence of theory of mind. They imply an ability to recognize that one person can have information that another does not and therefore that we can influence what other people think by withholding the truth. Researchers find that deception emerges earlier than success at the false belief task (Chandler, Fritz, & Hala, 1989). Perhaps lying and deception are better measures of theory of mind than false belief tasks. That said, recent findings indicate that training children on false belief as well as other theory of mind skills increases children's tendency to lie in the home (Ding et al., 2015). This indicates that even if false belief tasks do not herald the onset of theory of mind, they certainly are related to a wider conception of theory of mind (encompassing lying and deception for example).

THEORY OF MIND IN INFANCY

A significant revelation over the last decade which has sparked much debate and controversy has been that theory of mind abilities and even an appreciation of false belief may emerge well before three years of age (when children still typically fail the classic false belief task). The first demonstration of false belief understanding in infancy was made by Onishi and Baillargeon (2005), using the violation of expectation paradigm. They showed that prelinguistic 15-month-old infants appear surprised (look longer) when someone searches successfully for an object when they should have had a false belief (because they were unable to see where an object was finally hidden; see Box 9-5).

Research close-up

BOX 9-5   15-month-old infants understand other people's false beliefs

Source: Onishi and Baillargeon (2005).

Introduction:

Since Wimmer and Perner (1983), the standard method for determining whether children possess a theory of mind has been the false belief test. This has typically been presented to children in terms of a story in which children have to respond to the experimenter's questions and make a differentiation between their own belief and the belief of someone else (e.g. in the situation where the child has observed Maxi's chocolate being moved to a new location when Maxi was out of the room (see earlier in this chapter). Various versions of the false belief task have indicated that the earliest age at which children can pass such tasks is around 4 years of age. However, Onishi and Baillargeon set out to determine whether infants could express an understanding of false belief at a much younger age in a 'looking-time' task.

Method:

Onishi and Baillargeon tested 56 fifteen-month-old infants. They presented the false belief scenario in a visual display. First the infants were briefly familiarized to the apparatus that would constitute the false belief task (see Figure 9-13), two boxes (one green, one yellow), a toy (a toy piece of watermelon), and an observer wearing a visor. In this familiarization display, they saw the person place the toy in the green box. They were then presented with one of four different scenarios (belief induction trials). In the True Belief Green condition they watched as a person observed the boxes moving but with the toy remaining in the green box. In the True Belief Yellow condition, the infants watched as the person observed the toy moving from the green to the yellow box. So in both of these conditions, if the infants are able to represent the observer's mental state then they should understand that the observer thinks the watermelon is in the box in which the infants knows it to be. Two other groups of infants were placed into false belief induction trials. In the False Belief, Green condition, the infants saw the observer's view hidden, and then the watermelon moved to the yellow box without the observer knowing. In the False Belief Yellow condition, the infants saw the observer following the watermelon into the yellow box, but then saw the observer's view obscured and then the watermelon moving back into the green box. In both of these conditions, if infants are able to understand that other people can have different beliefs than themselves then they should be able to appreciate that the observer should have false beliefs about the whereabouts of the object. Lastly, the test trials presented infants with the observer reaching for the watermelon in either the yellow or the green box.

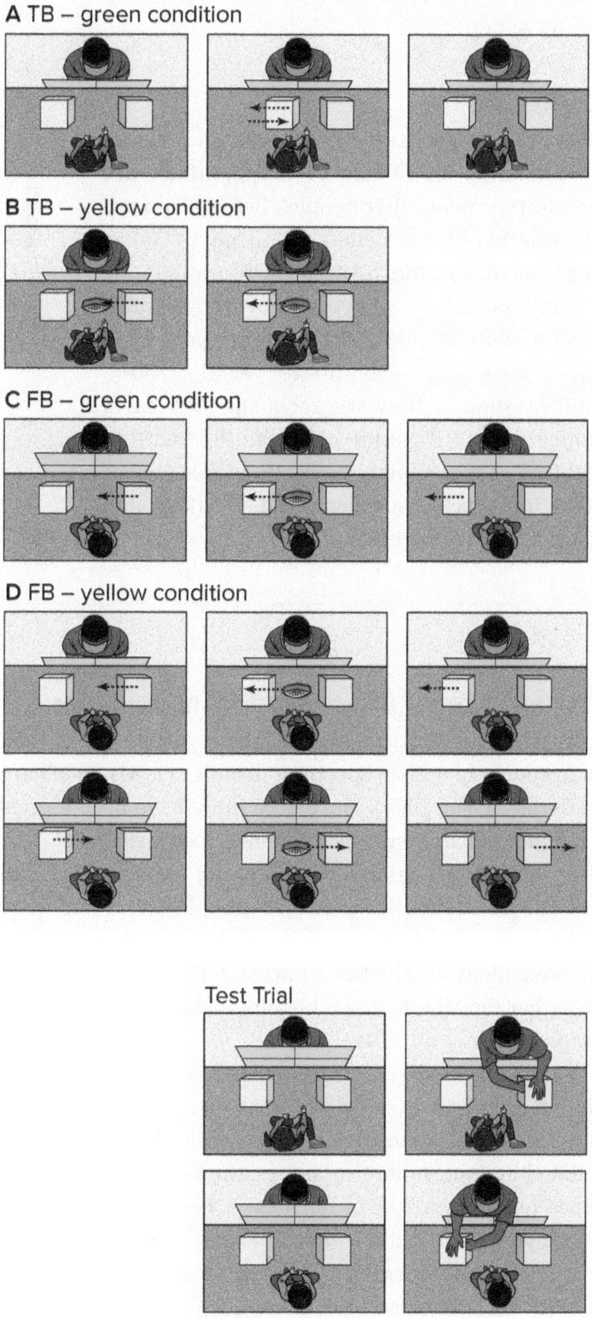

Figure 9-13   The experimental conditions in Onishi and Baillargeon's experiment

Source: Adapted from Onishi and Baillargeon (2005).

Results:

The results were very clear cut, the infants looked longer when the person reached into a box which violated what they should know from what the infants observed. If the infants saw the person receive a true belief that the watermelon was in the yellow box they would look longer if the observer reached incorrectly into the green box, and vice versa. If the infants had seen the person receive a false belief that the watermelon was in the yellow box, they would look longer if the observer searched correctly into the green box, and vice versa. Cross-reference to Figure 9-14.

Discussion:

These results are strong evidence that, even at the tender age of 15 months of age, infants are able to represent other people's beliefs, no matter whether those beliefs are true or false. There is much controversy surrounding this result, but others have uncovered similar results with slightly different methods and age-groups (e.g., Southgate et al., 2007). The question is how we reconcile this early competence in 15 month olds with the fact that children cannot answer correctly in false belief tasks until they are 4 years old. What do you think might explain this?

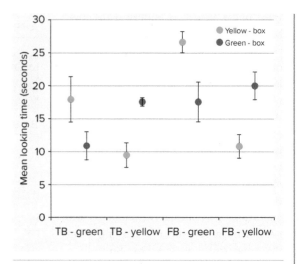

Figure 9-14 The results from Onishi and Baillargeon's experiment
Source: Adapted from Onishi and Baillargeon (2005).

Onishi and Baillargeon's (2005) study fuelled speculation that we may be genetically endowed with neural machinery dedicated to telling us about other people's minds (Leslie, 2005), and this has certainly chimed with accounts of autism spectrum disorder (ASD) which argue that such a capacity is impaired in this disorder (Baron-Cohen, 2005). Since 2005 there have been a great number of other studies which seem to confirm Onishi and Baillargeon's observation across a range of different kinds of task. For instance, Southgate et al. (2007) showed that infants will correctly anticipate with their eye movements where an actor with a false belief should search. Evidence of false belief predictions has now been reported in infants as young as 6 months of age (Southgate & Vernetti, 2014). Remarkably, it also seems that 18 month olds will modulate their predictions of whether an actor will search for an object with a true belief or a false belief depending on whether they knew that a blindfold that the actor was wearing was deceptive and could actually be seen through (Senju et al., 2011).

Despite the now significant number of studies which demonstrate false belief abilities in infancy using violation of expectation and anticipatory looking methods (Scott & Baillargeon, 2017), many researchers still believe that developments in conceptual understanding of mental states between 3 and 4 years of age underpin the shift from failure to success in the false belief task and remain sceptical about findings of earlier competence (take a look at Ruffman & Perner, 2005; Baillargeon, Scott, & He, 2010, Baillargeon, Buttelmann, & Southgate, 2018; Kulke et al., 2018 for a long argument about this).

It is clear that there is still much to do to fully understand the origins of theory of mind in early life. Nonetheless, regardless of whether they believe that such abilities are innate, develop in infancy or as a result of a conceptual change in early childhood, it is doubtless that researchers are united in the view that an ability to represent and interpret mental states is a particularly important ability, enabling us to identify with other human beings as mental agents with needs, desires and intentions that guide their behaviour. The potential for interacting with, and learning from, others that this capability makes possible is profound (Tomasello et al., 2005; Carpendale & Lewis, 2006).

Understanding other people's reliability and dispositions

A relatively recent focus of interest in the area of social cognitive development has been understanding how infants and children come to understand other people's roles and dispositions. In a now classic study in this area, Koenig, Clement, and Harris (2004) examined whether children would place more trust in people who they knew, from experience, to make more truthful assertions. They presented 3- to 4-year-old children with two people who labelled (i.e., named) objects either correctly or incorrectly (in a way so that the children would be able to identify which person was the more truthful). They then presented the truthful and the deceitful person, naming a new object which the children did not know, and did not know the name of. The children were much more likely to learn the name given by the more truthful person. So young children not only notice whether people are telling the truth, but then use that information to decide on whom they should base their trust.

Since Koenig et al.'s (2004) study, there have now been a great many studies published addressing the development of children's and even infants' understanding of the quality of different people's knowledge, and when to seek or provide knowledge or help. As discussed in the previous section, false belief tasks seem to demonstrate that infants in the second year of life understand when another person does or does not have knowledge about a certain event. But infants also seem to be able to decide whether to trust someone based on how reliable they are. Begus and Southgate (2012) have actually shown that 16 month olds are more likely to point to an object requesting information if the person they are with appears well informed than if they are accompanied by an unreliable adult (someone whom they previously observed to name objects incorrectly).

As well as seeking information from well-chosen adults, under certain circumstances infants will attempt to provide information or help to someone who knows less than they do. Knudsen and Liszkowski (2012) showed that 18 month olds will help an adult to find a hidden object, but only if that adult had been out of the room whilst the infant saw the object being moved from an expected location.

And so, even infants seem to have a keen sense of states of knowledge in other people, and know about the ways in which knowledge or help can be provided. Beyond infancy, children become increasingly sophisticated at taking into account various aspects of behaviour in adults and other children, which might have a bearing on the extent to which their knowledge or testimony can be relied upon (Harris et al., 2018). As we shall see in the next section, some authors have gone so far as to suggest that humans are provided and born with natural predispositions to learn from other people (Csibra & Gergely, 2009). It is possible that infants' and children's ability to differentiate between reliable and unreliable sources of information might be part of such an adaptation.

As well as determining whether another person might be a reliable or unreliable informant, an important way of understanding other people is to determine whether they are likely to want to help, or possibly hinder you. Hamlin, Wynn, and Bloom (2007) asked whether infants can discriminate helpers from hinderers. They showed infants a display involving an animated red circle that was trying to climb a hill (but failing). Infants then saw another shape 'helping' the red circle to climb the hill by pushing it up (the yellow triangle in Figure 9-15). In another display they saw yet another shape 'hindering' the red circle by pushing it back down the hill (the blue square in Figure 9-15). The infants were then given a choice of who they could pick up (the helper or the hinderer). Both age groups of children preferred to reach for the helper. So, according to Hamlin et al. (2007), even from 6 months of age, infants can make evaluations about others' social dispositions.

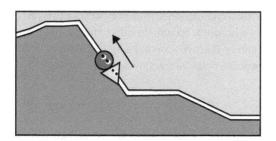 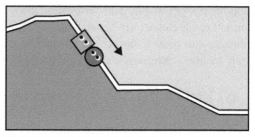

Figure 9-15   The displays 6- and 10-month-old infants saw in Hamlin et al.'s (2007) 'helper-hinderer' experiment

Infants either saw a helping event (left) or a hindering event (right). Both 6 and 10 month olds preferred to reach for the helping shape (the yellow triangle) rather than the hindering shape (the blue square).
Source: Based on Hamlin et al. (2007).

Evolutionary accounts of social cognition

The early abilities of infants and young children to understand other people's minds and dispositions has encouraged a number of researchers to propose that the human species has evolved cognitive mechanisms which enable us to understand others' minds, and to learn from other people in specific ways (e.g., Leslie, Friedman, & German, 2004; Csibra & Gergely, 2006, 2011). Indeed, the inability of children with autism to pass theory of mind tasks has been used by some to argue in favour of an account of theory of mind that relies substantially on inheritance.

A particularly influential recent account of early social cognition has argued that human infants are born with a predisposition to learn from relevant others (Csibra & Gergeley, 2006). Certainly as we shall discuss in the next chapter, we know that children are able to learn by observation. Some authors have argued that humans have evolved to be able to learn from observation in a special way: through imitation. But what makes imitation different from other kinds of observational learning? Some theorists have appealed to a distinction between imitation and emulation (Tennie, Call, & Tomasello, 2006). Both imitation and emulation can occur through an observer watching another person (or animal) succeeding at a task (e.g., pressing a lever to gain some juice), but, importantly, emulation learning concerns learning about how the object works (i.e., learning that a lever can move up and down), whereas imitation learning involves learning about how the other animal's action on the lever can lead to the reward. It is the prevalence of imitation in human behaviour that has led some authors to argue that imitation is unique to humans (Meltzoff & Moore, 1997). For instance, as we shall describe in the next chapter, young infants often imitate the facial gestures (e.g., tongue protrusion) made by adults (Meltzoff & Moore, 1977).

But how has this ability to imitate arisen, and is it really a uniquely human ability? There are some quite different opinions on this matter. Some developmental psychologists have argued that an ability to imitate is innate (Meltzoff & Moore, 1997; Csibra & Gergely, 2009). For instance, Meltzoff and Moore (1997) suggest that we have an evolved ability to perceive commonalities between what we see someone else do and what we can do ourselves, and actively make such matches, and that this allows imitation. On the other side of the argument, Celia Heyes (Heyes, 2005) thinks that an ability to imitate is mostly learned. Heyes argues that we can learn to produce responses to visually perceived behaviours in others, and that processes of associative learning could gradually shape our behaviours so that they become imitative.

But how can we tell between these interpretations? Those in favour of an innateness account point to the presence of imitation early in life (Meltzoff & Moore, 1997), and the absence of imitation in species that are not primates. Those in favour of learned imitation (Heyes, 2005) argue that it is difficult to find strong evidence for newborn imitation of facial gestures other than tongue protrusion. Heyes (2005) also points out that as well as imitation being observable in non-human primates (Custance, Whiten, & Bard, 1995; Gross, 2006), evidence suggests that even some bird species have been shown to imitate. The argument is that if a range of species are able to imitate, then this suggests that imitation is underpinned by a set of common learning mechanisms like classical and operant conditioning.

But how then can the learning account explain the higher prevalence of imitative behaviours in humans than any other species? Call and Tomasello (1996) show that chimpanzees who are born and grow up with substantial human contact are better imitators than those who grow up among other chimps only. This suggests that humans provide the culture in which imitation can be learned – perhaps by engaging in behaviours that draw infants' (chimpanzee and human) attention towards social interactions.

SUMMARY

In this chapter we have considered research and theory about the development of knowledge about ourselves and the physical and social world around us. Piaget and Vygotsky are two key theorists in this domain. According to Piaget, children actively seek out information and adapt it to the knowledge and conceptions of the world that they already have. In this *constructivist view*, children construct their understanding of reality from their own experiences, and organize their knowledge into increasingly complex cognitive structures called *schemas*. Piaget divided intellectual development into four stages that reflect changes in children's cognitive structures and the increasing complexity of the schemas they form. During the first two years of life, called the *sensorimotor period*, a child makes the transition from relying on reflexes to using internal representations of external events. Piaget divided this period into six substages, during which the child becomes able to explore his or her environment in increasingly more complex ways. The culmination of the sensorimotor period is an ability to think about the world in a symbolic way (i.e., in the absence of action). One particular interest of Piaget's was the infant's ability to appreciate *object permanence*. Critics have suggested that children may acquire object permanence, as well as other ideas about the properties of objects and such principles of the physical world as causality, earlier than Piaget thought. Recently, researchers have begun to use looking-time techniques to determine whether infants can represent aspects of the world before they are able to properly act on them. The findings of cognitive competence in early infancy have led researchers to argue that infants may possess innate *core knowledge* about the world.

The major developmental milestone during the *concrete operational period* is the ability to think about objects in a logical way. During the preoperational subperiod, children's thinking is limited by *animistic thinking*, the tendency to attribute lifelike characteristics to inanimate objects, and by *egocentrism*, a tendency to view things from one's own perspective and to have difficulty seeing things from another person's perspective. As the child begins to acquire logical thought (as they enter the concrete operations subperiod), they gain mastery of tasks like *conservation, transitive inference* and *class inclusion*. As with the sensorimotor period, critics have suggested that children may achieve mastery of these skills earlier than Piaget believed.

According to Piaget's framework, children in the *formal operational period* can use abstract reasoning, test mental hypotheses and consider multiple possibilities for the solution to a problem. Not all children or adults attain this stage. The nature of a problem and the opportunity to attend formal schooling that emphasizes this type of thinking are related to the use of formal operations.

Piaget's ideas have been very influential in the field of cognitive development. Despite limitations in his theorizing and methods, Piaget asked and proposed answers to important questions in an innovative way, stimulating the work of other investigators.

Vygotsky's theory emphasizes the critical role played by the social world in facilitating the child's development. According to his theory, children generally internalize thought processes that first occur through interaction with others in the social environment. Qualitative transitions between *elementary mental functions* and *higher mental functions* occur because of shifts in the use of *mediators* such as language and other symbols. The acquisition and use of language plays a primary role in children's developing intellectual abilities. Vygotsky's interest in the child's potential for intellectual growth led him to develop the concept of the *zone of proximal development*. In recent years, this concept has led to the study of *scaffolding*, an instructional process in which the teacher adjusts the amount and type of support offered to the child to suit the child's abilities, withdrawing support as the child becomes more skilled.

Two assumptions about cultural influence inform Vygotsky's theory. First, cultures vary widely in the kinds of institutions, settings and tools they offer to facilitate children's development. Second, in assessing children's cognitive development, we may seriously underestimate children's cognitive development unless we consider these variations and cultural contexts. Language also plays an important role in Vygotskian theory. As children begin to use social speech, *egocentric speech* and *inner speech*, they learn to communicate and to form thoughts and regulate intellectual functions.

Vygotsky's approach mainly offers a general outline that addresses unique and important questions about the nature and course of cognitive development. The theory's focus is on *microgenetic change*, for it examines change over a learning episode rather than change associated with age (*ontogenetic change*). Vygotsky's ideas, especially in their emphasis on the social and cultural aspects of learning and cognition, challenge future researchers to explore the role of context in greater depth.

In the last part of the chapter we discussed the development of social cognitive abilities, a topic which has been of particular interest over the last 20 to 30 years. Although Piaget did not emphasize how the child learns to distinguish self from others, his concepts of egocentrism and object permanence have clear implications for this process and the beginnings of social cognition. A shift away from egocentrism may be related to the development of social cognitive abilities such as an understanding of the self, role-taking abilities, and theory of mind. Research on children's *theory of mind* is uncovering when and how children come to understand the properties of the mind, including that the beliefs and desires guide a child's own behaviour and the behaviour of others. Interestingly, different kinds of tasks have revealed different findings. Researchers originally thought that children did not understand theory of mind until around 4 years of age, but new tasks using looking time as an index of understanding have pushed that achievement to as early as 6 months! It will be an important challenge to determine why such young infants cannot make use of their apparent knowledge until later in development.

Explore and Discuss

1. How do changes in infants' thinking, as described by Piaget, contribute to the infant's increasing ability to interact with people and objects in the world?

2. Imagine you are an educational consultant and you have been asked to consult at a primary school where several children are having difficulty understanding scientific concepts that involve the conservation of weight and volume. How would you explain this difficulty and what would you advise the teachers to do to help these children?

3. How could Vygotsky's ideas about culture and development be used to understand children's learning and development in a multicultural society such as ours?

4. Can you explain why young infants appear so competent in the looking-time task, but fail when asked to act on or articulate their understanding? What factors may account for this developmental lag?

Recommended Reading

Classic

Donaldson, M. (1978). *Children's minds*. Glasgow, Fontana Press.

Flavell, J. (1963). *The developmental psychology of Jean Piaget*. Princeton, NJ: D. van Nostrand Company.

Contemporary

Apperly, I. (2011). *Mindreaders: The cognitive basis of theory of mind*. Hove: Psychology Press.

Csibra, G., & Gergely, G. (2011). Natural pedagogy as evolutionary adaptation. *Philosophical Transactions of the Royal Society B, 366*, 1149–1157.

Mareschal, D., Quinn, P. C., & Lea, S. E. G. (eds) (2010). *The making of human concepts*. Oxford: Oxford University Press.

CHAPTER 10
The Development of Cognitive Functions

Introduction

Every day, children engage in activities that require thinking: deciding what to wear, remembering to take their homework to school, solving problems on a maths assignment, or trying to understand why their best friend is angry with them. This chapter focuses on the cognitive skills that children use when thinking, and the way these skills change across childhood. We focus on approaches to cognitive development that are based on an 'information-processing' view of cognition (Munakata, 2006).

The information processing perspective originated in the study of adult cognition, and several approaches to cognitive development are based on this perspective. In this chapter we will therefore use information processing models of adult cognitive function as a jumping-off point for considering the development of various cognitive processes.

The basic cognitive functions we will discuss in this chapter include attention, memory, executive functions (planning) and problem solving. We will also look at children's knowledge of their own mental capabilities; this is referred to as *metacognition*. The basic cognitive functions mentioned above are all referred to in models of adult cognitive function, such as Baddeley and Hitch's (1974) *Working Memory* model. However, we will start the chapter with a consideration of cognitive functions that have a more historical rooting in the field of developmental psychology and psychology more generally. We begin with the development of learning. As we will discuss (see also Chapter 2), prior to the emergence of cognitive psychology in the middle of the last century, the behaviourist school was particularly concerned with how humans and human children learn new behaviours.

As you study this chapter, keep in mind that the many different theories and approaches to cognitive development discussed in this chapter and in Chapter 9 do not necessarily compete directly with one another. In many cases, the theories address different aspects of cognitive development.

COGNITIVE PSYCHOLOGY AND DEVELOPMENTAL PSYCHOLOGY

An important, and often neglected, line of enquiry in developmental psychology is to consider how accounts of development relate to what we know about adult psychology (see Chapter 1). For instance, it is good practice for researchers studying cognitive development to refer to what we know about cognitive functioning in adults. Without this kind of contextualization it is difficult to make sense of what development is heading towards, and therefore predict trajectories of development and plan appropriate investigations. One key figure in developmental psychology who often neglected to do this was Piaget; indeed, as we saw in Chapter 9, many of the tasks Piaget presented to children were really quite difficult, challenging perhaps even for adults. But perhaps we cannot really blame Piaget. At the beginning of the twentieth century, when Piaget was developing his method and theories, the predominant framework for explaining human behaviour in adults and children was the behaviourist model; a way of thinking about behaviour and cognition that was fundamentally at odds with Piaget's approach.

Behaviourists such as Watson, Thorndike and Skinner chose to measure and explain psychological processes only in terms of the behaviours through which these could be observed. Early behaviourist theorists refused to acknowledge the existence of an internal (cognitive) representation, and this left little room for studying insightful or creative mental processes. The behaviourists explained changes in behaviour in terms of simple forms of learning, such as stimulus-response (S-R) pairing (also referred to as classical conditioning and operant conditioning) in which humans or animals learn to pair particular responses with a particular environmental stimulus (e.g., learning the response of crossing the road following the stimulus of seeing a green light). The impact that behaviourism had on developmental psychology was to reduce development to these simple S-R learning mechanisms. Thus, in a sense, adult learning and development were seen as the same process.

However, around the middle of the last century, the tide began to change, and many psychologists – both those studying mature processes (e.g., Lashley, 1951) and those studying development (e.g., Piaget and

Vygotsky, see Chapter 9) began arguing that we need to invoke the idea of *internal representations* in order to explain behaviour in adults and development. In this light, the behaviourist framework began to crumble; behaviourist models had a great deal of difficulty explaining insightful behaviours in learning and development, such as creative problem solving in chimpanzees (Köhler, 1926) and the stage-wise shifts in ability that Piaget had been describing in young children (see Chapter 9). Cognitive psychologists thus began to develop theories and models that addressed how internal representations and cognitive processes could give rise to human behaviours. It is important to remember, however, that learning processes are a crucial element of both adult and child cognition and development.

In this chapter we will discuss the development of such cognitive functions. First, however, we will take a look at the functions in which the behaviourists had so much faith: processes of learning.

LEARNING IN INFANTS AND CHILDREN

In Chapter 6, we showed how newborn infants arrive in the world prepared to interact in ways that promote their survival: they possess reflex reactions to particular kinds of sensory stimulation (e.g., they suck when a nipple is in their mouth, and they grasp when an object is placed in their hand). Importantly though, this range of reflexes is limited. Because we cannot have an innate reflex for every action we need in order to interact successfully with our environment, we need learning mechanisms. Learning mechanisms are a means for us to change and adapt our behaviours to new stimuli in the environment. Psychologists (and in particular the behaviourists) have been particularly interested in investigating how we learn through association, as in the case of classical and operant conditioning. In this section, we not only explore basic forms of associative learning, but also more simple forms of learning such as habituation learning, and more complex kinds, such as learning through imitation.

Habituation and sensitization in infancy

As we saw in Chapter 6, newborn infants habituate to visual stimuli which are presented for a certain period of time; they decrease their responses (e.g., their visual orienting) to repetitive, non-threatening stimuli. However, when presented with a stimulus that is perceived as new, infants often look longer at this novel stimulus compared to the habituated stimulus (this is called dishabituation). For researchers interested in infants' perceptual abilities this behaviour has been a boon – it allows us to set up experiments to determine whether infants can discriminate between different stimuli. However, habituation plays an important role besides this. The essence of habituation is that it functions as a learning mechanism which helps us orientate towards new information and away from the old. However, as well as habituating, infants also sensitize to perceptual information at the same time. We discuss both of these simple learning mechanisms here.

Habituation is a decrease in the strength of response to a repeated stimulus. It occurs across species ranging from humans to dragonflies to sea snails, and it occurs in the youngest infants (even before they are born), through development and into old age. This is a simple form of learning in that it occurs in response to only a single stimulus (in contrast to more complex forms of learning, discussed later in this section, in which two or more stimuli are associated in some way).

Sensitization is an increase in the strength of response to a repeated stimulus. Like habituation, sensitization is also classified as a simple learning mechanism as it occurs in response to only a single stimulus. Also like habituation, sensitization serves an adaptive function. There are some aspects of the environment which are important for us to attend to. Often, these stimuli are harmful to us in some way. When a stronger tactile stimulus is applied to sea snails, on repeated presentation they

habituation A form of learning instantiated in a decrease in the strength of response to a repeated stimulus.

sensitization An increase in the strength of response to a repeated stimulus. Like habituation, sensitization is also classified as a simple learning mechanism as it occurs in response to only a single stimulus.

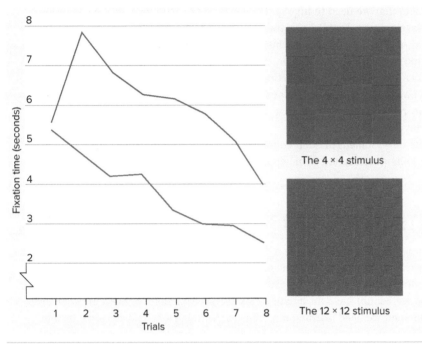

Figure 10-1 Stimuli examples and results

When a stimulus is interesting enough infants will initially sensitize to it (look for an increasing amount of time) and then later habituate. If the stimulus is less complex (in the case of the 4 × 4 grid), infants only show a pattern of habituation. Groves and Thompson (1970) argue that sensitization and habituation learning happen simultaneously.

will respond by withdrawing more parts of their body than they did initially (Kandel, 2004). The strength of their response increases on repeated presentation of the stimulus. This also happens when young infants view more complex visual stimuli, looking time increases on repeated presentations.

But what determines whether we habituate or sensitize to a stimulus? Groves and Thompson (1970) proposed that both sensitization and habituation happen at the same time, and compete to determine our behaviour. We can find corroboration for Groves and Thompson's (1970) theory when we look at young human infants' behaviour towards visual stimuli. As we saw in Chapter 6, infants' visual inspection of a stimulus usually habituates – they gradually look less and less (Fantz, 1964). However, if a stimulus is interesting enough, infants will first gradually increase in their looking towards it and then habituate (Bashinski, Werner, & Rudy, 1985; see Figure 10-1). This shows us that, in this case at least, both habituation and sensitization are at play; early on in learning sensitization has the greatest effect on behaviour (performance), whereas habituation wins later.

But why do we need habituation and sensitization? Both processes serve key adaptive functions. If an infant responded to every stimulus in its environment, it would rapidly become overwhelmed and exhausted. By learning not to respond (habituating) to uneventful familiar stimuli, infants conserve energy and can attend to other stimuli that are more important. However, there are clearly some situations where it is *not* useful for us to ignore stimuli – when we are learning a lot from them (e.g., when seeing a new person for the first time) or when they are a threat to our survival (e.g., if a blanket accidentally covers the face while an infant is in his cot).

Classical and operant conditioning

For years, psychologists have considered how early babies can learn and what they can learn through classical conditioning (Rovee-Collier & Gerhardstein, 1997). For a refresher on the mechanisms of classical conditioning, look at Figure 10-2, in which we depict the way a child might become conditioned to fear his doctor.

In Chapter 6 we described how newborns sleep a great deal more than later in development. Researchers have recently found that learning continues to happen during newborns' sleep.

Up until recently the evidence that newborns can learn by association or classical conditioning was somewhat limited. In one study some years ago now, babies as young as 2 hours old learned to associate a stroke on the head with delivery of a sugar solution to their mouths, until eventually the stroke alone elicited puckering and sucking responses (Blass, Ganchrow, & Steiner, 1984). However, newborns seem to have more difficulty learning associations that involve unpleasant stimuli, such as loud noises or things that are painful (Rovee-Collier, 1987).

Given the absence of strong evidence for the prevalence of classical conditioning in young infants (especially for negative), a number of writers have pondered whether classical conditioning may be less critical at an early age, because human

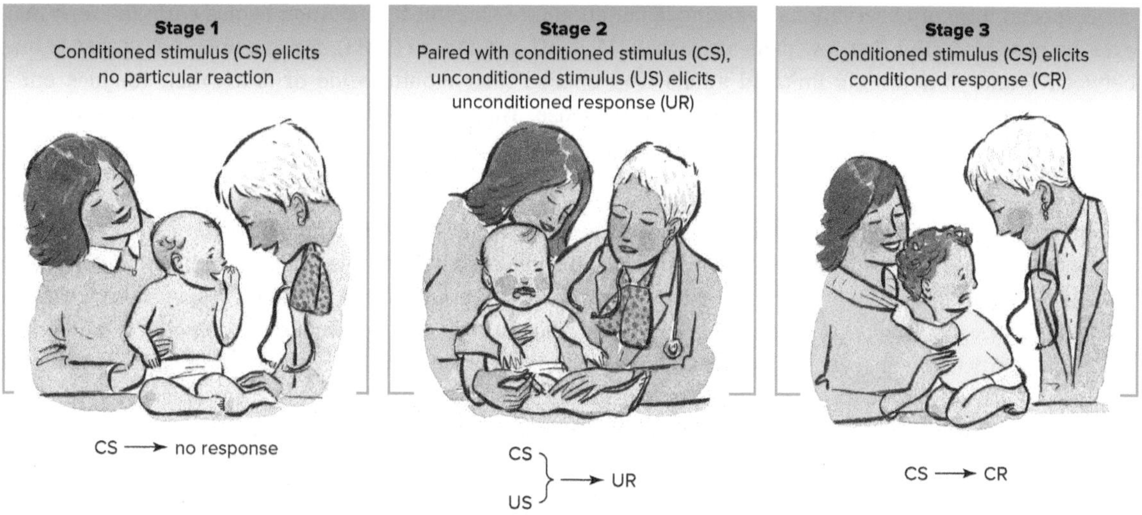

Figure 10-2   How a baby may be conditioned to fear a doctor

At their first meeting (stage 1), the baby may show no particular reaction to the doctor (the doctor is termed the conditioned stimulus, CS), but after the doctor (CS) gives the baby a painful injection (an unconditioned stimulus, US) that causes the baby to cry (an unconditioned response) (stage 2), the baby may learn to produce what is now a conditioned response (CR) of crying in the presence of the doctor (CS) (stage 3).

infants have parents to protect them (Rovee-Collier, 1987, 1999; Rovee-Collier & Shyi, 1992). However, recent findings have once more highlighted the importance of this means of learning in early life. Fifer et al. (2010) have demonstrated that newborns can learn to associate an eye-blink eliciting stimulus with the presentation of a tone. In the training group of babies a tone was presented just before a puff of air was made to one of the newborn's eyes. This led to conditioning whereby the tone by itself elicited an eye-blink response. Interestingly the researchers were able to demonstrate that this learning occurred even when the newborns were asleep (the puff of air was applied to the sleeping infants' eyelids, resulting in the same blink response; Tarullo et al., 2016). Given that newborns sleep a great deal (see Chapter 6), it may be that classical conditioning during sleep is particularly crucial to calibrate their body's physiological responses to the environment.

Operant conditioning is much easier to show in young infants. This learning situation involves learning to exhibit (or inhibit) a behavioural response to a stimulus because of the rewarding (or punishing) consequences it brings. Just as babies can be classically conditioned, they can also learn by operant conditioning (Gewirtz & Peláez-Nogueras, 1992). In some studies researchers condition infants to suck in response to seeing a particular stimulus by rewarding that sucking with a favourable stimulus (like an interesting cartoon moving on a screen). As in the case of classical conditioning, successful demonstrations of operant conditioning in newborns typically involve behaviours such as sucking or turning the head (related to the rooting reflex), behaviours that are components of feeding and thus of considerable importance to the baby's survival. Researchers take advantage of these early behaviours to investigate how infants learn specific behaviours.

Observational learning and imitation

Acquiring behaviours through classical or operant conditioning (displaying a behaviour, being rewarded, repeating the behaviour, being reinforced again, etc.) is uneconomical in terms of time and energy because, to be learned, the behaviour has to be experienced directly by the infant. Fortunately, infants are able to learn a great deal without any overt conditioning but simply by observing the behaviour of other people. As you learned in Chapter 2 (when we discussed Bandura's social learning theory) and in Chapter 9 (when we discussed social cognitive development), this is observational learning.

A special form of observational learning is imitation (see Chapter 9). Imitation begins early in life; it may even be possible in the first few days after birth. Meltzoff and Moore (1983), for example, found that babies between 7 and 72 hours old imitated adults who opened their mouths wide or stuck their tongues out – movements that are components of the sucking response. These findings are somewhat controversial.

THE NEONATAL IMITATION DEBATE

Recent studies have found it difficult to replicate the original newborn imitation findings (e.g., Jones, 2009; Oostenbroek et al., 2016), and others have argued that the most robust imitative skills which young infants seem to be showing are the result of processes other than imitation. For instance, Anisfeld (1996) has argued that an infant who sticks his tongue out at the sight of an adult doing the same thing may not be truly imitating another's behaviour, particularly as there is evidence that the sight of any protruding object may cause newborns to stick out their tongues. Perhaps this is not imitation but rather because the newborns see these objects as suckable. The response from the authors who originally published findings of neonatal imitation has been robust (Meltzoff et al., 2017). They view their results as accurate and replicable, but question whether the authors who failed to replicate their study (Oostenbroek et al., 2016) were using the optimal methods for eliciting imitative responses from young infants. Ooestenbroek et al. (in press) have, in their turn, questioned Meltzoff et al.'s critique of their methods. This is turning into a fascinating debate not just about the existence of neonatal imitation as a phenomenon, but about the use of methods more generally for inferring behavioural competence in newborn infants.

Irrespective of the current debate about neonatal imitation, it is clear that infants master imitation sooner or later (Meltzoff & Prinz, 2002). Six month olds can imitate a series of modelled behaviours (e.g.,

shaking plastic eggs filled with pebbles) immediately after seeing the behaviours, and 9 month olds can carry out these imitations both immediately after seeing them and after an interval of 24 hours, with no opportunity to practise the behaviours in between (Herbert, Gross, & Hayne, 2006). At 14 months of age, infants can delay (or defer) imitation for 1 week (Meltzoff, 1988), and between 14 and 18 months, they can not only defer imitation, but they can also generalize it to new settings. For example, children this age who saw a peer model a new behaviour at day care could imitate that behaviour 2 days later in their own homes (Hanna & Meltzoff, 1993). By 2 years of age, children can reproduce behaviours later even when the materials they use to carry out the behaviours have changed (Herbert & Hayne, 2000).

This man and his little son are playing an age-old game that's fun for dad and instructive for baby. Some theorists consider imitation to be a form of learning for which the human species is specialized.
© Shutterstock/Vitalinka

HOW DOES IMITATION DEVELOP AND WHAT IS IT FOR?

What mechanisms underlie the ability of babies to imitate behaviours that they see others perform? Meltzoff and Moore (2002) have argued that when newborns and older infants imitate behaviours they are engaging in something which they call *active intermodal matching* (AIM), in which the infant tries to match the feeling of a movement or gesture which they make with their face or hands, to the visual appearance of the observed movement or gesture. Meltzoff (2007) thinks that neonatal imitation through AIM is an innate adaptation of the human species which allows newborn infants access to the perspectives and minds of others. By imitating people they are able to empathize with their feelings, perspectives, and states of mind, providing a stepping stone into developing a fully fledged theory of mind (see Chapter 9).

> In Chapter 6 we discussed infants crossmodal abilities. These might be a fundamental ingredient in their ability to imitate.

In the context of the doubt surrounding findings of neonatal imitation, a number of alternatives to the active intermodal matching hypothesis have been proposed. Cecilia Heyes (e.g., Heyes, 2016) presents the argument that imitation can be learned associatively, through mechanisms like operant condition (see above), and that the learning of imitation in the context of social interactions is enough to explain its presence later in infancy. It is certainly an important point to make that imitation is a crucial learning mechanism through which infants, children, and indeed adults learn from others about what they can do in the world (Catmur & Heyes, 2017).

The usefulness of imitation for learning from the people around us has prompted some researchers to argue that we are not provided imitation as a means to perceive other people's mental states (Meltzoff, 2007), but rather as a means of making the best use possible from the people who surround us and offer advice about new ways to do things in the world. As we discussed at the end of Chapter 9, Csibra and Gergely (2009) have argued for an innate predisposition to learn from our social environment, a 'natural pedagogy', and they consider imitation as one of the means whereby this is achieved.

The idea that imitation serves the purpose of learning new behaviours from others, as proposed by the natural pedagogy account, is attractive for a number of reasons. Firstly, irrespective of whether the capacity to imitate has to be learned (Heyes, 2016) or is innately bestowed (Meltzoff & Moore, 2002), the drive to imitate is consistent with Bandura's broader social learning theory. Secondly, if imitation is an inherited ability, it is somehow more intuitive that it is inherited as a means of learning new actions, than of accessing mental states, as surely imitation is action. Lastly, the idea that imitation is for learning new ways of acting on the world, is a better way to account for some of the ways in which older children imitate. Gergely, Bekkering, and Király (2002) found that when 18-month-olds watch an adult undertake an unexplained (and palpably odd) action (bringing their head down to touch a book), they are more likely to imitate the precise action if the adult is able to use their hands rather than unable to use them (because their arms have restricted movement because of being wrapped under a shawl). Gergely et al.'s interpretation of this finding is that children have a drive to imitate actions if they are less able to find an explanation for them. If this is correct then it certainly supports the idea that imitation is for learning new ways of thinking about and acting on the world, rather than for placing oneself in the position of the person one is imitating.

Processes of learning, including habituation, sensitization, associative learning, observational learning and imitation are vital to human infants and children. They allow them to adapt to an ever-changing environment and make the best of the knowledge contained in the people surrounding them. Watson considered these learning abilities to be the most important function in human development. However, when the cognitive school arrived, emphases changed, and developmental psychologists began to consider the emergence of the internal workings of the mind in the absence of behaviour.

THE INFORMATION-PROCESSING ACCOUNT OF COGNITIVE DEVELOPMENT

Perhaps the most influential approach to understanding internal representations in adults and children was named the information-processing approach to the study of cognition. This approach, which came to the fore in the 1950s and 1960s was initially inspired by the emergence of computer technologies. And so information processing theorists often used the computer as an analogy for describing how the human mind works. In this account, the human mind, like a computer, is seen as an organized system that processes the information input that is presented to it, and through a set of computations transforms this into an appropriate output. Information processing theorists developed numerous models of cognitive functions such as memory, perception, attention, and executive function. A little later in the twentieth century developmental psychologists began adopting these models and the findings associated with them to examine the development of cognitive functions.

information processing approaches Theories of development that focus on the flow of information through the child's cognitive system and particularly on the specific operations the child performs between input and output phases.

An influential information-processing model of adult cognition, advanced in the early years of cognitive psychology, was Atkinson and Shiffrin's (1968) *modal model*. Atkinson and Shiffrin focused their model on the steps that the adult mind goes through as information is processed. As the modal model sets out these steps in a clear and systematic fashion it gives us a good jumping-off point for considering the development of various cognitive processes. The successor of the modal model, Baddeley and Hitch's *working memory* model was an advancement on the modal model, as it incorporated elements which captured the need for information processing resources to be flexibly and strategically deployed between different tasks. As we will see, the strategic 'central executive' component of the working memory model, absent in the modal model, is fairly crucial in capturing how cognitive development happens. However, we will also later consider a variety of more modern information-processing approaches that address more specifically the means by which information processing develops.

> **modal model** A model of information processing in which information moves through a series of organized processing units: *sensory register, short-term memory* and *long-term memory.* The modal model emphasizes the importance of storage capacity and duration.
>
> **sensory register** The mental processing unit that takes information from the environment and stores it in original form for brief periods of time.

Models of adult human information processing

The modal model (Atkinson & Shiffrin, 1968) describes how information enters and flows through the mind as it is processed. It describes information processing with a particular emphasis on the various types of storage systems that are involved (Figure 10-3). The first processing point involves the acquisition of information from the environment through our senses (see Chapter 6). This sensory information enters the system through the sensory register. In the modal model, this information in the sensory register is stored in its original form – that is, images are stored visually, sounds aurally, and so forth. This storage is very brief, lasting around a second only (Sperling, 1960).

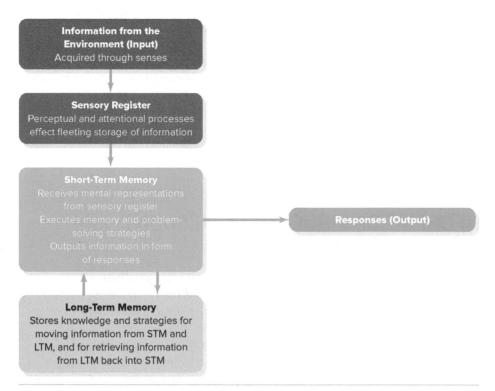

Figure 10-3   Atkinson and Shiffrin's (1968) modal model of information processing
A model of information processing that describes the flow of information through various stores of the cognitive system.
Note: The executive control process is discussed on pages 301-302.
Source: Based on Atkinson and Shiffrin (1968)

In the next step of processing in the modal model, information in the sensory register is transformed, or encoded, into a mental representation and then placed in the storage area referred to as short-term memory. Short-term memory can best be thought of as the conscious 'work space' of the mind (Bjorklund, 2005). Atkinson and Shiffrin characterized the short-term store as being limited with regard to the number of meaningful units or chunks of information that it can hold at any one time, as well as how long it can hold this information for, without any active effort to retain it. Without a specific effort, such as rehearsal, we generally lose information from short-term memory within 15 to 30 seconds (Brown, 1958; Peterson & Peterson, 1959).

Long-term memory is the term used to describe knowledge that is retained over a long period of time. Long-term memory contains episodic information about events (e.g., what I did on my 16th birthday) and more general *semantic* information about the world including things like vocabulary, rules, types of problems and ways to solve them. According to the modal mode, information transferred from short- to long-term memory can be retained for an indefinite period of time.

From the modal model to the working memory model

Because the modal model put such a great emphasis on storage parameters such as capacity and duration of storage, the first researchers to consider development in the context of information processing models naturally asked whether capacity changes over development. Such considerations were particularly important at the time, as many researchers (e.g., Bryant & Trabasso, 1971) were discovering that children would perform much better at Piagetian tasks if the storage demands were reduced. Researchers focused particularly on the capacity of the sensory and short-term stores. We will discuss these kinds of development later in our treatment of memory development. However, to cut a long story short, it turned out that the major developments in memory abilities appeared not to be so much in terms of the capacity and duration of short term memory, but rather in terms of the kinds of rehearsal strategies that children employed to enhance their storage abilities (e.g., Hitch & Towse, 1995).

The realization that cognitive development may be more about the acquisition of *ways of processing information* (e.g., using retention strategies like rehearsal) prompted a shift of focus towards the more recently developed working memory model (Baddeley & Hitch, 1974; Baddeley, 2012; Figure 10-4). The working memory does not emphasize stores, but rather cognitive 'thinking' processes which act on the information that the human is working with currently. Two important components of the working memory model are the

short-term memory
The mental processing unit in which information is stored temporarily; the 'work space' of the mind, where a decision is made to discard information, work on it or transfer it to permanent storage in *long-term memory.*

long-term memory
The mental processing unit in which information may be stored permanently, and from which it may later be retrieved.

working memory model Baddeley and Hitch's (1974) model of human information processing, which emphasizes dynamic thought processes rather than more basic parameters like storage duration and capacity.

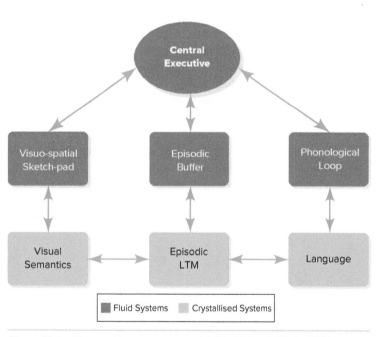

Figure 10-4 *The working memory model (Baddeley & Hitch, 1974)*
The working memory model replaced the modal model as a means of understanding human information processing. Notice the important role of the central executive. Changes in the central executive are better at explaining children's cognitive development than storage capacity changes.
Source: Based on Baddeley (2012).

visuospatial sketch-pad
A 'slave system' in the working memory model which deals with visual-spatial representations.

phonological loop
A 'slave system' in the working memory model that deals with speech sound information.

central executive
The overarching controller in the working model, which regulates the action of the various slave systems. This is similar to the concept of executive function.

visuospatial sketch-pad and the phonological loop. The visuospatial sketch-pad, as the name suggests, deals with visual information (e.g., imagine the shape of an object and you are using your visuospatial sketch-pad). The phonological loop deals with speech sounds (rehearse a phone number in your mind and that is your phonological loop in action). According to Baddeley and Hitch these 'slave systems' are controlled by the central executive, which controls and regulates the use of various thought processes. Today, much more emphasis is placed on the development of executive control, and thinking strategies rather than absolute measures of storage or capacity (although we will return to this when we cover memory). We will next discuss the development of the involvement of executive processes and strategies in cognitive functions.

A note on cognitive models and why they are helpful

You might be wondering at this point why we are talking about box and arrow 'models' based on musings about how computers work. Surely the brain is not a set of boxes and arrows, and likewise surely children do not think about the world like computers do. Well you probably have two good points. However, the strength of models is that they formalize our views of what the human and her brain needs to be able to do. Despite using our brains all the time, it is remarkably difficult for us to describe precisely what it is that we are doing when we're thinking. Cognitive psychologists have expended huge amounts of effort in attempting to put down their ideas about how the brain works onto paper. And so even if they turn out to be wrong it might be polite to hear them out. Even so, one of the great things about formal models like the modal model or the working memory model is that they do not have to be correct to be useful. Models make predictions, occasionally quite counterintuitive predictions, which can be tested with experiments. Even if a model turns out to be incorrect, which they often do, at least we now know they are incorrect and can now move on to the next model.

'OK,' you say, 'Fair enough. These models may be useful for cognitive psychologists. But what do they do for those of us who are interested in how cognitive abilities develop?' Well, as we said at the beginning of the chapter, we do actually as developmental psychologists need to understand what development is heading towards. Without that how can we figure out what questions to ask? But importantly, and this is often forgotten, this is not all about what cognitive psychologists can teach developmental psychologists. Development can also feature in models of cognitive functions. If our model of how the brain works could not possibly fit with the ways in which children develop their abilities to learn and reason, then it may be time to come up with another model.

And so developmental research is also crucial for understanding how it is that information is processed, even in the mature brain. We can see this clearly in the transition between the modal model and the working memory model. Findings about how memory abilities seemed to develop in childhood made researchers realize that there is probably more to memory than stores with particular durations and capacities. The biggest changes in memory abilities in childhood seem to be due to changes in executive control over cognitive strategies.

THE DEVELOPMENT OF EXECUTIVE FUNCTIONS AND COGNITIVE STRATEGIES

As we discussed in the last section, there appear to be some important changes in the ways children think about and control the information they are processing. Indeed, changes in the way we think about information appear to be more important than changes in more basic parameters of information processing like storage capacity and duration. But what are these changes in 'thinking'? Developmental psychologists refer to such processes in a range of ways. When talking about memory, these ways of thinking to improve memory performance are sometimes referred to as cognitive strategies (Pressley & Hilden, 2006). More recently, the use of cognitive strategies has been linked with a broader concept of executive function (sometimes referred to as executive control or cognitive control).

What is executive function? This is actually a rather difficult question to answer. Psychologists have been using the term executive function since around the 1970s. For instance, in Baddeley and Hitch's (1974) working memory model, the *central executive* was the overarching controller of the working memory system, determining and regulating the action of the various memory slave systems. So executive function has something to do with controlling. Actually these days researchers tend to describe executive functions as an umbrella term for various processes involved in controlling our information processing and behaviours. Executive functions include inhibition, planning, means-end coordination, task switching, attentional control and it is also probably substantially involved in problem solving. But what groups all of these functions together? First, as we have indicated, these functions all involve the regulation and control of information processing and behaviour. Secondly, many of these processes are substantially governed by a particular area of the brain: the pre-frontal cortex.

> cognitive strategies
> Cognitive activities used to enhance mental performance.
>
> executive function
> A cognitive system that is presumed to control and manage other cognitive processes.

As we discussed in Chapter 5, the prefrontal cortex is one of the last areas of the brain to fully mature, continuing to develop into adolescence and even early adulthood. Developmental psychologists think that the development of prefrontal cortical function is associated with improvements across a wide range of different tasks and competencies. Executive functions impinge, for instance, on social interactions, mathematics, memory and spatial navigation. Let's look at a few examples of this.

How does executive function affect development?

We'll start with short-term memory, which we'll refer to as working memory from this point given that our discussions of it will be largely structured around Baddeley and Hitch's working memory model. As we discussed in the last section, one of the particular advantages of the working memory model is that it includes a set of processes which can be deployed strategically by the central executive, and that the development of these systems better captures what improves in children's memory than did previous models which emphasized the storage capacity and duration of working memory (or short-term memory as it was referred to in that context). Let's see how this played out.

SHORT-TERM MEMORY DEVELOPMENT: IMPROVEMENTS IN CAPACITY OR EXECUTIVE FUNCTION?

Suppose you are asked to repeat a sequence of numbers beginning with three digits and then progressively more numbers are added. Eventually, you will be unable to repeat all the numbers correctly, for the sequence will have exceeded your memory span for this kind of information. The number of items of information that a person can keep in working memory at any one time is limited, but that limit changes with development. For example, memory span for a series of numbers (digit span) is about eight units for university students, six or seven units for 12 year olds, and four units for 5 year olds (Starr, 1923; Brener, 1940; Gathercole, 1999). However, there is an important problem in how we interpret these developments in short-term memory. Is it capacity that is improving with development or is something else changing? As we discussed in Chapter 2, the so-called Neo-Piagetian theorists explained improvements in memory span by appealing to increases in the number of items which could be stored in working (short-term) memory with development (Pascual-Leone, 1989).

> memory span   The amount of information one can hold in short-term memory.

However, findings emerged that did not support the idea of capacity change in development. For instance, Dempster (1985) showed that young children can remember more items from lists of things that interest them (e.g., toys). Such findings demonstrate that interest or motivation plays a role in memory span, and capacity changes may not be necessary to explain changes associated with age (Lindberg, 1980).

And so another possibility is that older children's and adults' greater memory span may be explained by better executive control of short-term memory capacity rather than its limits *per se*. What do we mean, though, by executive control of short-term memory? Let's think again about memory span tasks. One way to improve

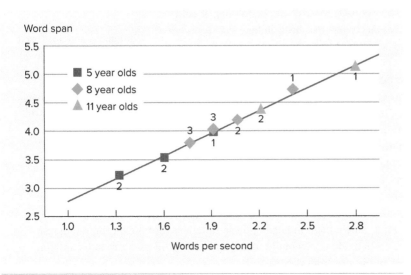

Figure 10-5   Memory skills improve with age

Experimenters asked children in three age groups to memorize a list of words. The older the child, the faster she could pronounce the words in rehearsing them, and the more words she could retain in working memory. (Numbers by data points indicate number of syllables in the word.) For example, 11 year olds could pronounce 2.8 single-syllable words per second and could remember about five single-syllable words, whereas 5 year olds could pronounce 1.9 single-syllable words per second and could remember about four single-syllable words.

Source: Adapted from Siegler and Aliball (2005).

short-term memory might be to employ strategies for encoding the information. For instance, in many cases adults organize or 'chunk' the information to be remembered into smaller, more easily remembered groups of numbers (Miller, 1956). Thus, whereas the young child may not be able to remember the sequence 1 4 9 2 1 7 7 6 1 8 1 2 because it is too long, the adult can recall the sequence because she chunks the numbers into meaningful groups: 1492, 1776, 1812. So, awareness of strategies, and deployment of them can improve short-term memory. Notice here that in order to use strategies for improving memory (in this case chunking) we need to have some understanding of the limits of our memory abilities. We will talk about this more later when we cover metacognition later in this chapter.

Another way in which children become better at storing information in short-term memory is through becoming better at rehearsing. Rehearsal involves repeating the information to be remembered, either mentally or out loud. Rehearsal has been shown to be very important in adults' short-term memory, but it is also predictive of children's short-term memory span. For instance, Hitch and Towse (1995) demonstrated that development in rehearsal abilities may account for much of the development in short-term memory across early childhood (see Figure 10-5).

> **rehearsal**   A memory strategy in which one repeats a number of times the information one wants to remember, either mentally or orally.

So, as we can see, the deployment of memory strategies benefits children's short-term memory abilities. Another key way in which working memory can be enhanced is through the application of knowledge from long-term memory. Having more knowledge about the world enables us to sort items into groups for instance, among other strategies. The use of long-term memory strategies to enhance working memory is pervasive in adults and older children. We will discuss a number of these in the next section, including elaboration and organization. Overall, then, a greater executive ability to plan and strategize appears to help their memory performance. But executive functions help us with more than just memory. Before we move on to look at some tasks which measure executive functions, let's look at another domain of cognitive development in which emerging executive control plays an important role: number, counting and maths.

NUMBER, COUNTING AND MATHS

In recent years, researchers have been surprised by the competence which young infants appear to show in representing number, and even in undertaking some basic arithmetic.

In a famous study by Wynn (1992), 5-month-old infants were shown simple subtraction and addition events (see Figure 10-6). For instance, in the 2–1 subtraction event, two objects were shown on a stage. Then a screen came up covering both objects, and a hand moved in behind the screen so that the infants saw it removing one of the objects. Then the screen came down to reveal either one object (which is the 'possible' outcome which we should expect), or the screen came down to reveal two objects (which is the 'impossible'

Do infants know that 2 - 1 = 1?

Steps 1 to 4

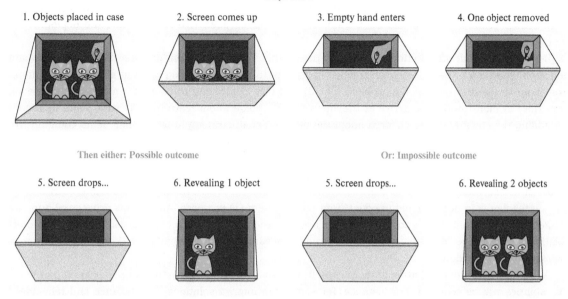

1. Objects placed in case   2. Screen comes up   3. Empty hand enters   4. One object removed

Then either: Possible outcome   Or: Impossible outcome

5. Screen drops...   6. Revealing 1 object   5. Screen drops...   6. Revealing 2 objects

Figure 10-6   Infants understand addition and subtraction

Five-month-old infants watch the sequence of events shown in steps 1 to 4. Then in step 5 they witness a 'possible' or 'impossible' event. Infants stare longer at the impossible event, suggesting that they were expecting only one object and are surprised to see two objects still there. In other words, they understand that 2 – 1 should equal 1. In another experiment, in steps 1 to 4, infants watch one object being added to another object. Then the screen is raised and lowered, revealing either two objects ('possible event') or just one object ('impossible event'). Once again, infants stare longer at the impossible event, suggesting that they understand that 1 + 1 should equal 2.
Source: Adapted from Wynn (1992).

outcome which we should not expect). In this 'violation of expectation' task, the 5 month olds looked longer at the impossible outcome for 2–1 events, 2+1 events, and 1+1 events, with the conclusion that at this tender age they were able to add and subtract.

However, as we have discussed in Chapter 9, there are some concerns with violation of expectation methods in that infants' looking preferences for particular scenes could be driven by other factors than a preference for the unexpected. These concerns have certainly been raised regarding Wynn's study (Cohen & Marks, 2002; Wakeley et al., 2000). However, recent eye tracking studies have shed some more light on this issue, showing that when infants observe possible and impossible arithmetical events their pattern of looking seems to show that they are intent on tracking the location and existence of all hidden objects in the scene (Bremner et al., 2017). This suggests that infants have a rudimentary ability with maths on small numbers of physical objects, but does not confirm Wynn's suggestion that young infants have an adult-like symbolic understanding of addition and subtraction.

Infants also have a sense of larger numbers at an early age. For instance, Starr et al. (2013), showed 6-month-old infants two screens which showed changes in pictures of arrays of different objects. On one side, the kinds of objects being shown, as well as the number of objects changed from screen to screen. On the other side, just the kinds of objects being shown and not the number of them changed from screen to screen. Starr et al. (2013) showed that the 6-month-olds would look longer at the screen where the number of objects was changing. They also showed that the infants' preference scores for the changing number screen versus the unchanging number screen predicted their maths and number abilities at 3.5 years of age when the same children were tested later in a longitudinal study. This relationship held true even when taking account of the different children's IQs. So it seems that early abilities in infancy to perceive numbers plays a role in numeracy and maths later in development.

Nonetheless, as any primary school teacher will be able to tell you, children do not just turn up at school able to count and do sums. So there seems to be something other than number discrimination and the basic conceptual understanding of addition and subtraction which explains the development of numeracy in the early school years. One important contributor to this is likely executive function and the deployment of cognitive strategies.

Let's look at children's addition as an illustration of this. When we present younger children with an addition problem such as 3 + 14, they will frequently attempt to solve it by using a 'count all' strategy, counting from 1 up to the first term of the problem (i.e., 3) and then continuing to count the number of the second term (i.e., 14 more) until they arrive at the answer of 17. Some might learn to start with 3 and then count on, adding the other 14. Older children adopt the more efficient strategy in which they begin counting from the larger of the two addends (14) and continue upwards, adding the amount of the smaller number, thus counting '14, 15, 16, 17' to arrive at the answer. The use of these strategies, as with memory span, is likely to be dependent on executive functions. For instance, one of the many abilities which are included under the umbrella of executive functions is *inhibition*. When children first learn to count, the obvious starting point for any teacher is to get the child to count from the first item (1) upwards. And so this procedural approach is likely to be invoked when addition problems are first encountered. As such, in order to learn to add efficiently, children have to inhibit previously learned procedures such as counting all, or counting from the lowest of the two addends.

As children get older and attempt more complicated sums, it seems likely that a greater variety of executive abilities will be required. For instance, for sums with interim solutions, maintenance and rehearsal in working memory is likely to be required to store the interim solution while carrying out the next steps. In addition, switching tasks between holding a number in mind in working memory and carrying out a mental computation on it is another taxing load on executive control (Bull & Lee, 2014).

And so, despite the surprising competence which infants appear to show with number and mathematics described above, it seems likely that the more gradual development of numeracy skills at school is due to the more extended development of executive functions (Cragg et al., 2017). Cragg and Gilmore (2014) outline a number of ways in which executive functions are likely to be involved in the development of numeracy and argue that the interface between executive function and mathematics needs closer attention in research and in the classroom.

And so, in line with the working memory model and its emphasis on executive control, it has become clear that the strategic deployment of information processing resources is one of the most important means by which children develop their cognitive abilities. We will discuss a numner of other areas in which executive functions play a role in cognitive development in the next section. For instance, selective attention, the strategic selection of which information to process in the first place, is intimately tied up with executive functions. First of all, though, let's take a look at the development of executive functions themselves in a bit more detail.

Executive functions

As we mentioned at the start of this chapter, executive functions include such functions as inhibition, working memory planning, means–end coordination, task switching, and attentional control. These functions are grouped together under this heading because: (a) they all involve the regulation and control of information processing and behaviour; and (b) they are substantially governed by the pre-frontal cortex.

THE DEVELOPMENT OF EXECUTIVE FUNCTION IN EARLY CHILDHOOD

Perhaps the most widely used measure of executive function in young children is the Dimension Change Card Sort task (DCCS; Zelazo, Frye, & Rapus, 1996; Kirkham, Cruess & Diamond, 2003). In this task, children are asked to sort cards that vary on two dimensions (e.g., red cars and blue rabbits) into piles according to one of those dimensions. For instance, the experimenter may ask the children to sort the cards first by colour. Children of 3 years can typically manage this quite well. After successfully sorting the cards by the first dimension, they are asked to switch to sorting by a second dimension (e.g., by shape not colour). Even though 3-year-old children know how to sort by shape (they are good at answering questions about this), they have a much harder time switching their sorting to that new rule. By 4 years, children are typically able to switch their sorting rule.

What makes tasks of executive function so difficult for young children? Well, one thing which might be challenging is that tasks like the DCCS involve more than one function at the same time. In this task, children have to hold the rules in *working memory*, they have to *switch* between playing by one set of rules and another, and they have to *inhibit* sorting the cards according to the rule they have just switched from.

Developmentalists disagree a great deal about just what it is that makes the DCCS tricky for children. Some have suggested that children have difficulty thinking about and selecting the two different rules (sort by shape, sort by colour; Zelazo, 2004; Simpson & Riggs, 2005). In agreement with this interpretation Box 10-1 describes a study indicating that children may be much better at tasks of executive function if they do not involve rules.

Others think that the children have no difficulty understanding and selecting the rules in the DCCS, but simply cannot stop doing something which they have started doing (they cannot *inhibit* the first sorting rule). What is *inhibition*? Inhibition is a cognitive process also thought to be subserved by the frontal lobe of the brain. It certainly improves in early life also. A famous test of inhibition in young children is the 'day–night' task (Gerstadt, Hong, & Diamond, 1994; Carlson & Moses, 2001; Simpson & Riggs, 2005). In this simple task an experimenter shows children a picture of a shining sun, or a moon surrounded by stars. The children's task is to say 'day' when they see the moon and stars, and 'night' when they see the sun. They have to inhibit what they would normally say and say the opposite. Between 3 and 5 years children also improve markedly on this task.

So – who is right? Modern thinking is that both inhibition and an ability to manipulate rules are related cognitive functions that develop at a similar time (Garon, Bryson, & Smith, 2008). Developments in executive control have wide-reaching implications on children's abilities. Some researchers have argued that these developments in executive control can explain why children get better at the *false belief* task of *theory of mind* as they get older (Carlson & Moses, 2001; Perner, Kloo, & Gornik, 2007; see Chapter 9).

> In Chapter 9 we discussed how children get better at false belief tests of theory of mind between 3 and 4 years of age. Some researchers think that these improvements are due to the development of executive control.

BOX 10-1 Two year olds can show cognitive control so long as they are not dealing with rules

Research close-up

Source: Based on Bremner et al. (2007).

Introduction:

As you have just read, some researchers have argued that the development of executive function in young children is particularly linked to their improving abilities to think about and select rules (Zelazo, 2004; Simpson & Riggs, 2005). This has been used to explain why young children (before 4 years of age) have difficulty switching a rule by which they are sorting cards in the DCCS task (Zelazo et al., 1996). Bremner and colleagues therefore reasoned that if the requirement to think about rules was taken away then young children should be better able to control their behaviours. They therefore developed a task like the DCCS where children learn one behaviour first, but then have to switch to a different behaviour. The key difference from the DCCS is that the behaviours children had to control were not based on rules they knew but on patterns of movement of the hand which they learned from the experimenter in an incidental way (i.e., they were not asked explicitly to learn these patterns of movements).

Method:

Sixty 2 year olds took part in the study. They were told that they were about to play a chasing game with a cat and dog. The experimenter picked up a model cat and placed it on one of four squares on a play-board (see Fig. 10-7), and then encouraged the child to chase the cat with a model dog to that same location. The experimenter then repeated this, but secretly followed a specific pattern of movement around the board (like 132412..132412..132412..). After the child had followed this repeating pattern several times the experimenter told them that the cat had been going a special way. Then the experimenter asked the child to this time be the cat and either run the same way as before around the board or to go a different way. This way the children were asked to generate a sequence of movements which was the same as what they had just learned or a different sequence. This requires an ability to exert control over a learned behaviour.

The graph shows that the children were able to respond to instructions to repeat the sequence of movements they had just learned (inclusion), or to produce a different sequence of movements (exclusion).

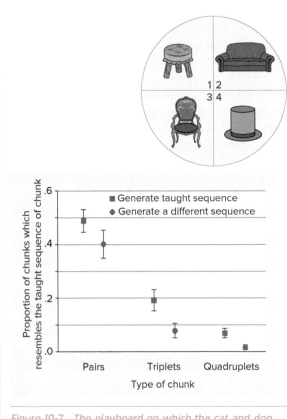

Results:

The experimenters analysed the sequences that the children had generated, looking for little segments of the sequence which resembled the taught sequence or which deviated from it. For example, if the children had been taught the sequence: 1-3-2-4-1-2-..1-3-2-4-1-2-.., then if they generated segments like 3-2 (a pair), or 2-4-1 (a triplet), then those would be classed as parts of the taught sequence. But if they generated segments like 4-3, or 3-1-4 then these would be classed as parts of a different sequence. Remarkably, the 2-year-olds were able to respond to the experimenter's instructions and either generate a sequence which was similar to that which they had learned, or produce a different sequence.

Discussion:

These findings show that even at the tender age of 2 years children are able to exert some executive control over their knowledge and behaviour in response to instructions. This stands in contrast to tasks like the DCCS which children have difficulty with until 4 years of age. Bremner et al. (2007) argued that the thing which makes this task easier for young children was that they did not have to deal with and think about rules.

Figure 10-7   The playboard on which the cat and dog chased around in Bremner et al.'s task

Source: Bremner et al. (2007)

PRECURSORS OF EXECUTIVE FUNCTION IN INFANCY

You might be forgiven for thinking, at this stage, that infants in their first year of life might have considerable difficulty with anything to do with executive control. However, some researchers have studied precursors to executive control in young infants. One particular task has come from Piaget's studies of young infants – this is the cloth pulling task. Remember that in Chapter 9, we described how Piaget considered means–end coordination to be an important acquisition in the sensorimotor period of development (the first two years of life). Means–end coordination requires infants, children or adults for that matter to recognize that a particular action can given rise to a particular occurrence or an event. In fact, means–end coordination is rather like an executive function task; it requires children or infants to inhibit their response to a goal and to focus on a subgoal. The cloth-pulling task was originally used by Piaget (1952), but has been developed by Willatts (1999). In this the infant is presented with an object which he or she would like to get hold of, for example, some shiny-looking keys. However, the keys are out of reach. Fortunately for the infant they have been placed on top of a cloth, and the infant can reach the edge of the cloth. If they can pull the cloth towards them, then that subgoal (means), will enable them to reach their goal (ends – the keys). Willatts (1999) observed that purposeful means–end coordination in this task emerges at around 8 months of age.

So, even though executive control develops substantially between 3 and 4 years of age, it appears that infants are laying down the ground-work in terms of means–end coordination well before that.

> **executive control process** A cognitive process that serves to control, guide and monitor the success of a problem-solving approach a child uses.

THE DEVELOPMENT OF EXECUTIVE FUNCTIONS INTO ADOLESCENCE AND ADULTHOOD

A recent focus of research has been the continued development of executive functions into adolescence and beyond, even into early adulthood. This has largely come about from observations that structural and functional changes in the brain, particularly in prefrontal areas, continue to take place well into adolescence and beyond (Blakemore, 2008; Blakemore & Choudhury, 2006; Giedd, 2004; Crone, 2009).

Compared with infancy and early childhood, overall brain growth slows from late childhood to adolescence (Sowell et al., 2001). Nonetheless, there are considerable increases in the myelination of neurons, in the establishment of new neural connections while at the same time pruning away of over-abundant synaptic connections formed during earlier years of explosive brain growth (Blakemore, 2008; Gogtay et al., 2004).

Neural restructuring is especially prominent in the prefrontal cortex and the limbic system, regions that play a key role in executive functions, and in controlling behaviours that satisfy motivational goals. As well as attempting to understand how these continued brain changes impact on executive functioning as well as a range of other cognitive abilities such as social perspective taking, psychologists are actively exploring how the interaction between social development and more slowly emerging executive functions might provide a basis for explaining the increase in risky behaviours (e.g., drug use, sensation seeking and aggression) which is often seen in adolescence (Blakemore & Choudhury, 2006; Braams, van Leijenhorst, & Crone, 2014; Steinberg, 2007).

One current line of research is investigating whether the brain and neural changes seen in adolescence are driven by the hormonal changes which come with puberty. Research shows that there are significant variations between individuals in both the timing of puberty and the ways in which the brain changes during adolescence (Foulkes & Blakemore, 2018). It also seems to be the case that pubertal stage is more strongly related to changes in brain structure than age is during adolescence (Blakemore, Burnett, & Dahl, 2010). The next stages in this field will be to undertake large-scale studies to investigate how changes in the brain are related to individual adolescent's circumstances, both hormonal and in their social environments.

How do executive functions and cognitive strategies develop?

So what developmental processes give rise to the emergence of an ability to control our behaviour and mental processes? This is a very difficult question to answer on the basis of what we currently know. One line of argument is that executive control somehow comes about through the maturation of prefrontal cortex (e.g., Diamond, 1988). However, this glosses over the question of how experience plays a role in the emergence of flexible behaviour and thought. One clue about this might come from Piaget. Although the term 'executive functions' was not being used during Piaget's time, we might consider his description of the origins of domain-general flexible (reversible) thinking in childhood (see Chapter 9), and means–end coordination in sensorimotor behaviour in infancy (see above) to capture much of what is involved in executive control of thought. As such, we might infer that Piaget's account of the origins of executive control might well explain this as an outcome of the child's active assimilation and accommodation of the environment and their progressively better organization of sensorimotor and mental schemas.

An important consideration is also how emerging executive abilities enable us to become ever more efficient thinkers and problem solvers. One perspective on executive functions is to argue that these provide us with cognitive strategies which decrease the load on the child's and later the adult's information-processing system by increasing its efficiency and thus freeing up space for the various tasks necessary for solving the problem. This is the question of how cognitive strategies become automatized.

AUTOMATIZATION AND GENERALIZATION OF COGNITIVE STRATEGIES

automatization The process of transforming conscious, controlled behaviours into unconscious and automatic ones.

script A mental representation of an event or situation of daily life, including the order in which things are expected to happen and how one should behave in that event or situation.

generalization The application of a strategy learned while solving a problem in one situation to a similar problem in a new situation.

Automatization involves making behaviours that once were conscious and controlled into unconscious and automatic ones. The transition from conscious to unconscious thinking enables children to free up resources so that cognitive tasks happen more efficiently. A good example of automatization is an adult learning to drive a car with a gear stick. At first, every gear shift is slow, with the driver concentrating on each aspect of shifting so as to get it right. With practice, however, the driver can shift gears quickly and efficiently, unaware of the individual steps involved and often unaware of shifting altogether. In the same way, the child who has developed a memorization strategy for calculating simple addition or multiplication problems is able, in time, to use this strategy without thinking about it (Siegler & Alibali, 2005). For example, a child who has memorized the mathematical formula that $2 + 2 = 4$ can use this stored knowledge in giving a quick answer to the question 'What is $2 + 2$?' In contrast, a child who hasn't memorized the formula may have to stop, think, and perhaps count on his fingers ($[1 + 1] + [1 + 1]$) to figure out the answer.

One of the ways in which we automatize our cognitive abilities is through the use of scripts. If we had to figure out, entirely on our own, what to do in every situation that is repeated day after day (e.g., bathing, dressing and eating meals) we would have little time or energy to devote to new events and activities. Scripts provide basic outlines of what one can expect in a particular situation and what one should do in that situation (Schank & Abelson, 1977; Nelson, 1993). Scripts function as a cognitive tool by freeing up space in the information-processing system so that an individual can pay attention to new or unexpected information that might come up within the course of a routine activity. As such, scripts function as an automatization tool that also helps organize children's memory and expectations of events. Over the course of development, they are increasingly part of the information that guides children's behaviour.

Initially, the strategies that children develop to solve a given problem tend to be quite specific to the task at hand. Through the process of generalization, children apply a strategy learned while solving a problem in one situation to a similar problem in a new situation. Generalization does not happen overnight, though, and children may need to gain familiarity with the use of a rule, using it many times over, before they can successfully generalize it to new situations. Suppose, for example, that the child who used the min rule in the earlier addition problem had arrived at this solution in school. Coming home after school, he finds that his mother has bought some jelly beans, and he decides to count the jelly beans so that he and his brother will have the same number of sweets. Even though he applied the min rule successfully at school, now that he is presented with a set of concrete objects – a different situation – he may revert to the less sophisticated and more time-consuming strategy of counting all the items. However, with time and experience, the more general use of a strategy across problem situations occurs.

And so, through automatization and generalization, we become more efficient thinkers, capitalizing on the hard work with which we have used our executive control in development to construct and select successful cognitive strategies.

DEVELOPMENTAL CHANGES IN SOME SIGNIFICANT COGNITIVE ABILITIES

In this section, we consider what has been learned about the development of some important cognitive abilities when they have been studied using an information-processing approach. These abilities include attention, memory, problem solving and reasoning. As you will see, the emerging executive functions which we discussed in the last section have a considerable role to play in the development of most cognitive abilities.

Attention

A group of children in the same situation do not necessarily take in the same information. Each child's attention may be focused on different aspects of the environment. Attention involves the identification and selection of particular sensory input for more detailed processing. For example, one child in a classroom who is focusing on the teacher will hear and understand the lesson, but another child who is more interested in a whispered message from a classmate may focus on that sound and regard the teacher's voice as background noise. How children's experiences affect them depends on what aspects of a situation children attend to and what meaning this information has for them. Attention is a complex process that can be divided into voluntary (controlled) and involuntary (automatic) components. The voluntary aspects of attention are particularly related to executive function. And so as you might expect given our discussion of executive functions in the last section, children have particular difficulty controlling the voluntary aspects of their attention when they are young, but this improves significantly through childhood, adolescence and into early adulthood (Waszak et al., 2010).

> **attention** The identification and selection of particular sensory input for more detailed processing.

LEARNING TO SHIFT ATTENTION IN INFANCY

Attention needs to be controlled in terms of where (and to what) we direct it, but we also need to be able to sustain it for a given period of time. Very young children can sustain their attention for only short periods. However, this ability increases steadily over development (Ruff & Rothbart, 1996). Interestingly, in the first months of life, young infants seem to have the opposite problem. They occasionally demonstrate 'sticky fixation' (sometimes referred to as 'obligatory attention'; Hood, 1995), a phenomenon in which they are unable to divert their attention away from something they are looking at, even if it is a very boring thing to look at.

During the first year of life, there are a number of changes in the flexibility with which infants can shift their attention. Between 2 and 3 months of age, the infant becomes more adept at disengaging their attention. Also, the focus of the infant's attention shifts from the external contours of objects towards their internal features (Colombo, 2001). Other attentional skills that infants gain during this period are an ability to smoothly track moving objects with their eyes and an ability to anticipate the appearance of a visual object with an eye-movement to where it is about to appear (Canfield & Haith, 1991). When explaining these early developments in attention researchers have often appealed to the maturation of cortical areas of the brain (Atkinson, 1984; Johnson, 2010; Richards, 2010)

A crucial aspect of attentional development is becoming able to attend to (select) perceptual objects or features which are relevant to what we are doing right now. An ability to shift attention in a way which is not just driven by the salience of objects and features in our environments is evident as early as 2 to 3 months of age. Whereas neonates may look longer at an object just because it is larger or brighter than another object, by 2 to 3 months of age, infants begin to select what to look at based more on the form or pattern of the information (Ruff & Rothbart, 1996; Colombo, 2001).

THE DEVELOPMENT OF VOLUNTARY ATTENTION IN CHILDHOOD

Research has shown that, in the school years, children improve markedly in their ability to focus and refocus their attention on task-relevant information. In one recent study, investigators (Cavallina et al., 2018), based on a well-known set of tasks (e.g., Enns, Brodeur, & Trick, 1998; Posner & Petersen, 1990) gave children a visual search task in which they had to search for a target (e.g., a cartoon dog's face) in amongst a cluttered cartoon scene. Before the scene was presented an auditory sound was presented just beforehand which was either on the same side as the subsequent target, or on a different side (this was called an invalid cue trial). The children and adults all performed better at searching for the target when the sound was on the correct side. However, the children (6 and 10 year olds) were particularly impaired compared to adults on the invalid cue trials when the sound occurred on the wrong side.

So, taking control of our attention, and shifting it away from salient but irrelevant information seems to be something which develops significantly across childhood. This is very likely due to the executive control which is needed to master these kinds of voluntary attentional skills. As Figure 10-8 shows, the processing

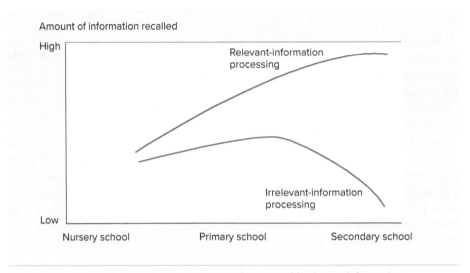

Figure 10-8 Children's changing attention to relevant and irrelevant information
Children steadily increase their attention to relevant information, but their concern with irrelevant information weakens and drops off quickly after primary school age.

CHRONOLOGY OF DEVELOPMENT
Some cognitive achievements as seen from the information-processing view

Age	Achievements
1 month	Still gaining control of eye movements – has difficulty disengaging fixation Able to remember sounds and visual patterns across several hours' delay
12 months	Can store the same number of items as adults in sensory memory Can plan a means–end sequence of action to retrieve an object Able to anticipate the appearance of objects with anticipatory fixations with the eyes
2 years	May be able to use basic category labels to help remember things May be able to draw very simple analogies Can correctly relocate objects after multiple hiding events, and long delays.
3 years	Can use two rules in combination Often distractible; when attention is fully engaged, may be quite attentive May use analogies in solving a problem Understands relations between scale models and real objects
4 years	Can combine two or more rules into a higher-order rule and shift between two tasks Knows that long lists are harder to remember than short lists Can memorize four units in a digit-span test
6 years	Begins to find audio content of TV programmes as interesting as the visual content With enough cues, may be able to plan an effective attentional strategy
7 years	With training, can score as well on a test of recall as 12 year olds
10 years	Becomes more selective in searching for information needed to make decisions Begins to improve at shifting attention away from irrelevant information
12 years	Can memorize six or seven units in a digit-span test

Note: Developmental events described in this and other Chronology of Development charts represent overall trends identified in research studies. Individual children vary greatly in the ages at which they achieve these developmental changes.

of relevant information increases steadily throughout the elementary and high school years. However, even preschoolers will use the relevance of items as a guide when they encode and process information (Blumberg, Torenberg, & Randall, 2005). Processing irrelevant information, however, increases slightly until the age of 11 or 12 and then decreases rapidly. Overall, children show increasing efficiency in how they use attention in processing information. Their developing executive abilities allow them to get better at targeting relevance and releasing themselves from the draw of distracting irrelevant information.

ATTENTION AND PLANNING

Greater executive control allows older children to develop more effective plans of action to guide their attention as they solve problems. With development, selective attention skills combine with planning, which is the deliberate organization of a sequence of actions orientated towards achieving a goal, and enables the child to solve increasingly more complex problems.

> **planning** The deliberate organization of a sequence of actions orientated towards achieving a goal.

A classic study by Elaine Vurpillot (1968) illustrated the coordination of attention and planning using the drawings of houses presented in Figure 10-9. Suppose you were asked to determine whether each pair of houses was identical. How might you approach this problem? Probably, you would compare the six pairs of corresponding windows in each pair of houses until you found a pair of windows in which the objects displayed did not match. If all the pairs matched, you would conclude that the houses were identical. When Vurpillot administered this task to children, she found that younger children were far less likely than older children to use a systematic plan to get the necessary information. Filming the children's eye movements as they made their comparisons, she found that younger children tended to look at the windows randomly and even made judgements without ever looking at the windows that were different.

Should we conclude from this research that young children are unable to plan an efficient use of their attention? Not necessarily. In a study with preschool-age children, Miller and Aloise-Young (1995) gave the children (ages 3 to 4) a task that required them to open doors to reveal two arrays of pictures and then to determine if the arrays were the same or different. When the task was embedded in an engaging story context, the children were able to attend to the appropriate contextual information and plan their solution more effec-

tively. However, even in meaningful contexts, preschoolers can run into difficulty regulating their attention while they plan because they are less able to inhibit or suspend action during activity, a behaviour that is critical to planning (Kochanska & Murray, 2000).

Planning is often done in social situations and, as we saw in Chapter 9, Vygotsky's theory considers social and cognitive development as closely linked. To explore social contributions to the development of planning, Gauvain and Rogoff (1989) used a model grocery store to compare the planning behaviours of 5 and 9 year olds working with a peer, an adult or alone. The older children were better at organizing their attentional resources and planning ahead, and children who planned in advance of action devised more efficient routes. Children were more likely to use attentional strategies and plan efficiently when they worked with a peer or adult partner, especially when the partners shared task responsibility. Sharing responsibility for carrying out a task helps children understand the problem from the perspective of another person. Learning about the thinking of another appears to enhance the child's own understanding of the problem.

Figure 10-9 A test of children's ability to gather and filter information

How quickly can you perform a task given to young children – to determine which pairs of houses, either pair (a) or pair (b), are identical?
Source: Adapted from Vurpillot (1968)

Memory

Memory is one of the most extensively studied topics in cognitive development. An interest in human memory and how it develops is not surprising if one considers what memory is. Everything you know you have remembered in some way. Thus, the terms *memory* and *knowledge* are interchangeable. Acts of memory range from rapid-fire, basic processes, such as face recognition, to the recall of complex knowledge systems and events, such as the rules of chess and how a family coped with a tragic event.

There are several different types of memory (Schneider & Bjorkland, 1998). We have already discussed short-term memory (more recently referred to as working memory) in the last section, particularly in its relation to executive functions. Working memory is the conscious workspace of memory. Long-term memory is where we store knowledge that we retain for long periods of time. We will cover sensory and working memory first and then proceed to long-term memory.

DEVELOPMENT OF SENSORY AND WORKING MEMORY

As we discussed in the last section, the main changes in working memory performance across childhood seem to involve the construction and use of strategies to aid maintenance, such as rehearsal, and chunking. However, before the development of executive control over short-term memory (we call this short-term memory rather than working memory in the absence of executive control processes), what is known about the basic parameters of short-term storage in infancy? Are we to assume that because memory strategies appear to be more important in childhood development that we have a fully developed short-term memory capacity from birth?

Memory storage parameters include the amount of information that can be held, referred to as memory span; the duration for which it can be held in memory; and speed of this processing. Research has shown that these basic capacities, in particular, processing speed, are related to each other across development and that changes in these have an impact on the effectiveness of working memory (Demetriou et al., 2002).

CAPACITIES OF SENSORY AND SHORT-TERM MEMORY

Researchers have investigated the capacity of sensory and short-term memory in young infants. In Box 10-2 we describe how they have found that sensory memory capacity is quite mature even in very young infants. Short-term memory capacity develops a little more slowly. For instance, Ross-Sheehy, Oakes, and Luck (2003) showed infants sets of objects on a screen, one of which changed from one moment to the next. They examined whether the infants would notice changes in the display when there were more or less items that could change. Early in the first year of life, infants seem to be limited to remembering the identity of only one item in visual short-term memory, but by the end of the first year they resemble adults by being able to remember four items (Ross-Sheehy, Oakes, & Luck, 2003; Kaldy & Leslie, 2005). So the current picture suggests that while short-term memory capacity develops early in life, we manage to improve our retention abilities dramatically by learning how to turn short-term memory into working memory by applying strategies for retention, such as rehearsal.

Research close-up | **BOX 10-2 Investigating the capacity of sensory memory in 6-month-old infants**

Source: Based on Blaser and Kaldy (2010).

Introduction:

iconic memory
Sensory memory for visual information. Of very short duration.

In their modal model, Atkinson and Shiffrin draw a distinction between short-term memory and sensory memory. Sensory memory is a very short-lived store which passes information on to short-term memory (Sperling, 1960; Atkinson & Shiffrin, 1968). When the sensory information is visual, then sensory memory is often referred to as iconic memory. Research has shown that the sensory store appears not to change much over childhood. For example, 5 year olds and adults have the same time limitations on their ability to store sensory information (Morrison, Holmes, & Haith, 1974), but we cannot conclude from this that iconic memory does not change earlier in development. Until very recently, no one had investigated the capacity of infant iconic memory. The way we test for iconic memory is different from the way we test for short-term memory. In sensory memory tests infants are shown a set of items, some of which disappear (there is no advance warning of which items will disappear). If infants (or adults) can detect changes in some of the disappearing items across a short gap then it is concluded that they had some iconic memory for all the items (as they could not predict which ones would disappear).

Method:

In Figure 10-10, we show the experiment that Blaser and Kaldy conducted. They examined whether 6-month-old infants would locate a change in a display of several items across a half-second gap. Only two items would disappear and those were chosen at random. The number of total items on the screen was either 2, 4, 6, 8 or 10. They used an eye-tracker (a machine which reflects light on the back of the infant's eye in order to determine where they are looking), and found that infants would reliably look towards the changed item in a set of stimuli, so long as there were not more than six items in the total set. The authors concluded that the infants have an iconic memory of at least five items. This is very similar to the sensory store capacity of mature adults.

Discussion:

Interestingly it seems that even 6-month-old infants have largely the same storage capacity as adults in their iconic memory (Blaser & Kaldy, 2010). Having a strong sensory (iconic) memory capacity will aid them in their ability to cope with remembering information about the world with smaller short-term memory capacities. Short-term memory capacity develops significantly over the first year of life. Beyond infancy, the most important developments are in memory strategies like rehearsal.

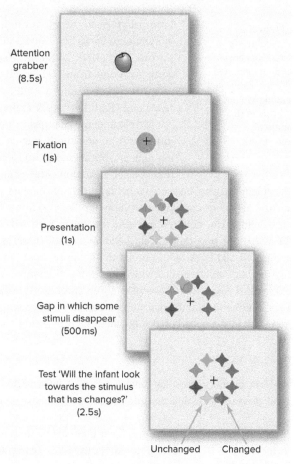

Attention grabber (8.5s)

Fixation (1s)

Presentation (1s)

Gap in which some stimuli disappear (500ms)

Test 'Will the infant look towards the stimulus that has changes?' (2.5s)

Unchanged   Changed

Source: Adapted from Blaser and Kaldy (2010)

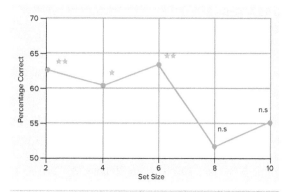

Figure 10-10   Sensory store capacity is adult-like at six months of age

Experimenters showed infants a set of visual stimuli, two of which disappeared across a short gap. When they reappeared one of them had changed. Six month olds were more likely to look towards the item that had changed, so long as there were no more than six items in the original set.
Source: Adapted from Blaser and Kaldy (2010)

PROCESSING SPEED

In Chapter 5 we discussed how the neurons in children's nervous systems become increasingly myelinated. Kail (1995) has suggested that this may play an important role in the development of processing speed.

Processing speed, which is often assessed by reaction time, is the time it takes an individual to carry out a given mental act, such as recognizing a stimulus or reading a word. Kail (1991, 2000) has demonstrated that speed of processing increases linearly with age from childhood to early adulthood. Processing speed is known to affect working memory abilities as well as a number of other abilities such as reasoning (Kail, Lervåg, & Hulme, 2016).

Developmental changes in processing speed are similar for tasks that are very different from one another, such as reading comprehension, mental addition, retrieving names from memory, and visual search (Kail, 1995). According to Kail, the fact that we see developmental changes in processing speeds in many different tasks with widely varying task components and requirements suggests that change in processing speed is a fundamental aspect of cognitive development. We also know that processing speed is not simply due to practice. With development, children increase the speed with which they accomplish tasks that they encounter regularly and those that they rarely encounter (and therefore have little opportunity to practice) (Kail, 1995). Finally, Kail and Park (1994) found the same relation between processing speed and age in Korean children and American children, but with some later indications that the development of processing speed is more rapid in East Asian than Western children (Kail et al., 2013). So, whilst the improvement of processing speed across childhood is universal across cultures, there may be cultural or genetic differences which lead to differences in the speed of development of processing speed.

LONG-TERM MEMORY

Long-term memory includes a vast array of information. It includes all the world knowledge and facts a person possesses, which is called semantic memory. It also includes knowledge of specific events, or episodic memory (Tulving, 2002; Bauer, 2006). Much of the latter is autobiographical in nature, for it includes memories of important events or experiences that have happened to an individual. Later, we discuss the development of autobiographical memory, which has been a more recent topic of research.

semantic memory
All the world knowledge and facts a person possesses.

episodic memory
Memory for specific events, often autobiographical in nature.

The act of remembering can be either intentional or unintentional. Much of everyday experience involves unintentional forms of remembering. It is rarely necessary to exert effort to recall such things as language (e.g., vocabulary) and behavioural routines (e.g., how to get ready for school in the morning). Much of the research on memory development focuses on the strategies children use to remember information intentionally such as rehearsal, organization and elaboration. However, before we turn to memory strategies, do we know much about the long-term memory abilities of infants?

Even very young infants can remember what they see and hear over relatively long time spans. Two researchers found that newborns could remember a previously seen visual event over a 24-hour period (Werner & Siqueland, 1978). The babies in this study altered their sucking patterns when the colour and pattern of a visual stimulus changed, even though they had not seen that stimulus for nearly a day. Other studies show that newborns can also remember speech sounds over a similar time period (Ungerer, Brody, & Zelazo, 1978; Swain, Zelazo, & Clifton, 1993; Bauer, 2006). In one study of mothers and their 14-day-old infants, the mothers repeated the words *tinder* and *beguile* to their babies 60 times a day for 13 days (780 exposures); as you may imagine, 2 week olds rarely hear these particular words. At 14 and 28 hours after this training ended, the researchers tested the babies' memory for the words. The infants showed not only that they remembered the words but that they also recognized them better than their own names.

Older babies have even more impressive memory capabilities. In one study, 3-month-old infants first learned to make a mobile move by kicking one leg, to which the researcher had attached a long ribbon that was also attached to the mobile suspension bar (see photos) (Rovee-Collier & Gerhardstein, 1997). Usually, babies this age will forget the connection between a kick and a bobbing mobile after about eight days. However, with a brief reminder before the testing period, infants could remember the connection for as long as four weeks. The reminder, provided about 24 hours before the memory test, consisted simply of letting the babies see the mobile bobbing up and down for three minutes. During the reminder session, the babies' legs were not attached to the mobile, so they could not relearn the connection. The visual reminder was enough, however. Babies who had experienced the reminder kicked their legs more often in the testing session (when the ankle ribbon was again attached) than babies who had learned the leg–mobile connection but who had been given no reminder of it in the interim. Another cue that helps babies remember is the context or setting in which the original learning took place (Rovee-Collier, 1999). Babies were able to remember better when tested in the same setting in which they originally learned, such as the day-care centre, rather than in a novel context, such as the laboratory (Hayne, McDonald, & Barr, 1997).

But do these long-term memories resemble long-term memories in adults? Are they episodic and tied to a particular event that the infant has encoded? Perhaps these conditioned behaviours in infants do not really tap the kinds of

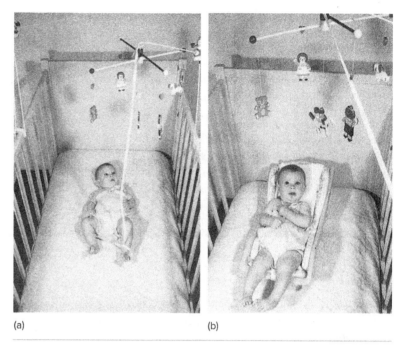

(a)   (b)

Memory lessons for babies: Rovee-Collier found that when she taught 3-month-old infants to make a mobile move by attaching the mobile to one of their legs with a ribbon (a) the babies forgot the association between kicking and moving the mobile after about a week. When this researcher gave these infants a 'reminder' session, however, during which she removed the ribbon so that they could look at the mobile but couldn't make it move (b) and then reattached the ribbon (as in a), she found that most babies were able to remember the association for as long as four weeks. Source: Handbook of Infant Development, 2nd edition, Rovee-Collier © 1987, Reproduced with permission of John Wiley & Sons, Inc.

memory encodings that cognitive psychologists describe as being episodic memories in adults. This is certainly a matter of controversy (Mandler, 1998). However, research by Bauer and colleagues (Bauer & Mandler, 1992; Bauer & Dow, 1994; Bauer, 2007) used a different technique, in which infants are demonstrated a sequence of events, and their imitation of that sequence is measured a few weeks later; this showed that by the end of the first year, infants use temporal information in recalling events (*put teddy in the tub, 'wash' teddy with a sponge, 'dry' teddy with the towel*). According to this method long-term memory emerges at the end of the first year of life, so certainly still quite early in development.

MEMORY STRATEGIES

As we have already discussed, memory strategies are procedures that help people carry out memory-related tasks. Strategies can be used for maintaining information in working memory, but the ability to store and retrieve information efficiently from long-term memory also relies on strategies. People use a wide range of strategies to remember. Some of these strategies involve external supports such as taking notes during lectures or writing down appointments on calendars. Other memory supports are internal or mental (e.g., repeating a person's name to yourself several times). Adults commonly use three memory strategies: rehearsal, organization and elaboration. Developmentalists have studied these three strategies to determine when and how they emerge in childhood and what role they may play in enhancing children's memory.

Although researchers tend to study these strategies separately, children often use more than one strategy at a time (Siegler, 1996; Schneider & Bjorkland, 1998). Children's use of multiple strategies was demonstrated in a study by Coyle and Bjorkland (1997). They presented second-, third- and fourth-grade children with sets

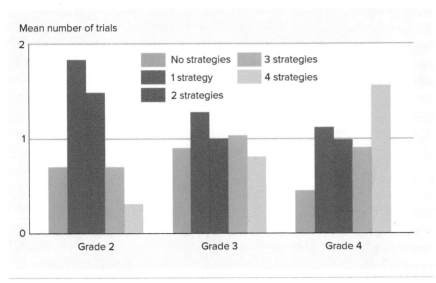

Mean number of trials

Figure 10-11 More strategies, more memory

In a memory task, the oldest children used more strategies and recalled more words. Quite a few of the youngest children used multiple strategies, but their recall was less accurate.

Source: Coyle and Bjorklund (1997)

of words (e.g., *house, pencil, carrot, bean, dog, book, cat, potato*) that could be organized into categories such as vegetables, animals or school-related items. Although the number of strategies children used to organize the words increased with age (Figure 10-11), even second graders used a variety of strategies.

One of the simplest memory strategies is to repeat the information to be remembered, either mentally or out loud. This is called rehearsal. Research has shown that the spontaneous use of rehearsal to aid memory increases with age (Flavell, Beach, & Chinsky, 1966). Young children tend not to rehearse unless told to do

rehearsal A memory strategy in which one repeats a number of times the information one wants to remember, either mentally or orally.

organization A memory strategy that involves putting together in some organized form the information to be remembered; usually entails categorization and hierarchical relations.

so, and they are less efficient than older children when they do rehearse. For example, younger children will repeat the items to be remembered only once or twice when more repetitions are needed, and they are less likely to repeat earlier items (Naus, 1982). However, even young children can employ and benefit from rehearsal strategies if instructed to use them (Keeney, Cannizzo, & Flavell, 1967).

In a classic study, John Flavell and his colleagues (1966) showed a series of pictures to a group of children ranging from kindergarteners to fifth graders and asked them to recall the sequence in which an experimenter pointed to a subset of the pictures. Watching the children's lip movements for a sign that they were rehearsing by naming the pictures to themselves, the researchers found that the children who used spontaneous verbal rehearsal had better memory for the pictures. They also found that the use of such rehearsal increased dramatically with age. Whereas only about 10% of kindergarten children rehearsed the names of the objects in the pictures, more than 60% of second graders and over 85% of fifth graders did so. Later research by Ornstein, Naus and Liberty (1975) modified this finding somewhat by showing that it was not the frequency of rehearsal that predicted performance differences in younger and older children. Rather, the style of rehearsal, which differs in younger and older children, explains the age differences in performance. Younger children are more likely to rehearse each item one at a time as it is presented to them. Older children are more likely to rehearse each item in a group with previously rehearsed items. It seems that the use of a more cumulative rehearsal strategy is more effective in aiding memory of items in a list. Although younger children can be trained to use a cumulative rehearsal strategy (Cox et al., 1989), older children are more likely to use this strategy spontaneously.

When we store information, we often organize it in a way that makes it more meaningful and thus easier to remember. How does the process of actively altering and rebuilding information change as children get older? An answer to this question is found in research on the use of the memory strategy known as organization, or the process of imposing an organization on the information to be remembered using categories and hierarchical relationships.

Over time, children make increasing use of organization to help them remember. The spontaneous use of organization to facilitate memory appears late in elementary school (Hasselhorn, 1992). By grade 4, most children use organizational strategies, such as categorizing and sorting (Bjorklund, 2005). Suppose we present a series of cards containing pictures of a *sweater, hat, apple, orange, jeans, sandwich, gloves, coat, milk* and *dress* to children of different ages. Older children would be more likely than younger ones to form the cards into two groups of similar objects: *apple, orange, sandwich* and *milk* as food items and *sweater, hat, jeans, gloves, coat* and *dress* as items of clothing (Schneider & Bjorklund, 1998). Children who use this strategy are better able to recall the items in a subsequent test (Best & Ornstein, 1986).

Are we to assume that young children are incapable of learning to use categorization? No, indeed, children as young as 2 or 3 years old have been found to use basic category labels to help them remember (Waxman, Shipley & Shepperson, 1991). Also, recall from Chapter 9 that assistance from more skilled people such as parents and teachers may enhance a child's cognitive performance. Researchers have been able to teach children as young as 7 to use organizational strategies like categorization. For example, Ackerman (1996) prompted 7 and 12 year olds to categorize a set of words (e.g., *horse, pig, cow*) by asking them 'Are all of these animals?' Older children generally recalled more than younger ones, but with training, 7 year olds did as well as their older peers.

Finally, children's engagement in a task can also influence the use of this strategy. Guttentag (1995) presented third graders with pictures of common objects to be recalled (25 pictures in five categories) and used these measures to explore how active participation (being allowed to place the pictures themselves) related to children's use of an organizational strategy. Active participation led children to use the organizational strategy and thereby facilitated their recall.

The strategy of elaboration involves adding to the information we want to remember to make it more meaningful and thus easier to remember. This is a useful strategy because, although it might seem to add to the information burden, we are much more likely to remember something that is meaningful to us (Kee, 1994). The *Peanuts* cartoon shows how Charlie Brown elaborates the numbers of his locker combination with major league players' numbers to provide a meaningful context for three seemingly random numbers. As with other strategies, children are more likely to use elaboration when they get older. However, even preschoolers can be instructed in elaboration strategies and how to use them to aid memory (Pressley & Hilden 2006).

> **elaboration** A memory strategy in which one adds to information to make it more meaningful and thus easier to remember.

THE INFLUENCE OF KNOWLEDGE, MEANINGFULNESS AND GOALS

Children obtain knowledge of the world in many ways: through their own experiences, through formal and informal instruction, and via information they obtain from their society and family. This knowledge also influences their memory abilities. Research based on Vygotsky's sociocultural view of development has focused on society's role in children's use of memory strategies and their memory performance (Gauvain, 2001). Unfortunately, a great deal of cross-cultural research investigating children's memory processes has applied experimental techniques commonly used in Western society to non-Western populations. As a result, children in non-Western communities, who are less familiar with these techniques, often perform poorly on them (Cole, 1996; Rogoff, 2003). However, when memory tasks draw on children's knowledge base, for example, when they are presented in culturally familiar contexts, children in non-Western cultures perform as well as, or better than, children tested in the West.

Rogoff and Waddell (1982) presented 9-year-old Mayan children in Guatemala and 9-year-old US children with a memory task. The children watched as 20 familiar objects were placed into a model of a town that contained familiar landmarks (each model was appropriate to the culture of the group being tested). These objects were placed in their appropriate locations – for example, boats on lakes and furniture in houses. The objects were then removed from the display and, after a short delay, the children were asked to re-create the display they had seen prepared. Rogoff and Waddell found that the Mayan children performed slightly better than the US children.

What led to the Mayan children's advantage? Rogoff (2003) speculates that the performance of the American children was hampered by the fact that about a third tried to use the strategy of rehearsal. However, this strategy, which is often taught in US schools, is best suited to memorizing unrelated lists of objects; it may be only minimally effective in this spatial reconstruction task. In contrast to the

US children, the Mayan children appeared to rely on visual memory; they used the spatial relationships of the objects to organize their memories, which seems to have enhanced their performance.

In Chapter 9 we discussed how Vygotsky argued that the knowledge we have is strongly influenced by the culture in which we develop.

In another study designed to explore how the goal of the activity affects children's memory, researchers (Rogoff, 1990; Mistry, Rogoff, & Herman, 2001) enlisted the help of the parents of a group of 4 year olds. In the 'lab' condition, parents presented their children with ten pictures of lunch-related items such as cheese, bread, juice and a napkin. After repeating the names of all ten items, they asked the children to go to the experimenter at the other side of the room and tell her all the items they remembered. In the 'lunch' condition, parents told the children that they were making a packed lunch and needed to get the ingredients from the 'grocer' (played by the experimenter). The parents showed the child the pictures of the ten items, and the child then went to the grocer and asked for the items. On average, children in the lab condition remembered only 2.7 items, whereas children in the lunch condition remembered 5.3 items. It seems that a clear and meaningful goal for the activity is important to children's remembering.

These findings echo Vygotsky's (1978) view that memory in everyday life occurs in the course of meaningful, goal-directed activities. In other words, to remember something in and of itself is rarely our goal. Instead, we usually remember something so that we can do something else. For example, we remember the items on a list so that we can assemble them for an event, like a meal. Often, when memory is tested in laboratory situations, remembering in and of itself is the goal of the activity. Therefore, children who have more experience with activities in which memory alone functions as a goal, which is frequent in school settings, do better on such tasks than children who have less experience with school. But when a laboratory task is designed to resemble a more everyday type of memory activity – one in which remembering is used to carry out a meaningful, goal-directed activity – the difference in memory performance between children who have much versus little experience with school is reduced or eliminated.

Despite the likelihood that a meaningful activity will improve memory performance, there are some situations in which a meaningful, goal-directed activity may not elicit optimal remembering in children. Consider the question of children's reliability as witnesses in the courtroom. Often, the cases in which children serve as witnesses involve domestic conflict or, worse, domestic and/or child abuse that is sometimes of a sexual nature. Although these situations are highly meaningful to children, as Box 10-3 suggests, other factors such as the influence of inaccurate suggestions by others and repeated questions may undermine memory performance (Eisen, Goodman, & Quas, 2002).

Applied Developmental Psychology

BOX 10-3 Should young children testify in court?

How accurate are children when asked to give testimony in a court of law? Research has indicated that suggestions by others, especially adults, may strongly influence a young child's reporting of past events (Bruck, Ceci, & Principe, 2006). Several investigators have explored this issue by having children listen to brief stories and then following up the presentation by introducing inaccurate information (e.g., Ceci, Ross, & Toglia, 1987; Doris, 1991; Ornstein, Gordon, & Larus, 1992). In general, these researchers have concluded that young children are more often affected by inaccurate information than older children are.

Ceci and his colleagues (Ceci & Bruck, 1998; Ceci, Leichtman, & White, 1998; Bruck & Ceci, 1999) undertook an extensive series of studies to explore these effects of suggestion on children's memory. In one study, the experimenters engaged preschool children in a game similar to Simon Says. A month later, an interviewer talked with each child about the activity. In one condition of the experiment, the interviewer was accurately informed about what happened during the activity, and in the other, the interviewer was given false information. When the interviewer was accurately informed, the children's recall was 93% accurate. However, when she was misinformed, 34% of children 3 to 4 years old and 18% of children 5 to 6 years old corroborated false statements about what had happened during the experiment itself. The experimenters concluded that the younger the child, the more likely she was to be influenced by false information.

On the premise that children testifying in sexual abuse cases are often exposed to statements such as 'X is bad' or 'X did bad things', these investigators designed another study to test the effects of such information on children's memories of an event (Leichtman & Ceci, 1995). In the first condition of this study, a stranger named 'Sam Stone' spent two minutes with 3- to 6-year-old children at their day-care centre. On four later occasions, an interviewer asked the children about Sam's visit, trying to elicit as much detail as possible but taking care not to ask questions that would suggest answers. On a fifth occasion, a new interviewer elicited the same information and then asked specifically about two events that had not occurred during Sam's visit. Only 10% of the youngest children confirmed that these events had occurred and, of these, 5% said they had not actually seen or heard these events. Only 2.5% insisted on confirming the events when challenged.

In this study's second condition, starting a month before Sam's visit, the experimenters told children specific stories about how clumsy Sam was. After Sam had visited with the children, during which time he showed none of the behaviours that had been described, the children were again interviewed four times. This time, however, on each occasion, the interviewer stated a number of untruths about Sam, such as that he ripped a book during his visit and marked a teddy bear with a crayon. On a fifth occasion, a new interviewer asked the children for a free narrative about Sam's visit. Among the youngest children, 72% reported seeing Sam perform one or more of the misdeeds they'd been told about after the fact. When the interviewer asked if they had actually seen Sam do these things, the percentage dropped to 44. Even when challenged, however, 21% maintained that they had seen these events.

Regardless of whether children's testimony is accurate or has been altered by suggestions from others, a jury's perception of a child witness is usually not favourable. Both laypeople and legal scholars believe that children make poor witnesses (Yarmey & Jones, 1983), considering them inferior to adults in recall memory. In one study, mock jurors believed that children under 11 could not provide accurate testimony (Leippe & Romanczyk, 1989). Paradoxically, these same adults believed that children make more honest witnesses than adults!

As yet, we have an uncertain picture of the child's ability to give an accurate account of past events (Saywitz & Lyons, 2002). As in the case of many other cognitive functions, a variety of factors affect recall. For example, an interviewer who is intimidating and forceful may well affect children's accuracy, but a kind and supportive interviewer may elicit accurate information from a child (Goodman et al., 1991). In addition, research has found that when a child has been an active participant in a situation, rather than a spectator, she is less likely to be susceptible to others' misleading suggestions (Rudy & Goodman, 1991; Lindberg et al., 2001). The type of question asked, and whether and how it is repeated, may also affect children's responses (Lyons, 2002).

Current research has moved beyond description to focus on the mechanisms that may account for children's ability to recall events accurately. Some cognitive mechanisms include strength of memory, semantic knowledge, knowledge of scripts and linguistic comprehension. For instance, Ricci and Beal (1998) showed that children who were more accurate in their original memory of an event were less likely to answer inaccurately when a question was repeated. Also playing a role are socioemotional factors, such as avoiding punishment or embarrassment, keeping promises made to others, eschewing personal gain if it involves being deceitful, and personality characteristics. As we have repeatedly noted, cognitive and social factors operate together in accounting for the kinds of effects we have discussed here. Finally, this work reminds us that the lines between basic and applied research are often blurred. Although the research reviewed tells us about children's testimony, it also informs us about children's cognitive and social development.

KNOWLEDGE OF THE SELF: AUTOBIOGRAPHICAL MEMORY

Here is how Ben, a 5-year-old boy, explained to his teacher how his 2.5-year-old brother Graeme sustained a bloody, but minor, cut to the head.

Teacher: *What did you do over the holidays?*
Ben: *There was an accident.*
Teacher: *Oh, what happened?*
Ben: *My brother jumped on the bed and cut his head on the table. And then, after he cut his head, then the paramedics came and two fire trucks and an ambulance.*
Teacher: *Oh, how awful! Then what happened?*
Ben: *Mommy went with him to the hospital in the ambulance. I stayed home with Nana.*

In this example, an adult, the child's teacher, elicited details that brought out more information about the event from the child's memory. She also defined an emotional context and steered the child along as he recounted the story. The child used the occasion to describe the aspects of the event that were important and understandable to him. He used the narrative form, an account of an event that is temporally sequenced and conveys meaning (Bruner, 1990). In his narrative, he described the event as well as information about himself, his family, and his own experience during the event. Even though what Ben said is

> **narrative form** A temporally sequenced account that conveys meaning about an event.

brief, he makes it clear that this was an emotionally arousing experience for him. Even a short narrative may have deep meaning or value for a child (Engel, 1995). This value is enhanced because memories such as this one are personal in an interesting way: they define an individual's own history. Because there are often social contributions to these memories as children discuss them with others, this history is shaped by other people who inform the child about what aspects of his memory are interesting or important to remember. Since the event in this example garnered interest and attention from an adult, it may increase the likelihood of Ben retelling the story and therefore rehearsing it, which will help him remember the event. Even the interpretations of others regarding an event may become part of the memory if the retelling triggers a certain response. For instance, if a child describes an experience that adults find amusing, the event may then be remembered not only in terms of the actions and the sequences of these actions but also in terms of its effect on others.

autobiographical memory A collection of memories of things that have happened to a person at a specific time or place.

problem-solving The identification of a goal and of steps to reach that goal.

A person's memories about things that happened to her at a specific time or place are part of the person's autobiographical memory (Bauer, 2006; Fivush, 2011). Autobiographical memory emerges in the early years of life, when a child is about 2.5 years old, and it develops substantially over the preschool years (Nelson & Fivush, 2004). Autobiographical memories are linked in both process and content to children's social experiences (Fivush, Haden, & Reese, 2006). Researchers estimate that, during family interaction, discussion of past events occurs as often as five to seven times an hour (Fivush et al., 1996). Parents talk directly to children about the past. Parents also talk to each other about the past in the presence of their children. Early in the child's life, shared memories are mostly one-sided, with the parent taking on much of the responsibility for reminiscing. But by the age of 3, children's contributions increase, and their memories begin to endure rather well. In fact, children as young as 3 years of age can remember specific event information over a fairly long time period (Fivush & Hamond, 1989).

Shared conversations about the past also help children have better memory for the event (Haden et al., 2001). The fact that these conversations typically tie these memories to something of personal significance helps children acquire knowledge about themselves, other people and the world in which they live (Engel & Li, 2004). This type of personal storytelling or shared reminiscence is not unique to particular families or cultures. This practice is culturally widespread and helps to communicate cultural values to children. Psychologists have observed interesting cultural variations in these conversations. Wang (2004) asked preschool and early school-age children from China and the United States to recount four autobiographical events. She found that the memories of the American children included lots of personal details that emphasized the child's own experiences and feelings. In contrast, the Chinese children recalled memories that concentrated on social aspects of their lives, such as social interactions and daily routines. These patterns are consistent with different emphases on autonomy and social connections and with the parenting styles in these two cultural communities, which have been studied by Ruth Chao and are discussed in Chapter 12.

During social interaction, children learn much about what to remember, how to formulate their memories, and how to retain them in a retrievable form (Bauer, 2006). These conversations also help children learn how to cope with difficult or emotional experiences such as an asthma attack or a hurricane or other environmental disaster (Fivush & Sales, 2004).

Such shared memory experiences carry much import in young children's lives (Nelson, 2007). They contribute to the development of the self and thereby help create what Nelson (1996) calls the historical self. They also contribute to the cultural self in that shared memories reflect the values and practices of the culture in which development occurs. Finally, they give children the opportunity to rehearse these memories and, in so doing, to learn some very important things about the process of remembering.

Problem solving and reasoning

Every day, people try to achieve many and varied goals. Some of these are modest, such as having a good breakfast. Some are grand, such as completing a long project at school or work. To reach these goals, people organize their actions in ways that are directed towards meeting their goals. Problem solving is the process of identifying an action goal and delineating steps or means to reach this goal. Problem solving is a central feature of human intelligence. In fact, some psychologists equate problem solving with thinking. But I suspect that by now you will also associate problem solving with executive function. An important feature of problem solving is overcoming obstacles or distractions that interfere with reaching the goal. Thus, problem solving usually involves a goal and one or more obstacles that need to be overcome to reach this goal. Sometimes, young children find problem solving difficult because they find it hard to inhibit their interest in the goal while avoiding obstacles or carrying out sub-goals.

During children's development, their problem-solving abilities become more sophisticated; the strategies they possess become better developed, and they acquire new strategies (Klahr, 2000; Garton, 2004). To illustrate the impact these changes have on children's problem-solving abilities, we examine development in four areas of problem solving: solving problems by using rules that guide thinking; solving problems by analogy, or using information from one problem to solve another; using cognitive tools, such as the structure of routine behaviours or forms of representation, to solve problems; and solving problems by deductive reasoning. We also discuss another type of reasoning that plays an important role in cognitive development and problem solving: numerical reasoning.

RULE-BASED PROBLEM SOLVING

Some types of problems are solved by applying rules that describe the properties or elements of the problem. An interesting aspect of the development of problem-solving skills is that children learn the various rules to solve problems at different points in childhood. This is because the rules often vary in complexity, so younger children understand and apply the simpler rules of the problem, whereas older children understand and apply the more complex rules. This developmental change lends itself well to observational analysis of the development of skills in rule-based problem solving, and Robert Siegler (1983, 1991) has conducted research examining this development. This research uses the balance-scale task developed by Inhelder and Piaget (1958) in which there is a balance beam with weights on either side of the fulcrum. Children are asked to predict which way a balance with different weights placed at different distances from the fulcrum will tilt when supports holding up the arms of the beam are released. As you can see from Figure 10-12, what makes this a difficult problem is the need to consider two dimensions at the same time: both the number of weights on each side of the balance's fulcrum and the distance from the fulcrum at which each set of weights lies. Based on their observations of children of different ages, researchers (Klahr & Siegler, 1978; van Rijn, van Someran, & van der Maas, 2003) have described four rules that children apply at various points in development as they go about solving the problem.

Siegler (1976, 1981) found that 3 year olds did not use rules at all; about half of 4 year olds used rule I, and all 5 year olds used rule I. Among 9 year olds, about half used rule II and half used rule III, and 13 and 17 year olds almost always used rule III. Interestingly, although rule IV embodies the reasoning Piaget attributed to the child in the period of formal operations, only a minority even of college students used it! When Siegler analysed the task carefully to try to discover why young children couldn't solve many of the balance-scale problems, he hypothesized that perhaps limited memory and/or lack of knowledge was at fault. When he allowed children to continue viewing the original balance arrangement (low memory demand) and gave them direct, detailed, and repeated instructions (knowledge), those as young as 5 were often able to solve the problems. In this case, social support or scaffolding, as research based on Vygotsky's ideas would predict, led to better task performance (Gauvain, 2001).

To understand the development of rule-based problem solving, it is important to notice that these rules are increasingly sophisticated in terms of how much information about the problem is considered in making a judgement about whether the beam will balance. Siegler's observations tell us that children are increasingly able with age to understand and apply these rules in solving this problem. It is important to appreciate that children are seeing and working with the same problem and that what distinguishes their approach to solving it is how children interpret or make sense of the problem. Not surprisingly, researchers have found that children use the more sophisticated rules as they get older. Although this general developmental pattern is consistent with other research in which older children perform better than younger children, what is important about this research is that it describes cognitive development in the area of problem solving as a logical

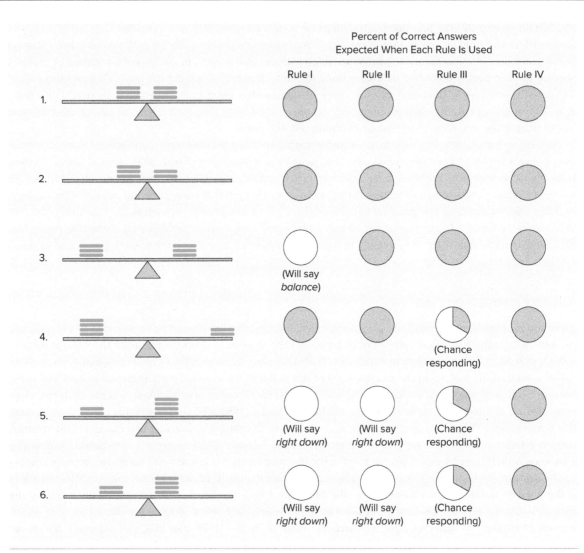

Figure 10-12 Balance-scale problems and strategies for solving them
On the right hand side the pie charts indicate the percentage of correct answers expected when each rule is used.
Filled circles equal 100%. White, empty, circles equal 0%.
Rule I: The side with more weights is heavier.
Rule II: If weights on both sides are equal, the side whose weights are farther from the fulcrum is heavier.
Rule III: If one side has more weights but the other's weights are farther from the fulcrum, you have to guess at
the answer.
Rule IV: Weights × distance from fulcrum equals torque; the side with greater torque is heavier.
Using Robert Siegler's rule IV will get you the correct answers on all these problems. Interestingly, your next best
chance to get as many correct answers as possible is to use rule II. Why?
Answers: Problems 1 and 6: balance; problems 2–5: left down.
Source: Adapted from Siegler and Aliball (2005)

and rule-based process of growth. As a result, it has interesting and important implications for understanding
the development of children's problem solving in a wide range of everyday and more school like and scientific
problems (Klahr, 2000).

Siegler (1996) and Siegler and Chen (2002) have extended this view by pointing out that not only do
children have rule-based reasoning, but they also have a variety of strategies for solving problems at any
given time. To solve a problem, children choose from the strategies they have available. What is important

developmentally is the kinds of strategy choices available at a particular point in development, how children decide which strategy or strategies to use, and the effectiveness with which children use these strategies during problem solving. Siegler (1996, 2006) calls this process an adaptive strategy choice approach to problem solving and learning because, with development, the child makes strategy choices that are an increasingly better fit, or adapted, to the task at hand.

SOLVING PROBLEMS BY ANALOGY

Suppose you are trying to learn how to use a personal computer and are having difficulty understanding how all the directories and files are organized. In this situation, drawing an analogy between the workings of the computer and that of an office filing system may be helpful. The computer can be thought of as the filing cabinet, and files are the documents inserted in the drawers of the cabinet.

The use of *analogy* – or the inference that if two or more objects or situations resemble each other in some respects, they are likely to resemble each other in other respects – is a powerful problem-solving strategy (Holyoak, 2005). In an analogy, there is one situation that is more familiar and one that is less familiar. When individuals use an analogy to help them solve a problem, they draw an inference between the *source analog*, or the familiar situation, and the *target analog*, or the unfamiliar situation (Gentner & Holyoak, 1997). Sometimes, children and even adults find it difficult either to think of or to make use of analogies (Gick & Holyoak, 1980). One reason may be that when analogies are presented in the classic form of A:B as C:? (e.g., 'foot is to leg as arm is to what?'), the important relations that need to be evaluated in the analogy may be unclear.

However, when simpler relations are used, even infants are able to use them to solve a problem (Goswami, 2001). For instance, Chen, Sanchez and Campbell (1997) showed that 13 month olds can use the perceptual similarity of different tools, such as boxes, cloths and strings, to pull toys closer to play with them. Using perceptual similarity is a very simple type of analogical reasoning, however – recognizing deeper relations across two pairs of objects is more difficult. Research has shown that young children can demonstrate reasoning involving deeper relations provided the relational information is clear and little distracting information is present (Richland, Morrison, & Holyoak, 2006). For instance, in a study with preschoolers, pictures were used to represent the A, B and C terms of the analogy – for example, chocolate (A):melted chocolate (B) as snowman (C):? (Goswami & Brown, 1990). The investigator would then show children five picture choices, one of which was of a melted snowman, and children would be asked to choose the picture that best represented the answer (D). Three year olds were correct 52% of the time on these types of problems, 4 year olds were correct 89% of the time and 5 year olds were correct 99% of the time.

Analogical reasoning may play an important role in knowledge acquisition in that it helps the child broaden and deepen his understanding of the relations between objects and across similar types of objects. Researchers have found that even though children do not often generate analogies on their own, cognitive support from another person can lead a child into identifying and using an analogy in an effective way to solve problems (Chen & Daehler, 1989). This has important implications for education. The type of relations that occurs in analogical reasoning seems particularly beneficial for learning subjects like mathematics, which require the application of abstract principles across similar problems (Novick & Bassok, 2005). Goswami and Bryant (2015) make the compelling case that children use analogy of speech sounds (especially the rhymes of particular words in relation to how they appear when written to learn to read.

In a cross-cultural analysis of 12-year-olds' mathematics lessons in Hong Kong, Japan and the United States, Richland, Zur and Holyoak (2007) found that teachers often include relational comparisons in their lessons, and the most effective lessons included cognitive supports such as the vividness of the relational comparison that is being used. Although teachers in the three countries presented analogies at similar rates, teachers in Hong Kong and Japan provided more cognitive supports for students in using this relational information than teachers in the United States did. These investigators suggest that one way to strengthen mathematics education is for teachers to provide more cognitive support in their lessons that include analogies.

DEDUCTIVE REASONING

Piaget placed great emphasis on children's ability to solve problems based on logical reasoning, such as conservation and class inclusion. These tasks rely on children's ability to use a form of logic called deductive reasoning. When individuals use deductive reasoning, they come to a conclusion based on a set of premises or statements that have already been laid out. A syllogism is a type of deductive reasoning problem that includes a major premise, a minor premise and a conclusion – for example, 'All virtues are good. Kindness is a virtue. Therefore, kindness is good.' Researchers have studied several types of deductive reasoning problems with children; we concentrate on three of these: propositional logic, transitive reasoning and hierarchical categorization. Each of these types of reasoning makes important contributions to mature thinking. However, as we shall see, they take a while to develop, and children often find problems based on deductive reasoning difficult.

> **deductive reasoning**
> Logical thinking that involves reaching a necessary and valid conclusion based on a set of premises.
>
> **propositional reasoning** Logical thinking that involves evaluating a statement or series of statements based on the information in the statement alone.
>
> **transitive inference**
> The mental arrangement of things along a quantitative dimension.

PROPOSITIONAL LOGIC

In propositional reasoning, the logic of a statement is evaluated based on the information in the statement alone, as in a syllogism. For example, the Russian psychologist Alexander Luria (1976) tested the propositional reasoning of adults who had varying experiences with schooling and literacy by using the following syllogism:

> *In the Far North, where there is snow, all bears are white.*
> *Novaya Zemlya is in the Far North and there is always snow there.*
> *What color are the bears there? (p. 108)*

Piaget considered logical syllogisms such as this quite difficult and claimed that solving them required formal operational thinking. However, simpler versions of logical syllogisms were presented to 4- and 5-year-old children by Hawkins and her colleagues (1984). Here's an example of these syllogisms.

> *Pogs wear blue boots.*
> *Tom is a pog.*
> *Does Tom wear blue boots? (p. 587)*

The children in this study performed very well on these types of syllogisms – for example, by stating that Tom wears blue boots because he is a pog, which suggests that some of the basic skills needed for deductive reasoning of the type that is tapped in logical syllogisms may start to appear in the late preschool years and, as is often the case, earlier than Piaget suggested (see Chapter 9).

TRANSITIVE REASONING

One of Piaget's reasoning tasks involves transitive inference, or the mental arrangement of things along a quantitative dimension. This type of inference is important for understanding information that falls along an ordered sequence, such as which is faster than or heavier than something else. For instance, recall from Chapter 9 that children younger than 6 or 7 could not deduce that Miranda was taller than Georgina when given the information 'Miranda is taller than Zoe and Zoe is taller than Georgina.' Piaget attributed this failure to an inability to use the logic of transitive inference. An alternative hypothesis (e.g., Bryant & Trabasso, 1971; Halford & Andrews, 2006), is that children do understand transitive inference but either use an incorrect strategy to solve this kind of problem or the memory load is too great, and therefore, it interferes with their performance. As we discussed in Chapter 9, if memory demands are reduced then children are able to pass transitive inference tasks at a much younger age (Bryant & Trabasso, 1971; Bryant & Kopytynska, 1976). But their strategies might also be incorrect. One strategy young children often use in this kind of task is to assume that the most recently mentioned object is also the largest; in this case, the strategy leads them to an incorrect inference. Another strategy is to assume automatically that one of the given objects is longer than the others, regardless of what the experimenter actually said (Brainerd & Reyna, 1990). Both these strategies reduce the child's memory load but often lead to erroneous conclusions. However, when a transitive inference task is presented in a simple or familiar form – for example, when children are asked to arrange the Mama, Papa and Baby Bears in the Goldilocks story in order of their size – even 4-year-old children do well (Goswami, 1995).

HIERARCHICAL CATEGORIZATION

The organization of concepts into levels of abstraction that range from the specific (e.g., *dog*) to the general (e.g., *animal*) is called hierarchical categorization, or class inclusion. It is one thing to know that there are dogs and there are collies; a much more sophisticated understanding of categorization involves knowing that a collie is a kind of dog, such that all collies are dogs but not all dogs are collies. Some evidence suggests that even very young children are capable of forming categories based on hierarchical relationships (Trabasso et al., 1978; Haith & Benson, 1998; Mandler, 1998).

> **hierarchical categorization** The organization of concepts into levels of abstraction that range from the specific to the general.

Mandler and Bauer (1988) studied 12-, 15- and 20-month-old infants' knowledge of categories using a method called *sequential touching*, which takes advantage of young children's tendency to touch and manipulate objects within their grasp. These experimenters recorded the order in which an infant reached for objects that were placed, as a group, within the child's reach. Ensuring that the infants viewed objects from both specific levels (*dogs* and *cars*) and general levels (*animals* and *vehicles*), they presented a child with, say, two dogs and a horse or two cars and a truck and found that children touched sequentially objects that belonged to the same hierarchical category (e.g., all the dogs). This pattern of sequential touch was strongest at the specific level and present to a lesser extent at more general levels. Thus, it appears that even infants have some knowledge of class-inclusion relations and, further, that they are able to use this information to form categories for familiar objects (Mandler, 1998; Quinn & Eimas, 1998). In Chapter 2 we described a connectionist model of young infants' categorization abilities. This suggested that infants glean their categorical knowledge of the environment from the structure of the environment rather than any predetermined knowledge (Maraschal et al., 2000).

Later in infancy, language development, especially names or labels for objects, contributes substantially to the ability of children to categorize objects hierarchically. Markman and Hutchinson (1994) gave 2- to 3-year-old children a set of three objects and asked them to sort the objects 'where they belong', sometimes labelling objects and sometimes giving them no labels. When the experimenters did not label an object (e.g., a police car), the children put it with either a same physical category object (another car) or a same thematic category object (a police officer), apparently at random. When the experimenters did apply labels to objects, they used nonsense words rather than an object's real name. For example, they referred to the police car as a *daz*. Given this label, most of the children placed the police car with another car, apparently seeing both as having the same category membership. Other researchers have replicated this effect (e.g., Mandler, 1998), and some have reported similar findings using Japanese words instead of nonsense syllables (Waxman & Gelman, 1986).

In summary, children's ability to form hierarchical categories is evident from a very young age. This ability, together with other deductive reasoning skills, contributes in significant ways to how children think and solve problems.

CHANGES IN MENTAL REPRESENTATIONS: IMPACTS ON INFORMATION PROCESSING

As we discussed in Chapter 9, the knowledge children have of the world around them changes dramatically in the first years of life. These changes in knowledge have an impact on the way children process information. Some of the changes are envisaged (e.g., by Piaget) as being due to necessary developments in the way the child thinks about the world (such as thinking about the world in a symbolic way), but others are due to some important cognitive tools provided by culture (such as number and language). As we shall see when

mental representation
Information stored mentally in some form (e.g. verbal, pictorial, procedural).

infantile amnesia The inability to remember any event or piece information encoded before the age of around 3 years.

In Chapter 9 we discussed how infants and young children's concepts about objects and people change dramatically as they get older. Could these changes explain infantile amnesia?

we return to a discussion of the acquisition of numerical knowledge, researchers do not always agree as to whether certain forms of knowledge are provided by the child's inheritance or by culture.

Developmental changes in mental representations

Mental representation is the term used to describe information that is stored mentally in some form (e.g., verbal, pictorial, procedural). A mental representation depends on the child's understanding that one thing (e.g., a word such as *chair*) can stand for or 'represent' something else (e.g., an actual chair). Some developmentalists have proposed that changes in the type and complexity of mental representations underlie much of cognitive development (Bjorklund, 2005).

INFANTILE AMNESIA

A strange phenomenon of cognitive development concerns the fact that we cannot remember anything which happened to us before around 2 to 3 years of life. This is termed infantile amnesia. One of the most sensible explanations of infantile amnesia concerns changes in the way we encode information and form mental representations between 2 to 4 years of age. There are crucial differences in the ways infants and older children think about the information coming into their cognitive systems. Young infants have a very limited vocabulary, they think about objects, people and events in a very different way to older children (see Chapter 9). Changes in these ways of encoding the world could mean that it becomes very difficult for an adult or even a 6 year old to access memories which were formed before these changes in encoding.

SYMBOLIC REPRESENTATIONS

One particularly important developmental change in the nature of mental representations concerns our ability to use symbols. Remember that Piaget considered this to be the culmination of the sensorimotor period of development. According to Judy DeLoache (2004), the ability to use symbolic representations, such as scale models and pictures, is a great aid in information processing. In her research on how children use models as representations of actual objects, DeLoache (1987) showed children who were 31 and 39 months old a furnished, normal-size living room and a miniature model of the same room, complete with furniture. She also showed them a normal-size doll and a miniature version of the doll. She hid the tiny doll in the model room while the children watched and then asked the children to find the larger version of the doll in the life-size living room, explaining that it was hidden in the same place in that room as the miniature doll was hidden in the model room.

The older children had no problem finding the doll, but the younger children could not do so, although by retrieving the miniature doll from the model room, they showed that they remembered where it had been hidden. DeLoache proposed that the problem for the younger children was their inability to form a *dual representation*. That is, they couldn't conceive of the model room both as an object in its own right and as a representation of the larger, real room. To test this hypothesis, DeLoache and her colleagues (DeLoache, Miller, & Rosengren, 1997) presented two groups of children with different accounts of the hidden doll problem. Both groups saw the full-size room and the doll hidden in this room. The researchers then presented the model room to the first group and hid the miniature doll. To the second group, however, they explained that 'a shrinking machine' had shrunk the full-size room, and then the researchers revealed the small, model room. The 2.5-year-old children in this study had no difficulty finding the miniature doll in the 'shrunken' room. DeLoache and her colleagues suggest that the shrunken room version of the task was easier for the children because it did not require them to understand that the small room stood for or represented the large room symbolically. Thus, the children in the second group did not need to understand the *relation* between two objects – the large and small rooms – as children in the first group did. Instead, children in the second group had only to recognize the room in its new, shrunken form.

For DeLoache and colleagues (DeLoache et al., 1997; DeLoache & Smith, 1999), the development of an ability to use symbolic representations has some massive implications concerning how children can process information. For instance, whereas it may be that teaching basic mathematics concepts by using blocks of different sizes to represent different numerical quantities may present difficulty for very young children, this kind of analogy will later become very useful for older children.

NUMERICAL REASONING

As we have already discussed earlier in this chapter, the ability to think about and use numbers to reason and solve problems is an important developmental achievement that has significant implications for children's success at school (Geary, 2006b). But the use of number involves a set of tools, one of which is counting. There is some disagreement over whether our counting abilities are learned from our environment or provided innately (e.g., Leslie et al., 2008; Nunes et al., 1996). However, it is clear that children know something about counting from quite an early age. Gelman and Gallistel (1978) have famously studied what preschool children do and do not understand about counting. Based on their findings, they proposed five basic principles of counting that lead to children's competence with numbers.

1. The one-one principle: Each object should be counted once and only once.
2. The stable-order principle: Always assign the numbers in the same order.
3. The cardinal principle: A single number can be used to describe the total of a set.
4. The abstraction principle: The other principles apply to any set of objects.
5. The order-irrelevance principle: The order in which objects are counted is irrelevant.

A simple example will show these principles in action. Suppose we show a child ten pennies, placed in a row, and ask her to count them. Pointing to each one, she proceeds to count them aloud, '1, 2, 3, 5, a, b, c, 10, 15, 12'. When she finishes, we ask her to count them again, starting from the other end. Again she counts all ten of the pennies, counting each one once and only once. 'How many pennies are there?' we ask. 'Twelve,' she replies. We then ask her to count 10 marbles. She repeats: '1, 2, 3, 5, a, b, c, 10, 15, 12'. Again, we ask, 'How many?' 'Twelve.'

Can we say that this child understands counting? Based on the principles just outlined, the answer is yes. Despite her use of an unconventional number sequence, she does seem to understand the critical principles of counting. She assigned only one number to each of the objects and always assigned the numbers in the same order, showing that she understood the one-one and stable-order principles. She had no problem switching the order in which she counted the objects, nor did she mind counting both pennies and marbles, demonstrating her command of the order-irrelevance and abstraction principles. Finally, when asked how many objects there were, she replied 'Twelve', showing that she understood the cardinal principle. Children may be competent in some or all of these principles at different points in their development. For example, a 3 year old may grasp the one-one principle and the cardinal principle. However, he may be able to apply the stable-order principle only to sets with five or fewer members.

In addition to learning to count, many other abilities are important to numerical reasoning. These abilities include the conservation of number, first described by Piaget (1965) and discussed in Chapter 9. This is the understanding that the amount of a set remains the same despite superficial transformations – for example, understanding that moving a line of eight counters closer together does not change the number of counters in the line.

Researchers have examined differences between cultures in the development of numeracy skills, partly to gain a more representative picture of development from across the world, but also in an attempt to understand whether our knowledge of number and counting is mediated by culture. Certainly, counting is at least partly a cultural tool in Vygotsky's terms, and the way in which that tool functions depends on variations between cultures, such as the ways in which language is used, or even the the counting system itself (e.g., whether it is base 10 or not). Evidence has also accumulated that Asian children display greater mathematical skills than American children do (Geary, Fan, & Bow-Thomas, 1992; Stevenson & Lee, 1990). Box 10-4 suggests that, as seen in Chinese and US children, this difference may begin to emerge very early in life and may reflect verbal as well as quantitative abilities.

Research close-up

BOX 10-4 It's easier to count in Chinese than in English

Source: Based on Miller et al. (1995).

Introduction:

Chinese-speaking children may have an advantage over English-speaking children when it comes to counting. According to Miller and colleagues (Miller et al., 1995), the Chinese language offers a more consistent 'base-10' naming system than the system used in English. This may make it easier for young children to learn to count.

As Miller and associates point out, the base-10 Arabic system of numbering (1, 2, 3 ... 10, 11, 12 ..., etc.) is now used throughout the world, but names for numbers in different languages reflect older and sometimes more complex number systems. These researchers divided the number-naming systems of both (Mandarin) Chinese and English into four segments of interest: 1 to 10, 11 to 19, 20 to 99, and 100 and above. In the first segment, Chinese and English do not differ in difficulty of learning, they propose, for both languages require children to master an unordered sequence of names. There's no way to predict, for example, that jiu follows ba or that nine follows eight. In the second segment, however, Chinese follows a consistent base-10 rule (e.g., in Mandarin Chinese, the number 11 is called, literally, 'ten-one'), whereas the English system is inconsistent and mixed: the names eleven and twelve seem to bear no relation to one and two, and the names for 13 through 19 both place unit values before the tens values and modify the names of both (*thir-teen, fif-teen*).

Between 20 and 99, both languages follow a base-10 approach in naming, but Chinese uses unmodified unit and tens names (e.g., 'two-ten-four', for 24) whereas English modifies the first unit name – but not the second – and the tens names (e.g., *twenty-four*). Finally, above 100, the naming systems in both languages are fairly consistent in using the base-10 format, with only a few exceptions.

Based on an early study in which they found some differences in mathematical skills favouring Chinese over US children entering school for the first time, Miller and colleagues formulated several hypotheses. If these differences in fact reflected a more easily comprehended number-naming system, then (a) Chinese children should show substantial skills advantages after all children begin to learn to count above 10, (b) US children should have more trouble with counting in the teens than Chinese children, and (c) differences should generally be related to the system of number names and not involve other aspects of counting.

Method:

Engaging 99 Chinese children and 98 US children – all between 3 and 6 years old – in a series of tasks that involved counting, these investigators confirmed their predictions.

Results:

As you can see from Figure 10-13, there were no substantial differences between the two groups in counting up to 10, but as children began to count in the teens, a significant difference between Chinese and US children emerged. This differential ability was evident until both groups began to count in the 100s, where they again performed similarly. Chinese children were somewhat more successful in counting actual displays of between 14 and 17 objects, but they did not differ from US children in the ability to solve simple mathematical problems or to count arrays of ten or fewer objects. Although this finding might seem to violate the researchers' third prediction, it is consistent with the notion that US children will have the greatest difficulty with number naming with values in the teens.

Discussion:

Given that neither the Chinese nor the English language is likely to change its number-naming system, how can we help American children acquire counting skills more efficiently and effectively? According to Miller and colleagues, obstacles that the English system presents can interfere with such mathematics operations as arithmetic carrying and borrowing. Other studies have suggested not only that Chinese children display more sophisticated addition strategies when they first enter school but also that

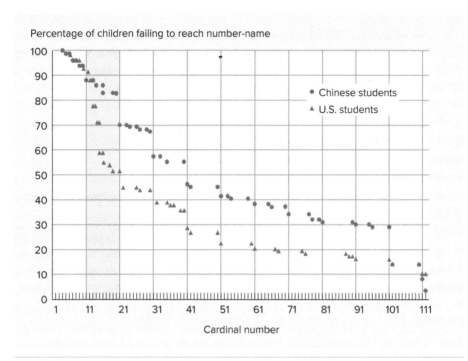

Figure 10-13   Counting in Chinese and English
The coloured band at the left of the graph highlights the numerical teens (11–19) where Chinese and US children begin to diverge in counting skills, possibly owing to the non-base-10 structure of English names for these numbers.
Source: Adapted from Miller et al. (1995).

counting strategies for certain kinds of problems predict adult performance on those problems. Although these researchers suggest that it may be important both to familiarize US children with Arabic numerals at an earlier age and to emphasize use of the digits over the use of number words, they also point out that this approach might interfere with other methods used to teach American children the 10s-structured addition method. Perhaps the answer lies in both parents and teachers – in the Vygotskian style – encouraging children more to learn mathematics skills.

METACOGNITION

As cognitive beings, we don't just remember things, solve problems, and form concepts; we also have an awareness of the strengths and limitations of our cognitive abilities. In other words, we have knowledge about knowing (Flavell, Green, & Flavell, 1995), or metacognition. The child's understanding of her cognitive abilities and processes and of the task situation will influence the strategies she uses in her learning. In turn, her abilities and her experience in learning will contribute to her knowledge about cognition and to her success or failure on cognitive tasks. Consequently, metacognitive skills have significant implications for children's success in the classroom (Bransford, Brown, & Cocking, 1999).

> **metacognition** The individual's awareness of and understanding about her or his cognitive abilities.

There are a number of developmental changes in metacognition. The child's own awareness of how much he knows and is able to remember changes with age. Older children have a more realistic and accurate picture of their own and others' memory abilities than do younger children (Flavell, Friedricks, & Hoyt, 1970; Yussen & Berman, 1981; Flavell, 1985). An older child recognizes, for example, that he doesn't learn well when tired or anxious.

In this section, we examine two important areas of research on metacognition: children's knowledge of tasks and their knowledge of specific strategies for learning and remembering. A broader set of metacognitive limitations, as described by Flavell et al. (1995) are summarized in Table 10-1. Whilst reading this section on metacognition, bear in mind that the development of a theory of mind (theory of one's own mind as well as that of others), discussed in Chapter 9, is closely related to metacognition.

Table 10-1   Limitations on young children's metacognition

Young children
Underestimate the amount of thinking which they and others do
Don't understand the concept of a 'stream of consciousness'
Fail to appreciate that someone sitting quietly and not obviously 'doing' something might be engaging in mental activity
Don't understand that activities such as looking, listening, or reading involve thinking. When someone is engaged in such an activity, preschoolers do not automatically understand that the person's mind is active. Similarly, they don't recognize that they have been thinking when engaging in these kinds of activities
Cannot infer what another person might be thinking about, even when they realize the person is thinking
Fail to understand that when you focus attention on one thing, you are often not able to think about other things
Have difficulty saying, when asked, whether they were thinking or what they were thinking about, even when their responses are prompted and facilitated
Tend to understand thinking in terms of its products rather than in terms of the process of thinking itself

Source: Based on Flavell et al. (1995).

Knowledge about the task

The ability to monitor one's comprehension is critical for a wide range of problem solving and communication tasks. Do I understand the directions to get to the party tomorrow? Do I understand the instructions for this week's science project? To process information effectively, the child has to be sensitive to her present state of knowledge so that she can seek out the information she needs to further her understanding.

One way that children get information about their present state of understanding is by monitoring their task performance. To study this type of knowledge, Markman (1977, 1979) assessed children's ability to monitor their comprehension of task instructions. In one study, Markman (1977) gave 5, 6, and 7 year olds inadequate instructions for playing a card game. The experimenter dealt each child four cards, which had letters on them, and explained the game.

We each put our cards in a pile. We both turn over the top card in our pile. We look at cards to see who has the special card. Then we turn over the next card in our pile to see who has the special card this time. In the end, the person with the most cards wins the game. How would you like to try to play this game with these instructions?

The experimenter made no mention either of what the 'special card' might be or of how one acquired more cards. The 5 year olds were far less likely to realize the inadequacy of the instructions than the second and third graders, who asked for more instructions before attempting to play the game. One quarter of the first graders never asked a question, and most recognized that a problem existed only when they were asked to repeat the instructions or when they began to flounder in playing the game.

Another aspect of knowledge of a task is an understanding of task demands. Do children realize that some things are harder to learn than others? Apparently, yes. Even 4 year olds know that a long list of objects is harder to remember than a very short list and that success on the harder task is more likely if one makes a greater effort (Wellman, 1978; Wellman, Collins, & Glieberman, 1981). Many preschoolers and 5 year olds know that it would be easier to relearn information (e.g., a list of birds) that one had forgotten than to learn it for the first time. Of course, younger children are not aware of some aspects of memory; for example, only older children appreciate that it is easier to retell a story in their own words than to repeat it verbatim, a realization that is relevant to children's courtroom testimony (Kurtz & Borkowski, 1987; Bruck et al., 2006).

Knowledge about strategies

Children know a great deal more about using strategies to help in memorizing and solving problems than we might think. They seem particularly sensitive to the value of external aids to memory – for example, leaving your books where you will see them in the morning and writing notes to yourself. According to Lovett and Pillow (1995), even children who were not yet literate suggested the latter ploy! Children are also aware of the value of associations in memory (e.g., jogging your memory of a birthday party by thinking about who was there) (Wellman, 1977). As children grow older, their understanding of what strategies are appropriate improves (O'Sullivan, 1996), and sometimes, they reveal a rather sophisticated understanding of memory strategies. When asked how she would remember a phone number, an 8-year-old responded:

> 'Say the number is 633-8854. Then what I'd do is – say that my number is 633, so I won't have to remember that, really. And then I would think, now I've got to remember 88. Now I'm 8 years old, so I can remember, say, my age two times. Then I say how old my brother is, and how old he was last year. And that's how I'd usually remember that phone number.'

> 'Is that how you would most often remember a phone number?' the experimenter asked.

> 'Well, usually I write it down.' (Kreutzer, Leonard, & Flavell, 1975, p. 11)

How can we define the relationship between metacognition and performance on cognitive tasks? Unfortunately, this relationship is not straightforward (Miller & Weiss, 1981). Some situations, for example, are more likely to engage the child's metacognitive abilities than others. Carr and Jessup (1995) found that 5, 6, and 7 year olds who understood which strategy they were using employed some strategies more correctly when solving maths problems. If children understand that a strategy like rehearsal is useful, do they actually use it in all situations? The answer is no. Although they would know to use it when doing maths, they wouldn't necessarily use it when trying to remember a shopping list, for instance. But it is important to remember that even adults don't always apply strategies they know to be effective in situations where they would be useful. It is unrealistic to expect children always to act at an optimal level of cognitive functioning when adults don't.

SUMMARY

This chapter focused on the development of the cognitive functions which help us think about the world around us, such as memory, attention and executive control. We highlighted the *information-processing approach*, which views the human mind as a system that processes information and attempts to understand how the limitations of the system impact on the way cognitive functions work. While early information processing accounts of cognitive development focused on changes in processing limitations (e.g., the capacity of short-term memory), more recently researchers have tried to consider developments in the executive control of the cognitive functions which children use for processing information (e.g., rehearsing in working memory) as they get older.

Executive control processes govern how we organize and use our various cognitive functions and strategies. Researchers have linked the development of executive function to the growth of prefrontal cortex. Tasks like the Dimension Change Card Sort indicate that executive control develops significantly between 3 and 4 years of age. Nonetheless, precursors of executive function emerge significantly before this in the first year of life. Researchers have disagreed over what emerging abilities explain the development of executive function. Some have suggested that inhibition is particularly important whereas others stress the importance of understanding and thinking about rules. More recently theorists have suggested that both of these developments may be important.

As children get older, and their executive abilities improve they become better at exerting control over their *attention,* to shift towards task relevant information and avoid distraction. Older children also implement more systematic or deliberate *planning* to focus their attention when gathering needed information.

Memory development is studied extensively, examining changes in sensory memory, working (or short-term) memory, and long-term memory. Long-term memory includes semantic memory, which concerns all the knowledge and facts about the world a child has, and *episodic memory*, which concerns memory for specific events. Our working *memory span*, or the amount of information we can hold in working memory, improves between infancy and adulthood. However, it is clear that beyond infancy this is largely due to improvements in executive control of working memory strategies and processes. For instance, the spontaneous use of verbal *rehearsal* as a memory strategy increases with age.

Problem solving involves a high level of executive control because it mobilizes perception, attention and memory to reach a solution. Over development, rule-based problem solving changes as children use different and more complex rules to guide their problem solving on logical tasks. *Analogy* is a powerful tool in problem solving, and may be an important means by which we learn to read and do maths. *Deductive reasoning* seems to develop later in childhood, though simple versions of such tasks have shown some early evidence of *propositional reasoning*, transitive *inference* and *hierarchical categorization*.

Lastly, we discussed the development of metacognitive abilities. *Metacognition* refers to the individual's knowledge and control of cognitive activities. Metacognitive knowledge, which develops over childhood, includes the child's knowledge about the self, her theory of mind, and her knowledge about the task and about specific strategies. Although young children understand how some features of a task may influence memory, even 6-year-olds are not good at monitoring their comprehension of information about a task. Young children are aware of the importance of memory strategies, and they are particularly sensitive to the use of external memory cues. However, older children have a more accurate and realistic view of their own memory abilities, and they are able to separate their own beliefs and desires from reality.

Explore and Discuss

1. When we reach 2.5 to 3 years of age and begin to use language rather effectively, we talk to other people quite a bit as we try to remember the events we have experienced. Do you think our early memories are actually memories of our own experiences and our reactions to them, or are they more like a social redefinition of these experiences? Explain your answer.

2. Given what you have read in this chapter about changes in thinking and problem-solving abilities in childhood, do you think it is a coincidence that formal schooling begins at around 6 to 7 years of age? Why or why not?

3. Think about when you use executive functions. Can you think up a test of executive functions for school-aged children and adults? Which components of executive function would it tap?

4. Child testimony is a very important and complex issue. What do you think might be the best way to interview a preschooler who is the only witness to a crime? Would you use a different interview approach if the child was 7 to 8 years of age? Why or why not?

Recommended Reading

Classic

Hitch, G. J., & Towse, J. N. (1995). Working memory: What develops? In F. E. Weinert & W. Schneider (eds), *Memory performance and competencies: Issues in growth and development* (pp. 3–21). Mahwah, NJ: Erlbaum.

Nunes, T., & Bryant, P. E. (1996). *Children doing mathematics.* Oxford: Blackwell.

Rovee-Collier, C. (1990). The 'memory system' of prelinguistic infants. *Annals of the New York Academy of Sciences, 608*, 517–542.

Siegler, R. (1998). *Emerging minds: The process of change in children's thinking.* Oxford: Oxford University Press.

Contemporary

Bornstein, M. H., & Lamb, M. E. (2011). *Developmental psychology: An advanced textbook.* Hove: Psychology Press.

Goswami, U. (2010). *The Wiley-Blackwell handbook of childhood cognitive development.* Winchester UK: Wiley-Blackwell.

Saxe, G. B. (2015). *Culture and cognitive development: Studies in mathematical understanding.* Hove: Psychology Press.

CHAPTER 11

Intelligence, Achievement and Learning

In this chapter, we examine how children's abilities and experiences influence their achievement and learning. We describe how scientists define and measure intelligence. We also identify the biological and experiential factors that affect intelligence and its development and discuss how these factors may be modified to improve intelligent behaviour. We will explore such questions as: 'Are differences in intelligence caused by genetic factors, environmental influences, or both?', 'Are these differences permanent, or can they be changed?' We then consider the matter of achievement, examining various factors that affect children's performance on intelligence tests and in the classroom. After considering the results of some interventions to improve cognitive functioning, and theories of learning and academic or intellectual achievement, finally we look at intellectual giftedness and mental retardation, and conclude with some ideas about creativity in young children.

THEORIES OF INTELLIGENCE

In attempting to formulate theories of intelligence scientists have focused on three main issues: whether intelligence is unitary or multifaceted, whether it is determined by genetic or environmental factors, and whether it predicts academic success and success outside school. The first of these questions, typically concerns whether intelligence is a single characteristic of a person that cuts across all aspects of behaviour or whether intelligence has many components so that a person can be intelligent in some, but not all, of these components. Today, it is generally accepted that intelligence is multifaceted, and that both genetic and environmental influences contribute to a person's intelligence. The argument is far from over. Contemporary debates concentrate on such issues as whether heredity is more influential than the environment or the other way around, and the degree to which inherited factors that contribute to intelligence may be altered by environmental conditions. The third question asks how important intelligence, as measured by IQ tests, is in predicting children's and adults' success in school, real-life situations and problem solving. Is it useful in predicting academic success, job stability, and good health and adjustment?

The factor analytic approach

It may seem obvious that intelligence has many components. We all know we are better at some things than at others. Early investigators believed that intelligence is a unitary or single ability that affects everything a person does. To test this idea, researchers have performed factor analysis on intelligence test performances of large samples of people. This approach is a statistical procedure that can determine which of several factors, or scores, are closely related to one another without overlapping one another's contribution. An early researcher who used factor analysis, Charles Spearman (1927), proposed that intelligence is composed of a *general factor* (*g*) and a number of *specific factors* (*s*). Spearman regarded *g* as general mental ability, which was involved in all cognitive tasks, and he saw *s* factors as unique to particular tasks. A person with a high *g* would be expected to do generally well on all tasks. Variations in her performance on different tasks could be attributed to the varying amounts of *s* factors she possesses.

> **factor analysis** A statistical procedure used to determine which of a number of factors, or scores, are both closely related to one another and relatively independent of other groups of factors, or scores.

This unitary concept of intelligence was challenged by Lewis Thurstone (1938), who proposed that seven primary skills comprise intelligence: verbal meaning, perceptual speed, reasoning, number, rote memory, word fluency and spatial visualization. Other researchers, such as Carroll (1993, 1997) and Johnson et al. (2004), have also argued for the existence of a general factor of cognitive ability. It seems that people who do well on one kind of cognitive test (e.g., reading comprehension) are indeed likely to do well on other such tests (e.g., listening comprehension or folding paper into specific shapes, as in Japanese origami). However, individuals still vary in their competence across different domains, such as vocabulary, basic mathematics skills or the ability to discriminate musical pitch. In other words, children vary both in overall level of intellectual ability and in how skilled they are in specific aspects of cognitive functioning.

However, it may be the case that there are alternative models that can explain some important findings in terms of intelligence without recourse to a concept of general intelligence (van der Maas et al., 2006). One possibility may be that different aspects of intelligence or cognitive abilities interact through the course of development to indicate higher 'general' intelligence scores when, in fact, there is no underlying factor. Thus positive associations between different aspects of intelligence or abilities give an illusion of a common, core factor. Van der Maas and colleagues argue that their dynamical model can explain other factors too, such as low predictability from early childhood and the Flynn effect.

How researchers (and children and adults) conceptualize intelligence has important implications in educational contexts because, as we shall see, it influences perceptions of self and the motivation to succeed at a task. How useful or appropriate the concept of general intelligence is remains a topic of considerable debate.

The information-processing approach: Sternberg's triarchic theory

Information-processing researchers focus on the processes involved in intellectual activity. They argue that to understand intelligence we must assess how individuals use information-processing capabilities, such as memory and problem-solving skills, to carry out intelligent activities (Das, 2004).

Sternberg's (1985, 2001, 2005) triarchic theory of intelligence is an important example of this approach. As this theory's name implies, it proposes three major components of intelligence: information-processing skills, experience with a given task, and ability to tailor one's behaviour to the demands of a particular context. These three components work together in organizing and guiding intelligent behaviour. *Information processing skills* are required to encode, store and retrieve varying kinds of information. *Experience,* the second component of Sternberg's model, considers how much exposure and practice an individual has had with a particular intellectual task. For example, if two children perform similarly on a mathematics test of long division but one child has never studied this topic and the other child has studied it for several years, we would make different judgements about these children's relative intelligence based on their performance on the test (Sternberg, Wagner, & Okagaki, 1993).

> **triarchic theory of intelligence** A theory that proposes three major components of intelligence: information-processing skills, experience with a task, and ability to adapt to the demands of a context.

Sternberg's third component, *context,* recognizes that intelligence cannot be separated from the situation in which it is used. Because people must function effectively in many different contexts, they must be able both to adapt to the requirements of a situation and to select and arrange situations to meet their own abilities and needs (Sternberg, 1985). Thus, one dimension on which the intelligence of a particular behaviour can be measured is its suitability and effectiveness in a particular setting (Sternberg & Wagner, 1994; Ceci, 1996).

Subsequently, Sternberg expanded his triarchic theory into a theory of *successful intelligence,* which considers intelligence in relation to the ability of an individual to meet her own goals and those of her society (Sternberg, 2001). Successful intelligence requires three abilities: analytical, creative and practical. *Analytical abilities* include those taught and tested in most schools and colleges, such as reasoning about the best answer to a test question. *Creative abilities* are involved in devising new ways of addressing issues and concerns. *Practical abilities* are used in everyday activities such as work, family life, and social and professional interactions. Much of practical knowledge we use is tacit. It is not explicitly formulated, and it is rarely taught directly to children; rather it is learned by observing others (Sternberg & Wagner, 1993). Nonetheless, this kind of practical, *tacit knowledge,* which is often referred to as common sense, is shared by many people and guides intelligent behaviour (Cianciolo et al., 2006). Sternberg (2001) found that tacit knowledge of this sort, though not associated with IQ score, predicted the salaries and job performance of adult workers.

Applications of Sternberg's triarchic theory in schools appear successful in helping children to learn academic material (Grigorenko, Sternberg, & Strauss, 2006) and in helping adolescents improve their scores on college entrance examinations (Stemler et al., 2006). Moreover, children who were given teaching materials and approaches based on the triarchic theory reported enjoying the material more than children taught the same information in a more traditional fashion. This research suggests that this approach to intelligence, when applied in the class setting, may benefit children's learning as well as enhance their motivation to learn.

Gardner's theory of multiple intelligences

> **theory of multiple intelligences** Gardner's multifactorial theory that proposes eight distinct types of intelligence.

Howard Gardner (2011) proposed a theory of multiple intelligences. He suggests that human beings possess eight kinds of intelligence: linguistic, logical-mathematical, spatial, musical, bodily kinaesthetic, intrapersonal, interpersonal, and naturalistic (see Table 11-1). He has also suggested a possible ninth form, which he called spirituality or existential intelligence (Gardner, 1999). Three of the types of intelligence – linguistic, logical-mathematical and spatial – are similar to the kinds of abilities assessed in traditional intelligence tests. The remaining types have been much less widely studied, yet according to Gardner they are equally important to human functioning. For example, interpersonal intelligence may be of crucial importance to a parent, a nurse or a teacher; bodily kinaesthetic intelligence may greatly facilitate the performance of a dancer or an athlete.

Table 11-1 Gardner's theory of multiple intelligences

Type of intelligence/description	Examples
Linguistic: Sensitivity to word meanings; mastery of syntax; appreciation of the ways language can be used	Poet, teacher
Logical-mathematical: Understanding of objects, symbols, the actions that can be performed on them and the interrelations among these actions; ability to operate in the abstract and to identify problems and seek explanations	Mathematician, scientist
Spatial: Accurate perception of visual world; ability to transform perceptions and mentally re-create visual experience; sensitivity to tension, balance, and composition; ability to detect similar patterns	Artist, engineer, chess player
Musical: Sensitivity to musical tones and phrases; ability to combine tones and phrases into larger rhythms and structures; awareness of music's emotional aspects	Musician, composer
Bodily kinaesthetic: Skilled and graceful use of one's body for expressive or goal-directed purposes; ability to handle objects skilfully	Dancer, athlete, actor
Intrapersonal: Access to one's own feelings; ability to draw on one's emotions to guide and understand behaviour	Novelist, psychotherapist, actor
Interpersonal: Ability to notice and distinguish among others' moods, temperaments, motives, and intentions; ability to act on this knowledge	Political or religious leader, parent, teacher, psychotherapist
Naturalist: Insight into the natural world; ability to identify different life forms and species and the relationships between them	Biologist, naturalist

Source: Gardner (1983, 1999); Torff and Gardner (1999)

Playing football requires a different form of kinaesthetic intelligence than, for example, dance or juggling
© moodboard/Alamy Stock Photo

Each type of intelligence is considered unique, with its own developmental path guided by its own forms of perception, learning and memory (Connell, Sheridan, & Gardner, 2003). For example, linguistic intelligence emphasizes verbal and memory abilities, and generally develops over years of educational experience. In contrast, bodily kinaesthetic intelligence, which emphasizes understanding of body mechanics and its coordination with perceptual abilities, may appear quite early in life and be less dependent on experience. Gardner also suggests that an individual can display different combinations of these intelligences, and different cultures or periods of history may emphasize or value some of these forms of intelligence more than others.

Although the approach has many positive and intuitively appealing elements, Gardner's intelligences may not all be entirely separate entities; some may be closely tied to others, whereas others may be distinct (e.g., Weinberg, 1989; Carroll, 1993). For instance, one might anticipate greater overlap between ability in logical-mathematical and spatial abilities than between logical-mathematical and interpersonal abilities. In addition there is a need for further empirical validation of the theory because comparatively few efforts have been made to evaluate Gardner's theory rigorously using standard assessment techniques or to develop tests based directly on the theory (Sternberg & Wagner, 1994; Benbow & Lubinski, 1996).

TESTING INTELLIGENCE

Although psychologists have become increasingly interested in the *processes* that contribute to intellectual functioning, the study and testing of intelligence have traditionally focused on its *products* – that is, on the specific knowledge and skills displayed on intelligence tests. On the basis of such tests, researchers have developed the intelligence quotient (IQ), an index of the way a person performs on a standardized intelligence test relative to the way others her age perform. Although the term IQ is widely used, it is often misunderstood: many people think IQ is innate and although we are able to do and understand more things as we get older, an individual's IQ does not change. But research has shown that an individual's IQ *can* change over the life span and can be modified both by experience and training. Moreover, because of doubts over its reliability and usefulness across educational contexts, the concept of IQ has proved somewhat controversial in terms of its usefulness in education and learning environments.

> **intelligence quotient (IQ)** An index of the way a person performs on a standardized intelligence test relative to the way others her age perform.

In discussing intelligence and intelligence testing, it is important to remember that we can only *infer* intellectual capacity from the results of an IQ test. Although we assume that capacity and performance are related, we can only directly measure how someone performs on a test. Moreover, there is always some discrepancy or gap between capacity and performance owing to the particular circumstances of a performance, such as the precise construction of a test or the test taker's emotional state during the test. How we interpret or explain the gap ends up being crucial to our evaluations of our own and other people's intelligence, a topic we discuss later in the chapter when we consider achievement motivation (Dweck, 2000, 2006).

Most existing intelligence tests predict academic achievement quite well. Predicting how well a person will succeed at a job is the second goal of intelligence testing, and according to Gottfredson (1997), such measures can be powerful predictors of overall work performance. A third use of intelligence testing is in assessing people's general adjustment and health. Many tests have been used to detect signs of neurological and serious intellectual problems, and emotional distress in infants and children as well as adults.

Unfortunately, intelligence tests do not make predictions as accurately for some groups in society as for others (Neisser et al., 1996). Critics have pointed out that these tests often require knowledge that children with fewer advantages than others, or less attentive parents, may not have. As a result, intelligence tests may unfairly classify some people or groups of people as less intelligent than they actually are. For some years now, researchers have been attempting to develop what are known as 'culture-fair tests' – that is, tests that attempt to exclude or minimize the kind of experientially or culturally biased content in IQ tests that could influence scores. The Raven Progressive Matrices Test, which requires people to identify, distinguish and match patterns of varying complexity, and the Kaufman test are examples of such tests.

More recently, researchers and educational psychologists have moved towards computer-based methods for delivering tests and assessing intelligence. For instance, Vrana and Vrana (2017) administered the Weschler Test online. One potential drawback of computer-based assessments is that they are not able to pick up on some of the subtleties of interaction or responses which human assessors are able to. However, the researchers argue that artificial intelligence is near to being able accurately to administer tests and assess intelligence on many standard measures.

Measuring infant intelligence

The *Bayley Scales of Infant Development*, or BSID (Bayley, 1969, 1993), are probably the best-known and most widely used of all infant development tests. Because these tests were designed to be used with the very young, they include many non-verbal test items chosen for their ability to measure specific developmental milestones. The Bayley scales are used with infants and children between 1 month and 3.5 years of age, and they are generally used to assess children suspected to be at risk for abnormal development. For example, the Bayley *mental* scale includes such things as looking for a hidden object and naming pictures, whereas the *motor* scale includes such items as grasping ability and jumping skills. Although these scales are useful in identifying infants at risk for unhealthy development, the Bayley scales and other tests of infant intelligence are poor predictors of later cognitive levels. This may be because they rely primarily on sensorimotor measures, or because aspects of higher intelligence are not adequately developed in infancy to be easily tested.

The development of motor and information processing skills from infancy onwards is discussed, in more detail, in Chapter 4.

Newer tests, such as the Fagan test, measure information-processing skills. The *Fagan Test of Infant Intelligence* assesses processes such as encoding the attributes of objects, seeing similarities and differences between objects, and forming and using mental representations (Fagan, 1992). The Fagan test examines an infant's intelligence by measuring the amount of time the infant spends looking at a new object compared with the time he spends looking at a familiar object (Fagan et al., 1991) – the habituation–dishabituation technique. Using a set of 20 photographs of human faces, arranged in pairs, the examiner begins by showing a baby one photograph of the first pair for 20 seconds. Then the examiner pairs that photograph with its mate, showing the baby the two photos together for 5 seconds, and then again for another 5 seconds, this time reversing the two photos left to right (to avoid any tendency for the infant to 'choose' one side). The score the infant receives is made up of the total time he spends looking at the novel photograph throughout a presentation of all ten pairs. In cross-cultural research, Fagan and his colleagues found that there were practically no differences between the average scores obtained by nearly 200 infants from America, Bahrain and Uganda, suggesting that the test is culture fair. However, although this test predicts later cognitive development better than older tests, the correlations with later development remain weak to moderate (Sternberg, Grigorenko, & Bundy, 2001; Tasbihsazan, Nettelbeck, & Kirby, 2003).

Measuring intelligence from infancy onwards

THE STANFORD-BINET TEST

The *Stanford-Binet Test* is the modern version of a test devised in the early 1900s by Binet and Simon to identify children who were unable to learn in traditional classroom settings and who would benefit from special education. Binet and Simon believed that intelligence was malleable and that children's academic performance could be improved with special programmes (Binet, 1973; Siegler, 1992). They were critical of earlier psychologists who had tried to assess intelligence by measuring simple sensory or motor responses, and so sought to examine higher mental functions, such as comprehension, reasoning and judgement, as well as skills taught in school, such as recalling the details of a story. In addition, because they recognized that as children grow they become able to solve increasingly complex problems, they built into their test age-related changes in children's learning with the aim of tapping children's competence at different age levels.

Piaget's early work was conducted with Binet in Paris. This connection and Piaget's later work are discussed more fully in Chapter 9.

Binet introduced the concept of *mental age*, which is an index of a child's actual performance compared with her true age. Thus, if a 6-year-old child gets as many items correct as the average 7 year old, the 6 year old's mental age is 7; that is, she performs as well as a child who is 7 years old. The mental age concept was later captured in the intelligence quotient, for which the German psychologist William Stern devised the following formula:

$$IQ = MA/CA \times 100$$

where IQ equals mental age (MA) divided by chronological age (CA), multiplied by 100. Thus, if a child's mental age equalled her chronological age, she would be performing like an average child her age, and her IQ would be 100. If her performance was better than other children her age, her IQ would be above 100. If it was inferior, her IQ would be less than 100. Today's Stanford-Binet test is an updated version of the Binet-Simon test. It includes language and mathematics skills as well as other indexes of intelligent performance.

THE WECHSLER SCALES

Wechsler Intelligence Scales Three intelligence tests for preschool children, school-age children and adults, which yield separate scores for verbal and performance IQ as well as a combined IQ score.

The Wechsler Intelligence Scales, developed by David Wechsler (1952, 1958), include the Wechsler Preschool and Primary Scale of Intelligence (WPPSI), the Wechsler Intelligence Scale for Children (WISC), and the Wechsler Adult Intelligence Scale (WAIS). These tests yield separate verbal and performance IQ scores as well as a combined, full-scale IQ score. The most recent update of the WISC, which is the fourth version (Wechsler, 2003), includes items related to how children process information such as memory, strategy use, and processing speed. Such items were added because they may be less influenced by experience with school or certain cultural or economic factors. The descriptions of the WISC subtests from this recent version are shown in Table 11-2.

Table 11-2   The Wechsler Intelligence Scale for Children, fourth edition (WISC-IV)

Subtests	Descriptions and some examples	Skills thought to tap
Similarities	The child is asked to tell how paired words are alike (e.g., *How are a cup and a glass alike?*)	Concept formation; categorization
Vocabulary	The child is asked to define each word in a list of words of increasing difficulty	Concept formation; long-term memory; vocabulary
Comprehension	A series of questions ask the child to explain why certain actions or practices are desirable (e.g., *What should you do if you lose a friend's toy?*)	Factual knowledge; long-term memory; intellectual interest
Information	For each item, the child answers questions that address a broad range of general knowledge topics (e.g., *How many days are there in a week?*)	Factual knowledge; long-term memory; intellectual interest
Word reasoning*	The child is given successive clues and asked to identify the common concept being described in a series of clues (e.g., *'This is squishy and full of holes'* or *'You use it to wash things with'*)	Verbal abstraction and comprehension; analogic and general reasoning ability; integration and synthesis of different types of information; domain knowledge; generation of alternative concepts
Block design	The child is shown a model of a red-and-white design or a picture of it and is asked to re-create the design, using blocks whose sides are either red, white, or half red and half white	Visual-motor coordination; concept formation; pattern recognition; spatial ability
Picture concepts*	The child is presented with two or three rows of pictures of familiar objects and must choose one from each row to form a group with a common characteristic (e.g., *things to eat or things to play with*)	Fluid reasoning; abstract categorical ability
Matrix reasoning*	The child looks at an incomplete matrix, a grid of four equal-size squares in which all but three of the squares are filled with designs. The child must look then at a separate display of five possible designs and choose the one that will complete the matrix	Visual information processing; abstract reasoning skills
Picture completion	The child is asked to look at a series of pictures and, for each one, to point out what is missing from the picture (e.g., *a car with a missing wheel; a rabbit with a missing ear*)	Visual organization; perceptual reasoning; concentration
Digit span	The examiner says several sequences of digits, each longer than the preceding one, and the child is asked to repeat them either in the order in which the examiner said them or in reverse order (e.g., *2-7-4; 3-1-9-6; 8-4-2-7-5*).	Mental alertness and attention; cognitive flexibility; short-term memory
Letter-number sequencing*	The examiner reads to the child a sequence of letters and numbers and asks the child to recall the numbers (in ascending order) and the letters (in alphabetical order)	Working memory – sequencing, mental manipulation, attention, short-term auditory memory, visual-spatial imaging, processing speed
Arithmetic	The child is asked to solve, without physical aids such as pencil and paper, arithmetic problems that the examiner presents orally (the test is timed)	Working memory; mathematical skills
Cancellation*	The child is shown an array of pictures of objects and asked to find and mark every picture of a certain class of objects as fast as possible (the test is timed) (e.g., *in an array of pictures of miscellaneous things such as flowers, furniture items, animals, cleaning implements, the child might be asked to find and mark all the pictures of animals*)	Visual selective attention; processing speed

* Subtests marked with an asterisk are new to the WISC in its fourth edition.

> **deviation IQ** An IQ score that indicates the extent to which a person's performance on a test deviates from age mates' average performance.

Rather than use mental age as a basis for estimating intelligence, Wechsler created the deviation IQ, which like the Binet IQ takes 100 as an average score. The deviation IQ is based on extensive testing of people of different ages and on the statistical computation of mean scores for each age group. In computing these average scores, psychologists use a statistic called the *standard deviation* to identify the extent to which scores deviate from the norm. As a result, an individual's score may be at the mean (average), or it may be one or more standard deviations above or below the average for their age group. This test has been standardized on samples in a number of countries around the world (Suzuki, 2007).

THE KAUFMAN ASSESSMENT BATTERY FOR CHILDREN

The *Kaufman Assessment Battery for Children (K-ABC)* (Kaufman & Kaufman, 1983, 2006) measures several types of information-processing skills grouped into two categories: *sequential processing* (solving problems in a step-by-step fashion) and *simultaneous processing* (examining and integrating a wide variety of materials in the solution of a problem). The test also assesses achievement in academic subjects, such as vocabulary and arithmetic, and efforts have been made to design the test items (many non-verbal) to be culture fair. In addition, the test designers used a wide and representative sample of many American cultural and socioeconomic groups in establishing norms for this test. An interesting innovation is that if a child fails early items on a subscale, the examiner teaches the child how to complete these items before the child does the rest of the subtest. According to the designers of the test, this ensures that no child who is capable of learning an unfamiliar task receives a failing score on it.

THE COGNITIVE ASSESSMENT SYSTEM

The *Cognitive Assessment System (CAS)* is a further test that is used in many different countries (Naglieri & Das, 1997). The test assesses different cognitive processes across childhood and adolescence. Assessment of *planning* relates to how people form, select and regulate plans of action. *Attention* processes are concerned with how cognitive resources and effort are distributed. *Simultaneous* and *successive* processing comprise the cognitive processes used in the acquisition, storage and retrieval of information. Researchers who use the test argue that these PASS processes are very important from an educational perspective and, although they relate to one another, are conceptually distinct. However, some (e.g., Kranzler & Keith, 1999) have argued that a general intelligence account is more useful and a better fit to explain data because the PASS processes are difficult to disentangle empirically, and may not be conceptually or functionally distinct.

RAVEN'S MATRICES

Raven's *Standard Progressive Matrices (SPM)*, *Advanced Progressive Matrices (APM)* and *Coloured Progressive Matrices (CPM)* are forms of test developed by John C. Raven. To complete the tests, participants need to complete a pattern or sequence (see Figure 11-1 for an example). These tests were initially devised to

Figure 11-1 Pattern from Raven's Standard Progressive Matrices
© Science & Society Picture Library/Getty Images

assess the ability to think clearly and logically about complex issues, and the ability to store and reproduce information. Often the tests are characterized as assessing analytic ability. The different forms of the matrix tests, which have been further developed over a number of years, are appropriate for different subpopulations. So, for instance, the SPM is used primarily for children, APM for adolescents and adults, and CPM for younger children.

Raven's matrices are used widely not only in educational contexts but also to assess the performance and reasoning abilities of individuals with psychological and other disorders such as autism and Asperger's syndrome (e.g., Hayashi et al., 2007). They have also helped to address questions about the genetic heritability of intelligence through the Minnesota Twin Study (Bouchard et al., 1990). In this study, the performance on Raven's SPM of twins who had been raised together was compared with twins who had been raised apart. Compared with dizygotic twins (non-identical twins who do have the same genetic make up), monozygotic (identical) twins showed much higher correlation between one another in IQ scores. Moreover, although the correlations were higher for monozygotic twins raised together (in the same household) than those raised apart, the difference was not substantial. Bouchard et al. concluded that around 70% of intelligence (measured using Raven's SPM) was genetically based.

Although widespread, Raven's matrices have been criticized as a measure of intelligence because they are based upon Spearman's model of general intelligence (g) and therefore multifaceted perspectives on intelligence are not covered by the test. In a similar vein, performance does appear to be susceptible to learning or training. In a study of 14 and 16 year olds in Central Africa, Irvine (1969b) found that variations in performance across the sample decreased when a training procedure was introduced that involved giving sample problems. A further criticism (Bortner, 1965) is that the tests can give an indication of level of performance, but are of little diagnostic use in establishing why people make errors.

The measurement of intelligence

DEVELOPMENT OF NORMS AND STANDARDS

A person's performance on an intelligence test is always described in relation to the performance on the same test of others in a particular group; the person's intelligence score (or IQ) can therefore be either average, above average, or below average. Age is a particularly critical factor when setting norms (average or typical performance) for children's test performance. Although children generally improve their test performance as they grow older, their score relative to the scores of other children of their age continues to be the significant factor in evaluating their intellectual development.

Psychometricians do not agree on whether comparison groups in intelligence testing should be equated on such factors as level of education, socioeconomic class or gender. Nevertheless, in evaluating test performance, we should always consider how closely the attributes and experiences of the person being tested approximate those of the group that was used to establish the test norms. For example, it would be inappropriate to use the same set of norms in evaluating the performance of children raised in an isolated Papua New Guinea tribal community without access to formal schooling that we use to evaluate the performance of middle-class, Swedish children. Because the conditions under which a test is administered may influence performance, it is extremely important that we subject a test to *standardization*, which means that on every testing occasion the procedures that examiners follow, the instructions they give to examinees and the test scoring are identical, or as nearly so as possible.

TEST VALIDITY AND RELIABILITY

For any test to provide useful information about an individual, it must be valid; that is, it must measure what it claims it measures. It must also be reliable; that is, an individual's scores must be consistent over different times of measurement.

In establishing the *validity* of an intelligence test, researchers and practitioners often correlate performance on the test with some other measure which is believed to reflect the capacity being tested. The most frequently used criteria for process of validation are achievement test scores, previous achievement or grades in school, teachers' ratings of cognitive ability, and performance on other intelligence tests. Intelligence tests are much more successful in predicting school performance than in predicting things like creativity or social skills. Even within school performance, intelligence test scores are more closely related to mathematical problem solving and reading comprehension than to ability in drama, art, or music.

Reliability – the extent to which a test yields consistent results over time or successive administrations – is also critical for evaluating the utility of an intelligence test. To be useful, a test's scores must not fluctuate unpredictably from one administration to another. This is because a chief goal of these tests is to *predict* the individual's performance *beyond a single administration of the test*. Although reliability captures how much a test is useful across administrations, a related but broader issue is that of the stability of intelligence, to which we turn next.

Stability of measured intelligence

Is intelligence an absolute quality that remains stable or fixed over time, or can it change as a function of experience? To answer this question, we need to understand many things about intelligence, intelligence testing, and the limitations of intelligence measures. Tests like the Binet and Wechsler scales, which focus on the products of intelligence and measure current performance, have generally demonstrated that IQ scores are not stable over time but fluctuate. In fact, as we will see, the evidence to date suggests that there are both stability and change in intellectual functioning over time.

PREDICTIVE VALUE OF INFANT TESTING

Most information on the consistency of performance on intelligence tests derives from longitudinal studies in which children – in some cases, as young as 1 month old – have been repeatedly tested over time. Some of these studies are the Berkeley Guidance Study, the Berkeley Growth Study and the Fels Longitudinal Study, in which individuals were followed for periods of time ranging from 20 to 50 years. These and other early studies have found no significant relation between intelligence test scores recorded in infancy and those attained later in childhood or even adulthood (Figure 11-2; see also McCall, Hogarty, & Hurlburt, 1972; Honzik, 1983; Lewis, 1983). However, as these early studies tended to compare infants' sensorimotor skills with later problem-solving and verbal skills, it may be that these two kinds of abilities have little relation to one another. From a developmental psychology perspective, getting information about base or trait intelligence is hampered by the abilities of infants and children to answer the same sorts of questions as older children, adolescents and adults. This has led some to question whether the concept of intelligence, as understood in many education contexts, is a useful one for developmental psychologists (e.g., Ma & Schapira, 2017).

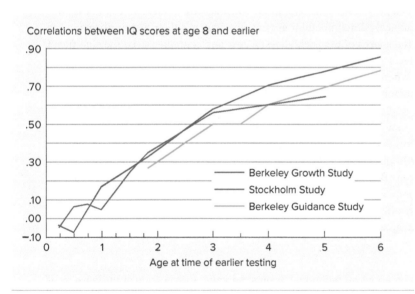

Correlations between IQ scores at age 8 and earlier

Figure 11-2   Predicting IQ scores
The height of each curve represents the degree to which children's early intelligence test scores correlated with their Stanford-Binet IQ scores when they were 8 years old. The longer the time lapse between earlier and later testing, the less predictive value the earlier score held. Notice that in the Berkeley Growth and Stockholm Studies, the earliest scores were actually negatively correlated with later ones.
Source: Honzik (1976, 1983).

Research using infant tests that mostly focus on information-processing abilities, especially attentional processes, has found higher correlations with later cognitive measures (e.g., Fagan, 1992; Rose & Feldman, 1995).

These studies have typically used methods such as habituation and recovery (the infant's ability to recognize and attend to a totally new stimulus) to assess information processing.

Fagan and his colleagues found significant but moderate correlations between infants' attention at 7 months of age and their intellectual functioning at 3 and 5 years (Fagan et al., 1991). Bornstein and Sigman (1986) also found moderately strong relations between such attentional measures in young infants and the scores these children achieved on intelligence tests at ages 3 to 6. Other researchers have found similar relations, sometimes extending even into adulthood (Rose et al., 1989; DiLalla et al., 1990). However, not all studies show such positive relations (Tasbihsazan et al., 2003).

Although we may be tempted to conclude that early individual differences in attention reflect genetic predispositions, the child's environment and other personal characteristics may be influential. In fact, one study found that attentional processing in 5 month olds was related to the responsivity of the infants' mothers (Bornstein & Tamis, 1986). Differences in attentional processing in infants may also reflect variation stemming from other factors, such as child temperament (Karass & Braungart-Rieker, 2004). Thus, parental behaviour and the other characteristics of the child probably have a significant impact on infant intelligence, as well as on later development into adulthood.

CHANGES IN CHILDREN'S IQ OVER TIME

IQ appears relatively stable from childhood onwards. A good deal of research indicates that, from the middle years of childhood, intelligence tests are fairly reliable predictors of later performance on such tests. For example, Honzik, MacFarlane, and Allen (1948) found a correlation of .70 between children's IQs at ages 8 and 18. Nonetheless, there is also evidence of variability in children's IQs. Many of the children tested in the Fels study, mentioned earlier, shifted considerably upward in IQ scores between the ages of 2.5 and 17 (McCall, Applebaum, & Hogarty, 1973). One of every three children scored higher by some 30 points, and one in seven shifted upward more than 40 points. On rare occasions, individuals have improved their IQ performance as much as 74 points. Investigators have also observed that high-IQ children are likely to show greater amounts of change than low-IQ children.

Some of the variability in IQ scores reflects the fact that different children develop cognitively at different rates of speed, just as they experience physical growth in spurts and at different ages (Garlick, 2003; Kanaya, Ceci, & Scullin, 2005). These variations in cognitive development affect the reliability of IQ scores. Experiential factors may also contribute to changes in IQ. Stressful life events, such as parental divorce or death or a change in schools, can cause at least temporary disruptions in cognitive performance. Indeed, children who show the most dramatic changes in IQ over time have often experienced major changes in their life circumstances, such as foster home placement or a serious illness (Honzik, 1983).

> In Chapter 16 we discuss whether intelligence declines or stays the same as people age.

INDIVIDUAL DIFFERENCES IN INTELLIGENCE
How much of intelligence is inherited?

There is considerable support for a component of heredity in intelligence. Most estimates of the heritability of intelligence – that is, the proportion of the variability in intelligence attributable to genetic factors – have suggested a figure of about 40% to 50% for middle-class European-Americans (McGue & Bouchard, 1987; Plomin, 1990; Plomin & Petrill, 1997). This suggests that the remaining 50% to 60% of the variability is due to environmental factors, including both social (family, peers, school) and non-social (dietary and disease factors, pollutants). However, any psychologists disagree with this 'more or less 50–50' proposition. Some, like Stephen Ceci (1996), hold that the estimates of the heritability of intelligence are too high; others, like Jensen, insist that they are too low; and still others argue that these estimates depend on the match and the interaction between genetic potential and environmental opportunities (Dickens & Flynn, 2001). Some, again, question the sense in which IQ captures a meaningful and stable psychological construct and whether it should be used in educational or other settings at all.

> The discussion over the heritability of IQ is another classic nature–nurture debate in psychology (see Chapter 1).

VIEWS THAT EMPHASIZE HERITABILITY OF IQ

associative learning
According to Jensen, lower-level learning tapped in tests of such things as short-term memorization and recall, attention, rote learning, and simple associative skills. Also called level I learning.

cognitive learning
According to Jensen, higher-level learning tapped in tests of such things as abstract thinking, symbolic processing and the use of language in problem solving. Also called level II learning.

The measures of intelligence used in studies to support arguments for high levels of heritability in IQ are often based on traditional views of intellectual functioning. For instance, Jensen (1969, 1993), the most outspoken proponent of the heritability position, proposes two types of learning, both inherited but each distinct from the other. Associative learning (*level I* learning) involves short-term memory, rote learning, attention, and simple associative skills. For example, we might ask a child to look at a group of familiar objects and then later to recall these objects. Cognitive learning (*level II* learning) involves abstract thinking, symbolic processes, conceptual learning, and the use of language in problem solving. An example of cognitive learning is the ability to answer questions like the following:

What should be the next number in the following series? 2, 3, 5, 8, 12, 17, …
How are an apple and a banana alike?

Most intelligence tests measure primarily cognitive learning abilities. Some, however, include some items that tap associative learning ability. Much of the work on variations in intelligence has focused on understanding differences in performance between different ethnic groups in North America. Jensen suggests that associative learning is equally distributed across all people but that level II learning is more concentrated in middle-class and European-American groups than in working-class or African-American groups (Herrnstein & Murray, 1994).

These conclusions have been called into question by studies comparing the IQs of people with differing numbers of genetic markers for African ancestry. Such studies have found no association between the number of markers of African ancestry and IQ (Nisbett et al., 2012). In addition, Williams and Ceci (1997) have shown that the IQ gap between ethnic groups has been decreasing, rather than increasing, in recent years. Van de Vijer and Phalet (2004) argue that care needs to be taken when assessing multicultural groups within a society, because not all individuals may have the same cultural understanding and sense of identification with the host culture (acculturation). Possible solutions to iron out cultural variations in test scores include: identifying what different norms are and making evaluations relative to these; adding corrections depending on how far an individual feels or belongs to a particular culture.

Twin studies also point to the importance of genetic factors in IQ. Van Leewen et al. (2007) explored how the high correlation in IQ scores among family members might be explained. The researchers focused on the concept of assortative mating – that is, the observation that individuals tend to choose partners with a similar IQ, therefore obscuring how far genes and how far environment (parenting factors) might explain their children's intelligence. Exploring the IQ correlations of monozygotic (MZ) and dizygotic (DZ) twins, and considering also the high correlation ($r = .33$) between parents' IQ, the analysis suggested that around 67% of variance in IQ was explained by genetic factor. Moreover, a further 9% was, claimed the researcher, due to gene–environment interaction; that is, the interrelation between genetic and environmental factors. Gene–environment interaction was particularly important for children with low IQs. These findings suggested, therefore, that only around 24% of IQ was due to environmental factors (broadly understood).

Some broad developmental theorists such as Brofenbrenner and Scarr have also suggested that genetic influences on IQ may be amplified in higher social economic groups where there is less scope for environment to affect development and intelligence negatively. However, much research giving support for this proposal comes from studies conducted in North America (e.g., Shanahan & Hofer, 2005). A study in Germany by Spengler et al. (2018) of 531 monozygotic and dizygotic twin pairs suggested that there was no influence of parental level of education on cognitive and non-verbal abilities, even for those with little shared environmental experiences. Environmental influences did positively influence verbal abilities for children raised by more educated parents. So, clearly genes and environment play a role but in often complex ways, and in different domains of development. To make simplistic statements about one or the other, or worse to use one or the other to guide education policy, would be a serious mistake.

Comparing intelligence scores across groups is a complex process. It is inappropriate to use estimates of the heritability of intelligence obtained from one group in interpreting findings based on the study of another group unless it can be demonstrated that the critical contributions from the environment to support the development of IQ are present *across* these groups. This is because environmental conditions will influence the extent to which an inherited ability can be expressed. Let's take as an example a person's height, a physical characteristic of human beings that, when children have good nutrition and are immunized against serious diseases, is essentially the result of inheritance (Kagan, 1969). However, all inherited characteristics interact with environmental forces to some degree, and so does height: in cultures with extremely adverse health and/ or nutritional factors, the genetic contributions to physical stature are lessened relative to more advantageous situations. This is why most starving children, if they live to adulthood, remain small of stature, regardless of the typical height of the ethnic groups to which they belong.

In the same fashion, heritability measures regarding intelligence for middle-class families with reasonably similar backgrounds and life circumstances may be quite different from such measures for working-class groups whose circumstances may differ dramatically from the middle-class groups. In short, genes depend on the environment for their expression (Moore, 2001). Poor nutrition, disease and stress due to myriad factors – for example, economic deprivation, overcrowded living quarters, homelessness, abuse, civil unrest, war – may overwhelm and thus minimize the genetic contribution to intellectual performance (Garcia Coll, 1990; Huston, McLloyd, & Garcia-Coll, 1994; Neisser, 1998).

Environmental factors

Even strong advocates for the genetic basis of human intelligence understand that children are brought up in circumstances that range from the most favourable to the most destructive. Furthermore, most scholars recognize that the quality and amount of stimulation offered to children in these varying conditions affect intellectual development.

PREGNANCY AND BIRTH

Factors such as poor maternal nutrition can have lasting effects on a child. Moreover, an extensive body of research details the negative effects on intellectual development of such things as maternal disease, such as AIDS, smoking, or a mother's use of alcohol or addiction to other drugs. In addition, events attending the process of birth, such as oxygen deprivation, can have destructive effects on a child's mental functioning. Deficits or defects traced to such factors are considered congenital, meaning that they occur during gestation or at birth. Rather than genetic in origin, they are either transmitted directly from the mother to the foetus or result from events during the birth process.

THE FAMILY

The child's first social environment, which is usually the family, has important influences on her intellectual functioning. A supportive, warm home environment that encourages a child to become self-reliant, to express her curiosity, and to explore has been linked to higher intellectual functioning (Petrill & Deater-Deckard, 2004). Parents who are emotionally and verbally responsive to their children, who provide an appropriate variety of learning experiences, and who encourage

Family members have a great influence on intellectual development; here parents are encouraging their daughter to read and helping her to progress.
© Shutterstock/ilkercelik

their children's interest in and efforts at learning tend to have children with higher IQ scores (Wachs, 2000; Bradley et al., 2001). It's important to note, however, that such family environments do not uniformly produce high-achieving children; even though children in the same family have many shared environmental influences, they are also subject to non-shared environmental stimuli that may counteract other influences and affect their intellectual development (Reiss et al., 2000; Rutter, 2006b).

BOX 11-1 Are there sex differences in IQ? Analysing data from the Scottish Mental Survey (1932)

Source: Based on Deary et al. (2003).

Introduction:

The question of whether there are sex differences in IQ is both contentious and enduring. The broad consensus for some time (e.g., Mackintosh, 1996) is that differences, if there are any, are small and restricted to certain aspects of intelligence tests (see Chapter 15 for a further discussion of these issues). The present paper explored the question of IQ differences between boys and girls using a historical database of a very large number of children. These data were collected as part of the Scottish Mental Survey (1932), which sought to establish the number of people in Scotland who were 'mentally deficient'. Most tests were taken on the same day: 1 June 1932.

Method:

The tests of cognitive ability were taken by 87,498 children; almost all 11 year olds (i.e., children who had been born in 1921) and roughly 95% of the relevant population. Children completed three tests – two picture tests (one a simple matching task and the other a classification task) and what was described as a verbal test (the Moray House Test, MHT, which assessed a variety of skills involving literacy and numeracy). Scores on the three tests were summed and children were then classified into 'IQ bands': 50 to <60, 60 to <65, then in bands of five up to the top band, 130 to 140. Once data had been checked for missing items or inconsistencies, the total sample included in the analysis was 79,376 (39,343 girls and 40,033 boys).

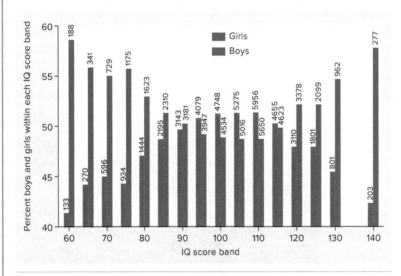

Figure 11-3 Numbers and percentages of boys and girls found within each IQ score band of the Scottish population born in 1921 and tested in the Scottish Mental Survey in 1932 at age 11

The y axis represents the percentage of each sex in each 5-point band of IQ scores. Numbers beside each point represent the absolute numbers of boys and girls in each 5-point IQ score band.
Source: Deary et al. (2003).

Results:

Boys' mean IQ score was 100.48, girls' mean score was 100.64. Although this was a huge sample size, this small difference was not statistically significant, $t(79,374) = 1.6$, $p = .11$. So boys' and girls' average IQ scores did not differ.

However, a Levene's test indicated there was a significant difference in the variance of boys' and girls' scores; that is, although boys and girls had very nearly the same average score, the distribution of scores around that average differed between the sexes. Figure 11-3 shows this variation and illustrates that more boys than girls scored either very low or very high marks on the test, whereas girls scored more marks close to the 100 average.

Discussion:

The findings from this study demonstrate that it is important to consider not only mean differences but also the ways in which data are distributed in different subpopulations. Deary and colleagues point to links between this pattern of variation and findings from studies with undergraduate students that indicate a similar pattern of achievement in university marks. That is, women tend to obtain more marks close to the mean and the distribution of marks for women is 'narrower', whereas men are over-represented in the top and bottom categories of marks awarded.

However, although the coverage of the dataset is impressive, the study is not without its problems. A key issue is the test itself. It may be that the test was in some way biased to producing this sex difference. This possibility remains, but there is good evidence that tests similar to the three used in the 1932 survey have reasonable predictive power in terms of IQ stability, and later academic and occupational success.

Moreover, because the home environment is not independent of inherited intelligence factors, the ways in which the family environment is related to children's intellectual functioning can be very difficult to disentangle from genetic effects.

SCHOOLS AND PEER GROUPS

Although more years of school and higher-quality schooling are related to increases in intelligence scores, the contrary is also true. Deficits in education may cause IQ scores to decline (Ceci, 1996; Ceci & Williams, 1997). Declines in intellectual skills have been associated with lack of formal education, dropping out and too much time off school. Numerous studies have also shown that children who have attended a high-quality preschool have higher skill levels than children who have not, even when the two groups are similar in socioeconomic status, family environment and prior skill levels (Wachs, 2000).

Poor and minority students in inner-city and rural areas in many countries often face a substantial disadvantage in school quality compared with those in wealthier areas. In addition, these students, due to a variety of environmental factors, are likely to enter school with no preschool experience and with lower levels of skills compared with their middle-class peers. Furthermore, disadvantaged students tend to fall further behind as they progress into middle and high school (Molfese & Martin, 2001; Turkheimer et al., 2003). Cultural differences and negative teacher attitudes may also hinder adjustment and learning for these children (Comer, 1996, 2004; Eccles, 2007).

THE COMMUNITY

The community as a cultural unit may have significant effects on a child's cognitive and intellectual development. For example, studies have shown that children living in isolated circumstances, such as rural areas, score lower on IQ tests than children in suburban or urban areas (Flynn, 1987; Ceci, 1991). Similarly, economically disadvantaged urban areas of modern cities are often associated with slowed intellectual development. The poor diets, unsafe housing, and high levels of violence and unemployment that characterize impoverished areas may all contribute to less adequate intellectual functioning (Pollitt, 1994; Garbarino, 1995; Bronfenbrenner et al., 1996; Evans, 2003).

It is important to stress, however, that in some cases environments stimulate and help children to develop intellectual abilities that are sophisticated, highly adaptive, and meaningful in their specific cultural circumstances (Sternberg, Grigorenko, & Bridglall, 2007). Intelligence tests devised to reveal intellectual capabilities in varying cultural contexts, such as regions in Africa (Serpell & Haynes, 2004) and the Eastern Mediterranean–Middle East (Gulgoz & Kagitcibasi, 2004), have been helpful in identifying how the construct of intelligence can be construed and measured in different cultural settings. This research indicates that concepts of intelligence can differ widely across cultures and that social factors, such as responsibility and sensitivity towards the family or community, are an important component of many of these conceptions. In recent years, the idea of social intelligence has even risen in prominence in discussions of intelligence (Goleman, 2006). Finally, other research has revealed intelligent actions that people carry out in their cultures and that are rarely tapped in typical tests of intelligence. For instance, the Pulawat islanders of Micronesia, who have little formal education or technology, have developed a navigational system that reveals a complex understanding of the relations among direction, winds, tides and currents, and that enables them to sail long distances out of the sight of land (Gladwin, 1970). Nevertheless, these skilled navigators would not perform well on a standard test of intelligence, despite the fact that their navigational skills evidence high levels of intelligence. Observations like these show us how important it is to analyse intellectual performance within the individual's cultural context (Ceci, 1996; Hutchins, 1996).

ETHNICITY, SOCIAL CLASS AND INTELLECTUAL PERFORMANCE

Some research has found somewhat controversial associations among ethnicity, social class and intellectual performance. In this section, we discuss these relations in greater depth. *Social class* is a broad term that includes such variables as education, occupation and income. The term *socioeconomic status* (or SES) is often used to refer to a combined assessment of these three variables (Benokraitis, 1996). Because these factors are frequently associated with one another, researchers tend to study them together. However, because they are closely associated, researchers often find it very difficult to disentangle one factor from another – for example, the effects of having a particular occupation from being poor.

Ethnicity presents particular problems of measurement and analysis because researchers tend to lump subcultures together. Thus, a study of 'Asians' may include Chinese, Filipinos, Indians, Pakistanis, Japanese, Koreans and Vietnamese as one group, and, as a result, the study will mask important differences among these groups. Another problem related to both ethnicity and social class is that researchers' assumptions may influence the kinds of questions they ask and the way they ask them.

Are intelligence tests biased against minority groups?

Those who argue that existing tests of intelligence are biased against certain social groups point out that the most widely used tests were standardized on European-American middle-class people (Valencia & Suzuki, 2001). They maintain that for this reason test items do not accurately measure the problem-solving abilities appropriate to the circumstances in which some members of ethnic groups live. These tests, their detractors insist, draw on the language, experience, and values of middle-class European-American children. For example, the vocabulary used on traditional IQ tests often differs from the dialect or even language some children use every day. On this view, some researchers have argued that the lower verbal scores of minority groups in the US and individuals in many other cultures may reflect cultural bias, not any lack of intelligence. In support of this position, tests such as the Kaufman battery, aimed at minimizing cultural bias, show less difference between the scores of African-American and European-American children than do standard IQ tests.

stereotype threat
Being at risk of confirming a negative stereotype about the group to which one belongs.

In his concept of stereotype threat, Claude Steele (1997) has offered yet another explanation for poor performance on IQ tests among ethnic minority youth. According to Steele, people are aware of the stereotypes that society holds about their particular groups – for example, the stereotype that certain ethnic groups are intellectually inferior to other ethnic groups. In situations in which this stereotype can be tested, Steele believes that individuals from the group for which there is a negative stereotype have self-doubt and worry about confirming the stereotype in their test performance. This self-doubt has the effect of hurting the individual's performance, which in turn confirms the stereotype. Stereotype threat has been found in children as young as 6 years of age and, by age 10, most children are aware of broadly held social stereotypes regarding certain stigmatized minority groups such as African-Americans and Latinos (McKown & Weinstein, 2003). Moreover, children in these minority groups are more aware of the stereotypes than children who are not in these groups. And, as Steele (1997) predicted, children in these minority groups who are aware of the stereotypes performed less well on cognitive tasks when they were told the purpose was to test their ability.

The conditions under which they are administered to minority children of lower socioeconomic status may also interfere with these children's ability to perform (Spencer, 2006). Recall that the newer, information-processing approaches to intelligence testing have pointed to the importance of context in children's intellectual performance (Das, 2004). Researchers influenced by these ideas have tried to familiarize children with the test environment and test materials, to encourage them on various tasks, and to use material rewards, such as candy, to motivate performance. These efforts have been successful with some low-income and minority-group children; in fact, they have been significantly more successful with economically deprived children than with middle-class children (Zigler et al., 1982). These findings support the view that intelligence tests do not measure the competencies of low-income and ethnic minority children as well as they measure the abilities of middle-class ethnic majority children.

Social-class influences on intellectual performance

Separating social class from intelligence and achievement is enormously challenging. Yet, if non-genetic factors contribute about 50% of the variation in IQ scores and intellectual performance, it is important to do this to gain a better understanding of the process of intellectual development. In this section, we look at some research efforts to isolate social-class factors in intellectual performance.

SOCIAL-CLASS FACTORS AND CUMULATIVE RISK

Investigators have described differences in performance on standardized intelligence tests among children from various social-class groups (Neisser et al., 1996; Huang & Hauser, 1998). In the United States, children in the lower socioeconomic classes score 10 to 15 IQ points below middle-class children (Brody, 1992). These differences are generally observed before children enter school and remain consistent throughout the school years (Kennedy, 1969; Moffitt et al., 1993). However, when factors such as family conditions and home environment are taken into account, the differences in scores are reduced somewhat (Brooks-Gunn et al., 2003). Longitudinal research in Scotland has revealed similar patterns in that children in families from the lowest social-class group in the study had IQ scores in the years of middle childhood that were significantly lower than children in families from higher SES groups (Lawlor et al., 2005).

> **cumulative risk** The notion that risk factors in children's life circumstances have cumulative negative effects on their intellectual performance.

The concept of cumulative risk may help us understand the significance of the effects of socioeconomic factors on intelligence and intellectual performance. If in the life circumstances of a given child only one of the many risk factors that may compromise healthy development, such as poverty, is present, many other factors in that child's environment may outweigh the risk that one factor poses. However, as more and more negative factors are added to the child's life experience, the risk of poor cognitive outcomes will increase (Sameroff & Fiese, 2000; Carmody et al., 2006). Major risk factors include poor maternal mental health, low maternal education, the head of the household being unemployed, father absent, minority group membership, families of more than four children, and a high incidence of stressful life events (Sameroff et al., 1993).

To test this notion, Sameroff and colleagues (Sameroff et al., 1987, 1993) identified specific environmental factors likely to present risks to children's cognitive development (Table 11-3) and then, among 215 four-year-old African American, European American and Puerto Rican children, examined the links between these risks and IQ scores. As you can see in Figure 11-4, the findings were striking.

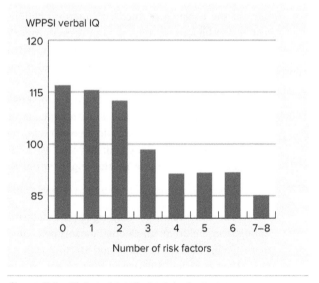

Figure 11-4 Risk and intellectual performance
This graph dramatically illustrates the relationship between risk factors and intellectual performance. The more risk factors (e.g., poverty, hunger, poor clothing, family stress) in the lives of these 4 year olds, the lower their scores on the Wechsler Preschool and Primary Scale of Intelligence.
Source: Based on Sameroff et al. (1993).

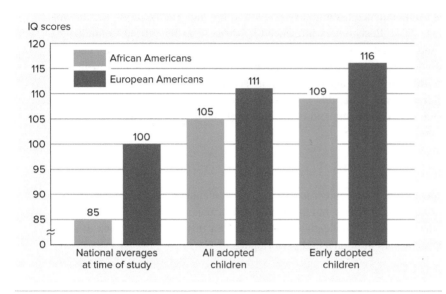

Figure 11-5   How do children adopted into middle-class European American homes fare?
Both African and European American children adopted into middle-class European American homes obtained IQ scores that were substantially above the national averages for their respective groups. And the earlier the child was adopted, the better the IQ score. It is not known why the European American adoptees fared somewhat better than the African Americans.
Source: Adapted from Scarr and Weinberg (1976).

Children with only one risk factor had verbal IQ scores well above average; an IQ of 115 is considered 'bright normal'. As the number of environmental risk factors increased, however, IQ scores dropped, and children whose life circumstances included seven or eight of the risk factors had IQs 30 points lower, putting them in the 'dull normal' range.

Social class did not appreciably affect these findings: the presence of several risk factors was associated with low IQs in families of both low and high socioeconomic status. However, any one of these factors was more likely to be present in low-income families than in families with more financial advantages. A follow-up study (Sameroff et al., 1993) of 152 of the same families when the children were 13 years old revealed a similar pattern: a 30- to 35-point IQ difference between the children whose risks were few and those who confronted many risk factors.

These findings argue for the notion that children who confront multiple risk factors face potential declines in their performance on intelligence tests (Grissmer et al., 1998). The findings also allow us to hypothesize that, in the absence of such risk factors, children should achieve higher test scores. Psychologists have tested this hypothesis by studying African-American children who were adopted by economically well-off European-American parents (Scarr & Weinberg, 1976). As you can see from Figure 11-5, adopted African American children achieved scores some 20 points above the national average for black children, and the younger they were at adoption, the higher their scores were. Follow-up studies (Scarr, 1997, 1998; Weinberg, Scarr, & Waldman, 1992) found that the adoptees experienced a gain in IQ similar to the gains of biological children of the adoptive parents. Although the adoptees' IQ scores more closely resembled those of their biological parents than their adoptive parents, their higher scores and continued gains showed the strong influence the environment may have on IQ and on the long-term maintenance of gains. Other adoption studies have echoed these results (e.g., Capron & Duyme, 1989).

SOCIAL CLASS AND PARENT–CHILD INTERACTIONS

Several investigators have suggested that maternal behaviour differs across social classes and may differentially affect children's intellectual performance in the school setting. For instance, middle-class mothers were more likely than lower-class mothers to speak in response to their babies' vocalizations (Lewis & Wilson, 1972; Hart & Risley, 1995), and their infants tended to stop vocalizing and listen when their mothers spoke. In contrast, lower-class children were more likely to continue vocalizing when their mothers were speaking (Lewis & Freedle, 1973). Some scholars have suggested that these early differences in the way infants attend to their mothers' speech may be related to later differences in the ease with which children learn from verbal information (Hoff, 2005).

Barnard, Bee, and Hammond (1984) found that mothers who had gone beyond a high school education were more highly involved with their infants than mothers who had not finished school; these differences, measured at several intervals before the

In Chapter 12 we discuss the role of parents and siblings in development across areas of psychology.

children reached age 2, were significantly related to the children's IQ scores at age 4. Specific behaviours that are important include reading to young children before they enter school. On average, 73% of young children whose mothers graduated from college were read to every day by a family member, compared with 60% of children whose mothers had some years of college, 49% of children whose mothers only finished high school, and 42% of children whose mothers had not finished high school (Federal Interagency Forum on Child and Family Statistics, 2007). These different rates are significant in that reading with an adult in the preschool years is associated with better reading achievement in the early school years (Bus, van Ijzendoorn, & Pelligrini, 1995).

In China, where there are relatively small differences in income across groups that vary in education, Tardif (1993) found that less educated parents used more commands with their toddlers than better-educated mothers. This style of interaction is likely to be associated with poorer cognitive development. Finally, many researchers have argued that stress, presumably more commonly experienced by lower-class parents than by middle-class parents, may directly influence parental styles of interaction – for example, leading parents to be more concerned with discipline than with positive emotional communication (Hess & Shipman, 1967; Goldstein, 1990; McLoyd, Hill, & Dodge, 2005).

BOX 11-2 How important for learning is personality? A study of students' grades in an undergraduate statistics class

Research close-up

Source: Based on Furnham and Chamorro-Premuzic (2004).

Introduction:

IQ is often associated with academic achievement, but other individual differences may also be important. For instance, certain personality types may be better suited to learning in formal or informal situations, or may prioritize learning over other activities. In this study, researchers explored the associations between intelligence, personality, and the statistics grades of undergraduate students at a British university. They also explore seminar performance such as attendance and contribution, as rated by seminar leaders.

Methods:

Participants were 91 (74 women, 17 men) undergraduate students (average age, 19.7 years). These students were given the NEO-FFI (Big Five) test of personality which gives a personality profile for individuals on five factors: neuroticism, extraversion, openness to experience, agreeableness, and conscientiousness. Three tests of intelligence (cognitive ability) were also applied. Statistics performance was assessed from two questions on a statistics end-of-year examination.

Results:

The researchers performed a hierarchical regression analysis to establish the relative contribution of different elements to statistics performance. The biggest contributor to performance on the test was the seminar leader's assessment of behaviour and attendance. Cognitive performance (intelligence) and personality also played a part. Unsurprisingly, those who performed better on the intelligence tests tended to perform better in the exam, but the relation was not as strong as might have been expected. In fact, personality seemed to be more important than intelligence in terms of its contribution to the statistics test score. Specifically, conscientious introverts did best.

Discussion:

Perhaps it is no surprise that this and other studies find that conscientiousness is a consistent predictor of academic performance. Indeed, the present study found high correlations between conscientiousness and seminar leader assessments of behaviour and attendance. Introversion may be a particular benefit in subjects such as statistics compared with, say, other areas of learning where collaboration or performance may be more pivotal to academic success. Certainly at university level, a good work ethic appears a very important aspect of academic performance.

The authors suggest selection for university entrance should consider personality as an important aspect in considering how students will succeed at that level, given the greater demands for self-motivation from, say, learning at school. The findings suggest, also, that a narrow focus on IQ can give an incomplete picture of what is often required for academic success.

PROCESSES OF LEARNING

Achievement motivation and intellectual performance

Children's academic performance is affected not only by their experiences in the family, school, peer group, and community but also by their own achievement motivation – that is, their tendency to strive for successful performance, to evaluate their performance against specific standards of excellence, and to experience pleasure as a result of having performed successfully (Wigfield, Eccles, & Schiefele, 2006). Variations in achievement motivation and intellectual performance are often related to a child's emotions and opinions of himself as a person and a learner – in short, to the sense of self (Dweck, 2000, 2006). Some children have negative feelings about specific learning tasks and may be convinced of their inability to learn in certain areas. Sometimes, a child's feelings and beliefs about his ability to succeed are sufficiently negative that they distract the learner from the task itself and may prevent him from learning (Bransford et al., 1999).

> **achievement motivation** A person's tendency to strive for successful performance, to evaluate her performance against standards of excellence, and to feel pleasure at having performed successfully.

Researchers have identified two different response patterns among children working on a challenging task at which they could fail (Heckhausen & Dweck, 1998). In an early study, 11- and 12-year-old children attempted to solve a series of difficult problems that resembled a game of Twenty Questions (Diener & Dweck, 1978). At first, the children were able to solve the problems, but then the experimenter presented several very difficult problems that they failed. Some children maintained or even improved their level of performance despite failure on some of the difficult problems; the researchers labelled these children mastery-orientated because they were focused on gaining skill or mastery at the problems. In contrast, other children tended to give up easily or to show marked performance deterioration when working on challenging problems; the researchers labelled these children helpless.

When mastery-orientated children performed poorly, they expressed neutral or even positive emotions, attributed their failure to insufficient effort rather than to lack of ability, and maintained high expectations for future success. Helpless children, on the other hand, expressed negative emotions such as frustration, blamed their own lack of ability for their performance, and expressed low expectations for future performance.

What might cause different children to react so differently to the same task? Helpless and mastery-orientated children do not differ in their actual ability levels; rather, they *think* differently about ability and achievement (Heckhausen & Dweck, 1998; Kamins & Dweck, 1999; Dweck, 2006). Mastery-orientated children tend to have *learning goals*. In other words, they are more concerned with improving their skills and learning new things than they are with specific judgements of their ability. Children who show the helpless pattern, on the other hand, tend to have *performance goals;* that is, they are concerned with 'looking smart', obtaining positive judgements, and avoiding negative judgements of their ability. Dweck and her colleagues have proposed that these different goals are associated with different beliefs about intelligence itself. That is, mastery-orientated children tend to hold an *incremental* view of intelligence, viewing intelligence as a body of skills and knowledge that can be increased with effort. In contrast, helpless children tend to hold an *entity* view of intelligence, believing, if implicitly, that intelligence is a fixed and unchangeable entity that people possess in varying degrees.

Dweck suggests that the two views of intelligence and the two goals orientate children to react very differently to achievement tasks. As Table 11-3 illustrates, when children are successful at tasks, they do not appear to differ in their behaviour; even children with an entity view and performance goals are likely to show the mastery-orientated pattern. However, when children fail at a task, their different views of intelligence lead to different forms of behaviour. Under these circumstances, mastery-orientated children may interpret their failure as an indication that they must work harder to learn more, whereas helpless children may see failure as evidence of their lack of ability and may give up. Of course, different situations can elicit different responses, and mastery-orientated children may occasionally show helpless responses when examiners or others put a lot of stress on performance goals (Dweck, 2001, 2006; Heckhausen & Dweck, 1998).

Table 11-3 Views of intelligence, goal orientations and behaviour patterns for high and low performance levels

View of intelligence	Goal orientation	Present performance level	Behaviour pattern
Entity (intelligence is fixed)	Performance (to gain positive, avoid negative judgements of competence)	High	Mastery-orientated (seeking challenge, persistence)
		Low	Helpless (avoiding challenge, low persistence)
Incremental (intelligence is malleable)	Learning (to increase competence)	High	Mastery-orientated (seeking challenge that fosters learning, persistence)
		Low	Mastery-orientated (seeking challenge that fosters persistence)

Source: Dweck and Leggett (1988); Dweck (2001).

Experience in the family in the preschool years may affect the development of these views of performance (Eccles, 2007). Children whose parents encouraged more mastery-orientated behaviour from them as toddlers – for example, by promoting independence and persistence in solving problems – show more mastery-orientated behaviours later on when they enter school (Pomerantz, Grolnick, & Price, 2005). In contrast, some environmental conditions may even promote helplessness in children. Evans (2003) found that children living in poverty who experienced a number of physical stresses (e.g., crowding and poor-quality housing) and psychosocial stresses (e.g., family turmoil or violence) were more likely to behave in a helpless manner when presented with a challenging puzzle task than were poor children who had fewer stresses in their lives.

Culture may also play a role. Chen and Stevenson (1995) found that European-American students tended to endorse 'having a good teacher' as the most important factor in their performance in mathematics, whereas Asian students reported that 'studying hard' was the most important factor. Chen and Stevenson and their colleagues (Chen & Stevenson, 1995; Stevenson, Lee, & Mu, 2000; Stevenson, 2001) found that, compared with Asian students and their parents, European-American students had lower standards for their academic work, and their parents more often attributed their children's performance to innate ability.

BOX 11-3 Making the grade in Japan, Taiwan and the United States

Applied Developmental Psychology

In recent years, the declining school achievement of US children has received substantial attention by the media. What can psychology tell us about children's academic achievement in the United States? Longitudinal studies by Harold Stevenson and his associates (Stevenson et al., 1990; Chen et al., 1995) have now provided evidence that in the earliest months of first grade, children in the United States already lag behind children who live in other parts of the world in academic achievement. Thus, although differences in academic performance may well reflect varying educational systems, the fact that these differences appear when children have had little exposure to formal education suggests more is involved than inadequate educational practices.

Over a ten-year period, Stevenson and colleagues administered tests of reading and mathematics ability to groups of first, fifth, and eleventh graders in classrooms in two US metropolitan areas (Minneapolis, Minnesota, and Fairfax County, Virginia), in two East Asian cities (Beijing, China, and Taipei, Taiwan), and in Japan (Sendai). The US students included four cultural groups – European, Chinese, African, and Latino American – although not

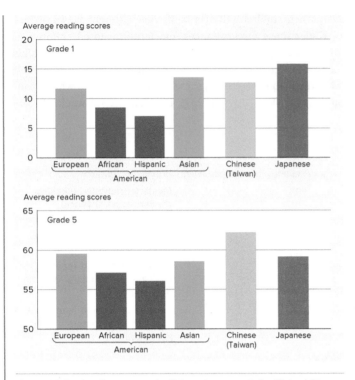

Figure 11-6   Reading scores in China, Japan and the United States
Across both first and fifth grades, Chinese and Japanese students tended to do better in reading than any of the US cultural groups. In first grade, Asian-American students ran second to Japanese students but, for some reason, dropped down by fifth grade. The relations among European, African and Latino American students remained fairly stable from first to fifth grade; these groups scored from higher to lower, respectively.
Source: Adapted from Chen et al. (1995).

all these groups were represented in every study. To the degree possible, the investigators retested the same students at different ages; over the ten-year span, Stevenson and his associates tested several thousand children. In each study, the researchers interviewed teachers, students, and students' mothers on a variety of topics, such as the value of education, beliefs about learning, attitudes towards school, and family involvement in children's schoolwork.

In one study, there were noticeable differences in reading test scores among seven groups of students even in the first grade (Figure 11-6). In first grade, Japanese students scored highest, followed fairly closely by Asian American, Taiwanese, and European American students; African American and Latino American students scored the lowest. By fifth grade, Taiwanese and European American students had jumped ahead of Japanese and Asian Americans. American students scored considerably below others on a mathematics test, and between first and fifth grade, these differences became more pronounced (Figure 11-6): at both times, Chinese (Beijing, Taiwan) and Japanese students had the highest scores, with Asian-Americans following close behind.

What could be contributing to these results? Stevenson and his colleagues found no evidence that the American children had lower intellectual levels, and parental education levels were highest among European American students. However, there were marked differences in parents' beliefs, their reported activities with their children, and the evaluations they made of their children and their educational systems. Chinese and Japanese mothers generally viewed academic achievement as the child's most important pursuit. Once children entered school, Chinese and Japanese families mobilized to help their children and to provide an environment conducive to achievement. Japanese mothers, in particular, were likely to see themselves as kyoiku mamas – that is, 'education mums' responsible for assisting, directing, and supervising their children's learning.

American mothers were less likely to be involved in helping their children with homework than mothers in other groups. They tended to put more emphasis on the role of innate ability in school performance and less on the role of effort. Mothers in all three countries viewed their children's academic performance as above average, but as Figure 11-8 shows, American mothers voiced the most positive views about their children's scholastic achievement and experience, even though they were aware of the country's low rank in comparative studies of children's performance.

American children spend significantly less time on homework and reading for pleasure and more time playing and doing chores than Japanese or Taiwanese children do. In one study, only 17% of first-grade and 28% of fifth-grade Taiwanese children did chores, in contrast to 90% and 95% of American first and fifth graders, respectively. When researchers asked one Taiwanese mother why she did not assign her children chores, she replied, 'It would break my heart. Doing chores would consume time that the child should devote to studying.'

American mothers appeared to be more interested in their children's general cognitive development than in their academic achievement per se, attempting to provide the children with experiences that fostered cognitive growth (Stevenson et al., 1990). These mothers reported reading more frequently to their young children, taking them on excursions, and accompanying them to more cultural events than did Chinese or Japanese parents.

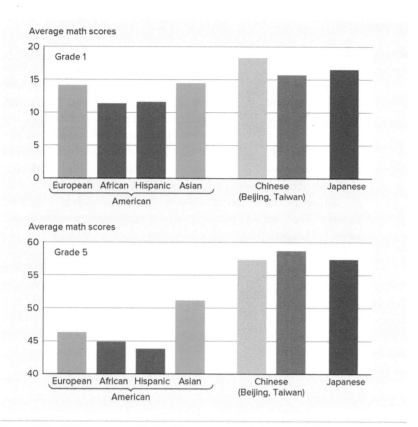

Figure 11-7   *Mathematics skills in China, Japan and the United States*

As in reading, Chinese and Japanese students outscored US students in mathematics. Although the differences were small in grade 1, they were large in grade 5, and Asian American students clearly led their American peers. *Source: Adapted from Chen et al. (1995).*

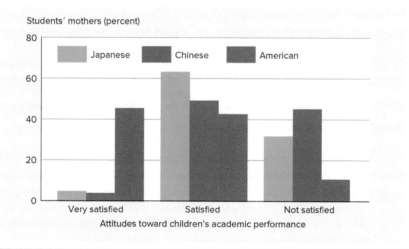

Figure 11-8   *Mothers' attitudes towards their children's academic performance*

In 1990, more Japanese and Chinese mothers than US mothers were 'satisfied' with their children's academic performance. However, more than 40% of American mothers, but fewer than 5% of Chinese and Japanese mothers, were 'very satisfied'.

Improving working memory and cognitive control

Cognitive psychologists have argued that intellectual performance and achievement can be improved by seeking to develop the underlying cognitive processes involved in learning. Gathercole and Alloway (2008) argue that a core ability in this respect is working memory. Working memory is considered to involve a number of different skills and subsystems for processing information, including the short-term storage of visual and verbal information and attentional processes. It is easy to see how working memory would play a crucial role in classroom learning where children need to take in and understand new information and integrate this into their existing knowledge and understanding. Poor working memory is associated with poor academic performance (Gathercole & Pickering, 2000).

> **working memory** A model of short-term memory processes incorporating a central executive, phonological loop (for storing auditory information), a visuospatial sketch-pad (for visual information) and an episodic buffer (for linking information across domains).

Gathercole (2008) identified several characteristics of a child with poor working memory. These include having a normal relationship with peers outside of the classroom, but becoming subdued or withdrawn in group learning activities; poor academic progress in reading and mathematics; difficulty in following instructions and activities that rely upon memory and information processing; short attention span and difficulties keeping a place (in reading for instance). Many children with these memory problems are often characterized as being unable to pay attention or concentrate. However, they are distinguished from children with behavioural problems (such as attention deficit hyperactivity disorder, ADHD) because they do not appear hyperactive or necessarily engage in disruptive or antisocial behaviour.

Gathercole suggests several principles to identify and address working memory problems in the classroom, outlined in Table 11-4.

Table 11-4 Principles of the classroom-based working memory approach

Principles	Further information
Recognition of working memory problems	Signs of difficulties in working memory may include failing to follow simple instructions, place-keeping errors, inability to persist at a task, problems with recalling all information accurately
Monitoring	Teachers need to be aware of the issue and look for warning signs. Ask the child if they are experiencing problems
Evaluate working memory loads	A clear sign is if children have difficulty with remembering or processing long sequences, new content or demanding cognitive activities
Reduce working memory loads	Reduce the amount and complexity of material to be remembered, or restructure complex tasks. Increasing the meaningfulness or familiarity of material can also help children with poor working memory to find other routes to process material
Repeat information	Repetition is an important technique for improving recall
Memory aids and strategies	Encouraging use of memory aids can help children with poor working memory to overcome some of the difficulties they may experience in the classroom and learning. These can be incorporated into classroom activities or the child herself can be encouraged to develop these skills such as self-rehearsal and note-taking

Source: Adapted from Gathercole (2008, p. 384).

Another important process that may well have implications for learning from preschool onwards is *cognitive control*, also sometimes referred to as *executive function* (EF). The control and management of cognitive systems is a vital skill for learning in the classroom that affects planning, the allocation of mental resources and other processes to explore and complete tasks. It is a useful concept for teachers and other educators both in terms of harnessing and developing children's higher cognitive functions, and in providing more focused assistance to children with learning disabilities (Meltzer, 2018).

A number of developmental disorders are associated with poor EF. In some instances, the links between EF and academic performance are not well known (for instance, in Autism Spectrum Disorder they may be associated with both inferior and superior academic performance compared with other children (St. John, Dawson, & Estes, 2018); whereas delays in language learning for children with Attention Deficit Hyperactivity Disorder, ADHD, are likely due to poor EF negatively impacting language processes (Berninger et al., 2016).

Executive functions develop rapidly from an early age and, as such, are strong predictors of early success in school (Blair & Razza, 2007). The 'Tools of the Mind' curriculum in the US (Diamond et al., 2007) seeks to develop EF skills in the preschool classroom to accelerate children's learning and engagement with school activities from a young age. Diamond and colleagues liaised with schools to give preschoolers (aged 5 years) either the Tools of the Mind curriculum, which was based on some of Vygotsky's ideas relating to EF, or another curriculum. Teaching the Tools of the Mind curriculum involved 40 activities such as getting a child to talk out loud to accompany an activity and engaging in dramatic play. These activities were designed to focus a child's attention on understanding how he controlled his own activities and regulated his own learning. The other curriculum was more conventional and preschoolers took part in balanced literary and thematic units, with no emphasis on developing EF skills.

Diamond and colleagues claim to seek marked improvements in EF for those children who were involved in the Tools of the Mind programme. They argue that giving preschool children a daily EF task is a little like taking regular exercise in that it prepares the mind for the attentional and cognitive demands of formal schooling. These may be especially important for children of families from low income groups who often experience the greatest difficulties adapting to school life early on. These early difficulties can lead to further academic failure.

> In Chapter 10 we discuss research into cognitive processes such as working memory and executive function.

LEARNING FROM TEACHERS AND LEARNING FROM PEERS
Sociocultural approaches

Although a good deal of research has focused on identifying how individual children's IQ relates to academic and intellectual achievement, broader theories of teaching focus on how best to educate and raise the performance of all children. Theories of school learning (and teaching) can be characterized as fitting into three broad approaches – behaviourist, constructivist and cognitive. These three approaches map on to different developmental theories. For instance, behaviourist approaches are closely based on classical behaviourist research in developmental and learning (see again Chapter 2). However, few teachers today would advocate the use of classical conditioning and there is recognition that learning is more than merely reproducing certain, reinforced or modelled behaviour. Rather, learning at school requires that the child thinks and understands something about a topic.

In fact, cognitive and constructivist approaches cover a range of approaches to teaching, because both emphasize the need to understand not only what children are learning but how they think about it. Constructivist approaches differ from cognitive approaches because the former emphasizes the child's own involvement in acquiring knowledge and learning, whereas the latter do not emphasize the importance of the child's own actions in these processes.

Both the developmental theories of Piaget and of Vygotsky map on to approaches to learning that could be described as constructivist. Typically, Vygotskian theory is regarded as more supported of formal models of teaching, whereby a child learns from a teacher (or expert) and internalizes this knowledge. However, it is important that this learning occurs within the Zone of Proximal Development – a sort of 'social space' where a child can work together with another individual on a level just above what he or she can do themselves already. Thus in some respects, for Vygotsky, the process of learning involves social action from not just the teacher but also the child.

Recent approaches to teaching and learning in a Vygotskian tradition have focused on these social aspects of communication, shared activity and apprenticeship. For instance, Lave and Wenger (1991) developed the concept of situated learning, based on case studies observing how individuals acquired new knowledge and skills in a variety of different cultures and contexts around the world. These contexts included observing tailors in Liberia, traditional midwives in Yucatan in Mexico, and quartermasters in the US Marine Corps. From these studies, Lave and Wenger suggested that not everyone who undertakes an activity (such as learning maths or delivering babies) can be an expert mathematician, but by learning he or she participates on the periphery of a learning community. The notion of legitimate peripheral participation is important here because it is through this participation – by *doing* knowledge and the things that make that knowledge meaningful – that individuals come to acquire relevant skills. Thus participation is legitimate because everyone accepts that people who are not qualified can do some low level skills (for example, a 4 year old can 'do' maths, but is unlikely to do so at the same level of a maths undergraduate). This participation is peripheral because they are not at the forefront of their field, but nevertheless engaged in the activity. From Lave and Wenger's perspective, merely taking part in an activity can be enough to stimulate learning and to separate learning about something from doing something is an error. This is, in many striking ways, a radically different model of schooling from what occurs in most classrooms. Even if we accept the need to understand these concepts in more formal, learning environments, the situated learning approach has interesting implications for how children come to identify themselves as learners and develop an academic identity, which need to be explored with further research.

A contrasting approach, yet also consistent with the thrust of Vygotskian theory, is that of Barbara Rogoff. Rogoff (1991) proposed the idea of apprenticeship in learning. In a series of careful studies exploring how children in different cultures acquired skills to become experts on a task, Rogoff argued that parents and other adults engage in social activity with children that scaffolds their development and allows them to enter a community of learners and experts together. Moreover, Rogoff suggests that Western 'schooling' really is just a formalization of these forms of practice that exist in a range of cultures: skills at calculus and reasoning may be valued in, for example, a northern European school system, but more practical skills in applying mathematical understanding are valued in another, less industrialized setting. Although Lave and Wenger explicitly reject the idea of simple apprenticeship models in their theory, both clearly have important implications for learning in a variety of contexts.

However, one concern with both Lave and Wenger's and Rogoff's proposals is that they are built upon studies with children and adults in very practical, sometimes physical, activities. Although the researchers argue that these sorts of learning environments and skills – tailoring, weaving – can tell us a good deal about how learning should and does happen at schools, it may be that the acquisition of knowledge about things is rather different from knowledge doing things.

Peer interaction and collaboration

Contemporary theories of teaching and learning emphasize the importance of social processes. While the approaches of Lave and Wenger and Rogoff and others draw inspiration from Vygotsky's work and point towards the importance of broad cultural norms, a further body of research has explored how interpersonal social processes might affect teaching, learning and development. This research has explored how children can advance in their knowledge through collaboration with peers.

Doise and Mugny (1984) reported a series of studies in which children were placed in groups and asked to make judgements about conservation problems together. The investigators found that, when non-conserving children discussed the task together, their reasoning and judgements showed advances compared with a control condition in which a child tried to solve the problems on his or her own. A number of other studies have found similar effects of peer interaction (e.g., Psaltis & Duveen, 2007; Leman & Björnberg, 2010), where there are benefits to learning even when no child involved in the interaction possesses expertise. Doise and Mugny suggested that the benefits of interaction were due to sociocognitive conflict; a little like Piaget's idea of cognitive conflict, children in interaction recognize that they have differing perspectives and this stimulates further consideration of the issue.

After Doise and Mugny, a number of researchers have sought to unpick further what makes for effective collaboration. In a series of fascinating studies Christine Howe and her colleagues (e.g., Howe, Tolmie & Rodgers, 1992; Howe, McWilliam & Cross, 2005) have systematically explored different factors that might be influential in classroom, collaborative learning. An important finding is that even when children do not show immediate gains after collaboration – and even when they sometimes get the answer wrong – the process of collaborating seems to stimulate a process of development over subsequent days or months that is associated with longer-term learning. In a series of studies concerning children's understanding of the factors that affect floating and sinking, Howe et al. (2005) found that peer collaboration may act to raise a child's awareness of a topic, and prime a child to be more sensitive and perhaps attentive to subsequent information on a topic. A further, related approach suggests that through talking together children develop argument and critical skills that help them to learn for themselves (Mercer, 2008).

BOX 11-4   Peer collaboration and learning: how much does task context matter?

Research close-up

Source: Based on Keogh et al. (2000).

Introduction:

Numerous studies have demonstrated how peer collaboration has positive benefits for children's learning. However, clearly other contextual factors matter, too. For instance, the gender of children engaging in interaction might be important if a boy dominates a girl in a task, or vice versa. Alternatively, two girls might work together in one way, and two boys in another way. So the dynamics of peer collaboration are important for learning, and teachers often seek to establish the best combination of children in pairs and groups to minimize disruption and make learning as effective as possible.

The present study sought to explore how school children interacted with one another depending on the gender of those involved. In addition to varying the gender of children involved in collaboration, the researchers were also interested to see if the task context was important: for instance, would gender have a different influence on interactions if the task was based on a computer, or if it involved the use of paper and pencils?

Method:

A total of 24 boys and 24 girls (aged 13 and 14 years) participated in the study. The researchers employed a mixed experimental design where gender and the gender mix of a pair (i.e., same-sex pairs or boy-girl pairs) were between participant factors and the task was a within participants factor. In other words, children participated in the same pair throughout the study, but all children completed computer and paper versions of the tasks.

For the task, children were given the lines of a poem in a random order, and they had to decide together how to rearrange these lines to make the correct, original poem. Two poems were presented – 'The Wife's Lament' by Nikolay Nekrasov, and 'On a Cat, Ageing' by Alexander Gray – and whether these were on the computer or on paper was varied so that all children completed each version of the task twice. Audiotaped recordings of children's conversations were coded to identify certain categories of speech: for instance, whether a child made a proposal to do something, or supported or disagreed with their partner.

Results:

There was a striking difference between boys and girls in the different versions of the task. In the computer version, in the mixed gender pairs, boys made more proposals, disagreed more and repeated their points more than they did in the same gender pair (i.e., with another boy). The opposite was true for the girls. They used fewer of these conversational elements in the mixed pair than when collaborating with a girl.

The researchers were also interested in how children in pairs took control of physical resources in the task. To assess this they explored how often children moved pieces of paper in the paper version or how often they controlled the computer mouse on the computer task. Although there were no differences between genders on the paper task, boys took control of the mouse more than girls in the computer task. In fact, on the computer task the boys controlled the mouse for an average of 752 seconds, compared to the girls, who controlled it for only an average 287 seconds, almost two and a half times as long!

Discussion:

Gender differences in interaction styles are well known and there appear to be differences even from preschool in the ways that boys and girls behave together. However, the present study demonstrates that this influence can extend to classroom problem solving, and that it interacts with the type of task involved. Specifically, for a paper-and-pencil task the differences between girls and boys exist but are less pronounced than on the computer task. One likely explanation for these task differences is that computers may be a more 'male labelled' classroom resource and hence the boys appropriate it more readily in collaboration. In this sense, these classroom differences might be an extension of stereotyped differences we see in preschoolers' toy choices (e.g., a car for a boy, a doll for a girl). Of course, though, this is potentially problematic if girls are being denied access to some resources and boys to other resources in that this can deny fair educational opportunities to one or other gender.

Teachers need to consider carefully the dynamics of children they may place in pairs or groups for classroom collaboration, and perhaps also the type of task involved.

Peer collaboration is now a common feature of many classrooms, yet there is still much to learn about when and why it is most fruitful (Howe, 2010). One reason for its importance may be that it allows children to learn in the less formal environment than is often found in more lecture-style, teacher–child instruction. However, that informality can cause additional problems if, for instance, gender, race or other aspects of children's interactions affect the dynamics of interaction and learning (Gummerum, Leman, & Hollins, 2014). Moreover, it may be that at different ages, children have a different understanding of the purposes and potential of learning with peers which, in turn, can influence whether and how collaboration is useful (Leman, 2015).

There is a role for many different types of learning in the classroom and the task of a skilled teacher is often to establish what form of teaching works best and in what situation for different children. So, for instance, in some circumstances peer collaboration may be very beneficial for learning, whereas in others children may engage in 'discovery learning' on an individual basis very productively. In others, still, children may benefit more from direct instruction (Klahr, 2005).

BEYOND THE NORMS: GIFTEDNESS AND INTELLECTUAL DEFICITS

Children vary greatly in the rate and manner in which they learn. Traditionally, specialists in intelligence testing have held that an IQ score above 130 signals intellectual giftedness; a score below 70, coupled with difficulty in coping with age-appropriate activities of everyday life, indicates mental retardation. Finally, some children, many of whom have normal or even high intelligence levels, have specific difficulties that interfere with learning, such as speech or language impairments or reading disabilities like dyslexia. These children are identified as having learning disabilities. We look first at the evidence on giftedness and then at the contemporary view of retardation and the prospects for fulfilling lives for those who fall into this category. Then we examine children with learning disabilities.

intellectual giftedness A characteristic defined by an IQ score of 130 or over; gifted children learn faster than others and may show early exceptional talents in certain areas.

mental retardation A characteristic defined by an IQ score below 70 together with difficulty in coping with age-appropriate activities of everyday life.

learning disabilities Deficits in one or more cognitive processes important for learning.

The intellectually gifted

Often gifted children show special interests and talents quite early, and they apply themselves to these interests with enthusiasm and perseverance (Winner, 2006). But are the cognitive processes these children use unique or different from what other children use? Dark and Benbow (1993) suggest that the processes that underlie the cognitive feats of gifted children are not unique; it's simply that such children use their cognitive skills more efficiently than the rest of us.

The question of how to educate and encourage exceptionally bright and talented children is controversial (Sternberg, 2006; Winner, 2006). Should these children be permitted to begin school early? Should they progress more quickly through school than other children? Some argue that these sorts of steps are necessary to maintain an exceedingly bright child's interest and motivation, but critics worry that these efforts may meet the child's intellectual needs at the expense of her social and emotional development, especially in terms of experiences and relationships with peers. Educational alternatives for gifted children include enrichment programmes, which attempt to provide these children with extra stimulation without advancing them to higher grades.

In another type of programme, the school sets up a special subject or activity meant to enrich the educational lives of a group of intellectually talented students – for example, a special class in science or social studies. A third type of enrichment programme offers gifted students instruction in creative writing or foreign languages or opportunities for study in the arts, such as painting and dance. Although some argue that the 'enrichment' offered by these types of programme may be mostly designed to keep these children occupied while others catch up, and are unrelated to the child's talent, enrichment programmes influenced by Gardner's notion of multiple intelligences are increasing in number. These programmes are designed to nurture the specific talents of gifted children (Moran & Gardner, 2006).

Children with intellectual deficits

In Chapter 5, we discussed three specific disorders that are accompanied by serious intellectual deficits: Down syndrome, phenylketonuria (PKU) and fragile X syndrome. Down and fragile X syndromes are chromosomal disorders, whereas the cause of PKU is lack of a specific enzyme for processing phenylalanine. Mental retardation that results from genetic causes or other factors that are clearly biological is referred to as *organic* retardation (Hodapp & Dykens, 2006). Intellectual deficits that derive from factors surrounding the birth process (e.g., lack of sufficient oxygen) and those that are the result of conditions of infancy or childhood (e.g., infections, traumas or lack of nurturance) are considered *familial* retardation. In general, organic retardation is more severe than familial retardation.

Mental retardation is diagnosed by two basic measures: assessments of the child's mental functioning and of his adaptive behaviour (American Association of Mental Retardation, 2002). Traditionally, an IQ score below 70, together with adaptive behaviour deficits, has indicated mental retardation. Each of four IQ score ranges reflects an increasingly serious degree of retardation: mild mental retardation, IQ 55 to 70; moderate mental retardation, IQ 40 to 54; severe mental retardation, IQ 25 to 39; and profound mental retardation, IQ below 20 or 25. In addition, according to the guidelines of the American Association on Mental Retardation (2002), to be classified as mentally retarded, children must show deficits in their ability to function in the real world. Young children who can dress themselves, find their way around the neighbourhood and use the telephone, for example, are less likely to be identified as mentally retarded than children with the same IQs who do not exhibit these practical competencies.

By far, the majority of people with mental retardation or intellectual disabilities (IDs) – some 95% of them – can learn and can hold jobs of more or less complexity, and live in the community. Children with mild disability (about 85% of all retarded children) usually acquire social and communicative skills during the preschool years and may be indistinguishable from other children until they reach their teens, at which time they may begin having difficulty with more advanced academic work. Children who are moderately intellectually disabled (about 10%) generally acquire communication skills in early childhood, and although they can benefit from vocational training, they are limited in their grasp of academic subjects. Young people in both of these groups may join the workforce and live in supervised settings or, in some cases, independently. Children with severe intellectual disabilities (3% to 4% of all retarded children) may learn to speak and communicate but have rarely progressed beyond reading a few words. Finally, children with profound IDs (1% to 2%) may learn communicative skills and some self-care. Both of the latter groups can learn to do some simple tasks with close supervision; young people in both these groups must live in supervised settings.

Children with learning disabilities

Not all children learn at the same pace or in the same way. Some learn faster than their classmates, but others with various learning disabilities may learn more slowly. Children identified as learning disabled are a very heterogeneous group in terms of the types of cognitive and social abilities they possess (National Joint Committee on Learning Disabilities, 1994). The diversity among children with learning disabilities makes it particularly difficult to know exactly what types of intervention are most useful for this group of children.

A major question in recent years has been whether these children with 'special needs' should be placed in separate classes or integrated into regular classrooms. Many schools have adopted the approach of *inclusion* (also called *integration* or *mainstreaming*), in which children of all ability levels are included in the same classroom. Other schools have placed children with learning disabilities and other special needs in separate special education classes. The success of these different approaches is still being debated (Berninger, 2006). Some argue that inclusion programmes enhance the academic achievement of children with learning disabilities (Buysse & Bailey, 1993), whereas others argue that such programmes put children at risk for peer rejection or inappropriate labelling (Greenberg, Kusche, & Riggs, 2004).

CREATIVITY

The nature of creativity and its relation to intelligence have long been of interest to psychologists. Some investigators, like Robert Sternberg, see intelligence and creativity as intertwined, but others, like Howard Gardner, see clear distinctions between the two. In this section, we look first at some of the definitions and theories of creativity, and then at some evidence on the distinctions between creativity and intelligence. We then consider children's creative behaviour and conclude with some thoughts on how to encourage creativity in children.

Definitions and theories

Defining creativity is just about as hard as defining intelligence; both are multifaceted qualities that vary as a function of personal characteristics (which are both inherited and learned), the context in which they are used, the risk factors that may inhibit them, and the environmental supports that may encourage and sustain them. The key to creativity is the notion of *uniqueness*. Most people – including most psychologists – would agree that the creative product is novel. In some way, it is unlike anything else in its class. But many authorities, such as Gardner (2006), also agree that a truly creative idea or product must be characterized by *usefulness*. It must be of benefit in some area of life, whether that be astrophysics, the visual arts (e.g., painting, sculpture), household products, literature, technology, music or another field of human endeavour. And still others argue that knowledge is crucial. For instance, Keegan (1996) discusses how Charles Darwin amassed an enormous body of knowledge of natural history before he offered his ideas about evolution to the world.

The relationship between creativity and intelligence

Are IQ and creativity related to each other? *Creativity* is defined as the ability to solve problems, create products or pose questions in a way that is different (novel) from the approaches most other people use

The notion of creativity is tied to that of intelligence. The distinct elements of creativity require novelty and uniqueness.
© Glow Images

(Gardner, 2006). To explore the relation of creativity to IQ, Wallach and Kogan (1965) administered WISC subtests and other intelligence tests as well as a set of tasks designed to tap creative modes of thinking to a group of fifth graders. The researchers found only minimal correlations between 'correct' answers on the intelligence tests and answers judged creative on the more open-ended tasks. The results suggested that the intelligent person excels at *convergent thinking*, or thinking with the goal of recognizing or remembering specific information or solving traditional problems for the correct answers, and the creative person excels at *divergent thinking*, or thinking that is imaginative and seeks variety, novelty and uniqueness. Thus, although highly creative people tend to be above average in intelligence, a higher IQ does not predict creativity (Gardner, 2006). Clearly, the true relationship between creativity and intelligence has yet to be determined. One thing people do agree on, however, is that both are desirable characteristics.

Are children creative?

According to some psychologists, very young children are not capable of true creativity. Although we know that children are capable of gathering significant bodies of knowledge, psychologists who specialize in creativity, such as Mark Runco (1996), hold that because young children often cannot distinguish between reality and fantasy, children cannot be truly creative until they reach preadolescence and can make this distinction. However, others point out that even though young children are not creative in the full sense of the term, their play – especially fantasy, or pretend, play – gives children a chance to practise the kind of divergent thinking that can lead them someday to invent new things or ideas (Russ, 2003; Moore & Russ, 2006). Vygotsky also thought that play facilitated creativity: 'The child's play activity is not simply a recollection of past experience but a creative reworking that combines impressions and construct-forming new realities addressing the needs of the child' (1967, p. 7).

If children may eventually be capable of creativity, are there ways that this creativity can be fostered or encouraged? Formal school instruction tends to focus on learning specific content, passing tests and advancing in grade. According to Albert (1996), a number of researchers have identified a period in middle childhood through to preadolescence when early signs of creativity seem to disappear as children concentrate on well-organized (and thus well-controlled) learning skills. Divergent thinking simply does not have much opportunity to flourish in the classroom. However, outside school, parents can contribute by encouraging their children's creative impulses (Russ, 2003).

Creativity in adolescence

Creativity is an important but often loosely used term and its significance in educational (and other) contexts is becoming increasingly understood. Many scientists believe that creative performance involves a particular mix of different psychological processes including fast, implicit and associative information processing and, simultaneously, more deliberate and logical processing (Chaiken & Trope, 1999). Broadly described, it is a combination of dual processes of cognitive flexibility and cognitive persistence (Förster, Friedman, & Lieberman, 2004).

Work on creative thinking into adolescence has identified not only social and contextual factors, but also the role of developmental changes in the brain as potentially important. For instance, Kleibeuker, De Dreu, and Crone (2016) suggest that changes in brain activity, when mapped on to performance on divergent thinking tasks, point to the frontal cortex as playing an important role in generating novelty and complexity. Emotion-related brain activity may also be involved in creative thinking in adolescence (Xia et al., 2017), but a darker side is that sensation-seeking behaviour may also be associated with higher levels of creativity which, in adolescence, may also lead to more risk-taking and impulsive behaviour.

SUMMARY

Most psychologists believe that intelligence is composed of multiple abilities and is not a single, general construct, although the existence of a general factor of cognitive ability, derived from Spearman's original *general factor (g)*, is often employed by researchers and can be a useful marker of broad cognitive ability. The middle-ground position, which also recognizes Spearman's concept of *specific factors (s)*, holds that children may vary both in overall intellectual power and in their proficiency in specific aspects of cognitive functioning. An information-processing approach to intelligence, Sternberg's *triarchic theory of intelligence* proposes that intelligence is built on information-processing skills, experience with particular kinds of tasks and problems, and the abilities to adapt to a particular context and to shape others to one's needs. Gardner's *theory of multiple intelligences* suggests that each of eight kinds of intelligence has its own developmental path and is guided by different forms of perception, learning, and memory.

Specialists in intelligence testing have generally described intelligence by means of an *intelligence quotient (IQ)*. However, it is important to remember that what is measured on an IQ test is performance; capacity cannot be directly measured. The widely used Bayley Scales of Infant Development and the Fagan Test of Infant Intelligence are designed for infants and very young children. The early intelligence test developed by Binet and Simon focused on verbal and problem-solving abilities. The Stanford-Binet Test is an adaptation of Binet's test. Binet developed the concept of *mental age*. The Wechsler Intelligence Scales (adult and child versions) are probably the most commonly used intelligence tests today. Their scoring is based on a *deviation IQ*. Other tests include the Kaufman Assessment Battery for Children (KABC), the Cognitive Assessment system (CAS) and Raven's Matrices.

Psychometricians establish *test norms* by administering a test to groups having particular characteristics, such as age. The stimuli, instructions, and scoring of test items are also carefully *standardized* so that the test procedures will be the same when administered by different people. Intelligence tests must have both *validity* and *reliability*. Most estimates of the heritability of intelligence have indicated that 40% to 50% of the variability in intelligence is due to genetic factors.

The concept of *cumulative risk* suggests that the more negative aspects of experience that are present in a child's life, and put the child at risk for unhealthy development, the more likely he is to score poorly on tests of intellectual skills. Varying styles of parent–child interactions in different social classes may influence a child's development of verbal and cognitive skills. Studies indicate that early differences in mothers' use of language and infants' attention to their mothers' speech may account for later differences in the use of verbal information. Research indicates that cultural differences in parents' attitudes and enthusiasm for education may affect children's performance on academic tasks. *Stereotype threat* may also interfere with the performance of ethnic minority youth on achievement tests.

Children's intellectual performance is influenced by their own *achievement motivation*, the emotions they associate with learning tasks, the ways they view themselves and their abilities, and their responses to success and failure. In one approach to understanding achievement motivation, children who see themselves as helpless tend to give up easily or show deterioration when working on hard problems. In contrast, mastery-orientated children use failure feedback to maintain or improve their performance. Helpless children may hold an entity view of intelligence, whereas mastery-orientated children may hold an incremental view.

Working memory and *executive function* (EF) or cognitive control are also processes that have been implicated as fundamental to effective learning. Interventions aimed at addressing or improving these processes appear to yield positive results in preparing children for school, and continuing on through school to educational success. Vygotskian approaches to developmental psychology often influence classroom teaching, and sociocultural theorists have developed these ideas to understand better how learning is embedded in social processes. *Peer collaboration* is also an important feature of many classrooms and has been demonstrated to be an effective means of learning.

Explore and Discuss

1. How important is IQ in education? What do IQ tests predict, and what do they not predict?

2. What is the Flynn effect and why does it happen?

3. Are there sex differences in intelligence? If not, why do men and women not perform equally in many education contexts?

4. Why are some IQ tests not so effective in estimating the abilities of ethnic-minority children and adults?

5. How can teachers help children to learn from preschool through to university and beyond?

6. How appropriate is a 'one size fits all' approach to education? If not, is IQ an appropriate means of establishing intellectual ability potential?

Recommended Reading

Classic

Dweck, C. S. (1986). Motivational processes affecting learning. *American Psychologist, 41*(10), 1040–1048.

Mackintosh, N. J. (1998). *IQ and human intelligence.* Oxford: Oxford University Press.

Spearman, C. (1927). *The abilities of man: Their nature and measurement.* New York: Macmillan.

Contemporary

Howe, C., & Littleton, K. (eds) (2010). *Educational dialogues: Understanding and promoting productive interaction.* Abingdon: Taylor & Francis.

Ma, C., & Schapira, M. (2017). *The Bell curve: Intelligence and class structure in American life.* New York: Taylor & Francis.

Sawyer, R. K., John-Steiner, V., Moran, S., Sternberg, R. J., Feldman, D. H., Nakamura, J., & Csikszentmihalyi, M. (eds.) (2003). *Creativity and development.* Oxford: Oxford University Press.

CHAPTER 12
Parents, Peers and Social Relationships

Introduction

Learning to understand and establish social relationships – with parents, perhaps siblings, peers and others – is a key developmental achievement. It is an achievement that is not only fundamental for successful cognitive development, but also for well-being and health. As they grow children come to develop friendships, acquaintances and associations with others whom they may encounter. This chapter focuses on how these relationships are acquired and develop, and how they may impact upon a child's psychological development.

The family is typically the earliest and the most sustained source of social contact for the child. The chapter begins by exploring the family and its influence on development. Family relationships often remain the most intense and enduring of all interpersonal and social bonds. Family members share not only their memories of the past but also their expectations of sharing future events and experiences. It is largely this continuity over time that makes the family relationship qualitatively different from the shorter-lived relationships children have with playmates and friends, teachers, neighbours and work colleagues. We explore the several subsystems of the family – including the relationships between and among marital partners, parents and children, and siblings – and examine how the family as a whole contributes to the child's and adolescent's socialization. The chapter examines systematic differences in parenting styles and the consequences of these for children. The chapter then turns to look at the effects of social class, socioeconomic status and ethnicity on the family and its role as socializing agent. Also considered is the development of children born to individuals who become parents either early or late in life.

After considering this social context to family life, the chapter considers children's relationships with peers, from infancy through to adolescence, and the differential contributions of parents and peers to developmental and social outcomes. Lastly, research on friendships and the change in these relations over time is examined.

THE FAMILY

Parents are usually the most important influence on a child's development, particularly in the early years. Yet while parents do indeed influence and direct their children, their children also influence them and, in fact, play an active role in their own socialization and development as an adult (Bronfenbrenner & Morris, 2006; Kuczynski & Parkin, 2007). In a complex family system in which members are interdependent, changes in structure or in the behaviour of a single member can affect the functioning of the entire family. Moreover, families do not function in isolation; they are influenced by the larger physical, cultural, social, and historical settings and events around them. Thus families are not static; they change, and the relationships between family members change, over time.

The ecological systems perspective

In Chapter 1 we outline Bronfenbrenner's 'ecological systems' perspective; considering the often competing influences of a child's parents, siblings and peers highlights how multiple different sources can exert an influence on psychological functioning and development.

The view of the family as an interdependent system that functions as a whole has two principal origins: the realization by psychotherapists that to change the behaviour of a troubled child one usually must change the family system as well (Minuchin, 2002) and Bronfenbrenner's ecological theory. This position is concerned both with the relationships between the child and the many nested systems within which she develops as well as with the relationships among these systems themselves, from the familiar microsystem to the larger social and cultural setting of the macrosystem (Bronfenbrenner & Morris, 2006). Because each family member and family subsystem influence and are influenced by each other member and subsystem, both cooperative behaviour and hostile or antisocial behaviour may have widespread effects on the system as a whole. Parents who have a good relationship with each other are more likely than not to be caring and supportive with their children, and in turn the children are likely to be cooperative and responsible. On the other hand, parents whose marriages are unhappy may become irritable with their children, and the children may exhibit antisocial behaviour that may in turn intensify problems in the parents' relationship.

Families tend to attain equilibrium, or *homeostasis*, in their functioning and to become resistant to forces that might alter this balance. This can be useful when routines and rituals help establish a sense of family history, identity and tradition, making interactions easier and more comfortable. On the other hand, adaptability is the central criterion of a well-functioning family; when family members are unbending in the face of parental dissension or family distress over an aggressive child, routines can solidify and intensify negative patterns of interaction (Katz & Gottman, 1997; Dishion & Bullock, 2002). In these circumstances, members may make no effort to communicate rationally, defuse anger, protect others or solve problems, and may become locked into a pattern of interaction that promotes or sustains maladaptive behaviour in one or more family members. Resistance to change can prevent parents or other family members from recognizing problems and can cause members to blame all family difficulties on one child, who becomes the target for everyone else.

Finally, families have *boundaries* that vary in how permeable or vulnerable they are to outside influences. A well-functioning family tends to have permeable boundaries that allow members to maintain satisfying relationships both within and outside the family itself (Kerig, 2008). If families are too rigidly bounded, members may have difficulty disengaging appropriately from the family as, for example, in adolescence, starting college, marrying or in time of need, making use of resources outside the family. Such families may have few positive community contacts and social supports and may be more likely than others to perceive their children negatively and be punitive and inconsistent with them (Wahler & Dumas, 1987). On the other hand, families whose boundaries are too permeable can be vulnerable to disruptions by external forces such as intrusive in-laws or peer groups whose behaviour is at odds with the family's own standards.

Parental behaviour

Attachment between parent and infant, as we discussed in Chapter 7, forms the foundation for later relationships. Although socialization begins at birth, it seems to become more conscious and systematic as the child achieves greater mobility and begins to use formal language. Parents cuddle and pet the child and praise her for all sorts of achievements that parents and society regard as desirable, such as learning to use a spoon, naming objects, and repeating new words. On the other hand, parents also impose and often enforce rules to ensure children behave by certain social and moral standards and do not expose themselves to danger or undue risk.

In Chapter 14 we discuss the development of children's moral understanding and development in more detail.

In teaching their children social rules and roles, parents rely on several of the learning principles we discussed earlier. For example, they use *reinforcement* when they explain acceptable standards of behaviour and then praise or discipline their children according to whether they conform to or violate these rules. Parents also teach their children by *modelling* behaviours they want the children to adopt. An important difference between these two approaches is that whereas parents knowingly use reinforcement techniques, observational learning may occur by chance. As a result, the modelled behaviour may not always be what they want to produce, especially if parents are inconsistent in the moral standards they apply to their own behaviour.

Parents also manage aspects of their children's environment that will influence their social development. They choose the neighbourhoods and home in which the child lives, decorate the child's room in a masculine or feminine style, provide the child with toys and books, and expose the child to television viewing. They also promote the child's social life and activities by arranging social events and enrolling the child in activities such as sports, art, music, and other social and skill enhancement programmes (Ladd & Pettit, 2002; Parke & Buriel, 2006).

Parenting patterns and styles tend to reflect two primary dimensions of behaviour. The first revolves around emotionality: Parents may be warm, responsive, and child-centred in their approach to their children, or they may be rejecting, unresponsive, and essentially uninvolved with their children and more focused on their own needs and wishes. The second dimension concerns the issue of control: parents may be very demanding of their children, restricting their behaviour, or they may be permissive and undemanding, pretty much allowing the child to do as he wishes. We discuss some aspects of these two dimensions and then consider four parental patterns of behaviour to which they contribute.

Warm and responsive parents are likely to have children who would be distressed to lose their approval. Children are therefore more likely to learn, accept and internalize parental standards.
Source: © rmarmion/123RF

Parental *emotionality* is crucial in the socialization process. When a parent is warm and loving, the child is likely to want to maintain the parent's approval and to be distressed at any prospect of losing the parent's love (Baumrind, 1991; Grusec & Davidov, 2007). If a parent is cold and rejecting, however, the threat of withdrawal of love is unlikely to be an effective mechanism of socialization. Warmth and nurturance are likely to be associated with parental responsiveness to the child's needs. Loving parents make children feel good about themselves, dispelling anxiety and building their sense of security and their self-esteem. Children with such parents are more likely to learn and to accept and internalize parental standards than children of rejecting parents (Kochanska & Murray, 2000). The high levels of tension and anxiety likely to be associated with hostile parents and frequent physical punishment may make it very difficult for the child to learn the social rules the parent is attempting to teach.

Successful socialization also enables the child to *control* her own behaviour and to make responsible choices and decisions. Two kinds of control have been identified: behavioural control and psychological control (Barber, 2002). Behavioural control involves setting reasonable rules and parental use of suggestions, reasoning, and possible alternative courses of action as well as monitoring of children's activities. Moderate levels of behavioural control (e.g., consistency of discipline and encouragement for the child to view compliance as self-initiated) lead children to be more likely to cooperate and to adopt or internalize their parents' standards (Barber & Harmon, 2002; Holden & Hawk, 2003).

Psychological control involves the use of emotion-directed tactics such as guilt or shame induction, withdrawal of love or affection, or ignoring or discounting a child's feelings. Use of this type of control often leads to lower self-esteem, higher anxiety and, possibly, depression (Barber & Harmon, 2002).

As the child gains in social and cognitive competence and becomes more autonomous, parents rely increasingly on reasoning, and the child engages more and more in active bargaining and negotiation with parents over rules and boundaries to behaviour (Kuczynski & Parkin, 2007). This gradual shift from control by parents and others to self-control becomes critical for the child as he begins to spend time out of the home. Parents' opportunities to monitor and control the child's activities directly decline markedly in the elementary school years and even more in adolescence (Mounts, 2000).

It is also worth noting that much of the research literature on parenting has tended to regard both parents as adopting a similar style or approach, or has tended to characterize different approaches as 'male' and 'female', and has led to less study into fathers' parenting styles (Cabrera, Volling, & Barr, 2018). Moreover, the types and dynamics of families change across culture and are changing across time. For instance, in many societies lesbian and gay parents are more common (more accepted) than they were in the past and there are many one parent families. In the case of the former, research demonstrates that there are very few negative outcomes for children, a few differences in aspects of children's gender knowledge (see chapter 13), compared with peers who have heterosexual parents (e.g., Farr, Bruun, Doss & Patterson, 2017). In the case of the latter, there is some evidence to suggest that children who grow up in a single parent family are at risk of more problems than those who grow up in a family when two parents are present (McLanahan & Sandefur, 1994).

In most single parent families it is the mother who is the sole caregiver. Statistics suggest that, looking across societies, the educational achievements of children from single parent families are lower than those from other families (Amato, Patterson, & Beattie, 2015). A single parent may also find it harder to deal with a child with mental health problems which could, in turn, exacerbate a situation and lead to further negative outcomes for the child or for other children in the household (McNeillis et al., 2017). However, broad statistics often mask other social and demographic factors that may influence children's outcomes or that may have led to the parent being sole caregiver in the first place. Moreover, it is almost impossible to identify a 'typical' family, including a single parent family who may be in that position through divorce, bereavement or another form of relationship breakdown. Fundamentally, any loving and caring environment that meets a child's social, emotional, physical, health and intellectual needs, and also offers the child some stability in growing up, is associated with generally favourable outcomes (Lee & McLanahan, 2015).

Parenting styles

Family systems theorists would argue that what is important in a child's socialization is not any particular parental dimension of behaviour but the overall combination of these behaviours. The four parenting styles shown in Table 12-1 – authoritative, authoritarian, permissive and uninvolved – are composed of different combinations of the warm–responsive/rejecting–unresponsive and the restrictive–demanding/permissive–undemanding dimensions discussed above. These dimensions were developed from research that has explored the relations among each parenting style and children's emotional, social and cognitive development.

Baumrind (1967) identified three parenting styles based on parental interviews and observations of parents interacting

Table 12-1   Baumrind's typology of parenting styles

| | Emotionality | |
Control	Warm, responsive	Rejecting, unresponsive
Restrictive, demanding	Authoritative	Authoritarian
Permissive, undemanding	Permissive	Uninvolved

Source: Based on Maccoby and Martin (1983).

with their children both at home and in the laboratory. Subsequently, Maccoby and Martin (1983) added a fourth, 'uninvolved' (also known as neglecting–rejecting).

Baumrind found that authoritative parenting correlated with the behaviour of energetic-friendly children, who exhibited positive emotional, social, and cognitive development. Authoritative parents were not intrusive and permitted their children considerable freedom. At the same time, they imposed restrictions in areas in which they had greater knowledge or insight, and they were firm in resisting children's efforts to get them to acquiesce to their demands. In general, warmth and moderate restrictiveness, with the parents expecting appropriately mature behaviour from their children, setting reasonable limits, but also being responsive and attentive to their children's needs, were associated with the children's development of self-esteem, adaptability, competence, internalized control, popularity with peers, and low levels of antisocial behaviour. Authoritative parenting continued to be associated with positive outcomes for adolescents, as it was with younger children; responsive, firm parent–child relationships were especially important in the development of competence in sons.

authoritative parenting
Parenting that is warm, responsive and involved yet unintrusive, and in which parents set reasonable limits and expect appropriately mature behaviour from their children.

In contrast, authoritarian parenting was linked with the behaviour of conflicted irritable children, who tended to be fearful, moody and vulnerable to stressors. These parents were rigid, power-assertive, harsh and unresponsive to their children's needs. In these families, children had little control over their environment and received little gratification. Baumrind proposed that these children often felt trapped and angry, but also fearful of asserting themselves in a hostile environment. Authoritarian child-rearing had more negative long-term outcomes for boys than for girls. Sons of authoritarian parents were low in cognitive and social competence. Their academic and intellectual performance was poor. They were unfriendly and lacked self-confidence, initiative and leadership in their relations with peers.

authoritarian parenting
Parenting that is harsh, unresponsive and rigid, and in which parents tend to use power-assertive methods of control.

permissive parenting
Parenting that is lax, and in which parents exercise inconsistent discipline and encourage children to express their impulses freely.

Permissive parenting, although it produced affectionate relationships between parents and children, was correlated with children's impulsive-aggressive behaviour. Excessively lax and inconsistent discipline and encouragement of children's free expression of their impulses were associated with the development of uncontrolled, non-compliant and aggressive behaviour in children. Table 12-1 summarizes Baumrind's findings on some major dimensions of parents' behaviours; parents of the energetic-friendly children scored highest on all these dimensions during home as well as in the more controlled, laboratory observations.

uninvolved parenting
Parenting that is indifferent and neglectful, and in which parents focus on their own needs rather than their children's needs. Also known as neglecting–rejecting parenting.

The fourth type, uninvolved parenting, identified by Maccoby and Martin (1983), characterized parents who were indifferent to or actively neglected their children and were 'motivated to do whatever is necessary to minimize the costs in time and effort of interaction with the child' (p. 48). Uninvolved parents are parent-centred rather than child-centred, and so frequently focus on their own needs over and above those of the child. Particularly when a child is older, these parents fail to monitor the child's activity or to know where she is, what she's doing or who her companions are.

Uninvolved parenting is sometimes found in mothers who are depressed (Goodman & Gotlib, 2002) and in people under the stress of such things as marital discord or divorce (Hetherington & Kelly, 2002). Their own anxiety and emotional neediness may drive some parents to pursue self-gratification at the expense and neglect of their children's welfare (Patterson & Capaldi, 1991). Table 12-2 summarizes the characteristics of parents who display the four parenting styles as well as the kinds of behaviours the children of each group of parents manifest.

Table 12-2   Relation between parenting styles and children's characteristics

Parenting style	Children's characteristics
Authoritative parent	*Energetic-friendly child*
Warm, involved, responsive; shows pleasure and support of child's constructive behaviour; considers child's wishes and solicits her opinions; offers alternatives	Cheerful
	Self-controlled and self-reliant
	Purposive, achievement orientated
Sets standards, communicates them clearly, and enforces them firmly; does not yield to child's coercion; shows displeasure at bad behaviour; confronts disobedient child	Shows interest and curiosity in novel situations
	Has high energy level
Expects mature, independent, age-appropriate behaviour	Maintains friendly relations with peers
Plans cultural events and joint activities	Cooperates with adults; is tractable
	Copes well with stress
Authoritarian parent	*Conflicted-irritable child*
Shows little warmth or positive involvement	Moody, unhappy, aimless
Does not solicit or consider child's desires or opinions	Fearful, apprehensive; easily annoyed
Enforces rules rigidly but doesn't explain them clearly	Passively hostile and deceitful
Shows anger and displeasure; confronts child regarding bad behaviour and uses harsh, punitive discipline	Alternates between aggressive behaviour and sulky withdrawal
Views child as dominated by antisocial impulses	Vulnerable to stress
Permissive parent	*Impulsive-aggressive child*
Moderately warm	Aggressive, domineering, resistant, non-compliant
Glorifies free expression of impulses and desires	Quick to anger but fast to recover cheerful mood
Does not communicate rules clearly or enforce them; ignores or accepts bad behaviour; disciplines inconsistently; yields to coercion and whining; hides impatience, anger	Lacks self-control and displays little self-reliance
	Impulsive
	Shows little achievement orientation
Makes few demands for mature, independent behaviour	Aimless; has few goal-directed activities
Uninvolved parent	*Neglected child*
Self-centred, generally unresponsive, neglectful	Moody, insecurely attached, impulsive, aggressive, non-compliant, irresponsible
Pursues self-gratification at expense of child's welfare	
Tries to minimize costs (time, effort) of interaction with child	Low self-esteem, immature, alienated from family
Fails to monitor child's activity, whereabouts, companions	Lacks skills for social and academic pursuits
May be depressive, anxious, emotionally needy	Truancy, association with troubled peers, delinquency and arrests, precocious sexuality
Vulnerable to marital discord, divorce	

Source: Baumrind (1967, 1991); Maccoby and Martin (1983).

Parental involvement plays a crucial role in the development of both social and cognitive competence in children. In infants, lack of parental involvement is associated with disruptions in attachment (Thompson, 2006b), and among preschool-age children, poor monitoring combined with coercive discipline predicted conduct problems in African American boys and girls at age 6 (Kilgore, Snyder, & Lentz, 2000). In older children, it is associated with impulsivity, aggression, non-compliance, moodiness, and low self-esteem (Baumrind, 1991). Children of uninvolved parents tend not only to be socially incompetent, irresponsible, immature, and alienated from their families but also show disruptions in cognitive development, achievement and school performance (Baumrind, 1991; Hetherington & Stanley-Hagan, 2002). Adolescents and young adults whose parents are uninvolved are likely to be truant, to spend time on the streets with friends whom the parents dislike, to be sexually active at a younger age than their peers, to drink excessively and to be delinquent (Dishion & Bullock, 2002).

Although the parenting styles approach is influential and widely used, the general approach has been criticized. First, more research is needed to establish how the components of each style contribute to their effectiveness in terms of children's development. Second, the parenting styles approach tends to neglect consideration of how much the child's temperament and behaviour may influence the parents' style or discipline techniques (Kochanska, 1997; Bates & Pettit, 2007). Finally, recent work has raised serious questions about how well these styles describe parenting across either socioeconomic or ethnic/cultural groups (Chao, 1994, 2001; McLoyd et al., 2007). There are two core issues here: do all groups use the parenting styles we've identified to the same degree, and are the advantages and disadvantages of each style for the child's development similar across groups? The answer to both of these questions seems to be no.

For one thing, where a child grows up and the norms and values prevalent in a parent's social circle seem to affect the kinds of socialization strategies parents adopt (Leventhal & Brooks-Gunn, 2000). For example, although an authoritative child-rearing style may promote social and academic competence in children living in low-risk environments (Baumrind, 1991; Steinberg, Dornbusch, & Brown, 1992), it may not work in other situations. Several studies have found that poor minority parents who used more authoritarian child-rearing practices, especially those who lived in dangerous areas, had better adjusted children than those who relied on authoritative strategies (Furstenberg et al., 1999; Parke et al., 2008). Parental social integration into the neighbourhood may also be an important predictor of more adequate parenting practices (Steinberg, Darling, & Fletcher, 1995). The more socially integrated the parents, the more vigilant they may be about their children's behaviour, although this probably holds true only when families reside in areas where 'good parenting' is the norm.

Culture also plays a part. Rudy and Grusec (2006) found no links between authoritarian parenting and negative feeling about the child or lack of warmth in Middle Eastern families living in Canada, but the ties between this style and negativity and low warmth were evident for Anglo-Canadian parents. Moreover, authoritarian style was associated with higher child self-esteem for Middle Eastern but not Anglo children. In summary, it is important to consider contextual and cultural issues in developing new concepts of parenting styles.

BOX 12-1 Parental child-rearing styles carry different meanings in different cultures

Applied Developmental Psychology

Chao (1994, 2001) points out that the term 'authoritarian' does not mean in Chinese what it means in English. Thus, when Chinese parents get such *high* authoritarian parenting scores, they may be expressing behaviour patterns that simply reflect a different set of norms, values and beliefs compared with Western ideas of authoritarianism described in Baumrind's typology. Whereas the Western concept of authoritarianism subsumes many quite negative beliefs, attitudes and behaviours, the Chinese style of parenting characterized by the concepts of *chiao shun* ('training') and *guan* ('to govern') requires a high degree of involvement with the child, physical closeness to the child, and devotion – mainly by the mother – of a great amount of time and effort. These concepts subsume teaching or educating children, focusing particularly on children's performance in school (for it is the Chinese belief that education is the key to success), and also connote 'loving' and 'caring for' the children. In this sense, these notions are antithetical to the concept of authoritarianism as it is defined in Western society. As Chao (1994) suggests, the seemingly restrictive behaviours that cause Asian parents to get high scores on Western scales may be equated with parental concern, caring and involvement, and Asian parental control may reflect a more organizational effort designed to keep the family running smoothly and to foster family harmony.

It seems likely that the Chinese concepts of *chiao shun* and *guan* may actually resemble authoritativeness more than authoritarianism. The major difference between Chinese and Western concepts is that in Western cultures adults often place an emphasis on encouraging a child's autonomy and independence: on soliciting the child's opinions, considering her wishes and offering her alternatives. As Chao (2001) points out, the Chinese notion of the self derives from the Confucian notion of *jen* ('humanity' or 'human kindness'), which holds that human beings are bound to one another and defined by their relationships with one another. For Chinese – and many other Asian – parents, adhering to social rules of conduct and interaction, and developing a sensitive knowledge of others and their expectations are more crucial than focusing on the free expression of internal attitudes, feelings and thoughts. Whereas the Western child is socialized to achieve according to some internalized standards of excellence, the Chinese child is encouraged to achieve according to family and social norms and expectations (Chao, 1995, 2001). These studies underscore the importance of recognizing how different cultures interpret various child-rearing practices.

To return to the suggestion by Steinberg and his colleagues that peer group support explains why Asian students excel in school despite their 'authoritarian' upbringing, it is just possible that the peer groups are reflecting the *chiao shun* and *guan* that these peers have received from their parents. In effect, then, they support a given child's motivation and endeavour to achieve because they have the same parent-taught motivation and belief in hard work.

Parental relationships

When partners offer each other emotional and physical support and comfort, the likelihood that they will provide the same kind of support and caring to their children is greatly increased. Research has shown that when partners are mutually supportive, they are more involved with their children, and their relationships with their children demonstrate affection, sensitivity, and competent child-rearing practices (Katz & Gottman, 1997; Cowan & Cowan, 2002, 2008).

Conflict between partners, however, can have seriously negative effects on both parents and children (Grych & Fincham, 2001; Cummings & Merrilees, 2008). Even when a family's children are infants or preschool age, conflict between parents has been found to reflect insecure attachments of the children to both parents (Frosch, Mangelsdorf, & McHale, 2000). Studying school-age children, Katz and Gottman (1993, 1996) found that not only the level of conflict but also the way adult partners manage their conflict can have deleterious effects on children. If marital partners handled disagreements in hostile or aggressive ways, children tended to display aggressive behaviour. In addition, fathers who had an angry and withdrawn style of dealing with marital disputes had children who were more likely to be depressed than others.

Parental relationships, particularly where conflict is involved, can influence children emotionally and affect their behavioural patterns. For example, children were more likely to display aggressive behaviour if marital partners behaved in a hostile or aggressive way in arguments.
Source: © Purestock/PunchStock

The effect of marital conflict on children takes two pathways: direct and indirect (Grych & Fincham, 2001; Cummings & Merrilees, 2008). Children may be affected by such conflict *indirectly* when marital difficulties cause parents to change their childrearing practices in unfamiliar ways. In the Katz and Gottman (1997) work, parents in conflicted marriages had a poor parenting style that was characterized as cold, unresponsive, angry and deficient in providing structure and setting limits; the children of these couples tended to display a lot of anger and non-compliance in interacting with their parents. Children may also be affected *directly* by marital conflict when they are actual witnesses to arguments and fights. In a series of studies, Cummings and his colleagues have shown children real or videotaped interactions between adult actors behaving like two parents in a home setting. For example, the actors might disagree about which movie to see or argue about who will wash the dishes. The more frequent and violent the conflict, and the more often the arguments were about something a child had done or said, the more likely the children were to show distress, shame, and self-blame (Frosch & Mangelsdorf, 2001; Cummings, Goeke-Morey, & Graham, 2002) (see Figure 12-1). Moreover, when the actors failed to settle their dispute, the children expressed more anger and distress than when the actors resolved a conflict. A clear implication of this work is that if partners handle their discussions constructively, showing respect for one another's opinions, they can reduce the harmful effects that their argument may have on their children as well as modelling healthy conflict negotiation for their children.

Boys appear much more susceptible to the negative effects of family disharmony than girls. Why should this be so? It seems that boys are more likely to be directly exposed to parental bickering and physical abuse than are girls (Hetherington & Stanley-Hagan, 2002). Parents quarrel more often and their quarrels are longer in the presence of their sons. If parents begin to disagree when daughters are present, they are more likely to raise their eyebrows,

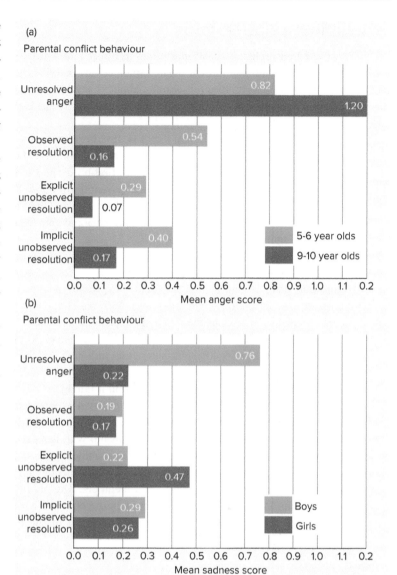

(a) Parental conflict behaviour

(b) Parental conflict behaviour

Figure 12-1 How children respond to parental conflict

Parents' failure to resolve an angry conflict was the most likely behaviour to arouse children's anger and caused the most displays of anger in older children (a). Such a failure was also more likely to trigger sadness in boys, but girls were more likely to be sad when parents resolved a conflict out of their presence and made only a brief reference to it later (b).
Source: Adapted from Cummings, Simpson, and Wilson (1993).

nod in the child's direction and mutter, 'We'll talk about this later'. Parents may simply be more protective of daughters than of sons, or boys' behaviour may lead to a greater need for discipline or greater parental disagreement.

Clearly, children can influence the relationship between their parents. For example, children who are temperamentally difficult are often the cause of heightened family stress that may translate into marital conflict. Couples who were satisfied with their relationship before the child's birth weather such pressures reasonably well, and their relationships show fewer disruptions than those of couples who were experiencing dissension before a child's arrival. Thus, although the presence of a difficult child may be enough to further undermine a fragile relationship (Hogan & Msall, 2002), the birth of a child rarely destroys a good relationship.

Sibling relationships

Most children probably spend more time in direct interaction with their siblings than with their parents or other people significant in their lives (Larson & Verma, 1999; Dunn, 2007). Interactions between siblings provide plenty of opportunities for learning about positive and negative behaviours, and the emotional intensity of these exchanges may be greater than that of exchanges with other family members and friends (Katz, Kramer, & Gottman, 1992).

A child's position in the family – that is, first-born or a later-born child – can affect siblings, parents and the interactions among all family members as well as the child too. Each child's experience and temperament is different, but the experience of the first-born child is unique because, at least for some period of time, a first-born child is the sole focus of parental attention. First-born children are generally more adult-orientated, helpful and self-controlled than their siblings; they also tend to be more studious, conscientious and serious, and to excel in academic and professional achievement (Zajonc & Mullally, 1997; Herrera et al., 2003) (see Figure 12-2).

Interestingly, however, research has found that second-born sons support innovative theories in major scientific controversies related to such issues as evolution, whereas first-born sons support the status quo (Sulloway, 1995). It may be that the greater expectations and demands parents typically place on their first-borns are responsible for some other, less desirable characteristics of first-borns. For example, they tend to be more fearful and anxious than their siblings, to experience more guilt, to have more difficulty coping alone with stressful situations, and to have less self-confidence. So birth order is associated with some trends in terms of positive and negative characteristics, although it is important to point out that these characteristics and outcomes are not inevitable or even true for every child; there are advantages and disadvantages to being the first, second, third or fourth child in a family.

An only child is exposed to the same high level of parental demands as other first-borns, but does not have to adapt to displacement and competition with siblings. Like first-borns, the only child tends to be a high achiever, sustained by her close relationship with her parents, but she tends to be less anxious and to show more personal control, maturity and leadership (Falbo & Polit, 1986).

As expected based on family systems theory, introducing a new sibling into the family mix changes the relationship dynamics among family members. The parents, to a great extent, determine whether the first-born child will find seriously distressing the changes wrought by the arrival of a sibling (Teti, 2002). If a mother continues to be responsive to the needs of the older child and helps him to understand the

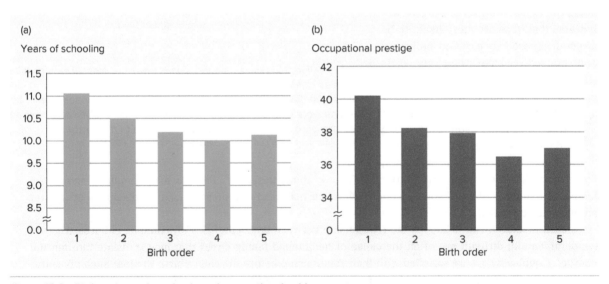

Figure 12-2   Birth order and academic and occupational achievement
This research showed a clear positive relationship between a person's rank in the family and her degree of achievement in academic endeavours and in working or professional life.
Source: Adapted from Herrera et al. (2003).

feelings of the younger child, intense sibling rivalry is unlikely to occur (Howe & Ross, 1990). And if a father becomes increasingly involved with his first-born child, this can also counter the child's feelings of displacement and jealousy. In fact, one positive effect of the birth of a second child may be that a father participates more in child care (Kramer & Ramsburg, 2002). Parents can help prepare their children for the arrival of a new sibling. Bringing the older sibling to visit mother and new baby in the hospital and providing maternal support both help with this transition (Kramer & Ramsburg, 2002). Friends, too, can serve as buffers in this potentially stressful transition. Kramer and Gottman (1992) found that pre-schoolers who had good friendships showed less upset than children who did not get along well with friends. Moreover, these preschoolers were more accepting and behaved more positively towards their new sibling.

Older siblings in large families are often assigned quasi-parental roles: warming a baby's bottle, changing nappies and comforting a distressed younger sibling. In many cultures, sibling caregivers are common (Weisner, 1993), and in still others – for example, Mexico – siblings rather than parents are the principal play partners (Zukow-Goldring, 2002).

Birth order also affects a child's interactions with his siblings. The eldest child is often expected to assume some responsibility for the younger sibling who has displaced him. Older siblings may function as tutors, managers or supervisors of their younger siblings' behaviour during social interactions, and may also act as gatekeepers who extend or limit siblings' opportunities to interact with other children outside the family (Edwards & Whiting, 1993; Parke & Buriel, 2006).

Eldest children inevitably focus on parents as their main sources of social learning, whereas younger children use both parents and older siblings as models and teachers (Dunn, 2007). Younger siblings, even infants as young as a year old, tend to watch, follow and imitate their older siblings (Pepler, Corter, & Abramovitch, 1982). Nor does their influence stop when children enter school, as 70% of children report getting help with homework from siblings, especially from older sisters (Zukow-Goldring, 2002). Older siblings can sometimes serve as deviant or negative influences, encouraging early sexual activity, drug use or delinquency in their brothers or sisters (East, 1996; Garcia et al., 2000).

Sibling relationships change with age. In adolescence, early overt sibling rivalry and ambivalence may diminish, and intimacy may arise in which a sibling serves as the most trusted confidant and source of emotional support. In concerns about appearance, peer relations, social problems and sexuality, siblings can often communicate more openly with each other than with peers or parents (Dunn, 2007). Female siblings often become closer over the lifespan.

BOX 12-2 Brothers and sisters can help the development of theory of mind

Research close-up

Source: Based on Perner, Ruffman, and Leekam (1994).

Introduction:

The development of children's understanding of the mind has been a major topic of interest for many years. An important aspect of this is that children acquire, at around 3 years of age, a 'theory of mind' – that is, the ability to attribute mental states to oneself and to other people, and to understand that other people have beliefs, desires and thoughts that are different from one's own. It is frequently tested using a 'false-belief' task (see Chapter 9 for more details). Based on the observation that practice and experience help the development of skills, Perner et al. suggested that theory of mind might develop more rapidly in children who had a number of siblings than in those who had none. Having siblings means that a child has more opportunity for various types of social interaction and so more opportunity to learn about other people's mental states. Therefore, they undertook two studies to investigate this. The first study used a false-belief task to test the hypothesis that children who had siblings would perform better on a false-belief task than children who did not. The second study investigated whether the age of the siblings would make a difference.

Method:

Study 1

A total of 76 children, aged 3–4 years, participated in this study. Each child completed a false-belief task, in which they were told a short story about a boy called Maxi, and then asked a series of questions. Half of the children were told a story in which Maxi helped his mother unpack some shopping and put some chocolate in a particular cupboard. He then went out to play. While he was outside, his mother moved the chocolate to a different cupboard. The children were asked questions about what Maxi knew and where he would look for the chocolate. Children who lack a theory of mind will wrongly judge that Maxi would know it had been moved, because they do not understand that Maxi will not have access to the same knowledge that they have. The other children were told a similar story but, in this version, Maxi was joined in the playground by his brother, Sam, who asked where the chocolate was. The children were asked the same questions, but about Sam.

Results of the study showed that children who had at least one sibling performed significantly better on this false-belief task than children who had no siblings, by showing a greater understanding of where Maxi thought the chocolate would be.

Study 2

This study aimed to examine the effect of age difference between the child and its sibling and whether it made a difference if the sibling was older or younger. This study had 43 participants, all of whom were in nursery or reception class and who had just one sibling. Each child carried out six false-belief tasks. In each, they were told a story about a girl called Katy, represented by a doll, who took an object to her grandmother. She put the object in a box and then went out to play. While she was out, the child was asked to replace the object with a different one. The child was then asked what Katy would think was in the box when she came back. This task was carried out six times, each time with a different pair of objects. In this study, 11 children gave all incorrect answers, while 25 gave all correct answers. However, overall, they showed that the age difference between the child and its sibling had no effect on performance; also, it made no difference whether the sibling was older or younger.

Discussion:

Study 1 shows that having at least one sibling helps the development of a child's theory of mind. The effect is so strong that, by the age of 3 or 4 years, when these children were tested, it was equivalent to approximately one year's development. However, Study 2 showed that the age of any siblings did not have an effect. These results support the hypothesis that increased social interactions due to having at least one sibling do help in the development of theory of mind. Consequently, they argue against explanations that suggest development of theory of mind relies only on internal maturation and support sociocognitive theories, such as that of Vygotsky, which emphasize social interaction as important for intellectual development.

THE SOCIAL CONTEXT OF FAMILY LIFE

Poverty and work

Parents and family life can be a major influence on educational achievement. We discuss parents' and teachers' roles in Chapter 11.

The broad social context in which family life takes place has a profound influence on children's development. In fact, from a social and political perspective, changes to this context are possibly the most effective means of promoting positive child development and improving outcomes for children who may be at risk in some way. In general, social-class differences are the strongest predictors of variation in family relations and parenting dynamics (Parke & Buriel, 2006). Childhood poverty is a particular concern. Being poor in early childhood is much more detrimental than being poor in middle childhood or adolescence (McLoyd et al., 2011). Poverty affects children in several ways. First, the quality of the home environment is often lower in poor families (Bradley et al., 2001). Children in poor homes have fewer physical resources (books, toys, educational games, computers); they also receive fewer learning opportunities and less cognitive stimulation (parents less often read to children or engage in other developmentally appropriate activities) than other children. Second, poor children are often placed in poorer quality child care settings. Third, poverty and economic stress are linked with parent–child conflict; this leads to lower grades and impairs emotional and social development. A fourth effect of poverty is that poor families often live in high-risk neighbourhoods characterized by social disorganization (crime, unemployment, low parental supervision) and limited resources (fewer playgrounds, after-school programmes, child care and health care facilities) which can adversely affect children's development (Leventhal & Brooks-Gunn, 2000). Finally, poor parents often suffer more physical and emotional problems that impair their parenting abilities.

Parents' and children's behaviour must always be understood in the context of the meanings and values of the individual's particular sociocultural niche (McLoyd et al., 2011; Parke & Buriel, 2006; Rothbaum & Trommsdorf, 2007). For example, in socializing their children, different cultures place different emphases on the continuity of ethnic values and worldviews and on social interdependence. In many cultures, we see reflections of such interdependence in the important role played by the extended family – the family inclusive of grandparents, aunts, uncles, nieces and nephews (McLoyd, Hill, & Dodge, 2005). This emphasis on interdependence is also reflected in a concern with cooperation, obligation, sharing and reciprocity, which often contrasts with typically Western ideals of self-reliance and competition. Often, the 'traditional' nuclear family – just parents and children – may move away from other family members, and thus lack wider social and family support.

> **extended family** A family that includes relatives such as grandparents, aunts, uncles, nieces and nephews within the basic family unit of parents and children.
>
> **nuclear family** A family composed of two parents and one or more children, in which the father is the breadwinner and the mother the homemaker.

There are other, gradual changes to the structure of family life. In Western countries, along with more distant extended family networks, family size is decreasing. For instance, the average number of children in a US family is 1.8, in Japan and the Netherlands the rate is 1.5, and in Germany it is 1.3 children per family (Bellamy, 2000). In these and other countries there are a greater number of single-adult households, which is attributable, in part, to delays in marriage, declines in birth rates and in remarriages, and an increase in the number of elderly people living alone.

Parental roles are changing, too. The number of working mothers has increased in Western societies and young mothers, poor mothers, and mothers from single-parent families are those most likely to enter the labour force because of economic need. As mothers spend more time on the job and less in the home, family roles and patterns of functioning are changing. One important shift may a growing similarity between the roles of the mother and father. When children more often see both of their parents as providing for the family and as participating actively in family and child-rearing tasks, the stereotypical roles of the breadwinning father and the homemaking mother may begin to fade away (Pleck & Masciadrelli, 2004). Note, however, that although father participation increases in dual-career families, currently mothers are still doing most of the child care and housework (Coltrane, 2000).

Working mothers report that time is their scarcest and most valued resource. Both working mothers and their school-age children complain that the mothers have too little time to spend with their children (Perry-Jenkins, Repetti, & Crouter, 2000; Booth et al., 2002). However, greater father involvement may compensate for some of these problems. In both dual-earner and single-earner families, high father involvement is associated with higher IQ and achievement test scores, as well as with greater social maturity in children (Gottfried, Gottfried, & Bathurst, 2002).

Children of working mothers have more egalitarian views of gender roles (Hoffman & Youngblade, 1999; Hoffman, 2000), and children in middle-class families whose mothers are employed have higher educational and occupational goals. Daughters are less likely to display traditional feminine interests and characteristics, and more often perceive the woman's role as involving freedom of choice, satisfaction and competence; daughters themselves are career- and achievement-orientated, independent and assertive, and high in self-esteem (Hoffman, 2000). The sons of working mothers, in contrast to sons of full-time homemaker mothers, not only perceive women as more competent but view men as warmer and more expressive.

It is not just whether one parent or the other works; the nature of the work situation determines the effects of parental employment on a child's development. As we have seen, maternal employment per se does not put children at risk. However, a parent's experience of stress on the job may take its toll on children, parents and marriages (Crouter & Bumpus, 2001). Fathers who worked in a high-stress occupation, air traffic control, withdrew from their wives and were more irritable with their children after a stressful day (Repetti, 1989, 1996). Similarly, mothers were more likely to withdraw from their children after particularly stressful workdays (Repetti & Wood, 1997). Finally, children of mothers who work non-standard schedules (evening, night, or rotating shifts) have poor early cognitive and language development (Han, 2005). In sum, it is not merely working or not working that matters but the conditions under which adults work that make a difference in children's lives.

Divorce and remarriage

Divorce and remarriage are not discrete events, but steps in a transition that modifies the lives and development of parents and children. Children's experiences in earlier family situations will modify their response to this transition: both divorce and remarriage force a restructuring of the household and changes in family roles and relationships (Hetherington & Kelly, 2002; Clarke-Stewart & Brentano, 2006).

Although divorce can be a positive solution to destructive family functioning, for many family members the transition period following separation and divorce is highly stressful. During the first year after a divorce, parents' feelings of distress and unhappiness, troubled parent–child relationships, and children's social and emotional adjustment actually get worse (Hetherington, 2006). In the second year, however, many parents experience a dramatic improvement in their sense of personal well-being, interpersonal functioning and family relations. In the long run, children in stable, well-functioning single-parent households are better adjusted than children in conflict-ridden families.

Some researchers have suggested that when parents delay divorcing – sometimes in the hope of protecting their children – those children show behavioural problems long before the divorce finally takes place. Moreover, these problems may be greater than those of children whose parents have some difficulties but remain in their marriage (Clarke-Stewart et al., 2000). It is possible that children respond adversely to the acrimony and conflict in a stressed marriage, particularly when it is suppressed, or behaviour problems in children may exacerbate difficulties in a troubled marriage and help to precipitate a divorce.

When divorced parents and their children do not experience additional stresses following divorce, most are coping reasonably well by the second or third year after a divorce. However, one-parent mother-headed households are at increased risk of encountering multiple stresses that make it difficult to raise children successfully, and in fact a period of diminished parenting often follows divorce (Hetherington & Stanley-Hagan, 2002). Custodial mothers may become self-involved, erratic, uncommunicative, non-supportive and inconsistently punitive in dealing with their children. They may also fail to control and monitor their children's behaviour adequately. Not uncommonly, children reciprocate in the immediate aftermath of divorce by being demanding, non-compliant and aggressive, or by whining and being overly dependent. However, Wolchick and colleagues (2000) found that when divorced mothers are high in warmth and consistent in their discipline, 8 to 15 year olds had fewer adjustment problems than their peers in less warm and consistent families.

Non-custodial as well as custodial parents can continue to play a significant role in their children's development. When divorced parents agree on child-rearing methods and maintain a reasonably friendly attitude towards each other, frequent visits between the children and the non-custodial parent may be associated with positive adjustment and self-control in the children. When the mother has custody, such visits are particularly helpful for sons. When there is continued conflict between parents, however, especially conflict where the child feels caught in the middle or when the parent is a non-authoritative parent or is poorly adjusted, frequent contact between the non-custodial parent and the child may be associated with disruptions in the child's behaviour (Buchanan, Maccoby, & Dornbusch, 1991; Buchanan & Heiges, 2001). Clearly, what counts is the quality of the contact with a non-custodial parent and the exposure of the child to conflict and stress.

Family members' experience in their original family setting greatly affects their response to remarriage. For divorced women, remarriage is the most common route out of poverty, and a new partner may give a custodial mother not only economic but emotional support as well as help in child-rearing. Children some-times resist the arrival of a step-parent, creating stress in the new marital relationship. Sons, who have often been involved in coercive relationships with their custodial mothers, may have little to lose and much to gain from a relationship with a caring stepfather. Daughters, on the other hand, may feel the intrusion of step-fathers into their close relationships with their mothers as more threatening and disruptive. Among preadolescent children, divorce seems to have more adverse consequences for boys, and remarriage seems to be more difficult for girls. Adolescents, regardless of gender, have a particularly difficult time accepting a parent's remarriage (Hetherington & Stanley-Hagan, 2002).

Over time, most boys and girls adjust reasonably well to their parents' marital transitions. Exhibiting remark-able resilience, some children actually become stronger through coping with divorce and remarriage. In fact, only about 25% have long-term problems (Hetherington & Kelly, 2002). Authoritative parenting is associated with more positive adjustment in children in divorced and remarried families, just as it is in non-divorced fami-lies. If divorce reduces stress and conflict and leads to better functioning on the part of the custodial parent, or if the child's loss of an uninvolved or incompetent father eventually results in the acquisition of a more accessible, responsive father figure, the child often benefits in the long run from divorce and remarriage. Preadolescent boys in particular may benefit from a close, caring relationship with a stepfather.

Early and late parenthood

The age at which an individual becomes a parent is, increasingly, being seen as an issue relevant to understanding children's development. Increasingly, people are becoming first-time parents at later ages. Although there may be many reasons for later parenthood, important factors are difficulty in conceiving and changing patterns of employment.

Delaying the decision to become parents sometimes means that a couple will have difficulty conceiving (Henig, 2004). Research to date suggests that children born via the technique of donor insemination, for example, function as well as chil-dren born in the usual manner (Patterson & Hastings, 2007). And recent study of the technique of surrogacy suggests not only that the offspring of surrogate mothers develop well but also that these children may benefit from parent–child relationships that are even more positive than many obtain in naturally conceived families. In part, this may be due to the eagerness of couples who must make extraordinary efforts to become parents (Golombok et al., 2004).

> In Chapter 4 we consider how a mother's age at the time of conception and birth can have a significant influence on the physical and psychological development of her child.

For both mothers and fathers, age of onset of parenting is linked with both parenting practices and knowledge. Between the teen years and 30, increasing age of first-time motherhood is related to greater satisfaction and higher parenting knowledge, as well as higher sensitivity and language stimulation in regard to their 20 month olds. However, after 30, few links with age were found, and some aspects of parenting are immune from age, such as parental investment and social play (Bornstein & Putnick, 2007). By age 30, moth-ers may be sufficiently settled in terms of their cognitive and emotional development that further shifts in their parenting are unlikely. The older father, with more flexibility and freedom in balancing the demands of work and family, is three times as likely as a younger father to have regular responsibility for some part of a preschool child's daily care (Daniels & Weingarten, 1988).

At the other extreme, very young parents are a source of concern both for the individuals themselves and for their child's development. Early sexual activity leads not just to unplanned pregnancies but also to declining school achievement and interest, and to sexually transmitted diseases (STDs). Many teenage mothers face personal, economic and social problems that make it very difficult for them to support and care for their children (Wakschlag et al., 2001). As a consequence, during the preschool years, signs of delays in children's cognitive development begin to emerge and tend to grow more evident as the children age. Preschool children of teenage mothers also tend to display higher levels of aggression and less ability to control impulsive behaviour. By adolescence, children of teenage mothers have, on the whole, higher rates of academic failure and more delinquency.

Teenagers whose own parents are educated and financially secure as well as warm and responsive to their children have a better chance at avoiding teen pregnancy. If the mother's situation changes for the better, and particularly if she moves off welfare, becomes economically independent, acquires more education or enters a stable relationship before her child becomes an adolescent, the child's adjustment and academic performance may be enhanced (Moore & Brooks-Gunn, 2002).

PEERS

Infancy: first social encounters

Babies are really curious about each other: in the first 6 months of life, they touch and look at each other and are surprisingly responsive to each other's behaviours. If one child cries, another may cry, too. But these early responses probably cannot be considered truly social in the sense that an infant seeks and expects a response from another child. It is likely not until the second half of their first year that infants begin to recognize a peer as a social partner (Brownell, 1990; Dunn, 2004). Between 6 and 12 months, an infant will start trying to influence another child by vocalizing, by looking at or waving at the child, or by touching them. Although babies do hit and push sometimes, a considerable amount of social behaviour among the baby crowd is friendly enough (Eckerman & Didow, 1988; Rubin, Bukowski, & Parker, 2006).

As children develop competence in interacting with peers, they shift towards increased social play and exhibit a clear preference for playing with peers rather than adults. In a classic study of social play in children between 10 months and 2 years of age, Eckerman, Whatley and Kutz (1975) found that older children engaged in significantly more social play than younger ones but were less interested than the younger children in playing with their mothers and more interested in playing with peers.

Social exchanges with mothers differ from those with peers (Vandell & Wilson, 1987; Dunn, 2004; Rubin et al., 2006). Babies find mothers more reliable and more responsive than infants. Exchanges with mothers are longer and more sustained, but the interchanges may be a bit one-sided. Mothers tend to bear the larger responsibility for maintaining the interaction, whereas in exchanges between infant peers, the two partners contribute more equally.

As children get older, they are more likely to move from associative play to cooperative play. For example, these children are engaged in associative play, where they are both colouring and interested in each other, but not creating a single drawing.
Source: © McGraw-Hill Education

> ▼ Vygotsky argued that play was a fundamental part of the developmental process during childhood. We discuss the role of play in his theory in Chapter 9.

Social exchange in early childhood

Between the ages of 1 and 2, children make gains in locomotion (their ability to move themselves around) and language. These advances increase the complexity of their social exchanges (Rubin et al., 2006). During this period, they also develop the capacity to engage in complementary social interaction (Howes, 1987). That is, partners take turns and exchange roles in their play. Peers also begin to imitate each other's activity and to show awareness that they're being imitated (Eckerman, 1993). Now, too, when children engage in positive social interactions, they're more likely to smile or laugh or display other kinds of positive affect (Mueller & Brenner, 1977), and their interactions last longer (Ross & Conant, 1992). In the late toddler period (25 to 36 months), the child's main social achievement is the ability to share meaning with a social partner (Dunn, 2004).

The complexity of toddlers' play increases with age: solitary play (e.g., when children play by themselves and generally ignore other children who are near) and parallel play (e.g., when two children play in similar activities, often side by side, but do not engage one another) diminish as the child grows older. Associative play (e.g., when children play with other children but are not fully engaged with each other in a joint project) and cooperative play (fully cooperative and reciprocal play) both increase in frequency with age. There is of course overlap: some 4 year olds are still engaging in solitary play, while some precocious 2.5 year olds are busily engaged in cooperative play bouts (Parten, 1932).

CHRONOLOGY OF DEVELOPMENT
Peer relationships and the development of friendships

0–6 months	Touches and looks at another infant, and cries in response to the other's crying
6–12 months	Tries to influence another baby by looking, touching, vocalizing or waving Interacts with other infants in a generally friendly way, but may sometimes hit or push another
13–24 months	Begins to adopt complementary behaviour (e.g., taking turns, exchanging roles) Engages in more social play throughout the period Begins to engage in imaginative play
25–36 months	In play and other social interaction, begins to communicate meaning (e.g., invites another to play or signals that it's time to switch roles) Begins to prefer peers to adults as companions
3 years	Begins to engage in complex cooperative and dramatic play Starts to prefer same-gender playmates
4 years	Shares more with peers than 3 year olds do
4.5 years	Begins to sustain longer play sequences Is more willing to accept roles other than protagonist
6 years	Reaches a peak in imaginative play
3–7 years	Main friendship goal: coordinated and successful play
7 years	Shows stable preference for same-gender playmates
7–9 years	Expects friends to share activities, offer help, be physically available
8–12 years	Main friendship goal: to be accepted by same-gender peers
9–11 years	Expects friends to accept and admire him or her, and to be loyal and committed to the relationship Is likely to build friendships on the basis of earlier interactions
11–13 years	Expects genuineness, intimacy, self-disclosure, common interests, and similar attitudes and values in friends Emergence of cliques
13–16 years	Important friendship goal: understanding of the self; beginnings of cross-gender relationships, often in group contexts Development of crowds in the high school years
16–18 years	Expects friends to provide emotional support; increase in dyadic romantic ties and development of exclusive romantic alliances

Note: Developmental events described in this and other Chronology of Development charts represent overall trends identified in research studies. Individual children vary greatly in the ages at which they achieve these developmental milestones.

Source: Dunn (2004); Ladd (2005); Collins and Van Dulmen (2006); Rubin et al. (2006).

As children develop, negative exchanges and conflict also increase (Hay & Ross, 1982; Dunn, 2004; Rubin et al., 2006). In fact, socializing and getting into conflicts seem to go together. As Brown and Brownell (1990) found, toddlers who frequently initiated conflicts with peers were also the most sociable and the most likely to initiate interactions. It takes a little time to learn how to manage your social interchanges effectively.

As children become familiar with each other, their early peer interactions tend to develop into relationships. In a relationship, two acquaintances share an ongoing

relationship A continuing succession of interactions between two people that are affected by their shared past interactions, and that also affect their future interactions.

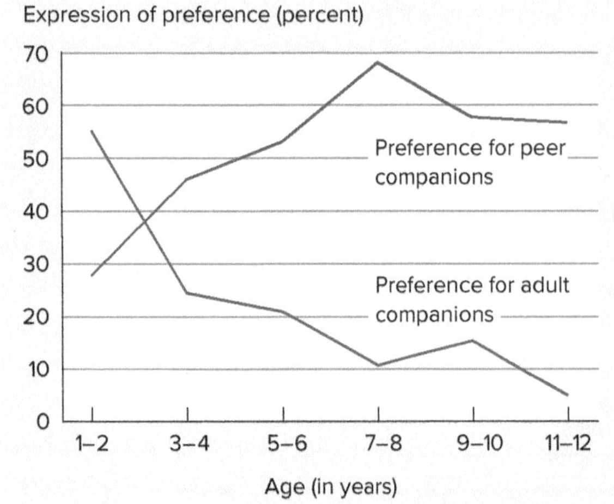

Expression of preference (percent)

Figure 12-3   Peers preferred

At about the age of 2.5, children begin to prefer other children as companions, and their choice of adults for companionship dwindles rapidly over time.
Source: Ellis et al. (1981)

succession of interactions that continues over time and that affects each other (Dunn, 2004; Rubin et al., 2006). That is, in every encounter between the partners, both their history of past interactions and their expectations of future interactions influence the nature and course of events. Toddlers develop relationships that are based on both positive and negative exchanges (Ross et al., 1992). In their simple give-and-take exchanges, these young peers display an elementary form of friendship. Interestingly, children between 1 and 2 develop preferences for particular playmates: it is a clear sign of early friendship formation that not just any other child will do. And these early social choices of special friends are not temporary: 50% to 70% of early friendships last over a year and, in some cases, over several years (Howes, 1996; Dunn, 2004). Nor are early relationships limited to just dyads: even 2 year olds can interact in a three-toddler group and exhibit not just dyadic but triadic, or three-way, interchanges as well (Ishikawa & Hay, 2006). Clearly, toddlers are capable of more complex social exchanges than previously thought.

As children move into preschool and the early years of school, they continue to seek and engage in more and more peer interactions. In their study of social interaction, Ellis, Rogoff, & Cromer (1981) found that the 400 children they observed were alone 26% of the time, with other children 46%, and with adults and peers 15% of the time. As Figure 12-3 shows, over time, children spend more hours with child companions and fewer with adults. These trends continue into adolescence, when children spend more time either alone or with friends (Larson, 1997).

However, there are some interesting cultural differences. Larson and Verma (1999) compared US, Korean and Japanese adolescents and found that the US teenagers spent more than twice as much time each day talking with each other (2.5 hours/day) than the Korean and Japanese teens (1.0 hours/day).

The kinds of peers children choose to spend time with change also. Age becomes a more important factor; for example, companionship with peers of the same age grows over time. Gender, too, begins to matter. Up to age 3 or 4, children choose same- and opposite-gender companions, but after this, both boys and girls prefer same- to opposite-gender play partners. Adolescence, of course, heralds a reversal, as cross-gender friendships begin to blossom once again (Richards et al., 1998; Rubin et al., 2006).

Peers play a role in socializing children, just as families do. Peers offer a perspective quite different from that of the family – the perspective of equals who share common abilities, goals, and problems. How does the peer group influence the child's development? In many of the same ways parents do – through modelling, reinforcement, and social comparison and by providing opportunities for learning and socializing.

Peers influence each other by serving as social models. Children can acquire knowledge simply by observing the behaviour and actions of their peers (Grusec & Abramovitch, 1982). Children also imitate older, more powerful, and more prestigious peer models (Bandura, 1989; Rubin et al., 2006). While imitation helps with social learning, it can often be an important way of maintaining social interaction. As Eckerman (1993) has shown, even in 2 year olds, imitation sustains joint play between partners and leads to more sophisticated forms of play in social games such as tossing a ball back and forth. Thus, through interactions with their peers, children learn to become social 'actors' and to take responsibility for themselves and their own actions, away from the watchful gaze of an adult.

As children develop, they also begin to reinforce their peers' behaviour. To *reinforce* is to pay attention to another's behaviour, to praise or criticize it, or to share in it. Imitation and reinforcement are not always forces for good: as the concept of 'peer pressure' implies, peers can convince children and adolescents to take risks and engage in deviant behaviour. Clearly, peers' influence can be harmful as well as beneficial. Throughout the preschool years, peers are increasingly likely to reinforce one another: one study found that

4 year olds praised, attended to or shared with their peers significantly more than 3 year olds did (Charlesworth & Hartup, 1967). And reciprocity begins to grow, as nursery schoolers reinforce the same peers who reinforce them (Hartup, 1983). The notion that peer reinforcement in the form of attention and approval affects a child's behaviour patterns has considerable research support. Peers' differential reinforcement can produce significant changes in the target child's behaviour (Furman & Gavin, 1989; Rubin et al., 2006).

Children respond to negative reinforcement, too. Just think of the looks and comments an adolescent who wears the wrong clothes is likely to elicit, or of the reactions preschoolers are likely to get if they play with toys regarded as meant only for the opposite gender. Older children can use other, less pleasant techniques for securing peer compliance – for example, by using biting comments or by ostracizing the child from the group (Lamb & Roopnarine, 1979).

Interaction with peers also provides an opportunity for specific instruction and learning (Zarbatany, Hartmann, & Rankin, 1990; Ladd, 2005). In Western cultures, one can see this in school games and sports and in tutorial arrangements, in which children teach each other and acquire new skills together. In some other cultures, such as those of India, Kenya and Mexico, both older peers and siblings teach and are caregivers for young children (Whiting & Edwards, 1988; Maynard, 2002; Rogoff, 2002).

Peers in later childhood and adolescence

In chapter 13 we will discuss, in some more detail, aspects of identity development and formation. The process of establishing a personal identity is increasingly important for individuals as they move in to adolescence, building on aspects of social identity which are formed early such as gender and ethnicity. Common wisdom is that a key influence in adolescence comes from a young person's friends and peer group. This influence is associated with positive factors including identity development and self-esteem. However, sometimes a peer group may place a young person at greater risk.

For instance, Mounts and Steinberg (1995) conducted a year-long longitudinal study comparing friendship groups and their relative influence on several outcomes and measures in adolescents (14–16 years), including school performance and drug use. The researchers found that both changes in school grades and substance use were associated with changes in friends' grades and substance use. In other words, friends in the same group tended to show the same patterns of change (improving grades, taking drugs). However, the researchers also noted that the influence of friends was moderated by parenting style: an adolescent with authoritative parents benefited more from having high achieving friends in terms of school performance; whereas an adolescent who had a drug-using friend was more likely to take drugs if their parents were less authoritative. Thus peer influence does appear to become increasingly important in adolescence, but parental influence does not disappear altogether and continues to frame a young person's behaviour.

It does appear that adolescence is a particularly vulnerable time in terms of negative peer influence, particularly in terms of taking risks. In an experimental study of peer influence on risk taking Gardner and Steinberg (2005) asked participants in three age groups – adolescents (13–16 years), youths (18–22 years) and adults (24 years and above) – to complete questionnaires on risk and some behavioural tasks in two randomly assigned conditions. In the first condition, participants completed the measures on their own. In the second, they completed them with two peers. The results indicated that participants made fewer risky decisions the older they were. Moreover, all participants took more risks and focused more on the benefits than the costs of actions when completing the task together with same-aged peers. Finally, peer influence on decisions was more pronounced for the adolescents and youths than for the adults. This study strongly suggests that in adolescence and perhaps into early adulthood young people are particularly susceptible to peer influence, and this influence particularly encourages young people to take more risks.

It may be that the shift to riskier decisions with peer influence is a consequence of an adolescent striving for more autonomy, independence and freedom as they get older. However, recent evidence suggests that risk-taking also derives from neurocognitive changes in the adolescent brain. Specifically, there is increasing evidence from imaging studies suggesting that adolescence sees changes in areas of the brain associated with the socioemotional reward system and executive functions or cognitive control (Albert, Chein, & Steinberg, 2015). It may be that adolescents are particularly good at ignoring or discounting social stimuli that are not relevant or do not align with their goals (i.e., conforming to peers' behaviour and disregarding other behaviour from a different social group) (McCormick, Perino, & Telzer, 2018). There is still much work to be done to understand how changes in brain anatomy and function influence reasoning and judgement in adolescence, and how these connect with peer influence and risky behaviour (Blakemore, 2018). However, this is an important task for developmental psychologists: as we argue in Chapter 16, much developmental research has tended to focus on infancy and childhood and has tended to ignore what might be profound and important developmental changes into adulthood. Understanding adolescence is a question at the front of many researchers' and many parents', minds!

Comparing parental and peer influence

Many writers have seen preadolescence and adolescence as highly stressful periods during which children are buffeted by the often conflicting behavioural standards of parents and contemporaries. Others have argued that these standards conflict far less frequently than is suggested and that, in fact, there is often remarkable agreement between parental and peer values (Brown & Huang, 1995; Collins et al., 2000; Vandell, 2007). A better question than whether peers or adults are more influential is: under what conditions and with what behaviours are peers or adults influential?

Peers and parents each have their own areas of expertise. Although peers are not generally the best advisers on occupational choices, parents are not the best source for the latest and best music recordings and videos. Peers exert more influence on teens' styles of interpersonal behaviour, their selections of friends, and their choices of fashions and entertainment. Parents have more impact on their teenagers' academic choices, their job preferences and their future aspirations (Hartup, 1996). Moreover, when adolescents are with parents and peers, they generally engage in very different types of activities – work and task activities with parents, recreation and conversation with peers (Larson & Richards, 1994; Larson & Verma, 1999).

Much of a child's behaviour reflects a mix of peer and parental influence (Elder & Conger, 2000; Ladd, 2005). Studying the use of marijuana, Kandel (1973) found that among teenagers whose best friends were non-users but whose parents were users, only 17% smoked marijuana. If friends used drugs, however, and parents did not, 56% of adolescents reported using marijuana. When both parents and peers were users, 67% of the adolescents used marijuana. Studies on the use of alcohol, tobacco and illegal drugs, and of early and risky sexual behaviour have reported similar numbers (Mounts & Steinberg, 1995; Dishion, Poulin, & Medici Skaggs, 2000). Thus, drug usage by parents and peers had a combined impact on adolescents' use of marijuana.

Although peers are often seen as a significant source of influence in adolescence, the impact of parents and peers may differ also in terms of long-term implications for behaviour. In a study of problem drinking among a large, longitudinal sample from the Netherlands, Poelen and colleagues (2007) explored how far having parents who drank heavily, and a peer network of heavy drinkers, affected problem drinking behaviour in adolescence right through into adulthood. Age and sex were key predictors of excessive alcohol use in early adolescence (older adolescents and boys drank more). Two years later, adolescents and young adults whose fathers drank frequently, and who had a large number of drinking friends, were most likely to be involved in problem drinking. Seven years later, however, the number of drinking friends was no longer related to problem drinking. However, a father's behaviour was still an influence on whether the (now) young adult – male or female – engaged in problem drinking.

The beliefs that parental influence is soon replaced by peer influence and that parenting really does not matter are very simply wrong. Although parental influence wanes as peer influence increases, both parents and peers play a significant role in determining the child's and adolescents' social development. It should not be forgotten, too, that children can have an influence on their parents' decisions, attitudes, choices and beliefs (Pardini, 2008). Part of the inevitable process of socialization is that children are learning to become,

Although important, peer influence in adolescence is much less than many think. In many circumstances, the influence of parents exceeds that of peers.
Source: © Shutterstock/Rawpixel.com

if not their parents' peers, active participants in an adult community of peers. Thus the relationships change into adulthood and when a child's parents enter the final years of their life the child may now assume the caregiver role for their own parents.

Peer acceptance

Children place enormous significance on being accepted by peers, and peer acceptance is of great importance to children's social development. Interacting with peers is the child's first experience of social behaviour beyond the family, and when this experience is positive, it can help lay the foundation for healthy adult social behaviour.

A common way of studying peer acceptance is to measure and compare the status of each child in a specific peer group. To do this, developmental psychologists generally use sociometric techniques in which they ask children to rate peers on scales of aggressiveness or helpfulness, or to compare peers in terms of likeability or to identify those whom they like best (Ladd, 2005).

Why do psychologists ask children, rather than teachers or other adults, to provide them with data on children's peer status? First, as insiders in the group, peers see a wider range of relevant behaviours than do adults. Second, peers have extended and varied experience with one another. And, third, by gathering data from many individuals who've interacted with the child who is the subject of study, we prevent any single individual's view from dominating our results.

One method of study is called the *nominations technique*, in which an investigator begins by asking each child in a group to name a specific number (usually three) of peers whom he likes 'especially' and the same number of peers whom he doesn't like 'very much'. Next the investigator sums the scores of all the 'like most' and 'like least' choices, and assigns children to one of several groups. Popular children are those who have received the greatest number of positive nominations and the fewest negative ones. Children whom their peers judge popular are friendly and assertive but not disruptive or aggressive. When they join a play group, they do it so smoothly that the ongoing action can continue without interruption (Black & Hazen, 1990; Newcomb, Bukowski, & Pattee, 1993). Children like this are good at communication; they help set the rules and norms for their groups, and they engage in more prosocial behaviour than less popular children.

Not all popular children fit this profile. Some children who are perceived as popular are also characterized as athletic, cool, dominant, arrogant, and both physically and relationally aggressive. These children and adolescents may wield high levels of social influence even though their actions are often manipulative in nature (Rodkin et al., 2000; Cillessen & Mayeux, 2004; Cillessen & Rose, 2005). In short, there is more than one pathway to popularity.

Average children receive some of both types of nomination, but are neither as well liked as popular peers nor as disliked as peers in other categories. Neglected children are isolated, often friendless children but aren't necessarily disliked by classmates; they receive few like or dislike votes. And children termed neglected are less aggressive, less talkative and more withdrawn. Controversial children receive many positive nominations but also a lot of negative ones. Rejected children receive many negative nominations. Aggressive rejected children are characterized by aggressiveness, poor self-control, and behaviour problems, whereas non-aggressive rejected children tend to be anxious, withdrawn and socially unskilled (French, 1990; Parkhurst & Asher, 1992; Ladd, 2005).

However, as we saw in our discussion of popular children, aggressive children who are competent and develop social networks are unlikely to be rejected and may even be popular (Cairns & Cairns, 1994; Rubin et al., 2006).

sociometric technique
A procedure for determining children's status within their peer group; each child in the group either nominates others whom she likes best and least, or rates each child in the group for desirability as a companion.

popular children
Children who are liked by many peers and disliked by very few.

average children
Children who have some friends but who are not as well liked as *popular children*.

neglected children
Children who are often socially isolated and, although they are not necessarily disliked by others, have few friends.

controversial children
Children who are liked by many peers but also disliked by many.

rejected children
Children who are disliked by many peers and liked by very few.

aggressive rejected children Rejected children who have low self-control, are highly aggressive and exhibit behaviour problems.

non-aggressive rejected children
Rejected children who tend to be anxious, withdrawn and socially unskilled.

Research close-up

BOX 12-3   A vicious cycle of peer rejection and poor social understanding

Source: Based on Banerjee, Watling, & Caputi (2011).

Introduction:

Although there is extensive research into the development of children's social understanding, relatively little work has been carried out into the relationship between this understanding and a child's position in their peer group. An earlier study by Banerjee and Watling (2005) found evidence that poor performance on a *faux pas* test of social understanding was associated with peer rejection and this current study was carried out in order to investigate this relationship further. A *faux pas* situation is one where a person unintentionally insults another because of a lack of some information about them; for example, they might say a painting is awful, not realizing they are speaking to the person who painted it. Banerjee et al. predicted that poor social understanding can lead to peer rejection but that the consequent lack of social interaction can further inhibit the development of this understanding. In this way, a vicious circle is maintained. This study therefore involved a longitudinal investigation into whether poor performance on the *faux pas* test was associated with peer rejection and, conversely, whether lack of social acceptance could lead to continued poor performance on the task.

Method:

The participants in this study were 210 children, in two separate age groups. Children in one group were aged approximately 6 years when they were first tested, while the children in the older group were approximately 9 years old. The children were tested twice more, at yearly intervals. On each occasion, each child was presented with four stories in which a character accidentally insulted another. They were then asked six questions about each story to test whether they had detected the *faux pas* and whether they understood the effect it would have had. In addition, each child was asked to identify the three people in the class that they most liked to play with and the three that they least liked to play with. This allowed the researchers to assess the level of social acceptance or rejection of each child.

Results:

The researchers found that peer rejection predicted relatively poorer *faux pas* understanding between 7 and 8 years of age and between 9 and 10 years of age. In other words, children who were poor at understanding *faux pas* were more likely to be classed as rejected by peers in subsequent testing sessions. Additionally, higher *faux pas* performance was associated with relatively increased peer acceptance scores from 9 to 10 years of age, and lower *faux pas* performance was associated with relatively increased peer rejection scores from 10 to 11 years of age.

Discussion:

The results of this study provide evidence of a two-way link between *faux pas* understanding and peer relations during the primary school years. They suggest that being rejected by one's peers makes it more difficult for a child to learn about the subtleties of social interaction. In turn, failure to gain this understanding can lead to further rejection. As well as adding to our knowledge about the relationship between peer relations and social understanding, these findings are important because they may also help us to develop strategies to support children who are socially rejected at school.

When they encounter someone new, children are just as likely as adults to base their impressions on the person's physical appearance (Langlois, 1985). People in general tend to attribute positive qualities to those who are physically attractive, and children and adolescents go right along with this tendency (Langlois et al., 2000; Hawley et al., 2007). Children expect to find characteristics such as friendliness, willingness to share, fearlessness and self-sufficiency in good-looking peers, and often think unattractive children are likely to be aggressive, antisocial and mean. Teenagers almost uniformly prefer good-looking partners.

Other social factors such as gender are very important too, and change throughout development, in terms of children's peer acceptance and friendship networks. The tendency to gender exclusivity increases throughout childhood (Maccoby, 1998), and it is not until adolescence that children once again choose opposite-gender companions. However, children who have cross-gender friendships as well as same-gender friendships are among the best-accepted, socially skilled children in the group (Kovacs, Parker, & Hoffman, 1996). In contrast, children whose primary friendships, or only friendships, were with opposite-gender peers were less well accepted, judged less skilled academically and socially, and tend to report lower self-esteem. Similarly, others have found that boys who had girls in their friendship networks reported greater intimacy with their same-gender best friends (Zarbatany, McDougall, & Hymel, 2000).

It is important not to exaggerate the differences in peer relationship styles of boys and girls (Underwood, 2004). Boys and girls participate in both cooperative and competitive activities and girls can be as aggressive as boys, although they generally express aggression differently. In addition, recent work has questioned the claim that boys' and girls' social networks are different in size or structure; for example, girls and boys are equally likely to be central members of their respective cliques (Cairns & Cairns, 1994; Bagwell et al., 2000). There are many similarities in the behaviours of boys and girls in their respective peer relationships.

> How does knowledge about gender tie in with children's developing social relationships? In Chapter 13 we consider cognitive and social influences on gender development.

In Western societies, play groups, especially those of young children, tend to be age delineated. Western children spend most of their time with same-age peers, playing less than a third of the time with children who are more than two years older or younger than themselves (Ellis et al., 1981). In contrast, in many other cultures, older children often play with younger ones as well as care for and teach them (Whiting & Edwards, 1988; Edwards, 1992; Zukow-Goldring, 2002). But children's typical preference for play with same-age peers does serve a special role in social development. After all, children share interests most closely with those who are at similar points in their cognitive, emotional, social, and physical development (Maccoby, 1998). And it is largely their peers with whom they will be interacting on a continuing basis in their schooling, their work and their communities.

Children are creative and cruel in the ways they reject the children whom they dislike. Sometimes, children exclude others from their group or activities and bully or dominate others in the classroom. In more direct action, children can deny others access to other people or objects, or directly attack a disliked peer, either verbally or physically. Many rejected children, especially those who are not aggressive, tend to be victimized by their classmates. For an exploration of this problem, see Box 12-4.

BOX 12-4   Are bullies just social 'oafs' or do they have a superior understanding of social skills?

Research close-up

Source: Based on Sutton, Smith, and Swettenham (1999).

Introduction:

The popular stereotype of a bully is of someone who is rather simple and oafish, but a different perspective suggests that, in fact, bullies can be highly skilled at understanding and manipulating other people's emotions, behaviour and mental states. A key aspect of this is the ability to attribute mental states to oneself and to other people, and to understand that other people have beliefs, desires and thoughts that are different from one's own. This is known as the theory of mind. Sutton et al. suggested that, far from being socially inept, bullies would display greater social cognition, as measured by theory of mind tasks, than their victims. In addition, bullying often takes place in a social context, where other people reinforce the behaviour by watching or generally encouraging the bully. Sutton et al. also hypothesized that bullies would show more advanced levels of social cognition than these 'followers'.

Method:

This study was carried out among 193 children aged between 7 and 10 years. Firstly, children were categorized according to their role when bullying took place, based on their own assessment of themselves and their peers. Roles were: Bully, Assistant, Reinforcer, Defender, Outsider and Victim. Each child was then asked to complete a theory of mind task. In this task, the researcher read 11 short stories. At the end of each story, the child was asked questions about the protagonist's behaviour in order to test their understanding of the protagonist's mental state or belief. For example:

> *Mike wants to go out with his friends, but he has a really bad tummy ache. He knows that if his Mum notices he is ill, she won't let him go out to play. Mike goes downstairs and asks his Mum 'Can I go out to play please?' The participant was then shown a series of pictures and asked: Which picture shows how Mike really feels? Which picture shows how Mike will look when he talks to his Mum?*

Results:

The child's score on each of the stories was added up to give a total social cognition score. Results showed that Bullies scored significantly higher on total social cognition scores than Victims and Followers (Assistants and Reinforcers). A second analysis looked for correlations between individual role score and total social cognition score. This showed that the Bully role was the most highly significantly positively correlated with total social cognition and that the Victim score was negatively correlated with total social cognition score. Assistant and Reinforcer scores were also positively correlated with total social cognition score, while Defenders were uncorrelated and Outsiders were negatively correlated.

Discussion:

This study showed that Bullies had a greater level of social cognition than their Followers and their Victims, which placed them at a considerable advantage for manipulating other people's feelings. On the other hand, having the weakest understanding put the Victims at a disadvantage. Despite having this superior understanding of the feelings of others, Bullies used this knowledge in a negative way and this indicates an inability or unwillingness to empathize with those feelings. However, their social cognition was no better than that of the Outsiders, who took no part in bullying, and the researchers suggest that investigation of the difference between Bullies and Outsiders could therefore be useful in developing resources for anti-bullying work. This study also suggests possible avenues of research to investigate bullies from a lifespan perspective and to develop possible strategies for intervention.

> In Chapter 14 we consider other strategies for reducing bullying and aggression and promoting positive peer relationships in schools.

Victimization and bullying

> **peer victimization** Ill treatment of one child by another (or by others) that can range from teasing to bullying to serious physical harm; typically, victimizing is a continuing behaviour that persists over time.
>
> **relational victimization** The attempt by a peer to damage or control another child's relationships with others.

Peer victimization occurs when a child is bullied by other peers. This kind of persecution can take several forms. Some children physically attack or threaten others, especially boys, with physical harm if they don't obey their peers (Perry, Hodges, & Egan, 2001). Girls, on the other hand, are more likely to be targets of relational victimization, in which peers try to damage or control their relationships with others. For example, a girl may be excluded from an important event such as a birthday party when she fails to comply with a peer request, or she may be the target of a hostile rumour within her peer group (Crick, Casas, & Ku, 1999; Underwood, 2004; Ostrov & Crick, 2006). Both of these forms of victimization have harmful consequences for children's adjustment. Victimized children are more anxious, depressed and lonely (Nangle et al., 2003). They are more likely to be rejected by peers, to hold more negative perceptions of their own competence, and to experience greater school adjustment problems and more loneliness and depression (Olweus, 2001; Ladd & Troop-Gordon, 2003). Not surprisingly, the longer a child is exposed to victimization, the greater the toll in terms of increasing internalizing difficulties (Goldbaum et al., 2003).

Some children are the regular targets of victimization, and it's unfortunate that, although we can often identify these victims of aggression early, they frequently remain victims throughout the school years (Khatri,

Kupersmidt, & Patterson, 1994; Kochenderfer-Ladd & Wardrop, 2001). Cross-national surveys suggest that from 6% to 22% of children report moderate to severe levels of peer abuse while in school or travelling to or from school (Nansel et al., 2001).

Who are these children that peers pick on, tease or attack? Some are children who, unwittingly, send implicit signals that they are unlikely to defend themselves or retaliate. These children may cry easily, they may exhibit anxiety or they may appear weak (Hodges & Perry, 1999). They tend to lack self-esteem and self-confidence, and they're often missing a sense of humour. And again, without realizing it, they may encourage their attackers by being submissive, by not being very good at persuading others, or by giving in to a bully's demands and surrendering possessions (Perry, Williard, & Perry, 1990; Crick et al., 1999; Juvonen, Graham, & Schuster, 2003).

Other victimized children are more outgoing in their responses: they argue, disrupt bullies' actions and attempt to return the attack; but even so, they aren't very effective. Instead, they somehow provoke and irritate other children without actually threatening them or giving them the idea that they'll follow through on their hostile displays. Olweus (2001) has termed these children 'provocative victims. Not surprisingly, such a child is also physically weak. If he were the school fullback, even bullies would leave him alone' (Olweus, 1999, 2001). Some children are both bullies and victims (or 'bully victims'): they are victimized by others, and they themselves act as bullies, often against weaker children.

Victimization takes its toll on children. Those who are victimized are likely to have lower social status and lower self-esteem, to experience more social anxiety, to be lonely, to avoid school and to show increasing depression over time (Hodges, Malone, & Perry, 1997; Smith et al., 1999; Juvonen et al., 2003). Further, in early adulthood, people who as young adolescents have been abused by peers report elevated depression and low self-esteem (Olweus, 1999, 2001). A study in Finland suggests that childhood bullying is even associated with increased risk of suicide (Brunstein Klomek et al., 2009), and interestingly this association appears more direct for women rather than men.

Bullying can occur in a variety of contexts: school is one of the typical places for it to occur (see Olweus, 1999) but it can occur outside of school and at home. A more recent forum for bullying is online, or virtual or 'cyber-bullying'. Cyber-bullying includes bullying by text message, email or phone, or displaying embarrassing video clips or photographs in public and widely accessible forums. Slonje and Smith (2007) argue that this type of bullying can be distinct from other forms of bullying and because it is online there is more possibility of children not making parents or other adults aware of its existence.

What factors protect or buffer children from being victimized? Hodges and colleagues (1997) tested the notion that children at risk of being attacked or bullied will be more likely to become victims if they lack friends or are rejected by their peers. Indeed, in these researchers' study, children who were at risk were increasingly less likely to be victimized as their numbers of friends grew. But not just any friend will do; it was children whose friends had characteristics that served a protective function (e.g., physical strength, aggressiveness) who were less likely to be victimized. Moreover, Hodges et al. (1999) found that friendship may not only protect children from victimization but may also increase the likelihood that a target child will maintain self-esteem and will not 'invite' attack or submit to it, at least over the year of these researchers' study. Although being victimized by peers can cause a child's social behaviour to become less effective, this is less likely to occur when she has a best friend. However, if you lose a best friend and fail to replace him or her by the end of the school year, a child is at increased risk for victimization by peers (Bowker et al., 2006).

Rejection by a peer group is another social risk factor related to increased victimization for children at risk. In other words, the link between each behavioural risk factor (e.g., physical weakness, showing anxiety, low self-confidence) and victimization was greater for peer-rejected children than for better accepted children. These findings support the notion that the expression of an individual's vulnerabilities often depends on social context factors (Hodges et al., 1997). Having friends – the right kind of friends – can serve to buffer the at-risk child from victimization.

The consequences of peer rejection

Being unpopular can lead to both short-term and long-term problems. Loneliness among children is one of the primary results of being rejected or ignored, and it has many faces. Unpopular children have often reported feeling lonely and socially dissatisfied (Cassidy & Asher, 1992; Hopmeyer & Asher, 1997; Bukowski, Brendgen, & Vitaro, 2007). Research suggests that although neglected children may be no lonelier than

Being unpopular as a child or adolescent can lead to loneliness or depression.
© Shutterstock/GagliardiImages

average children, rejected children are much more likely than average or neglected children to feel lonely (Asher, Hymel, & Renshaw, 1984). Being actively disliked by many of one's peers can lead to strong feelings of social isolation and alienation, although non-aggressive rejected children are likely to feel lonelier than aggressive rejected children (Parkhurst & Asher, 1992). Being verbally and physically victimized by peers rather than merely rejected is associated with even greater degrees of loneliness (Kochenderfer & Ladd, 1996; Kiesner, 2002; Ladd, 2005).

As social relationships change, feelings of loneliness can change, too. Renshaw and Brown (1993) tracked a group of Australian children in grades three through six for a year and found that those who showed considerable increases in loneliness over time were those who lost friends, became less accepted by peers, and made more remarks about how hard it was for them to make friends. However, even after victimization ceases, children often continue to feel lonely even when they are no longer being harassed by their peers (Kochenderfer-Ladd & Wardrop, 2001). It helps, though, to have at least one friend. Rejected children who have a stable friendship with just one other child may feel less lonely than rejected and totally friendless children (Sanderson & Siegal, 1991; Parker & Asher, 1993).

What are the long-term consequences for a child of being accepted by only a few of his peers? According to Asher and his co-workers (Parker & Asher, 1987; Asher & Paquette, 2003), these consequences are poor achievement, school avoidance and loneliness. These researchers found that children who were poorly accepted by their peers were less cooperative in the classroom than well-accepted children, and were also more likely to drop out of school entirely and to develop patterns of criminal activity. Moreover, chronically victimized children in late elementary school were more depressed at age 23 and at higher risk for being harassed by peers at work or school (Olweus, 2002). Even children who are shy and withdrawn follow a different life-course pattern than less shy children. Shy children were slower than non-shy children in establishing careers, marrying or becoming parents (Caspi, Elder, & Bem, 1988).

However, peer status is not necessarily a stable characteristic or inevitable outcome for certain children. In a study by Coie and Dodge (1983), both popular and neglected children were fairly stable in their social standing over a five-year span. Interestingly, though, popular children sometimes lost their high status and neglected children occasionally gained some social acceptance. In general, however, once a child was rejected, she was more likely than others to maintain this status over a considerable time span. It seems that poor peer relationships in childhood do have implications for later adjustment.

The stability of peer rejection is, in part, the result of reputational bias, or the tendency of children to interpret peers' behaviour on the basis of past encounters and feelings about these children (Hymel, Wagner, & Butler, 1990). When we ask children to judge a negative behaviour by a peer whom they earlier liked or disliked, they are likely to excuse the behaviour of a peer they earlier liked, giving her the benefit of the doubt, but not to excuse a peer they didn't like. Reputation colours children's interpretations of peers' actions and helps account for the stability of behaviour across time (Hymel, 1986).

reputational bias
Children's tendency to interpret peers' behaviour on the basis of past encounters with and feelings about them.

Reputation, however, is not the only component in peer-status stability. The behaviour and characteristics of the children who have experienced rejection are important, too. For example, Coie, Dodge, and Kupersmidt (1990) found that when boys were brought together into new and different social groups (whose members had no knowledge of the boys' earlier reputations), they tended to be assigned the same peer status they'd had before. This was as true of boys who'd been considered popular as of those who'd been rejected (Coie & Kupersmidt, 1983). As we said earlier, although peers' judgements of other children are often bound by relatively superficial and unimportant factors, like physical appearance, it is largely children's social skills that determine their social status. Clearly, we need to find ways to help children with lower status improve these skills and gain greater acceptance among their peers.

THE DEVELOPMENT OF FRIENDSHIP
Friendships in childhood and adolescence

In our discussions so far, we have focused on how well children may be accepted by their classmates or peer group. Although this group perspective is an important one, children also develop the close, dyadic relationships with a few peers that we call friendships. The essentials of a friendship, according to Hartup (1996), are reciprocity and commitment between people who see themselves more or less as equals.

> **friendship** A reciprocal commitment between two people who see themselves more or less as equals.

Children have certain expectations about relationships with friends (Schneider, 2000; Dunn, 2004). And these expectations about friends seem to change over time in three stages. Note, in the following list, that the expectations that emerge at each stage do not disappear with the next; in fact, those shown in italics tend to increase with age (Bigelow & LaGaipa, 1975; Bigelow, 1977).

1. **Reward-cost stage (7–9 years):** children expect friends to *offer help, share common activities*, provide stimulating ideas, be able to join in organized play, *offer judgements, be physically nearby*, and be demographically similar to them.
2. **Normative stage (10–11 years):** children now expect friends to *accept* and *admire* them, to bring *loyalty and commitment* to a friendship, and to express similar values and attitudes towards rules and sanctions.
3. **Empathic stage (12–13 years):** children begin to expect *genuineness* and the *potential for intimacy* in their friends; they expect friends to understand them and to be willing to engage in self-disclosure; they want friends to accept their help, to share *common interests*, and to hold similar attitudes and values across a range of topics (not just rules).

> **self-disclosure** The honest sharing of information of a very personal nature, often with a focus on problem solving; a central means by which adolescents develop friendships.

The obligations of friendship change as well. Studying 10 to 17 year olds, Youniss and his colleagues (Youniss, 1980; Smollar & Youniss, 1982) found that friendship obligations undergo marked shifts over adolescence. Although 80% of the 10 to 11 year olds thought friends should 'be nice to one another and help each other', only 11% of the 16 to 17 year olds indicated that this was a central obligation. In contrast, 62% of the 16 to 17 year olds thought that providing emotional support was important, but only 5% of the 10 to 11 year olds agreed. Reasons change, too. Young children view obligations as important 'so he'll be nice to you too' or 'to keep the relation going good'. Obligations are important to older children because they would benefit the other person ('because she'll be happier if you do') or because they define the relationship ('That's what friends are supposed to do'). Gender is also a factor: females at all ages are more likely than males to be concerned with emotional assistance and to stress reasons based on benefiting the other person (Schneider, 2000; Ladd, 2005).

Gottman and his colleagues (Gottman, 1983; Gottman & Parker, 1986; Parker & Gottman, 1989) explored how children come to be friends in a series of studies of children ranging in age from 3 to 7 years old. These researchers set up tape recorders in children's homes, and listened while some children played with their best friends and other children played with strangers. The study found that friends communicated more clearly, disclosed themselves more, had more positive exchanges, established common ground more easily, exchanged more information, and were able to resolve conflict more effectively than strangers. Interestingly, unacquainted children who got along well and were rated as likely to become friends scored higher on these dimensions than others in the stranger group.

Studies with other samples of children at varying ages confirm many of these findings. Not surprisingly, children spend more time with friends and express more positive affect in these interactions than they do with non-friends (Hartup, 1996; Schneider, 2000; Ladd, 2005). They share more with their friends (Jones, 1985), although when friends are tough competitors, sharing with each other may decrease somewhat (Berndt, 1986). Being friends does not mean never disagreeing (Hartup, 1996; Laursen, Hartup, & Koplas, 1996). In fact, friends disagree more than non-friends, but their conflicts are less heated and they're more likely to stay in contact after an argument than non-friends (Hartup et al., 1988). Friends are more likely to resolve conflicts in an equitable way and to ensure that the resolution preserves the friendship (Hartup, 1996; Laursen et al., 1996; Bowker et al., 2006). And friends, of course, are more intimate and self-disclosing with one another than with simple acquaintances (Berndt & Perry, 1990; Simpkins & Parke, 2001). Friends are more knowledgeable about each other than non-friends; they know one another's strengths and secrets as well as their wishes and weaknesses (Schneider, 2000; Dunn, 2004; Ladd, 2005). As someone once said, 'A friend is one who knows our faults but doesn't give a damn!'

Parker and Gottman (1989) suggest that the goals and central processes involved in successful friendship formation shift across age. For young children (ages 3 to 7 years), the goal of peer interaction is coordinated play, with all the social processes organized to promote successful play. In the second developmental phase – the 8- to 12-year period – the goal changes from playful interaction to a concern with being accepted by one's same-gender peers. Children are concerned with the norms of the group, working out which actions will lead to acceptance and inclusion and which to exclusion and rejection.

In the third developmental period (13 to 17 years), the focus shifts to understanding the self. Self-exploration and self-disclosure are the principal social processes this time, and they're accompanied by intense honesty and a lot of problem solving. Table 12-3 summarizes these developmental periods.

Table 12-3 How friendship patterns develop

	Early childhood (3–7 years old)	Middle childhood (8–12 years old)	Adolescence (13–17 years old)
Primary concerns	To maximize excitement, entertainment, and enjoyment through play	To be included by peers; to avoid rejection; to present oneself to others in a positive way	To explore oneself – to come to know oneself, define oneself
Main processes and purposes of communication	To coordinate play; to escalate and de-escalate play activity; talking about activities; resolving conflict	To share negative gossip with others	To disclose oneself to another or others; to solve problems
Emotional development	Learning to manage arousal during interaction	Acquiring rules for showing feelings; rejecting sentiment	Getting logic and emotion together; understanding the implications of emotions for relationships

Source: Adapted from Gottman and Mettetal (1986).

For most children, having friends is a positive accomplishment. As we saw earlier in the chapter, peers and friends provide support, intimacy and guidance. Children with friends are less lonely and depressed (Asher & Paquette, 2003; Dunn, 2004), and even their long-term outcomes are better.

But not all friendships are beneficial, for they may pose risks as well as offer protective factors (Bagwell, 2004). Even rejected children form friendships but, often, they choose as friends other rejected (and often aggressive) classmates. Moreover, compared with the friendships of non-rejected/non-aggressive children, the friendships of rejected children are often of poorer quality (i.e., they tend to be less satisfying, less intimate and more likely to be conflict ridden) (Poulin, Dishion, & Haas, 1999). Rejected children who are friends often encourage each other's deviant behaviour, such as cheating, aggression, and substance use or abuse (Bagwell, 2004). Thus, it is important to consider the common activities that form the basis of a friendship in addition to the quality of the relationship.

Romantic relationships

peer-group network
The cluster of peer acquaintances who are familiar with and interact with one another at different times for common play or task-orientated purposes.

As we all know, romance has its costs as well as its rewards. Adolescents in romantic relationships report more conflict, have more mood swings, and experience more symptoms of depression (Joyner & Udry, 2000; Larson & Richards, 1994; Laursen, 1995), especially around a break-up. But there are positive outcomes associated with romantic relationships, too. Being in such a relationship is linked with a feeling of self-worth, a sense of competence, and a feeling that one is part of a peer-group network (Kirtler, La Greca, & Prinstein, 1999; Connolly et al., 2004).

On the other hand, early dating with a large number of different partners may forecast relationships of poorer quality in young adulthood (Collins, 2003; Collins & Van Dulmen, 2006). Although these studies suggest that quality, timing and duration of relationships are all possible determinants of the long-term consequences of adolescent romantic ties, one recent report found no link between adolescent romantic involvement and adult adjustment (Roisman et al., 2004).

Adolescents at all ages develop romantic ties, but the romantic experience changes between early and late adolescence (Collins, 2003). Just as the frequency of romantic involvement increases across development, the length of time in a specific relationship also increases. Among 14 to 15 year olds, 35% were in relationships that lasted 11 months or more, whereas 55% of those 16 or older were in long-term relationships (Carver, Joyner, & Udry, 2003).

Romantic relationships increase in both frequency and time with age. Many adolescents are heavily influenced by their peers with regard to who it is appropriate to be in a relationship with.
Source: © Shutterstock/George Rudy

The peer group plays a major role in partner choice among young adolescents. You date partners that your peer network approves of or views as 'cool'. Appearance, clothes, status and other superficial features guide young adolescents' choices, but older adolescents focus more on characteristics that underlie intimacy and compatibility, such as personality, values and particular interests (Zani, 1993). Among older adolescents, there is more interdependence between partners in romantic relationships (Laursen & Jensen-Campbell, 1999). Older adolescents are more likely than younger ones to compromise with their partners as a way of solving problems.

In sum, romantic relationships do represent an important developmental milestone in adolescence. Romance is a harbinger of later adaptations; we need to accept and understand its importance to healthy adolescent development.

> Of course, social relationships, especially romantic relationships, continue into adulthood. In old age maintaining positive social relationships is particularly important for many aspects of happiness and well-being. We discuss this issue in more detail in Chapter 16.

Cliques and crowds

In middle childhood, children begin to form cliques, voluntary groups based on friendship (Schneider, 2000). A clique may range in size from three to nine children, and members usually are of the same gender and same race (Kindermann, McCollam, & Gibson, 1995). By the time children are 11, most of their interaction with peers is in the context of the clique. Membership in cliques enhances children's psychological well-being and their ability to cope with stress (Rubin et al., 2006), just as social acceptance and friendship are buffers against loneliness. Cliques are evident in adolescence as well but decline across the high school years (Shrum & Cheek, 1987), when they are superseded by crowds.

> **clique** A voluntary group formed on the basis of friendship.

A crowd is a collection of people who share attitudes or activities that define a particular stereotype – for example, jocks, brains, eggheads, loners, burnouts, druggies, populars and nerds – and who may or may not spend much time together (Brown & Klute, 2003). Crowd affiliation is assigned by consensus of the peer group; adolescents don't select it themselves (Rubin et al., 2006). The salience of crowds probably peaks in ninth or tenth grade and decreases throughout high school (Brown & Huang, 1995). Those who are in the populars or jocks crowds experience a drop in internalizing problems between childhood and adolescence, while the brains, a less popular group, experience an increase in internalizing problems (Prinstein & LaGreca, 2002). Like friendships, peer groups are not always beneficial to participants. In late adolescence, crowds tend to disband and are replaced by mixed-sex cliques or romantically orientated couples, as we saw in our exploration of romantic ties.

> **crowd** A collection of people whom others have stereotyped on the basis of their perceived shared attitudes or activities – for example, 'populars' or 'nerds'.

Applied Developmental Psychology

BOX 12-5   Cross-cultural variations in children's peer relationships

Cultures often differ in the way they view the relative importance of the individual or the group. In individual-orientated societies, like Canada, the United States and many countries of Western Europe, a person's identity is determined largely by personal accomplishments. In contrast, in group-orientated societies, like China and Japan, a greater proportion of a person's identity is related to his or her membership in the larger group (Schneider, 2000; Ladd, 2005). Just as adult relationships are shaped by these cultural orientations, so are children's peer relationships.

Studying children in China and Canada, Orlick, Zhou and Partington (1990) found several differences in the tendencies to be cooperative, to share, to engage in prosocial behaviour, to get involved in conflict, and to be aggressive. Among 5 year olds, 85% of Chinese children were cooperative with one another and more likely to help and share than Canadian children. And 78% of the 'individualistic' Canadian children were involved in conflict of one kind or another.

Across these two cultures, the behavioural correlates of peer acceptance showed both similarities and differences. In both China and Canada, middle-school-age children who were sociable and who engaged in prosocial behaviours were accepted by peers, whereas those who were aggressive were often not accepted (Chen & Rubin, 1994). At the same time, Canadian children 7 to 9 years old tended to reject other children who were shy and sensitive, whereas in China, the same characteristics were met with peer acceptance (Chen, Rubin, & Sun, 1992). Interestingly, however, these perceptions appear to change across development: Among 12-year-old Chinese children, shyness-sensitivity was related to peer rejection (Chen & Rubin, 1994). This shift is due in part to changing pressures from Chinese parents for achievement and academic excellence in the 11- to 13-year-old age group, as well as to the expectation that as children grow older, they must become more assertive.

Moreover, historical changes in China are modifying the links between shyness and peer acceptance. Chen et al. (2005) found that shyness was related to peer acceptance for 10 year olds in a 1990 study; in a 2002 sample of 10 year olds, shyness was related to peer rejection. Perhaps the changes towards a market economy in China with a focus on assertiveness and self-initiative are responsible for this shift.

Among Chinese Canadian children, those who were competitive in academic tasks were well liked, whereas those who were competitive in physical or athletic activities were disliked (Udvari et al., 1995). In contrast, non-Asian Canadian children who were competitive in athletics were well liked, and among these children, academic competition was unrelated to peer acceptance. These findings highlight the value that Chinese people place on educational attainment (recall our Chapter 10 discussion of cross-national studies of achievement by Stevenson and his colleagues). Clearly, in our efforts to understand peer relationships, we need to recognize the broader cultural contexts in which these relationships develop.

In some countries, peers play a more influential role, but in others, the family and adult agents are more important. Compared with American youth, adolescents in Japan spend less time with peers and more time at home (Rothbaum et al., 2000a). In Japan, parental values play a more prominent role than peer values in the formation and structure of adolescent peer groups than in the United States (Rothbaum et al., 2000b). In Mexico and Central America, parents often maintain this family orientation by directly discouraging peer interaction (Schneider, 2000; Ladd, 2005).

Finally, even styles of relating to peers vary cross-culturally. Research has suggested that Italian children are more likely than Canadian children to embrace debates and disputes with their friends (Casiglia, Lo Coco, & Zapplulla, 1998; Schneider et al., 1997). In these studies, Italian children's friendships were seen as stabler than those of Canadian children, and the investigators suggest that cultural differences in tolerance for conflict may account for this finding. There are even cultural differences in the factors that contribute to the formation of cliques. For example, an adolescent's academic achievement or standing is a stronger determinant of clique membership in China than it is in North America (Chen, Chang, & He, 2003).

SUMMARY

Parents, siblings, peers and teachers are major agents of *socialization*. They may influence the child by directly teaching standards, rules, and values; by providing role models; by making attributions about the child; and by creating the environment in which the child lives. The family is a complex system involving interdependent members whose functioning may be altered by changes in the behaviour of one member, or relationships among family members, and by changes over time. In addition, family functioning is influenced by the larger physical, cultural, and social setting in which the family lives.

Parental warmth and responsiveness are regarded as important to socialization, but some degree of parental control is necessary for positive social development. The goal is to teach self-regulation rather than continuing external control by the parents. Thus, discipline strategies that present alternatives and rely on reasoning are the most effective. The interaction of the dimensions of warmth and responsiveness with those of permissiveness and control creates a four-way typology: *authoritative, authoritarian, permissive* and *uninvolved parenting*. Baumrind found that authoritative parenting led to the most positive emotional, social, and cognitive development in children and adolescents. Critics of this typology have cited the need to identify the components of each style that contribute to its effects on the child, the need to recognize the role of the child's temperament and behaviour, and the question of the generalizability of the typology across cultures. The most effective Chinese style of parenting may fall somewhere between authoritative and authoritarian.

The functioning of the family is affected by the number, gender, and spacing of the children. These factors influence both parent–child and sibling interaction. As family size increases, parents and children have less opportunity for extensive contact, but siblings experience more contact. This may result in greater independence but lower self-esteem and academic achievement in children from large families.

Divorce, life in a one-parent family and remarriage should be viewed as part of a series of transitions that modify family roles and relationships and the lives of parents and children. In the first year following divorce, the children in single-parent households tend to be more disturbed, but in the long run, most are able to adapt to their parents' divorce. It can be difficult for adolescents to cope with a parent's – or both parents' – remarriage. Antisocial behaviour, depression and anxiety, school problems, and disruptions in peer relations have been associated with divorce and remarriage. In preadolescence, boys show the most negative responses to divorce, and girls show the most lasting resistance to remarriage; however, gender differences are rarely found in adolescence.

Children's interactions with peers are freer and more egalitarian than their interactions with their parents. This greater fluidity facilitates interpersonal exploration and encourages growth in social competence and the development of a sense of social justice.

During the second half of the first year, infants begin to recognize peers as social partners and attempt to influence one another by such means as vocalizing and touching. In the early toddler period, peers begin to exchange both turns and roles during social interactions; in the late toddler period, a major achievement is the ability to share meaning with a social partner. As children's competence with peers develops, they begin to form true *relationships*. After about age 7, children are more likely to choose same-gender rather than opposite-gender play partners; this remains the case until adolescence, when interest in the opposite gender begins.

Children acquire a wide range of knowledge and a variety of responses by observing and imitating the behaviours of their peers. Imitation may serve as a way to both learn social rules and maintain social interaction. Peers reinforce one another with increasing frequency throughout the preschool years, and reinforcement commonly is reciprocated. Peers also serve as standards against which children evaluate themselves. Research indicates that the use of *social comparison* with the peer group as a means of self-evaluation increases dramatically in the early elementary school years.

Researchers assess peer status with *sociometric techniques*, in which children identify peers they like and those they don't like. On the basis of these nominations, children have been classified as *popular* (those who receive many positive but few negative nominations), *rejected* (those who receive many negative but few positive nominations), *neglected* (those who receive few nominations in either direction), and *average* (those who have some friends but not as many as the popular group). *Controversial* children are liked by many peers but also disliked by many. Rejection occurs for a variety of reasons: *non-aggressive rejected* children tend to be withdrawn and to lack social skills; *aggressive rejected* children have low self-control and exhibit aggressive and other problem behaviours.

Parents and peers each have their own areas of expertise and influence in children's lives. Peers have more influence in the preadolescent and adolescent years, when they have a lot of impact on such things as selection of friends, styles of dress, and choices of entertainment. Parents have greater impact on academic choices and work, on job preferences, and on a child's aspirations for the future. In adolescence, peers become an increasingly influential source of information and this can interact with developing brain anatomy to lead adolescents to take more risks.

Children develop *friendships* with only a few peers. Expectations of a friend change during the elementary school years from someone who simply shares activities to someone who can also keep secrets and be understanding. Studies indicate that friends interact with each other in a way that differs from their interactions with unacquainted peers and that the goals of friendship appear to change with development. For young children (ages 3 to 7), the goal is coordinated play, and for older children (ages 8 to 12), the goal is establishing group norms and being accepted by peers. During this period, *self-disclosure* becomes important. By adolescence (ages 13 to 17), the focus shifts to understanding the self, making self-disclosure a critical component of friendship. Romantic involvements are different from family and other relationships and can have positive effects on the adolescent's development. Although the teenager may experience more conflict and more mood swings, she may also gain a sense of competence, heightened self-worth, and a feeling belonging to the peer group. In middle childhood, children may form *cliques*, which enhance their well-being and ability to cope with stress. Later, children may be assigned by their peers to *crowds*, whose salience decreases by the end of high school.

Explore and Discuss

1. How have family systems changed from one generation to the next, and what are the likely psychological consequences of this change?

2. Based on your own experience and observations, do you think parenting is influenced by culture? Explain your answer.

3. Divorce has many negative effects on children's adjustment. How can divorcing couples be helped to act in ways that minimize the potentially negative consequences of divorce on children? Is divorce always bad?

4. Are the same characteristics likely to make a child popular or rejected in all cultures?

5. Girls' and boys' friendships differ in a number of ways, but they also share some common characteristics. Discuss and differentiate the genders' friendship patterns and try to explain the reasons for their differences.

6. What do you think are the positive and negative effects of romantic relationships on adolescent development?

Recommended Reading

Classic

Baumrind, D. (1966). Effects of authoritative parental control on child behaviour. *Child Development, 37*(4), 887–907.

Hays, R. B. (1985). A longitudinal study of friendship development. *Journal of Personality and Social Psychology, 48*, 909–924.

Olweus, D. (1993). *Bullying at school: What we know and what we can do.* Oxford: Blackwell.

Contemporary

Blakemore, S. (2018). *Inventing ourselves: The secret life of the teenage brain.* New York: Random House.

Howe, C. (2010). *Peer groups and children's development.* Oxford: Wiley Blackwell.

Vandell, D. L., Belsky, J., Burchinal, M., Steinberg, L., & Vandergrift, N. (2010). Do effects of early child care extend to age 15 years? Results from the NICHD Study of Early Child Care and Youth Development. *Child Development, 81*, 737–756.

CHAPTER 13
Social Identities: Gender, Gender Roles and Ethnicity

Introduction

Our social roles (e.g., father, son, student, psychologist) have implications for our sense of who we are. Our sense of self, our identity, becomes increasingly important throughout development and into adulthood. Arguably the most significant aspects of this sense of self concern how individuals define themselves in terms of various social groups or 'categories'. Two of the most prominent and ubiquitous such categories in many societies are gender and ethnicity or race.

An individual's gender has important implications for her or his development. In most societies, men and women behave differently, are viewed and treated differently by others, and can play different roles. Similarly, ethnicity can have profound influences on individuals' lives, relationships, and well-being. Many issues of social inequality and discrimination are important societal, even political, questions. The challenge for psychologists is to determine how these differences and similarities originate in the developing child and to articulate the processes that contribute to specific patterns of behaviour.

This chapter will begin by discussing work on gender and gender roles, focusing on how children develop an understanding of these. It will consider, in turn, the distinction between sex and gender and the ways in which much of the adult world is often still divided along gender lines. The process of associating certain roles, behaviour, and even objects with different genders is known as gender-typing, and understanding gender typing is an important developmental skill for the child.

Biological influences on gender development will be considered, followed by cognitive-developmental approaches. The chapter will then turn to consider the array of possible social influences on gender typing in children: parents, siblings, peers, the media and school teachers. Finally, recent studies on gender, discrimination and opportunities for challenging gender stereotypes are discussed in the context of cultural differences in gender development.

The chapter will conclude by considering work on the development of ethnic identity, and ethnic group attitudes and prejudice. Although similar processes are often assumed to underpin the development of both ethnic and gender identity, there are also some differences between them. We consider recent work on the development of ethnic identity in the context of children's understanding of more general group-related processes, and recent theoretical work in the area.

SEX AND GENDER IN DEVELOPMENT

Defining sex and gender

Traditionally, the word *gender* has been used to refer to cognitive and social differences between males and females, and *sex* refers to biological and physiological differences. From a research perspective (because development often involves an interplay between biology and environment) there is frequent overlap between how these different terms are used in research. There is, however, fluidity in terms of both gender and sex, and while both designations pick out different processes it is still often the case that a child born female will be given a female gender identity as a child. Moreover, being identified as female means that the child may well grow up with a different set of expectations, messages and will experience different interactions than if she was identified as a boy. How these different ascriptions relate to sex and gender (to biology and environment) through development has been the subject of a great deal of research.

gender typing The process by which children acquire the values, motives and behaviours considered appropriate for their gender in their particular culture.

gender stereotypes Beliefs that members of a culture hold about how females and males should behave; that is, what behaviours are acceptable and appropriate for each sex.

The means by which children acquire the values, motives, and behaviours viewed as appropriate for males or females, referred to as gender typing, involves several interconnected processes (Ruble, Martin, & Berenbaum, 2006). Children begin by developing gender-based beliefs about what behaviours are appropriate. These beliefs are derived largely from gender stereotypes, which are the beliefs that members of an entire culture may hold about the attitudes and behaviours acceptable and appropriate for each sex. These stereotypes prescribe the way males and females should be and should act.

Gender roles are composites of the distinctive behaviours that males and females in a culture actually exhibit. They are, therefore, essentially the reflections of a culture's gender stereotypes. Early in life, children develop a gender identity, or a perception of themselves as either masculine or feminine and as having the characteristics and interests that are appropriate to their gender. And children develop gender-role preferences, or desires to possess certain gender-typed characteristics. Children's choices of toys and of play partners reflect these preferences. It is important to distinguish gender-related behaviour and preferences from sexual orientation, which describes whether someone is attracted to same- or opposite-gender individuals. Although there are some links between gender-role and sexual orientation, these are conceptually and behaviourally distinct.

gender roles Composites of the behaviours actually exhibited by a typical male or female in a given culture; the reflection of a gender stereotype in everyday life.

gender identity The perception of oneself as either masculine or feminine.

sexual orientation The preference for same- or opposite-gender sexual partners.

Gender roles and stereotypes across cultures

From birth, parents may treat a baby rather differently depending on gender; for instance decorating a room in gender-typed ways or anticipating certain behaviour differently for boys and girls (Maccoby, 1998). In fact, even before birth a child's gender can be an important consideration because parents may have a preference for one gender child over the other, or may choose gendered names if they know a child's sex from antenatal scans. As children grow, parents frequently dress male and female children in distinctive clothes, style their hair in different ways, select toys and activities for them that they deem gender appropriate, may promote children's association with same-gender playmates, and can react negatively when children behave in ways they consider gender inappropriate.

Gender is a social category that can have an enormous influence on a child's life. Even before birth, gender differences in foetal activity have been identified. See Chapter 5 for more information about the prenatal period.

Cultures are internally quite consistent with regard to their standards of 'appropriate' gender-role behaviour. The term *gender-appropriate* does not mean that it is considered necessarily 'desirable'; rather, it means that people in general think is appropriate, typical and socially normative. In many societies, the male role is seen, stereotypically, as charged with controlling and manipulating the environment. Men are expected to be independent, assertive, dominant and competitive in social and sexual relations. The female role is seen as emotionally supporting the family. Women are expected to be relatively passive, loving, sensitive and supportive in family and social relationships. In these societies, in general, people regard the expression of warmth in personal relationships, the display of anxiety under pressure, and the suppression of overt aggression and sexuality as more appropriate for women than for men (Ruble et al., 2006).

Although this description of male and female roles may strike a familiar chord for many, there are variations between and within cultures in these roles and stereotypes, how they are accepted and how they affect behaviour (Mead, 1935; Whiting & Edwards, 1988).

Gender differentiation and gender-typing has profound social and personal consequences. For instance, in North America and many European countries, the world of work remains stereotypically gendered. Strikingly, both children *and* adults still tend to think of mechanics and doctors as male and librarians and nurses as female (Liben & Bigler, 2002). Although there are some notable exceptions, beliefs in these particular stereotypical roles are widespread across a wide range of societies from North, South and Central America, Europe, Africa, Asia and Australia (Williams & Best, 1990; Wade & Tavris, 1999). More traditional cultures such as Middle Eastern nations (Saudi Arabia, Iraq) and some Asian societies (Taiwan) adhere to more rigid stereotypes for the two genders. For example, Lobel et al. (2001) found that 8- to 10-year-old Taiwanese children were more committed to maintaining gender-role stereotypes than were more westernized Israeli children.

The strength of these stereotypes also varies within cultures. One source of within-culture variation is ethnicity. African-American families are more likely to socialize children without strict boy–girl gender-role

Do children play with gender-specific toys because they choose to or because of social influence?
Source: © Ingram Publishing/SuperStock (L) © romrodinka/123RF.com (R)

distinctions, and the children are less likely to hold stereotypic views about women (Leaper, Tenenbaum, & Shaffer, 1999). Among Mexican Americans, gender-role socialization standards for boys and girls are much more clearly differentiated (Coltrane & Adams, 2008). Parents' values matter in other ways, too. Boys and girls whose mothers are employed in skilled occupations and professions are more likely than children whose mothers are full-time homemakers to think that acquiring an education and having a profession are appropriate for women and that it's also all right for men to assume housekeeping and child care tasks (see, again, Ruble et al., 2006).

Research from the United Kingdom indicates that children integrate quite sophisticated information about gender and ethnicity from around 5–6 years. For instance, children have different expectations about what sorts of toys and foods boys from South Asian, white (European) and black (African-Caribbean) groups will choose and like, and these expectations differ in turn from what girls from these ethnic groups will like (Lam & Leman, 2003, 2009). So children are able not only to understand about expectations relating to gender, but also see nuances in how other social factors can moderate these expectations in still more subtle ways. Lastly, age also affects gender-role expectations: young children between 3 and 6 years old appear to be especially rigid in their gender stereotyping (Ruble et al., 2006), whereas as they develop children become more flexible in their attitudes about a variety of concepts, including gender issues.

How accurately do gender stereotypes reflect differences in the actual behaviours of males and females? As Table 13-1 shows, although clear gender differences have been found in some characteristics, others involve more subtle differences or no differences at all. As you examine the table in detail, keep in mind that, even for the differences that have been observed consistently, the characteristics of males and females overlap. Some males are more compliant, verbal and interested in the arts than some females. Some women are stronger than the average male. So to make a general statement about gender differences can be misleading.

Developmental patterns of gender typing

Children develop gender-typed behaviour patterns at an early age (Ruble et al., 2006). Even before they can tell us about their gender-based preferences, infants and toddlers clearly express their choices through their looking behaviour. Using habituation techniques, Serbin and her colleagues (2001) found that from a very early age, boys and girls differ in their preferences for looking at pictures of dolls or cars. As Figure 13-1 shows, by the time they were a year old, girls had begun to show a greater preference for dolls than boys did, and this gender difference was even stronger by the time the children were 1.5 to 2 years old. In contrast, boys showed much stronger preferences for vehicles such as cars and trucks than girls did by the ages of 1.5 and 2. In a study of 1 to 3 year olds in a day-care centre, boys and girls expressed their preferences for gender-appropriate toys (O'Brien, Huston, & Risley, 1983). However, girls more often than boys also played with gender-inappropriate toys.

Table 13-1 Gender differences: real or myth?

SOME GENDER DIFFERENCES ARE REAL ...
Physical, motor and sensory development
At birth, girls are physically and neurologically more advanced. They walk earlier, and they attain puberty earlier. Boys have more mature muscular development and larger lungs and heart, and at birth, they are less responsive to pain. With increasing age, boys become superior at activities involving strength and gross motor skills. On the other hand, male foetuses are more likely to be miscarried, boys have a higher rate of infant mortality, and boys are more vulnerable to malnutrition, disease, and many hereditary anomalies. In terms of physiological vulnerability, females are clearly not the weaker sex.
Educational achievement
From infancy through to the early school years, girls display superior verbal abilities, including vocabulary acquisition, reading comprehension, and verbal creativity. From about age 10, boys display greater visual-spatial ability, which is involved in such tasks as reading maps, aiming at a target, and manipulating objects in two- or three-dimensional space. Beginning at about age 12, boys excel in some kinds of mathematic semantics, especially geometry although girls tend to perform better in exams throughout school. Many gender differences in academic performance continue into university and beyond, yet often they are also connected with differences in the sorts of subject girls and boys, men and women, choose to study at a more advanced level.
Social and emotional development
Even in early social play, boys are more often the aggressors and the victims of aggression, particularly physical aggression. From childhood, girls tend to use more indirect forms of aggression, such as excluding another child from social interaction. As early as age 2, girls are more likely to comply with the demands of parents and other adults. Boys are more variable in their responses to adult direction. Gender differences in compliance with peers are not consistent, but preschool boys are less likely to comply with girls' demands than with those of other boys, and they are also less likely than girls to comply with partners of either gender. Girls are more nurturant towards younger children.
Atypical development
Boys are more likely to have genetic defects, physical disabilities, mental retardation, reading disabilities, speech defects, and school and emotional problems.
OTHERS ARE MYTHS, OR A LITTLE MORE COMPLICATED THAN THEY FIRST APPEAR ...
Sociability
Boys and girls are equally social; they spend as much time with others and are equally responsive to others. There's no gender difference in the need for love and attachment. Males and females are equally capable of nurturance, although girls and women do more actual caring for children, relatives and friends.
Suggestibility and conformity
Girls and boys do not differ in suggestibility or in the tendency to conform to the standards of a peer group or to imitate the responses of others.
Learning style
Boys and girls are equally good at rote learning and simple repetitive tasks. They also display similar skills in tasks involving the inhibition of previously learned responses and in complex cognitive tasks. Girls and boys are equally responsive to visual and auditory stimuli.
Self-esteem
Boys and girls do not differ in global (overall) self-esteem. However, girls rate themselves as more competent in social skills, and boys view themselves as stronger and more powerful.
Verbal aggressiveness and hostility
Girls and boys engage equally in verbal aggression but use different approaches: girls tend to gossip and exclude others; boys are more directly verbally assaultive.

Source: Maccoby and Jacklin (1974); Hyde and Linn (1988); Hyde and Plant (1995); Maccoby (1998); Underwood (2003, 2004); Halpern (2004); Hyde (2005); Dodge, Coie, and Lynam (2006); Ruble, Martin, and Berenbaum (2006); Wigfield, Eccles, and Schiefele (2006); Halpern et al. (2007); Leaper and Friedman (2007).

These early differences may be partly a result of instinctive predispositions to certain kinds of object. But social influences doubtless play a part too, given how early children are presented with gender-specific information, and how gender distinctions are widespread and a common feature of everyday life. Boys are more likely to develop 'extremely intense interests' in some objects and activities than are girls, and these passionate interests of boys are often gender stereotyped (e.g., vehicles, machines,

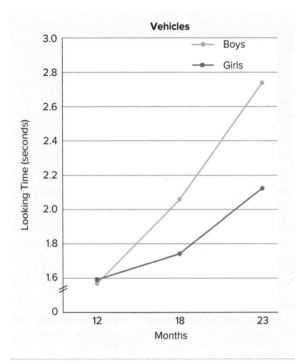
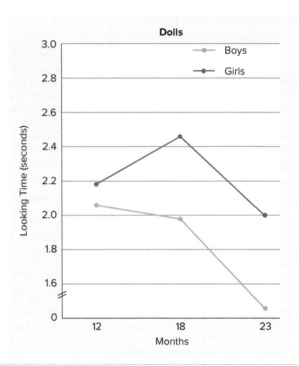

Figure 13-1   Toddlers prefer to look at gender-appropriate toys

By 18 months, boys and girls prefer to look at gender-reflective toys. Boys prefer looking at vehicles and girls prefer to look at dolls.

Source: Serbin et al. (2001).

> Toy choice and play is an important area for many developmental theorists: Vygotsky highlighted the importance of play for psychological development (Chapter 9). If toy choice and play is 'gendered', this could have important implications for children's developmental trajectories across domains.

trains) (DeLoache, Simcock, & Macari, 2007). Interestingly, boys' preferences for gender-stereotyped toys remained consistent across age (5 to 13), whereas girls' interest in play with gender-stereotyped toys decreased as the girls grew older (Cherney & London, 2006). This may be a consequence of greater social risks for boys (i.e., disapproval from parents and peers) who transgress gender-stereotypical boundaries. So there may be more negative social consequences for a boy who wishes to play with a doll than for a girl who wishes to play with a train or car.

Stability of gender typing

Although children develop masculine and feminine interests and behaviour early, as we have noted, many girls participate in both female and male pursuits during child-hood. With the onset of puberty, however, there is a movement back towards strict gender-typing (Larson & Richards, 1994; McHale et al., 2004). In one study, girls who claimed to be tomboys indicated that, at about age 12, they began to adopt more traditionally feminine interests and behaviours owing to pressures from both parents and peers, and to their own increasing interest in romantic relationships (Burn, O'Neil, & Nederend, 1996).

During adulthood, most people's masculine or feminine behaviour remains stable. In a longitudinal study, researchers found that 54% of adults continued to be rated similarly by observers over a 10-year period in terms of masculinity and femininity (Hyde, Krajnik, & Skuldt-Neiderberger, 1991). However, gender roles may shift as adults meet the demands of new situations and circumstances. One of the most important transitions is parenthood. Even among egalitarian couples committed to equal sharing of household tasks, the onset of parenthood generally heralds a return to traditional gender roles

(Cowan & Cowan, 2000; Parke, 2002). In these roles, women exhibit more expressive characteristics – they are more nurturing, concerned with feelings, empathic, and child orientated. Men exhibit more instrumental characteristics – they are more task and occupation orientated. Men tend to become more expressive and nurturing in old age, though. Women tend to become more autonomous as they get older, but return to a more feminine gender-role orientation in old age, perhaps because they become less self-sufficient and have a greater need for help (Hyde et al., 1991; Maccoby, 1998).

> **expressive characteristics** Presumably typical of females, these characteristics include nurturance and concern with feelings.
>
> **instrumental characteristics** Presumably typical of males, these characteristics include task and occupation orientation.

Gender differences in abilities

There are modest gender differences in abilities but also many similarities (Hyde, 2005). Boys tend to be more skilled than girls at manipulating objects, constructing three-dimensional forms, and mentally manipulating complex figures and pictures (Choi & Silverman, 2003). Boys also appear to be better in mental rotation tasks (where they have to imagine the rotation of an object in order to match it to another object) (Collaer & Hines, 1995). This difference in ability even appears at only 5 months of age (Moore & Johnson, 2008). Between the ages of 8 and 16, boys are more likely than girls to make correct judgements of spatial relations, as Figure 13-2 illustrates (Liben, 1991). However, this is not always the case: few gender differences in spatial abilities are found among children in poor families, which suggests that these differences are at least to some extent determined by environmental opportunities and socialization practices (Bower, 2005).

> ▼ How inevitable are gender differences in educational choices and achievement? We discuss some important research in education in Chapter 11.

Male superiority in mathematics is generally restricted to performance in geometry, a form of mathematics that requires spatial visualization skills (Hyde, 2005). In fact, girls do better in computational skills than boys, and there are no gender differences in girls' and boys' performance on tests of basic mathematical knowledge or algebra (Halpern, 2004; Hyde, Fennema, & Lamon, 1990). Moreover, boys' mathematics superiority only surfaces in the high school years, probably because of the lower expectations of teachers and parents for girls' mathematics skills (Hyde, 2005). Girls tend to speak and write earlier and to be better at grammar and spelling than boys (Halpern, 2000). Boys are more likely to suffer from social and communicative difficulties; autism is four times more frequent in boys than in girls (Baron-Cohen, 2003).

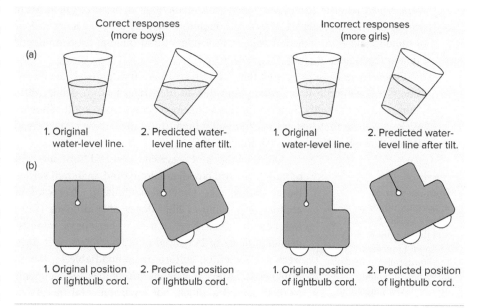

Figure 13-2   Boys' and girls' understandings of horizontal and vertical relations
Between the ages of about 8 or 9 to about 16 or 17, boys tend to make correct predictions of changes in horizontals and verticals following tilt, whereas girls are more likely to predict the results incorrectly. In general, boys seem to be more skilled at visual-spatial tasks.
Source: Based on Liben and Golbeck (1980).

BIOLOGY, COGNITION AND GENDER

The role of hormones

Hormones are powerful and highly specialized chemical substances produced by the cells of certain body organs and have a regulatory effect on the activities of certain other organs. Those hormones associated with sexual characteristics and with reproductive functions are present in differing concentrations in males and females from infancy through adulthood. Among male hormones, called androgens, testosterone is the principal and most potent one. Women's principal hormones are various forms of oestrogen and progesterone. However, each sex also has small amounts of the other's hormones: women have a little testosterone, and men have some oestrogen and progesterone. The differences in the concentrations of these hormones are not great in boys and girls of preschool and elementary school age, but they become quite pronounced after puberty.

Both the prenatal and the pubertal periods are critical in terms of the effect of hormonal action on development (Hines, 2004). In the prenatal period, foetal testosterone is the major determinant of the anatomic sex of the foetus, and hormones organize the foetus's biological and psychological predispositions to be masculine or feminine. The surge in hormones during puberty activates these early predispositions.

The effects of hormones have been demonstrated in animal studies. When pregnant monkeys were injected with testosterone, their offspring were females that exhibited masculine behaviours such as threatening gestures and rough-and-tumble play (Young, Goy, & Phoenix, 1967). When male hormones were injected into female monkeys after birth, they also became more assertive, sometimes even attaining prime dominance status in their monkey troop (Wallen, 1996). In human case studies, girls who were exposed to high levels of androgens prenatally exhibited masculine behaviours and interests – even if they were raised as girls (Hines, 2006). They enjoyed rough-and-tumble play and vigorous athletic activities, and showed little interest in playing with dolls, babysitting or caring for younger children. They preferred boys as playmates and chose toys usually preferred by boys. The greater the girl's exposure to androgen when a foetus, the stronger were her preferences for masculine play and activities (Berenbaum & Snyder, 1995). In other human case studies, genetic males born without a penis or with a very small one who underwent sex reassignment surgery and were raised as girls exhibited typical male behaviour such as rough-and-tumble play and had many male friends (Reiner & Gearhart, 2004). Although there is still no clear answer concerning the relative influences of biology and environmental factors, it is evident that biology plays an important role in gender-role development (Berenbaum, 2006).

Researchers have suggested that, at a critical period in prenatal development, sex hormones may determine a foetus's brain organization, and this, in turn, may lead to gender differences in males' and females' verbal and spatial skills. Support for this suggestion comes from studies showing that when prenatal androgen levels in female foetuses are exceptionally high, these girls have better visual-spatial skills than other girls (Hines, Ahmed, & Hughes, 2003; Hines, 2004).

> Hormones are an important influence on psychological functioning and development. Chapter 4 presents further details on the influence of biology across development.

Other methods of assessing prenatal hormone concentrations, including analysis of umbilical cord blood, amniotic fluid, maternal serum during pregnancy, and finger-length ratios, also show masculinizing effects of prenatal androgens on spatial abilities, especially at high doses of androgens (Cohen-Bendahan, van de Beek, & Berenbaum, 2005). Even if researchers have established a biological basis for the gender difference in spatial abilities, however, it does not mean that these abilities were unaffected by culture or unmodifiable by the environment (Berenbaum, 2006; Ruble et al., 2006). Hormonal differences between males and females may contribute to their spatial abilities, but environmental factors modify these biologically influenced patterns of differences between males and females.

Brain lateralization and gender differences

Another biological difference between males and females that may contribute to differences in cognitive abilities is the extent to which brain functioning is organized across the two cerebral hemispheres. In most people, the right hemisphere is more involved in processing spatial information and the left hemisphere in processing verbal information. However, there is some evidence that men's brains are more lateralized than women's; that is, their hemispheres are functionally more specialized than women's. Men whose left hemispheres are damaged are more likely than women with left hemisphere damage to experience verbal deficits, and men whose right hemispheres are damaged show more spatial deficits than women with right-hemisphere damage (Halpern, 2000).

Studies using brain-imaging techniques that detect blood flow in the brain as people perform different cognitive tasks confirm the greater lateralism among males. In a task in which men and women were asked to decide if nonsense words rhymed, both left and right sides of women's brains were activated; in men, however, only the left hemisphere was activated (Shaywitz et al., 1995). Even infants show this gender difference in patterns of brain activation in a word-comprehension task (Hines, 2004).

Socio-biological explanations

Researchers have asked what role biological 'programming' plays in shaping both gender-role standards and gender typing. For example, are women's abilities to have and to breast-feed a baby related to some kind of biological programming that causes girls to be more responsive than boys to the sights and signals of infants and children? Investigators have found that by the age of 4 or 5, girls interact more with babies and, when asked to care for a baby, are more likely to engage actively, whereas boys are inclined to watch the baby passively (Berman, 1987; Blakemore, 1990). These observations are consistent with the evolutionary theoretical perspective that argues that females are more committed to parental activities than males. Similarly, evolutionary theory suggests that males' greater visual-spatial ability is rooted in the distant past, when males' major activity was hunting (Buss, 2000; Geary, 2006b).

BOX 13-1 Foetal testosterone and autistic traits

Research close-up

Source: Based on Auyeung et al. (2009).

Introduction:

There is now a considerable body of research evidence suggesting that testosterone levels during pregnancy are associated with gender-related behaviours and other psychological and physical characteristics, once a child is born. Baron-Cohen has suggested that many of the features of autistic behaviour and cognitive function can be characterized as examples of an 'extreme male brain'. The present paper sought to test the hypothesis that a raised level of foetal testosterone (fT) would be associated with increased autistic characteristics during childhood.

Method:

The researchers used samples of amniotic fluid that had been collected from expectant mothers during amniocentesis. Amniocentesis is a procedure used to detect chromosomal abnormalities and infections of the foetus before birth. During the procedure, fluid is extracted from the amniotic sac that surrounds a foetus. This fluid contains the foetus's DNA which can then be analysed to detect abnormalities. It also gives information about hormonal levels, such as testosterone.

The researchers returned to these mothers between 6 and 10 years after the birth of their child and presented them with questionnaires about their child's behaviour and traits. These questionnaires assessed whether children displayed a number of characteristics of autism or behaviours on the autism spectrum.

Altogether, 950 women were considered but questionnaires were sent only to those who had not had a chromosomal abnormality detected during the amniocentesis, who did not have twins, where the pregnancy ended prematurely or the child died, or where medical information was missing or where doctors felt it would be inappropriate to contact the family. Altogether, 235 children had parents who had completed both questionnaires. IQ was also computed for a subset of children (using the WASI, a version of the Wechsler intelligence tests).

Results:

A key concern for the researchers was to establish any relationship between fT level and the display of autistic traits (according to mothers' reports). Unsurprisingly there was a strong correlation ($r = .63$, $p < .01$) between fT and the sex of the child, indicating that higher levels of fT were associated with male babies. Consistent with the researchers' hypothesis, there was significant correlation between fT and both autistic trait assessments ($r = .25$ and $r = .41$, both $p < .01$). But fT level showed no correlation with other variables such as maternal age or IQ, and was evident for both boys and girls.

Discussion:

The study provides support for the suggestion that prenatal androgen levels, specifically testosterone, are related to children exhibiting testosterone autistic traits. In addition, this might add weight to the 'extreme male brain' hypothesis of autism because testosterone is also associated with 'masculinizing effects' on sexually dimorphic traits such as social skills, language development, empathizing and visual-spatial skills. However, as the researchers conclude, clearly more research is required to understand why and how fT levels may vary and how these connect with complex psychological processes through pregnancy, into childhood and throughout life.

Socio-biological or evolutionary approaches to psychology stress the principles of natural selection and adaptation, and these concepts have been proposed to account for gender-related behaviours, especially behaviours that increase the likelihood that a person's genes will be passed across generations (Buss, 2003, 2007; Geary, 2006a). To be able to pass genes from one generation to the next, individuals need to have mating strategies that enhance their reproductive success. According to Buss (2000), males and females use different strategies to achieve reproductive success: males have developed aggressive and competitive skills to compete successfully with other males in attracting mates. Females have developed strategies for attracting and keeping males who are able to provide resources, including protection, for their offspring. The theory suggests that these two sets of strategies complement each other and have led to the evolution of gender differences in both animals and humans.

These behavioural tendencies, however, could as easily be due to cultural expectations. In adolescents and adults, they are more apparent when people know that someone is observing them (Berman, 1987). When experimenters have used subtle measures of responsiveness to an infant's crying, such as changes in blood pressure, electrical skin conductance or other responses of the autonomic nervous system, they have not detected any differences in mothers' and fathers' responses to a child (Lamb, 2004). Biological and evolutionary programming notwithstanding, culture has a considerable impact on males' and females' behaviour towards infants and children. Similarly, males' marginally superior visual-spatial ability is fostered (or even disproportionately nurtured) by culture, as boys are encouraged more often than girls to play with toys that involve spatial abilities, such as building sets, and to undertake mathematical and scientific endeavours (Beal, 1994). Experience with blocks, models, and video games, moreover, enhances spatial skills (Subrahmanyam et al., 2001).

Adolescence is also a period of rapid physical change, particularly with the onset of puberty. There may be, associated with this, sex differences in age-related changes in brain development (De Bellis et al., 2001). Moreover, females reach peak values of brain volumes earlier than males (Lenroot & Giedd, 2010). The significance of these developmental differences is yet to be fully understood. However, some researchers have suggested that specific links to psychopathologies associated with sex differences may be explained, in part, by different processes of brain development (see Hedman et al., 2012).

> Kohlberg's theory was derived from ideas in Piaget's account of human development (Chapter 9). Lawrence Kohlberg is best known for his work on the development of moral reasoning – see Chapter 14 for more details on Kohlberg's important contribution to developmental psychology in that area of research.

Kohlberg's cognitive developmental theory

Although biology and culture are important determinants of gender-typing, both approaches tend to assume gender differences are either inevitable or straightforwardly transmitted to the child. However, cognitive developmental theorists argue that children's own understanding of gender roles and rules contributes to the process of gender-role acquisition: in other words, à la Piaget, children themselves take an active role in constructing their own gender knowledge. In this section, we explore two dominant cognitive approaches to gender typing: Kohlberg's cognitive developmental theory and a more recent information-processing-based approach called Gender Schema Theory (GST).

In his cognitive developmental theory of gender typing, Lawrence Kohlberg (1966) proposed that children's differentiation of gender roles and their perception of themselves as more like same-gender than opposite-gender models begin very early. Children, using physical and behavioural clues such as hairstyle or playing with trucks, categorize people, including themselves, as male or female; they then find it rewarding to behave in a gender-appropriate manner and to imitate same-gender models. For example, a girl's thinking goes something like this: 'I am a girl because I am more like my mother and other girls than like boys; therefore, I want to dress like a girl, play girl games, and feel and think like a girl.' Consistency between the child's perceived gender and the way the child behaves is critical in sustaining self-esteem.

> **cognitive developmental theory** Kohlberg's theory that children use physical and behavioural clues to differentiate gender roles and to gender-type themselves very early in life, and that gender development is underpinned by the development of cognitive abilities.
>
> **gender stability** The notion that gender does not change; males remain male and females remain female.
>
> **gender constancy** The awareness that superficial alterations in appearance or activity do not alter gender.

Kohlberg believed that children go through three phases in gaining an understanding of gender. First, between the ages of 2 and 3, they acquire basic gender identity, recognizing that they are either male or female. Second, by the age of 4 or 5, they acquire the concept of gender stability, accepting that males remain male and females remain female. The little boy no longer thinks he might grow up to be a mother, and the little girl gives up her hopes of becoming Spider-Man. However, at this age children do not have a sense of gender constancy, and they fail to recognize that superficial changes in appearance or activities do not alter gender.

Kohlberg argued that this failure to appreciate gender constancy was a form of conservation error (see again Chapter 9 for a discussion of Piaget's initial work on conservation problems), and so reflected the immaturity of the child's cognitive abilities. By about 6 or 7, children reach the third stage and acquire this understanding, and so recognize that when a girl wears jeans or plays football, or when a boy wears long hair or has a burning interest in needlepoint, the child recognizes – and peers recognize, too – that gender remains the same.

Researchers who have tested Kohlberg's theory in several different countries have confirmed that both boys and girls acquire gender identity first, an understanding of stability next, and finally, an appreciation of consistency (Slaby & Frey, 1975; Martin & Little, 1990). However, culture and social factors clearly have some input: working-class children in the US and children in non-industrialized cultures generally reach these milestones about a year later than middle-class American children (Frey & Ruble, 1992).

Some researchers have suggested that the process by which children come to recognize males and females as distinct categories probably has its origins in infancy – well before babies can understand labels and language. For instance, 75% of 12-month-old infants were able to recognize male and female faces as belonging to distinctive categories (Leinbach & Fagot, 1992). This is not the same as recognizing that you yourself belong to one of these categories, but it does suggest that the process of understanding gender begins even earlier than Kohlberg originally thought.

The ability to understand gender labels such as boy and girl is not far behind. By the time they are 2 years old, children can correctly label their own gender, but they still have a very limited understanding of gender identity (Fagot & Leinbach, 1992). Young children have some understanding of gender words such as man and woman and recognize that some activities, objects and clothes are associated with each gender. It's not until they're about 3 years old, however, that they grasp the concept that they themselves, along with other children, belong to a gender class or group.

Genital knowledge is an important determinant of gender constancy (Ruble et al., 2006). Bem (1989, 1993) showed preschool children anatomically correct photos of a nude boy and girl and then showed the youngsters pictures of the same children dressed in either clothing appropriate to their gender or clothing appropriate to the opposite gender. Even when boys wore dresses or girls wore trousers, nearly 40% of the children correctly identified the gender of the child. When Bem then tested the preschoolers' understanding of genital differences between the sexes, she found that nearly 60% of the children who possessed genital knowledge, but only 10% of those who lacked it, had displayed gender constancy.

Research has shown that children who had developed gender identity engaged in more gender-typed play at age 2 than children who gained gender identity later; the boys were more likely to play with cars and trains, and the girls more likely to play with dolls (Fagot & Leinbach, 1989). Girls who had acquired gender stability chose to play with other girls more than did girls who had not (Smetana & Letourneau, 1984). And 5-year-old children who understood gender constancy were more attentive to same-sex characters on television than were children with less understanding of gender constancy (Luecke-Aleksa et al., 1995).

Gender-schema theory: an information-processing approach

Gender-Schema Theory
An information processing approach to gender development which suggests that schemas help children to organize and structure their experience related to gender differences and gender roles.

An important, more contemporary approach to understanding early gender differences, and in particular the interplay between social and biological forces, and cognitive processes, is Gender-Schema Theory (GST). According to GST, children develop *schemas,* or naive theories, about gender that help them organize and understand, organize and structure their social information and experiences that relate to gender differences and gender roles (Bem, 1998; Martin & Ruble, 2004). These schemas tell the child what kinds of information to look for in the environment and how to interpret such information. For instance, if a child sees that generally boys do not wear pink, that child will assimilate that information into the gender schema and in time may use it to guide his or her own behaviour.

Martin and Halverson (1983) demonstrated the importance of gender-role schemas by showing 5 and 6 year olds pictures of males and females involved in activities that were either gender consistent (e.g., a boy playing with a train) or gender inconsistent (e.g., a girl sawing wood). A week later, the researchers asked the children to recall the pictures. When they were asked to recall the gender-inconsistent pictures, children tended to distort information by changing the gender of the actor – presumably because they had schemas for what was gender appropriate.

Some children are particularly 'gender schematic' and are more attentive to gender cues. They are the ones who display better memories for gender-consistent information and are more likely to distort gender-inconsistent information (Levy, 1994). The degree to which children rely on gender schemas in interpreting their social world changes with age (Ruble et al., 2006). Preschool children rely more on gender schemas than elementary school children because older children have more complete and elaborate knowledge of gender roles, attach less importance to these roles, and are less rigid in applying their knowledge.

Children develop schemas through their own perceptions and based on information provided by parents, peers and cultural stereotypes. They use these gender schemas to evaluate and explain behaviour. For instance, when they were told about a child who spilled some milk, children evaluated the behaviour more negatively if the child was a boy because of the stereotype that boys are bad (Giles & Heyman, 2004; Heyman & Giles, 2006). They appraised the risk of injury as higher for girls than for boys because of the stereotype that girls are fragile – even though boys actually incur more injuries than girls do (Morrongiello, Midgett, & Stanton, 2000). The links between gender schemas and the child's own behaviour are presumed to occur through selective attention to and memory for own-sex relevant information and through motivation to be like same-sex others.

Gender schemas continue to develop and change into adolescence. Self-reflection and self-consciousness may also differ between genders, and may continue to be subject to greater influence from peer groups' and friends' gender norms and behaviours. Rankin et al. (2004) note that adolescence is often a period of intense self-reflection and self-discovery in terms of independence and autonomy (see chapter 12). Adolescent girls tend to show higher levels of public self-consciousness (awareness of one's roles in social situations), probably due to higher levels of social engagement among girls.

gender intensification
A particularly marked period (in early adolescence) of conformity to gender roles and norms.

Early adolescence also often sees young people experiencing gender intensification: an especially marked period of a need to conform to perceived gender norms and roles (Hill & Lynch, 1983). This period can lead to a hardening delineation between male and female friendship groups, and can also feed in to moral judgments (for instance, about decisions whether it is right or wrong to exclude someone from an activity based on their gender, e.g., Killen & Rutland, 2011). However, the concept of gender intensification has come under closer scrutiny. Priess, Lindberg, and Hyde (2009) argue that males and females appear to show rather different trajectories for intensification and, importantly, recent generations of adolescents may have different views on gender, sexuality and sexual orientation than previous generations.

SOCIAL INFLUENCES ON GENDER TYPING

Parents and gender typing

Parents have a significant impact on children's gender-role behaviours and gender typing: they may directly instruct children to behave in certain (gender typed) ways, or implicitly model or reinforce certain types of behaviour in children (McHale, Crouter, & Whiteman, 2003). Parents often speak differently to infant boys and girls, hold and move them differently, and choose different clothes and toys for them; and, as they get older, their parents encourage children in gender-appropriate activities and disapprove of their gender-inappropriate actions. Thus parents provide different opportunities for boys and girls to learn sex-typed behaviours by enrolling them in different gender-typed activities, clubs and sports (Leaper & Friedman, 2007) or encourage different academic and career routes (Tenenbaum, 2009).

Parents can, sometimes unintentionally, create gender distinctions that children pick up. Researchers have identified differences in the kinds of toys, decorations, furniture, and even the curtains and bedspreads that adorn the bedrooms of boys and girls between 1 month and 6 years old (Rheingold & Cook, 1975; Pomerleau et al., 1990): boys' rooms contained more vehicles, machines, army equipment, soldiers and sports equipment. In contrast, girls' rooms were more likely to house dolls and floral-patterned and ruffled furnishings. Parents also shape their children towards 'appropriate' gender roles by the way they dress them (Parke & Brott, 1999; Leaper & Friedman, 2007). When a group of researchers watched 1 to 13 month olds in a shopping centre, they found baby girls in pink, puffed sleeves, ruffles and lace. Boys wore blue or red but few bows or ribbons (Shakin, Shakin, & Sternglanz, 1985). Dressing a child in gender-typed clothing means that even strangers will respond to the child in gender-appropriate ways.

> Of course, parental and other social influences extend beyond gender although gender is one very important factor affecting all individuals' social relationships. Chapter 12 discusses the development of social relationships.

Parental behaviour can also differentiate between the genders. Both mothers and fathers tend to behave differently with their sons and daughters, but fathers are especially likely to treat them differently (Leaper & Friedman, 2007). From infancy, parents describe their newborn daughters as smaller, softer, cuter, more delicate and more finely featured than their sons. Fathers are even more likely than mothers to emphasize the size, strength, coordination and alertness of sons, and the fragility and beauty of daughters (Rubin, Provenzano, & Luria, 1974; Stern & Karraker, 1989). Researchers have found that adult strangers will play in more masculine ways with a baby they have been led to believe is a boy and in a gentler fashion with an infant they think is a girl, regardless of the infant's actual gender (Will, Self, & Datan, 1976).

Fathers are more likely to play and talk with infant sons than with daughters (Schoppe-Sullivan et al., 2006). As children grow older, fathers spend more time in play with male toddlers, tend to indulge in rough-and-tumble antics and may use more 'macho' language when speaking with them (Parke, 2002). In contrast, fathers are more likely to cuddle their infant daughters gently than to engage in active play with them.

Mothers tend to treat female and male babies in more similar ways (Siegel, 1987; Lytton & Romney, 1991; Leaper, 2002). But mothers still differentiate in some ways: both parents are more verbally responsive to girls, talk to them more, and use more supportive and directive speech with daughters than they do with sons (Leaper & Friedman, 2007).

As children grow older, parents often actively encourage and reinforce gender-stereotypic behaviour. Langlois and Downs (1980) observed how mothers and fathers reacted to their 3- and 5-year-old girls' and boys' play, purposely manipulating the children's choices of toys. Both 'masculine' toys, such as soldiers and a gas station, and 'feminine' toys, such as a dolls' house and kitchen utensils, were available to the children,

Parental behaviour and actions can impact on children's gender identity.
Source: © Design Pics/Con Tanasiuk (L) © Shutterstock/Ronnachai Palas (R)

but the researchers specifically told them to play with the toys that were either gender appropriate or not. They then recorded parents' reactions to their children's choices of toys, mothers in one session and fathers in another. Fathers consistently exerted pressure on their children – both boys and girls – to play with gender-typed toys. They were also quite consistent in rewarding both sons and daughters for play with gender-appropriate toys and in punishing them for play with opposite-gender toys. With daughters, mothers took the same approach, but their responses to their sons were inconsistent: they sometimes punished and sometimes rewarded them for playing with opposite-gender toys.

These findings are consistent with other evidence that men are more likely than women to gender-type toys and to purchase them, especially for boys (Fisher-Thompson, 1990). They also suggest that often the father is the principal agent of gender-role socialization and that the mother is less influential in this process (Parke, 2002).

Another difference in the way parents treat girls and boys is that they are more protective of girls' than of boys' physical well-being. Parents tend to encourage dependence and close family ties in girls and to put more emphasis on independence, early exploration, achievement and competition in boys (Ruble et al., 2006). Moreover, parents often communicate these messages quite directly: Pomerantz and Ruble (1998) found that parents were more likely to tell sons specifically that they were free to do certain activities than they were to grant such freedom to daughters.

Parents' gender-differentiated behaviour often seems to be associated with an interest in their children's achievement. Fathers, who are particularly prone to differentiate between boys and girls in this regard, are more likely to stress the importance of a career or occupational success for sons than for daughters. Differential treatment of boys and girls is particularly marked in the area of mathematical and scientific achievement (DeLisi & McGillicuddy-DeLisi, 2002). For example, parents are likely to encourage boys more often than girls to work on mathematics or science-related activities at home (Eccles et al., 2000). In one study, even when families visited a science museum, parents were more likely to explain interactive exhibits to their sons than to their daughters (Crowley et al., 2001). In another study, fathers of sons used more explanations and scientific vocabulary than fathers of daughters when instructing their child on a physical science task (Tennenbaum & Leaper, 2003).

Fathers of girls seem less concerned with performance and more concerned with interpersonal interactions with their daughters (Block, 1983). Even mothers, when reading bedtime stories, teach their boys more than their girls. They supply unfamiliar names to sons ('Look, here's a giraffe. Can you say giraffe?'), but with daughters, they emphasize enjoying the time spent with them (Weitzman, Birns, & Friend, 1985), or they focus on feelings and emotions rather than the cognitive aspects of the exchange (Cervantes & Callanan, 1998). When their parents endorse more gender-egalitarian attitudes and are more balanced in their treatment of boys and girls, girls do better (Updegraff, McHale, & Crouter, 1996; Leaper & Friedman, 2007).

The effect of parental absence on gender typing in girls is minimal. However, parental absence may have a delayed effect on girls' gender typing in adolescence. Father absence may cause adolescent daughters to have difficulties relating to other males; these difficulties may take different forms for daughters of widows and of divorcées. Adolescent girls from divorced homes have been observed to be more sexually precocious and assertive with males, whereas girls whose mothers were widowed were characterized as excessively anxious about sexuality and as shy and uncomfortable around males (Newcomer & Udry, 1987; Hetherington, 1991; Ellis et al., 2003).

Children reared in gay and lesbian families do not differ in gender-role behaviour from children reared in heterosexual households. Boys and girls in lesbian homes choose traditionally gender-orientated toys, activities, and friends are no more or less likely to develop a gay or a lesbian sexual orientation than their peers (Patterson & Hastings, 2007). Similarly, evidence suggests that boys raised by gay fathers are largely heterosexual in their sexual orientations and that this is true regardless of how long sons lived with their gay fathers (J. Bailey et al., 1995; Patterson, 2004).

Siblings and peers

Siblings as well as parents can influence children's gender choices, attitudes and behaviours. In a longitudinal study, researchers assessed whether the gender-role attitudes, leisure activities, and personality qualities of first-born children predicted these same outcomes in their second-born siblings two years later (McHale et al., 2001). They found that older siblings did indeed influence younger siblings' gender typing. Moreover, the links between siblings' attributes were stronger than the links between a child's attributes and those of the mother or father. Moreover, second-born children were more likely to model their older, first-born siblings than the other way around.

The sex of the older sibling matters, too. Children with sisters tend to develop more feminine qualities, whereas those with brothers generally develop more masculine qualities (Rust et al., 2000). In one study, brother–brother pairs engaged in more stereotypically masculine play (e.g., play with balls, vehicles or toy weapons); sister–sister or older sister–younger brother pairs engaged in more feminine play (e.g., art activities, play with dolls, playing 'mums and dads') (Stoneman, Brody, & MacKinnon, 1986). Children who had an older sibling of the other sex also had less stereotypical gender-role concepts.

In the early years, parents and siblings are important influences on a child's gender understanding, but as children become older peer influence becomes more important. Peers often serve as enforcers of society's gender-role standards, and they may also help to define them. In these roles, peers may help individual children define themselves and their gender identities (Rose & Rudolph, 2006; Leaper & Friedman, 2007). Observing 200 preschoolers at play over several months' time, Fagot (1985a) found that peers displayed marked reactions when children violated appropriate gender-role behaviour patterns. Boys who played with dolls rather than trucks had a tough time; their classmates criticized them five to six times more often than they heckled children who conformed. Peers weren't as harsh in their treatment of girls who would rather play firefighter than nurse, though; they tended to ignore rather than criticize these girls. When same-sex peers rewarded children for appropriate gender-role behaviour, the children tended to persist longer in the rewarded type of activity. Boys responded to feedback from boys but not from girls, and girls were more receptive to feedback from other girls. This pattern of responsiveness leads to gender segregation, which in turn provides additional opportunities to learn accepted gender roles (Fagot, 1985a; Maccoby, 1998).

These preferences in toy choice and gender-specific judgements are reinforced by their choice of playmates. In any school playground, you can see that children have a very strong tendency to associate and play with children of the same sex. When children are 4.5 years old, they spend nearly three times as much time with same-sex play partners as with children of the other sex. By age 6.5, the effect is even stronger: children spend 11 times as much time with same-gender as with opposite-gender partners (Maccoby, 1998). Gender segregation is particularly marked for boys (Benenson, Apostoleris, & Parnass, 1997). Children also like same-gender peers better than opposite-gender peers and are less likely to behave negatively towards them (Underwood, Galenand, & Paquette, 2001).

Martin and Fabes (2001) followed preschoolers throughout the school year. They found not only an increase in gender segregation but increasing gender differences in activities when children were in same-gender groups. The more time boys spent with other boys, the more active they became. They engaged in more and more rough-and-tumble play and overt aggression and spent less time with or near adults. In contrast, girls in groups with other girls showed a drop in activity level, their aggressive behaviour lessened, and they spent more time in proximity to adults. Consistent with these findings is the fact that preschool boys choose high-activity friends, whereas girls choose low-activity friends; in short, children choose friends that suit the level of activity that is within their comfort zone (Gleason et al., 2005). Similarly, girls are less competitive with their friends than are boys (Schneider et al., 2005).

These differences in activities in boys' and girls' groups led Maccoby (1998) to suggest a couple of reasons for gender segregation. First, girls view boys' rough-and-tumble play style and competition-dominance orientation as aversive; as a result, girls avoid interactions with boys. Second, girls find it difficult to influence boys. They influence each other successfully using their preferred method of making polite suggestions, but these tactics are not very effective with boys, who prefer more direct demands. Girls find it aversive to try to interact with children who are unresponsive, and they avoid such partners.

Similar gender segregation in childhood occurs across cultures including India, Europe and some African countries. It appears to occur without explicit adult encouragement, guidance or pressure, and reflects the spontaneous choices of children themselves. Thus children's choices of playmate are likely influenced by their gender-role knowledge and expectations, as well as by their preferences for certain types of activity. This gender-segregated play then maintains and builds upon these preferences, and peer group interaction becomes a major source of gender socialization. From preschool onwards, children tend to inhabit gender segregated play worlds that, in turn, encourage separate styles of interaction that are distinctly male and female (Leman, Ahmed, & Ozarow, 2005). Of course, gender segregation is not permanent; by adolescence, interest in opposite-sex partners is in full swing (Larson et al., 2002).

Media influence

There has been a shift towards more equal representation of boys and girls in children's books over the past several decades, but boys still appear more often in titles and in pictures than girls do (Purcell & Stewart, 1990; Gooden & Gooden, 2001). Moreover, books still often show females as more passive, dependent, and engaged in a narrower range of occupations than men and show males as more assertive and action orientated (Turner-Bowker, 1996). Males on television are more likely than females to be depicted as aggressive, decisive, professionally competent, rational, stable, powerful and tolerant. Females tend to be portrayed as warmer, more sociable, more emotional and happier. When women on television are aggressive, many times they are also seen as inept or unsuccessful, and they are more likely to be shown as victims than as initiators of violence. In television advertisements, males more often portray authorities and make more voice-over comments about a product's merits. Women are more likely to play the role of the consumer, displaying interest in product demonstrations (Coltrane, 1998). When women are shown as experts, they are likely to be discussing food products, laundry, soap, or beauty aids. These trends have been identified in a range of countries (Best & Williams, 1993; Singer & Singer, 2001).

The likelihood that these stereotypical presentations of male and female roles have a real impact on children is underscored by findings that children who are heavy TV viewers are more likely to have stereotypical notions of gender and race and to show conformity to culturally accepted gender-role typing (Berry, 2000; Ward & Friedman, 2006). When television was first introduced in a small town in Canada (see the discussion of natural experiments in Chapter 1), analysts recorded marked increases in traditional gender attitudes (Kimball, 1986; MacBeth, 1996). Moreover, experimental studies of TV advertisements that were targeted either to boys (action toys) or to girls (dolls, fashion, beauty) showed that the ads shaped children's toy requests (Robinson et al., 2001). The specific programmes children watch may be guided by their gender schemas, and what they watch may shape their gender beliefs (Leaper & Friedman, 2007). However, it is worth noting, too, that gender differentiation in advertisements at least partly reflects a recognition that boys and girls prefer different types of toys. So gender stereotyping in the media may be a consequence as well as a cause (or reinforcer) of gender-typed standards.

Television can also be used to change children's gender-role stereotypes. In one study, 5 and 6 year olds who were shown a cartoon in which the characters played non-traditional roles (girls helped boys build a clubhouse) subsequently expressed less conventional gender-role attitudes (Davidson, Yasuna, & Tower, 1979). However, the effects of most TV-based interventions have been relatively modest and short-lived and are more effective with younger than with older children (Bigler & Liben, 1992; Comstock & Scharrer, 2006).

Schools and teachers

Teachers and schools deliver a number of gender-related messages to children (Ruble et al., 2006; Leaper & Friedman, 2007). In several cultures, boys and girls are educated entirely separately. Even in mixed-sex schools and classes, teachers sometimes structure class-room activities by gender and provide differential rewards and punishments to boys and girls. Although teachers often seem to pay more attention to boys than to girls, the general culture of the classroom and the school in some ways favours girls. The school system tends to frown upon the inde-pendent, assertive, competitive and boisterous qualities that parents and the culture have encouraged in boys from infancy. Girls, who are more verbally orientated, generally better behaved and better at following rules,

Differences in classroom interaction by gender can cause different levels of academic performance and varying attitudes to school.
Source: © McGraw-Hill Education

typically experience greater acceptance from teachers who – at least in the early grades – are likely to be female. It is not surprising, then, that from the start girls tend to like school more than boys and to perform better in their academic work. Boys create more problems for teachers and elicit more criticism from them, and they often perform at a level that is lower than their female classmates (McCall, Beach, & Lan, 2000; Ruble et al., 2006). These gender differences in classroom interaction and attitudes may go some way to explaining variations in academic performance between boys and girls across the school system and into university (Leman, 1999, 2004).

Even in the preschool years, teachers respond differently to boys and girls, often reacting to them in gender-stereotypic ways (Fagot, 1985a). Researchers have found that teachers interrupt girls more frequently than boys during conversations and pay more attention to boys' assertive behaviour than to girls' pushing and shoving (Hendrick & Stange, 1991). They respond to girls' social initiatives, such as talking and gesturing, more than to these same behaviours in boys.

Teachers also influence how well children do in different school subjects. They encourage boys more than girls in mathematical pursuits and stress literature more for girls (Shepardson & Pizzini, 1992; Wigfield et al. 2006). Children pick up on teachers' belief that mathematics is a field for males. From childhood onwards, boys have greater interest in and higher expectations for success in mathematics and science than girls, whereas girls have more interest and self-perceived competence in reading and writing than boys (Evans, Schweingruber, & Stevenson, 2002). For instance, Muzzatti and Agnoli (2007) found that 10- and 11-year-old Italian boys are more confident than girls in their mathematics abilities in spite of similar abilities. As they get older, girls express a decreased liking for mathematics and, lacking any positive reinforcement for studying the subject, are more likely than boys to drop it when given the opportunity to do so (Shea, Lubinski, & Benbow, 2001). Thus gender stereotypes can affect students' and teachers' behaviour and perceptions of ability, and can have a profound and lasting affect on their academic and career choices.

Applied Developmental Psychology

BOX 13-2   Are single-sex or mixed-sex classrooms better?

There is often a common assumption that, although girls now perform rather better than boys academically in many countries, in mixed gender classrooms (i.e., those where there are boys and girls) boys tend to dominate time, apparatus and discussion, and boys' misbehaviour can distract the girls. This is a belief that is often voiced in relation to science subjects, where the comparative under-performance of girls in some science subjects, and the under-representation of girls and women studying science at university and pursuing science careers (Oakes, 1990; Spielhofer et al., 2002). In the UK, it has been argued that both boys and girls perform better, academically, when they are in single sex rather than mixed schools (Younger & Warrington, 2006).

Developmental, social and educational psychologists have sought to look behind these common assumptions to establish whether there are consistent differences in boys' and girls' classroom time and whether any differences impact upon learning or gender differences in achievement. The findings from this research have been used to inform teachers' classroom practices, materials and apparatus for work as well as discussions about educational policy.

A first source of gender differentiation in classroom dynamics comes from teachers themselves. Teachers often organize the classroom environment in ways that differentiate along gender lines – for instance, boys and girls have separate pegs in the classroom, and can engage in games and other activities in separate gender groups (Lloyd & Duveen, 1992). Teachers also appear to subtly differentiate between boys and girls in their interactions in the classroom. For instance, traditionally teachers tended to give more praise (and criticism), more response opportunities, initiate more interactions and ask more questions of boys than of girls, even though girls put their hands up more often than boys (Kelly, 1988).

Training now points teachers to be aware of the influence of gender stereotyping in the classroom (Skelton et al., 2009). A potentially more important source of influence on classroom dynamics, and children's learning, comes from children themselves. Often children will learn collaboratively and engage in joint activities such as working on science tasks together or sharing a computer. Studies suggest that gender is a major influence on interaction between children in some of these tasks. For instance, Keogh and colleagues (2000) looked at boys', girls' and cross-gender interactions when 13–14 year olds were asked to work together on a computer-based and then a paper-and-pencil version of an English language task. In cross-gender interaction (that is, interaction between a boy and a girl) on the computer task boys dominated interactions, often grabbing hold of the computer mouse. On the paper-and-pencil task, there was less dominance from the boys, suggesting that the task or activity context is an important determinant of social dynamics and collaboration style.

> In Chapter 5 we describe how research has shown that mixed-sex schools may be particularly problematic for girls who reach puberty earlier than their peers – leading them into more risky behaviours. How do you think physical sexual development and gender typing interact to affect social and academic development?

However, whether the differences in collaboration style feed into affect learning and achievement is less certain. Underwood, Underwood, and Wood (2000) observed similar effects of male dominance on a collaborative computer task at school, but the girls' more passive role in cross-gender interaction did not appear to affect their subsequent performance on a similar task. Other studies also suggest that boys' and girls' interaction styles do not appear to feed into gender differences in learning and development in any simple way (Barbieri & Light, 1992; Leman, Ahmed & Ozarow, 2005).

Lastly, these gender differences may also extend to university level where gender differences in achievement have also been attributed, among other causes, to men's dominance in tutorials and seminars (Mellanby, Martin, & O'Doherty, 2000).

Argument does not look likely to abate about whether boys and girls benefit from single sex education. Alongside the potential academic consequences for boys or girls, parents may also consider the social consequences of single- versus mixed-sex education. Although the research literature points towards the social, personal and academic benefits of single-sex education, certainly for girls, clearly other factors are important (Lee & Bryk, 1986; Spielhofer et al., 2002). What makes a good school or the best school for any child likely depends on other factors aside from the gender mix of the pupils in it. The psychological research also points to ways in which teachers can moderate their classroom behaviour and 'design out' gender as a factor affecting learning.

Challenging gender stereotypes

androgynous Possessing both feminine and masculine psychological characteristics.

Many psychologists believe that traditional ideas of masculinity and femininity have been socially and psychologically destructive. To speak and act as if each individual person is either 'masculine' or 'feminine' in interests, attitudes and behaviour makes little sense when we know that in reality most people possess a combination of characteristics traditionally viewed as masculine or feminine. Many people are androgynous; that is, they possess both masculine and feminine psychological characteristics (Bem, 1981, 1998; Spence & Buckner, 2000). Children, as well as adults, can be androgynous, and these children are less likely to make stereotyped choices of play, activities and occupations (Harter, 1989); they are better adjusted and more creative, too (Norlander, Erixon, & Archer, 2000). Children who are either masculine or androgynous in their gender identity have higher self-esteem than those with a feminine gender identity (Boldizar, 1991; Ruble et al., 2006). Children who are both accepting of themselves as a typical member of their own gender and feel that it is OK to cross gender boundaries are better adjusted than those who are not secure in their gender role (Egan & Perry, 2002; Carver, Egan, & Perry, 2004).

Can children be taught to be more androgynous? Can they learn that nurses and firefighters can be male or female? The study we discuss in Box 13-3 suggests that they can, but as the following exchange illustrates, the task may not be easy.

BOX 13-3   Does Barbie make girls want to be thin?

Research close-up

Source: Based on Dittmar, Halliwell, and Ive (2006a; see also Dittmar, Halliwell, and Ive, 2006b).

Introduction:

Although there are many potential sources of influence on children's gender stereotypes and knowledge, the types of toys that children play with may transmit subtle messages about gender roles and stereotypes. These messages may reinforce processes of gender socialization because, from a young age, children's emerging gender schemas influence the sorts of toys that children choose to play with. In an experimental study involving children from 5 to 8 years of age, Helga Dittmar and colleagues explored whether playing with one particular and widely found toy – the Barbie doll – had further, 'knock on' effects on girls' esteem and body image. The Barbie doll, although ubiquitous, is a deeply unrealistic representation of women's and girls' real body shapes. For instance, if a real woman had the same body proportions (e.g., waist, bust size) as Barbie her waist would be 39% smaller than that of individuals suffering from anorexia nervosa and her weight would be so low she would be unable to menstruate. The core question for the study was how far this unrealistic representation of body shape affects girls' feelings and beliefs about themselves.

Method:

The researchers used an experimental approach. Girls were aged between 5 and 8 years and were predominantly white, middle-class children from southern England, UK. Girls were, at random, placed in one of three experimental groups. In each group, girls were shown a series of pictures that made up a story book about a girl called 'Mira'. However, the images that accompanied the story varied for each group. For one group, pictures featured Barbie in various scenes – for example, wearing a top and jeans, or in a long, pink dress. Another group saw pictures of a different doll, Emme, in similar poses. Emme is a different type of doll whose body proportions better reflect real female figures. For instance, whereas Barbie would be the equivalent of a female, adult clothes size 2, Emme would be equivalent to size 16. The final group of girls heard the same story but saw images that did not include any information about body size; for instance, a picture of a window in a clothes shop or of a collection of shopping bags. Children were also asked a series of questions such as whether they like certain TV shows or films, which included questions on how they felt or others might feel about their looks or weight. Children indicated positive, neutral or negative responses by pointing to one of three face icons (happy, neutral or sad). One of the researchers also showed children pictures of various different body shapes (from thin to fat) and asked

The Barbie doll and her unrealistic proportions.
Source: © JuliaGrin/Shutterstock

children to colour the shape that looked most like them, and then colour the shape that they most wanted to look like. These two techniques were used to create measures of body esteem and body satisfaction or dissatisfaction, (the latter was calculated by subtracting the 'score' for the actual body shape from the ideal shape, see also Dittmar, Halliwell, & Ive, 2006b). Finally, girls were shown body shapes of adult women and were asked to colour in the shape they would most like to be as an adult (again, the actual score was subtracted from the ideal to give the satisfaction rating).

Results:

Older girls' responses suggested that they felt more dissatisfaction with their bodies than the younger girls. However, the older girls were generally less affected by the experimental manipulation than the younger ones. Girls in the two younger age groups (5.5–6.5 years and 6.5–7.5 years) showed more detrimental effects on body esteem and satisfaction after viewing the Barbie pictures compared with the control images, whereas there were no differences on these measures between girls who had seen the Emme doll pictures and the control images. The effects were particularly strong in the middle age group (i.e., 6.5–7.5 years). In the older age group (7.5–8.5 years) the Barbie condition had no effect on ratings of esteem and satisfaction. Unexpectedly, however, the girls who had seen pictures featuring the Emme doll showed greater discrepancy (dissatisfaction) between actual body shape and ideal shape as an adult, compared with those who had seen pictures featuring Barbie and the control condition.

Discussion:

The findings suggest that exposure to Barbie images has a negative impact on body esteem and satisfaction among younger girls. These effects may be particularly pronounced for girls around 6 to 8 years, indicating a sensitive period in terms of gender development and the acquisition of gender knowledge. This connects with a good deal of other research into gender development that suggests there are big changes in gender knowledge, roles, relationships and gender-related behaviour between 6 and 8 years that may be connected to underlying social and cognitive processes.

However, note that body dissatisfaction is higher for the older girls, particularly when girls expressed their most desirable body shape as an adult. Moreover, presenting the Emme doll as a potential role model seemed to have a negative effect for the older children, maybe because they imagined they did not want to end up having a fuller figure when older. Thus, while the immediate negative effects of Barbie may wane towards the end of middle childhood, the problem of body dissatisfaction for girls – and the 'thin ideal internalization' process – does not go away.

The research provides compelling evidence on the short-term effects of exposure to Barbie dolls. However, a shortcoming is that the study does not directly inform our knowledge about the longer-term outcomes of exposure. For instance, many girls in the study will already have had or seen Barbie dolls, and one important weakness in the methodology was that the researchers did not collect data on whether or not this was the case. However, the researchers argue that if such effects can be observed in the short term, for girls who already have experience of these toys, longer-term exposure to ideals of 'ultra-thinness' could have even more marked effects.

Work by Bigler and Liben (1990, 1992) suggests that children can learn to use fewer stereotypes. Using ten occupations that children view as typically masculine (e.g., dentist, farmer, builder) or feminine (e.g., beautician, flight attendant, librarian), these researchers tried to reduce children's stereotyping of these work roles. They taught the children, first, that gender is irrelevant. Then they focused the children's attention on two other ways of looking at job appropriateness: liking a job and having the skills needed for the job. For example, builders must like to build things, and they must acquire the skill to operate big machines. The investigators gave one group of children practice problems for which they had to specify why the job (e.g., builder) was a good match for the person. If the children based their answers on gender rather than on interest or skills, they received corrective feedback. In a control group, children participated in a group discussion about the roles of specific occupations within the community, with no emphasis on gender stereotyping. Children in the experimental group later gave more non-stereotyped answers not only for the occupations involved in the lessons but for a range of other occupations as well. For instance, when they were asked who could do various specific activities, such as police work and nursing, they gave more 'both men and women' responses. Children in the control group still argued that 'Girls can't be firefighters!'

Consistent with the theory of gender schemas, children in the experimental intervention showed better recall of counter-stereotypic information in a later memory test. Although children in both the experimental and control groups remembered stories about Frank the firefighter and Betty the beautician, children in the experimental group remembered stories about Larry the librarian and Ann the astronaut far better than did children in the control group. These findings suggest that children's ways of thinking about gender roles can be modified.

Clearly, gender roles and attitudes are modifiable. In several cultures, such as Sweden, where there is a deep-rooted commitment to gender equality, and the opportunities to observe males and females engaging in non-gender-stereotyped behaviours have resulted in some increases in androgynous attitudes among children (Coltrane & Adams, 2008; Tennenbaum & Leaper, 2002). In many other countries, attitudes towards gender roles are changing slowly and will likely continue to change as more and more individuals cross gender lines.

THE DEVELOPMENT OF ETHNIC GROUP UNDERSTANDING AND PREJUDICE

Ethnicity and prejudice

Ethnicity, like gender, is an important social category that has been associated with social inequality and discrimination. Ethnicity, like gender, picks out social and psychological characteristics; the term is generally used to denote the social, cognitive and cultural consequences of an individual's membership of one or other race group. In contrast, race, like sex, is typically used to pick out biological characteristics. Although both gender and ethnicity are social constructs and relate to social groups, a core difference is that while there are only two gender groups, ethnicity can be a more complex matter and children may meet individuals from many different ethnic groups, or from more than one ethnic group. It is perhaps not surprising, then, that children tend to be able to identify ethnic groups, or show ethnic awareness, a year or so later than they can identify gender groups (i.e., 4–5 years) and also that ethnic knowledge is at least partly influenced by the context or diversity of the social environment in which a child grows up.

Early research on ethnicity and ethnic prejudice was conducted in the USA in the context of racial segregation between African Americans and European Americans in parts of the country (e.g., Horowitz, 1939). These studies used a similar technique, which involved presenting children with dolls of different colour and asking various questions such as whether the child liked the black (brown) or white doll, whether they would like to play with the doll, and which one looked most like the child. Although far from being methodologically sophisticated, the findings from these studies suggest that younger children (up to around 7 years) give the most favourable assessments of the doll that relate to their own group, for instance, they would say that they like their own group most, and would like to play with the white doll most if they were a white child. Evidence suggests that these preferences for one's own ethnic group diminish (although do not entirely disappear) from middle childhood onwards (i.e., 8 years and above).

However, the picture is more complicated. In one famous 'doll study' conducted by Clark and Clark (1947), African American (black) and European American (white) children were asked questions about a black and white doll in two contrasting contexts: the then racially segregated South of the USA, and more liberal and racially mixed Massachusetts. In both locations, nearly two-thirds of the black

Gender stereotyping would result in most people assuming a firefighter is male. In this instance, would you assume the man is a doctor or a nurse? Does gender influence your assumption?
Source: © Blend Images/Alamy (T)
© Shutterstock/XiXinXing (B)

ethnic awareness The understanding of ethnicity as a social category.

prejudice An attitude, or set of attitudes, which is often based on stereotypes towards a particular group, and is usually negative.

In Chapter 11 we discuss the issue of whether intelligence tests are a fair assessment of the abilities of individuals from ethnic minorities, compared to majority group children. Ethnic differences in educational achievement are one likely consequence of negative stereotypes.

children thought the white doll was a 'nice colour', whereas barely a third thought that the black doll was a nice colour. In other words, the preference for one's own group was present for white children, but black children showed a more equivocal evaluation of the doll that represented their ethnic group. This finding has been replicated in New Zealand between indigenous Maori children and European, white children (Vaughan, 1964), German and Turkish children in Germany (Davey, 1983), and is evident from the interactions of UK children from white majority and ethnic minority groups (South Asian, African) (Leman & Lam, 2008).

Although attitudes among minority group members may be changing (see Vaughan, 1987), the general finding is that children from ethnic minority groups, or groups that are traditionally disadvantaged in society tend to make less favourable evaluations of their own ethnic group compared with children from the majority group. These findings suggest that children of all ethnic groups pick up messages from society about what is good, desirable, or normative and that this can entail damaging consequences for minority group children (Phinney, 1993). Unsurprisingly, a good deal of recent research has sought to explore how negative ethnic group attitudes can be eliminated among children, and these complement and have been used to inform interventions to improve attitudes and awareness among children (e.g., Abrams, Brown, & Jones, 2003).

How, then, a child comes to form an ethnic identity is closely connected with how their ethnic group membership(s) connect with their emerging knowledge about the roles, stereotypes, inequalities and injustices associated with ethnic groups, and in particular their own ethnic groups. Additionally, the attitudes they express are influenced by their growing knowledge of the world, society, and moral norms and values (chapter 14) which are closely linked to evaluations of their own ethnic identity and processes such as self-esteem. Finally, it also intersects with developing understanding of other social categories and other aspects of identity (e.g., Tenenbaum, Leman, & Aznar, 2017).

Theories of ethnic prejudice

Many children show a marked preference for their own ethnic group, at least in the early stages of childhood. It is not uncommon, and sometimes a little embarrassing, when a younger child expresses a negative ethnic group attitude about an individual from a different ethnic group, commenting perhaps on skin colour, clothes or language (accent). How far are these negative attitudes expressed by children a result of prejudice (a reflection of societal inequality and discrimination, perhaps) and how far are they merely the politically incorrect outbursts from a young, unknowing mind?

Aboud (1988) what she labelled 'social reflection' theories of prejudice. These theories, according to Aboud (1988), argue that children's attitudes are a simple reproduction of those they are exposed to or experience in their social environment. So, for instance, when white children in Clark and Clark's study said they thought the white doll was a 'nice colour' they merely reflected the attitudes of a society that often gives preference and higher value to the white ethnic majority group. Black children's responses were slightly more equivocal because their social experiences and immediate family context differed slightly, but they had nonetheless internalized some societal norms and information about ethnicity. According to social reflection theories, children merely absorb societal values: they start as naive, blank slates, and gradually acquire negative ethnic attitudes towards some ethnic groups.

Of course, Aboud is correct that there is more to the development of ethnic group attitudes than merely a reflection of those of society; for one thing, not all children grow up to reproduce the prejudices (or positive attitudes) of their parents. Most importantly, however, the finding that younger children often seem to hold more extreme negative ethnic attitudes, which become less negative as children approach adolescence, does not fit easily with simplistic, social reflection accounts.

Aboud argued that ethnic attitudes and prejudice were a consequence of children's underlying cognitive abilities, and a change in children's orientation to groups. Very young children's responses to individuals from other ethnic groups are fearful because such individuals are unfamiliar to the child. In early childhood this early fear response gives way to a focus on what is perceptually unfamiliar (for example, different-coloured skin, different-smelling food). This perceptual basis for ethnic group attitudes again emphasizes difference and is associated with negative ethnic attitudes towards unfamiliar groups. Only when children develop to understand that individual characteristics are important (e.g., not what ethnic group a person belongs to but what he or she is like, what attitudes he or she holds) do the childish negative attitudes of ethnic prejudice disappear or diminish.

Some evidence for Aboud's theory comes from studies of ethnic constancy, similar to those used by Kohlberg to demonstrate the cognitive basis of shifts in reasoning about gender. Aboud (1988) showed children photographs of a European child dressed in standard children's clothes (i.e., jeans and T-shirt) and children were able to identify the child as European (Aboud & Skerry, 1983). However, when the same child was shown wearing a native American headdress, children under 7 years said that the child's ethnicity had changed. Thus, overlapping changes in cognitive and social knowledge account for the demise of negative ethnic group attitudes and prejudice from middle childhood onwards.

> In Chapter 11 we discuss the issue of whether intelligence tests are a fair assessment of the abilities of individuals from ethnic minorities, compared to majority group children. Ethnic differences in educational achievement are one likely consequence of negative stereotypes.

Although Aboud's theory has received empirical support, some have argued that the role of social processes in it is not fully articulated. Indeed, Nesdale (2004) sought to link work on children's understanding of ethnicity and ethnic group attitudes with social psychological work in social identity theory (Tajfel, 1982). Nesdale's *social identity development theory (SIDT)* suggests that ethnic attitudes are largely learned from society, and that ethnic prejudice is the endpoint of a process of development where children's ethnic attitudes go through four phases or stages. These are: (i) undifferentiated, where children do not distinguish on the basis of ethnic groups; (ii) ethnic awareness, where children become aware of these distinctions; (iii) ethnic preference, which reflects the preference for one's own ethnic group found in previous research; and (iv) ethnic prejudice. Not all children will reach the final phase and develop prejudice, but most will end up showing some preference or other and, importantly, this will continue on to ethnic preference in adulthood. However, this sort of preference for one's own group is not dissimilar from the 'ingroup favouritism' observed by many social psychologists across a range of milieu. Whether a child develops ethnic prejudice in the longer term is largely a matter of what attitudes prevail in a particular ethnic group (Nesdale et al., 2003).

At first glance, SIDT would seem to sit uneasily with the observation that negative ethnic attitudes decline after 7 years of age. However, Nesdale argues that these negative attitudes do not decline but are merely 'driven underground' because children begin to appreciate that these attitudes are usually not considered socially desirable. Hence children will still show preference for their own ethnic group when they are not being asked explicitly to express their views (Baron & Banaji, 2006). So from 7 years children still show a bias towards their own ethnic group, but begin to realize that this is not a bias they should openly express.

BOX 13-4 Do children exhibit national group favouritism? Research close-up

Source: Based on Rutland (1999).

Introduction:

Although ethnic group differences have typically been studied as a course of prejudice in much of the developmental literature, there are plenty of other forms of prejudice such as homophobia and misogyny which also, presumably, relate to social and developmental processes. One area of research that has been a particular focus for European researchers is the development of national identity, favouritism towards one's own national group, and indifference or even hostility towards other national groups. The present study sought to explore the ages at which children's national group attitudes become positive or negative. Additionally, the study sought to test whether a prediction from cognitive developmental theory (Aboud, 1988) regarding ethnic group discrimination – that prejudice is the consequence of immature cognitive processing in younger children – holds for national group attitudes.

Method:

Participants were 329 white, British (English) children from 6 to 16 years of age. For the main part of the study, children took part in a photograph evaluation task. This task presented children with photographs of other children, and asked them to say how much they liked (or disliked) each child by placing each photograph in one of four cups, labelled from 1 ('I like very much') to 4 ('I dislike very much'). All the photographs were of white, European boys and girls of a similar age range to participants.

The study employed a repeated measures design. There were two different conditions. In one, children completed the evaluation task based on the pictures alone. In the other, the photographs each had labels which identified the child in the photograph as belonging to one of five national groups; British (the ingroup), and German, American, Russian and Australian (all outgroups). All children took part in both phases of the study (i.e., all rated the labelled and unlabelled photographs), but each session was conducted two weeks apart and the order of presentation of each condition was randomized. Lastly, participants also answered some open-ended questions about their identity and what made them proud to be British.

Results:

In analysis, Rutland compared the children's ratings in the unlabelled condition with the ratings in the labelled condition. Differences between these conditions indicated bias (or preference) for a national group. From 10 years of age children's responses indicated that they liked the child in the photograph more if they had a British label, compared with no label. Thus there was a clear preference for the ingroup (i.e., British children) at 10 years of age, which remained until 16 years, the oldest age group tested. For evaluations of outgroups, a different picture emerged. For the Americans, Russians and Australians there were no differences in evaluation at any age between the labelled and unlabelled photographs. However, from 10 years children consistently rated the photographs labelled as German as less liked than the no-label photographs. In other words, outgroup prejudice towards the Germans appeared from 10 years. Responses to the open-ended questions suggested that stereotypes appeared to get stronger as a child's identification with their own group increased.

Discussion:

The results do not fit easily with the prediction from cognitive developmental theory that young children display more negative attitudes than older children and adults. In some senses, national prejudice or preference appears to operate more like a classical intergroup process with preference for the ingroup and dislike of the outgroup. Both these processes appear to be acquired over time, probably through a process of socialization. However, the issue is not quite so clear-cut, because not all outgroups were rated negatively by children. Specifically, only the children with a German label were cast in unfavourable terms from 10 years. This suggests that contextual factors – history, relations, geographical proximity, perceived national characteristics and stereotypes – may make some national categories salient for children while others are not, or at least are not seen as salient in any threatening way. Thus children may be becoming sensitive not only to groups but also to the comparative context in which these groups operate.

Reducing ethnic prejudice

Considerable research effort has focused on establishing effective interventions for reducing ethnic prejudice and discrimination and many of these have focused on children. Generally, such programmes have proved effective, although the context and content of these interventions is important (Denson, 2009). If the social context and group norms that surround children are prejudicial, children may be more likely to acquire negative ethnic attitudes. For instance, in long-standing conflict situations children may come to associate very strongly with one group and attitudes can become entrenched (Muldoon, 2004). In a study from Italy, researchers found that children may also pick up negative ethnic attitudes and prejudices from parents, even if parents hold these attitudes implicitly (Castelli, Zogmaister, & Tomerelli, 2009).

If ethnic prejudice or even preference function on an implicit level, affecting behaviour but not being explicitly expressed, they may take longer to break down. McGlothlin, Killen, and Edmonds (2005) found that although children may not always exhibit bias in their moral judgements (that is, they will not try to exclude or upset a peer from one ethnic group more than a peer from another ethnic group), they did sharply distinguish between ethnic groups in terms of friendship potential. This supports other research which suggests that children from the same gender and ethnic groups tend to choose friends and playmates from their own ethnic group from an early age (see Finkelstein & Haskins, 1983; Leman & Lam, 2008) which, in turn, exacerbates ethnic division. Ethnic influences on friendship choice can be particularly insidious in terms of increasing prejudice because it reduces the opportunities for contact between children from different ethnic groups. Contact between groups has, traditionally, been proposed as a key means of reducing prejudice

(Allport, 1954; Pettigrew & Tropp, 2006), and even imagining contact with people from another ethnic group can have beneficial effects in terms of improving inter-ethnic attitudes and relations (Turner & Brown, 2008).

Internationally, research is beginning to identify other factors which can contribute to the development of prejudice in children. In a study in Portugal, researchers demonstrated that older children were less likely to exhibit prejudice against black individuals when there were marked anti-racist social norms in a group (Monteiro, de Franca & Rodrigues, 2009). In an experimental study in Australia using children placed in artificial groups, Nesdale et al. (2005) found that prejudice was greatest when a group norm was to exclude, and when that group felt under threat in some way. Younger children (7 years) tended to be more extreme in their dislike of other groups compared with 9 year olds, even when they did not threaten the child's own group. Thus, it is possible to see how social circumstances can interact with cognitive processes to foster prejudice in some groups of children, particularly when they are younger.

Understanding these processes better will help to build more effective programmes for reducing prejudice across a variety of contexts. The psychological research findings have helped greatly to inform programmes for reducing prejudice in childhood – and later in adulthood (e.g., Turner & Brown, 2008). Yet the context and causes of prejudice may well vary from one situation to another, and on-the-ground interventions to effect change often require a consideration of multiple factors. These interventions may well be particularly effective for children who have the potential to enjoy richer and a fuller range of peer relations if they acquire more tolerant attitudes from an early age.

SUMMARY

Biological and psychological factors influence gender development. The process by which children acquire the motives, values, and behaviours viewed as appropriate for males and females within a culture is called *gender typing*. Children develop *gender-based beliefs*, largely on the basis of *gender stereotypes*, which are reflected in *gender roles*. Children adopt a *gender identity* early in life. Of the many traditionally held differences between the behaviours of males and females, some are real, some are found only inconsistently, and some are not borne out by empirical evidence at all.

However, although differences exist, it is important to remember that the overlap between the distributions is always greater than the differences between them. In addition, noting the existence of the differences does not tell us why they exist. Clearly, girls and boys have many different experiences and opportunities as they develop, and these may either lead to divergent outcomes or highlight existing differences.

Children develop gender-typed patterns of behaviour and preferences before they are 2 years old. Girls tend to conform less strictly to gender-role stereotypes than do boys, possibly because parents and teachers exert greater pressure on boys to adhere to the masculine role. Girls may also imitate the male role because it has greater status and privilege in our culture. Although some boys and girls receive support for cross-gender behaviour, most are encouraged to behave according to traditional stereotypes. Gender-typed interests tend to remain stable from childhood to maturity. However, gender roles fluctuate across the life course as adults change to meet the demands of new situations and circumstances, such as child-rearing.

Biological factors that are thought to shape gender differences include hormones and lateralization of brain function. Hormones may organize a biological predisposition to be masculine or feminine during the prenatal period, and the increase in hormones during puberty may activate that predisposition. In addition, social experiences may alter the levels of such hormones as testosterone. Gender differences in the brain's organization may be reflected in the greater lateralization of brain functioning in males, which may help explain male success at spatial tasks. It may also explain female tendencies to be more flexible than males and to better withstand injury to the brain. Exceptionally high prenatal androgen levels in females may be correlated with greater visual-spatial skills later on. Environmental factors also influence both sexes' development of traditional and non-traditional gender-based abilities and interests.

Cognitive factors in children's understanding of gender and gender stereotypes may contribute to their acquisition of gender roles. Kohlberg's three-stage *cognitive developmental theory of gender typing* suggests that children begin by categorizing themselves as male or female, then feel rewarded by behaving in gender-consistent ways. To do this, they must develop gender identity, *gender stability*, and *gender constancy*. *Gender-schema theory* suggests that children need only basic information about gender to develop mental schemas that help them organize their experiences and form rules concerning gender. Some children are more 'gender schematic' than others.

Families play an active role in gender-role socialization in the way they organize their children's environment. They dress boys and girls differently, and give them different toys to play with. In addition, parents – especially fathers – treat girls and boys differently. Parents tend to see boys as stronger, even at birth, and to treat them more roughly and play with them more actively than with girls. As children grow older, parents protect girls more and allow them less autonomy than boys. Parents also expect boys to achieve more than girls in the areas of mathematics and careers. Because the father plays such a critical role in the development of children's gender roles, his absence may be related to disruptions in gender typing. Siblings can have an important impact on each other's gender socialization. Younger siblings tend to model their older siblings' behaviours; in addition, the sex of the older sibling may determine the character of his or her play with a younger sibling. This situation can result in the younger sibling's development of more or less stereotypical gender-role concepts.

Many extrafamilial influences affect gender-role typing. Male and female roles are portrayed in gender-stereotypic ways in many children's books and on television. Males are more likely than females to be portrayed as aggressive, competent, rational and powerful in the workforce. Females are more often portrayed as involved primarily in housework or caring for children. Peers also serve as an important source of gender role standards.

Ethnicity is another aspect of identity that has considerable social and psychological significance for the child. Like gender, ethnicity is often associated with stereotyping, prejudice and social injustice. Ethnic development occurs somewhat after gender development, maybe because there are more ethnic categories for children to learn in a multiethnic society, or because children have fewer experiences of children from other ethnic groups in more monocultural settings. Theories of ethnic prejudice have focused on cognitive and social processes. Recent research points to the importance of children's social group understanding in the development of prejudice. Increasing social contact between children is one effective way of reducing ethnic group prejudice.

Explore and Discuss

1. Girls and boys exhibit different levels of achievement in mathematics and computer-related activities. Do you believe that these differences are biologically based or the result of various cultural influences?

2. Do you think girls and boys should go to same-sex schools or classes?

3. Parents, peers, schools and the media all influence gender roles. Do you think one or more of these factors are more important than the others for children's learning of these roles? Or do you think each influence affects a particular aspect of gender-role learning? If so, which aspect does each impact?

4. How should we seek to reduce ethnic prejudice in children?

5. In what ways is the development of gender understanding similar to the development of ethnic identity, and in what way is it different?

Recommended Reading

Classic

Clark, K., & Clark, M. (1947). Racial identification and preference in Negro children. In T. Newcomb & E. Hartley (eds), *Readings in social psychology*. New York: Holt.

Kohlberg, L. (1966). A cognitive developmental analysis of children's sex role concepts and attitudes. In E. E. Maccoby (ed.). *The development of sex differences* (pp. 82–173). Stanford, CA: Stanford University Press.

Maccoby, E. E., & Jacklin, C.N. (1978). *The psychology of sex differences*. Stanford, CA: Stanford University Press.

Contemporary

Hines, M. (2011). Gender development and the human brain. *Annual Review of Neuroscience, 34,* 69–88.

Hyde, J. S. (2007). New directions in the study of gender similarities and differences. *Current Directions in Psychological Science, 16,* 259–263.

Martin, C. L., & Ruble, D. N. (2010). Patterns of gender development. *Annual Review of Psychology, 61,* 353–381.

CHAPTER 14

Morality, Altruism and Aggression

Introduction

Learning moral rules, and learning how to act according to them is a central part of children's development that feeds in to affect their relationships with others and their psychological well-being. It is frequently assumed that an understanding of right or wrong grows out of a child's interactions with others. However, there are many different interactions and very different types of social interaction that have a moral dimension. For instance, the threat of punishment from a parent and the opportunity to engage in a shared game with a peer offer very different contexts for moral learning.

This chapter considers how moral understanding and behaviour develops, and how this relates to children's prosocial reasoning and altruistic acts, and in turn to how children display or restrain themselves from acts of aggression. The chapter begins with a discussion of two classic theories of moral development – those of Piaget and Kohlberg. We explore the research evidence supporting these theories and some of the criticisms of them. In particular, the importance of cultural differences for our understanding of morality and moral development is considered. More recent approaches, which distinguish different domains of social reasoning are discussed, before turning to consider the links between moral reasoning, affect and behaviour.

The chapter then considers pro- and antisocial behaviour and its development, examining evidence of marked gender differences in each and how positive behaviour can be nurtured and encouraged, and negative behaviour diminished through development. We will discuss gender differences in how people display aggression, alongside questions about the origins of aggressive behaviour.

MORAL DEVELOPMENT

Every society has a system of rules about the rightness and wrongness of certain acts. In every culture, one of the most basic tasks of socialization is communicating ethical standards to the developing child and shaping and enforcing the practice of 'good' behaviour. Adults expect children to learn these rules and to act according to them. Such rules are vital for a well-functioning society and for maintaining good relationships between individuals.

Most adults (and children) will have a pretty good idea of what sorts of things are right and wrong (good and bad). However, deciding about the morally correct or fairest course of action in real-world situations can often be less than straightforward, and moral issues have great potential to generate heated discussion and conflict. Philosophers, judges and politicians spend considerable energy debating ethical issues or deciding on the most ethical course of action. The task of developing an understanding of morality is therefore a potentially complex one that requires that children grasp what the rules are, how they are justified, and when they should be applied. But it also requires an appreciation that people often have conflicting perspectives on an issue which sometimes cannot be easily resolved.

In Chapter 9 we discuss Piaget's theory in relation to cognitive processes; his work on moral judgement connects with this in terms of his interest in epistemological questions and constructivism in the theory. In Chapter 13, we also discuss some of Kohlberg's work outside of moral judgement, proposing a model for the development of gender understanding.

Only when children or adolescents have developed a certain level of moral understanding can society regard them as fully morally responsible. So many psychological approaches to the topic have focused on the development of moral reasoning and judgement. Of course, a child's (and indeed, an adult's) behaviour may not always be consistent with their moral understanding. Complementary research on self-control and conscience have explored the circumstances under which children may not always act as they know they should (e.g., Kochanska, 2002). We consider this research later in the chapter.

Empirical research into moral reasoning can be divided into three basic aspects of morality: cognitive, behavioural and emotional. The cognitive component involves knowledge of ethical rules and judgements of the 'goodness' or 'badness' of various acts. The behavioural component refers to people's actual behaviour in situations that invoke or relate to ethical issues. The emotional component focuses on people's feelings about situations and behaviours that involve moral and ethical decisions. As we will see, these same three components help us understand many aspects in the development of altruism and of aggression.

In general, studies of moral behaviour in children have investigated activities that most adults consider wrong, such as lying or cheating and failing to delay gratification, to resist temptation or to control aggression.

More recently, researchers have also studied positive behaviours, such as sharing, helping, cooperating, and performing prosocial or altruistic acts. Studies of the emotional dimension of morality have also traditionally focused on negative aspects, such as feelings of guilt after a transgression, but more recent work has focused on emotions such as empathy for other people's misfortunes or distress.

> empathy The capacity to experience the same emotion that someone else is experiencing.

Jean Piaget and Lawrence Kohlberg argued that moral development was fundamentally an issue of understanding moral rules. Piaget's explanations involved many of his principles and processes of cognitive growth we discussed in Chapter 9, although he emphasized the importance of children's social relations in moral reasoning and development. Kohlberg based his theory on Piaget's but, in contrast, argued that moral development was underpinned only by cognitive processes.

Piaget's theory of the development of moral judgement

Piaget proposed that the child's moral concepts evolve in an unvarying sequence through three stages. The first, *premoral* or *amoral stage* lasts until about the age of 5; the *stage of moral realism* lasts from about 6 to about 10 years of age; and the third stage of *morality of reciprocity,* or *autonomous morality,* lasts from age 11 onwards. One cannot reach the stage of moral reciprocity without first passing through the stage of moral realism. According to Piaget, mature morality includes both an understanding and acceptance of social rules and a concern for equality and reciprocity in human relationships; these qualities form the basis of justice. For Piaget, then, children's understanding of and involvement in social relations is fundamentally important to understanding moral rules. Piaget investigated children's developing moral judgement in several ways: first by studying how children come to grasp and understand how rules work in the games they play with one another, then by asking children to make and justify their moral judgements in response to moral vignettes. Piaget focused on how children understood the rules of games because, he argued, understanding the system of rules for a game was similar to understanding moral rules. In a game, the rules only make sense because they allow everyone to take part. If players no longer bother to follow the rules, the game becomes meaningless. From his early focus on rules of games, he moved on to look at more recognizable moral understanding.

> vignette A short story that depicts a scenario or situation about which the child has to comment, discuss or make a judgement.

> premoral stage Piaget's first stage of moral development, in which the child shows little concern for rules (also referred to as the amoral stage).

> moral realism Piaget's second stage of moral development, in which the child shows great respect for rules but applies them quite inflexibly.

In his theory Piaget proposed that preschool children are in a premoral stage; they show little concern for, or awareness of, rules. By the time they are 5 years, however, children move into the stage of moral realism, in which they develop great concern and respect for rules. For moral realists, rules come from authority figures, usually a child's parents. Children see rules as immutable, unchanging, and not to be questioned. The rigidity and inflexibility in children's views about rules mirrors children's attitudes to the rules of games. For instance, in a game of marbles or hopscotch, children would regard the rules as sacrosanct even if a new rule or adaptation would improve the game.

Children who are in the moral realism stage (also sometimes referred to as *moral heteronomy*) believe that the consequences of an action, or the likely reaction of an authority figure, are most relevant when deciding whether an act was right or wrong (good or bad); they don't consider the perpetrator's intentions (to do something good or bad) as the key issue in making moral judgements. This is because young children's moral realism is a consequence of *egocentric thinking* – the inability to perceive situations as others may – and they see morality as a one-way street; rules are given from an adult authority figure to a child. Older children, on the other hand, have a finer appreciation of the ways in which morality relates to subjectivity and mutual or reciprocal relations between people. In this sense, children who reason using a morality of reciprocity understand that morality is a two-way street; rules work because we all agree (and intend) to abide by them.

Piaget argued that the development of understanding of moral rules was similar to the ways in which children learned the rules of games.
Source: © Shutterstock/Karen Struthers (L) © Beau Lark/Glow Images (R)

Piaget argues that a morality of reciprocity begins to emerge in older children at about the age of 11. In terms of understanding rules of common games, children now believe that a rule can be changed to make the game better or more fun, but only if everyone agrees to it. They realize that obedience to authority is neither necessary nor always desirable. There is also a shift towards the peer group as a relevant concern in making moral judgements. It is this shift in terms of what morality

> **morality of reciprocity**
> Morality in which moral judgements should be made on the basis of equality and fairness between people, and equal justice for all.

is used for – from regulating adult–child to regulating peer relations – that is the important driver for development. For instance, from around 11 years children begin to regard peer solidarity as an important moral concern. This *autonomous morality* is characterized and underpinned by a belief in mutual respect for others, rather than the unilateral respect for adult authority that was evident in younger years. Children in this stage also believe in 'equalitarianism' – that is, they believe that there should be equal justice for all.

Some of the shifts in attitude from the stage of moral realism to the stage of moral reciprocity are vividly illustrated in Piaget's account of his investigations, *The Moral Judgment of the Child* (1932). Piaget would read paired stories (vignettes) to a child and then ask the child if the children in each story were equally guilty, which child was the naughtier, and why.

Story I.

A little boy who is called John is in his room. He is called to dinner. He goes into the dining room. But behind the door there [is] a chair, and on the chair there [is] a tray with 15 cups on it. John couldn't have known that there was all this behind the door. He goes in, the door knocks against the tray, 'bang' to the 15 cups and they all get broken!

Story II.

Once there was a little boy whose name was Henry. One day when his mother was out he tried to get some jam out of the cupboard. He climbed up on a chair and stretched out his arm. But the jam was too high up and he couldn't reach it and have any. But while he was trying to get it, he knocked over a cup. The cup fell down and broke. (Piaget, 1932, p. 122)

Clearly, Henry tried to deceive his mother. But the child in the stage of moral realism regards John as less ethical because he broke more cups, even though John's act was an accident and unintentional. This was because, for younger children, the child judged the rightness or wrongness on the likely reaction of the adult to the event, or on the amount of material damage done. So whether or not the children were being naughty or not, or were doing something they shouldn't, was not seen as morally 'relevant' for the younger children. For the older children, however, what was important was whether a child was intentionally doing something disobedient, rather than what reaction a parent may have to the events.

> We discuss the development of social relationships, a topic closely related to the development of moral understanding, in Chapter 13.

How well has Piaget's theory fared since 1932? In many studies investigators find regular age trends in the development of moral judgement from moral realism to reciprocity. Although these findings lend support to the general developmental sequence, some findings also suggest that Piaget underestimated the cognitive capacities of young children. This research suggests that in judging the behaviour of others even 6-year-old children are able to consider an actor's intentions when the situation is described in a way they can comprehend. For example, when Chandler, Greenspan, and Barenboim (1973) presented stories to 6 year olds by videotape rather than orally, the younger children responded to the intentions of the actors as well as older children did. Viewing the scenarios probably helps younger children by providing them with more information, such as facial expressions that signal emotional states; these additional clues can help younger ones better infer the actor's intentions. Indeed, recent research with infants (Woodward, 1998, 2005; Gergely & Csibra, 2003), shows that even 8 month olds are able to perceive the intentions of others. This suggests that the development of an ability to understand the intentions of others is unlikely to be the most important factor driving moral development between 5 and 11 years of age. However, it is important to remember that Piaget did not claim that young children could not understand an actor's intentions. Rather, they felt these were not relevant to moral judgements. Instead, younger children felt an adult's reaction was the important determinant of wrong or right.

Piaget's initial investigations may have some methodological flaws, but his key contribution is arguing that social and cognitive processes intersect in terms of moral development. At around 10–11 years, children move from the view of morality as a one-way street where adults dominate, to a two-way, reciprocal process where what is right or wrong depends on what we, as a society of equals, agree upon. This two moral worlds view (Youniss & Damon, 1992) does appear to correspond closely to age-related changes in children's social relationships. Piaget's early work on the topic also drew attention to the importance of rules and cognitive processes in moral judgement – themes that were subsequently picked up by Lawrence Kohlberg.

> **two moral worlds view**
> The view that there is a fundamental shift from heteronomous morality (morality is determined by adults and authority figures) to an autonomous morality (morality where we all participate and agree on moral rules as members of society).

Kohlberg's cognitive theory of moral development

Kohlberg (1969, 1985) based his theory of moral development on Piaget's. However, Kohlberg sought to refine and expand the stages involved in the developmental model, and also extended the age period covered. Like Piaget, Kohlberg believed that the child's cognitive capabilities determine the development of moral reasoning and that moral development builds on concepts grasped in preceding stages. However, unlike Piaget, Kohlberg did not believe that moral judgements and development were intimately connected to children's involvement in social relations.

To test his theory, Kohlberg began by interviewing boys between the ages of 10 and 16, presenting them with a series of moral dilemmas in which they had to choose either to obey rules and authority or to ignore them and respond to the needs and welfare of other people. Here is a representative story presented to Kohlberg's young participants.

> *Heinz needs a particular expensive drug to help his dying wife. The pharmacist who discovered and controls the supply of the drug has refused Heinz's offer to give him all the money he now has, which would be about half the necessary sum, and to pay the rest later. Heinz must now decide whether or not to steal the drug to save his wife; that is, whether to obey the rules and laws of society or to violate them to respond to the needs of his wife. What should Heinz do, and why?*

Development was a consequence of increasing cognitive ability and being able to resolve ethical dilemmas, or conflicts between moral rules, such as those in the *Heinz and the Druggist* dilemma above. On the basis of his findings, Kohlberg formulated a series of three broad levels of moral development and subdivided these into six stages. Each stage was based not only on participants' choices of either an obedient or a need-serving act but on the reasons participants gave and on the ways they justified their choices. Table 14-1 presents these levels and stages of moral development. Kohlberg argued that although the sequence of all six stages is fixed – that is, all people pass through the stages in the same order – they may occur in different people at different ages. Moreover, many people never attain the highest level of moral judgement, and even some adults continue to think in immature terms.

Kohlberg saw behaviour at the preconventional level as based on the desire to avoid punishment and gain rewards (see Table 14-1, Level I). At Level II, the conventional level, although children identify with their parents and conform to

> **preconventional level**
> Kohlberg's first level of moral development, in which he sees the child's behaviour as based on the desire to avoid punishment and gain rewards.

> **conventional level**
> Kohlberg's second level of moral development, in which the child's behaviour is designed to solicit others' approval and maintain good relations with them. The child accepts societal regulations unquestioningly and judges behaviour as good if it conforms to these rules.

Table 14-1 Kohlberg's stages of moral development

LEVEL I PRECONVENTIONAL MORALITY	
Stage 1	
Obedience and punishment orientation	To avoid punishment, the child defers to prestigious or powerful people, usually the parents. The morality of an act is defined by its physical consequences.
Stage 2	
Naive hedonistic and instrumental orientation	The child conforms to gain rewards. The child understands reciprocity and sharing, but this reciprocity is manipulative and self-serving.
LEVEL II CONVENTIONAL MORALITY: CONVENTIONAL RULES AND CONFORMITY	
Stage 3	
Good boy morality	The child's good behaviour is designed to maintain approval and good relations with others. Although the child is still basing judgements of right and wrong on others' responses, he is primarily concerned with their approval and disapproval. It is to maintain goodwill that he conforms to families' and friends' standards.
Stage 4	
Authority and morality that maintain the social order	The person blindly accepts social conventions and rules and believes that if society accepts these rules, they should be maintained to avoid censure. He now conforms not just to other individuals' standards but to the social order.
LEVEL III POSTCONVENTIONAL MORALITY: SELF-ACCEPTED MORAL PRINCIPLES	
Stage 5	
Morality of contract, individual rights, and democratically accepted law	Morality is based on an agreement among individuals to conform to norms that appear necessary to maintain the social order and the rights of others. However, because this is a social contract, it can be modified when people within a society rationally discuss alternatives.
Stage 6	
Morality of individual principles and conscience	People conform both to social standards and to internalized ideals. Their intent is to avoid self-condemnation rather than criticism by others. People base their decisions on abstract principles involving justice, compassion, and equality.

Source: Adapted from Kohlberg (1969).

postconventional level
Kohlberg's third level of moral development, in which the child's judgements are rational, and his conduct is controlled by an internalized ethical code that is relatively independent of the approval or disapproval of others.

what they regard as right or wrong, what they have internalized is the motive to conform, not the notion of ethical standards. It is only at Level III, the postconventional level, that moral judgement is rational and internalized and that conduct is controlled by an internalized ethical code that is relatively independent of others' approval or castigation. At this level, moral conflict is resolved in terms of broad ethical principles, and violating these principles results in guilt and self-condemnation.

In Kohlberg's studies (Kohlberg, 1985; Colby & Kohlberg, 1987), young children gave more preconventional (Level I) responses, and older children gave more post-conventional responses (Figure 14-1). Although as we've said, Kohlberg predicted no specific level of response at any particular age, the general sequence of stages was followed in these participants' responding. The sequence should be invariant across cultures, Kohlberg asserted, although the ultimate level attained may vary among cultures and for individuals within the same society. Once a person has attained a high level of moral cognition, especially Stage 6, he or she will not regress and go back to earlier stages.

Gilligan (1982) argued that Kohlberg failed to take account of possible differences in the moral orientations of females and males. Citing the fact that women usually score lower than men on Kohlberg's tests, and making the observation that Kohlberg's studies included only male participants, Gilligan (1982) suggested that 'the very traits that traditionally have defined the "goodness" of women are those that mark them as deficient in moral development' (p. 18). Researchers have rated most women's moral judgements on these tests at Stage 3. In this stage, the person is motivated primarily to maintain the goodwill and approval of others, although she or he is beginning to accept the notion of social regulations and to judge behaviours in terms of whether people conform to or violate these rules.

According to Gilligan, Kohlberg's theory focused too much on reason, rules and logic as the basis of moral judgements, partly because he studied only males. Gilligan argued that women tend to take a caring and interpersonal approach to moral judgements, whereas men tend to emphasize more abstract concepts such as individual rights and principles of justice. This is because boys and girls acquire different orientations – justice and care orientations respectively – through different socialization experiences. Because the primary caregiver is often female, girls more readily identify with an adult, and at an early age develop a focus on relationships. Boys lack the same opportunities for identification, and hence become more independent and focus less on rules rather than the socio-emotional aspects of relationships.

Gilligan's theory is intuitively appealing. It is

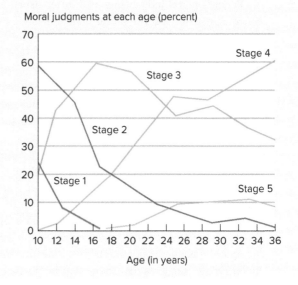

Moral judgments at each age (percent)

Age (in years)

Figure 14-1   How does moral reasoning evolve into adulthood?
Although Level I reasoning was significant in preadolescence, Stage 1 disappeared in the teens and Stage 2 had virtually disappeared by 30. At age 36, Level II, Stage 4 reasoning was the most common, and Level III was barely represented, with a small percentage of Stage 5 responses.
Source: Adapted from Colby et al. (1983).

certainly the case that Kohlberg's failure to include women in his research was a serious omission. However, studies using both hypothetical and real-life situations have yielded no clear baseline gender differences in moral reasoning (Jaffe & Hyde, 2000). In fact, the sort of issue under consideration, other contextual factors, and gender role – the social norms and stereotypes associated with gender – are better predictors of whether an individual will use care or justice orientations when making moral judgements (Sochting, Skoe, & Marcia, 1994; Haviv & Leman, 2002).

Although gender may pose problems for Kohlberg's theory, the notion that children proceed through the stages of moral judgement in an invariant fashion has received general, empirical support (Rest, Narvaez, & Thoma, 2000; Walker, Gustafson, & Hennig, 2001; Turiel, 2006). A powerful longitudinal study of participants' moral reasoning over 20 years (from childhood well into adulthood) using data from Kohlberg's original sample of boys, found that but two participants moved from lower to higher stages, and no one skipped stages (Colby et al., 1983). Although the vast majority stopped at Stage 4, a few (10%) continued to develop their moral reasoning in their twenties, reaching Stage 5 in young adulthood (Figure 14-1). None, however, reached Stage 6. The dominant pattern of moral reasoning in most adults appears to be conventional (Level II, Stage 3 or 4).

A more controversial claim is that the pattern of moral development is universal, Again, empirical support for Kohlberg's theory has been remarkably strong. For instance, studies in Turkey (Nisan & Kohlberg, 1982), Taiwan (Lei & Cheng, 1989), and Israel (Snarey, Reimer, & Kohlberg, 1985) showed that individuals, regardless of their cultural background, developed through the stage sequence in the same manner. In addition, few participants skipped a stage or regressed to a lower stage. However, there are cultural differences. In New Guinea, people place community obligations over individual rights; in India, people emphasize the sacredness of all forms of life. It is also important to note that in some cultures, particularly those in the developing world, moral reasoning levels are generally lower than in Western Europe and North America (Snarey, 1985). This has led some theorists to claim that Kohlberg's focus on individual rights and obligations may fail to recognize how moral understanding and moral norms differ between cultures, often in subtle yet important ways (Shweder et al., 1997; Snarey & Hooker, 2006).

People's moral judgements also differ depending on the way questions are presented. When an issue is couched in abstract form, rather than embedded in a realistic description of a particular situation or conflict, respondents are more likely to support the default position (Helwig, 2003, 2006). For example, when children were simply asked whether they endorsed freedom of speech and religion, nearly all said they did. However, when they were asked the same question in a context in which these freedoms conflicted with other liberties, such as freedom from physical and psychological harm, results were quite different. Fewer children endorsed freedom of speech. Moral judgements involve the need to balance competing moral issues, and Kohlberg's original stories oversimplified the nature of the dilemmas people face in everyday moral decision making.

There is also difficulty with Kohlberg's assertion that moral reasoning is underpinned by cognitive (rational) processes. Emler, Renwick, and Malone (1983) asked undergraduate students to complete a measure of moral reasoning and then scored their responses according to Kohlberg's scale. The researchers also asked the students to complete a questionnaire on political beliefs (e.g., right wing, centrist, left wing). Students who rated themselves as left wing scored higher on the moral reasoning measure than others. However, Emler and colleagues then asked the same students to complete the measure imagining they were the opposite political orientation. This time, the right-wing students (pretending to be left wing) scored higher. Emler's study suggests that there may be political bias in Kohlberg's measure. The study also demonstrates that Kohlberg's exclusive emphasis on cognitive processes neglects to consider how factors other than cognitive ability affect moral judgements and reasoning.

Distinguishing moral judgements from other social rules

social-convention rules Socially based rules about everyday conduct.

Children must learn many rules for behaviour. At the same time that they learn moral rules against cheating, lying, and stealing, they learn many other social-convention rules: table manners, kinds of dress, modes of greeting, forms of address, and other rules of etiquette. According to Elliot Turiel (1983, 2002, 2006), children make clear distinctions between these two kinds of rules. In one study of preschool-age children, researchers asked children how wrong it would be to hit someone, to lie, or to steal (moral rules) and how wrong it would be to address teachers by their first names, for a boy to enter a girls' bathroom, or to eat lunch with one's fingers (social-convention rules) (Nucci & Turiel, 1978). Children and adolescents from second grade to college consistently viewed the moral violations as more wrong than the violations of social convention. Even children as young as 3 can distinguish moral rules from social-convention rules (Smetana & Braeges, 1990). Children view moral violations as more wrong than conventional rule violations, and think that breaking moral rules should lead to more serious punishments.

Research confirms that children tend to identify the same set of core moral issues regardless of their culture, whereas social conventions are seen as more arbitrary, relative, and vary across cultures (Helwig 2006; Turiel, 2006). When asked if it would be acceptable to steal in a country that had no laws against stealing, children as young as 6 thought it was still wrong to steal. However, they thought that people in different countries could play games by different rules (Turiel, Killen, & Helwig, 1987). Cross-cultural research from many countries including Brazil, India, Indonesia, Korea, Nigeria and Zambia, suggests that children and adolescents make a consistent distinction between moral and social-conventional rules (Wainryb, 2006).

How do children learn to distinguish between moral and other transgressions? Children learn from their parents at a very early age that the consequences of eating your spaghetti with your hands or spilling your milk or wearing your shirt inside out are different from those of taking your brother's toy or pulling your younger sister's hair. Mothers of 2 year olds responded to social-convention violations with rules about social order and social regulation that focused on the disorder that the act created ('Look at the mess you made!'). They responded to moral transgressions by focusing on the consequences of the acts for other's rights and welfare or by making perspective-taking requests ('Think how you would feel if somebody hit you!') (Smetana, 1995). Children therefore learn to make the moral-conventional distinction by experience and observing a connection between acts and their consequences (Davidson, Turiel, & Black, 1983).

Parents influence adolescents as well as young children. Teenagers understand and accept that parents may legitimately regulate their moral behaviour (Smetana, 1995). They even accept some parental regulation of social-convention matters (Smetana, 2005). However, they do not agree that parents have a right to regulate personal matters such as their appearance, friendship choices and spending decisions. Conflicts most often arise in this area, and they arise with increasing frequency as the adolescent grows older (Smetana, 2000). Conflicts that mix social-convention and personal issues – for example, cleaning one's own room – are more intense.

Other socializing agents, including teachers and peers, play a part, too. Smetana (1997) found that 2- and 3-year-olds in a child-care centre reacted more emotionally and retaliated more often in the face of moral transgressions than when confronting social convention transgressions. The 3 year olds were likely to make statements about rights ('That's not fair' or 'The rules say that you can't do that'), a major accomplishment. In sum, children can distinguish among different kinds of violations and can do so at a surprisingly early age.

However, as with Kohlberg's theory, Turiel's approach has been criticized for a failure adequately to consider cross-cultural issues. Although there may well be core moral themes that occur in almost all societies, it is a rather different matter to say that the distinction between morality and convention is always the same. For instance, most cultures have a moral prohibition on killing, but how does this help us understand whether a society that has a death penalty for those convicted of murder (killing as a form of punishment or retribution) is a more just, humane, or ethical one than a society that does not? Moral judgements are almost always intermeshed with social, historical and other contextual factors which mean that a binary morality-convention distinction is always likely to be rather too simplistic. In this respect, Shweder, Mahapatra, and Miller (1987) point out that in some societies the boundaries between morality and convention are not so clear cut. How people understand and think about moral rules, and the personal significance of them, may well vary in subtle yet important ways across cultures. These concerns bring into question the usefulness of the morality-convention distinction.

BEHAVIOUR AND MORAL DEVELOPMENT

The maturity of the child's moral judgement does not necessarily predict how the child will actually behave; moral judgement and moral behaviour are often unrelated, especially in young children (Blasi, 1983; Straughan, 1986). Often, behaviour is impulsive and not guided by rational and deliberate thought (Burton, 1984; Walker, 2004). In older children and adults, moral judgements and moral behaviour are more likely to be linked (Kochanska et al., 2002). People who have reached Kohlberg's Level III (Stages 5 and 6) are less likely to cheat than those at lower levels, less likely to inflict pain on others, and more likely to endorse free speech and due process, and to oppose capital punishment (Kohlberg & Candee, 1984; Gibbs, Potter, & Goldstein, 1995; Judy & Nelson, 2000).

Rest et al. (2000) proposed a four-step process involved in executing a moral action. In Step 1, the child interprets the situation in terms of how other people's welfare could be affected by his or her possible actions. In Step 2, the child figures out what the ideally moral course of action would be, given the possibilities in Step 1. In Step 3, the child decides what to do and, finally, in Step 4, the child actually performs the action chosen. So far, we have considered Steps 1 and 2; in the next section, we explore Steps 3 and 4. That is, we focus on the action, or behavioural, component of moral development – deciding what to do and doing it.

Self-regulation and the delay of gratification

One goal for parents is to help children self-regulate, or control behaviour on their own, without reminders from others. The self-regulating aspect of moral development involves children learning to inhibit or direct their actions so as to conform to moral rules. Life is full of temptations, traps, and tugs that pull young children away from the right courses of action (as stipulated by moral rules). Children's ability to resist

> **self-regulation** The child's ability to control behaviour on her own without reminders from others.

these forces is most likely an interaction of both their own emerging cognitive and representational capacities and the guidance that parents, siblings, and other socializing agents provide.

How does this capacity to monitor and regulate one's own behaviour develop? According to Kopp (1982, 2002), it begins with a control phase, when 12- to 18-month-old children first initiate, maintain, modulate, or cease acts when an adult makes a demand. In this phase, children are highly dependent on the caregiver for reminder signals about acceptable behaviours. In the self-control phase, children gain the ability to comply with caregiver expectations in the absence of external reminders. Presumably, this is because the development of representational thinking and recall memory permits these children to remember family rules and routines. In the self-regulation phase, children become able to use strategies and plans to direct their behaviour and to help them resist temptation and to self-delay gratification. Kopp demonstrated these developmental changes by showing children attractive objects such as a toy telephone and telling them not to touch the objects right away. Children who were 18 months old were able to wait only 20 seconds, 24 month olds waited 70 seconds and 30 month olds waited nearly 100 seconds before touching the attractive but forbidden object (Vaughn, Kopp, & Krakow, 1984). Kopp and other researchers extended the study of self-regulation through the preschool period and confirmed the progression in self-control (Kochanska, Coy, & Murray, 2001; Kopp, 2002).

Although all children progress from control by others through self-control to self-regulation, some progress more rapidly and achieve higher levels of control than others. Some children reach the self-regulation phase by 4 or 5 years of age, whereas others continue to rely on adult control to comply with rules. Children who are self-regulators have a stronger sense of 'moral self'; they endorse and internalize parental values and rules, and they make conscious efforts to control their behaviour, even when it requires giving up or postponing pleasurable outcomes (Kochanska et al., 2001; Kochanska, 2002). When they were infants, self-regulators were better at inhibiting their actions.

control phase
According to Kopp, the first phase in learning self-regulation, when children are highly dependent on caregivers to remind them about acceptable behaviours.

self-control phase
According to Kopp, the second phase in learning self-regulation, when the child becomes able to comply with caregiver expectations in the absence of the caregiver.

self-regulation phase
According to Kopp, the third phase in learning self-regulation, when children become able to use strategies and plans to direct their own behaviour and to delay gratification.

self-delay gratification
To put off until another time possessing or doing something that gives one pleasure.

The development of self-control is also promoted by the actions of parents and other caregivers. Consistent and carefully timed punishment, as well as the provision of a rationale for compliance, helps increase children's resistance to temptation (Parke, 1977; Kuczynski et al., 1997). It also helps when an adult shifts their control strategies from physical techniques such as distraction to verbal modalities such as explanations, bargaining, and reprimands as the child grows older (Kuczynski et al., 1987). This adjusted parental input heightens the child's own abilities to use verbally based control strategies (Kopp, 2002). In addition, a mutually responsive orientation involving cooperation and shared positive affect between mother and child aids in conscience development. Children who, as toddlers, enjoyed this kind of mother–child or father–child relationship developed a higher level of conscience – internalized values and standards of behaviour – at 3 and 5 years of age than children in a less mutually responsive parent–child relationship (Kochanska et al., 2008; Kochanska & Murray, 2000).

conscience The child's internalized values and standards of behaviour.

The ability to self-regulate, and to delay or defer gratification, is associated with a raft of positive outcomes into adolescence (Shoda, Mischel, & Peake, 1990). While strategies for delaying gratification do improve (or are acquired) with age from around 5 years, the impulsivity that is associated with a poorer ability to delay gratification may endure across the lifespan. Thus, Mischel and Ayduk (2004) argue for a cognitive-affective personality system (CAPS) which sees an interplay of personality and cognitive factors to explain individual differences in impulsivity or sensation seeking (the need or drive for stimulation). Thus cognitive and affective processes may be dual and contrasting routes to decision-making and risk taking that contrast with self regulation (see Box 14-1). And it should be noted that people can learn to delay gratification with cognitive strategies such as self-distraction and cognitive reframing of tasks, which can allow more purposeful, 'cooler' cognitive processes to overcome the perceived, immediate benefits of not delaying.

BOX 14-1 Adolescent sensation seeking and self regulation across the world

Research close-up

Source: Based on Steinberg et al. (2018).

Introduction:

In Chapter 12 we saw how adolescence may be a time at which risk-taking behaviour is particularly evident. One factor that may well be involved in that is adolescents' relatively immature abilities to self-regulate. Steinberg (2008) has suggested that risk taking is a consequence of dual systems of incentive processing and cognitive control. In adolescence, an easily aroused reward system may be more likely to override self-regulatory mechanisms that can exert control (or inhibit) certain risky behaviours. The relative imbalance in these systems in adolescence is grounded in brain development, but also likely interacts with environmental factors which can frame risk or encourage risky behaviours in certain ways. For example, social expectations of adolescents, and what is and is not appropriate behaviour, may differ for a young person in China and Sweden, Italy and Cyprus. Parental discipline may also differ dramatically between cultures. The present study sought to explore whether sensation seeking and self-regulation are similar for adolescents in different countries, cultures or societies.

Method:

The international research team collected data from 5,404 participants between 10 and 30 years of age. Participants came from 11 different countries: Guang-Zhou and Shanghai in China; Medellin, Colombia; several cities in Sweden; Chang-Mai, Thailand; Nicosia, Cyprus; Delhi, India; Naples and Rome, Italy; Amman and Zarqa, Jordan; Mamila, Philippines; Kisumu, Kenya; Durham and Winston-Salem, United States. The study employed a cross-sectional design.

Participants were given a set of questionnaires including core demographic information and measures of intelligence, three measures of sensation seeking (e.g., a modified version of the Iowa Gambling Task; Bechara et al., 1994) and three measures of self-regulation (including a version of the Tower of London task).

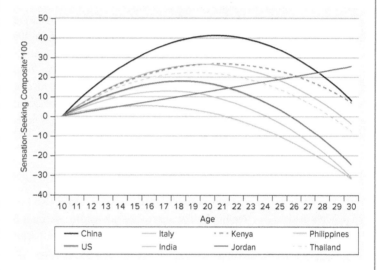

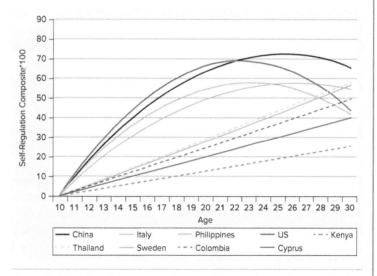

Figure 14-2   National differences in sensation seeking and self-regulation
Broadly, the age-related trajectories for sensation seeking and self-regulation were similar across countries
Source: Steinberg et al. (2018).

Results:

In all countries, and in line with previous work, sensation seeking was higher in adolescents in the samples, peaking at 19 years of age. Self-regulation, on the other hand, showed a steady growth across the sample from 10 years of age, continuing to develop until participants were in their mid-20s. Importantly, the patterns of age-related difference were surprisingly consistent across all the nations involved in the study: a peak in sensation seeking at around 19 years, and a gradual increase in self-regulation until the mid-20s. However, there were some variations in the magnitude of age differences, and four countries (Sweden, Jordan, Colombia and Cyprus) did not exhibit the inverted 'U' pattern of sensation seeking (i.e., peaking in later adolescence).

Discussion:

This study suggests that age-related patterns of self-regulation and sensation seeking behaviour are rather consistent, comparing across several different nations and cultures. However, there were four countries which did not evince the expected pattern of age-related changes in sensation seeking behaviour. All of these countries would appear, on the face of things, to be quite different in terms of opportunities and parenting styles and cultural norms. It is difficult to explain how and why these variations in sensation seeking occur: it may be that deeply embedded cultural practices or norms, or more specific parenting or social (generational) factors may underlie this variation. Future research is clearly needed to understand better how culture and context affects adolescence and adolescents' behaviour.

However, the study supported the aims of demonstrating, broadly, dual processes of incentive processing and cognitive control which exert different pressures or motivations for behaviour. In this respect, while adolescence is certainly a time in life where most adolescents across the world are exploring new experiences, it is also a time at which the ability to control impulsive behaviour is not fully developed.

The affective side of morality

Moral judgements also overlap with emotional processes. Moral transgressions or prosocial acts can lead to anxiety, fear, disgust and elation, to name just a few. Think about how the work on moral judgements and emotion connects with studies and theories of emotional development in Chapter 7.

The development of moral behaviour also involves emotions. We have all experienced 'feeling bad' when we break a rule. We may feel remorse, shame or guilt. Do children have these same emotional reactions? Kochanska, Murray, and Harlan (2002) tested young children at 22, 33 and 45 months. They presented each child with an object that belonged to the experimenter (e.g., a favourite stuffed animal the experimenter had kept from her childhood or a toy she had assembled herself) and asked the child to be very careful with it. However, the objects had been 'rigged' and fell apart as soon as a child began to handle them. Even at 22 months, children 'looked' guilty when the mishap occurred; they frowned, froze, or became upset. At older ages, children were better at masking their guilty reactions; they expressed fewer overt negative emotions. Instead, guilt leaked out in the form of subtle signs such as changes in posture, squirming, hanging the head, and other indications of arousal and upset. When they were later tested at 56 months, the children who had displayed more guilty reactions were less likely to play with forbidden toys than children who had not shown any guilty feelings.

Children who displayed more guilt in the Kochanska study were also more fearful in scary situations, such as climbing a ladder, falling backward on a trampoline, or interacting with a clown. In other research as well, 6- and 7-year-old children who were fearful as infants were rated by their parents as more prone to guilt and shame (Rothbart, Ahadi, & Hershey, 1994). Analyses of Kochanska's data suggested that fearful temperament contributes to guilt proneness, which in turn serves to inhibit children's tendency to violate rules. In contrast, fearless children do not experience remorse, guilt or shame if they violate rules, and because they feel no guilt, the lack of guilt does not deter them from future rule violations.

While we may like to think of ourselves as rational moral thinkers, it may well be the case that our moral judgements and behaviour are frequently affected by emotions and other, personal considerations. For instance, Wark and Krebs (1996) found that people tend to be more forgiving of a moral transgression when it concerns a personal issue than when they are making judgements of behaviour of others (i.e., in the third person). When making moral judgements about matters closer to home we may not be as objective and impartial as we would like to think. Moreover, emotions and intuitions may have a strong, hidden influence on our judgements. Haidt (2001) has proposed a *social intuitionist model* of moral reasoning and behaviour which argues that morals are frequently affected by social processes, are instinctive (intuitive), and are frequently underpinned by emotional considerations. Adults and children may often make up the reasons for a particular action afterwards to explain or justify behaviour, rather than thinking beforehand and then acting accordingly. Haidt's approach suggests that whilst we may use reason to explain or account for our moral judgements, the judgements themselves may stem from more automatic processes. Thus moral judgement may frequently be grounded in more basic, automatic, and even biological (or at least neurophysiological) processes (see Blair, 2003).

PROSOCIAL BEHAVIOUR AND ALTRUISM

Prosocial behaviour is behaviour that is intended to benefit another person or people. It may be motivated by self-interest, practical, moral or other concerns and is grounded in moral emotions including guilt and empathy. Altruistic behaviour is also behaviour that is designed to help someone else, but altruism is generally considered not to be motivated by self-interest. In common use, what distinguishes altruistic behaviour from prosocial behaviour is the willingness to help another without any thought of compensation. Altruistic acts are therefore motivated by internalized values, goals and self-rewards rather than by the expectation of concrete or social rewards. Research has demonstrated that we see the beginnings of prosocial behaviour in quite young children, whereas truly altruistic behaviour occurs only later on (Eisenberg et al., 2006).

> **prosocial behaviour** Behaviour designed to help or benefit other people.
>
> **altruism** An unselfish concern for the welfare of others.

Research suggests that the roots of prosocial behaviour appear very early in development (Warneken & Tomasello, 2009). Even infants show things to others or share their toys. Among 12- to 18-month-old children, showing and giving toys to a variety of other people (mothers, fathers and strangers) is common (e.g., Hay, 1994). Children engage in these early sharing activities spontaneously, without prompting or direction, and without being reinforced by praise.

Sharing and showing are not the only ways young children reveal their capacity for prosocial action. From an early age, children engage in a range of behaviour such as caring for siblings, helping with housework, or comforting others in distress (Hastings, Utendale, & Sullivan, 2007). Children between 10 and 12 months old typically become agitated or cry in response to another child's distress, but they make little effort to help the other child. By the time they're 13 or 14 months old, however, they often approach and comfort another child in distress. This comforting, though, may not be specific to the source of distress. By 18 months, children not only approach a distressed person but also offer specific kinds of help. For example, they may offer a toy to a child with a broken toy or comfort a mother who has hurt herself. By age 2, children engage in a wide range of prosocial actions, including verbal advice ('Be careful'), indirect helping (getting their mother to retrieve the baby's rattle), sharing (giving food to a sister), distraction (closing a picture book that has made their mother sad), and protection or defence (trying to prevent another from being injured, distressed or attacked) (Garner, Jones, & Palmer, 1994; Lamb & Zakhireh, 1997; van der Mark, van Ijzendoorn, & Bakermans-Kranenburg, 2002).

Children do not always show prosocial reactions to others' distress, and indeed they sometimes laugh or behave aggressively or even become distressed themselves (Radke-Yarrow & Zahn-Waxler, 1983; Zahn-Waxler, Robinson, & Emde, 1992; Lamb & Zakhireh, 1997). However, based on a *meta-analysis* of many relevant studies, Eisenberg et al. (2006) found clear evidence that as children grow older they are generally more likely to engage in prosocial behaviours. Specifically, prosocial behaviour increases from infancy and the preschool years through middle childhood to adolescence. Prosocial behaviour not only increases with age; it also appears to be linked with cognitive maturation. Toddlers who display self-recognition are more empathic and prosocial (Zahn-Waxler et al., 2001); preschool children who are able to take another person's perspective are more prosocial (Zahn-Waxler et al., 1995). Prosocial behaviour also increases as children learn to detect other people's emotional cues and realize that they need help (Eisenberg et al., 2006).

One way children exhibit prosocial behaviour is through the sharing of toys.

empathic Able to experience the same emotion that someone else is experiencing.

Consider how gender stereotypes are a strong influence on children's development across domains. These stereotypes can be communicated by parents, peers or the media. These same stereotypes may well underlie many gender differences in moral and prosocial behaviour. Chapter 13 discusses gender development in more detail.

Children's tendencies to donate to needy children, to assist an adult (e.g., by helping pick up paper clips), and to offer others help are consistent across the early years of schooling (Eisenberg et al., 2006). During adolescence, prosocial behaviour towards peers is relatively stable, as is young adults' valuing of concern for others (Malti & Dys, 2018). Thus preschoolers who are prosocial tend to continue to be prosocial throughout development (Baumrind, 1971).

There also appear to be gender differences in prosocial behaviour. However, gender influences vary depending on the type of prosocial behaviour (Fabes & Eisenberg, 1996). Girls tend to be more empathic than boys, especially as they get older (Zahn-Waxler et al., 2001). Yet it is interesting to note that gender differences are more pronounced when the data are derived from self-reports and reports by family members and peers than in data gathered by observational techniques (Hastings, Rubin, & Rose, 2005). This suggests that some gender differences reflect people's conceptions of what boys and girls are *supposed* to be like rather than how they actually behave (Hastings et al., 2007). Parents do stress the importance of politeness and prosocial behaviour more for daughters than for sons (Maccoby, 1998). Moreover, when girls behave prosocially, parents attribute such behaviours to inborn tendencies, whereas they attribute boys' prosocial behaviours to the influences of the environment and socialization. These findings do not mean that gender differences are *only* in the eye of the self or the beholder; rather, cultural stereotypes and beliefs that girls are in some way 'better behaved' contribute to the gender differences researchers have found (Hastings et al., 2007).

Another factor that contributes to gender differences in prosocial behaviour is culture. In particular, culture can modify how gender roles are viewed. For instance, Carlo et al. (1996) found that there was a clear association between a feminine gender role (i.e., how close an individual is in terms of their own beliefs and norms and stereotypes associated with gender) and prosocial reasoning in a Brazilian sample than there was in the USA. There are different cultural norms in terms of what sorts of prosocial behaviour men and women (boys and girls) should exhibit. For example, in Western societies children are typically given very few child-care responsibilities. However, girls tend to play with dolls and thus pick up nurturing skills which the boys rarely display. But in societies where women were expected to play an important role in agricultural work, both boys and girls look after younger siblings and there are few gender differences in nurturance (Whiting, 1983).

Cultural differences in parental practice are important too. Whiting (1983) also found that in a sample from Tarong, in the Philippines, where fathers give significant help to mothers in looking after children, there were few gender differences in boys' and girls' levels of nurturance. In contrast, girls rather than boys are very clearly expected to care for younger siblings in Juxtlaguaca in Mexico. In this context, where labour is strictly divided along gender lines, gender differences in children were greatest.

Determinants of prosocial development

Some evolutionary psychologists argue that human beings have a biological predisposition to respond with empathy and are biologically prepared to engage in prosocial behaviour because being part of a group provides additional protection and support, and increases the chances of individual survival (Sober & Wilson, 1998). As evidence of this, helping and sharing are seen among many infrahuman animals; for example, Preston and deWaal (2002) report both empathy and consoling behaviour in chimpanzees. It has also been claimed that the fact that human newborns cry in response to the cries of other infants is evidence of such a biological predisposition to behave in an empathic fashion (Hoffman, 1981, 2000).

BOX 14-2   Is altruism instinctive?

Source: Based on Warneken and Tomasello (2006).

Introduction:

Many researchers, philosophers and others have argued that the expression of altruism – helping others or performing a positive act with no immediate benefit to oneself – is unique to human beings. A key aim for the present study was to compare whether or how far young children and non-human primates (chimpanzees) offer assistance to someone who needs it. Most previous research with chimpanzees has suggested that they are highly competitive, rather than altruistic or cooperative in their behaviour. However, much of this research is based on studies that involve food – a highly desirable commodity for chimpanzees – which might obscure altruistic tendencies. Research evidence from studies with children and infants suggests that young children and infants appear to respond to other people's distress, sometimes trying to comfort them. However, a further key contribution from the present study was that the researchers sought to explore whether young children offer instrumental help – actively assisting someone to perform an action – when it is needed or desired.

Method:

Twenty-four 18-month-old infants (either prelinguistic or just linguistic) were presented with ten different situations. In each of these situations the adult male experimenter had difficulty achieving a goal. For instance, the adult tries without success to reach something he had dropped, or is blocked from putting some magazines away in a cupboard. Each situation was matched to a control task where the adult had no difficulty achieving the goal. The control tasks ensured that infants' responses were just due to a desire to see the adult repeat the task or put things back the way they were. The tasks were also repeated with three young chimpanzees (36, 54 and 54 months old) who had been raised in captivity by humans. In no tasks did infants or the chimpanzees receive or expect to receive any benefits for their help. Hence, helping behaviour could be interpreted as altruistic.

Results:

By comparing the infants' actions in the control and experimental versions of the task, the researchers showed that only two of the 24 human infants failed to help the adult at all, and this was significant in six of the ten tasks. This help took various forms, such as handing or retrieving objects that the adult couldn't reach, and opening the cabinet door. In contrast to the human infants, the chimpanzees engaged in instrumental help in some of the tasks, but only those that required reaching for an object.

Discussion:

The study demonstrates that infants offer instrumental help in a variety of different situations, and so have a strong capacity to behave in altruistic ways. The study also demonstrated instrumental helping in non-human primates, specifically chimpanzees. However, the chimpanzees only helped on reaching tasks, and this may be because trying to get an out-of-reach object offers clearer cues about the intentions or goals of the person requiring help. These strong cues mean that the reaching scenario amounted to a cognitively simpler task than the others. The authors conclude that there are certainly differences between humans and other species in terms of the level, frequency and types of cooperative behaviour that they display. However, there is evidence of helping behaviour in chimpanzees, human's closest evolutionary relatives, which suggests that the capacity for altruism is not uniquely human.

There is also evidence that individual differences in prosocial behaviour may have a genetic basis. Identical, or monozygotic, twins are more alike in prosocial behaviour (Davis, Luce, & Kraus, 1994) and empathic concern (Zahn-Waxler, Klimes-Dougan, & Kendizora, 1998) than are fraternal, or dizygotic, twins. Other studies of identical twins underscore the combined role of genetic and environmental factors in the development of children's prosocial behaviour (Hastings et al., 2005). For example, in a study of identical preschool-age twins, Deater-Deckard et al. (2001) found that both genetic and environmental factors (e.g., maternal supportive and punitive behaviours) contributed to children's prosocial behaviour. Further support for the genetic basis of prosocial behaviour comes from the study of children with genetic abnormalities. Children who have Williams syndrome (marked by loss of the long arm of chromosome 7) are more sociable, empathic, sympathetic and prosocial than children who do not have Williams (Mervis & Klein-Tasman, 2000; Semal & Rosner, 2003). Twin studies suggest that genetic influences become more important with age (Scourfield et al., 2004). In other words, genetically inherited tendencies to be more or less prosocial are more evident in older children.

Temperament (see Chapter 7) may also play a role in the likelihood of children's sympathetic responding and prosocial behaviour, just as it appears to influence children's ability to inhibit undesirable responses. For example, highly inhibited 2 year olds became more upset by another's distress than their less inhibited peers (Young, Fox, & Zahn-Waxler, 1999). Similarly, children who can regulate their emotions better, as indexed by measures of heart rate, are more likely to exhibit comforting behaviour (Eisenberg, Fabes, & Murphy, 1996).

Sources of environmental influence on prosocial behaviour include the family, peers and the media. Laboratory studies in which children see people donate to or share with others, as well as real-life situations in which parents, peers and others model prosocial behaviours, demonstrate that children acquire prosocial behaviours through social learning (e.g., Hay, 1994; Hart & Fegley, 1995). Daughters whose mothers are sensitive to their emotions, who try to find out why they feel bad and listen to them when they are anxious and upset, display more prosocial behaviour; for example, they will comfort an infant in distress (Eisenberg et al., 1993). The way that mothers talk about emotions matters, too. Preschoolers whose mothers explain their own feelings when they are sad display more prosocial behaviour (Denham, 1998; Denham et al., 2007). In addition, children who have opportunities to engage in prosocial actions, by volunteering at homeless shelters, for example, develop more prosocial attitudes and behaviour (Johnson et al., 1998; Metz, McLellan, & Youniss, 2003; Pratt et al., 2003).

As the study in Box 14-3 shows, parents' child-rearing practices also contribute to children's prosocial behaviour. Parents who use power-assertive techniques (e.g., physical punishment) and little reasoning and who show little warmth are unlikely to have altruistic children. In a study in the Netherlands, Dekovic and Janssens (1992) found that democratic parenting (parenting that is warm, supportive, and demanding and that provides guidance and positive feedback) was linked to more prosocial behaviour in children as rated by both teachers and peers. Studies in other countries have, similarly, indicated that when parents were negative and controlling and intolerant of children's distress, children were less empathic and prosocial (Asbury et al., 2003; Strayer & Roberts, 2004).

Applied
Developmental
Psychology

BOX 14-3 How parents can teach children prosocial behaviour

To find out how children learn to react in helpful ways when they have caused distress in another person or when they see another person suffering, Zahn-Waxler, Radke-Yarrow, and King (1979) devised a clever scheme. They trained mothers of 18 month olds to tape-record their children's reactions to others' distress that the children themselves either caused or witnessed. The mothers recorded both the child's and their own behaviour over a 9-month period, during which observers occasionally visited the home to check on the accuracy of the mothers' records. The researchers also asked the mothers to simulate distress from time to time: for example, mothers might pretend to be sad (sobbing briefly), to be in pain (bumping their feet or heads, saying 'Ouch' and rubbing the injured parts), or to suffer respiratory distress (coughing/choking).

How did the children respond to others' distress? Overall, whether they had hurt someone else or merely witnessed another person's distress, they reacted in a helpful fashion about a third of the time. However, some children responded in most distress situations (between 60% and 70%), whereas others failed to respond at all.

Mothers' reactions to their own children's harmful behaviour towards others, as well as to the sight of another person's distress, were related to their children's helpful behaviour in distress situations. Some mothers linked a child's behaviour with its consequences for the child's victim; the children of these mothers were more likely to respond in a helpful way when they caused harm to someone. These mothers might say, for example, in a clear but objective manner, 'Tom's crying because you pushed him.' Other mothers' discussions of distress situations had strong emotional overtones, and these explanations appeared to be even more effective. The children of these mothers were more likely to intervene in bystander situations when they did not cause any harm but saw that someone else was upset. These mothers might say something like, 'You must never poke anyone's eyes' or 'When you hurt me, I don't want to be near you. I am going away from you.'

More recent studies have confirmed these findings. For example, children of mothers who pointed out a peer's personal distress in an affectively charged manner tended to react in a sad fashion (Denham, Renwick-DeBardi, & Hewes, 1994). However, some maternal tactics were ineffective in encouraging prosocial behaviour. For example, physical restraint (simply moving away from the child or moving the child away from a victim), unexplained prohibitions ('Stop that!'), or physical punishment, may even interfere with the development of prosocial behaviour. These researchers also found that when mothers showed anger as they delivered their disciplinary reasoning and tried to induce guilt in children, preschoolers were unlikely to engage in parent-directed prosocial actions.

Prosocial and altruistic behaviour can begin early, and parents play an important role. They can facilitate and encourage the child's emerging altruistic behaviour by helping children make connections between their own actions and others' emotional states.

Parents who explicitly model prosocial behaviour and provide opportunities for children to perform these actions may be particularly successful in promoting altruism. A common way parents provide opportunities for learning prosocial behaviour is by assigning children responsibility for household tasks. Even 2 year olds will help adults in a variety of tasks such as cleaning, and setting tables (Rheingold, 1982). Allowing children to help in these ways may be important for their prosocial development.

Peers also act as models and shapers of children's prosocial behaviour. In one study, preschoolers who were exposed to prosocial peers at the beginning of the school year engaged in more prosocial peer interactions later in the year (Fabes, Martin, & Hanish, 2002). However, in general, children who were less prosocial spent their time with other less prosocial children, while highly prosocial children played together. As a result of this 'prosocial segregation', children who are low in prosocial behaviour have few chances to learn more prosocial practices from their prosocial peers. Moreover, preschoolers who initiated more altruism received more altruism from their peers a year later, although the converse was not true. Only the state of being the recipient was not related to increases in receiving altruistic behaviour from peers. Being an active participant in being helpful and kind probably led to reciprocity of prosocial acts from peers (Persson, 2005).

In some cultures, children are given more responsibility for taking care of siblings and performing household tasks. What effect does this have? Cross-cultural studies of children from a wide range of societies – Mexico, Japan, India and Kenya – suggest that children who perform more domestic chores and spend more time caring for their infant brothers, sisters and cousins are more altruistic (Whiting & Whiting, 1975; Whiting & Edwards, 1988). Similar results have been found in cultures that stress communal values, such as that of the Aitutaki of Polynesia, the Papago Indian tribe in Arizona, and many Asian cultures (Chen, 2000; Zaff et al., 2003; Eisenberg et al., 2006). Further evidence of the role of culture comes from studies of children raised in Israeli kibbutzim, which stress prosocial and cooperative values. Children reared in these communal settings are more prosocial than their city-reared peers (Aviezer et al., 1994).

Cultural norms, practices and traditions vary, and consequently prosocial behaviour and reasoning varies from one society to another (Hay, 1994). For instance, when given the choice of whether or how much money to distribute to unknown others, Chinese school children were slightly, but significantly, more generous than their German equivalents (Gummerum, Hanoch, & Keller, 2008). Given that both gender roles, and moral and prosocial reasoning vary across culture, it is perhaps unsurprising that these different environmental factors interrelate to affect the sorts of judgements that children and adults make. A major challenge for researchers is to unpick the ways in which social and cultural processes feed in to specific judgements and behaviour.

Perhaps understandably, because they are different sides of the same coin, there is also a link between prosocial behaviour and aggressive behaviour. However, the relation may not be quite as clear cut as one might think. Osbuth et al. (2015) studied 7–11 year olds' aggressive and prosocial behaviour in a longitudinal study. While higher aggressive behaviour predicted lower prosocial behaviour one year later, prosocial behaviour did not predict any changes in aggressive behaviour subsequently. Moreover, the link between aggressive and prosocial behaviour was mediated by peer difficulties (teacher ratings of whether a child was popular, isolated or victimized). This link was particularly pronounced in the first three years of schooling.

Prosocial behaviour is likely dependent on the broader social and cultural context (for instance, what values and behaviours are communicated and rewarded in school and at home), but is also increasingly connected with peer groups and friendships into adolescence (see chapter 12). Another, large longitudinal study (Di Giunta et al., 2018) of prosocial behaviour involved Italian boys and girls (10–14 years). Some of the sample was also subsequently followed up at 16–17 years of age. Children who were less prosocial and more aggressive at 10 years tended to follow a trajectory towards peer rejection later in their development. Boys who tended to be more rejected by peers at the later post-test showed high levels of delinquency and low levels of academic aspiration at the follow up when ages 16–17 years. Rejected girls showed low levels of academic aspiration and social competence at 16–17 years. And, being less attractive was associated with high levels of peer rejection at 10–14 years. These findings suggest a complex interplay where behaviours can lead to different social engagements and relationships which may (or may not) reinforce certain behaviours. Better understanding about how positive behaviours can buffer against peer rejection could be helpful in promoting interventions.

Prosocial reasoning

> **prosocial reasoning**
> Thinking and making judgements about prosocial issues.
>
> **hedonistic reasoning** Making a decision to perform a prosocial act on the basis of expected material reward.

Prosocial behaviour shifts in form and expression across development. These changes reflect changes in prosocial reasoning, which in turn reflect changes in children's cognitive development. Eisenberg and her colleagues (Eisenberg et al., 1999, 2001b, 2006) proposed a model of the development of prosocial reasoning that is similar to the Kohlberg model of the development of moral reasoning.

Eisenberg and her colleagues tested children when they were 4.5 and 11.5 years old, and again in early adulthood. As the children matured, they became less egocentric and more other orientated, and they became more capable of abstract reasoning about prosocial dilemmas. The first type of reasoning, shown in Table 14-2, was hedonistic reasoning, in which children based their decision to

Table 14-2 Evolution of prosocial reasoning

Level	Age group	Orientation	Mode of prosocial reasoning
1	Preschoolers and younger school children	Hedonistic, self-focused	Child is concerned with self-orientated consequences rather than moral considerations
2	Preschoolers and school children	Recognition of needs of others	Child expresses concern for the physical, material and psychological needs of others, even if these needs conflict with her own
3	School children and adolescents	Seeking others' approval and acceptance	Child uses stereotyped images of good and bad persons and behaviour and considerations of others' approval and acceptance in justifying prosocial or not helping behaviour
4	Older school children and adolescents	(a) Empathic	Child's judgements include evidence of sympathetic responding, self-reflective role taking, concern with the other's humanness, and guilt or positive affect related to the consequences of her actions
5	Minority of adolescents	(b) Transitional (empathic and internalized)	Child's justifications for helping or not helping involve internalized values, norms, duties or responsibilities, but may not be clearly expressed
6	Only a small minority of adolescents and virtually no school children	Strongly internalized	Child's justifications for helping or not helping are based on internalized values, norms or responsibilities, the desire to maintain individual and societal contractual obligations, and the belief in the dignity, rights, and equality of all individuals

Source: Adapted from Eisenberg, Lennon, and Roth (1983).

perform a prosocial act on the promise of material reward. This type of reasoning decreased with age. The second type of reasoning was needs-orientated reasoning. This was still a relatively simple type of reasoning in which children expressed concern for the needs of others, even though these needs conflicted with their own. It peaked in middle childhood and then levelled off. The higher types of reasoning listed in the table were empathic and prosocial; they all increased with age. Hedonistic reasoning was related to less sharing and empathy; needs-orientated reasoning was related to more prosocial behaviour; prosocial reasoning was related to more prosocial behaviour that required some cognitive reflection (Carlo et al., 2003).

needs-orientated reasoning Reasoning in which children express concern for others' needs even though their own needs may conflict with those needs.

Researchers have found that there are cultural differences in prosocial reasoning, as there are differences in prosocial behaviour. For example, in Asian countries, people are often considered to take a more collective approach to social and interpersonal behaviour compared with people in Europe and North America, placing emphasis on the welfare of the group rather than of the individual. However, even within Western countries there are differences in prosocial reasoning. In Germany and Israel, children are more likely than children in the United States to emphasize direct reciprocity, whereby they expect to receive payback for their prosocial actions (Eisenberg et al., 1985); in Brazil, urban adolescents are less likely to use high-level prosocial reasoning than US teens (Eisenberg et al., 2001). Clearly, cultural values not only shape prosocial behaviours but also organize the ways people think about their prosocial obligations to others.

THE DEVELOPMENT OF AGGRESSION

Aggression refers to behaviour that is intended to and does harm to other people by inflicting upset, pain or injury on them. For many years, psychologists have puzzled over the knotty problem of aggression. Why do some children attack others? Why do some adults cheat, rob, attack, and murder others? Do patterns of aggression change over time, and if so, how? What roles do genes, families, peers, and the mass media play in the development of aggression? From a more applied perspective, some researchers have asked, how can we control aggression in our children?

aggression Behaviour that intentionally harms other people by inflicting pain or injury on them.

instrumental aggression Quarrelling and fighting with others over toys and possessions.

A visit to any school will reveal striking age differences in the forms and frequency of aggressive behaviour. Preschool children are more likely to quarrel and fight over toys and possessions; this is instrumental aggression. Older children are more likely to exhibit hostile aggression – personally orientated aggressive acts in which the child criticizes, ridicules, tattles on, or calls the person names (Dodge, Coie, & Lynam, 2006). This shift from fighting over things to fighting over human characteristics and behaviour may occur as older children acquire a greater ability to infer the intentions and motives of others (Ferguson & Rule, 1980). When older children recognize that another person wants to hurt them, they are more likely to retaliate by a direct assault than by an indirect attack on the aggressor's possessions.

hostile aggression Directing aggressive behaviour at a particular person or group, criticizing, ridiculing, telling tales or calling names.

Children also differ in how accurately they can 'read' another person's intentions. Some children, especially those who are highly aggressive, have more difficulty judging other people's intentions (Crick & Dodge, 1994). This is especially helpful in ambiguous situations, when children's intentions are not clearly either aggressive or prosocial. In such situations, boys who are rated by their classmates as more aggressive are likely to react in a hostile way – as if the other person intended to be aggressive. Aggressive boys see the world as a threatening and hostile place. The reason for their negative views may be based on their experience: aggressive boys not only commit more unprovoked aggressive acts, but they are also the targets of more aggressive attacks (Dodge & Frame, 1982). Researchers have found that aggressive children make more hostile attributions about other people's behaviour (Graham & Hudley, 1994; Guerra & Huesmann, 2003).

reactive aggression
Aggressive behaviour as a response to attack, threat or frustration.

proactive aggression
The use of force to dominate another person or to bully or threaten others.

We can also characterize aggressive acts in terms of their causes, or in terms of who initiates them. Some children act aggressively only in response to being attacked, threatened or frustrated, displaying reactive aggression. These children are particularly likely to misinterpret others' intentions (Poulin & Boivin, 2000). Other children – playground bullies – show proactive aggression, using force to dominate another person or to threaten another to gain a prized object or possession. They are quite accurate in reading others' intentions, but they don't care about their intentions, just about dominating them. Like instrumental aggression, proactive aggression generally decreases across development (NICHD Early Child Care Research Network, 2004).

The ways children express their aggression also change over development. Toddlers rely more on physical attacks; older children, with their improved communication skills, are likely to be verbally rather than physically aggressive. This developmental shift is due not only to increased verbal skills but also to changes in adult expectations and rules. Most adults become less tolerant of physical aggression as children mature but are more likely to ignore a 'battle of words' even among older children. A few older children continue to express aggression physically, however; they fist fight at age 8, vandalize at age 12 and may commit even more serious aggressive acts into adulthood (Dodge et al., 2006).

Although in general the level of aggression declines as children grow older, and learn to solve problems and conflicts through more socially acceptable means, individual differences in aggressiveness are quite stable over time, and those who are particularly aggressive in childhood are likely to remain so into adulthood (Dodge et al., 2006). In one study of more than 600 children originally seen at 8 years of age, researchers found that the more aggressive 8 year olds were still more aggressive than their peers at age 30 (Huesmann et al., 1984; Bushman & Huesmann, 2001). The boys who were rated in childhood as aggressive were more likely as adults to have committed antisocial acts later in life such as being arrested for drunk driving, and abusing their wives; both boys and girls who were rated as aggressive as children were more likely to have criminal convictions by age 30 (see Figure 14-3). In other longitudinal studies,

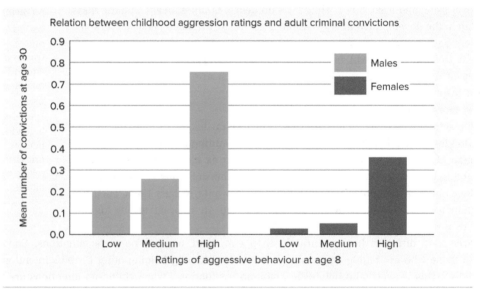

Figure 14-3   The relation between childhood aggression and adult criminal behaviour
Among males, the correlation between highly aggressive behaviour in childhood and the number of criminal convictions in later life was .75, which is extremely high. The same correlations for boys who showed little or only moderate aggressiveness in childhood were much lower, as were all the same correlations for females. Note, however, that among females we see the same tendency of rising correlations as the degree of early aggression escalates.
Source: Adapted from Huesmann et al. (1984)

too, young children who were ill-tempered at age 3 had more problems with aggression 6 years later (Campbell, 2000); ill-tempered 8- to 10-year-old boys experienced more erratic work lives and more marital instability than their even-tempered peers by the time they were 40; ill-tempered girls also experienced more marital instability and were less adequate and more ill-tempered mothers (Caspi, Elder, & Bem, 1987; Kokko & Pulkkinen, 2000). Clearly, an early pattern of aggressive behaviour has some continuity across the lifespan.

Gender differences in aggression

Although there are few gender differences in aggression in infancy, by the time they are toddlers, boys are more likely than girls to instigate and be involved in aggressive incidents (Maccoby, 1998). This gender difference is evident not only across socioeconomic groups and reappears in many different countries, including Britain, Canada, Ethiopia, India, Kenya, Switzerland, the Philippines, Mexico, New Zealand,

Girls are more likely to use verbal tactics when having a disagreement, rather than overt aggression. Boys are more physically aggressive.
Source: © Shutterstock/Iakov Filimonov

the USA, Sweden, Finland and Japan (Whiting & Whiting, 1975; Björkqvist, Österman, & Lagerspetz, 1993; Broidy et al., 2003; Dodge et al., 2006). Boys' and girls' aggression differs in important ways. Boys are more likely than girls to retaliate after being attacked (Darvill & Cheyne, 1981), and they are more likely to attack a male than a female (Barrett, 1979). Boys are more physically confrontational, and their expressions of physical aggression are more frequent than those of girls (Broidy et al., 2003; Ostrov & Crick, 2006). Boys are less likely than girls to engage in negative self-evaluation, they are less likely to anticipate parental disapproval for acting aggressively, and they are also more likely to approve of aggression (Perry, Perry, & Weiss, 1989; Huesmann & Guerra, 1997).

In attempting to resolve conflicts, girls tend to use such strategies as verbal objection and negotiation, methods that may make the escalation of a quarrel into overt aggression less likely (Eisenberg et al., 1994). However, this does not mean that girls are not aggressive. Rather, girls use different tactics to achieve their goals. At the start of schooling, girls often use what is called relational aggression, or the damaging or destruction of interpersonal relationships (Underwood, 2003; Ostrov & Crick, 2006). Relational aggression often includes attempts to exclude peers from group participation, spread nasty rumours and gossip about negative attributes. Often, children may seek to ostracize others, rather than directly confront them. As girls enter adolescence, they tend to make increasing use of the aggressive strategy of excluding others from social cliques (Crick et al., 1999, 2004; Underwood, 2003; Xie, Cairns, & Cairns, 2005). Although relational aggression becomes more common as girls get older, even preschool girls show significantly more relational aggression and are less overtly aggressive than boys (Crick, Casas, & Mosher, 1997).

> **relational aggression**
> Damaging or destroying interpersonal relationships by such means as excluding another or gossiping about or soiling another's reputation.

Relational aggression is significantly related to social and psychological maladjustment; boys and girls who engage in this type of aggression are more likely to be rejected by their peers (Crick et al., 2004; Ostrov & Crick, 2006). Although this kind of aggression may be less overt, other children notice it, and they may ostracize those who engage in it, creating a vicious cycle of conflict between cliques and groups. More girls than boys view this type of aggression as hurtful and even view it as being as hurtful as physical aggression (Galen & Underwood, 1997; Underwood, 2003). Boys tend to view physical aggression as more hurtful.

Table 14-3 and Figure 14-4 illustrate some of the differences between these two types of aggression and between girls' and boys' use of these behaviours.

Table 14-3   Some characteristics of overt and relational aggression in school children

Overt aggressors	Relational aggressors
Hit, kick, punch other children	Try to make other children dislike a certain child by spreading rumours
Say unkind things to insult others or put them down	Exclude another person from a group of friends
Tell other children that they will beat them up unless the children do what they say	Tell friends that they will stop liking them unless the friends do what they say
Push and shove others	Ignore the person or stop talking to him or her
Call other children nasty names	Try to keep certain people out of their own group during activity or play time

Source: Crick (1997); Ostrov and Crick (2006).

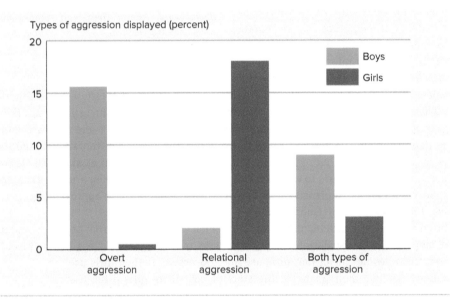

Figure 14-4   Aggression in boys and girls
Boys and girls do not differ greatly in the amount of aggression they express, but they express it in quite different ways.
Source: Based on Crick and Grotpeter (1995).

Biological origins of aggressive behaviour

There are many biological factors that can influence behaviour. This is certainly the case with aggressive behaviour. Our genetic inheritance ultimately starts this process, by giving rise to the proteins which cause the development of particular neural structures, and important chemicals in the body (hormones and neuro-transmitters). Nonetheless, the interaction between genes, environment and chemicals in the body is a complex one and by no means one way (e.g., hormones can also influence whether particular genes are 'switched on'. Nonetheless, studies of twins give support to the view that there is an important role for genetic factors in aggression (Rhee & Waldman, 2002; Dionne et al., 2003). Dionne and her colleagues found that, according to parents' ratings of aggressive behaviour, 18-month-old Canadian identical twins were more similar than non-identical twins. Research with adolescents yields similar findings. Research in the Netherlands,

Sweden and Britain has obtained similar results (Van Den Oord, Boomsma, & Verhulst, 1994; Eley, Lichtenstein, & Stevenson, 1999).

One of the important ways genes can influence aggression is through their interaction with hormones such as testosterone (e.g., by increasing their production, or increasing the nervous system's sensitivity to them). The link between hormones and aggression can be seen rather clearly in adolescence, when hormone levels rise (Moeller, 2001). Brooks and Reddon (1996) found that adolescent violent offenders had higher levels of testosterone than non-violent or even sexual offenders. In a study of 15- to 17-year-old boys in Sweden, Olweus et al. (1988) also found a link between testosterone and aggression. Boys whose blood showed higher levels of testosterone rated themselves as more likely to respond aggressively to provocations and threats from others and were also more impatient or irritable. This increased their readiness to engage in unprovoked and destructive kinds of aggressive behaviour (e.g., to start fights or say hostile things without provocation).

Tremblay et al. (1998) found another link between testosterone and aggression. In this case, testosterone was related to body mass, which in turn was linked to increased physical aggression. Even when researchers controlled for child-rearing practices, these hormonal effects held. Boys rated as tough and who were seen by their peers as social leaders had the highest testosterone levels, although they were not necessarily higher in everyday aggression. Tough, dominant boys, however, may be more likely to respond aggressively to provocation by lower status peers.

Hormones may affect aggression in girls as well (Brook et al., 2001). Levels of hormones, especially estradiol, that increase during puberty were positively linked with adolescent girls' expressions of anger and aggression during interactions with their parents (Inoff-Germain et al., 1988).

Interestingly, other work has suggested that there may be reciprocal effects; that is, dominance or success in conflict may lead to a rise in testosterone levels (Schaal et al., 1996). For example, winning a judo contest leads to increases in testosterone levels, but losing results in a drop in levels of this hormone (McCaul, Gladue, & Joppa, 1992; Dodge et al., 2006).

Serotonin, a neurotransmitter that is involved in emotional states and the regulation of attention, has also been linked with aggression in both humans and animals (Herbert & Martinez, 2001). Modulation of levels of serotonin and the brain's receptivity to it are another way genetic variation can influence levels of aggression. In one two-year study, Kruesi et al. (1992) found a negative relation between the severity of children's physically aggressive behaviour and levels of the neurotransmitter serotonin; the lower the level of serotonin, the higher the level of aggression. However, a combination of low levels of serotonin and a history of family conflict was evident in the most violent offenders, a reminder that the environment and biological factors operate together (Moffitt & Caspi, 2006).

Biological and environmental influences on aggressive behaviour

Temperament (itself influenced by biological and genetic factors) is also linked with aggressive behaviour. Infants with difficult temperaments – those who are irritable, whiny, unpredictable, hard to soothe, and prone to negative affect – are more likely to develop aggressive behaviour patterns at later ages (Rothbart & Bates, 2006).

However, it's very important to remember that biological factors do not act independently of the social environmental context; their influence on aggressive behaviour is exacerbated under certain conditions, such as a provoking and threatening situation or a high-risk environment (Raine, 2002; Dodge et al., 2006). A Swedish study of adopted children illustrates the interaction of biology and environment (Cloninger et al., 1978, 1982). When both the child's biological and adoptive parents were criminals, 40% of the adopted boys were likely to engage in criminal acts. If only the biological parent was a criminal, this declined to 12%; if only the adoptive parent was a criminal, it declined still further to 7%. If neither parent was a criminal, the proportion of adopted males who engaged in criminal acts dropped to only 3%. A similar gene–environment interaction was found for girls.

The debate over whether aggressive behaviour is caused by environmental or biological processes mirrors the nature–nurture debate throughout developmental psychology and introduced in Chapter 1.

A study of more than 4000 males in Denmark also illustrates the interaction of biology and environment on aggression. In this study, a combination of birth complications and early rejection by the mother predicted that adolescents would be involved in violent crime by the time they were 19 years old. Among the young offenders who had experienced both risk factors, 40% became violent, whereas only 20% of those who experienced only one risk factor committed violent crimes (Raine et al., 1998). Finally, a study of Australian 15 year olds tells a similar story: The most aggressive adolescents were those who were exposed to both biological risks (e.g., maternal smoking during pregnancy, low birth weight, and difficult temperament) and environmental risks (e.g., poverty, harsh discipline, family instability) (Brennan et al., 2003). This wealth of evidence clearly supports the view that biology and social environments operate together to produce aggressive children.

Research close-up

BOX 14-4 The changing relationship between internalizing and externalizing behaviour: shyness and aggression from childhood to early adulthood

Source: Based on Hutteman et al. (2009).

Introduction:

Aggression is often characterized as an *externalizing behaviour* – that is, difficulties or problems that are experienced by individuals are displayed or become evident in some sort of social or public settings, and the difficulties affect behaviour directed towards others. In contrast, *internalizing behaviour* is self-directed and entails consequences for the self. For instance, anxiety or depression would be an example of internalizing behaviour. A number of psychological disorders can be characterized as internalizing (e.g., avoidant personality disorder) or externalizing (e.g., antisocial personality disorder) while others such as borderline personality disorder involve both internalizing and externalizing behaviours.

Research suggests a complex developmental relation between internalizing and externalizing behaviour. For instance, some studies have found evidence to suggest that internalizing tendencies might protect children from developing externalizing problems. Other studies have found the two behaviours to co-occur with, for instance, both conduct problems and depression co-occurring over the course of childhood and adolescence.

The present study sought to explore the interplay between an externalizing behaviour, that is, aggressiveness, and an internalizing behaviour, that is, shyness.

Method:

The researchers recruited 230 boys and girls as participants from Munich, Germany. The main caregiver (usually the mother) rated their child on their shyness and aggressiveness when children were 4, 5, 6, 7, 8, 10 and 12 years of age. At 17 and 23 years of age both parents rated their child. Researchers also collected data from participants on the quality of their social relationships at age 17, and interviewed participants about transitions in their lives. The researchers used a cross-lagged design to explore the relationship between ratings at younger ages and subsequent ratings at older ages.

Results:

The association both within and between ratings of shyness and aggressiveness at the different ages are shown in Figure 14-5. In childhood, the pattern of the relation between shyness and aggressiveness (the internalizing and externalizing behaviours) remains fairly predictable. That is, children who were shy at age 6 years became less aggressive at 7 years; similarly, shy children at 8 years were less aggressive at 10 years. However, between 17 years and 23 years there was an interesting change in the direction of this relation. Specifically, the adolescents who had been shy at 17 years actually showed significant increases in their aggressiveness at 23 years. Moreover, interestingly, this finding of a shift between 17 and 23 years was only evident for adolescents who had low levels of support from their parents or who spent little time in part-time work.

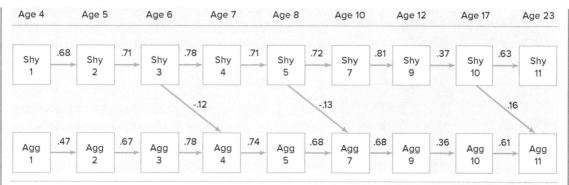

Figure 14-5   The cross-lagged model of stability and cascade effects between shyness and aggressiveness from age 4 to 23; all displayed paths are significant at p < .05

Discussion:

The study indicates that the way in which difficulties are expressed changes with development. The researchers argue that the results support the 'acting out' theory in that shyness in adolescence is subsequently revealed by showing aggression in adulthood. Moreover, environment and context may play an important role by interacting with individual differences. For instance, displays of aggression may be condoned more in certain contexts, and similarly some contexts may cause people to feel more social anxiety and be more shy than others. Clearly parental support and a sense of fulfilment from work are associated with problem behaviours outside the home in early adulthood. The findings also run against the 'failure theory', which suggests that externalizing behaviour results in failed social interactions which, in turn, can lead to social withdrawal and shyness.

This research has important implications for developmental and clinical psychology because it demonstrates how different forms of externalizing and internalizing behaviour are not fixed, but interrelate in often complex ways from childhood. Therapists need to consider these developmental changes, as well as the importance of person–environment interactions, when seeking to address problem behaviours.

Parenting and aggression

Although most parents do not view themselves as actively encouraging aggressive behaviour, some parents deliberately teach their children, especially boys, to 'defend' themselves or to 'be a man' (Anderson, 1998). But this is not the only way children learn aggression from their parents. When parents argue or fight with one another and, especially, fail to resolve their conflicts in positive ways, their children frequently notice, and may pick up subtle messages about the limits of acceptable behaviour.

In addition, parents' methods for punishing or disciplining their children may contribute to their children's aggression. Parents who use physical punishment such as smacking or slapping are likely to have aggressive, hostile children. This is especially the case when that punishment is inconsistent (Cohen & Brook, 1995; Patterson, 2002), or when the parent–child relationship lacks warmth (Deater-Deckard & Dodge, 1997; Caspi & Moffitt, 2006). Some researchers have suggested that the link between physical punishment and aggressive behaviour consists not so much in the physical act, but in the message that this form of punishment sends to a child about their relationship specifically, and norms in other relationships more generally (Lansford et al., 2004).

> The use of physical punishment is associated with certain forms of parenting such as authoritarian (in Baumrind's typology), which we discuss in more detail in Chapter 12.

In a meta-analysis of over 300 studies, Gershoff (2002) found that the use of physical punishment was associated with a raft of negative outcomes for the child, including higher levels of aggression and lower levels of moral reasoning and poorer mental health. The only, arguably, beneficial outcome was that children who had received this form of punishment were more quickly compliant than those who had not. Thus, there may be limited benefits of physical punishment in the short term, but it seems that these are benefits for the parent rather than for the child. The weight

Whether her parents have smacked her or a sibling in her presence, this little girl has clearly received the message that misbehaviour is to be physically punished
Source: © Monkey Business Images/Shutterstock

of evidence suggests that, in the longer term, physical punishment does damage. Consequently, many European countries now prohibit the use of physical punishment as a form of discipline.

Researchers have found that the family environments of aggressive and non-aggressive children are strikingly different (Patterson, 1982, 2002). Aggressive children's parents tend to be erratic and inconsistent in their use of punishment for deviant behaviours and ineffective in rewarding children for prosocial behaviours. They punish their sons more often, even when the children are behaving appropriately. Such inept parenting practices often lead to cycles of mutually coercive behaviour. Children are not passive victims in this process; they often develop behaviour patterns in which they quite purposely use aversive behaviours – such as whining and being difficult or committing directly aggressive acts – to coerce parents into giving them what they want. Children learn that such coercive behaviours can help them control the behaviour

of other family members, including that of siblings. When sibling pairs engage in coercive exchanges, especially if the older sibling is already delinquent, the younger sibling is more likely to become delinquent too (Slomkowski et al., 2001). A combination of rejecting parenting and sibling conflict is an especially potent recipe for later conduct problems (Garcia et al., 2000). The most appropriate model of discipline recognizes that parents, siblings and children all influence one another and all contribute to the development of aggression.

Parents not only influence their own children; their influence often continues across generations. Scaramella and Conger (2003) examined patterns of parent–adolescent interaction and then re-examined these same adolescents when they became parents themselves. The investigators found that adolescents who received hostile parenting were more likely to repeat this style of angry and coercive parenting with their 2 year olds. In turn, their toddlers exhibited more problem behaviours, including aggression. Cross-generational continuity was not inevitable, however. One factor that affected cross-generation consistency was the 2 year old's emotional reactivity (i.e., how much the child reacted to parental control with an angry emotional reaction). In families in which the young child was high in negative emotional reactivity, there was continuity in hostile parenting from one generation to the next, but when the child was less emotionally reactive, there was no link across generations.

Lack of parental monitoring is also associated with high rates of delinquency (Pettit et al., 2001; Patterson, 2004). Children's development of aggressive behaviour may depend as much on parents' awareness of activities in the surrounding community and their efforts to control negative aspects of these activities as on their direct child-rearing practices. Laird et al. (2003) found that when parents and adolescents spend more time together and have a more enjoyable relationship, monitoring is higher and antisocial behaviour is less likely.

Developmental trajectories of aggression

Patterson and his colleagues showed how children progress from aggression problems in early childhood to full-fledged delinquency in adolescence (Figure 14-6). A negative trajectory starts as a consequence of the early experience of poor parental disciplinary practices and lack of monitoring (Patterson, DeBarshyshe, & Ramsey, 1989). When these children enter school, two things typically happen: their peer group rejects them, and they experience academic failure (Ladd, Birch, & Buhs, 1999; Buhs & Ladd, 2001; Ladd, 2005). In late childhood and early adolescence, these now antisocial children seek out deviant peers who, in turn, provide further training in antisocial behaviour and opportunities for delinquent activities (Dishion, Poulin, & Burraston, 2001; Coie, 2004). Among adolescents, aggression is in some cases not only tolerated but admired and viewed as 'cool' (Cillessen & Mayeux, 2004b). In spite of their status among their peers, antisocial youth are more likely to be school dropouts, to experience marital problems and to end up in jail (Patterson & Bank, 1989).

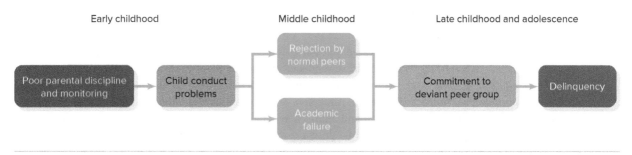

Figure 14-6   The origins and progression of antisocial behaviour
Note that parents, peers and school all play a role in the emergence of antisocial behaviour, but do so at different stages in development.
Source: Adapted from Patterson, DeBarshyshe, and Ramsey (1989)

If the family environment is already encouraging antisocial behaviour before children are 5 or 6 years old, they are more likely to develop serious and persistent delinquent behaviour than if they start on the deviance road at a later age – in middle to late adolescence (Dishion et al., 2001; Moffitt, 2003). These late starters may have avoided the social rejection and school failure common among early starters as well as early family encouragement of antisocial behaviour. Early starters also may be at greater risk owing to biological factors. Children who experience perinatal or birth complications, maternal illness during pregnancy, poor infant temperament, limited language understanding and deficits in executive functioning – combined with social risks such as poverty – are the most likely to be aggressive adolescents at age 15 (Brennan et al., 2003). Early starters are also ten times more often boys than girls (Moffitt et al., 2001; Moffitt, 2003).

Children may also learn about aggression from TV and other media. Several researchers have argued that exposure to aggressive models on TV can increase children's aggressive behaviour (Bushman & Huesmann, 2001; Comstock & Scharrer, 2006). Heavy doses of TV violence can also affect children's attitudes, leading them to view violence as an acceptable and effective way to solve interpersonal conflict (Dominick & Greenberg, 1972). There is a research consensus, from studies in several societies, of a link between TV violence and aggression; in Australia, Finland, Great Britain, Israel, the Netherlands and Poland (Huesmann & Miller, 1994; Bushman & Huesmann, 2001). Moreover, it seems that the total time spent watching TV in adolescence and early adulthood is positively associated with greater aggression (Johnson et al., 2002).

Other sources of aggressive behaviour

Although the idea of a link is broadly endorsed by researchers, a major challenge for research in the area is to demonstrate that viewing violent TV, and other media *causes* aggression in children. Many studies in the area rely on children's or their parents' reports of their viewing and aggression, or on observational techniques that are sometimes liable to bias or inaccuracy. Experimental studies are difficult to conduct ethically, and those that have been carried out tend to be based in laboratories that do not always satisfactorily mirror real-world viewing patterns or experiences. Research in the area often involves careful analysis of and longitudinal studies of viewing and behaviour. An example of one such study (Huesmann et al., 2003) examined the relations between TV violence and viewing at ages 6 to 10 years and participants' aggressive behaviour 15 years later as adults. The researchers found that exposure to violence as a child was associated with aggression in adulthood for both men and women. Aggression was also higher if participants identified with aggressive characters in a TV show, or if they perceived violence to be realistic. The association held even when other social factors such as socioeconomic status, intelligence and parenting were controlled.

Frequent viewers of TV violence may also become immune to violence on TV (i.e., they show less emotional reaction when viewing televised aggression) (Cantor, 2000) and indifferent to real-life violence (Drabman & Thomas, 1976). Exposure to TV violence affects children differently depending on their cognitive abilities. Children who were told that a violent film clip was real (a newsreel of an actual riot) later reacted more aggressively than children who believed that the film was a Hollywood production (Atkin, 1983).

As children develop and are able to make the fiction–reality distinction, many TV programmes may have less impact (Bushman & Huesmann, 2001).

Unsurprisingly, it has also been suggested that video and computer games influence aggressive behaviour as well (Comstock & Scharrer, 2006). Empirical evidence suggests a clear association between violent video games and aggressive behaviour (Krahe & Moller, 2004; Anderson, Gentile, & Buckley, 2007) as well as desensitization to actual violence (Carnagey, Anderson, & Bushman, 2007). Although there is a clear connection between TV and video game violence and aggressive behaviour, a further confounding factor in making causal links is that certain individuals may be drawn towards violent viewing and games. Thus, individuals predisposed to viewing violent content may seek out and watch more of it. For instance, video games that are designed for boys tend to be more violent, preferred by boys, and played more often.

Research close-up

BOX 14-5   Is aggression socially learned?

Source: Based on Bandura, Ross, and Ross (1961).

Introduction:

Bandura proposed that children learn through social processes such as social conditioning and from observation or adult models. How might this apply in the context of children's aggressive behaviour? Specifically, do children pick up aggressive behaviour from watching adults engaging in such behaviour? In a now classic study, Bandura tested the hypothesis that children would exhibit more aggressive behaviour if they observed an adult model behaving aggressively.

Method:

The researchers tested 36 girls and 36 boys who were enrolled at the Stanford University Nursery School, ranging in age from 37 to 69 months. On average the children involved were 52 months old (a little over 4 years). The experimenters matched children in terms of ratings of aggressive behaviour by a researcher and teacher at the nursery, based on their behaviour during interactions with other children at the nursery school.

Participants were divided into an *aggressive* and a *non-aggressive* condition, as well as a control group. Children were brought individually to a room and entered with an adult 'model'. The adult engaged in a task involving making potato prints and stickers to make a picture scene. There were both male and female adult models.

In the aggressive group, the adult model then went to another corner of the room where there were some other toys and a 3-foot tall Bobo doll (a doll that balances to remain upright, even when knocked over). The adult began by assembling the toys but after a minute began 'aggressing' towards the Bobo doll, punching it on the nose, hitting it on the head with a mallet and kicking it about the room. The sequence of events was repeated three times and was accompanied by the adult being verbally aggressive. The whole testing session lasted 10 minutes.

In the non-aggressive condition the adult model simply assembled the picture and then played with the toys. The children in the control group had no interaction with an adult model.

Children were given a brief aggression arousal procedure ostensibly to ensure that children had some motivation or stimulation to act in an aggressive way in the subsequent post-test. Children were then tested to see if they would imitate the adult model. The child was taken to another room containing a number of attractive toys, but after two minutes the experimenter returned and told the child she could no longer play with these toys. Instead, the experimenter told her that she could play with toys in another room. In this final room there were toys that might be used for aggressive or non-aggressive actions, including the Bobo doll, mallet and peg board, and a tether ball with a face painted on it, hanging from the ceiling. Children spent 20 minutes in the room, and their behaviour was observed and coded to identify imitative aggressive acts such as kicks and strikes towards the Bobo doll. Imitative non-aggressive acts and non-imitative acts of aggression and non-aggression were also assessed and coded.

Results:

The number of acts by boys and girls in each condition are detailed in Table 14-4. Often findings from this study are presented as indicating that all children simply followed the aggressive adult model. However, as the data in Table 14-4 show, the picture is rather more complicated than that. Statistical analyses showed that children in the aggression condition differed from non-aggressive and control children in their imitative physical, verbal and non-verbal behaviour in the post-test. For non-imitative aggression and partial imitation, however, results were less clear cut. It appears that children did imitate the adult model's aggression in quite specific ways.

Table 14-4   The mean aggression scores for experimental and control participants

| | Experimental groups | | | | Control |
| | Aggressive | | Non-aggressive | | |
	Female model	Male model	Female model	Male model	
Imitative physical aggression					
Girls	5.5	7.2	2.5	0.0	1.2
Boys	12.4	25.8	0.2	1.5	2.0
Imitative verbal aggression					
Girls	13.7	2.0	0.3	0.0	0.7
Boys	4.3	12.7	1.1	0.0	1.7
Mallet aggression					
Girls	17.2	18.7	0.5	0.5	13.1
Boys	15.5	28.8	18.7	6.7	13.5
Punches Bobo doll					
Girls	6.3	16.5	5.8	4.3	11.7
Boys	18.9	11.9	15.6	14.8	15.7
Non-imitative aggression					
Girls	21.3	8.4	7.2	1.4	6.1
Boys	16.2	36.7	26.1	22.3	24.6
Aggressive gun play					
Girls	1.8	4.5	2.6	2.5	3.7
Boys	7.3	15.9	8.9	16.7	14.3

Some other interesting findings were that boys seemed to show greater levels of aggression, and particularly when paired with an aggressive male model.

Discussion:

The study gives strong evidence to suggest that children copy adults in terms of displays of aggression. This appears to be particularly a matter of direct imitation of certain acts rather than some generalized aggression. However, there are important methodological considerations that could limit the applicability of the study to wider situations. The study was conducted in a laboratory-type setting and this may not mirror the sorts of day-to-day situations in which children might experience or witness adult aggression. Children may feel a greater need to comply with adult norms in such a situation. However, there would appear to be a good case to suggest that witnessing acts of aggression in a more natural setting or as a more commonplace act might lead to even more aggression from children than

Bobo doll.
© ImageZoo/Alamy Stock Photo

in this rather unusual environment. Wider testing of these processes in different contexts helps to secure the findings and inferences about processes of social learning of aggression that are found in this study.

Methodological refinements aside, it is unlikely that such a study could be conducted today because of ethical concerns. It is now widely accepted that adult aggression is associated with displays of aggression in children, or other psychological harm or damage. These ethical concerns are underscored by some observations from Bandura's own report where he noted how some children reacted with surprise to acts of aggression. Specifically, children tended to comment on the ways in which female aggressive adult models violated sex role norms. One remarked, for example, 'Who is that lady? That's not the way for a lady to behave. Ladies are supposed to act like ladies …' and 'You should have seen what that girl did in there. She was acting just like a man'. Although gendered expectations for physical aggression no doubt exist today, Bandura's study may be dated not only in approach to research ethics, but also to its attitudes to women's and men's behaviour.

Peers, especially deviant peers, can encourage other children's aggressive tendencies. Researchers have found that if a child's friends engage in disruptive behaviour (e.g., disobedience or truancy), the child is more likely to engage in either overt delinquent behaviour (e.g., fighting) or covert delinquent behaviour (e.g., stealing) both concurrently and a year later (Keenan et al., 1995; Thornberry et al., 2003). Displays of aggressive behaviour may also depend upon how far a young person feels part of a group, or how visible he or she is within a group (Ellis & Zarbatany, 2007). Peer group influence can become more marked in adolescence. There is some evidence suggesting that in adolescence children (especially boys) are, in fact, rather tolerant of indirect aggression – sometimes, it is even associated with greater peer acceptance and popularity (Salmivalli, Kaukiainen & Lagerspetz, 2000).

Other environmental conditions such as living in a poor, high-crime neighbourhood increase children's aggression, but these effects interact with other social contextual factors such as family functioning which, in turn, is associated with poverty and unemployment. In a study of children with an average age of 9 years, Kupersmidt et al. (1995) found that living in a middle-class neighbourhood acted as a protective factor in limiting the aggression displayed by children from high-risk families. However, there was a downside: these children tended to be more likely to be rejected by their peers, perhaps because their backgrounds and behaviour did not conform to the norms within the wider community.

Control of aggression

How can we control children's aggression? One of the most persistent beliefs about aggression is that if people have ample opportunity to engage in aggressive acts they will be less likely to act on hostile aggressive urges. This process, whether it is actual or symbolic, is known as catharsis. The central idea is that if aggressive urges build up in an individual a violent outburst will occur, unless this accumulating reservoir of aggressive energy is drained. The implications are clear: provide people with a safe opportunity to behave aggressively, and the likelihood of antisocial aggression will be reduced. In clinical circles, there is widespread belief in catharsis. People are often encouraged to express aggression in group therapy sessions. There are punching bags on many wards in mental hospitals and Bobo dolls, pounding boards, and toy guns and knives in play therapy rooms.

catharsis Discharging aggressive impulses by engaging in actual or symbolic aggressive acts that do not impinge on another person.

However, most studies suggest that aggressive experiences may promote rather than 'drain off' aggressive urges. In a classic test of the issue, Mallick and McCandless (1966) allowed third-grade children to shoot a toy gun after being frustrated by a peer who interfered with a task they were working on. Another group of children were allowed to work on arithmetic problems after the peer upset them. Then all the children were given a chance to express their aggression towards the peer who had upset them. The researchers used a rigged procedure in which children thought they were delivering a shock to the other child; in reality, of course, they were not delivering shocks to anyone. Whether the children, after being frustrated by the peer, had shot the toy gun or worked on math problems made little difference in their delivery of 'shocks'. Thus, catharsis did not explain any reduction in aggression.

Another group of methods that have been suggested to reduce aggressive behaviour are described as *cognitive modification strategies*. According to the social information-processing approach to aggression, aggressive children may behave in a hostile and inappropriate fashion because they are socially unskilled; that is, they're not very good at solving interpersonal problems (Dodge et al., 2006). In several studies, researchers who asked children and adolescents to come up with solutions to conflict problems in social situations found that aggressive participants in the studies offered fewer solutions than their non-aggressive peers (Crick & Dodge, 1994; Gifford-Smith & Rabiner, 2004). Moreover, the proposals that aggressive children and adolescents suggested were generally less effective than those less aggressive individuals offered.

> **socially unskilled**
> Being unskilled at solving interpersonal problems.

Making aggressive children and adolescents aware of the negative consequences of aggression for themselves and others through modelling and explanations can reduce aggression, and teaching and encouraging children to use alternative problem-solving behaviours such as cooperation or turn taking have also been found to reduce aggression (Chittenden, 1942; Guerra et al., 1997). One study found that teaching children how to read another person's behaviour more accurately – especially helping them to reduce if not wholly give up their biases towards making hostile attributions about other people and their behaviour – led to a decrease in aggression among African American boys (Hudley & Graham, 1993). This approach is especially effective with reactively aggressive children, who are poor at reading other people's intentions. Empathy and sympathy also play important roles in the control of aggression. There is a clear link between sympathy, empathy and lower levels of aggression in children, as well as less delinquency in adolescents (Laible, Carlo, & Raffaelli, 2000; Strayer & Roberts, 2004). Training children and adolescents to be more empathic and sensitive to the views, perspectives and feelings of others can be an effective way of reducing their aggression (Guerra et al., 1997).

Some psychologists are putting these findings into practical use. Curricula have been developed to improve the social problem-solving skills of aggressive children, and some success has been reported in studies in both the United States and Sweden (Weissberg & Greenberg, 1998; Stevahn et al., 2000). Researchers found that when teachers taught lessons in conflict resolution to their 6 and 12 year olds, these children were less aggressive over time (Aber et al., 2003). The children made fewer hostile attributions, showed fewer conduct problems, and exhibited less aggressive behaviour and more prosocial behaviour. Box 14-6 describes an example of a successful school-based intervention programme.

BOX 14-6 Reducing bullying in schools

Applied Developmental Psychology

Bullying is a worldwide problem (Smith, Pepler, & Rigby, 2004). What is bullying? 'Bullying is aggression directed repeatedly and specifically towards a specific victim who is, in most cases, weaker than the bully' (Schneider, 2000, p. 106). Between 15% and 30% of children report being victims of bullying (Fonzi et al., 1999; Smith et al., 2004). In fact, according to a Canadian observational study (Craig & Pepler, 1997), an incident of bullying occurs every seven minutes in a typical school. Physical or direct bullying (e.g., pushing, hitting) occurs more often among boys, whereas verbal or indirect bullying (e.g., name-calling, excluding others) is more common among girls. Bullying increases through the early years of schooling, up to adolescence and beyond. Bullying in the workplace is increasingly a concern. Not only is bullying hurtful to children who experience it at the time; both bullying and being bullied are related to poorer emotional and social adjustment (Juvonen et al., 2003).

What can be done about this problem? One of the most ambitious efforts comes from Dan Olweus (1993), who launched a nationwide campaign to reduce bullying in schools in Norway and Sweden. The programme enunciated four primary goals: (1) increase awareness of the problem of aggression among the general public and provide schools with information to increase their knowledge about aggressive behaviour; (2) get teachers and parents actively involved in the programme; (3) develop clear classroom rules to combat aggressive behaviour, such as *We will not bully others; We will help students who suffer bullying by others; We will include students who have been excluded*, and (4) provide support and protection for the victims of aggression.

Because it is well known that parents, teachers and children themselves may all contribute to the levels and kinds of aggressive behaviour children display, the programme was designed to target all three groups. The programme's main components were as follows.

- A booklet was prepared for school personnel that described the nature and scope of aggression in the schools and that offered practical suggestions about what teachers and other school personnel could do to control or prevent aggressive behaviour. For example, the booklet stressed the importance of increasing not only teachers' awareness of their responsibility to control interpersonal aggression in school but the awareness of other adult personnel as well and the importance of providing more adequate supervision of students during play times. The booklet encouraged teachers to intervene in bullying situations, and to give students the clear message that 'aggression is not acceptable in our school'. In addition, the booklet's guidelines advised teachers to initiate serious talks with victims, their aggressors and the children's parents if aggressive attacks persisted.
- A four-page folder was designed to address all parents, giving them basic information and in particular offering assistance to parents of both victims and aggressors.
- A video cassette was prepared, showing episodes from the everyday lives of two children who were victims of aggressive attacks.
- Students were asked to fill out a short questionnaire anonymously, providing information about the frequency of aggressor/victim problems in the school and describing the ways teachers and parents had responded, including how aware they were of the problem and how ready to take action to deal with it.

Although the programme was made available to all schools in Norway and Sweden, the researchers based their detailed evaluation of its effectiveness on data from about 2500 children in classes in 42 primary and junior high schools in Bergen, Norway. Did this multilevel cross-national campaign aimed at reducing aggression work? The answer was clearly yes.

Both 8 and 20 months after the intervention programme was initiated, the levels of aggressive behaviour the researchers reported were markedly reduced. Fewer children reported being attacked by others, and fewer children reported that they themselves had acted aggressively. Peer ratings told a similar story: classmates reported that both the 'number of students being bullied in the class' and 'the number of students bullying others' showed a marked drop. In addition, general antisocial behaviour such as vandalism, theft and truancy declined significantly, and student satisfaction with school life rose appreciably. Similar programmes have been launched in many countries with at least some success (Juvonen et al., 2003; Smith et al., 2004). Although we can't be sure just which aspects of these programmes (class rules, teacher awareness, parental intervention) were most important in achieving these effects, intervention clearly can make a difference in reducing this worrisome problem.

SUMMARY

The socialization of moral beliefs and behaviour is one of the main tasks in all cultures. Psychological research has focused on the three basic components of morality: cognitive, behavioural and emotional. Piaget proposed a three-stage approach: the *premoral stage*, the stage of *moral realism*, and the stage ruled by a *morality of reciprocity*, also called *autonomous morality*. Moral absolutism characterizes moral realism. In contrast, children in the stage of reciprocity recognize intentionality and the arbitrariness of social rules in their moral judgements. For Piaget, the essence of morality consisted in children's understanding of social relations and the rules that guided conduct within them.

Kohlberg proposed a theory of the development of moral judgement in which each of three levels contains two stages. The order of development is fixed and invariant, and movement is generally from lower levels – the *preconventional* and *conventional levels* – towards a higher one: postconventional level. Moral judgements continue to develop into adulthood, but few individuals reach the most advanced level (Stages 5 and 6). Gilligan suggested that Kohlberg's model emphasizes a masculine orientation, focusing on rights and logic, whereas an interpersonal and caring orientation may more accurately describe women's moral reasoning and judgements. Kohlberg's theory may be flawed in some ways. The theory's third level is controversial; relatively few people reach this level and, in particular, the sixth stage of moral reasoning. In addition, cross-cultural research suggests that Kohlberg's theory is culture-bound. *Social-convention rules*, such as table manners and forms of address, are distinct from moral rules and follow a different developmental course; in fact, children learn quite early to distinguish these kinds of rules from each other. Moral judgements do not always lead to moral behaviour, particularly among very young children.

Self-regulation, the ability to inhibit one's impulses and to behave according to social or moral rules, proceeds through three stages: the *control phase*, the *self-control phase* and the *self-regulation phase*. In the latter phase, children become capable of *delaying gratification*. Children can learn to use strategies and plans to help them postpone rewards and attend to a task at hand. The development of *conscience* is linked with children's achievement of self-regulatory capacities. Both self-regulation and conscience are linked with mother–child relationships that are positive, responsive and cooperative.

Prosocial behaviour begins very early; helping, sharing and exhibiting emotional reactions to the distress of others appear in the first and second years of life. *Altruism* may also appear quite early. Parents influence the emergence of *altruistic behaviour* by their direct teaching in 'distress' situations, by providing models, and by arranging for opportunities to behave in prosocial ways. Girls tend to be more prosocial than boys, but gender differences depend on the type of prosocial behaviour being expressed. Children's *prosocial reasoning* evolves over time through a number of stages, including *hedonistic reasoning* and *needs-orientated reasoning*, as values and norms become increasingly internalized.

Aggression undergoes important developmental shifts: younger children show more *instrumental aggression*, whereas older children display more person-orientated or *hostile aggression*. Children's ability to correctly infer intent in others – which varies among individual children – may account, in part, for these shifts. *Proactive aggression*, which is used to dominate another person, decreases across development more than *reactive aggression*, which occurs in response to being attacked. The expression of aggression changes over time, becoming more verbal as children mature, but the amount and quality of aggression remain fairly stable. Clear gender differences in aggression are evident, with boys instigating and retaliating more than girls. Girls are more likely to use *relational aggression* than boys, who are more likely to use physical aggression. Aggression is moderately stable over age for both sexes.

Certain parental disciplinary practices, especially ineffectual and erratic physical punishment, contribute to high levels of aggression in children. Lack of parental monitoring of children is another contributor to later aggressive behaviour or even serious delinquency. Biological influences on aggression include genetic, temperamental and hormonal factors. All of these factors find expression in interaction with the environment. Association with deviant peers can increase the possibility that a child will engage in aggressive or delinquent activities. Poverty and high-crime neighbourhoods can also promote aggressive behaviour.

Catharsis theory, the belief that behaving aggressively against a safe target can reduce aggression, has been seriously challenged by research evidence. Strategies that involve cognitive modification may be more successful. Some aggressive children who are *socially unskilled* may be helped to learn more prosocial behaviours through teaching them how to read others' behaviour more accurately and encouraging them to be more sensitive to the views and feelings of others. Increasing children's awareness of the harmful effects of aggression is an effective control technique, as are eliciting cooperation and improving the problem-solving skills of aggressive children.

---

1. Are there two moral worlds: one where children feel obliged to obey the rules of adults, and one where they can act more freely and make moral judgements for themselves?

2. Morality has behavioural, emotional and cognitive components. When a child is confronted with a moral problem, how do you think each of these components comes into play?

3. Altruistic behaviour involves helping or assisting others. Do you think acting in this manner has a positive effect on the actor? On the person receiving the help? Explain your answers.

4. Do children 'learn' aggression by watching adults behaving aggressively?

5. Violence in schools has received a great deal of attention in the mass media. How can we explain and reduce bullying?

Explore and Discuss

Classic

Bandura, A., Ross, D., & Ross, S.A. (1961). Transmission of aggression through imitation of aggressive behaviours. *Journal of Abnormal and Social Psychology, 63*, 575–582.

Kohlberg, L. (1969). Stages and sequences: The cognitive development approach to socialization. In D. A. Goslin, (ed.), *Handbook of socialization theory of research* (pp. 347–480). Chicago, IL: Rand McNally.

Piaget, J. (1932). *The moral judgement of the child.* London: Routledge & Kegan Paul.

Contemporary

Eisenberg, N., Morris, A. S., McDaniels, B., & Spinrad, T. L. (2009). Moral cognitions and prosocial responding in adolescence. In R. M. Lerner & L. Steinberg (eds), *Handbook of Adolescent Psychology* (pp. 229–265). Hoboken, NJ: Wiley.

Haidt, J. (2001). The emotional dog and its rational tail: A social intuitionist approach to moral judgement. *Psychological Review, 108*, 814–834.

Hymel, S., & Swearer, S. M. (2015). Four decades of research on school bullying: An introduction. *American Psychologist, 70*(4), 293–299. http://dx.doi.org/10.1037/a0038928

CHAPTER 15
Atypical Development

with Alice Jones

Introduction

Throughout the first 14 chapters of this book, we have focused on the normal or typical development of children. In this chapter, we turn to an intriguing but often painful and poorly understood area of development: disorders of developmental psychology. Shifting our focus from the 'typical' to what is considered 'atypical', we pursue an understanding of why some children develop problems that require special treatment and intervention. We ask such questions as: What is 'atypical development'? How are developmental disorders defined and identified? What is unique about a developmental approach to psychological disorders? How do risk factors, vulnerabilities and protective processes interact to promote or protect against atypical development? How should we classify the psychological disorders of childhood?

Some of the developmental disorders we discuss are not uncommon; others are relatively rare. Problems such as attention deficit/hyperactivity disorder (ADHD), in which children appear unable to control their own behaviour and are excitable, in constant motion and generally disruptive, are fairly widespread. Problems such as autism spectrum disorders (ASD), in which children evidence considerable difficulties that affect many spheres of functioning, are relatively rare, although notably increasing in prevalence.

In this chapter, as well as considering the best way to characterize developmental disorders, we will also address the developmental causes (or aetiologies) of disorders. Furthermore, we also address treatment approaches as well as the possibility of putting preventative measures in place to protect children at risk of disorder. To introduce you to the topics of this discussion and to illustrate the range of problems that children can experience, consider these short case studies.

Adam: *Adam had always been a handful. As an infant, he cried frequently, woke up at all hours, and was described by his (exhausted) parents as always being 'on the go'. As a toddler, he woke early and started the day wide-awake; always seeming to run when others walked. When he was 4, one of his favourite games was scrambling onto the roof of the family car and fearlessly diving off into his father's tired arms. During times like these, Adam's parents would try to discipline him by reasoning with him, but that strategy rarely worked. Instead, they would tolerate – and often secretly enjoy – his antics until they reached their limit, at which point they found it necessary to simply force Adam to comply. They describe having to shout and send Adam to his room. Although Adam exhausted them, his parents never considered him to have a real problem – until he started school. Bt the end of his first term in reception, Adam's teacher voiced concerns that Adam wasn't doing as well as his peers. The teacher said that Adam did not pay attention during class, often wandering away from his desk, or disrupting the other pupils. His teacher said that he required more supervision than she was able to give him. Adam's teacher suggested that Adam would benefit from being assessed by a community child psychology service, and that the school would support his academic progress by asking the school Special Educational Needs Coordinator to develop a programme for him.*

Sara: *Sara was beginning to worry her mother. She was a very well behaved and helpful 12 year old, but to her mother, Sara seemed unhappy. She really didn't have any close friends, and her mother wondered why the phone wasn't constantly ringing for Sara as it had for her when she was Sara's age. To her mother, Sara seemed to spend too much of her time alone in her room and not enough time socializing. More than that, her mother was concerned about Sara's schoolwork. Her As and Bs in her first year at secondary school had slipped down to mostly Cs and a couple of D grades for the first term in her second year at secondary school. Sara had also dropped out of the one thing that her mother thought she really seemed to enjoy – swimming team. Her mother wanted to talk with Sara about how she was feeling, but when she tried to approach her, Sara got angry at her mother 'interfering' and ran to her room in tears. Her mother blamed Sara's unhappiness on Sara's father and their divorce six years earlier. But what could she do about that now?*

Alfie: *Alfie was becoming a source of real worry to his parents. At age 3, he had not yet spoken his first clear word, and they could not ignore his unusual behaviour. He spent hours every day doing the same sort of play over and over again; lining up his toy cars, and* *becoming angrily upset if the cars were put away. Alfie showed very little interest in other children and would jerk away from his mother or father if they tried to give him a hug. Even as an infant, Alfie had resisted being held and stiffened at physical contact, and his mother could not remember a time when they had really cuddled. She commented that holding Alfie was more like holding a log than a baby since he did not mould or cling to her shoulder the way most babies do. His rejection of his parents didn't seem to be one of anger; rather, it almost seemed as if it was physically painful for Alfie to be touched by someone. Although Alfie had been a fairly quiet baby, his failure to speak and his endless repetitive play gradually became more distressing to his parents. At first, the paediatrician that Alfie saw had been reassuring, but by age three, she suggested that Alfie was referred for a specialist evaluation at a local hospital's psychology service. Alfie's parents were frightened by this possibility. Did this mean that their little boy would never catch up his peers? Would he ever learn to talk to his parents?*

All three of these children are exhibiting behaviour that concerns their parents. Adam's loving parents could tolerate and even appreciate his boundless energy, but his uncontrolled activity is causing trouble for him, his teacher and his classmates in school. Does Adam have a special problem that differentiates him from his peers and may require special attention? Does he need help from a specialist in order to be able to make academic progress? His teacher seems to think so. As for Sara, her apparent unhappiness may be a problem, but we don't really know how she feels about herself and her life. Is she feeling depressed, helpless and angry with her mother and father for getting divorced? Or is she going through a 'stage', feeling confused and lonely as she enters puberty? Perhaps Sara is simply experiencing the normal feelings of a quiet girl who is going through a transition to a new school. Of the three children, Alfie is exhibiting the most disturbing behaviour. But why is he behaving in this unusual manner? Does Alfie have a social communication disorder, or are his problems caused by a more general developmental delay? We will meet Adam, Sara and Alfie again as we explore the complexities of atypical development.

THE DEVELOPMENTAL APPROACH TO DEVELOPMENTAL DISORDERS

When a child appears to be developing differently to other children, to understand and help this young person we need to invoke principles of what is called developmental psychopathology. *Psychopathology* is the study of disorders of the *psyche* – that is, of the mind. Developmental psychopathology, which combines the study of psychopathology with the study of development, involves the investigation of the origins, course, changes, and continuities in atypical or maladaptive behaviour over the individual's lifespan. Although the principles of developmental psychopathology are relevant to individuals of all ages, here we are particularly concerned with understanding how biological, emotional, social and environmental factors play their roles in atypical development in infants and children.

> **developmental psychopathology** The investigation of the developmental origins, course, changes and continuities in disordered or maladaptive behaviour and thinking.

Principles of developmental psychopathology

The *developmental* approach to understanding psychopathology is embodied in a number of principles (Rutter & Sroufe, 2000; Cicchetti & Toth, 2006; Shiner & Allen, 2018). Here we will look at four of the most important principles.

First, *atypical behaviour or thinking in a child must be viewed in relation both to typical development and so considered in the context of the developmental changes that occur as children get older.*

By definition, psychopathology involves deviations from typical behaviour, and so developmental psychopathology involves deviations from typical development. A critical issue is how to distinguish between developmental disruptions within the normal range and those reflecting behaviour which should be classified as atypical (Rutter, 1996, 2003b). This is of course an issue for the study of psychopathology more generally, but the developmental angle adds an additional level of complexity to this. For example, although temper tantrums would be viewed as somewhat atypical in adolescents, they are common in 2 year olds.

An important implication of this principle is that our understanding of typical development contributes to our understanding of atypical development. Indeed, many authors now concur that developmental psychology and developmental psychopathology are intimately connected and mutually informative disciplines (e.g., Masten, 2006).

Second, *developmental disorders, like typical development can and should be understood at multiple levels of description*. In other words, atypical development can be understood at many levels of functioning including genetic contributions (e.g., an inherited genetic deletion), at the level of neurons and functional brain networks and areas (e.g., a damaged right cortical hemisphere), in terms of cognitive processes (e.g., working memory limitations), and in terms of social-cultural or interpersonal behaviours and functioning (e.g., an insecure attachment style). Importantly, these levels of functioning are not mutually exclusive, and developmental disorders occur at all these levels simultaneously.

Thirdly, and probably most importantly, because childhood disorders occur in a developing organism, we must *take into account the role of development when interpreting the symptoms, searching for the origins, and understanding the causes, of any given disorder.*

This principle captures the fact that the frequencies and patterns of symptoms in any given developmental disorder can vary considerably across the course of development. Let's illustrate this point with an example. Depression in adults is typically characterized by social withdrawal and a *dysphoric* (unhappy, dejected, anxious, and/or self-doubting) mood. Children can also present with depressive symptoms but it has not been until rather recently that clinicians have fully acknowledged that young (even 3-year-old) children can also present depressive symptoms which can continue into later life (Luby et al., 2014). Children – especially those between the ages of about 8 and 11 – do not seem to manifest the general slowing of mental and physical activity or the motivational deficits that adults with depression typically do (Gelfand & Drew, 2003), and early childhood depression may often be masked by other symptoms, often more behavioural in nature, such as hyperactivity, bed-wetting, learning problems and antisocial behaviour.

Depressive episodes are not uncommon during adolescence and may well be linked to the changes of puberty and the stresses and challenges of adolescence. Although depression is more common in girls, boys can also suffer. When depression lingers and is associated with expressions of guilt, low self-worth or suicidal ideation, however, knowledgeable adults need to intervene to prevent the adolescent from sinking into self-destructive behaviours such as substance abuse with alcohol or drugs.
© Shutterstock/tommaso79

In adolescents with depression, suicidal thoughts, which are quite uncharacteristic of younger children, begin to appear, and the depressed adult's symptoms of low self-worth, guilt, depressed mood, negative self-attributions, and inactivity also emerge (Goodman & Gotlib, 2002; Klein & Wender, 2005). Why do depressed mood and suicidal behaviours increase particularly in adolescence? There are a range of potential explanations for this, all of which rest on understanding developmental changes. Pubertal developmental changes, changes in brain development, advances in cognitive development, and the many stresses and adaptive challenges young people encounter in this developmental period seem likely to play into the different instantiations of depression at different points in development (Hammen, 1997, 2002).

However, understanding the role of development in developmental disorders is not simply about characterizing the different manners in which disorders are manifested at different ages. As Annette Karmiloff-Smith pointed out (Karmiloff-Smith et al., 2018), developmental disorders are products themselves of highly complex developmental processes. As the growing field of behavioural genetics has taught us (Knopik et al., 2016), our inherited characteristics and the environmental circumstances to which we are exposed interact with one another in complex ways, and underpin the emergence of both typical and atypical behaviour and thinking (see Chapter 5). As we shall discuss throughout this chapter, this means that it can be misleading to think of children with developmental disorders as having a fixed condition. Karmiloff-Smith (1994) among others has argued that developmental disorders should be considered as highly dynamic and complex phenomena because of the complex developmental interactions between our inheritance and experience at all levels of functioning (e.g., genetic, biological, social, interpersonal).

Because of the complex ways in which development (both typical and atypical development) occurs, there are multiple pathways to both typical atypical behaviour and thinking over the course of development (Cicchetti & Toth, 2006). This means that children with the same starting point can develop towards a range of different outcomes in response to the different environments which they experience (this is known as multifinality). It also means that children can end up with the same (typical or atypical) developmental outcome as a result of very different developmental trajectories (this is known as equifinality).

> **multifinality**
> multifinality captures the fact that children with the same developmental starting point can develop differently due to different environmental circumstances
>
> **equifinality**
> equifinality captures the fact that children can attain the same developmental outcome due to different developmental trajectories

Given the importance of developmental antecedents in the aetiology of developmental disorders, researchers are increasingly investigating developmental disorders at earlier stages in development. Although psychopathology is less clearly defined and less stable in younger children than in adults, early behaviours are often associated with later disturbances. In conduct disorder, two such early warning signs are non-compliant behaviours and rejection by peers. Although early non-compliance and rejection by peers are not necessarily pathological, they can be associated with more serious psychopathologies and antisocial behaviours such as substance abuse, criminal behaviour, mental health problems and poor-quality partner relationships (Fergusson, Horwood, & Ridder, 2005; Englund et al., 2008).

Tracing atypical development to its origins presents somewhat of a problem as many disorders, such as ASD, are difficult to diagnose in infancy. This has led to a rise in prospective longitudinal studies of developmental disorders in which infants at risk of a later diagnosis are studied. One such approach in the study of ASD has been to study children whose siblings have a diagnosis of ASD. It is know that there is around a 50% likelihood of ASD diagnosis in ASD siblings and so such studies can show which behaviours or even brain signatures can signal the emergence of an atypical diagnosis (Bussu et al., 2018; Ozonoff et al., 2010).

WHAT IS ATYPICAL DEVELOPMENT?

It is important to diagnose atypical behaviour and thinking when that behaviour or thinking pattern is unusual enough to cause disproportionate distress or disadvantage either to the child or to those with whom she or he interacts. However, defining abnormal psychological behaviour is not an easy task. Many cultural, societal, ethnic and personal values affect what we consider typical and atypical, and all of these values vary across regions, nations and cultures.

Consider another brief case history.

> *William is 11 years old and lives with his family in a quiet rural town. William also cares little for his personal appearance and is often described as 'scruffy'. His parents live in despair of his behaviour, often having to answer the doorbell to another furious neighbour, or repairing the damage caused to trampled gardens and broken windows. William spends the majority of his time with a gang of local boys who spend their time getting into trouble. He has also run away from home. There are also some concerns about animal cruelty, having once painted his dog blue.*

What can you conclude from this very brief account about the normality or abnormality of William's behaviour? Does he differ enough from the average to be considered abnormal according to the statistical model? Certainly, he deviates from many people's ideals, including, we might presume, the ideals of some of the people with whom William interacts. Put yourself in the position of a psychologist who has been asked to evaluate William's general adjustment. Are you suspicious that he is exhibiting some form of developmental psychopathology, or are you more inclined to dismiss his behaviour as nothing to worry about?

In weighing up your decision, you should know that William is actually Richmal Crompton's William Brown, or 'Just William'. At the time Crompton created this character in 1922, William was certainly not meant to be psychopathological or even atypical. Just the opposite: William represented a typical mischievous English boy. He was hardly a candidate for psychotherapy! But taken out of context and viewed by today's standards, William seems to show some behaviours that would worry many parents. Clearly, something other than a child's behaviour in any given situation affects people's social judgements as to what constitutes aypical behaviour.

Contextualizing judgements about whether a child is developing atypically

And so, in general, people's view of atypicality depends on their individual and cultural values. This yields some problems in making diagnoses. For example, different groups of people use different criteria to define atypicality, and these criteria may conflict. For example, one difference between teachers and parents is probably their ability to make comparative judgements. Teachers observe great variation in behaviour among their pupils, whereas it might be argued that parents lack this experience (Veenstra et al., 2008).

Because children rarely refer themselves for formal help but rather are identified as needing help by adults, psychologists must constantly be alert to factors other than simply the child's own behaviour. Thus, clinical and educational psychologists consider whether a child really has a problem or whether they have been referred because the referring adult has a distorted view of the child for some reason. Three sets of factors that may subtly influence a referring adult's perception of a child as developing typically or atypically are the characteristics of the child, the characteristics of the adult and contextual influences.

CHARACTERISTICS OF THE CHILD

Parents and other adults are more likely to perceive behaviour as deviant if it occurs in boys, in children who have been temperamentally difficult infants, in unattractive children, and in children with a history of other forms of deviance (Cummings, Davies, & Campbell, 2000; Rothbart & Bates, 2006). In addition, people are less likely to judge a behaviour displayed by a socially skilled child as atypical than they are if the child is socially unskilled (Gelfand & Drew, 2003). One reason that William would not likely be judged to have a psychological problem is that he has other, positive, qualities. He has a close-knit group of friends and shows that he cares very much about them.

CHARACTERISTICS OF THE REFERRING ADULT

Characteristics of the adult who identifies a child as having difficulties should also be taken into account. Adults, including teachers and health professionals, express views about children that, as well as reflecting something about the child can also reflect other contextual factors which may have more to do with the adult than the child. For instance, although it might seem that a parent would know their child better than anyone, it is not uncommon for a parent to have a rather narrow view of their child's behaviour and of their child's need for psychological help. For instance, parents who are depressed, anxious or abusive are likely to report their children's behaviour in a more negative light than other observations of the child's actual behaviour suggest (Hammen, 2005; Cicchetti & Toth, 2006; Veenstra et al., 2008). In one study (Bauer & Twentyman, 1985) it was found that abusive mothers were more likely to express negative expectations of their own children, and attributed failures to internal dispositions rather than external factors out of the child's control. Non-abusive mothers offered almost the exact opposite pattern of causal explanations: they emphasized their children's positive attributes as leading to success, and they suggested that either special circumstances or unusual behaviours were the causes of their children's transgressions.

THE CHILD'S ENVIRONMENT

The context in which adults observe a child's behaviour also influences their judgements of psychopathology. They may judge the same behaviour differently according to the demands of different situations. Adam's parents judged his inattentive and overactive behaviour as tiresome, but they accepted it in their home. But when Adam began school, the demands and stricter standards of the classroom context led teachers to judge his behaviour as atypical. Adam's disposition interacted with the new situation in ways which led to behaviour which the teachers considered atypical.

Contextual influences on the evaluation of children's psychological adjustment include still other factors. For example, a child's social background, race and prior behaviour can create contexts that influence the way adults judge a behaviour. Such factors often lead people to tag children with value-laden labels: 'naughty', 'a child from a broken home', 'lazy', 'high risk'. Unfortunately, such labels can create a context in which others perceive and respond to the child's behaviour in a way that has adverse consequences. For instance, black teenagers are up to three times more likely to be arrested than white teenagers (Huizinga et al., 2007). Lower-class ethnic minority individuals are more likely than middle-class white individuals to end up in court or custody, even when they are arrested for similar offences (Moeller, 2001; Dodge et al., 2006).

Models used for defining atypicality

Given the importance of contextual factors such as those described here, in determining whether children are judged to be typical or atypical, it is crucial that we have a robust means of determining whether a given child is developing atypically. Here we'll discuss how clinicians manage this tricky task. We will look at a few common views including the idea that atypicality can be defined as *different from average behaviours in the population of a given age group*.

A medical model of developmental disorders, one which is strongly related to practice in the field of psychiatry plays an important role in the consideration of the causes and treatments of developmental disorders. The medical model generally starts by characterizing psychological disorders in the same way as medicine characterizes a physical disease, as residing within the individual, that is, resulting from atypical biological or psychological processes. However, most developmental psychologists would consider the medical model is insufficient, by itself, for explaining atypical child behaviour and thinking. This is because of the importance of considering differences in how disorders are defined between different cultures and contexts. However, it is also because atypical behaviour and thinking is based not just in the individual but the interactions between individuals and their sociocultural environments (e.g., cast your mind back to the case study of Adam). This important point taken, it is nonetheless vital to recognize that many developmental disorders such as autism spectrum disorders and Down's syndrome have genetic roots in the individuals experiencing them (Pennington, 2005).

ATYPICAL DEVELOPMENT AS DEVIATION FROM THE STATISTICAL AVERAGE

The term *atypical* literally means 'not typical'; therefore, one way of defining atypicality is to view as atypical any behaviours or feelings that differ to some reasonably substantial degree from the average of the age group population. This method of defining atypicality is referred to as the *statistical model*. The statistical model for defining atypical development is often used as a guide to what constitutes atypical development. For example, intellectual disability is indicated by an IQ score of less than 70. On the Wechsler Intelligence Scale for Children–IV, a score of 100 is average, and one standard deviation is equal to 15 points; so an IQ of less than 70 is more than two standard deviations away from the mean.

The statistical model may seem appealing because it is so clear-cut, but it does yield some problems. Although it may work for intelligence, which is measured on a numerical scale and can be either lower than average or higher, it does not work so well for behaviours or experiences where there is no clearly agreed or measurable average (consider, for example the kinds of behaviours and experiences which vary considerably across cultures). Another problem with the statistical model is that it gives us no guidance as to how much of a difference from the average is atypical and under what circumstances differences matter. Why choose two standard deviations below the mean to determine mental retardation – why not one? or three? Moreover, deviation from a mean can go in either direction. By this rule, if we were to consider an IQ of 100 typical we would have to consider scores of both 69 and 131 atypical. It feels less clear cut that superior cognitive functioning should be considered as a developmental disorder.

OTHER DEFINITIONS OF ATYPICALITY

Given that there are many difficulties associated with defining what exactly is atypical behaviour or thinking, an alternative is to define atypicality as a deviation from the ideal. This approach starts by identifying ideal healthy behaviour and thinking and then considers what deviations from this ideal could be considered as atypical. The main problem with this approach of course is the question of how to define ideal mental health.

In Western cultures, the ideal tends to be that individuals can work hard, can be able to love and can be happy in achieving these two goals. When someone falls short of these cultural criteria, we become concerned. However, in other cultures other ideals may prevail.

Let's look at an example of cultural differences in the definition of atypical behaviour. Rates of hyperactivity in Hong Kong (Ho et al., 1996) have been reported to be double those reported in Western countries. Suppression of aggression, anger and strong emotions or overt behaviours is part of the Chinese culture. This aspect of Chinese culture may lead parents and teachers to have a lower threshold (or tolerance) for the hyperactive behaviour and therefore increased likelihood of reporting hyperactive and disruptive behaviours.

However, it is important to remember that there are some cross-cultural consistencies in ideal characteristics of healthy development. For instance, it seems likely that most cultures would agree that individuals who are developing healthily have a positive view of themselves, and are able to function adequately, performing the tasks that they need to in day-to-day living.

The continuity of atypicality over time

Whether or not a particular behaviour problem is viewed as atypical depends on the child's age and the probability that the behaviour will continue over time and be manifested in some form of adult disorder (Rutter, 1996). Some problems, such as bed-wetting, thumb-sucking, temper tantrums and tics, decline with age; others, such as nail-biting, increase from early childhood to adolescence; still others, such as disturbing dreams and nightmares, peak in preadolescence at about age 10 and then decline (Gelfand & Drew, 2003). Table 15-1 displays some problem behaviours that, when they occur at the ages indicated, are fairly common among normal children and thus not necessarily indicative of serious trouble. However, some problem behaviours give more cause for concern. As we will see, childhood disorders such as attention deficit hyperactivity disorder (ADHD), autism spectrum disorders (ASD), and overly aggressive and antisocial behaviours are more likely to be associated with later adult dysfunction (Gelfand & Drew, 2003; Dodge et al., 2006).

Longitudinal studies of behaviour allow us to follow children through adolescence and into adulthood to explore the effects of early behaviour and functioning over time. There are many longitudinal studies that help us to learn about different disorders, including the European-wide IMAGE project discussed in Box 15-2; the Twins Early Developmental Study (TEDS; Oliver & Plomin, 2007; Shakoor et al., 2018) and the Avon Longitudinal Study of Parents and Children (ALSPaC; Golding et al., 2001; Plant et al., 2017) in the UK; Twin Study of Child and Adolescent Development in Sweden (TCHAD; Lichtenstein et al., 2007) and the Tracking Adolescents' Individual Lives study in the Netherlands (TRAiLS; Huisman et al., 2008). Caspi and colleagues (2003) used the Dunedin Multidisciplinary Health and Development Study cohort (over 1000 babies born in 1972–73) to study the stability of behaviour in children who at age 3 had been categorized as falling into one of five temperament types.

1. Undercontrolled: impulsive, restless, negativistic, distractible, and labile in their emotional responses.
2. Inhibited: socially reticent, fearful, and easily upset by the examiner.
3. Confident: exceptionally friendly, somewhat impulsive, eager to explore the testing materials, displayed little or no concern about separating from their caregiver.
4. Reserved: timid and appearing somewhat shy.
5. Well-adjusted: capable of self-control, adequately self-confident.

Table 15-1 Common problem behaviours of children and adolescents

Problem behaviour	1.5–2 years	3–5 years	6–10 years	11–14 years	15–18 years
Inattentiveness	x				
Demanding attention constantly	x	x			
Refusal to do things when asked	x	x			
Overactivity	x	x	x		
Specific fears	x	x	x		
Temper tantrums	x	x	x	x	
Negativism		x			
Oversensitivity		x	x		
Lying		x	x		
Jealousy			x	x	
Withdrawn behaviour			x	x	
Moodiness				x	
School achievement problems			x	x	x
Truanting from school					x
Cheating on exams					x
Depression					x
Drinking					x
Smoking					x
Drug misuse					x
Early sexual activity					x
Trespassing					x
Shoplifting					x
Other minor law violations					x

Source: Adapted from Gelfand, Jensen, and Drew (1997).

These boys were followed up at age 26, where it was reported that these five temperament types were related to the big-5 personality types. For example, at age 3, children classified as 'undercontrolled' were described as irritable, impulsive and emotionally labile (prone to emotional outbursts and 'mood swings'). At age 26, these individuals were reported to be 'intolerant' and scored high on traits indexing Negative Emotionality; that is, they were easily upset, likely to overreact to minor events, and reported feeling mistreated, deceived, and betrayed by others. On the other hand, the 'well adjusted' children whose behaviour at age 3 was characterized as age- and situation-appropriate were described in a similar fashion at age 26. Put simply by Caspi et al. (2003), 'Well-adjusted children defined average adults' (p. 511).

CLASSIFYING DEVELOPMENTAL DISORDERS

Given the difficulties in defining atypical behaviour in children, it is not surprising that psychiatrists (medical doctors who specialize in psychological disorders), clinical psychologists and others disagree on how to classify the different forms of developmental psychopathology. Until the latter decades of the twentieth century, childhood psychological problems were viewed as variations of recognized adult disorders, and the diagnostic categories developed for adults were applied to children as well (Achenbach, 1995). Children are not simply small adults (Buitelaar, 2004), but the irony of viewing disturbed children as small people with adult problems is striking, for most theories of mental and emotional disturbance view psychological functioning during adult life as a product of child development!

Although it is broadly accepted that the seeds of abnormal development are sown in childhood, researchers and others have spent far less time studying abnormal behaviour in children than adult psychological disorders. Recent years have seen an increasing interest in the psychological problems unique to childhood. We look next at two important means of assessing and classifying developmental disorders: the diagnostic approach and the empirical method.

The diagnostic approach

> **diagnosis** The identification of a physical or mental disorder on the basis of symptoms and of knowledge of the cause or causes of the disorder and its common course. A diagnosis may also include information about effective forms of treatment.
>
> **aetiology** In medicine and psychiatry, the cause or causes of a specific disorder.

The diagnostic approach to assessing and classifying psychopathology is rooted in the medical tradition. In medicine, a diagnosis is useful or valid if it conveys information about the aetiology, or cause, of a disorder, about its likely course, or about the kind of treatment likely to be effective in curing or alleviating it. Because the classification of childhood psychopathology is still in its infancy, many diagnostic categories devised to characterize specific disorders are based largely on description – including such things as patterns of behaviour and specific kinds of thoughts and feelings – and few can make firm statements about either aetiology or treatment.

The diagnostic classification system most widely used in the field of psychiatry has been compiled by the American Psychiatric Association (APA). The current *Diagnostic and Statistical Manual* (American Psychiatric Association, 2013) is the fifth classification system that APA has developed (it is commonly referred to as *DSM-5*). Table 15-2 displays some examples of current *DSM* categories that relate specifically to childhood disorders. The emphasis on childhood disorders has increased significantly over the more than 65 years since *DSM-I* was published in 1952, a sign of the increased interest in psychological disorders of childhood. Today, *DSM-5* contains many diagnostic categories applicable to children, whereas *DSM-I* only had 2.

The *DSM* is not without its critics, however (Campbell, 1998, 2002; Insel, 2014). Some improvements in the reliability of the diagnostic criteria which *DSM* provides (i.e., the extent to which different clinicians can use the manual to provide the same diagnosis for a particular adult or child) have been noted for *DSM-5*. However, the biggest problem with *DSM-5* seems to be that its diagnostic categories lack validity. It is unclear whether the categories usefully describe the problems which people experience.

Table 15-2 Some examples of disorders in *DSM-5* that are particularly relevant to children

Intellectual disability
-Mild intellectual disability
-Moderate intellectual disability
-Severe intellectual disability
-Profound intellectual disability
Attention-deficit and disruptive behaviour disorders
-Attention deficit/hyperactivity disorder
-Conduct disorder
-Oppositional defiant disorder
Feeding and eating disorders of infancy or early childhood
-Avoidant/restrictive food intake disorder
-Anorexia nervosa
-Bulimia nervosa
-Binge eating disorder
Specific learning disorders
-Dyslexia
-Dyscalculia
-Disorder of written expression
Tic disorders (stereotyped motor movements or vocalizations)
-Tourette's disorder (multiple tics)
-Persistent motor or vocal tic disorder
-Provisional tic disorder
Motor skills disorders
-Developmental coordination disorder
Communication disorders
-Language disorder
-Speech sound disorder
-Childhood-onset fluency disorder (stuttering)
Elimination disorders
-Encopresis (incontinence of faeces)
-Enuresis (bed-wetting)
Autism spectrum disorders
-Asperger's syndrome
-Pervasive developmental disorder
-Childhood disintegrative disorder
Anxiety disorders
-Separation anxiety disorder
-Selective mutism
-Reactive attachment disorder

Source: Based on American Psychiatric Association (2013).

The empirical method

An alternative to the diagnostic approach is the empirical or rating-scale method (Achenbach, 1997; Achenbach & Rescorla, 2007). Using this method, an adult who is familiar with a child who displays signs of developmental difficulties – usually, a parent or a teacher – rates a large number of problem behaviours according to whether and to what degree the child displays the behaviours. Investigators then use statistical techniques to determine which problem behaviours are associated with one another. There is considerable overlap among the classifications arrived at by the diagnostic and the empirical methods, but there are also many disparities (Achenbach, 1995).

Both classification methods generally agree on the broader, major categories, such as 'intellectual disability', but often disagree – with each other and within their own systems – on narrower subcategories, such as 'mild intellectual disability' and 'moderate intellectual disability' (see Table 15-2). The finer the distinction one tries to draw between collections of symptoms and behaviours, the more difficult the task.

DEVELOPMENTAL DISORDERS

It is useful to discuss some representative child disorders in terms of the degree to which they reflect the nature of the control children exert over their behaviour. In externalizing disorders, the child fails to control behaviour in such a way as to suit the demands of a given environment. Examples of externalizing behaviours include non-compliance, disobedience, rule violation and aggression. Although these behaviours hurt the child, they can initially be most disturbing to other people around the child. Because externalizing behaviours are defined largely by this negative impact on others, and because most childhood psychological disorders are defined by adults' social judgements, it is not surprising that externalizing behaviour disorders are the most frequently reported of all the psychological problems of childhood. In this section, we discuss two of these types of disorders: conduct disorders and attention deficit/hyperactivity disorder.

In contrast to externalizing disorders, internalizing disorders tend to have a more adverse effect on the child, who seems to withdraw from others, lack spontaneity, and in general, not be the 'happy child' which parents hope for. Various negative emotions such as fear, anxiety and sadness characterize such children, who seem restrained and overly controlled in the way they relate to others. *Phobias* (excessive fears) may cause considerable discomfort for some children and their families; fortunately, research indicates that the majority of children's phobias disappear in a relatively short amount of time, even without treatment (Vanin, 2008). (Table 15-3 lists some fears that are common at different stages of normal development.) However, some fears and phobias are more long lasting, persisting across the lifespan. These include fear of heights and fear of physical illness. Childhood anxiety disorders are also predictive of a range of psychiatric problems in adolescence (Bittner et al., 2007).

> **externalizing disorders**
> A group of psychological disturbances in which a child appears to lack self-control in a variety of ways, through such behaviours as non-compliance, disobedience and aggression.

> **internalizing disorders**
> A group of psychological disturbances in which a child appears overly controlled, withdrawing from others, lacking spontaneity and generally appearing to be not a happy child.

Table 15-3   How children's fears change in development

Ages	Fears
0–12 months	Stranger anxiety; loud sounds; unexpected perceptual events
12–24 months	Stranger anxiety; parental separation; injury anxiety
24–36 months	Stranger anxiety; parental separation; fear of animals (e.g., large dogs); fear of the dark; injury anxiety
36 months–6 years	Stranger anxiety; parental separation; fear of animals; fear of the dark; injury anxiety
6–10 years	Fear of monsters (imaginary beings); fear of snakes; injury anxiety; fear of the dark; fear of being alone
10–12 years	Anxiety about social evaluations; fear of school failure; fear of thunderstorms; injury anxiety; death anxiety
Adolescence	Anxiety about social evaluations (especially by peers); fear of school failure; fear of disasters (e.g., war); fear of the future

Source: Drawing on Gelfand and Drew (2003).

As a representative of internalizing problems, we will discuss childhood depression. For several reasons, it is often difficult to identify internalizing problems in children. Because the definition of childhood psychopathology depends on an adult's social judgement, and because it is much more difficult for adults to evaluate children's inner feelings (e.g., sadness) than it is to judge their overt behaviour (e.g., aggression), the diagnostic

comorbidity The co-occurrence of two or more problem behaviours.

autism spectrum disorder (ASD) A lifelong disorder in which children's ability to communicate and interact socially is seriously impaired; children with ASD often have communicative and social difficulties, and often engage in repetitive and stereotyped kinds of behaviours.

labels for internalizing disorders are often vague and controversial. It is also the case that externalizing and internalizing behaviours often occur together. For example, the child who plays up and displays aggression may also experience depression and use drugs. So even though we discuss them separately, keep in mind that these problems often go together (Kim et al., 2003). Comorbidity is the term used to describe this co-occurrence of two or more problem behaviours (Pennington, 2005).

Although the problems of delinquency, hyperactivity, and depression are serious, some children exhibit forms of psychological difficulty that do not really fit under either the internalized or undercontrolled designations. The term autism spectrum disorders (ASD) describes a collection of disorders which are characterized by marked social difficulties as well as stereotyped behaviours. Children and adults with a diagnosis of ASD can vary widely in their abilities, behaviours and language abilities. Some children with ASD are non-verbal, not developing speech at all, some are able to communicate in limited phrases or conversations, while others have relatively normal language development. Children with ASD may also have difficulties processing sensory information, and have difficulties coping with loud noises or certain clothing or food textures.

conduct disorder A disorder characterized by a repetitive and persistent pattern of behaviour in which a young person violates the basic rights of others, or major age-appropriate societal norms or rules.

CONDUCT DISORDERS

A conduct disorder is characterized by a repetitive and persistent pattern of behaviour in which a child or adolescent violates the basic rights of others or major age-appropriate societal norms or rules (American Psychiatric Association, 2013). (See Table 15-4 for the *DSM-5* description of conduct disorders.) Thus, it is an *externalizing disorder*. Conduct disorder is more frequently diagnosed in males than females, and the prevalence of diagnosis increases across childhood (Maughan et al., 2004, Nock et al., 2007).

Table 15-4 *DSM-5* diagnostic criteria for conduct disorder

For a diagnosis of conduct disorder to be made, the individual has to show consistent behaviour in which they violate other people's rights or social norms, and this has to be seen in 3 out of the following 15 ways over the last year. Additionally, the aberrant behaviours have to cause significant social, work, or academic impairments.
Aggression
1. Bullying, threatening, intimidation
2. Physical conflicts
3. Use of a weapon that can cause serious harm to others (e.g., a knife)
4. Physical cruelty to people
5. Physical cruelty to animals
6. Theft which involved confronting a victim (e.g., mugging).
7. Sexual aggression
Destruction of property
8. Setting fire to property with the intent to damage or destroy
9. Destruction of someone else's property other than by arson
Lying or theft
10. Has broken and entered someone else's property (their home, other building, or car)
11. Lying to obtain something, either an item, or favours, or to avoid obligations
12. Theft of items of value without confronting a victim (e.g., shoplifting)
Serious infraction of rules
13. Staying out late without parental permission before 13 years of age
14. Running away from home
15. School truancy before age 13 years

Source: American Psychiatric Association (2013).

BOX 15-1 Psychopathic children? Applying the idea of psychopathic traits to conduct disorder research

Research close-up

Source: Based on Moffitt (2003).

Introduction:

Early onset antisocial behaviour carries a strong risk for persistent offending (Moffitt, 2003). Although a single diagnostic label, conduct disorder, is currently applied to children exhibiting antisocial behaviour, multiple routes to the same behavioural phenomena exist. One suggested way of subtyping conduct-disordered children is to highlight the differences between callous-unemotional (CU)/premeditated and reactive/threat-based antisocial behaviour.

Callous-unemotional traits can be thought of as being an early expression of the traits characterizing 'psychopathy' in adults. Typically, these involve the absence of empathy for victims and guilt for wrong-doing, and callous, or mean, treatment of others for personal gain (Frick et al., 1994). Over the past decade, a growing body of evidence has suggested a differential pathway to antisocial behaviour in children with CU traits and without.

Evidence from twin studies suggests that CU traits are highly heritable, that is, there is a strong genetic influence on the presence of these traits (Viding et al., 2005, 2008). Research using neuroimaging methods also suggest that there are differences in structure and function between children with CU traits and those without (Marsh et al., 2008; De Brito et al., 2009; Jones et al., 2009). fMRI studies on children with elevated levels of CU traits suggest that these traits are associated with weaker reactivity in the amygdala to 'fearful' stimuli (for example, photos of people showing fearful expressions). The amygdala is a part of the brain associated with understanding and development of fear, and other emotions.

CU traits have been associated with more severe antisocial behaviour and higher rates of recidivism (committing further crimes after the first arrest) for youth offenders (Loeber, Burke, & Lahey, 2002; Frick et al., 2005; Frick & Dickens, 2006).

Research has suggested that children with high levels of CU have specific deficits in emotion processing and empathy. CU traits are associated with a difficulty in recognizing facial expressions, sounds and postures of 'fear' (Blair & Viding, 2008; Munoz, 2009). They are also associated with a deficit in emotional empathy (caring about the feelings of others) (Jones et al., 2010).

These cognitive and affective deficits are likely to have some important implications for the way that we design treatments and interventions for children and adolescents with CU. One such study to examine the effects of CU on a behavioural intervention is that of Hawes and Dadds (2007).

Method:

Forty-nine families completed a well-validated parent training intervention. The intervention commenced with an initial assessment session, followed by nine weekly one-hour treatment sessions. Sessions addressed the use of positive reinforcement and reward-based strategies (for example, praising the child on appropriate behaviour), as well as methods for dealing with misbehaviour (for example, using time-out as a strategy). Participating parents gave ratings of their child's behaviour and levels of CU traits at three time points; pre-treatment, post-treatment and at six months follow-up.

Results:

It was predicted that CU traits would be largely unaffected by parent training and remain highly stable across the treatment and follow-up periods. However, approximately half the participants who scored in the highest 50% for CU scores at pre-treatment dropped below this median point by the end of the treatment. It was also showed that CU and antisocial behaviour scores at six-month follow-up were predicted by different variables. Antisocial behaviour scores at follow-up were associated with baseline antisocial scores, mothers' education and post-treatment CU scores. However, CU scores at follow-up were only predicted by pre-treatment CU scores. The group who had high-CU traits at all three time points showed the least behavioural improvement.

> **Discussion:**
>
> Previous research had shown that children with high levels of CU traits appear not to show the same kind of strong association between poor parenting practices and conduct problems that non-CU children show (Oxford, Cavell, & Hughes, 2003; Hipwell et al., 2007). Hawes and Dadds (2005) had also previously demonstrated that techniques like 'time out' have relatively little effect for high-CU children.
>
> This study provides some evidence that although CU traits and antisocial behaviour can be thought of as being different factors that follow different pathways, CU traits are not completely stable and intervention might offer a method for reducing the perceived levels of these traits in some children.
>
> Currently CU traits are being considered for inclusion into *DSM-5*, but there are still many opportunities for further research (Moffitt et al., 2008). One of the most important of these is what it might mean to be labelled 'CU' for a developing child – will such a diagnosis mean that this child will be seen as a 'psychopath in training', or will it allow a child to access the most effective type of help?

TREATING CONDUCT DISORDERS

time out Removing children from a situation or context in which they are acting inappropriately until they are able and ready to act appropriately.

The most successful approaches to treatment for conduct disorders have employed social learning and behavioural techniques (Reid, Patterson, & Snyder, 2002). Parents can be trained to teach and reinforce appropriate behaviour and to use non-reinforcement and time out – removing children from a situation or context in which they are acting inappropriately until they are able and ready to behave in an appropriate manner – to suppress undesirable behaviours. These approaches have been found to reduce rates of conduct disorders among boys showing conduct problems (Patterson, 2002; Cavell et al., 2007) as well as to reduce disruptive behaviour in classrooms (Walker, 1995). Parenting interventions have also shown promising results. One study targeted 6 year olds with high levels of conduct problems and engaged them and their parents on a 28-week intervention targeting parenting practices and child literacy (Scott et al., 2010). At follow-up parents allocated to the intervention used play, praise and rewards, and time out more often than control families, and reported using harsh discipline less often. Compared to control children, whose behaviour was not reported to change, intervention children's conduct problems reduced significantly, dropping from the 80th to the 61st percentile; oppositional defiant disorder (ODD) and ADHD symptoms also reduced significantly. Meanwhile, reading age improved by six months. However, it is interesting to note here that teacher ratings of behaviour did not change for the intervention group – it is unclear where this was because children's behaviour did not improve in the context of the school or because of some other rater-related reason.

A variety of other prevention and intervention programmes involving parent training, home visits, social skill training, academic tutoring and classroom intervention have also produced promising results (Weissberg & Greenberg, 1998; Patrikakou et al., 2005; Conduct Problems Prevention Research Group, 2004; Kress & Elias, 2006). However, as Box 15-1 shows, it is important to consider a range of individual differences in personality when considering implementing any intervention.

ATTENTION DEFICIT HYPERACTIVITY DISORDER (ADHD)

attention deficit/ hyperactivity disorder (ADHD) A childhood disorder characterized by a persistent pattern of inattention and hyperactivity or impulsivity that far exceeds such behaviours observed in children at comparable levels of development.

The essential feature of attention deficit/hyperactivity disorder (ADHD) is a persistent pattern of inattention and hyperactivity or impulsivity that is far in excess of such behaviours observed in children at comparable levels of development (American Psychiatric Association, 2013) (see also Table 15-5 for the *DSM* criteria for the diagnosis of ADHD). ADHD – another externalizing disorder – leads to difficulties in the home, the classroom, and the peer group (American Psychiatric Association, 2013; Barkley, 2000). Indeed, some authorities question whether ADHD differs from conduct disorder, although the diagnostic criteria are certainly distinct (see Table 15-5).

A variety of studies have demonstrated that hyperactive children not only experience more conflict with adults but also perform more poorly than other children in school, present serious classroom-management problems to the teacher, have difficult peer relations, and often have poorer self-esteem (Campbell, 2000). In at least 70% of these children, some of these problems persist into adolescence and early adulthood (Biederman et al., 2011). Attention deficit disorders occur more frequently and are more sustained in boys than in girls; however, it is important to consider that this prevalence difference may reflect some differences in presentation. One study reported that girls with ADHD were more likely than boys to have the predominantly inattentive type of ADHD, less likely to have a learning disability, and less likely to demonstrate inappropriate conduct in school or in their spare time. In addition, girls with ADHD were at less risk for comorbid major depression, conduct disorder and oppositional defiant disorder than boys with ADHD (Biederman et al., 2002). In girls, high rates of hyperactivity have been associated with greater incidence of school drop-out, early pregnancies and reliance on social welfare (Fontaine et al., 2008). Although some concern has been expressed that ADHD is increasing among the population in recent years, a fairly recent epidemiological study shows that any increases in diagnosis are due to the ways in which criteria have been used by clinicians and researchers rather than to increases in the disorder among the population (Polanczyk et al., 2014).

Table 15-5 *DSM-5* diagnostic criteria for ADHD (adapted for brevity)

Criterion	Description
Criterion 1	Consistent inattention and/or hyperactivity-impulsivity that causes problems in functioning or learning. *Inattention could include:* -Failing to attend to details and/or making careless mistakes in school work -Seeming not to listen when spoken to -Frequent loss of belongings which are important for tasks or activities (e.g., at school) *Hyperactivity-impulsivity could include:* -Frequent fidgeting -Excessive talking -Difficulties waiting
Criterion 2	Several of the above behaviours have to have been present before 12 years of age.
Criterion 3	Several of the behaviours in Criterion 1 have to have been present in two plus settings (e.g., at a club, at home, at school).
Criterion 4	The behaviours in Criterion 1 have to cause problems for social, academic, or work functioning.
Criterion 5	The behaviours in Criterion 1 are not better explained by other mental disorders such as schizophrenia or anxiety.

Source: American Psychiatric Association (2013).

CHARACTERISTICS OF THE DISORDER

Our case study of Adam exemplifies children with ADHD, who display over-activity, poorly sustained attention, impulsivity, and problems with adherence to instructions and rules. Probably the most marked symptom that parents and teachers notice about hyperactive children is their inappropriately high activity level. In free-play situations, hyperactive children are no more active than other children. But in structured situations like the classroom, which demand controlled, task-orientated behaviour, their activity is conspicuous (Barkley, 1998). They fidget, tap their feet, poke their neighbours and talk out of turn. A child who is engaged in the same amount of motor activity but who is diligently working is judged by the teacher to be normally active (Gelfand & Drew, 2003). The hyperactive child's behaviour disturbs peers and disrupts the class, which may help account for the fact that 50% to 60% of children with ADHD are rejected by their peers (Henker & Whalen, 1999).

Hyperactivity does tend to decrease during adolescence; unfortunately, other problems persist (Weiss, Hechtman, & Weiss, 1999). One of the most persistent problems is inattention, which becomes especially problematic in

A prime characteristic of children with ADHD is their inability to attend for long or to stay with a specific activity or task, particularly one that requires them to sit quietly and concentrate. This can be a particular problem in the classroom.
Source: © Suzanne Tucker/Shutterstock

school, where teachers may have to expend considerable effort to keep these children focused on a task (Campbell, 2000; DuPaul & Stoner, 2014).

Another persistent problem experienced by some hyperactive children is impulsivity. Hyperactive children often seem to act before they think. Impulsivity often presents as frequent accidents in preschoolers and poorly thought-out test answers in school age children. A higher incidence of accidental injury in childhood and car accidents in adolescents and adults are typically found among formerly hyperactive children (Rowe, Maughan, & Goodman, 2004; Barkley & Cox, 2007).

Children with attention deficit/hyperactivity disorder also find it difficult to follow rules such as, 'When your little brother takes one of your toys, don't hit him, or you will be sent to your room', possibly because they have problems *tracking* contingencies (Barkley, 1998).

As a result of all these problems with inattention, hyperactivity and impulsivity, it is not surprising that children with ADHD tend to do poorly in school. They often function 1 to 2 years below their peers' level despite having a normal IQ (Barkley, 1998; Pisecco et al., 2001).

A wealth of brain imaging studies in ADHD have indicated some brain differences, particularly in the frontal lobes. Based on the behavioural observation described above that many children with ADHD might appear to act younger than their years, researchers posited an immature brain might be at the root. This theory has been tested using neuroimaging methods, and has been found to present a helpful perspective. Longitudinal and cross-sectional structural MRI studies of over 150 children with ADHD scanned repeatedly between 5 and 20 years showed that children with ADHD are characterized by a non-progressive reduction in grey and white matter and cortical thickness (Castellanos et al., 2002; Shaw et al., 2007). These prefrontal regions that are delayed in structural maturation also have consistently been found to be smaller in structure and underactivated in ADHD children during tasks of cognitive control (e.g., Rubia et al., 2000, 2005, 2008).

As we shall see, ADHD is, to some extent, treatable with medication. Psychostimulant medications – drugs such as caffeine, amphetamine or methylphenidate (one brand name is Ritalin) (Whalen, 2001) – are a common treatment for children (and adults) with ADHD. These medications increase attention and, as a result, reduce extraneous activity, enabling the child to focus on a task and complete it. In line with the brain differences in ADHD discussed above, recent work has noted that psychostimulant medications have a direct effect on frontal brain regions in children with ADHD. Rubia et al. (2011) has shown that giving methylphenidate to a group of children with ADHD who had not previously been given psychostimulant medication resulted in an amelioration in brain activity, making prefrontal cortex activation indistinguishable from non-ADHD controls.

> **psychostimulant medications** Drugs, such as amphetamines and caffeine, that increase alertness and attention as well as psychomotor activity.

CAUSES OF ADHD

What is the cause of ADHD, and how can we help children with this disorder? Research on this topic has been complicated because so many explanations for the aetiology and treatment of hyperactivity have been offered. As with many disorders, it is likely that there are both biological and environmental contributes to the presentation of the disorder, most often these biological and environmental influences combine or interact to produce the observable constellation of symptoms. Some main theories of the causes of and influences on ADHD are described below.

Some researchers have suggested that ADHD may be environmentally caused. Diverse social and familial stressors such as poverty, low levels of education, marital discord and disruption, household disorganization and poor parenting practices have all been associated with ADHD (Campbell, 2000). Research focused on parent–child relations has found that the mothers of children with ADHD are generally more controlling and intrusive and less affectionate and reinforcing than the mothers of typically developing children. However, most investigators think that excessive parental control and lessened affectional response are likely reactions to the disorder rather than its cause (Barkley, 2000).

> Behavioural genetics research, discussed in Chapter 5 has investigated the causes of ADHD in gene-environment correlations.

Behavioural genetics research has initially yielded findings which emphasize the role of genetic contributions to ADHD (Stergiakouli & Thapar, 2010). Twin studies of ADHD indicate that it is one of the most heritable disorders, with heritability estimates resting somewhere between 60 and 91% (Thapar et al., 2007b). However, a crucial consideration here is that heritability estimates might be inflated by the role of gene-environment correlations (see Chapter 5). For instance, if the heritability of ADHD is high, then it is likely that the parents of children with ADHD may themselves experience problems with inattention and hyperactivity. The environments which such parents create in the home, which are potentially chaotic, and may be less well resourced due to the difficulties the parents face, could increase the development of ADHD behaviours in their children (Pennington et al., 2009; Wang et al., 2012). This avenue of research certainly seems important as it highlights the need for appropriate parenting interventions despite the high heritability of the condition, and it will be important to conduct more studies in this area to understand more precisely how ADHD comes about (Gould et al., 2018).

Despite the considerable contribution of inheritance to ADHD, there are a number of other environmental factors which have been implicated in the condition. Brain damage may cause hyperactivity in some instances, and environmental lead poisoning, or dietary agents may explain other cases. A number of arguments have been made that parental smoking may play a role. However, as we shall see in Box 15-2, this correlation between smoking parents and children with ADHD may in fact be better accounted for by a correlation between smoking in parents and heritable ADHD characteristics than by the effect of the smoke itself.

BOX 15-2   Effects of parental smoking on ADHD

Research close-up

Source: Based on Thapar et al. (2009).

Introduction:

This chapter has already made the case for ADHD being a complex disorder without a clear causal mechanism. While evidence from twin, adoption and molecular genetic studies indicate a strong genetic contribution to the development of the disease (Faraone & Khan 2006; Li et al., 2006), there are also environmental factors that make a significant contribution. Among the environmental factors that have been suggested to be relevant to ADHD are: complications during pregnancy and birth, low birth weight and exposure to toxins *in utero* (Banerjee, Middleton, & Faraone, 2007). Many studies have reported an increased risk for ADHD in children exposed to maternal and paternal smoking (e.g., Thapar et al., 2007a; Altink et al., 2009) However, recent evidence suggests that the association may not be as clear as once thought.

Method:

Thapar et al. (2009) utilized a novel design in family studies – recruiting women who had conceived via assisted reproduction methods at fertility clinics in the UK and USA. Over 800 families were recruited. Some of the mother–child pairs were genetically related, but others were not (e.g., mothers were surrogates). This interesting method allowed the researchers to compare the effects of maternal cigarette smoking between children who shared genetic make-up with their mothers and those who did not.

The link between smoking during pregnancy and ADHD might not be as clear cut as once thought. Although maternal smoking is associated with child ADHD, recent evidence suggests that this association might actually be mediated by a common genetic influence.
Source: © vchalup/123RF

Results:

The association between smoking and ADHD symptoms was found to be greater in the group where mothers and children were genetically related than for the non-related group.

Discussion:

This finding suggests that ADHD symptoms might represent an inherited, rather than environmental, risk effect. The fact that parents who have a preponderance towards heritable ADHD symptoms themselves are more likely to smoke, rather than to the effects of the smoke itself on child development. These findings lead to some interesting questions. Studies on maternal smoking continue to show an effect of smoking on low birth weight, and all studies were clear that it is important for expectant mothers to stop smoking during pregnancy due to the risk for low birth weight. However, these studies also tentatively suggest that smoking cessation during pregnancy may *not* actually work as a public health intervention strategy for reducing ADHD symptoms.

TREATING ADHD

Psychostimulant medication (e.g., Ritalin) improves the behaviour of about 80% of all children with ADHD, at least in the short term (Cunningham, 1999; Mehta, Sahakian, & Robbins, 2001). Of the 5% of children who receive a diagnosis of ADHD, many of these will be prescribed medication to help control their symptoms, especially in the United States (Visser, Lesesne, & Perou, 2007). However, there are differences in the method that different countries predominantly use to treat this disorder. In China, herbal treatments are widely accepted as a treatment option and are used as much as stimulant medications (Hinshaw et al., 2011). In recent years, in Germany and Norway in particular, the prevalence of individuals with ADHD treated with psychostimulant medication increased greatly (Hinshaw et al., 2011). However, there are concerns about using medication to treat developmental disorders. Some raise the philosophical-ethical question of whether altering children's behaviour with drugs is appropriate. Others raise concerns over the potential side effects of psychostimulants. Psychostimulants have been used for a number of decades, and most side effects (which may include loss of appetite, headaches, mood or emotional problems, or sleep disturbances (Tobaiqy et al., 2011) appear to be well tolerated by most children, even those taking medication on a long-term basis, although research in this area is still relatively scarce (Huang, Tsai, & Guilleminault, 2011; van de Loo-Neus, Rommelse, & Buitelaar, 2011).

> **behaviour therapy** A psychological form of treatment, often used in treating conduct disorders, which is based on such learning principles as reinforcement and social learning.

The major alternative treatment available for ADHD is behaviour therapy, a psychological intervention based on social learning principles, primarily reinforcement. In traditional behaviour therapy programmes, parents and teachers are taught to identify and monitor various specific, troublesome aspects of the ADHD child's behaviour (e.g., not completing class assignments on time) and to systematically reward the child for making improvements in the targeted problem area (Hardman, Drew, & Egan, 2002). In related behaviour therapy programmes, teachers and parents also work directly with the child in an attempt to teach cognitive self-control strategies. These cognitive-behavioural approaches have been shown to improve functioning in children with ADHD who have problematic symptoms even after trialling medication (Young & Amarasinghe, 2010; Ramsay, 2011).

To address the ongoing controversy of whether drugs, behavioural intervention, or both are the best way to treat children with ADHD, the National Institute of Mental Health in the USA launched a large clinical trial (Jensen et al., 2001; Wells, 2001). Nearly 600 children aged 7 to 9 with a primary diagnosis of ADHD were randomly assigned to one of four treatment conditions. One group received only medication; a second group received only psychosocial treatment consisting of parent training, teacher consultation, and cognitive-behavioural and behavioural treatments aimed at fostering academic, social, and sports skills. Children in the third group received a combination of both medication and psychosocial treatment, while those in the fourth group received only routine treatment from their community paediatrician or the school. Results indicated that children in all four treatment groups improved after the 14 months of treatment and 10 months of follow-up. Not only did ADHD symptoms decrease, but symptoms of oppositional defiant disorder and internalizing symptoms decreased as well. Moreover, social skills, academic achievement and parent–child relationships improved. But not all treatments were equally effective. Children receiving medication or the combined treatment (medication and psychosocial intervention) showed greater improvement than those receiving psychosocial treatment alone or community treatment, especially in ADHD symptoms. Moreover, children in the combined group showed the most impressive improvement on other measures, such as oppositional symptoms, internalizing symptoms, social skills and reading achievement.

CHILDHOOD DEPRESSION

Depression in childhood – an internalizing disorder – is diagnosed when a child has seemed depressed or has lost interest or pleasure in nearly all activities for at least two weeks. The dominant mood may be one of irritability and crankiness rather than sadness and dejection. Family members often notice social withdrawal or neglect of activities the child formerly enjoyed; for example, a child who used to enjoy playing football may begin to make excuses not to practise. Sara, from our earlier case study, was suffering from many of these symptoms. Depression often interferes with appetite and eating, and parents may note a failure of the child to make normal or expected weight gains. Another common effect of depression is an impaired ability to think, to concentrate, or to focus on a task; a precipitous drop in grades may signal depressive problems in a child or adolescent. Somatic complaints (e.g., headache, stomach ache) are not uncommon in children with depression. Table 15-6 lists some behaviours that are common in infants, children and adolescents with depression.

> **depression in childhood**
> Like adult depression, a mood disorder often manifested in a depressed mood and loss of interest in familiar activities, but also likely to be expressed as irritability and crankiness. Difficulty concentrating or focusing on tasks and concomitant drops in school grades are not uncommon, and children with depression often complain of physical problems such as headache.

Table 15-6 Depressive behaviours in children and adolescents

	Behaviours
Infants	Sad mood, crying, disinterest, delayed development of movement and other abilities, being sick, being irritable, feeding or sleeping problems
Toddlers and preschoolers	Being irritable, socially withdrawn, poor self-image, difficulty making friends, sad mood, weeping, disinterest, feeding or sleeping problems, aggressive behaviours, risky behaviours, incontinence, bed-wetting, asthma, eczema, desire to die
School children	Being irritable, disinterest, tiredness, feeding or sleeping problems, guilt, low self-esteem, schoolwork problems, aggressive behaviour, difficulty concentrating, anxiety, continued incontinence and/or bed-wetting, sad or depressed facial expression, suicidal thoughts
Adolescents	Difficulty sleeping, changes in appetite or weight, tiredness, disinterest, self-deprecation, difficulty concentrating, indecision, anxiety, continued incontinence and/or bed-wetting, emotional dependence, risky behaviours, suicidal thoughts or attempts

Source: Adapted from Gelfand and Drew (2003).

To be judged clinically depressed, a child must display changes in cognitive functioning and behaviour. Possible changes in cognitive functioning include guilt and feelings of worthlessness, complaints about inability to concentrate, slowed thinking, and recurrent thoughts of death and suicide. As we mentioned earlier in this chapter, the presentation of depression, like other developmental disorders, changes significantly with age. Pre-teen children do not seem to manifest the general slowing of mental and physical activity or the motivational deficits that adults with depression typically do (Gelfand & Drew, 2003), children with depression often present other more behavioural symptoms, such as hyperactivity, bed-wetting, learning problems and antisocial behaviour.

The traditional view has been that depression in childhood is low in frequency, and increases with age. And certainly, as Figure 15-1 shows, depression is rarely diagnosed among children at the age of 10, with the diagnosis rising in frequency quite dramatically among adolescent females from the age of 15 continuing into adulthood. The diagnosis rises for males as well at about 15 but levels off at about 18. Nearly twice as many girls as boys experience depression (Goodman & Gotlib, 2002; Hammen, 2005).

However, in recent years, researchers have begun to question whether depression might be present but not as evident in even earlier stages of development. In recent years clinicians have increasingly noted the presence of depressive symptoms in young (even 3-year-old) children which appear, revealed through longitudinal studies, to continue into later life (Luby et al., 2014). This is an important area of current research.

As with ADHD, there has been much concern of potentially rising incidences of depression among children in recent years. However, one study examining the prevalence of depression in childhood and adolescence across a 60-year period, has noted that the perceived 'epidemic' of depression compared to 60 years ago is unlikely (Costello, Erkanli, & Angold, 2006). This study noted that the rates of depression were about 2.8% for

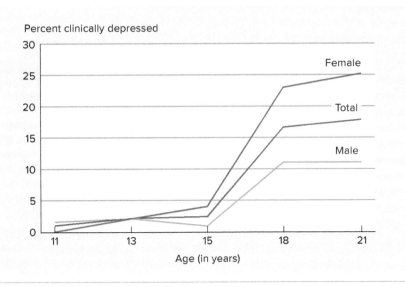

Percent clinically depressed

Figure 15-1   Clinical depression among children and adolescents

Clinical, or serious, depression is not seen often among children, but beginning at about the age of 15, it is diagnosed in a considerable number of young people. About twice as many females as males are found to be seriously depressed, and depression continues to rise slowly as young women enter adulthood.
Source: Hankin et al. (1998).

children under 13, and 5.6% for 13–18 year olds (5.9% for girls and 4.6% for boys). Costello and colleagues suggest that it is increased sensitivity, and better diagnosis of the problem that leads to the perception that depression in children is a modern problem. The fact that professionals diagnose depression in children more frequently as children grow older probably reflects both that difficulty and the fact that depressive disorder is experienced at its fullest only when the child's cognitive capacities reach the stage of formal operations.

One unfortunate consequence of the increased rate of depression during adolescence is a concomitant increase in the rate of suicide. Although suicide is very rare among children younger than 12, it is estimated to be the third leading killer of adolescents, following car accidents and homicide (Berman, Jobes, & Silverman, 2005; Centers for Disease Control and Prevention, 2007). However, reporting suicide rates for children across a wide age range (e.g., 5–14 years) is problematic. The suicidal intentions of children under 10 years of age are difficult to establish (Mishara, 1999) and potential misclassification of young deaths may lead to under- or over-reporting of suicide cases (Groholt & Ekeberg, 2003). Among university students, suicide is considered the second leading cause of death; about 10,000 individuals attempt suicide, and of those, 1000 succeed each year. One UK study examined suicides of young people aged between 10 and 19 between 1997 and 2003 (Windfuhr et al., 2008). In 2003, the rate of suicide was 2.47 per 100,000 young people, with rates of 3.42 per 100,000 for males and 1.46 per 100,000 for females. The majority of these cases had a history of self-harm (71%), and many had a history of substance misuse (also 71%). Almost one-third of these individuals had a diagnosis of an affective disorder (e.g., depression).

Culture plays a role in suicide as well as age and gender. Suicide rates are high in countries such as Japan, where there is a long tradition of viewing suicide as an honourable action. In Muslim and Catholic countries, where suicide is viewed as a violation of religious teachings, rates are low. Although depression and suicide are often linked, this is not always the case (Jellinek & Snyder, 1998). In one large study of adolescents, 42% of those who attempted suicide did *not* have a history of depression (Andrews & Lewinsohn, 1992). Suicide is related to a general sense of overwhelming hopelessness, although it also may result from the accumulation of adverse life events such as family conflicts; loss of a family member due to illness, death, or divorce; breakups or problems in romantic relationships or friendships; school failure; being apprehended in a delinquent, forbidden, or embarrassing act or situation; or real or imagined mental or physical illness (Jellinek & Snyder, 1998). Adolescents who attempt suicide often feel they have no source of emotional support. They frequently are alienated from their families and may have had disruptions or losses in intimate relations and relations with peers that give them an increasing sense of isolation and helplessness.

CAUSES OF CHILDHOOD DEPRESSION

Theories of the aetiology of depression are abundant. Like many human disorders, depression is very likely caused by multiple factors. Thus, in discussing biological, social and psychological, and cognitive accounts we should look not just for one answer but for many, and ask how such contributing factors interact.

One of the earliest theories of the causes of childhood depression linked it to the loss of maternal affection or failure to form a secure attachment (Bowlby, 1960). Although some research has supported this position, other factors, such as parental conflict, maternal depression, negative life events, lack of effective social supports and, especially for girls, problems with peers and unpopularity, have been linked with depression in children (Cummings et al., 2000; Hammen, 2005).

The link between depression in parents and children has received considerable attention in the research literature. Depression is more likely to occur in children of parents with clinical depression (Goodman & Gotlib, 2002; Cicchetti & Toth, 2006). Indeed, children of parents with depression are at risk for higher rates not only of depression but also of a wide range of other disorders such as anxiety, academic failure, attention deficit disorders and conduct disorders, especially if the parent's depression is chronic or sustained (Weissman et al., 1997; Embry & Dawson, 2002; Hammen, 2005).

Twin and adoption studies indicate that the association between depression in children and parents may in part be genetic (Franić et al., 2010). However, studies also show that the experiences of children with a depressed parent may differ from those with a non-depressed mother. Parents with depression are tenser, more disorganized, resentful and ambivalent, and less sensitive, communicative and affectionate with their children (Cummings et al., 2000; Goodman, 2008). Furthermore, they are more likely to perceive their children's behaviour negatively (Hammen, 2005). It is not surprising, then, that children of mothers with depression are more likely to be insecurely attached, fearful and lower in self-esteem, and to have problems in subsequent social relations (Lyons-Ruth et al., 2002; Cicchetti & Toth, 2006). Both paternal and maternal depression are associated with child depression (Jacob & Johnson, 1997).

A mother's depression and listlessness may lead the child to become depressed later on. Disruption in early attachment, as well as modelling, may contribute to the link between parent and child depression.
Source: © Golden Pixels LLC/Shutterstock

Peers can play a role in children's mental health, too. Primary-age school children who were socially anxious (shy, inhibited) and who were excluded by their peers were at higher risk for depression than non-anxious and better accepted classmates (Gazelle & Ladd, 2003). Life stressors also contribute to depression (Hammen, 2005). Finally, cultural expectations emphasizing achievement, success and wealth may contribute to the emergence of depression if children fail to meet them.

How do genetic and environmental contributions to depression act together? As with ADHD, at least one answer to this question comes from behavioural genetics studies which demonstrate that common genetic dispositions between parents and children can lead to children experiencing environments which affect their development in a particular way. For instance, the heritability of depression could mean that children who have a preponderance towards depression also develop in a parenting environment which is more negative (Jaffee & Price, 2007). Studies (e.g., Rice et al., 2013) of parents and children who are either biologically related or not, show that the intergenerational transmission of depression is largely due to the parenting environment.

TREATING CHILDHOOD DEPRESSION

Children and adolescents with depressive disorders benefit from a wide range of interventions. Antidepressant drugs such as fluoxetine (Prozac) and sertraline (Zoloft) are widely prescribed and somewhat effective. In one study, 56% of children with major depression improved with Prozac compared with only 33% of a placebo control group (Emslie et al., 1997). Unfortunately, antidepressant drugs are dangerous, and an overdose can be lethal (Gelfand & Drew, 2003). In 2004, the US government began to require that warning labels accompany these antidepressant drugs in light of the increased risk of suicide associated with their use in a small percentage of adolescents. However, the rates of suicide showed a sharp increase at the same time that the use of antidepressants among adolescents declined, which suggests that parents need to be aware of warning signs of suicide whether their teens are on antidepressant drugs or not (Centers for Disease Control and Prevention, 2007).

cognitive behaviour therapy A group therapy technique particularly useful in treating depression in adolescents. Therapeutic goals include reducing self-consciousness and feelings of being different, and teaching strategies for dealing with depressive moods and for acquiring a more positive outlook and improving social interactions.

Cognitive behaviour therapy is one of the most effective approaches for treating depression in adolescents (Hammen, 2005). This type of therapy is typically conducted in small groups of three to eight adolescents twice a week over a number of weeks. The goals are to reduce the teenagers' self-consciousness and feelings of being different, and to provide them with strategies such as relaxation techniques and self-control strategies to help them control their dark moods. The therapy also emphasizes positive strategies such as improving peer relations, setting realistic goals and learning how to get more fun out of activities. Results have been impressive. In one study that directly compared CBT with drug treatment for adolescents (aged around 14 years) with depression, 36 weeks after the onset of treatment, the CBT group had achieved 64% remissions from depressive symptoms, compared to 55% in the medication only condition (Kennard et al., 2009). For children and adolescents with depression that is not responding to medication, adding a course of CBT can improve remission rates by over 50% (Brent et al., 2008).

Prevention programmes have been effective in reducing depression, too. In one study, children at risk for depression were given training in cognitive and problem-solving skills (Gillham et al., 1995). Two years later, when researchers evaluated these children, they found fewer depressive symptoms than in a control group.

AUTISM SPECTRUM DISORDERS (ASD)

Following Leo Kanner's description of autism in the 1940s (Kanner, 1943), this puzzling disorder was characterized by Lorna Wing (Wing, 1981) as a 'triad of impairments':

- *Impairments in reciprocal social interactions.* This has been characterized as extreme autistic aloneness, expressed as a lack of interest in other people that sometimes appears to be an actual aversion to contact with other human beings.
- *Impaired communication,* ranging from an absence of speech to repeating others' exact words rather than replying or engaging in conversation.
- *Restricted interests and attempts to preserve sameness* in the environment that may lead to repetitive behaviours or total and extended concentration on one activity or perceptual sensation (e.g., a spinning top).

Our earlier case study, Alfie, displayed many of these behaviours.

Since the publication of *DSM-5* in 2013, however (American Psychiatric Association, 2013), autism has come to be defined a little differently. In *DSM-IV*, a range of disorders which were similar to autism, and included autism were covered. One such disorder, *Asperger's syndrome,* shares some of the social and affective deficits associated with autism, but children with Asperger's do not show significant language delays and are often able to progress in school at a satisfactory rate (Volkmar et al., 2004; Pennington, 2005). In *DSM-5*, autism and Asperger's syndrome are now grouped together as part of a broader diagnostic category of *Autism Spectrum Disorders (ASD).* Furthermore, the diagnostic criteria for ASD have moved away from the triad of impairments, grouping communicative and social impairments together under one heading, and keeping separate from that the requirement of 'restricted interests and repetitive behaviours'. Another change has been to include sensory abnormalities as one of the potential markers of restricted interests and repetitive behaviours.

How prevalent are these disorders? In the early 1980s autism (now known as ASD) was considered a rare disorder. However, following an increased awareness of the condition, diagnoses in the UK increased five-fold between 1988 and 1996. From 1996 diagnoses have remained fairly stable to the current decade (Taylor, Jick, & MacLaughlin, 2013) with a prevalence of about 3.8/1000 boys and 0.8/1000 girls at 8 years of age. In the US, rates of diagnosis have increased more dramatically to around 1 in every 88 children (Center for Disease Control and Prevention, 2012)! The increases in diagnosis over the last decades owe not only to better awareness and detection but also to the use of broader diagnostic criteria.

It is difficult to imagine just how pervasive the difficulties associated with autism can be. If two children with ASD are placed side by side in a room full of toys, they may well ignore each other. Children with ASD often seem to prefer inanimate objects to human interaction. Children with autism often appear to be unaware of other people and even of themselves. Children with autism show deficits in self-recognition. Children typically develop the ability to recognize their mirror images as themselves around the age of 2 using the rouge test (see Chapter 6). When researchers in one study showed children with autism a mirror, 31% failed to demonstrate recognition of their mirror images (Spiker & Ricks, 1984). These children also were likely to lack speech. However, even the children who showed self-recognition demonstrated little emotional response – unlike typically developing children.

Researchers using subtle measures of attention, such as heart rate, have shown that children with ASD are aware of the presence of other people (Baron-Cohen, 1995). However, they may not reflect this knowledge in their overt behaviour. Many children with ASD manifest a lack of attachment and understanding of others' thoughts and feelings in social relations. They also seem unable to understand that mental states such as knowledge, beliefs and expectations exist and are connected to people's behaviour (Baron-Cohen, 1995, 2003; Siegler & Alibali, 2005). This difficulty with 'theory of mind' makes it difficult for children with ASD to anticipate and predict others' responses and thus makes it hard

Children with autism often fail to develop a useful means of communication with others, whether verbal or non-verbal. Such children may be highly resistant to change and to new patterns of behaviour. At the same time, because these children often seem to prefer inanimate objects to human interaction, psychologists are exploring the approach of teaching children with autism to communicate by means of a computer.
Source: © Washington Post/Getty Images

for them to engage in effective social interactions. Most children with ASD fail to develop normal friendships and many risk becoming socially isolated (American Psychiatric Association, 2013; Baron-Cohen, 2003).

Children with ASD display deficits in both non-verbal and verbal communication. Many show difficulties understanding facial expressions of emotion and integrating or using gestures such as those meaning 'be quiet' or 'come here' or 'look' (Baron-Cohen, 2003, 2007). They are less likely than normal children to respond when called by name or to respond to an adult's point and gaze (Dawson et al., 2004). They display less attention to the distress of another person. In addition, some 50% of children with autism never develop meaningful, useful speech, and most others have limited and sometimes bizarre means of verbal expression.

Many children with autism master only a few of the tasks necessary to function in the world and need constant help with feeding, dressing, toileting and cleaning. Although their senses function adequately when tested, children with autism behave as if they have sensory deficits. For example, they spend their time engaging in obsessive self-stimulatory behaviour such as repetitively spinning objects, switching lights on and off, or flapping their hands in front of their eyes (Pennington, 2005). It is thought that the primary purpose of this bizarre-appearing behaviour may be to provide sensory stimulation.

> Children with autism display behaviours which suggest that they have an impaired theory of mind. In Chapter 9 we discuss how theory of mind develops in typical children.

> **obsessive self-stimulatory behaviour** Behaviour common in children with autism in which they engage in repetitive actions that seemingly have no purpose.

Some children with autism show a type of intelligence traditionally associated with the *savant*. This is a person who has some unusual talent – for example, in the area of mathematical and computer abilities – such as being able to quickly and accurately predict the day of the week on which some date far in the future will fall, or in art or music, such as the detailed architectural drawings produced by Stephen Wiltshire. Some children with autism show remarkable memory, such as the ability to repeat television commercials verbatim. About one in ten children with autism have been described to have special talents or abilities (Pring, 2005). However, about 70% of children with autism score in the retarded range on commonly used measures of intelligence, and this below-average performance is quite stable over time (Kauffman, 2001).

CAUSES OF AUTISM

At present, the cause of autism is unknown, however, it is clear that it is a strongly heritable disorder. Twin studies find a much higher incidence of the disorder in monozygotic than in dizygotic twins (Ronald &

Hoekstra, 2011; Tick et al., 2016). Behavioural genetics research demonstrating this strong role of inheritance, has thankfully pushed into the background the traditional and unhelpful view that ASD was due to children having cold and aloof 'refrigerator parents'.

Despite the knowledge that ASD has a strong heritability, we are still a long way from understanding what the specific genetic drivers of the disorder are, although researchers have shown that the precise genetic make-up of ASD is likely to be highly complex (Happé et al., 2006). Interestingly, chromosomal abnormalities have also been found in some children with autism (Kumar & Christian, 2009) as well as alterations in brain chemistry (Friedman et al., 2003, 2006). There is increasing evidence that it is likely that multiple potential influences interact to disrupt the development and function of several brain systems that are implicated in social and non-social behaviours that are characteristic of ASDs (Charman et al., 2011; Happé et al., 2006). These brain regions include the frontal and temporal neocortex, caudate and cerebellum (Abrahams & Geschwind, 2010).

It is clear that environmental factors can also play a role in the aetiology of ASD. There are differences in autistic symptoms within monozygotic twin pairs, which suggest that environmental influences play a role in shaping the form that autism will assume (Pennington, 2005; Rutter, 2007).

As well as understanding environmental and genetic causes of ASD, it is also crucial to consider the ways in which the disorder develops in the individual in cognitive terms. Indeed, it has been argued that understanding the cognitive phenotype of ASD plays a crucial role in linking genes, brain development and behaviour (Charman et al., 2011).

There have been several 'cognitive' accounts of ASD, and these are outlined in Table 15-7.

Table 15-7   Descriptions of some of the main cognitive theories of autism

Account	Description
Theory of Mind (ToM) Baron-Cohen et al. (1985)	Suggests that individuals with ASD had a deficit, or a delay, in understanding the thoughts and feelings of other people. Tested using 'false belief' tasks, requiring individuals to correctly state what another person would say the location of an object was if they had not seen it being moved. False belief tasks are passed by a significant subset of individuals with ASD. Likelihood of passing is also highly associated with verbal mental age. More advanced ToM tasks have also been trialled (e.g., Reading the Mind in the Eyes, Strange Stories); individuals with ASD do show a deficit, but do not always fail outright.
Executive Dysfunction Hill (2004) Ozonoff et al. (1991)	Derived from the observation that ASD behaviours were similar to some individuals with brain injury. Symptoms such as need for sameness, difficulties switching attention and disinhibition were not readily explained by ToM account. These difficulties are also common in individuals with frontal lobe damage. The Executive Dysfunction hypothesis can explain many of the features of ASD. However, its limitations are that not all individuals with autism show executive problems and those who do may have differing profiles of executive dysfunction. Executive difficulties are also not unique to ASD and are seen in other disorders (e.g., schizophrenia, ADHD).
Weak Central Coherence (WCC) and Enhanced Perceptual Functioning Frith (1989); Happé and Frith (2006); Mottron et al. (2006)	Suggests that individuals with autism process things in a detail-focused or piecemeal way – processing the constituent parts, rather than the global whole. In contrast, typically developing individuals process information by extracting overall meaning or gist. Evidence for WCC cites tests of visuo-spatial and perceptual functioning (including copying a pattern of blocks and finding a particular shape in a larger picture – the embedded figures task). Argued that better performance on these tasks is due to attention to detail, and lack of attention to the 'global whole'. This theory was extended by Mottron et al. (2006), who argued that although individuals with ASD could process both local and global information, there was some deficit which led to global information not taking priority (as for typically developing individuals).
Enhanced Systemizing Baron-Cohen et al. (2005)	Also known as the 'extreme male brain' theory of autism. Based on work in typically developing samples that suggested that females have a relative strength in empathizing (e.g., emotion recognition, social sensitivity), while males have a relative systemizing strength (e.g., visuo-spatial processing, making predictions according to rules). A pattern of enhanced 'systemizing' and decreased 'empathizing' abilities are also reported in individuals with ASD. Baron-Cohen et al. (2005) has linked this cognitive style with differences at the level of the brain and has suggested a link with exposure to prenatal androgens (e.g., testosterone).

These accounts aim to provide some explanation for all of the behaviours seen in ASD. However, more recent accounts have accepted that ASD is a highly heterogeneous disorder (that is, it can present differently across different individuals) and theories now aim to explain particular aspects of behaviour instead of the whole disorder (Happé et al., 2006).

BOX 15-3 Using home videos to learn about early identification of autism spectrum disorders

Applied Developmental Psychology

For over 30 years, there has been an interest in family home movies of infants who are subsequently diagnosed with ASD. It is now common in many countries for autism to be diagnosed at age 2 or 3, but home videos have been used to help researchers and clinicians learn more about how ASDs may present before they are formally diagnosed.

The primary motivation for identifying the earliest possible symptoms of emerging ASD is so that early tests and preventative or ameliorative strategies can be developed to attempt to change the course of development, and perhaps reduce the impact of an ASD on the child.

There are many advantages of using home videos to examine early behaviours in ASDs. Videos allow observers to have an insight into behaviour in a naturalistic setting and observe parent–child interactions that are not influenced by being in a clinical situation. It is also possible to have videos rated by coders who are blind to the eventual diagnosis of the child; many studies have compared behaviours between children who are later given a diagnosis of ASD and children who are considered typically developing. However, home videos do also suffer from some limitations. The information cannot be standardized, so it may be difficult to compare across different contexts, and parents may choose to videotape their children when the children are at their best and not necessarily while manifesting some of the behaviours that may be of most interest to researchers studying the early emergence of ASDs (Yirmiya & Charman, 2010).

Clifford, Young and Williamson (2007) analysed home videos of infants who were later diagnosed with ASDs; infants who had developmental or language delays; and typically developing infants between the ages of 12 months and 24 months. Videos were sourced from families and were rated by researchers who were not aware of the eventual diagnosis of the infant.

Clifford et al. indicated a range of social behaviours that discriminated the infants who were later diagnosed with ASDs from the other two groups. These behaviours included:

- eye contact quality
- positive affect (e.g., smiling)
- nestling
- gaze aversion (e.g., avoiding eye contact)
- interest in other children
- conventional social games and anticipatory postures (e.g., 'peek-a-boo')
- proto-declarative showing (pointing to show an adult something).

© santypan/Shutterstock

Clifford and colleagues suggest that between the first and second birthdays, infants with a later diagnosis of ASDs were distinguishable from infants with developmental delays on a number of basic dyadic social behaviours (e.g., eye contact, expressions of emotion). Home videos have provided an interesting method of observing early abnormalities in social behaviours, even before a child's first birthday, that have allowed researchers and clinicians an insight into those early behaviours that characterize ASD in young infants.

TREATING AUTISTIC DISORDER

Autism is a difficult disorder to treat. Professionals treating children with autism have increasingly used medications – especially medication designed to reduce serotonin levels – but although such medications have shown moderate success in reducing some problem behaviours, such as hyperactivity, they have not succeeded in dealing with the core symptoms, primarily self-injurious behaviour (Myers, 2007). Moreover, these medications are often accompanied by adverse side effects (Drew & Hardman, 2000).

operant behaviour therapy A form of behaviour therapy in which behaviour is carefully monitored and consistently rewarded with such things as food.

Of the host of treatments tried, operant behaviour therapy appears to be most effective (McEachin, Smith, & Lovaas, 1993; Clarke, 2001). By carefully monitoring the autistic child's behaviour, and by systematically rewarding appropriate behaviour with such things as food, operant behaviour therapy programmes have been quite successful in teaching children with autism basic self-care skills. However, these time-consuming treatments are not usually able to improve a child's adaptive skills to an age-appropriate level (Clarke, 2001). Such techniques are not guaranteed to produce generalizable language skills (Cantwell, Baker, & Rutter, 1978; Lovaas, 1987), and it may be that using a sign-based social form of teaching language may also be useful. For example, the Picture Exchange Communication System (PECS; Bondy & Frost, 2001) is one example of a socially based approach to teaching language. Rather than pointing to a picture of a desired item, children must hand the appropriate picture to an adult, who then reinforces the request with the actual item. Regardless of the type of intervention used, it is recognized that intervening at earlier ages, involving parents in training programmes, and working with children in their natural environment are the most important factors for effective intervention (Clarke, 2001).

One particular line of current research on ASD interventions has been to identify children at risk of developing ASD (as they are a sibling of a child with a diagnosis) and introduce intervention programmes during infancy (Green et al., 2015; 2017). Early results of these approaches are promising and further outcomes in these longitudinal studies will be important for determining their efficacy.

SUMMARY

Children exhibit a wide array of atypical behaviours and patterns of thinking, some of which are relatively common while others are quite rare. Whereas some of these behaviours are marked by a lack of control or inhibition (externalizing behaviours) others are characterized by excessive internalizing of troublesome issues.

Developmental psychopathology involves the study of the origins, changes, and continuities in maladaptive behaviour over the lifespan. The main tenet of developmental psychopathology has been that developmental disorders must not be considered as static impairments, but as outcomes of the complex process of development which individuals go through.

Two major ways of assessing and classifying developmental psychopathology are the diagnostic approach and the empirical method. Diagnoses are based on descriptions of clusters of behaviours and disturbing thoughts or feelings classified into various diagnostic categories. A *diagnosis* must convey information about the *aetiology* and course of a disorder to be useful. The most widely used diagnostic classification system is the American Psychiatric Association's *DSM-5*. Although this system has been revised several times, it still presents problems of validity. The empirical approach involves having adults familiar with the child rate a large number of problem behaviours and then using statistical techniques to determine which disorders are related.

Externalizing disorders, such as conduct and attention deficit/hyperactivity disorders, are the most frequently reported of all psychological problems of childhood and have considerable impact on the child's social environment. *Internalizing disorders*, such as childhood depression, have a greater effect on children themselves, who bottle up their feelings and concerns.

Children with *conduct disorders* repeatedly violate the rights of others or age-appropriate societal norms. Conduct disorders have a range of aetiologies (or causes), but the antisocial behaviours can cause children to become socially and academically excluded. Behavioural techniques, including reinforcement of appropriate behaviour and the *time-out method*, are among the most successful treatments for conduct disorders. Prevention programmes that involve both family and school show promise.

Attention deficit/hyperactivity disorder, often not diagnosed until children enter the structured environment of school, is characterized by overactivity, impulsivity, poor attention and difficulties with rule-governed behaviour. Although the inappropriate activity of hyperactive children tends to diminish with age, some problems may persist, resulting in poor academic performance. There is a strong genetic component in the causes of ADHD and it is often treated by *psychostimulant medications, behaviour therapy* or a combination of the two.

Depression in childhood may be characterized by depressed mood, changes in cognitive functioning such as inability to concentrate, behavioural signs such as irritability and withdrawal, and such physical problems as loss of appetite and weight loss. Depression in children is hard to diagnose because children may not be able or willing to talk about feelings of overwhelming sadness until they have reached a certain level of cognitive maturity. Diagnoses of depression increase dramatically in adolescence, as does the rate of suicidal thinking and actual suicide attempts. A number of causes of depression have been hypothesized.

Autism spectrum disorder (ASD) is characterized by a lack of interest in other people, various language abnormalities and a desire to engage in repetitive behaviours and to preserve sameness in the environment. Children with autism sometimes exhibit specific talents (savant abilities) in mathematics or the ability to repeat television commercials verbatim, but score in the learning disability range on IQ tests. ASD is highly heritable. Treatment, which has included medication and *operant behaviour therapy*, has met with limited success. Although treatment allows the children to develop many skills they would not otherwise acquire, their range of abilities can remain quite limited.

Explore and Discuss

1. Are developmental problems of childhood culturally specific or do children in all cultures show all of the same kinds of problems? If you believe these problems are culturally specific, support your answer with examples.

2. Some developmental disorders such as ASD seem more prevalent than they were a decade ago. What do you think may be some of the reasons for the increased incidence of this kind of developmental disorder?

3. Why do you think boys are more prone to externalize problems – for example, to engage in aggressive behaviour that is often physical – whereas girls are more likely to internalize their concerns and then to express them in anxiety and depression?

Recommended Reading

Classic

Rutter, M. (2000). Developmental psychopathology: Concepts and challenges. *Development and Psychopathology, 12*, 265–296.

Sameroff, A. J., Lewis, M., & Miller, S. (2000). *Handbook of developmental psychopathology* (2nd edn). New York, NY: Kluwer Academic.

Sroufe, A. L. (1997). Psychopathology as an outcome of development. *Development and Psychopathology, 9*, 251–268.

Contemporary

Cicchetti, D., & Toth, S. L. (2006). *Developmental psychopathology and preventive intervention.* In W. Damon and R. M. Lerner (eds), *Handbook of child psychology.* Hoboken, NJ: John Wiley & Sons.

Dodge, K. A. & Rutter, M. (2011). *Gene–environment interactions in developmental psychopathology.* New York, NY: Guilford Press.

Frick, P. J. & Viding, E. (2009), Antisocial behavior from a developmental psychopathology perspective. *Development and Psychopathology, 21*, 1111–1131.

Karmiloff-Smith, A., Thomas, M. S., & Johnson, M. H. (2018). *Thinking developmentally from constructivism to neuroconstructivism: Selected works of Annette Karmiloff-Smith.* Abingdon: Routledge.

CHAPTER 16
Development in Adulthood

Throughout most of its history, developmental psychology has focused on changes in infants' and children's reasoning and behaviour; that is, most development researchers have tried to explain how thoughts, feelings and behaviour change from infancy and into early adolescence. It is not until comparatively recently that a significant proportion of research in developmental psychology has moved to explore psychological processes of development outside of this period. This chapter focuses on the latter aspect; that is, what (if any) psychological development happens throughout adulthood, and how this development happens.

Introduction

We begin by exploring in more depth why the topic of development in adults has traditionally been rather neglected by researchers and theorists. The focus then moves to the physiological and neurological changes that occur throughout adulthood and into old age. The chapter then considers the reasons for variations in life expectancy, and introduces some basic definitions or categories of adulthood to provide a chronological framework for research in the area. Research findings on the links between ageing and cognitive processes, such as intelligence and memory are then presented. Reasons for the observed increases in memory problems with age in some individuals are discussed. To conclude the chapter, the changing role of social relationships across the lifespan is examined, including friendships, marriages, families, parenthood and grandparenting.

There are several different reasons for what might appear, at first glance, to be a very narrow focus on development through childhood to the exclusion of development across adulthood (and prenatal development). Many early theorists (such as Piaget and Vygotsky) were primarily interested in explaining cognitive change and so focused their research efforts on exploring that change in an age group in which it was most pronounced. In addition, there may have been little demand for research in changes through adulthood. However, some researchers have argued that historically, developmental psychology has simply ignored a set of processes of life-long social and psychological change in favour of more basic cognitive and social changes in the early years of life.

Many of the issues of development and psychological change in later adulthood (old age) have come to the fore more recently as the number of older adults in the population increases in the many developed countries. The increasing numbers of elderly people that may require social and other support in the future raises important social issues. At the same time, many older adults are more active and visible than in previous generations, and so have a significant societal 'voice'.

THE IMPORTANCE OF A LIFESPAN PERSPECTIVE

Much traditional developmental psychology research has focused heavily on development from birth to adolescence. For instance, Piaget explored the reasoning and behaviour of infants and children, and sometimes those of early adolescents (up to around 15 years of age). According to Piaget (1950a) once children have acquired formal operational reasoning (in early adolescence) as this, the structure of thinking does not change. In other words, once a child or young adolescent has grasped formal operations she can think about more complex problems and in more intricate ways, but will always apply the same basic scientific methods to solve them. Vygotsky's research emphasis was also on childhood and children's cognitive development. This work focused on development, primarily viewed in terms of children's education (Wozniak, 1996). Vygotsky shared Piaget's belief that psychological (cognitive) development was most pronounced in the earlier years and so this was the most fruitful age group to study developmental processes (Vygotsky, 1978).

However, the view that psychological development is pretty much completed by the middle of adolescence implies that adult reasoning and behaviour is the endpoint of development. But adults are not a homogenous group, and adult reasoning and behaviour is rarely perfect or complete. The idea that children are, in some way, incomplete adults necessarily limits the scope of developmental psychology and excludes any psychological and social changes that might occur throughout adulthood. Thus what might be considered developmental changes in adults' behaviour

In Chapter 9 we discuss Piaget's and Vygotsky's theories, applied to infant and child development, in more detail. We discuss other theoretical perspectives in Chapter 2.

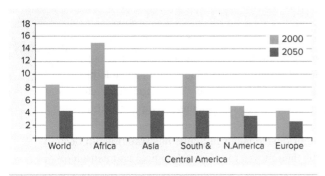

Figure 16-1   Young-old numbers (number of 15–64 year olds for every individual age 65+ years in 2000 and projected 2050)
Source: Based on data from United Nations (2017).

have tended to become the remit of other disciplines such as behavioural economics and sociology (e.g., Gummerum et al., 2008).

Concerns that a focus only on certain types of development has limited the scope of developmental psychological research have led some 'critical psychologists' to question the notion of development altogether (e.g., Morss, 1996). Central to these criticisms is the idea that any developmental framework makes unwarranted assumptions that some forms or aspects of reasoning or behaviour are superior to other forms. Rather, children's behaviour is merely a reflection of their adaptation to their environment: one that adults, in positions of power and authority, have created for them.

However, even if we do not accept the radical critical perspective, there are compelling, practical reasons for considering development in adulthood as an important research area for psychologists today. These stem from the social challenges that have arisen from demographic changes in many societies with an increasingly large, and ageing population who are living longer than in previous generations. Improvements in health care mean that more adults will live into old age. This means there will be a set of age-related medical conditions that affect a large number of individuals, which leads to associated increases in health care and related costs. Financially, the problem may be exacerbated by a decrease in birth rate such that there are fewer adults of working age to pay for and support an ageing population. As Figure 16-1 indicates, the population of many countries is ageing rapidly, and the proportion of elderly individuals (compared with children and young people) is increasing too, due to a diminishing birth rate.

> **gerontology**   The study of the social, biological and psychological aspects of ageing.

Most gerontologists divide adulthood into three broad stages. *Early adulthood* lasts from 18/19 years to 40 years of age. *Middle adulthood*, from 40 to around 60 or 65 years of age, and *late adulthood* from 60 or 65 years onwards. The boundaries between these stages are somewhat blurred. For instance, retirement from work is usually viewed as the boundary between middle and late adulthood, and this varies from country to country. Similarly, 'coming of age' is around 18/19 years in many countries, but not all adult 'privileges' are afforded to young people at the same age, even within the same society. So, for instance, young people may be able to drive a car at 17 years, vote at 18 years, but not purchase alcohol until 21 years of age. The boundaries between these stage classifications are therefore rather porous and often depend on social or societal norms, rules and regulations. In the present chapter we use the above definitions when discussing different stages of adulthood.

PHYSICAL CHANGES THROUGH ADULTHOOD

Earlier in this book, we outlined the rapid physical and psychological changes that happen from conception through to adolescence. This change is stage-like; development progresses in a non-linear fashion with infants and children achieving various milestones and consolidating particular achievements, skills or knowledge, before moving on to start to attain another milestone or stage of development. Physical development in adulthood appears smoother and less stage-like than during infancy and childhood. Much ageing is characterized by a slow but steady decline in abilities and skills, and where there are sudden drops in performance or competence these are typically a consequence of some sort of trauma such as accident or injury. However, some sudden significant physical changes do occur throughout life, some of which cannot be easily predicted (e.g., illness) and some of which can be expected (e.g., menopause). These events also have the potential to greatly influence psychological processes and well-being.

Early adulthood, the period roughly between the ages of 18 and 40 years, is the period at which people are generally in their best physical health. They are usually free from disease having outgrown childhood allergies and developed a strong immune system that can fight off minor ailments (such as flu and colds). Visual acuity, hearing and other senses are at an optimal level. Muscular strength and manual dexterity are at a peak between 25 and 30 years (Kallman, Plato, & Tobin, 1990).

From adolescence through to the end of middle adulthood, people are also at the pinnacle in terms of their reproductive capacity. However, there is a notable drop in women's fertility from the mid-thirties onwards, and associated with this an increased risk of complications with pregnancy and birth defects among children born to women who conceive beyond this age

Health is a key component of psychological well-being and this peaks in early adulthood.
Source: © Shutterstock/Mangostar

(Lewis, Legato, & Frisch, 2006). Men's reproductive capacity dips from around 40 years onwards, where there is a drop in the number of viable sperm produced.

Relatively minor deterioration in physical capacity begins towards the end of early adulthood, and continues into middle adulthood. Sometimes this may become noticeable but, more often than not, changes are so minor that they are not detected or noticeable. However, the senses become progressively less acute, with *presbyopia* (far-sightedness) in many adults during this phase. Hearing loss (*presbycusis*), which for men begun in the late twenties becomes progressively more acute, and from 55 years, this loss is more pronounced for men than women. One reason that deterioration often goes unnoticed is that in middle adulthood people can still do almost all of the everyday activities that people in early adulthood can. Only additional, strenuous activities or activities that push the body to its physical limits are no longer possible or cannot be carried out to the same level. Thus the body begins to lose its reserve capacity, but core functions remain comparatively unaffected.

A key physiological change for women in middle adulthood is the menopause. There is wide variation in the onset of this period of life, when a woman stops ovulating and menstruating and ceases to be able to reproduce. Generally women's menopause occurs at around 50 years of age, but this can vary widely. As with the age of onset, there is variation in the length of the menopause but for most women it lasts somewhere between two and five years. From a physiological perspective, the menopause occurs because of a marked decline in the body's production of the hormone oestrogen. The most distinctive physical symptoms are hot flushes – unwanted and unexpected sensations of heat. Probably due to its link with hormones, the experience of the menopause is often assumed to have negative psychological consequences such as greater variations in mood. There is some evidence that women with existing psychological disorders such as obsessive-compulsive disorder (Labad et al., 2008) and bipolar disorder (Freeman et al., 2002) experience greater difficulties associated with their disorder during the menopause. However, for the majority of women there appear to be no negative psychological consequences (Matthews et al., 1990).

Throughout middle adulthood both sexes begin to reduce their interest in sexual activity, and there is a reduction in men's production of the hormone testosterone (the 'male' hormone) from around the late twenties onwards. A cluster of physical symptoms that are often reported by men during middle adulthood include tiredness, irritability and also, occasionally, hot flushes. However, the decline in testosterone for men is far more gradual than the decline in oestrogen for women during the menopause. This has led to some controversy over whether the male menopause – the andropause – exists at all.

reserve capacity The capacity to push one's body a little further if undertaking strenuous physical activities.

menopause A biological change in women during middle adulthood where the ovaries cease functioning and women can no longer conceive children.

andropause The 'male menopause', linked to a decline in the production of testosterone but with varying symptoms and not universally acknowledged to exist.

Although there is a link between reductions in testosterone and depression in men, this link is noteworthy only for elderly males (i.e., 60 years and older) (Margolese, 2000). Moreover, the psychological characteristics of the andropause may well be explained by social or psychological processes rather than by hormones. For instance, traditionally male self-esteem has been closely linked to career and sexual success. If a middle-aged man begins to lose interest in sex, or if his career does not turn out as he had hoped, he might become depressed or begin a major reappraisal of himself, his values and ambitions (Lazarus & DeLongis, 1983). It is not surprising, then, that the andropause is also sometimes described as a 'mid-life crisis'. Whatever its causes, there is widespread acknowledgement that many men go through a major appraisal of their life and role at some stage during middle adulthood.

The physical decline that begins in middle adulthood accelerates in late adulthood. Although the declines in vision that lead to far-sightedness stabilize around 60 years, there is increasing hearing loss. Hearing loss affects around a third of individuals aged 65–74 years and half of those 75–79 years. Senses of smell and taste decline significantly from 60 years. The loss of taste, in particular, is a source of concern because older adults often complain that food is tasteless and, as a consequence, may not eat properly, lose weight and suffer from malnutrition (Fisher, 1990). Into old age, muscle strength progressively diminishes, reactions slow, and the body takes longer to recover from injury and illness. However, there is wide variation in both the extent and the nature of physical decline: many octogenarians remain in good physical health.

The ageing brain

In adulthood, changes with age in the physical characteristics of the brain also occur. These changes include brain shrinkage and a loss of neuron connections and plasticity. However, few studies have managed to link age-related changes in the brain with specific decline in cognitive functions in adulthood. Throughout adulthood, there is a gradual and steady reduction of around 2% for each decade of life in the weight and volume of the brain. This reduction is constant across adulthood and does not accelerate in later years. The observation that cognitive and other processes can be impoverished in old age is, therefore, a likely consequence of an accumulation of years of graduation deterioration (although, clearly, sudden brain traumas such as stroke and injury can lead to sudden problems with cognition). Brain shrinkage is partly due to the loss of neurons, but also due to the neurons themselves shrinking in size. This shrinkage is not uniform: areas most frequently affected are the frontal lobes and hippocampus (areas associated with memory processes). As neurons are lost and shrink, the complex connections between neurons across the brain are also lost. These lost connections may not be replaced or new connections are not so easily formed. Levels of key biochemical neurotransmitters such as dopamine also decline with age, further compromising the brain's ability to maintain efficient connections between neurons.

Research close-up

BOX 16-1 Age-related cognitive changes involve some parts of the brain more than others

Source: Based on MacPherson, Phillips, and Della Sala (2002).

Introduction:

Current neuropsychological models suggest that the age-related decline in some cognitive functions is related to a deterioration of the frontal lobes of the brain. However, when the performance of healthy ageing individuals is compared with that of patients with damage to the frontal lobes, there seems to be some inconsistency. MacPherson et al. suggested that this might be because the frontal lobes can be subdivided into two discrete areas which perform different functions and which age differently. From a structural perspective, the frontal lobes can be divided into the dorsolateral (DL) and ventromedial (VM) regions and there is some physical evidence, for example from autopsy studies, that the DL area ages faster than the VM area. From a functional perspective, the DL region is considered to be important for the cognitive abilities known as executive function, and for working memory. The VM area is considered to be involved in the processing of emotions and for control of social behaviour. The researchers therefore hypothesized that there should be a faster deterioration in performance on tasks which mainly involve executive function or working memory than on tasks which mainly involve emotional processing or social decision making.

Method:

This study compared participants in three different age groups: 20–38 years; 40–59 years; and 61–80 years. There were 15 men and 15 women in each age group. Each participant performed eight different tasks. Three of the tasks were chosen because they were known to involve mainly the DL region; these were the Wisconsin Card Sorting test, the Self-Ordered Pointing Test and a Delayed-Response Task. A further three tasks were chosen to test VM function; these were a Gambling task, a Faux Pas task and an Emotion Identification task. In addition, two tasks that tested the function of the medial temporal lobes were performed. These were required because there is some evidence that the medial temporal lobes deteriorate with healthy ageing and it was important to account for the effect of this on participants' performance.

Results:

Results showed that participants in the older age group performed significantly less well than the younger or middle-aged participants on all tasks thought to be dependent on DL function. However, there was no difference between the groups on the tasks dependent on VM function.

Discussion:

This study shows that the effect of ageing on cognitive abilities can be better understood by thinking of the frontal lobes as two distinct areas rather than just one. There is not a uniform global deterioration in the function of the frontal lobes. Instead, the dorsolateral prefrontal region, which supports executive function and working memory, seems to physically deteriorate more quickly than the ventromedial prefrontal area, responsible for emotional and social processing. This physical deterioration is reflected in functional performance. MacPherson et al. point out that the different areas of the brain are closely interconnected and, therefore, interpretation of results of this type of test should always be undertaken with caution; however, this study does offer a useful way to advance our understanding of age-related cognitive changes.

These neurophysiological consequences of ageing are the most likely factor in any deterioration in cognitive processes that is evident in the elderly. However, it is important to remember that not all elderly individuals show impoverished cognitive performance. Indeed, many octogenarians can function at the highest intellectual levels. Individual differences in physiology may play a part, but lifestyle differences are an important part too. For instance, diet and general physical health and an active mental and social life into old age may help to maintain connections in the brain and cognitive functioning.

In Chapter 4 we discuss the nervous system and its role in development from before birth in fuller detail.

Brain plasticity may also explain why many older adults are able to resist cognitive decline due to physical changes in the brain that are associated with age. In this respect, the brain can compensate for loss of neurons or connections in one area by finding an alternative process or pathway that achieves the same cognitive function. Imaging studies indicate that compensation may operate, partly, by decreasing brain specialization such that more areas are activated in response to particular stimuli in the old, compared with younger adults (e.g., Jonides et al., 2000). Moreover, Cabeza et al. (2002) found less asymmetry in prefrontal cortex activity of older adults who performed as well as younger adults on word recall tasks. In contrast, older adults who were significantly worse at the tasks showed the same asymmetry of activity as the younger adults. The high-performing older adults used more visual processing than the younger adults and low-performing older adults. Thus older adults' brains appeared to show the signs of adjusting to find alternative ways of solving the tasks.

BOX 16-2 Werner's syndrome: a window into the biological basis of ageing?

Werner's syndrome, also known as 'adult progeria', is a very rare autosomal, recessive disorder, which leads sufferers to prematurely age from puberty onwards. First identified by German scientist Otto Werner in 1904, research into the psychological functioning of Werner's syndrome patients suggests that cognitive function, generally, remains unimpaired (see Sild et al., 2006), while physical ageing is accelerated with early greying of hair, wrinkling skin, and age-related disorders such as diabetes, cardiovascular disease, cancer, cataracts and osteoporosis. There is also evidence that the normal body repair processes such as the ability to repair DNA fails to function properly in Werner syndrome patients (Yu et al., 1996). Although development is normal up until puberty, most individuals with Werner's syndrome do not survive beyond 50 years of age. Adult sufferers tend to have shorter than normal stature with a thick body trunk but thin arms and legs (Epstein et al., 1996). Werner's syndrome has a genetic basis and is associated with mutations in the WRN gene, although the precise nature of the mutation is complex and not fully understood (Ozgenc & Loeb, 2005).

The observation that physical ageing is accelerated while cognitive functions appear relatively unimpaired is intriguing because it suggests that there is, on some level, dissociation between these two elements in the normal ageing process (Goto, 1997). This has led some researchers to search the WRN gene for evidence of genes that may relate to cognitive functioning and ageing. For instance, Bendixen et al. (2004) examined data from 426 dizygotic twins aged 70–90 years from the 'Longitudinal study of Danish Twins'. The researchers were interested to see if they could understand a genetic basis for why cognition deteriorated more in some twins compared with others. Dizygotic twins were chosen because the researchers first conducted an unpaired analysis to see if they could find a general relationship between certain cognitive and physical characteristics and specific gene markers. They then hoped to follow up these findings to see if they could identify twins who differed in these characteristics, and then narrow down particular variations in order to establish precise genetic markers of specific features of ageing. The first, unpaired part of the analysis was successful and the researchers (confirming previous research; Kyng et al., 2003) found a 91% concordance in expression profile – that is, the measurement of how many cells operating together affect performance – between Werner and aged cells. Failure to maintain DNA (or DNA repair processes) was implicated in the ageing process. To their surprise, however, the strongest association was for cognitive profile even though cognitive decline is one area of normal ageing that is assumed to be unaffected in Werner's syndrome.

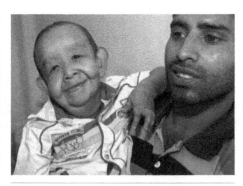

Werner's syndrome patient at 15 and 48 years
Source: © CrowdSpark/Alamy Stock Photo

However, the second part of the analysis, which planned to compare twins, was not successful, probably because there were too few suitable pairs to make powerful statistical comparisons. This underscores the difficulty in conducting this type of research. Bendixen et al. suggest that their findings, although tentative, have significance for two reasons. First, they support a notion that normal ageing is partly due to failings in DNA maintenance (see 'Theories of ageing', below). Second, from a more practical perspective, the authors argue that the effects of ageing could be delayed in many people by targeting those most likely to show early decline and give these individuals training and interventions, such as physical training and tailored exercise regimes, to slow this decline.

Studies with individuals with Werner's syndrome may also help to identify the onset and causes of age-related psychological disorders such as psychosis (Barak et al., 2001). However, Werner's syndrome really is extremely rare. Estimates are that there are around 300 cases per 100,000,000! So although data may be valuable, it is no easy matter identifying a suitable sample. Consequently, it may take a good deal of time for insights from Werner's syndrome to inform our understanding of the processes involved in normal ageing.

Theories of ageing

Why do we age? The pre-programmed theory of ageing proposes that we are genetically pre-programmed to reach a certain age and no more. Wear-and-tear theories, or damage-based theories, of ageing (e.g., Holliday, 2004; Kirkwood, 2005) suggest that ageing is a consequence of the body getting worn down through use, accidents, the build up of toxins, various types of abuse and poor diet and/or inefficient cellular repair processes to reverse this damage.

There is no question that our bodies deteriorate, get less efficient, and have less capacity and power as we age. However, simple wear and tear is not really enough to explain the phenomenon of ageing. The body's own repair processes, for example fighting an infection, mending a broken bone, or forming a scab and growing new skin over a wound, become less effective into old age. So it is unclear whether it is failure of the repair systems of wear and tear (and affecting the ability to repair the body) that is the main cause of ageing. The failure of body systems for maintaining and repairing DNA is often cited as a likely causal factor in ageing (e.g., de Boer et al., 2002).

However, although doubtless wear and tear causes some of the features of ageing, evidence from contrasting ageing processes in different animal species strongly suggests that there are genetic factors at play too. A starfish will often re-grow a limb that is lost. However, other animal species (such as mammals) do not replace lost body parts, at least not through the body's own physiological processes. For instance, although human teeth may be lost through accident (e.g., a well-aimed punch) or disease (e.g., tooth decay), human teeth are not replaced when they fall out in adulthood (Williams, 1957). In contrast, sharks' teeth also suffer from wear and tear, but sharks continue to replace teeth throughout their lifespan. These differences between species suggest that wear and tear alone does not explain ageing processes. Rather, the genetic make-up of the species must determine some aspects of ageing.

Genetic or pre-programmed theories view ageing as inevitable (e.g., Medvedev, 1990). The view, also referred to as 'developmental theories of ageing' or 'Dev-Age' (Bowen & Atwood, 2004), stems from observations and studies with various animal species. The central idea is that each species has a certain lifespan through which development progresses, and this is determined by genes. Ageing is a feature of the organism, not just a consequence of time or wear and tear. For instance, many insect species have distinct phases in their development (e.g., egg, caterpillar (larva), pupa, butterfly). Often, progression from one phase to the next (e.g., from pupa into butterfly) is not determined just by the length of pupation but also by certain external, environmental triggers such as temperature, humidity, and so on. In one case the organism may remain in its pupa form for a week, but in another case of the same species it may remain in this state for a month or two months. In the latter case we can say that development has been 'arrested' or delayed in some way. Importantly, however, this does not affect the length of time the organism survives as a butterfly. So the period as a pupa does not necessarily subtract from the period of lifespan spent as a butterfly. The conclusion drawn in terms of the process of human ageing is that lifespan is pre-programmed in terms of development rather than a specific period of time.

Another factor, which has also been implicated as a key factor in ageing, is the endocrine system, which regulates the body's hormones, (Gosden, 1996). As we have seen, hormone levels decline with age. Certainly, many anti-ageing cosmetics and medications such as hormone replacement therapy (HRT) target the body's hormonal levels to try and stave off some of the effects of ageing. However, while hormones can undoubtedly affect some consequences of ageing, such as reproductive capacity, it is less clear whether these are symptoms of or contributors to an underlying ageing process. However, an interesting recent phenomenon is that modern medical techniques mean that women can now bear children into old age (for instance, in 2009 a 70-year-old woman gave birth to a baby in Pakistan (Ramesh, 2009)), suggesting that human control over aspects of their own evolutionary destiny may complicate such accounts still further. Moreover, the age of onset of the menopause, in Western societies at least, appears to be getting later (perhaps due to changes in diet and health; Varea et al., 2000; Rödström et al., 2003). Increases in the age at which women can bear children may provide more information about how hormones relate to the ageing process.

> **pre-programmed theory** (or Dev-Age) The theory that our rate of physical ageing is set by our genes, and is therefore, in large part, inevitable.
>
> **wear-and-tear theory** The theory that ageing is due to environmental or external factors (such as injury or illness).

primary ageing The gradual deterioration in physical ability due to genetic or 'pre-programmed' factors.

secondary ageing The deterioration of the body in light of injuries and illnesses over time.

Most theorists agree that ageing is a combination of overlapping influences of genes and wear and tear to the body over time. Consequently a frequently used distinction is between primary and secondary ageing. Primary ageing refers to the gradual process of deterioration in the body's physical ability and power; secondary ageing refers to deterioration in the body due to disease, accidents and abuse (including diet). Nothing can be done to slow the progress of primary ageing. But improved medical care, lifestyles, and sensible behaviour such as taking regular exercise and eating a balanced diet can go a long way to slowing the progress of secondary ageing over a lifespan.

COGNITIVE AND BEHAVIOURAL CHANGE IN ADULTHOOD

Intelligence and problem-solving

The *age differentiation hypothesis* (Garrett, 1946) predicted that from childhood to adolescence factors other than 'natural' ability or intelligence (*g*) became increasingly important when explaining cognitive and educational performance. Such factors might include education, social class, or gender. In contrast, the *age de-differentiation hypothesis* (Balinsky, 1941) predicted that from early adulthood to old age, external factors became less important than *g*, as the early and more pronounced effects of environment stabilized or diminished.

The topic of IQ and whether it is a useful test of intelligence is a controversial one as we discuss in Chapter 11. Issues relating to IQ in adulthood, and in particular IQ changes, are no less controversial.

In fact, by and large, research now converges on agreement that there are no changes in differentiation of the structure of intelligence across adulthood (e.g., Escorial et al., 2002). However, there are changes in intelligence into late adulthood. In a major research study exploring changes in a range of intellectual abilities across a 50-year period, Schaie and colleagues (e.g., Willis & Schaie, 2005) reported data from a research programme that had begun as part of Werner Schaie's doctoral dissertation in the University of Washington (Seattle, USA), in 1956. By following a specific cohort of individuals and testing them every seven years from early adulthood onwards, Schaie was able to explore age-related changes longitudinally, across adulthood. This revealed a fairly constant level of intelligence throughout early and middle adulthood and into late adulthood. There was, however, a steady and marked decline in IQ from around 70 years onwards in Schaie's sample. The findings from this robust test of age differences in intelligence indicate that across most of adult life intelligence remains relatively stable.

fluid intelligence The capacity for abstract reasoning, such as spotting patterns of numbers or sequences.

crystallized intelligence Aspects of intelligence related to knowledge, education and experience, such as knowing what a particular word means.

Although general intelligence appears to remain stable there are marked age-related changes in different components of intelligence. Horn (1982) proposed that different types of intelligence – fluid and crystallized intelligence – show different developmental trajectories throughout adulthood. Fluid intelligence refers to a set of core capacities that relate, among other things, to abstract and 'logical' reasoning. For instance, letter and number sequence tasks are often used to assess fluid intelligence. Crystallized intelligence, in contrast, refers to aspects of intelligence that are dependent on learning, education or experience. For instance, being able to name three objects that are usually yellow or knowing the meaning of a word, or knowing how to perform a skill that you have learned. Studies indicate that crystallized intelligence rises from adolescence into early adulthood and remains stable across early and middle adulthood with some diminishing capacity into old age. However, evidence (for instance, from Schaie's Seattle Longitudinal Study) suggests that fluid intelligence declines from early adulthood and falls steadily across middle adulthood.

Changes in fluid and crystallized intelligence may correspond to differing life demands as much as to a general decline in cognitive ability. For instance, fluid skills may be more suited to an educational environment or to instances where individuals need to learn new skills and knowledge quickly, and organize this to understand it. Adults in middle adulthood may be in relatively stable careers or at least have come to exploit the skills that they have learned at a younger age. Thus middle adulthood may be a period where individuals come to use their mastery of certain cognitive (and physical) skills more efficiently.

A final area in which adults in middle and late adulthood appear to outperform younger adults is practical problem-solving. When solving everyday problems younger adults may have greater manual skills and physical abilities, but middle aged and older adults are better able to use experience and knowledge and to take a more efficient or strategic view to solve a problem (Wagner, 2000). Middle-aged and older adults also often take more responsibility or initiative, or display great autonomy when solving problems in everyday life (Denney, 1990).

During middle adulthood, individuals use their mastery of certain cognitive skills more efficiently, particularly within a work environment.
Source: © Shutterstock/Paisit Teeraphatsakool

BOX 16-3   Are older people wiser about social conflicts?

Research close-up

Source: Based on Grossmann et al. (2010).

Introduction:

Although it is generally accepted that there are significant age-related declines in many areas of cognitive processing, there is also a belief that older people are wiser than younger people. Wisdom can be described as the ability to deal with life problems, including the ability to appreciate different perspectives and values; therefore it is reasonable to believe that people gain more wisdom as they grow older, based on increased experience of life. Previous research in this area has been problematic because there were often methodological problems such as unrepresentative samples or poor stimulus materials. Therefore the researchers carried out two studies that they felt would overcome these problems. They expected to find that wisdom would increase throughout the lifespan.

Method and results:

Study 1

A sample of 247 participants was recruited from a county in Michigan, USA, covering the full range of social classes. There were approximately equal numbers of both sexes and of each of three age groups: 25–40, 41–59 and 60+. Each participant read three articles, each of which described an intergroup conflict between two strong groups. The topics of conflict were immigration, ethic tensions and natural resources. These are summarized in Table 16-1.

Table 16-1   The topics of intergroup conflict stories provided to Grossman and colleagues' participants

Topic/country	Summary
Immigration/ Tajikistan	Because of the economic growth of Tajikistan, many people from Kyrgyzstan immigrate to the country. Whereas Kyrgyz people try to preserve their customs, Tajiks want Kyrgyz people to assimilate fully and abandon their customs.
Natural resources/Chuuk	Huge crude oil resources have been discovered in the economically disadvantaged Chuuk state. Because of governmental restrictions, many interested firms cannot establish the required infrastructure for production. On the one side, government tries to preserve the ancient laws. On the other side, there are also a huge number of people in Chuuk who would like to eliminate the regulations entirely.
Ethnic tensions/ Djibouti	Two ethnic groups in Djibouti, the Issa and the Afari, have completely different perspectives on politics. Whereas one group tries to preserve traditions, the other group wants to alter the society entirely. Both groups are very strong.

Each participant was then asked, 'What do you think will happen after that?' and 'Why do you think it will happen this way?' Participants' responses were coded on six dimensions of wisdom: change, compromise, flexibility, perspective, resolution and uncertainty. For instance, a participant who responded to the immigration story that both sides should try to preserve a bit of each culture could be seen as reasoning using a high level of compromise reasoning, whereas consideration of different points of view would encompass perspective-shifting. In addition, each participant completed tests of crystallized intelligence (based on acquired knowledge) and fluid intelligence (ability to solve problems).

Results showed a decline in fluid intelligence with increasing age, but showed no age-related decline in crystallized intelligence. As predicted, older participants scored significantly higher than younger or middle-aged participants on each dimension of wisdom, as well as on a composite score of overall wisdom.

Study 2

In this second study, the researchers investigated interpersonal conflict and 200 of the original participants took part. Each participant read three authentic letters that had been written to an advice columnist, detailing conflicts between siblings, friends and spouses. As in the first study, each participant was interviewed and asked how they thought each situation would develop. Responses were coded on the six dimensions of wisdom used in Study 1.

Results showed that older people scored significantly higher than younger or middle-aged participants on all dimensions except conflict resolution and uncertainty.

Overall analysis

The aggregate wisdom score from the two studies was obtained and, again, the effect of age was substantial. Older people were significantly over-represented in the top 20% on wisdom performance. The average age of participants in this top 20% was 64.9 years, while the average age of people in the bottom 80% was 45.5 years. Further analyses also showed that wisdom was positively correlated with crystallized intelligence and that the age effect of wisdom held true regardless of social class or education.

Discussion:

Grossmann et al.'s study suggests that social reasoning, or wisdom, increases with advancing age despite a decrease in fluid intelligence. Compared to younger and middle-aged people, older people showed more understanding of multiple perspectives, the need for compromise and the limits of knowledge. Thus, older adults may well be using their experience (crystallized intelligence) to resolve conflict. As a result, Grossmann et al. suggest that older individuals could play a valuable role in key social roles such as making legal decisions, counselling and intergroup negotiations.

Characterizing intellectual development in early adulthood

The intellectual demands faced by young adults are significant and, maybe, qualitatively different from those they experienced at school. For instance, at university or in a new job, individuals may need to learn to work independently or take initiatives to solve problems for themselves. Labouvie-Vief (1980, 1990) has argued that after the grasp of Piagetian formal operations or fully scientific thinking, young adults need to learn how to apply their knowledge, to specialize and become experts, and to learn to apply that knowledge in socially responsible ways.

Labouvie-Vief (1985) gave people aged 10 to 40 a series of dilemmas or problems which required that they find a solution to somewhat ambiguous situations. Each situation had one or other possible logical conclusion or solution, but there were possible alternatives which could be more desirable or more adequate situations if some of the relevant context was also taken into consideration when making a judgement. Adolescents used logical reasoning to resolve the dilemmas, often taking extreme or idealistic actions. In contrast, young adults modified their use of logic and gave more consideration to the various possibilities in a real-life situation. Labouvie-Vief argued that these young adults exhibited postformal thinking because they recognized the complexity of the problem and the need to take into account different peoples' experiences, perspectives and values.

Sinnott (1998) argues that postformal thinkers are more flexible in the ways that they apply logic to solve problems. They can shift between idealistic and practical solutions to problems and recognize better the areas of greyness that often exist in real-world dilemmas and social judgements.

An alternative approach to intellectual development across the lifespan was developed by Schaie (1977). Schaie suggested a stage-like model of development across adulthood that focused on how information was used rather than on how information was acquired. Before adulthood children are gathering information for use later in development, hence they are acquiring knowledge. From young adulthood achievement becomes more important and they begin to apply their knowledge to achieving long-term goals such as developing a career. In middle adulthood intelligence is used both for looking after one's family and offspring (responsibility) and also for making a broader societal contribution and fulfilling a social role (executive stage). Late adulthood is associated with a reintegrative stage when reflection on personal meaning and the significance of one's life and contribution to society becomes important.

> **postformal thinking**
> Thought based on logical solutions but recognizing the role of relative perspectives and context in making judgements.

> Both Piaget and Vygotsky contend that significant psychological development does not extend beyond adolescence (see Chapter 9), but many lifespan theorists disagree.

Memory changes

In Chapter 10 we examined how memory changes through the earlier years of development. However, deterioration of memory is often thought of as a problem linked to age. However, there are at least two important reasons why this simple assumption is misleading. First, as with many psychological and physical processes, there is tremendous variation in memory processes across the population and in whether memory declines or remains stable with age for each individual (Craik, Byrd, & Swanson, 1987). Second, it is clear that there are many different types of memory and while some of these may decline with age, others may remain stable over the lifespan. So, for instance, semantic (memory for meanings) and procedural (remembering how to do something) memory may show no or minimal decline with age (Fleischmann et al., 2004). Episodic memory (memory for events, linked in a specific order) appears to undergo a marked decline with age (Nilsson, 2003).

There appears to be some minor decline in general memory ability throughout middle adulthood, but it is usually only into older (late) adulthood that there is notably slower recall (Babiloni et al., 2004). The capacity for short-term memory (STM, also known as 'working memory') is also often significantly reduced in older adults. Short-term memory is the ability to hold items in one's memory at one time. In a now classic study, West and Crook (1990) showed participants aged 18 to 85 years a series of telephone numbers containing seven or ten digits. After they had seen the numbers, participants had to dial the number on a key pad. However, some of the time they got a 'number busy' or engaged tone, and had to redial. Dialling immediately (i.e., no busy tone) led to the highest levels of recall for both age groups, although there was steady decline in recall from middle adulthood (around 50 years) onwards for the seven-digit version of the immediate recall task. Decline in recall for the ten-digit task also declined steadily from middle adulthood onwards, but the decline from the start of late adulthood was more marked. On the delayed recall task, when participants had to redial after the busy signal, performance was generally poorer as the researchers had predicted. However, the decline in performance with age was also more rapid than in the seven-digit immediate recall task, and particularly marked on the ten-digit, delayed recall condition.

West and Crook's findings suggest that information processing becomes less efficient or has a reduced capacity with age. This loss of efficiency may be largely a consequence of a more general age-related reduction in the speed with which neurons pass information around the central nervous system (Salthouse, 2004). However, factors other than neurological degeneration also explain why memory sometimes gets worse with age and why there is considerable variation in the memory abilities of older adults.

One important factor that is associated with memory problems in older adults is diet (Nyberg & Pudas, 2019). The connection between diet and cognitive decline (including Alzheimer's disease and also other forms of memory loss such as 'Mild Cognitive Impairment' (MCI)) has been demonstrated in several studies. Panza et al. (2004) examined diet and its effect on cognitive function in elderly populations in several European countries. They found that high levels of consumption of mono-unsaturated fatty acids (found in foods like nuts and olive oil) stemmed age-associated cognitive decline in a southern Italian sample, and eating white fish and cereals was associated with reduced levels of Alzheimer's disease in European and North American populations. Lastly, the risk of dementia was lower in a sample of French older adults who drank three or four glasses of wine a day, compared with those who did not drink any alcohol! Ponza and colleagues suggest a complex collection of factors including diet and, in particular, the presence of anti-oxidant molecules that prevent or slow down the oxidation of other molecules, may help to stem some age-related cognitive decline. Diet alone is unlikely to explain all of the variation in memory decline in older adults. More plausible is the suggestion that cognitive processes are the consequence of a complex mix of factors, social, cognitive and biological.

Research close-up

BOX 16-4   Explaining cultural and environmental influences on dementia: the Honolulu-Asia Ageing Study

Source: Based on White et al. (1996).

Introduction:

Occasionally, historical events or situations throw up opportunities to explore psychological phenomena from an intriguing or novel perspective. One classic study of ageing and dementia was conducted by White et al. (1996) on the Hawaiian island of Honolulu. The researchers used data that had been collected as part of the Honolulu-Asia Ageing Study (HAAS). This study involved a large sample of Japanese-American men born between 1900 and 1919. All of these men were born in Japan but had emigrated to Honolulu by the time they were 19 years old. They were living on the Hawaiian island of Oahu in 1965 when the survey began. The body of study data had been collected to measure the effects of living in Honolulu (USA) by comparing these men with a similar cohort of men who remained in Japan. However, the large dataset made it possible to explore other factors related to the ageing of these different groups. Thus the aim of the study was to compare the rates of dementia among the Japanese-American men (those born in Japan, but living most of their adult life in the USA) with rates of dementia in this Japanese comparison group.

Method:

Participants were 3734 Japanese-American men aged between 71 and 93 years. Data were collected from these individuals using a variety of cognitive tests and diagnoses as part of large study comparing various physiological and other effects of ageing across a wider population. The researchers used a stratified, random sampling technique. Specifically, participants were given a version of the Cognitive Abilities Screening Instrument (CASI) which tests several abilities such as memory and problem-solving. Tests were conducted in three phases – a first phase across the sample, and a second phase where 948 participants who had low scores on the CASI were then asked to come for further, neurological examination and an informant (usually the participant's wife) was interviewed to explore the extent of any cognitive decline over the past ten years. A third phase involved giving further tests to 426 individuals who had shown the most marked decline in the previous years, according to participant informants. For phase 3, interviewers were blind to findings from the first two stages and sought to make a clear diagnosis of dementia.

Results:

The researchers compared participants' responses in terms of two criteria for establishing dementia – Cummings and Benson's criteria and DSM-III-R. On both measures, rates of dementia in the Japanese-American sample were similar to those of the general US population (Cummings and Benson, 10.3%; DSM-III-R, 7.6%) for men in a similar age range. However, comparable Japanese data show prevalence rates for Japanese men who remain living in Japan throughout their adult life significantly lower, between 4% and 6%. Thus the Japanese-American men in the present study showed dementia levels approaching those of European and American populations.

Discussion:

The findings strongly suggest that environmental or cultural factors are influential in causing dementia, rather than solely genetic causes. Both the Japanese men living in Japan and those who had moved to Honolulu for most of their adult life share a similar genetic heritage. So something about their lifestyle or the experience of living in the USA had influenced dementia rates. At the same time, data show that factors involved with cardiovascular disease remain relatively unaffected. So what in the cultural experiences of these men in the USA differs from those in Japan and may therefore have led to the increased chances of dementia during old age? Many factors are implicated, including education and cultural expectations, whether an active or

Hanauma Bay, Oahu, Hawaii.
Source: © Shutterstock/Juancat

inactive lifestyle was encouraged or required or diet. The researchers suggest these possible explanations for their findings. However, further research was required to identify possible causes with more certainty.

Explaining age-related cognitive change

It is likely that there are some basic biological precursors of ageing that impact on the development (and decline) of cognitive processes in adulthood. These may be identifiable at an early age. In a longitudinal study, Flensborg-Masden and Mortensen (2018) identified several of 32 developmental milestones, achieved between 0 and 3 years of age, that were associated with intelligence in adulthood. Interestingly, those that related to early motor achievements were the strongest predictors of adult intelligence including standing, walking and language development. Why might these motor skills relate to cognitive processes later in life? It could be that there is a basic relationship in early maturation of certain brain functions. However, it could be more complex and due to complex factors including interactions with the environment and the methods used: for example, it might be that some forms of parenting or some types of social environment encouraged earlier motor achievements, or that these were better recorded for children from more affluent (and better supported) social groups. While longitudinal studies such as these offer the possibility of strong, causal information about development across the lifespan, caution is needed in inferring hard-and-fast causes and effects given the complexity of interactions and environmental interactions that an individual may encounter across the lifespan.

brain reserve hypothesis The suggestion that social and cognitive stimulation can help to build up reserves of ability, and improve brain function and performance in older adults.

Memory problems and cognitive decline also appear to be linked to other lifestyle factors including social class, health-related behaviour such as smoking and excessive drinking, and education (White et al., 1996). Valenzuela and Sachdev (2006) have explored what is known as the brain reserve hypothesis. This hypothesis proposes that social and cognitive stimulation can help to protect against the negative effects of ageing on cognitive functions. Numerous studies have sought to explore the brain reserve hypothesis. Most notably, perhaps, Snowdon (e.g., Snowdon, 2003) explored the effects of ageing on 678 nuns at the School Sisters of Notre Dame in Kentucky, USA. In the 'Nun Study', Snowdon and colleagues compared lifestyle and biological factors, seeking to understand what lay behind long life and why there was such great variation in cognitive decline with age. Snowdon (2001) suggests that findings from the nun studies demonstrate that diet, exercise, social and cognitive activity can act as sources of resistance to displaying the symptoms of biologically determined cognitive decline.

There is also a link between age-related cognitive decline and marital status. A study in the Kuopio and Joensuu regions of eastern Finland (Håkansson et al., 2009) explored participants' responses to a variety of measures over a 21-year gap; that is, during mid-life (average age 50 years) and later life (average age 71 years). The authors note that although genetic factors are also important, a rich social network – that is having lots of friends and acquaintances with whom one meets regularly – was an important component that was associated with lower rates of dementia among elderly individuals. In particular, individuals who were widowed or divorced in mid-life and did not remarry had a three times greater risk of displaying MCI in later life than those who remained in a relationship with a partner. For those who had lost a spouse or partner twice, either through death or divorce, this risk increased to over seven times the risk for those who remained married.

Håkansson and colleagues' study can be considered as further evidence for the brain reserve hypothesis because it suggests that the cognitive and social stimulation provided by a partner may help to inoculate genetically 'at risk' individuals against the chances of age-linked cognitive decline. However, the authors note the hypothesis would predict that those who had never married (i.e., remained single all their lives) would show the highest risk of impairment with age. Yet this was not the case; risk for those who had been single (unmarried) all of their life was lower than for those who had been divorced or who had experienced the death of a spouse or partner.

There seems to be something about loss or bereavement, and the associated rapid change in behaviour and day-to-day life, that leads to more pronounced cognitive decline. In a similar vein, in a long-term relationship partners may come to depend on one another in particular ways, or may take on particular roles. Thus one partner may take a leading role in managing household finances, while the other partner organizes social and family events. If partners get set into these roles they may find it difficult to take up another, unfamiliar set of responsibilities when one of them passes away.

It is clear that marital relationships are one of a complex network of factors that can increase the risk of accelerated cognitive decline. These factors include social, cognitive and biological processes. The brain reserve hypothesis suggests that biological and social factors can help individuals to resist the consequences of an ageing brain. However, a slightly different explanation was proposed by Baltes and Baltes (1990). They describe their model of selective optimization with compensation (SOC) whereby adults take a more strategic approach to tasks that involve cognitive (or other) effort. For instance, an ageing adult who has a failing memory may make lists or actively engage in rehearsal of information to stave off or compensate for these negative effects. Along with this compensation for failing abilities, adults will also seek to optimize those abilities and skills that are useful or functioning well. Thus older adults learn to become more strategic or efficient (or 'wiser', see Baltes & Kunzmann, 2003) in deploying their abilities, and can use these to fend off the effects of ageing and neurophysiological decline.

selective optimization with compensation (SOC) The theory that, as people age and cognitive capacities decline, they seek to compensate for this decline by finding alternative ways of completing tasks.

SOCIAL DEVELOPMENT IN ADULTHOOD

Well-being and happiness

As adults get older they, generally, become happier. Research indicates that positive affect (happiness) increases from something of a low in early adulthood to old age, although this may level off or even decrease slightly after 70 years of age (Diener, 1984). Mroczek and Kolarz (1998) found that this positive association between age and happiness holds regardless of other factors that can also influence levels of happiness such as gender, education, stress, personality and health.

Some social processes are associated with variations in positive (and negative) affect. Although married individuals tend to be happier than those who are unmarried, both married and unmarried people get happier as they get older. However, for men (but not for women) the relationship between happiness and age is influenced by personality and marital status. Men who are introverted and remain unmarried all their lives seem to show particularly marked increases in happiness with age.

The observation that happiness tends to increase with age has proved consistent over a number of years. Yang (2008), for instance, noting a similar result, suggests that this trend persists despite some cohort effects; that is, people born in certain periods of time or eras are slightly happier than in some other periods of time. It seems fairly obvious that social and historical conditions in different eras in history probably explain cohort effects such as these. Individuals born in times of war or difficult economic or social conditions will doubtless have a very different quality of life than those born into times of relative affluence and peace. However, the relation between social or societal factors and happiness is not always straightforward. For instance, Layard (2005) notes that general rates of happiness declined in many affluent Western societies during a period of economic growth in the latter half of the twentieth century. For sure, happiness does not depend only on material well-being but also an individual's perception of themselves and their relative well-being compared with others in a society. As we age, we may become more reflective, more content with our lives, and more accepting of our social position, which helps to increase positive, rather than negative, evaluations of one's own well-being.

Time and social changes influence affective processes in other ways too. Yang also noted that gender differences in happiness (women are generally happier than men) and ethnic differences (African Americans are less happy than European Americans) become less marked as individuals age (reminiscent of the age de-differentiation hypothesis of intelligence). However, gender differences in happiness diminished over the last 30 years of Yang's study for all cohorts, suggesting that underlying changes in societal conceptions of gender and gender roles may change in terms of their impact on how people evaluate and feel about their lives. Ethnic differences, however, appear to be more enduring.

Differences in social roles, social relationships, and expectations may explain some age differences in happiness. On the face of things, it might seem odd that early adulthood is typically a period of optimal physical well-being and fitness but also of relative unhappiness compared with later life. However, young adulthood is also often a period of considerable transition in people's lives in terms of establishing a career, moving away from the parental home, developing autonomy and life skills, and starting intimate relationships. These challenges and changes may cause stress and unhappiness. Or it may be that younger adults have not developed the ability to reflect on challenges and negative life events in a positive way.

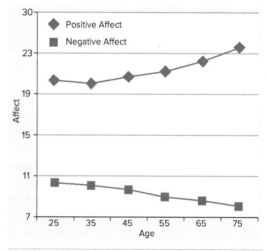

Figure 16-2 Plotted regression lines showing the relation between positive affect and age (diamonds) and negative affect and age (squares)
Positive and negative affect scores have a possible range of 6 to 30, with higher scores indicating higher levels of affect. The lines are based on the following equations: positive affect _ 22.38 _ age(_.14) _age2(.002); negative affect _ 10.94 _ age(_.03).
Source: Adapted from Mroczek and Kolarz (1998).

> Consider again our discussion of the development of emotion in Chapter 7. How do these early developmental processes relate to the sorts of changes in emotion seen across adulthood?

One significant cause of unhappiness in early adulthood may be the failure of romantic relationships; the course of true love does not always run smooth, and loneliness can be a significant source of unhappiness in early adulthood, where individuals may desire a long-term, intimate relationship but are unable to find one. Rokach (2001) found that the emotional distress caused by loneliness increases steadily during the teenage years and peaks in early adulthood. Although many older adults will experience loss of friends, a spouse or partner, it appears that with age people develop strategies for coping with loneliness or may expect less of their relationships (or expect fewer relationships) than younger adults (Rokach & Neto, 2006). Men are more negatively affected by loneliness than women, perhaps because men form fewer friendships and disclose less intimate information to friends (Stroebe & Stroebe, 1996).

Negative emotions and psychological disorders

Age and gender variations are also evident in the expression of negative affect across the lifespan. Older adults (over 65 years) report fewer depressive symptoms (Gallo, Anthony, & Muthén, 1994). This may be due to specific aspects of depression becoming more or less salient with age. Goldberg, Breckenridge, and Sheikh (2004) tested a sample of 178 male war veterans, aged 21–83 years and confirmed the finding of age differences in depression (there was significantly less depression in men aged 60 years and older). However, the age difference was specifically in the cognitive-affective symptoms of depression, and not in somatic-performance symptoms. Cognitive affective symptoms include low mood, impaired cognitive functioning and a negative attributional style; somatic performance symptoms include loss of sleep, and loss of interest in pleasurable activities such as sex. Older men showed fewer cognitive-affective symptoms than younger men. In other words, younger men appeared to ruminate more, and felt stronger negative affect.

Research into age differences in anxiety shows some correspondence with these findings. Brenes et al. (2008) found that among a sample of adults (19–87 years), who were under treatment for anxiety or anxiety-related problems, older adults reported less worry than younger adults, although age was not related to other symptoms of anxiety. One explanation for these age differences in clinical symptoms is that older adults may have developed coping strategies or a greater capacity for resilience when dealing with negative life events in a more sanguine way.

Gender is a further important source of variation in depression that also varies with age. In a review of research studies, Jorm (1987) examines a common assumption that women are more prone to depression than men, but observes that this relationship varies with age. Specifically, while rates of depression in men remain fairly constant across adulthood, rates of depression in women rise quite dramatically from childhood to adulthood, but drop back again among older adults. Jorm suggests that these age and gender variations are a consequence of differing social roles: in the workplace, women have traditionally held fewer positions of power and responsibility and have been paid less than their male contemporaries. Moreover, many women who choose to raise children often report feeling that society undervalues this role. These perceived differences in status may lead to frustration and depression during adult working years, but subside when older adults retire.

However, others have suggested a biological explanation for gender differences in depression and have observed that the decrease in reported depression among women often subsides after the menopause (Bebbington et al., 2003). Yet this review remains contested (Cairney & Wade, 2002), with studies suggesting that undertaking hormone replacement therapy (HRT), which is assumed to stave off many of the effects of the menopause, does not affect levels of depression. Conflicts and difficulties caused by competing social roles and challenging social circumstances remain a core likely cause of depression in women during early and middle adulthood (McKinlay, McKinlay, & Brambilla, 1987).

A number of other psychological disorders have an age of onset during early adulthood, although their origins may of course lie in childhood experiences or in biological or genetic processes. For instance, personality disorders such as borderline personality disorder and antisocial personality disorder are usually evident in mid- to late adolescence and become increasingly problematic throughout early adult life unless adequately treated. Schizophrenia typically begins in late adolescence or early adulthood although age of onset (or diagnosis) is a few years earlier for men than women and can be linked to a life stressor such as a new job or family bereavement. Bipolar disorder, similarly, appears between 15 and 29 years of age in most instances (Joyce, 1984).

Social relationships in adulthood

Throughout childhood and into adolescence, there is an increasing recognition of the importance of peer relationships with age, and some corresponding decrease in the importance of parents as sources of knowledge, expertise and influence. In adulthood, the changes in friendships and relationships, and how these impact on the structure of a person's life, are no less profound. However, across adulthood these changes are spaced across a longer time period than in the earlier years of life.

Adolescence and early adulthood is a period often marked by a number of significant transitions; for instance, from school to university or work, moving away from the family home, or in with a partner. As we shall see later on, how individuals cope with transitions is an important feature of some theories of adult development and arguably some of these patterns are set in childhood (e.g., Bryant et al., 2017). Early adulthood is a significant period of transition that could set an individual's life course, physical and mental health for their future adult life. Deventer et al. (2018) explored how personality affected relationships (and vice versa) during the transition from adolescence to early adulthood. Across three waves of study, the main direction of transfer was from personality to social relationships; that is, personality was more likely to influence new friendship choices some time after the transition, not immediately after leaving high school.

From adolescence (Chapter 12) friends become an increasingly important source of support and influence on individuals, and across life friends often remain an important source of support for individuals. There is good evidence that friendship can help to buffer negative life events and perhaps even the cognitive and physical effects of biological ageing processes. Indeed, some studies suggest that strong social bonds throughout life can decrease morality rates by up to 50% (Holt-Lunstad, Smith, & Layton, 2010; House, Landis, & Umberson, 1988).

Romantic relationships and love

For many people, early adulthood is an important period for establishing romantic and intimate relationships. During the early adult years, intimate relationships may begin to supplant strong friendships and family ties as individuals move towards making longer-term commitments such as marriage and cohabitation. In strong intimate relationships partners disclose more to each other than to others (Meeus et al., 2007).

In Western societies heterosexual men and women tend to look for different characteristics in a partner (Buss, 2008). Men place more emphasis on a woman's appearance, and women more on power, status or a man's prospects of providing financial security. Regardless of sexual orientation, men tend to find individuals of their preferred sex more attractive if they are slightly younger, whereas women prefer those who are slightly older than they are (Silverthorne & Quinsey, 2000). However, the most important characteristic for both men and women in a partner is mutual attraction and a similar desire for relationship satisfaction (Buss, 2008).

According to Sternberg's popular triangular theory of love (e.g., Sternberg, 1986), the ideal in loving relationships (and what most people seek to achieve) is described as 'consummate love' and includes three components: intimacy includes a sense of closeness and connectedness in loving relationships; passion includes sexual and physical attraction; decision or commitment involves a short-term decision that one loves another, and a longer-term intention and desire to maintain that love. Consummate love is more likely to result in a lasting relationship because all three

> In Chapter 12 we consider the development of relationships over childhood and adolescence, and explore some theories in the area. How far might these theories apply to developmental changes in adults' relationships?

triangular theory of love Sternberg's model of loving relationships, which includes three components – intimacy, commitment and passion – that vary in different relationship types.

consummate love The ideal love, in Sternberg's theory, including intimacy, passion and commitment

infatuation A relationship based only on passion (i.e. without intimacy or commitment).

romantic love Intimacy and passion without commitment.

fatuous love Passion and commitment without intimacy.

construal level theory of psychological distance The theory that the ways in which we think about people, events or objects is more or less abstract depending on our psychological distance from them.

elements from the triangle are included. Other forms of love, such as infatuation, include only some elements. As a result, infatuation (only passion), romantic love (intimacy and passion without commitment) and fatuous love (passion and commitment without intimacy) are ultimately not as rewarding for individuals (see Sternberg, 1997). There has been some empirical support for Sternberg's proposal, but this research also suggests that other psychosocial factors such as the perceived empathy of a partner are important in developing long-term loving relationships, too. Importantly, these other aspects are helpful in protecting against the negative consequences of failed or failing relationships (Cramer & Jowett, 2010).

A more recent account for the development of love in relationships stems from the construal level theory of psychological distance (see Trope & Liberman, 2010). Construal level theory proposes that objects, events or individuals can be perceived as close or distant in terms of 'psychological space' (e.g., a long time ago or how far into the future an event may occur, or how much an experience is to do with oneself or to do with others). According to the theory, more distant objects tend to evoke more abstract, intangible and broad thinking. In contrast, closer objects lead to more concrete, specific thinking about discrete features.

Förster, Epstude, and Ozelsel (2009) explored how construal level theory might apply to romantic relationships and the development of love. The researchers conducted two experiments. In the first, participants were either asked to think about love (for instance, some participants imagined going on a romantic walk with a partner), or to orientate their attention to sex (imagining, for instance, casual sex with someone). Participants then completed a series of tasks that required creative solutions to problems, such as how a person could determine that a coin was a fake or real. Participants also completed tasks that required the application of logical rules to solve a problem. The set of participants who orientated their attention towards love performed well on the creative task, which is associated with abstract construal; that is construal of things that are psychologically distant (Friedman & Förster, 2008). However, participants who orientated their attention towards sex performed well on the logical problem-solving task that is associated with concrete construal and psychologically closer objects, people and events.

The second study confirmed the thrust of the findings from the first. Specifically, thinking about love (as opposed to casual, loveless sex) inclined participants to use more global and abstract patterns of thinking and problem solving, whereas thinking about casual sex led to a focus on the more specific details of a problem.

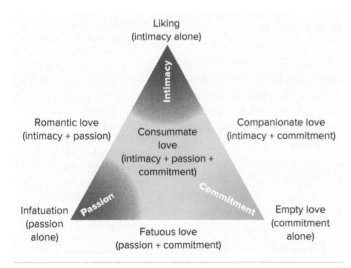

Figure 16-3 Triangular theory of love
Source: From Passer et al. (2009).

Construal level theory appears to offer a convincing explanation for some of the features (or symptoms) associated with love, but more needs to be known about the motivations or causes of falling in love in the first place! Indeed, the triangular theory and implications from construal level theory both offer some window to explain how love develops and endures. Other factors, such as hormones, may be involved as well. However, as Berscheid (2010) notes, theories of love and the development of loving relationships require further empirical support. In particular there is a need for clarity in explicating and defining the concept of love. This future work is important because a better understanding of love can help to understand what makes romantic relationships work well and endure because relationship breakdowns are a significant source of personal distress and sometimes impact children, as well as partners.

BOX 16-5   Love stinks!

Research close-up

Source: Based on Lundström and Jones-Gotman (2009).

Introduction:

The development of romantic relationships is one of the most important events in many young adults' lives. The processes involved doubtless have a social dimension, but biological processes might equally be involved as well. In particular, given the importance of mutual physical attraction, hormones would seem a likely factor to be involved, at least at the start of romantic relationships. The present study sought to explore whether hormones play a part in helping intimate partners to remain committed to each other. In particular the researchers tested two complementary hypotheses: that on the one hand love leads to greater attention towards a partner, and corresponding attention away from others members of the opposite sex. The focus was on the role of hormones in increasing or deflecting attention.

Method:

The researchers assessed women's ability to identify body odours originating from their boyfriend, a same-sex friend and an opposite-sex friend. They then examined the relationship between this ability to identify the odour and the degree of romantic love expressed towards their boyfriend on a questionnaire. The researchers had two key hypotheses: first, they predicted that an increase in attention towards one's partner would lead to positive correlation between identification of a boyfriend's body odour and degree of romantic love; second, they hypothesized that attention deflected away from other potential partners would lead to a negative correlation between identification of an opposite-sex friend's body odour and degree of romantic love for the boyfriend.

Participants were 20 women in heterosexual relationships (average age, 21 years). Body odours were collected from partners, opposite-sex friends (i.e., not partners) and a same-sex friend, by asking each 'odour donor' to sleep for seven consecutive nights alone in a cotton T-shirt with odourless cotton nursing pads that were sewn into the underarm area. Odour donors also followed some very clear instructions from the experimenters to minimize contact with other individuals and pets, and engage in a limited personal hygiene routine and diet.

At test, along with identifying which odour belonged to which person, participants rated the intensity of the odour.

Results:

There was a negative correlation between participants' ratings of love for their boyfriend and their ability to identify an opposite-sex (male) friend's odour. Specifically, the more a woman said she loved her boyfriend, the worse she was at identifying the male friend's odour. However, there was no correlation between ratings of love and ability to identify her boyfriend's or her same-sex friend's odour.

Discussion:

These findings support the deflection hypothesis relating hormones to romantic love. In other words, the more a woman loved her partner the more she was deflected away from identifying the odour of a male friend. However, there was no support for the increased attention hypothesis.

The endocrine system has been previously linked with romantic love and is also closely linked to the olfactory system (smell). So the link between smell and romantic love is not as spurious as it might at first seem. However, it is probably important also to note that women are rather better than men at identifying information about individuals from their personal odours. So it remains to be seen if the same type of correlation would exist for men.

Marriage

In many societies, intimate and romantic relationships in early adulthood progress towards marriage or cohabitation. For heterosexual couples the path to marriage and formalization of the relationship has been enshrined in social and religious ceremonies for many centuries. More recently, in contemporary societies, homosexual relationships too may result in marriage although in many other societies a considerable degree of discrimination against homosexual relationships of any kind still exists. Although the norm in many Western societies is for individuals to find a partner themselves, in other societies or in certain ethnic groups within Western societies, marriage and adult romantic relationships are seen as being more closely enmeshed with community and family life (Buss et al., 2001). In many cases marriages may be arranged by members of an extended family.

There is a dearth of reliable research data concerning the psychological consequences of arranged marriages. What evidence there is suggests that men and women involved in arranged marriages are not necessarily less happy than those in other marriages (what are, perhaps misleadingly, termed 'love marriages'). For instance, Yelsma and Athappilly (1988) compared marriage satisfaction and communication between Indian couples in arranged and love marriages. They found that men and women in the arranged marriages displayed higher marriage satisfaction scores than those in love matches and a comparative sample of American men and women. In contrast, however, Xiaohe and Whyte (1990) report greater dissatisfaction among women in arranged marriages in a Chinese sample. The cultural context, and how accepting of it both partners are, would appear to be an important influence on the success of a marriage and each partner's satisfaction with it. This context may influence not just expectations of romantic love, but of acceptance of gender roles, personal goals and family support.

We discuss attachment in Chapter 7. How far do you think the attachments formed with parents during infancy feed in to our approach to close relationships in adulthood?

The basis of marital and other, long-term intimate relationships into middle adulthood and beyond may be formed, at least in part, in early attachment relationships with a caregiver (see again Bowlby, 1969, 1980) where *internal working models* are set up that guide conduct in and expectations of close relationships. Adults who report secure attachment relationships as a child reported more satisfactory, stable and secure relationships as adults compared with those who report anxious or avoidant caregiver relationships as a child (Kirkpatrick & Davis, 1994). Individuals with an avoidant working model tended to close themselves off from potentially rewarding relationships as adults, and distance themselves from partners. Adults with an anxious internal model formed early in life tended to be clingy, too dependent, or to ruminate on aspects of the relationship in a negative way which led to negative consequences for their relationships with a partner.

Evidence suggests that marriage (or at least long-term, stable, romantic partnerships) has a positive influence on well-being (Robles et al., 2014). Of course, not all marriages are beneficial in this respect, and other types of relationships can also offer the same positive outcomes for different individuals. In this respect the benefits of marriage may be linked to separate but inter-connected processes of partner responsiveness and adult attachment style (Slatcher & Selcuk, 2017), which can be evident across relationships and perhaps across different cultures.

Parenting and grandparenting

Of course, not all partners marry or have children. But, for those that do, the middle adult years represent a set of challenges associated with parenting and a new set of close relationships and associated demands. Parenting involves not only a considerable increase in work required within the family but also a marked change in identity and roles (Cowan & Cowan, 2000). In fact, expectant mothers may begin to experience changes in identity and an increased sense of 'connectedness' to an unborn child throughout pregnancy (Smith, 1999). We discuss later how changes such as becoming a parent can have a significant impact on development across the lifecourse. There is also some evidence to suggest that the life changes a new baby may bring to a couple's relationship are influenced by partners' evaluations of their experiences as children (specifically, of their parents' relationship; Belsky & Isabella, 1985).

Changes in relationships and roles across adulthood, such as new parenthood and working relationships, point to how developmental researchers have tended to focus on these more social frames in development outside of childhood. Thus much research in the area is more qualitative or to do with understanding people's experiences of their own lives, roles, identities and relationships. Nevertheless, parenthood, unemployment and changing working roles are certainly important and sometimes dramatic influences on people's lives. Into adulthood, however, people often follow different pathways (e.g., having children, not having children) so the challenge for developmental psychologists is to recognize this diversity while identifying general developmental psychological trends across ages.

From 70 years of age the number of friends with whom people have regular social contact begins to fall (Carstensen, Isaacowitz, & Charles, 1999). This may be due to increased physical difficulty in visiting friends, or to death of friends. A significant loss, obviously, is that of a partner or spouse, yet as we have seen older adults can often employ very successful coping strategies to overcome the negative effects of this loss in the longer term (see again Stroebe & Stroebe, 1993). However, the later the age at which a man or woman is widowed, the less successful the recovery both in terms of affect and the cognitive and physical symptoms associated with bereavement (Lund & Caserta, 2004).

As adults age, their own children leave home and have children. Older adults' roles as grandparents are influenced by culture: in many societies grandparents are seen as part of an extended family and are often and frequently actively involved in their grandchildren's care and upbringing. Grandparents can have a very positive influence on children's development by offering an additional source of practical and emotional support to the child and parent (Adkins, 1999). Moreover, grandchildren can have a positive influence on grandparents too because they can be a significant source of satisfaction and well-being (Smith & Drew, 2002). Having and caring for grandchildren appears to be especially beneficial for women (Thiele & Whelan, 2008) perhaps because, given historical female roles as primary caregivers in many societies, female grandparents can feel they are more useful or helpful to their own children.

Cherlin and Furstenberg (1985) classified three different grandparenting styles. Most grandparents (around half) in their study of American grandparents across the social spectrum displayed *compassionate relationships* with their grandchildren. That is, they engaged in very loving relationships with their grandchildren, although not always taking full responsibility for discipline. The relationship between grandparent and grandchild was warm and mutually rewarding. Around a third of grandparents were *remote*; that is, they had little involvement in their grandchild's life. One in six grandparents was in an *involved relationship* with their grandchild or grandchildren. These grandparents took on something akin to the parenting role, with responsibility for everyday aspects of life and care.

> **grandparenting styles** Different types of grandparenting relationship identified as compassionate, involved and remote, depending on the degree of involvement with a grandchild and the quality of the relationship.

The quality of grandparents' involvement with their grandchildren is clearly dependent on several factors including geographical distance, socioeconomic status, and the grandparents' marital status. A further important factor is the relationship between a child's parents and grandparents. The quality of this relationship can influence whether and how much a parent asks a grandparent to help with childcare and other domestic activities (Mueller & Elder, 2003). Generally, the better the relationship between parent and grandparent the better the quality and extent of grandparent's involvement with the child (Barnett et al., 2010). This association is especially strong in terms of grandparents' relationships with a child's mother.

Grandparents do not provide just instrumental support. They may also act as a link across generations to ensure family continuity and identity. Moreover, it is not just in the early years that grandparents have influence but also into adolescence, where grandparents may be a useful sounding board for young people when difficulties with parent–child relationships arise (see, for instance, Tan et al., 2010).

The role and significance of grandparents in development is only recently becoming recognized by researchers. This may, at least in part, be a feature of changing societal and economic demands and family dynamics. Similarly, the importance of becoming a grandparent in terms of an older individual's social roles and relationships is an area where further research is required in order to understand better its impact on development in adulthood.

Death and dying

The inevitability of the end of life – the ending of the physical body at least – is often treated as a taboo or a topic of discussion to be avoided. Most religions and cultures tend not to view death as the end of existence, and incorporate ideas such as afterlife and reincarnation into their belief systems (Lobar, Youngblut, & Brooten, 2006). Contemplating our own death, the death of loved ones, or even just the abstract idea of death, can be disturbing at any age. Yet for elderly adults, who may themselves be close to death or have seen partners and friends dying, death is a prospect that they need to confront.

Perhaps surprisingly, it is not older adults who show most fear of death, but those in middle adulthood (Kalish & Reynolds, 1976). This may be because older adults have more experience of others' death and spend more time contemplating the issue which reduces anxiety about the unknown, or are more accepting of its inevitability. It may also be that, in middle age, many adults feel anxious contemplating the possibility that they may no longer be able to actively care for dependent children and others.

There are notable age differences in individuals' knowledge about and attitudes towards death. Young children frequently have little experience of death or dying, but by 6–7 years most children have a rudimentary concept of the biological basis of life and death. However, it is not until around 9 years that most children understand that death is irreversible (Cuddy-Casey & Orvaschel, 1997). Experience appears to play an important part. For instance, Slaughter and Lyons (2003) found that teaching children about the characteristics and processes involved in life enhanced knowledge about death and its causes. Again, children who have experienced the death of a close relative are more likely to understand about its permanence than those who have not (Stambrook & Parker, 1987; Hunter & Smith, 2008). There may also be some cultural influences on beliefs about death. In a study comparing American and Swedish adolescents, Wenestam and Wass (1987) asked participants to draw pictures representing what they thought of when they heard the words 'death' or 'dying'. Although there were broad similarities between cultures, more Swedish participants tended to draw images of religion or religious symbols, whereas more US teenagers drew pictures of violent deaths.

It does not appear that older adults talk or think less about death, but that they find the idea less frightening and, possibly, have greater acceptance of the inevitable end of their life (Cicirelli, 2006). Fear of death is also affected by personal beliefs, and in particular religious beliefs. Those with religious beliefs are reported to fear death less than those without (Kalish, 1985). People who feel their lives have been worthwhile, or who feel they have achieved personal goals, also seem to experience less anxiety about death as they age (Ardelt & Koenig, 2006).

Beliefs and attitudes towards death may go some way to helping people to cope with their own and others' deaths. Alongside inevitable physiological deterioration and medical complications, people suffering with terminal illnesses face particular emotional and psychological challenges. Elisabeth Kübler-Ross (Kübler-Ross, 1969, 1974) developed an account of the stages of dying and approaches to coping with death. The stages were built upon analysis of responses to interviews from cancer patients who were terminally ill. Table 16-2 summarizes these stages of dying.

Table 16-2   Kübler-Ross's stages of dying

Stage	Individual's reaction to dying
Denial	An initial, temporary psychological defence against contemplating one's own death is to deny the diagnosis. This initial period does not usually last very long – maybe just a few days – but may act as a buttress against the emotional trauma of the news.
Anger	Denial gives way to anger in response to the realization that the diagnosis is accurate and death is inevitable. Anger can be directed outwardly towards others: God, medics and nurses, and healthy family members.
Bargaining	When anger subsides, individuals begin a sort of mental negotiation phase where they may try to find ways of prolonging life or delaying death, or focus on a particular future event that act as a motivation for surviving longer. Bargains can be struck with doctors, God or others including the patient themselves.
Depression	Once the bargaining phase is completed, patients face the inevitability of their own, imminent death and become depressed. The patient may refuse to see relatives or loved ones. This stage, according to Kübler-Ross, is a normal and necessary one for reaching the final stage.
Acceptance	The final stage of dying. Individuals now finally accept their fate and grieve for what they will lose, but achieve a sense of peace having fully come to terms with death.

Source: Kübler-Ross (1969).

Kübler-Ross's stage theory has been influential in the psychological treatment and counselling of terminally ill patients. Although presented as a stage model, she suggested that these stages do not form the same invariant sequence for all individuals, and not all people will experience all five. However, according to Kübler-Ross, individuals who are dying will always experience at least two, and the stages are universal (that is, they do not vary between cultures). Often there may be a 'rollercoaster' ride, with people moving rapidly between anger and depression, denial and bargaining.

However, although it has proved influential for therapeutic work with dying and other trauma victims, the attempt to chart dying as a series of stages has come in for considerable criticism in light of subsequent research. Kastenbaum (2000), for instance, argues that no two individuals are similar and no two contexts for dying are the same. Moreover, empirical support for the stage model is thin, and the methods used for selecting interviewees did not always have regard for ages and other important details such as the extent of illness and diagnosis. Kastenbaum also argues that Kübler-Ross fails to consider how contextual factors – support from friends, family, the institution in which they die – influence the dying process. Lastly, the claim that the stages of dying are universal does not fit easily with observations of widespread differences in coping with death between cultures (see again, Lobar et al., 2006). It is also unclear why some people go through some stages while others do not. Perhaps there is no 'right' or 'correct' way to die and all individuals will have their own means of coping. Certainly, it seems that not all individuals reach a phase of acceptance before their death (Schneidman, 1980).

The style of coping with a diagnosis of a serious illness is not just important for considering the quality of life of the terminally ill. Coping strategies of patients with diagnoses of serious, life-threatening illnesses may also relate to the chances of surviving the illness. Greer (1991) reported a study that involved interviewing over 60 women who had been diagnosed with early stage breast cancer in the 1970s. Interviews were used to establish how women coped with the diagnosis. For instance, some women entered denial (ignoring the severity of the illness, akin to Kübler-Ross's first stage), others developed a 'fighting spirit', still others were fatalistic, anxious or felt helpless about the illness, stoically accepting the diagnosis and likelihood of death. Researchers then followed up to establish how these styles related to survival after 5, 10 and 15 years, making sure that they compared survival rates of women with similar diagnoses at the outset. By far the greatest majority stoically accepted the diagnosis – in the 1970s death rates from breast cancer were considerably higher than today – and of these 76% had died from cancer 15 years later. However, those women who were in denial about the illness or adopted a fighting spirit fared much better: 15 years later, only 35% had died from the cancer.

The role of coping strategies in surviving diagnoses of serious illness is probably complex. For instance, fighting spirit may work well for cancer but not so well in combating chronic heart disease. Moreover, there are always difficulties in establishing causal links because not enough is yet known about the genetic or physiological mechanisms that underpin personality, coping and risk of illnesses such as cancer. Social support (from family, friends, or social welfare bodies and charities) has also been linked to increased likelihood of surviving serious illness (Spiegel et al., 1989). Moreover, counsellors and others need to be wary of giving a message that adopting one coping style or another may help a patient to avoid death because it may prevent them from fully coming to terms with or accepting their death, which may have negative consequences for well-being and dying in a dignified way.

SUCCESSFUL AGEING

There is considerable diversity in terms of how, or how well, people age. Some will grow old before their time and others will remain physically, socially and mentally active until well into their 90s. Given the increased number of individuals living to an older age, there has been considerable research effort aimed at identifying the characteristics of the 'successful ager' (e.g., Kensinger & Gutchess, 2017). That is, researchers have sought to identify what it is that leads some individuals to lead active and satisfying lives into old age both to improve older adults' quality of life but also because many years of illness and dependency into old age presents a significant personal and social challenge for many others.

disengagement theory The theory that successful ageing involves a gradual retreat and withdrawal from many activities.

Disengagement theory (Cummings & Henry, 1961) proposes that successful ageing is partly a matter of gradually withdrawing from the world. This is both physical, intellectual and social withdrawal, as elderly people engage less with the world around them and show less interest in it. Disengagement theory suggests that this disengagement is mutual; few societies have, traditionally, had a central role for the very old (although several societies venerate the elderly). Moreover, this disengagement is not necessarily a negative process because older adults can be freer to do what they want without having to worry too much about social norms and expectations, and they can focus their energies and activities where they most want or will receive the most enjoyment.

Disengagement may be a successful strategy for some but not others (Bergstrom & Holmes, 2000), for instance it may be a poor strategy after the loss of a spouse if an older adult has few other relationships or has been in a highly co-dependent relationship. An alternative is activity theory. Activity theory proposes that rather than disengagement and gradual withdrawal, retaining interest and activity in life is important in successful ageing (Bell, 1978). Thus older adults who keep high levels of activity will be happiest and will successfully age.

activity theory The theory that successful ageing involves maintaining interest in activities into late adulthood.

In fact, both activity theory and disengagement theory are perhaps a little simplistic. While total disengagement will rarely lead to a satisfying life maintaining high levels of activity even when these may be impossible due to a reduction in the body's physical capabilities would also appear to be a recipe for dissatisfaction. Most theorists now agree that a mixture of the two – continuity theory – best explains what is required for successful ageing. Continuity theory proposes that activity is important but only insofar as it ensures happiness. Thus some gradual disengagement is probably inevitable as people age, but so long as there is a focus on enjoying life ageing can be said to be successful (Atchley & Barusch, 2004).

continuity theory The theory that maintaining activity to a level that ensures life satisfaction is optimal for successful ageing.

Rowe and Kahn (1998) suggest there are three elements that help individuals to age successfully. These are:

1. maintaining good physical health
2. retaining cognitive abilities
3. continuing to engage with social and productive activities.

Ensuring that these three elements are in place will, according to Rowe and Kahn, help to avoid or lessen age-related deterioration in health and well-being.

Maintaining good physical health is important throughout life and a good pattern of exercise in early adulthood, particularly exercise geared towards improving or maintaining cardiovascular health, has beneficial effects in old age. However, remaining physically active is important for those in old age where recovery from injury make take longer. In addition, a lack of engagement with life, physical disability or fear of crime may make the elderly less likely to leave home, walk and take regular physical exercise. Retaining cognitive abilities is also important, too, for successful ageing. Activities such as completing a daily crossword, or taking up a new hobby or educational challenge may help to keep individuals both socially and mentally active. Learning something new might assist the brain to establish new neuron connections or to resist the effects of age-related neuron loss.

Successful ageing is most likely to involve both activity and some gradual disengagement in both physical and social aspects; regardless, the important thing for achieving successful ageing is a focus on enjoying life.
Source: © Shutterstock/Monkey Business Images

Elderly individuals may find it more difficult to maintain an active network of friends and acquaintances, and so may find that they engage in fewer social and productive activities as they age, especially if a partner or a number of friends pass away. Maintaining a social network can help with intellectual stimulation and maintaining a sense of purpose in life and life satisfaction (Lachman et al., 2008).

The core message from many researchers interested in promoting successful ageing is 'use it or lose it' – that is, use your abilities while you still have them in order to maintain them. For instance, Hultsch et al. (1999) assessed data from the Victoria Longitudinal Study – a study based in Canada. The researchers tested 250 middle-aged and older adults over a period of six years, and found a relationship between changes in intellectually related activities such as doing a regular crossword or taking a new course of study, and changes in cognitive functioning. Briefly, those who maintained intellectually related activities retained much of their cognitive function.

> **'use it or lose it'** The idea that, to avoid cognitive or physical decline into old age, people must continue to use cognitive and physical abilities as much as possible.

While there is broad agreement that all these elements are important, some researchers contend that leading a physically active lifestyle – proper nutrition and avoidance of harmful activities such as smoking – is of primary importance (Franklin & Tate, 2009). However, social and cultural influences are also, clearly, important. For instance, Hess, Emery, and Queen (2009) found that exposing older American adults to stereotype-related words and phrases about the elderly before encoding began impaired subsequent memory performance compared with a control condition where there were no stereotyped words. Hess and colleagues' findings correspond to the more general finding of 'stereotype threat' (see Steele & Aronson, 1995) which is based on the observation that presenting people with stereotype information (for instance, telling women that they perform more poorly on a maths task than men) often produces the stereotyped effect (that is, women perform more poorly) even if there is no truth in the stereotype information that is given. Thus, people are sensitive to information about the groups to which they belong and often behave in ways that are consistent with this information, and older adults are no exception to this social pressure.

Stereotypes are important because cultures differ in how they consider older adults. For instance, in Japan there is considerably more reverence paid to older adults than in North America and European societies. In several societies the elder members remain deeply involved in decision-making and governance of a community or group (see Fry, 1985). Challenging negative stereotypes of the elderly may well have a beneficial effect on the elderly in terms of self-perceptions and, in turn, physical health and well-being.

> Stereotype threat plays an important role in understanding theories of gender and ethnic differences in educational performance (see Chapter 11).

A further perspective for successful ageing comes from Baltes's selective optimization with compensation (SOC) perspective. Baltes and Freund (2003) suggest an integrated approach combining wisdom, SOC and goals to lead to optimal human development. The foundations for proactive ageing, argues Baltes, are set in childhood. Building upon these early steps individuals can use the wisdom that they acquire throughout life to determine what goals they desire to pursue for their own and others' good. To achieve these goals individuals can use SOC to manage their life (lifestyle) effectively and efficiently. To ensure happiness and satisfaction with life, individuals also need to think realistically about what goals can be achieved to avoid too much disappointment from failure. Baltes's perspective emphasizes that retaining good physical and cognitive functioning is a means to an end. In later life, individuals may also seek a sense of purpose or meaning from their life and look to their legacy.

Conceptualizing identity change in adults

As discussed at the start of this chapter, the traditional focus in developmental psychology has been with development from infancy through childhood. Adolescent, and certainly adult development, has been somewhat neglected. Consequently, many core theoretical approaches have not sought to encompass developmental change beyond childhood. However, a handful of theorists have attempted to conceptualize development into adulthood, or have charted patterns of change across the adult years.

One of the best-known theorists, who sought to extend Freud's psychosexual theory to explain development across the lifespan, was Erik Erikson (Erikson, 1950, 1968, 1975). Like Freud, Erikson argued that developmental change was stimulated by a series of conflicts which children and adults need to resolve. Erikson focused on the development of social (and self) understanding, playing down the emphasis on drives and sexuality in Freud's account. Perhaps Erikson's most significant contribution was to add three stages of

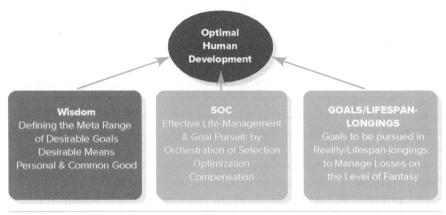

Figure 16-4 Research on composing one's life
Source: Baltes and Freund (2003).

adult conflict and development. These stages correspond, broadly, to early, middle and late adulthood respectively.

In early adulthood, the focus is on establishing life partnerships and intimate relationships. Here young adults experience conflict between *intimacy* (involvement with a partner on the one hand) and *isolation* (failure to find such a partner). In middle adulthood the conflict is between *generativity* and *stagnation*. Generativity (passing on your ideas and values) is typically achieved through parenting and successful child-rearing. Erikson viewed the concept more generally to refer to the production of anything that could ensure continuity to the next generation and into the future. Thus not just in family life, but also through work and other forms of activity middle adults can fulfil this need. Failure to achieve generativity results in stagnation, a sense in which they have not achieved anything of significance or worth. Late adulthood sees a final conflict between *integrity* and *despair*. Older adults have the opportunity to reflect on their lives and a sense of achievement and satisfaction with their life helps to give a sense of integrity. However, feelings of missed opportunities, failure and general dissatisfaction when reflecting on life can lead to despair.

Erikson's model was rooted in the psychoanalytic tradition, and although the approach has the merit of extending development across the age range, it suffers from some of the same weaknesses. For instance, some of the central concepts may be intuitively appealing but can be difficult to test empirically. In all instances, the conflicts experienced by individuals may be rather more complex and sophisticated than described by Erikson.

Erikson seeks to capture broad themes in an individual's life, and as we have seen the roles one takes on often change across adulthood. Duvall (1962) described eight stages in the development of family roles (see Figure 16-5). The developmental 'task' for an individual is to fulfil these roles and cope with the distinct challenges they present. Thus, an early change in adulthood (for many when Duvall was developing his theory) is the addition of the spousal role. Here the individual enters a new partnership that possesses a significance and level of involvement that he or she may not have experienced before. This may present challenges and new experiences which the individual has to accept and meet. The role changes progressively as the family grows.

For example, the newly married man becomes a husband and accordingly adopts a new aspect to his identity by virtue of this new role. When a mother gives birth to her first child, her role and identity change. Families develop and change in response to these different life phases which are associated with different social and personal demands and roles.

Duvall's model has the advantage of considering the family unit, and the individual in terms of their relationships with others, as important. However, the model is also rather narrow and excludes diverse forms of family such as divorced couples, families who do not have children, and those who are not part of a family at all. Moreover, the model appears to be insensitive to other factors such as gender and ethnicity, which may have a profound effect on roles and development. In addition, while it provides an account of

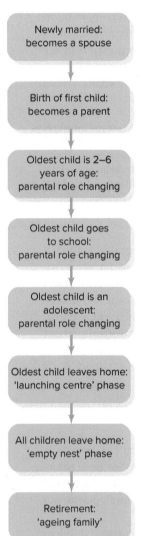

Figure 16-5 Duvall's role theory
Source: Duvall (1962).

family life it does not address other aspects of life that may be very important for individual and identity development such as work roles and careers.

Daniel Levinson considered adult development as made up of periods of transition and stability. Levinson (1978, 1990) coined the idea of life structures. A life structure is the set of important aspects of an individual's life, at a given time, that includes aspects of her relationships, roles in society, and challenges, obstacles and issues she faces at that time. Stable periods in life describe periods where an individual is settled and has made and reconciled choices about their life. These are followed by periods of transition where the individual moves to the next phase or stage of life.

> **life structure** The underlying pattern of an adult's life at a particular point in life.

A great deal of life satisfaction depends on how far dreams and ambitions, held during early adulthood, are realized throughout the life course. These dreams may or may not be realized but require that the man adapts to differing periods or phases. A little like Duvall's role theory. In early adulthood, after transition into the adult world, Levinson identified initial choices in love and lifestyle were important, but by 33 years the theory focused on individuals who have settled down both in family and career terms. The mid-life transition (between 40 and 45 years) led to a re-evaluation of life and role, often characterized by some sense of crisis or uncertainty about the future.

Levinson's characterization of 'seasons of life' (Figure 16-6) picks out some of the important social and personal changes that may be aspects of development in adulthood for many people, although a clear criticism of Levinson's work was his emphasis exclusively on men's life courses. He subsequently also produced a model of stage-like progression for women's seasons of life (Levinson & Levinson, 1996). However, although Levinson belatedly attempted to address this omission in his theory, herein lies a major problem with Levinson's work: by focusing on the sorts of conflicts, dilemmas and issues that men and women face in their lives Levinson seeks (perhaps implicitly) to provide a universal framework for adult development. Yet maybe what marks out much of psychological and social development in adulthood, and what distinguishes it from models of development through childhood, is its diversity. While men's and women's lives may follow broad seasonal patterns they may be dictated more by the world men and women live in than by any underlying cognitive processes. Thus we may well find aspects of Levinson's theory that resonate with our own lives, or with the lives of people we know. But the question of how far this remains development, or just change, remains to be seen.

An important question for developmental psychologists who are interested in adult development is how we construe a relevant process of change. If we focus on development as fundamentally a process of learning and intellectual advancement, then adulthood is perhaps better understood as a period where the emphasis is on social rather than cognitive aspects of advancement. Yet, without doubt, important changes happen in adulthood, and these changes have significance for the behaviour, reasoning and well-being of individuals.

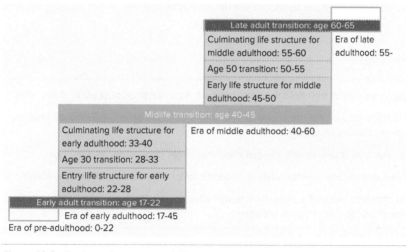

Figure 16-6   Levinson's seasons of life

SUMMARY

Throughout much of the history of developmental psychology, theories and research have tended to focus on developmental change in infancy, childhood and adolescence. While this is certainly a period of more pronounced changes in reasoning and behaviour, researchers now appreciate that some meaningful psychological development happens in adulthood and across the lifespan. Some adult developmental theories view patterns of behaviour that are formed during childhood as determining adult psychological functioning. Recently, however, *gerontology* has sought to understand how humans function psychologically as they age, and this is an important perspective in terms of society where the numbers of older adults are growing progressively and in proportion to the number of younger adults. Most gerontologists divide adult development into three phases: early adulthood from around 18 to 40 years, middle adulthood from 40 to 65 years, and late adulthood from 65 years onwards.

There are important physical changes that happen across the lifespan. In early adulthood most people are in their physical peak. In middle adulthood, most people remain in good physical condition although there is some loss of *reserve capacity* – the energy and physical resources that are available to push oneself a little further in terms of physical activity. Theories of ageing distinguish *pre-programmed* or *Dev-age* accounts from *wear-and-tear* theories. The former argues that ageing is the consequence of genetic factors, whereas the latter argues that ageing occurs through environmental stressors such as illness and injury. Clearly, both factors play a part and many researchers prefer to identify both *primary* (pre-programmed) and *secondary* (wear and tear) ageing.

How far *intelligence* changes throughout adulthood has been the attention of considerable research focus. Some argue that environmental factors become more important with age (dedifferentiation hypothesis) while others argue that they become less important than 'natural' intelligence (or *g*, the differentiation hypothesis). In fact, in most cases intelligence appears to change little across the lifespan, although some different capabilities (e.g., *fluid intelligence*) may diminish with age while others (e.g., *crystallized intelligence*) increase progressively throughout adult life. Age-related decline in *memory* abilities in adulthood appears to be more marked for some types of memory (e.g., short-term memory) than others. Moreover, there is great variability in the extent of memory decline. This variability is probably due to several factors including genetics, lifestyle and diet.

Individuals who 'age successfully' seem to engage in some activity while withdrawing from aspects of life they no longer enjoy, or are no longer able to participate in. This middle ground approach is described as *continuity theory*. Generally, maintaining an active social, physical and intellectual lifestyle is important. The principle of *selective optimization with compensation* also describes an approach to successful ageing. Coping with identity change, such as becoming a parent or becoming retired, is important in adult life. This may be achieved by resolving conflicts between contrasting social identities or by adopting different family and social roles as one ages. The hopes and dreams we had as young adults may also affect our life plans and lead to different seasons of life as we develop and mature.

Explore and Discuss

1. Does any meaningful psychological development occur after adolescence? If so, what?

2. What factors account for the changes in memory function across adulthood? How can we avoid problems with memory in old age?

3. Why do you think that many people believe that people get less happy as they age?

4. How should we explain the development of romantic love? Can we ever explain it scientifically?

5. What are the characteristics of successful ageing? Why do you think so many older adults cease to engage in a full range of social and physical activities?

Classic

Baltes, P. B., & Baltes, M. M. (1990). Psychological perspectives on successful ageing: The model of selective optimization with compensation. In P. B. Baltes & M. M. Baltes (eds), *Successful ageing* (pp. 1–34). Cambridge, Cambridge University Press.

Erikson, E. H. (1975). *Life history and the historical moment*. New York: Norton.

Hetherington, E. M., & Clingempeel, W. G. (1992). Coping with marital transitions: A family systems perspective. *Monographs of the Society for Research in Child Development, 57,* 2–3.

Contemporary

Baltes, P. B., & Freund, A. M. (2003). Human strengths as the orchestration of wisdom and selective optimization with compensation. In L. G. Aspinwall & U. M. Staudinger (eds), *A psychology of human strengths: Perspectives on an emerging field.* Washington, DC: American Psychological Association.

Franklin, N. C., & Tate, C. A. (2009). Lifestyle and successful ageing: An overview. *American Journal of Lifestyle Medicine, 3,* 6–11.

Mejía, S. T., Ryan, M. H., Gonzalez, R., & Smith, J. (2017). Successful aging as the intersection of individual resources, age, environment, and experiences of well-being in daily activities. *The Journals of Gerontology: Series B, 72,* 279–289, https://doi.org/10.1093/geronb/gbw148

Recommended Reading

Glossary

accommodation Modifying an existing schema to fit a new experience.

achievement motivation A person's tendency to strive for successful performance, to evaluate her performance against standards of excellence, and to feel pleasure at having performed successfully.

active gene–environment correlation A situation in which people's genes encourage them to seek out particular kinds of experiences.

activity theory The theory that successful ageing involves maintaining interest in activities into late adulthood.

aetiology In medicine and psychiatry, the cause or causes of a specific disorder.

age cohort People born within the same generation.

age of viability The age of 22 to 26 weeks from conception, at which point the foetus's physical systems are advanced enough that it has a chance to survive if born prematurely.

aggression Behaviour that intentionally harms other people by inflicting pain or injury on them.

aggressive rejected children Rejected children who have low self-control, are highly aggressive and exhibit behaviour problems.

allele Alleles are alternative forms of a gene. An individual typically has two alleles – one from the mother and one from the father.

altruism An unselfish concern for the welfare of others.

amniotic sac A membrane that contains the developing organism and the amniotic fluid around it; sac and fluid protect the organism from physical shocks and temperature changes.

androgynous Possessing both feminine and masculine psychological characteristics.

andropause The 'male menopause', linked to a decline in the production of testosterone but with varying symptoms and not universally acknowledged to exist.

animistic thinking The attribution of life to inanimate objects.

approach/avoidance behaviour A pattern of interaction in which the infant or child shows an inconsistent pattern of approaching and retreating from a person or an object.

assimilation Applying an existing schema to a new experience.

associative learning According to Jensen, lower-level learning tapped in tests of such things as short-term memorization and recall, attention, rote learning, and simple associative skills. Also called level I learning.

attachment A strong emotional bond that forms between infant and caregiver in the second half of the child's first year.

Attachment Q Sort (AQS) An assessment method in which a caregiver or observer judges the quality of a child's attachment based on the child's behaviour in naturalistic situations, often including brief separations from parents.

attention The identification and selection of particular sensory input for more detailed processing.

attention deficit/hyperactivity disorder (ADHD) A childhood disorder characterized by a persistent pattern of inattention and hyperactivity or impulsivity that far exceeds such behaviours observed in children at comparable levels of development.

authoritarian parenting Parenting that is harsh, unresponsive and rigid, and in which parents tend to use power-assertive methods of control.

authoritative parenting Parenting that is warm, responsive and involved yet unintrusive, and in which parents set reasonable limits and expect appropriately mature behaviour from their children.

autism spectrum disorder (ASD) A lifelong disorder in which children's ability to communicate and interact socially is seriously impaired; children with ASD often have communicative and social difficulties, and often engage in repetitive and stereotyped kinds of behaviours.

autobiographical memory A collection of memories of things that have happened to a person at a specific time or place.

automatization The process of transforming conscious, controlled behaviours into unconscious and automatic ones.

autosomes The 22 paired non-sex chromosomes.

average children Children who have some friends but who are not as well liked as popular children.

basic reflex activity An infant's exercise of, and growing proficiency in, the use of innate reflexes.

Bayesian modelling A form of computational modelling which rests on conditional probabilistic relationships between items of information. Bayesian modelling is used to model the development of children's understanding of the relationships between many things, including events, words and objects.

Bayes's theorem Bayes's theorem describes conditional probability; that is, the probability of an event based on prior knowledge that something else which might be related to the event is the case or has occurred.

behaviour therapy A psychological form of treatment, often used in treating conduct disorders, which is based on such learning principles as reinforcement and social learning.

behavioural genetics The field of study that examines the role of genetics in human (and animal) behaviour.

behavioural genetics The study of the relative influences of heredity and environment on the evolution of individual differences in traits and abilities.

behaviourism A school of psychology prominent in the early twentieth century, which emphasized the role of learning in human behaviour and attempted to describe behaviour in such terms.

binocular disparity The sense of a third spatial dimension, that of depth, produced by the brain's fusion of the separate images contributed by each eye, each of which reflects the stimulus from a slightly different angle.

brain hemispheres The two halves of the brain's cerebrum, left and right.

brain reserve hypothesis The suggestion that social and cognitive stimulation can help to build up reserves of ability, and improve brain function and performance in older adults.

Brazelton Neonatal Assessment Scale A scale containing a battery of tests used to measure an infant's sensory and perceptual capabilities, motor development, range of states and ability to regulate these states, as well as whether the brain and central nervous system are properly regulating involuntary responses.

Caesarean delivery The surgical delivery of a baby; the baby is removed from the mother's uterus through an incision made in her abdomen and uterus in a procedure also known as Caesarean section.

canalization The genetic restriction of a phenotype to a small number of

developmental outcomes, permitting environmental influences to play only a small role in these outcomes.

case study A form of research in which investigators study an individual person or group very intensely.

catch-up growth The tendency for human beings to regain a normal course of physical growth after injury or deprivation.

categorical speech perception The tendency to perceive as the same a range of sounds belonging to the same phonemic group.

catharsis Discharging aggressive impulses by engaging in actual or symbolic aggressive acts that do not impinge on another person.

central executive The overarching controller in the working model, which regulates the action of the various slave systems. This is similar to the concept of executive function.

cephalocaudal The pattern of human physical growth in which development begins in the area of the brain and proceeds downwards to the trunk and legs.

cerebral cortex The covering layer of the cerebrum that contains the cells that control specific functions such as seeing, hearing, moving and thinking.

cerebrum The two connected hemispheres of the brain.

Chromosomes Threadlike structures, located in the nucleus of a cell, that carry genetic information to help direct development.

classical conditioning A type of learning in which two stimuli are repeatedly presented together until individuals learn to respond to the unfamiliar stimulus in the same way they respond to the familiar stimulus.

clique A voluntary group formed on the basis of friendship.

codominance A genetic pattern in which heterozygous alleles express

the variants of the trait for which they code simultaneously and with equal force.

cognition The mental activity through which human beings acquire and process knowledge.

cognitive behaviour therapy A group therapy technique particularly useful in treating depression in adolescents. Therapeutic goals include reducing self-consciousness and feelings of being different, and teaching strategies for dealing with depressive moods and for acquiring a more positive outlook and improving social interactions.

cognitive developmental theory Kohlberg's theory that children use physical and behavioural clues to differentiate gender roles and to gender-type themselves very early in life, and that gender development is underpinned by the development of cognitive abilities.

cognitive developmental view of attachment The view that to form attachments infants must differentiate between mother and stranger, and understand that people exist independent of the infant's interaction with them.

cognitive learning According to Jensen, higher-level learning tapped in tests of such things as abstract thinking, symbolic processing and the use of language in problem solving. Also called level II learning.

cognitive neuroscience The field in which scientists study the biological machinery and processes which underpin cognition.

cognitive strategies Cognitive activities used to enhance mental performance.

community of learners An approach to classroom learning in which adults and children work together in shared activities, peers learn from one another, and the teacher serves as a guide.

comorbidity The co-occurrence of two or more problem behaviours.

concrete operations Subperiod in which the child is able to reason logically about materials that are physically present.

conduct disorder A disorder characterized by a repetitive and persistent pattern of behaviour in which a young person violates the basic rights of others, or major age-appropriate societal norms or rules.

connectionist models Connectionist models are a class of computational model used to make explicit theoretical accounts of human cognition and development.

conscience The child's internalized values and standards of behaviour.

conservation The understanding that altering an object's or a substance's appearance does not change its basic attributes or properties.

construal level theory of psychological distance The theory that the ways in which we think about people, events or objects is more or less abstract depending on our psychological distance from them.

constructivism The idea that children actively create their understanding of the world as they engage with new information and attempt to understand it.

consummate love The ideal love, in Sternberg's theory, including intimacy, passion and commitment

continuity theory The theory that maintaining activity to a level that ensures life satisfaction is optimal for successful ageing.

continuous development A pattern of development in which abilities change in a gradual and smooth way.

control group In an experiment, the group that is not exposed to the treatment, or the *independent variable.*

control phase According to Kopp, the first phase in learning self-regulation, when children are highly dependent on caregivers to remind them about acceptable behaviours.

controversial children Children who are liked by many peers but also disliked by many.

conventional level Kohlberg's second level of moral development, in which the child's behaviour is designed to solicit others' approval and maintain good relations with them. The child accepts societal regulations unquestioningly and judges behaviour as good if it conforms to these rules.

coordination of secondary circular reactions An infant's combination of different schemas to achieve a specific goal (sometimes referred to as means–end coordination).

core knowledge Ways of reasoning about ecologically important objects and events, such as the solidity and continuity of objects.

corpus callosum The band of nerve fibres that connects the two hemispheres of the brain.

correlational method A research design that permits investigators to establish relations among variables as well as assess the strength of those relations.

critical period A period of development (age range) at which specific experiences are vital for development to occur in a typical way.

cross-sectional method A research method in which researchers compare groups of individuals of different age levels at approximately the same point in time.

crossing over The process by which equivalent sections of homologous chromosomes switch places randomly, shuffling the genetic information each carries.

crossmodal matching paradigms Tasks that examine whether participants can match an object according to its unimodal properties. For instance, one could examine if an infant can match a cube presented to his hands with a visual cube by examining where he looks when presented with both a cube and a distracter stimulus, such as a triangle.

crowd A collection of people whom others have stereotyped on the basis of their perceived shared attitudes or activities – for example, 'populars' or 'nerds'.

crystallized intelligence Aspects of intelligence related to knowledge, education and experience, such as knowing what a particular word means.

cumulative risk The notion that risk factors in children's life circumstances have cumulative negative effects on their intellectual performance.

debriefing Communicating the findings of research, or its purpose, to participants after a study has been completed.

deductive reasoning Logical thinking that involves reaching a necessary and valid conclusion based on a set of premises.

deferred imitation Mimicry of an action some time after having observed it; requires that the child have some sort of mental representation of the action.

deoxyribonucleic acid (DNA) A ladder-like molecule that stores genetic information in cells and transmits it during reproduction.

dependent variable The variable, or factor, that researchers expect to change as a function of change in the independent variable.

depression in childhood Like adult depression, a mood disorder often manifested in a depressed mood and loss of interest in familiar activities, but also likely to be expressed as irritability and crankiness. Difficulty concentrating or focusing on tasks and concomitant drops in school grades are not uncommon, and children with depression often complain of physical problems such as headache.

developmental psychology A field of study that seeks to understand and explain change in individuals' cognitive, social and other capacities, first by describing changes in the child's observed behaviours and second by uncovering the processes that underlie these changes.

developmental psychopathology The investigation of the developmental origins, course, changes and continuities in disordered or maladaptive behaviour and thinking.

deviation IQ An IQ score that indicates the extent to which a person's performance on a test deviates from age mates' average performance.

diagnosis The identification of a physical or mental disorder on the basis of symptoms and of knowledge of the cause or causes of the disorder and its common course. A diagnosis may also include information about effective forms of treatment.

discontinuous development A pattern of development in which changes occur suddenly, resulting in qualitatively different stages (periods) of development.

disengagement theory The theory that successful ageing involves a gradual retreat and withdrawal from many activities.

dizygotic Characterizing fraternal twins, who have developed from two separate fertilized eggs.

domain-general development The idea that developments can have an impact on a wide range of abilities.

domain-specific development The idea that the development of various abilities occurs independently (separately) and has little impact on skills in other domains.

dominant The more powerful of two alleles in a heterozygous combination.

dopamine A neurohormone involved in the motivation of motor behaviour.

dynamic systems accounts of development Dynamic systems are an area of study in mathematics which attempts to describe complex systems with many inputs which interact in complex ways. Developmental psychologists have tried to explain development in this way.

dyslexia (b) A learning disability that impairs the ability to read and spell fluently.

ecological perspective A perspective that stresses the importance of understanding not only the relationships between organisms and various environmental systems but also the relations among such systems themselves.

ecological validity The degree to which a research study accurately represents events or processes that occur in the natural world.

ego In Freudian theory, the rational, controlling component of the personality, which tries to satisfy needs through appropriate, socially acceptable behaviours.

egocentric speech According to Vygotsky, a form of self-directed dialogue by which the child instructs herself in solving problems and formulating plans; as the child matures, this becomes internalized as *inner speech*.

egocentrism The tendency to view the world from one's own perspective and to have difficulty seeing things from another's viewpoint.

elaboration A memory strategy in which one adds to information to make it more meaningful and thus easier to remember.

elementary mental functions Psychological functions with which the child is endowed by nature, including attention, perception and involuntary memory, which emerge spontaneously during children's interaction with the world.

embryo The developing organism, which, implanted in the uterus wall, undergoes rapid cell division resulting in the differentiation of the major physiological structures and systems.

embryonic stage The period of prenatal development lasting from the second to around the eighth week of gestation.

emotional display rules Rules that dictate which emotions one may appropriately display in particular situations.

emotional script A complex scheme that enables a child to identify the emotional reaction likely to accompany a particular sort of event.

emotions Subjective reactions to the environment that are usually experienced cognitively as either pleasant or unpleasant, generally accompanied by physiological arousal, and often expressed in some visible form of behaviour.

empathic Able to experience the same emotion that someone else is experiencing.

empathy The capacity to experience the same emotion that someone else is experiencing.

empiricism The idea that development is primarily determined by environmental influences.

epigenetics The study of how genetic material is expressed.

episodic memory Memory for specific events, often autobiographical in nature.

equal-environment assumption Twin methods in behavioural genetics assume that monozygotic and dizygotic twins receive equal exposure to environmental influences which determine their behaviour. Some researchers have criticized this assumption, but most research demonstrates that it holds up.

equifinality equifinality captures the fact that children can attain the same developmental outcome due to different developmental trajectories

ethnic awareness The understanding of ethnicity as a social category.

ethological theory A theory which holds that behaviour must be viewed and understood as occurring in a particular context and as having adaptive or survival value.

ethological theory of attachment Bowlby's theory that attachment derives from the biological preparation of both infant and parents to respond to one another's behaviours in such a way that parents provide the infant with care and protection.

evocative gene–environment correlation Genetic influence on the environment through an individual's inherited tendencies to evoke certain environmental responses; for example, a child's smiling may elicit smiles from others.

evolutionary psychology An approach which holds that critical components of psychological functioning reflect evolutionary changes and are critical to the survival of the species.

executive control process A cognitive process that serves to control, guide and monitor the success of a problem-solving approach a child uses.

executive control structure According to Case, a mental blueprint or plan for solving a class of problems.

executive function A cognitive system that is presumed to control and manage other cognitive processes.

expansion A technique adults use in speaking to young children in which they imitate and expand or add to a child's statement.

experimental group In an experiment, the group that is exposed to the treatment, or the *independent variable.*

expressive characteristics Presumably typical of females, these characteristics include nurturance and concern with feelings.

extended family A family that includes relatives such as grandparents, aunts, uncles, nieces and nephews within the basic family unit of parents and children.

externalizing disorders A group of psychological disturbances in which a child appears to lack self-control in a variety of ways, through such behaviours as non-compliance, disobedience and aggression.

factor analysis A statistical procedure used to determine which of a number of factors, or scores, are both closely related to one another and relatively independent of other groups of factors, or scores.

fatuous love Passion and commitment without intimacy.

field experiment An experiment in which researchers deliberately create a change in a real-world setting and then measure the outcome of their manipulation.

fluid intelligence The capacity for abstract reasoning, such as spotting patterns of numbers or sequences.

foetal alcohol syndrome A disorder of the developing foetus caused by the ingestion of alcohol by the foetus's mother during gestation. It is characterized by stunted growth, a number of physical and physiological abnormalities and, often, mental retardation.

foetus The developing organism from the third month of gestation through delivery; during the foetal period, bodily structures and systems develop to completion.

formal operations stage Stage in which the child becomes capable of abstract thinking, complex reasoning and hypothesis testing.

fragile X syndrome A form of chromosomal abnormality, more common in males than in females, in which an area near the tip of the X chromosome is narrowed and made fragile due to a failure to condense during cell division. Symptoms include physical, cognitive and social problems.

friendship A reciprocal commitment between two people who see themselves more or less as equals.

fusiform face area An area of the temporal lobes that is strongly involved in face recognition.

gender constancy The awareness that superficial alterations in appearance or activity do not alter gender.

gender identity The perception of oneself as either masculine or feminine.

gender intensification A particularly marked period (in early adolescence) of conformity to gender roles and norms.

gender roles Composites of the behaviours actually exhibited by a typical male or female in a given culture; the reflection of a gender stereotype in everyday life.

Gender Schema Theory An information processing approach to gender development which suggests that schemas help children to organize and structure their experience related to gender differences and gender roles.

gender stability The notion that gender does not change; males remain male and females remain female.

gender stereotypes Beliefs that members of a culture hold about how females and males should behave; that is, what behaviours are acceptable and appropriate for each sex.

gender typing The process by which children acquire the values, motives and behaviours considered appropriate for their gender in their particular culture.

gene A portion of DNA located at a particular site on a chromosome and that codes for the production of specific kinds of proteins.

generalization The application of a strategy learned while solving a problem in one situation to a similar problem in a new situation.

genetic epistemology the genesis of knowledge; this was the term which Piaget used to describe what he was attempting to study and to capture in his constructivist theory of development

genetic transmission The biological process in which genetic material from both parents is combined into a new organism's genetic inheritance at conception via the conjoining of reproductive cells (gametes).

genital herpes A common viral infection spread primarily through sexual contact; if contracted by an infant during birth, it can cause blindness, motor abnormalities, cognitive delay and a wide range of neurological disorders.

germinal stage The stage of pregnancy beginning with the zygote being formed by the fertilization of the egg, and finishing when the zygote is implanted in the wall of the uterus (about seven days later).

gerontology The study of the social, biological and psychological aspects of ageing.

gestation The carrying of an embryo/foetus during pregnancy, usually for nine months in humans.

glial cell A nerve cell that supports and protects neurons, and serves to encase them in myelin sheaths.

grammar The structure of a language; consists of *morphology* and *syntax*.

grandparenting styles Different types of grandparenting relationship identified as compassionate, involved and remote, depending on the degree of involvement with a grandchild and the quality of the relationship.

guided participation Learning that occurs as children participate in activities of their community and are guided in their participation by the actions of more experienced partners in the setting.

habituation A form of learning instantiated in a decrease in the strength of response to a repeated stimulus.

haptic perception The active use of touch to encode and recognize objects and surface properties, which relies on inputs from both cutaneous (skin) receptors and proprioception (muscle receptors).

hedonistic reasoning Making a decision to perform a prosocial act on the basis of expected material reward.

hemispheric specialization Differential functioning of the two cerebral hemispheres; the left controlling the right side of the body, the right controlling the left side.

heritability factor A statistical estimate of the contribution heredity makes to a particular trait or ability.

heterozygous The state of an individual whose alleles for a particular trait from each parent are different.

hierarchical categorization The organization of concepts into levels of abstraction that range from the specific to the general.

higher mental functions Psychological functions, such as voluntary attention, complex memory processes and problem solving, that entail the coordination of several cognitive processes and the use of *mediators*.

holophrase A single word that appears to represent a complete thought.

homozygous The state of an individual whose alleles for a particular trait from each parent are the same.

horizontal décalage The term Piaget used to describe unevenness in children's thinking within a particular stage; for example, in developing an understanding of conservation, children conserve different objects or substances at different ages.

hormones Powerful and highly specialized chemical substances that are produced by the cells of certain body organs and that have a regulatory effect on the activity of certain other organs.

hostile aggression Directing aggressive behaviour at a particular person or group, criticizing, ridiculing, telling tales or calling names.

iconic memory Sensory memory for visual information. Of very short duration.

id In Freudian theory, the person's instinctual drives; the first component of the personality to evolve, the id operates on the basis of the *pleasure principle*.

imprinting The process by which birds and other infrahuman animals develop a preference for the person or object to which they are first exposed during a brief, critical period after birth.

independent variable The variable, or factor, that researchers deliberately manipulate in an experiment.

infant state A recurring pattern of arousal in the newborn, ranging from alert, vigorous, wakeful activity to quiet, regular sleep.

infant-directed, or child-directed, speech A simplified style of speech parents use with young children, in which sentences are short, simple and often repetitive, and the speaker enunciates especially clearly, slowly and in a higher-pitched voice, often ending with a rising intonation. Also called *motherese*.

infantile amnesia The inability to remember any event or piece information encoded before the age of around 3 years.

infatuation A relationship based only on passion (i.e. without intimacy or commitment).

information processing approaches Theories of development that focus on the flow of information through the child's cognitive system and particularly on the specific operations the child performs between input and output phases.

informed consent Agreement, based on a clear and full understanding of the purposes and procedures of a research study, to participate in that study.

inner speech Internalized egocentric speech that guides intellectual functioning.

insecure-avoidant attachment A type of attachment shown by babies who seem not to be bothered by their mothers' brief absences but specifically avoid them on their return, sometimes becoming visibly upset.

insecure-disorganized attachment A type of attachment shown by babies who seem disorganized and disorientated when reunited with their mothers after a brief separation.

insecure-resistant attachment A kind of attachment shown by babies who tend to become very upset at the departure of their mothers and who exhibit inconsistent behaviour on their return, sometimes seeking contact, sometimes pushing their mothers away.

instrumental aggression Quarrelling and fighting with others over toys and possessions.

instrumental characteristics Presumably typical of males, these characteristics include task and occupation orientation.

intellectual giftedness A characteristic defined by an IQ score of 130 or over; gifted children learn faster than others and may show early exceptional talents in certain areas.

intelligence quotient (IQ) An index of the way a person performs on a standardized intelligence test relative to the way others her age perform.

intent community participation Children's participation in the authentic activities of their community with the purpose of learning about the activity.

internal working model According to Bowlby, a person's mental representation of himself as a child, his parents and the nature of his interaction with his parents, as he reconstructs and interprets that interaction; also referred to as an *attachment representation*.

internalizing disorders A group of psychological disturbances in which a child appears overly controlled, withdrawing from others, lacking spontaneity and generally appearing to be not a happy child.

interposition The sense that one object is in front of another, provided by the partial occlusion of the further object by the nearer object.

inventing new means by mental combination Children begin to combine schemas mentally, and rely less on physical trial and error.

iron-deficiency anaemia A disorder in which inadequate amounts of iron in the diet causes listlessness, and may retard a child's physical and intellectual development.

laboratory experiment A research design that allows investigators to determine cause and effect by controlling variables and treatments, and assigning participants randomly to treatments.

language A communication system in which words and their written symbols combine in rule-governed ways and enable speakers to produce an infinite number of messages.

language acquisition device (LAD) Chomsky's proposed mental structure in the human nervous system, which incorporates an innate concept of language.

language acquisition support system (LASS) A collection of strategies and tactics that environmental influences – initially, a child's parents or caregivers – provide to the language-learning child.

lateralization The process by which each half of the brain becomes specialized for certain functions – for example, the control of speech and language by the left hemisphere and of visual-spatial processing by the right.

learning disabilities Deficits in one or more cognitive processes important for learning.

learning theory of attachment The theory that infants become attached to their mothers because a mother provides food, or primary reinforcement, and thus becomes a secondary reinforcer.

level of explanation The way in which we choose to describe psychological abilities (and the developments of those abilities). Levels of explanation can include biological, behavioural, social and emotional.

life structure The underlying pattern of an adult's life at a particular point in life.

lifespan perspective A view of development as a process that continues throughout the life cycle, from infancy through adulthood and old age.

linear perspective The manner in which patterns of light fall on the eye from objects that recede in depth.

long-term memory The mental processing unit in which information may be stored permanently, and from which it may later be retrieved.

longitudinal method A method in which investigators study the same people repeatedly at various times in the participants' lives.

low birth weight A term describing a premature baby who may be born close to its due date but who weighs significantly less than would be appropriate to its gestational age.

maturational approach An early approach to explaining development in terms of maturational timetables, predetermined by genetic inheritance.

mediators Psychological tools and signs – such as language, counting, mnemonic devices, algebraic symbols, art and writing – that facilitate and direct thinking processes.

meiosis The process by which a cell divides to produce new reproductive cells with only half the normal complement of chromosomes; thus male and female reproductive cells (sperm and ovum) each contain only 23 chromosomes so that, when they unite, the new organism they form will have 46 chromosomes, half from each parent.

memory span The amount of information one can hold in short-term memory.

menarche In females, the beginning of the menstrual cycle.

menopause A biological change in women during middle adulthood where the ovaries cease functioning and women can no longer conceive children.

mental representation Information stored mentally in some form (e.g. verbal, pictorial, procedural).

mental retardation A characteristic defined by an IQ score below 70 together with difficulty in coping with age-appropriate activities of everyday life.

messenger ribonucleic acid (mRNA) Molecules that transcribe the genetic code in DNA in the nucleus of the cell, and then travel to the body of the cell, where they are then used to synthesize protein.

metacognition the individual's awareness of and understanding about her or his cognitive abilities

metalinguistic awareness The understanding that language is a rule-bound system of communicating.

microcephaly A condition in which an infant is born with a head and brain which are smaller than normal.

microgenetic change Changes associated with learning that occur over the time of a specific learning experience or episode.

miscarriage The natural or spontaneous end of a pregnancy before the infant is capable of survival outside the womb. Human infants are generally unable to survive outside the uterus prior to 20 weeks' gestation.

mitosis The process in which a body cell divides in two, first duplicating its chromosomes so that the new daughter cells produced each contain the usual 46 chromosomes.

modal model A model of information processing in which information moves through a series of organized processing units: *sensory register, short-term memory* and *long-term memory*. The modal model emphasizes the importance of storage capacity and duration.

Molyneux's question William Molyneux asked the seventeenth-century British philosopher John Locke whether a blind person who had their sight restored might be able to see and recognize objects which they had previously learned about through touch alone.

monozygotic Characterizing identical twins, who have developed from a single fertilized egg.

moral realism Piaget's second stage of moral development, in which the child shows great respect for rules but applies them quite inflexibly.

morality of reciprocity Morality in which moral judgements should be made on the basis of equality and fairness between people, and equal justice for all.

morphology The study of morphemes, language's smallest units of meaning.

motion parallax A cue to depth emerging from the fact that, when we move, objects that are further away move across our visual field more slowly than do objects that are closer to us.

multifinality multifinality captures the fact that children with the same developmental starting point can develop differently due to different environmental circumstances

multisensory perception The process of perceiving objects and events in a unified way across more than one modality.

myelination The process by which glial cells encase neurons in sheaths of the fatty substance myelin.

narrative form A temporally sequenced account that conveys meaning about an event.

nativism The idea that development is primarily determined by inherited factors (i.e. genetics).

natural experiment An experiment in which researchers measure the results of events that occur naturally in the real world.

needs-orientated reasoning Reasoning in which children express concern for others' needs even though their own needs may conflict with those needs.

neglected children Children who are often socially isolated and, although they are not necessarily disliked by others, have few friends.

neo-Piagetian theories Theories of cognitive development that reinterpret Piaget's concepts from an information-processing perspective.

neonatal abstinence syndrome A withdrawal syndrome in newborn infants experienced following exposure to drugs of dependence *in utero*.

neonate A newborn baby.

neural migration The movement of neurons within the brain, which ensures that all brain areas have a sufficient number of neural connections.

neural proliferation The rapid formation of neurons in the developing organism's brain.

neural tube This structure, which is formed by the ectoderm (a layer of cells in the embryo) folding in on itself, develops into the nervous system, via a process of cell differentiation, along its extent.

neuron A cell in the body's nervous system, consisting of a cell body, a long projection called an axon and several shorter projections called dendrites; neurons send and receive neural impulses, or messages, throughout the brain and nervous system.

neuronal death The death of some neurons that surround newly formed synaptic connections among other neurons; also called programmed cell death.

niche picking Seeking out or creating environments compatible with one's genetically based predispositions.

non-aggressive rejected children Rejected children who tend to be anxious, withdrawn and socially unskilled.

non-shared environment A set of conditions or activities experienced by one child in a family but not shared with another child in the same family.

nuclear family A family composed of two parents and one or more children, in which the father is the breadwinner and the mother the homemaker.

nucleotide A compound containing a nitrogen base, a simple sugar and a phosphate group. The order in which the 4 types of nitrogen base contained within the nucleotide is sequenced in our DNA is the genetic code which contains our inheritance.

obesity A condition in which a person's weight is significantly in excess of the average weight for his or her height and frame. In the UK, childhood obesity is defined as being above the 95th centile compared to norms in 1990.

object permanence The notion that entities external to us, such as objects and people, continue to exist independent of our seeing or interacting with them.

observation A method in which researchers go into settings in the natural world or bring participants into the laboratory to observe behaviours of interest.

observational learning Learning that occurs through observing the behaviour of others.

observer bias The tendency of observers to be influenced in their judgements by their knowledge of the hypotheses guiding the research.

obsessive self-stimulatory behaviour Behaviour common in children with autism in which they engage in repetitive actions that seemingly have no purpose.

oestrogens Hormones that, in the female, are responsible for sexual maturation.

operant behaviour therapy A form of behaviour therapy in which behaviour is carefully monitored and consistently rewarded with such things as food.

operant conditioning A type of learning that depends on the consequences of behaviour; rewards increase the likelihood that a behaviour will recur, whereas punishment decreases that likelihood.

operations Schemas based on internal mental activities.

organization (b) A memory strategy that involves putting together in some organized form the information to be remembered; usually entails categorization and hierarchical relations.

overextension The use, by a young child, of a single word to cover many different things.

overregularization The application of a principle of regular change to a word that changes irregularly.

ovum The female reproductive cell, or egg.

parahippocampal place area An area in the temporal lobe (surrounding the hippocampus), which is strongly involved in forming representations of visual scenes.

passive gene–environment correlation The associations between the genetic inheritance a

child receives and the environment in which they are raised.

peer victimization Ill treatment of one child by another (or by others) that can range from teasing to bullying to serious physical harm; typically, victimizing is a continuing behaviour that persists over time.

peer-group network The cluster of peer acquaintances who are familiar with and interact with one another at different times for common play or task-orientated purposes.

perinatal complications Difficulties surrounding the birth of a child, which can lead to developmental difficulties.

perinatal risk factors Factors that can contribute to perinatal complications.

permissive parenting Parenting that is lax, and in which parents exercise inconsistent discipline and encourage children to express their impulses freely.

phenylketonuria (PKU) A disease caused by a recessive allele that fails to produce an enzyme necessary to metabolize the protein phenylalanine; if untreated immediately at birth, damages the nervous system and causes mental retardation.

phonological awareness The understanding of the sounds of a language and of the properties, such as the number of sounds in a word, related to these sounds.

phonological loop A 'slave system' in the working memory model that deals with speech sound information.

phonology The system of sounds that a language uses.

Piagetian theory A theory of cognitive development that sees the child as actively seeking new information.

pituitary gland A so-called master gland, located at the base of the brain, which triggers the secretion of hormones by all other hormone-secreting (endocrine) glands.

Placeholder Definition version 2

placenta A fleshy, disk-like structure formed by cells from the lining of the uterus and from the *zygote* that, together with the *umbilical cord*, serves to protect and sustain the life of the growing organism.

planning The deliberate organization of a sequence of actions orientated towards achieving a goal.

plasticity The capacity of the brain, particularly in its developmental stages, to respond and adapt to input from the external environment.

pleiotropy A gene is pleiotropic if it is expressed differently in different parts of the brain.

popular children Children who are liked by many peers and disliked by very few.

postconventional level Kohlberg's third level of moral development, in which the child's judgements are rational, and his conduct is controlled by an internalized ethical code that is relatively independent of the approval or disapproval of others.

postformal thinking Thought based on logical solutions but recognizing the role of relative perspectives and context in making judgements.

pragmatics A set of rules that specify appropriate language for particular social contexts.

pre-programmed theory (or Dev-Age) The theory that our rate of physical ageing is set by our genes, and is therefore, in large part, inevitable.

preconventional level Kohlberg's first level of moral development, in which he sees the child's behaviour as based on the desire to avoid punishment and gain rewards.

prejudice An attitude, or set of attitudes, which is often based on stereotypes towards a particular group, and is usually negative.

premoral stage Piaget's first stage of moral development, in which the child shows little concern for rules (also referred to as the amoral stage).

preoperational representations In this subperiod, the ability to use symbols facilitates the learning of language; this stage is also marked by pre-logical reasoning, egocentricity – in which the child sees the world from her own point of view – and intuitive behaviour, in which the child can solve problems using mental operations but cannot explain how she did so.

preterm A term describing a premature baby that is born before its due date and whose weight, although less than that of a full-term infant, may be appropriate to its gestational age.

primary ageing The gradual deterioration in physical ability due to genetic or 'pre-programmed' factors.

primary circular reactions Behaviours focused on the infant's own body that the infant repeats and modifies because they are pleasurable and satisfying.

proactive aggression The use of force to dominate another person or to bully or threaten others.

problem-solving The identification of a goal and of steps to reach that goal.

productive language The production of speech.

progesterone A hormone that, in females, helps regulate the menstrual cycle, and prepares the uterus to receive and nurture a fertilized egg.

propositional reasoning Logical thinking that involves evaluating a statement or series of statements based on the information in the statement alone.

prosocial behaviour Behaviour designed to help or benefit other people.

prosocial reasoning Thinking and making judgements about prosocial issues.

protodeclarative A gesture that an infant uses to make some sort of statement about an object.

protoimperative A gesture that either an infant or a young child may use to get someone to do something she or he wants.

proximal-distal The pattern of human physical growth wherein development starts in central areas, such as the internal organs, and proceeds to more distant areas, such as arms and legs.

psychoanalytic theory of attachment Freud's theory that babies become attached first to the mother's breast and then to the mother herself as a source of oral gratification.

psychodynamic theory In this view of development, which is derived from Freudian theory, development occurs in discrete stages and is determined largely by biologically based drives shaped by encounters with the environment and through the interaction of the personality's three components: the id, ego and superego.

psychosocial theory Erikson's theory of development, which sees children developing through a series of stages largely through accomplishing tasks that involve them in interaction with their social environment.

psychostimulant medications Drugs, such as amphetamines and caffeine, that increase alertness and attention as well as psychomotor activity.

puberty The onset of sexual maturity.

random assignment The technique by which researchers assign individuals randomly to either an *experimental* or *control group*.

range of reaction The notion that the human being's genetic makeup establishes a range of possible developmental outcomes, within which environmental forces largely determine how the person actually develops.

reactive aggression Aggressive behaviour as a response to attack, threat or frustration.

recast A technique adults use in speaking to young children in which they render a child's incomplete sentence in a more complex grammatical form.

receptive language Understanding the speech of others.

recessive The weaker of two alleles in a heterozygous combination.

reciprocal instruction A tutoring approach based on the ideas of the *zone of proximal development* and *scaffolding*.

reflex An involuntary response to external stimulation.

reflex smile A smile seen in the newborn that is usually spontaneous and appears to depend on some internal stimulus rather than on something external such as another person's behaviour.

regulation factor A substance that influences non-protein-coding DNA to regulate transcription of protein-coding DNA into mRNA and, later, protein.

rehearsal A memory strategy in which one repeats a number of times the information one wants to remember, either mentally or orally.

rejected children Children who are disliked by many peers and liked by very few.

relational aggression Damaging or destroying interpersonal relationships by such means as excluding another or gossiping about or soiling another's reputation.

relational victimization The attempt by a peer to damage or control another child's relationships with others.

relationship A continuing succession of interactions between two people that are affected by their shared past interactions, and that also affect their future interactions.

REM sleep REM, or rapid eye movement, sleep is characterized by rapid, jerky movements of the eyes and, in adults, is often associated with dreaming.

representativeness The degree to which a sample actually possesses the characteristics of the larger population it represents.

reputational bias Children's tendency to interpret peers' behaviour on the basis of past encounters with and feelings about them.

reserve capacity The capacity to push one's body a little further if undertaking strenuous physical activities.

reversibility The understanding that the steps of a procedure or operation can be reversed, and that the original state of the object or event can be obtained.

romantic love Intimacy and passion without commitment.

sample A group of individuals who are representative of a larger population.

scaffolding An instructional process in which the more knowledgeable partner adjusts the amount and type of support he offers to the child to fit with the child's learning needs over the course of the interaction.

schema An organized unit of knowledge that the child uses to try to understand a situation; a schema forms the basis for organizing actions and thoughts in response to the environment.

scientific methods The use of measurable and replicable techniques in framing hypotheses, and collecting and analysing data to test a theory's usefulness.

script A mental representation of an event or situation of daily life, including the order in which things are expected to happen and how one should behave in that event or situation.

secondary ageing The deterioration of the body in light of injuries and illnesses over time.

secondary circular reactions Behaviours focused on objects outside the infant's own body that the infant repeatedly engages in because they are pleasurable and satisfying.

secondary reinforcer A person or other stimulus that acquires reinforcing properties by virtue of repeated association with a primary reinforcer.

secular trend A shift in the normative pattern of a characteristic, such as height, that occurs over a historical time period, such as a decade or century.

secure attachment A kind of attachment displayed by babies who are secure enough to explore novel environments, who are minimally disturbed by brief separations from their mothers, and who are quickly comforted by their mothers when they return.

secure base According to Ainsworth, a caregiver to whom an infant has formed an attachment, and whom the child uses as a base from which to explore and as a safe haven in times of stress.

selective optimization with compensation (SOC) The theory that, as people age and cognitive capacities decline, they seek to compensate for this decline by finding alternative ways of completing tasks.

self-control phase According to Kopp, the second phase in learning self-regulation, when the child becomes able to comply with caregiver expectations in the absence of the caregiver.

self-delay gratification To put off until another time possessing or doing something that gives one pleasure.

self-disclosure The honest sharing of information of a very personal nature, often with a focus on problem solving; a central means by which adolescents develop friendships.

self-regulation The child's ability to control behaviour on her own without reminders from others.

self-regulation phase According to Kopp, the third phase in learning self-regulation, when children become able to use strategies and plans to direct their own behaviour and to delay gratification.

self-report Information that people provide about themselves, either in a direct interview or in some written form, such as a questionnaire.

semantic memory All the world knowledge and facts a person possesses.

semantics The study of word meanings and word combinations.

sensitive care Consistent and responsive caregiving that begins by allowing an infant to play a role in determining when feeding will begin and end, and at what pace it will proceed.

sensitive period A period of development (age range) at which particular experiences are important for typical development. If those experiences do not occur during that period, typical development may still occur.

sensitization An increase in the strength of response to a repeated stimulus. Like habituation, sensitization is also classified as a simple learning mechanism as it occurs in response to only a single stimulus.

sensorimotor period Piaget's name for the first stage of cognitive development that he described, during which children's abilities are rooted in their physical interactions with objects.

sensory register The mental processing unit that takes information from the environment and stores it in original form for brief periods of time.

separation protest An infant's distress reaction to being separated from his or her mother, which typically peaks at about 15 months of age.

sequential method A research method that combines features of both the *cross-sectional* and the *longitudinal methods*.

sex chromosomes In both males and females, the 23rd pair of chromosomes, which determine the individual's sex and are responsible for sex-related characteristics; in females, this pair normally comprises two X chromosomes, in males an X and a Y chromosome.

sexual orientation The preference for same- or opposite-gender sexual partners.

sexual reproduction The production of a new living organism by the combination of genetic material from two individuals of different sexes (the biological mother and father). This occurs via the fusion of two gametes originating from the mother (ovum) and the father (sperm).

shared environment A set of conditions or experiences shared by children raised in the same family; a parameter commonly examined in studies of individual differences.

short-term memory The mental processing unit in which information is stored temporarily; the 'work space' of the mind, where a decision is made to discard information, work on it or transfer it to permanent storage in *long-term memory*.

social learning theory A learning theory that stresses the importance of observation and imitation in the acquisition of new behaviours, with learning mediated by cognitive processes.

social referencing The process of 'reading' emotional cues in others to help determine how to act in an uncertain situation.

social-convention rules Socially based rules about everyday conduct.

socially unskilled Being unskilled at solving interpersonal problems.

sociocultural theory A theory of development, proposed by Lev Vygotsky, that sees development as emerging from children's interactions with more skilled people, and the institutions and tools provided by their culture.

sociometric technique A procedure for determining children's status within their peer group; each child in the group either nominates others whom she likes best and least, or rates each child in the group for desirability as a companion.

sperm The male reproductive cell.

spermarche In males, the first ejaculation of sperm-containing ejaculate.

stereotype threat Being at risk of confirming a negative stereotype about the group to which one belongs.

Strange Situation A testing scenario in which mother and child are separated and reunited several times; enables investigators to assess the nature and quality of a mother–infant attachment relationship.

stranger distress A fear of strangers that typically emerges in infants around the age of 9 months.

structured observation A form of observation in which researchers structure a situation so that behaviour(s) they wish to study is/ are more likely to occur.

sudden infant death syndrome (SIDS) The sudden, unexplained death of an infant while sleeping; also called *cot death*.

superego In Freudian theory, the personality component that is the repository of the child's internalization of parental or societal values, morals and roles.

symbolic representation The ability to use symbols, such as images, words and gestures, to represent objects and events in the world.

symbolic thought The use of mental images and concepts to represent people, objects and events.

synapse A specialized site of intercellular communication where information is exchanged between nerve cells, usually by means of a chemical neurotransmitter.

synaptic pruning The brain's disposal of the axons and dendrites of a neuron that is not often stimulated.

synaptogenesis The forming of synapses.

syntax The part of grammar that prescribes how words may combine into phrases, clauses and sentences.

telegraphic speech Two-word utterances that include only the words essential to convey the speaker's intent.

teratogen An environmental factor, such as a drug, medication, dietary imbalance or polluting substance, that may cause developmental deviations in a growing human organism; teratogens are most threatening in the embryonic stage but are also capable of causing abnormalities in the foetal stage.

teratology The study of abnormalities in physical development and how they arise. Teratologists often investigate the influence of teratogens on prenatal and postnatal development.

tertiary circular reactions Behaviours in which infants experiment with the properties of external objects and try to learn how objects respond to various actions.

testosterone A hormone that, in males, is responsible for the development of primary and secondary sex characteristics, and is essential for the production of sperm.

thalidomide A drug once prescribed to relieve morning sickness in pregnant women but discontinued when found to cause serious foetal malformations. Current controversy surrounds its possible use in treating symptoms of such diseases as AIDS, cancer and Hansen's disease (leprosy).

theory of mind A person's beliefs about the 'mind' and the ability to understand mental states.

theory of multiple intelligences Gardner's multifactorial theory that proposes eight distinct types of intelligence.

time out Removing children from a situation or context in which they are acting inappropriately until they are able and ready to act appropriately.

transitive inference The mental arrangement of things along a quantitative dimension.

triangular theory of love Sternberg's model of loving relationships, which includes three components – intimacy, commitment and passion – that vary in different relationship types.

triarchic theory of intelligence A theory that proposes three major components of intelligence: information-processing skills, experience with a task, and ability to adapt to the demands of a context.

two moral worlds view The view that there is a fundamental shift from heteronomous morality (morality is determined by adults and authority figures) to an autonomous morality (morality where we all participate and agree on moral rules as members of society).

umbilical cord A tube that contains blood vessels connecting the growing organism and its mother by way of the *placenta*; it carries oxygen and nutrients to the growing infant, and removes carbon dioxide and waste products.

underextension The use, by a young child, of a single word in a restricted and individualistic way.

uninvolved parenting Parenting that is indifferent and neglectful, and in which parents focus on their own needs rather than their children's needs. Also known as neglecting-rejecting parenting.

'use it or lose it' The idea that, to avoid cognitive or physical decline into old age, people must continue to use cognitive and physical abilities as much as possible.

vestibular system A sensory system residing in the inner ear which provides cues to gravity and movement which enable us to balance and coordinate our movements.

vignette A short story that depicts a scenario or situation about which the child has to comment, discuss or make a judgement.

visual acuity Sharpness of vision; the clarity with which fine details can be detected.

visual cliff An apparatus that tests an infant's depth perception by using patterned materials and an elevated, clear glass platform to make it appear that one side of the platform is several feet lower than the other.

visuospatial sketch-pad A 'slave system' in the working memory model which deals with visual-spatial representations.

wear-and-tear theory The theory that ageing is due to environmental or external factors (such as injury or illness).

Wechsler Intelligence Scales Three intelligence tests for preschool children, school-age children and adults, which yield separate scores for verbal and performance IQ as well as a combined IQ score.

working memory A model of short-term memory processes incorporating a central executive, phonological loop (for storing auditory information), a visuospatial sketch-pad (for visual information) and an episodic buffer (for linking information across domains).

working memory model Baddeley and Hitch's (1974) model of human information processing, which emphasizes dynamic thought processes rather than more basic parameters like storage duration and capacity.

X-linked genes Genes that are carried on the X chromosome and that, in males, may have no analogous genes on the Y chromosome.

Zika virus A teratogenic virus which can be passed from mother to foetus. Infants born with the Zika virus can have microcephaly, severe brain malformations and other birth defects.

zone of proximal development (ZPD) The region of sensitivity for learning characterized by the difference between the developmental level of which a child is capable when working alone and the level she is capable of reaching with the aid of a more skilled partner.

zygote The developing organism from the time sperm and egg unite to about the second week of gestation, during which the zygote undergoes rapid cell division.

References

Abel, E. L. (1998). *Fetal alcohol abuse syndrome.* New York: Plenum Press.

Aber, J. L., Brown, J. L., & Jones, S. M. (2003). Developmental trajectories toward violence in middle childhood: Course, demographic differences and response to school-based interventions. *Developmental Psychology, 39,* 324–348.

Abitz, M., Damgaard-Nielsen, R., Jones, E. G., Laursen, H., Graem, N., & Pakkenberg, B. (2007). Excess of neurons in the human newborn mediodorsal thalamus compared with that of the adult. *Cerebral Cortex, 17,* 2573–2578.

Aboud, F. (1988). *Children and prejudice.* London: Blackwell Publishers.

Aboud, F. E., & Skerry, S. A. (1983). Self and ethnic concepts in relation to ethnic constancy. *Canadian Journal of Behavioral Science, 15,* 14–26.

Abrahams, B. S., & Geschwind, D. H. (2010). Connecting genes to brain in the autism spectrum disorders. *Archives of Neurology, 67,* 395–399.

Achenbach, T. M. (1995). Developmental issues in assessment, taxonomy and diagnosis of child and adolescent psychopathology. In D. Cicchetti & D. J. Cohen (eds), *Developmental psychopathology: Vol. 1. Theory and methods* (pp. 57–82). New York: Wiley.

Achenbach, T. M. (1997). What is normal? What is abnormal? Developmental perspectives on behavioral and emotional problems. In S. S. Luthar, J. A. Burack, D. Cicchetti, & J. R. Weisz (eds), *Developmental psychopathology perspectives on adjustment, risk and disorder* (pp. 93–114). New York: Cambridge University Press.

Achenbach, T. M., & Rescorla, L. A. (2007). *Multicultural understanding of child and adolescent psychopathology: Implications for mental health assessment.* New York: Guilford Press.

Ackerman, B. P. (1996). Induction of a memory retrieval strategy by young children. *Journal of Experimental Child Psychology, 62,* 243–271.

Acredolo, L. P. (1978). Development of spatial orientation in infancy. *Developmental Psychology, 14*(3), 224.

Adamson, L. B. (1995). *Communication development during infancy.* Madison, WI: Brown & Benchmark.

Adamson, L. B., & Bakeman, R. (1991). The development of shared attention during infancy. In R. Vasta (ed.), *Annals of child development* (Vol. 8, pp. 1–41). London: Kingsley.

Adamson, L. B., & Frick, J. E. (2003). The still face: A history of a shared experimental paradigm. *Infancy, 4,* 451–473.

Adkins, V. K. (1999). Grandparents as a national asset: A brief note. *Activities; Adaptation & Aging, 24,* 13–18.

Adolph, K. (2008). Motor and physical development: Locomotion. In M. M. Haith & J. B. Benson (eds.), *Encyclopedia of infant and early childhood development.* New York: Academic Press.

Adolph, K. E. (2005). Learning to learn in the development of action. In J. Lockman, J. Reiser & C. Nelson (eds), *Minnesota symposium on child psychology* (Vol. 33, pp. 91–133). Mahwah, NJ: Erlbaum.

Adolph, K. E., & Berger, S. E. (2010). Physical and motor development. In M. H. Bornstein & M. E. Lamb (eds.), *Developmental science: An advanced textbook* (4th edn, pp. 223–281). Hillsdale, NJ: Erlbaum.

Adolph, K. E., & Eppler, M. A. (2002). Flexibility and specificity in infant motor skill acquisition. In J. W. Fagen & H. Hayne (eds), *Progress in infancy research* (Vol. 2, pp. 121–167). Mahwah, NJ: Lawrence Erlbaum Associates.

Adolph, K. E., Hoch, J. E., & Cole, W. E. (2018). Development (of walking): 15 suggestions. *Trends in Cognitive Sciences,* https://doi.org/10.1016/j.tics.2018.05.010

Adolph, K. E., Vereijken, B., & Denny, M. A. (1998). Learning to crawl. *Child Development, 69,* 1299–1312.

Adolph, K., & Berger, S. E. (2006). Motor development. In W. Damon & R. M. Lerner (Series eds) & D. Kuhn & R. Siegler (Vol. eds), *Handbook of child psychology: Vol. 2. Perceptual and cognitive development* (6th edn, pp. 161–213). New York: Wiley.

Agras, W. S. (1988). Does early eating behavior influence later adiposity? In N. A. Krasnegor, G. D. Grave & N. Kretchmer (eds), *Childhood obesity: A biobehavioral perspective* (pp. 49–66). Caldwell, NJ: Telford Press.

Ahmed, N. U., Zeitlin, M. F., Beiser, A. S., Super, C. M., & Gershoff, S. N. (1993). A longitudinal study of the impact of behavioural change intervention on cleanliness, diarrhoeal morbidity and growth of children in rural Bangladesh. *Social Science and Medicine, 37,* 159–171.

Ainsworth, M. D. (1963). The development of infant-mother interaction among the Ganda. In D. M. Foss (ed.), *Determinants of infant behavior* (Vol. 2, pp. 67–104). New York: Wiley.

Ainsworth, M. D. (1973). The development of infant-mother attachment. In B. Caldwell & H. Ricciuti (eds), *Review of child development research* (Vol. 3, pp. 1–94). Chicago: University of Chicago Press.

Ainsworth, M. D., Blehar, M., Waters, E., & Wall, S. (1978). *Patterns of attachment*. Hillsdale, NJ: Erlbaum.

Albert, D., Chain, J. & Steinberg, L. (2015). Peer influences on adolescent decision making. *Current Directions in Psychological Science*, 2013 Apr; 22(2): 114–120.

Albert, D., Chein, J., & Steinberg, L. (2015). Peer influences on adolescent decision making. *Current Directions in Psychological Science*, 22(2): 114–120. doi: 10.1177/0963721412471347

Albert, R. S. (1996, Summer). Some reasons why childhood creativity often fails to make it past puberty into the real world. In M. A. Runco (ed.), *Creativity from childhood through adulthood: The developmental issues* [Special issue]. *New Directions for Child Development*, 72, 43–56.

Alderson-Day, B., & Fernyhough, C. (2015). Inner speech: Development, cognitive functions, phenomenology, and neurobiology. *Psychological Bulletin*, 141(5), 931–965.

Aldridge, M. A., Braga, E. S., Walton, G. E., & Bower, T. G. R. (1999). The intermodal representation of speech in newborns. *Developmental Science*, 2(1), 42–46.

Aldwin, C. M., & Werner, E. E. (2007). *Stress, coping, and development: An integrative perspective* (2nd edn). New York: Guilford Press.

Alessandri, S. M. & Lewis, M. (1996) Differences in pride and shame in maltreated and nonmaltreated preschoolers. *Child Development*, 67, 1857–1869.

Allen, J. P., McElhaney, K. B., Land, D. J., Kuperminc, G. P., **Moore, C. W., O'Beirne-Kelly, H. et al.** (2003). A secure base in adolescence: Markers of attachment security in the mother-adolescent relationship. *Child Development*, 74, 292–307.

Allport, G. W. (1954). *The nature of prejudice*. Cambridge, MA: Addison-Wesley.

Als, H., Gilkerson, L., Duffy, F. H., McAnulty, G. B., Buehler, D. M., Vandenberg, K. et al. (2003) A three-center, randomized, controlled trial of individualized developmental care for very low-birthweight preterm infants: Medical, neurodevelopmental, parenting, and caregiving effects. *Journal of Developmental and Behavioral Pediatrics*, 24, 399–408.

Althaus, N., & Plunkett, K. (2015). Timing matters: The impact of label synchrony on infant categorisation. *Cognition*, 139, 1–9.

Altink, M. E., Slaats-Willemse, D. I. E., Rommelse, N. N. J., Buschgens, C. J. M., Fliers, E. A., Arias-Vásquez, A. et al. (2009). Effects of maternal and paternal smoking on attentional control in children with and without ADHD. *European Child and Adolescent Psychiatry*, 18, 465–475.

Amato, P. R., Patterson, S., & Beattie, B. (2015). Single-parent households and children's educational achievement: A state-level analysis, *Social Science Research*, 53, 191–202.

American Association of Mental Retardation (2002). *Mental retardation: Definition, classification, and systems of supports* (10th edn). Annapolis, MD: Author.

American Psychiatric Association (2013). *Diagnostic and statistical manual of mental disorders (DSM-5®)*. Washington, DC: American Psychiatric Association.

Amsterdam, B. (1972). Mirror self-image reactions before age two. *Developmental Psychobiology*, 5(4), 297–305.

Anderson, C. A., Gentile, D. A., & Buckley, K. E. (2007). *Violent video game effects on children and adolescents: Theory, research, and public policy*. New York: Oxford University Press.

Anderson, E. (1998). The social ecology of youth violence. In M. Tenry & M. H. Moore (eds), *Youth violence: Crime and justice* (pp. 65–104). Chicago: University of Chicago Press.

Anderson, P., Doyle, L. W., Callahan, C., Carse, E., Casalaz, D., Charlton, M. P. et al. (2003). Neurobehavioral outcomes of school-age children born extremely low birth weight or very preterm in the 1990s. *Journal of American Medical Association*, 289, 3264–3272.

Andrews, J. A. & Lewinsohn, P. M. (1992) Suicidal attempts among older adolescents: Prevalence and co-occurrence with psychiatric disorders. *Journal of American Academy of Child and Adolescent Psychiatry*, 31, 655–662.

Anhert, L., Gunnar, M. R., Lamb, M. E. & Barthel, M. (2004) Transition to child care: Associations with infant–mother attachment, infant negative emotion and cortisol elevations. *Child Development*, 75(3), 639–650.

Anisfeld, E., Casper, V., Nosyce, M., & Cunningham, N. (1990). Does infant-carrying promote attachment? An experimental study of the effects of increased physical contact on the development of attachment. *Child Development*, 61, 1617–1627.

Anisfeld, M. (1991) Neonatal imitation. *Developmental Review*, 11, 60–97.

Anisfeld, M. (1996). Only tongue protrusion modeling is matched by neonates. *Developmental Review*, 16(2), 149–161.

Anneken, K., Konrad, C., Drager, B., Breitenstein, C., Kennerknecht, L., Ringelstein, E. B. et al. (2004). Familial aggression of strong hemispheric language lateralization. *Neurology, 63*, 2433–2435.

Apgar, V. (1953). A proposal for a new method of evaluation of the newborn infant. *Current Research in Anesthesia and Analgesia, 32*, 260–267.

Ardelt, M., & Koenig, C. (2006). The role of religion for hospice patients and relatively healthy older individuals. *Research on Aging, 28*, 184–215.

Aries, P. (1962) *Centuries of childhood.* New York: Knopf.

Armstrong L. (2013). *Epigenetics.* New York: Garland Science.

Arsenio, W. F., & Kramer, R. (1992). Victimizers and their victims: Children's conceptions of mixed emotional consequences of moral transgressions. *Child Development, 63*, 915–927.

Arterberry, M. E., & Bornstein, M. H. (2001). Three-month-old infants' categorization of animals and vehicles based on static and dynamic attributes. *Journal of Experimental Child Psychology, 80*, 333–346.

Arterberry, M. E., Bensen, A. S., & Yonas, A. (1991). Infants' responsiveness to static-monocular depth information: A recovery from habituation approach. *Infant Behavior and Development, 14*, 241–251.

Asbury, K., Dunn, J. F., Pike, A., & Plomin, R. (2003). Nonshared environmental influences on individual differences in early behavioral development: A monozygotic twin differences study. *Child Development, 74*, 933–943.

Asher, S. & Hopmeyer, A. (2001) Loneliness in childhood. In G. G. Baer, K. M. Minke & A. Thomas (eds) *Children's needs: Development, problems and alternatives* (pp. 279–292) Silver Spring, MD: National Association of School Psychologists.

Asher, S. R., & Paquette, J. A. (2003). Loneliness and peer relations in childhood. *Current Directions in Psychological Science, 12*, 75–78.

Asher, S. R., Hymel, S., & Renshaw, P. D. (1984). Loneliness in children. *Child Development, 55*, 1456–1464.

Aslin, R. (1987). Visual and auditory development in infancy. In J. Osofsky (ed.), *Handbook of infant development* (2nd edn, pp. 5–97). New York: Wiley.

Aslin, R. N., Jusczyk, P. W., & Pisoni, D. B. (1998). Speech and auditory processing during infancy: Constraints on and precursors to language. In W. Damon (Series ed.), D. Kuhn & R. Siegler (Vol. eds), *Handbook of child psychology: Vol. 2. Cognition, perception and language* (pp. 147–198). New York: Wiley.

Aslin, R. N., Woodward, J. Z., LaMendola, N. P., & Bever, T. G. (1996). Models of work segmentation in fluent maternal speech to infants. In J. L. Morgan & K. Dermuth (eds), *Signal to syntax* (pp. 117–134). Hillsdale, NJ: Erlbaum.

Atchley, R. C., & Barusch, A. (2004). *Social forces and aging* (10th edn). Belmont, CA: Wadsworth.

Atkin, C. (1983). Effects of realistic TV violence vs. fictional violence on aggression. *Journalism Quarterly, 60*, 615–621.

Atkinson, J. (1984). Human visual development over the first 6 months of life: A review and a hypothesis. *Human Neurobiology, 3*(2), 61–74.

Atkinson, J., & Braddick, O. J. (1981). Acuity, contrast sensitivity and accommodation in infancy. In R. N. Aslin, J. R. Alberts, & M. R. Petersen (eds), *The development of perception* (Vol. 2, pp. 245–278). New York: Academic Press.

Atkinson, R. C., & Shiffrin, R. M. (1968). Human memory: A proposed system and its control processes. In K. W. Spence & J. Spence (eds), *Advances in the psychology of learning and motivation: Research and theory* (Vol. 2, pp. 1–35). New York: Academic Press.

Auyeung, B., Baron-Cohen, S., Ashwin, E., Knickmeyer, R., Taylor, K., & Hackett, G. (2009). Fetal testosterone and autistic traits. *British Journal of Psychology, 100*, 1–22.

Aviezer, O., Sagi, A., Joels, T., & Ziv, Y. (1999). Emotional availability and attachment representations in kibbutz infants and their mothers. *Developmental Psychology, 35*, 811–821.

Aviezer, O., Van Ijzendoorn, M. H., Sagi, A., & Schuengel, C. F. (1994). 'Children of the dream' revisited: 70 years of collective early child care in Israeli kibbutzim. *Psychological Bulletin, 116*, 99–116.

Avis, J., & Harris, P. L. (1991). Belief-desire reasoning among Baka children: Evidence for a universal conception of mind. *Child Development, 62*(3), 460–467.

Axia, G., Bonichini, S., & Benini, F. (1999). Attention and reaction to distress in infancy, a longitudinal study. *Developmental Psychology, 35*, 500–504.

Azar, S. T. (2002) Parenting and child maltreatment. In M. Bornstein (ed.), *Handbook of parenting* (Vol. 4, pp. 361–388) Mahwah, NJ: Erlbaum.

B

Babiloni, C., Babiloni, F., Carducci, F., Cappa, S. F., Cincotti, F., Del Percio, C., et al. (2004). Human cortical rhythms during visual delayed choice reaction time tasks: A high-resolution EEG study on normal aging. *Behavioral Brain Research, 153*, 261–271.

Bablioni, C. et al. (2004) Human cortical rhythms during visual delayed choice reaction time tasks: A high-resolution EEG study on normal aging. *Behavioral Brain Research, 153*, 261–271.

Baddeley, A. (2012). Working memory: Theories, models, and controversies. *Annual Review of Psychology, 63*, 1–29.

Baddeley, A. D., & Hitch, G. (1974). *Working memory.* In G.H. Bower (ed.), *The psychology of learning and motivation: Advances in research and theory* (Vol. 8, pp. 47–89). New York: Academic Press.

Bagwell, C. L. (2004). Friendships, peer networks and antisocial behavior. In J. B. Kupersmidt & K. A. Dodge (eds), *Children's peer relations* (pp. 37–57). Washington, DC: American Psychological Association.

Bagwell, C. L., Coie, J. D., Terry, R. A., & Lochman, J. E. (2000). Peer clique participation and social status in preadolescence. *Merrill-Palmer Quarterly, 46,* 280–305.

Bahrick, L. E., & Lickliter, R. (2014). Learning to attend selectively: The dual role of intersensory redundancy. *Current Directions in Psychological Science, 23*(6), 414–420.

Bahrick, L. E., & Watson, J. S. (1985). Detection of intermodal proprioceptive–visual contingency as a potential basis of self-perception in infancy. *Developmental Psychology, 21*(6), 963.

Bahrick, L. E. (2010). Intermodal perception and selective attention to intersensory redundancy: Implications for typical social developmental and autism. In J. G. Bremner & T. D. Wachs (eds.), *The Wiley-Blackwell handbook of infant development* (2nd edn, pp. 120–166). Oxford: Wiley-Blackwell.

Bahrick, L. E., & Lickliter, R. (2000). Intersensory redundancy guides attentional selectivity and perceptual learning in infancy. *Developmental Psychology, 36,* 190–201.

Bailey, A., LeCouteur, A., Gottesman, I., Bolton, P., Simonoff, E., Yuzda, F. Y. et al. (1995a) Autism as a strongly genetic disorder: Evidence from a British twin study. *Psychological Medicine, 25,* 63–77.

Bailey, J., Bobrow, D., Wolfe, M., & Mikach, S. (1995). Sexual orientation of adult sons of gay fathers [Special Issue: Sexual orientation and human development.] *Developmental Psychology, 31,* 124–129.

Baillargeon, R. (1986). Representing the existence and the location of hidden objects: Object permanence in 6- and 8-month-old infants. *Cognition, 23,* 21–41.

Baillargeon, R. (1993). The object concept revisited: New directions in the investigation of infants' physical knowledge. In C. E. Granrud (ed.), *Visual perception and cognition in infancy* (pp. 265–315). Hillsdale, NJ: Erlbaum.

Baillargeon, R. (2004). Infants' reasoning about hidden objects: Evidence for event-general and event-specific expectations. *Developmental Science, 7,* 391–424.

Baillargeon, R., & Wang, S. (2002) Event categorization in infancy. *Trends in Cognitive Science, 6,* 85–93.

Baillargeon, R., Scott, R. M., & He, Z. (2010). False-belief understanding in infants. *Trends in Cognitive Science, 14*(3), 110–118.

Baillargeon, R., Spelke, E. S., & Wasserman, S. (1985). Object permanence in five-month-old infants. *Cognition, 20,* 191–208.

Baillargeon, R., Buttelmann, D., & Southgate, V. (2018). Interpreting failed replications of early false-belief findings: Methodological and theoretical considerations. *Cognitive Development, 46,* 112–124.

Bainum, C. K., Lounsbury, K. R., & Pollio, H. R. (1984). The development of laughing and smiling in nursery school children. *Child Development, 55,* 1946–1957.

Baird, A. A., Kagan, J., Gaudette, T., Walz, K. A., Hershlag, N. & Boas, D. A. (2002) Frontal lobe activation during object permanence: data from near-infrared spectroscopy. *Neuroimage, 16*(4), 1120–1126.

Baird, G., Simonoff, E., Pickles, A., Chandler, S., Loucas, T., et al. (2006) Prevalence of disorders of the autism spectrum in a population cohort of children in South Thames: the special needs and autism project (SNAP). *Lancet, 368,* 210–25.

Bakeman, R., & Gottman, J. (1997). *Observing behavior* (2nd edn). New York: Cambridge University Press.

Bakermans-Kranenburg, M. J., van Ijzendoorn, M. H. & Juffer, F. (2003) Less is more: Meta-analyses of sensitivity and attachment interventions in early childhood. *Psychological Bulletin, 129,* 195–215.

Balinsky, B. (1941). An analysis of the mental factors of various age groups from nine to sixty. *Genetic Psychology Monographs, 23,* 191–234.

Baltes, P. B., & Baltes, M. M. (1990). Psychological perspectives on successful aging: The model of selective optimization with compensation. In P. B. Baltes & M. M. Baltes (eds.), *Successful aging: Perspectives from the behavioral sciences* (pp. 1–34). Cambridge: Cambridge University Press.

Baltes, P. B., & Freund, A. M. (2003). Human strengths as the orchestration of wisdom and selective optimization with compensation. In L. G. Aspinwall & U. M. Staudinger (eds), *A psychology of human strengths: Perspectives on an emerging field* (pp. 23–35). Washington, DC: American Psychological Association.

Baltes, P. B., & Kunzmann, U. (2003). Wisdom. *The Psychologist, 16,* 131–133.

Baltes, P. B., Lindenberger, U., & Staudinger, U. M. (2006). Life span theory in developmental psychology. In W. Damon & R. M. Lerner (Series eds) & R. M. Lerner (Vol. ed.), *Handbook of child psychology: Vol. 1. Theoretical models of human development* (6th edn, pp. 569–664). New York: Wiley.

Bandura, A. (1989). Social cognitive theory. In R. Vasta (ed.), *Annals of child development: Six theories of child development* (Vol. 6, pp. 1–60). Greenwich, CT: JAI Press.

Bandura, A. (1997). *Self-efficacy.* New York: Freeman.

Bandura, A., Ross, D., & Ross, S. A. (1961). Transmission of aggression through imitation of aggressive behaviours. *Journal of Abnormal and Social Psychology, 63,* 575–582.

Banerjee, R. Watling, D. & Caputi, M. (in press) Peer relations and the understanding of faux pas: Longitudinal evidence for bidirectional associations. *Child Development.*

Banerjee, R., & Watling, D. (2005). Children's understanding of faux pas: Associations with peer relations. In special issue on 'Theory of Mind', *Hellenic Journal of Psychology, 2*(1), 27–45.

Banerjee, R., & Yuill, N. (1999). Children's understanding of self-presentational display rules: Associations with mental-state understanding. *British Journal of Developmental Psychology, 17,* 111–124.

Banerjee, R., Watling, D., & Caputi, M. (2011). Peer rejection and the understanding of faux pas: Longitudinal evidence for bi-directional associations. Child Development, 82(6), 1887–1905.

Banerjee, T. D., Middleton, F. & Faraone, S. V. (2007). Environmental risk factors for attention-deficit hyperactivity disorder. *Acta Paediatrica, 96,* 1269–1274.

Banish, J. T. (1998) Integration of information between the cerebral hemispheres. *Current Directions in Psychological Science, 7,* 32–37.

Banks, M. S., & Salapatek, P. (1983). Infant visual perception. In M. H. & J. Campos (eds), *Handbook of child psychology: Biology and infancy* (pp. 435–571). New York: Wiley.

Banks, M. S., & Shannon, E. (1993). Spatial and chromatic visual efficiency in human neonates. In C. Granrud (ed.), *Visual perception and cognition in infancy* (pp. 1–46). Hillsdale, NJ: Erlbaum.

Banks, M. S., Aslin, R. N., & Letson, R. D. (1975). Sensitive period for the development of human binocular vision. *Science, 190,* 675–677.

Barak, Y. Sirota, P., Kimhi, R., & Slor, H. (2001). Werner's syndrome (adult progeria): An affected mother and son presenting with resistant psychosis, *Comprehensive Psychiatry, 42,* 508–510.

Barber, B. K. (ed.) (2002). *Intrusive parenting: How psychological control affects children and adolescents.* Washington, DC: American Psychological Association.

Barber, B. K., & Harmon, E. (2002). Parental psychological control of children and adolescents. In B. K. Barber (Ed)., *Intrusive parenting: How psychological control affects children and adolescents* (pp. 15–52). Washington, DC: American Psychological Association.

Barbieri, S., & Light, P. (1992). Interaction, gender and performance on a computer-based problem-solving task. In H. Mandel, E. De Corte, S.N. Bennett, & H. F. Friedrich (eds), *Learning and instruction: European research in international contexts.* Oxford: Pergamon.

Barglow, P., Vaughn, B. E., & Molitor, N. (1987). Effects of maternal absence due to employment on the quality of infant–mother attachment in a low-risk sample. *Child Development, 58,* 945–954.

Baringa, M. (1996) Learning defect identified in the brain. *Science, 273,* 867–868.

Barkley, R. A. (1998). *Attention deficit/hyperactivity disorder: A handbook for diagnosis and treatment* (2nd edn). New York: Guilford Press.

Barkley, R. A. (2000). *Taking charge of ADHD.* New York: Guilford Press.

Barkley, R. A., & Cox D. (2007). A review of driving risks and impairments associated with attention-deficit/hyperactivity disorder and the effects of stimulant medication on driving performance. *Journal of Safety Research, 38,* 113–128.

Barnard, K. E., & Bee, H. L. (1983). The impact of temporally patterned stimulation on the development of preterm infants. *Child Development, 54,* 1156–1167.

Barnard, K. E., Bee, H. L., & Hammond, M. A. (1984). Home environment and cognitive development in a healthy, low-risk sample: The Seattle study. In A. W. Gottfried (ed.), *Home environment and early cognitive development* (pp. 117–149). Orlando, FL: Academic Press.

Barnas, M. V., & Cummings, E. M. (1994). Caregiver stability and toddlers' attachment-related behavior towards caregivers in day care. *Infant Behavior and Development, 17,* 141–147.

Barnett, M. A., Scaramella, L. V., Neppl, T. K., Ontai, L., & Conger, R. D. (2010). Intergenerational relationship quality, gender, and grandparent involvement. *Family Relations, 59,* 28–44.

Baron, A. S. & Banaji, M. R. (2006) The development of implicit attitudes: Evidence of race evaluations from ages 6 and 10 and adulthood. *Psychological Science, 17,* 53–58.

Baron-Cohen, S. (1995). *Mindblindness: An essay on autism and theory of mind.* Cambridge, MA: MIT Press.

Baron-Cohen, S. (2000) Theory of mind and autism: A fifteen year review. In S. Baron-Cohen, H. Tager-Flusberg & D. J. Cohen (eds), *Understanding other minds* (pp. 3–20) Oxford: Oxford University Press.

Baron-Cohen, S. (2003). *The essential difference: Male and female brains and the truth about autism.* New York: Basic Books.

Baron-Cohen, S. (2007). The rise of autism and the digital age. https://www.edge.org/response-detail/10669

Baron-Cohen, S. (2000). Theory of mind and autism: A fifteen year review. In S. Baron-Cohen, H. Tager-Flusberg, & D. J. Cohen (eds), *Understanding other minds* (pp. 3–20). Oxford: Oxford University Press.

Baron-Cohen, S., Knickmeyer, R. C., & Belmonte, M. K. (2005). Sex differences in the brain: Implications for explaining autism. *Science, 310*(5749), 819–823.

Baron-Cohen, S., Leslie, A. M., & Frith, U. (1985). Does the autistic child have a 'theory of mind'? *Cognition, 21*(1), 37–46.

Baron-Cohen, S., Ring, H., Moriarty, J., Shmitz, P., Costa, D., & Ell, P. (1994). Recognition of mental state terms: A clinical study of autism, and a functional neuroimaging study of normal adults. *British Journal of Psychiatry, 165*, 640–649.

Barr, H. M., Steissguth, A. P., Darby, B. L., & Sampson, P. D. (1990). Prenatal exposure to alcohol, caffeine, tobacco, and aspirin: Effects on fine and gross motor performance in 4-year-old children. *Developmental Psychology, 26*, 339–348.

Barrett, D. E. (1979). A naturalistic study of sex differences in children's aggression. *Merrill-Palmer Quarterly, 25*, 193–203.

Barry, G., & Mattick, J. S. (2012). The role of regulatory RNA in cognitive evolution. *Trends in Cognitive Sciences, 16*, 497–503.

Bartocci, M., Bergqvist, L. L., Lagercrantz, H., & Anand, K. J. S. (2006). Pain activates cortical areas in the preterm newborn brain. *Pain, 122*(1–2), 109–117.

Bashinski, H., Werner, J., & Rudy, J. (1985). Determinants of infant visual attention: Evidence of a two-process theory. *Journal of Experimental Child Psychology, 39*, 580–598.

Bates, E. (1976). *Language and context: The acquisition of pragmatics.* New York: Academic Press.

Bates, E. (1999). On the nature of language. In R. Levi-Montalcini, D. Baltimore, R. Dulbecco, & F. Jacob (Series eds), and O. E. Bizzi, P. Calissano & V. Vorterra (Vol. eds), *The brain of Homo sapiens.* Rome: Giovanni Trecami.

Bates, E., Thal, D., Whitsell, K., Fenson, L., & Oakes, L. (1989). Integrating language and gesture in infancy. *Developmental Psychology, 25*, 1004–1019.

Bates, J., & Pettit, G. (2007). Temperament, parenting, and socialization. In J. Grusec & P. Hastings (eds), *Handbook of socialization* (pp. 153–177). New York: Guilford Press.

Bauer, P. J. & Wewerka, S. S. (1997) Saying is revealing: Verbal expression of event memory in the transition from infancy to early childhood. In P. W. van den Broek, P. J. Bauer & T. Bourg (eds), *Developmental spans in event comprehension and representation: Bridging fictional and actual events* (pp. 139–168). Hillsdale, NJ: Erlbaum.

Bauer, P. J. (2002) Long-term recall memory: Behavioral and neuro-developmental changes in the first 2 years of life. *Current Directions in Psychological Science, 11*, 137–141.

Bauer, P. J. (2006). Event memory. In W. Damon & R. M. Lerner (Series eds) & D. Kuhn & R. Siegler (Vol. eds), *Handbook of child psychology: Vol. 2. Cognition, perception, and language* (6th edn, pp. 373–425), Hoboken, NJ: John Wiley & Sons.

Bauer, P. J. (2007). Recall in infancy: A neurodevelopmental account. *Current Directions in Psychological Science, 16*, 142–146.

Bauer, P. J., & Dow, G. A. (1994). Episodic memory in 16- and 20-month-old children: Specifics are generalized but not forgotten. *Developmental Psychology, 30*, 403–417.

Bauer, P. J., & Mandler, J. M. (1992). Putting the horse before the cart: The use of temporal order in recall of events by one-year-old children. *Developmental Psychology, 28*, 441–452.

Bauer, W. D. & Twentyman, C. T. (1985) Abusing, neglectful, and comparison mothers' responses to child-related and non-child-related stressors. *Journal of Consulting and Clinical Psychology, 53*, 335–343.

Baumeister, A. A. (1967). The effects of dietary control on intelligence in phenylketonuria. *American Journal of Mental Deficiency, 71*, 840–847.

Baumrind, D. (1967). Child care practices anteceding three patterns of preschool behavior. *Genetic Psychology Monographs, 75*, 43–88.

Baumrind, D. (1971). Current patterns of parental authority. *Developmental Psychology Monographs, 1*, 1–103.

Baumrind, D. (1991). Effective parenting during the early adolescent transition. In P. A. Cowan & E. M. Hetherington (eds), *Family transitions* (pp. 111–164). Hillsdale, NJ: Erlbaum.

Bayley, N. (1969). *Bayley scales of infant development.* New York: Psychological Corporation.

Bayley, N. (1993). *Bayley scales of infant development* (rev. edn). New York: Psychological Corporation.

Beal, C. R. (1994) *Boys and girls: The development of gender roles.* New York: McGraw-Hill.

Bebbington, P., Dunn, G., Jenkins, R., Lewis, G., Brugha, T., Farrell, M., & Meltzer, H. (2003). The influence of age and sex on the prevalence of depressive conditions: Report from the National Survey of Psychiatric Morbidity. *International Review of Psychiatry, 15*, 74–83.

Bechara, A., Damasio, A., Damasio, H., & Anderson, S. W. (1994). Insensitivity to future consequences following damage to the prefrontal cortex. *Cognition, 50*, 7–15.

Beckett, C., Maughan, B., Rutter, M., Castle, J., Colvert, E., Groothues, C. et al. (2006). Do the effects of early severe deprivation on cognition persist into early adolescence? Findings from the ERA study. *Child Development, 77*, 696–711.

Bedard, J. & Chi, M. T. H. (1992) Expertise. *Current Directions in Psychological Science, 1*, 135–139.

Begum Ali, J., Spence, C., & Bremner, A. J. (2015). Human infants' ability to perceive touch in external space develops postnatally. *Current Biology, 25*(20), R978–R979.

Begus, K., & Southgate, V. (2012). Infant pointing serves an interrogative function. *Developmental Science, 15*(5), 611–617.

Beilin, H. (1992). Piaget's enduring contribution to developmental psychology. *Developmental Psychology, 28*, 191–204.

Belin, P., Zatorre, R. J., Lafaille, P., Ahad, P., & Pike, B. (2000). Voice-selective areas in human auditory cortex. *Nature, 403*(6767), 309.

Bell, J. Z. (1978). Disengagement versus engagement—a need for greater expectation. *Journal of American Geriatric Sociology, 26*, 89–95.

Bell, S. & Ainsworth, M. D. (1972) Infant crying and maternal responsiveness. *Child Development, 43*, 1171–1190.

Bellamy, C. (2000). *The state of the world's children*. New York: Oxford University Press.

Belsky, J. (1999). Interactional and contextual determinants of attachment security. In J. Cassidy &

P. Shaver (eds), *Handbook of attachment* (pp. 249–264). New York: Guilford Press.

Belsky, J., & Cassidy, J. (1994). Attachment: Theory and evidence. In M. Rutter, D. Hay, & S. Baron-Cohen (eds), *Developmental principles and clinical issues in psychology and psychiatry*. Oxford: Blackwell.

Belsky, J., & Isabella, R. A. (1985). Marital and parent-child relationships in family of origin and marital change following the birth of a baby: A retrospective analysis. *Child Development, 56*, 342–349.

Belsky, J., & Rovine, M. (1988). Nonmaternal care in the first year of life and infant- parent attachment security. *Child Development, 57*, 1224–1231.

Belsky, J., Spritz, B., & Crnic, K. (1996). Infant attachment security and affective-cognitive information processing at age 3. *Psychological Science, 7*(2), 111–114.

Belsky, J., Steinberg, L., & Draper, P. (1991). Further reflections on an evolutionary theory of socialization. *Child Development, 62*, 682–685.

Belsky, J., Vandell, D. L., Burchinal, M., Clarke-Stewart, K. A., McCartney, K., Owen, M. T., & the NICHD Early Child Care Research Network (2007). Are there long-term effects of early child care? *Child Development, 78*(2), 681–701.

Bem, S. L. (1981). Gender schema theory: A cognitive account of sex typing. *Psychological Review, 88*, 354–364.

Bem, S. L. (1989). Genital knowledge and gender constancy in preschool children. *Child Development, 60*, 649–662.

Bem, S. L. (1993). *The lenses of gender: Transforming the debate on sexual inequality*. New Haven, CT: Yale University Press.

Bem, S. L. (1998). *An unconventional family*. New Haven, CT: Yale University Press.

Benbow, C. P., & Lubinski, D. J. (eds) (1996). *Intellectual talent: Psychometric and social issues*. Baltimore, MD: Johns Hopkins University Press.

Bendixen, M. H. Nexöa, B. A., Bohr, V. A., Frederiksen, H., McGue, M., Kölvraa, S., & Christensen, K. (2004). A polymorphic marker in the first intron of the Werner gene associates with cognitive function in aged Danish twins. *Experimental Gerontology, 39*, 1101–1107.

Benenson, J. F., Apostoleris, N. H., & Parnass, J. (1997). Age and sex differences in dyadic and group interaction. *Developmental Psychology, 33*, 538–543.

Benloucif, S., Bennett, E. L., & Rosenzweig, M. R. (1995). Norepinephrine and neural plasticity: The effects of Xylamine on experience-induced changes in brain weight, memory and behavior. *Neurobiology of Learning and Memory, 63*, 33–42.

Benokraitis, N. V. (1996). *Marriages and families: Changes, choices, and constraints* (2nd edn). Upper Saddle River, NJ: Prentice Hall.

Benson, E. S. (2004). Behavior genetics: Meet molecular biology. *Monitor on Psychology, 35*, 42–45.

Berenbaum, S. A. (2006). Psychological outcome in children with disorders of sex development: Implications for treatment and understanding typical development. *Annual Review of Sex Research, 17*, 1–38.

Berenbaum, S. A., & Snyder, E. (1995). Early hormonal influences on childhood sex-typed activity and playmate preferences: Implications for the development of sexual orientation. *Developmental Psychology, 31*(1), 31–42.

Bergstrom, M. J. & Homes, M. E. (2000) Lay theories of successful aging after the death of a spouse: A network analysis of bereavement advice. *Health Communication, 12*, 377–406.

Berk, L. E. (1992). Children's private speech: An overview of theory and the status of research. In R. M. Diaz & L. E. Berk (eds), *Private speech: From social interaction to self-regulation* (pp. 17–53). Hillsdale, NJ: Erlbaum.

Berk, L. E., Mann, T. D., & Ogan, A. T. (2006). Make-believe play: Wellspring for development of self-regulation. In D. G. Singer, R. M. Golinkoff, & K. Hirsh-Pasek (eds), *Play-learning: How play motivates and enhances children's cognitive and social-emotional growth*. New York: Oxford University Press.

Berkeley, G. (1709). An essay towards a new theory of vision. In M. R. Ayers (ed.), *A new theory of vision and other writings, George Berkeley*. London: Everyman Library, J. M. Dent, 1975.

Berlin, L. J., & Cassidy, J. (1999). Relations among relationships: Contributions from attachment theory and research. In J. Cassidy & P. Shaver (eds), *Handbook of attachment* (pp. 688–712). New York: Guilford Press.

Berman, A. L., Jobes, D. A., & Silverman, M. M. (2005). *Adolescent suicide: Assessment and intervention* (2nd edn). Washington, DC: American Psychological Association.

Berman, P. W. (1987). Children caring for babies: Age and sex differences in response to infant signals and to the social context. In N. Eisenberg (ed.), *Contemporary topics in developmental psychology* (pp. 25–51). New York: Wiley.

Berndt, T. J., & Perry, T. B. (1990). Distinctive features and effects of adolescent friendships. In R. Montemeyer, G. R. Adams, & T. P. Gullotta (eds), *From childhood to adolescence: A transition period?* (pp. 269–287). London: Sage.

Berninger, V. W. (2006). A developmental approach to learning disabilities. In W. Damon & R. M. Lerner (Series eds) & K. A. Renninger & I. E. Siegel (Vol. eds), *Handbook of child psychology: Vol. 4. Child psychology in practice* (6th edn, pp. 420–452). New York: Wiley.

Berninger, V., Abbott, R., Cook, C. R., & Nagy, W. (2016). Relationships of attention and executive functions to oral language, reading, and writing skills and systems in middle childhood and early adolescence. *Journal of Learning Disabilities, 50*(4), 434–449.

Berry, G. (2000). Multicultural media portrayals and the changing demographic landscape: The psychosocial impact of television representations on the adolescent of color. *Journal of Adolescent Health, 275*, 57–60.

Berscheid, E. (2010). Love in the fourth dimension. *Annual Review of Psychology, 61*, 1–25.

Bertenthal, B. I., & Clifton, R. K. (1998). Perception and action. In W. Damon (Series ed.) & D. Kuhn & R. Siegler (Vol. eds), *Handbook of child psychology: Vol. 2. Cognition, perception and language* (pp. 51–102). New York: Wiley.

Bertenthal, B. I., Campos, J. J., & Kermoian, R. (1994). An epigenetic perspective on the development of self-produced locomotion and its consequences. *Current Directions in Psychological Science, 3*, 140–145.

Bertenthal, B. I., Proffitt, D. R., & Cutting, J. E. (1984). Infant sensitivity to figural coherence in biomechanical motions. *Journal of Experimental Child Psychology, 37*, 213–230.

Bertenthal, B. I., Proffitt, D. R., & Kramer, S. J. (1987). The perception of biomechanical motions: Implementation of various processing constraints. *Journal of Experimental Psychology: Human Perception and Performance, 13*, 577–585.

Bertenthal, B. I., & Davis, P. (1988). Dynamical pattern analysis predicts recognition and discrimination in biomechanical motions. *Proceedings of the Annual Meeting of the Psychonomic Society*. Psychonomic Society Publications, Austin, Texas.

Berthier, N. E., DeBlois, S., Poirier, C. R., Novak, J. A., & Clifton, R. K. (2000). Where's the ball? Two- and three-year-olds reason about unseen events. *Developmental Psychology, 36*, 394–401.

Best, D. L. (1993) Inducing children to generate mnemonic organizational strategies: An examination of long-term retention and materials. *Developmental Psychology, 29*, 324–336.

Best, D. L., & Ornstein, P. A. (1986). Children's generation and communication of mnemonic organizational strategies. *Developmental Psychology, 22*, 845–853.

Best, D. L., & Williams, J. E. (1993). A cross-cultural viewpoint. In A. E. Beall & R. J. Sternberg (eds), *The psychology of gender* (pp. 215–248). New York: Guilford Press.

Bialystok, E. (1991). Metalinguistic dimensions of bilingual language proficiency. In E. Bialystok (ed.), *Language processing in bilingual children* (pp. 113–141). Cambridge: Cambridge University Press.

Bialystok, E. (1997). Effects of bilingualism and biliteracy on children's emerging concepts of print. *Developmental Psychology, 33*, 429–440.

Bialystok, E. (1999). Cognitive complexity and attentional control in the bilingual mind. *Child Development, 70*, 636–644.

Bialystok, E. (2006). Effect of bilingualism and computer video game experience on the Simon task. *Canadian Journal of Experimental Psychology, 60*, 68–79.

Bialystok, E., & Viswanathan, M. (2009). Components of executive control with advantages for bilingual children in two cultures. *Cognition, 112*, 494–500.

Bickerton, D. (1983). Creole languages. *Scientific American, 249*, 116–122.

Bickerton, D. (1990). *Language and species*. Chicago: University of Chicago Press.

Bickerton, D. (2008). *Bastard tongues: A trailblazing linguist finds clues to our common humanity in the world's lowliest languages*. New York: Hill & Wang.

Biederman, J., Mick, E., Faraone, S. V., Braaten, E., Doyle, A., Spencer, T., Wilens, T. E., Frazier, E., & Johnson, M. A. (2002). Influence of gender on attention deficit hyperactivity disorder in children referred to a psychiatric clinic. *American Journal of Psychiatry, 159*, 36–42.

Biederman, J., Petty, C. R., Clarke, A., Lomedico, A., & Faraone, S. V. (2011). Predictors of persistent ADHD: An 11-year follow-up study. *Journal of Psychiatric Research, 45*, 150–155.

Bigelow, B. J. (1977). Children's friendship expectations: A cognitive-developmental study. *Child Development, 48*, 246–253.

Bigelow, B. J., & LaGaipa, J. J. (1975). Children's written descriptions of friendship: A multidimensional analysis. *Developmental Psychology, 11*, 857–858.

Bigler, R. S., & Liben, L. S. (1990). The role of attitudes and interventions in gender-schematic processing. *Child Development, 61*, 1440–1452.

Bigler, R. S., & Liben, L. S. (1992). Cognitive mechanisms in children's gender stereotyping: Theoretical and educational implications of a cognitive-based intervention. *Child Development, 63*, 1351–1363.

Bilger, B. (2004, April 5). The height gap. *New Yorker*, 38–45.

Binet, A. (1973). *Les idées modernes sur les enfants*. Paris: Flammarion. (Original work published 1909.)

Biological reviews of the Cambridge Philosophical Society, 65, 375–398.

Biringen, Z., Emde, R. N., Campos, J. J., & Appelbaum, M. I. (1995). Affective reorganization in the infant, the mother, and the dad: The role of upright locomotion and its timing. *Child Development, 66*, 499–514.

Birnbaum, G. E., & Reis, H. T. (2019). Evolved to be connected: The dynamics of attachment and sex over the course of romantic relationships. *Current Opinion in Psychology, 25*, 11–15.

Bishop, D. V. M. (2006). What causes specific language impairment in children? *Current Directions in Psychological Science, 15*(5), 217–221. http://doi.org/10.1111/j.1467-8721.2006.00439.x

Bittner, A., Egger, H. L, Erkanli, A., Costello, E. J, Foley, D. L., & Angold, A. (2007). What do childhood anxiety disorders predict? *Journal of Child Psychology and Psychiatry, 48*, 1174–1183.

Bivens, J. A. & Berk, L. E. (1990) A longitudinal study of the development of elementary school children's private speech. *Merrill-Palmer Quarterly, 36*, 443–463.

Bivens, J. A., & Berk, L. E. (1990). A longitudinal study of the development of elementary school children's private speech. *Merrill-Palmer Quarterly (1982-)*, 443–463.

Bjorklund, D. F. (2005). *Children's thinking: Developmental function and individual differences* (4th edn). Belmont, CA: Wadsworth.

Bjorklund, D. F., & Pelligrini, A. D. (2002). *The origins of human nature: Evolutionary developmental psychology*. Washington, DC: American Psychological Association.

Bjorklund, D. F., Miller, P. H., Coyle, T. R. & Slawinski, J. L. (1997) Instructing children to use memory strategies: Evidence of utilization deficiencies in memory training studies. *Developmental Review, 17*, 411–441.

Bjorklund, D. F., Schneider, W., Cassel, W. S. & Ashley, E. (1994)

Training and extension of a memory strategy: Evidence for utilization deficiencies in the acquisition of an organizational strategy in high- and low-IQ children. *Child Development, 65*, 951–965.

Björkqvist, K., Österman, K., & Lagerspetz, K. M. J. (1993). Sex differences in covert aggression among adults, *Aggressive Behaviour, 20*, 27–33.

Black, B., & Hazen, N. (1990). Social status and patterns of communication in acquainted and unacquainted preschool children. *Developmental Psychology, 26*, 379–387.

Black, J. E., Jones, T. A., Nelson, C., & Greenough, W. T. (1998). Neuronal plasticity and the developing brain. In N. E. Alessi, J. T. Coyle, S. I. Harrison, & S. Eth (eds.), *Handbook of child and adolescent psychiatry: Vol. 6. Basic psychiatric treatment and science* (pp. 31–53). New York: John Wiley and Sons.

Black, M., Schuler, M., & Nair, P. (1993). Prenatal drug exposure: Neurodevelopmental outcome and parenting environment. *Journal of Pediatric Psychology, 18*, 605–620.

Blair, C., & Razza, R. P. (2007), Relating effortful control, executive function, and false belief understanding to emerging math and literacy ability in kindergarten. *Child Development, 78*, 647–663.

Blair, R. J. R. (2003). Neurobiological basis of psychopathy. *British Journal of Psychiatry, 182*, 5–7.

Blair, R. J. R., & Viding, E. (2008). *Psychopathy*. In M. Rutter, D. Bishop, D. Pine, S. Scott, J. Stevenson, E. Taylor, & A. Thapar (eds), *Rutter's child and adolescent psychiatry* (5th edn, pp. 852–863). Chichester: John Wiley & Sons.

Blakemore S. J., Burnett, S., & Dahl R. E. (2010). The role of puberty in the developing adolescent brain. *Human Brain Mapping, 31*(6), 926–933.

Blakemore, J. E. O. (1990). Children's knowledge about babies: The influence of gender and gender-role development. Paper presented at the annual meeting of the Midwestern Psychological Association, Chicago, IL.

Blakemore, S. (2018). *Inventing ourselves: the secret life of the teenage brain*. London: Doubleday/Penguin Random House

Blakemore, S. J. (2008). The social brain in adolescence. *Nature Reviews Neuroscience* 9(4), 267–277.

Blakemore, S. J. (2008). The social brain in adolescence. *Nature Reviews Neuroscience*, 9(4), 267.

Blakemore, S. J., & Choudhury, S. (2006). Development of the adolescent brain: Implications for executive function and social cognition. *Journal of Child Psychology and Psychiatry*, 47(3–4), 296–312.

Blakemore, S. J., & Choudhury, S. (2006). Development of the adolescent brain: Implications for executive function and social cognition. *Journal of Child Psychology and Psychiatry*, 47(3–4), 296–312.

Blakemore, S. J., Burnett, S., & Dahl, R. E. (2010). The role of puberty in the developing adolescent brain. *Human Brain Mapping*, 31(6), 926–933.

Blaser, E., & Kaldy, Z. (2010). Infants get five stars on iconic memory tests: A partial report test of 6-month-old infants' iconic memory capacity. *Psychological Science*, 21, 1643–1645.

Blasi, A. (1983). Moral cognition and moral action: A theoretical perspective. *Developmental Review*, 3, 178–210.

Blass, E., Ganchrow, J. R., & Steiner, J. E. (1984). Classical conditioning in newborn humans 2–48 hours of age. *Infant Behavior and Development*, 7, 223–234.

Block, J. H. (1983). Differential premises arising from differential socialization of the sexes: Some conjectures. *Child Development, 54*, 1335–1354.

Bloom, L. (1970). *Language development: Form and function in emerging grammars*. Cambridge, MA: MIT Press.

Bloom, L. (1976). An interactive perspective on language development. Keynote address presented at the Child Language Research Forum, Stanford University, Stanford, CA.

Bloom, L. (1991). *Language development from two to three*. New York: Cambridge University Press.

Bloom, L. (1993). *The transition from infancy to language*. New York: Cambridge University Press.

Bloom, L. (1998). Language acquisition in its developmental context. In W. Damon (Series Ed.) & R. Siegler & D. Kuhn (Vol. eds), *Handbook of child psychology: Vol. 2. Cognition, perception, and language* (5th edn, pp. 309–370). New York: Wiley.

Bloom, L., & Tinker, E. (2001). The intentionality model and language acquisition. *Monographs of the Society for Research in Child Development, 66*(4, Serial No. 267).

Bloom, L., Lifter, K., & Broughton, J. (1985). The convergence of early cognition and language in the second year of life: Problems in conceptualization and measurement. In M. Barrett (ed.), *Single word speech* (pp. 149–181). London: Wiley.

Bloom, P. (2000). *How children learn the meanings of words*. Cambridge, MA: MIT Press.

Blum, L. M. (2000). *At the breast: Ideologies of breastfeeding and motherhood in the contemporary United States*. Boston: Beacon Press.

Blumberg, F. C., Torenberg, M., & Randall, J. D. (2005). The relationship between preschoolers' selective attention and memory for location strategies. *Cognitive Development*, 20, 242–255.

Blumberg, M. S., Marques, H. G., & Iida, F. (2013). Twitching in sensorimotor development from sleeping rats to robots. *Current Biology, 23*(12), R532–R537.

Bobb, A. J., Castellanos, F. X., Addington, A. M., & Rapoport, J. L. (2006). Molecular genetic studies of ADHD: 1991 to 2004. *American Journal of Medical Genetics Part B 141B*, 551–565.

Boccia, M., & Campos, J. (1989). Maternal emotional signals, social referencing, and infants' reactions to strangers. In N. Eisenberg (ed.), *Empathy and related emotional responses: New directions for child development* (pp. 25–49). San Francisco: Jossey-Bass.

Bogartz, R. S., Shinskey, J. L., & Schilling, T. H. (2000). Object permanence in five-and-a-half-month-old infants? *Infancy, 1*, 403–428.

Bohannon, J. N., III & Warren-Leubecker, A. (1988) Recent developments in child-directed speech: We've come a long way, baby talk. *Language Sciences, 10*, 89–110.

Bohannon, J. N., III, & Stanowicz, L. (1988). The issue of negative evidence: Adult responses to children's language errors. *Developmental Psychology, 24*, 684–689.

Bohlin, G., & Hagekull, B. (1993). Stranger wariness and sociability in the early years. *Infant Behavior and Development, 16*, 53–67.

Boismier, J. D. (1977) Visual stimulation and wake-sleep behavior in human neonates. *Developmental Psychobiology, 10*, 219–227.

Boismier, J. D. (1977). Visual stimulation and wake-sleep behavior in human neonates. *Developmental Psychobiology: The Journal of the International Society for Developmental Psychobiology, 10*(3), 219–227.

Boldizar, J. P. (1991). Assessing sex typing and androgyny in children: The children's sex role inventory. *Developmental Psychology, 27*, 505–515.

Bonawitz, E., Denison, S., Griffiths, T. L., & Gopnik, A. (2014). Probabilistic models, learning algorithms, and response variability: Sampling in cognitive development. *Trends in Cognitive Sciences*, *18*(10), 497–500.

Bond, T. G. (1998). Fifty years of formal operational research: The empirical evidence. *Archives de Psychologie, 66*, 221–238.

Bondy, A., & Frost, L. (2001). *The picture exchange communication system*. Cherry Hill, NJ: Pyramid Educational Consultants.

Booth, A. E., Pinto, J., & Bertenthal, B. I. (2002a). Perception of the symmetrical patterning of human gait by infants. *Developmental Psychology, 38*, 554–563.

Booth, C. A., Clarke-Stewart, K. A., Vandell, D. L., McCartney, K., & Owen, M. T. (2002). Child-care usage and mother–infant 'quality time'. *Journal of Marriage and Family, 64*, 16–26.

Borke, H. (1971). Interpersonal perception of young children: Egocentrism or empathy. *Developmental Psychology, 5*, 263–269.

Borke, H. (1975). Piaget's mountains revisited: Changes in the egocentric landscape. *Developmental Psychology, 11*, 240–243.

Bornstein, M. H., & Kessen, W. (Eds.). (2017). *Psychological development from infancy: Image to intention* (Vol. 2). Routledge.

Bornstein, M. H., & Putnick, D. L. (2007). Chronological age, cognitions, and practices in European American mothers: A multivariate study of parenting. *Development Psychology, 43*, 850–864.

Bornstein, M. H., & Sigman, M. D. (1986). Continuity in mental development from infancy. *Child Development, 57*, 251–274.

Bornstein, M. H., & Tamis, C. (1986). *Origins of cognitive skills in infants*. Paper presented at the International Conference on Infant Studies, Los Angeles.

Bornstein, M. H., Hahn, C.-S., Putnick, D. L., & Pearson, R. (2018). Stability of child temperament: Multiple moderation by child and mother characteristics. *British Journal of Developmental Psychology*. Online first: 23 July, https://doi.org/10.1111/bjdp.12253

Bornstein, M. H., Tal, J., & Tamis-LeMonda, C. S. (1991). Parenting in cross-cultural perspective: The United States, France, and Japan. In M. H. Bornstein (ed.), *Cultural approaches to parenting* (pp. 69–90). Hillsdale, NJ: Erlbaum.

Bortner, M. (1965). Review of the progressive matrices. In O. K. Buros (ed.), *Sixth mental measurements yearbook* (pp. 761–765). Highland Park, NJ: Gryphon Press.

Bouchard, C. (1994). *The genetics of obesity*. Boca Raton, FL: CRC Press.

Bouchard, T. J. Jr, Lykken, D. T., McGue, M., Segal, N. L., & Tellegen, A. (1990). 'Sources of human psychological differences: The Minnesota Study of Twins Reared Apart'. *Science 250* (4978), 223–228.

Bowen, R. L., & Atwood, C. S. (2004). Living and dying for sex. A theory of aging based on the modulation of cell cycle signalling by reproductive hormones. *Gerontology, 50*, 265–290.

Bower, B. (2005). Mental meeting of the sexes: Boys' spatial advantage fades in poor families. *Science News, 168*, 323–324.

Bower, T. G. R., & Wishart, J. G. (1972). The effects of motor skill on object permanence. *Cognition, 1*, 165–172.

Bowker, J. C. W., Rubin, K. H., Burgess, K. H., Booth-LaForce, C., & Rose-Krasnor, L. (2006). Behavioral characteristics associated with stable and fluid best friendship patterns in childhood. *Merrill-Palmer Quarterly, 52*, 671–693.

Bowlby, J. (1944). Forty-four juvenile thieves: Their characters and home-life. *International Journal of Psychoanalysis, 25*, 19–52.

Bowlby, J. (1958). The nature of the child's tie to his mother. *International Journal of Psychoanalysis, 39*, 350–373.

Bowlby, J. (1960). Grief and mourning in infancy and early childhood. *The Psychoanalytic Study of the Child, 15*, 9–52.

Bowlby, J. (1969). *Attachment and loss: Vol. 1. Attachment*. New York: Basic Books.

Bowlby, J. (1973). *Separation and loss*. New York: Basic Books.

Bowlby, J. (1980). *Attachment and loss: Vol. 3. Loss: Sadness and depression*. International Psycho-analytical Library No. 109. London: Hogarth Press.

Boyum, L., & Parke, R. D. (1995). Family emotional expressiveness and children's social competence. *Journal of Marriage and the Family, 57*, 593–608.

Braams, B. R., van Leijenhorst, L., & Crone, E. A. (2014). Risks, rewards, and the developing brain in childhood and adolescence. In V. F. Reyna & V. Zayas (eds), *Bronfenbrenner series on the ecology of human development. The neuroscience of risky decision making* (pp. 73–91). Washington, DC: American Psychological Association.

Bradley, R. H., Corwyn, R. F., Burchinal, M., McAdoo, H. P., & Garcia-Coll, C. (2001). The home environments of children in the United States. Part II: Relations with behavioral development through age thirteen. *Child Development, 72*, 1868–1886.

Bradley, R. H., Whiteside, L., Mundfrom, D. J., Casey, P. H., Kelleher, K. J., & Pope, S. K. (1994). Early indications of resilience and their relation to experiences in the home environments of low birthweight, premature infants living in poverty. *Child Development, 65,* 346–360.

Brain and Cognition, 72(1), 46–55.

Brainerd, C. J., & Reyna, V. F. (1990). Inclusion illusions: Fuzzy trace theory and perceptual salience effects in cognitive development. *Developmental Review, 10,* 365–403.

Bransford, J. D., Brown, A. L., & Cocking, R. R. (1999). *How people learn: Brain, mind, experience, and school.* Washington, DC: National Academy Press.

Braungart-Rieker, J. M., Garwood, M. M., Powers, B. P., & Wang, X. (2001). Parental sensitivity, infant affect and affect regulation: Predictors of later attachment. *Child Development, 72,* 252–270.

Brazelton, T. B., Nugent, J. K., & Lester, B. M. (1987). Neonatal behavioral assessment scale. In J. Osofsky (ed.), *Handbook of infancy* (2nd edn, pp. 780–817). New York: Wiley.

Breedlove, S. M., & Watson, N. V. (2013). *Biological psychology: An introduction to behavioral, cognitive, and clinical neuroscience* (7th edn). Sunderland, MA: Sinauer.

Bremner, A. J. (2016). Developing body representations in early life: Combining somatosensation and vision to perceive the interface between the body and the world. *Developmental Medicine & Child Neurology, 58,* 12–16.

Bremner, A. J., & Mareschal, D. (2004). Reasoning . . . what reasoning? *Developmental Science, 7,* 419–421.

Bremner, A. J., & Spence, C. (2017). The development of tactile perception. *Advances in Child Development and Behavior, 52,* 227–268.

Bremner, A. J., Doherty, M. J., Caparos, S., Fockert, J., Linnell, K. J., & Davidoff, J. (2016). Effects of culture and the urban environment on the development of the Ebbinghaus illusion. *Child Development, 87*(3), 962–981.

Bremner, A. J., Holmes, N. P., & Spence, C. (2008). Infants lost in (peripersonal) space? *Trends in Cognitive Sciences, 12,* 298–305.

Bremner, A. J., Lewkowicz, D. J., & Spence, C. (2012). The multisensory approach to development. In A. J. Bremner, D. J. Lewkowicz, & C. Spence (eds.) *Multisensory development.* Oxford: Oxford University Press.

Bremner, A. J., Lewkowicz, D. J., & Spence, C. (eds) (2012a). *Multisensory development.* Oxford: Oxford University Press.

Bremner, A. J., Lewkowicz, D. J., & Spence, C. (2012b). The multisensory approach to development. In A. J. Bremner, D. J. Lewkowicz, & C. Spence (eds), *Multisensory development.* Oxford: Oxford University Press.

Bremner, A. J., Mareschal, D., Destrebecqz, A., & Cleeremans, A. (2007). Cognitive control of sequential knowledge in 2-year-olds: Evidence from an incidental sequence-learning and generation task. *Psychological Science, 18,* 261–266.

Bremner, A. J., Mareschal, D., Lloyd-Fox, S. & Spence, C. (2008). Spatial localization of touch in the first year of life: Early influence of a visual spatial code and the development of remapping across changes in limb position. *Journal of Experimental Psychology: General, 137*(1), 149–162.

Bremner, A. J., Mareschal, D., Lloyd-Fox, S., & Spence, C. (2008). Spatial localization of touch in the first year of life: Early influence of a visual spatial code and the development of remapping across changes in limb position. *Journal of Experimental Psychology: General, 137*(1), 149–162.

Bremner, A. J. (2017). The origins of body representations in early life. In A. Alsmith & F. De Vignemont (eds.), *The subject's matter.* Cambridge, MA: MIT Press.

Bremner, A. J., Bryant, P. E., Mareschal, D., & Volein, Á. (2007). Recognition of complex object-centred spatial configurations in early infancy. *Visual Cognition, 15,* 1–31.

Bremner, A. J., Lewkowicz, D. J., & Spence, C. (2012). The multisensory approach to development. In A.J. Bremner, D.J. Lewkowicz, and C. Spence (Eds.), Multisensory development. Oxford, UK: Oxford University Press.

Bremner, A. J., Lewkowicz, D. J., & Spence, C. (2012). The multisensory approach to development. In A. J. Bremner, D. J. Lewkowicz, & C. Spence (eds.), *Multisensory development.* Oxford: Oxford University Press.

Bremner, J. G. (1978). Egocentric versus allocentric spatial coding in nine-month-old infants: Factors influencing the choice of code. *Developmental Psychology, 14,* 346–355.

Bremner, J. G., & Bryant, P. E. (1977). Place vs. response as the basis of spatial errors made by young infants. *Journal of Experimental Child Psychology, 23,* 162–171.

Bremner, J. G., Slater, A. M., Hayes, R. A., Mason, U. C., Murphy, C., Spring, J., . . . & Johnson, S. P. (2017). Young infants' visual fixation patterns in addition and subtraction tasks support an object tracking account. *Journal of experimental child psychology, 162,* 199–208.

Brener, R. (1940). An experimental investigation of memory span. *Journal of Experimental Psychology, 33,* 1–19.

Brenes, G. A., Penninx, B. W. J. H., Judd, P. H., Rockwell, M. D., Sewell, D. D., & Loebach Wetherell, J. (2008). Anxiety, depression and disability across the lifespan. *Aging Mental Health, 12*(1), 158–163.

Brennan, P. A., Hall, J., Bor, W., Najman, J. M., & Williams, G. (2003). Integrating biological and social processes in relation to early-onset persistent aggression in boys and girls. *Developmental Psychology, 32*, 309–323.

Brent, D., Emslie, G., Clarke, G., Wagner, K. D., Asarnow, J. R., Keller, M., et al. (2008). Switching to another SSRI or to venlafaxine with or without cognitive behavioral therapy for adolescents with SSRI-resistant depression: The TORDIA randomized controlled trial. *Journal of the American Medical Association, 299*, 901–913.

Bretherton, I. (2005). In pursuit of the working model construct and its relevance to attachment relationships. In K. E. Grossmann, K. Grossmann, & E. Waters (eds), *Attachment from infancy to adulthood* (pp. 13–47). New York: Guilford Press.

Bretherton, I., & Munholland, K. A. (1999). Internal models in attachment relationships: A construct revisited. In J. Cassidy & P. Shaver (eds), *Handbook of attachment* (pp. 89–114). New York: Guilford Press.

Bridges, L. J., & Grolnick, W. S. (1995). The development of emotional self-regulation in infancy and early childhood. In N. Eisenberg (ed.), *Social development. Review of personality and social psychology* (pp. 185–211). Thousand Oaks, CA: Sage.

Briggs, G. G., Freeman, R. K., Towers, C. V., & Forinash, A. B. (2017). *Drugs in pregnancy and lactation: A reference guide to fetal and neonatal risk* (11th edn). New York: Wolters Kluwer Health.

Briones, T. L., Klintsova, A. Y., & Greenough, W. T. (2004). Stability of synaptic plasticity in the adult rat visual cortex induced by complex environment exposure. *Brain Research, 1018*, 130–135.

Brockington, I. (1996) *Motherhood and mental health.* Oxford: Oxford University Press.

Brody, N. (1992). *Intelligence* (2nd edn). San Diego, CA: Academic Press.

Broidy, L. M., Nagin, D. S., Tremblay, R. E., Bates, J. E., Brame, B., Dodge, K. A., et al. (2003). Developmental trajectories of childhood discipline behaviors and adolescent delinquency: A six-site, cross-national study. *Developmental Psychology, 39*, 222–245.

Bronfenbrenner, U. (1979). *The ecology of human development.* Cambridge, MA: Harvard University Press.

Bronfenbrenner, U., & Morris, P. (2006). The ecology of developmental processes. In W. Damon & R. M. Lerner (Series eds) and R. M. Lerner (Vol. ed.), *Handbook of child psychology* (6th edn, Vol. 1, pp. 793–828). New York: Wiley.

Bronfenbrenner, U., McClelland, P., Wethington, E., Moen, P., & Ceci, S. J. (1996). *The state of Americans: This generation and the next.* New York: Free Press.

Bronner, M. E., & Simões-Costa, M. (2016). The neural crest migrating into the twenty-first century. In *Current topics in developmental biology* (Vol. 116, pp. 115–134). New York: Academic Press.

Brook, J. S., Zheng, L., Whiteman, M. & Brook, D. W. (2001). Aggression in toddlers: associations with parenting and marital relations. *The Journal of Genetic Psychology, 162*(2), 228–241.

Brooks, J. H., & Reddon, J. R. (1996). Serum testosterone in violent and non-violent young offenders. *Journal of Clinical Psychology, 52*, 475–483.

Brooks-Gunn, J. (1988). Antecedents and consequences of variations in girls' maturational timing. *Journal of Adolescent Health Care, 9*, 1–9.

Brooks-Gunn, J., & Warren, W. P. (1985). The effects of delayed menarche in different contexts: Dance and nondance students. *Journal of Youth and Adolescence, 14*, 285–300.

Brooks-Gunn, J., Klebanov, P. K., Smith, J., Duncan, G. J., & Lee, K. (2003). The black-white test score gap in young children: Contributions of test and family characteristics. *Applied Developmental Science, 7*, 239–252.

Brown, A. L. (1975) The development of memory: Knowing, knowing about knowing, and knowing how to know. In H. W. Reese (ed.), *Advances in child development and behavior* (Vol. 10, pp. 103–152) New York: Academic Press.

Brown, A. L. (1994). The advancement of learning. *Educational Researcher, 23*, 4–12.

Brown, A. L., & Campione, J. C. (1997). Designing a community of young learners: Theoretical and practical lessons. In N. M. Lambert & B. L. McCombs (eds), *How students learn: Reforming schools through learner-centered education* (pp. 153–186). Washington, DC: American Psychological Association.

Brown, B. B. & Huang, B. (1995). Examining parenting practices in different peer contexts: Implications for adolescent trajectories. In L. J. Crockett & A. C. Crouter (eds), *Pathways through adolescence: Individual development in relation to social contexts* (pp. 151–177). Mahwah, NJ: Erlbaum.

Brown, B. B., & Klute, C. (2003). Friends, cliques, and crowds. In G. R. Adams & M. D. Berzonski (eds), *Blackwell handbook of adolescence* (pp. 330–348). Malden, MA: Blackwell.

Brown, E., & Brownell, C. A. (1990). Individual differences in toddlers' interaction styles. Paper presented at International Conference on Infant Studies, Montreal.

Brown, J. (1958). Some tests of the decay theory of immediate memory. *Quarterly Journal of Experimental Psychology, 10*, 12–21.

Brown, R. (1973). *A first language: The early stages.* Cambridge, MA: Harvard University Press.

Brown, R., & Hanlon, C. (1970). Derivational complexity and order of acquisition in child speech. In J. Hayes (ed.), *Cognition and the development of language* (pp. 11–54). New York: Wiley.

Brown, S. A. (2004) Measuring youth outcomes from alcohol and drug treatment. *Addiction, 99*, 38–46.

Brownell, C. A. (1990) Peer social skills in toddlers: Competencies and constraints illustrated by same age and mixed-age interaction. *Child Development, 61*, 838–848.

Bruck, M., & Ceci, S. J. (1999). The suggestibility of children's memory. *Annual Review of Psychology, 50*, 419–439.

Bruck, M., Ceci, S. J., & Principe, G. F. (2006). The child and the law. In W. Damon & R. M. Lerner (Series eds) & K. A. Renninger & I. E. Siegel (Vol. eds), *Handbook of child psychology: Vol. 4. Child psychology in practice* (6th edn, pp. 776–816). New York: Wiley.

Bruner, J. (1990). *Acts of meaning.* Cambridge, MA: Harvard University Press.

Bruner, J. S. (1966). On cognitive growth. In J. S. Bruner, R. R. Olver, & P. M. Greenfield (eds), *Studies in cognitive growth* (pp. 1–67). New York: Wiley.

Bruner, J. S. (1983). The acquisition of pragmatic commitments. In R. Golinkoff (ed.), *The transition from prelinguistic to linguistic communication* (pp. 27–42). Hillsdale, NJ: Lawrence Erlbaum.

Brunstein Klomek, A., Sourander, A., Nielmela, S., Kumpulainen, K., Phia, J., Tamminen, T., Almqvist, F., & Gould, M. (2009). Childhood bullying behaviours as risk for suicide attempts and completed suicides: A population-based birth cohort study. *Journal of the American Academy of Child and Adolescent Psychiatry, 48*, 254–261.

Bryant, P. E., & Kopytynska, H. (1976). Spontaneous measurement by young children. *Nature, 260.*

Bryant, P. E., & Trabasso, J. (1971). Transitive inferences and memory in young children. *Nature, 232*, 456–458.

Bryant, R., Creamer, M., O'Donnell, M., Forbes, D., Felmingham, K., Silove, D., et al. (2017). Separation from parents during childhood trauma predicts adult attachment security and post-traumatic stress disorder. *Psychological Medicine, 47*, 2028–2035. doi: 10.1017/S0033291717000472

Bryden, M. P. (1988) Does laterality make any difference? Thoughts on the relation between asymmetry and reading. In D. L. Molfese & S. J. Segalowitz (eds), *Brain lateralization in children* (pp. 509–525) New York: Guilford Press.

Buchanan, C. M., & Heiges, K. L. (2001). When conflict continues after the marriage ends: Effects of postdivorce conflict on children. In J. Grych & F. D. Fincham (eds), *Interparental conflict and child development* (pp. 337–362). New York: Cambridge University Press.

Buchanan, C. M., Maccoby, E. E. & Dornbusch, S. M. (1991) Caught between parents: Adolescents' experience in divorced homes. *Child Development, 62*, 1008–1029.

Buck, R. (1975). Nonverbal communication of affect no children. *Journal of Personality and Social Psychology, 31* (4), 644–653.

Buckingham-Howes, S., Berger, S. S., Scaletti, L. A., & Black, M. M. (2013). Systematic review of prenatal cocaine exposure and adolescent development. *Pediatrics*, peds-2012.

Bugental, D. B., & Happaney, K. (2004). Predicting infant maltreatment in low-income families: The interactive effects of maternal attributions and child status at birth. *Developmental Psychology, 40*, 234–243.

Bugental, D., & Grusec, J. (2006). Socialization processes. In W. Damon & R. M. Lerner (Series eds) & N. Eisenberg (Vol. ed.), *Handbook of child psychology* (6th edn, Vol. 3, pp. 366–428). New York: Wiley.

Buhs, E. S., & Ladd, G. W. (2001). Peer rejection as an antecedent of young children's school adjustment: An examination of mediating processes. *Developmental Psychology, 37*, 550–560.

Buitelaar, J. K., Barton, J., Danckaerts, M., Friedrichs, E., Gillberg, C., Hazell, P. L. et al. (2006) A comparison of North American versus non-North American ADHD study populations. *European Child and Adoelscent Psychiatry, 15*, 177–181.

Buitelaar, J. K. (2004, June). Children are not simply small adults! *ECNP matters, 7.*

Bukowski, W. M., Brendgen, M. & Vitaro, F. (2007) Peers and socialization: Effects on externalizing and internalizing problems. In J. Grusec & P. D. Hastings (eds), *Handbook of socialization: Theory and research* (pp. 355–381) New York: Guilford Press.

Bull, R., & Lee, K. (2014). Executive functioning and mathematics achievement. *Child Development Perspectives, 8*(1), 36–41.

Bullinger, A., & Chatillon, J. (1983). Recent theory and research of the Genevan school. In P. H.

Mussen (Series ed.) & J. H. Flavell & E. M. Markman (Vol. eds) *Handbook of child psychology* (Vol. 3, pp. 231–262). New York: Wiley.

Bullock, D. (1983) Seeking relations between cognitive and social-interactive transitions. In K. W. Fischer (ed.), *Levels and transitions in children's development: New directions in child development* (pp. 97–108) San Francisco: Jossey-Bass.

Bullock, D., & Merrill, L. (1980). The impact of personal preference on consistency through time: The case of childhood aggression. *Child Development, 51*, 808–814.

Bullock, M. (1985) Animism in childhood thinking: A new look at an old question. *Developmental Psychology, 21*, 217–225.

Burbach, J. P. H. (2016). Unraveling a pathway to autism. *Science, 351*, 1153–1154.

Burden, M. J., Jacobson, S. W., & Jacobson, J. L. (2005). Relation of prenatal alcohol exposure to cognitive processing speed and efficiency in childhood. *Alcoholism: Clinical and Experimental Research, 29*, 1473–1483.

Burkitt, E., & Watling, D. (2013). The impact of audience age and familiarity on children's drawings of themselves in contrasting affective states. *International Journal of Behavioral Development, 37*(3), 222–234.

Burn, S. M., O'Neil, A. K., & Nederend, S. (1996). Childhood tomboyism and adult androgyny. *Sex Roles, 34*, 419–428.

Burnett, S., Sebastian, C., Kadosh, K. C., & Blakemore, S. J. (2011). The social brain in adolescence: evidence from functional magnetic resonance imaging and behavioural studies. *Neuroscience & Biobehavioral Reviews, 35*(8), 1654–1664.

Burns, K. A., Deddish, R. B., Burns, K., & Hatcher, R. P. (1983). Use of oscillating waterbeds and rhythmic sounds for premature infant stimulation. *Developmental Psychology, 19*, 746–751.

Burton, R. V. (1984). A paradox in theories and research in moral development. In W. M. Kurtines & J. L. Gewirtz (eds), *Morality, moral behavior, and moral development* (pp. 193–207). New York: Wiley.

Bus, A. G., van Ijzendoorn, M. H., & Pelligrini, A. D. (1995). Joint book reading makes for success in learning to read: A meta-analysis on intergenerational transmission of literacy. *Review of Educational Research, 65*, 1–21.

Bushman, D., & Huesmann, L. R. (2001). Effects of televised violence on aggression. In D. Singer & J. Singer (eds), *Handbook of children and the media* (pp. 223–254). Thousand Oaks, CA: Sage.

Buss, D. (2000). Evolutionary psychology. In A. Kazdin (ed.), *Encyclopedia of psychology*. Washington, DC: American Psychological Association and Oxford University Press.

Buss, D. (2003). *The evolution of desire: Strategies of human mating*. New York: Basic Books.

Buss, D. (2007). *Evolutionary psychology: The new science of the mind* (2nd edn). New York: Basic Books.

Buss, D. M. (2008) *Evolutionary psychology: The new science of mind*. Boston: Allyn & Bacon.

Buss, D. M., Shackleford, T. K., Kirkpatrick, L. A., & Larsen, R. J. (2001). A half century of mate preferences: The cultural evolution of values. *Journal of Marriage and Family, 63*, 491–503.

Bussu, G., Jones, E. J., Charman, T., Johnson, M. H., Buitelaar, J. K., & BASIS Team. (2018). Prediction of autism at 3 years from behavioural and developmental measures in high-risk infants: A longitudinal cross-domain classifier analysis. *Journal of Autism and Developmental Disorders, 48*(7), 2418–2433.

Butler, S. C., Berthier, N. E., & Clifton, R. K. (2002). Two-year-olds' search strategies and visual tracking in a hidden displacement task. *Developmental Psychology, 38*, 581–590.

Buttelmann, D., Baillargeon, R., & Southgate, V. (2018). Interpreting failed replications of early false-belief findings: Methodological and theoretical considerations. *Cognitive Development*. doi: 10.1016/j.cogdev.2018.06.001

Buttelmann, D., Baillargeon, R., & Southgate, V. (2018). Interpreting failed replications of early false-belief findings: Methodological and theoretical considerations. *Cognitive Development*.

Butterfield, E. C., & Siperstein, G. N. (1972). Influence of contingent auditory stimulation upon non-nutritional suckle. In J. F. Bosoma (ed.), *Third symposium on oral sensation and perception: The mouth of the infant* (pp. 313–333). Springfield, IL: Charles C Thomas.

Butterworth G, & Castillo M, (1976), Coordination of auditory and visual space in newborn human infants, *Perception, 5*(2) 155–160.

Buysse, V., & Bailey, D. B. (1993). Behavioral and developmental outcomes in young children with disabilities in integrated and segregated settings: A review of comparative studies. *Journal of Special Education, 26*, 434–461.

Cabeza, R., Dolcos, F., Graham, R., & Nyberg, L. (2002). Similarities and differences in the neural correlates of episodic memory retrieval and working memory. *Neuroimage, 16*(2), 317–330.

Cabrera, N. J., Volling, B. L., & Barr, R. (2018). Fathers are parents, too! Widening the lens on parenting for children's development. *Child Development Perspectives*, https://doi.org/10.1111/cdep.12275

Cain, K. (2010). *Reading development and difficulties*. Oxford: Wiley.

Cairney, J., & Wade, T. J. (2002). The influence of age on gender differences in depression: Further population-based evidence on the relationship between menopause and the sex difference in depression. *Social Psychiatry and Psychiatric Epidemiology*, *37*, 401–408.

Cairns, R. B. & Cairns, B. D. (2006) The making of developmental psychology. In W. Damon & R. M. Lerner (Series eds) & R. M. Lerner (Vol. Ed.), *Handbook of child psychology: Vol. 1. Theoretical models of human development* (6th edn, pp. 89–165) New York: Wiley.

Cairns, R. B., & Cairns, B. D. (1994). *Lifelines and risks: Pathways of youth in our time*. Cambridge: Cambridge University Press.

Call, J., & Tomasello, M. (1996). The effect of humans on the cognitive development of apes. In A. E. Russon, K. A. Bard, & S. T. Parker (eds), *Reaching into thought* (pp. 371–403). New York: Cambridge University Press.

Callanan, M. A., & Oakes, L. M. (1992). Preschoolers' questions and parents' explanations: Causal thinking in everyday activity. *Cognitive Development*, *7*, 213–233.

Campbell, S. B. (1998). Developmental considerations in child psychopathology. In T. Ollendick & M. Hersen (eds), *Handbook of child psychopathology* (3rd edn, pp. 1–35). New York: Plenum Press.

Campbell, S. B. (2000). Developmental perspectives on attention deficit disorder. In A. Sameroff, M. Lewis, & S. Miller (eds), *Handbook of child psychopathology* (2nd edn, pp. 383–401). New York: Plenum Press.

Campbell, S. B. (2002). *Behavior problems in preschool children: Clinical and developmental issues* (2nd edn). New York: Guilford Press.

Campos, J. J., & Bertenthal, B. I. (1989). Locomotion and psychological development in infancy. In F. Morrison, C. Lord, & D. Keating (eds), *Applied developmental psychology* (Vol. 2, pp. 230–258). New York: Academic Press.

Campos, J. J., Anderson, D. I., Barbu-Roth, M. A., Hubbard, E. M., Hertenstein, M. J., & Witherington, D. (2000). Travel broadens the mind. *Infancy, 1*, 149–219.

Campos, J. J., Anderson, D. I., Barbu-Roth, M. A., Hubbard, E. M., Hertenstein, M. J., & Witherington, D. (2000). Travel broadens the mind. *Infancy, 1*(2), 149–219.

Campos, J. J., Bertenthal, B., & Kermonian, R. (1992). Early experience and emotional development: The emergence of wariness of heights. *Psychological Science, 3*, 61–64.

Campos, J., Hiatt, S., Ramsey, D., Henderson, C., & Svejda, M. (1978). The emergence of fear on the visual cliff. In M. Lewis & L. Rosenblum (eds), *The origins of affect*. New York: Plenum Press.

Camras, L. A., Malatesta, C., & Izard, C. (1991). The development of facial expressions in infancy. In R. Feldman & B. Rime (eds), *Fundamentals of nonverbal behavior* (pp. 73–105). New York: Cambridge University Press.

Canfield, R. L., & Haith, M. M. (1991). Young infants' visual expectations for symmetrical and asymmetrical sequences. *Developmental Psychology, 27*, 198–208.

Cantor, N. (2000). Life task problem solving: Situational affordances and personal needs. In E. T. Higgins, A. W. Kruglanski, & W. Arie (eds), *Motivational science: Social and personality perspectives. Key readings in social psychology* (pp. 100–110). New York: Psychology Press.

Cantwell, D. P., Baker, L., & Rutter, M. (1978). Family factors. In M. Rutter & E. Schopier (eds), *Autism: A reappraisal of concepts and treatment* (pp. 269–296). New York: Plenum Press.

Cantwell, D. P., Russell, A. T., Mattison, R. & Will, L. A. (1979) A comparison of *DSM-II* and *DSM-III* in the diagnosis of childhood psychiatric disorders. *Archives of General Psychiatry, 36*, 1208–1228.

Caparos, S., Ahmed, L., Bremner, A. J., de Fockert, J. W., Linnell, K. J., & Davidoff, J. (2012). Exposure to an urban environment alters the local bias of a remote culture. *Cognition, 122*(1), 80–85.

Capron, C., & Duyme, M. (1989). Assessment of effects of socioeconomic status on IQ in a crossfostering study. *Nature, 340*, 552–554.

Cardon, L. R. (1994). Height, weight, and obesity. In J. C. DeFries, R. Plomin & D. W. Fulker (eds), *Nature and nurture during middle childhood* (pp. 46–65). Oxford: Blackwell.

Carey, S. (1994). Does learning a language require the child to reconceptualize the world? In L. Gleitman & B. Landau (eds), *The acquisition of the lexicon* (pp. 143–168). Cambridge, MA: Elsevier/MIT Press.

Carey, S. (2009). The origin of concepts. Oxford, UK: Oxford University Press.

Carlo, G., Hausmann, A., Christiansen, S., & Randall, B. A. (2003). Sociocognitive and behavioral correlates of a measure of prosocial tendencies for adolescents. *Journal of Early Adolescence, 23*, 107–134.

Carlo, G., Koller, S. H., Eisenberg, N., Da Silva, M. S., & Frohlich, C. B. (1996). A cross-national study on the relations among prosocial moral reasoning, gender role orientations, and prosocial behaviors. *Developmental Psychology, 32*, 231–240.

Carlson, E. A., Sroufe, L. A. & Egeland, B. (2004) The construction of experience: A longitudinal study of representation and behavior. *Child Development, 75*, 66–83.

Carlson, S. M., & Moses, L. J. (2001). Individual differences in children's inhibitory control and theory of mind. *Child Development, 72*, 1032–1053.

Carlson, S. M., Moses, L. J. & Hix, H. R. (1998) The role of inhibitory processes in young children's difficulties with deception and false belief. *Child Development, 60*(3), 672–691.

Carlson, V., Cicchetti, D., Barnett, D., & Braunwald, K. (1989). Disorganized/disoriented attachment relationships in maltreated infants. *Developmental Psychology, 25*, 525–531.

Carmody, D. P., Bendersky, M., Dunn, S. M., DeMarco, J. K., Hegyi, T., Hiatt, M. et al. (2006) Early risk, attention, and brain activation in adolescents born preterm. *Child Development, 77*, 384–394.

Carnagey, N. C., Anderson, C. A., & Bushman, B. J. (2007). The effect of videogame violence on physiological desensitization to real-life violence. *Journal of Experimental Social Psychology, 43*, 489–496.

Carpendale, J., & Lewis, C. (2006). *How children develop social understanding.* Malden, MA: Blackwell.

Carr, M., & Jessup, D. L. (1995). Cognitive and metacognitive predictors of mathematics strategy use. *Learning and Individual Differences, 7*, 235–247.

Carraher, T. N., Schliemann, A. D., & Carraher, D. W. (1988). Mathematical concepts in everyday life. *New Directions for Child Development, 41*, 71–87.

Carroll, J. B. (1993). *Human cognitive abilities: A survey of factor analytic studies.* New York: Cambridge University Press.

Carroll, J. B. (1997). Psychometrics, intelligence, and public perception. *Intelligence, 24*, 25–52.

Carroll, J. M., Snowling, M. J., Hulme, C., & Stevenson, J. (2003). The development of phonological awareness in preschool children. *Developmental Psychology, 39*, 913–923.

Carson, R. C. (1991) Dilemmas in the pathway of the *DSM-IV. Journal of Abnormal Psychology, 100*, 302–307.

Carstensen, L. L., Isaacowitz, D., & Charles, S. T. (1999). Taking time seriously: A theory of socioemotional selectivity. *American Psychologist, 54*, 165–181.

Carter, C. S., Freeman, J. H., & Stanton, M. E. (1995). Neonatal medial prefrontal lesions and recovery of spatial delayed alternation in the rat: Effects of delay interval. *Developmental Psychobiology, 28*, 269–279.

Carver, K., Joyner, K., & Udry, J. R. (2003). National estimates of adolescent romantic relationships. In P. Florsheim (ed.), *Adolescent romantic relations and sexual behavior: Theory, research, and practical implications* (pp. 23–56). Mahwah, NJ: Erlbaum.

Carver, P. R., Egan, S. K., & Perry, D. G. (2004). Children who question their heterosexuality. *Developmental Psychology, 40*, 43–53.

Case, R. (1984). The process of stage transition: A neo-Piagetian view. In R. Sternberg (ed.), *Mechanisms of cognitive development* (pp. 19–44). New York: Freeman.

Case, R. (1992). Neo-Piagetian theories of child development. In R. J. Sternberg & C. A. Berg (eds), *Intellectual development* (pp. 161–196). New York: Cambridge University Press.

Case, R. (1996) Modeling the dynamic interplay between general and specific change in children's conceptual understanding. *Monographs of the Society for Research in Child Development, 61*(1–2, Serial No. 246) 156–188.

Case, R. (1998). The development of conceptual structures. In W. Damon (Series Ed.) & D. Kuhn & R. S. Siegler (Vol. eds), *Handbook of child psychology: Vol. 2. Cognition, perception, and language* (5th edn, pp. 745–800). New York: Wiley.

Case, R., Hayward, S., Lewis, M., & Hurst, P. (1988). Toward a neo-Piagetian theory of cognitive and emotional development. *Developmental Review, 8*, 1–51.

Cashon, C. H., & Cohen, L. B. (2000). Eight-month-old infants' perception of possible and impossible events. *Infancy, 1*, 429–446.

Casiglia, A. C., Lo Coco, A., & Zapplulla, C. (1998). Aspects of social reputation and peer relationships in Italian children: A cross-cultural perspective. *Developmental Psychology, 34*, 723–730.

Caspi, A., & Moffitt, T. E. (2006). Gene-environment interactions in psychiatry: Joining forces with neuroscience. *Nature Reviews Neuroscience, 7*, 583–590.

Caspi, A., & Moffitt, T. E. (1991). Individual differences are accentuated during periods of social change: The sample case of girls at puberty. *Journal of Personality and Social Psychology, 61*, 157–168.

Caspi, A., Elder, G. H., & Bem, D. J. (1987). Moving against the world: Life course patterns of explosive children. *Developmental Psychology, 23*, 308–313.

Caspi, A., Elder, G. H., & Bem, D. J. (1988). Moving away from the world: Life-course patterns of shy children. *Developmental Psychology, 24*, 824–831.

Caspi, A., Harrington, H. L., Milne, B., Amell, J. W., Theodore, R. F., & Moffitt, T. E. (2003). Children's behavioral styles at age 3 are linked to their adult personality traits at age 26. *Journal of Personality, 71*, 495–513.

Caspi, A., Lyman, D., Moffitt, T. E., & Silva, P. A. (1993). Unraveling girls' delinquency: Biological, dispositional and contextual contributors to adolescent misbehavior. *Developmental Psychology, 29*, 19–30.

Caspi, A., Williams, B., Kim-Cohen, J., Craig, I. W., Milne, B. J., Poulton, R. et al. (2007). Moderation of breastfeeding effects on the IQ by genetic variation in fatty acid metabolism. *Proceedings of the National Academy of Sciences, 104*, 18860–18865.

Cassiba, R., Coppola, G., Sette, G., Curci, A., & Costantini, A. (2017). The transmission of attachment across three generations: A study in adulthood. *Developmental Psychology, 53*, 396–405.

Cassidy, J. (1999). The nature of the child's ties. In J. Cassidy & P. R. Shaver (eds), *Handbook of attachment: Theory, research, and clinical applications* (pp. 3–20). New York: Guilford Press.

Cassidy, J., & Asher, S. R. (1992). Loneliness and sociometric status among young children. *Child Development, 63*, 350–365.

Cassidy, J., & Berlin, L. J. (1994). The insecure/ambivalent pattern of attachment: Theory and research. *Child Development, 65*, 971–991.

Cassidy, J., Kirsh, S. J., Scolton, K. L., & Parke, R. D. (1996). Attachment and representations of peer relationships. *Developmental Psychology, 32*, 892–904.

Castellanos, F. X., Lee, P. P., Sharp, W., Jeffries, N. O., Greenstein, D. K., Clasen, L. S., et al. (2002). Developmental trajectories of brain volume abnormalities in children and adolescents with attention-deficit/hyperactivity disorder. *Journal of American Medical Academy, 288*, 1740–1748.

Castelli, L., Zognmaister, C., & Tomerelli, S. (2009). The transmission of racial attitudes within the family. *Developmental Psychology, 45*, 586–591.

Catmur, C., & Heyes, C. (2017). Mirroring 'meaningful' actions: Sensorimotor learning modulates imitation of goal-directed actions. *Quarterly Journal of Experimental Psychology*, 1–38.

Cavallina, C., Puccio, G., Capurso, M., Bremner, A. J., & Santangelo, V. (2018). Cognitive development attenuates audiovisual distraction and promotes the selection of task-relevant perceptual saliency during visual search on complex scenes. *Cognition, 180*, 91–98.

Cavell, T. A., Hymel, S., Malcolm, K. T., & Seay, A. (2007). Socializing and interventions for antisocial youth. In J. Grusec & P. Hastings (eds), *Handbook of socialization* (pp. 42–69). New York: Guilford Press.

CDC Division of News & Electronic Media (404) 639–3286. http://www.cdc.gov/media/releases/2012/p0329_autism_disorder.html.

Ceci, S. J. (1991). How much does schooling influence general intelligence and its cognitive components? A reassessment of the evidence. *Developmental Psychology*, 27, 703–722.

Ceci, S. J. (1996). *On intelligence: A bioecological treatise on intellectual development* (Exp. ed.). Cambridge, MA: Harvard University Press.

Ceci, S. J., & Williams, W. (1997). Schooling, intelligence, and income. *American Psychologist, 52*, 1051–1058.

Ceci, S. J., Leichtman, M. D. & White, T. (1998) Interviewing preschoolers' remembrance of things planted. In D. P. Peters (ed.), *The child witness in context: Cognitive, social and legal perspectives*. Dordrecht, The Netherlands: Kluwer.

Ceci, S. J., Leichtman, M. D., & White, T. (1998). Children's testimony: Applied and basic issues. In W. Damon (Series Ed.), I. Sigel & K. A. Renninger (Vol. eds), *Handbook of child psychology* (Vol. 4, pp. 713–774). New York: Wiley.

Ceci, S. J., Ross, D. F., & Toglia, M. P. (1987). Suggestibility of children's memory: Psycholegal implications. *Journal of Experimental Psychology: General, 116*, 38–49.

Centers for Disease Control and Prevention (2007, September 8). *Morbidity and morality*. Weekly Report. Atlanta, GA: Teen CDC.

Centers for Disease Control and Prevention (2012). CDC estimates 1 in 88 children in United States has been identified as having an autism spectrum disorder. Division of News & Electronic Media (404) 639–3286. http://www.cdc.gov/media/releases/2012/p0329_autism_disorder.html.

Cervantes, C. A., & Callanan, M. (1998). Labels and explanations in mother-child emotion talk: Age and gender differentiation. *Developmental Psychology, 34*, 88–98.

Chabris, C. F., Lee, J. J., Cesarini, D., Benjamin, D. J., & Laibson, D. I. (2015). The fourth law of behavior genetics. *Current Directions in Psychological Science, 24*(4), 304–312.

Chaiken, S., & Trope, Y. (eds) (1999). *Dual-process theories in social psychology*. New York: Guilford Press.

Chandler, M. J., Greenspan, S., & Barenboim, C. (1973). Judgments of intentionality in response to videotaped and verbally presented moral dilemmas: The medium is the message. *Child Development, 44,* 315–320.

Chandler, M. J., Lalonde, C. E., Sokol, B. W. & Hallett, D. (2003) Personal persistence, identity development, and suicide. *Monographs of the Society for Research on Child Development, 68*(1, Serial No. 273).

Chandler, M., Fritz, A. S., & Hala, S. (1989). Small scale deceit: Deception as a marker of two-, three-, and four-year-olds' early theories of mind. *Child Development, 60,* 1263–1277.

Chao, R. K. (1994). Beyond parental control and authoritarian parenting style: Understanding Chinese parenting through the cultural notion of training. *Child Development, 65,* 1111–1119.

Chao, R. K. (1995). Chinese and European American cultural models of the self reflected in mothers' childrearing beliefs. *Ethos, 23,* 328–354.

Chao, R. K. (2001). Extending research on the consequences of parenting style for Chinese Americans and European Americans. *Child Development, 72,* 1832–1843.

Charlesworth, R., & Hartup, W. W. (1967). Positive social reinforcement in the nursery school peer group. *Child Development, 38,* 993–1002.

Charlton, A. (1994). Children and passive smoking: A review. *Journal of Family Practice, 38,* 267–277.

Charman, T., Jones, C. R., Pickles, A., Simonoff, E., Baird, G., & Happé, F. (2011). Defining the cognitive phenotype of autism. *Brain Research, 1380,* 10–21.

Chase, W. G. & Simon, H. A. (1973) The mind's eye in chess. In W. G. Chase (ed.), *Visual information processing* (pp. 215–281) New York: Academic Press.

Chen, C., & Stevenson, H. W. (1995). Motivation and mathematics achievement: A comparative study of Asian-American, Caucasian-American and East Asian high school students. *Child Development, 66,* 1215–1234.

Chen, C., Stevenson, H. W., Hayward, C., & Burgess, S. (1995). Culture and academic achievement: Ethnic and cross-national differences. In P. Pintrich & M. Maehr (eds), *Advances in motivation and achievement: Vol. 9. Culture, race, ethnicity, and motivation.* New York: Plenum.

Chen, X. (2000) Growing up in a collectivist culture: Socialization and socioemotional development in Chinese children. In A. L. Comunian & U. P. Gielen (eds), *Human development in cross-culture perspective* (pp. 331–353) Padua, Italy: Cedam.

Chen, X., & Rubin, K. H. (1994). Family conditions, parental acceptance, and social competence and aggression in Chinese children. *Social Development, 3,* 269–290.

Chen, X., Cen, G., Li, D., & He, Y. (2005). Social functioning and adjustment in Chinese children: The imprint of historical time. *Child Development, 76,* 182–195.

Chen, X., Chang, L., & He, Y. (2003). The peer group as context: Mediating and moderating effects on relations between academic achievement and social functioning in Chinese children. *Child Development, 74,* 710–727.

Chen, X., Rubin, K. H., & Sun, Y. (1992). Social reputation and peer relationships in Chinese and Canadian children: A cross-cultural study. *Child Development, 63,* 1336–1343.

Chen, Z., & Daehler, M. W. (1989). Positive and negative transfer in analogical problem solving by 6-year-old children. *Cognitive Development, 4,* 327–344.

Chen, Z., Sanchez, R. P., & Campbell, T. (1997). From beyond to within their grasp: The rudiments of analogical problem solving in

10- and 13-month-olds. *Developmental Psychology, 33,* 790–801.

Cherlin, A., & Furstenberg, F. F. (1985). Styles and strategies of grandparenting. In V. L. Bengtson & J. F. Robertson (eds), *Grandparenthood.* Beverly Hills, CA: Sage.

Cherney, I. D., & London, K. (2006). Gender-linked differences in toys, television shows, computer games, and outdoor activities of 5- to 13-year-old children. *Sex Roles, 54,* 717–726.

Chess, S., & Thomas A. (1987). Temperamental individuality from childhood to adolescence. *Journal of Child Psychiatry, 16,* 218–226.

Chi, M. T. H. & Koeske, R. D. (1983) Network representation of a child's dinosaur knowledge. *Developmental Psychology, 19,* 29–39.

Chi, M. T. H. (1976) Short term memory limitations in children: Capacity or processing deficits? *Memory and Cognition, 4,* 559–572.

Chi, M. T. H. (1978) Knowledge structures and memory development. In R. S. Siegler (ed.), *Children's thinking: What develops?* (pp. 73–96) Hillsdale, NJ: Erlbaum.

Chiang, C., Soong, W., Lin, T., & Rogers, S. J. (2008). Nonverbal communication skills in young children with autism. *Journal of Autism and Developmental Disorders, 38* (10), 1898–1906.

Childers, J. B., & Tomasello, M. (2002). Two-year-olds learn novel nouns, verbs, and conventional actions from massed or distributed exposure. *Developmental Psychology, 38,* 967–978.

Chittenden, G. E. (1942). An experimental study in measuring and modifying assertive behavior in young children. *Monographs of the Society for Research in Child Development, 7* (Serial No. 31).

Choi, J., & Silverman, I. (2003). Processes underlying sex differences in route-learning strategies in children and adolescents. *Personality and Individual Differences, 34*, 1153–1166.

Chomitz, V. R., Cheung, L. W. Y. & Lieberman, E. (2000) The role of lifestyle in preventing low birthweight. In K. L. Freiberg (ed.), *Human development* 00/01 (28th edn, pp. 18–28) Guilford, CT: Duskin/McGraw-Hill.

Chomsky, N. (1965). *Aspects of the theory of syntax.* Cambridge, MA: MIT Press.

Chomsky, N. (1968). *Language and mind.* New York: Harcourt, Brace & World.

Cianciolo, A. T., Matthew, C., Sternberg, R. J., & Wagner, R. K. (2006). Tacit knowledge, practical intelligence, and expertise. In K. A. Ericsson, N. Charness, P. J. Feltovich, & R. R. Hoffman (eds), *The Cambridge handbook of expertise and expert performance* (pp. 613–632). New York: Cambridge University Press.

Cicchetti, D., & Toth, S. L. (2006). Developmental psychopathology and preventive intervention. In W. Damon & R. M. Lerner (Series eds) & K. A. Renninger & I. E. Sigel (Vol. eds), *Handbook of child psychology: Vol. 4. Child psychology and practice* (6th edn, pp. 497–547). New York: Wiley.

Cicero, T. J. (1994). Effects of paternal exposure to alcohol on offspring development. *Alcohol Health and Research World, 18*, 37–41.

Cicirelli, V. (2006). Fear of death in mid old age. *Journal of Gerontology: Psychological Sciences and Social Sciences, 61*, 75–81.

Cillessen, A. H. N., & Marjeaux, L. (2004b). From censure to reinforcement: Developmental changes in the association between aggression and social status. *Child Development, 75*, 147–163.

Cillessen, A. H. N., & Mayeux, L. (2004a). Sociometric status and peer group behavior: Previous findings and current directions. In J. B. Kupersmidt & K. A. Dodge (eds), *Children's peer relations* (pp. 3–20). Washington, DC: American Psychological Association.

Cillessen, A. H. N., & Rose, A. J. (2005). Understanding popularity in the peer system. *Current Directions in Psychological Science, 14*, 102–105.

Clancy, P. (1985). Acquisition of Japanese. In D. I. Slobin (ed.), *The cross-linguistic study of language acquisition: Vol. 1. The data* (pp. 323–524). Hillsdale, NJ: Erlbaum.

Clark, E. V. (1983). Meanings and concepts. In P. H. Mussen (Series Ed.) & J. H. Flavell & E. M. Markman (Vol. eds), *Handbook of child psychology* (Vol. 3, pp. 787–840). New York: Wiley.

Clark, K. B., & Clark, M. P. (1947). Racial identification and preference in Negro children. In T.M. Newcomb & E.L. Hartley (Eds.), *Reading in social psychology.* New York: Holt, Rinehart & Winston.

Clarke, D. J. (2001). Treatment of schizophrenia. In A. Dosen & K. Day (eds), *Treating mental illness and behavior disorders in children and adults with mental retardation* (pp. 183–200). Washington, DC: American Psychiatric Press.

Clarke-Stewart, A. & Brentano, C. (2006) *Divorce: Causes and consequences.* New Haven, CT: Yale University Press.

Clarke-Stewart, K. A. (1978) And daddy makes three: The father's impact on mother and young child. *Child Development, 49*, 466–478.

Clarke-Stewart, K. A. (1989). Infant day care: Maligned or malignant? *American Psychologist, 44*, 266–273.

Clarke-Stewart, K. A., & Allhusen, V. D. (2002). Nonparental caregiving. In M. Bornstein (ed.), *Handbook of parenting* (2nd edn, pp. 215–252). Mahwah, NJ: Erlbaum.

Clarke-Stewart, K. A., & Allhusen, V. D. (2005). *What we know about childcare.* Cambridge, MA: Harvard University Press.

Clarke-Stewart, K. A., Vandell, D. L., McCartney, K., Owen, M. T., & Booth, C. (2000). Effects of parental separation and divorce on very young children. *Journal of Family Psychology, 14*(2), 304–326.

Clearfield, M. W., & Niman, L. C. (2012). SES affects infant cognitive flexibility. *Infant Behavior and Development, 35*(1), 29–35.

Cleveland, H. H. & Wiebe, R. P. (2003) The moderation of adolescent to peer similarity in tobacco and alcohol use by school levels of substance abuse. *Child Development, 74*, 279–291.

Clifford, S., Young, R., & Williamson, P. (2007). Assessing the early characteristics of autistic disorder using video analysis. *Journal of Autism and Developmental Disorders, 37*, 301–313.

Clifton, R. K. (1992) The development of spatial hearing in human infants. In L. A. Werner & E. W. Rubel (eds), *Developmental psychoacoustics* (pp. 135–157) Washington, DC: American Psychological Association.

Cloninger, C. R., Christiansen, K. O., Reich, T., & Gottesman, I. I. (1978). Implications of sex differences in the prevalences of antisocial personality, alcoholism, and criminality for familial transmission. *Archives of General Psychiatry, 35*, 941–951.

Cloninger, C. R., Sigvardsson, S., Bohman, M., & van Knoring, A. L. (1982). Predisposition to petty criminality in Swedish adoptees: II. Cross-fostering analyses of gene-environmental interactions. *Archives of General Psychiatry, 39*, 1242–1247.

Cochi, S. L., Edmonds, L. E., Dyer, K., Grooves, W. L., Marks, J. S., Rovira, E. Z. et al. (1989). Congenital rubella syndrome in the

United States, 1970–1985: On the verge of elimination. *American Journal of Epidemiology, 129,* 349–361.

Cohen Kadosh, K., Cohen Kadosh, R., Dick, F., & Johnson, M. H. (2010). Developmental changes in effective connectivity in the emerging core face network. *Cerebral Cortex, 21*(6), 1389–1394.

Cohen Kadosh, K., Cohen Kadosh, R., Dick, F., & Johnson, M. H. (2011). Developmental changes in effective connectivity in the emerging core face network. *Cerebral Cortex, 21*(6), 1389–1394.

Cohen, L. B. & Cashon, C. H. (2006) Infant cognition. In W. Damon & R. M. Lerner (Series eds) & D. Kuhn & R. S. Siegler (Vol. eds), *Handbook of child psychology: Vol. 2. Cognition, perception, and language* (6th edn, pp. 214–251) New York: Wiley.

Cohen, L. B., & Marks, K. S. (2002). How infants process addition and subtraction events. *Developmental science, 5*(2), 186–201.

Cohen, L. B., & Younger, B. A. (1983). Perceptual categorization in the infant. In E. Scholnick (ed.), *New trends in conceptual representation* (pp. 197–220). Hillsdale, NJ: Erlbaum.

Cohen, L., & Younger, B. A. (1984). Infant perception of angular relations. *Infant Behaviour and Development, 7,* 37–47.

Cohen, P., & Brook, J. S. (1995). The reciprocal influence of punishment and child behavior disorder. In J. McCord (ed.), *Coercion and punishment in long-term perspectives* (pp. 154–164). New York: Cambridge University Press.

Cohen-Bendahan, C. C. C., van de Beek, C., & Berenbaum, S. A. (2005). Prenatal sex hormone effects on child and adult sex-typed behavior: Methods and findings. *Neuroscience & Biobehavioral*

Reviews. Special Issue: Prenatal Programming of Behavior, Physiology and Cognition, 29, 353–384.

Cohen-Kadosh, K., Cohen Kadosh, R., Dick, F., & Johnson, M. H. (2013). Developmental changes in effective connectivity in the emerging core face network. *Cerebral Cortex, 21*(6), 1389–1394.

Cohen-Kadosh, K., Henson, R. N. A., Cohen-Kadosh, R., Johnson, M. H., & Dick, F. (2010) Task-dependent activation of face-sensitive cortex: An fMRI adaptation study. *Journal of Cognitive Neuroscience, 22,* 903–917.

Coie, J. D. (2004). The impact of negative social experiences on the development of antisocial behavior. In J. B. Kupersmidt, K. A. Dodge (eds), *Children's peer relations: From development to intervention, Decade of behavior* (pp. 243–267). Washington, DC: American Psychological Association.

Coie, J. D., & Dodge, K. A. (1983). Continuities and changes in children's social status: A five-year longitudinal study. *Merrill-Palmer Quarterly, 29,* 261–282.

Coie, J. D., & Kupersmidt, J. B. (1983). A behavioral analysis of emerging social status in boys' groups. *Child Development, 54,* 1400–1416.

Coie, J. D., Dodge, K. A. & Kupersmidt, J. (1990) Peer group behavior and social status. In S. R. Asher & J. D. Coie (eds), *Peer rejection in childhood* (pp. 17–59) New York: Cambridge University Press.

Colby, A., & Kohlberg, L. (1987). *The measurement of moral judgment* (Vols 1–2). New York: Cambridge University Press.

Colby, A., Kohlberg, L., Gibbs, J., & Lieberman, M. (1983). A longitudinal study of moral judgment. *Monographs of the*

Society for Research in Child Development, 48(Serial No. 200).

Cole, M. (1996). *Cultural psychology: A once and future discipline.* Cambridge, MA: Harvard University Press.

Cole, M. (2006). Culture and cognitive development in phylogenetic, historical and ontogenetic perspective. In W. Damon & R. M. Lerner (Series eds) & D. Kuhn & R. Siegler (Vol. eds), *Handbook of child psychology* (Vol. 2, 6th edn, pp. 636–683). New York: Wiley.

Cole, P. M., & Tan, P. Z. (2007). Emotion socialization from a cultural perspective. In J. E. Grusec & P. Hastings (eds), *Handbook of socialization* (pp. 516–542). New York: Guilford Press.

Cole, P. M., Bruschi, C. J., & Tamang, B. L. (2002). Cultural differences in children's emotional reactions to difficult situations. *Child Development, 73,* 983–996.

Cole, P. M., Martin, S. E., & Dennis, T. A. (2004). Emotion regulation as a scientific construct: Methodological challenges and directions for child development research. *Child Development, 75*(2), 317–333.

Cole, T. J. (2000). Secular trends in growth. *Proceedings of the Nutrition Society, 59,* 317–324.

Colin, V. L. (1996). *Human attachment.* New York: McGraw-Hill.

Collaer, M. L., & Hines, M. (1995). Human behavioural sex differences: A role for gonadal hormones during development? *Psychological Bulletin, 118,* 55–107.

Collins, W. A. (2003). More than myth: The developmental significance of romantic relationships during adolescence. *Journal of Research on Adolescence, 13,* 1–24.

Collins, W. A., & Repinski, D. J. (2001). Parents and adolescents as transformers of relationships: Dyadic adaptation to developmental change. In J. R. M. Gerris (ed.), *Dynamics of parenting* (pp. 429–444). Leuven, Belgium: Garant.

Collins, W. A., & Van Dulman, M. (2006). The course of true love(s): Origins and pathways in the development of romantic relationships. In A. C. Crouter & A. Booth (eds), *Romance and sex in adolescence and emerging adulthood: Risks and opportunities* (pp. 63–86). Mahwah, NJ: Erlbaum.

Collins, W. A., Maccoby, E. E., Steinberg, L., Hetherington, E. M., & Bornstein, M. H. (2000). Contemporary research on parenting: The case for nature and nurture. *American Psychologist, 55,* 218–232.

Colombo, J. (2001). The development of visual attention in infancy. *Annual Review of Psychology, 52,* 337–367.

Coltrane, S. (1998). *Gender and families.* Thousand Oaks, CA: Pine Forge Press.

Coltrane, S. (2000) Research on household labor: Modeling and measuring the social embeddedness of routine family work. *Journal of Marriage and the Family, 62,* 1208–1233.

Coltrane, S., & Adams, M. (2008). *Gender and families* (2nd edn). Lanham, MD: Rowman & Littlefield.

Comer, J. (1996). Improving psychoeducational outcomes for African American children. In M. Lewis (ed.), *Child and adolescent psychiatry: A comprehensive textbook* (pp. 176–201). Baltimore, MD: Williams & Wilkins.

Comer, J. P. (2004). *Leave no child behind: Preparing today's youth for tomorrow's world.* New Haven, CT: Yale University Press.

Comstock, G., & Scharrer, E. (2006). Media and pop culture. In W. Damon & R. M. Lerner (Series eds), K. A. Renninger & I. Sigel (Vol. eds), *Handbook of child psychology* (Vol. 4, 6th edn). New York: Wiley.

Conduct Problems Prevention Research Group (2004). The Fast Track experiment: Translating the developmental model into a prevention design. In J. B. Kupersmidt & K. A. Dodge (eds), *Children's peer relations: From development to intervention* (pp. 181–208). Washington, DC: American Psychological Association.

Conel, J. L. (1975). *The postnatal development of the human cerebral cortex* (Vols I–VIII). Cambridge, MA: Harvard University Press. (Originally published in 1939.)

Conger, J. J., & Petersen, A. C. (1984). *Adolescence and youth* (3rd edn). New York: Harper & Row.

Conklin, H., Luciana, M., Hooper, C., & Yarger, R. (2007). Working memory performance in typically developing children and adolescents: Behavioral evidence of protracted frontal lobe development. *Developmental Neuropsychology, 31,* 103–128.

Connell, M. W., Sheridan, K., & Gardner, H. (2003). On abilities and domains. In R. J. Sternberg & E. Grigorenko (eds), *Perspectives in the psychology of abilities, competencies and expertise* (pp. 126–155). New York: Cambridge University Press.

Connolly, J. A., Craig, W., Goldberg, A., & Pepler, D. (2004). Mixed-gender groups, dating, and romantic relationships in early adolescence. *Journal of Research on Adolescence, 14,* 185–207.

Connolly, K. J. & Dalgleish, M. (1989) The emergence of tool-using skill in infancy. *Developmental Psychology, 25,* 894–912.

Connor, P. D., Sampson, P. D., Bookstein, F. L., Barr, H. M., & Streissguth, A. P. (2001). Direct and indirect effects of prenatal alcohol damage on executive function. *Developmental Neuropsychology, 18,* 331–354.

Conrad, M. E. (2006). *Iron deficiency anemia.* Retrieved November 28, 2007, from http://www.emedicine.com.

Conrod, P. J, Stewart, S. H., Comeau, N. & Maclean, A. M. (2006) Efficacy of Cognitive–Behavioral Interventions Targeting Personality Risk Factors for Youth Alcohol Misuse. *Journal of Clinical Child and Adolescent Psychology, 35,* 550–563.

Contreras, J. M., Kerns, K., Weimer, B. L., Gentzler, A. L., & Tomich, P. L. (2000). Emotional regulation as a mediator of association between motherchild attachment and peer relationships in middle childhood. *Journal of Family Psychology, 14,* 111–124.

Cooper, M. L. (1994) Motivations for alcohol use among adolescents: Development and validation of a four-factor model. *Psychological Assessment, 6,* 117–128.

Cooper, M. L., Frone, M. R., Russell, M. & Mudar, P. (1995) Drinking to regulate positive and negative emotions: A motivational model of alcohol use. *Journal of Personality and Social Psychology, 69,* 990–1005.

Cooper, R. P., & Aslin, R. N. (1990). Preference for infant directed speech in the first month after birth. *Child Development, 61,* 1584–1595.

Coovadia, H. (2004) Antiretroviral agents—how best to protect infants from HIV and save their mothers from AIDS. *The New England Journal of Medicine, 351,* 289–292.

Coren, S. (1992) *The left-hander syndrome: The causes and consequences of left-handedness.* New York: Free Press.

Cornell, E. H., Hadley, D. C., Sterling, T. M., Chan, M. A., & Boechler, P. (2001). Adventure as a stimulus for cognitive development. *Journal of Environmental Psychology, 21,* 219–231.

Corsaro, W. (1990). The underlife of the nursery school: Young children's social representations of adult rules.

In G. Duveen and B. Llyod (eds), *Social Representations and the Development of Knowledge* (pp. 11–26). Cambridge: Cambridge University Press.

Cosgrove, J. M., & Patterson, C. J. (1977). Plans and the development of listener skills. *Developmental Psychology, 13*, 557–564.

Cosmides, L., & Tooby, J. (1987). From evolution to behavior: Evolutionary psychology as the missing link. In J. Dupre (ed.), *The latest and best essays on evolution and optimality* (pp. 277–306). Cambridge, MA: MIT Press.

Costall, A. (2004). From Darwin to Watson (and cognitivism) and back again: The principle of animal–environment mutuality. *Behaviour and Philosophy, 32*, 179–195.

Costello, E. J., Erkanli, A. & Angold, A. (2006) Is there an epidemic of child or adolescent depression? *Journal of Child Psychology and Psychiatry. 47*, 1263–1271.

Cowan, C. P., & Cowan, P. A. (2000). *When partners become parents: The big life change for couples.* Mahwah, NJ: Erlbaum.

Cowan, P. A., & Cowan, C. P. (2002). What an intervention design reveals about how parents affect their children's academic achievement and behavior problems. In J. Borkowski, S. L. Ramey & M. Bristol-Power (eds), *Parenting and the child's world* (pp. 75–98). Mahwah, NJ: Erlbaum.

Cowan, P. A., & Cowan, C. P. (2008). From prevention science to public policy: How working with couples fosters children's development. In M. Schultz, M. K. Pruett, P. Kerig, & R. D. Parke (eds), *Feathering the nest: Couples relationships, couples interventions, and children's development.* Washington, DC: American Psychological Association.

Cowen, E. L, Pederson, A., Babigian, H., Izzo, L. D, & Trost, M. A. (1973) Long-term follow-up of early detected vulnerable children. *Journal of Consulting and Clinical Psychology, 41*, 438–446.

Cowie, D., McKenna, A., Bremner, A. J., & Aspell, J. E. (2018). The development of bodily self-consciousness: Changing responses to the Full Body Illusion in childhood. *Developmental Science, 21*(3), e12557.

Cox, B. C., Ornstein, P. A., Naus, M. J., Maxfield, D., & Zimler, J. (1989). Children's concurrent use of rehearsal and organizational strategies. *Developmental Psychology, 25*, 619–627.

Cox, M. (1991). *The child's point of view*, Hemel Hempstead: Harvester/Wheatsheaf.

Coyle, T. R., & Bjorklund, D. F. (1997). Age differences in, and consequences of, multiple and variable-strategy use on a multitrial sort-recall task. *Developmental Psychology, 33*, 372–380.

Cragg, L., & Gilmore, C. (2014). Skills underlying mathematics: The role of executive function in the development of mathematics proficiency. *Trends in Neuroscience and Education, 3*(2), 63–68.

Cragg, L., & Nation, K. (2010). Language and the development of cognitive control. *Topics in Cognitive Science, 2*(4), 631–642.

Cragg, L., Keeble, S., Richardson, S., Roome, H. E., & Gilmore, C. (2017). Direct and indirect influences of executive functions on mathematics achievement. *Cognition, 162*, 12–26.

Craig, W., & Pepler, D. J. (1997). Observations of bullying and victimization in the schoolyard. *Canadian Journal of School Psychology, 13*, 41–57.

Craik, F. I. M., Byrd, M. & Swanson, J. M. (1987). Patterns of **memory** loss in three elderly samples, *Psychology and Aging, 2*, 79–86.

Crain-Thoreson, C., & Dale, P. S. (1992). Do early talkers become early readers? Linguistic precocity, preschool language and emergent literacy. *Developmental Psychology, 28*, 421–429.

Cramer, D. & Jowett, S. (2010) Perceived empathy, accurate empathy and relationship satisfaction in heterosexual couples *Journal Of Social And Personal Relationships, 27*, 327–349.

Cratty, B. J. (1999). *Movement behavior and motor learning.* Ann Arbor, MI: Books on Demand.

Crick, N. R. & Bigbee, M. A. (1998) Relational and overt forms of peer victimization: A multi-informant approach. *Journal of Consulting and Clinical Psychology, 66*, 337–347.

Crick, N. R. (1997). Engagement in gender normative versus non-normative forms of aggression: Links to social-psychological adjustment. *Developmental Psychology, 33*, 610–617.

Crick, N. R., & Dodge, K. A. (1994). A review and reformulation of social information processing mechanisms in children's social adjustment. *Psychological Bulletin, 115*, 74–101.

Crick, N. R., & Grotpeter, J. K. (1995). Relational aggression, gender, and social-psychological adjustment. *Child Development, 66*, 710–722.

Crick, N. R., Casas, J. F., & Ku, H. (1999). Relational and physical forms of peer victimization in preschool. *Developmental Psychology, 35*, 376–385.

Crick, N. R., Casas, J. F., & Mosher, M. (1997). Relational and overt aggression in preschool. *Developmental Psychology, 33*, 579–588.

Crick, N. R., Ostrov, J. M., Appleyard, K., Jansen, E. A., & Casas, J. F. (2004). Relational aggression in early childhood: 'You can't come to my birthday party unless.' In M. Puttalaz & K. L. Bierman (eds), *Aggression,* *antisocial behavior, and violence among girls* (pp. 71–89). New York: Guilford Press.

Crockenberg, S. B. (1981). Infant irritability, mother responsiveness and social support influences on the security of infant-mother attachment. *Child Development, 52,* 857–865.

Crone, E. A. (2009). Executive functions in adolescence: Inferences from brain and behavior. *Developmental Science, 12,* 825–830.

Crone, E. A. (2009). Executive functions in adolescence: Inferences from brain and behavior. *Developmental Science, 12*(6), 825–830.

Crouter, A. C., & Bumpus, M. F. (2001). Linking parents' work stress to children's and adolescents' psychological adjustment. *Current Directions in Psychological Science, 10,* 156–159.

Crowell, J. A., Treboux, D., & Waters, E. (2002). Stability of attachment representations: The transition to marriage. *Developmental Psychology, 38,* 467–479.

Crowley, K., Callahan, M. A., Tennenbaum, H. R., & Allen, E. (2001). Parents explain more often to boys than to girls during shared scientific thinking. *Psychological Science, 12,* 258–261.

Csibra, G., & Gergely, G. (2006). Social learning and social cognition: The case for pedagogy. In Y. Munakata & M. H. Johnson (eds), *Processes of change in brain and cognitive development. Attention and performance XXI* (pp. 249–274). Oxford: Oxford University Press.

Csibra, G., & Gergely, G. (2009). Natural pedagogy. *Trends in Cognitive Sciences, 13,* 148–153.

Csibra, G., & Gergely, G. (2011). Natural pedagogy as evolutionary adaptation. *Philosophical Transactions of the Royal Society B, 366,* 1149–1157.

Csibra, G., & Gergely, G. (2011). Natural pedagogy as evolutionary adaptation. *Philosophical Transactions of the Royal Society B: Biological Sciences, 366*(1567), 1149–1157.

Csibra, G., & Gergely, G. (2011). Natural pedagogy as evolutionary adaptation. *Philosophical Transactions of the Royal Society of London B: Biological Sciences, 366*(1567), 1149–1157.

Csibra, G., Davis, G., Spratling, M. W., & Johnson, M. H. (2000). Gamma oscillations and object processing in the infant brain. *Science, 290,* 1582–1585.

Cuddy-Casey, M., & Orvaschel, H. (1997). Children's understanding of death in relation to child homocidality and suicidality. *Death Studies, 17,* 33–45.

Cumming, E., & Henry, W. E. (1961). *Growing old.* New York: Basic Books.

Cummings, E. M., & Merrilees, C. E. (2008). Identifying the dynamic processes underlying links between marital conflict and child adjustment. In M. Schultz, M. K. Pruett, P. Kerig, & R. D. Parke (eds), *Feathering the nest: Couples relationships, couples interventions, and children's development.* Washington, DC: American Psychological Association.

Cummings, E. M., Davies, P., & Campbell, S. (2000). *Developmental psychopathology and family process.* New York: Guilford Press.

Cummings, E. M., Goeke-Morey, M. C., & Graham, M. A. (2002). Interparental relations as a dimension of parenting. In J. Borkowski, S. L. Ramey, & M. Bristol-Power (eds), *Parenting and the child's world* (pp. 251–264). Mahwah, NJ: Erlbaum.

Cummings, E. M., Simpson, K. S., & Wilson, A. (1993). Children's responses to interadult anger as a function of information about resolution. *Developmental Psychology, 29,* 978–985.

Cunningham, C. E. (1999), In the wake of the MTA: Charting a new course for the study and treatment of children with attention-deficit hyperactivity disorder. *Canadian Journal of Psychiatry, 44,* 999–1006.

Cunningham, F. G., MacDonald, P. C., & Grant, N. F. (1993). *Williams obstetrics.* Norwalk, CT: Appleton & Lange.

Curtiss, S. (1989). The independence and task-specificity of language. In M. H. Bornstein & J. S. Bruner (eds), *Interaction in human development* (pp. 105–138). Hillsdale, NJ: Erlbaum.

Curzi-Dascalova, L., Giganti, F., & Salzarulo, P. (2008). Neurophysiological basis and behaviour of early sleep development. In C. Marcus (ed.), *Sleep in children: Developmental changes in sleep patterns.* New York: Informa Healthcare USA.

Custance, D. M., Whiten, A., & Bard, K. A, (1995), Can young chimpanzees (Pan Troglodytes) imitate arbitrary actions? Hayes & Hayes (1952) revisited. *Behaviour, 132*(11/12), 837–859.

D'Souza, H., Cowie, D., Karmiloff-Smith, A., & Bremner, A. J. (2017). Specialization of the motor system in infancy: From broad tuning to selectively specialized purposeful actions. *Developmental Science, 20*(4).

D'Souza, H., Cowie, D., Karmiloff-Smith, A., & Bremner, A. J. (2017). Specialization of the motor system in infancy: from broad tuning to selectively specialized purposeful actions. *Developmental Science, 20*(4), e12409.

Dahl, A., Campos, J. J., Anderson, D. I., Uchiyama, I., Witherington, D. C., Ueno, M., . . . & Barbu-Roth, M. (2013). The epigenesis of wariness of heights. *Psychological Science, 24*(7), 1361–1367.

Dale, P. S. (1976). *Language development: Structure and function* (2nd edn). New York: Holt.

Daniels, H., Cole, M., & Wertsch, J. V. (2007). *The Cambridge companion to Vygotsky*. Cambridge: Cambridge University Press.

Daniels, P., & Weingarten, K. (1988). The fatherhood click: The timing of parenthood in men's lives. In P. Bronstein & C. P. Cowan (eds), *Fatherhood today: Men's changing role in the family* (pp. 36–52). New York: Wiley.

Dark, V. J., & Benbow, S. P. (1993). Cognitive differences among the gifted: A review and new data. In D. K. Detterman (ed.). *Current topics in human intelligence* (Vol. 3, pp. 85–120). Norwood, NJ: Ablex.

Darling-Churchill, K., & Lippman, L. (2016). Early childhood social and emotional development: Advancing the field of measurement. *Journal of Applied Developmental Psychology*, *45*, 1–7. doi: 10.1016/j.appdev.2016.02.002

Darvill, D., & Cheyne, J. A. (1981). Sequential analysis of response to aggression: Age and sex effects. Paper presented at the biennial meeting of the Society for Research in Child Development, Boston.

Darwin, C. (1872). *The expression of emotions in animals and man*. London: John Murray.

Darwin, C. (1877). A biographical sketch of an infant. *Mind*, *2*(7), 285–294.

Das, J. P. (2004). Theories of intelligence: Issues and applications. In G. Goldstein, S. R. Beers, & M. Hersen (eds), *Comprehensive handbook of psychological assessment: Vol. 1. Intellectual and neuropsychological assessment* (pp. 5–23). Hoboken, NJ: Wiley.

Dasen, P. R. (1984). The cross-cultural study of intelligence: Piaget and the Baoulé. *International Journal of Psychology*, *19*, 407–434.

Dasen, P. R., Inhelder, B., Lavallée, M., & Retschitzki, J. (1978). *Naissance de l'intelligence chez l'enfant Baoulé de Côte d'Ivoire*. Berne, Switzerland: Hans Huber.

Davey, A. G. (1983). *Growing up in multi-ethnic Britain*. London: Edward-Arnold.

Davidson, E. S., Yasuna, A., & Tower, A. (1979). The effects of television cartoons on sex role stereotyping in young girls. *Child Development*, *50*, 597–600.

Davidson, P., Turiel, E., & Black, A. (1983). The effect of stimulus familiarity on the use of criteria and justifications in children's social reasoning. *British Journal of Developmental Psychology*, *1*, 49–65.

Davidson, R. J. (1994). Temperament, affective style, and frontal lobe asymmetry. In G. Dawson & K. W. Fischer (eds), *Human behavior and the developing brain* (pp. 518–536). New York: Guilford Press.

Davis, M. H., Luce, C., & Kraus, S. J. (1994). The heritability of characteristics associated with dispositional empathy. *Journal of Personality*, *62*, 369–391.

Davis, S. C., Leman, P. J. & Barrett, M. (2007) Children's implicit and explicit ethnic group attitudes, ethnic group identification, and self esteem. *International Journal of Behavioural Development*, *31*, 514–525.

Dawson, G. & Sterling, L. (2008) Autism spectrum disorders. In M. Haith & J. Benson (eds), *Encyclopedia of infant and early childhood development*. Oxford: Elsevier.

Dawson, G. (1994). Development of emotional expression and regulation in infancy. In G. Dawson & K. W. Fischer (eds), *Human behavior and the developing brain* (pp. 346–379). New York: Guilford Press.

Dawson, G., Meltzoff, A. N., Osterling, J. & Rinaldi, J. (1998) Neuropsychological correlates of early symptoms of autism. *Child Development*, *19*, 1276–1285.

Dawson, G., Toth, K., Abbott, R., Osterling, J., Munson, J., Estes, A., et al. (2004). Early social attention impairments in autism: Social orienting, joint attention, and attention to distress. *Developmental Psychology*, *40*, 271–283.

Day, N. L., & Richardson, G. A. (1994). Comparative teratogenicity of alcohol and other drugs. *Alcohol Health and Research World*, *18*, 42–48.

De Bellis, M. D., Keshavan, M. S., Beers, S. R., Hall, J., Frustaci, K., Masalehdan, A., Noll, J., & Boring, A. M. (2001). Sex differences in brain maturation during childhood and adolescence, *Cerebral Cortex*, 11(6), 552–557.

De Boer, J., Andressoo, J. O., de Wit, J., Huijmans, J., Beems, R. B., van Steeg, H., et al. (2002). Premature aging in mice deficient in DNA repair and transcription, *Science*, *296* (5571), 1276–1279.

De Boysson-Bardies, B., Vihman, M., Roug-Hellichius, L., Durand, C., Landberg, I., & Arao, F. (1992). Material evidence of infant selection from target language: A cross-linguistic study. In C. A. Ferguson, L. Menn, & C. Stoel-Gammon (eds), *Phonological development* (pp. 369–391). Timonium, MD: York Press.

De Brito, S. A., Hodgins, S., McCrory, E., Mechelli, A., Wilke, M., Jones, A. P., & Viding, E. (2009). Structural neuroimaging and the antisocial brain: Main findings and methodological challenges. *Criminal Justice and Behavior*, *36*, 1173–1186.

De Haan, M., Johnson, M. H., & Halit, H. (2003). Development of face-sensitive event-related potentials during infancy: A review. *International Journal of Psychophysiology*, *51*, 45–58.

de Houwer, A. (1995). Bilingual language acquisition. In P. Fletcher & B. MacWhinney (Eds.), *The handbook of child language* (pp. 219–250). Oxford: Basil Blackwell.

de Villiers, P. A. & de Villiers, J. G. (1979) *Early language.* Cambridge, MA: Harvard University Press.

de Villiers, P. A., & de Villiers, J. G.(1992). Language development. In M. E. Lamb & M. H. Bornstein (eds), *Developmental psychology: An advanced textbook* (3rd edn, pp. 313–373). Hillsdale, NJ: Erlbaum.

Deacon, S. H., Wade-Woolley, L., & Kirby, J. (2007). Crossover: The role of morphological awareness in French immersion children's reading. *Developmental Psychology, 43,* 732–746.

Deák, G. O. (2006). Do children really confuse appearance and reality? *Trends in Cognitive Sciences,* 10(12), 546–550.

Dean, R. S., & Anderson, J. L. (1997). Lateralization of cerebral function. In A. M. Horton, D. Wedding & J. Webster (eds), *The neuropsychology handbook* (Vol. 1, pp. 138–139). New York: Springer.

Deary, I. J., Thorpe, G., Wilson, V., Starr, J. M., & Whalley, L. J. (2003). Population sex difference in IQ at age 11: The Scottish Mental Survey 1932. *Intelligence, 31,* 533–542.

Deater-Deckard, K., & Dodge, K. A. (1997). Externalizing behavior problems and discipline revisited: Nonlinear effects and variation by culture, context, and gender. *Psychological Inquiry, 8,* 161–175.

Deater-Deckard, K., Pike, A., Petrill, S. A., Cutting, A. L., Hughes, C., & O'Connor, T. G. (2001). Nonshared environmental processes in social-emotional development: An observational study of identical twin differences in the preschool period. *Developmental Science, 4,* F1–F6.

DeCasper, A. J., & Spence, M. (1986). Newborns prefer a familiar story over an unfamiliar one. *Infant Behavior and Development, 9,* 133–150.

DeCasper, A., & Fifer, W. (1980). Of human bonding: Newborns prefer their mothers' voices. *Science, 12,* 305–317.

Decety, J., Michalska, K. J., & Akitsuki, Y. (2008). Who caused the pain? An fMRI investigation of empathy and intentionality in children. *Neuropsychologia,* 46(11), 2607–2614.

DeCorte, E. & Verschaffel, L. (2006) Mathematical thinking and learning. In W. Damon & R. M. Lerner (Series eds) & K. A. Renninger & I. E. Siegel (Vol. eds), *Handbook of child psychology: Vol. 4. Child psychology in practice* (6th edn, pp. 103–152) New York: Wiley.

Deen, B., Richardson, H., Dilks, D. D., Takahashi, A., Keil, B., Wald, L. L., . . . & Saxe, R. (2017). Organization of high-level visual cortex in human infants. *Nature Communications, 8,* 13995.

Dehaene-Lambertz, G., Dehaene, S., & Hertz-pannier, L. (2002). Functional neuroimaging of speech perception in infants. *Science, 298,* 2013–2015.

Dekaban, A. S., & Sadowsky, D. (1978). Changes in brain weights during the span of human life: Relation of brain weights to body heights and body weights. *Annals of Neurology,* 4(4), 345–356.

Dekker, M. C., Ferdinand, R. F., van Lang, N. D., Bongers, I. L., van der Ende, J., Verhulst, F. C. et al. (2007) Developmental trajectories of depressive symptoms from early childhood to late adolescence: gender differences and adult outcome. *Journal of Child Psychology and Psychiatry, 48,* 657–666.

Dekovic, M., & Janssens, J. M. (1992). Parents' child-rearing style and child's sociometric status. *Developmental Psychology, 28,* 925–932.

Del Giudice, M. (2011). Alone in the dark? Modeling the conditions for visual experience in human fetuses. *Developmental Psychobiology,* 53(2), 214–219.

Del Giudice, M., & Colle, L. (2007). Differences between children and adults in the recognition of enjoyment smiles. *Developmental Psychology, 43,* 796–803.

DeLisi, R., & McGillicuddy-DeLisi, A. V. (2002). Sex differences in mathematical abilities and achievement. In A. V. McGillicuddy & R. DeLisi (eds), *Biology, society and behavior: The development of sex differences in cognition* (pp. 155–182). Westport, CT: Ablex.

DeLoache, J. S. & Brown, A. L. (1983) Very young children's memory for the location of objects in a large-scale environment. *Child Development, 54,* 888–897.

DeLoache, J. S. (1987) Rapid change in symbolic functioning of very young children. *Science, 238,* 1556–1557.

DeLoache, J. S. (2004). Becoming symbol minded. *Trends in Cognitive Science, 8,* 66–70.

DeLoache, J. S., & Smith, C. M. (1999). Early symbolic representation. In I. E. Sigel (ed.), *Development of mental representation: Theories and applications* (pp. 61–86). Mahwah, NJ: Erlbaum.

DeLoache, J. S., Miller, K., & Rosengren, K. (1997). The credible shrinking room: Very young children's performance in symbolic and non-symbolic tasks. *Psychological Science, 8,* 308–314.

DeLoache, J. S., Simcock, G., & Macari, S. (2007). Planes, trains, automobiles—and tea sets: Extremely intense interests in very young children. *Developmental Psychology, 43,* 1579–1586.

Demaree, H. A., Everhart, D. E., Youngstrom, E. A., & Harrison, D. W. (2005). Brain lateralization of emotional processing: historical roots and a future incorporating 'dominance'. *Behavioral and Cognitive Neuroscience Reviews,* 4(1), 3–20.

Demetriou, A., Christou, C., Spanoudis, G., & Platsidou, M. (2002). The development of mental processing: Efficiency, working memory, and thinking. *Monographs of the Society for Research in Child Development, 67*(1, No. 268).

Dempster, F. N. (1985). Proactive interference in sentence recall: Topic similarity effects and individual differences. *Memory and Cognition, 13*, 81–89.

Denham, S. A. (1998). *Emotional development in young children.* New York: Guilford Press.

Denham, S. A., Bassett, H. H., & Wyatt, T. (2007). The socialization of emotional competence. In J. E. Grusec & P. Hastings (eds), *Handbook of socialization* (pp. 516–542). New York: Guilford Press.

Denham, S. A., Renwick-DeBardi, S., & Hewes, S. (1994). Emotional communication between mothers and preschoolers: Relations with emotional competence. *Merrill-Palmer Quarterly, 40*, 488–508.

Denmark, F., Russo, N. F., Frieze, I. H., & Sechzer, J. A. (1988). Guidelines for avoiding sexism in psychological research. *American Psychologist, 43*, 582–585.

Denney, N. W. (1990). Adult age differences in traditional and practical problem-solving. *Advances in Psychology, 72*, 329–349.

Dennis, W. (1940). Does culture appreciably affect patterns of infant behavior? *Journal of Social Psychology, 12*, 305–317.

Denson, N. (2009). Do curricular and co-curricular diversity activities influence racial bias? A meta-analysis. *Review of Educational Research, 72*, 805–838.

Derks, E. M., Dolan, C. V., & Boomsma, D. I. (2006). A test of the equal environment assumption (EEA) in multivariate twin studies. *Twin Research and Human Genetics, 9*(3), 403–411.

Deventer, J., Wagner, J., Lüdtke, O., & Trautwein, U. (2018). Are personality traits and relationship characteristics reciprocally related? Longitudinal analyses of codevelopment in the transition out of high school and beyond. *Journal of Personality and Social Psychology.* Advance online publication.

Dewey, K. (2001). Nutrition, growth and complementary feeding of the breastfed infant. *Pediatric Clinics of North America, 48*, 87–104.

Di Giorgio, E., Lunghi, M., Simion, F., & Vallortigara, G. (2017). Visual cues of motion that trigger animacy perception at birth: The case of self-propulsion. *Developmental Science, 20*(4), e12394.

Di Giorgio, E., Lunghi, M., Simion, F., & Vallortigara, G. (2017). Visual cues of motion that trigger animacy perception at birth: The case of self-propulsion. *Developmental Science, 20*(4), e12394.

Di Giunta, L., Pastorelli, C., Thartori, E., Bombi, A. S., Baumgartner, E., Fabes, R. A., et al. (2018). Trajectories of Italian children's peer rejection: Associations with aggression, prosocial behavior, physical attractiveness, and adolescent adjustment, *Abnormal Child Psychology, 46*(1), 1021–1035.

Diamond A. (1988). Abilities and neural mechanisms underlying AB performance. *Child Development, 59*, 523–527.

Diamond, A., Barnett, W. S., Thomas, J., & Munro, S. (2007). Preschool program improves cognitive control. *Science, 318*, 1387–1388.

Diaz, R. M. (1983). Thought and two languages: The impact of bilingualism on cognitive development. *Review of Research in Education, 10*, 23–54.

Diaz, R. M. (1985). Bilingual cognitive development: Addressing three gaps in current research. *Child Development, 56*, 1376–1388.

Dickens, W. T., & Flynn, J. R. (2001). Heritability estimates versus large environmental effects: The IQ paradox resolved. *Psychological Review, 108*, 346–369.

Diener, C. I., & Dweck, C. S. (1978). An analysis of learned helplessness: Continuous changes in performance, strategy and achievement cognitions following failure. *Journal of Personality and Social Psychology, 36*, 451–462.

Diener, E. (1984). Subjective well-being. *Psychological Bulletin, 95*, 542–572.

Dietrich, K. N., Berger, O. G., Succop, P. A., Hammond, P. B., & Bornschein, R. L. (1993). The developmental consequences of low to moderate prenatal and postnatal lead exposure: Intellectual attainment in the Cincinnati Lead Study cohort following school entry. *Neurotoxicology and Teratology, 13*, 37–44.

DiLalla, L. F., Thompson, L. A., Plomin, R., Phillips, K., Faga, J. F., Haith, M. M. et al. (1990). Infant predictors of preschool and adult IQ: A study of infant twins and their parents. *Developmental Psychology, 26*, 759–769.

Ding, X. P., Wellman, H. M., Wang, Y., Fu, G., & Lee, K. (2015). Theory-of-mind training causes honest young children to lie. *Psychological Science, 26*(11), 1812–1821.

Dionne, G., Tremblay, R., Boivin, M., Laplante, D., & Perusse, D. (2003). Physical aggression and expressive vocabulary in 19-month-old twins. *Developmental Psychology, 39*, 261–273.

DiPietro, J. A. (2004). The role of prenatal maternal stress in child development. *Current Directions in Psychological Science, 13*, 71–74.

DiPietro, J., Novak, M. F., Costigan, K. A., Atella, L. D., & Reusing, S. P. (2006). Maternal psychological distress during pregnancy in relation to child development at age 2. *Child Development, 77*, 573–587.

Dishion, T. J., Poulin, F., & Burraston, B. (2001). Peer group dynamics associated with iatrogenic effects in group interventions with high-risk young adolescents. In D. W. Nangle & C. A. Erdley (eds), *The role of friendship in psychological adjustment: New directions for child and adolescent development, No. 91* (pp. 79–92). San Francisco: Jossey-Bass.

Dishion, T. J., Poulin, F., & Medici Skaggs, N. (2000). The ecology of premature autonomy in adolescence: Biological and social influences. In K. A. Kerns & A. M. Neal-Barnett (eds), *Family and peers: Linking two social worlds* (pp. 27–45). Westport, CT: Praeger.

Dishion, T., & Bullock, B. M. (2002). Parenting and adolescent problem behavior: An ecological analysis of the nurturance hypothesis. In J. Borkowski, S. L. Ramey, & M. Bristol-Power (eds), *Parenting and the child's world* (pp. 231–249). Mahwah, NJ: Erlbaum.

Dittmar, H., Halliwell, E., & Ive, S. (2006a). Does Barbie make girls want to be thin? The effect of experimental exposure to images of dolls on the body image of 5–8-year-old girls. *Developmental Psychology, 42*, 283–292.

Dittmar, H., Halliwell, E., & Ive, S. (2006b). Correction to Dittmar, Halliwell, and Ive (2006). *Developmental Psychology, 42*, 1258.

Dittrichova, J. (1969). The development of premature infants. In R. J. Robinson (ed.), *Brain and early development*. London: Academic Press.

Dobson, V., & Teller, D. Y. (1978). Visual acuity in human infants: A review and comparison of behavioral and electrophysiological studies. *Vision Research, 18*(11), 1469–1483.

Dodge, K. A., & Frame, C. L. (1982). Social cognitive biases and deficits in aggressive boys. *Child Development, 53*, 620–635.

Dodge, K., Coie, J., & Lynam, D. (2006). Aggression. In W. Damon & R. L. Lerner (Series eds) & N. Eisenberg (Vol. ed.), *Handbook of child psychology* (Vol. 3, 6th edn, pp. 719–788). New York: Wiley.

Dodge, N. C., Jacobson, J. L., & Jacobson, S. W. (2014). Protective effects of the alcohol dehydrogenase-ADH1B* 3 allele on attention and behavior problems in adolescents exposed to alcohol during pregnancy. *Neurotoxicology and Teratology, 41*, 43–50.

Doherty, M. (2008). *Theory of mind: How children understand others' thoughts and feelings*. Hove: Psychology Press.

Doherty-Sneddon, G. (2003). *Children's unspoken language*. London: Jessica Kingsley.

Doise, W., & Mugny, G. (1984). *The social development of the intellect*. Cambridge: Cambridge University Press.

Dominick, J. R., & Greenberg, B. S. (1972). Attitudes toward violence: The interaction of television exposure, family attitudes, and social class. In G. A. Comstock & E. A. Rubenstein (eds), *Television and social behavior: Television and adolescent aggressiveness* (Vol. 3, pp. 314–335). Washington, DC: Government Printing Office.

Donaldson, M. (1978). *Children's minds*. New York: Norton.

Doolittle, W. F. (2013). Is junk DNA bunk? A critique of ENCODE. *Proceedings of the National Academy of Sciences USA, 110*, 5294–5300.

Doris, J. (ed.) (1991). *The suggestibility of children's recollections*. Washington, DC: American Psychological Association.

Drabman, R. S., & Thomas, M. H. (1976). Does watching violence on television cause apathy? *Pediatrics, 52*, 329–331.

Drew, C. J., & Hardman, M. L. (2000). *Mental retardation: A life cycle approach* (7th edn). Columbus, OH: Merrill.

Dubowitz, L., & Dubowitz, V. (1981). *The neurological assessment of the preterm and fullterm newborn infant*. Philadelphia: Lippincott.

Dunbar, R. I., & Shultz, S. (2007). Evolution in the social brain. *Science, 317*(5843), 1344–1347.

Dunham, P. J., Dunham, R., & Curwin, A. (1993). Joint-attentional states and lexical acquisition at 18 months. *Developmental Psychology, 29*, 827–831.

Dunn, J. (1988). *The beginnings of social understanding*. Cambridge, MA: Harvard University Press.

Dunn, J. (2004). *Children's friendships*. Oxford: Blackwell.

Dunn, J. (2007). Siblings and socialization. In J. E. Grusec & P. Hastings (eds), *Handbook of socialization* (pp. 309–327). New York: Guilford Press.

Dunn, J., & Hughes, C. (1998). Young children's understanding of emotions within close relationships. *Cognition and Emotion, 12*, 171–190.

Dunn, J., & Hughes, C. (2001). I got some swords and you're dead! Violent fantasy, antisocial behavior, friendship, and moral sensibility in young children. *Child Development, 72*,491–505.

Dunn, J., & Kendrick, C. (1982). The speech of two- and three-year-olds to infant siblings: 'Baby talk' and the context of communication. *Journal of Child Language, 9*, 579–595.

Dunn, J., & Plomin, R. (1991). Why are siblings so different? The significance of differences in sibling experiences within the family. *Family Process, 30*, 271–283.

Dunn, J., Brown, J. R., & Maguire, M. (1995). The development of children's moral sensibility: Individual differences and emotional understanding. *Developmental Psychology, 31*, 649–659.

Dunn, K., & Bremner, J. G. (2017). Investigating looking and social looking measures as an index of infant violation of expectation. *Developmental Science, 20*(6), e12452.

DuPaul, G. J., & Stoner, G. (2014). *ADHD in the schools: Assessment and intervention strategies* (3rd edn). New York: Guilford Press.

Duvall, E. M. (1962). *Family development*. Philadelphia: J. B. Lippincott.

Dweck, C. (2006). *Mindset: The new psychology of success*. New York: Random House.

Dweck, C. S. (2000). *Self-theories*. Philadelphia: Taylor & Francis.

Dweck, C. S. (2001). Caution—Praise can be dangerous. In K. L. Frieberg (ed.), *Human development 01/02* (9th edn, pp. 105–109). Guilford, CT: Dushkin/McGraw-Hill.

Dweck, C. S., & Leggett, E. L. (1988). A social-cognitive approach to motivation and personality. *Psychological Review, 95*, 256–273.

East, P. L. (1996). The younger sisters of childrearing adolescents: Their attitudes, expectations, and behaviors. *Child Development, 67*, 953–963.

Eberhart-Phillips, J. E., Frederick, P. D., & Baron, R. C. (1993). Measles in pregnancy: A descriptive study of 58 cases. *Obstetrics and Gynecology, 82*, 797–801.

Eccles, J. (2007). Families, schools and developing achievement-related motivation and engagement. In J. Grusec & P. Hastings (eds), *Handbook of socialization* (pp. 665–691). New York: Guilford Press.

Eccles, J. S., Freedman-Doan, C., Frome, P., Jacobs, J., & Yoon, K. S. (2000). Gender socialization in the family: A longitudinal approach.

In T. Ecker & H. Trautner (eds), *The developmental social psychology of gender* (pp. 333–365). Mahwah, NJ: Erlbaum.

Eccles, J. S., Jacobs, J., Harold, R., Yoon, K. S., Abreton, A. & Freedman-Doan, C. (1993) Parents' and gender-role socialization during the middle childhood and adolescent years. In S. Oskamp & M. Costanzo (eds), *Gender issues in contemporary society* (pp. 59–83) Newbury Park, CA: Sage.

Eckerman, C. O. (1993). Imitation and toddlers' achievement of coordinated action with others. In J. Nadel & L. Camaioni (eds), *New perspectives in early communicative development* (pp. 116–156). New York: Routledge.

Eckerman, C. O., & Didow, S. M. (1988). Lessons drawn from observing young peers together. *Acta Paeditrica Scandinavica, 77*(Suppl. 344), 55–70.

Eckerman, C. O., Whatley, J. L. & Kutz, S. L. (1975) Growth of social play with peers during the second year of life. *Developmental Psychology, 11*, 42–49.

Edge, https://www.edge.org/response-detail/10669

Edwards, C. P. (1992). Cross-cultural perspectives on family-peer relations. In R. D. Parke & G. W. Ladd (eds), *Family-peer relationships: Modes of linkage* (pp. 285–316). Hillsdale, NJ: Erlbaum.

Edwards, C. P., & Whiting, B. B. (1993). 'Mother, older sibling, and me': The overlapping roles of caregivers and companions in the social world of two- and three-year-olds in Ngeca, Kenya. In K. MacDonald (ed.), *Parent-child play: Descriptions and implications* (pp. 305–329). Albany, NY: State University of New York Press.

Egan, S. K., & Perry D. G. (2002). Gender identity: A multidimensional analysis with implications for psychosocial adjustment. *Developmental Psychology, 17*, 451–463.

Eilers, R. E., Oller, D. K., Levine, S., Basinger, D., Lynch, M. P., & Urbano, C. (1993). The role of prematurity and socioeconomic status in the onset of canonical babbling in infants. *Infant Behavior and Development, 16*, 297–315.

Eisen, M., Goodman, G., & Quas, J. (2002). *Memory and suggestibility in the forensic interview*. Hillsdale, NJ: Erlbaum.

Eisenberg, N. (1992). *The caring child*. Cambridge, MA: Harvard University Press.

Eisenberg, N., Boehnke, K., Schuhler, P., & Silbereisen, R. K. (1985). The development of prosocial behavior and cognitions in German children. *Journal of Cross-Cultural Psychology, 16*, 69–82.

Eisenberg, N., Cumberland, A., Spinard, T. L., Fabes, R. A., Shepard, S. A., Reiser, M., et al. (2001b). The relation of regulation and emotionality to children's externalizing and internalizing problem behavior. *Child Development, 72*, 1112–1134.

Eisenberg, N., Fabes, R. A., & Murphy, B. C. (1996). Parents' reactions to children's negative emotions: Relations to children's social competence and comforting behavior. *Child Development, 67*, 2227–2247.

Eisenberg, N., Fabes, R. A., & Spinrad, T. (2006). Prosocial development. In W. Damon & R. M. Lerner (Series eds) & N. Eisenberg (Vol. Ed.), *Handbook of child psychology* (Vol. 3, 6th edn, pp. 646–718). New York: Wiley.

Eisenberg, N., Fabes, R. A., Carlo, G., Speer, A. L., Switzer, G., Karbon, M. et al. (1993). The relations of empathy-related emotions and maternal practices to children's comforting behavior. *Journal of Experimental Child Psychology, 55*, 131–150.

Eisenberg, N., Fabes, R. A., Nyman, M., Bernzweig, J., & Pinuelas, A. (1994). The relations of emotionality and regulation to children's anger-related reactions. *Child Development, 65,* 109–128.

Eisenberg, N., Gershoff, E. T., Fabes, R. A., Shepard, S. A., Cumberland, A. J. et al. (2001a) Mothers' emotional expressivity and children's behavior problems and social competence: Mediation through children's regulation. *Developmental Psychology, 37,* 475–490.

Eisenberg, N., Guthrie, I. K., Murphy, B. C., Cumberland, A., & Carlo, G. (1999). Consistency and development of prosocial dispositions. *Child Development, 70,* 1370–1372.

Eisenberg, N., Lennon, R., & Roth, K. (1983). Prosocial development: A longitudinal study. *Developmental Psychology, 19,* 846–855.

Eisenberg, N., Zhou, Q., & Koller, S. (2001). Brazilian adolescents' prosocial moral judgments and behavior: Relations to sympathy, perspective taking, gender-role orientation, and demographic characteristics. *Child Development, 72,* 518–534.

Ekman, P. (1994). Strong evidence for universals in facial expression: A reply to Russell's mistaken critique. *Psychological Bulletin, 115,* 268–287.

Ekman, P. (2003). *Emotions revealed.* New York: Times Books.

Ekman, P., Davidson, R., & Friesen, W. V. (1990). The Duchenne smile: Emotional expression and brain physiology. *Journal of Personality and Social Behavior, 58,* 342–353.

Ekman, P., Friesen, W. V., O'Sullivan, M., Chan, A., Diacoyanni-Tarlatzis, I., Heider, K., et al. (1987). Universals and cultural differences in the judgments of facial expressions of emotion. *Journal of Personality and Social Psychology, 52,* 712–717.

Elam, K. K., Chassin, L., Lemery-Chalfant, K., Pandika, D., Wang, F. L., Bountress, K., . . . & Agrawal, A. (2017). Affiliation with substance-using peers: Examining gene-environment correlations among parent monitoring, polygenic risk, and children's impulsivity. *Developmental Psychobiology, 59*(5), 561–573.

Elbers, L., & Ton, J. (1985). Playpen monologues: The interplay of words & babbles in the first words period. *Journal of Child Language, 12,* 551–565.

Elder, G. H., & Conger, R. D. (2000). *Children of the land.* Chicago: University of Chicago Press.

Eldredge, L. & Salamy, A. (1988). Neurobehavioral and neurophysiological assessment of healthy and 'at risk' full-term infants. *Child Development, 59,* 186–192.

Eley, T. C., Lichtenstein, P., & Stevenson, J. (1999). Sex differences in the etiology of aggressive and nonaggressive antisocial behavior: Results from two twin studies. *Child Development, 70,* 155–168.

Ellis, B. J. (2004). Timing of pubertal maturation in girls: An integrated life history approach. *Psychological Bulletin, 130,* 920–958.

Ellis, B. J., & Essex, M. J. (2007). Family environments, adrenarche, and sexual maturation: A longitudinal test of a life history model. *Child Development, 78,* 1799–1817.

Ellis, B. J., Bates, J. E., Dodge, K. A., Fergusson, D. M., Horwood, L. J., Pettit, G. S. et al. (2003). Does father absence place daughters at special risk for early sexual activity and teenage pregnancy? *Child Development, 74,* 801–821.

Ellis, B. J., McFadyen-Ketchum, S., Dodge, K. A. Pettit, G. S., & Bates, J. E. (1999). Quality of early family relationships and individual differences in the timing of pubertal maturation in girls: A longitudinal test of an evolutionary model. *Journal of Personality and Social Psychology, 77,* 387–401.

Ellis, S., Rogoff, B., & Cromer, C. (1981). Age segregation in children's social interactions. *Developmental Psychology, 17,* 399–407.

Ellis, W. E., & Zarbatany, L. (2007). Peer group status as a moderator of group influence on children's deviant, aggressive, and prosocial behaviour. *Child Development, 78,* 1240–1254.

Ellsworth, C. P., Muir, D. W., & Hains, S. M. J. (1993). Social competence and person–object differentiation. An analysis of the still-face effect. *Developmental Psychology, 29,* 63–73.

Elman, J. L., Bates, E. A., Johnson, M. H., Karmiloff-Smith, A., Parisi, D., & Plunkett, K. (1997). *Rethinking innateness: A connectionist perspective on development.* Cambridge, MA: MIT Press.

Elman, J. L., Bates, E., Johnson, M. H., Karmiloff-Smith, A., Parisi, D., & Plunkett, K. (1996). Rethinking nativism: A connectionist perspective on development. Cambridge, MA: MIT Press.

Elman, J. L., Bates, E., Johnson, M. H., Karmiloff-Smith, A., Parisi, D., & Plunkett, K. (1996). *Rethinking nativism: A connectionist perspective on development.* Cambridge, MA: MIT Press.

Eluvathingal T. J., Chugani H. T., Behen M. E., et al. (2006). Abnormal brain connectivity in children after early severe socioemotional deprivation: A diffusion tensor imaging study. *Pediatrics, 117,* 2093–2100.

Embry, L., & Dawson, G. (2002). Disruptions in parenting related to maternal depression: Influences on children's behavioral and psychobiological development. In J. G. Borkowski, S. Ramey, & M. Bristol-Power (eds), *Parenting and the child's world* (pp. 203–213). Mahwah, NJ: Erlbaum.

Emde, R. N., Gaensbauer, T. J., & Harmon, R. J. (1976). Emotional expression in infancy: A biobehavioral study. *Psychological Issues, 10* (Serial No. 37).

Emler, N., Renwick, S., & Malone, B. (1983). The relationship between moral reasoning and political orientation. *Journal of Personality and Social Psychology, 45,* 1073–1080.

Emons, J. A. M., Boerama, B., Baron, J., & Wit, J. M. (2005). Catch-up growth: Testing the hypothesis of delayed growth plate senescence in humans. *Journal of Pediatrics, 14,* 843–846.

Emory, E. K., Schlackman, L. J., & Fiano, K. (1996). Drug-hormone interactions on neurobehavioral responses in human neonates. *Infant Behavior and Development, 19,* 213–220.

Emslie, G. J., Rush, A. J., Weinberg, W. A., Kowatch, R. A., Hughes, C. W., Carmody, T., et al. (1997). A double-blind, randomized, placebo-controlled trial of fluoxitine in children and adolescents with depression. *Archives of General Psychiatry, 54,* 1031–1037.

Engel, S. (1995). *The stories children tell: Making sense of the narratives of childhood.* New York: Freeman.

Engel, S., & Li, A. (2004). Narratives, gossip, and shared experience: How and what young children know about the lives of others. In J. M. Lucariello, J. A. Hudson, R. Fivush, & P. J. Bauer (eds), *The development of the mediated mind: Sociocultural context and cognitive development* (pp. 151–174). Mahwah, NJ: Erlbaum.

Englund, M. M., Egeland, B., Oliva, E. M., & Collins, W. A. (2008). Childhood and adolescent predictors of heavy drinking and alcohol use disorders in early adulthood: A longitudinal developmental analysis. *Addiction, 103,* 23–35.

Enns, J. T., Brodeur, D. A., & Trick, L. M. (1998). Selective attention over the life span: Behavioral measures. In J. Richards (ed.), *Cognitive neuroscience of attention: A developmental perspective* (pp. 393–418). Mahwah, NJ: Lawrence Erlbaum.

Entwisle, D. R., & Alexander, K. L. (1987). Long-term effects of cesarean delivery on parents' beliefs and children's schooling. *Developmental Psychology, 23,* 676–682.

Entwisle, D. R., & Frasure, N. E. (1974). A contradiction resolved: Children's processing of syntactic cues. *Developmental Psychology, 10,* 852–857.

Epstein, C. J., Martin, G. M., Schultz, A. L., & Motulsky, A. G. (1996). Werner's syndrome: A review of its symptomatology, natural history, pathologic features, genetics and relationships to the natural aging process. *Medicine, 45,* 172–221.

Epstein, J. A., Griffin, K. W. & Botvin, G. J. (2001) Risk taking and refusal assertiveness in a longitudinal model of alcohol use among inner-city adolescents. *Prevention Science, 2,* 193–200.

Epstein, R., Harris, A., Stanley, D. & Kanwisher, N. (1999). The parahippocampal place area: Recognition, navigation, or encoding? *Neuron, 23,* 115–125.

Erikson, E. H. (1950). *Childhood and society.* New York: Norton.

Erikson, E. H. (1968). *Identity: Youth and crisis.* New York: Norton.

Erikson, E. H. (1975). *Life history and the historical moment.* New York: Norton.

Ervin-Tripp, S. (1979). Children's verbal turn taking. In E. Ochs & B. Schieffelin (eds), *Developmental pragmatics* (pp. 391–414). New York: Academic Press.

Escorial, S., Juan-Espinosa, M. García, L. F., Rebollo, I., & Colom, R. (2002). Does *g* variance change in adulthood? Testing the age de-differentiation hypothesis across sex. *Personality and Individual Differences, 34,* 1525–1532.

Evans, D. W., & Gray, F. L. (2000). Compulsive-like behavior in individuals with Down syndrome: Its relation to mental age level, adaptive and maladaptive behavior. *Child Development, 71,* 288–300.

Evans, E. M., Schweingruber, H., & Stevenson, H. W. (2002). Gender differences in interest and knowledge acquisition: The United States, Taiwan and Japan. *Sex Roles, 47,* 153–167.

Evans, G. (2004). The environment of childhood poverty. *American Psychologist, 59,* 77–92.

Evans, G. W. (2003). A multimethodological analysis of cumulative risk and allostatic load among rural children. *Developmental Psychology, 39,* 924–933.

F

Fabes, R. A. & Eisenberg, N. (1996) *An examination of age and sex differences in prosocial behavior and empathy.* Unpublished data, Arizona State University.

Fabes, R. A., Eisenberg, N., Smith, M. C., & Murphy, B. (1996). Getting angry at peers: Associations with liking of the provocateur. *Child Development, 67,* 942–956.

Fabes, R. A., Martin, C. L. & Hanish, L. D. (2002, October). *The role of sex segregation in young children's prosocial behavior and disposition.* Paper presented at the Groningen Conference on Prosocial Dispositions and Solidarity, Groningen, The Netherlands.

Fabrizi, L., Slater, R., Worley, A., Meek, J., Boyd, S., Olhede, S., & Fitzgerald, M. (2011). A shift in sensory processing that enables the developing human brain to discriminate touch from pain. *Current Biology, 21*(18), 1552–1558.

Fagan, J. F., III (1992). Intelligence: A theoretical viewpoint. *Current Directions in Psychological Science, 1,* 82–86.

Fagan, J. F., III, Drotar, D., Berkoff, K., Peterson, N., Kiziri-Mayengo, R., Guay, L. et al. (1991). The Fagan test of infant intelligence: Cross-cultural and racial comparisons. *Journal of Developmental and Behavioral Pediatrics, 12,* 168.

Fagot, B. I. (1985a). Beyond the reinforcement principle: Another step toward understanding sex role development. *Developmental Psychology, 21,* 1097–1104.

Fagot, B. I. (1985b) Changes in thinking about early sex role development. *Developmental Review, 5,* 83–98.

Fagot, B. I., & Leinbach, M. D. (1989). The young child's gender schema: Environmental input, internal organization. *Child Development, 60,* 663–672.

Fagot, B. I., & Leinbach, M. D. (1992). Gender-role development in young children: From discrimination to labeling. *Developmental Review, 13,* 205–224.

Fairhurst, M. T., Löken, L., & Grossmann, T. (2014). Physiological and behavioral responses reveal 9-month-old infants' sensitivity to pleasant touch. *Psychological Science, 25*(5), 1124–1131.

Falbo, T., & Polit, D. F. (1986). Quantitative review of the only child literature: Research evidence and theory development. *Psychological Bulletin, 100,* 176–189.

Fantz, J. F. (1964). Visual experience in infants: Decreased attention to familiar patterns relative to novel ones. *Science, 146.*

Fantz, R. (1963) Pattern vision in newborn infants. *Science, 140,* 296–297.

Fantz, R. L. (1961). The origin of form perception. *Scientific American, 204,* 66–72.

Fantz, R. L. (1964). Visual experience in infants: Decreased attention to familiar patterns relative to novel ones. *Science, 146*(3644), 668–670.

Faraone, S. V., & Khan, S. A. (2006). Candidate gene studies of attention-deficit/ hyperactivity disorder. *Journal of Clinical Psychiatry, 67,* 13–20.

Farmer, H., Ciaunica, A., & Hamilton, A. F. de C. (2018). The functions of imitative behaviour in humans. *Mind & Language, 33*(4), 378–396.

Farr, R. H., Bruun, S. T., Doss, K. M., & Patterson, C. J. (2017). Children's gender-typed behavior from early to middle childhood in adoptive families with lesbian, gay, and heterosexual parents. *Sex Roles, 78,* 528–542.

Farroni, T., Csibra, G., Simion, F., & Johnson, M. H. (2002). Eye contact detection in humans from birth. *Proceedings of the National Academy of Sciences, 99*(14), 9602–9605.

Federal Interagency Forum on Child and Family Statistics (2007). Retrieved from http://www.childstats.gov/pubs.asp

Feinberg, M., & Hetherington, M. E. (2001). Differential parenting as within-family variable. *Journal of Family Psychology, 15,* 22–37.

Feinman, S., & Lewis, M. (1983). Social referencing at ten months: A second-order effect on infants' responses to strangers. *Child Development, 54,* 878–887.

Feiring, C., & Lewis, M. (1987). The ecology of some middle class families at dinner. *International Journal of Behavioral Development, 10,* 377–390.

Feldman, R., & Eidelman, A. I. (2003). Skin-to-skin contact (kangaroo care) accelerates autonomic and neurobehavioral maturation in preterm infants. *Developmental Medicine and Child Neurology, 45,* 274–281.

Fennell, C. T., Byers-Heinlein, K., & Werker, J. F. (2007). Using speech sounds to guide word learning: The case of bilingual infants. *Child Development, 78,* 1510–1525.

Fenson, L., Dale, P. S., Reznick, J. S., Bates, E., Thal, D. J., & Pethick, S. J. (1994). Variability in early communicative development. *Monographs of the Society for Research in Child Development, 59*(Serial No. 242).

Ferguson, T. J., & Rule, B. G. (1980). Effects of inferential sex, outcome severity and basis of responsibility on children's evaluations of aggressive acts. *Developmental Psychology, 16,* 141–146.

Fergusson, D. M., Horwood, L. J., & Ridder, E. (2005). Show me the child at seven: The consequences of conduct problems in childhood for psychosocial functioning in adulthood. *Journal of Child Psychology & Psychiatry, 46,* 837–849.

Fernald, A. (1992). Meaningful melodies in mothers' speech to infants. In H. Papousek, U. Jurgens & M. Papousek (eds), *Nonverbal vocal communication* (pp. 262–282). Cambridge: Cambridge University Press.

Fernald, A., & Kuhl, P. K. (1987). Acoustical determinants of infant preference for motherese speech. *Infant Behavior and Development, 10,* 279–293.

Fernald, A., & Mazzie, C. (1991). Prosody and focus in speech to infants and adults. *Developmental Psychology, 27,* 209–221.

Fernald, A., & Morikawa, H. (1993). Common themes and cultural variations in Japanese and American mothers' speech to infants. *Child Development, 64,* 636–637.

Fernandes, O., Sabharwal, M., Srailey, T., Pastuszak, A., Koren, G. & Einarson, T. (1998) Moderate to heavy caffeine consumption during pregnancy and relationship to spontaneous abortion and abnormal fetal growth: A meta-analysis. *Reproductive Toxicology, 12,* 435–444.

Fernyhough, C., & Fradley, E. (2005). Private speech on an executive task: Relations with task difficulty and task performance. *Cognitive Development, 20*(1), 103–120.

Field, T. M. (1978). Interaction behaviors of primary versus secondary caretaker fathers. *Developmental Psychology, 14,* 183–184.

Field, T. M. (1986). Affective responses to separation. In T. B. Brazelton & M. W. Yogman (eds), *Affective development in infancy* (pp. 125–144). Norwood, NJ: Ablex.

Field, T. M. (1990). *Infancy.* Cambridge, MA: Harvard University Press.

Field, T. M. (2001a) Massage therapy facilitates weight gain in preterm infants. *Current Directions in Psychological Science, 10,* 51–54.

Field, T. M. (2001b). *Touch.* Cambridge, MA: MIT Press.

Field, T. M., Diego, M., & Hernandez-Reif, M. (2007). Massage therapy research. *Developmental Review, 27,* 75–89.

Field, T. M., Schanberg, S. M., Scafidi, F., Bauer, C. R., Vega-Lahr, N., Garcia, R., . . . & Kuhn, C. M. (1986). Tactile/kinesthetic stimulation effects on preterm neonates. *Pediatrics, 77*(5), 654–658.

Field, T. M., Woodson, R., Greenberg, R., & Cohen, D. (1982). Discrimination and imitation of facial expression by neonates. *Science, 218*(4568), 179–181.

Fifer, W. P., Byrd, D. L., Kaku, M., Eigsti, I. M., Isler, J. R., Grose-Fifer, J., . . . & Balsam, P. D. (2010). Newborn infants learn during sleep. *Proceedings of the National Academy of Sciences, 107*(22), 10320–10323.

Filippetti, M. L., Johnson, M. H., Lloyd-Fox, S., Dragovic, D., & Farroni, T. (2013). Body perception in newborns. *Current Biology, 23*(23), 2413–2416.

Finkelstein, N. W., & Haskins, R. (1983). Kindergarten children prefer same color peers. *Child Development, 54,* 502–508.

Fisher, C., Hall, D. G., Rakowitz, S., & Gleitman, L. (1994). When it is better to receive than to give: Syntactic and conceptual constraints on vocabulary growth. In L. Gleitman & B. Landau (eds), *The acquisition of lexicon* (pp. 333–376). Cambridge, MA: MIT Press/Elsevier.

Fisher, J. (1990). Low body weight and weight loss in the aged. *Journal of the American Dietetic Association, 90,* 1697–1706.

Fisher-Thompson, D. (1990). Adult gender typing of children's toys. *Sex Roles, 23,* 291–303.

Fivush, R. (2011). The development of autobiographical memory. *Annual Review of Psychology, 62,* 559–582.

Fivush, R., & Hamond, N. R. (1989). Time and again: Effects of repetition and retention interval on two year olds' event recall. *Journal of Experimental Child Psychology, 47,* 259–273.

Fivush, R., & Sales, J. M. (2004). Children's memories of emotional events. In D. Reisberg & P. Hertel (eds), *Memory and emotion* (pp. 242–271). New York: Oxford University Press.

Fivush, R., Haden, C. & Reese, E. (1996) Remembering, recounting, and reminiscing: The development of autobiographical memory in social context. In D. C. Rubin (ed.), *Remembering our past: Studies in autobiographical memory* (pp. 341–359) Cambridge: Cambridge University Press.

Fivush, R., Haden, C. A., & Reese, E. (2006). Elaborating on elaborations: Role of maternal reminiscing style in cognitive and socioemotional development. *Child Development, 77,* 1568–1588.

Fivush, R., Hudson, J. & Nelson, K. (1984) Children's long-term memory for a novel event: An exploratory study. *Merrill-Palmer Quarterly, 30,* 303–316.

Flavell, J. H. (1963). *The developmental psychology of Jean Piaget.* Princeton, NJ: Van Nostrand.

Flavell, J. H. (1985). *Cognitive development.* Englewood Cliffs, NJ: Prentice Hall.

Flavell, J. H., Beach, D. R., & Chinsky, J. M. (1966). Spontaneous verbal rehearsal in a memory task as a function of age. *Child Development, 37,* 283–299.

Flavell, J. H., Friedricks, A. G., & Hoyt, J. D. (1970). Developmental changes in memorization processes. *Cognitive Psychology, 1,* 324–340.

Flavell, J. H., Green, F. L., & Flavell, E. R. (1995). Young children's knowledge about thinking. *Monographs of the Society for Research in Child Development, 60,* 243–256.

Flavell, J. H., Green, F. L., & Flavell, E. R. (1986). Development of knowledge about the appearance-reality distinction. *Monographs of the Society for Research in Child Development, 51(1),* i-v, 1–87.

Flavell, J. H., Miller, P. H. & Miller, S. A. (1993) *Cognitive development* (3rd edn). Englewood Cliffs, NJ: Prentice-Hall.

Fleischman, D. A., Wilson, R. S., Gabrieli, J. D. E., Bienias, J. L., & Bennett, D. A. (2004). Abstract: A longitudinal study of implicit and explicit memory in old persons. *Psychology and Aging, 19,* 617–625.

Fleming, A. S., Corter, C., Stallings, J., & Steiner, M. (2002). Testosterone and prolactin are associated with emotional responses to infant cries in new fathers. *Hormones and Behavior, 42,* 399–413.

Fleming, P., & Blair, P. S. (2007). Sudden infant death syndrome and parental smoking. *Early Human Development, 83*(11), 721–725.

Fleming, R. W. (2014). Visual perception of materials and their properties. *Vision research, 94,* 62–75.

Flensborg-Madsen, T., & Mortensen, E. L. (2018). Developmental milestones during the first three years as precursors of adult intelligence. *Developmental Psychology, 54*(8), 1434–1444.

Flynn, E., Pine, K. & Lewis, C. (2006). The microgenetic method: Time for change? *The Psychologist, 19* (3), 152–155.

Flynn, J. R. (1987). Massive IQ gains: What IQ tests really measure. *Psychological Bulletin, 101,* 171–191.

Flynn, J. R. (2007) *What is intelligence? Beyond the Flynn effect.* Cambridge: Cambridge University Press.

Fodor, J. A. (1983). *The modularity of mind.* Cambridge, MA: MIT Press.

Fogel, A. (1993). *Developing through relationships: Origins of communication, self, and culture.* Chicago: University of Chicago Press.

Fogel, A., Hsu, H., Shapiro, A. F., Nelson-Goens, G. C., & Secrist, C. (2006). Effects of normal and perturbed play on the duration and amplitude of different types of infant smiles. *Developmental Psychology, 42,* 459–473.

Fonagy, P. (2018). Attachment, trauma, and psychoanalysis: Where psychoanalysis meets neuroscience. In J. Canestri (ed.), *Early development and its disturbances.* London: Routledge.

Fonagy, P., Gergely, G., Jurist, E. L., & Target, M. (2002). *Affect regulation, mentalization and the development of the self.* Oxford, UK: Routledge.

Fonagy, P., Steele, H. & Steele, M. (1991) Maternal representations of attachment during pregnancy predict organization of infant-mother attachment at one year of age. *Child Development, 62,* 891–905.

Fontaine, N., Carbonneau, R., Barker, E. D., Vitaro, F., Hébert, M., Côté, S. M., et al. (2008). Girls' hyperactivity and physical aggression during childhood and adjustment problems in early adulthood. *Archives in General Psychiatry, 65,* 320–328.

Fonzi, A. F., Genta, M. L., Menesini, E., Bacchini, D., Bonino, S., & Constabile, A. (1999). Italy. In P. K. Smith, Y. Morita, J. Junger-Tas, D. Olweus, R. Catalano, & P. Slee (eds), *The nature of school bullying: A cross-national perspective* (pp. 140–156). New York: Routledge.

Förster, J., Epstude, K., & Ozelsel, A. (2009). Why love has wings and sex has not: How romantic reminders of love and sex influence creative and analytic thinking. *Personality and Social Psychology Bulletin, 35,* 1479–1491.

Förster, J., Friedman, R. S., & Liberman, N. (2004). Temporal construal effects on abstract and concrete thinking: Consequences for insight and creative cognition. *Journal of Personality and Social Psychology, 87*(2), 177–189.

Foulkes L., & Blakemore S. J. (2018). Studying individual differences in human adolescent brain development. *Nature Neuroscience, 21*(3), 315–323.

Foulkes, L., & Blakemore, S. J. (2018). Studying individual differences in human adolescent brain development. *Nature Neuroscience, 21,* 315–323.

Fox, H. E., Steinbrecher, M., Pessel, D., Inglis, J., Medvid, L., & Angel, E. (1978). Maternal ethanol ingestion and the occurrence of human fetal breathing movements. *American Journal of Obstetrics and Gynecology, 132,* 1327–1328.

Fox, N. A. (1991). If it's not left, it's right: Electroencephalograph asymmetry and the development of emotion. *American Psychologist, 46,* 863–872.

Fox, N. A., & Calkins, S. (2003). The development of self-control of emotions: Intrinsic and external influences. *Motivation and Emotion, 27,* 7–26.

Fox, N. A., & Davidson, R. J. (1988). Patterns of brain electrical activity during facial signs of emotion in 10-month-old infants. *Developmental Psychology, 24,* 230–236.

Fox, N. A., Calkins, S. D., & Bell, M. A. (1994). Neural plasticity and development in the first two years of life: Evidence from cognitive and socioemotional domains. *Development and Psychopathology, 6,* 677–696.

Francis, P. L., Self, P. A., & Horowitz, F. D. (1987). The behavioral assessment of the neonate: An overview. In J. Osofsky (ed.), *Handbook of infancy* (2nd edn). New York: Wiley.

Francks, C., Maegawa, S., Lauren, J., Abrahams, B., Velayos-Baeza, A., Medland, S. E. et al. (2007) LRRTMI on chromosome 2p12 is a maternally suppressed gene that is associated with handedness and schizophrenia. *Molecular Psychiatry, 12,* 1129–1139.

Franco, F., & Butterworth, G. (1996). Pointing and social awareness: Declaring and requesting in the second year. *Journal of Child Language, 23,* 307–336.

Franco, S. J., & Müller, U. (2013). Shaping our minds: Stem and progenitor cell diversity in the mammalian neocortex. *Neuron, 77*(1), 19–34.

Franić, S., Middeldorp, C. M., Dolan, C. V., Ligthart, L., & Boomsma, D. I. (2010). Childhood and adolescent anxiety and depression: Beyond heritability. *Journal of the American Academy of Child & Adolescent Psychiatry, 49*(8), 820–829.

Franklin, A. V., King, M. K., Palomo, V., Martinez, A., McMahon, L. L., & Jope, R. S. (2014). Glycogen synthase kinase-3 inhibitors reverse deficits in long-term potentiation and cognition in fragile X mice. *Biological Psychiatry, 75,* 198–206.

Franklin, N. C., & Tate, C. A. (2009). Lifestyle and successful aging: An overview. *American Journal of Lifestyle Medicine, 3,* 6–11.

Fredrickson, D. D. (1993). Breastfeeding research priorities, opportunities, and study criteria: What have we learned from the smoking trail. *Journal of Human Lactation, 3,* 147–150.

Freeman, M. P., Smith, K. W., Freeman, S. A., McElroy, S. L., Kmetz, G. E., Wright, R., & Keck, P. E. Jr (2002). The impact of reproductive events on the course of bipolar disorder in women. *Journal of Clinical Psychiatry, 63,* 284–287.

French, D. C. (1990). Heterogeneity of peer rejected girls. *Child Development, 61,* 2028–2031.

French, R. M., Mareschal, D., Mermillod, M., & Quinn, P. C. (2004). The role of bottom-up processing in perceptual categorization by 3- to 4-month old infants: Simulations and data. *Journal of Experimental Psychology: General, 133,* 382–397.

Frey, K. S., & Ruble, D. N. (1992). Gender constancy and the 'cost' of sex-typed behavior: A test of the conflict hypothesis. *Developmental Psychology, 28,* 714–721.

Frick, P. J., & Dickens, C. (2006). Current perspectives on conduct disorder. *Current Psychiatry Reports, 8,* 59–72.

Frick, P. J., Stickle, T. R., Dandreaux, D. M., Farrell, J. M., & Kimonis, E. R. (2005). Callous-unemotional traits in predicting the severity and stability of conduct problems and delinquency. *Journal of Abnormal Child Psychology, 33,* 471–487.

Frick, P., O'Brien, B., Wootton, J., & McBurnett, K. (1994). Psychopathy and conduct problems in children. *Journal of Abnormal Psychology, 103,* 700–707.

Friedman, J. M. & Polifka, J. E. (1996) *The effects of drugs on the fetus and the nursing infant.* Baltimore: Johns Hopkins University Press.

Friedman, R., & Förster, J. (2008). Activation and measurement of motivational states. In A. Elliott (ed.), *Handbook of approach and avoidance motivation* (pp. 235–246). Mawah, NJ: Lawrence Erlbaum Associates.

Friedman, S. D., Shaw, D. W., Artru, A. A., Dawson, G., Petropoulos, H., & Dager, S. R. (2006). Gray and white matter brain chemistry in young children with autism. *Archives of General Psychiatry, 63*(7), 786–794.

Friedman, S. D., Shaw, D. W., Artru, A. A., Richards, T. L., Gardner, J., Dawson, G., et al. (2003). Regional brain chemical alterations in young children with autism spectrum disorder. *Neurology, 60,* 100–107.

Friedrich, L. K., & Stein, A. H. (1973). Aggressive and prosocial television programs and the natural behavior of preschool children. *Monographs of the Society for Research in Child Development, 38* (Serial No. 151).

Frith, C. D. (2007). The social brain? *Philosophical Transactions of the Royal Society of London B: Biological Sciences, 362*(1480), 671–678.

Frith, C. D. (2007). The social brain?. *Philosophical Transactions of the Royal Society of London B: Biological Sciences, 362*(1480), 671–678.

Frith, U. (1989). *Autism: Explaining the enigma.* Oxford: Blackwell.

Frosch, C. A., & Mangelsdorf, S. C. (2001). Marital behavior, parenting behavior and multiple reports of preschoolers' behavior problems: Mediation or moderation. *Developmental Psychology, 37,* 502–519.

Frosch, C. A., Mangelsdorf, S., & McHale, J. L. (2000). Marital behavior and the security of preschool-parent attachment relationships. *Journal of Family Psychology, 14,* 1438–1449.

Fry, C. L. (1985). Culture, behaviour, and aging in the comparative perspective. In J. E. Birren & K. W. Schaie (eds), *Handbook of the psychology of aging* (pp. 216–244). New York: Van Nostrand Reinhold.

Furman, W., & Gavin, L. A. (1989). Peers influence on adjustment and development. In T. J. Berndt & G. W. Ladd (eds), *Peer relationships in child development* (pp. 319–340). New York: Wiley.

Furman, W., Simon, V. A., Shaffer, L., & Bouchey, H. A. (2002). Adolescents' working models and styles for relationships with parents, friends, and romantic partners. *Child Development, 73,* 241–255.

Furnham, A., & Chamorro-Premuzic, T. (2004). Personality and intelligence as predictors of statistics examination grades. *Personality and Individual Differences, 37,* 943–955.

Furstenberg, F. F., Cook, T., Eccles, J., Elder, G., & Sameroff, A. (1999). *Managing to make it.* Chicago: University of Chicago Press.

Fusaro, M., & Harris, P. L. (2008). Children assess informant reliability using bystanders' non-verbal cues. *Developmental Science, 11,* 771–777.

Galen, B. R., & Underwood, M. K. (1997). A developmental investigation of social aggression among children. *Developmental Psychology, 33*, 589–600.

Gallace, A., & Spence, C. (2014). *In touch with the future: The sense of touch from cognitive neuroscience to virtual reality.* Oxford: Oxford University Press.

Gallaway, C., & Richards, B. J. (1994). *Input and interaction in language acquisition.* Cambridge: Cambridge University Press.

Gallo, J. J., Anthony, J., & Muthén, B. (1994). Age differences in the symptoms of depression: A latent trait analysis. *Journals of Gerontology: Psychological Sciences, 49*, 251–264.

Ganger, J., & Brent, M. R. (2004). Reexamining the vocabulary spurt. *Developmental Psychology, 40*, 621–632.

Garbarino, J. (1982) Sociocultural risk: Dangers to competence. In C. Kopp & J. Krakow (eds), *Child development in a social context* (pp. 630–685) Reading, MA: Addison-Wesley.

Garbarino, J. (1995). *Raising children in a socially toxic environment.* San Francisco: Jossey-Bass.

Garber, J. & Martin, N. C. (2002) Negative cognitions in offspring of depressed parents: Mechanisms of risk. In S. H. Goodman & I. N. Gotlib (eds), *Children of depressed parents* (pp. 121–154) Washington, DC: American Psychological Association.

Garcia Coll, C. T. (1990). Developmental outcome of minority infants: A process-oriented look into our beginnings. *Child Development, 61*, 270–289.

Garcia, M. M., Shaw, D. S., Winslow, E. B., & Yaggi, K. E. (2000). Destructive sibling conflict and the development of conduct problems in young boys. *Developmental Psychology, 36*, 44–53.

Gardner, H. (1983; 1993). *Frames of mind: The theory of multiple intelligences.* New York: Basic Books.

Gardner, H. (1999). *Intelligence reframed.* New York: Basic Books.

Gardner, H. (2004) *Frames of mind: The theory of multiple intelligences.* New York: Basic Books.

Gardner, H. (2006). *Multiple intelligences: New horizons.* New York: Basic Books.

Gardner, H. (2011). *Frames of mind: The theory of multiple intelligences.* New York: Basic Books.

Gardner, M., & Steinberg, L. (2005). Peer influence on risk taking, risk preference, and risky decision making in adolescence and adulthood: An experimental study. *Developmental Psychology, 41*, 625–635. doi: 10.1037/0012-1649.41.4.625

Gardner, R. J. M. & Sutherland, G. R. (1996) *Chromosome abnormalities and genetic counseling* (2nd edn). Oxford: Oxford University Press.

Garlick, D. (2003). Integrating brain science research with intelligence research. *Current Directions in Psychological Science, 12*, 185–189.

Garner, P. W., & Power, T. G. (1996). Preschoolers' emotional control in the disappointment paradigm and its relation to temperament, emotional knowledge and family expressiveness. *Child Development, 67*, 1406–1429.

Garner, P. W., Jones, D. C., & Palmer, D. (1994). Social cognitive correlates of preschool children's sibling caregiving behavior. *Developmental Psychology, 30*, 905–911.

Garon, N., Bryson, S. E., & Smith, I. M. (2008). Executive function in preschoolers: A review using an integrative framework. *Psychological Bulletin, 134*(1), 31–60.

Garrett, A. S., Menon, V., Mackenzie, K., & Reiss, A. (2004). Here's looking at you kid: Neural systems underlying face and gaze processing in fragile X syndrome. *Archives of General Psychiatry, 61*, 281–288.

Garrett, H. E., (1946). A developmental theory of intelligence. *American Psychologist 1*, 372–378.

Garthe, A., Roeder, I., & Kempermann, G. (2016). Mice in an enriched environment learn more flexibly because of adult hippocampal neurogenesis. *Hippocampus, 26*(2), 261–271.

Garton, A. F. (2004). *Exploring cognitive development: The child as problem solver.* Malden, MA: Blackwell.

Garvey, C. (1990). *Play.* Cambridge, MA: Harvard University Press.

Gathercole, S. (2008). Working memory in the classroom. *The Psychologist, 21*, 382–385.

Gathercole, S. E. (1999). Cognitive approaches to the development of short-term memory. *Trends in Cognitive Sciences, 3*(11), 410–419.

Gathercole, S., & Alloway, T. (2008). *Working memory and learning: A practical guide for teachers.* London: Sage.

Gathercole, S., & Pickering, S. J. (2000). Working memory deficits in children with low achievements in the national curriculum at 7 years of age. *British Journal of Educational Psychology, 70*, 177–194.

Gauvain, M. (1992). Social influences on the development of planning in advance and during action. *International Journal of Behavioral Development, 15*, 377–398.

Gauvain, M. (2001). *The sociocultural context of cognitive development.* New York: Guilford Press.

Gauvain, M. (2005). Sociocultural contexts of learning. In *Learning in cultural context* (pp. 11–40). Boston, MA: Springer.

Gauvain, M., & Perez, S. M. (2007). The socialization of cognition. In J. Grusec & P. Hastings (Eds.), *Handbook of socialization: Theory and research*(pp. 588–613). New York: Guilford.

Gauvain, M., & Rogoff, B. (1989). Collaborative problem solving and children's planning skills. *Developmental Psychology, 25*, 139–151.

Gazelle, H., & Ladd, G. W. (2003). Anxious solitude and peer exclusion: A diathesis-stress model of internalizing trajectories in childhood. *Child Development, 74*, 257–278.

Ge, X., Brody, G., Conger, R., Simons, R., & Murry, V. M. (2002). Contextual amplification of pubertal transition effects on deviant peer affiliation and externalizing behavior among African-American children. *Developmental Psychology, 38*, 42–54.

Ge, X., Conger, R. D., & Elder, G. H., Jr. (2001a). Pubertal transition, stressful life events, and the emergence of gender differences in adolescent depressive symptoms. *Developmental Psychology, 37*, 404–417.

Ge, X., Conger, R., & Elder, G. (1996). Coming of age too early: Pubertal influences on girls' vulnerability to psychological distress. *Child Development, 62*, 3386–3400.

Ge, X., Conger, R., & Elder, G. H. (2001b). The relation between puberty and psychological distress in adolescent boys. *Journal of Research on Adolescence, 11*, 49–70.

Geary, D. C. (2006a). Coevolution of paternal investment and cuckoldry in humans. In T. K. Shackelford & S. Platek (eds), *Female infidelity and paternal uncertainty* (pp. 14–34). New York: Cambridge University Press.

Geary, D. C. (2006b). Development of mathematical understanding. In W. Damon & R. M. Lerner (Series eds) & D. Kuhn & R. S. Siegler (Vol. eds), *Handbook of child psychology: Vol. 2. Cognition, perception, and language* (6th edn, pp. 777–810). New York: Wiley.

Geary, D. C., Fan, L., & Bow-Thomas, C. C. (1992). Numerical cognition: Loci of ability differences comparing children from China and the United States. *Psychological Science, 3*, 180–185.

Gelfand, D. M., & Drew, C. J. (2003). *Understanding child behavior disorders* (4th edn). Belmont, CA: Wadsworth.

Gelfand, D. M., Jensen, W. R., & Drew, C. J. (1997). *Understanding child behavior disorders* (3rd edn). Fort Worth, TX: Harcourt Brace.

Gelman, R., & Baillargeon, R. (1983). A review of some Piagetian concepts. In P. H. Mussen (Series Ed.) & J. H. Flavell & E. M. Markman (Vol. eds), *Handbook of child psychology: Cognitive development* (Vol. 3, pp. 167–230). New York: Wiley.

Gelman, R., & Gallistel, C. R. (1978). *The child's understanding of number*. Cambridge, MA: Harvard University Press.

Gelman, R., & Shatz, M. (1977). Appropriate speech adjustments: The operation of conversational restraints on talk to two-year-olds. In M. Lewis & L. Rosenblum (eds), *Interaction, conversation and the development of language* (pp. 27–61). New York: Wiley.

Gentner, D. (1982). Why nouns are learned before verbs: Linguistic relativity versus natural partitioning. In S. A. Kuczaj II (ed.), *Language development: Vol. 2. Language, thought, and culture* (pp. 301–332). Hillsdale, NJ: Erlbaum.

Gentner, D., & Holyoak, K. J. (1997). Reasoning and learning by analogy: Introduction. *American Psychologist, 52*, 32–34.

Gergely, G. & Csibra, G. (2003). Teleological reasoning in infancy: The naive theory of rational action. *Trends in Cognitive Sciences, 7*, 287–292.

Gergely, G., Bekkering, H., & Király, I. (2002). Developmental psychology: Rational imitation in preverbal infants. *Nature, 415*(6873), 755.

Gergely, G., Bekkering, H., & Király, I. (2002). Rational imitation in preverbal infants. *Nature, 415*(6873), 755.

Gershoff, E. T. (2002) Corporal punishment by parents and associated child behaviors and experiences: A meta-analytic and theoretical review. *Psychological Bulletin, 128*, 539–579.

Gerstadt, C. L., Hong, Y. J., & Diamond, A. (1994). The relationship between cognition and action: Performance of 3.5–7 years old on Stroop-like day–night test. *Cognition, 53*, 129–153.

Gervain, J., Mehler, J., Werker, J. F., Nelson, C. A., Csibra, G., Lloyd-Fox, S., Shukla, M., & Aslin, R. A. (2011). Near-infrared spectroscopy: A report from the McDonnell infant methodology consortium. *Developmental Cognitive Neuroscience, 1*(1), 22–46.

Gesell, A., & Ames, L. B. (1940). The ontogenetic organization of prone behavior in human infancy. *The Journal of Genetic Psychology, 56*, 247–263.

Gessell, A., & Ilg, F. L. (1949). *Child development: An introduction to the study of human growth, Volumes 1-2.* New York: Harper.

Gewirtz, J. L. (1967). The course of infant smiling in four childrearing environments in Israel. In B. M. Foss (ed.), *Determinants of infant behavior* (Vol. 3, pp. 105–248). London: Methuen.

Gewirtz, J. L. (1969). Mechanisms of social learning: Some roles of stimulation and behavior in early human development. In D. A. Goslin (ed.), *Handbook of socialization theory and research* (pp. 121–162). Chicago: Rand McNally.

Gewirtz, J. L., & Peláez-Nogueras, B. F. (1992). Skinner's legacy to human infant behavior and development. *American Psychologist, 47*, 1411–1422.

Gibbs, J. C., Potter, G. B., & Goldstein, A. P. (1995). *The EQUIP program: Teaching youth to think and act responsibly through a peer helping approach.* Champaign, IL: Research Press.

Gibson, E. J., & Walk, R. D. (1960). The 'visual cliff'. *Scientific American, 202*, 64.

Gibson, E. J. (1969). *Principles of perceptual learning and development.* New York: Appleton-Century-Crofts.

Gibson, J. J. (1979). *The ecological approach to visual perception.* Boston: MA: Houghton Mifflin.

Gick, M. L., & Holyoak, K. J. (1980). Analogical problem solving. *Cognitive Psychology, 12*, 306–355.

Giedd, J. N. (2004). Structural magnetic resonance imaging of the adolescent brain. *Annals of the New York Academy of Sciences, 1021*(1), 77–85.

Giedd, J. N., Blumenthal, J., Jeffries, N. O., Castellanos, F. X., Liu, H., Zijdenbos, A., . . . & Rapoport, J. L. (1999). Brain development during childhood and adolescence: A longitudinal MRI study. *Nature Neuroscience, 2*(10), 861.

Gifford-Smith, M. E., & Rabiner, D. L. (2004). Social information processing and children's social adjustment. In J. Kupersmidt & K. A. Dodge (eds), *Children's peer relations: From development to intervention to policy: A festschrift to honor John D. Coie* (pp. 61–79). Washington, DC: American Psychological Association.

Giles, J. W., & Heyman, G. D. (2004). When to cry over spilled milk: Young children's use of category information to guide inferences about ambiguous behavior. *Journal of Cognition and Development, 5*, 359–382.

Gillham, J. E., Reivich, K. J., Jaycox, L. H., & Seligman, M. E. (1995). Prevention of depressive symptoms in schoolchildren: Two-year follow-up. *Psychological Science, 6*, 343–351.

Gilligan, C. (1982). *In a different voice.* Cambridge, MA: Harvard University Press.

Gilliland, F. D., Li, Y. F., & Peters, J. M. (2001). Effects of maternal smoking during pregnancy and environmental tobacco smoke in asthma and wheezing in children. *American Journal of Respiratory and Critical Care Medicine, 163*, 429–436.

Gilliom, M., Shaw, D., Beck, J. E., Shonberg, M., & Lukon, J. L. (2002). Anger regulation in disadvantaged preschool boys: Strategies, antecedents, and the development of self-control. *Developmental Psychology, 38*, 222–235.

Giusti, R. M., Iwamoto, K. & Hatch, E. E. (1995) Diethylstilbestrol revisited: A review of the long-term health effects. *Annals of Internal Medicine, 122*, 778–788.

Gladwin, T. (1970). *East is a big bird.* Cambridge, MA: Harvard University Press.

Gleason, T. R., Gower, A. L., Hohmann, L. M., & Gleason, T. C. (2005). Temperament and friendship in preschool-aged children. *International Journal of Behavioral Development, 29*, 336–344.

Gleitman, L. (1990). The structural sources of verb meanings. *Language Acquisition, 1*, 3–55.

Glucksberg, S., Krauss, R., & Higgins, E. T. (1975). The development of referential communication skills. In F. D. Horowitz (ed.), *Review of child development research* (Vol. 4, pp. 305–345). Chicago: University of Chicago Press.

Goddings, A. L., Mills, K. L., Clasen, L. S., Giedd, J. N., Viner, R. M., & Blakemore, S. J. (2014). The influence of puberty on subcortical brain development. *Neuroimage, 88*, 242–251.

Gogtay, N., Giedd, J. N., Lusk, L., Hayashi, K. M., Greenstein, D., Vaituzis, A. C., . . . & Rapoport, J. L. (2004). Dynamic mapping of human cortical development during childhood through early adulthood. *Proceedings of the National Academy of Sciences, 101*(21), 8174–8179.

Goksan, S., Hartley, C., Emery, F., Cockrill, N., Poorun, R., Moultrie, F., . . . & Clare, S. (2015). fMRI reveals neural activity overlap between adult and infant pain. *Elife, 4*.

Goldbaum, S., Craig, W. M., Pepler, D., & Connolly, J. (2003). Developmental trajectories of victimization: Identifying risk and protective factors. *Journal of Applied School Psychology, 19*, 59–68.

Goldberg J. H., Breckenridge J. N., & Sheikh J. I. (2004). Age differences in symptoms of depression and anxiety: Examining behavioral medicine outpatients. *Journal of Behavioral Medicine, 26*, 119–132.

Goldberg, S., & DeVitto, B. (2002). Parenting children born premature. In M. Bornstein (ed.), *Handbook of parenting* (Vol. 1, 2nd edn, pp. 329–354) Mahwah, NJ: Erlbaum.

Golding, J., Pembrey, M., Jones, R., & ALSPAC Study Team (2001). ALSPAC—the Avon Longitudinal Study of Parents and Children. I. Study methodology. *Paediatric and Perinatal Epidemiology, 15*, 74–87.

Goldin-Meadow, S. (2006). Nonverbal communication: The hand's role in talking and thinking. In W. Damon & R. M. Lerner (Series eds) & D. Kuhn & R. Siegler (Vol. eds), *Handbook of child psychology* (Vol. 2, 6th edn, pp. 336–371). New York: Wiley.

Goldin-Meadow, S. (2007). Pointing sets the stage for language learning and creating language. *Child Development, 78*, 741–745.

Goldstein, N. (1990, January). Explaining socioeconomic differences in children's cognitive test scores. Unpublished manuscript, Malcolm Weiner Center for Social Policy, J. F. Kennedy School of Government, Harvard University.

Goleman, D. (1995) *Emotional intelligence*. New York: Bantam Books.

Goleman, D. (2006). *Social intelligence: Beyond IQ, beyond emotional intelligence*. New York: Bantam Books.

Golinkoff, R. M. (1983). The preverbal negotiation of failed messages: Insights into the transition period. In R. M. Golinkoff (ed.), *The transition from prelinguistic to linguistic communication* (pp. 57–78). Hillsdale, NJ: Erlbaum.

Golinkoff, R. M., & Hirsh-Pasek, K. (1999). *How babies talk*. New York: Penguin Group.

Golinkoff, R. M., Hirsh-Pasek, K. & Schweisguth, M. A. (2001). A reappraisal of young children's knowledge of grammatical morphemes. In J. Weissenborn & B. Hoehle (eds), *Approaches to bootstrapping: Phonological, syntactic, and neurophysical aspects of early language acquisition* (pp. 167–188). Amsterdam & Philadelphia: John Benjamins.

Golinkoff, R. M., Hirsh-Pasek, K., Bailey, L. M., & Wenger, N. R. (1992). Young children and adults use lexical principles to learn new words. *Developmental Psychology, 28*, 99–108.

Golombok, S., Murray, C., Jadva, V., MacCallum, F., & Lycett, E. (2004). Families created through surrogacy arrangements: Parent-child relationships in the first year of life. *Developmental Psychology, 40*, 400–411.

Gomez, J. C. (2004). *Apes, monkeys, children, and the growth of mind*. Cambridge, MA: Harvard University Press.

Goncz, L., & Kodzopeljic, J. (1991). Exposure to two languages in the preschool period: Metalinguistic development and the acquisition of reading. *Journal of Multilingual and Multicultural Development, 12*, 137–142.

Gooden, A. M., & Gooden, M. A. (2001). Gender representation in notable children's picture books: 1995–1999. *Sex Roles, 45*, 89–101.

Goodglass, H. (1993). *Understanding aphasia*. New York: Academic Press.

Goodman, G. S., Bottoms, B. L., Schwartz-Kenney, B. M., & Rudy, L. (1991). Children's testimony for a stressful event: Improving children's reports. *Journal of Narrative and Life History, 1*, 69–99.

Goodman, J. C. (1989). The development of context effects of spoken word recognition. Unpublished doctoral dissertation, University of Chicago.

Goodman, J. H. (2008). Influence of maternal postpartum depression on fathers and on father-infant interaction. *Infant Mental Health Journal, 29*, 624–643.

Goodman, S. H., & Gotlib, I. N. (eds) (2002). *Children of depressed parents*. Washington, DC: American Psychological Association.

Gopnik, A. (2017). How babies think. *Scientific American, 26*, 48–53.

Gopnik, A., & Astington, J. W. (1988). Children's understanding of representational change and its relation to the understanding of false belief and the appearance-reality distinction. *Child Development, 59*(1), 26–37.

Gopnik, A., & Astington, J. W. (1988). Children's understanding of representational change and its relation to the understanding of false. *Child Development, 59*(1).

Gopnik, A., & Tenenbaum, J. B. (2007). Bayesian networks, Bayesian learning and cognitive development. *Developmental Science, 10*(3), 281–287.

Gopnik, A., & Wellman, H. M. (2012). Reconstructing constructivism: Causal models, Bayesian learning mechanisms, and the theory theory. *Psychological Bulletin, 138*(6), 1085.

Gosden, R. (1996). *Cheating time: Science, sex, and aging*. New York: W. H. Freeman & Co.

Gosselin, P., Perron, M., Legault, M., & Campanella, P. (2002). Children's and adults' knowledge of the distinction between enjoyment and non-enjoyment smiles. *Journal of Nonverbal Behavior, 26*, 83–108.

Goswami, U. & Bryant, P. (1990) *Phonological skills and learning to read*. Hillsdale, NJ: Erlbaum.

Goswami, U. (1995). Transitive relational mappings in 3- and 4-year-olds: The analogy of Goldilocks and the Three Bears. *Child Development, 66*, 877–892.

Goswami, U. (2001). Analogical reasoning in children. In D. Gentner, K. Holyoak & B. Kokinov (eds), *Analogy: Interdisciplinary perspectives* (pp. 437–470). Cambridge, MA: MIT Press.

Goswami, U., & Brown, A. L. (1990). Higher-order structure and relational reasoning: Contrasting analogical and thematic relations. *Cognition, 36*, 207–226.

Goswami, U., & Bryant, P. (2015). *Phonological skills and learning to read* (Classic edn). Abingdon: Routledge.

Gotlieb, I. H., Joormann, J., Minor, K. L. & Cooney, R. E. (2006) Cognitive and biological functioning in children at risk for depression. In T. Canli (ed.), *Biology* *of personality and individual differences.* New York: Guilford Press.

Goto M. (1997). Hierarchical deterioration of body systems in Werner's syndrome: Implications for normal aging. *Mechanisms of Aging and Development 98,* 239–254.

Gottesman, I. I. (1963). Genetic aspects of intelligent behavior. In N. Ellis (ed.), *Handbook of mental deficiency: Psychological theory and research* (pp. 79–96). New York: McGraw-Hill.

Gottfredson, L. S. (ed.) (1997). Intelligence and social policy [Special issue]. *Intelligence, 24,* 1–320.

Gottfried, A. E., Gottfried, A. W., & Bathurst, K. (2002). Maternal and dual-earner employment status and parenting. In M. Bornstein (ed.) *Handbook of parenting* (rev. edn, pp. 207–230). Mahwah, NJ: Erlbaum.

Gottlieb, G. (1971). Ontogenesis of sensory function in birds and mammals. E. Tobach, L. R. Aronson, & E. Shaw (eds.) *The biopsychology of development* (pp. 67–128). New York: Academ

Gottlieb, G. (1991). Experiential canalization of behavioral development theory. *Developmental Psychology, 27,* 4–13.

Gottlieb, G. (1992). *Individual development and evolution: The genesis of novel behavior.* New York: Oxford University Press.

Gottlieb, G. (1995). Some conceptual deficiencies in 'developmental' behavior genetics. *Human Development, 38,* 131–141.

Gottlieb, G. (2007). Probabilistic epigenesis. *Developmental Science, 10,* 1–11.

Gottlieb, G., & Lickliter, R. (2004). The various roles of animal models in understanding human development. *Social Development, 13,* 311–325.

Gottman, J. M. (1983). How children become friends. *Monographs of the Society for Research in Child Development, 48* (Serial No. 201).

Gottman, J. M., & Mettetal, G. (1986). Speculations about social and affective development: Friendship and acquaintanceship through adolescence. In J. M. Gottman & J. G. Parker (eds), *Studies in emotion and social interaction. Conversations of friends: Speculations on affective development* (pp. 192–237). New York: Cambridge University Press.

Gottman, J. M., & Parker, J. G. (eds) (1986). *The conversations of friends.* New York: Cambridge University Press.

Gottman, J. M., Katz, L., & Hooven, C. (1996). *Meta-emotion.* Mahwah, NJ: Erlbaum.

Gould, E., Reeves, A. J., Graziano, M. S., & Gross, C. G. (1999). Neurogenesis in the neocortex of adult primates. *Science, 286,* 548–555.

Gould, K. L., Coventry, W. L., Olson, R. K., & Byrne, B. (2018). Gene-environment interactions in ADHD: The roles of SES and chaos. *Journal of Abnormal Child Psychology, 46*(2), 251–263.

Graham, G. G. (1966). Growth during recovery from infantile malnutrition. *Journal of the American Medical Women's Association, 21,* 737–742.

Graham, S., & Hudley, C. (1994). Attributions of aggressive and nonaggressive African-American male early adolescents: A study of construct accessibility. *Developmental Psychology, 30,* 365–373.

Graham, S., Doubleday, C., & Guarino, P. A. (1984). The development of relations between perceived controllability and the emotions of pity, anger, and guilt. *Child Development, 55*(2), 561–565.

Granrud, C. E., & Yonas, A. (1984). Infant's perception of pictorially specified interposition. *Journal of Experimental Child Psychology, 37,* 500–511.

Grantham-McGregor, S. M., Powell, C. A., Walker, S. P. & Hines, J. H. (1991) Nutritional supplementation, psychological stimulation and mental development of stunted children: The Jamaican study. *Lancet, 338,* 1–5.

Gray, L., Watt, L., & Blass, E. M. (2000). Skin-to-skin contact is analgesic in healthy newborns. *Pediatrics, 105*(1), e14.

Green, J., Charman, T., Pickles, A., Wan, M. W., Elsabbagh, M., Slonims, V., . . . & Jones, E. J. (2015). Parent-mediated intervention versus no intervention for infants at high risk of autism: A parallel, single-blind, randomised trial. *The Lancet Psychiatry, 2*(2), 133–140.

Green, J., Pickles, A., Pasco, G., Bedford, R., Wan, M. W., Elsabbagh, M., . . . & Charman, T. (2017). Randomised trial of a parent-mediated intervention for infants at high risk for autism: longitudinal outcomes to age 3 years. *Journal of Child Psychology and Psychiatry, 58*(12), 1330–1340.

Greenberg, M. (1999). Attachment and psychopathology in childhood. In J. Cassidy & P. Shaver (eds), *Handbook of attachment* (pp. 449–456). New York: Guilford Press.

Greenberg, M. T., Kusche, C. A., & Riggs, N. (2004). The PATHS curriculum: Theory and research on neuro-cognitive development and school success. In J. E. Zins, R. P. Weissberg, M. C. Wang, & H. J. Walberg (eds), *Building academic success on social and emotional learning: What does the research say?* (pp. 170–188). New York: Teachers College Press.

Greenfield, P. M., & Childs, C. P. (1991). Developmental continuity in biocultural context. In R. Cohen & A. W. Siegel (eds.), *Context and*

development (pp. 135–160). Hillsdale, NJ: Erlbaum.

Greer, S. (1991). Psychological response to cancer and survival. *Psychological Medicine, 21,* 43–49.

Gregory, A. M. (2018). *Nodding off.* London: Bloomsbury Press.

Grella, C. (2006) The Drug Abuse Treatment Outcome Studies: Outcomes with adolescent substance abusers. In H. A. Liddle & C. L. Rowe (eds), *Adolescent substance abuse: Research and clinical issues.* (pp. 148–173) New York: Cambridge University Press.

Grief, E. B., & Gleason, J. B. (1980). Hi, thanks, and goodbye: More routine information. *Language in Society, 9,* 159–166.

Griffin, P. B., & Griffin, M. B. (1992). Fathers and childcare among the Cagayan Agta. In B. Hewlett (ed.), *Father-child relations: Cultural and biosocial contexts* (pp. 297–320). New York: Aldine de Gruyther.

Grigorenko, E. L., Sternberg, R. J., & Strauss, S. (2006). Practical intelligence and elementary-school teacher effectiveness in the United States and Israel: Measuring the predictive power of tacit knowledge. *Thinking Skills and Creativity, 1,* 14–33.

Grissmer, D. W., Williamson, S., Kirby, S. N., & Berends, M. (1998). Exploring the rapid rise in black achievement scores in the United States (1970–1990). In U. Neisser (ed.), *The rising curve: Long-term gains in IQ and related measures* (pp. 251–285). Washington, DC: American Psychological Association.

Gritz, E. R. (2004) Smoking and friendship influence in three ethnic groups. *Nicotine and Tobacco Research, 11,* 109–115.

Groen, G. J. & Parkman, J. M. (1972) A chronometric analysis of simple addition. *Psychological Review, 79,* 329–343.

Groholt, B., & Ekeberg, O. (2003). Suicide in young people under 15 years: Problems of classification. *Nordic Journal of Psychiatry, 57,* 411–417.

Gross, L. (2006) Evolution of neonatal imitation. *PLoS Biol.* **4**(9).

Grossman, I., Na, J., Varnum, M. E. W., Park, D. C., Kitayama, S. & Nisbett, R. E. (2010) Reasoning about social conflicts improves into old age. *PNAS, 107,* 7246–7250.

Grossmann, I., Na, J., Varnum, M. E. W., Park, D. C., Kitayama, S., & Nisbett, R. E. (2010). Reasoning about social conflicts improves into old age. *Proceedings of the National Academy of Sciences of the United States of America, 107,* 7246–7250.

Grossmann, K., Grossmann, K. E., & Kindler, H. (2005). Early care & the roots of attachment and partnership representations: The Bielefeld and Regensburg Longitudinal studies. In K. E. Grossmann, K. Grossmann & E. Waters (eds), *Attachment from infancy to adulthood* (pp. 98–136). New York: Guilford Press.

Groundwater-Smith, S., Dockett, S., & Bottrell, D. (2015). *Participatory research with children and young people.* London: Sage.

Groves, P. M., & Thompson, R. F. (1970). Habituation: A dual-process theory. *Psychological Review, 77,* 419–450.

Grusec, J. E., & Abramovitch, R. (1982). Imitation of peers and adults in a natural setting: A functional analysis. *Child Development, 53,* 636–642.

Grusec, J. E., & Davidov, M. (2007). Socialization in the family: The role of parents. In J. E. Grusec & P. Hastings (eds), *Handbook of socialization* (pp. 284–308). New York: Guilford Press.

Grych, J., & Fincham, F. F. (eds) (2001). *Interparental conflict and child development: Theory, research, and applications.* New York: Cambridge University Press.

Guedes, M., Santos, A. J., Ribeiro, O., Freitas, M., Rubin, K. H., & Veríssimo, M. (2018). Perceived attachment security to parents and peer victimization: Does adolescent's aggressive behaviour make a difference?

Guerra, N. G., & Huesmann, R. (2003). A cognitive-ecological model of aggression. *Revue Internationale de Psychologie Sociale, 17,* 177–203.

Guerra, N. G., Eron, L. D., Huesmann, L. R., Tolan, P. H., & Van Acker, R. (1997). A cognitive-ecological approach to the prevention and mitigation of violence and aggression in inner-city youth. In D. P. Fry & K. Bjorkqvist (eds), *Cultural variation in conflict resolution: Alternatives to violence* (pp. 199–213). Mahwah, NJ: Erlbaum.

Gulgoz, S., & Kagitcibasi, C. (2004). Intelligence and intelligence testing in Turkey. In R. J. Sternberg (ed.), *International handbook of intelligence* (pp. 248–269). New York: Cambridge University Press.

Gummerum, M., Hanoch, Y., & Keller, M. (2008). When child development meets economic game theory: An interdisciplinary approach to investigating social development. *Human Development, 51,* 235–261.

Gummerum, M., Leman, P. J., & Hollins, T. S. (2014). How do children share information in groups? *Developmental Psychology, 50,* 2105–2114. doi: 10.1037/a0037144

Gunnar, M. (1980). Control, warning signals and distress in infancy. *Developmental Psychology, 16,* 281–289.

Gunnar, M. (1998). Quality of early care and buffering of neuroendocrine stress reactions: Potential effects on the developing human brain. *Preventive Medicine, 27,* 208–211.

Gunnar, M. R., Malone, S. M., Vance, G., & Fisch, R. O. (1985). Coping with aversive stimulation in the neonatal period: Quiet sleep and plasma cortisol levels during recovery from circumcision. *Child Development, 56,* 824–834.

Gunnar, M., Leighton, K., & Peleaux, R. (1984). The effects of temporal predictability on year-old infants' reactions to potentially frightening toys. Unpublished manuscript, University of Minnesota, Minneapolis.

Guthrie, R., & Bickel, H. (1996). The introduction of newborn screening for phenylketonuria. *European Journal of Pediatrics, 155,* S4-S5.

Guttentag, R. E. (1995). Mental effort and motivation: Influences on children's memory strategy use. In F. E. Weinert & W. Schneider (eds), *Memory performance and competencies: Issues in growth and development* (pp. 207–224). Mahwah, NJ: Erlbaum.

Guyll, M., Spoth, R. L., Chao, W., Wickrama, K. A. S. & Russell, D. (2004) Family-focused risk moderations of substance use trajectories. *Journal of Family Psychology, 18,* 293–201.

Haden, C. A., Ornstein, P. A., Eckerman, C. O., & Didow, S. M. (2001). Mother-child conversational interactions as events unfold: Linkages to subsequent remembering. *Child Development, 72,* 1016–1031.

Haidt, J. (2001). The emotional dog and its rational tail: A social intuitionist approach to moral judgment. *Psychological Review, 108,* 814–834.

Haith, M. M., & Benson, J. (1998). Infant cognition. In W. Damon (Series ed.), D. Kuhn & R. Siegler (Vol. eds), *Handbook of child psychology: Vol. 2. Cognition, perception and language* (pp. 199–254). New York: Wiley.

Haith, M. M., Hazen, C. & Goodman, G. S. (1988) Expectation and anticipation of dynamic visual events by 3.5-month-old babies. *Child Development, 59,* 467–479.

Håkansson, K., Rovio, S., Helkala, E.-L., Vilska, A.-R., Winblad, B., Soininen, H., et al. (2009). Association between mid-life marital status and cognitive function in later life: Population based cohort study. *British Medical Journal, 339,* b2462.

Hakuta, K. (1986). *Mirror of language: The debate on bilingualism.* New York: Basic Books.

Halberstadt, A. G., Denham, S. A., & Dunsmore, J. C. (2001). Affective social competence. *Social Development, 10,* 79–119.

Halford, G. S., & Andrews, G. (2006). Reasoning and problem solving. In D. Kuhn & R. S. Siegler (Series eds) and W. Damon & R. M. Lerner (Vol. eds), *Handbook of child psychology: Vol. 2. Cognition, perception, and language* (6th edn, pp. 557–608). Hoboken, NJ: John Wiley & Sons.

Halit, H., de Haan, M., & Johnson, M. H. (2003). Cortical specialisation for face processing: Face-sensitive event-related potential components in 3- and 12-month-old infants. *NeuroImage 19*(3), 1180–1193.

Hall, G. S. (1898). Some aspects of the early sense of self. *The American Journal of Psychology, 9,* 351–395.

Halliday, M. A. K. (1975). *Learning how to mean: Exploration in the development of language.* London: Arnold.

Halpern, D. F. (2000). *Sex differences in cognitive abilities* (3rd edn). Mahwah, NJ: Erlbaum.

Halpern, D. F. (2004). A cognitive-process taxonomy for sex differences in cognitive abilities. *Current Directions in Psychological Science, 13,* 135–139.

Halpern, D. F., Benbow, C. P., Geary, D. C., Gur, R. C., Hyde, J. S., & Gernsbacher, M. A. (2007). The science of sex differences in science and mathematics. *Psychological Science in the Public Interest, 8,* 1–51.

Halverson, L. E., & Williams, K. (1985). Developmental sequences for hopping over distance: A prelongitudinal screening. *Research Quarterly for Exercise and Sport, 56,* 37–44.

Hamlin, J. K., Wynn, K., & Bloom, P. (2007). Social evaluation of preverbal infants. *Nature, 450,* 557–559.

Hammen, C. (1997). *Depression.* Washington, DC: Brunner/Mazel.

Hammen, C. (2002). Context of stress in families with depressed parents. In S. H. Goodman & I. Gotlib (eds), *Children of depressed parents* (pp. 175–202). Washington, DC: American Psychological Association.

Hammen, C. (2005). Stress and depression. *Annual Review of Clinical Psychology, 1,* 293–319.

Hammond, S. I. (2014). Children's early helping in action: Piagetian developmental theory and early prosocial behavior. *Frontiers in Psychology, 5,* 759.

Han, W. (2005). Maternal nonstandard work schedules and child cognitive outcomes. *Child Development, 76,* 137–154.

Hankin, B. L., Abramson, L. Y., Moffit, T. E., Silva, P. A., McGee, R., & Angell, K. E. (1998). Development of depression from preadolescence to adulthood: Emerging gender differences in a 10 year longitudinal study. *Journal of Abnormal Psychology, 107,* 128–140.

Hanna, E., & Meltzoff, A. N. (1993). Peer imitation by toddlers in laboratory, home, and day-care contexts: Implications for social learning and memory. *Developmental Psychology, 29,* 701–710.

Happé, F., & Frith, U. (2006). The weak coherence account: Detail-focused cognitive style in autism spectrum disorders. *Journal of Autism and Developmental Disorders, 36*(1), 5–25.

Happé, F., Ronald, A., & Plomin, R. (2006). Time to give up on a single explanation for autism. *Nature neuroscience, 9*(10), 1218.

Hardman, M. L., Drew, C. J., & Egan, M. W. (2002). *Human exceptionality: Society, school and family* (7th edn). Newton, MA: Allyn & Bacon.

Hare, R. D. (1985) *Scoring manual for the psychopathy checklist.* Unpublished manuscript. University of British Columbia, Vancouver, Canada.

Harkness, S., & Super, C. (2002). Culture and parenting. In M. Bornstein (ed.), *Handbook of parenting* (Vol. 2, 2nd edn, pp. 253–280). Hillsdale, NJ: Erlbaum.

Harland, T. (2003) Vygotsky's Zone of Proximal Development and Problem-based Learning: linking a theoretical concept with practice through action research. *Teaching in Higher Education, 8*, 263–272.

Harlow, H. F., & Zimmerman, R. R. (1959). Affectional responses in the infant monkey. *Science, 130*, 421–432.

Harris, B. (1979). Whatever happened to little Albert? *American Psychologist, 34*(2), 151–160.

Harris, J. (1995) Where is the child's environment? A group socialization theory of development. *Psychological Review, 102*, 458–489.

Harris, M., & Butterworth, G. (2002). *Developmental psychology: A student's handbook.* Hove: Psychology Press.

Harris, P. L. (1989). *Children and emotion.* New York: Basil Blackwell.

Harris, P. L. (2006). Social cognition. In W. Damon, R. M. Lerner, D. Kuhn, & R. Siegler (eds), *Handbook of child psychology: Vol. 2. Cognition, perception, and language* (pp. 811–858). New York: John Wiley & Sons.

Harris, P. L., Koenig, M. A., Corriveau, K. H., & Jaswal, V. K. (2018). Cognitive foundations of learning from testimony. *Annual Review of Psychology, 69.*

Harris, P. L., Olthof, T., Meerum Terwogt, M., & Hardman, C. E. (1987). Children's knowledge of the situations that provide emotions. *International Journal of Behavioral Development, 10*, 319–343.

Harrison, L. J., & Ungerer, J. A. (2002). Maternal employment and infant-mother attachment security at 12 months postpartum. *Developmental Psychology, 38*, 758–773.

Hart, B., & Risley, T. R. (1995). *Meaningful differences in the everyday experience of young American children.* Baltimore, MD: Brookes.

Hart, B., & Risley, T. R. (1999). *The social world of children learning to talk.* Baltimore, MD: Brookes.

Hart, D., & Fegley, S. (1995). Prosocial behavior and caring in adolescence: Relations to self-understanding and social judgment. *Child Development, 66*, 1346–1359.

Hart, S., Field, T., DelValle, C., & Letourneau, M. (1998). Infants protest their mothers attending to an infant-size doll. *Social Development, 7*, 54–61.

Harter, S. (1989). The development of self-representations. In W. Damon, N. Eisenberg (eds), *5th ed. vol 3, Handbook of child psychology, Social, emotional, and personality development* (pp. 553–617). Hoboken, NJ 2002: John Wiley & Sons.

Harter, S. (2006). The self. In W. Damon & R. M. Lerner (Series eds) & N. Eisenberg (Vol. ed.), *Handbook of child psychology* (6th edn, Vol. 3, pp. 505–570). New York: Wiley.

Harter, S., & Buddin, B. J. (1987). Children's understanding of the simultaneity of two emotions: A five-stage developmental acquisition sequence. *Developmental Psychology, 23*, 388–399.

Hartup, W. W. (1983). The peer relations. In E. M. Hetherington (ed.), P. H. Mussen (series ed.), *Handbook of child psychology: Vol. 4. Socialization, personality and social development* (pp. 103–196). New York: Wiley.

Hartup, W. W. (1996). The company they keep: Friendships and their developmental significance. *Child Development, 67*, 1–13.

Hartup, W. W., Laursen, B., Stewart, M. I., & Eastenson, A. (1988). Conflict and the friendship relations of young children. *Child Development, 59*, 1590–1600.

Harwood, L., & Fergusson, D. (1998). Breastfeeding and later cognitive and academic outcomes. *Pediatrics, 101*, 1–7.

Hasselhorn, M. (1992). Task dependency and the role of category typicality and metamemory in the development of an organizational strategy. *Child Development, 63*, 202–214.

Hastings, P. D., Rubin, K., & De Rose, L. (2005). Links among gender, inhibition, and parental socialization in the development of prosocial behavior. *Merrill-Palmer Quarterly, 51*, 501–527.

Hastings, P. D., Utendale, W. T., & Sullivan, C. (2007). The socialization of prosocial behavior. In J. Grusec & P. Hastings (eds), *The handbook of socialization* (pp. 638–664). New York: Guilford Press.

Haviv, S., & Leman, P. J. (2002). Moral decision-making in real life: Factors affecting moral orientation and behaviour justification. *Journal of Moral Education, 31*, 121–140.

Hawes, D. J., & Dadds, M. R. (2005). The treatment of conduct problems in children with callous-unemotional traits. *Journal of*

Consulting & Clinical Psychology, *73*, 737–741.

Hawes, D. J., & Dadds, M. R. (2007). Stability and malleability of callous-unemotional traits during treatment for childhood conduct problems. *Journal of Clinical Child and Adolescent Psychology, 35,* 347–355.

Hawkins, J., Pea, R. D., Glick, J., & Scribner, S. (1984). 'Merds that laugh don't like mushrooms': Evidence for deductive reasoning by preschoolers. *Developmental Psychology, 20,* 584–594.

Hawley, P. H., Johnson, S. E., Mize, J. A., & McNamara, K. A. (2007). Physical attractiveness in preschoolers: Relationships with power, status, aggression and social skills. *Journal of School Psychology, 45,* 499–521.

Hawslett, B., & Samter, W. (1997). *Children communicating: The first 5 years.* Mahwah, NJ: Erlbaum.

Hay, D. F. & Ross, H. S. (1982) The social nature of early con-flict. *Child Development, 53,* 105–113.

Hay, D. F. (1994). The development of prosocial behaviour. *Journal of Child Psychology and Psychiatry and Allied Disciplines, 35,* 29–71.

Hayashi, M. L., Rao, B. C., Seo, J., Choi, H., Dolan, B., Choi, S. et al. (2007). Inhibition of P21 activated kiase rescues symptoms of fragile X syndrome symptoms in mice. *Proceedings of the National Academy of Sciences, USA, 104,* 11489–11494.

Hayne, H., McDonald, S., & Barr, R. (1997). Developmental changes in the specificity of memory over the second year of life. *Infant Behavior and Development, 20,* 233–245.

Haynie, D. L. (2003). Contexts of risk? Explaining the link between girls' pubertal development and their delinquency involvement. *Social Forces, 82,* 355–397.

Healy, B. (1995) *A new perspective for women's health.* New York: Viking.

Heath, S. B. (1998). Working through language. In S. M. Hoyle & C. Temple Adger (eds), *Kids' talk: Strategic language use in later childhood* (pp. 217–240). Oxford: Oxford University Press.

Heckhausen, J., & Dweck, C. S. (eds) (1998). *Motivation and self-regulation across the life span.* New York: Cambridge University Press.

Hecox, K., & Deegan, D. M. (1985). Methodological issues in the study of auditory development. In G. Gottlieb & N. A. Krasnegor (eds), *Measurement of audition and vision in the first year of postnatal life: A methodological overview.* Norwood, NJ: Ablex.

Hedman, A. M., van Haren, N. E., Schnack, H. G., Kahn, R. S., & Hulshoff Pol, H. E. (2012). Human brain changes across the life span: A review of 56 longitudinal magnetic resonance imaging studies. *Human Brain Mapping, 33,* 1987–2002.

Helm, P., & Grolund, J. (1998). A halt in the secular trend toward earlier menarche in Denmark. *Acta Obstetrics and Gynecology Scandinavia, 77,* 198–200.

Helwig, C. C. (2003). Culture and the construction of concepts of personal autonomy and democratic decision making. In J. E. Jacobs & P. A. Klaczynski (eds), *The development of judgment and decision making in children and adolescents* (pp. 181–212). Mahwah, NJ: Erlbaum.

Helwig, C. C. (2006). Rights, civil liberties, and democracy across cultures. In M. Killen & J. G. Smetana (eds), *Handbook of moral development* (pp. 185–210). Mahwah, NJ: Erlbaum.

Hendrick, J., & Stange, T. (1991). Do actions speak louder than words? An effect of the functional use of language on dominant sex role behavior in boys and girls. *Early Childhood Research Quarterly, 6,* 565–576.

Henig, R. M. (2004). *Pandora's baby: How the first test tube baby sparked the reproductive revolution.* New York: Ecco.

Henker, B., & Whalen, C. K. (1999). The child with attention deficit/hyperactivity disorder in school and peer settings. In H. C. Quay & A. E. Hogan (eds). *Handbook of disruptive behavior disorders* (pp. 157–178). New York: Plenum Press.

Henrich, J., Heine, S. J., & Norenzayan, A. (2010). Most people are not WEIRD. *Nature, 466*(7302), 29.

Hepper, P. (1992) Fetal psychology: An embryonic science. In J. Niijhuis (ed.), *Fetal behavior: Developmental and perinatal aspects* (pp. 129–156) New York: Oxford University Press.

Hepper, P. (2004. July). *Handedness in the womb.* Paper presented at the Forum of European Neuroscience, Lisbon, Portugal.

Herbert, J., & Hayne, H. (2000). Memory retrieval by 18- to 30-month olds: Age-related changes in representational flexibility. *Developmental Psychology, 36,* 473–484.

Herbert, J., & Martinez, M. (2001). *Neural mechanisms underlying aggressive behaviour.* New York: Cambridge University Press.

Herbert, J., Gross, J., & Hayne, H. (2006). Age-related changes in deferred imitations between 6 and 9 months of age. *Infant Behavior and Development, 29,* 136–139.

Herman, L. M., & Uyeyama, R. K. (1999). The dolphin's grammatical competency: Comments on Kako. *Animal Learning and Behavior, 27,* 18–23.

Hermann, E., Call, J., Hernandez-Lloreda, M. V., Hare, B. & Tomasello, M. (2007). Humans have evolved specialized skills of social cognition: The cultural intelligence hypothesis. *Science, 317,* 1360–1366.

Herrera, N. C., Zajonc, R. B., Wieczorkowska, G., & Cichomski, B. (2003). Beliefs about birth rank and their reflection in reality. *Journal of Personality and Social Psychology, 85*, 142–150.

Herrnstein, R., & Murray, C. (1994). *The bell curve: Intelligence and class structure in American life.* New York: Basic Books.

Herting, M. M., & Sowell, E. R. (2017). Puberty and structural brain development in humans. *Frontiers in Neuroendocrinology, 44*, 122–137.

Hespos, S. J., & Baillargeon, R. (2001). Infants' knowledge about occlusion and containment events: A surprising discrepancy. *Psychological Science, 12*, 140–147.

Hess, E. H. (1959). Imprinting. *Science, 130*, 133–141.

Hess, R. D., & Shipman, V. (1967). Cognitive elements in maternal behavior. In J. Hill (ed.), *Minnesota symposia on child psychology* (pp. 57–81). Minneapolis: University of Minnesota Press.

Hess, T. M., Emery, L., & Queen, T. L. (2009). Task demands moderate stereotype threat effects on memory performance.

Hesse, E. (1999). The adult attachment interview: Historical and current perspectives. In J. Cassidy & P. Shaver (eds), *Handbook of attachment* (pp. 395–433). New York: Guilford Press.

Hetherington, E. M. (1966) Effects of paternal absence on sex-typed behaviors in Negro and white preadolescent males. *Journal of Personality and Social Psychology, 4*, 87–91.

Hetherington, E. M. (1991). Families, lies and videotapes. *Journal of Adolescent Research, 1*(4), 323–348.

Hetherington, E. M., & Kelly, J. (2002). *For better or for worse.* New York: Norton.

Hetherington, E. M., & Stanley-Hagan, M. (2002). Parenting in divorced, single-parent, and stepfamilies. In M. H. Bornstein (ed.), *Handbook of parenting* (2nd edn, pp. 287–316). Mahwah, NJ: Erlbaum.

Hetherington, E. M. (2006). The influence of conflict, marital problem solving, and parenting on children's adjustment in non-divorced, divorced, and remarried families. In A. Clarke-Stewart & J. Dunn (eds), *Families count* (pp. 203–237). New York: Cambridge University Press.

Hewlett, B. S. (2004). *Fathers in forager, farmer, and pastoral cultures.* Hoboken, NJ: Wiley.

Heyes, C. (2016). Imitation: Not in our genes. *Current Biology, 26*(10), R412–R414.

Heyes, C. (2016a). Imitation: Not in our genes. *Current Biology, 26*(10), R412–R414.

Heyes, C. (2016b). Born pupils? Natural pedagogy and cultural pedagogy. *Perspectives on Psychological Science, 11*(2), 280–295.

Heyes, C. M. (2005). Imitation by association. In S. Hurley & N. Chater (eds), *Perspectives on imitation: From mirror neurons to memes.* Cambridge, MA: MIT Press.

Heyman, G. D., & Giles, J. W. (2006). Gender and psychological essentialism. *Enfance, 58*, 293–310.

Higgins, A. T. & Turnure, J. E. (1984) Distractibility and concentration of attention in children's development. *Child Development, 55*, 1799–1810.

Hill, E. L. (2004). Executive dysfunction in autism. *Trends in Cognitive Sciences, 8*(1), 26–32.

Hill, J. P., & Lynch, M. E. (1983). The intensification of gender-related role expectations during early adolescence. In J. Brooks-Gunn & A. Petersen (eds), *Girls at puberty: Biological and psychosocial perspectives* (pp. 201–228). New York: Plenum.

Hinde, R. A. (1994). Developmental psychology in the context of the other behavioral sciences. In R. D. Parke, P. Ornstein, J. Reisen, & C. Zahn-Waxler (eds), *A century of developmental psychology* (pp. 617–644). Washington, DC: American Psychological Association.

Hines, M. (2004). *Brain gender.* New York: Oxford University Press.

Hines, M. (2006). Prenatal testosterone and gender-related behaviour. *European Journal of Endocrinology, 155*.

Hines, M., Ahmed, S. F., & Hughes, I. A. (2003). Psychological outcomes and gender-related development in complete androgen insensitivity syndrome. *Archives of Sexual Behavior, 32*, 93–101.

Hinshaw, S., Scheffler, R. M., Fulton, B. D., Aase, H., Banaschewski, T., Cheng, W., et al. (2011). International variation in treatment procedures for ADHD: Social context and recent trends. *Psychiatric Services, 62*, 459–464.

Hipwell, A. E., Pardini D. A., Loeber, R., Sembower, M., Keenan, K., & Stouthamer-Loeber, M. (2007). Callous-unemotional behaviors in young girls: Shared and unique effects relative to conduct problems. *Journal of Clinical Child and Adolescent Psychology, 36*, 293–304.

Hirsch, J., & Kim, K. (1997). New views of early language. *Nature, 103*, 1141–1143.

Hirsh-Pasek, K., Zosh, J. M., Golinkoff, R. M., Gray, J. H., Robb, M. B., & Kaufman, J. (2015). Putting education in 'educational' apps: Lessons from the science of learning. *Psychological Science in the Public Interest, 16*(1), 3–34.

Hitch, G. J., & Towse, J. N. (1995). Working memory: What develops? In F. E. Weinert & W. Schneider (eds), *Memory performance and competencies: Issues in growth and development* (pp. 3–21). Mahwah, NJ: Erlbaum.

Hitch, O. J. and Baddeley, A. D. (1976) Verbal reasoning and working memory, *Quarterly Journal of Experimental Psychology 28*: 603–21.

Ho, T. P., Leung, P. W. L., Luk, E. S. L., Taylor, E., Bacon-Shone, J., & Lieh-Mak, F. (1996). Establishing the constructs of childhood behavioral disturbances in a Chinese population: A questionnaire study. *Journal of Abnormal Child Psychology, 24,* 417–431.

Hodapp, R. (2002). Parenting children with Down syndrome and other types of mental retardation. In M. Bornstein (ed.), *Handbook of parenting* (2nd edn, pp. 355–382). Mahwah, NJ: Erlbaum.

Hodapp, R. M., & Dykens, E. M. (2006). Mental retardation. In W. Damon & R. M. Lerner (Series eds) & K. A. Renninger & I. E. Siegel (Vol. eds), *Handbook of child psychology: Vol. 4. Child psychology in practice* (6th edn, pp. 453–496). New York: Wiley.

Hodges, E. V. E., & Perry, D. G. (1999). Personal and interpersonal antecedents and consequences of victimization by peers. *Journal of Personality and Social Policy, 76,* 677–685.

Hodges, E. V. E., Boivin, M., Vitaro, F. & Bukowski, W. M. (1999) The power of friendship: Protection against an escalating cycle of peer victimization. *Developmental Psychology, 35,* 94–101.

Hodges, E. V. E., Malone, M. J., & Perry, D. G. (1997). Individual risk and social risk as interacting determinants of victimization in the peer group. *Developmental Psychology, 33,* 1032–1039.

Hoehl, S. (2016). The development of category specificity in infancy: What can we learn from electrophysiology? *Neuropsychologia, 83,* 114–122.

Hoeve, M., Stams, G. J. J. M., van der Put, C. E., Dubas, J. S., van der Laan, P. H., & Gerris, J. R. M. (2012). A meta-analysis of attachment to parents and delinquency. *Journal of Abnormal Child Psychology, 40*(5), 771–785.

Hoff, E. (2005). *Language development* (3rd edn). Belmont, CA: Wadsworth/Thomson.

Hoff-Ginsberg, E., & Shatz, M. (1982). Linguistic input and the child's acquisition of language. *Psychological Bulletin, 92,* 3–26.

Hoffman, L. W. (2000). Maternal employment: Effects of social context. In R. D. Taylor & M. C. Wang (eds), *Resilience across contexts: Family, work, culture and community* (pp. 147–176). Mahwah, NJ: Erlbaum.

Hoffman, L. W., & Youngblade, L. M. (1999). *Mothers at work: Effects on children's well-being.* New York: Cambridge University Press.

Hoffman, M. L. (1981). Is altruism part of human nature? *Journal of Personality and Social Psychology, 40,* 121–137.

Hoffman, M. L. (2000) *Empathy and moral development: Implications for caring and justice.* Cambridge: Cambridge University Press.

Hogan, D., & Msall, M. E. (2002). Family structure and resources and the parenting of children with disabilities and functional limitations. In J. G. Borkowski, S. L. Ramey, & M. Bristol-Power (eds), *Parenting and the child's world* (pp. 311–328). Mahwah, NJ: Erlbaum.

Hohne, E. A. & Jusczyk, P. W. (1994) Two-month-old infants' sensitivity to allophonic differences. *Perception and Psychophysics, 56,* 613–623.

Holden, G. W. (1988). Adults' thinking about a child-rearing problem: Effects of experience, parental status and gender. *Child Development, 59,* 1623–1632.

Holden, G. W., & Hawk, C. K. (2003). Meta-parenting in the journey of child rearing: A cognitive mechanism for change.

In L. Kuczynski (ed.), *Handbook of dynamics of parent-child relations* (pp. 189–210). Thousand Oaks, CA: Sage.

Holditch-Davis, D. (1990). The development of sleeping and waking states in high-risk preterm infants. *Infant Behavior and Development, 13,* 513–531.

Hollich, G. J., Hirsh-Pasek, K., & Golinkoff, R. M. (2000). Breaking the language barrier: An emergentist coalition model for the origins of word learning. *Monographs of the Society for Research in Child Development, 65*(3) (Serial no. 262).

Hollich, G., Golinkoff, R. M., & Hirsch-Pasek, K. (2007). Young children associate novel words with complex objects rather than salient parts. *Developmental Psychology, 43,* 1051–1061.

Holliday, R. (2004). The multiple and irreversible causes of aging. *Journal of Gerontology. Series A, Biological Sciences and Medical Sciences, 59*(6), B568–B572.

Holt-Lunstad, J., Smith, T. B., & Layton, J. B. (2010). Social relationships and mortality risk: A meta-analytic review. *PLOS Medicine, 7,* e1000316. doi: 10.1371/journal.pmed.1000316

Holyoak, K. J. (2005). Analogy. In K. J. Holyoak & R. G. Morrison (eds), *The Cambridge handbook of thinking and reasoning* (pp. 117–142). New York: Cambridge University Press.

Honzik, M. (1983). Measuring mental abilities in infancy: The value and limitations. In M. Lewis (ed.), *Origins of intelligence: Infancy and early childhood* (2nd edn, pp. 67–105). New York: Plenum Press.

Honzik, M. P., MacFarlane, J. W., & Allen, L. (1948). The stability of mental test performance between two and eighteen years. *Journal of Experimental Education, 17,* 309–324.

Honzik, M. P. (1976). Value and limitations of infant tests: An overview. In M. Lewis (ed.), *Origins of intelligence*. New York: Plenum Press.

Hood, B. M. (1995). Shifts of visual attention in the human infant: A neuroscientific approach. In L. Lipsett & C. Rovee-Collier (eds), *Advances in infancy research* (Vol. 9, pp. 163–216). Norwood, NJ: Ablex.

Hood, B., Carey, S., & Prasada, S. (2000). Predicting the outcomes of physical events: Two-year-olds fail to reveal knowledge of solidity and support. *Child Development, 71*(6), 1540–1554.

Hopkins, B., & Westra, T. (1988). Maternal handling and motor development: An intracultural study. *Genetic Psychology Monographs, 14*, 377–420.

Hopkins, B., & Westra, T. (1990). Motor development, maternal expectations, and the role of handling. *Infant Behavior and Development, 13*, 117–122.

Hopmeyer, A., & Asher, S. R. (1997). Children's responses to peer conflicts involving a rights infraction. *Merrill-Palmer Quarterly, 43*, 235–254.

Hoppu, U., Kalliomaki, M., Laiho, K., & Isolauri, E. (2001). Breast milk—immunomodulatory signals against allergenic disease. *Allergy, 56*, 23–26.

Horn, J. L. (1982). The theory of fluid and crystallized intelligence in relation to concepts of cognitive psychology and aging in adulthood. In F. I. M. Craik & S. Trehub (eds), *Aging and cognitive processes* (pp. 237–278). New York: Plenum Press.

Horowitz, D. L. (1939). *Ethnic groups in conflict*, Berkeley, CA: University of California Press.

Hossain, Z., Field, T., Gonzalez, J., Malphurs, J., De Valle, C., & Pickens, J. (1994). Infants of depressed mothers interact better with their non-depressed fathers. *Infant Mental Health Journal, 15*, 348–357.

Houdé, O., Rossi, S., Lubin, A., & Joliot, M. (2010). Mapping numerical processing, reading, and executive functions in the developing brain: An fMRI meta-analysis of 52 studies including 842 children. *Developmental Science, 13*, 876–885.

House, J. S., Landis, K. R., & Umberson, D. (1988). Social relationships and health. *Science, 241*, 540–545. doi: 10.1126/

Howe, C. (2010). *Peer groups and children's development*. Oxford: Blackwell.

Howe, C., McWilliam, D., & Cross, G. (2005). Chance favours only the prepared mind: Incubation and the delayed effects of peer collaboration. *British Journal of Psychology, 96*, 67–93.

Howe, C., Tolmie, A., & Rodgers, C. (1992). The acquisition of conceptual knowledge in science by primary school children: Group interaction and the understanding of motion down an inclined plane. *British Journal of Developmental Psychology, 10*, 113–130.

Howe, N., & Ross, H. S. (1990). Socialization, perspective taking and the sibling relationship. *Developmental Psychology, 26*, 160–165.

Howe, P. E., & Schiller, M. (1952). Growth responses of the school child to changes in diet and environment factors. *Journal of Applied Physiology, 5*, 51–61.

Howes, C. (1987). Social competence with peers in young children. Developmental sequences. *Developmental Review, 7*, 252–272.

Howes, C. (1996). The earliest friendships. In W. M. Bukowski, A. F. Newcomb, & W. W. Hartup (eds), *The company they keep: Friendship in childhood and adolescence* (pp. 66–86). New York: Cambridge University Press.

Howes, C. (1999). Attachment relationships in the context of multiple caregivers. In J. Cassidy & P. R. Shaver (eds), *Handbook of attachment: Theory, research, and clinical applications* (pp. 671–687). New York: Guilford Press.

Howes, C., & Ritchie, S. (2003). *A matter of trust*. New York: Columbia University Press.

Hser, Y. I., Grella, C. E., Hubbard, R. L., Hsieh, M. S., Fletcher, B., Brown, B. C. et al. (2001) An evaluation of drug treatment for adolescents in four U.S. cities. *Archives of General Psychiatry, 58*, 689–695.

Hsiao, Y., & Nation, K. (2018). Semantic diversity, frequency and the development of lexical quality in children's word reading. *Journal of Memory and Language, 103*, 114–126.

Huang, M.-H., & Hauser, R. M. (1998). Trends in black-white test-score differentials: II. The WORDSUM Vocabulary Test. In U. Neisser (ed.), *The rising curve: Long-term gains in IQ and related measures* (pp. 303–332). Washington, DC: American Psychological Association.

Huang, Y. S., Tsai, M. H., & Guilleminault, C. (2011). Pharmacological treatment of ADHD and the short and long term effects on sleep. *Current Pharmaceutical Design, 17*(15), 1450–1458.

Huber, B., Tarasuik, J., Antoniou, M. N., Garrett, C., Bowe, S. J., Kaufman, J., & Swinburne BabyLab Team (2016). Young children's transfer of learning from a touchscreen device. *Computers in Human Behavior, 56*, 56–64.

Hudley, C., & Graham, S. (1993). An attributional intervention to reduce peer-directed aggression among African-American boys. *Child Development, 64*, 124–138.

Huesmann, L. R., & Guerra, N. G. (1997). Children's normative beliefs about aggression and aggressive behavior. *Journal of Personality and Social Psychology, 72*, 408–419.

Huesmann, L. R., & Miller, L. S. (1994). Long-term effects of repeated exposure to media violence in childhood. In L. R. Huesmann (ed.), *Aggressive behavior: Current perspectives* (pp. 153–186). New York: Plenum Press.

Huesmann, L. R., Eron, L. D., Lefkowitz, M. M., & Walder, L. O. (1984). The stability of aggression over time and generations. *Developmental Psychology, 20,* 1120–1134.

Huesmann, L. R., Moise-Titus, J., Podolski, C., & Eron, L. D. (2003). Longitudinal relations between children's exposure to TV violence and their aggressive and violent behavior in young adulthood: 1977–1992. *Developmental Psychology, 39*(2), 201–221.

Hughes, M. (1975). *Egocentrism in pre-school children.* Unpublished doctoral dissertation, University of Edinburgh, Scotland.

Huisman, M., Oldehinkel, A. J., de Winter, A., Minderaa, R. B., de Bildt, A., Huizink, A. C., Verhulst, F. C., & Ormel, J. (2008). Cohort profile: The Dutch 'Tracking Adolescents' Individual Lives' Survey'; TRAILS. *International Journal of Epidemiology, 7,* 1227–1235.

Huizinga, D., Thornberry, T. P., Knight, K. E., Lovegrove, R. L., Hill, K., & Farrington, D. P. (2007). *Disproportionate minority contact in the juvenile justice system: A study of differential minority arrest/referral to court in three cities. A report to the Office of Juvenile Justice and Delinquency Prevention* (NCJ Rept. No. 219743). Retrieved from National Criminal Justice Reference System website: http://www.ncjrs.gov/pdffiles1/ojjdp/grants/219743.pdf.

Huizink, A., Mulder, E., & Buitelaar, J. (2004). Prenatal stress and risk for psychopathology. *Psychological Bulletin, 130,* 115–142.

Hultsch, D. F., Hertzog, C., Small, B. J., & Dixon, R. A. (1999). Use it or lose it: Engaged lifestyle as a buffer of cognitive decline in aging? *Psychology and Aging, 14,* 245–263.

Humphrey, M. M. (1982) Children's avoidance of environmental, simple task internal, and complex task internal distracters. *Child Development, 53,* 736–745.

Hunt, C. E. (2001). Sudden infant death syndrome and other causes of infant mortality: Diagnosis, mechanisms and risk of recurrence for siblings. *American Journal of Respiratory and Critical Care Medicine, 164,* 346–357.

Hunter, S. B., & Smith, D. E. (2008). Predictors of children's understandings of death: Age, cognitive ability, death experience and maternal communicative competence. *Omega-Journal of Death and Dying, 57,* 143–162.

Huston, A. C., & Wright, J. C. (1998). Mass media and children's development. In W. Damon (Series ed.), I. E. Sigel & K. A. Renninger (Vol. eds), *Handbook of child psychology: 5th edn, Vol. 4. Child psychology in practice* (pp. 999–1058). New York: Wiley.

Huston, A. C., McLloyd, V., & Garcia-Coll, C. (1994). Children and poverty: Issues in contemporary research. *Child Development, 65,* 275–282.

Hutchins, E. (1980). *Culture and inference: A Trobriand case study.* Cambridge, MA: Harvard University Press.

Hutchins, E. (1996). *Cognition in the wild.* Cambridge, MA: MIT Press.

Hutteman, R., Denissen, J. J. A., Asendorpf, J. B., & van Aken, M. A. G. (2009). Changing dynamics in personality: A multiwave longitudinal study of the relationship between shyness and aggressiveness from childhood to early adulthood. *Development and Psychopathology, 21,* 1083–1094.

Huttenlocher, J. (1974). The origins of language comprehension. In R. L. Solso (ed.), *Theories in cognitive psychology.* Hillsdale, NJ: Erlbaum.

Huttenlocher, J., & Lui, F. (1979). The semantic organization of some simple nouns and verbs. *Journal of Verbal Learning and Verbal Behavior, 18,* 141–162.

Huttenlocher, J., & Smiley, P. (1987). Early word meanings: The case of object names. *Cognitive Psychology, 19,* 63–89.

Huttenlocher, J., Haight, W., Bryk, A., Seltzer, M., & Lyons, T. (1991). Early vocabulary growth: Relation to language impact and gender. *Developmental Psychology, 27,* 236–248.

Huttenlocher, J., Smiley, P., & Charney, R. (1987). Emergence of action categories in the child: Evidence from verb meanings. *Psychological Review, 90,* 72–93.

Huttenlocher, J., Vasilyeva, M., Waterfall, H. R., Vevea, J. L., & Hedges, L. V. (2007). The varieties of speech to young children. *Developmental Psychology, 43,* 1062–1083.

Huttenlocher, P. R. (1994). Synaptogenesis, synapse elimination, and neural plasticity in human cerebral cortex. In C. A. Nelson (ed.), *Threats to optimal development. The Minnesota Symposia on Child Psychology* (Vol. 27, pp. 35–54). Hillsdale, NJ: Erlbaum.

Huttenlocher, P. R., & Dabholkar, A. J. (1997). Regional differences in synaptogenesis in the human cerebral cortex. *Journal of Comparative Neurology, 387,* 167–178.

Huttunen, M., & Niskanen, P. (1978). Prenatal loss of father and psychiatric disorders. *Archives of General Psychiatry, 35,* 429–431.

Hwang, C. P. (1986). Behavior of Swedish primary and secondary caretaking fathers in relation to mothers' presence. *Developmental Psychology, 22,* 749–751.

Hyde, J. S. (2005). The gender similarities hypothesis. *American Psychologist, 60,* 581–592.

Hyde, J. S., & Linn, M. C. (1988). Gender differences in verbal ability: A meta-analysis. *Psychological Bulletin, 104*, 53–69.

Hyde, J. S., & Plant, E. A. (1995). Magnitude of psychological gender differences. *American Psychologist, 50*, 159–161.

Hyde, J. S., Fennema, E., & Lamon, S. J. (1990). Gender differences in mathematics performance: A meta-analysis. *Psychological Bulletin, 107*, 139–155.

Hyde, J. S., Krajnik, M., & Skuldt-Neiderberger, K. (1991). Androgyny across the life span: A replication and longitudinal follow-up. *Developmental Psychology, 27*, 516–519.

Hymel, S. (1986). Interpretations of peer behavior: Affective bias in childhood and adolescence. *Child Development, 57*, 431–445.

Hymel, S., Wagner, E., & Butler, L. (1990). Reputational bias: View from the peer group. In S. R. Asher & J. D. Coie (eds), *Peer rejection in childhood* (pp. 156–188). New York: Cambridge University Press.

Hymes, D. H. (1972). Models of the interaction of language and social life. In J. Gumprez & D. Hymes (eds), *Directions in sociolinguistics: The ethnography of communication* (pp. 35–71). New York: Holt, Rinehart & Winston.

Hyson, M., Copple, C., & Jones, J. (2006). Early childhood development and education. In W. Damon & R. M. Lerner (Series eds) & K. A. Renninger & I. E. Siegel (Vol. eds), *Handbook of child psychology: Vol. 4. Child psychology in practice* (6th edn, pp. 3–47). New York: Wiley.

In J. J. Volpe (ed.) *Volpe's neurology of the newborn* (6th edn, pp. 176–188). Philadelphia, PA: Elsevier.

In W. J. Livesley & R. Larstone (eds), *Handbook of personality disorders: Theory, research, and treatment* (2nd edn, pp. 309–323). New York: Guildford Press.

Ingersoll, E. W., & Thoman, E. B. (1999). Sleep/wake states of preterm infants: Stability, developmental change, diurnal variation, and relation with caregiving activity. *Child Development, 70*, 1–10.

Ingram, D. (1989). *First language acquisition.* New York: Cambridge University Press.

Inhelder, B., & Piaget, J. (1958). *The growth of logical thinking from childhood to adolescence.* New York: Basic Books.

Inoff-Germain, G., Arnold, G. S., Nottleman, E. D., Susman, E. J., Cutler, G. B., & Chrousos, G. P. (1988). Relations between hormone levels and observational measures of aggressive behavior of young adolescents in family interactions. *Developmental Psychology, 24*, 129–139.

Insel, T. R. (2014). The NIMH research domain criteria (RDoC) project: Precision medicine for psychiatry. *American Journal of Psychiatry, 171*(4), 395–397.

International Human Genome Sequencing Consortium. (2004) Finishing the euchromatic sequencing of the human genome. *Nature, 431*, 931–945.

Irvine, S. H. (1969a). Factor analysis of African abilities and attainments: Constructs across cultures. *Psychological Bulletin, 71*, 20–32

Irvine, S. H. (1969b). Figural tests of reasoning in Africa. Studies in the use of Raven's Progressive Matrices across cultures. *International Journal of Psychology, 4*, 217–228.

Isabella, R. (1993). Origins of attachment: Maternal interactive behavior across the first year. *Child Development, 64*, 605–621.

Ishikawa, F. & Hay, D. F. (2006) Triadic interaction among newly acquainted 2-year-olds. *Social Development, 15*, 145–168.

Izard, C. E. (1994). Innate and universal facial expressions: Evidence from developmental and cross-cultural research.

Psychological Bulletin, 115, 288–299.

Izard, C. E., Fantauzzo, C. A., Castle, J. M., Haynes, O. M., & Slomine, B. S. (1995). The morphological stability and social validity of infants' facial expressions. Unpublished manuscript, University of Delaware.

Izard, C. E., Hembree, E., & Huebner, R. (1987). Infants' emotional expressions to acute pain: Developmental changes and stability of individual differences. *Developmental Psychology, 23*, 105–113.

Izard, V., Sann, C., Spelke, E. S., & Streri, A. (2009). Newborn infants perceive abstract numbers. *Proceedings of the National Academy of Sciences, 106*(25), 10382–10385.

Jackson, I., & Sirois, S. (2009). Infant cognition: Going full factorial with pupil dilation. *Developmental Science, 12*(4), 670–679.

Jackson, K. M. & Sher, K. J. (2003) Alcohol use disorders and psychological distress: A prospective state-trait analysis. *Journal of Abnormal Psychology, 112*, 599–613.

Jackson, L. A., von Eye, A., Biocca, F. A., Barbatsis, G., Zhao, Y., & Fitzgerald, H. E. (2006). Does home Internet use influence the academic performance of low-income children? *Developmental Psychology, 42*, 429–435.

Jacob, T., & Johnson, S. L. (1997). Parent-child interaction among depressed fathers and mothers: Impact on child functioning. *Journal of Family Psychology, 11*, 391–409.

Jacobs, B. L. (2004) Depression: The brain finally gets into the act. *Current Directions in Psychological Science, 13*, 103–106.

Jacobsen, T., & Hofmann, V. (1997). Children's attachment representations: Longitudinal relations to school behavior and academic competency in middle childhood and adolescence. *Developmental Psychology, 33,* 703–710.

Jacobson, J. L. & Jacobson, S. W. (2004) Prenatal exposure to polychlorinated biphenyls and attention at school age. *Obstetrical and Gynecological Survey, 59,* 412–413.

Jacobson, J. L., & Jacobson, S. W. (1996). Prospective longitudinal assessment of developmental neurotoxicity. *Environmental Health Perspectives, 104,* 275–283.

Jaekel, J., Pluess, M., Belsky, J., & Wolke, D. (2015). Effects of maternal sensitivity on low birth weight children's academic achievement: A test of differential susceptibility versus diathesis stress. *Journal of Child Psychology and Psychiatry, 56*(6), 693–701.

Jaffe, S., & Hyde, J. (2000). Gender differences in moral orientation: A meta-analysis. *Psychological Bulletin, 126,* 703–726.

Jaffee, S. R., & Price, T. S. (2007). Gene–environment correlations: A review of the evidence and implications for prevention of mental illness. *Molecular Psychiatry, 12*(5), 432.

Jaffee, S. R., Moffitt, T. E., Caspi, A., & Taylor, A. (2003). Life with (or without) father: The benefits of living with two biological parents depend on the father's antisocial behavior. *Child Development, 74,* 109–126.

Jakobson, R. (1968). *Child language, aphasic, and phonological universals.* Hague, The Netherlands: Mouton.

Jamain, S., Quach, H., Betancur, C., Råstam, M., Colineaux, C., Gillberg, I. C., . . . & Bourgeron, T. (2003). Mutations of the X-linked genes encoding neuroligins NLGN3 and NLGN4 are associated with autism. *Nature Genetics, 34,* 27–29.

James, W. (1890). *The principles of psychology, Vol. 1.* New York: Henry Holt.

Jaruratanasirikul, S., & Sriplung, H. (2015). Secular trends of growth and pubertal maturation of school children in Southern Thailand. *Annals of Human Biology, 42*(5), 447–454.

Jeffrey, R. W. (2001) Public health strategies for obesity treatment and prevention. *American Journal of Health Behavior, 25,* 252–259.

Jellinek, M. B., & Snyder, J. B. (1998). Depression and suicide in children and adolescents. *Pediatric Review, 19,* 255–264.

Jensen, A. R. (1969). How much can we boost IQ and scholastic achievement? *Harvard Educational Review, 39,* 1–123.

Jensen, A. R. (1993). Test validity: 'g' versus 'tacit knowledge.' *Current Directions in Psychological Science, 2,* 9–109.

Jensen, P. S., Hinshaw, S. P., Swanson, J. M., Greenhill, L. L., Conners, C. K. & Arnold, L. E., et al. (2001). Findings from the NIMH multimodal treatment study of ADHD (MTA): Implications and applications for primary care providers. *Journal of Developmental and Behavioral Pediatrics, 22,* 60–73.

Johnson, G. J. Cohen, P. Smailes, E. M. Kasen, S., & Brook, J. S. (2002). Television viewing and aggressive behaviour during adolescence and adulthood, *Science, 295* (5564), 2468–2471.

Johnson, M. H. (2011). Interactive specialization: A domain-general framework for human functional brain development? *Developmental Cognitive Neuroscience, 1,* 7–21.

Johnson, M. H. (2011). Interactive specialization: A domain-general framework for human functional brain development? *Developmental Cognitive Neuroscience, 1*(1), 7–21.

Johnson, M. H., & Morton, J. (1991). *Biology and cognitive development: The case of face*

recognition. Oxford: Basil Blackwell.

Johnson, M. H., & Munakata, Y. (2005). Processes of change in brain and cognitive development. *Trends in Cognitive Sciences, 9*(3), 152–158.

Johnson, M. H., Dziurawiec, S., Eills, H., & Morton, J. (1991). Newborn's preferential tracking of face-like stimuli and its subsequent decline. *Cognition, 40,* 1–19.

Johnson, M. H. (2010). Functional brain development during infancy. In J. G. Bremner & T. Wachs (eds), *The Wiley-Blackwell handbook of infant development* (2nd edn). Oxford: Wiley-Blackwell.

Johnson, M. H., & de Haan, M. (2010). *Developmental Cognitive Neuroscience.* 3rd Edition. Wiley-Blackwell.

Johnson, M. H., & de Haan, M. (2015). *Developmental cognitive neuroscience: An introduction* (4th edn). Oxford: Wiley-Blackwell.

Johnson, M. H., Dziurawiec, S., Ellis, H., & Morton, J. (1991). Newborns' preferential tracking of face-like stimuli and its subsequent decline, *Cognition, 40,* 1–19.

Johnson, M. K., Beebe, T., Mortimer, J. T., & Snyder, M. (1998). Volunteerism in adolescence: A process perspective. *Journal of Research on Adolescence, 8,* 309–332.

Johnson, W., Bouchard, T. J., Krueger, R. F., McGue, M., & Gottesman, I. I. (2004). Just one *g:* Consistent results from three test batteries. *Intelligence, 32,* 95–107.

Johnson, W., Emde, R. N., Pannabecker, B., Stenberg, C., & Davis, M. (1982). Maternal perception of infant emotion from birth through 18 months. *Infant Behavior and Development, 5,* 313–322.

Johnston, L. D., O'Malley, P. M. & Bachman, J. G. (1997) National survey results on drug use from the Monitoring the Future study, 1975–1995. Rockville, MD: National Institutes of Health.

Jones, A. P., Happé, F., Gilbert, F., Burnett, S., & Viding, E. (2010). Feeling, caring, knowing: Different types of empathy deficit in boys with psychopathic tendencies and autism spectrum disorder. *Journal of Child Psychology & Psychiatry, 51*, 1188–1197.

Jones, A. P., Laurens, K. R., Herba, C. M., Barker, G. J., & Viding, E. (2009). Amygdala hypoactivity to fearful faces in boys with conduct problems and callous-unemotional traits. *American Journal of Psychiatry, 166*, 95–102.

Jones, D. C. (1985). Persuasive appeals and responses to appeals among friends and acquaintances. *Child Development, 56*, 757–763.

Jones, G., Riley, M., & Dwyer, T. (2000). Breastfeeding early in life and bone mass in prepubertal children: A longitudinal study. *Osteoporosis International, 11*, 146–152.

Jones, M. C., & Bayley, N. (1950). Physical maturing among boys as related to behavior. *Journal of Educational Psychology, 41*, 129–148.

Jones, S. S. (2009). The development of imitation in infancy. *Philosophical Transactions of the Royal Society of London B: Biological Sciences, 364*(1528), 2325–2335.

Jones, T. A., & Greenough, W. T. (1996). Ultrastructural evidence for increased contact between astrocytes and synapses in rats reared in a complex environment. *Neurobiology of Learning and Memory, 65*, 48–56.

Jonides, J., Marshuetz, C., Smith, E. E., Reuter-Lorenz, P. A., Koeppe, R. A., & Hartley, A. (2000). Age differences in behavior and PET activation reveal differences in interference resolution in verbal working memory. *Journal of Cognitive Neuroscience, 12*, 188–196.

Jorm, A. F. (1987). Sex and age differences in depression: A quantitative synthesis of published research. *Australian and New Zealand Journal of Psychiatry, 21*(1), 46–53.

Jouen, F. & Molina, M. (2005) Exploration of the newborn's manual activity: A window onto early cognitive processes. *Infant behavior and development, 28*(3), 227–239.

Jouen, F., & Molina, M. (2005). Exploration of the newborn's manual activity: A window onto early cognitive processes. *Infant Behavior & Development, 28*, 227–239.

Jourdan, C. (1991). Pidgins and creoles: The blurring of categories. *Annual Review of Anthropology, 20*, 187–209. *Journal of Adolescence, 65*, 196–206. *Journals of Gerontology, Series B: Psychological Sciences and Social Sciences, 64B* (4), 482–486.

Joyce, P. R. (1984). Age of onset in bipolar affective disorder and misdiagnosis as schizophrenia. *Psychological Medicine, 14*, 145–149.

Joyner, K., & Udry, J. R. (2000). You don't bring me anything but down: Adolescent romance and depression. *Journal of Health and Social Behavior, 41*, 369–391.

Judy, B., & Nelson, E. S. (2000). Relations between parents, peers, morality, and theft in an adolescent sample. *High School Journal, 83*, 31–42.

Jusczyk, P. W., Friederici, A. D., Wessels, J., Svenkerud, V. Y., & Jusczyk, A. M. (1993). Infants' sensitivity to the sound patterns of native language words. *Journal of Memory and Language, 32*, 402–420.

Jusczyk, P. W., Rosner, B. S., Cutting, J. E., Foard, F., & Smith, L. B. (1977). Categorical perception of non-speech sounds by two-month-old infants. *Perception and Psychophysics, 21*, 50–54.

Jusczyk, P., Houston, D. M., & Newsome, M. (1999). The beginnings of word segmentation in English-learning infants. *Cognitive Psychology, 39*(3–4), 159–207.

Juvonen, J., Graham, S., & Schuster, M. A. (2003). Bullying among young adolescents: The strong, the weak, and the troubled. *Pediatrics, 112*, 1231–1237.

Kagan, J. (1969). Inadequate evidence and illogical conclusions. *Harvard Educational Review, 39*, 274–277.

Kagan, J. (1998). Biology and the child. In W. Damon (Series ed.) & N. Eisenberg (Vol. ed.), *Handbook of child psychology* (Vol. 3, pp. 177–235). New York: Wiley.

Kagan, J., & Moss, H. A. (1962). *Birth to maturity: A study in psychological development.* New York: Wiley.

Kagan, J., & Snidman, N. (2004). *The long shadow of temperament.* Cambridge, MA: Harvard University Press.

Kagan, J., Kearsley, R. B., & Zelazo, P. R. (1978). *Infancy: Its place in human development.* Cambridge, MA: Harvard University Press.

Kail, R. (1991). Development of processing speed in childhood and adolescence. In H. W. Reese (ed.), *Advances in child development and behavior* (Vol. 23). San Diego, CA: Academic Press.

Kail, R. (1995). Processing speed, memory, and cognition. In F. E. Weinert & W. Schneider (eds), *Memory performance and competencies: Issues in growth and development* (pp. 71–88). Mahwah, NJ: Erlbaum.

Kail, R. (2000). Speed of information processing: Developmental change and links to intelligence. *Journal of School Psychology, 38*, 51–61.

Kail, R. V., Lervåg, A., & Hulme, C. (2016). Longitudinal evidence linking processing speed to the development of reasoning. *Developmental Science,* *19*(6), 1067–1074.

Kail, R. V., McBride-Chang, C., Ferrer, E., Cho, J. R., & Shu, H. (2013). Cultural differences in the development of processing speed. *Developmental Science, 16*(3), 476–483.

Kail, R. V., McBride-Chang, C., Ferrer, E., Cho, J. R., & Shu, H. (2013). Cultural differences in the development of processing speed. *Developmental Science, 16*(3), 476–483.

Kail, R. (1995) Processing speed, memory, and cognition. In F. E. Weinert & W. Schneider (eds), *Memory performance and competencies: Issues in growth and development* (pp. 71–88) Mahwah, NJ: Erlbaum.

Kail, R., & Park, Y. (1994). Processing time, articulation time, and memory span. *Journal of Experimental Child Psychology, 57,* 281–291.

Kako, E. (1999). Elements of syntax in the systems of three language-trained animals. *Animal Learning and Behavior, 27,* 1–15.

Kaldy, Z., & Leslie, A. (2005). A memory span of one? Object identification in 6.5-month-old infants. *Cognition, 57,* 153–177.

Kalish, R. A. (1985). The social context of death and dying. In R. H. Binstock & E. Shanas (eds), *Handbook of aging and the social sciences* (2nd edn, pp. 149–170). New York: Van Rostrand Reinholt.

Kalish, R. A., & Reynolds, D. K. (1976). *An overview of death and ethnicity.* Farmingdale, NY: Baywood.

Kallman, D. A., Plato, C. C., & Tobin, J. D. (1990). The role of muscle-loss in the age-related decline of grip strength: Cross-sectional and longitudinal perspectives. *Journal of Gerontology: Medical Sciences, 45,* 82–88.

Kaltiala-Heino, R., Rimpelä, M., Rissanen, A., & Rantanen, P.

(2001). Early puberty and early sexual activity are associated with bulimic-type eating pathology in middle adolescence. *Journal of Adolescent Health, 28,* 346–352.

Kamins, M. L., & Dweck, C. (1999). Person-versus-process praise and criticism: Implications for contingent self-worth and coping. *Developmental Psychology, 35,* 835–847.

Kanaya, T., Ceci, S. J., & Scullin, M. H. (2005). Age differences with secular IQ trends: An individual growth modeling approach. *Intelligence, 33,* 613–621.

Kandel, D. (1973). Adolescent marijuana use: Role of parents and peers. *Science, 181,* 1067–1070.

Kandel, E. R. (2004). Nobel Lecture: The molecular biology of memory storage: A dialogue between genes and synapses. *Bioscience Reports, 24,* 477–522.

Kandel, E. R., Schwartz, J. H., & Jessell, T. M. (2000). *Principles of neuroscience* (4th edn). New York: McGraw-Hill.

Kanner, L. (1943). Autistic disturbances of affective contact. *Nervous Child, 2*(3), 217–250.

Kanwisher, N., McDermott, J., & Chun, M. (1997). The fusiform face area: A module in human extrastriate cortex specialized for the perception of faces. *Journal of Neuroscience, 17,* 4302–4311.

Karass, J., & Braungart-Rieker, J. M. (2004). Infant negative emotionality and attachment: Implications for preschool intelligence. *International Journal of Behavioral Development, 28,* 221–229.

Karmiloff-Smith, A. (1994). Précis of Beyond modularity: A developmental perspective on cognitive science. *Behavioral and Brain Sciences, 17*(4), 693–707.

Karmiloff-Smith, A. (1995). *Beyond modularity: A developmental perspective on cognitive science.* Cambridge, MA: MIT Press.

Karmiloff-Smith, A. (1995). *Beyond modularity: A developmental perspective on cognitive science.* Cambridge, MA: MIT Press/Bradford Books.

Karmiloff-Smith, A., & Inhelder, B. (1975). If you want to get ahead, get a theory. *Cognition, 3* (3), 195–212.

Karmiloff-Smith, A., Doherty, B., Cornish, K., & Scerif, G. (2016). Fragile X Syndrome as a multilevel model for understanding behaviorally defined disorders. In D. Cicchetti (ed.), *Developmental psychopathology: Vol. 3. Maladaptation and psychopathology* (pp. 68–80). Hoboken, NJ: John Wiley & Sons.

Karmiloff-Smith, A., Thomas, M. S., & Johnson, M. H. (2018). *Thinking Developmentally from constructivism to neuroconstructivism: Selected works of Annette Karmiloff-Smith.* Abingdon: Routledge.

Kass, L. (2002). *Life, liberty, and the defense of dignity.* San Francisco: Encounter Books.

Kastenbaum, R. J. (2000). *The psychology of death* (3rd edn). New York: Springer.

Katz, L. F., & Gottman, J. M. (1993). Patterns of marital conflict predict children's internalizing and externalizing behaviors. *Developmental Psychology, 29,* 940–950.

Katz, L. F., & Gottman, J. M. (1996). Spillover effects of marital conflict: In search of parenting and co-parenting mechanisms. In J. P. McHale & P. A. Cowan (eds), *Understanding how family-level dynamics affect children's development: Studies of two-parent families* (pp. 57–76). San Francisco: Jossey-Bass.

Katz, L. F., & Gottman, J. M. (1997). Buffering children from marital conflict and dissolution. *Journal of Clinical Child Psychology, 26,* 157–171.

Katz, L. F., Kramer, L., & Gottman, J. M. (1992). Conflict and emotions in marital, sibling, and peer relationships. In C. U. Shantz & W. W. Hartup (eds), *Conflict in child and adolescent development* (pp. 122–149). Cambridge: Cambridge University Press.

Kauffman, J. (2001). *Characteristics of emotional and behavioral disorders of children and youth* (7th edn). Columbus, OH: Merrill/Prentice Hall.

Kaufman, A. S., & Kaufman, N. L. (1983). *Kaufman assessment battery for children: Interpretive manual.* Circle Pines, MN: American Guidance Service.

Kaufman, A. S., & Kaufman, N. L. (2006). *KBIT: Kaufman Brief Intelligence Test* (2nd edn). Toronto: Pearson Education.

Kaufman, J. & Needham, A. (in press) Spatial expectations of young human infants following passive movement. *Developmental Psychobiology.*

Kaufman, J., & Needham, A. (1999). Objective spatial coding in 6.5-month-old infants in a visual dishabituation task. *Developmental Science, 2*(4), 432–441.

Kaufman, J., & Needham, A. (2011). Spatial expectations of young human infants, following passive movement. *Developmental Psychobiology, 53*(1), 23–36.

Kaufman, J., Csibra, G., & Johnson, M. H. (2003). Representing occluded objects in the human infant brain. *Proceedings of the Royal Society,* London B (Suppl.), *270,* 140–143.

Kaufman, R. H., Adam, E., Hatch, E. E., Noller, K., Herdst, A. L., Palmer, J. R. et al. (2000) Continued follow-up of pregnancy outcomes for diethylstilbestrol-exposed offspring. *Obstetrics and Gynecology, 96,* 483–489.

Kaye, K. L. & Bower, T. G. R. (1994) Learning and intermodal transfer of information in newborns. *Psychological Science, 5,* 286–288.

Keating, D. P. (1990). Adolescent thinking. In J. Adelson (ed.), *Handbook of adolescent psychology* (pp. 54–89). New York: Wiley.

Kee, D. W. (1994). Developmental differences in associative memory: Strategy use, mental effort, and knowledge-access interaction. In H. W. Reese (ed.), *Advances in child development and behavior* (Vol. 25, pp. 7–32). New York: Academic Press.

Keefer, C. H., Dixon, S., Tronick, E. Z., & Brazelton, T. B. (1991). Cultural mediation between newborn behavior and later development: Implications for methodology in cross-cultural research. In J. K. Nugent, B. M. Lester & T. B. Brazelton (eds), *The cultural context of infancy: Vol. 2. Multicultural and interdisciplinary approaches to parent-infant relations* (pp. 39–61). Norwood, NJ: Ablex.

Keegan, R. T. (1996, Summer). Creativity from childhood to adulthood: A difference of degree and not of kind. In M. A. Runco (ed.), *Creativity from childhood through adulthood: The developmental issues* [Special issue]. *New Directions for Child Development* (72), 57–66.

Keen, R. (2003). Representation of objects and events: Why do infants look so smart and toddlers look so dumb? *Current Directions in Psychological Science, 12,* 79–83.

Keen, R., Carrico, R. L., Sylvia, M. R., & Berthier, N. E. (2003). How infants use perceptual information to guide action. *Developmental Science, 6*(2), 221–231.

Keenan, K., Loeber, R., Zhang, Q., Stouthamer-Loeber, M., & Van Kammen, W. B. (1995). The influence of deviant peers on the development of boys' disruptive and delinquent behavior: A temporal analysis. *Development and Psychopathology, 7,* 715–726.

Keeney, T. J., Cannizzo, S. R., & Flavell, J. H. (1967). Spontaneous and induced rehearsal in a recall task. *Child Development, 38,* 953–966.

Keller, M. B., Klein, D. N., Hirsh-field, R. M., Kocsis, J. H., McCullough, M. (1995) Results of the *DSM-IV* mood disorders field trial. *American Journal of Psychiatry, 152,* 843–849.

Kellman, P. J., & Arterberry, M. E. (2006). Infant visual perception. In W. Damon & R. M. Lerner (Series eds) & D. Kuhn & R. Siegler (Vol. eds), *Handbook of child psychology* (Vol. 2, 6th edn, pp. 109–160). New York: Wiley.

Kelly, A. (1988). Gender differences in teacher-pupil interactions: A meta-analytic review. *Research in Education, 39,* 1–23.

Kelly, Y., Sacker, A., Gray, R., Kelly, J., Wolke. D, & Quigley, M. A. (2009) Light drinking in pregnancy, a risk for behavioural problems and cognitive deficits at 3 years of age? *International Journal of Epidemiology, 38,* 129–140.

Kendler, K. S., Neale, M. C., Kessler, R. C., Heath, A. C., & Eaves, L. J. (1993). A test of the equal-environment assumption in twin studies of psychiatric illness. *Behavior Genetics, 23*(1), 21–27.

Kennard, B. D., Clarke, G. N., Weersing, V. R., Asarnow, J. R., Shamseddeen, W., Porta, G., et al. (2009). Effective components of TORDIA cognitive behavioral therapy or adolescent depression. *Journal of Consulting and Clinical Psychology, 77,* 1033–1041.

Kennare, R. (2007). Risks of adverse outcomes in the next birth after a first cesarean delivery. *Obstetrics and Gynecology, 109,* 270–276.

Kennedy, W. A. (1969). A followup normative study of Negro intelligence and achievement. *Monographs of the Society for Research in Child Development, 34*(2) (Serial no. 126).

Kensinger, E. A., & Gutchess, A. H. (2017). Cognitive aging in a social and affective context: Advances over the past 50 years, *Journals of Gerontology: Series B, 72*(1), 61–70, https://doi.org/10.1093/geronb/gbw056

Keogh, T., Barnes, P., Joiner, R., & Littleton, K. (2000). Gender, pair composition and computer versus paper presentations of an English language task. *Educational Psychology, 20*, 33–43.

Kerig, P. K. (2008). Boundary dissolution in the family context: The search for the ties that bind marriage, parenting, and child development. In M. Schultz, M. K., Pruett, P. Kerig, & R. D. Parke (eds), *Feathering the nest: Couples relationships, couples interventions, and children's development*. Washington, DC: American Psychological Association.

Khatri, P., Kupersmidt, J., & Patterson, C. (1994, April). *Aggression and peer victimization as predictors of self-report of behavioral and emotional adjustment*. Poster presented at the biennial meeting of the Conference in Human Development, Pittsburgh, PA.

Kiesner, J. (2002). Depression symptoms on early adolescence: Their relations to classroom problem behavior and peer status. *Journal of Research on Adolescence, 12*, 463–478.

Kilgore, K., Snyder, J., & Lentz, C. (2000). The contribution of parental discipline, parental monitoring and school risk to early-onset conduct problems in African American boys and girls. *Developmental Psychology, 36*, 835–845.

Killen, M., & Rutland, A. (2011). *Children and social exclusion: Morality, prejudice and group identity*. Oxford: Wiley.

Killen, M., & Rutland, A. (2011). *Children and social exclusion: Morality, prejudice and group identity*. Oxford: Wiley-Blackwell.

Kim, J. K., Conger, R. D., Elder, G. H. & Lorenz, F. O. (2003) Reciprocal influences between stressful life events and adolescent internalizing and externalizing problems. *Child Development, 74*, 127–143.

Kimball, M. M. (1986). Television and sex role attitudes. In T. M. Williams (ed.), *The impact of television: A natural experiment in three communities* (pp. 265–301). Orlando, FL: Academic Press.

Kindermann, T. A., McCollam, T. L., & Gibson, E., Jr (1995). Peer networks and students' classroom engagement during childhood and adolescence. In K. Wentzel & J. Juvonen (eds), *Social motivation: Understanding children's school adjustment* (pp. 279–312). New York: Cambridge University Press.

Kinney, H. C., & Volpe, J. J. (2017). Organizational events. *Volpe's neurology of the newborn e-Book*, 145.

Kinney, H. C., & Volpe, J. J. (2018). Myelination events. In J. J. Volpe (ed.) *Volpe's neurology of the newborn* (6th edn, pp. 176–188). Philadelphia, PA: Elsevier.

Kinney, H. C., & Volpe, J. J. (2018). Myelination events.

Kirk, E., & Pine, K. J. (2010). I hear what you say but I see what you mean: The role of gestures in children's pragmatic comprehension. *Language and Cognitive Processes, 26*(2), 149–170.

Kirkham, N. Z., Cruess, L. M., & Diamond, A. (2003). Helping children apply their knowledge to their behavior on a dimension-switching task. *Developmental Science, 6*(5), 449–467.

Kirkpatrick, L. A., & Davis, K. E. (1994). Attachment style, gender, and relationship stability: A longitudinal analysis. *Journal of Personality and Social Psychology, 66*, 502–512.

Kirkwood, T. B. L. (2005). Understanding the odd science of aging. *Cell, 120*, 437–447.

Kirtler, A. F., La Greca, A. M., & Prinstein, M. J. (1999). Friendship qualities and social-emotional functioning of adolescents with close, cross-sex friendships. *Journal of Research on Adolescence, 93*, 339–366.

Kisilevsky, B. S., & Muir, D. W. (1991). Human fetal and subsequent newborn responses to sound and vibration. *Infant Behavior and Development, 14*, 1–26.

Klahr, D. (2000). *Exploring science: The cognition and development of discovery processes*. Cambridge, MA: MIT Press.

Klahr, D. (2005). The equivalence of learning paths in early science instruction: Effects of direct instruction and discovery learning. *Psychological Science, 15*, 661–667.

Klahr, D., & Siegler, R. S. (1978). The representation of children's knowledge. In H. W. Reese & L. P. Lipsitt (eds), *Advances in child development and behavior* (Vol. 12, pp. 61–116). New York: Academic Press.

Klaus, M. H., & Kennell, J. H. (1976). *Maternal-infant bonding*. St Louis, MO: C.V. Mosby.

Klaus, M. H., & Kennell, J. H. (1982). *Parent-infant bonding*. St. Louis, MO: Mosby.

Klaus, M. H., Kennell, J. H. & Klaus, P. H. (1995) *Bonding: Building the foundations of secure attachment and independence*. Reading, MA: Addison-Wesley.

Klebanoff, M. A., Levine, R. J., Der Simonian, R., Clemens, J. D. & Wilkins, D. G. (1999) Maternal serum paraxanthine, a caffeine metabolite and the risk of spontaneous abortion. *The New England Journal of Medicine, 341*, 1639–1644.

Klebanov, P. K., Brooks-Gunn, J., & McCormick, M. C. (2001). Maternal coping strategies and emotional distress: Results of an early intervention program for low-birthweight young children. *Developmental Psychology, 37,* 654–667.

Kleibeuker, S. W., De Dreu, C. K. W., & Crone, E. A. (2016). Creativity development in adolescence: Insight from behavior, brain, and training studies. *New Directions for Child and Adolescent Development, 151,* 73–84.

Klein, D. I., & Wender, P. H. (2005), *Understanding depression: A complete guide to its diagnosis and treatment.* New York: Oxford University Press.

Knafo, A., & Jaffee, S. R. (2013). Gene–environment correlation in developmental psychopathology. *Development and Psychopathology, 25,* 1-6.

Knopik, V. S., Neiderhiser, J. M., DeFries, J. C., & Plomin, R. (2016). *Behavioral genetics.* Macmillan Higher Education.

Knopik, V. S., Neiderhiser, J. M., DeFries, J. C., & Plomin, R. (2016). *Behavioral genetics.* New York: Macmillan Higher Education.

Knopik, V. S., Neiderhiser, J. M., DeFries, J. C., & Plomin, R. (2016). *Behavioral genetics.* New York: Worth.

Knudsen, B., & Liszkowski, U. (2012). 18-month-olds predict specific action mistakes through attribution of false belief, not ignorance, and intervene accordingly. *Infancy, 17*(6), 672–691.

Kochanska, G. (1997). Multiple pathways to conscience for children with different temperaments: From toddlerhood to age 5. *Developmental Psychology, 33,* 228–240.

Kochanska, G. (2002). Committed compliance, moral self and internalization: A mediational model. *Developmental Psychology, 38,* 339–351.

Kochanska, G., & Murray, K. T. (2000). Mother-child mutually responsive orientation and conscience development: From toddler to early school age. *Child Development, 71,* 417–431.

Kochanska, G., Aksan, N., Prisco, T. R., & Adams, E. E. (2008). Mother-child and father-child mutually responsive orientation in the first two years and children's outcomes at preschool age: Mechanisms of influence. *Child Development, 79,* 30–44.

Kochanska, G., Coy, K. C., & Murray, K. T. (2001). The development of self-regulation in the first four years of life. *Child Development, 72,* 1091–1111.

Kochanska, G., Gross, J. N., Mei-Hua, L., & Nichols, K. E. (2002). Guilt in young children: Development, determinants, and relations with a broader system of standards. *Developmental Psychology, 73,* 461–482.

Kochanska, G., Murray, K., & Harlan, E. T. (2000). Effortful control in early childhood: Continuity and change, antecedents, and implications for social development. *Developmental Psychology, 36,* 220–232.

Kochenderfer, B. J., & Ladd, G. W. (1996). Peer victimization: Manifestations and relations to school adjustment. *Journal of School Psychology, 34,* 267–283.

Kochenderfer-Ladd, B., & Wardrop, J. (2001). Chronicity and instability in children's peer victimization experiences as predictors of loneliness and social satisfaction trajectories. *Child Development, 72,* 134–151.

Koenig, M. A., Clement, M., & Harris, P. L. (2004). Trust in testimony: Children's use of true and false statements. *Psychological Science, 15,* 694–698.

Koeppen-Schomerus, G., Eley, T. C., Wolke, D., Gringras, P., & Plomin, R. (2000). The interaction of prematurity with genetic and environmental influences on cognitive development in twins. *Journal of Pediatrics, 137*(4), 527–533.

Kohlberg, L. (1966). A cognitive developmental analysis of children's sex-role concepts and attitudes. In E. E. Maccoby (ed.), *The development of sex differences* (pp. 82–173). Stanford, CA: Stanford University Press.

Kohlberg, L. (1969). *Stages in the development of moral thought and action.* New York: Holt.

Kohlberg, L. (1985). *The psychology of moral development.* San Francisco: Harper & Row.

Kohlberg, L., & Candee, D. (1984). The relationship of moral judgment to moral action. In W. M. Kurtines & J. L. Gewirtz (eds), *Morality, moral behavior and moral development* (pp. 52–73). New York: Wiley.

Köhler, W. (1926). *The mentality of apes.* New York: Harcourt, Brace & Company.

Köhler, W. (1947). *Gestalt psychology: An introduction to new concepts in modern psychology.* New York: Liveright Publication.

Kokko, K., & Pulkkinen, L. (2000). Aggression in childhood and long-term unemployment in adulthood: A cycle of maladaptation and some protective factors. *Developmental Psychology, 36,* 463–472.

Kolb, B., Gorny, G., Li, Y., Samaha, A., & Robinson, T. E. (2003). Amphetamine or cocaine limits the ability of later experience to promote structural plasticity in the neocortex and nucleus accumbens. *Proceedings of the National Academy of Sciences, 100,* 10523–10528.

Kollar, E., & Fisher, C. (1980). Tooth induction in chick epithelium: Expression of quiescent genes tor enamel synthesis. *Science, 20,* 993–995.

Koopman, P. & Ames, E. W. (1968) Infant's preferences for facial arrangements: A failure to replicate. *Child Development, 39,* 481–487.

Kopp, C. B. (1982). The antecedents of self-regulation. *Developmental Psychology, 18,* 199–214.

Kopp, C. B. (1994). *Baby steps: The 'whys' of your child's behavior in the first two years.* New York: Freeman.

Kopp, C. B. (2002). Commentary: The co-development of attention and emotional regulation. *Infancy, 3,* 199–208.

Korner, A. (1974). The effect of the infant's state, level of arousal, sex and ontogenic stage on the caregiver. In M. Lewis & L. Rosenblum (eds), *The effect of the infant on its caregiver* (pp. 187–214). New York: Wiley.

Korner, A. F. (1989). Infant stimulation: The pros and cons in historical perspective. *Bulletin of National Center for Clinical Infant Programs, 10,* 11–17.

Kosik, K. S. (2006). The neuronal microRNA system. *Nature Reviews Neuroscience, 7,* 911–920.

Kovacs, D. M., Parker, J. G., & Hoffman, L. W. (1996). Behavioral, affective and social correlates of involvement in cross-sex friendship in elementary school. *Child Development, 67,* 2269–2286.

Kovas, Y., & Plomin, R. (2006). Generalist genes: Implications for the cognitive sciences. *Trends in Cognitive Sciences, 10*(5), 198–203.

Kozulin, A. (1990). *Vygotsky's psychology: A biography of ideas.* Cambridge, MA: Harvard University Press.

Kraebel, K. S., & Gerhardstein, P. C. (2006). Three-month-old infants' object recognition across changes in viewpoint using an operant learning procedure. *Infant Behavior and Development, 29*(1), 11–23.

Krahe, B., & Moller, I. (2004). Playing violent electronic games, hostile attributional style, and aggression-related norms in German adolescents. *Journal of Adolescence, 27,* 53–69.

Kramer, L., & Gottman, J. M. (1992). Becoming a sibling—with a little help from my friends. *Developmental Psychology, 28,* 685–699.

Kramer, L., & Ramsburg, D. (2002). Advice given to parents on welcoming a second child: A critical review. *Family Relations, 51,* 2–14.

Kranzler, J. H., & Keith, T. Z. (1999). Independent confirmatory factor analysis of the Cognitive Associatgion System (CAS): Further evidence challenging the construct validity of the CAS. *School Psychology Review, 28,* 117–144.

Kress, J. S., & Elias, M. J. (2006). School based social and emotional learning programs. In W. Damon & R. Lerner (Series eds) & K. A. Reninger & I. Sigel (Vol. eds), *Handbook of child psychology* (Vol. 4, 6th edn, pp. 592–618). New York: Wiley.

Kreutzer, M. A., Leonard, C., & Flavell, J. H. (1975). An interview study of children's knowledge about memory. *Monographs of the Society for Research in Child Development, 40,* 1–60.

Kristiansen, M., & Ham, J. (2014). Programmed cell death during neuronal development: The sympathetic neuron model. *Cell Death and Differentiation, 21*(7), 1025.

Kromm, H., Färber, M., & Holodynski, M. (2015). Felt or false smiles? Volitional regulation of emotional expression in 4-, 6-, and 8-year-old children. *Child Development, 86*(2), 579–597.

Kruesi, M. J., Hibbs, E. D., Zahn, T. P., & Keysor, C. S. (1992). A 2-year prospective follow-up study of children and adolescents with disruptive behavior disorders: Prediction by cerebrospinal fluid 5-hydroxyindoleacetic acid, homovanillic acid and autonomic measures? *Archives of General Psychiatry, 49,* 429–435.

Kübler-Ross, E. (1969). *On death and dying.* New York: Macmillan.

Kübler-Ross, E. (1974). *Questions and answers on death and dying.* New York: Macmillan.

Kuczynski, L. (ed.) (2003). *Handbook of dynamics in parentchild relations.* Thousand Oaks, CA: Sage.

Kuczynski, L., & Parkin, C. M. (2007). Agency and bidirectionality in socialization. In J. E. Grusec & P. Hastings (eds), *Handbook of socialization* (pp. 259–283). New York: Guilford Press.

Kuczynski, L., Kochanska, G., Radke-Yarrow, M., & Girnius-Brown, O. (1987). A developmental interpretation of young children's noncompliance. *Developmental Psychology, 23,* 799–806.

Kuczynski, L., Marshall, S. & Schell, K. (1997) Value socialization in a bidirectional context. In J. E. Grusec & L. Kuczynski (eds), *Parenting and children's internalization of values: A handbook of contemporary theory* (pp. 23–50) New York: Wiley.

Kuhl, P. K., Andruski, J. E., Christovich, I. A., Christovich, L. A., Kozhovnikova, E. A., Ryskina, V. L. et al. (1997). Cross-language analysis of phonetic units in language addressed to infants. *Science, 277,* 685–686.

Kuhl, P. K., Williams, K. A., Lacerda, F., Stevens, K. N., & Lindblom, B. (1992). Linguistic experience alters phonetic perception in infants by 6 months of age. *Science, 255,* 606–608.

Kuhn, D. (1995). Microgenetic study of change: What has it told us? *Psychological Science, 6,* 133–139.

Kuhn, D., & Franklin, S. (2006). The second decade: What develops (and how?). In W. Damon & R. M. Lerner (Series eds), D. Kuhn & R. Siegler (Vol. eds), *Handbook of child psychology* (Vol. 2, 6th edn, pp. 953–994). New York: Wiley.

Kulke, L., von Duhn, B., Schneider, D., & Rakoczy, H. (2018). Is implicit theory of mind a real and robust phenomenon? Results from a systematic replication study. *Psychological Science*, doi: 10.1177/0956797617747090.

Kumar, R. A., & Christian, S. L. (2009). Genetics of autism spectrum disorders. *Current Neurology and Neuroscience Reports, 9,* 188–197.

Kupersmidt, J. B., Griesler, P. C., DeRosier, M. E., Patterson, C. J., & Davies, P. W. (1995). Childhood aggression and peer relations in the context of family and neighborhood factors, *Child Development, 66,* 360–375.

Kupersmidt, J., & Dodge, K. A. (eds) (2004). *Children's peer relations: From development to intervention.* Washington, DC: American Psychological Association.

Kurtz, B. E., & Borkowski, J. G. (1987). Development of strategic skills in impulsive and reflective children: A longitudinal study of metacognition. *Journal of Experimental Child Psychology, 43,* 129–148.

Kyng, K. J., May, A., Kòlvraa, S., & Bohr, V. A. (2003). Gene expression profiling in Werner syndrome closely resembles that of normal aging. *Proceedings of the National Academy of Science USA, 100,* 12259–12264.

La Barbera, J. D., Izard, C. E., Vietze, P. & Parisi, S. A. (1976) Four- and six-monthold infants' visual responses to joy, anger, and neutral expressions. *Child Development, 47,* 535–538.

Labad, J., Menchon, J. M., Alonso, P., Segalas, C., Jimenez, S. Jaurrieta, N., et al. (2008). Gender differences in obsessive–compulsive symptom dimensions. *Depression and Anxiety,* 25(10), 832–838.

Labouvie-Vief, G. (1980). Beyond formal operations: Uses and limits of pure logic in lifespan development. *Human Development, 23,* 141–161.

Labouvie-Vief, G. (1985). Intelligence and cognition. In J. E. Birren & K. W. Schaie (eds), *Handbook of the psychology of aging* (2nd edn, pp. 500–530). New York: Van Nostrand Reinhold.

Labouvie-Vief, G. (1990). Modes of knowledge and organisation of development. In M. L. Commons, L. Kohlberg, F. Richards, & J. Sinnott (eds), *Beyond formal operations (3) Models and methods in the study of adult and adolescent thought.* New York: Praeger.

Lachman, M. E., Rocke, C., Rosnick, C., & Ryff, C. D. (2008). Realism and illusion in Americans' temporal views of their life satisfaction: Age differences in reconstructing the past and anticipating the future. *Psychological Science, 19,* 889–897.

Ladd, G. W. (2005). *Peer relationships and social competence of children and youth.* New Haven, CT: Yale University Press.

Ladd, G. W., & Pettit, G. S. (2002). Parents and children's peer relationships. In M. Bornstein (ed.), *Handbook of parenting* (Vol. 4, 2nd edn, pp. 377–409). Hillsdale, NJ: Erlbaum.

Ladd, G. W., & Troop-Gordon, W. (2003). The role of chronic peer difficulties in the development of children's psychological adjustment problems. *Child Development, 74,* 1344–1367.

Ladd, G. W., Birch, S. H., & Buhs, E. S. (1999). Children's social and scholastic lives in kindergarten: Related spheres of influence? *Child Development, 70,* 1373–1400.

LaFrance, M., Hecht, M. A., & Levy Paluck, E. (2003). The contingent smile: A meta-analysis of sex differences in smiling. *Psychological Bulletin, 129,* 305–334.

LaFreniere, P. J. (2000). *Emotional development: A biosocial perspective.* Belmont, CA: Wadsworth/Thompson Learning.

Laible, D. (2007). Attachment with parents and peers in late adolescence: Links with emotional competence and social behavior. *Personality and Individual Differences,* 43(5), 1185–1197.

Laible, D. J., & Thompson, R. A. (1998). Attachment and emotional understanding in preschool children. *Developmental Psychology, 34,* 1038–1045.

Laible, D. J., Carlo, G., & Raffaelli, M. (2000). The differential relations of parent and peer attachment to adolescent adjustment. *Journal of Youth and Adolescence, 29,* 45–59.

Laird, R. D., Pettit, G. S., Dodge, K. A., & Bates, J. E. (2003). Change in parents' monitoring knowledge: Links with parenting, relationships quality, adolescent beliefs and antisocial behavior. *Social Development, 12,* 401–419.

Lam, V. L., & Leman, P. J. (2003). The influence of gender and ethnicity on children's inferences about toy choice. *Social Development, 12,* 269–287.

Lam, V. L., & Leman, P. J. (2009). Children's gender- and ethnicity-based reasoning about foods. *Social Development, 18,* 478–496.

Lamb, M. E. (1997). *The role of the father in child development* (3rd edn). New York: Wiley.

Lamb, M. E. (ed.) (1987) *The father's role: Cross-cultural perspectives.* New York: Wiley.

Lamb, M. E. (ed.) (2004). *The role of the father in child development* (4th edn). New York: Wiley.

Lamb, M. E., & Ahnert, L. (2006). Childcare and youth programs. In W. Damon & R. L. Lerner (Series eds) & K. A. Renninger & I. E. Sigel (Vol. eds). *Handbook of child psychology: Vol. 4. Child psychology and practice* (6th edn, pp. 950–1016). New York: Wiley.

Lamb, M. E., & Roopnarine, J. L. (1979). Peer influences on sex role development in preschoolers. *Child Development, 50*, 1219–1222.

Lamb, M. E., Suomi, S. J., & Stephenson, G. R. (1979). *Social interaction analysis: Methodological issues.* Madison, WI: University of Wisconsin Press.

Lamb, S., & Zakhireh, B. (1997). Toddlers' attention to the distress of peers in a day care setting. *Early Education and Development, 8*, 105–118.

Lambert, K., & Spinath, B. (2018). Conservation abilities, visuospatial skills, and numerosity processing speed: Association with math achievement and math difficulties in elementary school children. *Journal of Learning Disabilities, 51*(3), 223–235.

Lambert, S. R., & Drack, A. V. (1996). Infantile cataracts. *Survey of Ophthalmology, 40*, 427–458.

Lambert, W. E. (1987). The effects of bilingual and bicultural experiences on children's attitudes and social perspectives. In P. Homel, M. Palij, & D. Aranson (eds), *Childhood bilingualism* (pp. 197–221). Hillsdale, NJ: Erlbaum.

Lampl, M., Johnson, M. L., & Frongillo, E. A., Jr (2001). Mixed distribution analysis identifies saltation and stasis growth. *Annals of Human Biology, 28*, 403–411.

Lampl, M., Veldhuis, J. D., & Johnson, M. L. (1992). Saltation and stasis: A model of human growth. *Science, 258*(5083), 801–803.

Lane, H. (1976). *The wild boy of Aveyron.* Cambridge, MA: Harvard University Press.

Langlois, J. H., & Downs, C. A. (1980). Mothers, fathers and peers as socialization agents of sex-typed play behaviors in young children. *Child Development, 51*, 1237–1247.

Langlois, J. H., Kahakanis, L., Rubenstein, A. J., Larson, A., Hallam, N., & Smoot, M. (2000). Maxims or myths of beauty: A meta-analytic and theoretical review. *Psychological Bulletin, 126*, 390–423.

Langlois, R. N. (1985). Knowledge and rationality in the Austrian School: An analytical survey, *Eastern Economic Journal* 9(4), 309–330.

Lansford, J. E., Deater-Deckard, K., Dodge, K. A., Bates, J. E., & Pettit, G. S. (2004). Ethnic differences in the link between physical discipline and later adolescent externalizing behavior. *Journal of Child Psychology and Psychiatry, 45*, 801–812.

Larson, R. (1997). The emergence of solitude as a constrictive domain of experience in early adolescence. *Child Development, 68*, 80–93.

Larson, R. W., & Verma, S. (1999). How children and adolescents spend time across the world: Work, play and developmental opportunities. *Psychological Bulletin, 125*, 701–736.

Larson, R., & Richards, M. H. (1994). *Divergent realities: The emotional lives of mothers, fathers and adolescents.* New York: Basic Books.

Larson, R., & Verma, S. (1999). How children and adolescents around the world spend time: Work, play, and developmental opportunities. *Psychological Bulletin, 125*, 701–736.

Larson, R., Monetia, G., Richards, M. H., & Wilson, S. (2002). Continuity, stability, and change in daily emotional experience across adolescence. *Child Development, 73*, 1151–1165.

Lashley, K. (1951). The problem of serial order in behaviour. In L. A. Jeffress (ed.), *Cerebral mechanisms in behaviour* (pp. 112–136). New York: John Wiley.

Laursen, B. (1995). Conflict and social interaction in adolescent relationships. *Journal of Research on Adolescence, 5*, 55–70.

Laursen, B., & Jensen-Campbell, L. A. (1999). The nature and functions of social exchange in adolescent romantic relationships. In W. Furman, B. Brown & C. Feiring (eds), *The development of romantic relationships in adolescence. Cambridge studies in social and emotional development* (pp. 50–74). New York: Cambridge University Press.

Laursen, B., Hartup, W. W., & Koplas, A. L. (1996). Towards understanding peer conflict. *Merrill-Palmer Quarterly, 42*, 76–102.

Lave, J., & Wenger, E. (1991). *Situated Learning: Legitimate Peripheral Participation.* Cambridge: Cambridge University Press (First published in 1990 as Institute for Research on Learning Report 90-0013.)

Lawlor, D. A., Batty, G. D., Morton, S. M. B., Deary, I. J., Macintyre, S., Ronalds, G. et al. (2005) Early life predictors of childhood intelligence: Evidence from the Aberdeen children of the 1950s study. *Journal of Epidemiology and Community Health, 59*, 656–663.

Layard, R. (2005). *Happiness: Lessons from a new science.* London: Penguin Press.

Lazarus, R. S., & De Longis, A. (1983). Psychological stress and coping in aging. *American Psychologist*, April, 245–254.

Leaper, C. (2002). Parenting girls and boys. In M. Bornstein (ed.) *Handbook of parenting* (2nd edn, Vol. 1, pp. 189–226). Mahwah, NJ: Erlbaum.

Leaper, C., & Friedman, C. K. (2007). The socialization of gender. In J. Grusec & P. Hastings (eds), *Handbook of socialization* (pp. 561–587). New York: Guilford Press.

Leaper, C., Tenenbaum, H. R., & Shaffer, T. G. (1999). Communication patterns of African American girls and boys from low-income, urban background. *Child Development, 70*, 1485–1503.

LeCanuet, J.-P., Fifer, W., Krasnegor, N. & Smotherman, W. (1995) *Fetal development: A psychobiological perspective.* Hillsdale, NJ: Erlbaum.

LeDoux, J. (2002) *Synaptic self: How our brains become who we are.* New York: Viking Press.

Lee, D., & McLanahan, S. (2015). Family structure transitions and child development: Instability, selection, and population heterogeneity. *American Sociological Review, 80.* https://doi.org/10.1177/0003122415592129

Lee, V. E., & Bryk, A. S. (1986). Effects of single-sex secondary schools on student achievement and attitudes. *Journal of Educational Psychology, 78,* 381–395.

Lefrancois, G. R. (1973). *Of children.* Belmont, CA: Wadsworth.

Lei, T., & Cheng, S. (1989). A little but special light on the universality of moral judgment development. In L. Kohlberg, D. Candee, & A. Colby (eds), *Rethinking moral development.* Cambridge, MA: Harvard University Press.

Leichtman, M. D., & Ceci, S. J. (1995). The effects of stereotypes and suggestions on preschoolers' reports. *Developmental Psychology, 31,* 758.

Leinbach, M. D., & Fagot, B. I. (1992). Gender-schematic processing in infancy: Categorical habituation to male and female faces. Unpublished manuscript, University of Oregon, Eugene.

Leippe, M. R., & Romanczyk, A. (1989). Reactions to child (versus adult) eyewitnesses: The influence of jurors' preconceptions and witness behavior. *Law and Human Behavior, 13,* 103–132.

Leman, P. J. & Björnberg, M. (2010). Conversation, development, and gender: A study of changes in children's concepts of punishment. *Child Development, 81,* 958–972.

Leman, P. J. (2004). And your chosen specialist subject is . . . *The Psychologist, 17*(4), 196–198.

Leman, P. J. (2015). How do groups work? Age differences in performance and the social outcomes of peer collaboration. *Cognitive Science, 39,* 804–820. doi: 10.1111/cogs.1217

Leman, P. J. (1999). The role of subject area, gender, ethnic origin and school background in the degree results of Cambridge University undergraduates. *The Curriculum Journal, 10,* 231–252.

Leman, P. J., & Lam, V. (2008). The influence of race and gender on children's conversations and playmate choices. *Child Development, 79,* 1329–1343.

Leman, P. J., Ahmed, S., & Ozarow, L. (2005). Gender, gender relations, and the social dynamics of children's conversations. *Developmental Psychology, 41,* 64–74.

Lemerise, E. A., & Arsenio, W. F. (2000). An integrated model of emotion process and cognition in social information processing. *Child Development, 71,* 107–118.

Lengua, L. J. (2002). The contribution of emotionality and selfregulation to the understanding of children's response to multiple risk. *Child Development, 73,* 144–161.

Lenneberg, E. H. (1967). *Biological foundations of language.* New York: Wiley.

Lenneberg, E. H., Rebelsky, F. G., & Nichols, I. A. (1965). The vocalizations of infants born to deaf and hearing parents. *Human Development, 8,* 23–37.

Lenroot, R. K., & Giedd, J. N. (2010). Sex differences in the adolescent brain, *Brain and Cognition, 72*(1), 46–55.

Leslie, A. M. (2005). Developmental parallels in understanding minds and bodies. Research Focus. *Trends in Cognitive Sciences, 9,* 459–462.

Leslie, A. M., & Thaiss, L. (1992). Domain specificity in conceptual development: Neuropsychological evidence from autism. *Cognition, 43,* 225–251.

Leslie, A. M., Friedman, O., & German, T. P. (2004). Core mechanisms in 'theory of mind'. *Trends in Cognitive Sciences, 8,* 528–533.

Leslie, A. M., Gelman, R., & Gallistel, C. R. (2008). The generative basis of natural number concepts. *Trends in cognitive sciences, 12*(6), 213–218.

Lester, B. M. (1988). Neurobehavioral assessment of the infant at risk. In P. Vietze & H. G. Vaughan (eds), *Early identification of infants with developmental disabilities* (pp. 96–120). New York: Grune & Stratton.

Lester, B. M., Boukydis, C. F. Z., & Twomey, J. E. (2000). Maternal substance abuse and child outcome. In C. H. Zeanah (ed.), *Handbook of infant mental health* (pp. 161–175). New York: Guilford Press.

Leung, G. M., Lai-Ming, H., Tin, K. Y. K., Schooling, C. M., & Lam, T. (2007). Health consequences of cesarean birth during the first 18 months of life. *Epidemiology, 18,* 479–484.

Leventhal, T., & Brooks-Gunn, J. (2000). The neighborhoods they live in: The effects of neighborhood residence on child and adolescent outcomes. *Psychological Bulletin, 126,* 309–337.

Levine, L. J. (1995). Young children's understanding of the causes of anger and sadness. *Child Development, 66,* 697–709.

Levinson, D. (1978). *The seasons of a man's life.* New York: Knopf.

Levinson, D. (1990). A theory of life structure development in adulthood. In N. Alexander & E. Langer (eds), *Higher stages of human development: Perspectives on adult growth* (pp. 35–53). New York: Oxford University Press.

Levinson, D. J., & Levinson, J. D. (1996). *Seasons of a woman's life.* New York: Knopf.

Levitt, M. J., Weber, R. A., & Clark, M. C. (1986). Social network relationships as sources of maternal support and well-being. *Developmental Psychology, 22,* 310–316.

Levy, G. D. (1994) High and low gender schematic children's release from proactive interference. *Sex Roles, 30,* 93–108.

Lewis, B. H., Legato, M., & Fisch, H. (2006). Medical implications of the male biological clock. *Journal of the American Medical Association, 296,* 2369–2371.

Lewis, C., & Osborne, A. (1990). Three-year-olds' problems with false belief: Conceptual deficit or linguistic artifact? *Child Development, 9,* 397–424.

Lewis, M. & Brooks-Gunn, J. (1979) *Social cognition and the acquisition of self.* New York: Plenum Press.

Lewis, M. (1983) On the nature of intelligence: Science or bias? In M. Lewis (ed.), *Origins of intelligence: Infancy and early childhood* (pp. 1–24) New York: Plenum Press.

Lewis, M. (1992). *Shame: The exposed self.* New York: Free Press.

Lewis, M. (1995). Embarrassment: The emotion of self-exposure and evaluation. In J. P. Tangney & K. Fischer (eds), *Self-conscious emotions* (pp. 198–218). New York: Guilford Press.

Lewis, M. (1998). Emotional competence and development. In D. Pushkar, W. M. Bukowski, A. E. Schwartzman, D. M. Stack & D. R. White (eds), *Improving competence across the lifespan* (pp. 27–36). New York: Plenum Press.

Lewis, M. (2000). Self-conscious emotions: Embarrassment, pride, shame, and guilt. In M. Lewis & J. Haviland (eds), *Handbook of emotions* (2nd edn, pp. 623–636). New York: Guilford Press.

Lewis, M., & Brooks, J. (1974). Self, other, and fear: Infants' reactions to people. In M. Lewis & L. Rosenblum (eds), *The origins of fear* (pp. 195–227). New York: Wiley.

Lewis, M., & Freedle, R. (1973). Mother-infant dyad: The cradle of meaning. In P. Pilner, L. Kranes, & T. Holoway (eds), *Communication and affect: Language and thought* (pp. 127–155). New York: Academic Press.

Lewis, M., & Michaelson, L. (1985). *Children's emotions and moods.* New York: Plenum Press.

Lewis, M., & Ramsay, D. (2002). Cortisol response to embarrassment and shame. *Child Development, 73,* 1034–1045.

Lewis, M., & Wilson, C. D. (1972). Infant development in lower-class American families. *Human Development, 15,* 112–127.

Lewis, M., Alessandri, S., & Sullivan, M. W. (1992). Differences in shame and pride as a function of children's gender and task difficulty. *Child Development, 63,* 630–638.

Lewkowicz, D. J., & Hansen-Tift, A. M. (2012). Infants deploy selective attention to the mouth of a talking face when learning speech. *Proceedings of the National Academy of Sciences, 109*(5), 1431–1436.

Lewkowicz, D. J., & Turkewitz, G. (1980). Cross-modal equivalence in early infancy: Auditory-visual intensity matching. *Developmental Psychology, 16,* 597–607.

Lewkowicz, D. J., Leo, I., & Simion, F. (2010). Intersensory perception at birth: Newborns match nonhuman primate faces and voices. *Infancy, 15*(1), 46–60.

Li, D., Sham, P. C., Owen, M. J., & He, L. (2006). Meta-analysis shows significant association between dopamine system genes and attention deficit hyperactivity disorder (ADHD). *Human Molecular Genetics, 15,* 2276–2284.

Liben, L. S. (1991). Adults' performance on horizontality tasks: Conflicting frames of reference. *Developmental Psychology, 27,* 285–294.

Liben, L. S., & Bigler, R. S. (2002). The developmental course of gender differentiation. *Monographs of the Society for Research in Child Development, 67*(269, Pt 2).

Liben, L. S., & Golbeck, S. L. (1980). Sex differences in performance on Piagetian spatial tasks: Differences in competence or performance. *Child Development, 51,* 594–597.

Liberman, I. Y., Shankweiler, D., Liberman, A. M., Fowler, C. & Fischer, F. W. (1976) Phonetic segmentation and recoding in the beginning reader. In A. S. Reber & D. Scarborough (eds), *Reading: Theory and practice* (pp. 207–226) Hillsdale, NJ: Erlbaum.

Lichtenstein, P., Tuvblad, C., Larsson, H., & Carlström, E. (2007). The Swedish Twin study of Child and Adolescent Development: The TCHAD-study. *Twin Research and Human Genetics, 10,* 67–73.

Liddle, H. A. & Rowe, C. L. (eds) (2006) *Adolescent substance abuse: Research and clinical issues.* New York: Cambridge University Press.

Liebal, K., Behne, T., Carpenter, M., & Tomasello, M. (2009). Infants use shared experience to interpret pointing gestures. *Developmental Science, 12*(2), 264–271.

Liebert, R. M., & Baron, R. A. (1972). Some immediate effects of televised violence on children's behavior. *Developmental Psychology, 6,* 469–475.

Lifshitz, F., Finch, N., & Lifshitz, J. (1991). *Children's nutrition.* Boston, MA: Jones & Bartlett.

Lillard, A. S. (1993). Pretend play skills and the child's theory of mind. *Child Development, 64,* 348–371.

Lillard, A. S. (1998). Ethnopsychologies: Cultural variations in theory of mind. *Psychological Bulletin, 123,* 3–33.

Lillard, A. S. (2005). *Montessori: The science behind the genius.* Oxford: Oxford University Press.

Lillard, A. S. (2006) The socialization of theory of mind: Cultural and social class differences in behavior explanation. In A. Antonietti, O. Liverta-Simpio & A. Marchetti (eds), *Theory of mind and language in developmental contexts* (pp. 65–76) New York: Springer.

Lin, C., Verp, M. S., & Sabbagha, R. E. (1993). *The high risk fetus: Pathophysiology, diagnosis, management.* New York: Springer/Verlag.

Lindberg, M. (1980). Is knowledge base development a necessary and sufficient condition for memory development? *Journal of Experimental Child Psychology, 30,* 401–410.

Lindberg, M. A., Jones, S., McComas-Collard, L., & Thomas, S. W. (2001). Similarities and differences in eyewitness testimonies of children who directly versus vicariously experience stress. *Journal of Genetic Psychology, 162,* 314–333.

Linn, S., Lieberman, E., Schoenbaum, S. C., Monson, R. R., Stubblefield, P. G. & Ryand, K. J. (1988) Adverse outcomes of pregnancy in women exposed to diethylstilbestrol in utero. *Journal of Reproductive Medicine, 33,* 3–7.

Linnell, K. J., Bremner, A. J., Caparos, S., Davidoff, J., & de Fockert, J. W. (2018). Urban experience alters lightness perception. *Journal of Experimental Psychology: Human Perception and Performance, 44*(1), 2.

Linsell, L., Malouf, R., Morris, J., Kurinczuk, J. J., & Marlow, N. (2015). Prognostic factors for poor cognitive development in children born very preterm or with very low birth weight: A systematic review. *JAMA Pediatrics, 169*(12), 1162–1172.

Lipsitt, L. P. (2002). The newborn as informant. In J. W. Fagan & H. Hayne (eds), *Progress in infancy research,* Vol. 2. Mahwah, NJ: Lawrence Erlbaum.

Lipsitt, L. P. (2003). Crib death: A biobehavioral phenomenon? *Current Directions in Psychological Science, 12,* 164–170.

Little, R. (1975) *Maternal alcohol use and resultant birth weight.* Unpublished doctoral dissertation. Johns Hopkins University, Baltimore.

Liu, S. (2007). Maternal mortality and severe morbidity associated with low-risk planned cesarean delivery versus planned vaginal delivery at term. *Canadian Medical Association Journal, 176,* 455–460.

Lloyd, B., and Duveen, G. (1992). *Gender identities and education: The impact of starting school.* Hemel Hempstead: Harvester Wheatsheaf.

Lloyd-Fox, S., Begus, K., Halliday, D., Pirazzoli, L., Blasi, A., Papademetriou, M., . . . & Elwell, C. E. (2017). Cortical specialisation to social stimuli from the first days to the second year of life: A rural Gambian cohort. *Developmental Cognitive Neuroscience, 25,* 92–104.

Lloyd-Fox, S., Blasi, A., Volein, A., Everdell, N., Elwell, C. E., & Johnson, M. H. (2009). Social perception in infancy: A near infrared spectroscopy study. *Child Development, 80,* 986–999.

Lloyd-Fox, S., Wu, R., Richards, J. E., Elwell, C. E., & Johnson, M. H. (2015). Cortical activation to action perception is associated with action production abilities in young infants. *Cerebral Cortex, 25*(2), 289–297.

Lobar, S. L., Youngblut, J. M., & Brooten, D. (2006). Cross-cultural beliefs, ceremonies and rituals surrounding the death of a loved one. *Pediatric Nursing, 32,* 44–50.

Lobel, T. E., Gruber, R., Govrin, N. & Mashraki-Pedhatzur, S. (2001) Children's gender-related inferences and judgments: A cross cultural study. *Developmental Psychology, 37,* 839–846.

Locke, J. (1894). *An essay concerning human understanding.* Ed. A. C. Fraser. Oxford, UK: Clarendon Press.

Locke, J. (1960) In P.H. Nidditch (ed), *An essay concerning human understanding,* Oxford University Press, Oxford.

Loeber, R., Burke, J. D., & Lahey, B. B. (2002). What are adolescent antecedents to antisocial personality disorder? *Criminal Behaviour & Mental Health, 12,* 24–36.

Loehlin, J. C. (2016). What can an adoption study tell us about the effect of prenatal environment on a trait? *Behavior Genetics, 46*(3), 329–333.

Lorenz, K. (1937). The companion in the bird's world. *Auk, 54,* 245–273.

Lorenz, K. (1952). *King Solomon's ring.* New York: Crowell.

Lourenço, O., & Machado, A. (1996). In defense of Piaget's theory: A reply to ten common criticisms. *Psychological Review, 103*(1), 143–164.

Lovaas, O. I. (1987). Behavioral treatment and normal educational and intellectual functioning in young autistic children. *Journal of Consulting and Clinical Psychology, 55,* 3–9.

Lovett, S. B., & Pillow, B. H. (1995). Development of the ability to distinguish between comprehension and memory: Evidence from strategy-selection tasks. *Journal of Educational Psychology, 87,* 523–536.

Lowe, X., Eskenazi, B., Nelson, D. O., Kidd, S., Alme, A., & Wyrobek, A. J. (2001). Frequency of XY sperm increases with age in fathers of boys with Klinefelter syndrome. *American Journal of Human Genetics, 69,* 1046–1054.

Lozoff, B., Jimenez, E., & Smith, J. B. (2006). Double burden iron deficiency in infancy and low socioeconomic status. *Archives of*

Pediatrics and Adolescent Medicine, 160, 1108–1113.

Luby, J. L., Gaffrey, M. S., Tillman, R., April, L. M., & Belden, A. C. (2014). Trajectories of preschool disorders to full DSM depression at school age and early adolescence: Continuity of preschool depression. *American Journal of Psychiatry, 171*(7), 768–776.

Luecke-Aleksa, D., Anderson, D. R., Collins, P. A., & Schmitt, K. L. (1995). Gender constancy and television viewing. *Developmental Psychology, 31*, 773–780.

Lund, D. A., & Caserta M. S. (2004). Older men coping with widowhood. *Geriatrics & Aging, 7*, 29–33.

Lundström, J. N., & Jones-Gotman, M. (2009). Romantic love modulates women's identification of men's body odors. *Hormones and Behavior, 55*, 280–284.

Luo, Y. (2011). Do 10-month-old infants understand others' false beliefs? *Cognition, 121*(3), 289–298.

Luo, Y., & Baillargeon, R. (2010). Toward a mentalistic account of early psychological reasoning. *Current Directions in Psychological Science, 19*(5), 301–307.

Luria, A. R. (1976). *Cognitive development: Its cultural and social foundation.* Cambridge, MA: Harvard University Press.

Luthar, S. S. (2007). Conceptual issues in studies of resilience: Past, present, and future research. In B. M. Lester, A. S. Masten & B. McEwen (eds), *Resilience in children* (pp. 105–115). New York: Blackwell.

Luthar, S. S., Cicchetti, D., & Becker, B. (2000). The construct of resilience: A critical evaluation and guidelines for future work. *Child Development, 71*, 543–562.

Lykken, D. T., McGue, M., Tellegen, A., & Bouchard, T. J., Jr (1992). Genetic traits that may not run in families. *American Psychologist, 47*(12), 1565–1577.

Lynch, M. P., Eilers, R. E., Oller, D. K., & Urbano, R. C. (1990). Innateness, experience, and music perception. *Psychological Science, 1*, 272–276.

Lyons, T. D. (2002). Applying suggestibility research to the real world: The case of repeated questions. *Law and Contemporary Problems, 65*, 97–126.

Lyons-Ruth, K., & Jacobvitz, D. (1999). Attachment disorganization. In J. Cassidy & P. Shaver (eds), *Handbook of attachment* (pp. 520–554). New York: Guilford Press.

Lyons-Ruth, K., Lyubchik, A., Wolfe, R., & Bronfman, E. (2002). Parental depression and child attachment: Hostile and helpless profiles of parent and child behavior among families and risk. In S. H. Goodman & I. Gotlib (eds), *Children of depressed parents* (pp. 89–120). Washington, DC: American Psychological Association.

Lytton, H., & Romney, D. M. (1991). Parents' differential socialization of boys and girls: A meta-analysis. *Psychological Bulletin, 109*, 267–296.

Ma, C., & Schapira, M. (2017). *The bell curve.* London: Macat Library.

MacBeth, T. M. (1996). Indirect effects of television: Creativity, persistence, school achievement, and participation in other activities. In T. M. MacBeth (ed.), *Tuning in to young viewers: Social science perspectives on television* (pp. 149–219). Thousand Oaks, CA: Sage.

Maccoby, E. E. (1998). *The two sexes.* Cambridge, MA: Harvard University Press.

Maccoby, E. E., & Jacklin, C. N. (1974). *The psychology of sex differences.* Stanford, CA: Stanford University Press.

Maccoby, E. E., & Martin, J. A. (1983). Socialization in the context of the family: Parent-child interaction. In E. M. Hetherington (ed.), *Socialization, personality, and social development: Vol. 4. Handbook of child psychology* (pp. 1–102). New York: Wiley.

MacDonald, K. & Parke, R. D. (1986) Parent-child physical play: The effects of sex and age of children and parents. *Sex Roles, 15*, 367–378.

MacFarlane, J. A. (1975) Olfaction in the development of social preferences in the human neonate. In M. A. Hofer (ed.), *Parent-infant interaction* (pp. 103–117) New York: Elsevier.

Machluf, K., & Bjorklund, D. F. (2015). Evolutionary developmental psychology. In J. Wright (ed.) *International encyclopedia of the social and behavioral sciences* (2nd ed., pp. 420–429). Amsterdam: Elsevier. DOI: 10.1016/B978-0-08-097086-8.81018-1

Mackintosh, N. J. (1996) Sex differences and IQ. *Journal of Biosocial Science, 28*, 559–571.

Macpherson, F. (ed.) (2011). *The senses: Classic and contemporary philosophical perspectives* (Vol. 11). Oxford: Oxford University Press.

MacPherson, S. E., Phillips, L. H., & Della Sala, S. (2002). Age, executive function, and social decision making: A dorsolateral prefrontal theory of cognitive ageing. *Psychology and Ageing, 17*(4), 598–609.

Magai, C., & McFadden, S. H. (1995). *The role of emotions in social and personality development.* New York: Plenum Press.

Magnusson, D. & Stattin, H. (2006) The person in context: A holistic-interactionistic approach. In W. Damon & R. M. Lerner (Series eds) & R. M. Lerner (Vol. ed.), *Handbook of child psychology: Vol. 1. Theoretical models of human development* (6th edn, pp. 400–464) New York: Wiley.

Magnusson, D. (1988). *Individual development from an interactional perspective*. Hillsdale, NJ: Erlbaum.

Magnusson, D. (1996). Towards a developmental science. In D. Magnusson (ed.), *The lifespan development of individuals* (pp. xv–xviii). Cambridge: Cambridge University Press.

Mahon, B. Z., & Caramazza, A. (2009). Concepts and categories: A cognitive neuropsychological perspective. *Annual Review of Psychology, 60*, 27–51.

Main, M. (1973). Exploration, play and level of cognitive functioning as related to child-mother attachment. Unpublished doctoral dissertation. Johns Hopkins University, Baltimore.

Main, M., & Cassidy, J. (1988). Categories of response to reunion with the parent at age 6: Predictable from infant attachment classification and stable over a 1-month period. *Developmental Psychology, 24*, 415–426.

Main, M., & Goldwyn, R. (1985/1991). Adult attachment scoring and classification system. Unpublished manuscript, University of California, Berkeley.

Main, M., & Hesse, E. (1990). Parents' unresolved traumatic experiences are related to infant disorganized attachment status: Is frightened and/or frightening parental behavior the linking mechanism? In M. T. Greenberg, D. Cicchetti, & E. M. Cummings (eds), *Attachment in the preschool years: Theory, research, and intervention* (pp. 161–182). Chicago: University of Chicago Press.

Main, M., & Weston, D. (1981). The quality of the toddler's relationship to mother and father: Related to conflict behavior and readiness to establish new relationships. *Child Development, 52*, 932–940.

Main, M., Hesse, E., & Kaplan, N. (2005). Predictability of attachment behavior and representational processes at 1, 6, and 19 years of age: The Berkeley Longitudinal Study. In K. E. Grossmann, K. Grossmann, & E. Waters (eds), *Attachment from infancy to adulthood* (pp. 245–304). New York: Guilford Press.

Main, M., Kaplan, N., & Cassidy, J. (1985). Security in infancy, childhood, and adulthood: A move to the level of representation. *Monographs of the Society for Research in Child Development, 50*, 66–104.

Maitre, N. L., Key, A. P., Chorna, O. D., Slaughter, J. C., Matusz, P. J., Wallace, M. T., & Murray, M. M. (2017). The dual nature of early-life experience on somatosensory processing in the human infant brain. *Current Biology, 27*(7), 1048–1054.

Malatesta, C. Z. (1982). The expression and regulation of emotion: A lifespan perspective. In T. Field & A. Fogel (eds), *Emotion and early interaction* (pp. 1–24). Hillsdale, NJ: Erlbaum.

Malatesta, C. Z., Culver, C., Tesman, J. & Shepard, B. (1989) The development of emotional expression during the first two years of life: Normative trends and patterns of individual differences. *Monographs of the Society for Research in Child Development, 54*, 1–2.

Malcolm, L. A. (1970). Growth of the Asai child of the Madang district of New Guinea. *Journal of Biosocial Science, 2*, 213–226.

Mallick, S. K., & McCandless, B. R. (1966). A study of catharsis of aggression. *Journal of Personality and Social Psychology, 4*, 591–596.

Malti, T., & Dys, S. P. (2018). From being nice to being kind: Development of prosocial behaviors. *Current Opinion in Psychology, 20*, 45–49.

Mandler, J. M. (1998). Representation. In W. Damon (Series Ed.) & D. Kuhn & R. S. Siegler (Vol. eds), *Handbook of child psychology: Vol. 2. Cognition, perception, and language* (pp. 255–308). New York: Wiley.

Mandler, J. M., & Bauer, P. J. (1988). The cradle of categorization: Is the basic level basic? *Cognitive Development, 3*, 247–264.

Mangelsdorf, S. C., Shapiro, J. R., & Marzolf, D. (1995). Developmental and temperamental differences in emotion regulation in infancy. *Child Development, 66*, 1817–1828.

Mangelsdorf, S., Watkins, S., & Lehn, L. (1991, April). *The role of control in the infant's appraisal of strangers*. Paper presented at the biennial meeting of the Society for Research in Child Development, Seattle, Washington.

Manuck, S. B., & McCaffery, J. M. (2014). Gene-environment interaction. *Annual Review of Psychology, 65*, 41–70.

Maratsos, M. (1983) Some current issues in the study of the acquisition of grammar. In P. H. Mussen (ed.), *Handbook of child psychology* (Vol. 3, pp. 707–786) New York: Wiley.

Maratsos, M. (1989). Innateness and plasticity in language acquisition. In M. Rice & R. Schiefelbusch (eds), *The teachability of Language*. Baltimore: Paul Brooks.

Maratsos, M. (1993). Discussion in the symposium *Issues in the acquisition of inflectional processes*, presented at the meetings of the Society for Research in Child Development, New Orleans, LA.

Maratsos, M. (1998). The acquisition of grammar. In W. Damon (Series Ed.) & D. Kuhn & R. S. Siegler (Vol. eds), *Handbook of child psychology: Vol. 2. Cognition, perception, and language* (5th edn, pp. 421–466). New York: Wiley.

Marco, E. J., & Skuse, D. H. (2006). Autism-lessons from the X chromosome. *Social Cognitive and Affective Neuroscience, 1*, 183–193.

Marcovitch, S., & Zelazo, P. D. (2009). A hierarchical competing systems model of the emergence and early development of executive function (Target article with commentaries). *Developmental Science, 12*, 1–18.

Marcus, G. F. (1995). Children's overregularization of English plurals: A quantitative analysis. *Journal of Child Language, 22*, 447–460.

Marcus, L., Lejeune, F., Berne-Audéoud, F., Gentaz, E., & Debillon, T. (2012). Tactile sensory capacity of the preterm infant: Manual perception of shape from 28 gestational weeks. *Pediatrics, 130*, e88–e94.

Marean, G. C., Werner, L. A., & Kuhl, P. K. (1992). Vowel categorization by very young infants. *Developmental Psychology, 28*, 396–405.

Mareschal, D. (2000). Object knowledge in infancy: Current controversies and approaches. *Trends in Cognitive Sciences, 4*(11), 408–416.

Mareschal, D., French, R., & Quinn, P. (2000). A connectionist account of asymmetric category learning in early infancy. *Developmental Psychology, 36*, 635–645.

Mareschal, D., Johnson, M. H., Sirois, S., Spratling, M., Thomas, M., & Westermann, G. (2007). *Neuroconstructivism, Vol. I: How the brain constructs cognition, Vol. 2 Perspectives and prospects.* Oxford, UK: Oxford University Press.

Margolese, H. (2000). The male menopause and mood: Testosterone decline and depression in the aging male—is there a link? *Journal of Geriatric Psychiatry and Neurology, 13*, 93–101.

Markman, E. M. (1977). Realizing that you don't understand: A preliminary investigation. *Child Development, 48*, 986–992.

Markman, E. M. (1979). Realizing that you don't understand: Elementary school children's awareness of inconsistencies. *Child Development, 50*, 643–655.

Markman, E. M. (1989). *Categorization and naming in children.* Cambridge, MA: MIT Press.

Markman, E. M. (1994). Constraints on word meaning in early language acquisition. In L. Gleitman & B. Landau (eds), *The acquisition of the lexicon* (pp. 199–229). Cambridge, MA: MIT Press/Elsevier.

Markman, E. M., & Hutchinson, J. E. (1994). Children's sensitivity to constraints on word meaning: Taxonomic versus thematic relations. *Cognitive Psychology, 16*, 1–27.

Marlow, N., E. M. Hennessy, Bracewell, M., & Wolke, D. (2007). Motor and executive function at 6 years of age after extremely preterm birth. *Pediatrics, 120*(4), 793–804.

Marsh, A., Finger, E., Mitchell, D., Reid, M., Sims, C., Kosson, D. et al. (2008). Reduced amygdala response to fearful expressions in children and adolescents with callous-unemotional traits and disruptive behavior disorders. *American Journal of Psychiatry, 165*(6), 712–720.

Martin, C. L., & Fabes, R. (2001). The stability and consequences of young children's same-sex peer interactions. *Developmental Psychology, 37*, 431–446.

Martin, C. L., & Halverson, C. F. (1983). The effects of sex-typing schemas on young children's memory. *Child Development, 54*, 563–574.

Martin, C. L., & Little, J. K. (1990). The relation of gender understanding to children's sex-typed preferences and gender stereotypes. *Child Development, 61*, 1427–1439.

Martin, C. L., & Ruble, D. N. (2004). Children's search for gender cues. *Current Directions in Psychological Science, 13*, 67–70.

Martinez, F. D., Wright, A. L. & Taussig, L. M. (1994) The effect of paternal smoking on the birthweight of newborns whose mothers do not smoke. *American Journal of Public Health, 84*, 1489–1491.

Martini, F. H. (1995). *Fundamentals of anatomy and physiology* (3rd edn). Upper Saddle River, NJ: Prentice Hall.

Martini, M., & Kirkpatrick, J. (1981). Early interactions in the Marquesas Islands. In T. M. Field, A. M. Sostek, P. Vietze, & P. H. Leiderman (eds), *Culture and early interactions* (pp. 189–214). Hillsdale, NJ: Erlbaum.

Martorell, R. (1984). Genetics, environment and growth: Issues in the assessment of nutritional status. In A. Velasquez & H. Bourges (eds), *Genetic factors in nutrition* (pp. 373–392) Orlando, FL: Academic Press.

Massey, C. M., & Gelman, R. (1988). Preschooler's ability to decide whether a photographed unfamiliar object can move itself. *Developmental Psychology, 24*, 307–317.

Masten, A. S. (2006). Developmental psychopathology: Pathways to the future. *International Journal of Behavioral Development, 30*(1), 47–54.

Masten, A. S. (2015). *Ordinary magic: Resilience in development.* Guilford Publications.

Masten, A. S., & Labella, M. H. (2016). Risk and resilience in child development. *Child psychology: A handbook of contemporary issues*, 423–450.

Matas, L., Arend, R., & Sroufe, L. A. (1978). Continuity of adaptation in the second year: The relationship between quality of attachment and later competence. *Child Development, 49*, 547–556.

Matthen, M. (ed.) (2015). *The Oxford handbook of philosophy of perception.* Oxford: Oxford University Press.

Matthews, K. A., Wing, R. R., Kuller, L. H. Meilahn, E. N., Kelsey, S. F., Costello, E. J., &

Caggiula, A. W. (1990). Influences of natural menopause on psychological characteristics and symptoms of middle-aged healthy women. *Journal of Consulting and Clinical Psychology, 58,* 345–351.

Maughan, B., Rowe, R., Messer, J., Goodman, R., & Meltzer, H. (2004). Conduct disorder and oppositional defiant disorder in a national sample: Developmental epidemiology. *Journal of Child Psychology and Psychiatry, 45,* 609–621.

Maurer, D. & Barrera, M. E. (1981). Infants' perception of natural and distorted arrangements of a schematic face. *Child Development, 52*(1), 196–202.

Maurer, D., & Maurer, C. (1988). *The world of the newborn.* New York: Basic Books.

Maurer, D., & Salapatek, P. (1976). Developmental changes in scanning of faces by young infants. *Child Development, 47,* 523–527.

Maurer, D., Stagner, C. L., & Mondlach, C. J. (1999). Crossmodal transfer of shape is difficult to demonstrate in one-month-olds. *Child Development, 70,* 1047–1057.

Maynard, A. E. (2002). Cultural teaching: The development of teaching skills in Maya sibling interactions. *Child Development, 73,* 969–982.

McCall, R. B., Applebaum, M. I., & Hogarty, P. S. (1973). Developmental changes in mental performance. *Monographs of the Society for Research in Child Development, 38*(3), (Serial no. 150), 1–84.

McCall, R. B., Hogarty, P. S., & Hurlburt, N. (1972). Transitions in infant sensorimotor development and the prediction of childhood IQ. *American Psychologist, 27,* 728–748.

McCall, R., Beach, S. R., & Lan, S. (2000). The nature and correlates of underachievement among elementary school children in Hong Kong. *Child Development, 71,* 785–801.

McCarty, M. E., Clifton, R. K., Ashmead, D. H., Lee, P. & Goubet, N. (2001). How infants use vision for grasping objects. *Child Development 72,* 973–987.

McCaul, K. D., Gladue, B. A., & Joppa, M. (1992). Winning, losing, mood, and testosterone. *Hormones and Behavior, 26,* 486–504.

McClelland, J. L., Botvinick, M. M., Noelle, D. C., Plaut, D. C., Rogers, T. T., Seidenberg, M. S., & Smith, L. B. (2010). Letting structure emerge: Connectionist and dynamical systems approaches to cognition. *Trends in Cognitive Sciences, 14*(8), 348–356.

McCormick, E. M., Perino, M. T., & Telzer, E. H. (2018). Not just social sensitivity: Adolescent neural suppression of social feedback during risk taking. *Developmental Cognitive Neuroscience, 30,* 134–141. doi: 10.1016/j.dcn.2018.01.012

McCrory, E., Puetz, V. B., & Viding, E. (2017). The neuroscience and genetics of childhood maltreatment. In D. Skuse, H. Bruce, & L. Dowdney (eds), *Child Psychology and Psychiatry: Frameworks for Clinical Training and Practice,* 3rd ed., 187–194. Chichester: Wiley.

McDowell, D. J., & Parke, R. D. (2000). Differential knowledge of display rules for positive and negative emotions: Influences from parents influences on peers. *Social Development, 9,* 415–432.

McDowell, D. J., O'Neil, R., & Parke, R. D. (2000). Display rule application in a disappointing situation and children's emotional reactivity: Relations with social competence. *Merrill-Palmer Quarterly, 46,* 306–324.

McEachin, J. J., Smith, T., & Lovaas, O. I. (1993). Long-term outcome for children with autism who receive early intensive behavioral treatment. *American Journal on Mental Retardation, 97,* 359–372.

McGarrigle, J., & Donaldson, M. (1975). Conservation accidents. *Cognition, 3*(4), 341–350.

McGlothlin, H., Killen, M., & Edmonds, C. (2005). European-American children's intergroup attitudes about peer relationships. *British Journal of Developmental Psychology, 23,* 227–249.

McGraw, M. (1940). Neuromuscular development of the human infant as exemplified in the achievement of erect locomotion. *Journal of Pediatrics, 17,* 747–771.

McGraw, M. B. (1935). *Growth: A study of Johnny and Jimmy.* New York: Appleton Century Crofts.

McGue, M., & Bouchard, T. J. (1987). Genetic and environmental determinants of information processing and special mental abilities: A twin analysis. In R. J. Sternberg (ed.), *Advances in the psychology of human intelligence* (Vol. 5, pp. 7–45). Hillsdale, NJ: Erlbaum.

McGuire, S. (2001) Nonshared environment research: What is it and where is it going? *Marriage and Family Review, 33,* 31–56.

McHale, S. M., Crouter, A. C., & Whiteman, S. D. (2003). Family contexts of gender development in childhood and adolescence. *Social Development, 12,* 125–148.

McHale, S. M., Shanahan, L., Updegraff, K. A., Crouter, A. C., & Booth, A. (2004). Developmental and individual differences in girls' sex-typed activities in middle childhood and adolescence. *Child Development, 75,* 1575–1593.

McHale, S. M., Updegraff, K. A., Helms-Erikson, H., & Crouter, A. C. (2001). Sibling influences on gender development in middle childhood and early adolescence: A longitudinal study. *Developmental Psychology, 37,* 115–125.

McIntire, D. D., Bloom, S. L., Casey, B. M., & Leveno, K. J. (1999). Birthweight in relation to morbidity and mortality among newborn infants. *The New England Journal of Medicine, 340,* 1234–1238.

McKinlay, J. B., McKinlay, S. M., & Brambilla, D. (1987). The relative contributions of endocrine changes and social circumstances to depression in mid-aged women. *Journal of Health and Social Behavior, 28,* 345–363.

McKown, C., & Weinstein, R. S. (2003). The development and consequences of stereotype consciousness in middle childhood. *Child Development, 74,* 498–515.

McLanahan, S., & Sandefur, G. (1994). *Growing up with a single parent: What hurts, what helps?* Cambridge, MA: Harvard University Press.

McLoyd, V. C., Hill, N., & Dodge, K. (eds) (2005). *African American family life: Ecological and cultural diversity.* New York: Guilford Press.

McLoyd, V. C., Kaplan, R., Hardaway, C., & Wood, D. (2007). Does endorsement of physical discipline matter? Assessing moderating influences on the maternal and child psychological correlates of physical discipline in African American families. *Journal of Family Psychology, 21,* 165–175.

McLoyd, V. C., Kaplan, R., Purtell, K. M., & Huston, A. C. (2011). Assessing the effects of a work-based antipoverty program for parents on youths' future orientation and employment experiences. *Child Development, 82,* 113–132.

McNeilis, J., Maughan, B., Goodman, R., & Rowe, R. (2018). Comparing the characteristics and outcomes of parent- and teacher-reported oppositional defiant disorder: Findings from a national sample. *Journal of Child Psychology and Psychiatry, 59,* 659–666. doi: 10.1111/jcpp.12845

Mead, M. (1935). *Sex and temperament in three primitive societies.* New York: Morrow.

Medvedev, Z. A. (1990). An attempt at a rational classification of theories of aging. *Biological reviews of the Cambridge Philosophical Society, 65,* 375–398.

Meeus, W. H. J., Branje, S. J. T., van der Valk, I., & de Wied, M. (2007). Relationships with intimate partner, best friend, and parents in adolescence and early adulthood: A study of the saliency of the intimate partnership. *International Journal of Behavioral Development, 31,* 569–580.

Mehler, J., Jusczyk, P., Lambertz, G., Halsted, N., Bertoncini, J., & Amieltison, C. (1988). A precursor of language acquisition in young infants. *Cognition, 29,* 143–178.

Mehler, J., Morton, J., & Jusczyk, P. W. (1984). On reducing language to biology. *Cognitive Neuropsychology, 1,* 83–116.

Mehta, M. A., Sahakian, B. J., & Robbins, T. (2001). Comparative psychopharmacology of methylphenidate and related drugs in human volunteers, patients with ADHD, and experimental animals. In M. V. Solanto, A. F. T. Arnsten, & F. X. Castellanos (eds), *Stimulant drugs and ADHD: Basic and clinical neuroscience* (pp. 303–331). New York: Oxford University Press.

Meisel, J. M. (1995). Parameters in acquisition. In P. Fletcher & B. MacWhinney (eds), *The handbook of child language* (pp. 10–35). Oxford: Blackwell.

Mellanby, J, Martin, R. M. A., & O'Doherty, J. (2000). The gender gap in final examination results at Oxford University. *British Journal of Psychology, 91,* 377–390.

Meltzer, L. (2018). *Executive function in education.* New York: Guildford Press.

Meltzoff, A. N. (1981) Imitation, intermodal coordination and representation in early infancy. In G. Butterworth (ed.), *Infancy and epistemology* (pp. 85–114) Brighton: Harvester Press.

Meltzoff, A. N. (1988). Infant imitation after a 1-week delay: Long-term memory for novel acts and multiple stimuli. *Developmental Psychology, 24,* 470–476.

Meltzoff, A. N. (1990) Towards a developmental cognitive science. *Annals of the New York Academy of Sciences, 608,* 1–37.

Meltzoff, A. N. (2007). 'Like me': A foundation for social cognition. *Developmental Science, 10*(1), 126–134.

Meltzoff, A. N., & Borton, R. W. (1979). Intermodal matching by human neonates. *Nature, 282,* 403–404.

Meltzoff, A. N., & Moore, M. K. (1977). Imitation of facial and manual gestures by human neonates, *Science, 198,* 75–78.

Meltzoff, A. N., & Moore, M. K. (1983). Newborn infants imitate adult facial gestures. *Child Development, 54,* 702–709.

Meltzoff, A. N., & Moore, M. K. (1997). Explaining facial imitation: A theoretical model. *Early Development and Parenting, 6,* 179–192.

Meltzoff, A. N., & Moore, M. K. (2002). Imitation, memory, and the representation of persons. *Infant Behavior and Development, 25*(1), 39–61.

Meltzoff, A. N., & Prinz, W. (eds) (2002). *The imitative mind: Development, evolution and brain.* New York: Cambridge University Press.

Meltzoff, A. N., & Prinz, W. (Eds.). (2002). *The imitative mind: Development, evolution and brain bases* (Vol. 6). Cambridge University Press.

Meltzoff, A. N., Murray, L., Simpson, E., Heimann, M., Nagy, E., Nadel, J., . . . & Subiaul, F. (2018). Re-examination of Oostenbroek et al. (2016): Evidence for neonatal imitation of tongue protrusion. *Developmental Science, 21*(4), e12609.

Meltzoff, A. N., & Borton, R. W. (1979). Intermodal matching by human neonates. *Nature, 282*, 403–404

Mendle, J., Turkheimer, E., & Emery, R. E. (2007). Detrimental psychological outcomes associated with early pubertal timing in adolescent girls. *Developmental Review, 27*, 151–171.

Mennella, J. A. & Beauchamp, G. K. (1993) The effects of repeated exposure to garlic-flavored milk on the nursling's behavior. *Pediatric Research, 34*, 805–808.

Mennella, J. A. & Beauchamp, G. K. (1996) The human infants' response to vanilla flavors in mother's milk and formula. *Infant Behavior and Development, 19*, 13–19.

Menzies, L., Goddings, A. L., Whitaker, K. J., Blakemore, S. J., & Viner, R. M. (2015). The effects of puberty on white matter development in boys. *Developmental Cognitive Neuroscience, 11*, 116–128.

Mercer, J. R. (1971) Sociocultural factors in labeling mental retardates. *Peabody Journal of Education, 48*, 188–203.

Mercer, N. (2008). Talk and the development of reasoning and understanding. *Human Development, 51*(1), 90–100.

Merewood, A. (2000). Sperm under siege. In K. L. Freiberg (ed.), *Human development 00/01* (28th edn, pp. 41–45) Guilford, CT: Dushkin/McGraw-Hill.

Merriman, W. E., Evey-Burkey, J. A., Marazita, J. M., & Jarvis, L. H. (1996). Young two-year-olds' tendency to map novel verbs onto novel actions. *Journal of Experimental Child Psychology, 63*, 466–498.

Merriman, W., & Bowman, L. (1989), The mutual exclusivity bias in children's word learning. *Monographs of the Society for Research in Child Development, 54* (Serial no. 220).

Mervis, C. B., & Klein-Tasman, B. P. (2000). Williams syndrome: Cognition, personality, and adaptive behavior. *Mental Retardation and Developmental Disabilities Research Review, 6*, 148–158.

Mervis, C. B., & Mervis, C. A. (1982). Leopards are kitty cats: Object labeling by mothers for their thirteen-month-olds. *Child Development, 53*, 267–273.

Messinger, D. S., & Lester, B. M. (2006). Prenatal substance exposure and human development. In A. Fogel, B. J. King & S. Shanker (eds), *Human development in the 21st century: Visionary policy ideas from systems scientists* (pp. 225–232) Bethesda, MD: Council on Human Development.

Messinger, D. S., Fogel, A., & Dickson, K. L. (2001). All smiles but some smiles are more positive than others. *Developmental Psychology, 37*, 642–653.

Metz, E., McLellan, J., & Youniss, J. (2003). Types of voluntary service and adolescents' civic development. *Journal of Adolescent Research, 18*, 188–203.

Miller, G. A. (1956). The magical number seven, plus or minus two: Some limits on our capacity for processing information. *Psychological Review, 63*(2), 81–97.

Miller, J. D., Wier, C. C., Pastore, R. E., Kelley, W. J., & Dooling, R. J. (1976). Discrimination and labeling of noise-buzz sequences with varying noise-lead times: An example of categorical perception. *Journal of the Acoustic Society of America, 60*, 410–417.

Miller, J. L., & Eimas, P. D. (1994). Observations on speech perception, its development, and the search for a mechanism. In J. C. Goodman & H. C. Nusbaum (eds), *The development of speech perception: The transition from speech sounds to spoken words* (pp. 37–56). Cambridge, MA: MIT Press.

Miller, K. F., Smith, C. M., Zhu, J., & Zhang, H. (1995). Preschool origins of cross-national differences in mathematical competence: The role of number-naming systems. *Psychological Science, 6*, 56–60.

Miller, L. T. & Vernon, P. A. (1997) Developmental changes in speed of information processing in young children. *Developmental Psychology, 33*, 549–554.

Miller, P. H. (1990) The development of strategies of selective attention. In D. F. Bjorklund (ed.), *Children's strategies: Contemporary views of cognitive development* (pp. 157–184) Hillsdale, NJ: Erlbaum.

Miller, P. H. (2002). *Theories of developmental psychology* (4th edn). New York: Worth.

Miller, P. H., & Aloise-Young, P. A. (1995). Preschoolers' strategic behavior and performance on a same-different task. *Journal of Experimental Child Psychology, 60*, 284–303.

Miller, P. H., & Weiss, M. G. (1981). Children's attention allocation, understanding of attention, and performance on the incidental learning task. *Child Development, 52*, 1183–1190.

Miller, P. H., Seier, W. L., Probert, J. S. & Aloise, P. A. (1991) Age differences in the capacity demands of a strategy among spontaneously strategic children. *Journal of Experimental Child Psychology, 52*, 149–165.

Miller, P., & Sperry, L. L. (1987). The socialization of anger and aggression. *Merrill-Palmer Quarterly, 33*, 1–31.

Mills, J. L. (1999). Cocaine, smoking, and spontaneous abortion. *The New England Journal of Medicine, 340*, 380–381.

Milstein, R. M. (1980). Responsiveness in newborn infants of overweight and normal parents. *Appetite, 1*, 65–74.

Minami, M., & McCabe, A. (1995). Rice balls and bear hunts: Japanese and North American family narrative patterns. *Journal of Child Language, 22*, 423–446.

Mindell, J. A., Leichman, E. S., DuMond, C., & Sadeh, A. (2017). Sleep and social-emotional development in infants and toddlers. *Journal of Clinical Child & Adolescent Psychology, 46*(2), 236–246.

Minuchin, P. (2002). Looking toward the horizon: Present and future in the study of family systems. In J. McHale & W. Grolnick (eds), *Retrospect and prospect in the psychological study of families* (pp. 259–278). Mahwah, NJ: Erlbaum.

Mischel, W., & Ayduk, O. (2004). Willpower in a cognitive-affective processing system: The dynamics of delay of gratification. In R. F. Baumeister & K. D. Vohs (eds), *Handbook of self-regulation: Research, theory, and applications* (pp. 99–129). New York: Guilford Press.

Mishara, B. L. (1999). Conceptions of death and suicide in children ages 6–12 and their implications for suicide prevention. *Suicide & Life-Threatening Behavior, 29*, 105–118.

Mistry, J., Rogoff, B., & Herman, H. (2001). What is the meaning of meaningful purpose in children's remembering? Istomina revisited. *Mind, Culture, and Activity, 8*, 28–41.

Mitchell, E. A., Ford, R. P. K., Stewart, A. W., Taylor, B. J., Bescroft, D. M., Thompson, J. M. P. et al. (1993). Smoking and the sudden infant death syndrome. *Pediatrics, 91*, 893–896.

Mitchell, P. (1997). *Introduction to theory of mind.* London: Arnold.

Moeller, T. G. (2001). *Youth aggression and violence.* Mahwah, NJ: Erlbaum.

Moffitt, A. R. (1971). Consonant cue perception by twenty- to twenty-four week old infants. *Child Development, 42*, 717–732.

Moffitt, T. E. (2003). Life course persistent and adolescence-limited antisocial behavior: A 10-year research review and a research agenda. In B. B. Lahey, T. E. Moffitt, & A. Caspi (eds), *Causes of conduct disorders and juvenile delinquency* (pp. 49–75). New York: Guilford Press.

Moffitt, T. E., & Caspi, A. (2006). Evidence from behavioral genetics for environmental contributions to antisocial conduct. In J. E. Grusec & P. Hastings (eds), *Handbook of socialization* (pp. 259–283). New York: Guilford Press.

Moffitt, T. E., Arseneault, L., Jaffee, S., Kim-Cohen, J., Koenen, K., Odgers, C., et al. (2008). Research review: DSM-V conduct disorder: research needs for an evidence base. *Journal of Child Psychology and Psychiatry, 49*, 3-33.

Moffitt, T. E., Caspi, A., Belsky, J., & Silva, P. A. (1992). Childhood experience and the onset of menarche: A test of a sociobiological model. *Child Development, 63*, 47–58.

Moffitt, T. E., Caspi, A., Harkness, A. R., & Silva, P. A. (1993). The natural history of change in intellectual performance: Who changes? How much? Is it meaningful? *Journal of Child Psychology and Psychiatry and Allied Disciplines, 34*, 455–506.

Moffitt, T. E., Caspi, A., Rutter, M., & Silva, P. A. (2001). *Sex differences in antisocial behavior.* Cambridge: Cambridge University Press.

Moffitt, T. E. (1993). Life-course-persistent and adolescence-limited antisocial behaviour: A developmental taxonomy. *Psychological Review, 100*, 674–701.

Molfese, D. L. (1973). Cerebral asymmetry in infants, children, and adults: Auditory evoked responses to speech and musical stimuli. *Journal of the Acoustical Society of America, 53*, 363.

Molfese, D. L., & Betz, J. C. (1988). Electrophysiological indices of the early development of lateralization for language and cognition, and their implications for predicting later development. In D. L. Molfese & S. J. Segalowitz (eds), *Brain lateralization in children: Developmental implications* (pp. 171–190). New York: Guilford Press.

Molfese, D. L., & Molfese, V. J. (1985). Electrophysiological indices of auditory discrimination in newborn infants: The bases for predicting later language development? *Infant Behavior and Development, 8*, 197–211.

Molfese, D. L., Morse, P. A., & Peters, C. J. (1990). Auditory evoked responses to names for different objects: Cross-modal processing as a basis for infant language acquisition. *Developmental Psychology, 26*, 780–795.

Molfese, V. J., & Martin, T. B. (2001). Intelligence and achievement: Measurement and prediction of developmental variations. In D. L. Molfese & V. J. Molfese (eds), *Developmental variations in learning* (pp. 1–22). Mahwah, NJ: Erlbaum.

Molina, J., Chotro, M. & Dominguez, H. (1995) Fetal alcohol learning resulting from contamination of the prenatal environment. In J.-P. le Canuet, W. Fifer, N. Krasnegor & W. Smotherman (eds), *Fetal development: A psychobiological perspective* (pp. 419–438) Hillsdale, NJ: Erlbaum.

Money, J. (1993). Specific neurocognitive impairments associated with Turner (45, X) and Klinefelter (47, XXY) syndromes: A review. *Social Biology, 40*, 147–151.

Monk, C., Fifer, W. P., Myers, M. M., Sloan, R. P., Trien, L. & Hurtado, A. (2000) Maternal stress responses and anxiety during pregnancy: Effects on fetal heart rate. *Developmental Psychology, 36*, 67–77.

Montague, D. P. F., & Walker-Andrews, A. S. (2002). Mothers, fathers, and infants: The role of person familiarity and parental involvement in infants' perception of emotion expressions. *Child Development, 75,* 1339–1352.

Monteiro, M. B., de Franca, D. X., & Rodrigues, R. (2009). The development of intergroup bias in childhood: How social norms can shape children's racial behaviours, *International Journal Of Psychology, 44,* 29–39.

Moon, R. Y., Horne, R. S. C., & Hauck, F. R. (2007). Sudden infant death syndrome. *Lancet, 370* (9598), 1578–1587.

Moore, C., & Fry, D. (1986). The effect of experimenter's intention on the child's understanding of conservation. *Cognition, 22,* 283–298.

Moore, D. S. (2001). *The dependent gene: The fallacy of 'nature vs. nurture'.* New York: Freeman.

Moore, D. S., & Johnson, S. P. (2008). Mental rotation in human infants: A sex difference. *Psychological Science, 19*(11), 1063–1066.

Moore, K. L. (1989). *Before we are born.* Philadelphia, PA: Saunders.

Moore, K. L., Persaud, T. V. N., & Torchia, M. G. (2016). *Before we are born* (9th edn). Philadelphia, PA: Elsevier.

Moore, M. R., & Brooks-Gunn, J. (2002). Adolescent parenthood. In M. H. Bornstein (ed.), *Handbook of parenting* (2nd edn, vol. 3, pp. 173–214). Mahwah, NJ: Erlbaum.

Moore, M., & Russ, S. W. (2006). Pretend play as a resource for children: Implications for pediatricians and health professionals. *Journal of Developmental and Behavioral Pediatrics, 27,* 237–248.

Moran, S., & Gardner, H. (2006). Extraordinary achievements: A developmental and systems analysis. In W. Damon & R. M. Lerner (Series

eds) & D. Kuhn & R. S. Siegler (Vol. eds), *Handbook of child psychology: Vol. 2. Cognition, perception, and language* (6th edn, pp. 905–949). New York: Wiley.

Morelli, G., & Tronick, E. Z. (1992). Male care among Efe foragers and Lese farmers. In B. Hewlett (ed.), *Father-child relations: Cultural and biosocial contexts* (pp. 231–262). New York: Aldine de Gruyther.

Morelli, G., Rogoff, B., & Angellio, C. (2003). Cultural variation in young children's access to work or involvement in specialised child-focused activities. *International Journal of Behavioral Development, 27,* 264–274.

Morgan, G. A., & Ricciuti, H. (1969). Infants' responses to strangers during the first year. In B. M. Foss (ed.), *Determinants of infant behavior* (Vol. 4, pp. 253–272). London: Methuen.

Morgan, J. L. (1990). Input, innateness, and induction in language acquisition. *Developmental Psychology, 23,* 661–678.

Morgan, J. L. (1994). Converging measures of speech segmentation in preverbal infants. *Infant Behavior and Development, 17,* 387–403.

Morgan, J. L., & Saffran, J. R. (1995). Emerging integration of sequential and suprasegmental information in preverbal speech segmentation. *Child Development, 16,* 911–936.

Morris, A. S., Criss, M. M., Silk, J. S., & Houltberg, B. J. (2017). The impact of parenting on emotion regulation during childhood and adolescence. *Child Development Perspectives, 11*(4), 233–238.

Morrison, F. J., Holmes, D. L., & Haith, M. M. (1974). A developmental study of the effect of familiarity on short-term visual memory. *Journal of Experimental Child Psychology, 18,* 412–425.

Morrongiello, B. A., Hewitt, K. L. & Gotowiec, A. (1991) Infant

discrimination of relative distance in the auditory modality: Approaching versus receding sound sources. *Infant Behavior Development, 14,* 187–208.

Morrongiello, B. A., Midgett, C., & Stanton, K. (2000). Gender biases in children's appraisals of injury risk and other children's risk-taking behaviors. *Journal of Experimental Child Psychology* [Special Issue: *Sex and gender development*], *77,* 317–336.

Morss, J. R. (1996). *Growing critical: Alternatives to developmental psychology.* London: Routledge.

Moshman, D. (1998). Cognitive development beyond childhood. In W. Damon (Series ed.) & D. Kuhn & R. S. Siegler (Vol. eds), *Handbook of child psychology: Vol. 2. Cognition, perception, and language* (pp. 947–978). New York: Wiley.

Moss, H. (1967). Sex, age and state as determinants of mother-infant interaction. *Merrill-Palmer Quarterly, 13,* 19–36.

Mottron, L., Dawson, M., Soulieres, I., Hubert, B., & Burack, J. (2006). Enhanced perceptual functioning in autism: An update, and eight principles of autistic perception. *Journal of Autism and Developmental Disorders, 36*(1), 27–43.

Mounts, N. S. (2000). Parental management of adolescent peer relationships: What are its effects on friend selection? In K. Kerns, J. Contreras, & A. M. Neal-Barnett (eds), *Family and peers: Linking two social worlds* (pp. 169–194). Westport, CT: Praeger.

Mounts, N. S., & Steinberg, L. (1995). An ecological analysis of peer influences on adolescent grade point average and drug use. *Developmental Psychology, 31,* 915–922.

Mounts, N. S., & Steinberg, L. (1995). An ecological analysis of peer influence on adolescent grade point average and drug use. *Developmental Psychology, 31*(6),

915–922. http://dx.doi.org/ 10.1037/0012-1649.31.6.915

Mroczek, D. K., & Kolarz, C. M. (1998). The effect of age on positive and negative affect: A developmental perspective on happiness. *Journal of Personality and Social Psychology, 75,* 1333–1349.

Mueller, E., & Brenner, J. (1977). The origins of social skills and interaction among playgroup toddlers. *Child Development, 48,* 854–861.

Mueller, M. M., & Elder, G. H. (2003). Family contingencies across the generations: Grandparent-grandchild relationships in holistic perspective. *Journal of Marriage and Family, 65,* 404–417.

Muldoon, O. T. (2004). Children of the troubles: The impact of political violence in Northern Ireland. *Journal of Social Issues, 60, 3,* 453–468.

Mullen, M. K., & Yi, S. (1995). The cultural context of talk about the past: Implications for the development of autobiographical memory. *Cognitive Development, 10,* 407–419.

Mumme, D. L., Fernald, A., & Herrera, C. (1996). Infants' responses to facial and vocal emotional signals in a social referencing paradigm. *Child Development, 67,* 3219–3237.

Munakata, Y. (2001) Graded representations in behavioral dissociations. *Trends in Cognitive Sciences, 5*(7), 309–315.

Munakata, Y. (2006). Information processing approaches to development. In W. Damon & R. M. Lerner (Series eds) & D. Kuhn & R. S. Siegler (Vol. eds), *Handbook of child psychology: Vol. 2. Cognition, perception, and language* (6th edn, pp. 426–463). New York: Wiley.

Munakata, Y., McClelland, J. L., Johnson, M. J., & Siegler, R. S. (1997). Rethinking infant knowledge: Toward an adaptive

process account of successes and failures in object permanence tasks. *Psychological Review, 104,* 686–713.

Mundy, P., Sigman, M., Kasari, C., & Yirmiya, N. (1988). Nonverbal communication skills in Down Syndrome children. *Child Development, 59* (1), 235–249.

Mundy, P., Sigman, M., Ungerer, J., & Sherman, T. (1987). Nonverbal communication and play correlates of language development in autistic children. *Journal of Autism and Developmental Disorders, 17*(3), 349–364.

Munoz, L. C. (2009). Callous-unemotional traits are related to combined deficits in recognizing afraid faces and body poses. *Journal of the American Academy of Child & Adolescent Psychiatry, 48,* 554–562.

Munroe, R. H., Munroe, R. L., & Brasher, A. (1985). Precursors of spatial ability: A longitudinal study among the Logoli of Kenya. *Journal of Social Psychology, 125,* 23–33.

Murata, M. (2000). Secular trends in growth and changes in eating patterns of Japanese children. *American Journal of Clinical Nutrition, 72,* 1379S–1383S.

Murray, T. A. (1996). *The worth of a child.* Berkeley, CA: University of California Press.

Muzzati, B., & Agnoli, F. (2007). Gender and mathematics: Attitudes and stereotype threat susceptibility in Italian children. *Developmental Psychology, 43,* 747–759.

Myers, S. M. (2007). The status of pharmacotherapy for autism spectrum disorders. *Expert Opinion of Pharmacotherapy, 8*(11), 1579–1603.

Myles-Worsley, M., Cromer, C. C. & Dodd, D. H. (1986) Children's preschool script reconstruction: Reliance on general knowledge as memory fades. *Developmental Psychology, 22,* 22–30.

Naglieri, J. A., & Das, J. P. (1997). *Cognitive assessment system interpretive handbook.* Itasca, IL: Riverside.

Naigles, L. (1990). Children use syntax to learn verb meanings. *Journal of Child Language, 17,* 357–374.

Nangle, D. W., Erdley, C. A., Newman, J. E., Mason, C. A., & Carpenter, E. M. (2003). Popularity, friendship, quantity, and friendship quality: Interactive influences on children loneliness and depression. *Journal of Clinical Child and Adolescent Psychology, 32,* 546–555.

Nansel, T. R., Overpeck, M., Pilla, R. S., Ruan, W. J., Simons-Morton, B., & Scheidt, P. (2001). Bullying behaviors among U.S. youth. *Journal of the American Medical Association, 285,* 2094–2100.

Nash, J. M. (1997, February 3). Fertile minds. *Time,* pp. 49–62.

National Center for Health Statistics (2006a). Health and longevity in the United States. Retrieved 27 October, 2006, from http:// www. cdc.gov

National Center for Health Statistics (2006b). *Health in America, 2006.* Hyattaville, MD: Author.

National Joint Committee on Learning Disabilities (1994). Learning disabilities: Issues on definition, a position paper of the National Joint Committee on Learning Disabilities. In *Collective perspectives on issues affecting learning disabilities: Position papers and statements.* Austin, TX: Pro-Ed.

Naus, M. J. (1982). Memory development in the young reader: The combined effects of knowledge base and memory processing. In W. Otto & S. White (eds), *Reading expository text* (pp. 49–74). New York: Academic Press.

Nazzi, T., & Gopnik, A. (2001). Linguistic and cognitive abilities in infancy: When does language become a tool for categorization? *Cognition, 80,* 30–37.

Neal, M. (1968). Vestibular stimulation and developmental behavior of the small, premature infant. *Nursing Research Reports, 3,* 2–5.

Neisser, U. (1967). *Cognitive psychology.* New York: Appleton-Century-Crofts.

Neisser, U. (1998). *The rising curve: Long-term gains in IQ and related measures.* Washington, DC: American Psychological Association.

Neisser, U., Boodoo, G., Bouchard, T. J., Boykin, A. W., Brody, N., Ceci, S. J. et al. (1996). Intelligence: Knowns and unknowns. *American Psychologist, 51,* 77–101.

Nelson, C. A., & Bosquet, M. (2000). Neurobiology of fetal and infant development: Implications for infant mental health. In C. Zeanah (ed.), *Handbook of infant mental health* (pp. 37–59). New York: Guilford Press.

Nelson, C. A., & Luciana, M. (eds) (2001). *Handbook of developmental cognitive neuroscience.* Cambridge, MA: MIT Press.

Nelson, C. A., Thomas, K. M. & de Haan, M. (2006). Neural bases of cognitive development. In W. Damon & R. M. Lerner (Series eds) & D. Kuhn & R. S. Siegler (Vol. eds), *Handbook of child psychology. Vol. 2: Cognition, perception, and language* (pp. 3–57). New York: Wiley.

Nelson, K. (1973). Structure and strategy in learning to talk. *Monographs of the Society for Research in Child Development, 38*(1, 2).

Nelson, K. (1989). Strategies for first language teaching. In M. L. Rice & R. L. Schiefelbusch (eds), *The teachability of language* (pp. 263–310). Baltimore, MD: Brooks/Cole.

Nelson, K. (1993). Events, narratives, memory: What develops? In C. A. Nelson (ed.), *Memory and affect in development: The Minnesota symposia on child psychology* (Vol. 26, pp. 1–24). Hillsdale, NJ: Erlbaum.

Nelson, K. (1996) *Language in cognitive development: The emergence of the mediated mind.* New York: Cambridge University Press.

Nelson, K. (1998). *Language in cognitive development: The emergence of the mediated mind.* Cambridge: Cambridge University Press.

Nelson, K. (2007). *Young minds in social worlds: Experience, meaning, and memory.* Cambridge, MA: Harvard University Press.

Nelson, K. E., Carskadden, G., & Bonvillian, J. D. (1973). Syntax acquisition: Impact of experimental variation in adult verbal interaction with the child. *Child Development, 44,* 497–504.

Nelson, K. E., Welsh, J., Camarata, S. M., Butkovsky, L., & Camarata, M. (1995). Available input for language-impaired children and younger children of matched language levels. *First Language, 15,* 1–17.

Nelson, K., & Fivush, R. (2004). The emergence of autobiographical memory: A social cultural developmental theory. *Psychological Review, 111,* 486–511.

Nesdale, D. (2004). Social identity processes and children's ethnic prejudice. In M. Bennett & F. Sani (eds), *The development of the social self* (pp. 219–245). New York: Psychology Press.

Nesdale, D., Durkin, K., Maass, A., & Griffiths, J. (2005). Threat, group identification and children's ethnic prejudice. *Social Development, 14,* 189–205.

Nesdale, D., Maass, A., Griffiths, J., & Durkin, K. (2003). Effects of ingroup and outgroup ethnicity on children's attitudes towards members of the ingroup and outgroup. *British Journal of Developmental Psychology, 21,* 177–192.

Nesi, J., & Prinstein, M. J. (2015). Using social media for social comparison and feedback-seeking: Gender and popularity moderate associations with depressive symptoms. *Journal of Abnormal Child Psychology, 43*(8), 1427–1438.

Neumann, C. G., Murphy, S. P., Gewa, C., Grillenberger, M., & Bwibo, N. O. (2007). Meat supplementation improves growth, cognitive, and behavioral outcomes in Kenyan children. *Journal of Nutrition, 137,* 1119–1123.

Neville, B., & Parke, R. D. (1997). Waiting for paternity: Interpersonal and contextual implications of the timing of fatherhood. *Sex Roles, 37,* 45–59.

Neville, H. J. (1991). Neurobiology of cognitive and language processing: Effects of early experience. In K. R. Gibson & A. C. Petersen (eds), *Brain maturation and cognitive development: Comparative and cross-cultural perspectives* (pp. 355–380). New York: Aldine de Bruyter.

Neville, H. J., & Bruer, J. T. (2001). Language processing: How experience affects brain organization. In D. B. Bailey, J. T. Bruer, F. J. Simons & J. W. Lichtman (eds), *Critical thinking about critical periods* (pp. 151–172). Baltimore, MD: Broker.

Nevin, M. M. (1988) Dormant dangers of DES. *The Canadian Nurse, 84,* 17–19.

Newcomb, A. F., Bukowski, W. M., & Pattee, L. (1993). Children's peer relations: A meta-analytic review of popular, rejected, neglected, controversial, and average sociometric status. *Psychological Bulletin, 113,* 99–128.

Newcomer, S., & Udry, J. R. (1987). Parental marital status effects on adolescent sexual behavior. *Journal of Marriage and the Family, 48,* 235–240.

Newell, K., Scully, D. M., Mc Donald, P. V., & Baillargeon, R. (1989). Task constraints and infant grip configurations. *Developmental Psychobiology, 22*, 817–832.

Newman, J. (1995). How breast milk protects newborns. *Scientific American, 273*, 76–79.

NICHD Early Child Care Research Network (2004). Trajectories of physical aggression from toddlerhood to middle childhood: Predictors, correlates, and outcomes. *Monographs of the Society for Research in Child Development.*

NICHD Early Child Care Research Network (2004b) Trajectories of physical aggression from toddlerhood to middle childhood: Predictors, correlates, and outcomes. *Monographs of the Society for Research in Child Development.*

NICHD Early Child Care Research Network (1997). The effects of infant child care on infant-mother attachment security: Results of the NICHD Study of Early Child Care. *Child Development, 68*, 860–879.

Nielsen, M., & Haun, D. (2016). Why developmental psychology is incomplete without comparative and cross-cultural perspectives. *Phil. Trans. R. Soc. B, 371*(1686), 20150071.

Nightingale, E. O., & Meister, S. B. (1987). *Prenatal screening, policies, and values: Three examples of neural tube defects.* Cambridge, MA: Harvard University Press.

Nilsson, L-G. (2003). Memory function in normal aging. *Acta Psychologica Scandanavika, 107*, 7–13.

Ninio, A., & Snow, C. (1996). *Pragmatic development.* Boulder, CO: Westview Press.

Nisan, M., & Kohlberg, L. (1982). Universality and variation in moral judgment: A longitudinal and cross-sectional study in Turkey. *Child Development, 53*, 865–876.

Nisbett, R. E., Aronson, J., Blair, C., Dickens, W., Flynn, J., Halpern, D. F., & Turkheimer, E. (2012). Intelligence: New findings and theoretical developments. *American Psychologist, 67*(2), 130–159.

Nock, M. K., Kazdin, A. E., Hirpi, E., & Kessler, R. C. (2007). Lifetime prevalence, correlates, and persistence of oppositional defiant disorder: Results from the National Comorbidity Survey Replication. *Journal of Child Psychology and Psychiatry, 48*, 703–713.

Norlander, T., Erixon, A., & Archer, T. (2000). Psychological androgyny and creativity: Dynamics of gender roles and personality traits. *Social Behavior and Personality, 28*, 423–435.

Novick, L. R., & Bassok, M. (2005). Problem solving. In K. J. Holyoak & R. G. Morrison (eds), *The Cambridge handbook of thinking and reasoning* (pp. 321–349). New York: Cambridge University Press.

Novosad, C. & Thoman, E. B. (2003) The Breathing Bear: An intervention for crying babies and their mothers. *Journal of Developmental and Behavioral Pediatrics, 24*, 89–95.

Nucci, L. P., & Turiel, E. (1978). Social interactions and the development of social concepts in preschool children. *Child Development, 49*, 400–407.

Nugent, J. K., Lester, B. M., & Brazelton, T. B. (1991). *The cultural context of infancy, Vol. 2: Multicultural and interdisciplinary approaches to parentinfant relations.* Westport, CT: Ablex.

Nunes, T., & Bryant, P. (1996). *Children doing mathematics.* Oxford: Blackwell.

Nunes, T., Bryant, P., & Dunn, J. (1996). *Children doing mathematics.* Oxford: Blackwell.

Nwokah, E. E., Hsu, H., Dobrowolska, O., & Fogel, A. (1994). The development of laughter in mother-infant communication:

Timing parameters and temporal sequences. *Infant Behavior and Development, 17*, 23–35.

Nyberg, L., & Pudas, S. (2019). Successful memory ageing. *Annual Review of Psychology, 70.* https://doi.org/10.1146/annurev-psych-010418-103052

O'Brien, M., Huston, A. C., & Risley, T. (1983). Sex-typed play of toddlers in a day care center. *Journal of Applied Developmental Psychology, 4*, 1–9.

O'Connor, T. G., Ben-Sholmoy, Y., Heron, J., Golding, J., Adams, D., & Glover, V. (2005). Prenatal anxiety predicts individual differences in preadolescent children. *Biological Psychiatry, 58*, 211–217.

O'Sullivan, J. T. (1996). Children's metamemory about the influence of conceptual relations on recall. *Journal of Experimental Child Psychology, 62*, 1–29.

Oakes, J. (1990). Opportunities, achievement, and choice: Women and minority students. *Review of Research in Education, 16*, 153–222.

Oakes, L. M., & Madole, K. L. (2003). Principles of developmental change in infants' category formation. In D. H. Rakison & L. M. Oakes (eds), *Early category and concept learning* (pp. 132–158). New York: Oxford University Press.

Obsuth, I., Eisner M. P., Malti, T. & Ribeaud, D. (2015). The developmental relation between aggressive behaviour and prosocial behaviour: A 5-year longitudinal study, *BMC Psychology, 3*, 16. https://doi.org/10.1186/s40359-015-0073-4

Ochs, E. (1988). *Culture and language development.* Cambridge: Cambridge University Press.

Oehler, J. M., Eckerman, C. D. & Wilson, W. H. (1988) Social stimulation and the regulation of premature infants' state prior to term age. *Infant Behavior and Development, 12,* 341–356.

Ohlsson, A., & Jacobs, S. E. (2013). NIDCAP: A systematic review and meta-analyses of randomized controlled trials. *Pediatrics, 131*(3), e881–e893.

Ohno, S. (1972). So much 'junk' DNA in our genome. *Brookhaven Symposia in Biology, 23,* 366–370.

Oktay-Gür, N., Schulz, A., & Rakoczy, H. (2018). Children exhibit different performance patterns in explicit and implicit theory of mind tasks. *Cognition, 173,* 60–74.

Oliver, B. R., & Plomin, R. (2007). Twins' Early Development Study (TEDS): A multivariate, longitudinal genetic investigation of language, cognition and behavior problems from childhood through adolescence. *Twin Research and Human Genetics, 10,* 96–105.

Oller, D. K., Wieman, L. A., Doyle, W. J., & Ross, C. (1976). Infant babbling and speech. *Journal of Child Language, 3,* 1–11.

Olney, D. K., Pollitt, E., Kariger, P. K., Khalfan, S. S., Ali, N. S., Tielsch, J. M. et al. (2006). Combined iron and folic acid supplementation with or without zinc reduces time to walking unassisted among Zanzibari infants 5- to 11-months old. *Journal of Nutrition, 136,* 2427–2434.

Olweus, D. (1993). *Bullying and school: What we know and what we can do.* Oxford: Blackwell.

Olweus, D. (1999). Bullying in Norway. In P. K. Smith, Y. Morita, J. Junger-Tas, D. Olweus, R. Catalano, & P. Slee (eds), *The nature of school bullying: A cross-national perspective* (pp. 28–48). New York: Routledge.

Olweus, D. (2001). Peer harassment: A critical analysis and some important issues. In: J. Juvonen, S. Graham, (eds) *Peer*

harassment in school: The plight of the vulnerable and victimized (pp. 3–20). New York: Guilford Press. p 3–20.

Olweus, D. (2002). Gewalt in der Schule: Was Lehrer und Eltern wissen sollten - und tun können. 3.,korr. Auflage. Bern: Huber.

Olweus, D., Mattson, A., Schalling, D., & Low, H. (1988). Circulating testosterone levels and aggression in adolescent males: A causal analysis. *Psychosomatic Medicine, 50,* 261–272.

Ong, K. K. & Loos, R. J. (2006) Rapid infancy weight gain and subsequent obesity: Systematic reviews and hopeful suggestions. *Acta Paediatrica, 95,* 904–908.

Onishi, K. H., & Baillargeon, R. (2005). Do 15-month-old infants understand false beliefs? *Science, 308,* 255–258.

Onishi, K. H., & Baillargeon, R. (2005). Do 15-month-old infants understand false beliefs? *Science, 308*(5719), 255–258.

Oostenbroek, J., Redshaw, J., Davis, J., Kennedy-Costantini, S., Nielsen, M., Slaughter, V., & Suddendorf, T. (in press). Re-evaluating the neonatal imitation hypothesis. *Developmental Science.*

Oostenbroek, J., Suddendorf, T., Nielsen, M., Redshaw, J., Kennedy-Costantini, S., Davis, J., . . . & Slaughter, V. (2016). Comprehensive longitudinal study challenges the existence of neonatal imitation in humans. *Current Biology, 26*(10), 1334–1338.

Orlick, T., Zhou, Q., & Partington, J. (1990). Co-operation and conflict within Chinese and Canadian kindergarten settings. *Canadian Journal and Behavioural Science, 22,* 20–25.

Ornstein, P. A., Gordon, B. N., & Larus, D. M. (1992). Children's memory for a personally experienced event: Implications for testimony. *Applied Cognitive Psychology, 6,* 49–60.

Ornstein, P. A., Naus, M. J., & Liberty, C. (1975). Rehearsal and organizational processes in children's memory. *Child Development, 46,* 818–830.

Ostrov, J. M., & Crick, N. R. (2006). How recent developments in the study of relational aggression and close relationships in early childhood advance the field. *Journal of Applied Developmental Psychology, 27,* 189–192.

Ottosson, H., Ekselius, L., Grann, M., & Kullgren, G. (2002) Cross-system concordance of personality disorder diagnoses of DSM-IV and diagnostic criteria for research of ICD-10. *Journal of Personality Disorders, 16,* 283–292.

Overton, W. F., & Byrnes, J. P. (1991). Cognitive development. In R. M. Lerner, A. C. Petersen & J. Brooks-Gunn (eds), *Encyclopedia of adolescence* (Vol. 1, pp. 151–156). New York: Garland Press.

Oxford, M., Cavell, T., & Hughes, J. (2003). Callous-unemotional traits moderate the relation between ineffective parenting and child externalizing problems: A partial replication and extension. *Journal of Clinical Child & Adolescent Psychology, 32,* 577–585.

Ozgenc, A., & Loeb, L. A. (2005). Current advances in unravelling the function of the Werner syndrome protein. *Mutation Research, 577,* 237–251.

Ozonoff, S., Iosif, A. M., Baguio, F., Cook, I. C., Hill, M. M., Hutman, T., . . . & Steinfeld, M. B. (2010). A prospective study of the emergence of early behavioral signs of autism. *Journal of the American Academy of Child & Adolescent Psychiatry, 49*(3), 256–266.

Ozonoff, S., Losif, A. M., Baguio, F., Cook, I. C., Hill, M. M., Hutman, T., . . . & Steinfeld, M. B. (2010). A prospective study of the emergence of early behavioral signs of autism. *Journal of the American Academy of Child & Adolescent Psychiatry, 49*(3), 256–266.

Ozonoff, S., Pennington, B. F., & Rogers, S. J. (1991). Executive function deficits in high-functioning autistic individuals: Relationship to theory of mind. *Journal of Child Psychology and Psychiatry, 32*(7), 1081–1105.

Paley, B., Cox, M. J., Burchinal, M. R., & Payne, C. C. (1999). Attachment and family functioning: Comparison of spouses with continuous-secure, earned-secure, dismissing and preoccupied attachment stances. *Journal of Family Psychology, 13,* 580–597.

Palincsar, A. S. & Brown, A. L. (1984) Reciprocal teaching of comprehension-fostering and comprehension-monitoring activities. *Cognition and Instruction, 1,* 117–175.

Panza, F., Solfrizzi, V., Colacicco, A. M., D'Introno, A., Capurso, C., Torres, F., et al. (2004). Mediterranean diet and cognitive decline. *Public Health Nutrition, 7,* 959–963.

Papalia, D. E., & Olds, S. W. (1996). A child's world (4th edn). McGraw-Hill: New York.

Pardini, D. A. (2008). Novel insights into longstanding theories of bidirectional parent-child influences: Introduction to the special section, *Journal of Abnormal Child Psychology, 36*(5), 627–631.

Parke, R. D. (1977). Punishment in children: Effects, side effects and alternative strategies. In H. Hom & P. Robinson (eds), *Psychological processes in early education* (pp. 71–97). New York: Academic Press.

Parke, R. D. (1996). *Fatherhood.* Cambridge, MA: Harvard University Press.

Parke, R. D. (2002). Fatherhood. In M. Bornstein (ed.), *Handbook of parenting* (2nd ed., pp. 27–74). Mahwah, NJ: Erlbaum.

Parke, R. D., & Brott, A. (1999). *Throwaway dads.* Boston, MA: Houghton-Mifflin.

Parke, R. D., & Buriel, R. (2006). Socialization in the family: Ethnic and ecological perspectives. In W. Damon & R. M. Lerner (Series eds) & N. Eisenberg (Vol. Ed.), *Handbook of child psychology: Vol. 3. Social, emotional and personality development* (6th edn, pp. 429–504). New York: Wiley.

Parke, R. D., & O'Neil, R. (2000). The influence of significant others on learning about relationships: From family to friends. In R. S. L. Mills & S. Duck (eds), *The developmental psychology of personal relationships* (pp. 15–47). New York: Wiley.

Parke, R. D., Lio, S., Schofield, T., Tuthill, L., Vega, E., & Coltrane, S. (2008). Neighborhood environments: A multi-measure, multi-level approach. In L. C. Mayes & M. Lewis (eds), *The environment of human development: A handbook of theory and measurement.* New York: Cambridge University Press.

Parke, R. D., McDowell, D. J., Cladis, M., & Leidy, M. S. (2005). Family-peer relationships: The role of emotional regulatory processes. In D. K. Snyder, J. A. Simpson & J. N. Hughes (eds), *Emotional regulation in families: Pathways to dysfunction and health* (pp. 143–162). Washington, DC: American Psychological Association.

Parker, F. L., Boak, A. Y., Griffin, K. W., Ripple, C. & Peay, L. (1999) Parent-child relationship, home learning environment, and school readiness. *School Psychology Review, 28*(3), 413–425.

Parker, J. G. & Asher, S. R. (1993) Friendship and friendship quality in middle childhood: links with peer group acceptance and feelings of loneliness and social dissatisfaction. *Developmental Psychology, 29*(4), 611–621.

Parker, J. G., & Asher, S. R. (1987). Peer acceptance and later personal adjustment: Are low-accepted children at risk? *Psychological Bulletin, 102,* 357–389.

Parker, J. G., & Gottman, J. M. (1989). Social and emotional development in a relational context: Friendship interaction from early childhood to adolescence. In T. J. Berndt & G. W. Ladd (eds), *Peer relationships in child development* (pp. 95–132). New York: Wiley.

Parker, S. W., Nelson, C. A., & The Bucharest Early Intervention Project Core Group (2005). The impact of early institutional rearing on the ability to discriminate facial expressions of emotion: An event-related potential study. *Child Development, 76,* 54–72.

Parkhurst, J. T., & Asher, S. R. (1992). Peer rejection in middle school: Subgroup differences in behavior, loneliness and interpersonal concerns. *Developmental Psychology, 28,* 231–241.

Parten, M. (1932). Social play among preschool. *Journal of Abnormal and Social Psychology, 28,* 231–241.

Pascalis, O., de Haan, M., & Nelson, C. A. (2002). Is face processing species-specific during the first year of life? *Science, 5,* 427–434.

Pascalis, O., De Schonen, S., Morton, J., Deruelle, C., & Fabre-Grenet, M. (1995). Mother's face recognition by neonates: A replication and extension. *Infant Behavior and Development, 18,* 79–85.

Pascual-Leone, J. A. (1989). Constructive problems for constructive theories: The current relevance of Piaget's work and a critique of information processing simulation psychology. In H. Spada & R. Kluwe (eds), *Developmental models of thinking.* New York: Academic Press.

Passer, M. W., Smith, R. E., Holt, N., Bremner, A., Sutherland, E., & Vliek, M. (2009). *Psychology: The science of mind and behaviour.* Maidenhead: McGraw-Hill Higher Education.

Passive addiction and teratogenic effects. In J.J. Volpe (ed.) *Volpe's neurology of the newborn* (6th edn, pp. 1149–1189). Philadelphia, PA: Elsevier.

Patrikakou, E. N., Weissberg, R. P., Redding, S., & Walberg, H. J. (2005). School-family partnerships: Enhancing the academic, social, and emotional learning of children. In E. N. Patrikakou, R. P. Weissberg, S. Redding, & H. J. Walberg (eds), *School-family partnerships for children's success* (pp. 1–17). New York: Teachers College Press.

Patterson A. & Rafferty, A. (2001) Making it work: Towards employment for the young adult with autism. *International Journal of Language and Communication Disorders, 36*(Suppl.), 475–480.

Patterson, C. (2004). Gay fathers. In M. E. Lamb (ed.), *The role of the father in child development* (pp. 397–416). New York: Wiley.

Patterson, C. J., & Hastings, P. D. (2007). Socialization in the context of family diversity. In J. Grusec & P. D. Hastings (eds), *Handbook of socialization* (pp. 328–351). New York: Guilford Press.

Patterson, C. J., & Kister, M. C. (1981). Development of listener skills for referential communication. In W. P. Dickerson (eds), *Children's oral communication skills* (pp. 143–166). New York: Academic Press.

Patterson, G. R. (1982). *Coercive family process*. Eugene, OR: Castalia Press.

Patterson, G. R. (1996). Some characteristics of a developmental theory for early-onset delinquency. In M. F. Lenzenweger & J. J. Haugaard (eds), *Frontiers of developmental psychopathology* (pp. 81–124). New York: Oxford University Press.

Patterson, G. R. (2002). The early development of coercive family processes. In J. B. Reid, G. R. Patterson, & J. Snyder (eds), *Antisocial behavior in children and adolescents* (pp. 25–44). Washington, DC: American Psychological Association.

Patterson, G. R., & Bank, L. (1989). Some amplifying mechanisms for pathologic processes in families. In M. Gunnar & E. Thelen (eds), *Systems and development: The Minnesota Symposium on Child Psychology* (Vol. 22, pp. 167–209). Hillsdale, NJ: Erlbaum.

Patterson, G. R., & Capaldi, D. M. (1991). Antisocial parents: Unskilled and vulnerable. In P. A. Cowan & E. M. Hetherington (eds), *Family transitions* (pp. 195–218). Hillsdale, NJ: Erlbaum.

Patterson, G. R., DeBarshyshe, B., & Ramsey, R. (1989). A developmental perspective on antisocial behavior. *American Psychologist, 44*, 329–335.

Pearson, B. Z., Fernandez, S. C., & Oller, D. K. (1993). Lexical development in bilingual infants and toddlers: Comparison to monolingual norms. *Language Learning, 43*, 93–120.

Pearson, B. Z., Fernandez, S. C., Lewedeg, V., & Oller, D. K. (1997). The relation of input factors of lexical learning by bilingual infants (ages 8 to 30 months). *Applied Psycholinguistics, 18*, 41–58.

Pegg, J. E., Werker, J. F. & McLeod, P. J. (1992) Preference for infant-directed over adult-directed speech: Evidence from 7-week-old infants. *Infant Behavior and Development, 15*, 325–345.

Pennington, B. F. (2005). *The development of psychopathology: Nature and nurture*. New York: Guilford Press.

Pennington, B. F., McGrath, L. M., Rosenberg, J., Barnard, H., Smith, S. D., Willcutt, E. G., & Olson, R. K. (2009). Gene x environment interactions in reading disability and attention-deficit/hyperactivity disorder. *Developmental Psychology, 45*(1), 77.

Pepler, D., Corter, C., & Abramovitch, R. (1982). Social relations among children. Comparisons of siblings and peer interaction. In K. Rubin & H. S. Ross (eds), *Peer relationships and social skills in childhood* (pp. 209–227). New York: Springer-Verlag.

Pepperberg, I. M. (2000). *The Alex studies: Cognitive and communicative abilities of grey parrots*. Cambridge, MA: Harvard University Press.

Perfors, A., Tenenbaum, J. B., Griffiths, T. L., & Xu, F. (2011). A tutorial introduction to Bayesian models of cognitive development. *Cognition, 120*(3), 302–321.

Perner, J., Kloo, D., & Gornik, E. (2007). Episodic memory development: Theory of mind is part of re-experiencing experienced events. *Infant & Child Development, 16*, 471–490.

Perner, J., Leekam, S. R., & Wimmer, H. (1987). Three-year-olds' difficulty with false belief: The case for a conceptual deficit. *British Journal of Developmental Psychology, 5*(2), 125–137.

Perner, J., Ruffman, T., & Leekam, S. R. (1994). Theory of mind is contagious: You can catch it from your sibs. *Child Development, 65*, 1228–1238.

Perry, B. D. (1997). Incubated in terror: Neurodevelopmental factors in the 'cycle of violence'. In J. D. Osofsky (ed.), *Children in a violent society* (pp. 124–149). New York: Guilford Press.

Perry, D. G., Hodges, E. V., & Egan, S. (2001). Determinants of chronic victimization by peers: A review and new model of family influence. In J. Juvonen & S. Graham (eds), *Peer harassment in school: The plight of the vulnerable and victimized* (pp. 73–104). New York: Guilford Press.

Perry, D. G., Perry, L. C., & Weiss, R. J. (1989). Sex differences in the consequences children anticipate for aggression. *Developmental Psychology, 25*, 312–320.

Perry, D. G., Williard, J. C., & Perry, L. C. (1990). Peers' perceptions of the consequences that victimized children provide aggressors. *Child Development, 61*, 1310–1325.

Perry-Jenkins, M., Repetti, R., & Crouter, A. C. (2000). Work and family in the 1990s. *Journal of Marriage and the Family, 62*, 981–998.

Persson, G. E. B. (2005). Young children's prosocial and aggressive behaviors and their experiences of being targeted for similar behaviors by peers. *Social Development, 14*, 206–228.

Peters, A. M. (1983). *The units of language.* New York: Cambridge University Press.

Petersen, A. C. & Taylor, B. (1980) The biological approach to adolescence: Biological change and psychological adaptation. In J. Adelson (ed.), *Handbook of adolescent psychology* (pp. 117–155) New York: Wiley.

Peterson, L. R., & Peterson, M. J. (1959). Short-term retention of individual verbal items. *Journal of Experimental Psychology, 58*, 193–198.

Petitto, L. A., & Marenette, P. (1991). Babbling in the manual mode: Evidence for the ontogeny of language. *Science, 251*, 1493–1496.

Petitto, L. A., Holowka, S., Sergio, L. E., & Ostry, D. (2001). Language rhythms in baby hand movements. *Nature, 413*, 35–36.

Petrill, S. A., & Deater-Deckard, K. (2004). Task orientation, parental warmth and SES account for a significant proportion of the shared environmental variance in general cognitive ability in early childhood: Evidence from a twin study. *Developmental Science, 7*, 25–32.

Pettigrew, T. F. & Tropp, L. R. (2006) A meta-analytic test of intergroup contact theory. *Journal of Personality and Social Psychology, 90*, 751–783.

Pettit, G. S., Laird, R. D., Dodge, K. A., Bates, J. E., & Criss, M. N. (2001). Antecedents and behavior problem outcomes of parental monitoring and psychological control in early adolescence. *Child Development, 72*, 583–598.

Phillips, J. L. (1969). *The origins of intellect: Piaget's theory.* San Francisco, CA: W. H. Freeman and Co.

Phillips, R. B., Sharma, R., Premachandra, B. R., Vaughn, A. J., & Reyes-Lee, M. (1996). Intrauterine exposure to cocaine: Effect on neurobehavior of neonates. *Infant Behavior and Development, 19*, 71–81.

Phinney, J. (1993). A three-stage model of ethnic identity development. In M. Bernal & G. Knight (eds), *Ethnic identity: Formation and transmission among Hispanics and other minorities* (pp. 61–79) Albany, NY: State University of New York Press.

Piaget, J. (1923). *Le langage et al pensée chez l'enfant.* Neuchátal, Paris: Delachauz and Niestlé.

Piaget, J. (1926). *Language and thought of the child.* London: Kegan Paul, Trench & Trubner.

Piaget, J. (1929/1952). *The child's conception of the world.* London: Kegan Paul, Trench & Trubner.

Piaget, J. (1932) *The moral judgment of the child.* New York: Harcourt, Brace.

Piaget, J. (1950). *The psychology of intelligence.* London: Kegan Paul, Trench & Trubner.

Piaget, J. (1950). *The psychology of intelligence.* Routledge.

Piaget, J. (1950a). *Introduction ã l'Épistémologie Génétique.* Paris: Presses Universitaires de France.

Piaget, J. (1951). *The psychology of intelligence.* London: Routledge and Kegan Paul.

Piaget, J. (1952). *The origins of intelligence in the child.* London: Routledge & Kegan-Paul (Originally published in French in 1936.)

Piaget, J. (1954). *The construction of reality in the child.* London: Routledge & Kegan-Paul (originally published in French in 1937).

Piaget, J. (1965). *The child's conception of number.* New York: Norton.

Piaget, J. (1985). *The equilibration of cognitive structures.* Chicago: University of Chicago Press.

Pine, K. J., Lufkin, N., Kirk, E., & Messer, D. (2007). A microgenetic analysis of the relationship between speech and gesture in children: Evidence for semantic and temporal asynchrony. *Language and Cognitive Processes, 22*(2), 234–246.

Pinker, S. (1994). *The language instinct: How the mind creates language.* London: Allen Lane.

Pinker, S., & Jackendoff, R. (2005). The faculty of language: What's special about it? *Cognition, 95*, 201–236.

Pisecco, S., Baker, D. B., Silva, P. A., & Brooke, M. (2001). Boys with reading disabilities and/or ADHD: Distinctions in early childhood. *Journal of Learning Disabilities, 43*, 98–106.

Plant, D. T., Jones, F. W., Pariante, C. M., & Pawlby, S. (2017). Association between maternal childhood trauma and offspring childhood psychopathology: Mediation analysis from the ALSPAC cohort. *British Journal of Psychiatry, 211*(3), 144–150.

Pleck, J. H., & Masciadrelli, B. P. (2004). *Paternal involvement by U.S. residential fathers: Levels, sources, and consequences.* Hoboken, NJ: Wiley.

Plomin, R. (1990). *Nature and nurture: An introduction to human behavioral genetics.* Pacific Grove, CA: Brooks/Cole.

Plomin, R. (1995). Genetics and children's experiences in the family. *Journal of Child Psychology and Psychiatry, 36*, 33–68.

Plomin, R. (2011). Commentary: Why are children in the same family so different? Non-shared environment three decades later. *International Journal of Epidemiology*, *40*(3), 582–592.

Plomin, R., & Deary, I. J. (2015). Genetics and intelligence differences: Five special findings. *Molecular Psychiatry*, *20*, 98–108.

Plomin, R., & Rutter, M. (1998). Child development, molecular genetics and what to do with genes once they are found. *Child Development*, *69*, 1223–1242.

Plomin, R., DeFries, J. C., Knopik, V. S., & Neiderhiser, J. M. (2016). Top 10 replicated findings from behavioral genetics. *Perspectives on Psychological Science*, *11*(1), 3–23.

Plomin, R., DeFries, J. C., Knopik, V. S., Neiderhiser, J. M. (2013). *Behavioral genetics, 6th Ed.* New York: Worth Publishers.

Plomin, R., DeFries, J. C., McClearn, G. E. & McGuffin, P. (2001) *Behavioral genetics* (4th edn). New York: Worth.

Plomin, R., DeFries, J. C., McClearn, G. E., & Rutter, M. (1997). *Behavior genetics* (3rd edn). New York: Freeman.

Poduri, A., & Volpe, J. J. (2017). Neuronal proliferation. *Volpe's neurology of the newborn e-Book*, 100.

Poelen E. A. P., Engels, R. C. M. E., Van Der Vorst, H., et al. (2007). Best friends and alcohol consumption in adolescence: A within-family analysis. *Drug and Alcohol Dependence*, *88*, 163–173.

Polanczyk, G. V., Willcutt, E. G., Salum, G. A., Kieling, C., & Rohde, L. A. (2014). ADHD prevalence estimates across three decades: An updated systematic review and meta-regression analysis. *International Journal of Epidemiology*, *43*(2), 434–442.

Polderman, T. J., Benyamin, B., De Leeuw, C. A., Sullivan, P. F.,

Van Bochoven, A., Visscher, P. M., & Posthuma, D. (2015). Meta-analysis of the heritability of human traits based on fifty years of twin studies. *Nature Genetics*, *47*(7), 702.

Pollak, S. D., & Sinha, P. (2002). Effects of early experience on children's recognition of facial displays of emotion. *Developmental Psychology*, *38*, 784–791.

Pollitt, E. (1994). Poverty and child development: Relevance of research in developing countries to the United States. *Child Development*, *65*, 283–295.

Pollitt, E., Gorman, K., & Metallinos-Katsaras, E. (1992). Long-term developmental consequences of intrauterine and postnatal growth retardation in rural Guatemala. In G. J. Suci & S. R. Robertson (eds), *Future directions in infant development research* (pp. 43–70). New York: Springer-Verlag.

Pomerantz, E. M., & Ruble, D. N. (1998). A multidimensional perspective of control: Implications for the development of sex differences in self-evaluation and depression. In J. Heckhausen & C. Dweck (eds), *Motivation and self-regulation across the life span* (pp. 159–184). New York: Cambridge University Press.

Pomerantz, E. M., Grolnick, W. S., & Price, C. E. (2005). The role of parents in how children approach achievement: A dynamic process perspective. In A. J. Elliot & C. S. Dweck (eds), *Handbook of competence and motivation* (pp. 229–278). New York: Guilford Press.

Pomerleau, A., Bolduc, D., Malcuit, G., & Cossette, L. (1990). Pink or blue: Environmental gender stereotypes in the first two years of life. *Sex Roles*, *22*, 359–367.

Pons, F., Harris, P. L., & de Rosnay, M. (2004). Emotion comprehension between 3 and 11 years: Developmental periods and hierarchical organization. *European*

Journal of Developmental Psychology, *1*, 127–152.

Posada, G., Gao, Y., Wu, F., Posada, R., Tascon, M., Schelmerich, A., et al. (1995). The secure-base phenomenon across cultures: Children's behavior, mothers' preferences, and experts' concepts. In E. Waters, B. E. Vaughn, G. Posada, & K. Kondo-Ikemura (eds), *Caregiving, cultural, and cognitive perspectives on secure-base behavior and working models: New growing points of attachment theory and research. Monographs of the Society for Research in Child Development*, *60*(2–3), (Serial no. 244).

Posada, G., Jacobs, A., Richmond, M. K., Carbonell, O. A., Alzate, G., Bustamante, M. R. et al. (2002). Maternal caregiving and infant security in two cultures. *Developmental Psychology*, *38*, 67–78.

Posner, M. I., & Petersen, S. E. (1990). The attention system of the human brain. *Annual Review of Neuroscience*, *13*(1), 25–42.

Postlethwait, J. H., & Hopson, J. L. (1995). *The nature of life* (3rd edn). New York: McGraw-Hill.

Poulin, F. & Boivin, M. (2000) The role of proactive and reactive aggression on the formation of boys' friendships. *Developmental Psychology*, *36*, 233–240.

Poulin, F., Dishion, T., & Haas, E. (1999). The peer influences paradox: Friendship quality and deviancy training within male adolescents. *Merrill-Palmer Quarterly*, *45*, 42–61.

Povinelli, D. J., Bering, J., & Giambrone, S. (2000). Toward a science of other minds: Escaping the argument by analogy. *Cognitive Science*, *24*, 509–541.

Pratt, M. W. & Fiese, B. H. (eds) (2004) *Family stories and the life course.* Mahwah, NJ: Erlbaum.

Pratt, M. W., Hunsberger, B., Prancer, S. M., & Alisat, S. (2003). A longitudinal analysis of personal values socialization: Correlates of a moral self-ideal in late adolescence. *Social Development, 12*, 563–585.

Prechtl, H. F. R. (1984). Continuity of neural functions from prenatal to postnatal life. *Clinics in Developmental Medicine, 94.* Oxford: Blackwell Scientific.

Premack, D. G., & Woodruff, G. (1978). Does the chimpanzee have a theory of mind? *Behavioral and Brain Sciences, 1,* 515–526.

Pressley, M., & Hilden, K. (2006). Cognitive strategies. In W. Damon & R. M. Lerner (Series eds) & D. Kuhn & R. S. Siegler (Vol. eds), *Handbook of child psychology: Vol. 2. Cognition, perception, and language* (6th edn, pp. 511–556). New York: Wiley.

Preston, S. D., & de Waal, F. B. M. (2002). Empathy: Its ultimate and proximate bases. *Behavioral and Brain Sciences, 25*, 1–72.

Price, T. S., & Jaffee, S. R. (2008). Effects of the family environment: Gene-environment interaction and passive gene-environment correlation. *Developmental Psychology, 44*(2), 305–315.

Price-Williams, D. R., Gordon, W., & Ramirez, M., III. (1969). Skill and conservation: A study of pottery-making children. *Developmental Psychology, 1*, 769.

Priess, H. A., Lindberg, S. M., & Shibley Hyde, J. (2009). Adolescent gender-role identity and mental health: Gender intensification revisited. *Child Development, 80*(5), 1531–1544.

Pring, L. (2005), Savant talent. *Developmental Medicine & Child Neurology, 47*, 500–503.

Prinstein, M. J., & LaGreca, A. M. (2002). Peer crowd affiliation and internalizing distress in childhood and adolescence: A longitudinal follow-back study. *Journal of Research on Adolescence, 12*, 325–351.

Provenzi, L., Guida, E., & Montirosso, R. (2018). Preterm behavioral epigenetics: A systematic review. *Neuroscience & Biobehavioral Reviews, 84*, 262–271.

Psaltis, C., & Duveen, G. (2007). Conversation types and conservation: Forms of recognition and cognitive development. *British Journal of Developmental Psychology, 25*, 79–102.

Purcell, P., & Stewart, L. (1990). Dick and Jane in 1989. *Sex Roles, 22*, 177–185.

Pysanenko, K., Bureš, Z., Lindovský, J., & Syka, J. (2018). The effect of complex acoustic environment during early development on the responses of auditory cortex neurons in rats. *Neuroscience, 371*, 221–228.

Quinn, P. C., & Eimas, P. D. (1998). Perceptual cues that permit categorical differentiation of animal species by infants. *Journal of Experimental Child Psychology, 63*, 189–211.

Quinn, P. C., Eimas, P. D., & Rosenkrantz, S. L. (1993). Evidence for representations of perceptually similar natural categories by 3-month-old and 4-month-old infants. *Perception, 22*, 463–475.

Radke-Yarrow, M. & Zahn-Waxler, C. (1983) Roots, motives and patterns in children's prosocial behavior. In J. Reykowski, T. Karylowski, D. Bar-Tal & E. Staub (eds), *Origins and maintenance of prosocial behaviors* (pp. 81–99) New York: Plenum Press.

Radziszewska, B., & Rogoff, B. (1988). Influence of adult and peer collaborators on the development of children's planning skills. *Developmental Psychology, 24*, 840–848.

Raine, A. (2002). Biosocial studies of antisocial and violent behavior in children and adults: A review. *Journal of Abnormal Child Psychology, 30*, 311–326.

Raine, A., Stoddard, J., Bihrle, S., & Buchsbaum, M. (1998). Prefrontal glucose deficits in murderers lacking psychosocial deprivation. *Neuropsychiatry, Neuropsychology and Behavioral Neurology, 11*, 1–7.

Rakic, P. (1988). Specification of cerebral cortical areas. *Science, 241*, 170–176.

Rakic, P. (1995). Corticogenesis in human and nonhuman primates. In M. S. Gazzaniga (ed.), *The cognitive neurosciences* (pp. 127–145). Cambridge, MA: MIT Press.

Rakison, D. H. (2007). Fast tracking: Infants learn rapidly about object trajectories. *Trends in Cognitive Sciences, 11*, 140–142.

Ramchandani, P., Stein, A., Evans, J. & O'Connor, T. G. (2005). Paternal depression in the postnatal period and child development: a prospective population study. *Lancet, 365*, 2201–2205.

Ramesh, R. (2009). The world's oldest mother. *Guardian*, 6 March.

Ramsay, J. R. (2011). CBT is effective in reducing symptoms in adults with ADHD whose symptoms persist following pharmacotherapy. *Evidence Based Mental Health, 14*, 28.

Rankin, J. L., Lane, D. J., Gibbons, F. X., & Gerrard, M. (2004). Adolescent self-consciousness: Longitudinal age changes and gender differences in two cohorts. *Journal of Research on Adolescence, 14*(1), 1–21.

Rao, G. (2006). *Child obesity*. New York: Prometheus Books.

Ray, J. W., & Klesges, R. C. (1993). Influences on the eating behavior of children. In C. L. Williams & S. Y. S. Kimm (eds), *Prevention and treatment of childhood obesity* (pp. 57–69). New York: New York Academy of Sciences.

Raynor, H. A., & Epstein, L. H. (2001). Dietary variety, energy regulation, and obesity. *Psychological Bulletin, 127,* 325–341.

Reese, H. W, (1962) Verbal mediation as a function of age level.*Psyuchological bulletin,* 59, 502–509.

Reid, J. B., Patterson, G. R., & Snyder, J. J. (eds) (2002). *Antisocial behavior in children and adolescents.* Washington, DC: American Psychological Association.

Reid, V. M., Dunn, K., Donovan, T., & Young, R. J. (2018). Response to Scheel et al. *Current Biology, 28*(10), R596–R597.

Reid, V. M., Dunn, K., Young, R. J., Amu, J., Donovan, T., & Reissland, N. (2017). The human fetus preferentially engages with face-like visual stimuli. *Current Biology, 27*(12), 1825–1828.

Reilly, T. W., Entwisle, D. R., & Doering, S. G. (1987). Socialization into parenthood: A longitudinal study of the development of self evaluations. *Journal of Marriage and the Family, 49,* 295–308.

Reiner, W. G., & Gearhart, J. P. (2004). Discordant sexual identity in some genetic males with cloacal exstrophy assigned to female sex at birth. *The New England Journal of Medicine, 350,* 333–341.

Reiss, D., Neiderhiser, J. M., Hetherington, E. M., & Plomin, R. (2000). *The relationship code: Deciphering genetic and social influences on adolescent development.* Cambridge, MA: Harvard University Press.

Renninger, K. A. & Sigel, I. E. (eds) (2006) *Child psychology in practice* (Vol. 4) In W. Damon & R. M. Lerner (Series eds), *Handbook of child psychology.* New York: Wiley.

Renshaw, P. D., & Brown, P. J. (1993). Loneliness in middle childhood: Concurrent and longitudinal predictors. *Child Development, 64,* 1271–1284.

Repetti, R. (1989). Effects of daily workload on subsequent behavior during marital interaction: The roles of withdrawal and spouse support. *Journal of Personality and Social Psychology, 57,* 651–659.

Repetti, R. (1996). Short-term and long-term linking job stressors to father child interaction. *Social Development, 1,* 1–15.

Repetti, R., & Wood, J. (1997). The effects of stress and work on mothers' interactions with preschoolers. *Journal of Family Psychology, 1,* 90–108.

Rescorla, L. A. (1980). Overextension in early language. *Journal of Child Language, 7,* 321–335.

Rest, J. R., Narvaez, D., & Thoma, S. J. (2000). *Postconventional moral thinking: A neo-Kohlbergian approach.* Mahwah, NJ: Erlbaum.

Revelle, G. L., Wellman, H. M., & Karabenick, J. D. (1985). Comprehension monitoring in preschool children. *Child Development, 56,* 654–663.

Reznick, J. S., Corley, R., & Robinson, J. (1997). A longitudinal twin study of intelligence in the second year. *Monographs of the Society for Research in Child Development, Serial no. 249.*

Rhee, S. H., & Waldman, I. D. (2002). Genetic and environmental influences on antisocial behavior: A meta-analysis of twin and adoption studies. *Psychological Bulletin, 128,* 490–529.

Rheingold, H. L. & Cook, K. V. (1975) The content of boys' and girls' rooms as an index of parent behavior. *Child Development, 46,* 459–463.

Rheingold, H. L. (1982). Little children's participation in the work of adults, a nascent prosocial behavior. *Child Development, 53,* 114–125.

Rheingold, H. L., & Eckerman, C. (1970). The infant separates himself from his mother. *Science, 168,* 78–83.

Rheingold, H. L., & Eckerman, C. O. (1973). The fear of strangers hypothesis: A critical review. In H. Reese (ed.), *Advances in child development and behavior* (Vol. 8, pp. 185–222). New York: Academic Press.

Ricci, C. M., & Beal, C. R. (1998). Effect of questioning techniques and interview setting on young children's eyewitness memory. *Expert Evidence, 6,* 127–128.

Rice, F., Lewis, G., Harold, G. T., & Thapar, A. (2013). Examining the role of passive gene–environment correlation in childhood depression using a novel genetically sensitive design. *Development and Psychopathology, 25*(1), 37–50.

Richards, J. E. & Anderson, D. R. (2004) Attentional inertia in children's extended looking at television. In R. V. Kail (ed.), *Advances in child development and behavior* (Vol. 32, pp. 163–212) San Diego, CA: Elsevier.

Richards, J. E. (2010). The development of attention to simple and complex visual stimuli in infants: Behavioral and psychophysiological measures. *Developmental Review, 30,* 203–219.

Richards, M. H., Crowe, P. A., Larson, R. & Swarr, A. (1998) Developmental patterns and gender differences in the experience of peer companionship during adolescence. *Child Development, 69,* 154–163.

Richardson, L. (2015). Space, time and Molyneux's question. In J. Stazicker, (ed.), *The structure of perceptual experience* (pp. 125–147). Chichester: Wiley.

Richland, L. E., Morrison, R. G., & Holyoak, K. J. (2006). Children's development of analogical reasoning: Insights from scene analogy problems. *Journal of Experimental Child Psychology, 94,* 249–273.

Richland, L. E., Zur, O. & Holyoak, K. J. (2007) Cognitive supports for analogies in the mathematics classroom. *Science, 316,* 1128–1129.

Riciutti, H. N. (1993). Nutrition and mental development. *Current Directions in Psychological Science, 2*, 43–46.

Rigato, S., Ali, J. B., van Velzen, J., & Bremner, A. J. (2014). The neural basis of somatosensory remapping develops in human infancy. *Current Biology, 24*(11), 1222–1226.

Rigato, S., Banissy, M. J., Romanska, A., Thomas, R., van Velzen, J., & Bremner, A. J. (2017). Cortical signatures of vicarious tactile experience in four-month-old infants. *Developmental Cognitive Neuroscience.* https://doi.org/10.1016/j.dcn.2017.09.003.

Rinn, J. L., & Chang, H. Y. (2012). Genome regulation by long noncoding RNAs. *Annual Review of Biochemistry, 81*. doi: 10.1146/annurev-biochem-051410-092902.

Rivera, S. M., Wakeley, A., & Langer, J. (1999). The drawbridge phenomenon: Representational reasoning or perceptual preference? *Developmental Psychology, 35*, 427–435.

Robinson, J. L., Kagan, J., Reznick, J. S., & Corley, R. (1992). The heritability of inhibited and uninhibited behavior. A twin study. *Developmental Psychology, 28*, 1030–1037.

Robinson, T. N., Saphir, M. N., Kraemer, H. C., Varady, A., & Haydel, K. F. (2001). Effects of reducing television viewing on children's requests for toys: a randomized controlled trial. *Journal of Developmental Pediatrics, 22*, 179–184.

Robles, T. F., Slatcher, R. B., Trombello, J. M., & McGinn, M. M. (2014). Marital quality and health: A meta-analytic review. *Psychological Bulletin, 140*, 140–187. doi: 10.1037/

Rochat, P. (1998). Self-perception and action in infancy. *Experimental Brain Research, 123*(1–2), 102–109.

Rochat, P. (2010). The innate sense of the body develops to become a public affair by 2–3 years. *Neuropsychologia, 48*(3), 738–745.

Roche, A. F. (ed.) (1979). Secular trends: Human growth, maturation, and development. *Monographs of the Society for Research in Child Development, 44*, (Serial no. 179).

Rodkin, P. C., Farmer, T. W., Pearl, R., & Van Acker, R. (2000). Heterogeneity of popular boys: Antisocial and prosocial configurations. *Developmental Psychology, 30*, 14–24.

Rödström, K., Bengtsson, C., Milsom, I., Lissner, L., Sundh, V., & Bjoürkelund, C. (2003). Evidence for a secular trend in menopausal age: A population study of women in Gothenburg. *Menopause, 10*, 538–543.

Roffwarg, H. P., Muzio, J. N., & Dement, W. C. (1966). Ontogenetic development of the human sleep-dream cycle. *Science, 152*, 604–619.

Roggman, L. A., Langlois, J. H., Hubbs-Tait, T. L., & Rieser-Danner, L. A. (1994). Infant day-care attachment and the 'file drawer problem'. *Child Development, 65*, 1429–1443.

Rogoff, B. & Mistry, J. (1990) The social and functional context of children's remembering. In R. Fivush & J. A. Hudson (eds), *Knowing and remembering in young children* (pp. 197–222) New York: Cambridge University Press.

Rogoff, B. & Morelli, G (1989). Perspectives on Children's development from cultural psychology. *American Psychologist, 44*, 343–348.

Rogoff, B. (1990). *Apprenticeship in thinking: Cognitive development in social context.* New York: Oxford University Press.

Rogoff, B. (1991). Social interaction as apprenticeship in thinking: Guidance and participation in spatial planning. In

L. B. Resnick, J. M. Levine, & S. D. Teasley (eds), *Perspectives on socially shared cognition.* Washington, DC: American Psychological Association.

Rogoff, B. (1998). Cognition as a collaborative process. In D. Kuhn & R. Siegler (eds) & W. Damon (Series ed.), *Handbook of child psychology: Vol. 2. Cognition, perception and language* (5th edn, pp. 679–744). New York: Wiley.

Rogoff, B. (2002). How can we study cultural aspects of human development? *Human Development, 45*, 387–389.

Rogoff, B. (2003). *The cultural nature of human development.* New York: Oxford University Press.

Rogoff, B. (2003). *The cultural nature of human development.* Oxford: Oxford University Press.

Rogoff, B. (2016). Culture and participation: A paradigm shift. *Current Opinion in Psychology, 8*, 182–189.

Rogoff, B., & Waddell, K. J. (1982). Memory for information organized in a scene by children from two cultures. *Child Development, 53*, 1224–1228.

Rogoff, B., Callanan, M., Gutiérrez, K. D., & Erickson, F. (2016). The organization of informal learning. *Review of Research in Education, 40*(1), 356–401.

Rogoff, B., Paradise, R., Mejia Arauz, R., Correa-Chavez, M., & Angelillo, C. (2003). Firsthand learning through intent participation. *Annual Review of Psychology, 54*, 175–203.

Roisman, G. I., Masten, A. S., Coatsworth, J. D., & Tellegen, A. (2004). Salient and emerging development tasks in the transition to adulthood. *Child Development, 75*, 123–133.

Roisman, G. I., Padron, E., Sroufe, L. A., & Egeland, B. (2002). Earned-secure attachment states in retrospect and prospect. *Child Development, 73*, 1204–1219.

Rokach, A. (2001). Perceived causes of loneliness in adulthood. *Journal of Social Behaviour and Personality, 15,* 1281–1289.

Rokach, A., & Neto, F. (2006). Age, culture, and coping with loneliness. *Psychology and Education, 43,* 1–21.

Rolls, E. T. & Treves, A. (1998) *Neural networks and brain function.* Oxford: Oxford University Press.

Rolls, E. T., & Treves, A. (1998). *Neural networks and brain function.* Oxford, UK: Oxford University Press.

Romski, M. A., & Sevcik, R. A. (1996). *Breaking the speech barrier: Language development through augmented means.* Baltimore, MD: Brookes.

Ronald, A., & Hoekstra, R. A. (2011). Autism spectrum disorders and autistic traits: A decade of new twin studies. *American Journal of Medical Genetics B: Neuropsychiatric Genetics, 156B,* 255–274.

Roopnarine, J. (2004). African American and African Caribbean fathers: Level, quality and meaning of involvement. In M. E. Lamb (ed.), *The role of the father in child development* (4th edn, pp. 58–97). Hoboken, NJ: Wiley.

Rose, A. J., & Rudolph, K. D. (2006). A review of sex differences in peer relationship processes: Potential trade-offs for the emotional and behavioral development of girls and boys. *Psychological Bulletin, 132,* 98–131.

Rose, S. A., & Blank, M. (1974). The potency of context in children's cognition: An illustration through conservation. *Child Development, 45,* 199–502.

Rose, S. A., & Feldman, J. F. (1995). Prediction of IQ and specific cognitive abilities at 11 years from infancy measures. *Developmental Psychology, 31,* 685–696.

Rose, S. A., Feldman, J. F., Wallach, I. F., & McCarton, C. (1989). Infant visual attention: Relation to birth status and developmental outcome during the first 5 years. *Developmental Psychology, 25,* 560–576.

Rose, S. A., Jankowski, J. J. & Feldman, J. F. (2002) Speed of processing and face recognition at 7 and 12 months. *Infancy, 3,* 435–455.

Rosen, M. L., Sheridan, M. A., Sambrook, K. A., Dennison, M. J., Jenness, J. L., Askren, M. K., et al. (2018). Salience network response to changes in emotional expressions of others is heightened during early adolescence: Relevance for social functioning. *Developmental Science, 21,* e12571. https://doi.org/10.1111/desc.12571

Rosenblum, T., & Pinker, S. (1983). Word magic revisited: Monolingual and bilingual children's understanding of the word-object relationships. *Child Development, 54,* 773–780.

Rosenstein, D. & Oster, H. (1988) Differential facial response to four basic tastes in newborns. *Child Development, 59,* 1555–1568.

Rosenzweig, M. R. (2003). Effects of differential experience on brain and behavior. *Developmental Neuropsychology, 24,* 523–540.

Rosenzweig, M. R., Leiman, A. S., & Breedlove, S. M. (1996). *Biological psychology.* Sunderland, MA: Sinauer.

Roshanfekr, P., Gharibzadeh, S., Mohammadinia, L., Sajedi, F., Habibi, E., & Malekafzali, H. (2017). Involving mothers in child development assessment in a community-based participatory study using ages and stages questionnaires. *International Journal of Preventive Medicine, 8,* 102. http://doi.org/10.4103/ijpvm. IJPVM_268_17

Ross, H. S., & Conant, C. L. (1992). The social structure of early conflict: Interactions, relationships, and alliances. In C. U. Shantz & W. W. Hartup (eds), *Conflict in child and adolescent development* (pp. 153–185). Cambridge: Cambridge University Press.

Ross, H. S., Conant, C., Cheyne, J. A. & Alevizos, E. (1992) Relationships and alliances in the social interactions of kibbutz toddlers. *Social Development, 1,* 1–17.

Ross-Sheehy, S., Oakes, L. M., & Luck, S. J. (2003). The development of visual short-term memory capacity in infants. *Child Development, 74,* 1807–1822.

Rothbart, M. K., Ahadi, S. A., & Hershey, K. L. (1994). Temperament and social behavior in childhood. *Merrill-Palmer Quarterly, 40,* 21–39.

Rothbart, M., & Bates, J. (2006). Temperament. In W. Damon & R. Lerner (Series eds) & N. Eisenberg (Vol. ed.), *Handbook of child psychology* (Vol. 3, 6th edn, pp. 99–166). New York: Wiley.

Rothbaum, F., & Trommsdorff, G. (2007). Do roots and wings complement or oppose one another? The socialization of relatedness and autonomy in cultural context. In J. E. Grusec & P. Hastings (eds), *The handbook of socialization* (pp. 461–189). New York: Guilford Press.

Rothbaum, F., Pott, M., Azuma, H., Miyake, K., & Weisz, J. (2000b). The development of close relationships in Japan and the United States: Paths of symbiotic harmony and generative tension. *Child Development, 71,* 1121–1142.

Rothbaum, F., Weisz, J., Pott, M., Miyake, K., & Morelli, G. (2000a). Attachment and culture: Security in the United States and Japan. *American Psychologist, 35,* 1093–1104.

Rousseau, J.-J. (1762) *Emile,* London: Dent.

Rovee-Collier, C. K. (1987). Learning and memory in infants. In J. D. Osofsky (ed.), *Handbook of infant development* (pp. 98–148). New York: Wiley.

Rovee-Collier, C. K. (1999). The development of infant memory. *Current Directions in Psychological Science, 8*, 80–85.

Rovee-Collier, C. K., & Gerhardstein, P. (1997). The development of infant memory. In C. Nelson & C. Hulme (eds), *The development of memory in childhood: Studies in developmental psychology* (pp. 5–39). Hove: Psychology Press.

Rovee-Collier, C. K., & Lipsitt, L. P. (1982). Learning, adaptation and memory in the newborn. In P. Stratton (ed.), *Psychobiology of the human newborn* (pp. 147–190). New York: Wiley.

Rovee-Collier, C. K., & Shyi, G. (1992). A functional and cognitive analysis of infant long-term retention. In C. J. Brainard, M. L. Howe, & V. Reyna (eds), *Development of long-term retention* (pp. 3–55). New York: Springer-Verlag.

Rowe, J., & Kahn, R. (1998). *Successful aging.* New York: Pantheon.

Rowe, M., Leech, K. A., & Cabrera, N. (2017). Going beyond input quality: Wh- questions matter for toddlers' language and cognitive development. *Cognitive Science, 41*, 162–179.

Rowe, R., Maughan, B., & Goodman, R. (2004). Childhood psychiatric disorder and unintentional injury: Findings from a national cohort study. *Journal of Pediatric Psychology, 29*, 119–130.

Rubia, K., Halari, R., Cubillo, A., Smith, A. B., Mohammad, A. M., Brammer, M. & Taylor, E. (2011) Methylphenidate normalizes fronto-striatal underactivation during interference inhibition in medication-naive boys with attention-deficit hyperactivity disorder. *Neuropsychopharmacology, 36*, 1575–1586.

Rubia, K., Halari, R., Cubillo, A., Smith, A. B., Mohammad, A. M., Brammer, M., & Taylor, E. (2011). Methylphenidate normalizes fronto-striatal underactivation during interference inhibition in medication-naive boys with attention-deficit hyperactivity disorder. *Neuropsychopharmacology, 36*(8), 1575.

Rubia, K., Halari, R., Smith, A. B., Mohammad, M., Scott, S., Giampietro, V., Taylor, E., & Brammer, M. E. (2008). Dissociated functional brain abnormalities of inhibition in boys with pure conduct disorder and in boys with pure attention-deficit/hyperactivity disorder. *American Journal of Psychiatry, 165*, 889–897.

Rubia, K., Overmeyer, S., Taylor, E., Brammer, M., Williams, SCR, Simmons, A., Andrew, C., & Bullmore, E. T. (2000). Frontalisation with age: Mapping neurodevelopmental trajectories with fMRI. *Neuroscience Biobehavioural Review, 24*, 13–21.

Rubia, K., Smith, A. B., Brammer, M. J., Brian Toone, B., & Taylor, E. (2005). Medication-naïve adolescents with attention-deficit hyperactivity disorder show abnormal brain activation during inhibition and error detection. *American Journal of Psychiatry, 162*, 1067–1075.

Rubin, J. Z., Provenzano, F. J., & Luria, A. (1974). The eye of the beholder: Parents' views on sex of newborns. *American Journal of Orthopsychiatry, 43*, 720–731.

Rubin, K. H., Bukowski, W. M., & Parker, J. G. (2006). Peer interactions, relationships, and groups. In W. Damon & R. M. Lerner (Series eds) & N. Eisenberg (Vol. ed.), *Handbook of child psychology: Vol. 3. Social, emotional, and personality development* (6th edn, pp. 571–645). New York: Wiley.

Ruble, D., Martin, C., & Berenbaum, S. (2006). Gender development. In W. Damon & R. M. Lerner (Series eds) & N. Eisenberg (Vol. ed.), *Handbook of child psychology: Vol. 3. Social, emotional, and personality development* (6th ed, pp. 858–932). New York: Wiley.

Rudy, D. & Grusec, J. E. (2006) Authoritarian parenting in individualistic and collectivist groups: Associations with maternal emotion and cognition and children's self-esteem. *Journal of Family Psychology, 20*, 68–78.

Rudy, G. S., & Goodman, G. S. (1991). The effects of participation on children's reports: Implications for children's testimony. *Developmental Psychology, 27*, 527–538.

Ruff, H. A. & Capozzoli, M. C. (2003) Development of attention and distractibility in the first 4 years of life. *Developmental Psychology, 39*, 877–890.

Ruff, H. A., & Rothbart, M. K. (1996). *Attention in early development: Themes and variations.* New York: Oxford University Press.

Ruffman, T., & Perner, J. (2005). Do infants really understand false belief? *Trends in Cognitive Sciences, 9*(10), 462–463.

Ruffman, T., Perner, J., Naito, M, Parkin, L., & Clements, W. A. (1998). Older (but not younger) siblings facilitate false belief understanding. *Developmental Psychology, 34*(1), 161–174.

Rumelhart, D. E., McClelland, J. L., and the PDP research group. (1986). *Parallel distributed processing: Explorations in the microstructure of cognition. Volume I.* Cambridge, MA: MIT Press.

Runco, M. A. (1996, Summer). Personal creativity: Definition and developmental issues. In M. A. Runco (ed.), *Creativity from childhood through adulthood: The developmental issues* [Special issue] *New Directions for Child Development, 72*, 3–30.

Russ, S. (2003). Play and creativity: Developmental issues. *Scandinavian Journal of Educational Research, 47*, 291–303.

Russell, A., Russell, G., & Midwinter, D. (1991). Observer effects on mothers and fathers: Self-reported influence during a home observation. *Merrill-Palmer Quarterly, 38*, 263–283.

Rust, J., Golombok, S., Hines, M., Johnston, K., Golding, J., & the ALSPAC Study Team (2000). The role of brothers and sisters in the gender development of preschool children. *Journal of Experimental Child Psychology, 77*, 292–303.

Rutland, A. (1999). The development of national prejudice, in-group favouritism and self-stereotypes in British children. *British Journal of Social Psychology, 38*, 55–70.

Rutter, M. (1992). Nature, nurture and psychopathology. In B. Tizard & V. Varma (eds), *Vulnerability and resilience in human development* (pp. 21–38). London: Jessica Kingsley.

Rutter, M. (1996). Transitions and turning points in developmental psychopathology: As applied to the age span between childhood and mid-adulthood. *International Journal of Behavioral Development, 19*, 603–626.

Rutter, M. (2003b). Crucial paths from risk indicator to causal mechanism. In B. B. Lahey, T. E. Moffitt, & A. Caspi (eds), *Causes of conduct disorder and juvenile delinquency* (pp. 3–24). New York: Guilford Press.

Rutter, M. (2006a). *Genes and behavior*. New York: Blackwell.

Rutter, M. (2006b). The psychological effects of early institutional rearing. In P. Marshall & N. Fox (eds), *The development of social engagement: Neurobiological perspectives* (pp. 355–391). Oxford: Oxford University Press.

Rutter, M. (2007, September). *Autism research: Lessons from the past and prospects for the future.* Presentation at the New York University Child Study Center.

Rutter, M. (ed.) (2003a) *Autism: Neural basis and treatment possibilities.* London: Novartis.

Rutter, M., & Sroufe, L. A. (2000). Developmental psychopathology: Concepts and challenges. *Development and Psychopathology, 12*(3), 265–296.

Rutter, M., Beckett, C., Castle, J., Kreppner, J., Stevens, S., & Sonuga-Barke, E. J. (2009). *Policy and practice implications from the English and Romanian Adoptees (ERA) Study: Forty two key questions.* London: BAAF.

Rutter, M., Kreppner, J., O'Conner, T. & the English & Romanian Adoptees (ERA) Study Team (2001) Risk and resilience following profound early global privation. *British Journal of Psychiatry, 179*, 97–103.

Rymer, R. (1993). *Genie: A scientific tragedy.* New York: HarperCollins.

Saarni, C. (1999). *The development of emotional competence.* New York: Guilford Press.

Saarni, C., Campos, J. J., & Camras, L. (2006). Emotional development. In W. Damon & R. M. Lerner (Series eds) & N. Eisenberg (Vol. ed.), *Handbook of child psychology: Vol. 3. Social, emotional, and personality development* (6th edn, pp. 226–299). New York: Wiley.

Sachs, J. (1985) Prelinguistic development. In J. Berko-Gleason (ed.), *The development of language.* Columbus, OH: Merrill.

Sadeh, A. (1996). Stress, trauma, and sleep in children. *Child and Adolescent Psychiatric Clinics of North America, 5*, 685–700.

Sadeh, A. (2008). Sleep. In M. M. Haith & J. B. Benson (eds), *Encyclopedia of infant and early childhood development* (pp. 174–185). Oxford: Elsevier.

Sadeh, A., De Marcas, G., Guri, Y., Berger, A., Tikotzky, L., & Bar-Haim, Y. (2015). Infant sleep predicts attention regulation and behavior problems at 3–4 years of age. *Developmental neuropsychology, 40*(3), 122–137.

Sadeh, A., Tikotzky, L., & Scher, A. (2010). Parenting and infant sleep. *Sleep Medicine Reviews, 14*(2), 89–96.

Saffran, J. R., & Griepentrog, G. J. (2001). Absolute pitch on infant auditory learning: Evidence for developmental reorganization. *Developmental Psychology, 37*, 74–85.

Saffran, J. R., Aslin, R. N., & Newport, E. L. (1996). Statistical learning by 8-month-old infants. *Science, 274*, 1926–1928.

Saffran, J. R., Werker, J., & Werner, L. A. (2006). The infant's auditory world. In W. Damon & R. M. Lerner (Series eds) & D. Kuhn & R. Siegler (Vol. eds), *Cognition, perception & language* (Vol. 2, 6th edn, pp. 58–108). New York: Wiley.

Sagi, A., van Ijzendoorn, M. H., Aviezer, O., Donnell, F., & Mayseless, O. (1994). Sleeping out of home in a kibbutz community arrangement: It makes a difference for infant-mother attachment. *Child Development, 65*, 992–1004.

Sagi-Schwartz, A., and Aviezer, O. (2005). Correlates of attachment to multiple caregivers in kibbutz children from birth to emerging adulthood: The Haifa longitudinal study. In K. E. Grossmann, K. Grossmann, & E. Waters (eds), *Attachment from Infancy to Adulthood* (pp. 165–197). New York: Guilford Press.

Sagiv, S. K., Tolbert, P. E., Altshul, L. M., and Korrick, S. A. (2007) Organochlorine exposures during pregnancy and infant size at birth. *Epidemiology, 18*, 120–129.

Saigal, S., & Doyle, L. W. (2008). An overview of mortality and sequelae of preterm birth from infancy to adulthood. *The Lancet, 371*(9608), 261–269.

Salapatek, P., & Kessen, W. (1966). Visual scanning of triangles by the human newborn. *Journal of Experimental Child Psychology, 3*, 155–167.

Salmivalli, C., Kaukiainen, A., & Lagerspetz, K, (2000). Aggression and sociometric status among peers: Do gender and type of aggression matter? *Scandinavian Journal of Psychology*, 24.

Salthouse, T. A. (2004). What and when of cognitive aging. *Current Directions in Psychological Science*, *13*, 140–144.

Sameroff, A. J. (2007). Biopsychosocial influences on the development of resilience. In B. Lester, A. Masten & B. McEwen (eds) *Resilience in children* (pp. 116–124). New York: Blackwell.

Sameroff, A. J., & Chandler, M. J. (1975). Reproductive risk and the continuum of caretaking casualty. In F. Horowitz (ed.), *Review of child development research* (Vol. 4, pp. 187–244). Chicago: University of Chicago Press.

Sameroff, A. J., & Fiese, B. H. (2000). Transactional regulation: The developmental ecology of early intervention. In J. P. Shonkoff & S. J. Meisels (eds), *Handbook of early childhood intervention* (2nd edn, pp. 135–159). New York: Cambridge University Press.

Sameroff, A. J., Seifer, R., Baldwin, A., & Baldwin, C. (1993). Continuity of risk from childhood to adolescence. Unpublished manuscript, University of Rochester.

Sameroff, A. J., Seifer, R., Barocas, R., Zax, M., & Greenspan, S. (1987). Intelligence quotient scores of 4-year-old children: Social-environmental risk factors. *Pediatrics*, *79*, 343–350.

Sampaio, R. & Truwit, C. (2001) Myelination in the developing human brain. In C. Nelson & M. Luciana (eds), *Handbook of developmental cognitive neuroscience* (pp. 35–44) Cambridge, MA: MIT Press.

Samson, D., Apperly, I. A., Braithwaite, J. J., Andrews, B. J., & Bodley Scott, S. E. (2010). Seeing it their way: Evidence for rapid and involuntary computation of what other people see. *Journal of Experimental Psychology: Human Perception and Performance, 36*(5), 1255.

Sanders, L. D., Weber-Fox, C. M., & Neville, H. J. (2007). Varying degrees of plasticity in different subsystems of language. In J. R. Pomerantz & M. Crair (eds), *Topics in integrative neuroscience: From cells to cognition* (pp. 125–153). New York: Cambridge University Press.

Sanderson, J. A., & Siegal, M. (1991). Loneliness in young children. Unpublished manuscript. University of Queensland, Brisbane, Australia.

Sann, C., & Streri, A. (2007). Perception of object shape and texture in human newborns: evidence from cross-modal transfer tasks. *Developmental Science, 10*(3), 399–410.

Savage-Rumbaugh, S. & Shanker, S. (1998) *Apes, language, and the human mind.* New York: Oxford University Press.

Saxe, G. B. (1979) Developmental relations between notational counting and number conservation. *Child Development, 50*, 180–187.

Saxe, G. B. (1991). *Culture and cognitive development: Studies in mathematical understanding.* Hillsdale, NJ: Erlbaum.

Saywitz, K. J., & Lyons, T. D. (2002). Coming to grips with children's suggestibility. In M. Eisen, G. Goodman, & J. Quas (eds), *Memory and suggestibility in the forensic interview* (pp. 85–113). Hillsdale, NJ: Erlbaum.

Scaramella, L. V & Conger, R. D. (2003) Intergenerational continuity of hostile parenting and its consequences: The moderating influence of children's negative emotional reactivity. *Social Development, 12*, 420–439.

Scarr, S. (1996). How people make their own environments: Implications for parents and policy makers. *Psychology, Public Policy and Law, 2*, 204–228.

Scarr, S. (1997). Behavior-genetic and socialization theories of intelligence: Truce and reconciliation. In R. J. Sternberg & E. Grigorenko (eds), *Intelligence, heredity, and environment* (pp. 3–41). New York: Cambridge University Press.

Scarr, S. (1998). How do families affect intelligence? Social-environmental and behavior-genetic predictions. In J. J. McArdle & R. W. Woodcock (eds), *Human cognitive abilities in theory and practice* (pp. 113–136). Mahwah, NJ: Erlbaum.

Scarr, S., & McCartney, K. (1983). How people make their own environments: A theory of genotype environment effects. *Child Development, 54*, 424–435.

Scarr, S., & Weinberg, R. A. (1976). IQ test performance of black children adopted by white families. *American Psychologist, 31*, 726–739.

Scarr, S., & Weinberg, R. A. (1983). The Minnesota adoption studies: Genetic differences and malleability. *Child Development, 54*, 260–267.

Schaal, B. (2015). Prenatal and postnatal human olfactory development: Influences on cognition and behavior. In R. L. Doty (ed.), *Handbook of olfaction and cognition* (3rd edn, pp. 305–335). Hoboken, NJ: John Wiley & Sons.

Schaal, B., & Durand, K. (2012). The role of olfaction in human multisensory development. In A. J. Bremner, D. J. Lewkowicz, & C. Spence (eds), *Multisensory development* (pp. 29–62). New York: Oxford University Press.

Schaal, B., Marlier, L., & Soussignan, R. (2000). Human foetuses learn odours from their pregnant mother's diet. *Chemical Senses, 25*(6), 729–737.

Schaal, B., Tremblay, R. E., Soussignan, R., & Susman, E. J. (1996). Male testosterone linked to high social dominance but low physical aggression in early adolescence. *Journal of the American Academy of Child and Adolescent Psychiatry, 19,* 1322–1330.

Schaffer, H. R. (1971) *The growth of sociability.* London: Penguin.

Schaffer, H. R. (1974). Cognitive components of the infant's response to strangeness. In M. Lewis & L. A. Rosenblum (eds), *The origins of fear.* New York: Wiley.

Schaffer, H. R. (1977). *Mothering.* Cambridge, MA: Harvard University Press.

Schaffer, H. R. (1996). *Social development.* Cambridge, MA: Blackwell.

Schaffer, H. R., & Emerson, P. E. (1964). The development of social attachments in infancy. *Monographs of the Society for Research in Child Development, 29*(3, Serial No. 94).

Schaffer, H. R. (1996). *Social Development.* Oxford: Blackwell

Schaie, K. W. (1977). Toward a stage model of adult cognitive development. *Journal of Aging and Human Development, 8,* 129–138.

Schank, R. C., & Abelson, R. P. (1977). *Scripts, plans, goals and understanding.* Hillsdale, NJ: Erlbaum.

Scharf, M. (2001). A 'natural experiment' in childrearing ecologies and adolescents' attachment and separation representations. *Child Development, 72,* 236–251.

Scheel, A. M., Ritchie, S. J., Brown, N. J., & Jacques, S. L. (2018). Methodological problems in a study of fetal visual perception. *Current Biology, 28*(10), R594–R596.

Schellenberg, E. G., & Trehub, S. E. (1996). Natural musical intervals: Evidence from infant listeners. *Psychological Science, 7,* 272–277.

Schicke, T., & Röder, B. (2006). Spatial remapping of touch: Confusion of perceived stimulus

order across hand and foot. *Proceedings of the National Academy of Sciences, 103*(31), 11808–11813.

Schieffelin, B. B., & Ochs, E. (1987). *Language socialization across cultures.* New York: Cambridge University Press.

Schneider, B. H. (2000). *Friends and enemies: Peer relations in childhood.* London: Arnold.

Schneider, B. H., Atkinson, L., & Tardif, C. (2001). Child-parent attachment and children's peer relations: A quantitative review. *Developmental Psychology, 37,* 86–100.

Schneider, B. H., Smith, A., Poisson, S. E., & Kwan, A. B. (1997). Cultural dimensions of children's peer relations. In S. Duck (ed.), *Handbook of personal relationships* (2nd edn, pp. 121–146). New York: Wiley.

Schneider, B. H., Woodburn, S., del Toro, M. P. S., & Udvari, S. J. (2005). Cultural and gender differences in the implications of competition for early adolescent friendship. *Merrill-Palmer Quarterly, 51,* 163–191.

Schneider, W., & Bjorklund, D. F. (1998). Memory. In W. Damon (Series ed.), and D. Kuhn & R. S. Siegler (Vol. eds), *Handbook of child psychology: Vol. 2. Cognition, perception, and language* (pp. 467–521). New York: Wiley.

Schneidman, E. (1980). *Voices of death.* New York: Harper & Row.

Scholl, T. O., Heidiger, M. L. & Belsky, D. (1996) Prenatal care and maternal health during adolescent pregnancy: A review and meta-analysis. *Journal of Adolescent Health, 15,* 444–456.

Schoppe-Sullivan, S. J., Diener, M. L., Magelsdorf, S. C., Brown, G. L., McHale, J. L., & Frosch, C. A. (2006). Attachment and sensitivity in family context: The roles of parent and infant gender. *Infant and Child Development, 15,* 367–385.

Schultz, J., Friston, K. J., O'Doherty, J., Wolpert, D. M., & Frith, C. D. (2005). Activation in posterior superior temporal sulcus parallels parameter inducing the percept of animacy. *Neuron, 45*(4), 625–635.

Schwartz, R. G., & Leonard, L. B. (1984). Words, objects, and actions in early lexical acquisition. *Journal of Speech, Language, and Hearing Research, 27*(1), 119–127.

Scott, R. M., & Baillargeon, R. (2017). Early false-belief understanding. *Trends in Cognitive Sciences, 21*(4), 237–249.

Scott, S., Sylva, K., Doolan, M., Price, J., Jacobs, B., Crook, C., and Landau, S. (2010). Randomised controlled trial of parent groups for child antisocial behaviour targeting multiple risk factors: The SPOKES project. *Journal of Child Psychology and Psychiatry, 51,* 48–57.

Scourfield, J., John, B., Martin, N., & McGuffin, P. (2004). The development of prosocial behaviour in children and adolescents: A twin study. *Journal of Child Psychology and Psychiatry, 45*(5), 927–935.

Seligman, M. E. P. (1974) Depression and learned helplessness. In R. J. Friedman & M. M. Katz (eds), *The psychology of depression: Contemporary theory and research* (pp. 83–113) Washington, DC: Winston-Wiley.

Selman, R. L. (1980). *The growth of interpersonal understanding.* New York: Academic Press.

Selman, R. L., & Byrne, D. F. (1974). A structural-developmental analysis of levels of role taking in middle childhood. *Child Development, 45,* 803–806.

Selman, R. L., & Dray, A. (2006). Risk and prevention: Building bridges between research and practice. In W. Damon & R. L. Lerner (Series eds) & K. A. Renninger & I. E. Sigel (Vol. eds), *Handbook of child psychology: Vol. 4. Child psychology and practice* (6th edn, pp. 378–419). New York: Wiley.

Selman, R. L., & Jacquette, D. (1978). Stability and oscillation in interpersonal awareness: A clinical-developmental analysis. In C. B. Keasey (ed.), *The 25th Nebraska symposium on motivation.* Lincoln: University of Nebraska Press.

Semel, E., & Rosner, S. R. (2003). *Understanding Williams syndrome: Behavioral patterns and interventions.* Mahwah, NJ: Erlbaum.

Senghas, A., & Coppola, M. (2001). Children creating language: How Nicaraguan sign language acquired a spatial grammar. *Psychological Science, 12*(4), 323–328.

Senju, A., Southgate, V., Snape, C., Leonard, M., & Csibra, G. (2011). Do 18-month-olds really attribute mental states to others? A critical test. *Psychological Science, 22*(7), 878–880.

Serbin, L. A., Poulin-Dubois, K. A., Colburne, K. A., Sen, M. G., & Eichstedt, J. A. (2001). Gender stereotyping in infancy: Visual preferences for and knowledge of gender-stereotyped toys in the second year. *International Journal of Behavioral Development, 25,* 7–15.

Serpell, R., & Hatano, G. (1997). Education, schooling, and literacy. In J. W. Berry, P. R. Dasen, & T. S. Saraswathi (eds), *Handbook of cross-cultural psychology: Vol. 2. Basic process and human development* (2nd edn, pp. 339–376). Boston: Allyn & Bacon.

Serpell, R., & Haynes, B. P. (2004). The cultural practice of intelligence testing: Problems of international export. In R. J. Sternberg & E. L. Grigorenko (eds), *Culture and competence: Contexts of life success* (pp. 163–185). Washington, DC: American Psychological Association.

Shakin, M., Shakin, D., & Sternglanz, S. H. (1985). Infant clothing: Sex labeling for strangers. *Sex Roles, 12,* 955–963.

Shakoor, S., McGuire, P., Cardno, A. G., Freeman, D., & Ronald, A. (2018). A twin study exploring the association between childhood emotional and behaviour problems and specific psychotic experiences in a community sample of adolescents. *Journal of Child Psychology and Psychiatry, 59*(5), 565–573.

Shanahan, M. J., & Hofer, S. M. (2005). Social context in gene-environment interactions: Retrospect and prospect. *Journals of Gerontology Series B: Psychological Sciences and Social Sciences, 60,* 65–76.

Shatz, M. (1983). Communication. In P. H. Mussen (ed.), *Handbook of child psychology* (Vol. 3, pp. 841–889). New York: Wiley.

Shatz, M. (1994). Theory of mind and the development of sociolinguistic intelligence in early childhood. In C. Lewis & P. Mitchell (eds), *Children's early understanding of mind: Origins and development* (pp. 311–329). Hillsdale, NJ: Erlbaum.

Shatz, M., & Gelman, R. (1973). The development of communication skills: Modifications in the speech of young children as a function of listener. *Monographs of the Society for Research in Child Development, 38*(5), (Serial no. 152), 1–37.

Shaw, P., Eckstrand, K., Sharp, W., Blumenthal, J., Lerch, J. P., Greenstein, D., et al. (2007). Attention-deficit/hyperactivity disorder is characterized by a delay in cortical maturation. *Proceedings of the National Academy of Sciences, 104,* 19649–19654.

Shaywitz, B. A., Shaywitz, S. E., Pugh, K. R., & Constable, R. T. (1995). Sex differences in the functional organization of the brain for language. *Nature, 373,* 607–609.

Shea, D. L., Lubinski, D., & Benbow, C. P. (2001). Importance of assessing spatial ability in intellectually talented young adolescents: A 20-year longitudinal study. *Journal of Educational Psychology, 93,* 604–614.

Sheeber, L., Davis, B. & Hops, H. (2002) Gender-specific vulnerability to depression in children of depressed mothers. In S. Goodman & I. Gotlib (eds), *Children of depressed mothers* (pp. 253–274) Washington, D.C: American Psychological Association.

Shepardson, D. P., & Pizzini, E. L. (1992). Gender bias in female elementary teachers' perceptions of the scientific ability of students. *Science Education, 76*(2), 147–153.

Sher, K. J., Bartholow, B. D. & Wood, M. D. (2000) Personality and substance use disorders: A prospective study. *Journal of Consulting and Clinical Psychology, 68,* 818–829.

Sherif, M., & Sherif, C. W. (1953). *Groups in harmony and tension.* New York: Harper & Row.

Shi, Z., & Mueller, H. J. (2013). Multisensory perception and action: Development, decision-making, and neural mechanisms. *Frontiers in Integrative Neuroscience, 7,* 81.

Shiffman, S. (1993) Smoking cessation treatment: Any progress? *Journal of Consulting and Clinical Psychology, 61,* 718–722.

Shiner, R. L., & Allen, T. A. (2018). Developmental psychopathology. In W. J. Livesley & R. Larstone (eds), *Handbook of personality disorders: Theory, research, and treatment* (2nd edn, pp. 309–323). New York: Guildford Press.

Shinskey, J. L., & Munakata, Y. (2001). Detecting transparent barriers: Clear evidence against the means-end deficit account of search failures. *Infancy, 2,* 395–404.

Shinskey, J. L., & Munakata, Y. (2010). Something old, something new: A developmental transition from familiarity to novelty preferences with hidden objects. *Developmental Science, 13,* 378–384.

Shoda, Y., Mischel, W., & Peake, P. K. (1990). Predicting adolescent cognitive and social competence from preschool delay of gratification: Identifying diagnostic conditions. *Developmental Psychology, 26,* 978–986.

Shoda, Y., Mischel, W., & Peake, P. K. (1990). Predicting adolescent cognitive and self-regulatory competencies from preschool delay of gratification: Identifying diagnostic conditions. *Developmental Psychology, 26*(6), 978–986.

Shoda, Y., Mischel, W., & Peake, P. K. (1990). Predicting adolescent cognitive and social competence from preschool delay of gratification: Identifying diagnostic conditions. *Developmental Psychology, 26*, 978–986.

Shonkoff, J., & Phillips, D. (eds) (2000). *From neurons to neighborhoods*. Washington, DC: National Academy Press.

Shrum, W., & Cheek, N. H. (1987). Social structure during the school years: Onset of the degrouping process. *American Sociological Review, 52*, 218–223.

Shultz, T. R. (2013). Computational models in developmental psychology. In P. D. Zelazo (Ed.), *Oxford handbook of developmental psychology, Vol. 1: Body and mind* (pp. 477–504). New York: Oxford University Press.

Shusterman, A., Lee, S. A., & Spelke, E. (2008). Young children's spontaneous use of geometric information in maps. *Developmental Science, 11*(2), F1–F7.

Shweder, R. A., Goodnow, J. J., Hatano, G., LeVine, R. A., Markus, H. R., & Miller, P. J. (2006). The cultural psychology of development: One mind, many mentalities. In W. Damon & R. M. Lerner (Series eds) & R. M. Lerner (Vol. ed.), *Handbook of child psychology: Vol. 1. Theoretical models of human development* (6th edn, pp. 716–792). New York: Wiley.

Shweder, R. A., Mahapatra, M. & Miller, J. G. (1987) Culture and moral development. In J. Kagan & S. Lamb (eds), *The emergence of morality in young children*. Chicago: University of Chicago Press.

Shweder, R. A., Much, N. C., Mahapatra, M., & Park, L. (1997). The 'big three' of morality (autonomy, community, divinity) and the 'big three' explanations of suffering. In A. M. Brandt & P. Rozin (eds), *Morality and health* (pp. 119–169). Florence, KY: Taylor & Frances/Routledge.

Siddiqui, A. (1995). Object size as a determinant of grasping in infancy. *Journal of Genetic Psychology, 156*, 345–358.

Siegel, M. (1987). Are sons and daughters treated more differently by fathers than mothers? *Developmental Review, 7*, 183–209.

Siegler, R. S. & Chen, Z. (2002) Development of rules and strategies: Balancing the old and new. *Journal of Experimental Child Psychology, 81*, 446–457.

Siegler, R. S. (1976). Three aspects of cognitive development. *Cognitive Psychology, 8*, 481–520.

Siegler, R. S. (1981). Developmental sequences within and between concepts. *Monographs of the Society for Research in Child Development, 46*(2), (Whole No. 189).

Siegler, R. S. (1983). How knowledge influences learning. *American Scientist, 71*, 631–638.

Siegler, R. S. (1991). Strategy choice and strategy discovery. *Learning and Instruction, 1*, 89–102.

Siegler, R. S. (1992). The other Alfred Binet. *Developmental Psychology, 28*, 179–190.

Siegler, R. S. (1996). *Emerging minds*. Oxford: Oxford University Press.

Siegler, R. S. (1996). *Emerging minds: The process of change in children's thinking*. New York: Oxford University Press.

Siegler, R. S. (2000). The rebirth of children's learning. *Child Development, 71*, 26–36.

Siegler, R. S. (2006). Microgenetic analysis of learning. In W. Damon & R. M. Lerner (Series eds) & D. Kuhn & R. S. Siegler (Vol. eds), *Handbook of child psychology: Vol. 2. Cognition, perception, and language* (6th edn, pp. 464–510). New York: Wiley.

Siegler, R. S. (2016). Continuity and change in the field of cognitive development and in the perspectives of one cognitive developmentalist. *Child Development Perspectives, 10*(2), 128–133.

Siegler, R. S., & Alibali, M. W. (2005). *Children's thinking* (4th edn). Upper Saddle River, NJ: Prentice Hall.

Siegler, R., & Crowley, K. (1991). The microgenetic method: A direct means for studying cognitive development. *American Psychologist, 46*, 606–620.

Siegler, R. S. (1995). How does change occur: A microgenetic study of number conservation. *Cognitive Psychology, 25*, 225–273.

Sigman, M. (1995). Nutrition and child development: More food for thought. *Current Directions in Psychological Science, 4*, 52–55.

Silberg, J. L., Rutter, M. & Eaves, L. J. (2001) Genetic and environmental influences on the temporal association between early anxiety and later depression in girls. *Biological Psychology, 49*, 1040–1049.

Sild, M., Koca, C., Bendixen, M. H., Frederickson, H., McGue, M., Kòlvraa, S., Christensen, K., & Nexò, B. (2006). Possible associations between successful aging and polymorphic markers in the Werner gene region. *Annals of the New York Academy of Sciences, 1067—Understanding and Modulating Aging*, 309–310.

Silverthorne, Z. A., & Quinsey, V. L. (2000). Sexual partner age preferences of homosexual and heterosexual men and women. *Archives of Sexual Behavior, 29*, 676–76.

Simion, F., Regolin, L., & Bulf, H. (2008). A predisposition for biological motion in the newborn baby. *Proceedings of the National Academy of Sciences, USA, 105,* 809–813.

Simmons, R. G., & Blyth, D. A. (1987). *Moving into adolescence: The impact of pubertal change and school context.* Hawthorne, NY: Aldine.

Simpkins, D., & Parke, R. D. (2001). The relations between parental friendships and children's friendships: Self-report and observational analysis. *Child Development, 72,* 569–582.

Simpson, A., & Riggs, K. J. (2005). Inhibitory and working memory demands of the day–night task in children. *British Journal of Developmental Psychology, 23,* 471–486.

Singer, D., & Singer, J. (eds) (2001). *Handbook of children and the media.* Thousand Oaks, CA: Sage.

Sinnot, D. (1998). *The development of logic in adulthood: postformal thought and its applications.* New York: Plenum Press.

Sirois, S., & Mareschal, D. (2002). Models of habituation in infancy. *Trends in Cognitive Sciences, 6,* 293–298.

Skelton, C., Carrington, B., Francis, B., Hutchings, M., Read, B., & Hall, I. (2009). Gender 'matters' in the primary classroom: Pupils' and teachers' perspectives. *British Educational Research Journal, 35,* 187–204.

Skinner, B. F. (1957). *Verbal behavior.* New York: Appleton-Century-Crofts.

Slaby, R. G., & Frey, K. S. (1975). Development of gender constancy and selective attention to same-sex models. *Child Development, 46,* 849–856.

Slatcher, R. B., & Selcuk, E. (2017). A social psychological perspective on the links between close relationships and health. *Current Directions in Psychological Science, 26*(1), 16–21.

Slater, A. & Morison, M. V. (1985) Shape constancy and slant perception at birth. *Perception, 14,* 337–344.

Slater, A. M., Mattock, A., Brown, E., & Bremner, J. G. (1991). Form perception at birth: Cohen and Younger (1984) revisited. *Journal of Experimental Child Psychology, 51,* 395–405.

Slater, A. M., Mattock, A., Brown, E., & Bremner, J. G. (1991). Form perception at birth: Cohen and Younger (1984) revisited. *Journal of Experimental Child Psychology, 51,* 395–405.

Slater, A., & Morison, V. (1985). Shape constancy and slant perception at birth. *Perception, 14*(3), 337–344.

Slater, A., Mattock, A. & Brown, E. (1990) Size constancy at birth: Newborn infants' responses to retinal and real size. *Journal of Experimental Child Psychology, 49,* 314–322.

Slater, A., Mattock, A., & Brown, E. (1990). Size constancy at birth: Newborn infants' responses to retinal and real size. *Journal of Experimental Child Psychology, 49*(2), 314–322.

Slater, A. M. & Findlay, J. M. (1975). Binocular fixation in newborn baby. *Journal of Experimental Child Psychology, 20*(2), 248–273.

Slater, A. M., Morison, V., & Rose, D. (1983). Perception of shape by the newborn baby. *British Journal of Developmental Psychology, 1,* 135–142.

Slaughter, V., & Lyons, M. (2003). Learning about life and death in early childhood. *Cognitive Development, 46,* 1–30.

Slobin, D. I. (1979). *Psycholinguistics.* Glenview, IL: Scott, Foresman.

Slobin, D. I. (1982). Universal and particular in the acquisition of language. In E. Wanner & L. R. Gleitman (eds), *Language acquisition: The state of the art*

(pp. 128–170). New York: Cambridge University Press.

Slobin, D. I. (1985). *The cross-linguistic study of language acquisition* (Vols. 1 & 2). Hillsdale, NJ: Erlbaum.

Slobin, D. I. (ed.) (1992). *The cross-linguistic study of language acquisition* (Vol. 3). Hillsdale, NJ: Erlbaum.

Slomkowski, C., Rende, R., Conger, K. J., Simons, R. L., & Conger, R. D. (2001). Sisters, brothers, and delinquency: Evaluating social influence during early and middle adolescence. *Child Development, 72,* 271–283.

Slonje, R., & Smith, P. K. (2007). Cyberbullying: Another main type of bullying? *Scandinavian Journal of Psychology, 49,* 147–154.

Smetana, J. G. (1995). Morality in context: Abstractions, ambiguities, and applications. In R. Vasta (ed.), *Annals of child development* (Vol. 10, pp. 83–130). London: Jessica Kingsley.

Smetana, J. G. (1997) Parenting and the development of social knowledge reconceptualized: A social domain analysis. In J. E. Grusec & L. Kuczynski (eds), *Parenting and children's internalization of values* (pp. 162–192) New York: Wiley.

Smetana, J. G. (2000) Middleclass African American adolescents' and parents' conceptions of parental authority and parenting practices: A longitudinal investigation. *Child Development, 71,* 1672–1686.

Smetana, J. G. (ed.) (2005) *Changing conceptions of parental authority: New directions for child development.* San Francisco, CA: Jossey-Bass.

Smetana, J. G., & Braeges, J. L. (1990). The development of toddler's moral and conventional judgments. *Merrill-Palmer Quarterly, 36,* 329–346.

Smetana, J. G., & Letourneau, K. J. (1984). Development of gender constancy and children's sex-typed free play behavior. *Developmental Psychology, 20,* 691–696.

Smith, B. C. (2015). The chemical senses. In M. Matthen (ed.), *The Oxford handbook of philosophy of perception.* Oxford: Oxford University Press.

Smith, C. L. (1979). Children's understanding of natural language hierarchies. *Journal of Experimental Child Psychology, 27,* 437–458.

Smith, D. (2001) Prevention: Still a young field. *Monitor on Psychology, 3,* 70–72.

Smith, J. A. (1999). Towards a relational self: Social engagement during pregnancy and psychological preparation for motherhood. *British Journal of Social Psychology, 38,* 409–426.

Smith, L. (2000). Learning how to learn words: An associative crane. In R. M. Golinkoff, K. Hirsh-Pasek, L. Bloom, L. Smith, A. Woodward, N. Akhtar et al. (eds), *Becoming a word learner: A debate on lexical acquisition* (pp. 51–80). New York: Oxford University Press.

Smith, L. B., & Thelen, E. (2003). Development as a dynamic system. *Trends in Cognitive Sciences, 7*(8), 343–348.

Smith, L., & Gasser, M. (2005). The development of embodied cognition: Six lessons from babies. *Artificial Life, 11*(1–2), 13–29.

Smith, P. K., & Drew, L. M. (2002). Grandparenthood. In M. H. Bornstein (ed.), *Handbook of parenting* (Vol. 3, 2nd edn, pp. 141–169). Mahwah, NJ: Lawrence Erlbaum.

Smith, P. K., Morita, Y. M., Junger-Tas, J., Olweus, D., Catalano, R. F., & Slee, P. (eds) (1999). *The nature of school bullying: A cross-national perspective.* New York: Routledge.

Smith, P. K., Pepler, D., & Rigby, K. (eds) (2004). *Bullying in schools: How successful can*

intervention be? New York: Cambridge University Press.

Smith, T. M. (1994). Adolescent pregnancy. In R. Simeonsson (ed.), *Risk, resilience and prevention: Promoting the well-being of all children.* Baltimore, MD: Brooks Publishing.

Smollar, J., & Youniss, J. (1982). Social development through friendship. In K. H. Rubin & H. S. Ross (eds), *Peer relationships and social skills in childhood* (pp. 279–298). New York: Springer-Verlag.

Snarey, J. R., Reimer, J., & Kohlberg, L. (1985). Development of social-moral reasoning among kibbutz adolescents: A longitudinal cross-cultural study. *Developmental Psychology, 21,* 3–17.

Snarey, J., & Hooker, C. (2006). Lawrence Kohlberg. *Encyclopedia of spiritual and religious development* (pp. 251–255). Thousand Oaks, CA: Sage.

Snarey, J. R. (1985). Cross-cultural universality of social-moral development: A critical review of Kohlbergian research. *Psychological Bulletin, 97*(2), 202–232.

Snow, C. E. (1989). Understanding social interaction and language acquisition: Sentences are not enough. In M. H. Bornstein & J. S. Bruner (eds), *Interaction in human development* (pp. 83–104). Hillsdale, NJ: Erlbaum.

Snowdon, D. A. (2001). *Aging with grace: What the nun study teaches us about leading longer, healthier, and more meaningful lives.* New York : Bantam Books.

Snowdon, D. A. (2003). Healthy aging and dementia: Findings from the Nun Study. *Annals of Internal Medicine, 139,* 450–454.

Snowling, M. J., & Hulme, C. (2011). Evidence-based interventions for a reading and language difficulties: Creating a virtuous circle. *British Journal of Educational Psychology, 81,* 1–23.

Sober, E., & Wilson, D. S. (1998). *Unto others: The evolution and psychology of unselfish behavior.* Cambridge, MA: Harvard University Press.

Sochting, I., Skoe, E. E., & Marcia, J. E. (1994). Care-oriented moral reasoning and prosocial behaviour—a question of gender or sex-role orientation. *Sex Roles, 3,* 131–147.

Sokolov, J. L. (1993). A local contingency analysis of the fine-tuning hypothesis. *Developmental Psychology, 29,* 1008–1023.

Solomon, J., & George, C. (1999). The measurement of attachment security in infancy and childhood. In J. Cassidy & P. Shaver (eds), *Handbook of attachment* (pp. 287–318). New York: Guilford Press.

Somogyi, E., Jacquey, L., Heed, T., Hoffmann, M., Lockman, J. J., Granjon, L., . . . & O'Regan, J. K. (2017). Which limb is it? Responses to vibrotactile stimulation in early infancy. *British Journal of Developmental Psychology.* doi: 10.1111/bjdp.12224

Sostek, A. M., & Anders, T. F. (1981). The biosocial importance and environmental sensitivity of infant sleep-wake behaviors. In K. Bloom (ed.), *Prospective issues in infancy research* (pp. 99–118). Hillsdale, NJ: Erlbaum.

Southgate, V., & Vernetti, A. (2014). Belief-based action prediction in preverbal infants. *Cognition, 130*(1), 1–10.

Southgate, V., Johnson, M. H., Osborne, T., & Csibra, G. (2009). Predictive motor activation during action observation in human infants. *Biology Letters, 5,* 769–772.

Southgate, V., Senju, A., & Csibra, G. (2007). Action anticipation through attribution of false belief by 2-year-olds. *Psychological Science, 18*(7), 587–592.

Sowell, E. R., Peterson, B. S., Thompson, P. M., Welcome, S. E., Henkenius, A. L., & Toga, A. W. (2003). Mapping cortical change across the human life span. *Nature Neuroscience, 6*, 309–315.

Sowell, E. R., Thompson, P. M., Tessner, K. D., & Toga, A. W. (2001). Mapping continued brain growth and gray matter density reduction in dorsal frontal cortex: Inverse relationships during postadolescent brain maturation. *Journal of Neuroscience, 21*(22), 8819–8829.

Spangler, G., & Grossman, K. E. (1993). Biobehavioral organization in securely and insecurely attached infants. *Child Development, 64*, 1439–1450.

Spearman, C. (1927). *The abilities of man.* New York: Macmillan.

Spelke, E. (1976). Infants' intermodal perception of events. *Cognitive Psychology, 8*(4), 553–560.

Spelke, E. (2000). Core knowledge. *American Psychologist, 55*, 1233–1243.

Spelke, E. S. & Cortelyou, A. (1981) Perceptual aspects of social knowing: Looking and listening in infancy. In M. E. Lamb & L. R. Sherrod (eds), *Infant social cognition* (pp. 6–84) Hillsdale, NJ: Erlbaum.

Spelke, E. S. (1998). Nativism, empiricism, and the origins of knowledge. *Infant Behavior and Development, 21*(2), 181–200.

Spelke, E. S., & Kinzler, K. D. (2007). Core knowledge. *Developmental Science, 10*(1), 89–96.

Spelke, E. S., Breinlinger, K., Macomber, J., & Jacobson, K. (1992). Origins of knowledge. *Psychological Review, 99*(4), 605–632.

Spence, C. (2017). *Gastrophysics: The new science of eating.* London: Penguin.

Spence, J., & Buckner, C. (2000). Instrumental and expressive traits, trait stereotypes, and sexist attitudes. *Psychology of Women Quarterly, 24*, 44–62.

Spencer, J. P., & Thelen, E. (2000). Spatially specific changes in infants' muscle coactivity as they learn to reach. *Infancy, 1*, 275–302.

Spencer, M. B. (2006). Phenomenology and ecological systems theory: Development of diverse groups. In W. Damon & R. M. Lerner (Series eds) & R. M. Lerner (Vol. ed), *Handbook of child psychology: Vol. 1. Theoretical models of human development* (6th edn, pp. 829–893). New York: Wiley.

Spengler, M., Gottschling, J., Hahn, E., Tucker-Drob, E. M., Harzer, C., & Spinath, F. M. (2018). Does the heritability of cognitive abilities vary as a function of parental education? Evidence from a German twin sample. *PLoS ONE, 13*(5): e0196597.

Sperling, G. (1960). The information available in brief visual presentations. *Psychological Monographs: General and Applied, 74*(11), 1–29.

Spiegel, D., Bloom, J. R., Kraemer, H. C., & Gottheil, E. (1989). Effect of psychosocial treatment on survival of patients with metastatic breast cancer. *The Lancet,* 14 October, 888–891.

Spielhofer, T., O'Donnell, L., Benton, T., Hagen, S., & Shagen, I. (2002). *The impact of school size and single sex education on performance.* Slough: National Foundation for Educational Research.

Spiker, D. & Ricks, M. (1984) Visual self-recognition in autistic children: Developmental variations. *Child Development, 55*, 214–225.

Spittle, A., Orton, J., Anderson, P. J., Boyd, R., & Doyle, L. W. (2015). Early developmental intervention programmes provided post hospital discharge to prevent motor and cognitive impairment in preterm infants. *The Cochrane Library.*

Spoth, R. L., Redmond, C. & Shin, C. (2001). Randomized trial of brief family interventions for general populations: Adolescent substance use outcomes 4 years following baseline. *Journal of Consulting and Clinical Psychology, 69*, 627–642

Spoth, R., Redmond, C. & Shin, C. (2003) Randomized trial of brief family interventions for general populations: Adolescent substance use outcomes four years following baseline. *Journal of Consulting and Clinical Psychology, 69*, 627–642.

Springer, S. P., & Deutsch, G. (1993). *Left brain, right brain.* New York: Freeman.

Spruit, A., Wissink, I., Noom, M. J., Colonnesi, C., Polderman, N., Willems, L., . . . Stams, G. J. J. M. (2018). Internal structure and reliability of the Attachment Insecurity Screening Inventory (AISI) for children age 6 to 12. *BMC Psychiatry, 18*, 30.

Sroufe, L. A. (1996). *Emotional development: The organization of emotional life in the early years.* New York: Cambridge University Press.

Sroufe, L. A. (2005). Attachment and development: A prospective, longitudinal study from birth to adulthood. *Attachment & Human Development, 7*(4), 349–367.

Sroufe, L. A., & Wunsch, J. P. (1972). The development of laughter in the first year of life. *Child Development, 43*, 1326–1344.

Sroufe, L. A., Waters, E., & Matas, L. (1974). Contextual determinants of infant affectional response. In M. Lewis & L. Rosenblum (eds), *Origins of fear* (pp. 49–72). New York: Wiley.

St. John, T., Dawson, G., & Estes, A. (2018). Brief report: Executive function as a predictor of academic achievement in school-aged children with ASD. *Journal of Autism and Development Disorders, 48*(1), 276–283. https://doi.org/10.1007/s10803-017-3296-9

Stambrook, M., & Parker, K. C. H. (1987). The development of the concept of death in childhood: A review of the literature. *Merrill-Palmer Quarterly, 33*, 133–158.

Stams, G. J. M., Juffer, F., & van Ijzendoorn, M. H. (2002). Maternal sensitivity, infant attachment and temperament in early childhood predict adjustment in middle childhood: The case of adopted children and their biologically unrelated parents. *Developmental Psychology, 38*, 806–821.

Starr, A. S. (1923). The diagnostic value of the audio-vocal digit memory span. *Psychological Clinic, 15*, 61–84.

Starr, A., Libertus, M. E., & Brannon, E. M. (2013). Number sense in infancy predicts mathematical abilities in childhood. *Proceedings of the National Academy of Sciences, 110*(45), 18116–18120.

Stattin, H., & Magnusson, D. (1990). *Pubertal maturation in female development* (Vol. 2) Hillsdale, NJ: Erlbaum.

Steckel, R. (1997, 2 June) Ohio State University. As reproduced in '2000: The millennium notebook', *Newsweek*, p. 10.

Steele, C. M. (1997). A threat in the air: How stereotypes shape intellectual identity and performance. *American Psychologist, 52*, 613–629.

Steele, C. M., & Aronson, J. (1995). Stereotype threat and the intellectual test performance of African Americans. *Journal of Personality and Social Psychology, 69*, 797–811.

Stein, B. E. (ed.) (2012). *The new handbook of multisensory processing.* Cambridge, MA: MIT Press.

Steinberg, L. (1987). Impact of puberty on family relations: Effects of pubertal status and pubertal timing. *Developmental Psychology, 23*, 451–460.

Steinberg, L. (2007). Risk taking in adolescence: New perspectives from

brain and behavioral science. *Current Directions in Psychological Science, 16*(2), 55–59.

Steinberg, L. (2008). A social neuroscience perspective on adolescent risk-taking. *Developmental Review, 28*, 78–106.

Steinberg, L., Darling, N. E., & Fletcher, A. C. (1995). Authoritative parenting and adolescent adjustment: An ecological journey. In P. Moen, G. H. Elder Jr, & K. Luscher (eds), *Examining lives in contest: Perspectives on the ecology of human development* (pp. 423–466). Washington, DC: American Psychological Association.

Steinberg, L., Dornbusch, S. M., & Brown, B. B. (1992). Ethnic differences in adolescent achievement: An ecological perspective. *American Psychologist, 47*, 723–729.

Steinberg, L., Icenogle, G., Shulman, E. P., Breiner, K., Chein, J., Bacchini, D., et al. (2018). Around the world, adolescence is a time of heightened sensation seeking and immature self-regulation. *Developmental Science, 21*, e12532. doi: 10.1111/desc.1253

Steiner, J. E. (1979) Human facial expression in response to taste and smell stimulation. In H. W. Reese & L. P. Lipsitt (eds), *Advances in child development and behavior* (Vol. 13, pp. 257–295) New York: Academic Press.

Steinschneider, A. (1975). Implications of the sudden infant death syndrome for the study of sleep in infancy. In A. D. Pick (ed.), *Minnesota symposia on child psychology* (Vol. 9, pp. 106–133). Minneapolis: University of Minnesota Press.

Stellwagen, D., & Shatz, C. J. (2002). An instructive role for retinal waves in the development of retinogeniculate connectivity. *Neuron, 33*, 357–367.

Stemler, S. E., Grigorenko, E. L., Jarvin, L., & Sternberg, R. J.

(2006). Using the theory of successful intelligence as a basis for augmenting AP exams in psychology and statistics. *Contemporary Educational Psychology, 31*, 344–376.

Stenberg, C., & Campos, J. (1989). The development of anger expressions during infancy. Unpublished manuscript, University of Denver, CO.

Stenberg, C., Campos, J., & Emde, R. N. (1983). The facial expression of anger in seven-month-old infants. *Child Development, 54*, 178–184.

Stephan, K. E., Marshall, J. C., Friston, K. J., Rowe, J. B., Ritzl, A., Zilles, K. et al. (2003). Lateralized cognitive processes and lateralized task control in the human brain. *Science, 301*, 384–386.

Stergiakouli, E., & Thapar, A. (2010). Fitting the pieces together: Current research on the genetic basis of attention-deficit/hyperactivity disorder (ADHD). *Neuropsychiatric Disease and Treatment, 6*, 551–560.

Stern, M., & Karraker, K. H. (1989). Sex stereotyping of infants: A review of gender labeling studies. *Sex Roles, 20*, 501–522.

Sternberg, R. J. (1985). *Beyond IQ: A triarchic theory of human intelligence.* Cambridge: Cambridge University Press.

Sternberg, R. J. (1986). A triangular theory of love. *Psychological Review, 93*, 119–135.

Sternberg, R. J. (1988) *The triarchic mind.* New York: Viking Press.

Sternberg, R. J. (1997). Construct validation of a triangular love scale. *European Journal of Social Psychology, 27*, 313–335.

Sternberg, R. J. (2001). Successful intelligence: Understanding what Spearman had rather than what he studied. In J. M. Collis & S. Messick (eds), *Intelligence and personality* (pp. 347–373). Mahwah, NJ: Erlbaum.

Sternberg, R. J. (2005). The triarchic theory of successful intelligence. In D. P. Flanagan & P. L. Harrison (eds), *Contemporary intellectual assessment: Theories, tests, and issues* (pp. 103–119). New York: Guilford Press.

Sternberg, R. J. (2006). The nature of creativity. *Creativity Research Journal* [Special Issue: A Tribute to E. Paul Torrance], *18*, 87–98.

Sternberg, R. J., & Wagner, R. K. (1993). The geocentric view of intelligence and job performance is wrong. *Current Directions in Psychological Science, 2*, 1–6.

Sternberg, R. J., & Wagner, R. K. (1994). *Mind in context.* New York: Cambridge University Press.

Sternberg, R. J., Grigorenko, E. L., & Bridglall, B. L. (2007). Intelligence as a socialized phenomenon. In E. W. Gordon & B. L. Bridglall (eds), *Affirmative development: Cultivating academic ability* (pp. 49–72). Lanham, MD: Rowman & Littlefield.

Sternberg, R. J., Grigorenko, E. L., & Bundy, D. A. (2001). The predictive value of IQ. *Merrill-Palmer Quarterly, 47*, 1–41.

Sternberg, R. J., Wagner, R. K., & Okagaki, L. (1993). Practical intelligence: The nature and role of tacit knowledge in work and at school. In H. W. Reese & W. Puckett (eds), *Advances in lifespan development* (pp. 205–227). Hillsdale, NJ: Erlbaum.

Stevahn, L., Johnson, D. W., Johnson, R. T., Oberle, K., & Wahl, L. (2000). Effects of conflict resolution training integrated into a kindergarten curriculum. *Child Development, 71*, 772–784.

Stevenson, H. W. & Lee, S. Y. (1990) Context of achievement. *Monographs of the Society for Research in Child Development, 55* (Serial no. 221).

Stevenson, H. W. (2001). Schools, teachers, and parents. In A. Thornton (ed.), *The well-being of children and families: Research and data needs* (pp. 341–355). Ann Arbor, MI: University of Michigan Press.

Stevenson, H. W., Lee, S., & Mu, X. (2000). Successful achievement in mathematics: China and the United States. In C. F. M. Van Lieshout & P. G. Heymans (eds), *Developing talent across the life span* (pp. 167–183). Philadelphia: Psychology Press.

Stevenson, H. W., Lee, S.-y., Chen, C., Lummis, M., Stigler, J., Fan, L., & Ge, F. (1990). Mathematics achievement of children in China and the United States. *Child Development, 61*, 1053–1066. doi: 10.1111/j.1467-8624.1990.tb02841.x

Stevenson-Hinde, J. (2005). The interplay between attachment, temperament, and maternal style: A Madingley perspective. In K. E. Grossmann, K. Grossmann, & E. Waters (eds), *Attachment from infancy to adulthood* (pp. 198–222). New York: Guilford Press.

Stice, E., Cameron, R. P., Hayward, C., Killen, J. D., & Taylor, C. B. (2000) Body-image and eating disturbances predict onset of depression among female adolescents: A longitudinal study.- *Journal of Abnormal Psychology, 109*(3) 438–444.

Stice, E., Presnell, K., & Bearman, S. K. (2001). Relation of early menarche to depression, eating disorders, substance abuse, and comorbid psychopathology among adolescent girls. *Developmental Psychology, 37*, 608–619.

Stiles, J., Reilly, J. S., Levine, S. C., Trauner, D. A., & Nass, R. (2012). *Neural plasticity and cognitive development: Insights from children with perinatal brain injury.* New York, NY: Oxford University Press.

Stoch, M. B., Smyth, P. M., Moodie, A. D., & Bradshaw, D. (1982). Psychological outcome and findings after gross undernourishment during infancy: A 20-year developmental study.

Developmental Medicine and Child Neurology, 24, 419–436.

Stoneman, Z., Brody, G., & MacKinnon, C. E. (1986). Same sex and cross-sex siblings: Activity choices, roles, behavior, and gender stereotypes. *Sex Roles, 15*, 495–511.

Storey, A. E., Walsh, C. J., Quinton, R. L., & Wynne-Edwards, K. E. (2000). Hormonal correlates of paternal responsiveness in new and expectant fathers. *Evolution and Human Behaviour, 21*, 79–95.

Straughan, R. (1986). Why act on Kohlberg's moral judgments? (or how to reach stage 6 and remain a bastard). In S. Modgil & C. Modgil (eds), *Lawrence Kohlberg: Consensus and controversy* (pp. 149–157). Philadelphia: Falmer Press.

Strayer, J., & Roberts, W. (2004). Children's anger, emotional expressiveness, and empathy: Relations with parents' empathy, emotional expressiveness, and parenting practices. *Social Development, 13*, 229–254.

Streissguth, A. P. (1997). *Fetal alcohol syndrome.* New York: Oxford University Press.

Streissguth, A. P. (2007). Offspring effects of prenatal alcohol exposure from birth to 25 years: The Seattle Prospective Longitudinal Study. *Journal of Clinical Psychology in Medical Settings, 14*, 81–101.

Streri, A. & Pecheux, M. (1986) Tactual habituation and discrimination of form in infancy: A comparison with vision. *Child Development, 57*, 100–104.

Streri, A., & Gentaz, E. (2003). Cross-modal recognition of shape from hand to eyes in human newborns. *Somatosensory and Motor Research, 20*(1), 13–18.

Streri, A., & Gentaz, E. (2004). Cross-modal recognition of shape from hand to eyes and handedness in human newborns. *Neuropsychologia, 42*, 1365–1369.

Streri, A., Lhote, M., & Dutilleul, S. (2000). Haptic perception in newborns. *Developmental Science, 3*, 319–327.

Stroebe, M., & Stroebe, W. (1993). *Handbook of bereavement: Theory, research and intervention.* Cambridge: Cambridge University Press.

Stroebe, W., & Stroebe, M. (1996). The social psychology of social support, in E. T. Higgins and A. W. Kruglanski (eds), *Social psychology: Handbook of basic principles* (pp. 597–621). New York: Guildford Press.

Stromswold, K. (2006). Why aren't identical twins linguistically identical? Genetic, prenatal and postnatal factors. *Cognition, 101*(2), 333–384.

Stunkard, A. J., Foch, T. T., & Hrubeck, Z. (1986a). A twin study of human obesity. *Journal of the American Medical Association, 256*, 51–54.

Stunkard, A. J., Sorenson, T. I., Hanis, C., Teasdale, T. W., Chakraborty, R., Schull, W. J. et al. (1986b). An adoption study of human obesity. *The New England Journal of Medicine, 314*, 193–198.

Subrahmanyam, K., Kraut, R. E., Greenfield, P. M. & Gross, E. F. (2001)/ New forms of electronic media: The impact of interactive games and Internet on cognition, socialization, and behavior. In D. Singer & J. Singer (eds), *Handbook of children and the media* (pp. 73–99)/ Thousand Oaks, CA: Sage.

Sugita Y. (2009). Innate face processing. *Current Opinion in Neurobiology, 19*, 39–44.

Sulloway, F. J. (1995). Birth order and evolutionary psychology: A meta-analytic overview. *Psychological Inquiry, 6*, 75–80.

Super, C. M., & Harkness, S. (1981). The infant's niche in rural Kenya and metropolitan America. In L. L. Adler (ed.), *Cross-cultural research at issue* (pp. 47–55). New York: American Press.

Super, C. M., Herrera, M. G., & Mora, J. O. (1990). Long-term effects of food supplementation and psychosocial intervention on the physical growth of Columbian infants at risk of malnutrition. *Child Development, 61*, 29–49.

Surtees, A. D., & Apperly, I. A. (2012). Egocentrism and automatic perspective taking in children and adults. *Child Development, 83*(2), 452–460.

Susman-Stillman, A., Kalkoske, M., Egeland, B., & Waldman, I. (1996). Infant temperament and maternal sensitivity as predictors of attachment security. *Infant Behavior and Development, 19*, 33–47.

Sutton, J., Smith, P. K., & Swettenham, J. (1999). Social cognition and bullying: Social inadequacy or skilled manipulation? *British Journal of Developmental Psychology, 17*, 435–450.

Suzuki, L. A. (2007). Review of *Culture and children's intelligence: Cross cultural analysis of the WISC-III. Journal of Psychoeducational Assessment, 25*, 101–104.

Swaiman, K. F., & Phillips, J. (2017). Neurological examination of the term and preterm infant. In K. Swaiman et al. (eds.), *Swaiman's pediatric neurology* (6th edn). Edinburgh: Elsevier.

Swain, I. U., Zelazo, P. R., & Clifton, R. K. (1993). Newborn infants' memory for speech sounds retained over 24 hours. *Developmental Psychology, 29*, 312–323.

Tager-Flusberg, H. (1997). Putting words together: Morphology and syntax in the preschool years. In J. Berko-Gleason (ed.), *The development of language* (pp. 159–209). Boston: Allyn & Bacon.

Tajfel, H. (1982). Social psychology of intergroup relations. *Annual Review of Psychology, 33*, 1–39.

Tamis-LeMonda, C. S., Bornstein, M. H., & Baumwell, L. (2001). Maternal responsiveness and children's achievement of language milestones. *Child Development, 72*, 748–767.

Tan, J-P., Buchanan, A., Flouri, E., Attar-Schwartz, S., & Griggs, J. (2010). Filling the parenting gap? Grandparent involvement with UK adolescents. *Journal of Family Issues, 31*, 992–1015.

Tangney, J. P. (1998). How does guilt differ from shame? In J. Bybee (ed.), *Guilt and children* (pp. 1–17). San Diego, CA: Academic Press.

Tangney, J. P., & Fischer, K. W. (eds) (1995). *Self-conscious emotions.* New York: Guilford Press.

Tanner, J. M. (1970). Physical growth. In P. H. Mussen (ed.), *Carmichael's manuscript of child psychology* (Vol. 1, pp. 77–155). New York: Wiley.

Tanner, J. M. (1978). *Fetus into man: Physical growth from conception to maturity.* Cambridge, MA: Harvard University Press.

Tanner, J. M. (1990). *Fetus into man: Physical growth from conception to maturity* (2nd edn). Cambridge, MA: Harvard University Press.

Tapper, K., & Boulton, M. J. (2002). Studying aggression in school children: The use of a wireless microphone and micro-video camera. *Aggressive Behavior 28*, 356–365.

Tardif, T. (1993). Audit-to-child speech and language acquisition in Mandarin Chinese. Unpublished doctoral dissertation, New Haven, CT: Yale University Press.

Tardif, T. (1996). Nouns are not always learned before verbs: Evidence from Mandarin speakers' early vocabularies. *Developmental Psychology, 32*, 492–504.

Tarullo, A. R., Isler, J. R., Condon, C., Violaris, K., Balsam, P. D., & Fifer, W. P. (2016). Neonatal eyelid conditioning during sleep. *Developmental Psychobiology, 58*(7), 875–882.

Tasbihsazan, R., Nettelbeck, T., & Kirby, N. (2003). Predictive validity of the Fagan test of infant intelligence. *British Journal of Developmental Psychology, 21,* 585–597.

Taylor, B., Jick, H., & MacLaughlin, D. (2013). Prevalence and incidence rates of autism in the UK: Time trend from 2004–2010 in children aged 8 years. *BMJ Open, 3*(10), e003219.

Teasdale T. W. & Owen D. R. (1987) National secular trends in intelligence and education: a twenty year cross-sectional study. *Nature, 325,* 119–121.

Teasdale T. W. & Owen D. R. (2008). Secular declines in cognitive test scores: A reversal of the Flynn Effect. *Intelligence, 36*(2), 121–126.

Tenenbaum, H. R. (2009). 'You'd be good at that': Gender patterns in parent-child talk about courses. *Social Development, 18,* 447–463.

Tenenbaum, H. R., & Leaper, C. (2003). Parent-child conversations about science: The socialization of gender inequalities. *Developmental Psychology, 39,* 34–47.

Tenenbaum, H., Leman, P., & Aznar, A. (2017). Children's reasoning about peer and school segregation in a diverse society. *Journal of Community and Applied Social Psychology: Growing Up with Diversity: A Social Psychological Perspective, 27*(5), 358–365.

Tennenbaum, H., & Leaper, C. (2002). Are parents' gender schemas related to their children's gender-related cognitions? A meta-analysis. *Developmental Psychology, 38*(4), 615–630.

Tennie, C., Call, J., & Tomasello, M. (2006). Push or pull: Imitation versus emulation in human children and great apes. *Ethology, 112,* 1159–1169.

Tessier, R., Cristo, M. B., Velez, S., Giron, M., Line, N., Figueroa de Calume, Z., et al. (2003). Kangaroo mother care: A method for protecting high-risk low-birth weight and premature infants against developmental delay. *Infant Behavior Development, 26,* 384–397.

Tessier, R., Nadeau, L., Boivin, M., & Tremblay, R. E. (1997). The social behaviour of 11- to 12-year-old children born as low birthweight and/or premature infants. *International Journal of Behavioral Development, 21,* 795–811.

Teti, D. M. (2002). Retrospect and prospect in the study of sibling relationships. In J. McHale & W. Grolnick (eds), *Retrospect and prospect in the psychological study of families* (pp. 193–224). Mahwah, NJ: Erlbaum.

Thapar A., Rice F., Hay D., Boivin J., Langley K., & van den Bree M. (2009). Prenatal smoking might not cause attention-deficit/hyperactivity disorder: Evidence from a novel design. *Biological Psychiatry, 66,* 722–727.

Thapar, A., Fowler, T., Rice, F., Scourfield, J., Van den Bree, M., Thomas, H., Harold, G., & Hay, D. (2003). Maternal smoking during pregnancy and attention deficit hyperactivity disorder symptoms in offspring. *American Journal of Psychiatry, 160,* 1985–1989.

Thapar, A., Harold, G., Rice, F., Langley, K., & O'Donovan, M. (2007a). The contribution of gene–environment interaction to psychopathology. *Development and Psychopathology, 19,* 989–1004.

Thapar, A., Langley, K., Owen, M. J., & O'Donovan, M. C. (2007b). Advances in genetic findings on attention deficit hyperactivity disorder. *Psychological Medicine, 37,* 1681–1692.

Thelen, E. & Fisher, D. M. (1982). Newborn stepping: An explanation for a 'disappearing reflex'. *Developmental Psychology, 18,* 760–775.

Thelen, E. & Smith, L. B. (1994) *A dynamic systems approach to the development of cognition and action.* Cambridge, MA: MIT Press.

Thelen, E. (1995). Motor development: A new synthesis. *American Psychologist, 50, 79–95.*

Thelen, E., & Smith, L. (2006). Dynamic systems theory. In W. Damon & R. L. Lerner (Series eds) & R. L. Lerner (Vol. ed.), *Handbook of child psychology: Vol. 1. Theoretical models of human development* (6th edn, pp. 258–312). New York: Wiley.

Thelen, E., Schoner, G., Scheier, C., & Smith, L. B. (2001) The dynamics of embodiment: A field theory of infant perseverative reaching. *Behavioral and Brain Sciences, 24,* 1–34.

Thevenin, D. M., Eilers, R. E., Oller, D. K., & LaVoie, L. (1985). Where's the drift in babbling drift? A cross-linguistic study. *Applied Psycholinguistics, 6,* 3–15.

Thiele, D. M., & Whelan, T. A. (2008). The relationship between grandparent satisfaction, meaning, and generativity. *International Journal of Aging and Human Development, 66,* 21–48.

Thiessen, E. D., & Saffran, J. D. (2003). When cues collide: Use of stress and statistical cues to word boundaries by 7- to 9-month-old infants. *Developmental Psychology, 39,* 706–716.

Thoman, E. B. (1987) Self-regulation of stimulation by prematures with a breathing blue bear. In J. Gallagher & C. Ramey (eds), *The malleability of children.* Baltimore/London: Brookes.

Thoman, E. B. (2005) Sleeping behavior and its impact on psychosocial child development. *Encyclopedia on early childhood development.* Montreal: Center of Excellence for Early Childhood Development.

Thoman, E. B., Hammond, K., Affleck, G. & DeSilva, H. N. (1995) The breathing bear with preterm infants: Effects on sleep, respiration, and affect. *Infant Mental Health Journal, 16,* 160–168.

Thompson, R. A. (1989). Causal attributions and children's emotional understanding. In C. Saarni & P. L. Harris (eds), *Children's understanding of emotions* (pp. 117–150). New York: Cambridge University Press.

Thompson, R. A. (2006a). Emotional regulation in children. In J. Gross (ed.), *Handbook of emotional regulation* (pp. 249–268). New York: Guilford Press.

Thompson, R. A. (2006b). The development of the person: Social understanding, relationships, self, conscience. In W. Damon & R. M. Lerner (Series eds) & N. Eisenberg (Vol. ed.), *Handbook of child psychology* (6th edn, Vol. 3, pp. 24–98). New York: Wiley.

Thompson, R. A., Lamb, M. E. & Estes, D. (1982) Stability of infant-mother attachment and its relationship to changing life circumstances in an unselected middle-class sample. *Child Development, 53,* 144–148.

Thornberry, T. P., Krohn, M. D., Lizotte, A. J., Smith, C. A., & Tobin, K. (2003). *Gangs and delinquency in developmental perspective.* New York: Cambridge University Press.

Thurber, C. A., & Weisz, J. R. (1997). 'You can try or you can just give up': The impact of perceived control and coping style on childhood homesickness. *Developmental Psychology, 33,* 508–517.

Thurstone, L. L. (1938). *Primary mental abilities.* Chicago: University of Chicago Press.

Tick, B., Bolton, P., Happé, F., Rutter, M., & Rijsdijk, F. (2016). Heritability of autism spectrum disorders: A meta-analysis of twin studies. *Journal of Child Psychology and Psychiatry, 57*(5), 585–595.

Tinsley, B. J., Holtgrave, D. R., Erdley, C. A. & Reise, S. P. (1997) A multi-method analysis of risk perceptions and health behaviors in children. *Educational and Psychological Measurement, 57,* 197–209.

Titus-Ernstoff, L., Troisi, R., Hatch, E. E., Wise, L. A., Palmer, J., Hyer, M. et al. (2006) Menstrual and reproductive characteristics of women whose mothers were exposed in utero to diethylstilbestrol (DES). *International Journal of Epidemiology, 35,* 862–868.

Tobaiqy, M., Stewart, D., Helms, P. J., Williams, J., Crum, J., Steer, C., & McLay, J. (2011). Parental reporting of adverse drug reactions associated with attention-deficit hyperactivity disorder (ADHD) medications in children attending specialist paediatric clinics in the UK. *Drug Safety, 34,* 211–219.

Tobin-Richards, M. H., Boxer, A. M., & Petersen, A. C. (1983). The psychological significance of pubertal change: Sex differences in perceptions of self during early adolescence. In J. BrooksGunn & A. C. Petersen (eds), *Girls at puberty: Biological and psychosocial perspectives* (pp. 127–154). New York: Plenum Press.

Tomalski, P., Moore, D. G., Ribeiro, H., Axelsson, E. L., Murphy, E., Karmiloff-Smith, A., . . . & Kushnerenko, E. (2013). Socioeconomic status and functional brain development–associations in early infancy. *Developmental Science, 16*(5), 676–687.

Tomasello, M. (1995). Language is not an instinct. *Cognitive Development, 10,* 131–156.

Tomasello, M. (1996) Do apes ape? In: Social learning in animals: The roots of culture (Ed. by Heyes, C. M. & Galef, B. G., Jr.), pp. 319–346. San Diego, CA, USA: Academic Press, Inc.

Tomasello, M. (1996) Do apes ape? In: Social learning in animals: The roots of culture (Ed. by Heyes, C. M. & Galef, B. G., Jr.), pp. 319–346.

Tomasello, M. (2003). *Constructing a language: A usage-based theory of language acquisition.* Cambridge, MA: Harvard University Press.

Tomasello, M. (2006). Acquiring metalinguistic constructions. In W. Damon & R. M. Lerner (Series eds) & D. Kuhn & R. Siegler (Vol. eds), *Handbook of child psychology* (Vol. 2, 6th edn, pp. 255–298). New York: Wiley.

Tomasello, M. (ed.) (1998). *The new psychology of language: Cognitive and functional approaches to language structure.* Mahwah, NJ: Erlbaum.

Tomasello, M., & Farrar, J. (1986). Joint attention and early language. *Child Development, 57,* 1454–1463.

Tomasello, M., Carpenter, M., & Liszkowski, U. (2007). A new look at infant pointing. *Child Development, 78,* 705–722.

Tomasello, M., Carpenter, M., Call, J., Behne, T., & Moll, H. (2005). Understanding and sharing intentions: The origins of cultural cognition. *Behavioral and Brain Sciences, 28,* 675–735.

Tomlinson, M., Cooper, P., & Murray, L. (2005). The mother–infant relationship and infant attachment in a South African peri-urban settlement. *Child Development, 76,* 1044–1054.

Topál, J., Gergely, G., Miklósi, Ý., Erdőhegyi, Ý., & Csibra, G. (2008). Infants' perseverative search errors are induced by pragmatic misinterpretation. *Science, 321*(5897), 1831–1834.

Torff, B., & Gardner, H. (1999). The vertical mind—the case for multiple intelligences. In M. Anderson (ed.), *The development of intelligence: Studies in developmental psychology* (pp. 139–159). Hove: Psychology Press/Taylor & Francis.

Towers, H., Spotts, E., & Reiss, D. (2003). Unraveling the complexity of genetic and environmental influences on family.

In F. Walsh (ed.), *Normal family processes* (3rd edn, pp. 608–631). New York: Guilford Press.

Trabasso, T., Issen, A. M., Dolecki, P., McLanahan, A., Riley, C., & Tucker, T. (1978). How do children solve class-inclusion problems? In R. S. Siegler (ed.), *Children's thinking: What develops?* Hillsdale, NJ: Erlbaum.

Trainor, L. J. (1996). Infant preferences for infant-directed versus non-infant directed playsongs and lullabies. *Infant Behavior and Development, 19*, 83–92.

Trehub, S. E., & Trainor, L. J. (1993). Listening strategies in infancy: The roots of music and language development. In S. McAdams & E. Bigand (eds.), *Thinking in sound: The cognitive psychology of human audition* (pp. 278–327). New York: Oxford University Press.

Tremblay, R. E., Schall, B., Boulerice, B., Arsonault, L., Soussignan, R. G., & Paquette, D. (1998). Testosterone, physical aggression, and dominance and physical development in adolescence. *International Journal of Behavioral Development, 22*, 753–777.

Troller-Renfree, S., Zeanah, C. H., Nelson, C. A., & Fox, N. A. (2018). Neural and cognitive factors influencing the emergence of psychopathology: Insights from the Bucharest Early Intervention Project. *Child Development Perspectives, 12*(1), 28–33.

Tronick, E. Z., Messinger, D. S., Weinberg, M. K., Lester, B. M., LaGasse, L., Seifer, R. et al. (2005). Cocaine exposure is associated with subtle compromises of infants' and mothers' social-emotional behavior and dyadic features of their interaction in the face still face paradigm. *Developmental Psychology, 41*, 711–722.

Tronick, E. Z., Morelli, G. A., & Ivey, P. K. (1992). The Efe forager infant and toddler's pattern of social relationships: Multiple and simultaneous. *Developmental Psychology, 28*, 568–577.

Trope, Y., & Liberman, N. (2010). Construal level theory of psychological distance. *Psychological Review, 117*, 440–463.

Trouton, A., Spinath, F. M., & Plomin, R. (2002). Twins Early Development Study (TEDS): A multivariate longitudinal genetic investigation of language, cognition, and behaviour problems in childhood. *Twin Research, 5*, 444–448.

True, M. M., Pisani, L., & Oumar, F. (2001). Infant-mother attachment among the Dogan of Mali. *Child Development, 72*, 1451–1466.

Tulving, E. (2002). Episodic memory: From mind to brain. *Annual Review of Psychology, 53*, 1–25.

Turiel, E. (1983). *The development of social knowledge: Morality and convention*. New York: Cambridge University Press.

Turiel, E. (2002). *The culture of morality*. New York: Cambridge University Press.

Turiel, E. (2006). The development of morality. In W. Damon & R. M. Lerner (Series eds) & N. Eisenberg (Vol. ed.), *Handbook of child psychology* (Vol. 3, 6th edn, pp. 789–857). New York: Wiley.

Turiel, E., Killen, V. & Helwig, F. (1987) Morality: Its structure, functions and vagaries. In J. Kagan and S. Lamb (eds), *The emergence of morality in young children* (pp. 155–244) Chicago: University of Chicago Press.

Turkheimer, E. (2000). Three laws of behavior genetics and what they mean. *Current Directives in Psychological Science, 9*, 160–164.

Turkheimer, E., Haley, A., Waldron, M., D'Onofrio, B., & Gottesman, I. I. (2003). Socioeconomic status modifies heritability of IQ in young children. *Psychological Science, 14*, 623–628.

Turner, J. S. & Rubinson, L. (1993) *Contemporary human sexuality*. Englewood Cliffs, NJ: Prentice Hall.

Turner, R. N., & Brown, R. J. (2008). Improving children's attitudes towards refugees: An evaluation of a multicultural curricula and anti-racist intervention. *Journal of Applied Social Psychology, 38*, 1295–1328.

Turner-Bowker, D. M. (1996). Gender stereotyped description in children's picture books: Does 'Curious Jane' exist in literature? *Sex Roles, 35*, 461–488.

Turnure, J. E. (1970) Children's reactions to distractors in a learning situation. *Developmental Psychology, 2*, 115–122.

Udvari, S., Schneider, B. H., Labovitz, G., & Tassi, F. (1995, August). A multidimensional view of competition in relation to children's peer relations. Paper presented at the meeting of the American Psychological Association, New York.

UNAIDS. (2006) Overview of the global AIDS epidemic. In 2006 *Report on the global AIDS epidemic*. Retrieved 1 May 2008 from http://www.unaids.org/en/KnowledgeCentre/HIVData/GlobalReport/

UNAIDS. (2017). UNAIDS data 2017. Retrieved 19 April 2018 from http://www.unaids.org/sites/default/files/media_asset/20170720_Data_book_2017_en.pdf

Underwood, J., Underwood, G., & Wood, D. (2000). When does gender matter? Interactions during computer-based problem solving. *Learning and Instruction, 10*(5), 447–462.

Underwood, M. K. (2003). *Social aggression among girls*. New York: Guilford Press.

Underwood, M. K. (2004). Gender and peer relations. In J. Kupersmidt & K. A. Dodge (eds), *Children's peer*

relations (pp. 21–36). Washington, DC: American Psychological Association.

Underwood, M. K., Galenand, B. R., & Paquette, J. A. (2001). Top ten challenges for understanding gender and aggression in children: Why can't we all just get along? *Social Development, 10*(2), 248–266.

Ungerer, J. A., Brody, L. R., & Zelazo, P. R. (1978). Long-term memory for speech in 2- to 4-week-old infants. *Infant Behavior and Development, 7,* 177–186.

United Nations (2017). *World population prospects: Key findings and advance tables.* New York: United Nations. https://population. un.org/wpp/Publications/Files/ WPP2017_KeyFindings.pdf

Updegraff, K. A., McHale, S. M., & Crouter, A. C. (1996). Gender roles in marriage: What do they mean for girls' and boys' school achievement? *Journal of Youth and Adolescence, 25,* 73–88.

Uzgiris, I. C. (1989). Infants in relation: Performers, pupils and partners. In W. Damon (ed.), *Child development: Today and tomorrow* (pp. 288–311). San Francisco: Jossey-Bass.

Valencia, R. R., & Suzuki, L. A. (2001). *Racial and ethnic minority psychology.* Thousand Oaks, CA: Sage.

Valenzuela, M. J., & Sachdev, P. (2006). Brain reserve and dementia: A systematic review. *Psychological Medicine, 36,* 441–454.

Valian, V. (1986). Syntactic categories in the speech of young children. *Developmental Psychology, 22,* 562–579.

Valiente, C., & Eisenberg, N. (2006). Parenting and children's adjustment: The role of children's emotional regulating. In D. K. Snyder, J. A. Simpson & J. N. Hughes (eds), *Emotion regulation*

in couples and families (pp. 123–142). Washington, DC: American Psychological Association.

Van de Loo-Neus, G. H., Rommelse, N., & Buitelaar, J. K. (2011). To stop or not to stop? How long should medication treatment of attention-deficit hyperactivity disorder be extended? *European Neuropsychopharmacology, 21,* 584–589.

Van de Vijer, F. J. R., and Phalet, K. (2004). Assessment in multicultural groups: The role of acculturation. *Applied Psychology, 53,* 215–236.

Van Den Bergh, B. R. H. (1992). Maternal emotions during pregnancy and fetal and neonatal behavior. In J. G. Nijhuis (ed.), *Fetal behavior: Development and perinatal aspects* (pp. 157–178). New York: Oxford University Press.

Van den Boom, D. C. (1994). The influence of temperament and mothering on attachment and exploration: An experimental manipulation of sensitive responsiveness among lowerclass mothers with irritable infants. *Child Development, 65,* 1457–1477.

Van Den Oord, E. J., Boomsma, I., & Verhulst, F. C. (1994). A study of problem behaviors in 10- to 15-year-old biologically related and unrelated international adoptees. *Behavior Genetics, 24,* 193–205.

Van der Maas, H. L. J., Dolan, C. V., Grasman, R. P. P. P., Wicherts, J. M., Huizenga, H. M., & Raijmakers, M. E. J. (2006). A dynamical model of general intelligence: The positive manifold of intelligence by mutualism. *Psychological Review, 113*(4), 842–861.

Van der Mark, I. L., van Ijzendoorn, M. H., & Bakermans-Kranenburg, M. J. (2002). Development of empathy in girls during the second year of life: Associations with parenting, attachment, and temperament. *Social Development, 11,* 451–468.

Van Ijzendoorn, M. H. (1995). Adult attachment representations, parental responsiveness, and infant attachment: A meta-analysis on the predictive validity of the Adult Attachment Interview. *Psychological Bulletin, 117*(3), 387–403.

Van Ijzendoorn, M. H., & Sagi, A. (1999). Cross-cultural patterns of attachment: Universal and contextual dimensions. In J. Cassidy & P. Shaver (eds), *Handbook of attachment* (pp. 713–734). New York: Guilford Press.

Van Ijzendoorn, M. H., Sagi, A., & Lamberman, M. W. E. (1992). The multiple caretaker paradox: Data from Holland and Israel. In R. C. Planta (ed.) *Beyond the parent: The role of other adults in children's lives* (pp. 5–24). San Francisco: Jossey-Bass.

Van Ijzendoorn, M. H., Vereijken, C. M. J. L., Bakermans-Kranenburg, M. J., & Riksen-Walraven, J. M. (2004). Assessing attachment security with the attachment Q sort: Meta-analytic evidence for the validity of the observer AQS. *Child Development, 75,* 1188–1213.

Van Leeuwen, M., van den Berg, S. M., Hoekstra, R., & Boomsma, D. I. (2007). Endophenotypes for intelligence in children. *Intelligence, 35,* 369–380.

Van Os, J., & Selton, J. (1998). Prenatal exposure to maternal stress and subsequent schizophrenia. *British Journal of Psychiatry, 172,* 324–326.

Van Rijn, H., van Someran, M., & van der Maas, H. (2003). Modeling developmental transitions in the balance scale task. *Cognitive Science, 27,* 227–257.

Vandell, D. L. (2007). Early child care: The known and the unknown. In G. Ladd (ed.), Appraising the human development sciences essays in honor of Merrill-Palmer Quarterly (pp. 300–328). Detroit, MI: Wayne State University Press. (Reprinted from *Merrill-Palmer Quarterly, 50*(3), 387–414.)

Vandell, D. L., & Wilson, K. (1987). Infants' interactions with mother, siblings and peer contacts and relations between interaction systems. *Child Development, 58,* 176–186.

Vandell, D. L., Henderson, V. K., & Wilson, K. S. (1988). A longitudinal study of children with varying quality day care experiences. *Child Development, 59,* 1286–1292.

Vander, A. J., Sherman, J. H., & Luciano, D. S. (1994). *Human physiology* (6th edn). New York: McGraw-Hill.

Vanin, J. R. (2008). Specific phobia. In J. R. Vanin & J. D. Helsley (eds), *Current clinical practice. Anxiety disorders: A pocket guide for primary care* (pp. 149–157). Totowa, NJ: Humana Press.

Varea, C., Bernis, C., Montero, P., Arias, S. Barroso, A., & Gonzalez, B. (2000). Secular trend and intrapopulational variation in age at menopause in Spanish women. *Journal of Biological Science, 32,* 383–393.

Varela, F. J., Thompson, E., & Rosch, E. (2017). *The embodied mind: Cognitive science and human experience.* Cambridge, MA: MIT Press.

Varnum, M. E., Grossmann, I., Kitayama, S., & Nisbett, R. E. (2010). The origin of cultural differences in cognition: The social orientation hypothesis. *Current Directions in Psychological Science, 19*(1), 9–13.

Vaughan, G. M. (1964). *Ethnic awareness and attitudes in New Zealand,* Wellington: Victoria University of Wellington Publication in Psychology No. 17.

Vaughan, G. M. (1987). A social psychological model of ethnic identity development. In J. S. Phinney & M. J. Rotheram (ed.), *Children's ethnic socialization: Pluralism and development* (pp. 73–91). Beverly Hills, CA: Sage.

Vaughn, B. E., & Bost, K. K. (1999). Attachment and temperament. In J. Cassidy & P. Shaver (eds), *Handbook of attachment* (pp. 198–225). New York: Guilford Press.

Vaughn, B. E., Kopp, C. B., & Krakow, J. B. (1984). The emergence and consolidation of self-control from eighteen to thirty months of age: Normative trends and individual differences. *Child Development, 55,* 990–1004.

Veenstra, R., Lindenberg, S., Oldehinkel, A. J., De Winter, A. F., Verhuslt, F. C., & Ormel, J. (2008). Prosocial and antisocial behavior in preadolescence: Teachers' and parents' perceptions of the behavior of girls and boys. *International Journal of Behavioral Development, 32,* 243–251.

Venter, J. C., Adams, M. D., Myers, E. W., Li, P. W., Mural, R. J., Sutton, G. G. et al. (2001) The sequence of the human genome. *Science, 291,* 1304–1351.

Veuillet, E., Magnan, A., Ecalle, J., Thai-Van, H. & Collet, L. (2007) Auditory processing disorder in children with reading disabilities: Effect of audiovisual training. *Brain, 130,* 2915–2928.

Vidal, F. (1994) *Piaget before Piaget.* Cambridge: Harvard University Press.

Viding, E., Blair, R. J. R., Moffitt, T. E., & Plomin, R. (2005). Evidence for substantial genetic risk for psychopathy in 7-year-olds. *Journal of Child Psychology & Psychiatry, 46,* 592–597.

Viding, E., Jones, A. P., Frick, P., Moffitt, T. E., & Plomin, R. (2008). Heritability of antisocial behaviour at age nine: Do callous-unemotional traits matter? *Developmental Science, 11,* 17–22.

Visser, S. N., Lesesne, C. A., & Perou, R. (2007). National estimates and factors associated with medication treatment for childhood attention-deficit/hyperactivity disorder. *Pediatrics, 119,* 99–106.

Volkmar, F. R., Lord, C., Bailey, A., Schultz, R. T., & Klin, A. (2004). Autism and pervasive developmental disorders. *Journal of Child Psychology and Psychiatry, 45,* 135–170.

Volling, B. L., McElwain, N. L., & Miller, A. L. (2002). Emotion regulation in context: The jealousy complex between young siblings and its relations with child and family characteristics. *Child Development, 73,* 581–600.

Von Hofsten, C. (2004). An action perspective on motor development. *Trends in Cognitive Science 8,* 266–272.

von Hofsten, C., & Fazel-Zandy, S. (1984). Development of visually guided hand orientation in reaching. *Journal of Experimental Child Psychology 38,* 208–219.

von Hofsten, C., & Rönnquist, L. (1988). Preparation for grasping an object: A developmental study. *Journal of Experimental Psychology: Human Perception and Performance 14,* 610–621.

Von Stumm, S., & Plomin, R. (2015). Breastfeeding and IQ growth from toddlerhood through adolescence. *PloS One, 10*(9), e0138676.

Voorhees, C. V. & Mollnow, E. (1987) Behavioral teratogenesis: Long-term influences on behavior from early exposure to environmental agents. In J. D. Osofsky (ed.), *Handbook of infant development* (2nd edn, pp. 913–971) New York: Wiley.

Vrana, S. R., & Vrana, D. T. (2017). Can a computer administer a Wechsler Intelligence Test? *Professional Psychology: Research and Practice, 48*(3), 191–198. http://dx.doi.org/10.1037/pro0000128

Vurpillot, E. (1968). The development of scanning strategies and their relation to visual differentiation. *Journal of Experimental Child Psychology, 6,* 632–650.

Vygotsky, L. S. (1934) *Thought and language.* Cambridge, MA: MIT Press.

Vygotsky, L. S. (1967). *Vaobraszeniye i tvorchestvo v deskom voraste* [Imagination and creativity in childhood]. Moscow: Akademii Izdatel'stvo Pedagogicheskikh Nauk. (Original work published 1930.)

Vygotsky, L. S. (1978). *Mind in society: The development of higher psychological functions.* Cambridge, MA: Harvard University Press.

Wachs, T. D. & Kohnstamm, G. A. (eds) (2001) *Temperament in context.* Mahwah, NJ: Erlbaum.

Wachs, T. D. (2000). *Necessary but not sufficient: The respective roles of individual and multiple influences on individual development.* Washington, DC: American Psychological Association.

Waddington, C. H. (1962). *New patterns in genetics and development.* New York: Columbia University Press.

Waddington, C. H. (1966). *Principles of development and differentiation.* New York: Macmillan.

Wade, C., & Tavris, C. (1999). Gender and culture. In L. A. Peplau, S. C. De Bro, R. Veniegas, & P. L. Taylor (eds), *Gender, culture and ethnicity: Current research about women and men.* Mountain View, CA: Mayfield.

Wagner, R. K. (2000). Practical intelligence. In R. J. Sternberg (ed.), *Handbook of intelligence* (pp. 380–395). Cambridge: Cambridge University Press.

Wahler, R. G. (1967). Infant social attachments: A reinforcement theory interpretation and investigation. *Child Development, 38,* 1079–1088.

Wahler, R. G., & Dumas, J. E. (1987). Family factors in childhood

psychology: Toward a coercion-neglect model. In T. Jacob (ed.), *Family interaction and psychopathology: Theories, methods, and findings* (pp. 581–625). New York: Plenum Press.

Wainryb, C. (2006). Moral development in culture: Diversity, tolerance, and justice. In M. Killen & J. Smetana (eds), *Handbook of moral development* (pp. 211–240). Mahwah, NJ: Erlbaum.

Wakeley, A., Rivera, S., & Langer, J. (2000). Can young infants add and subtract?. *Child Development, 71*(6), 1525–1534.

Wakschlag, L. S., Gordon, R. A., Lahey, B. B., Loeber, R., Green, S. M., & Leventhal, B. L. (2001). Maternal age at first birth and boys' risk for conduct disorders. *Journal of Research on Adolescence, 10,* 417–441.

Walden, T. (1991). Infant social referencing. In J. Garber & K. Dodge (eds), *The development of emotional regulation and dysregulation* (pp. 69–88). New York: Cambridge University Press.

Walker, H. M. (1995). *The acting out child: Coping with classroom disruption.* Longmont, CO: Sopris West.

Walker, L. J. (2004). Gus in the gap: Bridging the judgment–action gap in moral functioning. In D. K. Lapsley & D. Narvaez (eds), *Moral development, self, and identity* (pp. 1–20). Mahwah, NJ: Erlbaum.

Walker, L. J., Gustafson, P., & Hennig, K. H. (2001). The consolidation/transition model in moral reasoning development. *Developmental Psychology, 37,* 187–197.

Walkowiak, J., Weiner, J., Fastabend, A., Heinzow, H., Kramer, U., Schmidt, E. et al. (2001) Environmental exposure to polychlorinated biphenyls and quality of the home environment: Effects on psychodevelopment in early childhood. *The Lancet, 358,* 1602–1607.

Wallach, M. A., & Kogan, N. (1965). *Modes of thinking in young children: A study of the creativity-intelligence distinction.* New York: Holt, Rinehart & Winston.

Wallen, K. (1996). Nature needs nurture: The interaction of hormonal and social influences on the development of behavioral sex differences in rhesus monkeys. *Hormones and Behavior, 30,* 364–378.

Waller, T., & Bitou, A. (2011). Research *with* children: Three challenges for participatory research in early childhood. *European Early Childhood Education Research Journal, 19*(1), 5–20, doi: 10.1080/1350293X.2011.548964

Walton, G. E., Bower, N. J. A., & Bower, T. G. R. (1992). Recognition of familiar faces by newborns. *Infant Behavior and Development, 15,* 265–269.

Wang, Q. (2004). The emergence of cultural self-constructs: Autobiographical memory and self-description in European American and Chinese children. *Developmental Psychology, 40,* 3–15.

Wang, Z., Deater-Deckard, K., Petrill, S. A., & Thompson, L. A. (2012). Externalizing problems, attention regulation, and household chaos: A longitudinal behavioral genetic study. *Development and Psychopathology, 24*(3), 755–769.

Ward, L. M., & Friedman, K. (2006). Using TV as a guide: Associations between television viewing and adolescents' sexual attitudes and behavior. *Journal of Research on Adolescence, 16,* 133–156.

Wark, G. R., & Krebs, D. L. (1996). Gender and dilemma differences in real-life moral judgment. *Developmental Psychology, 32,* 220–230.

Warneken, F., & Tomasello, M. (2006). Altruistic helping in human infants and young chimpanzees. *Science, 311,* 1301–1303.

Warneken, F., & Tomasello, M. (2009). The roots of human altruism. *British Journal of Psychology, 100,* 455–471.

Wartner, A. G., Grossman, K., Fremmer-Bombik, E., & Suess, G. (1994). Attachment patterns at age six in South Germany: Predictability from infancy and implications for preschool behavior. *Child Development, 49,* 483–494.

Waszak, F., Li, S. C., & Hommel, B. (2010). The development of attentional networks: Cross-sectional findings from a life span sample. *Developmental Psychology, 46*(2), 337.

Waters, E. (1995). The attachment Q Set, Version 3.0. In E. Waters, B. Vaughn, G. Posada, & K. Kondo Ikemura (eds), Caregiving, cultural, and cognitive perspectives on securebase phenomena and working models: New growing points of attachment theory and research. *Monographs of the Society for Research in Child Development, 60*(2–3), (Serial no. 244), 133–145.

Waters, E., Merrick, S., Treboux, D., Crowell, J., & Albersheim, L. (2000). Attachment security in infancy and early childhood: A twenty-year longitudinal study. *Child Development, 71,* 684–689.

Waters, E., Vaughn, B. E., Posada, G. & Kondo-Ikemura, K. (1995) Caregiving, cultural, and cognitive perspectives on secure-base behavior and working models: New growing points of attachment theory and research. *Monographs of the Society for Research in Child Development, 60*(2–3), (Serial no. 244).

Watson, J. B. (1930). *Behaviorism* (rev. edn). New York: Norton.

Watson, J. B., & Rayner, R. (1920). Conditioned emotional reactions. *Journal of Experimental Psychology, 3,* 1, 1–14.

Watts, T. W., Duncan, G. J., & Quan, H. (2018). Revisiting the Marshmallow Test: A conceptual replication investigating links between early delay of gratification and later outcomes. *Psychological Science,* doi: 0956797618761661.

Waxman, S. R., & Gelman, R. (1986). Preschoolers' use of superordinate relations in classification and language. *Cognitive Development, 1,* 139–156.

Waxman, S. R., & Lidz, J. L. (2006). Early word learning. In W. Damon & R. M. Lerner (Series eds) & D. Kuhn & R. Siegler (Vol. eds), *Handbook of child psychology* (Vol. 2, 6th edn, pp. 299–335). New York: Wiley.

Waxman, S. R., Shipley, E. F., & Shepperson, B. (1991). Establishing new subcategories: The role of category labels and existing knowledge. *Child Development, 62,* 127–138.

Wechsler, D. (1952). *Wechsler Intelligence Scale for Children.* New York: Psychological Corporation.

Wechsler, D. (1958). *The measurement and appraisal of adult intelligence* (4th edn). Baltimore, MD: Williams & Wilkins.

Wechsler, D. (2003). *Wechsler Intelligence Scale for Children* (4th edn). New York: Psychological Corporation.

Weinberg, M. K., & Tronick, E. Z. (1998). *Infant and caregiver engagement phases system.* Boston, MA: Harvard Medical School.

Weinberg, R. A. (1989). Intelligence and IQ: Landmark issues and great debates. *American Psychologist, 44,* 98–104.

Weinberg, R. A., Scarr, S., & Waldman, I. D. (1992). The Minnesota Transracial Adoption Study: A follow-up of IQ test performance at adolescence. *Intelligence, 16,* 117–135.

Weinraub, M., & Lewis, M. (1977). The determinants of children's responses to separation. *Monographs of the Society for Research in Child Development, 42* (Serial no. 172).

Weisner, T. S. (1993). Overview: Sibling similarity and difference in different cultures. In C. W. Nuckolls (ed.), *Siblings in South Asia: Brothers and sisters in cultural context* (pp. 1–17). New York: Guilford Press.

Weisner, T., & Gallimore, R. (1977). My brother's keeper: Child and sibling caretaking. *Current Anthropology, 18,* 169–190.

Weiss, M., Hechtman, L. T. & Weiss, G. (1999) *ADHD in adulthood: A guide to current theory, diagnosis and treatment.* Baltimore: Johns Hopkins University Press.

Weissberg, R., & Greenberg, M. T. (1998). School and community competence-enhancement and prevention programs In W. Damon (Series ed.) & I. Sigel & K. A. Renninger (Vol. eds), *Handbook of child psychology: Vol. 4. Child psychology in practice* (6th edn, pp. 877–954). New York: Wiley.

Weissman, M., Warner, V., Wickramaratne, P., Moreau, D., & Olfson, M. (1997). Offspring of depressed parents: Ten years later. *Archives of General Psychiatry, 54,* 932–940.

Weitzman, E. D., & Graziani, L. J. (1968). Maturation and topography of the auditory evoked response of the prematurely born infant. *Developmental Psychobiology, 1*(2), 79–89.

Weitzman, N., Birns, B., & Friend, R. (1985). Traditional and nontraditional mothers' communication with their daughters and sons. *Child Development, 56,* 894–898.

Weizman, Z. O., & Snow, C. E. (2001). Lexical output as it relates to children's vocabulary acquisition: Effects of sophisticated exposure as a support for meaning. *Developmental Psychology, 37,* 265–279.

Wellens, R., Malina, R. M., Beunen, G., & Lefevre, J. (1990). Age at menarche in Flemish girls:

Current status and secular change in the 20th century. *Annals of Human Biology, 17,* 145–152.

Wellman, H. M. (1977). Preschoolers' understanding of memory relevant variables. *Child Development, 48,* 1720–1723.

Wellman, H. M. (1978). Knowledge of the interaction of memory variables: A developmental study of metamemory. *Developmental Psychology, 14,* 24–29.

Wellman, H. M., & Lempers, J. D. (1977). The naturalistic communicative abilities of two-year-olds. *Child Development, 48,* 1052–1057.

Wellman, H. M., Collins, J., & Glieberman, J. (1981). Understanding the combinations of memory variables: Developing conceptions of memory limitations. *Child Development, 52,* 1313–1317.

Wellman, H. M., Cross, D., & Watson, J. (2001). Meta-analysis of theory-of-mind development: The truth about false belief. *Child Development, 72,* 655–684.

Wells, K. C. (2001). Comprehensive versus matched psychosocial treatment in the MTA study: Conceptual and empirical issues. *Journal of Clinical Child Psychology, 30,* 131–135.

Wendland-Carro, J., Piccinini, C. A., & Miller, W. S. (1999). The role of an early intervention on enhancing the quality of mother-infant interaction. *Child Development, 70,* 713–721.

Wenestam, C. G., & Waas, H. (1987). Swedish and US children's thinking about death: A qualitative study and cross-cultural comparison. *Death Studies, 11,* 99–121.

Werker, J. F. & Vouloumanos, A. (2001) Speech and language processing in infancy: A neurocognitive approach. In C. A. Nelson & M. Luciana (eds), *Handbook of developmental cognitive neuroscience* (pp. 269–280) Cambridge, MA: MIT Press.

Werker, J. F. (1989). Becoming a native listener. *American Scientist, 77,* 54–59.

Werker, J. F., Pegg, J. E., & McLeod, P. J. (1994). A crosslanguage investigation of infant preference for infant-directed communication. *Infant Behavior and Development, 17,* 323–333.

Werker, J., & Polka, L. (1993). Developmental changes in speech perception: new challenges and new directions. *Journal of Phonetics, 21,* 83–101.

Werner E. E., & Smith R. S. (1982). *Vulnerable but invincible: A longitudinal study of resilient children and youth.* New York: McGraw-Hill.

Werner, E. (1995). Resilience in development. *Current Directions in Psychological Science, 4,* 81–85.

Werner, E. E. (1984). Resilient children. *Young Children, 40,* 68–72.

Werner, E. E., & Smith, R. S. (2001). *Journeys from childhood to midlife: Risk, resilience, and recovery.* New York: Cornell University Press.

Werner, E. E., Bierman, J. M., & French, F. F. (1971). *The children of Kauai.* Honolulu: University of Hawaii Press.

Werner, J. S., & Siqueland, E. R. (1978). Visual recognition memory in the preterm infant. *Infant Behavior and Development, 1,* 79–84.

Wertsch, J. V., & Tulviste, P. (1992). L. S. Vygotsky and contemporary developmental psychology. *Developmental Psychology, 28,* 543–553.

Wertsch, J. V., McNamee, J. D., McLane, J. B., & Budwig, N. A. (1980). The adult–child dyad as a problem-solving system. *Child Development, 51,* 1215–1221.

West, R. L., & Crook, T. H. (1990). Age differences in everyday memory: Laboratory analogues of telephone number recall. *Psychology and Aging, 5,* 520–529.

Westermann, G., & Mareschal, D. (2014). From perceptual to language-mediated categorization. *Philosophical Transactions of the Royal Society of London B: Biological Sciences, 369*(1634), 20120391.

Whalen, C. K. (2001). ADHD treatment in the 21st century: Pushing the envelope. *Journal of Clinical Child Psychology, 30,* 136–140.

Whitall, J., & Clark, J. E. (1994). The development of bipedal interlimb co-ordination. In S. P. Swinnen, J. Massion & H. Heuer (eds), *Interlimb coordination: Neural, dynamical and cognitive constraints* (pp. 391–411). San Diego, CA: Academic Press.

White, L., Petorvitch, H., Wevser-Ross, G., Masaki, K. H, Masaki, K. H. Abbott, R. D., et al. (1996). Prevalence of dementia in older Japanese-American men in Hawaii: The Honolulu-Asia Aging Study. *Journal of the American Medical Association, 276,* 955–960.

Whitehurst, G. J., & Lonigan, C. J. (1998). Child development and emergent literacy. *Child Development, 69,* 848–872.

Whiting, B. B., & Whiting, J. W. M. (1975). *Children of six cultures: A psychocultural analysis.* Cambridge, MA: Harvard University Press.

Whiting, B., & Edwards, C. (1988). *Children of different worlds: The formation of social behavior.* Cambridge, MA: Harvard University Press.

Whiting, B. B. (1983). The genesis of prosocial behaviour. In D. L. Bridgeman (ed.), *The nature of prosocial development* (pp. 221–242). New York: Academic Press.

Whitlock, J. L., Powers, J. L., & Eckenrode, J. (2006). The virtual cutting edge: The internet and adolescent self-injury. *Developmental Psychology, 42,* 407–417.

WHO Summary (2007). *The challenge of obesity in the WHO European Region and the strategies for response: Summary.* F. Branca, H. Nikogosian, & T. Lobstein (eds). Geneva: World Health Organization.

Wicks-Nelson, R. & Israel, A. C. (2000) *Behavior disorders in childhood.* Upper Saddle River, NJ: Prentice Hall.

Wiesenfeld, A., Malatesta, C., & DeLoache, L. (1981). Differential parental response to familiar and unfamiliar infant distress signals. *Infant Behavior and Development, 4,* 281–295.

Wigfield, A., Eccles, J., & Schiefele, U. (2006). Motivation. In W. Damon & R. M. Lerner (Series eds) & N. Eisenberg (Vol. ed.), *Handbook of child psychology* (Vol. 3, 6th edn, pp. 933–1002). New York: Wiley.

Wilcox, A. J., Baird, D. D., Weinberg, C. R., Hornsby, P. P. & Herbst, A. L. (1995) Fertility in men exposed prenatally to diethylstilbestrol. *The New England Journal of Medicine, 332,* 1411–1416.

Will, J. A., Self, P. A., & Datan, N. (1976). Maternal behaviour and perceived sex of infant. *American Journal of Orthopsychiatry, 46,* 135–139.

Willatts, P. (1999). Development of means-end behavior in young infants: Pulling a support to retrieve a distant object. *Developmental Psychology, 35,* 3.

Willford, J. A., Leach, S. H., & Day, N. L. (2006). Moderate alcohol exposure and cognitive status of children at age 10. *Alcoholism: Clinical and Experimental Research, 30,* 1051–1059.

Williams, G. C. (1957). Pleiotropy, natural selection, and the evolution of senescence. *Evolution, 11,* 398–411.

Williams, J. E., & Best, D. L. (1990). *Measuring sex stereotypes: A multinational study* (rev edn). Newbury, CA: Sage.

Williams, W. M., & Ceci, S. J. (1997). Are Americans becoming more or less alike? Trends in race, class, and ability differences in intelligence. *American Psychologist, 52,* 1226–1235.

Willis, S. L., & Schaie, K. W. (2005). Cognitive trajectories in midlife and cognitive functioning in old age. In S. L. Willis & M. Martin (eds). *Middle adulthood: A lifespan perspective* (pp. 243–276). Thousand Oaks, CA: Sage.

Willis, T. A. & Yaeger, A. M. (2003) Family factors and adolescent substance use: Models and mechanisms. *Current Directions in Psychological Science, 12,* 222–226.

Wilson, B. J. & Weiss, A. J. (1993) The effects of sibling coviewing on preschooler's reactions to a suspenseful movie scene. *Communication Research, 20,* 214–248.

WIlson, J. G. (1973). *Environment and birth defects.* New York: Academic Press.

Wilson, M. (2002). Six views of embodied cognition. *Psychonomic Bulletin & Review, 9*(4), 625–636.

Wimmer, H. (1980) Children's understanding of stories: Assimilation by a general schema for actions or coordination of temporal relations. In F. Wilkening, J. Becker & T. Trabasso (eds), *Information integration by children* (pp. 267–290) Hillsdale, NJ: Erlbaum.

Wimmer, H., & Perner, J. (1983). Beliefs about beliefs: Representation and constraining function of wrong beliefs in young children's understanding of deception. *Cognition, 13,* 103–128.

Windfuhr, K., While, D., Hunt, I., Turnbull, P., Lowe, R., Burns, J., et al. (2008). Suicide in juveniles and adolescents in the United Kingdom. *Journal of Child Psychology and Psychiatry, 49,* 1155–1165.

Wing, L. (1981). Language, social, and cognitive impairments in autism and severe mental retardation. *Journal of Autism and Developmental Disorders, 11*(1), 31–44.

Winner, E. (2006). Development in the arts: Drawing and music. In W. Damon & R. M. Lerner (Series eds) & D. Kuhn & R. S. Siegler (Vol. eds), *Handbook of child psychology. Vol. 2: Cognition, perception, and language* (pp. 859–904). New York: Wiley.

Wintre, M. G., & Vallance, D. D. (1994). A developmental sequence in the comprehension of emotions: Intensity, multiple emotions and valence. *Developmental Psychology, 30,* 509–514.

Witelson, S. F. (1983) Bumps on the brain: Neuroanatomical asymmetries as a basis for functional symmetries. In S. Segalowitz (ed.), *Language functions and brain organization* (pp. 117–144) New York: Academic Press.

Wolchik, S. A., Wilcox, K. L., Tein, J.-Y., & Sandler, I. N. (2000). Maternal acceptance and consistency of discipline as buffers of divorce stressors on children's psychological adjustment problems. *Journal of Abnormal Child Psychology, 28,* 87–102.

Wolff, P. H. (1966). The causes, controls and organizations of behavior in the neonate. *Psychological Issues, 5*(1), (Whole no. 17).

Wolff, P. H. (1987). *The development of behavioral states and the expression of emotions in early infancy: New proposals for investigation.* Chicago: University of Chicago Press.

Wolke, D. (1998). The psychological development of prematurely born children. *Archives of Disease in Childhood, 78,* 567–570.

Wood, D., Bruner, J., & Ross, G. (1976). The role of tutoring in problem solving. *Journal of Child Psychology and Psychiatry, 17,* 89–100.

Woodward, A. L. (1998). Infants selectively encode the goal object of an actor's reach. *Cognition, 69,* 1–34.

Woodward, A. L. (2005) The infant origins of intentional understanding. In R. V. Kail (ed.) *Advances in Child Development and Behavior,* (vol 33), (pp. 229–262). Oxford: Elsevier.

Woodward, J. Z. & Aslin, R. N. (1990, April). *Segmentation cues in maternal speech to infants.* Paper presented at the seventh biennial meeting of the International Conference on Infant Studies, Montreal, Quebec, Canada.

Woodward, L. J., McPherson, C. C., & Volpe, J. J. (2018). Passive addiction and teratogenic effects. In J. J. Volpe (Ed.), *Volpe's Neurology of the Newborn, 6th Ed.* (pp. 1149–1189). Elsevier Health Science.

Woodward, L. J., McPherson, C. C., & Volpe, J. J. (2018). Passive addiction and teratogenic effects. In J. J. Volpe (ed.) *Volpe's neurology of the newborn* (6th edn, pp. 1149–1189). Philadelphia, PA: Elsevier.

Woodward, L. J., McPherson, C. C., & Volpe, J. J. (2018). Passive Addiction and Teratogenic Effects. In *Volpe's Neurology of the Newborn (Sixth Edition)* (pp. 1149–1189).

Woodward, L. J., McPherson, C. C., & Volpe, J. J. (2018).

Wozniak, R. H. (1996). Qu'est-ce que l'intelligence? Piaget, Vygotsky and the 1920s crisis in psychology. In A. Tryphon & J. Voneche (eds), *Piaget-Vygotsky: The social genesis of thought* (pp. 11–23). Hove: Psychology Press.

Wright, J. C., & Huston, A. C. (1995). *Effects of educational TV viewing of lower income preschoolers on academic skills, school readiness, and school adjustment one to three years later.* Report to Children's Television Workshop, Center for Research on the Influences of Television on Children, University of Kansas, Lawrence.

Wynn, K. (1992). Addition and subtraction by human infants. *Nature, 358*(6389), 749–750.

Wyrobek, A. J., Eskenazi, B., Young, S., Arnheim, N., Tiemann-Boege, I., Jabs, E. W., et al. (2006). Advancing age has differential effects on DNA damage, chromatin integrity, gene mutations, and aneuploidies in sperm. *Proceedings of the National Academy of Sciences, USA, 103,* 9601–9606.

Wyshak, G., & Frisch, R. E. (1982). Evidence for a secular trend in age of menarche. *The New England Journal of Medicine, 306,* 1033–1035.

Xia, Y., Zhuang, K., Sun, J., Chen, Q., Wei, D., Yang, W., & Qiu, J. (2017). Emotion-related brain structures associated with trait creativity in middle children. *Neuroscience Letters, 658,* 182–188. https://doi.org/10.1016/j.neulet.2017.08.008

Xiaohe, X., & Whyte, M. K. (1990). Love matches and arranged marriages: A Chinese replication. *Journal of Marriage and the Family, 52,* 709–722.

Xie, H., Cairns, B. D., & Cairns, R. B. (2005). The development of aggressive behavior among girls: Measurement issues, social functions, and differential trajectories. In D. J. Pepler, K. C. Madsen, C. Webster, & K. S. Levene (eds), *The development and treatment of girlhood aggression* (pp. 105–136). Mahwah, NJ: Erlbaum.

Yale, M. E., Messinger, D. S., Cobo-Lewis, A. B., & Delgado, C. F. (2003). The temporal coordination of early infant communication. *Developmental Psychology, 39,* 815–824.

Yang, J., Kanazawa, S., Yamaguchi, M. K., & Motoyoshi, I. (2015). Pre-constancy vision in infants. *Current Biology, 25,* 3209–3212.

Yang, Y. (2008). Social inequalities in happiness in the united states, 1972 to 2004: An age-period-cohort analysis. *American Sociological Review, 73,* 204–226.

Yarmey, A. D., & Jones, H. P. (1983). Accuracy of memory of male and female eyewitnesses to a criminal assault and rape. *Bulletin of the Psychonomic Society, 21,* 89–92.

Yaylaci, F. T., Cicchetti, D., Rogosch, F. A., Bulut, O., & Hetzel, S. R. (2017). The interactive effects of child maltreatment and the FK506 binding protein 5 gene (FKBP5) on dissociative symptoms in adolescence. *Development and Psychopathology, 29*(3), 1105–1117.

Yelsma, P., & Athappilly, K. (1988). Marital satisfaction and communication practices—comparisons among Indian and American couples. *Journal of Comparative Family Studies, 19,* 37–54.

Yirmiya, N., & Charman, T. (2010). The prodrome of autism: Early behavioral and biological signs, regression, peri- and post-natal development and genetics. *Journal of Child Psychology and Psychiatry, 51,* 432–458.

Yonas, A. & Granrud, C. (1985). The development of sensitivity to kinetic binocular and pictorial depth information in human infants. In D. Ingle, M. Jeannerod, & D. Lee (Eds.), *Brain Mechanisms and Spatial Vision* (pp. 113–145). Amsterdam: Martinus Nijhoff Press.

You, H., Gaab, N., Wei, N., Cheng-Lai, A., Wang, Z., Jie, J., Song, M., Meng, X., & Ding, G. (2011). Neural deficits in second language reading: fMRI evidence from Chinese children with English reading impairment. *Neuroimage, 57,* 670–770.

Young, L. J., & Wang, Z. (2004). The neurobiology of pair bonding(Review). *Nature Neuroscience, 7*(10), 1048–1054.

Young, S. K., Fox, N. A., & Zahn-Waxler, C. (1999). The relations between temperament and empathy in two-year-olds. *Developmental Psychology, 35,* 1189–1197.

Young, S., & Amarasinghe, J. A. (2010). Practitioner review: Non-pharmacological treatments for ADHD—A lifespan approach. *Journal of Child Psychology and Psychiatry, 51,* 116–133.

Young, W. C., Goy, R. W., & Phoenix, C. H. (1967). Hormones and sexual behavior. *Science, 143,* 212–218.

Younger, M., & Warrington, M. (2006). Would Harry and Hermione have done better in single-sex classes? A review of single-sex teaching in coeducational secondary schools in the United Kingdom, *American Educational Research Journal, 43,* 579–620.

Youniss, J. (1980). *Parents and peers in social development.* Chicago: University of Chicago Press.

Youniss, J., and Damon, W. (1992). Social construction in Piaget's theory. In H. Beilin and P. Pufall (eds), *Piaget's theory: Prospects and possibilities* (pp. 267–286). Hillsdale, NJ: Erlbaum.

Yu, C-E., Oshima, J., Fu, Y-H., Wijsman, E. M., Hisama, F., Alisch, R., Matthews, S., Nakura, J., Miki, T., Ouais, S., Martin, G. M., Mulligan, J., & Schellenberg, G. D. (1996). Positional cloning of the Werner's syndrome Gene, *Science, 272,* 258–262.

Yuill, N., & Oakhill, J. (1988). Effects of inference training on poor reading comprehension.

Applied Cognitive Psychology, 2, 33–45.

Yuill, N., & Pearson, A. (1998). The development of bases for trait attribution: Children's understanding of traits as causal mechanisms based on desire. *Developmental Psychology, 34,* 574–586.

Yussen, S. R., & Berman, L. (1981). Memory predictions for recall and recognition in first, third, and fifth grade children. *Developmental Psychology, 17,* 224–229.

Zaff, J. F., Moore, K. A., Papillo, A. R., & Williams, S. (2003). Implications of extracurricular activity participation during adolescence on positive outcomes. *Journal of Adolescent Research, 18,* 599–630.

Zahn-Waxler, C., Cole, P. M., Welsh, J. D., & Fox N. A. (1995). Psychophysiological correlates of empathy and prosocial behaviors in preschool children with problem behaviors. *Development and Psychopathology, 7,* 27–48.

Zahn-Waxler, C., Klimes-Dougan, B., & Kendizora, K. T. (1998). The study of emotion socialization: Conceptual, methodological, and developmental considerations. *Psychological Inquiry, 9,* 313–316.

Zahn-Waxler, C., Radke-Yarrow, M., & King, R. A. (1979). Child rearing and children's prosocial initiations toward victims of distress. *Child Development, 50,* 319–330.

Zahn-Waxler, C., Robinson, J. L., & R. Emde, N. (1992). The development of empathy in twins. *Developmental Psychology, 28,* 1038–1047.

Zahn-Waxler, C., Schiro, K., Robinson, J. L., Emde, R. N., & Schmitz, S. (2001). Empathy and prosocial patterns in young MZ and DZ twins: Development and genetic and environmental influences.

In R. N. Emde & J. K. Hewitt (eds), *Infancy to early childhood* (pp. 141–162). New York: Oxford University Press.

Zajonc, R. B., & Mullally, P. R. (1997). Birth order: Reconciling conflicting effects. *American Psychologist, 52,* 685–699.

Zani, B. (1993). Dating and interpersonal relationships in adolescence. In S. Jackson & H. Rodriguez-Tome (eds), *Adolescence and its social worlds* (pp. 95–119). Hillsdale, NJ: Erlbaum.

Zarbatany, L., Hartmann, D. P., & Rankin, D. B. (1990). The psychological functions of preadolescent peer activities. *Child Development, 61,* 1067–1080.

Zarbatany, L., McDougall, P., & Hymel, S. (2000). Gender-differentiated experience in the peer culture: Links to intimacy in preadolescence. *Social Development, 9,* 62–69.

Zeanah, C. H., Smyke, A. T., & Settles, L. D. (2006). *Orphanages as a developmental context for early childhood.* Malden, MA: Blackwell.

Zelazo, N. A., Zelazo, P. R., Cohen, K. M., & Zelazo, P. D. (1988, April). Specificity of practice effects on elementary neuromotor patterns. Paper presented at the International Conference on Infant Studies, Washington, DC.

Zelazo, P. D. (2004). The development of conscious control in childhood. *Trends in Cognitive Sciences, 8,* 12–17.

Zelazo, P. D., Frye, D. & Rapus, T. (1996). An age-related dissociation between knowing rules and using them. *Cognitive Development, 11,* 37–63.

Zelazo, P. R. (1983). The development of walking: New findings and old assumptions. *Journal of Motor Behavior, 15,* 99–137.

Zelazo, P. R., Zelazo, N. A., & Kolb, S. (1972). 'Walking' in the newborn. *Science, 176*, 314–315.

Zigler, E., Abelson, W. D., Trickett, P. K., & Seitz, V. (1982). Is an intervention program necessary in order to improve economically disadvantaged children's IQ scores? *Child Development, 53*, 340–348.

Zukow-Goldring, P. (2002). Sibling caregiving. In M. H. Bornstein (ed.), *Handbook of parenting* (Vol. 3, pp. 177–208). Mahwah, NJ: Erlbaum.

Zwicker, A., Denovan-Wright, E. M., & Uher, R. (2018). Gene–environment interplay in the etiology of psychosis. *Psychological Medicine*, 1–12. doi: 10.1017/S003329171700383X

Author Index

Subject Index

Boldface page numbers indicate key terms. *Italic* page numbers indicate figures or tables